FOURTH EDITION

SPECIAL & EDUCATION

STUDENT DISABILITY

AN INTRODUCTION

TRADITIONAL, EMERGING, AND ALTERNATIVE PERSPECTIVES

EDITED BY

EDWARD L. MEYEN

THOMAS M. SKRTIC

THE UNIVERSITY OF KANSAS

LOVE PUBLISHING COMPANY®
Denver, Colorado 80222

Photographs on pages 486 and 523 are courtesy of the American Printing House for the Blind.

Fourth Edition
Previous editions titled
Exceptional Children and Youth: An Introduction

Library of Congress Catalog Card Number 92-74811

Copyright © 1995, 1988, 1982, 1978 by Love Publishing Company
Printed in the U.S.A.
ISBN 0-89108-231-X

For my family—thanks again!

—ELM

For Cathy Skrtic, whose friendship means everything to me.

—TMS

C*ONTENTS*

INTRODUCTION TO PART TWO   565
ALTERNATIVE PERSPECTIVES

*F*IGURES

TABLES

PREFACE

The first edition of this book was published in 1978. Like most survey texts in special education, it was organized according to categories of disability or exceptionality and, as such, was meant to provide a state of the art review of the psychology and education of exceptional children and youth. Appearing shortly after implementation of Public Law 94–142 and the introduction of mainstreaming, it also introduced readers to changes that were occurring in special education practice as a result of the law and the new service delivery model. The second edition, which was published in 1982, also was organized categorically. It focused on the impact of PL 94–142 and mainstreaming to that point and added chapters on three new topics—early intervention, career/vocational education, and individualized instructional planning—that cut across categories of exceptionality.

When the third edition of the text was published in 1988, not much had changed with respect to the nature and effects of student exceptionality. And new legislation, while significant, largely built on earlier legislative initiatives. Two things had changed, however. First, PL 94–142 and mainstreaming had come under attack by advocates of the Regular Education Initiative, who questioned the ethics and efficacy of contemporary special education practices. Second, and more important, the theoretical grounding of special education practice had been called into question by revolutionary developments in philosophy and the social sciences, developments which, we argued, undercut the legitimacy of special education theory and practice and the professions themselves.

As a result of these developments, we felt that it was no longer sufficient for a survey text to focus exclusively on the nature and effects of existing special education programs and practices and the characteristics of the students served. Although the bulk of the third edition followed the traditional format for special education survey texts, we added an entirely new section that addressed the Regular Education Initiative and, more importantly, challenged the conventional way of conceptionalizing the field of special education and the notion of disability itself. The section began with a chapter on the nature of the professions and professional knowledge and an introduction to the developments in philosophy and the social sciences that had called the legitimacy of professions like special education into question. This chapter presented a rationale for considering alternative perspectives on special education and the very notion of student disability, and was followed by three chapters that criticized the traditional perspective and provided alternative ways to conceptualize the field and its clients.

The present edition follows the same general format. Part One is a state-of-the-art treatment of the field of special education and the nature and needs of the students it serves. New chapters that cut across areas of exceptionality have been added, and all of the categorical chapters have been revised and updated. This part of the book is meant to orient students of special education to the latest developments in the field, as well as to some important related developments in public education and society. Part Two addresses the continuing challenge to the field posed by advocates of inclusive education who, like those of the Regular Education Initiative, are questioning the ethics and efficacy of the current system of special education. More important, however, the Part Two chapters challenge the traditional theories and assumptions upon which the field of special education is premised, and thus question the way special educators conceive of their field and its practices and clients. The chapters in this part of the book also have been revised and updated, and a new chapter has been added. Together, the Part Two chapters argue for and present alternative ways to conceptualize the field and its clients as well as the social world that gives meaning to social practices and concepts like special education and student disability.

The fourth edition juxtaposes traditional, emerging, and alternative interpretations of special education and disability. Much of the content is new, and some is complex. But today's students of special education, we believe, are not only intellectually capable and curious, but also bring with them a common set of experiences based on working in and around schools and living in the contemporary world. One can hardly participate in modern society without being aware of the ongoing struggle of many groups—including persons with disabilities—for equity in the quality of life. We believe the alternative perspectives presented in this book will provide our readers with new insights for understanding these struggles and doing something about them. In any event, the content of this volume is a snapshot in time of a still emerging profession and the challenges it must face.

Edward L. Meyen

Thomas M. Skrtic

ACKNOWLEDGMENTS

Theory and practice in professional fields evolve largely through the efforts of those who share their ideas in the literature. We are grateful to these people, especially to those whose ideas we have borrowed. There are many others whose work, although not cited in the text, has had a significant impact on us and this book. Our gratitude goes out to them as well. We also want to acknowledge the readers of this book who will reflect on its contents and, through their own thought and action, improve upon what we are attempting to achieve.

We are indebted to the chapter authors for contributing their talents and energies to this project, and particularly for their willingness to share the risks inherent in setting what we believe is a new direction for teaching textbooks in special education. Many other colleagues and students offered insightful criticism of the manuscript and thus, each in their own way, contributed to the final product. They deserve a great deal of credit for helping to shape our thinking and the book.

As is true in all projects of this nature, there are those who contribute behind the scenes as well. Although computer technology has eliminated the role of a single individual who "prepares" the manuscript, we wish to acknowledge the faculty and staff of the Department of Special Education at the University of Kansas for taking up the slack while we focused our attention on the book. Finally, we want to thank Holly Rumpler, Senior Editor at Love Publishing, for her commitment to this project and for keeping us and the book moving forward.

*I*NTRODUCTION TO PART ONE

*T*RADITIONAL AND *E*MERGING PERSPECTIVES

*T*he special education community is engulfed in its second round of self-criticism in 30 years. The first round began in the 1960s, when the field's traditional special classroom model was called into question, and largely subsided in 1975 with enactment of the Education for All Handicapped Children Act (Public Law 94–142) and introduction of the mainstreaming model. Although both of these innovations were presumed to provide solutions to the problems associated with the special classroom approach, a second round of self-criticism began shortly after 1975 and has continued with increasing intensity. It rejects PL 94–142 and mainstreaming and calls for yet another approach—the inclusive education model—which is presumed to be a solution to the new problems associated with PL 94–142 and mainstreaming. Whereas the first round of self-criticism ultimately increased the field's certainty in its professional knowledge and practices, the current round has had just the opposite effect. After more than a decade of debating the ethics and efficacy of PL 94–142 and mainstreaming, the special education community is less certain about its professional knowledge and practices than ever before.

Of course, special education professionals are not alone in their uncertainty. Following publication of *A Nation At Risk* by the National Commission on Excellence in Education in 1983, the level of uncertainty throughout the institution of public education has been unprecedented. Special educators may take some comfort in the knowledge that other educators share their uncertainty, but we have far more to be concerned about than either we or our education colleagues may realize. The very legitimacy of the professions has been called into question because of a far more pervasive sense of uncertainty spreading throughout intellectual and cultural life. This larger uncertainty is affecting every discipline of study and field of practice, including the professions of education and special education. The substance and format of this text reflect our attempt to address the implications of this development for the field of special education and for children and youth who have special educational needs.

This book has been written as a resource for students of special education during this unique period of cultural and professional uncertainty. It is a unique time in the history of Western civilization, and thus a unique period in the development of the institution of public education and the field of special education. Because unique times require extraordinary measures, this book is intended to accomplish two largely contradictory purposes. On one hand, it is intended to be an authoritative teaching textbook for inculcating students with the field's established way of viewing the world and its practices and clients. This is the more common of the book's two purposes, since all teaching textbooks in the professions are written with this purpose in mind. On the other hand, however, this book introduces students to the idea that special education and the very notion of student disability can and should be viewed from alternative perspectives—perspectives that challenge the field's traditional way of viewing itself and its practices and clients.

Although this second purpose is far less common than the first one, it is by no means original with this book. There is a substantial body of literature that challenges special education's traditional perspective. In fact, the decision to organize the book as we have—rather than writing a separate book of alternative perspectives—was based on the fact that historically the alternative perspectives literature has had little, if any, impact on special education's traditional perspective. Most often these criticisms are written by persons outside the field of special education, which has meant that their insights could be written off as uninformed. To help avoid this possibility we have included a discussion of alternative perspectives within a largely traditional presentation of special education knowledge and practices. In addition, we have included a separate chapter on the professions and the nature of professional knowledge, as well as one on the nature and implications of special education professional knowledge and practices. These chapters present our arguments for the possibility and importance of considering alternative interpretations of special education and student disability.

Before reviewing the book's contents, it will be helpful to explain what we mean by traditional, emerging, and alternative perspectives. Special education's traditional perspective is the field's existing, time-honored pattern of knowledge, beliefs, and practices. This is the type of information that is presented in virtually all teaching textbooks in special education. By emerging perspectives we mean new ideas, knowledge, and practices that have been (or most likely will be) accepted as legitimate by the professional community but do not challenge the grounds of the traditional perspective. As such, emerging perspectives can be viewed as state of the art refinements and extensions of knowledge and practice *within* the traditional frame of reference. Alternative perspectives, by contrast, challenge the most fundamental aspects of the traditional perspective and seek to replace it with an entirely new way of understanding special education and the notion special educational needs.

The text has been organized into two parts. Part One contains both traditional and emerging perspectives on special education and student disability. The chapters are organized around the traditional notion of "categorical areas of exceptionality," and each one provides a comprehensive state-of-the-art treatment of one of these areas. As such, each chapter presents contemporary and emerging perspectives built upon a foundation of traditional and emerging special education knowledge and beliefs. In addition to the categorical chapters, Part One includes four introductory chapters covering material that cuts across the traditional categorical areas.

Part Two is reserved for what we call alternative perspectives. Chapter 14 considers the nature of the professions and professional knowledge and discusses the implications of a changing conceptualization of science and knowledge for the validity of professional knowledge and, thus, the legitimacy of the professions. It provides both an argument for considering alternative interpretations of special education and disability and a framework for understanding and evaluating available alternative perspectives. Chapter 15 extends this discussion and focuses it more sharply on the professional knowledge and practices of the field of special education. The remaining chapters in Part Two provide three alternative perspectives for viewing special education and disability. Of course, these chapters represent only three of many possible ways to view special education and disability, but the purpose of Part Two is not to present every alternative perspective. Rather, it is intended to demonstrate that special education and disability can be viewed from alternative perspectives and, more important, to show that different perspectives have different implications for the children and youth the field of special education exists to serve.

A

COMMENTARY ON

SPECIAL EDUCATION

EDWARD L. MEYEN

*C*hange seems to be the word of today. Schools are changing in response to public calls for reform to improve the quality of education. The economy is causing national policymakers to question earlier commitments to social causes as they strive for equity in the face of declining resources. States and large cities are facing major capital outlays as they work to rebuild their infrastructures. Special education is undergoing major shifts in philosophy and practice. Even the demographics of students defined as disabled are changing. While these changes are occurring all around us, world politics are undergoing dramatic changes that also are influencing our quality of life.

All these circumstances and the way they interact with each other must be understood as new policies are formulated and practices adopted. In studying special education today, students must be willing to invest the effort necessary to understand the needs of children and youth with disabilities from the broader perspective of social change. They also must be willing to entertain ideas that contradict what they see in practice. Students aspiring to be professionals with responsibilities for enhancing the education of young people with disabilities must prepare themselves to analyze critically their experiences and practices and to participate in the philosophical debate on how best to meet the needs of students with disabilities.

For the past two decades, policymakers concerned about students with special needs have focused on improving the conditions under which these children and youth are educated, creating better employment opportunities for them as adults, and working toward equity in their treatment as family members and citizens. Practices to prevent conditions that contribute to disabilities or help reduce the consequences of disabilities also have been implemented. Although progress can be cited in each of these areas, they remain in need of further study, as many aspirations and desired outcomes continue to be unmet.

To assume that the advocacy movement on behalf of students with disabilities will continue to become more refined and more effective as we enter the 21st century may be unreasonable. Many of the goals of this movement since it began to evolve in the 1970s—the rights of persons with disabilities to a free and appropriate education, access to public facilities and places, public policies to assure nondiscrimination practices— have been achieved. How these rights will operationalize into routine practices of public agencies and everyday behaviors of citizens, however, is unknown. Equally unknown is how the current reform initiatives in special education will eventually blend with those in general education. Some evidence suggests that the reform movement may result in a single system of education for all students. If and how the blending occurs will depend largely on how successful advocates for students with disabilities are in making special education integral to the overall reform movement in general education.

Because the rights of people with disabilities related to public access and nondiscrimination have parallels in the larger arena of civil rights, many sources of influence that will affect the public response to educational reform are already in place. The challenge today, therefore, is to keep the advocacy movement for students with disabilities alive, and policymakers responsive. The latter is particularly problematic because the turnover of incumbents in public office necessitates constantly educating policymakers about the needs and rights of people with disabilities. Some time in the future, when public attitudes and understandings have become more positive and we hold the same expectations for the quality of life of persons with disabilities as we do for all citizens, this will be less of a concern.

The circumstances in our schools and society's concerns for education have changed so drastically over just the last 10 years that predicting what special education will be like in the year 2000 is extremely difficult. Only by placing in perspective how we arrived at our current practices and contrasting that knowledge with what is anticipated in the 21st century can we project what might happen in the future. The only predictable observation we can make about education in the 21st century is that it undoubtedly will be different and that the expected changes will come from a number of sources.

The results may not be positive for students with disabilities. Most educational reform initiatives aimed at improving American education are driven by economic motives that have evolved from concerns related to the labor force, international competitiveness, and global economics. Although proponents of most of these reforms imply that they are intended to benefit all students, the benefits of most of these initiatives seem unconvincing, at best, for students considered at risk academically. Students with disabilities typically fall in this at-risk group. Any discussion of how the educational needs of students with disabilities will be accommodated in the 21st century must address the dynamics of what is occurring today in social, economic, and educational reform.

As a professional, you will share the responsibility for completing the story on special education in the 1990s and into the 21st century. Your inquiry skills and ability to integrate information, coupled with your personal experiences, must be brought into play as you strive to understand the attributes of exceptional students, their evolving equality as citizens, the dynamics of educational and social change, and the expanding knowledge base.

Special education is in transition. The social conditions that impact the life span of people with disabilities are changing and, most important, education is changing. Students and professionals interested in special education must be willing to make an extra personal effort to integrate what they learn from the literature and their personal experiences with what is occurring around them. This personal commitment adds both to the challenge and the excitement of the field.

Students who want to understand what influences the quality of life for individuals with disabilities know that we no longer can separate educational and social issues according to the needs of one segment of the population from those affecting the population in general. Although the way in which certain groups are assimilated may vary, overall the values and expectations our society holds for its people are intended to help *all* citizens achieve their potential.

Constant monitoring and modification of our social conscience are necessary as society continually responds to shifts in world views, changes in the economy and, more specifically, what society expects of education as the primary vehicle for positioning our country for the future. In the education reform movement's push to contribute to a stronger economy, we must ensure that groups, such as children and youth requiring special education, are not overlooked.

Given the changing conditions in education and society, you must develop a frame of reference for understanding and questioning the practices and policies that govern the way special education services are delivered today. Such probing may raise doubts about the validity or desirability of some or many of today's policies and practices, but a degree of doubt is necessary if one is to recognize where changes may be needed and to become familiar with the forces behind these changes. You first will be introduced to the emergent reform agenda in general education. It will serve as background for understanding the emergent trends within special education, and developments in general and special education will serve as a context for examining the broader change in world view that is behind many of the changes taking place in society today.

Special education will be described here, in Part One, in terms of traditional and emerging perspectives—the perspectives that have shaped the field and its policies and practices historically (traditional), as well as those that have begun to reshape the field's policies and practices in the 1980s and 1990s (emerging). The traditional perspective is based on the time-honored pattern of knowledge, beliefs, and practices of the special education professional community. Emerging perspectives are new ideas, knowledge, and practices that have been (or most likely will be) accepted by the members of the special education community but do not challenge the most fundamental aspects of the traditional perspective.

THE EMERGENT REFORM AGENDA

"Organizing for results" is an inherently attractive concept. It implies a deliberate attempt to plan and conduct essential activities so as to accomplish our aims successfully—in other words, purposefully doing what we set out to do. From my perspective, that means having all students learn well, not just the fastest, the brightest, or the most advantaged. Unfortunately, our educational systems, schools, and instructional programs are not organized to achieve or ensure successful results; instead, they are organized primarily for student custody and administrative convenience. If we were to organize for results, we would have to make major changes in our philosophy, purpose, operations, and structures. (Spady, 1988, p. 4)

Although Spady was writing about outcomes-based education (OBE), a specific reform initiative, his message characterizes much of what is expected of educational reform today. The public expects schools to restructure in ways that will result in all students learning more and also learning what is most important to be prepared for the 21st century.

The report, *A Nation at Risk* (National Commission on Excellence in Education, 1983), is viewed as the benchmark for the current reform movement. Even though it stimulated districts to examine their educational practices and motivated many to form local "Nation-at-Risk" committees, the report had a greater impact by causing professional associations, private-sector groups, governmental agencies at all levels, and special-interest groups to conduct their own studies and release their own reports. Over the past 10 years hundreds of reports have been published, each setting forth its own analysis of the problems inherent in American education and proposed solutions. Some have gained visibility and helped set state and national agendas; others have had only nominal effect. Among the many reports receiving considerable attention by the public and professional groups are four issued in 1991 and early 1992:

- *America 2000: An Education Strategy*, U.S. Department of Education, 1991.
- *The National Education Goals Report: Building a Nation of Learners*, National Education Goals Panel, 1991.
- *What Work Requires of Schools: A SCANS Report for America 2000*, Secretary's Commission on Achieving Necessary Skills, U.S. Department of Labor, 1991.
- *Raising Standards for American Education: A Report to Congress, the Secretary of Education, the National Education Goals Panel, and the American People*, National Council on Education Standards and Testing, 1992.

Although each report has its own orientation and purpose, certain issues are common to all. For example, they all (a) call for educational programs that will enhance achievement of higher-order thinking skills; (b) acknowledge diversity among students; (c) present improved education as the primary solution to the nation's declining competitiveness in international markets; (d) generalize higher expectations for student performance to all students; and (e) make only nominal mention of the needs of students with disabilities.

The emerging view seems to be one of tying the economic woes of the country to the perception that the educational establishment has not been responsive to the needs of students or of the nation. The evidence cited is typically comparative data on how American students compare with their peers in other developed nations. These comparisons seldom take into consideration cultural differences, the population served by the schools, the presence of a national curriculum and associated testing in most other countries, the problems of our large cities, or the family structure in America.

In addition, many of the proposed reforms are only peripheral to teaching and learning. Yet, they are presented as if they individually represent powerful interventions for change. The reforms most visible in the media tend to be those that evolve from the political process. This makes it more difficult to determine what is valid and has the highest probability of bringing about significant improvement in American education.

The intent of the reform movement is to improve education, but how the reform agenda will benefit students now served through special education is not clear. Although references to "all" students are present in almost all reports, rarely do the authors address how all student will meet their proposed reform or even benefit them. The assumption is that referring to *all* students implies a level of equity. Besides, politically, focusing on all students is beneficial. Proposed reforms, however, often are weakened when their application to all students is examined. This is true particularly for special education students. From a policy perspective, the question of what is meant by "all" is being examined; yet, authors of reform initiatives continue to use the term freely. Discussing the allusions too often made in the reform literature to including all students, Kauffman and Hallahan (1993) stated:

> The implicit and explicit meanings of "all" are critical for understanding political and educational dialogue because one typically assumes that the freedoms, rights, and responsibilities addressed in these exchanges are limited, not absolute. The user of the word "all" does not usually intend that it be interpreted literally because either tradition or rational discourse (or both) suggests exceptions, meaning that "all usually represents only an approximation—and sometimes not a very close approximation—of every individual. "All," then, is frequently understood to exclude certain individuals, sometimes for reasons that are justifiable and sometimes for reasons that are not. The varied meanings of "all" are therefore of considerable consequence to those who may be tacitly excluded (pp. 74–75).

Because special education has a long history of attempting to bring about reform in general education to best meet the needs of students with disabilities, the reference to *all* students in today's reform literature can be misleading. When the recommendations of a reform report address all students, this does not necessarily mean that all students were considered. Nor does it mean that the advocacy movement for special education has been so successful that references to *all* reflect how well policymakers or others proposing educational reforms understand the needs of special education students.

To understand the implications of the emerging educational reform movement for special education, we must ensure that the reference to *all* is real, or at least qualified, and also place in perspective the performance expectations being articulated as national goals for all students. These expectations are driven largely by assumptions about what is required to be successful in the labor force. Given that independent living is central to the goals of special education and that employment is critical to independent living, these expectations have to be examined as special education programs become part of education reform.

Performance expectations (largely in the area of academic achievement) are included in most reform reports, and the four reports noted above address this issue most directly. The relevance of each of these reports to special education will be outlined briefly.

NATIONAL EDUCATION GOALS REPORT

The National Education Goals, presented in Table 1.1, have particular relevance to special education. At first glance, these goals may seem too high for special education students. Reviewing them in the context of what is important for students with disabilities, however, makes their applicability more apparent. Clearly, the goal that all students start to school ready to learn is important. This is important for all students, and it may be even more important for youngsters with disabilities than for any other group. The emphasis on early childhood education for children with disabilities clearly is an avenue for ensuring that children with disabilities are ready to learn when they begin school.

Increasing the graduation rate to 90% also would benefit students with special educational needs, as the drop-out rate is much higher among special education students than their nondisabled peers. Too often, students with severe learning problems elect to leave school before meeting high school graduation requirements.

The proposed academic achievement expectations for students in grades 4, 8, and 12, outlined in the third goal, may be seen by some to be excessive for many special education students. The paradigm of the past has been largely to expect many special education students to achieve in self-help and independent living skills. If the old paradigm is set aside or replaced by one that articulates higher expectations, the results might be different. How the academic performance of students with disabilities can be positively influenced, given new curricula, instructional approaches, and expectations,

---

● **TABLE I.I**

National education goals

By the year 2000:
1. All children in America will start school ready to learn.
2. The high school graduation rate will increase to at least 90%.
3. American students will leave grades 4, 8, and 12 having demonstrated competency in challenging subject matter including English, mathematics, science, history, and geography; and every school in America will ensure that all students learn to use their minds well, so they may be prepared for responsible citizenship, further learning, and productive employment in our modern economy.
4. U. S. students will be first in the world in science and mathematics achievement.
5. Every adult American will be literate and will possess the knowledge and skills necessary to compete in a global economy and exercise the rights and responsibilities of citizenship.
6. Every school in America will be free of drugs and violence and will offer a disciplined environment conducive to learning.

The four-part AMERICA 2000 education strategy will enable every community to achieve these goals.

Source: From National Council on Education Standards and Testing, *Raising Standards for American Education: A Report to Congress, the Secretary of Education, the National Goals Panel, and the American People* (Washington, DC: Author, 1992).

remains to be seen. The key is to create the instructional conditions and higher expectations essential to enhancing the probabilities that students with disabilities can meet higher academic performance standards.

Being first in the world in the sciences and mathematics will require more than better instruction in these subjects. It will require reassessing who is to be included in the comparisons. If special education students are to be included, they, too, must benefit from improved instruction in these subjects.

As for goal 5, employment skills and effective citizenship are central to the goals of special education just as they are for nondisabled individuals. The key consideration relates to how the skills needed for employment will change and how those changes will affect individuals with disabilities. Drug- and violence-free environments certainly are vital to all students. Again, this goal has particular relevance for special education students, many of whom are particularly vulnerable to substance and physical abuse.

Balancing these national goals with what is reasonable for students served through special education does not lend itself to generalizations. Certainly, given appropriate instructional support, many students receiving special education can achieve more than today's evidence might suggest. Others, with severe and multiple disabilities, may be able to achieve more than is currently the case, but probably not at the level reflected in the National Goals.

Knowing the expectations for the new labor force is valuable for all students and their teachers. Thus, expectations of what skills will be required to be employable in the 21st century are as critical to curriculum planning in special education as in general education. Table 1.2 contrasts the characteristics of today's workplace with what is anticipated in the future. The comparison clearly shows that the roles for which many persons with disabilities historically have been prepared are less present in the projected workforce. As a result, the traditional view of the jobs that people with disabilities are capable of performing must change. If the educational programs and life experiences provided have limited their abilities, new curricula and instructional approaches may result in their meeting the demands of the workplace in the 21st century.

SCANS REPORT FOR AMERICA 2000

The SCANS report is concerned only with that part of the curriculum that prepares students for the world of work. Although the report does not call for a work-focused curriculum, it does set forth the competencies required to meet workplace demands in the 21st century. The report identifies five competencies that, when combined with what is described as a three-part foundation of skills and personal qualities, represent what is required in work performance to be successful today.

The SCANS competencies presented in Table 1.3 are not specific to the technical skills required for specific careers but, rather, are generalizable across roles. Specifically, they represent skills that require reasoning, problem-solving, and generalization skills beyond what often is included in instructional programs for special education

● *TABLE 1.2*

Characteristics of today's and tomorrow's workplace

Traditional Model	High-Performance Model

Strategy

Traditional Model	High-Performance Model
• mass production	• flexible production
• long production runs	• customized production
• centralized control	• decentralized control

Production

Traditional Model	High-Performance Model
• fixed automation	• flexible automation
• end-of-line quality control	• on-line quality control
• fragmentation of tasks	• work teams, multiskilled workers
• authority vested in supervisor	• authority delegated to worker

Hiring and Human Resources

Traditional Model	High-Performance Model
• labor-management confrontation	• labor-management cooperation
• minimal qualifications accepted	• screening for basic skills abilities
• workers as a cost	• workforce as an investment

Job Ladders

Traditional Model	High-Performance Model
• internal labor market	• limited internal labor market
• advancement by seniority	• advancement by certified skills

Training

Traditional Model	High-Performance Model
• minimal for production workers	• training sessions for everyone
• specialized for craft workers	• broader skills sought

Source: From Office of Technology Assessment, *Competing in the New International Economy* (Washington, DC: Office of Technology Assessment, 1990).

students. The question is not whether the proposed competencies accurately reflect what will be required in the 21st century; instead, the concern is how we can best ensure that special education students have an opportunity to achieve competencies to the extent their abilities allow.

RAISING STANDARDS FOR AMERICAN EDUCATION

As American businesses strive to improve their international competitiveness, the issue of a national curriculum often emerges as a reform proposal. The assumption is that a national curriculum is an answer to a better prepared workforce. Proponents point to

● *TABLE 1.3*

Five competencies from SCANS report

Resources: Identifies, organizes, plans, and allocates resources
A. Time: Selects goal-relevant activities, ranks them, allocates time, and prepares and follows schedules
B. Money: Uses or prepares budgets, makes forecasts, keeps records, and makes adjustments to meet objectives
C. Material and facilities: Acquires, stores, allocates, and uses materials or space efficiently
D. Human resources: Assesses skills and distributes work accordingly, evaluates performance, and provides feedback

Interpersonal: Works with others
A. Participates as member of a team: contributes to group effort
B. Teaches others new skills
C. Serves clients/customers: works to satisfy customers' expectations
D. Exercises leadership: communicates ideas to justify position, persuades and convinces others, responsibly challenges existing procedures and policies
E. Negotiates: works toward agreements involving exchange of resources, resolves divergent interests
F. Works with diversity: works well with men and women from diverse backgrounds

Information: Acquires and uses information
A. Acquires and evaluates information
B. Organizes and maintains information
C. Interprets and communicates information
D. Uses computers to process information

Systems: Understands complex interrelationships
A. Understands systems: knows how social, organizational, and technological systems work, and operates effectively with them
B. Monitors and corrects performance: distinguishes trends, predicts impacts on system operations, diagnoses deviations in system performance, and corrects malfunctions
C. Improves or designs systems: suggests modifications to existing systems and develops new or alternative systems to improve performance

Technology: Works with a variety of technologies
A. Selects technology: chooses procedures, tools, and equipment including computers and related technologies
B. Applies technology to task: understands overall intent and proper procedures for set-up and operation of equipment
C. Maintains and troubleshoots equipment: prevents, identifies, or solves problems with equipment, including computers and other technologies

Source: From Secretary's Commission on Achieving Necessary Skills, *What Work Requires of Schools: A SCANS Report for AMERICA 2000* (Washington, DC: U. S. Department of Labor, 1991).

the adoption of a national curriculum in many developed nations, including Japan.

To date, however, the concept of a national curriculum in the United States has been largely rejected both by professional educators and the public. In general, a national curriculum is not compatible with the American emphasis on local control of public education. Adopting a national curriculum likely would improve American students' performance in international comparisons if the curriculum were to result in more emphasis on academics and implementation of a national assessment system designed to measure mastery of skills taught through the national curriculum. At the same time, it would require some trade-offs that most Americans are not willing to make. Particularly, these relate to the importance communities place on determining what will be taught in their schools and most communities' lack of willingness to restrict the broad array of responsibilities now assigned to public schools. For example, American schools provide more services to students and more extracurricular activities than most countries with a national curriculum. American schools also offer a broader range of courses and choices. In addition, less curricular tracking means more diversity among American students in terms of their instructional needs.

Congress charged the National Council on Education Standards and Testing (1992) to advise on the desirability and feasibility of national standards and tests, as well as to recommend long-range policies and assessment systems. If implemented, these recommendations will move the country toward curricula that will have some of the merits of a national curricula while still protecting local and state control. Focusing on the teaching fields of history, geography, English, math, and science, the council recommended a voluntary approach to national standards at a world-class level and national testing with an emphasis on four types of standards:

- *Content standards* that describe the knowledge, skills, and other understandings that schools should teach in order for students to attain high levels of competency in challenging subject matter.
- *Student performance standards* that define various levels of competence in the challenging subject matter set out.
- *School delivery standards* developed by the states collectively from which each state could select the criteria it finds useful for the purpose of assessing a school's capacity and performance.
- *System performance standards* that provide evidence about the success of schools, local school systems, states, and the nation in bringing all students, leaving no one behind, to high performance standards. (pp. E4–E5)

Even though strong arguments can be made in favor of setting national standards, application of national standards to the education of students with disabilities must be carefully analyzed and questioned. For example, the Council for Exceptional Children (CEC), in its testimony before the Subcommittee on Elementary, Secondary and Vocational Education of the U. S. House of Representatives, on March 18, 1992, acknowledged the need for improving educational outcomes for all students and concurred that if world-class standards were to be set, these should be inclusive of all students. CEC, however, raised several issues related to the application of world-class standards to the education of students with disabilities:

Will students with severe disabilities be expected to meet world-class standards in the five core subjects? If yes, will they be expected to reach the same standards as the majority of the school-age population? If not, what performance standards will they be expected to meet? We cannot accept an answer that students with severe disabilities are "exempt" from meeting world-class standards.

In terms of national testing, the National Council on Education Standards and Testing (1992) recommended a national system designed to assess performance relative to the national standards. The system would contain the following features:

- *Multiple assessments, not a single test.* It will be up to states, individually or in groups, to adopt assessments linked to the national standards. States can design the assessments or they may acquire them.
- *Voluntary, not mandatory.* State participation in the national system of assessments will be voluntary. The federal government will not require that states adopt any particular tests.
- *Developmental, not static.* The system should be developmental. It should change and evolve over time, maintaining alignment with the national content and performance standards and incorporating improved assessment techniques as these are developed. (p. 15)

If a system designed to assess the performance of students on national standards evolves, a basic question must be addressed: Should students with disabilities be exempt from these assessments? During the 1970s and 1980s, when most states were implementing minimum-competency testing programs, students with disabilities typically were exempted from taking the tests. The reasons were largely twofold: (a) special education students frequently require special accommodations when taking exams; and (b) standardized tests often lack validity for special education students who follow a curriculum that is different from that of their nondisabled peers. To counter these problems, the National Council on Education Standards and Testing proposes developing alternative forms of assessment that would address the test-taking needs of all students.

The pros and cons of including or excluding students with disabilities in national testing against national standards are just emerging. If national standards become a reality, many federal and state funding initiatives tied to national standards may follow. One could argue that exempting students with disabilities from national testing could mean that programs for these students may lose out in terms of future federal educational reform initiatives. Specifically, the major group of students requiring alternative forms of assessment are special education students. Therefore, exempting special education students would reduce the need to invest in researching alternative forms of assessment and needed alternative assessment forms might not be developed. On the other hand, higher expectations stimulated by national standards tied to national testing might bring about more effective curriculum and instructional changes for special education students.

Arguments against application of standards and national testing to students with disabilities include the views that setting standards can be arbitrary; may not be appropriate for students with disabilities; and will negatively affect the self-esteem of students who fail to achieve national standards. Attempts to develop alternative forms of assessment have not been successful. Further, the varied placement practices of special education students in general education classes would complicate decisions on which grade level to test special education students.

To analyze the implications of these arguments requires one to set aside traditional views of special education instructional programs and assessment. Development of national standards and national testing over the next decade will have major implications for special education. The extent to which these implications benefit students will depend on how effectively special education convinces policymakers to invest in (a) researching the effects of applying national standards to special education students, (b) designing alternative forms of assessment, and (c) broadening the range of teaching fields for which standards will be developed to include areas of importance to special education students. Central to broadening the original five teaching fields is the general area of independent living skills. The bottom line on adopting national standards and applying them to all students is to provide assurance that all students have an opportunity to learn the skills, knowledge, and behaviors essential to meet the standards. Further, assessment structures must allow all students to demonstrate what they know.

ANALYZING THE PROPOSALS

The reform movement of the 1980s is best described as an assortment of independent initiatives. Some were motivated by assumed economies, others by the political belief that change in itself will make a difference. Still others were based on well-founded assumptions and principles. The problem is that each initiative tends to be promulgated in the media and debated in statehouses on equal merit of presumed substance, making it difficult for the public to sort out which are substantive and are most likely to positively affect student performance. Few reform initiatives address what students should be taught or what they should learn as a result of their school experience. Most relate to organizational entry into the profession or financial issues.

The public's confusion in trying to analyze all the arguments for or against the various reform initiatives is compounded as many reform issues take on a life of their own. For example, a reform may be born in one state and fade after a couple of years, only to reappear in another state and be promoted for different reasons. An illustration is *alternative certification*. Some states have argued that alternative certification represents a viable approach to solving teacher shortages. Other states maintain that alternative certification would allow people with subject-matter expertise to enter the teaching profession without completing a professional education preparation program. Still others argue that alternative certification represents an employment opportunity for professionals in fields with an oversupply of personnel, individuals who wish to change careers, and retirees with specific areas of expertise.

On the surface, most proposals for reform have some merit, particularly when considered as general concepts. Even the more substantive ones, however, are vulnerable when their benefit for students with disabilities are more closely examined. Table 1.4 briefly describes selected reform proposals that have gained public attention in recent years and continue to receive national attention. No judgment of merit or lack of merit is implied. Instead, the list illustrates the need to examine every reform initiative in terms of its implications for special education. Reform initiatives, regardless of their ultimate merit, may contribute to special education merely by forcing us to examine current policies and practices. In addition, reform proposals should not necessarily be judged useless if they disadvantage a certain group or fail to benefit a group of students as long as they can be modified to maximize their value to the majority of students while protecting the interests of all.

EMERGING SPECIAL EDUCATION PRACTICES

Special education has a history of pushing the boundaries of education. Initially the emphasis was on expanding the range of students the public considers to be the responsibility of the schools. Next came advocacy for a broader definition of curriculum, followed by efforts to make public education more equitable relative to students with special educational needs. Today some special educators are calling for a new approach to special education, one based on the belief that our educational system can be rendered capable of meeting the needs of all students without the special organizational arrangements characterizing previous efforts to serve special populations of students. This new approach was initially referred to as the *regular education initiative* (REI) and, more recently, as the *inclusive education movement* (see Chapter 15 for a more comprehensive review).

As a professional field, special education has demonstrated the capacity *to change its practices and policies when they were shown to be wanting.* Nevertheless, the field has tenaciously, if implicitly, retained two guiding assumptions (see Skrtic, 1986, 1991b).

1. The belief that disabilities are conditions that students have; that disabilities are inherent human pathologies. This assumption stands behind the field's traditional diagnostic-prescriptive approach to special education identification and intervention. Although the assumption of human pathology has guided research in the field, stimulated the development of instructional strategies and curriculum, and shaped special education personnel preparation programs, it is being challenged today.
2. The belief that schools, and thus their special education programs, are rational entities. The assumption of organizational rationality underwrites the way special education professionals, advocates, and policymakers have conceptualized the nature and functioning of schools, and ultimately the way they have structured the special education system.

The capacity of special education to change and to play a major role in bringing about change in the broader arena of education is illustrated in the pattern of how educational services have been delivered to children and youth with exceptionalities over time. Special schools for such students began to appear in the United States in the

● **TABLE 1.4**

Reform proposals and their implications for special education

Reform Proposal	Special Education Questions
1. *Choice:* Allowing parents to select which district or school to send their children.	Will all districts/schools accept students with severe disabilities? Will participating districts implement inclusion policies?
2. *Site-based management:* Empowering teachers and parents to assume more direct responsibility for allocating instructional resources and general program operation at the school level (attendance site).	Will local policies supersede districtwide policies regarding special education practices? Will changing the composition of the decision-making process to include parents and professionals require efforts to help these parties understand the needs of students with disabilities? Will the needs of students with disabilities diminish as priorities when building-level board/councils have other special interests?
3. *Alternative certification:* Allowing individuals with subject-field knowledge but without a major in education to enter the teaching profession. A limited amount of professional education preparation and required experience under a mentor typically is required to achieve alternative certification.	Will special education be exempt from alternative certification programs? Will individuals approved to teach in regular education through alternative certification programs be prepared sufficiently to accommodate the needs of students with disabilities who will be integrated in their classes?
4. *Outcomes-based accreditation:* An approach to accrediting public schools based on outputs (i.e., specified performance criteria largely in the form of student achievement). This replaces the traditional emphasis on inputs (e.g., facilities, programs, resources, personal ratios).	Will districts set outcomes and indicators appropriate to the needs of students with disabilities? Will the admission criteria, program requirements, special appropriation, and required training of special education personnel be affected by a shift to outcomes accreditation? Will a sufficient investment be made in researching outcomes and indicators to ensure quality control of special education services/intervention, thereby protecting the welfare of students with disabilities?

5. *Higher-order thinking skills:* Increasing the curriculum and instructional emphasis for all students to stress the teaching of skills such as problem-solving, critical thinking, and generalization.

In the design of curriculum for students with disabilities, will higher-order thinking skills be emphasized in addition to practical skills?

Will the focus on higher-order thinking skills take instructional time away from teaching functional skills to special education students whose needs call for a functional curriculum?

6. *High-stakes testing:* Placing consequences on students for failing to meet performance expectations. For example, to be promoted or admitted to college, students would be required to earn specific scores on exams. The responsibility shifts from the school and parents to the student.

Will schools provide assurance that all students have an opportunity to learn what is assessed via tests?

Will sufficient alternative forms of assessments be available to ensures that all students, including students with disabilities, are able to demonstrate what they know?

7. *National standards:* Setting national curriculum standards in subject-matter fields, along with standards of performance expectations in curriculum areas where such standards are established.

Will the standards set be achievable by students with disabilities?

Will standards be validated as essential to meeting labor force and postsecondary education requirements?

Will standards be developed for functional curriculum areas in addition to academic fields?

8. *National testing:* Administering similar tests to all students in selected subject-fields. The results of national testing would be used to assess how American students perform in selected subject-fields. These data would help tailor instruction to the needs of individual students and make comparisons across peer groups.

Will alternative tests be designed to ensure that students with disabilities are able to demonstrate what they know?

Will students with disabilities be included in national testing, and will the results of their performance be aggregated with the results of nondisabled students?

9. *Restructuring:* Changing how education is delivered (changing the organization of schools, giving teachers more involvement in resource decisions, increasing parental involvement in education, shared decision-making, extended school calendar, etc.).

Will restructuring result in a weakening of administrative support for special education?

Will restructuring extend to state education agencies and cause deregulation or elimination of categorical financial aid for special education?

19th century (Hewett, 1974). The first special class was established in 1869 in Boston for deaf students and in 1896 in Chicago for blind students (Hewett, 1974).

Evolvement of the special class within public schools increased significantly with the inception of the intelligence test. The French Ministry of Education in 1904 commissioned Alfred Binet to develop a test for assessing the performance of children with particular attention to determining if low-functioning children should be placed in programs for students labeled "mentally deficient." Binet's work had a lasting effect on diagnosis, classification, and educational planning (Doll, 1962).

In the United States, Lewis Terman revised Binet's test in 1916 and standardized it on American children. This set the conditions for establishing special education programs for students with mental retardation and, more recently, students with learning disabilities. Although the nature and sophistication of assessment and diagnostic instruments changed and improved over time, Binet's early work has had considerable influence on adoption of the "diagnostic/prescriptive" paradigm that has guided special education for much of its history in the United States. This perception of how evaluation, classification, prescription, and intervention decisions should be made has prevailed even when changes were occurring in the way educational services were delivered.

For the first 65 years of special education in this country, the segregated special classroom was the dominant format for delivering special education services. Students typically were referred for testing to determine their eligibility, and if they met eligibility criteria set by the state, they were placed in a special class. Once placed, few special education students returned to the general education class on a full-time basis.

During this era, the principle of *normalization* emerged with reference to the care and treatment of individuals with mental retardation. Wolfensberger (1972) described the normalization principle as "utilization of means which are as culturally normative as possible, in order to establish and/or maintain personal behaviors and characteristics which are as culturally normative as possible" (p. 28). The principle of normalization significantly influenced the development of community-based services for people with mental retardation and generally caused people to think differently about the way special education services should be structured. It is the guiding principle behind the concept of *least restrictive environment* (LRE) and the practice of mainstreaming, both of which are premised on educational placements that are most "normal," given the learner's special educational needs.

Paralleling the emphasis on normalization in programs for individuals with mental retardation was the appearance of the resource room and itinerant services as instructional options for students with mild disabilities. Although the special classroom continued as an option, the emphasis for students with mild disabilities shifted to placement in general education classes with the option of receiving services from a resource or an itinerant teacher. Within this model, students were "pulled out" for part-time placement in resource rooms, or an itinerant teacher came to the general education classroom to provide remedial assistance to the student or to assist the classroom teacher.

Collectively, the normalization principle, as well as the resource and itinerant delivery models, set the stage for the more dramatic shift that began in the early 1970s and was central to the Education for All Handicapped Children Act of 1975, PL 94–142 (now Individuals with Disabilities Education Act). Mainstreaming—the integration of special education students with their nonhandicapped peers in social and educational settings—quickly became the goal of most school districts as state and federal regulations supporting the principles of mainstreaming came into being. The same legislation that created the conditions essential to mainstreaming also mandated educational opportunities for students who were judged to have severe and profound handicaps, although the segregated special classroom remained the preferred placement for these students.

By the mid-1980s special education no longer relied on segregated special classes to serve students with special needs. Although a variety of instructional options were employed, the focus on diagnosis, prescription, and intervention continued to be central to determining eligibility and making placement decisions. Thus, although special education practices had changed, the grounding assumptions of human pathology and organizational rationality were not questioned. At the same time, concerns were being expressed about the efficacy of PL 94–142 in achieving quality programs. The following statement by Reynolds, Wang, and Walberg (1987) reflects the nature of the criticism that was beginning to emerge and the discourse that was to follow:

> Unless major structural changes are made, the field of special education is destined to become more of a problem, and less of a solution, in providing education for children who have special needs. This is our conclusion following a broad review of research in special education. Our remarks refer to programs for "mildly" or "judgementally" handicapped children, more than three-fourths of the clients of special educators. (p. 391)

These challenges to PL 94–142 as a solution to the educational needs of students with disabilities helped shape the emerging views of the 1980s and 1990s. The legislative process of the 1970s was generally recognized to have established as public policy the principles that (a) all handicapped children should be served in the public schools; (b) testing should be nondiscriminatory; (c) related services were needed; and (d) individualized planning was necessary to ensure education appropriate to the needs of students with handicapping conditions. Many in the special education community, however, began to see that, despite these successes, students' needs were not being met, either by the special education system of in the general education program. This concern with the efficacy of the current approach raised questions about how best to assure a quality and equitable education for students with disabilities and spawned the current push for a more inclusive approach to special education programming.

The disenchantment of many special educators with the current approach to special education provided a basis for challenging current practices and policies and also spawned a number of proposals for reform. For example, Gartner and Lipsky (1987) characterized the current system as "inadequate because it is...not integrated" (p. 368) and recommended that "we must learn from our mistakes and attempt to create a new type of unitary system, one which incorporates quality education for all students" (p. 368). Their proposal for a new model of special education programming is premised on integrating virtually all students with disabilities into general education programs at the building level (see Chapters 15 and 18).

Reynolds et al. (1987) also called for major reforms in how students now served in special education should be educated in the future. Their proposal was based on the belief that the categories used in special education for students with mild handicaps are neither reliable nor valid as indicators of particular forms of education. Instead, they proposed "an initiative involving the joining of demonstrably effective practices from special, compensatory, and general education to establish a general education system that is more inclusive and that better serves all students, particularly those who require greater-than-usual educational support" (p. 394). To achieve the objectives of this model, the authors acknowledged that waivers from current state and federal categorical regulations may be necessary.

More recently, the Office of Special Education Programs of the U.S. Department of Education convened a group of special education professionals and advocates that produced a mission statement and action plan entitled *A National Agenda for Achieving Better Results for Children with Disabilities* (1993). Basic to this agenda are four purposes that, although they do not go as far as the inclusive special education models noted previously at least do recognize the need for reform and attempt to tie special education reform to the current reform movement in general education. The purposes are:

- To ensure that education of students with disabilities is fully included in overall educational reform, which has as its goal the improvement of educational outcomes for *all* students.
- To guide program and policy development activities relative to students with disabilities within the overall reform framework.
- To promote restructuring of schools to meet the needs of *all* students.
- To empower each child and youth with disabilities to become a caring, competent, contributing citizen in an integrated, changing, and diverse society.

What the 21st century holds for special education is speculative at best. The only certainty is that changes will take place. Special education clearly has demonstrated the capacity to change. What is encouraging about the current process of change in special education, compared to that of the past, is that general education also is changing. Thus, many of the proposed changes in special education call for parallel changes in general education, making widespread change more likely in how all students are educated. At a minimum, current reform efforts in special and general education hold the promise of reinforcing the principle that public education is ultimately responsible for the education of all students. Central to the challenge of reforming today's system of education is to question the traditional practice of referring students out of general education on the assumption that they are not the responsibility of general education but of some other educational entity. Instead, the emerging assumption is that excellence and equity can be achieved under a system that is committed to all students and that does not encourage alternatives that result in separate programs.

THE EMERGENT WORLD VIEW

The reform movements in education and special education in many ways reflect a larger development in society—a questioning of the basic beliefs that have shaped social practices for the past 200 years or so. Assumptions and beliefs about "what works" in society tend to take on a life of their own. They attract advocates, become institutionalized, and are resistant to change. Even though challenges to conventional thinking may emerge, they tend to be targeted at certain social practices. These challenges may alter some practices, but to a large extent they have little influence on underlying assumptions and basic beliefs. Although changes in specific practices seldom represent a clear break with the past, things are different today. Over the past 30 years, scholars in the social sciences and humanities have begun to realize that Western civilization is experiencing one of those rare instances in which basic beliefs actually do change, and they have begun to speculate on the nature of the new world view that is emerging.

THE EMERGENT PARADIGM OF THOUGHT AND BELIEF

A world view, or a paradigm, is a shared pattern of basic beliefs and assumptions about the nature of the world and how it works. These beliefs and assumptions tell us what is real and what is not; they provide us with a sense of collective identity and justify our actions. Thus, paradigms are both enabling and normative. They are enabling because they unrandomize the complexity of social life, permitting us to act in the world. At the same time, paradigms are normative; they guide our actions without requiring prolonged considerations of the nature of reality or the validity of knowledge. As Patton (1978) pointed out, this dual aspect of paradigms is what constitutes both their strength and their weakness—"their strength in that it makes action possible, their weakness in that the very reason for action is hidden in the unquestioned assumptions of the paradigm" (p. 203).

We rarely are conscious of the assumptions that underlie our world view because they are implicit; we take them for granted. Instead, paradigms and their underlying assumptions tend to surface mainly when they are changing. Western civilization is uncertain and uneasy just now because we are in the midst of a paradigm shift—a fundamental change in the beliefs that guide and justify what we do.

Until the 17th century Western civilization's world view was based on the Aristotelian model of organic growth, which collapsed under the weight of the new ideas of the Enlightenment. In essence, the revolutionary discoveries in science during the Enlightenment eventually replaced the Aristotelian paradigm of organic change with the Newtonian paradigm of mechanical change. The Newtonian paradigm gave us new models and metaphors for understanding the world: the acorn becoming an oak was replaced by billiard balls, clocks, and pendulums. Ultimately, the new way of understanding the world became part of our cultural, social, and political systems. It became embedded in our language, in the sciences, arts and humanities, and in what were to become the professions.

Although we tend to think of the massive change in world view associated with the Enlightenment as a one-time event, we are becoming more and more aware that such a pattern of change is underway again in the 20th century.

There is strong evidence that a number of the underpinnings of our basic beliefs are under challenge....from a multifaceted revolution of the sort that we have experienced only a few times in the course of our civilization's history: the revolution that began more than a century ago and has gathered momentum ever since involves as great a change as the Copernican revolution or the emergence of the Enlightenment. (Schwartz & Ogilvy, 1980, p. 2)

Schwartz and Ogilvy (1979, 1980) argued that the dimensions of the emergent world view are visible today in the revolutionary discoveries in the sciences and the humanities over the last 100 years. Through a systematic analysis of these manifestations in physics, chemistry, brain theory, ecology, evolution, mathematics, philosophy, politics, psychology, linguistics, religion, consciousness, and the arts, Schwartz and Ogilvy characterized the emergent world view according to the seven dimensions of change presented in Table 1.5.

The seven terms—complexity, heterarchy, holographic, indeterminacy, mutual causality, morphogenesis, and perspective—describe the major dimensions of the new world view that is emerging in Western civilization. Schwartz and Ogilvy argued that we will come to see the world, our place in it, and ourselves differently as these basic beliefs replace the older Newtonian ideas of simplicity, hierarchy, mechanical, determinancy, linear causality, assembly, and objectivity, which underwrite our current world view.

As significant as the recognition of a fundamental change in world view might be, there is even more here to cause Western civilization to feel uncertain and uneasy. Although we have experienced a change in world view before, the current change is more revolutionary because this time the patterns of change themselves have changed.

Neither the teleological interpretation of organic growth [the Aristotelian paradigm] nor the causal account of physical mechanism [the Newtonian paradigm] is adequate any longer. And we know it.

Further, we know that we know it. We know that we have accomplished a break from our previous paradigms. *We know that there are such things as paradigms* [emphasis added]. Before our era, most people didn't think of themselves as being caught within a paradigm. Having never consciously experienced a shift of paradigms, the very existence of paradigms could not be perceived. Now, however, not only do we appear to be on the edge of a new paradigm, but in addition, we know that there *are* paradigms. Precisely, *that* awareness is part of the new paradigm, that meta-leap to a self-reflective stance on all of one's thoughts, and how it is, finally, that thought thinks about itself. (Schwartz & Ogilvy, 1980, p. 6)

Thus, the key element in the emergent world view is an "appreciation of the importance of the stance or perspective of the knower or perceiver" (Schwartz & Ogilvy, 1980, p. 6). This "reflection on the reflector," or "meta-awareness," is unique because our current paradigm amounts to the view that there are no such things

● *TABLE I.5*

Changes in basic beliefs—conventional versus emergent paradigm

Conventional	Emergent	Explanatory Quotations
From	*Toward*	
Simple	Complex	1. *From simple to complex.* The task of most knowledge processes has been to reduce that which is studied to its simplest relationships. These are called fundamentals and basic laws.... We can no longer treat the actual word as simple;...diversity, interaction, and open systems are the nature of things. The world is composed of diverse things, all of which interact; and it is in principle impossible to separate a thing from its interactive environment. (pp. 10–12)
Hierarchy	Heterarchy	2. *From hierarchy to heterarchy.* The old conception of order was hierarchical; there exists a "pecking order," a chain of command, higher- and lower-order principles, and so on. The emergent order is heterarchical. There may be vertical orderings, but there are many on a comparable level; there is no one person, principle, or object at the top of everything. There may be peaks to these pyramids, and which one comes into play and its relationship to the others depend on the situation. (p. 13)
Mechanical	Holographic	3. *From mechanical to holographic.* The relationships among parts were once found in analogies to simple machines such as the lever.... A more useful metaphor may be the hologram. With the holographic metaphor come several important attributes. We find that the image in the hologram is created by a dynamic process of interaction and differentiation. We find that information is distributed throughout—that at each point information about the whole is contained in the part.... everything is interconnected..., having been generated by the same dynamic process and containing the whole in the part. (pp. 13–14)
Determinate	Indeterminate	4. *From determinate to indeterminate.* The success of the mechanistic description of the actual world gave a strong foundation to the argument for a deterministic view of the world.... Those simplistic notions were laid to rest by Heisenberg's Indeterminacy Principle, which tells us that (1) at a subatomic level the future state of a particle is in principle not predictable, and (2) the act of experimentation to find its state will itself determine the observed state. Qualitatively, the implication of this is that there are no causal linkages between past, present, and future; rather, in complex systems possibilities can be known but precise

Linearly Casual	Mutually Casual
Assembly	Morphogenesis
Objective	Perspective

outcomes cannot be predicted. It means that *ambiguity* about the future is the state of nature. (p. 14)

5. *From linear to mutual causality.* The indeterminacy in nature is mirrored in the evolution of causal models. The simplest causal model is linear; that is, a simple action always leads to the same predictable result. Thermodynamics introduced probabilities into causality.... Cybernetics gave us feedback, but with a concentration on negative feedback.... Such a system tends toward stability. The new paradigm adds positive feedback, which means that the feedback signal from B affects A in a fashion such that A tends to increase B. In the simplest and most negative form, that is called a vicious circle. When it is of mutual benefit for A and B, however, it is like symbiosis. Both A and B evolve and change together, each affecting the other in such a way as to make the distinction between cause and effect meaningless. (p. 14)

6. *From assembly toward morphogenesis.* Our old metaphor for change is that of a construction project. We have components being assembled according to a plan with a predictable outcome.... [But] if a system is complex...and...open to external inputs, then it can change morphogenetically. A new form, unpredicted by any of its parts, can arise in such a system.... Not just any form is possible. The components constrain, but they do not determine the exact form.... The requirements for morphogenesis are diversity, openness, complexity, mutual causality, and indeterminacy. When these conditions exist, we have the ingredients for qualitative change. (p. 14)

7. *From objectivity toward perspective.* Until this century, we were taught to believe that the way to know about the world was to stand outside it somehow and observe it objectively. We assumed that our mental processes, our experimental instruments, and our disciplines were neutral. But we've discovered that none of these are neutral to the world.... If objectivity is an illusion, is subjectivity the only alternative? We suggest that perspective is a more useful concept. Perspective connotes a view at a distance from a particular focus. Where we look from affects what we see. This means that any one focus or observation gives only a partial result; no single discipline ever gives a complete picture. (p. 15)

Source: Adapted from *The Emergent Paradigm: Changing Patterns of Thought and Belief* (Analytic Rep. No. 7, Values and Lifestyle Program) by P. Schwartz and J. Ogilvy (Menlo Park, CA: SRI International, 1980), p. 13. Quotations drawn from pp. 10–15, as compiled in Skrtic, Guba, and Knowlton (1985), pp. 7–10.

as paradigms. It asserts that we can discover objective truth about reality in the form of "facts" and that these facts will speak for themselves. In essence, the assumption is that seeing is believing. In contrast, the revolutionary discoveries in the sciences and understandings in the humanities are forcing us to begin to appreciate the proposition that what we believe—our current world view or paradigm—largely determines what we see.

Over the same 100-year period during which the Newtonian world view began to lose its relevance in the physical sciences, the social disciplines fought to gain recognition as genuine sciences by adopting the Newtonian world view that was falling out of favor. In effect, representatives of the developing social sciences claimed they could use the methods of the physical sciences, which were assumed to be a value-free means of producing "objective" knowledge about reality, to study and improve society. Indeed, the notion of value-free, objective empirical research applied to the problems of the social world lies at the heart of the liberal tradition in the social disciplines.

But the emergent world view—with its recognition of the importance of the perspective of the knower—is challenging this most basic assumption of the social sciences. Rather than a neutral, technical activity, science has been recognized as a form of interaction between an object of study and an observer who is conditioned to see the object in a certain way by his or her paradigm, world view, or frame of reference. As such, what is "observed" or "discovered" in the object is as much a product of this interaction as it is of the object itself. As Morgan (1983) noted, this means that knowledge is "a potentiality resting in an object of investigation" (p. 13), and science, rather than a process that yields objective knowledge, is a form of human engagement that is "concerned with the realization of potentialities—of possible knowledges" (p. 13).

The idea that science produces "possible knowledges" rather than "objective knowledge" has profound implications for the professions. This is so because the dominant model of professional knowledge conceptualizes all professional knowledge as being built upon a foundation of scientific knowledge, which is assumed to be value-free, objective knowledge about reality. The way the professions think about the world and themselves and, more important, they way they act toward their clients is shaped by their disciplinary foundation of scientific knowledge (see Skrtic, 1986).

The nature of professional knowledge and its relationship to scientific knowledge is discussed at length in Part Two. The key idea to grasp here is the significance of a new conceptualization of knowledge for the nature and validity of professional knowledge. For the field of special education, the logical implication is that its professional knowledge is only a particular type of knowledge based on a particular frame of reference. This means that current professional knowledge in special education is not inherently correct; it is not objective knowledge about reality (Skrtic, 1991a). Consistent with this view, the substance and format of this book address the implications of recognizing current special education knowledge as but one of a number of possible knowledges.

Summary

The situation in the field of special education today is similar to the effects of a paradigm shift on civilization and culture as a whole. Perhaps Berry (1978) said it best:

> It's all a question of story. We are in trouble just now because we do not have a good story. We are in between stories. The Old Story—the account of how the world came to be and how we fit into it—is not functioning properly, and we have not learned the New Story. The Old Story sustained us for a long period of time. It shaped our emotional attitudes, provided us with a life purpose, energized action. It consecrated suffering, integrated knowledge, guided education. We awoke in the morning and knew where we were. We could answer the questions of our children. We could identify crime, punish criminals. Everything was taken care of because the story was there. It did not make men good, it did not take away the pains and stupidities of life, or make for unfailing warmth in human association. But it did provide a context in which life could function in a meaningful manner. (cited in Schwartz & Ogilvy, 1980, p. 1)

Using Berry's analogy, special education is "between stories." There is the "old story"—special education's time-honored foundation of grounding beliefs and assumptions—and there is the "new story" which, at this point, is just being written. With a new story as a frame of reference, special education professionals will think and act differently in the future. Because the field of special education is between stories just now, however, people entering the field today will need to know the old story and be open to—and help write—the new story that will be written during their professional careers. Part One of this book is devoted to the old story, the time-honored beliefs and assumptions that underwrite special education's traditional and emerging perspectives. Part Two questions the old story and provides some intellectual resources to support the task of writing the new story.

Understanding what is occurring today in special education and placing this understanding in perspective requires a broad knowledge base. Merely understanding special education's traditional perspective and practices, or even the emerging conceptualizations of disability, assessment, and instructional programming associated with the inclusive education reform movement, is no longer sufficient. Nor is it enough to know the policies and regulations that govern special education, or even to be familiar with current research findings. Serious students of the field also must be concerned with educational reform more broadly, and ultimately with the nature and implications of a changing world view.

References

Berry, T. (1978, Winter). Comments on the origin, identification and transmission of values. *Anima*.

Doll, E. (1962). A historical survey of research and management of mental retardation in the United States. In E. P. Trapp & P. Himmelstein (Eds.), *Reading on the exceptional child: Research and theory* (pp. #). New York: Appleton-Century-Crofts.

Gartner, A., & Lipsky, D. K. (1987). Beyond special education: Towards a quality system for all students.

Harvard Educational Review, 57(4), 367–390.

Hewett, F. M., with Forness, S. R. (1974). *Education of exceptional learners.* Boston: Allyn and Bacon.

Kauffman, J. M., & Hallahan, D. P. (1993). Toward a comprehensive delivery system: The necessity of identity, focus, and authority for special education and other compensatory programs. In J. I. Goodlad & T. C. Lovitt (Eds.), *Integrating general and special education.* Columbus, OH: Charles E. Merrill.

Morgan, G. (Ed.). (1983). *Beyond method: Strategies for social research.* Beverly Hills, CA: Sage.

National Agenda for Achieving Better Results for Children with Disabilities. (1993). Forum Briefing Materials. Charlottesville, VA. Supported by the U.S. Department of Education.

National Commission on Excellence in Education. (1983). *A nation at risk: The imperative for educational reform.* Washington, DC: U.S. Government Printing Office.

National Council on Education Standards and Testing. (1992). *Raising standards for American education: A report to Congress, the Secretary of Education, the National Goals Panel, and the American people.* Washington, DC: U.S. Government Printing Office.

National Education Goals Panel. (1991). *The national education goals report: Building a nation of learners.* Washington, DC: Author.

Office of Technology Assessment. (1990). Competing in the new international economy. Washington, DC: U.S. Government Printing Office.

Patton, M. Q. (1978). *Utilization-focused evaluation.* Beverly Hills, CA: Sage.

Reynolds, M. C., Wang, M. C., & Walberg, H. J. (Eds.). (1987). The necessary restructuring of special and regular education. *Exceptional Children, 53*(5), 391–398.

Schwartz, P., & Ogilvy, J. (1979). *The emergent paradigm: Changing patterns of thought and belief* (Analytic Rep. No. 7, Values and Lifestyle Program). Menlo Park, CA: SRI International.

Schwartz, P., & Ogilvy, J. (1980, June). *The emergent paradigm: Toward an aesthetics of life.* Paper presented at ESOMAR Conference, Barcelona, Spain.

Secretary's Commission on Achieving Necessary Skills. (1991). *What work requires of schools: A SCANS report for America 2000.* Washington, DC: U.S. Department of Labor.

Skrtic, T. M. (1986). The crisis in special education knowledge: A perspective on perspective. *Focus on Exceptional Children, 18*(7), 1–16.

Skrtic, T. M. (1991a). *Behind special education: A critical analysis of professional culture and school organization.* Denver: Love Publishing.

Skrtic, T. M. (1991b). The special education paradox: Equity as the way to excellence. *Harvard Educational Review, 61*(2), 148–206.

Skrtic, T. M., Guba, E. G., & Knowlton, H. E. (1985). *Interorganizational special education programming in rural areas* (Technical report on the Multisite Nationalistic Field Study). Washington, DC: National Institution of Education.

Spady, W. G. (1988, October). Organizing for results: The basis of authentic restructuring and reform. *Educational Leadership*, pp. 4–8.

U.S. Department of Education. (1991). *America 2000: An education strategy.* Washington, DC: Author.

Wolfensberger, W. (1972). *Normalization: The principle of normalization in human services.* Toronto, Ontario, Canada: National Institute on Mental Retardation.

LEGISLATIVE AND

PROGRAMMATIC

FOUNDATIONS OF

SPECIAL EDUCATION

EDWARD L. MEYEN

*T*he late 1970s and early 1980s represent an era of change for students with disabilities and their families. During this time, students with disabilities who historically had been in special programs in the schools became fully participating members of regular classrooms. Even children whose disabilities were multiple and severe were included in the public schools. The term "handicapped" gave way to "disability" in an attempt to focus attention on the abilities of all individuals. Also, the unprecedented individualized education program (IEP) came into being. Parents took part in planning instruction for their children. For the first time, needed services were identified, detailed objectives were specified, and specific responsibilities of education to meet the needs of students with disabilities were designated. Finally, due process procedures were established to ensure that the rights of students with disabilities as well as their parents were clearly communicated and honored. Although these changes were designed to benefit students with disabilities, all of education benefited.

The school bureaucracy also changed during this time, as addressing the needs of exceptional children and youth through an administrative structure dedicated to special education only was no longer feasible. As a result, special and general educators came to share decisions concerning placement, service delivery, and resource allocation. Collaboration emerged as the professional approach to bringing about change through restructuring in the schools.

Also during this period, public policy regarding the education of students with disabilities was articulated, implemented, and challenged. Until the early 1970s, public policy evolved as a consequence of practice rather than purposeful development through the legislative process. Consequently, federal laws now require that a free and appropriate education be provided to all children of school age with disabilities. Many states have elected to extend that age range from birth to age 21. According to the *Fourteenth Annual Report to Congress*, prepared by the Office of Special Education and Rehabilitative Services, U.S. Department of Education (1992), 367,083 handicapped children 3–5 years old and 4,549,351 ages 3–21 were served in 1990–91.

Initiatives begun in the 1970s with passage of the Education for All Handicapped Children Act continue to shape public policy. For example, PL 99–457 in 1986 amended PL 94–142 to include early intervention programs for infants and toddlers with handicaps and their families. In 1990, the law was renamed the Individuals with Disabilities Education Act (IDEA, PL 101–476). Table 2.1 notes this legislation. In the same year, the Americans with Disabilities Act (ADA, PL 101–336), designed to end discrimination against persons with disabilities, was signed into law. Although not precisely an education act, as a standard of public policy, ADA complements the

35

● **TABLE 2.1**

Educational implications of major federal legislation on education of the handicapped

Law	Date Passed	Implications	Comments
PL 93–516	1974	Amended Section 504 of the Rehabilitation Act of 1973 to cover a broader array of services for handicapped children and adults. The nondiscrimination provisions of this law are almost identical to the nondiscrimination provisions related to race in Title VI of the Civil Rights Act of 1964 and to Title IX of the Education Amendments of 1972.	This is the first federal civil rights law to specifically protect the rights of children and adults with handicaps. Section 504 provides one basis for enforcing PL 94–142.
PL 93–380	1974	Extended and amended the Elementary and Secondary Act of 1965 to establish equal educational opportunity for all citizens as national policy. Section 613(A) set forth the due process procedures that became the basis for many of the provisions in PL 94–142.	This law likely will be considered an historical statement of public social policy.
PL 94–142	1975	The Education for All Handicapped Children Act is an amendment to PL 93–380. 1. It mandates a free and appropriate public education (FAPE) for all handicapped children and youth. Related services include speech pathology, audiology, psychological and counseling services, physical and occupational therapy, recreation, medical services (for diagnosis and evaluation only). 2. An individualized education program (IEP) must be developed (in conference with parents	This law sometimes is referred to as the "Bill of Rights for the Handicapped." Rules and regulations were published in the *Federal Register*, August 1977. Gifted children are not included in the definition of "handicapped," unless a gifted child also is handicapped. See Chapter 3 for a detailed discussion of the IEP.

Law	Date Passed	Implications	Comments
PL 94–142	1975	present) and maintained for each handicapped student. The law sets specific requirements on IEP content and the manner in which it is to be developed.	
		3. A special feature of PL 94–142 (and PL 93–380) is the principle of least restrictive environment (LRE), which states that, to the maximum extent appropriate, handicapped children, including children in public and private facilities, are to be educated with children without handicaps.	This revises the previous pattern of relaying solely on the segregated special class as the primary placement for most handicapped students.
		4. Due process procedures include requirements such as the following:	If due process procedures do not result in a program that is satisfactory to the parent or guardian, an impartial due process hearing must be provided as an option.
		a. Parents are allowed to examine all records pertaining to the school's examination of their child.	
		b. Parents may obtain evaluation from examiners independent of the school.	Parents also may exercise the option of pursuing civil action through the court judicial system after they have a due process hearing. Schools may require these hearings.
		c. Surrogate parents must be appointed if the child's parents or guardians are not known or available, or if the child is a ward of the state.	
		d. Notice in written form and the native language of the parent or guardian must be provided to the parent or guardian whenever the school proposes a change in identification, evaluation, or educational placement of the handicapped child.	
		e. A process must be provided whereby parents are able to present complaints on any matter relating to identification,	

Law	Date Passed	Implications	Comments
		evaluation, or educational placement of their child. f. Protection is afforded against the use of discriminatory tests.	
PL 98–199 Sec. 1419 and 1423	1983	This amendment to the Education of the Handicapped Act replaced the State Implementation Grants (SIGs) with the Early Childhood State Grant Program (from birth through age 5). The planning grants are of three types: (a) needs assessment, (b) plan development, and (c) implementation and evaluation of state plans.	In 1984, 23 grants for the planning stage were awarded, two for development and one for implementation. By 1983, many states had begun to serve children with disabilities 3–5 years of age. The group from birth through age 2 represents the population that is either not served or underserved.
Sec. 1402, 1424(a), and 142		The 1983 amendment also addressed the transition from school to adulthood, allowing for programs to be developed and disseminated for postsecondary education, delivery of transitional services, and creation of a national clearinghouse on postsecondary education for the handicapped.	
PL 99–457 Sec. 671, 673, 676, 680, and 682	1986	The bill amends the Education of the Handicapped Act by establishing new federal discretionary programs to assist states in developing and implementing a comprehensive, coordinated, interdisciplinary program of early intervention services for handicapped infants and toddlers and their families; strengthens incentives for states to serve all handicapped children aged 3–5; amends Part B evaluations; and amends and extends the authority for discretionary programs under Parts C through G.	Research supports the advantages of early intervention for infants and toddlers with disabilities. These amendments represent a significant change from the authorizations in the 1983 amendment in terms of services to young children with disabilities.

Law	Date Passed	Implications	Comments
PL 101–476	1990	Amends the Education of the Handicapped Act and renames it the Individuals with Disabilities Education Act (IDEA). The act revises and extends parts C through G of EHA. It continues the provisions of funds to state and local education agencies that comply with conditions of the law. It also clarifies several definitions, particularly with reference to who is entitled to benefits as a results of the law. Specific attention is directed to students with autism, traumatic brain injury, and those who are deaf-blind. The reference to underrepresented groups is broadened. Attention also is given to requirements in the language in describing transitional services and applying assistive technological devices and services. The involvement of parents is clarified and strengthened.	Changing the name to replace "handicapped" with "disability" represents a major change. It reflects progress in achieving more acceptable terminology. The law basically establishes a zero-reject model. By broadening the definition of underrepresentation, the law provides improved conditions for ensuring that students with disabilities from minority groups receive an appropriate education. Attention to transitional programs will encourage greater community participation by persons with disabilities. Attention deficit disorder (ADD) is not included, but the Department of Education is required to solicit public comment on the need to provide special education to students with ADD.

evolution of education policy pertaining to individuals with disabilities.

Current public policies on the education of children with disabilities are based in federal and state legislation. Over a 30-year span, public policy has evolved from statements of intent, leaving to the discretion of the schools whether children with disabilities would be served, to mandates requiring provision of services and also the nature of services to be provided, as well as the protection of due process.

The evolving public policy for individuals with disabilities has benefited greatly from the experience of policymakers in the area of civil rights and the legislative precedents to prevent discrimination. These new public policies are intended to assure equal rights for persons with disabilities. The true meaning of "equal rights," however, is still evolving, as courts try cases and agencies put into practice their interpretation of what they perceive those rights to be.

A sophisticated advocacy movement for people with disabilities has also evolved. No longer are advocacy organizations loose networks of parent groups. Instead, they are organizations with broad constituencies that have gained credibility among legislators as a consequence of their long-term investment in learning how to use the legislative process. Their power rests on the advocacy resources they provide legislators in positions of political influence.

This advocacy base recently has been strengthened further by the presence of those with disabilities, who increasingly are becoming self-advocates. The emergence of adults and youth with disabilities as an advocacy force was a major influence in passing ADA, for example. Without the precedent of the civil rights movement and the 30-year history of advocacy for individuals with disabilities, the Americans with Disabilities Act would not have passed in 1990.

Given these legislative achievements, one would assume that all is well with the education of exceptional children and youth. Unquestionably, the quality of life for people with disabilities is better than it was in the 1970s. Efforts continue to develop effective instructional interventions and nondiscriminatory assessment methodologies and to implement programs to serve the 0–5 age group. When the programs of the mid-1980s are compared to the legislative intent of the mid-1970s, however, there is little evidence that the latter has been fully achieved.

With the addition of the Americans with Disabilities Act as a public policy, the conditions are set to eliminate practices in all aspects of life that have discriminated against persons with disabilities. As has been true with each new law, however, it takes time for the specifics to become routine practice. The law will be challenged in public debates, but over time the courts will assure implementation and progress toward uniform interpretation.

A PERSPECTIVE ON TERMINOLOGY

Special educators established a professional language that is useful for communicating among the disciplines that collectively study and serve exceptional children and youth. As advocacy groups began to develop public policy, however, our language fell short. Scientific and historical terms took on social meaning (see Chapter 16), and advocates became more assertive in calling for socially acceptable and respectful references to people with disabilities. As a result, professionals and the public have become more sensitive to their written and spoken language.

Terms such as "atypical," "special needs," "special students," "exceptional," "handicapped," "disabled," and, more recently, "challenged" have been advanced. Each label had its merits, depending on one's perspective of its value as a descriptor. Attempts to come up with terms devoid of negative meaning continue to be hampered by the limitations of our language. The search for an acceptable language has meant replacing certain terms with others that more adequately reflect the times. The public—particularly those who make policy—must be comfortable with the labels we use, especially if we are to gain public support for the policies they develop. Only recently, however, has attention been given to the impact of these labels on the individuals they designate.

"EXCEPTIONAL" VERSUS "HANDICAPPED"

To achieve essentially the same meaning, the terminology of today includes "exceptional children," used in education, and "handicapped," used frequently by the federal government, but which is in the process of changing to "disabled." Advocates who want to emphasize persons as individuals rather than focusing on their limitations are successfully beginning to shift the public emphasis to "persons with disabilities" or the "challenged."

Use of the term "exceptional" is not recent. For example, it appeared in the name of the International Council for the Education of Exceptional Children (now the Council for Exceptional Children), founded in 1922. In his *Introduction to Exceptional Children*, Baker (1953) stated that "exceptional" is more inclusive than "handicapped" as it covers children at the extremes of various scales of mental ability (p. 12). It includes the gifted and people with mental retardation, whereas the term "handicapped" excludes the gifted.

This differentiating between the two primary terms ("exceptional" and "handicapped") continues today. The general public tends to interpret "exceptional" as applicable only to the gifted, resulting in some confusion outside the field. Some professionals, too, question "exceptional" as a label for individuals with mental retardation.

"HANDICAP" VERSUS "DISABILITY"

"Handicap" and "disability" also are differentiated. *Disability* refers to a condition, such as loss of a limb, whereas *handicap* describes the consequences of the disability. People are handicapped because of their disability. If a disability does not hamper a person in daily life, the current preference would be not to refer to the person as having a handicap.

The term "handicapped" was used in federal legislation (e.g., the Education for All Handicapped Children Act). Although variations exist, states tend to use terms that are compatible with federal legislation. For this reason, through the 1980s most public policies at the state level mirrored the language of the federal government, using "handicap" as the standard of policy language. With passage of IDEA in 1990, the federal government substituted "disability" for "handicap."[1]

---

[1] Because this book is a primary reference in special education, we are obligated to use the terms "exceptional," "handicapped," and "disabled" in their appropriate context. As a general practice, however, we would rather use "with a disability" or "exceptional" than describe a person as "disabled" or "handicapped." Some groups advocate the term "challenged" to further avoid sounding pejorative. We, too, are concerned with the way society views people with disabilities and, therefore, recommend cautious use of labels in communicating about individuals with disabilities.

Labels only serve our need to communicate. They do not reflect some absolute truth. Yet, the way professionals define labels may perpetuate their meaning. Definitions must serve the needs of exceptional individuals, but we must recognize that the definitions themselves are social creations, and therefore subject to variance as knowledge increases and circumstances change.

THE ELIGIBILITY DILEMMA: A MATTER OF DEFINITION

Deciding who is exceptional, and who is not, or who does or does not have a disability poses a major dilemma. Before special programs were available, students with disabilities were described by their characteristics and by the instructional challenges they presented. When education agencies began to respond to the needs of each emerging group of students, services were established and eligibility criteria determined. From that point on, a child was identified (for school purposes) as "exceptional" if he or she met the eligibility criteria for a given program or service. This process was repeated as each new group was presented—for example, the learning disabled during the 1960s, the severely/profoundly handicapped during the 1970s, and, more recently, infants and toddlers with disabilities. Children with attention deficit disorder may be the new group in the 1990s.

Obviously, instruction must relate to learners' characteristics, but the question is: How does one characterize children with special needs for purposes of instruction? The tendency has been to have a rigid interpretation of eligibility criteria, causing educators to be concerned primarily with the limitations of the student with special needs. Recently this tendency has been challenged. Instead of developing definitions based on ideology or personal attributes, educators prefer to focus on the consequences of disabilities and their implications for learning.

Even as educators are moving away from reliance on definitions, definitions continue to be essential for educational placement and access to certain instructional activities. This need for definitions is logically explained as: (a) definitions differentiate among learners; and (b) definitions communicate among personnel. Both explanations are necessary in providing services, and on the surface they are defensible. One must identify students who require differentiated instruction, and participants in educational programs must understand the terminology. Little is gained, however, if definitions and criteria do not ultimately lead to improved instruction. This is especially true for exceptional children.

In an attempt to more precisely match interventions with students' needs while minimizing reliance on definitions, a compromise was reached. Schools used definitions to determine eligibility; states used definitions to approve programs and placement. Typically, a general definition of exceptional children was stated, accompanied by more specific definitions for each area of exceptionality. Schools, however, were allowed flexibility in the descriptions applied to programs serving groups of students with similar attributes.

Eligibility criteria obviously are necessary when attached to the provision of programs for specific groups of students for which additional financial support is required. Because they affect the allocation of financial aid, definitions are couched in the context of federal law or state regulations and, thus, greatly influence users. For example, if educators read in a state regulation that a child with an IQ below 50 is "moderately mentally retarded," they may adhere too strictly to that requirement when making placement decisions. (During the 1950s and 1960s, many state regulations were that specific.)

Establishing eligibility criteria as a basis for supplemental financial aid to districts significantly impacts public school services to exceptional children and decisions on whether to serve certain children. For instance, a state can reduce the need for funds by making criteria more restrictive; in time, taking this step makes fewer children eligible for special services and, hence fewer funds are needed.

THE NEGATIVE EFFECTS OF LABELS

Using definitions as the basis for eligibility has, in the judgment of many professionals, negatively influenced the development of educational programs for exceptional children. At least three examples can be cited.

First, definitions enabled teachers to refer exceptional children out of the regular classroom more readily if they found them too difficult to teach. Aimed at getting the exceptional child out of the regular class, the referral process often resulted in the child's being excluded from school.

Second, definitions emphasized limitations rather than strengths: low intelligence, inability to hear or see, physical disabilities, or generally unacceptable social behavior. The children were classified according to what they could not do instead of considering ways to develop their capabilities. Even though a given label may have made the child eligible for a specific service, it carried with it a stigma that frequently influenced the child far beyond the educational program by causing others to view the child differently.

The self-fulfilling prophecy, "exceptional children are expected to perform according to their label," was described by Rosenthal and Jacobson (1968). Although their work was criticized for methodological shortcomings, those authors offered the theory that teachers can influence a student's performance by the way they interpret the label applied to the student. If the information shared with a teacher focuses on the child's limitations, the teacher may expect the child to perform less well and, in turn, the student may perform at the level of expectations.

Traditionally, students with disabilities were tested and teachers were presented with detailed negative data on the children's performance. One might reasonably assume that teachers' expectations are influenced greatly by the information presented to them and by their experience in working with the child. To date, the research in this area is inconclusive. The key factor is how flexible the teacher is. Can a teacher's expectations of a student's performance change following interaction with the student?

Third, student performance historically has been associated with definition. If a child is classified as "exceptional," he or she will remain not only exceptional but always in need of special education services. Treatment of students identified as educable mentally retarded prior to the 1970s is a good example. Once so identified, these children generally were placed in special classes and rarely returned to the regular classes. Their placement became permanent, as did the label. Many believe the emphasis on definitions and labels is the primary contributor to the permanency of educational placement.

THE BENEFITS OF LABELS

Using labels to define eligibility criteria offers some benefits, but because labels are of a general nature, the individuals so labeled do not always directly experience them. For example, establishing specific programs based on labels allowed such programs to grow. Further, the categorical approach (the development of educational programs for children identified as having similar handicapping conditions) allowed special-interest groups to be specific in promoting their programs, thereby facilitating legislative efforts. In this way, exceptional children gained visibility within the broader context of general education. Although teachers' perceptions often were inappropriate, separate programs based on assumed needs and defined characteristics contributed to the evolvement of special education and the development of many specialized instructional practices. Later approaches referred to as "noncategorical" emerged. These programs largely ignored students' specific handicapping conditions, focusing instead on educational needs that students may have in common.

Thus, despite current restructuring in education, as well as philosophical changes, the categorical approach, whose popularity is declining, deserves some credit for attracting policymakers' attention to the educational needs of students with disabilities. Greater social responsibility for people with disabilities is largely a result of categorical approaches as well as the social climate created by the civil rights movement. A public policy evolved, setting the stage for special education for all exceptional children.

CONTINUING CHALLENGES

In spite of progress, major issues in defining exceptional children and youth remain:

1. Characteristics of exceptional individuals are not always present at birth. They may appear at any time, making identification difficult. Further, characteristics often overlap. Even among those with the same characteristics, then, instructional needs vary.
2. Like all students, exceptional children change, and their educational needs change accordingly. Not all disabilities are permanent. This state of flux complicates the use of definitions.

3. Cultural differences cloud the identification/eligibility issue. Some students, for cultural reasons, respond differently in testing and instructional situations. Progress is being made in developing nondiscriminatory assessment instruments and instructional resources that accommodate cultural differences.

EXAMPLES OF DEFINITIONS

Today, individual differences are accommodated more effectively in regular classes, and we no longer need to remind society of its educational obligations to all children. Access to due process and legislation prohibiting discrimination, however, are recent, and practices that have the effect of discrimination persist. Consequently, we must continue to focus the attention of educators and the general public on children and youth for whom education, as typically provided, is still inappropriate. Further, we must continue to define populations of students who, because of their disabilities or their unusual abilities or talents, require accommodation in education.

Several examples of contemporary definitions are offered. For example, consider the term "exceptional":

> The term "exceptional" refers to physical, social, and intellectual uniqueness; the term "learners" refers to individuals who are waiting to be taught; and the term "special education" refers to adaptations of typical teaching approaches made to accommodate the uniqueness of the exceptional learner. (Hewett & Forness, 1984, p. 5)

> School personnel use the term "exceptional" to refer to students whom they consider to be abnormal. Students are exceptional who differ either positively or negatively from normal students. Students may be considered abnormal statistically, medically, or socially. Typically, exceptional students are classified or categorized and grouped for instructional purposes. (Ysseldyke & Algozzine, 1984, p. 13)

> The term "exceptional" is much more comprehensive than "handicapped" and refers to any individual whose physical or behavioral performance deviates so substantially from the norm, either higher or lower, that additional educational and other services may be necessary to meet the individual's needs. An exceptional person is not necessarily a handicapped person. (Hardman, Drew, & Egan, 1984, p. 23)

> The term "exceptional" is a label for those with disabilities and impairments, as well as for the gifted and talented.... "Normal" and "exceptional" are relative terms. Like all labels, they tell us little about the individuals involved.... The exceptional population includes people of all ages. Special education is not limited to what is traditionally thought of as the school-age population. For normal people learning is a lifelong activity that begins at birth and continues through adulthood. The same is true for the exceptional population. Many exceptional individuals need special educational services from infancy through adulthood to enable them to learn from and adapt to their environments. (Haring & McCormick, 1986, pp. 1, 2)

Two decades have passed since passage of PL 94–142. In the past, safeguards had to be established at the program level to prevent practices such as overrepresenting minority children in special education programs, using culturally based assessment instruments, and excessively referring children for special education placement. Today, regulations exist to minimize (if not control) the probability that these practices will occur. As a result, definitions now can be more general, as long as they are couched in the context of specific rules and regulations that place boundaries on the decisions of educators and other human service providers.

The current law, IDEA, includes within its definition of children with disabilities those who are mentally retarded, hard of hearing, deaf, speech or language impaired or other health-impaired, autistic, deaf-blind, multihandicapped, or those with specific learning disabilities or traumatic brain injury. To be eligible for services under IDEA, a child must need special education or related services because of one or more of these disabilities. This law defines each disability from the perspective of eligibility for special education or related services.

In the years preceding PL 94–142, attempts were made to define students eligible for special education services to ensure that *only* students requiring special education services received them. Expressing concern about overreferral and inappropriate placement, Dunn (1963), in an attempt to bring about change in the 1960s, defined exceptional children as those:

> (1) who differ from the average to such a degree in physical or psychological characteristics, (2) that school programs designed for the majority of children do not afford opportunity for all-around adjustment and optimum progress, (3) and who therefore need either special instruction or, in some cases, special ancillary services, or both, to achieve at a level commensurate with their respective abilities. (p. 3)

In the second edition of his book (just prior to passage of PL 94–142 in 1975), Dunn (1973) offered a more restrictive definition:

> An exceptional pupil is so labeled only for that segment of his school career (1) when his deviating physical or behavioral characteristics are of such a nature as to manifest a significant learning asset or disability for special education purposes and, therefore, (2) when, through trial provisions, it has been determined that he can make greater all-around adjustment and scholastic progress with direct or indirect special education services than he could with only a typical regular school program. (p. 7)

A marked improvement over the first definition, the second contributed significantly to the literature. It is a conservative definition, introducing the concept of "trial placement" as a condition of determining exceptionality and calling for close monitoring of the exceptional child's program. Dunn's definition recognizes a direct relationship between the child labeled exceptional and the superiority of the special education services over regular class placement alone. In addition, it addresses the schools' responsibility to students identified as exceptional, not only in the identification process but also after placement.

Through regulations to implement the Education for All Handicapped Children Act and the Individuals with Disabilities Education Act, the U.S. Department of Education set forth specific definitions for groups considered to be handicapped within the context of the law. The primary change in IDEA with regard to students served involves those with autism and traumatic brain injury. The terms were removed from the definition for "seriously emotionally disturbed" and now are included in the definition for "other health impaired."

As mentioned, changes in definitions influence the eligibility criteria for special education services established for state education agencies. As disabling conditions evolve, the question is raised as to which new groups should be covered by public policy pertaining to the education of children with disabilities. For example, IDEA covers children with AIDS. Turnbull (1993) reported that, "People with AIDS are considered to be disabled under Section 504 and may be considered disabled under IDEA if the disability causes them to need special education or related services" (p. 63).

The following EHA definitions continue to be used:

(a) As used in this part, the term "handicapped children" means those children evaluated in accordance with Regs. 300.530–.534 as being mentally retarded, hard of hearing, deaf, speech impaired, visually handicapped, seriously emotionally disturbed, orthopedically impaired, other health impaired, deaf-blind, multihandicapped, or as having specific learning disabilities, who because of those impairments need special education and related services.

(b) The terms used in this definition are defined as follows:

(1) "Deaf" means a hearing impairment which is so severe that the child is impaired in processing linguistic information through hearing, with or without amplification, which adversely affects educational performance.

(2) "Deaf-blind" means concomitant hearing and visual impairments, the combination of which causes such severe communication and other developmental and educational problems that they cannot be accommodated in special education programs solely for deaf or blind children.

(3) "Hard of hearing" means a hearing impairment, whether permanent or fluctuating, which adversely affects a child's educational performance but which is not included under the definition of "deaf" in this section.

(4) "Mentally retarded" means significantly subaverage general intellectual functioning existing concurrently with deficits in adaptive behavior and manifested during the developmental period, which adversely affects a child's educational performance.

(5) "Multihandicapped" means concomitant impairments (such as mentally retarded-blind, mentally retarded-orthopedically impaired, etc.), the combination of which causes such severe educational problems that they cannot be accommodated in special education programs solely for one of the impairments. The term does not include deaf-blind children.

(6) "Orthopedically impaired" means a severe orthopedic impairment which adversely affects a child's educational performance. The term includes impairments caused by congenital anomaly (e.g., clubfoot, absence of some member, etc.), impairments caused by disease (e.g., poliomyelitis, bone tuberculosis, etc.), and impairments from other causes (e.g., cerebral palsy, amputations, and fractures or burns which cause contractures).

(7) "Other health impaired" means

(i) having an autistic condition, which is manifested by severe communication and other developmental and educational problems; or

(ii) having limited strength, vitality, or alertness, due to chronic or acute health problems such as a heart condition, tuberculosis, rheumatic fever, nephritis, asthma, sickle cell anemia, hemophilia, epilepsy, lead poisoning, leukemia, or diabetes, which adversely affect a child's educational performance.

(8) "Seriously emotionally disturbed" is defined as follows:

(i) The term means a condition exhibiting one or more of the following characteristics over a long period of time and to a marked degree, which adversely affects educational performance:

(A) an inability to learn which cannot be explained by intellectual, sensory, or health factors;

(B) an inability to build or maintain satisfactory interpersonal relationships with peers and teachers;

(C) inappropriate types of behavior or feelings under normal circumstances;

(D) a general pervasive mood of unhappiness or depression; or

(E) a tendency to develop physical symptoms or fears associated with personal or school problems.

(ii) The term includes children who are schizophrenic. The term does not include children who are socially maladjusted, unless it is determined that they are seriously emotionally disturbed.

(9) "Specific learning disability" means a disorder in one or more of the basic psychological processes involved in understanding or in using language, spoken or written, which may manifest itself in an imperfect ability to listen, think, speak, read, write, spell, or to do mathematical calculations. The term includes such conditions as perceptual handicaps, brain injury, minimal brain dysfunction, dyslexia, and development aphasia. The term does not include children who have learning problems which are primarily the result of visual, hearing, or motor handicaps, of mental retardation, of emotional disturbance, or of environmental, cultural, or economic disadvantage.

(10) "Speech impaired" means a communication disorder such as stuttering, impaired articulation, a language impairment, or a voice impairment, which adversely affects a child's educational performance.

(11) "Visually handicapped" means a visual impairment which, even with correction, adversely affects a child's educational performance. The term includes both partially seeing and blind children.

Under separate legislation (the Gifted and Talented Children's Education Act of 1978), Congress defined gifted and talented children as follows:

"Gifted and talented children" means children, and whenever applicable, youth, who are identified at the preschool, elementary, or secondary level as possessing demonstrated or potential abilities that give evidence of high performance capability in areas such as intellectual, creative, specific academic, or leadership ability, or in the performing and visual arts, and who by reason thereof, require services or activities not ordinarily provided by the school. (Sec. 902)

IMPLICATIONS OF CLASSIFICATION

Labeling children who demonstrate similar behavioral, learning, or physical character-istics has been debated throughout the history of special education. The rationale behind labeling is the need to group children with similar instructional needs for purposes of teaching. Until the 1970s, however, the overriding concern was to make visible the unique needs of students with various handicapping conditions. Before that time, no effective coalition had advocated for the needs of exceptional or handicapped children as a total group. Instead, each area of disability had its own constituency and advocacy base.

State legislation during the 1960s and 1970s allowed (and in some cases, mandat-ed) children with disabilities to receive special education services. Although more programs for children with disabilities were being developed, few qualitative gains were being achieved. For the most part, the program needs were the same; that is, instructional interventions were insufficient, assessment practices lacked precision, many students were not being served or were underserved, and related services often were not available. A later focus on the needs of *all* handicapped children, rather than on those from separate categorical groups, made reforms in educational practices and public policy achievable.

These advances in public policy were possible largely because of the earlier classification approach. Classifying children by disability provided a structure for establishing financial aid programs and a basis for certifying teachers. In addition, it attracted the interest of commercial producers of instructional materials and, to a certain extent, stimulated a stronger interest among researchers in the disabled popula-tion.

To weigh the above benefits of classification against the negative aspects of labeling is difficult. Being identified as mentally retarded and placed in a special education class affects a child's self-concept and self-image—the way the child is perceived by peers. Further, the process is suspected of affecting the child's achieve-ment in school, although research on the subject is equivocal.

Among others, MacMillan, Keogh, and Jones (1986) reviewed the literature on the effects of placement on self-concept, specifically, the results of placing students with mild mental retardation in self-contained classes and in regular classrooms. These students seemed to profit from the protection of the special class. Because none of the studies in the review reported better self-concept among the educable mentally re-tarded (mildly mentally retarded) students in regular classes, the authors suggested that placement with a peer group permits favorable self-comparisons and, therefore, en-hances self-concept. MacMillan, Jones, and Aloia (1974) stated that "the [reason for the] low self-concept of EMR pupils in special classes is...that children are labeled 'mentally retarded' prior to being placed, and may incorporate these negative evalua-tions in their self-perceptions" (p. 701).

To empirically substantiate the negative impact of labeling on a handicapped child is difficult. Nevertheless, widespread concern about the social implications is reflected in the professional literature and in the activities of advocacy groups alike.

Writing in *Issues in the Classification of Children*, Goldstein et al. (1975) placed the issue in perspective:

> The classification of handicapped children for educational purposes has always been a controversial matter among educators. Recently, however, the parents of handicapped children, national and state associations of parents, and social scientists have extended the controversy—even to the point of involving the courts in efforts to arrive at actions that will be most equitable for handicapped children in public education.

> Essentially, the controversy over classification as a decision point in public education centers on the following questions: (1) Are the schools justified in using classification systems to deny some children access to education? (2) Are systems of classification so porous that misclassification is as possible as classification, with the result that some children are assigned to educational settings inconsistent with their inherent capabilities and thus are denied an appropriate education? (3) Are classification criteria so flexible that available educational settings can be used as repositories for children, irrespective of the child's needs? (4) Are classification systems substituted for the real descriptors of children's characteristics to the extent that teachers and administrators are responding to labels rather than data as they portray children's educational needs?

> The traditional points of departure for classifying handicapped children in education are in regard to their sensory, intellectual, physical, and behavioral status and, more recently, combinations of these. Obviously, these categories are too gross to be of any real service as indices to educational intervention today. Nevertheless, one by one they took shape over the 200 years or so that formal education has been operative in Europe and the United States. (pp. 4–6)

> Although some might agree that present systems for classifying handicapped children in the public schools have some value to administration in that they provide pegs upon which funding and management procedures can be hung, their value to the educational enterprises is less pronounced. Their limited relationship to teaching/learning activities, along with their ambiguities, makes possible educational practices that are unproductive and frequently unjust. To put it another way, they give minimum direction in decision making about day-to-day instructional needs of children; at the same time, they permit children who require interventions other than those typical of special education to be sidetracked into these classes. Moreover, they often are inaccurate and can be distracting and misleading to some teachers. (p. 55)

Goldstein and his colleagues recommended that labels and classification systems be abandoned in favor of more precise descriptions of individual children, as these would have implications for classroom interaction. If implemented, the recommendation could result in developing another classification system, which would be used for educational decisions and would reduce any negative impact of labeling and classification on the individual.

Also reporting on definitional issues, the Council for Exceptional Children (1977) stated that, regardless of the classification system used, definitions must be based on criteria designed to facilitate identification, evaluation, and educational programming and placement. This position seems compatible with that of Goldstein et al. and also is consistent with PL 94–142 and IDEA requirements regarding identification, due process, and the individualized education program (IEP).

Despite progress, the definition/classification issue persists. Addressing this dilemma requires implementation of a continuum of educational and service alternatives; individualization of instruction; and elimination of the dichotomy between serving exceptional and serving nonexceptional students. As long as the government must reimburse or supplement local districts' costs, however, eligibility criteria will continue to exert undue influence on educational decisions. Only when districts are able to offer a full array of instructional service options and are free to match those options with learner needs without regard for why the learner has such needs, and whether he or she is exceptional, can the assumed stigma of labels be minimized and the value derived from decisions based on learner-specific information maximized.

The schools continue to be the primary agencies placing labels on children. Although criticizing the schools is easy, the issue goes far beyond that. All agencies, and, to a certain extent, all people, engage in labeling. In discussing bias and classification, Turnbull (1986) stated:

> Consider the disabled person. The characteristic of the person on which intervention usually is predicated is "disabled," not "person." Disabled people are seen to be qualitatively different in this important and debilitating sense: They are "deviant." For example, the retarded newborn is commonly called a "defective child." (p. 85)

As Turnbull pointed out, the emphasis is on the individual's disability or limitations rather than his or her capabilities. If, on the other hand, the emphasis were on ability to learn and individual learning style, negative labels might disappear or be replaced by designations that affirmatively approach teaching and learning.

Often the potentially negative effects associated with labeling are compounded by overidentification or mislabeling. When this occurs, students are identified as eligible for and receive special education or related services when in reality they do not meet the requirements. If labeling a child results in a negative impact, mislabeling is particularly serious (see Chapter 16). Prior to the emphasis on developing nondiscriminating tests and the use of multiple criteria, students from minority groups commonly were misidentified, often leading to a disproportionate number of minority students in programs for the mildly disabled.

PL 94–142 and, more recently, IDEA have addressed nondiscriminating testing and evaluation. As states have become more specific in prescribing procedures for preventing discrimination through testing and placement practices, researchers and instructional developers have had more success in creating assessment instruments and instructional resources that more accurately measure student performance. As a result, the probability of mislabeling is lower. Sec 300. 532 of IDEA states:

(a) Tests and other evaluation materials
   (1) Are provided and administered in the child's native language or other mode of communication, unless it is clearly not feasible to do so;
   (2) Have been validated for the specific purpose for which they are used;
   (3) Are administered by trained personnel in conformance with instructions from the producer;

(b) Tests and other evaluation materials include those tailored to access specific areas of educational need and not merely those which are designed to provide a single general intelligence quotient;

(c) Tests are selected and administered so as best to insure that when a test is administered to a child with impaired sensory, manual, or speaking skills, the test results accurately reflect the child's aptitude or achievement level or whatever other factor the test purports to measure, rather than reflecting the child's impaired sensory, manual, or speaking skills (except where those skills are the factors which the test purports to measure);

(d) No single procedure is used as the sole criterion for determining an appropriate educational program for a child and placement;

(e) The evaluation is made by a multidisciplinary team or group of persons, including at least one teacher or other specialist with knowledge in the area of suspected disability;

(f) The child is assessed in all areas related to the suspected disability, including, where appropriate, health, vision, hearing, social and emotional status, general intelligence, academic performance, communicative status, and motor abilities.

PREVALENCE OF EXCEPTIONAL CHILDREN AND YOUTH

The terms "prevalence" and "incidence" have different meanings; yet, unfortunately, they often are used interchangeably. Simply stated, prevalence refers to the current number of exceptional children, whereas incidence refers to the number of children who, at some time in their life, might be considered exceptional. Of the two, the latter figure obviously is much higher and much more difficult to substantiate.

States are required to report annually the prevalence of children (by handicapping condition) receiving special education services so the Office of Special Education and Rehabilitative Services (OSERS) can monitor the impact of PL 94–142 and PL 101–476. The figures are conservative because, as defined, prevalence refers only to students currently receiving special education services. Further, evidence suggests that some students with handicapping conditions are not being served (Skrtic, Guba, & Knowlton, 1985). In addition, the data do not include infants and toddlers with disabilities, who are served in some states.

ANNUAL REPORTING

Even though annual reporting enhances accountability, it contributes to practices such as overplacement. In the 1950s and 1960s, significant numbers of students who had learning problems but were not handicapped, particularly children from minority groups, were placed in special education programs. This occurred largely because teachers were inclined to refer failing students out of their classrooms, and special education programs were inclined to respond to their needs. Also, because state funding was based largely on the numbers of children served and personnel costs, the school district received more aid if it had more students.

Today, state and federal eligibility regulations are more restrictive. In addition, diagnostic procedures and conditions in regular education have improved, and educators are increasingly recognizing what may happen if a student is placed inappropriately in a special education program. Therefore, more school districts are taking a methodical and conservative approach to identifying students with handicapping conditions.

Another factor contributing to this trend is the cost of providing special education, which far exceeds the cost of educating students without handicaps, especially because of the necessarily low pupil-teacher ratio. Because state and federal financial aid seldom is sufficient to cover the excess, local education agencies (LEAs) must cover the difference. Some evidence suggests that, to control costs, some districts restrict special education services, particularly if costs are high.

According to state and federal reporting procedures, a child with more than one disability can be reported only once, which keeps the prevalence rates lower. Some school administrators believe this is unduly restrictive. For example, if a child needs the services of both a resource room teacher and a speech and language pathologist, the costs rise accordingly. Thus, they argue, the child should be counted twice. The situation is particularly acute for severely/profoundly handicapped children, who generally need several types of services.

Until recently, most figures were derived from needs-assessment studies conducted in specific geographic areas. Therefore, generalization must be viewed carefully. For example, more children are identified as having mild mental retardation when unfavorable socioeconomic conditions prevail. Similarly, an outbreak of rubella in one part of the country likely would increase the number of children with hearing problems in that area, compared to an unaffected area of similar size.

PREVALENCE SHIFTS AND NATIONAL VARIATIONS

Even the quality and level of special education services can influence the number of exceptional children enrolled. Several years ago I was employed in a state education agency in the Midwest. In one community, far more children were placed in programs for trainable mentally retarded (TMR) children than would be expected based on known estimates. The reason for the inflated numbers related to the community's long history of operating comprehensive TMR services and the ability to attract families seeking these programs.

OSERS reported 4,370,244 handicapped children served in 1990–91 (U.S. Department of Education, 1992). Figure 2.1 compares children served, by disability, between 1976–77 and 1990–91. Note the relative change by category. For example, the number and proportion of learning disabled children served increased significantly compared to only a modest increase for emotionally disturbed students. At the same time, the numbers of mentally retarded and other health impaired students declined.

Major shifts in the proportion of children served can be expected from one year to the next. If changes do occur, they likely will result from more children with disabili-

Percent

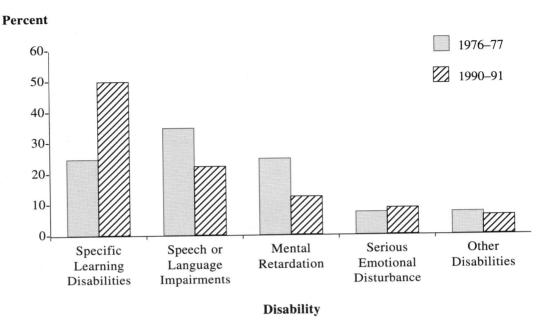

Source: From U.S. Department of Education, Office of Special Education Programs, Data Analysis System (DANS).

● **FIGURE 2.1**

Changes in the distribution of specific disabilities for children ages 6–21 served under IDEA, Part B: School years 1976–77 and 1990–91

ties being served in the 0–5 age group, changes in state funding policies, and new categories related to disease or medical conditions. In the latter group, shifts may stem from better medical care and longer survival rates or an increase in the incidence of conditions causing birth defects or disabilities. The total proportion of children served in special education can be assumed to remain at around 10%–11% of the school enrollment nationally. At the same time, variances across states likely will continue.

LEGISLATION AND PUBLIC POLICY

Progress in special education has been a consequence largely of the law, regulations, and the courts. The same is true for the educational history of African Americans. Whereas for African Americans the concern has shifted from a concern for access to education to a concern for educational equality, however, the concern for the children with disabilities is for access to educational opportunity *and* equality.

Many educators entering the field of special education today may have difficulty understanding why formalized due process procedures must be adhered to, why state education agencies regularly review schools' compliance with federal and state regulations, and why much of the professional literature is devoted to interpretations of law or court cases. The same is not true in the education of students without disabilities, even though general education also is based on law and governed by federal, state, and local regulations.

Almost two decades after PL 94–142, with implementation of the IDEA amendments, one would expect that a child no longer would have to rely on the courts for equal educational opportunity. Yet, in many communities this remains the primary recourse for children with AIDS, for example. Negative public reaction often evolves from lack of information. Moreover, attitudes, once formed, do not necessarily change when information becomes available, particularly when they relate to presumed hazards to one's children. Thus, some parents believe contact with children with AIDS poses a risk to their own children, despite professional opinion to the contrary. This reaction is similar to that of many parents when children with mental retardation were first enrolled in public schools. Just as significant progress has been made in recent years toward achieving better understanding of the educational needs of children with mental retardation, the same can be anticipated for children with AIDS. Although progress will be enhanced by legislation, advocates will have to persevere to ensure that public policy becomes practice.

Changes in the education of African American children and of children with disabilities came about through effective advocacy and court action, not through educational leadership. Because of this historical reliance on the courts, we must understand the underlying legislation and be able to relate today's educational practices to the law. Some day, perhaps the principles of educational equality for children with handicaps will be so integral to our culture that a discussion like this no longer will be necessary in introductory books on special education.

ADVOCACY CONTRIBUTIONS

Most, if not all, of the progress in special education can be attributed to the efforts of parents and advocacy groups. Dissatisfied with their children's educational experiences (or lack thereof), parents of children with disabilities began to organize during, and particularly after, the major civil rights initiative on behalf of minorities. A number of the issues raised on behalf of students with disabilities overlapped with those of minorities, such as the need for more appropriate education, better employment opportunities, and public access. Also of mutual concern were some school districts' exclusion policies to avoid having to provide needed programs. Other issues included discriminatory testing, disproportionate representation of minority children in special education classes, insufficient funding for needed programs, and frequent failure to provide due process when making placement decisions.

These concerns were compounded by the schools' lack of responsiveness to the needs of subgroups such as children with multiple or severe handicaps. Another issue involved providing a broader range of instructional programs to include preschool through young adulthood.

Already experienced in negotiating with education agencies, parents and advocacy groups now lobbied at state and federal levels to capitalize on the power of the courts. Although not originally planned on, litigation aided the legislative process greatly. Thus, clear interpretation of the laws came about through the courts. This continues as parents seek clarification on aspects of the law they think might help them meet the needs of their children with disabilities.

LEGISLATION IN PERSPECTIVE

Laws are intended to correct unjust situations and protect people's rights. Legislation relating to human services is not an exception. For example, laws mandating school attendance have been in effect since the early part of the century. Historically, though, boards of education and school administrators have exercised provisions to exclude a significant portion of children with moderate and severe handicaps. In addition, many who were served in the schools did not receive an appropriate education. If laws on educability had included children with disabilities, PL 94–142 would not have been necessary.

Throughout the 1950s and 1960s, parents, individually and in groups, tried to persuade local school administrators and boards of education to allow a broader range of children with disabilities to be served in the public schools and to improve the quality of services available to them. As a result, some communities developed exemplary programs and others passed legislation to enhance program development and establish a firm financial base for providing supplemental support to local districts. For large numbers of handicapped children, however, access to educational equality depended on where they lived. To obtain needed resources, many families had to move to resort to private resources. By the 1970s, to bring about change, federal legislation was seen as the *only* solution.

The result of these efforts was five landmark pieces of legislation in the 1970s and on into the 1990s: the Education for All Handicapped Children Act (PL 94–142); related laws such as the Education of the Handicapped Amendments (PL 93–380); Section 504 of the Rehabilitation Act of 1973 (PL 93–516); PL 101–476, the 1990 amendments that renamed the Education of the Handicapped Act (EHA) as the Individuals with Disabilities Education Act (IDEA), and the Americans with Disabilities Act (ADA).

Between 1827 and passage of PL 94–142 in 1975, 175 federal laws specific to the handicapped were enacted, 61 of them between March 1970 and March 1975 (Weintraub, Abeson, Ballard, & LaVor, 1976). (Table 2.1 summarizes the major legislation since 1975 and illustrates the major features of Section 504 of PL 93–516, PL 93–380, PL 94–142, and the 1983 and 1986 amendments to the Education of the Handicapped Act, IDEA and ADA.)

Enactment of legislation does not guarantee that sufficient funds are appropriated or that needed programs are always available. For example, Congress never has fulfilled its funding commitment to EHA or IDEA. Although EHA authorized 40% reimbursement, actual appropriations did not exceed 10%, and states and local communities had to cover the burden of costs for special education. Further, legislation does not guarantee that compliance will be enforced.

Proper implementation of laws governing human services depends on clear regulations, responsive public and professional advocacy groups, significant sanctions for failure to comply, and a court system that ensures due process. Safeguards have not always protected legislation pertaining to persons with disabilities. Even though they do today, they are effective only if fully implemented. In discussing Section 504 and IDEA, Turnbull (1993) stated:

> The effect of IDEA and Section 504, then, is to assure that children with disabilities receive a free appropriate education and are not discriminated against in or by any public agencies furnishing special education services. Together, the two laws cover all disabled children without regard to where they live in the state (whether in the community or in an institution, for example) or which state or local agency serves them (whether a department of public education or a department of human resources, for example). There is no real escape from these Acts for state and local agencies. The two Acts seal all the cracks in services and carry out policies of zero reject and nondiscrimination. (p. 21)

PL 94–142 received considerable public attention during the 1970s and 1980s and initially was referred to as the "Bill of Rights for the Handicapped" (Goodman, 1976). As a result, many new professionals in special education and health-related fields at first overlooked the significance of Section 504 of the Rehabilitation Act. Section 504, however, is the legislation that actually provides the basic source of enforcement for PL 94–142 and, in turn, for PL–101–476 (IDEA).

Originally, Section 504 applied primarily to employment. As a result of the passage in 1974 of PL 93–516, however, it was amended to cover a broader array of services for individuals with handicaps. Ultimately, including people with handicaps in the provisions covered by Section 504 made equal rights for people with handicaps part of the broader public policy on civil rights.

Because PL 94–142 is referred to as the Education for All Handicapped Children Act and PL 101–476 is referenced as the Individuals with Disabilities Education Act, many assume these are independent acts. Actually, however, PL 94–142 is an amendment to PL 93–380, passed in 1974 to extend and amend the Elementary and Secondary Education Act of 1965, whereas PL 101–476 is an amendment to PL 94–142. Each act is significant to the history of education for students with disabilities. From a public policy perspective, however, PL 93–380 was the first act to address the concept of education for all:

> Sec. 801. Recognizing that the Nation's economic, political, and social security require a well educated citizenry, the Congress (1) reaffirms, as a matter of high priority, the Nation's goal of equal educational opportunity, and (2) declares it to be the policy of the

United States of America that every citizen is entitled to an education to meet his or her full potential without financial barriers.

Congress set 1978 as the deadline for implementation of PL 94–142. During the interim, states were required to revise their statutes to comply. In anticipation of the act, some states already had revised old legislation, but many had to initiate major new legislative processes to ensure that policies and procedures would be compatible with new federal laws. Although PL 94–142 did not include the gifted, many states defined special education services to include services for gifted and talented students. This explains why school programs typically include gifted students in special services, even though the law refers to "handicapped" or "disabled" rather than "exceptional" students.

As shown in Table 2.1, the principles of these three acts and the requirements they set forth are specific and detailed, dictating a wide array of responses from the public schools. For example, to implement PL 94–142 and now IDEA, schools must do more than identify all students with disabilities and provide for their education at public expense. They must offer instruction that requires clear assessment of instructional needs and implement interventions that are designed to enhance the performance of students with disabilities. According to many administrators, the regulations designed to implement the principles of these laws are restrictive. Others, however, recognize that, without specific regulations, school districts would differ greatly in how they implement principles, making monitoring for compliance difficult, if not impossible.

MAJOR PROVISIONS OF EHA

Although provisions of PL 94–142, the Education of the Handicapped Act (EHA), are subsumed under the provisions of PL 101–476, the Individuals with Disabilities Education Act (IDEA), the original provision of PL 94–142 will be described here. Discussing PL 94–142 as independent legislation and then presenting the changes to these provisions as incorporated in IDEA places the changes in perspective and highlights the historical significance of PL 94–142. The fact that these laws are amendments illustrates the evolutionary nature of public policy and evidences the progress being made.

PL 94–142 and its subsequent amendments (see Table 2.1) represent a comprehensive law, which collectively has been abbreviated as the EHA and now is incorporated in IDEA. From a policy-analysis perspective, at least five major provisions can be identified: due process, free and appropriate public education (FAPE) or "zero reject," least restrictive environment (LRE), the individualized education program (IEP), and nondiscriminatory testing.

Due process. A basic provision of EHA suggested in IDEA is the establishment of procedural due process for handicapped children (and/or their parents or advocates) so actions (or nonactions) of educational agencies that result in discriminatory practices may be challenged. To comply, therefore, school districts must establish due process procedures in accordance with the conditions of state and federal laws and make them known to parents, who, in turn, must be able to exercise their right of protest.

The due process requirements are technical and highly specific: the right to appeal, the right to cross-examine, and the right to representation by counsel. Translating the legal language into procedures that are easily understood and result in quality instruction has been difficult. Nevertheless, educators have found ways to communicate more effectively the meaning and utility of due process, particularly to parents.

If due process procedures do not lead to a program that is satisfactory to the parent or guardian, the law allows for an impartial hearing. Hearings can be initiated either by parents or by the school district. Depending on the state, hearings may be held by the local school district, an intermediate school district, or the state education agency.

If school personnel respond appropriately, convincing parents of their concern for all students, due process will be effective, making a hearing or an appeal unnecessary. The child's best interests are served when parents and school personnel reach decisions cooperatively. This does not mean that school personnel are always right. All parties should use the required procedures to effect quality education. When due process procedures are seen only as legal requirements to be met, parents, advocates, and schools may become adversaries. In these instances, the students' needs often go unmet.

Due process procedures are costly, and the paperwork involved can be burdensome. The impact of the EHA and IDEA, however, is clear: The quality of services has improved; parents are more involved in educational decisions; discriminatory practices are being prevented or corrected; and an appropriate education now prepares students with disabilities for adult life.

Free and appropriate public education (FAPE). The FAPE requirement addresses both access to education and quality of education. Enforcement of the Fourteenth Amendment (equal protection of the law) is enhanced, and school districts no longer can exclude children from an appropriate education because of disability (the zero reject principle):

> Nothing is clearer in the EHA and IDEA than the intent of Congress that no handicapped child be excluded from school by recipients of federal funds for education of the handicapped, and that all involved agencies follow a policy of zero reject. Finding, as the courts did, that both total and functional exclusion existed (Section 1400)(B)(3) and (4), and concluding that it was in the national interest to provide programs to meet the needs of handicapped children and thereby assure them equal protection of the law (Section 1400)(B)(9), Congress declared the purpose of the EHA to provide a free appropriate education to the handicapped (Section 1400)(C) and acted in numerous ways to implement the zero reject policy. (Turnbull, 1986, p. 40)

The appropriateness of education obviously is difficult to substantiate. In part, the requirement is tied to related services and the individualized education program (IEP), which defines appropriate education. Parents or guardians must agree to the IEP and it must be monitored and evaluated over time (see Chapter 3).

In many ways, the zero reject principle is the most significant provision of the law. Schools no longer can place children with disabilities on waiting lists for a program opening but must begin to provide the most appropriate education program as soon as the student is identified, or risk litigation and loss of federal aid. In contrast, prior to PL 94–142, there was no real consequence for the school if a special education student was inappropriately placed or did not receive an appropriate education.

Individualized education program (IEP). The IEP requirement establishes a basis for accountability and quality control. The action by Congress to define and require an instructional plan for each student receiving special education is unprecedented. Prior to PL 94–142, special educators based instruction on assessment data and used behaviorally stated objectives to develop instructional plans. Practices varied, and rarely was the process systematic or programs closely coordinated with related services. As a result, continuity in the instructional planning and record-keeping process was lacking. When special education students moved to other communities or were transferred to another school within the same district, therefore, the new teachers had to devote an extraordinary amount of time to determine the student's level of functioning, verify the previous curriculum resources, and establish a meaningful and effective program. The student was the loser.

The IEP is not like a daily lesson plan; rather, the focus is on structuring the student's overall educational program (see Chapter 3). The required IEP components are instructionally sound and include the following:

1. *Current performance.* An assessment must be made of the student's current level of performance. Assessment should cover school-related performance and the need for related services, if necessary.
2. *Annual goals.* These goals relate to the student's current performance level and specify what the student should be able to accomplish after 12 months in the program.
3. *Short-term objectives.* These are intended to be intermediate, or enroute, objectives between the student's current performance level and those suggested by the long-term goals. Although not as detailed as instructional objectives used in daily planning, short-term objectives are specific to areas of performance. They are to be used in measuring progress.
4. *Related services.* The goals and objectives should include the needed related services. In identifying related services, attention must be given to specifying the amounts of service needed (e.g., time in speech therapy). The education agency responsible for the student is required to provide the related service or to contract for its provision.
5. *Evaluation criteria.* The long-term goals and short-term objectives serve as the evaluation criteria. A timeline need not be set for each short-term objective, but evaluation procedures must be linked to the short-term objective. If IEP goals or objectives are to be changed, an IEP meeting must be held. The IEP provides a mechanism for parents' input in planning their child's educational program. Under some circumstances, the student also is afforded an opportunity to participate. In addition to serving as an educational plan, the IEP becomes a source of accountability in determining if a student is receiving a free and appropriate public education.

IDEA amends PL 94–142 to expand the requirements of the IEP so it now must include a transition services statement for each student by age 16. If assistive technology devices or assistive technology services will benefit a student, they, too, should be included in the IEP.

Nondiscriminatory testing. Testing has become the major means of establishing eligibility for special education programs. The reasons for testing are threefold: (a) to substantiate the need for special education services; (b) to provide a basis for planning; and (c) to establish a baseline for measuring progress. The form of testing depends on the nature of the disability. In assessing sensory impairments, for example, available tests are considered to be reasonably accurate: they can be calibrated and, unless the student is multiply handicapped, yield rather precise measures. Available instruments for measuring cognitive abilities and deviant behavior, however, are less precise and therefore are vulnerable to error. This is especially true for people with severe handicaps.

Tests of intelligence frequently are alleged to be racially or culturally discriminatory, especially if they are used to establish the eligibility of students with mild handicaps (children with mild mental retardation). Many tests in the 1950s and 1960s were designed and standardized largely for white, middle-class children, and single test scores determined eligibility for placement. Children who were unable to comprehend what was expected of them in the testing situation often received lower test scores and, therefore, inappropriate placement.

Historically, minority children have been overrepresented in special education programs for students with mental retardation (see Chapter 6). These children, although functionally performing like their special-class peers, were disadvantaged by the design and standardization of the tests used to establish their eligibility. In some cases, the disadvantage was related to language; in others, to culture.

Test bias is not limited to minority groups. Students with multiple handicaps often are discriminated against by tests that do not take into consideration their language or their motor, perceptual, or behavioral attributes. The consequences of discriminatory testing are serious: Students may be denied needed services or may be placed inappropriately. To guard against discrimination, specific requirements (Sec. 300.530-534) were included in the regulations governing implementation of PL 94–142:

(a) Tests and other evaluation materials
  (1) Are provided and administered in the child's native language or other mode of communication, unless it is clearly not feasible to do so;
  (2) Have been validated for the specific purpose for which they are used;
  (3) Are administered by trained personnel in conformance with instructions from the producer.
(b) Tests and other evaluation materials include those tailored to access specific areas of educational need and not merely those which are designed to provide a single general intelligence quotient;
(c) Tests are selected and administered so as best to insure that when a test is administered to a child with impaired sensory, manual or speaking skills, the test results accurately reflect the child's aptitude or achievement level or whatever other factor the test

purports to measure, rather than reflecting the child's impaired sensory, manual or speaking skills (except where those skills are the factors which the test purports to measure);

(d) No single procedure is used as the sole criterion for determining an appropriate education program for a child and placement;

(e) The evaluation is made by a multidisciplinary team, or group of persons, including at least one teacher or other specialist with knowledge in the area of suspected disability;

(f) The child is assessed in all areas related to the suspected disability, including, where appropriate, health, vision, hearing, social and emotional status, general intelligence, academic performance, communicative status, and motor abilities.

The nondiscriminatory testing provision has influenced the attitudes and practices of test developers, who have become more sensitive to bias in test construction for all children. Unfortunately, few bias-free tests have been produced, and the concern remains.

1983 AND 1986 AMENDMENTS

In spite of early attempts to alter PL 94–142 and, in some cases, weaken its provisions, no amendments were passed until 1983. Passage of PL 98–199 in that year made two significant contributions to public policy by expanding services to handicapped children beginning at birth and by strengthening programs designed to enhance the transition from school to employment. As was true for PL 94–142 itself, several states had anticipated the federal initiative and passed similar legislation prior to action by Congress. Thus, programs for handicapped infants and toddlers, as well as transitional programs, were operational in many states prior to 1983.

Services to preschool handicapped children. PL 94–142 did not mandate services for handicapped infants and toddlers. In 1975, however, Congress authorized grants to state education agencies (SEAs) to extend special education and related services to handicapped children ages 3–5.

The Incentive Grant Program was preceded by the Handicapped Children's Early Education Assistance Act (HCEEAA) (PL 90–538) in 1968. It was designed to support activities demonstrating the effectiveness of strategies to serve preschool handicapped children and their families. A major outcome of the program was the development of models to guide establishment of local programs.

Based in part on the success of the HCEEAA, Congress created the State Implementation Grant (SIG) program in 1976 to aid states in planning and coordinating comprehensive preschool service delivery systems. A study conducted by the National Association of State Directors of Special Education (1983) reported that the SIG program successfully helped states initiate planning and create structures to enhance the provision of services statewide.

The 1983 amendment provides three types of early childhood state grants, each serving a designated purpose for a specified time.

1. *Planning grants*. To provide support to SEAs in coordinating needs assessment of

designs for the development of state plans.
2. *Development grants.* To provide support for the development of comprehensive state plans with an emphasis on interagency collaboration.
3. *Implementation grants.* To provide support for implementation and evaluation of comprehensive state plans for early education of handicapped children.

Although PL 98–199 stimulated the development of programs for children with disabilities beginning at birth, it did not necessarily create new kinds of services. What did evolve between the 1983 and the 1986 amendments, in addition to expanded services, were effective interagency collaborative arrangements. This was necessitated by the varied needs of infants and toddlers (ages 0–2) with disabilities and the lack of a single state- or community-level agency responsible for this age group.

In most states, public schools assume responsibility for preschool-aged children 3–5. Families seeking services for a 4-year-old child with a physical disability, for example, approach the schools and at that point gain access to available services. If they are unfamiliar with the schools, their physician or a social agency in the community likely will refer them to the schools as a source of service.

The search for appropriate services for infants with disabilities, however, may be more difficult. Only recently have early intervention programs for infants and toddlers emerged, and no standard structure for services exists yet. Parent training and intervention are common to all programs, though.

The range of services infants with handicaps require is influenced greatly by parents' needs. If parents are able to provide good care and implement interventions learned through special training programs, the need for programs outside the home may be minimal. If both parents work or if other circumstances prevent the family from providing the needed care and intervention, however, the child's development will depend on services in the community. Examples of services are:

Family

Referral source	Genetic counseling
Case management	Crisis intervention
Family counseling	Nutritional planning

Child

Health care	Occupational therapy
Dental care	Day care
Diagnosis	Respite care
Assessment	Language development
Physical therapy	Education
Speech therapy	

Parents often have difficulty finding an agency that is willing to accept a child with a disability. For example, many daycare centers are not staffed to provide the kind of care young children with handicaps may require. Another, more serious, problem faces many parents—how to find an agency capable of coordinating (or willing to coordinate) the services their child needs. The ideal is a single referral source, linked to all available services, which also assures family and child access to a continuum of service. Such agencies continue to be scarce.

PL 99–457 amends the EHA by (a) establishing new federal discretionary programs to assist states in developing and implementing a comprehensive, coordinated, interdisciplinary program of early intervention services for handicapped infants and toddlers and their families; (b) strengthening the incentives for states to serve all handicapped children aged 3–5 inclusively; and (c) amending Part B evaluations, as well as amending and extending the authority for the discretionary programs under Parts C through G. This landmark piece of legislation is responsive to the needs of families and young handicapped children.

The 1986 amendments reflect the success of advocacy groups in convincing Congress of the need to extend the concepts of a free and appropriate public education to include all handicapped children from birth. These amendments define handicapped infants and toddlers as:

> ...individuals from birth to age two, inclusive, who need early intervention services because they are (1) experiencing developmental delays, as measured by appropriate diagnostic instruments and procedures, in one or more of the following areas: cognitive development, physical development, language and speech development, psychosocial development, or self-help skills, or (2) having a diagnosed physical or mental condition which has a high probability of resulting in development delay.

States also may serve infants and toddlers considered to be at risk and not otherwise covered by the general definition previously cited. The 1986 amendments repeal the incentive program of PL 94–142, creating a new preschool grant program. This represents a national initiative:

> ...to provide federal financial assistance to states to: develop and implement a statewide, comprehensive, coordinated, multidisciplinary interagency program of early intervention services for all handicapped infants and toddlers and their families; facilitate coordination of payments for early intervention services from various public and private sources; and enhance its capacity to provide quality early intervention services and expand and improve existing services.

The *early intervention services* in the act include case management services; health services necessary for children to benefit from early intervention services; services related to physical development, psychosocial development, and self-help skills; family training, counseling, and home visits; special instruction; speech pathology and audiology; occupational therapy; and psychological services.

For infants and toddlers, family involvement in intervention is essential. As a result, one of the most important sections of the 1986 amendments related to infants and toddlers with disabilities pertains to the individualized family service plan (IFSP), which must:

1. Include a multidisciplinary assessment of needs.
2. Include the identification of required services.

3. Be in written form.
4. Be reviewed at least every 6 months.
5. Be developed within a reasonable time following assessment.

The written individualized family service plan further must include:

1. Levels of development.
2. Family strengths and needs.
3. Expected major outcomes for infants and toddlers and families.
4. Description of needed intervention services.
5. Dates services are to be provided.
6. Name of case manager.
7. Steps for transition to special education services, if needed, following intervention.

PL 101–456 (IDEA) calls for improving early identification of disabled infants and toddlers and those at risk for having developmental disabilities. Transition from medical care to early intervention programs also is identified as a priority service. Technology in the form of assistive devices and services is included as a requirement when appropriate. In discussing the range of services preschool-age handicapped children and their families need, Peterson (1987) built on the work of Evans (1975). (Table 2.2 illustrates the comprehensiveness of services, types of care providers, and types of settings in which interventions are offered.) When the service needs are combined with delivery settings and service providers (intervention agents), the continuum of care preschool-age children with disabilities require obviously is far more difficult to meet than that of school-aged children with handicaps.

Provision of services to preschool handicapped children is complicated by at least three factors: (a) it often is not clear how and where to enter the service system; (b) in contrast to the school-aged population for whom mandatory attendance laws apply, access to services by preschool handicapped children has depended largely on parents' initiative or on the alertness of health care-providers; and (c) services to this population typically have been provided by a number of different agencies that may or may not be part of a coordinated system.

Services to handicapped youth. PL 98–194 also acknowledged that, through employment, most persons achieve independence. For many persons with disabilities, however, special assistance and support are necessary to reach this goal. Historically, programs to prepare and train individuals with handicaps for meaningful adult employment have been nonexistent or ineffective at best. For example, early rehabilitative programs focused on individuals with sensory and physical impairments, whereas vocational and rehabilitation services for those with mental retardation or behavior disorders occurred much later. Program options are just beginning to evolve for people with severe or profound handicaps.

The evolution of vocational and employment-related programs has been incongruously slow, considering the goals of special education and the needs of this population. The magnitude of this problem was made particularly clear when in 1992 for the first time, the Fourteenth Annual Report to Congress (U.S. Department of Education, 1992)

● **TABLE 2.2**

Issues in selecting service delivery approaches for early intervention

Elements defining a service delivery approach

(WHO) Target of service	(WHEN) Beginning point of intervention	(WHAT) Services to be provided	(WHERE) Setting for intervention program	(BY WHOM) Primary intervention agent	(WITH WHOM) Social context of services	(THROUGH WHOM) Agencies providing service(s)
Child	Birth	Case finding and screening services	Home-based	Paraprofessional	Individual program	Public schools
Mother	Infancy	Diagnostic services	Center-based	Parent	Group program	Private schools
Father	Toddler years	Education program	Classroom	Teacher	Segregated	State/local government agencies
Both parents	Preschool years	Therapy services	Clinic	Therapist	Mainstreamed	agencies
Family	Kindergarten	Speech and language	Combination of center-based and home-based	Social services personnel	Integrated	Churches
		Physical		Multidisciplinary team	Reverse-mainstreamed	Nonprofit service organizations
		Occupational				Profit-making agencies
		Other special therapies		Combination of intervention agents		Multi-agency consortium
		Parent education and training				
		Family counseling				
		Social services				
		Nutritional services				
		Medical services				
		Transportation				

Source: From Nancy L. Peterson, 1987, *Early Intervention for Handicapped and At-Risk Children*, p. 353, Denver: Love.

reported the number of students exiting from programs; 212,000 students age 16 and older were reported to have left the educational system. In addition to insufficient vocational training and employment opportunities, few resources are available to facilitate the transition from special education (school) to employment (the community).

Once a handicapped youth leaves school, getting and keeping a job rely on cooperation among agencies and the family's initiative or personal resourcefulness. The primary goal in special education is to prepare individuals with disabilities for a productive life after leaving school. Too many handicapped students are not ready, though, a great disadvantage in achieving independence.

Several federal initiatives have been targeted at improving the employment conditions of young adults with disabilities. For example, Section 626 of Part C of EHA, as amended by PL 98–199 in 1983, authorizes the Secondary Education and Transitional Services for Handicapped Youth Program. Specifically, this amendment authorizes support for projects that (a) assist in preparing handicapped youth for the transition from school to competitive and supportive employment, postsecondary education and training, and adult services; and (b) stimulate the development and improvement of secondary special education programs.

Madeline Will (1985), Assistant Secretary for OSERS, stated in the first issue of *News in Print*: "Because one of the major problems facing handicapped youth is a lack of a continuum of service to provide an effective bridge between school and work, transition becomes a pressing issue for disabled youth, their families and educators and service professionals" (p. 1). As for preschool-aged children, seldom is a single agency responsible for coordinating services for youth with disabilities.

Similarly, Ballantyne, McGee, Patton, and Cohen (1985) noted:

> Providing a coordinated continuum of service to aid disabled youth in moving from school into competitive employment can be accomplished only through interagency collaboration. The reasons for this are well documented. Vocational services, like other services for other disabled persons, are fragmented and duplicative. Professionals working with handicapped youth must look to other agencies if they wish to meet the full range of client needs.
>
> Interagency cooperation to deliver services to secondary-age students encourages the development of new strategies. It also establishes mechanisms for ongoing support after graduation. For youth leaving the school system without jobs, coordination is critical to ensure that they do not fall between the cracks of the service delivery system. (p. i)

Effective transition from school to employment and, ultimately, independent living is impossible without a continuum of services for disabled youth, particularly those with more severe disabilities. Schools are pivotal in preparing youth with disabilities for employment and in fostering interagency collaborative arrangements to facilitate transition. A well developed career and vocational education curriculum, however, is insufficient if no support system is in place. The nature of needed support depends on the individual's unique attributes. For example, a person with the "right" attitudes, values, and habits may demonstrate incompetent personal or work behaviors. Likewise, a person can be adept in human relationships, yet be unskilled in daily living;

or be knowledgeable about the world of work but unable to maintain employment because of poor social behavior (Clark, 1982).

Wehman, Moon, and McCarthy (1986) identified five alternatives to the current status of youth services: (a) adult activity centers and sheltered workshops, (b) supported employment, (c) supported competitive employment, (d) enclaves in industry, and (e) mobile work crews.

Adult activity centers offer recreation, instruction in daily living skills, and opportunities to develop work skills. In contrast, *sheltered workshops* provide work experiences for which clients are paid. Both tend to be segregated facilities, emphasizing the buildings, not the staff.

Supported employment, though not appropriate for all youths with severe handicaps, is a reasonable goal for most individuals with handicapping conditions. The foundations of supported employment are paid employment, integration into the community, necessity of ongoing support, and presence of severe disability.

Supported competitive employment—a goal for many disabled youth—has not been widely achieved by persons with disabilities. To be effective, this model requires that a job coach be accessible for individualized one-to-one training and follow-up, as the emphasis is on structured assistance in job placement and job-site training (Wehman & Melia, 1985).

The *enclave model* involves groups of disabled clients working under supervision in a business or industry. *Mobile work crews* perform (under supervision) at different locations of a building or in the community. Both models provide employment to disabled individuals who have been unsuccessful in, or excluded from, other employment opportunities.

As a result of the efforts of OSERS, transition from school to work now has become a national priority for youths with disabilities, as reflected in IDEA, which requires that a transition service statement be included within each student's IEP by age 16.

MAJOR PROVISIONS OF INDIVIDUALS WITH DISABILITIES EDUCATION ACT

Congress revised EHA in 1990, creating the Individuals with Disabilities Education Act (IDEA). The most visible and, many would agree, the most significant change was in renaming the act from the Education of the Handicapped Act to the Individuals with Disabilities Education Act. Previously the federal government had tended to rely on the word "handicapped" to identify persons with disabilities. As public reference for other terms evolved, the government continued to use "handicapped," both in legislation for infants with disabilities and for adults. The current change in language represents progress in communication and also will assist in continuing efforts to alter attributes and to minimize the negative connotation that tends to be associated with former terms describing attributes of individuals with disabilities.

As an amendment to EHA, Congress sought through IDEA to correct omissions and to provide clarification where needed. In replacing EHA, IDEA did not make philosophical changes in public policy. Rather, Congress sought to provide further assurances that the educational and related service needs of children and youth with disabilities would be met as a matter of public policy. Summarizing the changes, IDEA:

- Renamed the law. Substituted the term "disability" for "handicapped."
- Defined transition services.
- Clarified the inclusion of students with autism and traumatic brain injury.
- Added the definition of "assistive technology device" and "assistive technology service"; also clarified the search devices and services to be delineated on IEPs when appropriate.
- Provided assurances and clarification regarding the inclusion of therapeutic recreation, social work services, and rehabilitation counseling as related services.
- Included students attending Bureau of Indian Affairs schools as eligible for the benefits of IDEA if they have a disability.
- Redefined "underrepresented" to include students with limited-English proficiency, minority students, and poor students with disabilities.
- Redefined "deaf-blind" and clarified the responsibilities of schools for providing transitional services to students who are deaf-blind.
- Clarified and expanded early education services (ages 3–5); broadened parental involvement and clarified transition services for infants and toddlers into early education.
- Created opportunities for extended school-year programs.
- Established an emphasis on transition services with a focus on independent living and community programming; also required a transitional statement for students by age 16.

When combined with Section 504 and the Americans with Disabilities Act (ADA), IDEA offers the most favorable public policy to date for ensuring equity for students with disabilities and their families. It adds significantly to the quality of life throughout the life span of persons with disabilities. The broader coverage of public policy makes even more significant the provisions of IDEA in achieving equity in education for students with disabilities.

MAJOR PROVISIONS OF AMERICANS WITH DISABILITIES ACT

Whereas EHA and IDEA emphasize education, the Americans with Disabilities Act (ADA) provides the most encompassing civil rights public policy affecting the lives of persons with disabilities to date. It sets forth detailed and enforceable standards prohibiting discrimination against persons with disabilities of all ages and types of disabilities, and it recognizes that discrimination must be prevented in the private as well as the public sector. Thus far, much of the legislation intended to prevent discrimination against persons with disabilities has been limited to the public sector where public funds are involved. ADA addresses discrimination in the private sector.

In describing ADA, Turnbull (1993) stated:

> Consistent with its goals, the ADA extends its civil rights nondiscrimination protection to the following sectors of American life: employment in the private sector; privately owned public accommodations (for example, theaters, hotels, restaurants, shopping centers, and grocery stores); services provided by state and local governments, including public and private transportation services; and telecommunication services (for people with hearing or visual impairments). (p. 24)

In addressing the needs of persons with disabilities in the private and public sectors, ADA has major implications for the outcomes of special education. For example, a discrimination-free employment environment changes dramatically the curricular expectations of special education. Further, banning discrimination in public accommodations and private programs removes barriers to services and community participation for persons with disabilities of all ages. This, in turn, should contribute significantly to students with disabilities entering school ready to learn and successfully transitioning from school to the world of work and independent living as adults. In selected provisions of the act, ADA:

- Covers persons with AIDS but includes some limitations relative to required accommodation by employers and service providers.
- Covers individuals who have successfully completed a drug rehabilitation program.
- Prohibits discrimination against individuals with a disability who are otherwise qualified; this provision applies if an employer makes reasonable accommodation.
- Prohibits all state and local governments from discrimination against persons with disabilities.
- Bans all discrimination by private service providers (e.g., retail stores, doctors' offices, hotels, restaurants, libraries, private schools).
- Prohibits discrimination in public and private transportation on the basis of disability; also provides regulations to ensure accessibility.
- Requires that telecommunication services available to the general public include special accommodations for people who are deaf.

ADA went into effect in 1992. Because of the comprehensiveness of the act and the costs involved, the law sets forth special provisions for implementation, particularly to assist small businesses in achieving compliance. Because many public agencies and private businesses have had little experience in developing accommodations for persons with disabilities, training and consulting services designed to assist in implementation have emerged. The initial focus of the training has been on the provision of the law. In addition, technical assistance is being provided regarding accommodations in the workplace.

INFLUENCE OF THE COURTS

While legislation has created the legal base for educational services to benefit students with disabilities, the courts have provided the needed clarification and enforcement. As parents and advocates sought to ensure that the intent of law was implemented on behalf of individual students, these efforts often were met with inaction or claims that the laws were not clear on certain points. Then it became necessary to pursue available due process. If due process procedures did not prove satisfactory, the responses were challenged in the courts.

The history of court cases in this area provides a chronology of progress as specific aspects of the law were challenged and solutions achieved. Each case has contributed to clarifying the law and, in many instances, created the opportunities the law was intended to guarantee to students with disabilities and their families. See Table 2.3 for a detailed list of court cases that have helped make operational several laws, beginning in 1954, that have been passed to achieve educational equity on behalf of students with disabilities.

SERVICES

As schools have broadened the range of services offered and as advocacy groups have been successful in amending legislature to include new groups of students with special needs, special education has been redefined. To date, this redefinition has been largely in the form of services to be offered and the students to be served. The intended outcomes underlying special education remain the same even though the prevailing approach to meeting the educational needs of students with disabilities has shifted to retaining their primary placement in regular classrooms.

Special education can be defined as *a complement of services designed to meet the educational needs of children and youth with handicapping conditions.* Educational needs beyond instruction include services to assure access to instruction and to enhance educational performance. The specific services provided depend on the needs of the individual child. In the past, handicapped children were defined as those who were unable to profit from regular classroom instruction or who needed special therapies. Locally, this often was interpreted to mean special classes or services "currently" available. This circular approach assessed the students only within the range of services a district had to offer, with little attention to the needs the district was unable to meet.

PL 94–142 and subsequent amendments established student need, not availability of services, as the primary determinant of services. As a result, schools no longer can postpone establishing programs or hiring special personnel until a sufficient number of students warrants specific services. For example, students who need specialized interventions (such as catheterization) to attend school can no longer be excluded. To serve students with specialized needs, therefore, districts must be creative, form collaborative relationships with other agencies, or rethink their organizational structure. They must alter their traditional approach to determining who participates in regular classroom instruction. At times, they must even look to the private sector as a vendor of needed services and enter into contractual agreements.

School districts typically have been independent, governed by state standards but,

● *TABLE 2.3*

Selected legal cases related to special education

Case	Precedent
Brown v. Board of Education, 347, U.S. 483 (1954)	■ Established the right to an equal educational opportunity based upon the Fourteenth Amendment, which provided that people could not be denied "equal protection of the laws" or deprived of "life, liberty, or property" without due process. ■ Recognized that educating any "class of children" separately, even if done in equal facilities, was intrinsically unequal because of the stigma attached to segregation and because of the denial of association with children from other classes.
Pennsylvania Association for Retarded Children (PARC) v. Commonwealth of Pennsylvania, 334 F. Supp. 1257, 343 F. Supp. 279 (E.D. Pa. 1971, 1972)	■ Established that students with mental retardation have the right to an appropriate education. ■ Required state and local districts to place all children with mental retardation in a "free public program of education and training appropriate to the child's capacity." ■ Established that the State must engage in extensive efforts to locate and evaluate all student with mental retardation.
Mills v. D.C. Board of Education, 348 F. Supp. 866 (D.D.C. 1972)	■ Established that children with disabilities other than mental retardation have the right to an appropriate education, regardless of the degree of mental, physical, or emotional disability. ■ Established that children with disabilities receive a supported education suited to their needs, including compensatory services.
Larry P. v. Riles, 343 F. Supp. 1306, (N.D. Cal. 1972) aff'd 502 F. 2nd 963 (9th Cir. 1974)	■ Established that using intelligence tests as the sole basis for diagnosing mental retardation for placement in special education classes is inappropriate.
Allen v. McDonough, No. 14,948 (Mass. Super. Ct., Suffolk County, consent decree June 23, 1976)	■ Established that appropriate education for children with disabilities consisted of timely and sufficient evaluations, individualized programs, and reviews of the programs.
Frederick L. v. Thomas, Civ. Act. No. 74-52 (E.D. Pa., Memo. Order Aug. 2, 1976)	■ Established that students with learning disabilities should be provided an appropriate education. ■ Established that screening and evaluation procedures be designed and implemented to identify students with learning disabilities.

Case	Precedent
Lora v. New York City Board of Education, 456 F. Supp. 1211 (E.D.N.Y. 1978)	■ Established that evaluation procedures for entrance into special education classes or schools should not violate the student's right to treatment and due process.
Stuart v. Nappi, 443 F. Supp. 1235 (D. Conn. 1978)	■ Established that a school may not expel a student with a disability without providing an appropriate alternative program.
New York State Association for Retarded Children, Inc. et al. v. Carey et al., 466 F. Supp. 479 (E.D., NY 1978), aff'd 612 F. 2nd 644 (2nd Cir. 1979)	■ Established that segregation of students with mental retardation carrying hepatitis B within the public schools constituted unlawful discrimination under Section 504 of the Rehabilitation Act because nonhandicapped student carriers are not similarly restricted.
PASE (Parents in Action in Special Education) v. Hannon, 506 F. Supp. 831 (N.D. Ill. 1980)	■ Established that the use of standardized intelligence tests are valid when used in multifaceted, multidisciplinary evaluations.
Battle v. Commonwealth, (629 F. 2nd 269, 3rd Cir. 1980)	■ Established that the denial of a free public education for students with disabilities would violate the Education for All Handicapped Children Act.
S-1 v. Turlington, 635 F. 2nd 342 (5th Cir. 1981)	■ Established that schools must determine if a student's misconduct is handicap-related and, if so, any disciplinary action that would result in a change of placement must be conducted under the review procedures of PL 94–142.
Mattie T. v. Holladay, Vic. No. D.C.-75-31-S (N.D. Miss., filed Apr. 25, 1975), further proceedings, 522 F. Supp. 72 (N.D. Miss. 1981)	■ Established that the state goal of providing an appropriate education for children with disabilities should be met in the least restrictive environment possible.
Board of Education v. Rowley, 458 U.S. 176, 102 S. Ct. 3034, 73L. Ed., 2nd 690 (1982)	■ Established that an "appropriate" education is found when a program of special education and related services is comparable to that given a child without disabilities.
Irving Independent School District v. Tatro, 468 U.S. 833, 104 S. Ct. 3371, 82 L. Ed. 2nd 664 (1984)	■ Established that catheterization is a "related service" when it is simple to provide and medical assistance is not necessary to provide it.

Case	Precedent
School Board of Nassau County v. Arline, (107 S. Ct. 1123, 1987)	■ Established that contagious diseases are considered a disability under section 504 of the Rehabilitation Act and that individuals with them are protected from discrimination if they are qualified in every other way (risk to others may disqualify the individual).
Honig v. Doe, (108 C. Ct. 592, 1988)	■ Established that expulsion from school exceeding ten days constitutes a change in placement for which all due process provisions must be met; temporary removals are permitted in emergencies.
New Hampshire School District v. Timothy W., (1st Cir. 1989)	■ Established that a child with disabilities must be served under EHA regardless of the severity of his or her disability, even if the school deems that the child is incapable of benefiting from the provided education.
W.G. v. Target Range School District No. 23 Board of Trustees, 17 EHLR 277 (D. Mont. 1990)	■ Established that a parent is entitled to private school cost reimbursement when a school district is in violation of EHA.
Community Consolidated School District No. 21 v. Illinois State Board of Education, 18 IDELR 43 (6th Cir. 1991)	■ Established that the hostility of parents is of "obvious and direct relevance" in determining the benefits of an educational placement.
Strongsville City School District v. Theado, 17 EHLR 514 (Ohio 1991)	■ Established that compensatory education may be awarded to an individual with disabilities after the age of 21 in the case that they were denied an appropriate education during their tenure in public education.
Board of Education, Sacramento City Unified School District v. Rachel Holland, Civ. S-90-1171-DFL Order.	■ Established that any placement, other than a regular class placement, can be made only after determining that the regular class placement will be unsuccessful.
Oberti v. Board of Education of the Borough of Clementon School District, C.A. No. 91-2818. D.N.J. 8/17/92.	■ Established inclusion as a right, not a privilege, and found that in order to learn to function effectively all children with disabilities need integrated experiences. ■ Established that children with disabilities may be harmed by segregated experiences with inappropriate role models.

Source: From *National Agenda for Achieving Better Results for Children with Disabilities*, Forum Briefing Materials. U.S. Department of Education, 1993, p. 6–8.

for the most part, accommodating the needs of their students within their own educational resources. Only occasionally might an able student with a disability go to a nearby college or a disabled student be bused to an adjacent district to participate in a cooperative program. In general, these students were dealt with individually.

PL 94–142 and IDEA challenged school districts' conventional organizational structure and operational policies. Because of the nature of required services and the low incidence of some handicapping conditions, most districts no longer could fulfill their obligations to their communities independently. Instead, they had to determine the needs of all handicapped children and adjust organizationally to meet these needs and, in some cases, added responsibilities. Most districts were neither prepared nor anxious to build consortia and make similar arrangements. As discussed in Chapter 1, the organizational demands placed on the schools may have exceeded their ability to respond.

How special education services are delivered is influenced greatly by the beliefs of those responsible for services. This is why the types of services provided have not changed as much as *how* services are delivered and *who* receives services. For example, in the 1950s, most students receiving special education instruction were placed in special classes. The special class today remains a service delivery option, but far fewer students are placed in special classes. Instead, the special class model now is used largely to provide education for students with severe disabilities. In both applications the focus is on education, but beliefs have changed relative to the students for whom special class placement is most appropriate.

MOVEMENTS INFLUENCING SERVICE DELIVERY

Throughout the development of special education programs in the 1950s and early 1960s, the general belief was that students with disabilities were best educated when grouped with students with similar attributes. This belief contributed to policies and practices suggesting placement in *self-contained special classes*.

In the 1960s, the emphasis began to shift more to *integration* in regular classes for purposes of instruction. *Resource rooms* became available, and students with mild disabilities began to spend more time in resource rooms and regular classes.

During this era, institutions came under scrutiny, and deinstitutionalization (returning people in residential facilities to the community) became a priority. The movement toward integration set the stage for trends in the 1970s and 1980s that would shift much of the responsibility for instruction of students with disabilities to regular classroom teachers.

In the late 1960s and early 1970s, the principle of *normalization* gained popularity. Wolfensberger (1972), an early leader in espousing the principle of normalization, focused initially on people with mental retardation. According to the basic tenet of normalization, people with disabilities should be treated like others in society; they should be allowed to live a "normal" life, and programs for them should be developed with normalization as a goal.

Normalization was extended to all activities of life, including living arrangements, work, play, and education. Even though the early research on normalization was carried out for the most part with adults having mental retardation, this work provided the basis for much of what is described today as inclusion of students with disabilities in the schools.

Even though many students with disabilities were in regular classes (during the 1950s, for example) because special education programs were unavailable, *mainstreaming* as an instructional strategy emerged in the early 1960s and gained popularity during the 1970s. Many viewed the delivery system of mainstreaming as an extreme from what characterized special education at the time. In contrast to a model based largely on segregation, mainstreaming called for integration.

Introduction of the least restrictive environment (LRE) principle as part of PL 94–142 supported the concept of purposeful integration of students with disabilities in regular classes. Integration of students with disabilities into classes with nondisabled students as a planned approach, however, occurred largely for philosophical reasons rather than for presumed academic benefits. Many argue that the social benefits of mainstreaming were sufficient to justify the practice. Research has tended to focus as much on the weakness of the special class model as on the advantages of mainstreaming. As the belief system among special education changed and support for mainstreaming grew, the value of the special class model declined (Wang, Reynolds, & Walberg, 1989).

In contrast to the mainstreaming movement, the *regular education initiative (REI)* emerged in the 1980s as a special education reform during the early stages of what in the 1990s has become a major reform movement in general education. All of education is being scrutinized, and significant restructuring is being called for by the public and private sectors alike. The REI movement goes beyond mainstreaming and takes on the attributes of a fully integrated system of education. With its emphasis on the abilities of all students, the REI minimizes the need for special instructional programs based on the consequences of disability. Rather, the assumption is that the regular classroom environment allows for effective instruction to meet the needs of all students.

Skrtic (1991) differentiated the REI from the mainstreaming movement in part on the basis of where the educational problem of disability lies. According to Skrtic, proponents of REI assign responsibility for students' disability to the general educational program and traditional school organization, whereas proponents of mainstreaming sought greater access to the general education program within the traditional organization of schools. For the goals of REI to be achieved, general education must change. In summarizing the status of REI in the context of general education, Skrtic (1991) stated:

> The REI proponents and opponents agree that most mild disabilities are not pathological and that the mildly handicapped designation is neither objective nor useful. However, their disagreement over the rationality of the special education system and the nature of progress has resulted in total disagreement about an appropriate course of ameliorative action. Given the negative evidence on the ethics and efficacy of special education practices and the nonadaptability of the general education system, the REI proponents believe that the special education diagnostic and instructional practices associated with the EHA and

mainstreaming models should be eliminated. As a replacement they propose a new system in which all or most students are eligible for in-class assistance, which is to be created by restructuring the current general education and special education systems into a single adaptable system. Given the same negative evidence on the ethics and efficacy of special education practices, however, the REI opponents believe that the diagnostic and instructional practices of EHA and mainstreaming models should be retained for political purposes, given the nonadaptability and political inequity of the general education system. And, because they recognize the inadequacies of the current system, they propose to improve it incrementally through additional research and development. Thus, because the proponents and opponents agree that the current system has serious problems and must be resolved, the REI debate turns to the question of the nature of school organizations and how to go about changing them. (pp. 68–69)

In the current reform movement to restructure public education, the term "all" finds its way into almost every reform initiative, often without the authors of the initiative having thought through implications of the concept (Meyen, 1992). This is occurring in general education, whereas reference to "full inclusion" is appearing in the special education literature. Underlying the current reference to "all students" is the belief that *all* students can learn.

The reform literature reveals a tendency to promote inclusion without clarification, however, leading to questions about what constitutes reasonable expectations of the general education system. For example, in *Raising Standards for American Education*, a report from the National Council on Education Standards and Testing (1992), the term "all" is used in discussing equitable educational opportunities:

> High national education standards and a system of assessments to measure their attainment can play a vital role in raising expectations, especially for youngsters from groups that have historically experienced less academic access. While the Council recognizes that new standards and assessments alone are not a complete education reform strategy, world-class standards and quality assessments can be powerful catalysts for implementing the systemic change necessary to bring all students, leaving no one behind, to high performance standards. (p. 10)

In many ways, the implied commitment of the general education reform initiatives to all students creates a climate of receptivity to the principles and practices proposed by the proponents of REI and inclusion. Clarification of what reformists mean when referring to "all students," however, is essential to the credibility of the reforms proposed. Kauffman and Hallahan (1993) described the meaning of "all" as follows:

> The implicit and explicit meanings of *all* are critical for understanding political and educational dialogue because one typically assumes that the freedoms, rights and responsibilities addressed in these exchanges are limited, not absolute. The user of the word *all* does not usually intend that it be interpreted literally because either tradition or rational discourse (or both) suggests exceptions, meaning that *all* usually represents only an approximation (and sometimes not a very close approximation) of every individual. *All*, then, is frequently understood to exclude certain individuals, sometimes for reasons that are justifiable and sometimes for reasons that are not. The varied meanings of *all* are therefore of considerable consequence to those who may be tacitly excluded. (p. 74)

During the 1990s, the reform of general and special education may well come together as the emphasis on *all students* becomes operational as a major priority. Although the outcomes of such a "merger" may not be full inclusion in the mainstream of regular classrooms for students with disabilities, the range of children served in regular classrooms likely will be broadened and full inclusion in the context of the responsibility of general education achieved. If so, the challenge for special education will consist more of integration of professional roles than of students.

STRUCTURE OF EDUCATION AGENCIES

No other area of education is as highly controlled by governmental regulations as special education. As illustrated through EHA and IDEA, Congress created a significant federal role in the education of handicapped children. This role was designed to be twofold: (a) to ensure that all children and youth with disabilities receive a free and appropriate education, and (b) to provide financial assistance to states and local education agencies in meeting their obligations to this population of students. Although the regulatory function has been enforced, however, the fiscal commitment has not been met.

Federal involvement has resulted in clarification of roles and responsibilities related to special education services. For example, the Office of Special Education and Rehabilitative Services (OSERS) represents the federal level, and education agencies operate at the state (SEA) and local (LEA) levels.

Although most students in the United States attends school in densely populated districts, a large percentage attend school in sparsely populated areas. The low incidence of students with disabilities combined with the sparse population in some rural areas has led many districts to rely on cooperative arrangements or the services of intermediate units to effectively meet the needs of students with disabilities. Thus, the intermediate education unit (IEU) has evolved as a major contributor to the education of children and youth with disabilities. In some rural areas, cooperative agreements among local districts (not fully developed IEUs) have been reached to provide specific services.

Table 2.4 illustrates the responsibilities education agencies typically assume in providing special education services. The organizational structure varies by state. Some states do not have formal IEUs; others differ in the types of services the IEUs and cooperatives provide and in how they are formed. States also employ different terms to identify IEUs and cooperative arrangements.

The regulatory function to ensure compliance with rules and legislation usually is carried out by federal and state agencies. If resources are applied appropriately, and if rules and regulations are adhered to, the result should be *appropriate, quality education*. Full compliance with state and federal regulations, however, does not ensure high-quality service. Quality is influenced by a number of locally controlled variables, including history of special education services, staff attitudes and expectations, continuity of programs offered, communities served, and enrichment experiences provided.

● **TABLE 2.4**

Responsibilities of education agencies

Agency	Function
U. S. Department of Education Office of Special Education and Rehabilitative Services (OSERS)	Serves as a resource to Congress in legislation. Enforces implementation of federal laws.
Office of Special Education (OSE)	Provides leadership in coordinating national responses toward meeting the needs of exceptional children and youth. Administers federal funds to state and local education agencies. Provides leadership in stimulating research and personnel training.
State education agencies (SEAs)	Establish rules and regulations for the approval of local educational programs serving exceptional children and youth. Serve as a resource to the state legislature on matters relating to exceptional children and youth. Provide leadership in developing and implementing comprehensive statewide plans to ensure equal educational opportunity for exceptional students. Serve as the major appeal source in disputes involving the education of exceptional children and youth. Serve in a liaison role with other state agencies in coordinating the services to exceptional students and their families. Monitor compliance of local districts in meeting state and federal requirements. Provide leadership to local districts in development of inservice training. Maintain data on numbers of exceptional children served and identified and on program expenditures.
Local education agencies (LEAs)	Provide appropriate educational programs and services for all exceptional children and youth. Implement programs in compliance with state and federal regulations. Conduct inservice training to assure that all educational personnel are effective in meeting the needs of exceptional students. Maintain due process procedures. Serve as liaison with community agencies in coordinating programs for exceptional children and youth. Operate long-range comprehensive planning programs to assure quality programs for exceptional children and youth.
Intermediate education units (IEUs) (An IEU is an organizational structure between the local education agency and the state education agency. In several states IEUs are set up by county boundaries. Others encompass several counties. Other states ignore county lines and allow adjoining districts to organize as IEUs. Intermediate education units vary in the services they provide. Some have taxing powers; others obtain funds from SEAs and by contracting with LEAs).	May provide direct services to exceptional children and youth. Frequently offer support services to LEAs. Comply with state and federal regulations governing the education of exceptional children and youth. Often contract with LEAs to provide transportation for exceptional children and youth. Generally operate inservice training programs as part of an instructional materials center.

SERVICE DELIVERY MODELS

In the 1960s, professionals began to intensify their interest in philosophical and conceptual issues related to serving students with disabilities appropriately. As long as the self-contained class was the preferred educational model for educating children with disabilities, the emphasis was on what to teach. The configuration of services was not an issue; nor was much attention given to the changing needs of students with disabilities. Options were few, and placement tended to be permanent.

As states began to pass legislation mandating special education, schools were asked to assume responsibility for children with severe disabilities, many of whom were not attending school or receiving services. At the same time, research began to focus on early intervention, and the efficacy of special education came into question. In response, service delivery system design became more complex. Also during this period, graduate programs in universities trained researchers, administrators, and other professionals with an orientation toward studying the larger question of how the needs of students with disabilities are best met in our society.

New conceptual approaches to service provision gradually evolved, along with principles to guide their implementation. Emerging delivery models constituted a set of decision rules designed to support approaches to identification, placement, and education of children with disabilities. Services were planned according to beliefs about how children with disabilities should be served versus matching children to the capabilities of existing services. These conceptual changes made possible the subsequent implementation of the LRE, due process, and the IEP. In addition, they provided a construct for considering the current emphasis on REI and inclusion.

Some service delivery models proposed over the past 20 years have been criticized for being too abstract and, in some cases, lacking in practical value. For the most part, however, the growing emphasis on service delivery models has been positive. Specifically, a focus on the child as the primary source of learning and behavior problems has been replaced by an emphasis on instructional environments, teaching methods, and the child's instructional history.

The models not only directed debate to how services should be delivered but also provided a base for research and evaluation of services. Much of the legislation passed in the 1970s, 1980s, and into the 1990s has evolved from modifications of delivery models originally designed in the 1970s.

Zero reject model. Lilly (1970), one of the first to focus on instructional accountability, proposed a zero reject model in which no child can be separated administratively from the regular class once placed there. Although it forces administrators to examine instructional options within the regular class, this approach is not fully compatible with the LRE principle because it does not allow for full-time placement outside the regular class, which is a consideration for students with severe disabilities. IDEA comes close to making the zero reject model a reality. Certainly, it makes it difficult for a student with a disability to be excluded from school.

Deno's cascade system. Probably the most frequently cited service delivery model is the cascade system proposed by Deno (1970). This model is based on a hierarchy of levels of service options, ranging from the most segregated and noneducational to the most fully integrated class placement. The cascade model enhances the match between program alternatives and student needs. Although a number of more recent adaptations of this model have been proposed, the original one is most instructional in a review of delivery models.

Application of Deno's model requires that the student be served in the least restrictive environment. If a student is placed in a Level III program after careful study, the child should be transferred to a Level II program as soon as performance warrants. The goal is to place all students in the regular class setting of a Level I program if they can be served appropriately at that level. Students may be moved to a more segregated arrangement, but only when necessary, and only until they can be returned to a less restrictive placement.

Deno's cascade system appeared early in the mainstreaming, or least restrictive environment, movement. As a conceptual model, it has become a frame of reference for local districts, reflecting a philosophy compatible with public school settings and with the intent of PL 94–142.

Dunn's inverted pyramid. Dunn (1973) modified Deno's cascade model to include four basic types of exceptional pupils and increased the number of placement options from 8 to 11. Dunn's descriptions of pupil classifications and placement options constitute a useful reference for districts in structuring service delivery plans and setting placement criteria. Dunn's is also one of the classic service delivery models. The four types of exceptional children are:

> A Type I exceptional pupil is so classified for that segment of his school career (1) when he is enrolled in the regular program of the public day schools, (2) but the teachers in that program have failed in teaching him to such a degree (3) that special supplementary instructional materials and equipment have been made available to him and/or special education consultive services to the regular teachers who work with him; special educators are not directly teaching child.

> A Type II exceptional pupil is so classified for that segment of his school career (1) when the regular teachers have failed in teaching him to such a degree (2) that he is receiving direction from one or more special educators, (3) though he continues to receive part of academic instruction in the regular program, and (4) may be enrolled in either a regular or special class.

> A Type III exceptional pupil is so classified for that segment of his school career (1) when he is receiving no academic instruction in the regular program of the public day schools, but (2) is in a separate self-contained special education day program in the local school system.

> A Type IV exceptional pupil is so classified for that segment of his school career (1) when he is unable to attend any type of day school program provided by the local school system, but (2) is in a special boarding school or on hospital or homebound instruction. (pp. 38–39)

Current emphases of delivery models. Today, many districts are concerned that their delivery systems accommodate their practices, thereby contributing to quality instruction *and* meeting the principles of zero reject, least restrictiveness, or full inclusion, as well as due process requirements. During the past decade, agencies have conducted compliance checks to ensure that local education agencies adhere to state and federal regulations.

From the perspective of some local agencies, these reviews are interruptive and tend to focus on procedural, not qualitative, aspects of programming. When viewed in the larger context, however, compliance checks have been relatively successful. Thus, federal mandates clearly have influenced policies and practices governing delivery of special education services. In the future, though, current investments in compliance reviews should shift to documentation of quality practices.

The concept of a least restrictive and full-inclusion environment is largely philosophical; it guides rather than prescribes decision making. No precise procedures are set forth for making easy decisions on placement and delivery of services. Placement decisions must take into consideration the nature of the instruction/treatment and the individual's attributes. Further, the level of restrictiveness is determined not by the environment but, rather, by the individual's needs and abilities.

The characteristics of the environment are matched to the student. For example, a child requiring medical treatment may be placed initially in a hospital school or a residential center, but once the medical problem is controlled, the original setting may be considered too restrictive and, therefore, inappropriate. Similarly, a student may need the structure offered by part-time placement in a special class, but because of a strong need for identification with nonhandicapped peers, she may be served best through regular class placement and tutoring until the benefits of working with the special classroom teacher have been clearly established.

Least restrictiveness for a given student cannot always be determined at the time the placement decision is made. How the student responds is often a key factor. The levels of restrictiveness are arbitrary. They merely demonstrate how placement alternatives vary from what is considered normal or routine in the education of nonhandicapped students without considering the needs of specific students or measuring restrictiveness. Restrictiveness increases as the child requires additional instructional resources and services. The levels in Figure 2.2 are as follows:

Level 1: The *regular class* represents the primary source of instruction. This level represents the ultimate attributes of REI or inclusion with the needs of all students being accommodated in regular classes.

Level 2: The *special class* represents the primary source of instruction. Students may be integrated into regular classes, but their instructional base remains the special class.

Level 3: Assignment to a *special day school* (public or private) in the community is significantly more restrictive than the special class in a neighborhood attendance center. If the student resides outside the home, the environment is considered to be more restrictive.

Level 4: Settings that involve *24-hour care* outside the home are the most restrictive. Instruction becomes several treatment programs as the student requires.

In many ways, LRE placements are determined more easily for students who have

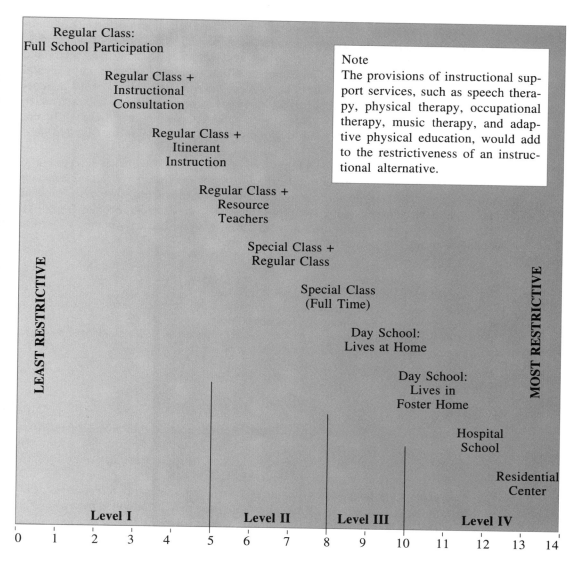

Regular Class:
Full School Participation

Regular Class +
Instructional
Consultation

Regular Class +
Itinerant
Instruction

Regular Class +
Resource
Teachers

Special Class +
Regular Class

Special Class
(Full Time)

Day School:
Lives at Home

Day School:
Lives in
Foster Home

Hospital
School

Residential
Center

Note
The provisions of instructional support services, such as speech therapy, physical therapy, occupational therapy, music therapy, and adaptive physical education, would add to the restrictiveness of an instructional alternative.

LEAST RESTRICTIVE

MOST RESTRICTIVE

Level I   Level II   Level III   Level IV

0   1   2   3   4   5   6   7   8   9   10   11   12   13   14

[a]This figure illustrates the comparative restrictiveness of settings, but placement decisions should be based on the needs of the learner as well as characteristics of the alternative settings.

Source: From E. L. Meyen (Ed.), 1982, *Exceptional Children in Today's Schools: An Alternative Resource Book*, Denver: Love.

● FIGURE 2.2

Instructional placement environments based on level of restrictiveness[a] severe handicaps, because fewer effective options are available to this population. For students with mild handicaps, on the other hand, recommendations for regular class placement, although least restrictive, do not always recognize conditions that could mitigate effective instruction. For example, although a student with mild mental retardation may benefit socially from being placed in a regular class, his instructional needs may not be met if he is required to satisfy the same requirements as nondisabled students in the class. Another student with mild retardation may have sufficient independent study skills to respond to group instructional techniques or limited individualized attention.

Most students with mild handicaps require intense individualized instruction. Therefore, basing an LRE placement decision solely on the features of the environment is unreasonable. Instead, conditions favorable to intense instruction must be considered first. If an environment is not conducive to intense instruction, it becomes restrictive and, in turn, inappropriate. Meyen and Lehr (1980) described environments that are conducive to intense instruction characterized by:

- the consistency and duration of time on task
- the timing, frequency, and nature of feedback to the student, based on the student's immediate performance and cumulative progress
- regular and frequent communication to the student that the teacher expects the student to master the task and demonstrate continuous progress
- a pattern of interaction in which the teacher responds to student initiatives and uses consequences appropriate to the student's response. (p. 6)

SERVICE DELIVERY OPTIONS

Local and state education agencies both use various terms to identify special education services and service providers, in part because of attempts to minimize stigma. Also, efforts are being made to ensure that services are described functionally within the broad range of educational services the school offers. In spite of the lack of uniformity, some generic terms and descriptions are used.

A service does not depend on the title or terms used. In general, terms reflect what is most applicable to local or state situations. Services may be provided by a district, a private school, an intermediate education unit, a consortium of school districts, or, in some cases, a state agency. The following is a brief description of services/personnel.

Regular class placement. Placement of students with disabilities in regular classes assumes that the regular classroom teacher is trained in how to adapt materials and methods to the student's unique needs and has access to resource materials and consultation. Today, there is disagreement regarding the severity of learning problems that teachers in the regular class can accommodate.

Self-contained special class placement. Designed to provide full-time assignment outside the regular class, self-contained placement is not a main option for most exceptional children today. It is limited primarily to students with moderate to severe handicapping conditions. Until the late 1960s, however, special classes served students with mild handicaps.

Within this setting, children with similar characteristics typically are assigned to a teacher who is responsible for planning and executing the educational program. The teacher may be assisted by an aide or a paraprofessional, and students may receive services from other specialists as well. For the most part, however, instruction is delivered by the special classroom teacher.

Part-time special class placement. Particularly for students with mild mental retardation, part-time placement in a special class has been used extensively. It differs from resource placement (below) in that the student spends at least half the school day in the special class. In the movement to eliminate or reduce special classes, students likely will receive special instruction in basic skill subjects in these settings but be integrated into regular classes for other experiences. At the secondary level, students may attend selected regular classes and receive assistance with academic and job readiness skills in the special class.

This placement option has advantages for exceptional children who have problems working with several teachers. It also offers advantages for regular classroom teachers who have difficulty accommodating the exceptional student's instructional needs while simultaneously meeting the needs of their nonhandicapped students. The special classroom teacher spends more time with the student and is able to both counsel and teach. In many districts, part-time special class placement is a transitional phase between full-time special class placement and regular class placement. If inclusion is successful, this placement option will diminish in importance.

Resource room (teacher). The resource room or teacher continues to be among the most popular of the options, especially for students who have learning disabilities. Students typically are referred to a specially trained teacher on the basis of assessed academic difficulties. The resource teacher may work with students in small groups. Mainly, though, teaching is highly individualized, and remedial or supplemental instruction is based on prescribed objectives for individual students. The resource teacher also assumes major responsibilities for assessment and for developing prescriptions. Communication is established and maintained with regular classroom teachers of the students assigned to the resource room.

Placement is short-term, and the student is returned to full-time placement in the regular class when sufficient progress is noted. For many students, a combination of resource room and regular class placement remains the least restrictive alternative. Thus, a student may be assigned to a resource room throughout the elementary and early secondary grades.

Class-Within-a-Class. Currently, the fastest growing model in the country, class-within-a-class (CWC) is designed to include students with mild or moderate disabilities in the general education classroom with agemates. Although it meets the requirements of inclusion, CWC is not a full inclusion model. Within its emphasis on instructional delivery, the model involves *equally shared responsibility* between general and special education, including collaborative teaching, planning, and evaluating. Five components make up the model: integrated classroom; collaborative teaching/planning; effective teaching strategies; learning strategies for students; and enhanced and parallel curriculum.

Resource center. The resource center takes a variety of forms. Usually, it is organized as one or two rooms staffed by two or more teachers who work with students with various handicapping conditions. Working cooperatively, these teams make available more instructional resources to meet individual student needs. Students are referred to the centers for specific instruction and may be assigned for one or more periods per day, but rarely more than three. Most instruction is delivered on an individual basis, with considerable emphasis on independent work. Although occasionally used at the elementary level, resource centers are found most frequently at the secondary level.

Itinerant teacher. Itinerant teachers are not responsible for a classroom but, instead, provide services directly to the students assigned to a regular class or other setting. Itinerant teachers offer tutorial instruction that supplements the instruction offered by the regular teacher, who may initiate a referral for a student. These teachers work to a considerable extent with students who have visual handicaps, assisting them in learning braille, preparing materials in braille, and providing general support services so these students can maintain themselves in regular classes.

The term "itinerant" applies to a wide range of personnel—speech clinicians, school psychologists, rehabilitation counselors, social workers—who service students at various times. In this discussion, "itinerant teacher" describes teachers who provide direct instructional assistance to students with disabilities while the students remain in the regular or special class. In contrast to the resource room, where the students go to the teacher, the itinerant teacher takes the service to the students. By working with the students in class, these teachers can coordinate instruction closely with the regular teacher and observe the student in the routine classroom setting.

Consulting teacher. Various titles are conferred on the consulting teacher. Basically, consulting teachers are professionals who consult with regular classroom teachers and other personnel involved in the exceptional child's program. Unlike itinerant teachers, consulting teachers do not directly instruct students except when demonstrating an instructional technique to a teacher. The intent of most districts is to make available to regular classrooms these specialized teachers who are experienced in special instructional techniques, understand exceptional children, and are skilled in the consultation process but do not supervise. In addition, consulting teachers typically are skilled in facilitating collaboration among teachers and related services personnel. (Collaboration is discussed further in Chapter 3.) This service option is expected to become more widespread because of the growing emphasis on expanding the regular classroom teacher's responsibility in meeting the needs of exceptional students.

Child/study/diagnostic/evaluation/prescriptive/teaching center. No standard term describes the comprehensive evaluation center that combines testing, experimental instruction, family counseling, and instructional planning. Programs composed of highly coordinated referral, evaluation, and instructional planning services are designed to observe students while responding to newly prescribed programs or services. Changes can be made before students are placed in a recommended program. These centers offer many advantages for interdisciplinary planning. For example, they sometimes work with parents in instructional planning to help them better understand their child's capabilities.

Homebound instruction. Some students may be confined to the home for some time. To minimize interruption to the student's education, special teachers provide tutoring. Assigned a caseload, teachers visit students regularly and assist the regular teacher in preparing instruction. This option is intended for short-term confinement. Under unusual circumstances, however, it may be the student's primary source of instruction.

Hospital instruction. The extent of instruction offered to a hospitalized student varies according to the child's condition. Some large children's hospitals maintain small instruction staffs in cooperation with local school districts. The goal is to help students maintain progress in school programs.

RELATED SERVICES

Many students with disabilities require specialized services in addition to instruction. For some, the services are essential to their ability to participate in educational programs. Other services are more general but still supportive. Referred to in EHA and IDEA as "related services," they are defined as *direct services* provided by specialists (speech and language pathologists, school psychologists, physical therapists) or *support services* (resource teacher, itinerant teacher, special class teacher). "Support services" means special services other than educational placement or the student's primary assignment (included in the previous descriptions). For example, a child may be assigned to a regular class and a resource room; in this situation, the resource room functions as the support service. For another student, it may serve as the primary assignment. Related or support services include transportation, parent training or counseling, medical treatment counseling, adaptive physical education, and music therapy.

Direct services are offered by the following specialists. IDEA added rehabilitation counseling and social work services as related services.

School psychologist. Early in the history of special education, school psychologists provided only testing services. Although they continue to assume major responsibilities in diagnosis, school psychologists are becoming more involved in curriculum planning, consultation with teachers and parents, case management, and coordination of the IEP process. Districts frequently assign responsibility for chairing IEP conferences to the school psychologist.

Speech and language pathologist. Speech and language problems are common. More exceptional children receive speech therapy than any other special education service.

And a mentally retarded or emotionally disturbed child, for example, may have an accompanying speech problem. The speech and language pathologist helps children who have articulation or language difficulties as well as those who have more serious speech disorders. Many students receive speech therapy as an additional service. Others who have no other handicaps require only speech therapy. Therapy is provided in individual or group sessions or, in many cases, through consultation with the student's teacher.

Recently, districts have started to employ language specialists. Emphasis on language services can be expected to continue, but no pattern has yet been established in the nature of the services or the professional training involved. The language specialist may evolve as a person trained in both speech therapy and learning disabilities.

Physical therapist. Upon a physician's prescription, physical therapists provide treatment in motor performance, focusing on correction, development, and prevention. As more programs for students with severe/profound handicaps and preschool handicapped children are developed in the public schools, the availability of physical therapy in these settings will increase.

Occupational therapist. Occupational therapists are not routinely employed in public schools. Yet, occupational therapy is important to many exceptional children. For example, individual and group activities enhance physical, social, psychological, and cognitive development. Occupational therapy is a major service at most rehabilitation centers. Recent attention has been given to occupational therapy with exceptional preschool children.

Social worker. Now a major resource in programming for exceptional children, social workers provide a link between the school staff and the family. Services include assistance in interpreting evaluation reports and recommendations. In some districts, social workers chair child study committees and help special educators interact with community agencies.

Rehabilitation counselor. The early involvement of rehabilitative counseling services centered largely on people with physical disabilities. Now these counselors deal with all disabilities that require rehabilitative services. Specifically, rehabilitative counseling is concerned with assessing the abilities of individuals with disabilities; preparing for their employment, including transition from school to employment; and facilitating their independence.

TRANSITION SERVICES

IDEA has given additional impetus to transitional services by placing priority on these services for at-risk and disabled infants and youth. The emphasis for infants is on transition from medical care to early intervention services and on moving from early intervention services to preschool programs. For disabled youth, IDEA calls for the provision of transitional services from age 14 until students leave school. IDEA defines transition services as a "coordinated set of activities." In discussing transitional activities, Turnbull (1993) stated:

> This set of activities "shall include instruction, community experience, the development of employment and other post-school adult living objectives, and, when appropriate, acquisition of daily living skills and functional vocational evaluation." This requirement makes three commands. First, it tells local educational agencies to use specified means ("instruction, community experience," etc.) in order to achieve the outcomes (results, ends) that the transition provisions specify. Thus, the law sets out both the ends and the means. Second, it tells local educational agencies that "acquisition of daily living skills and functional vocational evaluation" are appropriate in transition plans for some, but not for all, students. Thus, the law sets a general rule in favor of employment or other post-school adult living objectives for most students. Third and finally, it tells local educational agencies that they should use community-referenced, community-based, and community-delivered instruction. Thus, it acknowledges the principles of generalization and durability (students learn best when they must actually use their skills), and it acknowledges that skill development should take place in the least restrictive, most normal settings. (p. 126)

Through IDEA, the expectations of transitional services have become more explicit. Outcomes, rather than process, are emphasized, calling for the schools to state transitional activities as part of the IEP process and also to create experiences in the community and workplace that will enhance student performance. Independent living and success in the workplace are clearly tied to the outcomes of transitional services.

In implementing transitional services for disabled youth, the schools must work with community agencies that define their mission as serving persons with disabilities, as well as with general or generic agencies that serve the general population. In the past, the latter have largely left to specialized agencies the responsibility for serving persons with disabilities. In some ways, current efforts represent the extension of mainstreaming, LRE, REI, and inclusion to the community and to meeting the life span needs of persons with disabilities.

OPPORTUNITIES OF TECHNOLOGY

Most current computer applications in education stem from attempts to design educational uses for known technology rather than a deliberate effort to seek technological solutions to existing problems. More and more, however, models pose a problem and then develop a technological response to it. Current technology cannot address all instructional challenges, however, and efforts in this area often fail because of the high cost of technology.

Students with disabilities present special challenges to technology. A few minutes of observing children and youth with severe disabilities, for example, is sufficient to develop a "want list" of technology applications that challenge research and development. Even when applications are available (communicative devices, speech synthesizers, print-reading computers), some individuals are precluded from effective use of current technology because of their specific disabilities or living circumstances.

Over time, technology may contribute to the quality of life for people with disabilities as much as did the policies of EHA and IDEA. Many seriously disabled individuals now have no control over their environment. Some are unable to communicate their wants and needs. In the future, computers may allow these individuals to interact with others and enjoy the dignity that comes from having control over one's life.

Others with mild disabilities need only the assistance of technology to achieve full employment and their potential for attaining the quality of life available to nondisabled persons. Computers now can read print, communicate, and, through remote switching capabilities, control the environment.

The extent to which technology contributes to the quality of life of people with disabilities depends largely on how effectively special educators apply available technologies, advocate for needed new technologies, and conduct research. Recreational and daily living applications are as important as instructional applications and probably represent areas in which the most significant quality-of-life contributions will occur.

Most of the current special educators and related service professionals began their careers before colleges and universities offered courses in computer literacy and programming. As a result, they must show personal initiative to achieve confidence and competence in the technological arena. They need to be able to operate microcomputers, evaluate and select software, create environments conducive to computer use in educational and treatment settings, do simple programming, and recognize needs that translate into applications.

Most, if not all, technology can be applied to students with disabilities. Many special educators invest significant resources and time to ensure that existing technology is being used with their students when appropriate. Computer-aided instruction (CAI), instructional management systems, databases, computer games, simulations, and research needs are examples. In many cases, existing software and peripheral devices can be used; in others, modifications may be necessary.

Assistive technology devices and services. IDEA incorporates the definition of assistive technology devices and assistive technology services from PL 100–407, the Technology-Related Assistance for Individuals with Disabilities Act of 1988. By including assistive devices and services as requirements of IDEA, a student's needs for devices or services become part of the student's IEP. IDEA defines assistive technology devices and assistive technology services in the following:

> The term "assistive technology device" means any item, piece of equipment, or product system, whether acquired commercially, off the shelf, modified, or customized, that is used to increase, maintain, or improve functional capabilities of individuals with disabilities. (Sec. 1401)(a)(25)

> The term "assistive technology service" means any service that directly assists an individual with a disability in the selection, acquisition, or use of an assistive technology device. Such terms include:
> (A) the evaluation of the needs of an individual with a disability, including a functional

evaluation of the individual in the individual's customary environment;

(B) purchasing, leasing or otherwise providing for the acquisition of assistive technology devices by individuals with disabilities;

(C) selecting, designing, fitting, customizing, adapting, applying, maintaining, repairing, or replacing of assistive technology devices;

(D) coordinating and using other therapies, interventions, or services with assistive technology devices, such as those associated with existing education and rehabilitation plans and programs;

(E) training or technical assistance for an individual with disabilities, or, where appropriate, the family of an individual with disabilities; and

(F) training or technical assistance for professionals (including individuals providing education and rehabilitation services), employers, or other individuals who provide services to, employ, or are otherwise substantially involved in the major life functions of individuals with disabilities.

Assistive devices. Although the necessary expertise and technology are available for applying many assistive devices and services, costs are excessive and the market thin. Like orphan drugs, developed to treat rare serious disorders, a device that will benefit only a few people does not receive the same development support as one intended for a larger population. Nevertheless, specialized assistive devices can greatly improve the quality of life for disabled individuals who need them.

Despite the appeal and potential of technology, all problems of students with disabilities cannot be solved through technology. IDEA provides the stimulus to explore application of technology to learning by students with disabilities and to enhancing their performance during transitions. This is true particularly for youth with disabilities as they make the transition from school to the world of work. In addition, ADA will be helpful as employers are required to make accommodations in the workplace.

Technology represents an unprecedented opportunity to address some of the most significant needs of children and youth with severe disabilities. As programs in bioengineering evolve, more technology may become available for students with disabilities than for typical students. This raises a number of concerns. For example, a substantial portion of existing educational software involves individualizing instruction with minimal interpersonal interaction. Some assistive devices, though benefiting the person, could create a technology-dependent environment. How does this mesh with our beliefs about least restrictiveness, normalization, and nondiscrimination? Technology to address the needs of people with disabilities is still in its infancy. As it matures, its capabilities for enhancing independence, building dependence (on technology), and influencing the interpersonal nature of the person's environment increase. The significance of these issues is largely a personal perspective. Special educators should ask:

■ Are there any limits to how technology may be applied to the lives of persons with disabilities?

■ Should special education instructional software contain interpersonal, interactive features?

■ What is the risk of a person with a disability becoming too dependent on technology?

■ How does the use of technology with children who have disabilities interface with our beliefs about normalization and least restrictiveness?

Technology may hold the key to addressing some of the most significant challenges facing individuals with severe handicapping conditions. It further may represent an instructional resource of unprecedented potential for developing educational interventions for students with mild disabilities. Some risks are involved, however, not the least of which is the need to ensure that technology is applied to the *specific needs* of children and youth with disabilities. If appropriate technologies are to evolve, attention must be directed to developing partnerships between educators and related professionals and representatives from industry and technology-intensive fields.

Clearly, opportunities to improve the quality of life for people with disabilities are increasing as a result of advancements in technology. The future must be guided by reasonable thought. What can, and what should, technology do for children, youth, and adults with disabilities to enhance their quality of life and facilitate their participation in the mainstream of their communities?

SUMMARY AND PROJECTIONS

The underpinnings of legislation affecting people with disabilities are the Civil Rights Act of 1964 and Section 504 of the Rehabilitation Act of 1973, which set the stage for the Education for All Handicapped Children Act of 1975 and its subsequent amendments extending services to preschool children and infants and toddlers. The Individuals with Disabilities Education Act (IDEA) of 1990 renamed the EHA in keeping with sensitivity to the terminology of "handicapped," which denoted a condition and placed the onus on the individual, to "with disabilities," which transfers more responsibility to the educational milieu—fitting the system to the individual rather than the individual to the system. The usage "exceptional" in some state legislation extends services to the gifted, expanding the population to include everyone who differs significantly from the norm.

The Americans with Disabilities Act (ADA), passed in 1990, is civil rights legislation prohibiting discrimination against persons with disabilities in both the public and private sectors, and has ramifications for the working environment. This and other legislation has come about largely from advocacy efforts of parents and other citizen groups and has been bolstered by court rulings that provided needed clarification and enforcement.

The conceptual foundations for service delivery are Lilly's zero reject model, Deno's cascade system, and Dunn's inverted pyramid, the latter two incorporating the important concept of least restrictive environment. Over the years, services have been delivered, first in separate schools, later in self-contained segregated classes (the typical form before the 1960s), giving way to preference for the resource room/teacher, an option that remains popular today, to primary placement in the regular classroom, except for those with severe and profound disabilities, including significant, mental retardation. Most recently, the REI and inclusion of *all* children are at the forefront of discussion and policymaking.

Services are delivered by state and local education agencies (SEAs and LEAs). In some sparsely populated areas, intermediate education units (IEUs) have been established to pool resources and thereby ensure adequate services. Other placement alternatives include the class-within-a-class, the resource center, itinerant teacher, consulting teacher, and diagnostic center, the latter of which has a variety of terminology. In addition, homebound and hospital instruction are provided for those who are unable to attend school for some period. *Related services* can be either direct or indirect. Specialists involved include the school psychologist, speech and language pathologist, physical therapist, occupational therapist, social worker, and rehabilitation counselor.

IDEA has given impetus to transitional services, both when entering and exiting the school system. Technology represents exciting possibilities for individuals with disabilities. Other assistive devices and services likewise are being developed to aid people with disabilities in living skills, communication, and workplaces.

Most, perhaps all, of what special education is today reflects what schools are doing in response to legislation. Some of these responses are perceived as sound educational practices; others stem from the consequences of noncompliance. When placed in the larger context, the benefits resulting from EHA and, most recently, IDEA are significant. What is questionable, however, is whether what is now occurring is most appropriate given the knowledge base of today.

This official perspective on special education is solidified by the power of rules and regulations. Without the structure they offer, what exists today could not have been achieved. The time will come, though, when these rules will no longer serve us.

We are reminded daily that current programs and policies are not necessarily an "ideal" way to accommodate the needs of children and youth with disabilities. For instance, it would be better if children did not have to be labeled to receive an appropriate education; if parents did not have to monitor the schools to ensure compliance; or if schools would adjust their organizational structure so special education programs no longer would differ from "plain good" instructional practice.

As changes come about, new issues will emerge, and other perspectives will take over. Our frame of reference will expand beyond individual children and youth to the larger ecological context within which "disabilities" and "exceptionalities" are created, recognized, and defined. This transformation, however gradual, will take us where we ought to be if least restrictiveness, normalization, REI, or inclusion are to mean anything in the evolution of special education.

An uneasiness is evolving because of widespread uncertainty about the world and the place of humans in it. Every discipline, including education, is affected. Although the official story of special education remains protected by the rules and regulations that have created it, the beliefs of many—including professionals, advocates, and disabled people themselves—are changing. Much of what is practiced today is being challenged. What the future holds for students with disabilities will depend largely on the reforms of general education. The decade of the 1990s will see restructuring in how schools operate and, if the view of those who argue for REI and inclusion prevail, restructuring will bring about significant changes in special education. These changes may result in the bureaucracy of special education becoming invisible as the needs of all learners are addressed without the need for legislative intervention for students who meet eligibility criteria.

REFERENCES

Baker, H. J. (1953). *Introduction to exceptional children.* New York: Macmillan.

Ballantyne, B., McGee, M., Patton, S., & Cohen, D. (1985). *Cooperative programs for transition from school to work.* Washington, DC: U.S. Department of Education, Office of Special Education & Rehabilitative Services, National Institute of Handicapped Research.

Clark, G. M. (1982). Career and vocational programming. In E. L. Meyen (Ed.), *Exceptional children and youth: An introduction* (2nd ed.). Denver: Love Publishing.

Council for Exceptional Children. (1977, August). *An analysis of categorical definitions, diagnostic methods, diagnostic criteria, and personnel utilization in the classification of handicapped children.* Discussion draft pursuant to grant from Bureau of Education for the Handicapped, U.S. Office of Education, Washington, DC.

Deno, E. (1970). Special education as developmental capital. *Exceptional Children, 37*(3), 229–237.

Dunn, L. M. (1963). *Exceptional children in the schools: Special education in transition* (1st ed.). New York: Holt, Rinehart & Winston.

Dunn, L. M. (1973). *Exceptional children in the schools: Special education in transition* (2nd ed.). New York: Holt, Rinehart & Winston.

Evans, E. D. (1975). *Contemporary influences in early childhood education* (2nd ed.). New York: Holt, Rinehart & Winston.

Goldstein, H., Arkell, C., Ashcroft, S. C., Hurley, O. L., Lilly, M. S., & Schools, M. S. (1975). In N. Hobbs (Ed.), *Issues in the classification of children.* San Francisco: Jossey-Bass.

Goodman, L. V. (1976). A bill of rights for the handicapped. *American Education, 12*(6), 6–8.

Hardman, M. L., Drew, C. J., & Egan, E. M. (1984). *Human exceptionality: Society, school and family.* Boston: Allyn & Bacon.

Haring, N. G., & McCormick, K. L. (1986). *Exceptional children and youth* (4th ed.). Columbus, OH: Charles E. Merrill.

Hewett, F. M., & Forness, S. R. (1984). *Education of exceptional learners* (3rd ed.). Boston: Allyn & Bacon.

Kauffman, J. M., & Hallahan, D. P. (1993). Toward a comprehensive delivery system: The necessity of identity, focus, and authority for special education and other compensatory programs. In J. I. Goodlad & T. C. Lovitt (Eds.), *Integrating general and special education.* Columbus, OH: Charles E. Merrill.

Lilly, M. S. (1970). Special education: A tempest in a teapot. *Exceptional Children, 37,* 43–49.

MacMillan, D. L., Jones, R. L., & Aloia, G. F. (1974). The mentally retarded label: A theoretical analysis and review of research. *American Journal of Mental Deficiency, 79,* 241–261.

MacMillan, D. L., Keogh, C. K., & Jones, R. L. (1986). Special education research on mildly handicapped learners. In M. C. Wittrock (Ed.), *Handbook of research on teaching* (3rd ed.). New York: Macmillan.

Meyen, E. L. (1982). *Exceptional Children in Today's Schools: An Alternative Resource Book.* Denver: Love Publishing.

Meyen, E. L. (1992). Educational reform: The intent and the risks. *The Kansas Journal of Law Public Policy, 2*(2) (1992 Symposium Issue).

Meyen, E. L., & Lehr, D. H. (1980, March). Least restrictive environment: Instructional implications. *Focus on Exceptional Children, 12*(7), 1–8.

National Association of State Directors of Special Education. (1983). Alexandria, VA: Author.

National Council on Education Standards and Testing. (1992). Raising standards for American education: *A report to Congress, the Secretary of Education, the National Education Goals Panel, and the American People*. Washington, DC: U.S. Government Printing Office.

Peterson, N. L. (1987). *Early intervention for handicapped and at-risk children*. Denver: Love Publishing.

Rosenthal, R., & Jacobson, L. (1968). *Pygmalion in the classroom*. New York: Holt, Rinehart & Winston.

Skrtic, T. M., Guba, E. G., & Knowlton, H. E. (1985). *Interorganizational special education programming in rural areas* (Technical report on the multisite naturalistic field study). Washington, DC: National Institute of Education.

Skrtic, T. M. (1991). *Behind special education*. Denver: Love Publishing.

Turnbull, H. R. (1986). *Free appropriate public education: The law and children with disabilities*. Denver: Love Publishing.

Turnbull, H. R. (1993). *Free appropriate public education: The law and children with disabilities* (4th ed.). Denver: Love Publishing.

U.S. Department of Education. (1993). *National Agenda for Achieving Better Results for Children with Disabilities*, Forum Briefing Materials. Washington, DC: U.S. Government Printing Office.

U.S. Department of Education, Office of Special Education and Rehabilitative Services (1992). *Fourteenth annual report to Congress on the implementation of the Education for the Handicapped Act*. Washington, DC: U.S. Government Printing Office.

U.S. House of Representatives, Committee on Education and Labor. (1983). *Report Accompanying the Education of the Handicapped Amendments of 1984*, H.R. 3435 (H.R. Rept. No. 98-410). Washington, DC: U.S. Government Printing Office.

Wang, M. C., Reynolds, M. C., & Walberg, H. J. (1989). Who benefits from segregation and murky water? *Phi Delta Kappan, 71*(1), 64–67.

Wehman, P., & Melia, R. (1985). The job coach: Function in transition and supported employment. *American Rehabilitation, 11*(2), 4–7.

Wehman, P., Moon, M. S., & McCarthy, P. (1986). Transition from school to adulthood for youth with severe handicaps. *Focus on Exceptional Children, 18*(5).

Weintraub, F. J., Abeson, A., Ballard, J., & LaVor, M. L. (Eds.). 1976). *Public policy and the education of exceptional children*. Reston, VA: Council for Exceptional Children.

Will, M. (1985). Transition: Linking disabled youth to a productive future. *OSERS New in Print, 1*(1).

Wolfensberger, W. (1972). *Normalization: The principle of normalization in human services*. Toronto, Ontario, Canada: National Institute on Mental Retardation.

Ysseldyke, J., & Algozzine, B. (1984). *Introduction to special education*. Boston: Houghton Mifflin.

CURRENT AND EMERGING

INSTRUCTIONAL

PRACTICES

EDWARD L. MEYEN

*P*roponents of educational reforms are calling for higher expectations of all students. They expect performance at levels that reflect world-class standards without taking into consideration the range of student attributes. Further, the emphasis is shifting from functional expectations to performance in disciplines such as math, science, geography, English, and history. In addition, skills for the workplace have been redefined to focus on higher-order thinking skills to produce workers with problem-solving skills that will enhance their performance as lifelong learners in a changing work environment.

The goals of special education historically have been to assist students with disabilities in reaching their potential. As education has become accessible to all students with disabilities, independent living has become a central theme, with considerable emphasis on functional curricular goals. If, as an adolescent, a student with moderate mental retardation is unable to read sufficiently, his or her instructional program acquires a more practical orientation aimed at continued training and work experience in the community after leaving school. This approach contrasts with continuing intense instruction in reading and other basic skills with the assumption that, given more time and instruction, students eventually will learn regardless of their abilities.

The education reform movement has not evolved to the point at which expectations are being differentiated based on abilities. Instead, the prevailing assumption is that all children can learn and that all students will benefit from being subjected to higher expectations, particularly in the subject-matter fields. As reasonable as these beliefs are, until they become operationally defined and revised curricula are in place, teachers of students with disabilities likely will be expected to respond to the proposed reforms without having access to the necessary instructional support. In addition, they may encounter unrealistic expectations of their ability to raise their students' academic performance.

The difficulties in implementing instructional programs for students with disabilities that are responsive to the reform movement in general education are compounded by the full inclusion and regular education initiatives (REI). Even though these approaches seem to be compatible with the overall reform movement, significant disagreement continues as to how realistic either of these approaches is and whether conditions in the regular classroom can be structured to ensure an appropriate education for students with disabilities.

If the barriers separating students with disabilities and those without disabilities are to be eliminated, instruction and other services must be provided in natural settings where all students are included. The question that remains to be answered is: Will students with disabilities benefit maximally from instruction in fully integrated classroom settings?

Today Johnny walks out of Mr. Gallo's sixth-grade classroom down the hall to Mrs. Brown's resource room for students with mild disabilities. He is considered to have mild disabilities and, as such, is participating in a special education program. Maria arrives at school in a special van. It is equipped with a lift that lowers Maria to the sidewalk. She wheels her way to Mrs. Wilcox's special class for students with severe multiple disabilities. Fifty miles away, Sara, who, like Maria, has multiple disabilities, is entering a regular fourth-grade class. She is a little older than her peers, but the fourth grade is her class. Each of these students is participating in a special education program. Each benefits from special education services. Each also is identified as a student with disabilities by virtue of his or her participation in the program. Many children like Johnny, Maria, and Sara are present in today's schools.

Maria and Sara would not be receiving special education services 25 years ago. As recent as 5 years ago, Sara would not have been attending a regular class. Today, because of IDEA, public policy assures all students with disabilities access to regular and special education programs. Which placement is most appropriate and effective, however, is not certain. The professional educators in Johnny and Maria's district assume these students are receiving a free and appropriate education because they have been identified as eligible for special services. Individualized education programs (IEPs) were developed and approved for these children, and they were placed in a program based on the staff's professional judgment and in accordance with the district's due process guidelines. Sara resides in a district committed to full inclusion. The district is in the implementation stage of this delivery model and is experimenting with instructional strategies to assist the regular class teacher in accommodating the instructional needs of students with disabilities.

If one of the educators involved in these scenarios were to question the appropriateness of the program, the district would point to (a) the initial referral, which called attention to the students' probable need for special education; (b) results of various tests confirming their cognitive abilities; (c) in the case of Maria and Sara, medical records identifying health needs requiring special consideration; and (d) an IEP for each, describing their current level of performance, needed related services, and a list of objectives detailing specific interventions essential to meeting their needs. This evidence would be well documented by test scores, anecdotal information, and examples of schoolwork.

Further, the skeptical educator likely would be reminded that the students' parents had signed their IEPs, indicating approval of both the placement and the program itself. The educator, however, likely would not get clear documentation of how effective the different instructional interventions are, or information on why these interventions were deemed more appropriate than others.

Given the state of reform in education, to determine how appropriate an educational program is in terms of its adherence to procedural requirements is much easier than to establish its qualitative merits or to argue the philosophical benefits of one placement over another. At some point, however, verifying *appropriateness* becomes essential, in terms of effectiveness, not procedural compliance or philosophy. How effectively did intervention remedy Johnny's learning deficits? Or enhance Maria's and Sara's achievement commensurate with their potential? As a planning tool, the IEP does not consistently shape the instruction offered children and youth with disabilities. Besides, we cannot assume that it will assure appropriate education. Yet, the IEP remains a focal point for decisions concerning instruction and services.

As a person who is preparing for a professional role in education, or is interested in the study of exceptional children and youth, you will encounter varying opinions about the effectiveness of the IEP process. School districts encountered a variety of problems in the early years of implementing the IEP. They knew that their responsiveness to the requirements would be monitored and that, if they were found to be noncompliant, they would be subject to litigation. The requirements, however, were largely procedural. The result was more paperwork and record keeping than schools had been accustomed to (see Skrtic, Guba, & Knowlton, 1985; Wright, Cooperstein, Reneker, & Padilla, 1982).

The purpose of the IEP, as initially mandated by PL 94–142 in 1975 and refined by IDEA in 1990, is that a written plan of instruction be prepared for each child receiving special services. Often perceived as a procedural or an administrative process rather than as an instructional planning system, the IEP meant little more than a lot of extra paperwork for teachers who already were under pressure. With too little time to instruct as it was, they now also had to attend conferences, interact with other professionals, and follow a prestructured format in developing their instructional plans. In addition, they had to negotiate with administrators, parents, and sometimes students. Decision making became a group process.

Amid all these changes, instructional decisions remained the primary responsibility of the special education and regular classroom teachers, who too often had to make decisions within the bureaucratic, if not political, arena the IEP process created. In many instances, once the student was placed and an IEP was completed, compliance was simply a matter of ensuring that the IEP was on file and that it was updated regularly. Through the IEP, however, some programs have been able to center on instruction and management while minimizing the procedural aspect and maintaining accountability. The principles underlying the IEP are sound. The challenge is to keep the focus on the instructional direction offered by the IEP and its potential as a source of individual instructional accountability.

THE INSTRUCTIONAL ENVIRONMENT

The scenario involving Johnny, Maria, and Sara is not solely a consequence of PL 94–142 or IDEA. Special education also has tended to attend primarily to identification, assessment/diagnosis, determination of eligibility, and, ultimately, placement. The instructional planning sequence has become formalized as a consequence of the IEP requirements in PL 94–142 and the accompanying public concern for due process. In contrast, instructional intervention—presumably the special student's basic need—seldom receives as much attention. Once a student is placed in an appropriate instructional setting (special class, resource room, regular class), the teacher somehow "knows" what is best instructionally for the student. This assumes the teacher has access to necessary resources and is capable of implementing the intervention successfully.

As Skrtic points out in Chapter 14, the special education process often has been compared to the medical model, which consists of symptoms, diagnosis, prescription, and treatment intervention. Medicine, however, emphasizes the design and improvement of treatment intervention, whereas in special education instructional planning based on assessment has too often received insufficient attention. The emphasis has been largely on ensuring access to needed services (sometimes referred to as "educational equity") and refining assessment instruments. Instructional decisions too often focus on appropriate educational settings rather than on strengthening the power and precision of intervention. The teacher is expected to develop instructional interventions most appropriate to the student's needs. The assessment data used to develop the IEP may not be as useful for instructional planning as for placement decisions. One of the byproducts of the reform movement is the emphasis on development of assessments intended to drive instructional decisions.

Despite its weaknesses, the IEP is viewed as the vehicle for changing the instructional environment for students with disabilities. Through the IEP, decisions are to be made that determine where children will receive their education, what the expectations for their performance are, and who is responsible for their program.

It is often difficult for new professionals, and possibly even more difficult for veteran special educators, to distinguish concern for equal rights, which has been the target of special education for years, from concern for a pragmatic determination of the educational needs of children with disabilities as individuals. Prior to PL 94–142, children with disabilities were subjected to considerable discrimination. Given a lack of resources, districts often were unable to meet many students' needs. As a result, they excluded these children, prevented their enrollment, or maintained them in regular classes without provisions for special needs. No penalty was assessed of school districts that chose not to provide special services or provided inappropriate services.

The "equal rights" or "educational equity" movement probably did more to ease the conscience of society than it did to meet the specific needs of the current generation of children and youth with disabilities. This perspective is not a criticism of the movement, nor does it downplay the positive benefits of PL 94–142 and IDEA. Rather, it draws attention to an important reality: The key to an appropriate education is the nature and quality of the student-teacher interaction. Due process only allows the interaction to occur; it does not define, or assure, the delivery of an appropriate instructional intervention.

*T*HE LEAST RESTRICTIVE INSTRUCTIONAL ENVIRONMENT

During the last decade, the concept of appropriateness has been confounded. As a result of philosophical arguments, the concept of LRE, REI, or inclusion often is interpreted as regular class placement for students with handicapping conditions.

Theoretically, decisions on least restrictive placement are reached after carefully studying each student's instructional needs and placement options. The practice of placing children with disabling conditions in regular classes whenever possible is carried out under the rubric of LRE. Consequently, to suggest that this placement is not in all children's best interest is viewed by many as heresy. If sufficient evidence suggests that some other arrangement—such as full-time special class placement—is warranted, that accommodation is made. Such a decision is not easily achieved, however, because settings that do not involve participation in regular education meet with so much resistance these days.

In the case of students with mild disabilities like Johnny, it is interesting to see how regular class placement comes about. The assumption is that the needs of students with learning disabilities, mental retardation, and emotional disturbance are met best in the regular classroom through arrangements with special personnel. As a result, recommendations for placement other than the regular class must be backed by strong evidence and persuasive argument.

Separate programming still tends to be the norm for students with moderate and severe disabilities, and for those with multiple disabilities, but this placement option is

Instruction for special children in inclusive classrooms will require well-trained, innovative teachers.

changing as inclusion gains favor. Today a recommendation for regular class placement of students with multiple disabilities also must be backed by strong evidence and persuasive arguments. The assumption is that the serious nature of their needs disrupts the educational process for nondisabled children or that the special needs of students with disabilities cannot be met in the regular classroom environment.

Both groups, theoretically, are treated equally according to the philosophy of least restrictiveness, but the emphasis tends to be on the setting and opportunities to interact with nondisabled peers, not on the conditions necessary for effective instructional intervention. Consequently, the question goes unanswered: What setting will allow the teacher to most effectively assist these children in achieving their capabilities? How one answers this question depends largely on the value one places on cognitive development versus socialization, and on one's perception of what LRE means. Too often the emphasis is on social rather than educational needs.

The primary goal of special education should be to create optimum learning experiences and, in turn, enhance educational achievement. To this end, another perspective might alter how LRE is perceived: the conditions required for the most effective student-teacher interaction.

Students considered to have mild disabilities (like Johnny) typically are placed in regular classrooms. To develop their reading skills, they may require intense instruction for sustained periods. Regular classroom teachers, however, are responsible for 25 to 30 students at a time, making such intense instruction for two or three students unlikely. Therefore, the special student may be scheduled for intense reading instruction with a resource teacher. If similar intense instruction also is needed in math, social studies, or other curriculum areas entailing still more instruction by the resource teacher, the appropriateness of regular class placement becomes questionable. Is the placement based on a perceived need for social interaction with nondisabled peers or on a need for special instruction? When making placement decisions, attention must be given to the student's instructional needs, and high priority must be placed on the conditions essential for providing the necessary instructional intervention. Shifting the emphasis from placement to instructional intervention will require considerable initiative on the part of new and experienced professionals alike.

HISTORICAL ANTECEDENTS OF THE IEP

Many special education practitioners, building principals, regular classroom teachers, members of boards of education, and teacher educators have entered the field since passage of PL 94–142 in 1975. To comply with prevailing beliefs and practices emanating from this law, those whose induction predates that era have had to rethink their orientation. Today, as a result of the inclusion movement, *all* educators are being challenged to readjust or alter their views. In addition to the historical context, the new professional has to understand why establishing the concept of a free and appropriate education was essential.

The logic underlying the IEP requirements seems so basic that one would assume the legislation was enacted merely to confirm prevailing practice. After all, the development of short- and long-term objectives, based on an assessment of a disabled child's current performance level, and with input from the child's parents, is not very innovative. Certainly, teaching students with known disabling conditions and a history of underachievement warrants an investment in individualizing their instruction.

Although some students with disabilities need special therapies, prostheses, technical resources, and specially designed materials, most are disadvantaged educationally simply because of the impact of their disabling condition on their learning. The IEP represents a reasoned, educationally sound approach to instructional planning.

Almost two decades after implementation of the IEP, most educators agree that the intent of special education and related services is to create circumstances that will enhance the efforts of students with disabling conditions to realize their capabilities. In addition and more important, is to prepare them for a full, quality life. This change from a perspective of custodial care to one of advocacy for educational equity is relatively recent in the history of American education.

Special educators who entered the profession after 1970 have witnessed an evolution that, given the short time span, is atypical within the educational realm. Up to that time, the needs of children and youth with disabilities were not always of interest to legislators, policymakers, local boards of education, advisory groups, and professional educational associations. In addition, parents had not always been willing to take on the risks associated with confronting educational and social policy establishments.

Educational programs for students with mental retardation provide a frame of reference for understanding the significance of the IEP requirement. This group of students was the focal point of much of the early special education legislation and represented the first population of children with special needs that the public schools were called upon to serve. Their needs are primarily instructional; they need assistance to learn. Early programs were institutional, developed in response to a public concern for protecting society from these "abnormal" citizens. The motivation behind services was based on a need for their custodial care, not a concern for their education or development. Parents typically shielded the children from society, and the schools denied having any responsibility for them. Eventually, programs for students with mild mental retardation became the target for special education. Half a century passed before the schools accepted responsibility for individuals with severe and multiple handicaps.

PROGRAM DEVELOPMENT

During the middle and late 1800s, there was a movement toward demonstrating the capabilities of children with mental retardation. After migrating to the United States, Seguin introduced what was to be described as a physiological educational process for educating mentally retarded people (Doll, 1962). Others, such as Samuel Gridley Howe and Harvey B. Wilbur, attracted attention by training "idiots." Howe's work with these individuals, who also were blind, further illustrated that the "hard to teach" can be taught. Much of the instruction during this era stemmed from Seguin's work, though. It was based on the assumption that "the brain could be developed only as an integral part of the nervous system. It was based upon stimulation of the muscles and senses, imitation, reflection, and synthesis" (Doll, 1962). Despite the pedagogical merits of work by Seguin and others, institutional programs continued to be custodial in nature.

The early work of Binet in Paris in 1904 was aimed at developing an assessment scale to select "defective" children for special classes. His pioneer work in assessing intelligence led to significant educational changes in the United States. Building on the work of Binet, Henry Goddard of the Vineland Training School developed an American translation and standardization of Binet's scale. This gave momentum to the normative testing movement, which soon evolved as a mainstay in special education. Although special education classes for the mentally disabled were reported as early as 1875 in Cleveland, growth prior to the 1900s was slow. The availability of normative tests to assess intellectual ability provided a tool that stimulated development of educational programs for individuals with mental retardation.

Special education classes. The rationale for developing classes for students with mental retardation continued to be as much for separating them from others for the benefit of society as for the benefit of the people with mental retardation themselves. Children served in the schools under the label of "mentally retarded" largely had mild mental and borderline retardation, with IQs between 60 and 80. Many were referred to as "slow learners." In general, they were higher functioning than the students with mental retardation served today through special education.

Special classes, referred to by various names such as "opportunity rooms" and "self-contained rooms," gained popularity beginning in the 1920s. The Stanford-Binet Intelligence Scale, developed by Terman at Stanford University in 1916, added to the schools' ability to differentiate instruction on the basis of assessed ability. To a large extent, the scale is a reliable way to differentiate low-functioning children from those who are more able. Though probably unfounded, this sense of confidence or security is credited for the early growth in special classes for students with mild retardation. It also allowed educators to deny participation in public education to students not perceived as "educable."

Compulsory education. Paralleling the early movement to develop special education programs and to use normative tests to exclude children from education was a movement to support compulsory education. Writing about the origins of special education, Chambers and Hartman (1983) noted that, "It is hard to overestimate the impact of an expanding, ultimately compulsory, system of schooling on the origins of special education. Schools that all were compelled to attend converted the problem of how to educate dependent and deviant children from a familial to a school concern." Compulsory education, as a public policy, resulted in handicapped children becoming the responsibility of the public schools, not by design but by circumstance. In reality, most disabled children continued to be served inappropriately, with many being excluded from school or placed in institutions. Later, the compulsory education law became a major resource for initiatives aimed at educational equity for children and youth with special needs.

Along with assessment "technology" to differentiate children on the basis of their measured ability, the movement toward compulsory education brought a more heterogeneous group of children to the public schools, setting the conditions for the ultimate development of special education. Specifically, programs for students with visual impairment, hearing impairment, and physical disabilities began to evolve, in addition to programs for students with mild mental retardation. Programs for students with moderate mental retardation (trainable or TMR) were not to gain support until the 1950s, those with learning disabilities in the late 1960s and 1970s, and children with severe and multiple handicaps in the middle 1970s and throughout the early 1980s.

Advocacy. At least two major influences contributed significantly to development of the contemporary concept of special education and, ultimately, the IEP mandate: (a) the parent advocacy movement, which gained strength during the 1950s with emergence of the National Association for Retarded Children (NARC), and (b) the civil rights movement of the 1960s. The parent movement raised the consciousness of professionals and the public, leading to changes in state legislation favoring development of special education programs. The civil rights movement, in turn, created a social climate that made civil rights initiatives on behalf of disabled persons achievable. Further, it sensitized Congress to the needs of special groups and made advocacy an acceptable, if not essential, process for social change. Without these movements, PL 94–142 probably would not have been written, and certainly not passed.

Program growth. As individual states began to mandate special education in the 1950s and 1960s, financial aid programs based on the principle of excess cost came into being as a means of stimulating program development. Expansion in the 1950s, 1960s, and 1970s emphasized starting new classes and broadening the range of children with handicapping conditions who warranted special instruction and related services. The demand for special education resulting from this growth quickly exceeded the supply of specially trained teachers.

To meet this demand, and to avoid slowing down the growth in classes, the practice of employing temporarily certified teachers and allowing less than fully trained teachers to be employed became common. Continuing through the early 1970s, administrators still utilized this option when the need exceeded supply. Although this stop-gap measure allowed school districts to meet their program obligations, it did little to improve the quality of instruction. This compromise in personnel standards characterizes the value placed on growth of programs versus quality of instructional intervention.

The growth of the 1960s took place while school district reorganization was occurring in many states. States were reducing the number of school districts by mergers to create larger, more efficient units. As a result of district reorganization, many regular classroom teachers who had been teaching without degrees in small districts were unable to continue teaching in their home districts. Many of them, however, were recruited to meet the demand for teachers in special education. No data are available on the proportion of special class teachers for the mentally retarded employed during the 1950s and 1960s who were fully certified, compared to those teaching with temporary certification; however, the number of teachers without full certification was substantial.

CURRICULUM DEVELOPMENT

Although overshadowed by the concern for program expansion during the last two decades, curriculum development did receive attention during the first half of the 20th century, primarily in the form of objectives for students with mental retardation. Developed mostly by educators or psychologists who were interested in curriculum, objectives were general, emphasizing areas of content or skills to be taught. They were not always behaviorally stated, nor were they necessarily useful as criteria for assessment. For the most part, they were intended to serve as guidelines for teachers in determining what to teach rather than as a technology for providing individualized instruction. This initial emphasis on curriculum planning signaled the beginning of instructional planning in special education, leading to more purposeful efforts in the 1950s and 1960s, and eventually setting the stage for the IEP.

Inskeep (1928) was one of the first to formulate a comprehensive listing of educational objectives for students with mental retardation. She developed a typology of curriculum objectives that included general goals, contributing objectives, a number of operationally defined correlates, and suggested techniques. Objectives were clustered around five topical areas: health, social living, getting and holding a job, thrift, and efficient use of leisure time. Decoeudres (1928) stressed teaching principles rather than objectives. In contrast to Inskeep, she focused more directly on academic skills, including knowledge of tool subjects, application of basic skills, and specific subjects such as reading, spelling, writing, English, and work study skills. Duncan (1943) published a curriculum outline based on his work at the Lankhills Schools in England. The content outline, though not in the form of instructional objectives, provided teachers with a curriculum structure that helped them prepare objectives.

In his book, Teaching the Slow Learner, Featherstone (1951) argued that little can be gained from listing specific objectives, based on the rationale that there were already too many and that knowledge of what constituted reasonable expectations for slow learners was insufficient. He did, however, propose content areas to be considered in teaching students with mental retardation. During the 1950s, when growth in special classes was increasing significantly in the public schools, a number of curriculum publications emerged. They included works by Featherstone (1951), Kirk and Johnson (1951), and Wallin (1955). These initiatives continued to emphasize curriculum content as guidelines to aid teachers in developing their instructional programs.

A lack of commercially available curriculum and instructional resource materials designed for students with mild mental retardation historically placed special class teachers in the position of having to develop their own curricula. Few teachers, however, were adequately prepared to assume this responsibility. In the 1950s, state departments of education and large school districts began to address the need for more detailed curriculum resources and inservice training needs of special class teachers. Thus, during the late 1950s and early 1960s, "curriculum guides" came of age. These often were developed by state departments of education, school districts, and universities. The materials were intended only as guidelines, but teachers often used them as "cookbooks." Examples included curriculum guides published by the State of Illinois (1958) and Kansas (Thorsell, 1969). Similarly, the Cincinnati Public Schools (1964) published an extensive curriculum guide for slow learners. The curriculum development movement gave rise to the widespread development of curriculum guides for teaching mentally retarded students.

The evolving curriculum development efforts were based on Ingram's (1935) work in unit teaching. Most of the curriculum guides developed during this early period were redundant. Each state or district, however, capitalized on the opportunity to involve teachers in the development process and to reflect the specific needs of the state or district. For example, from 1965 to 1968, the Special Education Curriculum Development Center (SECDC) at the University of Iowa developed more than 30 curriculum guides for teachers, combining objectives, content guidelines, and teaching strategies on specific curriculum topics (Meyen et al., 1968). Also during this era, Lynch (1967) published *Instructional Objectives and the Mildly Retarded Child.* This systematic approach to stating objectives offered curriculum developers a model for developing curriculum for the mildly mentally retarded.

Federal initiatives. Probably the most significant curriculum development initiative in the history of special education occurred in the middle to late 1960s, when the Bureau of Education for the Handicapped (BEH), the office in the federal government responsible for federal limitations pertaining to handicapped children, funded a number of long-term curriculum development projects to fill the void in the area of curriculum resources for teaching students with mild mental retardation. The curriculum development that had taken place before then was largely in response to immediate concerns rather than conceptual in nature. This was reflected in the emphasis of state education agencies and local districts on developing curriculum guides in response to teachers' obvious need for direction in what to teach.

By the late 1960s, the growth in special classes had created a demand for specially trained teachers. The federal government responded in the form of stipends for students in teacher training programs. As the number of special classes increased, and as teacher training programs began to evolve, the lack of curriculum for teaching students with mental retardation became a serious concern. Curriculum guides were useful to teacher educators in their methods courses, and also helpful to special class teachers, but they were insufficient as a basis upon which to teach curriculum development skills. As local programs matured, they too experienced a need for more sophisticated guidelines for local curriculum development.

Although BEH had funded projects addressing curriculum questions prior to 1965, these earlier projects were not intended to yield instructional products. Instead, the results took the form of final reports on research activities, and while adding to the literature, they did not help resolve the need for specially designed curricula. Between

1965 and 1970, BEH funded a number of large curriculum development projects, most of them subject-matter-oriented and designed for students with mild mental retardation. The BEH curriculum development projects were funded prior to 1968, a time when the self-contained special class was the dominant instructional delivery model.

Commercial challenges. When the curriculum products resulting from the BEH projects reached the commercial market, the shift toward least restrictive environment resulting from PL 94–142 was occurring. Although most of the products were applicable to individualizing instruction, several were designed largely for group instruction situations. The shift to LRE reduced the market for these products because of the growing need for material that paralleled the curriculum in regular classes.

Commercial vendors soon faced a serious dilemma. On the one hand, curriculum materials for students with mild mental retardation clearly were needed. On the other hand, the movement to teach these students in regular classrooms, with supplemental support for resource room teachers, was on the horizon, and many districts were moving toward noncategorical models. Further, many teacher training programs were considering noncategorical training models, replacing methods courses for the mentally retarded with methods courses for the broader classification of mildly handicapped, for example.

Also, although districts were beginning to receive federal support for special education, they were not accustomed to spending several thousand dollars for curriculum materials for special education students. Meanwhile, the practice of buying math or reading basal series for regular grades was well established. The dilemma operationalized into one of having well-tested and well-designed products, a demonstrated need, and potential purchasing power, but a lack of commitment on the part of education agencies to spend resources on instructional materials for special education programs.

Currently, few curricula are designed to accommodate the instructional needs of students with disabilities in regular classrooms. As REI and inclusion programs become more prevalent, however, private enterprise will be more responsive. Fortunately in special education, research has preceded curriculum development, but demonstrating the profitability of marketing instructional resources for students with disabilities has been difficult. "Thin" markets should be greatly reduced if the principles of REI and inclusion are adopted, as all schools will require curricula that can be modified to accommodate students with disabilities.

Shift in BEH focus. The BEH investment in curriculum development was short-lived. Immediately following passage of PL 94–142 in 1975, federal research and development resources were directed to assessing the impact of the law. As a result, the first decade of PL 94–142 was similar to the late 1950s and early 1960s, when the emphasis was on increasing the numbers of children served and establishing classes (programs) rather than curriculum. Compliance with the IEP requirement routinely took the form of ensuring that IEPs were on file, contained the necessary information, and were agreed to by parents. Qualitative accounting for appropriateness of the educational program for given students gave way to procedural compliance. In essence, progress came to be measured by access and receipt of services rather than by the substance of instruction offered. The assumption seemed to be that the IEP would stimulate local investments in curriculum and instructional planning.

To suggest that the shift away from investing in curriculum was attributable totally to PL 94–142 would be unfair. Nor would it be fair to imply that continuing the emphasis on curriculum development was more important than implementing PL 94–142. Certainly the benefits derived for students with disabilities during the first decade of the law were significant. The law was unquestionably successful in changing public policy. Nevertheless, the conditions created by the law, in terms of the timeline for compliance, emphasis on procedures, and potential consequences for noncompliance, were such that the substance of what was to be taught and the instructional interventions were easily slighted.

The lack of attention to curriculum development could have been explained at the time as resulting from compelling needs for procedural compliance and the need for all handicapped students to be "appropriately" served. In retrospect, it can be argued that implementation of PL 94–142 would have been smoother, and the intended benefit realized more fully, if federal resources for curriculum development had continued or even increased.

When the definition questions were resolved and related eligibility criteria were established, the pivotal question of what constitutes appropriate education remained. Definitions and eligibility criteria can be changed arbitrarily, but the student's educational need remains constant until it is met. Specifically, service delivery, administrative models, labels, professional roles, due process procedures, and policies are all variables that can be manipulated without resolving a student's instructional needs. In truth, merely changing any one of these variables could exacerbate a student's problem. All of them, however, are tangible variables in that the profession creates them. Some might speculate that they are created as issues and pursued as causes, because decisions about variables are achieved more readily than the development of needed instructional interventions. Questions of eligibility also are problems of an objective nature on which agreements can be reached by altering or confirming one's own beliefs. Curriculum development in the form of instructional interventions, however, is more than a set of beliefs upon which agreement can be reached. It requires long-term commitment of research and systematic development.

INDIVIDUALIZED INSTRUCTION

Antecedents of the IEP have their origin within the larger context of program development. As program structures moved from residential or institutional to self-contained special classes, resource rooms, and eventually regular class placement with supplemental support, teachers' ability to individualize instruction also was refined. Whether changes in the structure of delivering education stimulated refinements in the process of individualizing instruction or whether improvements in curriculum design and teaching methods were the primary contributors is not clear. In any event, throughout the history of special education, attention clearly has been given to individualizing instruction.

The learning, social, physical, and, in some cases, linguistic characteristics of students with disabilities have been pivotal in deciding what constitutes needed special education services for a given student. The IEP is the logical outcome of a century of progress, beginning with the development of residential institutions in the late 1800s.

Admittedly, the motivation for establishing institutions was not based totally on a desire to address the personal needs of individuals with disabilities. There was also the assumption that mentally retarded persons would be better served if they were separated from society. The later inception of special classes, together with the development of teacher training programs to prepare teachers with specialized skills, probably represents the first substantive initiative to accommodate the individualized needs of students with disabilities. As special classes gained in popularity, and as special teachers were employed, attention began to shift to adapting and developing curriculum for students with disabilities. This resulted in additional resources to bring instructional offerings closer to the needs of these students.

More recently, the roles of instructional specialists—resource teachers, consulting teachers, and special education consultants—have emerged in the delivery of instruction. At the same time, assessment instruments in the form of intelligence, achievement, aptitude, and diagnostic tests became more sophisticated in providing teachers with useful data on the strengths and weaknesses of individual children. In addition, professionals from related disciplines were becoming members of child study teams, adding input to the schools' capabilities to further refine services for students' needs.

Paralleling the development of individualized instruction within special education was an emphasis in general education on techniques for individualizing instruction. Teaching by objectives, criterion measures, domain testing, mastery learning, programmed instruction, applied behavioral analysis, and, more recently, computer-assisted instruction (CAI) are all examples of strategies that evolved as aids in individualizing instruction for disabled and nondisabled students.

For the most part, individualized instruction has been defined operationally by state-of-the-art techniques at the time, or by initiatives that have found acceptance in the classroom. These take the form of assessment strategies, ability grouping plans, instructional materials, technologies, and philosophies or beliefs about teaching and learning. Through individualized instruction, teachers attempt to control variables essential to structuring instruction in a way that offers maximum benefits to the learner. The extent to which it is achieved depends on a number of variables, most of which are changing constantly—the teachers' repertoire of teaching skills, students' response patterns and needs, the teaching environment, materials, and prevailing expectations of educational outcomes.

The literature provides a number of definitions of individualized instruction. Most are useful; many are redundant; and they largely reflect professional concern with quality instruction. While philosophically committed to individualized instruction, special education has not been the sole contributor to methods, techniques, and materials designed to help teachers individualize instruction. Although the mandate of individualized instruction (IEP) was a special education initiative, general educators have carried out much of the most significant work in individualizing instruction.

Through a project funded by the Office of Special Education and Rehabilitative Services in 1984 to examine the contributions of research to special education practices, the Council for Exceptional Children (CEC) identified individualized instruction as the first practice to be investigated. In reviewing definitions of individualized instruction, Pheeney and Prehm (1985) reported:

> It would be difficult to arrive at a single definition of individualized instruction whose precise wording would satisfy all educators. Nevertheless, defining the broad boundaries of common agreement is a feasible task. At one end of the continuum is a generic family of definitions which center upon the notion of adapting instruction to meet the needs of individual learners—whatever form of individual or group learning experience that adaptation may take (Chastain, 1975; Clem, 1932; Dunn, 1971; Reynolds & Rosen, 1976; Weisgerber, 1971). Among the most succinctly stated of these definitions is Cooley and Glaser's (1969) reference to individualized education as "essentially the adaptation of instructional practices to individual requirements" (p. 574). (To substitute the word "instruction" for education does not distort either the intent or the interpretation.) Another typical definition is that of Clymer and Kearney (1962), who describe individualization of instruction as "the steps taken to meet the needs of pupils, each of whom is a unique individual" (p. 268). Even more broad, perhaps, is Musgrave's (1975) assertion that "anytime...the school situation is focusing on the individual student in the teaching-learning process, another step is being made toward the ultimate goal of individualization of instruction" (p. x).

From these general definitions, one can infer a philosophical orientation and a set of parameters. The emphasis is on matching student needs to instructional options with concern for adapting resources—altering the instructional environment when necessary to accommodate learner needs. Parameters include what is known about the learner, the teacher's ability to adapt, access to instructional resources that address specific skills or content, and an environment conducive to individual instruction or individualizing instruction within a group.

AN INSTRUCTIONAL PLANNING PERSPECTIVE FOR THE IEP

From an educational perspective, the IEP is consistent with sound instructional planning principles. In teaching students with special needs, educators must be able to design instructional activities based on assessment information and to establish a performance baseline against which progress can be measured. Also important is to ensure that services such as speech and language therapy and occupational therapy, as well as other related services, are provided as part of a student's educational program. Assigning responsibility for delivering the individual's program and involving parents adds a much needed dimension to quality instruction. The intent of the IEP in many ways thus provides an instructional accountability system.

Requirements of the IEP have had a major impact on American education. Schools have established procedures for developing IEPs, large numbers of parents have used them to involve themselves in their children's education, and teacher trainers (preservice and inservice) have restructured methods to include preparation in skills related to the IEP. Although educators, parents, and advocacy groups continue to disagree on the effectiveness of the IEP as presently implemented, they generally agree that the principles underlying the IEP are educationally sound.

Through teachers' efforts the IEP can be made integral to instructional planning. IEP requirements for setting long- and short-term goals, assessing performance, and making team decisions with parental participation represent the basic features of instructional planning. Some districts limit use of the IEP to that of an administrative management tool to account for the student's receiving special services. This approach is not conducive to developing an effective instructional planning system. The purpose of instructional planning is to ensure that decisions about a student's program consider all information pertaining to the learner's needs. This requires systematic planning.

The relative severity of learning problems of exceptional children further dictates that planning be continuous, not done only when a problem interferes with instruction. Equally important, the IEP must not lock the teacher into a single, static mode of instruction. The teacher must be able to change course, based on the student's exhibited needs, as the intervention progresses. IEPs that are seen as mechanistic straightjackets are counterproductive.

PLANNING NEEDS OF STUDENTS WITH DISABILITIES

Some exceptional children enter school having been identified already as possessing characteristics that likely will interfere with their school performance. In general, the most serious handicapping conditions are congenital. These include impaired vision, defective hearing, physical problems, and multiple handicaps. If children have been identified as handicapped before entering school, instructional planning specific to their needs can be initiated upon enrollment. Under these circumstances, the teacher probably has the advantage of being familiar with the child's preschool history.

Most children with disabilities, however, are not identified until they are in school, where the demands on them are too great. Once a student is identified as having a problem, specific instructional plans are developed. Whether the child has a "disability" that produces this inability to cope, or whether the current school organization sets up situations that become "handicapping contexts" for some children, is a major issue. (Skrtic addresses this issue in Chapter 15.) Here, let us assume that current practices in regular education are adequate and that the child who cannot cope has a "disability"— in the sense that he or she cannot cope with the demands of the regular classroom without some type of special assistance.

A child whose teacher notices the difficulties before they become too serious is fortunate. Conditions resulting in the identification of a child as "exceptional" are many: social inadequacies, undeveloped language skills, academic requirements beyond the child's ability, specific learning tasks for which the child is not yet ready, and minor vision or hearing problems that affect school performance. If students demonstrate these problems, instructional planning must be broadened to include identification of behaviors that suggest potential learning difficulties. The planning process for exceptional children should begin before their special needs are identified.

No single set of planning procedures applies to all instructional settings. Teachers have varying preferences for planning, as in their teaching methodologies. Available resources also influence the instructional planning approach. Nevertheless, certain general principles and planning concepts have broad application and, if followed, increase the opportunities for quality instruction. Ideally, planning produces instruction that is appropriate to learner needs. Within this context, at least four objectives can be set forth:

1. To make use of available information about learner characteristics and instructional options in planning specific teacher activities.
2. To establish short-range objectives within a long-term plan that can be implemented as intended, often by persons other than the teacher responsible for the original plan.
3. To allow for collecting evaluative evidence that illustrates the student's cumulative performance.
4. To provide a base for instructional decisions regarding programs for individual students.

To be most effective, instructional planning for exceptional children must go beyond merely specifying objectives and activities and measuring their effects on student performance. Consideration also must be given to identifying behaviors that suggest learning problems and to becoming familiar with procedures for referring children to the appropriate resource personnel. Though these concerns go beyond the actual instructional process, they are critical to instructional planning aimed at situating the exceptional child most appropriately. For the nonhandicapped child, instructional placement decisions rarely are made as he or she progresses through the grade system. Although placement decisions are important, they serve primarily to set the conditions for instructional decisions.

SUGGESTED PLANNING STEPS

Five sequential steps comprise the basic guidelines for planning for exceptional children: (a) identification of potential problems, (b) referral, (3) assessment, (4) instructional and placement decisions, and (5) implementation.

Identifying potential problems. This first step should be preceded by a discussion on how to prevent children from developing learning problems. Thus, when describing a planning process applicable to exceptional children, the importance of the regular class teacher in the identification process must be stressed.

Exceptional children typically are first identified as having learning problems by concerned regular classroom teachers who initiate a referral for assistance. The regular class teacher is in an ideal position to observe students under a variety of circumstances. In addition to understanding typical patterns of child development in social, cognitive, and physical areas, the teacher must be a skilled observer. Even though some children are identified through planned screening procedures (e.g., to detect vision, hearing, speech, and language impairments), teachers already should have identified behaviors suggesting possible problems in these areas.

To identify children with learning difficulties, teachers use many techniques, including criterion measures, informal tests, skill inventories, diagnostic tests, and observation scales. Even though these testing devices are helpful, skilled teachers also are alert to day-to-day and task-to-task variations in pupil performance.

If a teacher is sensitive to cues that suggest learning problems, a student's problem need not become serious before being identified. Detection of potential problems is an important first step in instructional planning.

Initiating a referral. Although special education personnel often are involved in referrals for reevaluation or supplementary assistance for children with mild handicaps, the regular classroom teacher is the primary referral source. Exceptional children, therefore, often depend upon the regular classroom teacher's skill, first in identifying the problem and then in providing the necessary remediation or initiating a request, or referral, for assistance.

Originally, referral of a student suspected of needing special education meant first removing the child from the regular class and then relieving the regular classroom teacher from further instructional responsibility. The current emphasis on least restrictive alternatives, mainstreaming, and integration, however, makes the referral process the first step toward assisting the regular teacher in meeting a pupil's instructional needs. Although the referral may result in part- or full-time placement outside the regular class, more often it results in increased resources available to the regular class teacher. These resources may be in the form of diagnostic information, consultation, access to special materials or equipment, or actual assistance in teaching the child.

Once the teacher has decided to request assistance in addressing a child's problem, he or she must initiate the referral. Most districts have established referral procedures, generally involving a form for recording the reason for referral, among other things. Through inservice training or a detailed special service manual, specific directions may be given regarding whom to contact for each problem encountered.

An effective referral sets into motion the instructional planning process. That is, through referral, decisions are made to conduct evaluations and to involve parents. Teachers must be able to convey their concerns for the student's performance by specifying good referral questions and sharing information. If the child's problem is not related to academic performance but, rather, to social behavior or a physical or medical condition, the information should report this. Again, the teacher remains responsible for clearly communicating the nature of the problem.

Besides communicating an interpretation of the child's problems and the expectation for assistance, the teacher must prepare the child for referral. Most districts have due process procedures that begin with obtaining parental permission for testing. These procedures tend to be administrative and are not concerned with helping the child understand why testing is necessary or why other people are interested in his or her school performance. In some cases, the student's only experience with special person-nel has been in a group. In any referral that results in testing, observation, or consulta-tion with the student, the teacher should explain what will take place and why. The student's attitude clearly can influence test performance. Teachers should be alert to any cues that suggest anxiety about the test or consultation. Emphasis should be placed on helping the student in the area causing difficulty. The goal is to prepare the student to perform optimally during the testing or consultation. Information acquired during the referral influences subsequent decisions in the instructional planning process.

Assessment. The level and kind of assessment vary according to the reason for referral. If the referral is related to health, the school nurse or physician may be involved. If the problem is related to hearing, speech, or language, the audiologist or speech clinician may be called in. If the reason for referral primarily involves academic performance, the school psychologist or a person identified as an educational diagnostician may be consulted. Frequently, several resource staff members participate.

In evaluation activities specific to academic problems, diagnostic procedures typically are employed . Although the diagnostic procedure used in other types of referrals may vary, the series of evaluation activities usually is similar.

The first priority of the educational diagnosis is to clarify the reason for referral and to substantiate the presence of an instructional problem. This generally involves a conference with the referring teacher and a review of anecdotal and related information specific to the suspected problem. Also, the diagnostician may observe the student in the classroom, confer with parents, or consult with other resource personnel before determining what instructional steps to follow. The objective here is to determine the nature of the problem and to obtain the necessary information to prescribe an effective educational program.

Formal testing may or may not be required. When the referral involves a child suspected of having a handicap, the evaluation process frequently results in a recom-mendation, either for the regular class teacher to use specific instructional techniques or for the student to be placed in special programs on a part- or full-time basis. In such cases, specific procedures must be applied.

Having confirmed that an instructionally related problem exists, the diagnostician or school psychologist usually assumes responsibility for several areas:

1. Determining what evaluation information is necessary to provide appropriate remediation.
2. Obtaining required approvals for testing.
3. Administering or arranging for administration of appropriate evaluation instru-ments.
4. Compiling needed information from appropriate sources (teachers, other profes-sionals, records, parents).
5. Observing the student in natural and structured settings.
6. Analyzing test results and data collected.
7. Organizing test results and data into a report format the review committee can use.
8. Formulating recommendations.

9. Translating diagnostic information into information teachers or parents can use.
10. Initiating procedures for IEP conferences, if indicated.

If a child is found not to be handicapped, the diagnostician may work directly with the regular class teacher to implement a remediation program. PL 94–142 requires a handicapped child to have an IEP developed in a formal conference. The conference committee then becomes responsible for making instructional and placement decisions.

Making instructional and placement decisions. If the student's problems are identified first in the regular class, the child remains enrolled in the regular class while the referral is being processed, and the teacher continues to make instructional decisions as effectively as possible. After the evaluation process, recommendations are made regarding needed program changes. These may involve having the regular teacher use special techniques or materials, or it may entail placement in a special program on a part- or full-time basis.

The instructional placement decision is a critical step in the general planning. If appropriate decisions are to be made, evaluative and descriptive data specific to the child must be available. Decisions regarding instructional options and placement initially should involve the resource specialists and teachers most directly involved in the child's program. Because of the number of children referred for evaluation, time rarely permits more than one conference per referral to make instructional or placement decisions. A clear set of directives should result from the conference, covering instructional methods, programming materials to be used, evaluation guidelines, and follow-up suggestions.

No plan can describe all of the skills, concepts, and information a child should be taught. Even if possible, this would not be desirable. Instead, planning must allow for on-the-spot decision making. Learners' responses to tasks vary, and too many directives pose the risk that a teacher may adhere to a detailed plan even when evidence shows a child's changing needs warrant modification.

On the other hand, sufficient planning on the teacher's part is important. For example, it must be decided how detailed a plan should be in terms of skills, activities, and materials. In general, the more serious the learner's problem, the more precise is the planning required. Another major consideration pertains to whether persons other than the teacher should help carry out the plan. Thus, the plan should provide sufficient information for appropriate interpretation and implementation by everyone involved.

The plan's content and provisions for remediation, not its organizational format, determine how appropriate it is for a given student. The organization and the recording format of instructional plans, however, influence the success of planning efforts. An organized plan simplifies matching instructional options to learner characteristics. To ensure uniformity, districts often adopt or design a specific planning system. Some advantages accrue from having all teachers use a similar format: A uniform approach simplifies the administrator's role in evaluating the effectiveness of teacher planning, and uniformity in format enhances communication among teachers. Finally, in most cases, forms designed to make planning more convenient save time.

Implementation. Presumably, teacher and student both benefit from the planning process. The extent to which the teacher benefits depends in part on his or her effectiveness in the planning process. If the teacher clearly communicates information about the child's problem in the referral, is responsive when conferring with the diagnostician, and is an effective conference participant, the implementation step should prove beneficial.

The teacher who initiates the referral may have full responsibility for implementation or may share it with a resource teacher or other support personnel. Under some circumstances, implementation involves transferring the student to a special class, in which case the teacher is responsible for the transfer process. Situations in which the student remains with the referring teacher part- or full-time require implementing specific recommendations and continuing the planning process.

In deciding on instructional planning procedures, two primary factors must be considered: (a) the impact of instructional planning on student programming, and (b) the demands the planning process places on teachers. If procedures are too complex and time-consuming, the teacher may not be able to plan and teach effectively. On the other hand, if the plan is simplistic, few pupil benefits may be gained.

Although the initial goal is to design procedures that allow for efficiency and enhance instructional decision making specific to students' needs, the ultimate goal is to employ learning procedures that result in benefits for the learner. If program questions can be answered by an instructional planning process that does not add substantially to the teacher's workload, that process should be considered.

During implementation, the teacher must monitor the student's daily progress, assessing appropriateness of the child's placement and effectiveness of the instructional techniques employed. The teacher also must determine when additional assistance is needed and when to refer the student for reevaluation.

Further, the teacher is responsible for maintaining student performance records. An important facet of maintaining records is to provide a cumulative perspective on student progress, one that permits optimum review of student responses to specific teaching techniques and materials. Effective instructional planning depends on the availability of data on the student's performance in response to planned activities.

THE IEP CONFERENCE

PL 94–142 mandates that special IEP conferences be held. From the perspective of team decision making, the conference concept is not new. Special educators have been using the team or conference approach to make placement decisions about exceptional children for many years. The changes created by PL 94–142 relate to the greater number of children affected, parent participation, and requirements of a written plan.

Prior to 1975, conferences usually were held primarily in difficult cases or when several special services were needed. The results were mostly placement decisions and general recommendations. The number of conferences depended upon program vacancies for children, number of referrals, and time available for staff to participate.

Although parents might have been consulted, rarely were they invited to participate. Frequently, the conference was lengthy or involved a series of sessions. Today, with the IEP requirement applying to all handicapped children, considerable attention must be given to efficient use of time. Also, careful decisions must be made regarding data collection and organization of reports in advance of the conference.

The goal of the IEP conference is to develop an IEP that is most appropriate for a given student. Each person involved must be prepared to participate. The member assigned to chair the conference is obligated to moderate the discussion objectively and to encourage full participation. One of the most difficult tasks chairpersons of IEP conferences face is to help the group reach an agreement on the IEP. Two main strategies—staff preparation and communication with parents before the conference—can help achieve this goal.

Parents are expected to report their concerns and expectations for their child. To suggest that they tend to be defensive would be unfair, but in many cases they need encouragement to participate, particularly in their informative role. Teachers, regular and special alike, often have the most difficult role. They must advocate for the most appropriate IEP; but at the same time they may not have access to information acquired by the specialist until the time of the conference.

Prematurely incorporating recommendations into the IEP merely to gain support from the parent or to reach agreement on the IEP should be avoided. The law does not hold the school liable if the child fails to achieve IEP objectives. Also, the risk is always present that unreasonable expectations will emerge from an IEP conference. On the one hand, the IEP may exceed the student's capabilities; on the other hand, the

Parent participation in IEP decisions is essential.

short-term objectives may be within the student's repertoire of skills already.

When participating in a conference, teachers must keep in mind that they are responsible for implementation. If they knowingly agree to an IEP they believe is unsuitable, they are not being fair to themselves or to the student. Although changes in the IEP can and should be made when needed, to begin with the most appropriate program possible is best. Teachers who are willing to assume advocacy roles can help guard against premature decisions in an attempt to reach agreement on the IEP. Because of the large number of conferences held and the time required to monitor IEPs, the conference may become routine. This could contribute to decisions made in advance and programs designed with objectives having unrealistically high or low expectations for the child.

PARENTAL INVOLVEMENT

The systematic involvement of parents in instructional decision making, coupled with the required written plan, represents a bold step. In general, parents vary in how they communicate with school personnel. Too often the communication between parents and school personnel has evolved from conflict. For example, poor discipline and underachievement often are reasons for interaction between parents and educators. In the case of parents of handicapped students, the reason often centers on the school's failure to provide needed services.

The IEP process has evolved as a meaningful vehicle for establishing communication between the school and the home. Specifically, parents are encouraged to think about their child's performance, as well as what they believe the student is capable of achieving. School personnel must refine their assessment procedures and be able to relate assessed needs to proposed interventions. In addition, they must attend to communicating effectively with parents and to creating a conference environment conducive to parental participation. Participation, of course, means more than attendance. Parents should interact as well. Therefore, they should be encouraged to relate information, ask questions, and challenge the opinions of professionals.

Research on parent participation in IEP conferences indicates generally passive involvement in decision making (Turnbull, Turnbull, Summers, Brotherson, & Benson 1986). The reasons may relate to what was or was not done during the first decade of implementing PL 94–142. The emphasis on procedural compliance may mean that conferences have been held and that an IEP has been completed, but the qualitative aspects of conference may be neglected.

Several elements help make a conference more conducive to parent participation: scheduling the conference at a time convenient to both parents; keeping the number of attendees to only those with significant contributions to developing the IEP; preparing parents to participate by routinely sharing information prior to the conference; and ensuring that the person chairing the conference is sensitive to parents' concerns and encourages their participation.

Turnbull et al. (1986) offered specific suggestions for involving parents in IEP conferences. These suggestions are presented because parental effectiveness in advocating for instructional needs is influenced greatly by how they participate in the initial and subsequent conferences.

GUIDELINES

A. *Preconference Preparation*

1. Appoint a conference chair to coordinate all aspects of the conference. The conference chair should assume responsibility for coordinating preconference preparation, chairing the conference, and coordinating follow-up.
2. Solicit information from parents on their preferences related to their participation: persons who should attend, convenient time, convenient location, needed assistance (child care, transportation), and the type of information they would like to receive in advance....
3. Specify the persons appropriate to attend the IEP conference in light of parent and professional preferences. Be sure to consider carefully the possibility of including the student.
4. Arrange a convenient time and location for the meeting.
5. If needed, assist parents with logistics such as child care and transportation.
6. Inform parents (in writing or verbally) of the purpose, time of conference, location, and names of participants.
7. In light of parents' preferences, share information...they believe will help them prepare for participation—e.g., evaluation reports, evaluation checklists to complete, list of subject areas school personnel think should be covered by the IEP, summary of child's strengths and weaknesses in each subject area, ideas from school personnel on possible goals and objectives, information on legal rights, and information on placement options and related services.
8. If several placements are being considered for the student, encourage parents to visit each program prior to the conference.
9. Discuss the conference purpose and the procedures with students, and assist them in specifying their own preferences for educational programming. Encourage students to discuss their preferences with their parents.
10. Encourage parents to share any information with school personnel...that they believe will be helpful during the preparation period.
11. Gather all information from school personnel that will help prepare for the IEP conference.
12. Prepare an agenda to cover each of the remaining five conference components.

B. *Initial Conference Proceedings*

1. Greet and welcome parents upon arrival, and welcome anyone the parents bring with them.
2. Introduce all conference participants, and share sufficient information to identify roles and areas of responsibility. If parents are being introduced to several professionals for the first time, consider the use of name tags, or make a list of the names and positions of conference participants for the parents.
3. State the purpose of the conference and review the agenda. Ask the parents and their guests if they would like to add any issues to the agenda.

4. Ask participants the amount of time they have available for the conference. State the intention to use time wisely but to avoid rushing through important decisions. Share the option of rescheduling another meeting if necessary.
5. Ask parents and their guests if they would like to have a clarification of legal rights. If so, fully provide the information they request.

C. *Review of Formal Evaluation and Current Levels of Performance*

1. If a formal evaluation of the student has been conducted, and a separate evaluation conference to review results has not been held, ask the appropriate diagnostic personnel to identify the tests administered, the specific results of each, and the options for consideration, based on the evaluation results.
2. After evaluation information has been shared, summarize the major findings and encourage parents to point out areas of agreement and disagreement and their corresponding reasons.
3. Ask parents if they would like to have a written copy of evaluation results. If so, provide it to them.
4. If a formal evaluation has not been conducted (must be conducted every 3 years), review the child's developmental progress and present levels of performance subject area.
5. Identify current implications of all test results for instructional programming and future implications for the child's next life-cycle stage.
6. Clarify any diagnostic jargon used.
7. Solicit parental input on the student's current performance levels. Identify areas of agreement and disagreement.
8. Strive to resolve disagreement through discussion or examples of student performance. If your disagreement cannot be resolved within the conference, develop a plan for collecting further evaluation information by school personnel or an independent evaluator. Solicit parents' suggestions on the procedures to follow in collecting further information.
9. Proceed with development of the IEP only when you and the parents agree on the student's type of exceptionality and current levels of performance.

D. *Development of Goals and Objectives*

1. Based on the current levels of performance, identify all subject areas requiring specially designed instruction. For each subject area, collaboratively specify appropriate goals and objectives.
2. Encourage parents and their guests to share goals and objectives they believe are important for current and future functioning in the home, school, or community environment
3. Prioritize goals and objectives in light of relevance for the student. Discuss future educational and vocational options for the student to ensure that the goals and objectives provide sufficient preparation for future needs.
4. If the student receives instruction from two or more teachers, clarify the manner in which the responsibility for teaching the objectives will be shared.
5. Ask parents if they are willing to assume responsibility for teaching or reviewing some of the objectives with their son or daughter at home. If so, discuss their preferences for which goals and objectives they will work on.
6. Insure that evaluation procedures and schedules are identified for goals and objectives.

7. Explain to parents that including goals and objectives in the IEP does not represent a guarantee that the student will achieve them; rather, it represents a good-faith effort that school personnel will teach these goals and objectives.

E. *Determination of Placement and Related Services*

1. Based on the student's current levels of performance and the goals and objectives deemed appropriate, review the full continuum of viable placement options by identifying benefits and drawbacks of each. Solicit parent input on benefits and drawbacks, from an academic and social perspective, of the different placement options for their child.
2. If parents have not already visited possible placement, encourage them to do so. Agree on a "tentative placement" until the parents can visit and confirm its appropriateness.
3. Select the placement option consistent with the goals and objectives to be taught. The placement should be as close as possible to that of peers who do not have exceptionalities. Specify the extent of the student's participation in the regular education program.
4. Identify the related services the student needs. Discuss the benefits and drawbacks of each service and options for scheduling (i.e., frequency, the portion of class that will be missed).
5. Specify the dates for initiating each related service and the anticipated duration of each.
6. If the parents have not had an opportunity to meet the teacher of the selected placement or the related service providers, share the names and qualifications of these professionals.

F. *Concluding the Conference*

1. Summarize to review major decisions and follow-up responsibility. Take notes to record this summary.
2. Assign follow-up responsibility for any task (e.g., arranging for physical therapy) requiring attention.
3. Review with parents the responsibility (teaching objectives, increasing socialization opportunities during after-school hours, visiting adult programs) they have expressed interest in assuming.
4. Set a tentative date for reviewing the IEP document on at least an annual basis and preferably more frequently.
5. Identify strategies for ongoing communication with parents, in light of the preferences of all involved parties.
6. Express appreciation for the shared decision making that occurred, and reiterate to parents how much their participation is valued.*

During the next decade the quality and the appropriateness of educational programs for handicapped students may be as dependent on the role of parents in IEP conferences as on improvements in available instructional interventions. Extending educational experiences for handicapped students beyond the typical school day or school year will necessitate that the family become a true partner in the educational

---

*From *Families, Professionals, and Exceptionality: A Special Partnership* by A. P. Turnbull, H. R. Turnbull, J. A. Summers, M. J. Brotherson, and H. A. Benson, 1986 (p. 75), Columbus, OH: Charles E. Merrill. Reprinted by permission of the publisher.

process. This will require better communication between educators and parents and, above all, mutual respect. Parents represent a major teaching resource. Failure to involve them in the education of handicapped children and youth is to underutilize available resources, the net result being less than appropriate education.

Inclusion of the IEP as a requirement in PL 94–142 in 1975, and its continuation as a central feature of IDEA, reflects the history of special education in individualizing instruction. Specifically, assessing performance, setting instructional goals based on the student's assessed level of performance, and measuring the results of instruction historically have characterized the education of students with disabilities. Although this approach to instruction typically was called prescriptive or individualized, it is similar to what is called outcomes-based curriculum today. In fact, the IEP combined with the IEP conference(s) may provide more instructional accountability than outcomes-based education as applied in regular education. Today, outcomes-based instructional models are being prepared in many states as a preferred approach to education for all students.

IMPLICATIONS OF THE OUTCOMES MOVEMENT FOR SPECIAL EDUCATION

A common feature of the reform movement initiatives discussed in Chapter 1 is the emphasis on increasing expectations for student performance and shifting the evidence of educational progress to results or outcomes. The focus on results is aimed at students and schools. The two reform initiatives that are likely to have the most dramatic effect on the education of students with disabilities may be the movement of states to outcomes-based accreditation (OBA) and the instructional practice of outcomes-based education (OBE).

Although each is independent, these initiatives are interrelated and built on a few common principles, including (a) all students can learn, (b) indicators of performance that serve as indices of performance by students and schools can be identified, (c) measures tailored to outcomes can be used to assess indicators of student and school performance, and (d) education is more effective if it is based on expected results rather than inputs in the form of services and resources. The latter does not deny the importance of resources and services but calls for restructuring the way schools determine what is required or a student to benefit maximally from education.

OUTCOMES-BASED ACCREDITATION

Historically, states have accredited schools based on various types of inputs, including faculty-students ratios, quality and sufficiency of facilities, number of books in libraries, availability of special personnel, curricular offerings, and other quantifiable indices. Within this context, accreditation teams on a cycle of 5 or 10 years would review data provided by schools and make recommendations to the state education agency on the schools' qualifications for accreditation.

By comparison, outcomes-based accreditation (OBA) calls for districts to identify and provide evidence of results in specified areas of performance. Currently, states implement the OBA model in various ways. For example, the Kansas (1992) plan has implemented a model called *quality performance accreditation.* In designing the model, the state board of education set forth four general areas of outcomes: (a) outcomes related to effective schools, (b) outcomes related to high standards of performance through an integrated curricular approach, (c) outcomes related to human resource development/staff training and retraining, and (d) outcomes related to community-based outreach programs—the learning-working community concept.

The four outcomes apply to all districts and, in turn, to all students. The board recognizes that districts will vary in how they propose to achieve the outcomes and in the evidence they offer as indicators of success. Rather than presenting the indicators as standards to be met, districts are asked to develop school improvement plans. Within the structure of their plans, schools are to communicate, by adhering to state indicators and developing and achieving local indicators, how they will meet the intent of the outcomes model. The Kansas plan allows districts to develop outcomes within the four areas specified and to identify their own indictors. Although these must be approved, the approach allows districts some control over determining what is important to their community schools and setting expectations for what they judge to be evidence of their own success. Districts also have flexibility in determining how they will meet the outcomes.

Because special education has operated for several years somewhat independently of general education and because few states have experience with the outcomes model, some are concerned about how students with disabilities will be accommodated in an outcomes approach to accreditation. This concern translates into two specific issues: (a) Will general and special educators work collaboratively to ensure that the outcomes, indicators, and assessments are appropriate for all students and not disadvantage students with disabilities? (b) What assurances will be provided that the services and conditions students with disabilities require will continue to be available when the emphasis shifts to outcomes? The underlying problem is that, as OBA is implemented, several years will be required to determine if the model works. In the interim, inputs in the form of services and special provisions now available to students with disabilities may receive less priority as districts strive to implement interventions that they assume will enhance their students' success on measures designed to assess performance on their stated outcomes.

Schools typically are accredited as districts and not as programs. This underlines the importance of special educators' working closely with general educators at state and local levels to assure appropriate outcomes, indicators, and assessment measures. Research currently is being conducted on special education outcomes and indicators by Ysseldyke and his associates at the National Center on Educational Outcomes, University of Minnesota. An example of special education indicators is the Oregon system developed by Halpern and Nelson (1990) for secondary special education programs. The following excerpt from Halpern and Nelson illustrates the indicators they have validated in the areas of curriculum/instruction and transition.

Curriculum and Instruction Indicators

1. Students with disabilities receive appropriate academic instruction, which prepares them for functioning in their community, including the possibility of postsecondary education.
2. Students with disabilities receive appropriate vocational instruction, which prepares them for jobs in their community.
3. Students with disabilities receive appropriate instruction in independent living, which prepares them for functioning independently in their community.
4. Students with disabilities receive appropriate instruction in social/interpersonal skills, which prepares them for interacting effectively with people in their community.
5. Students with disabilities receive appropriate instruction in leisure and recreation skills, which prepares them for leisure opportunities within their communities.
6. Community-based instruction is available as one option within the special education program offerings.
7. Instructional procedures for students with disabilities are designed to ensure that students can perform skills they have learned in new settings (generalization), and also remember how to use their skills over time (maintenance).
8. Appropriate curriculum materials are available for providing instruction to students with disabilities.
9. Procedures exist for placing students into an instructional program tailored to their individual needs.

Transitional Indicators

1. Information exists on community services currently available for school leavers with disabilities.
2. Transition goals are addressed as part of the planning process for students with disabilities.
3. A process exists for enhancing collaboration between special education and relevant adult agencies to facilitate successful transition of students.

The challenge in implementing outcomes-based accreditation for programs serving students with disabilities stems more from the current trends in special education than from student attributes or needs. As many students with disabilities are being assigned primarily to regular classrooms, the responsibility for instructional decisions and data collection shifts largely to regular classroom teachers with support from specialists. For these collaborative arrangements to be effective in setting outcomes, identifying indicators, and collecting supportive evidence requires a major investment in staff development. However sound it may be, imposing an outcomes-based accreditation model on schools where mainstreaming, REI, or inclusion are still maturing is likely to increase frustration among instructional personnel. This frustration could interact with the outcomes-based accreditation process and hamper implementation when, in reality, the attitude of personnel toward placement of students with disabilities in regular classrooms rather than the accreditation model, is the source of concern. Positively influencing attitudes is a far more difficult task than gaining acceptance of an outcomes approach to accreditation.

The change in attitudes and responsibilities and the creation of new ways to make educational decisions are the essence of the organizational change called for by the reform movement. We do not suggest that states should retreat from insisting that programs serving students with disabilities be incorporated as an integral part of the OBA process. They should be incorporated and be viewed as an integral part of the student population when reference is made to *all* students. Setting the practical realities of applying an outcomes-based accreditation model may be complicated because of the transition occurring in the schools today relative to how special education students are being educated (Meyen et al., 1991).

OUTCOMES-BASED EDUCATION

Outcomes-based education (OBE) is built on three basic premises (Spady and Marshall, 1991):

> "All students can learn and succeed (but not all on the same day in the same way). Success breeds success. School controls the conditions of success." (p. 67)

Almost all of the major reform and policy reports on education in the last 5 years have emphasized higher expectations for student performance and the importance of schools' adopting instructional models that focus on outcomes. Although the language used to describe outcomes may vary, the intent is clear: Schools should give more attention to addressing the results of teaching and learning and provide some form of evidence tied to predetermined goals or expectations. Outcomes-based education is not a new approach to instruction. After increasing significantly in popularity since 1985, it is now going through a period of transformation. As specific methodologies are applied in practice, refinements and adjustments are made. Table 3.1 illustrates what is referred to as transformational OBE.

In contrast to outcomes-based accreditation, which focuses largely on programs or the aggregate performance of students, outcomes-based education is targeted to individual student performance. It involves setting expected outcomes for individual students, identifying appropriate indicators of progress toward those outcomes, and applying appropriate measures for assessing performance. The educational outcomes are intended to reflect the educational philosophy of the local school and the specific needs and capabilities of individual students. As in outcomes-based accreditation, communities exercise considerable influence over setting outcomes. In setting outcomes for OBA, however, representatives of the community participate directly, whereas in setting outcomes for individual students through OBE, the community creates the philosophy and sets the general expectations within which individual outcomes are set. Typically, parents, teachers, and students collectively set outcomes for individual students. Setting outcomes as expectations for students becomes a process integrated with curriculum and instructional decisions. Teachers plan the instructional program for the students assigned to them by first addressing the needs of individual students and then the needs shared among groups of students.

● *TABLE 3.1*

What is transformational OBE?

Transformational OBE is not:	Transformational OBE is:
1. Calendar defined (schools, programs, processes, credentialing, and decision-making priorities);	Outcome defined (schools, programs, processes, credentialing, and decision-making priorities);
2. Constrained in opportunity (which limits time for teaching and successful learning to occur);	Expanded in opportunity (which enables successful teaching and learning for all to occur);
3. Custodial in credentialing (credit based on seat-time attendance and ambiguous criteria);	Based on performance credentialing (credit through accomplishment, using clear criteria, and demonstrating success of priority outcomes);
4. Tied to curriculum coverage (approach to teaching and testing);	Aided by instructional coaching (fostering successful performance for all students on essential outcomes);
5. Segmented in content (curriculum structure, instructional delivery, testing, and credentialing);	Integrated in concepts (cross-curriculum approach to outcomes, curriculum structure, instructional delivery, and assessment);
6. Based on cumulative achievement (approach to curriculum planning, teaching, testing, and grading);	Based on culminating achievement ("end-result" approach to outcomes, curriculum design, instruction, assessment, and grading);
7. Selection oriented (opportunity structures, grading, and curriculum tracking);	Oriented to inclusionary success (structure of curriculum cross-groupings, learning, assessment, and credentialing opportunities);
8. Characterized by contest learning (students compete for scarce rewards);	Characterized by cooperative learning (to foster learning success for all);
9. Dependent on comparative evaluation (emphasizing relative quality of work accomplished and grades assigned);	Confirmed by criterion validation (expectations of high-level performance on clearly defined outcomes and standards);
10. Composed of cellular structures (school and curriculum organization, learning environments, and credentialing).	Formed on collaborative structures (for curriculum planning, instructional delivery, and student learning).

Source: Excerpt from "Beyond Traditional Outcome-Based Education," by W. G. Spady and K. J. Marshall. October 1991, *Educational Leadership*, p. 68.

Further, though outcomes-based accreditation is largely an accountability system, OBE takes on the form of a curriculum/instructional strategy. OBE does provide a base for instructional accountability, but much of its power lies in the decision making specific to instruction and curriculum central to setting outcomes and identifying indicators for individual students. In many respects, OBE is compatible with the instructional approaches that historically have characterized special education. Specifically, attention to individual needs and to developing instructional interventions tailored to the needs of students with disabilities has been the basis for special education. Further, the IEP model provides a construct upon which OBE can be developed for students with disabilities. The IEP itself is not an example of outcomes-based education, but it contributes to an instructional climate conducive to application of OBE. The IEP has to be made more specific and integral to daily instructional decisions to enhance its contribution to a program based on outcomes-based education principles.

Even though special education has extensive experience in individualizing instruction, only limited progress has been made in developing assessment instruments and strategies that are sufficiently reliable and valid for assessing student performance on specific outcomes. Standardized tests, though useful for many purposes, are not useful to teachers in carrying out OBE. Therefore, as outcomes are set for individual students with disabilities and as indicators are identified, attention must be given to the development or selection of assessment measures.

Curriculum-related outcomes should be measured by curriculum-based assessment or criterion-referenced testing, or both, as students are to be measured against what they have been taught. Hudson et al. (1989) defined curriculum-based assessment as any assessment that uses the material to be learned as the basis for assessing the extent to which it has been learned. Yet, much of the assessment conducted today relies heavily on standardized measures and tests, often of poor technical adequacy. A student's present level of performance is best measured by assessing down the hierarchy of skills prescribed for a curriculum area until the student demonstrates 100% mastery. At this point, present level of performance has been established and the instructional planning is simplified by teaching up the hierarchy of specified skills. This concept of *test down teach up* (Hudson et al., 1989) lends itself to the outcomes-based assessment/instructional process.

If the instructional and curricular needs of students with disabilities were the same as those of their nondisabled peers, both OBA and OBE would be achieved more easily. Certainly, that would be true for outcomes-based accreditation, in which the emphasis is primarily on the aggregate performance of students in the district. With an OBE instructional approach, however, the variability in instructional needs among students with disabilities can be accommodated more readily. In programs in which students with disabilities are integrated in regular classes, the challenge is to ensure that the curriculum and the outcomes are appropriate to the needs of individual students with disabilities. As illustrated in Table 3.2, this is achieved more easily for students with mild disabilities, whereas students with severe disabilities require greater accommodation to meet their instructional and curricular needs.

For students with disabilities who receive the same or similar curriculum as that of their nondisabled peers (although their instructional programs may involve different strategies), the outcomes and indicators may be the same as those specified for all students. Nevertheless, their performance is assessed by the content and the instructional level at which they are being taught rather than at the grade/age level at which they are placed. Primarily through such a strategy, a valid outcomes assessment can be made. Otherwise, students would be assessed on content and skills unrelated to the curriculum they have experienced, resulting in an unfair assessment and confounded outcomes data.

Though OBE is compatible with the instructional principles of the individualized instruction special education teachers typically employ, OBE also is embedded in a philosophy of instruction and curriculum. With the movement toward inclusion and with OBE gaining popularity in regular education, special educators must develop a broader understanding of OBE as applied in regular classrooms.

● **TABLE 3.2**

Curricular suggestions for setting outcomes and standards for students with disabilities

General Curriculum	Adapted Curriculum	Functional Curriculum
When the curriculum content for students with disabilities is the same for a nondisabled student, the outcomes measures *must* be the same. It there is a significant delay when content is taught, "off-grade" testing is permissible. Outcomes measurements are different only when curriculum requires change.	The pupil can benefit from the same content and, to some extent, curriculum sequences of general education. At this level, however, instructional needs are so significantly different from peers that the emphasis is on modifying the general content to match the student's ability or functioning level. This includes means such as adapting the access or response modes (e.g., listening rather than reading content or speaking instead of writing), simplifying subject-matter content to focus on its most relevant	Curriculum is substantially different from general education curriculum. When students are assigned to this level, a decision has been made that they cannot benefit from remediation or adaptation of content normally taught in general education.
Instructional and curriculum needs are essentially the same as for students in the general education program. In this case, educational performance may be quite low but still within the lower variation limits that can be		Instruction focuses on functional academics, prevocational or vocational training. Instructional content such as managing money, making sensible purchases, and skills associated with independent living are examples of curriculum content. These skills, primarily addressing daily

General Curriculum	Adapted Curriculum	Functional Curriculum

accommodated in general instructional settings. Also, the student probably has needs in other areas, such as affective or social, that may or may not be addressed in a general curriculum.

Emphasis at this level may be on remediation or enhancement of basic skills in core curriculum areas (i.e., reading, math, language arts, social studies). It also may focus on access to general education through methods such as signing, braille tests, or computer-enhanced augmentative devices.

Special education services focus on reducing or maintaining the existing educational gap between a student and age-equivalent peers. Remediating education deficits, enhancing educational strengths and improving learning and study strategies are emphasized at this level. Educational content is consistent with the curriculum in general education. Progress is measured with the same criterion-referenced/norm-referenced tests used with all students. Supplemental measures also could be used to reflect additional or special individual goals.

features, or emphasizing general educational content but at a significantly off-grade level.

Learning strategies are still stressed at this level, but the essential feature is that subject content is substantially off-grade.

Outcome measures are the same for the general curriculum, but "off-grade." Academic gains of an upper elementary pupil are measured with a primary achievement battery.

Additional measure should be used at this level based on specific individual goals.

living and vocational needs, are those necessary for everyday functioning and usually are learned by general education students through experience or develop as generalizations from basic school subjects.

Specific criterion-reference tests must be developed at this level.

Source: From E. L. Meyen et. al., 1991, *Policy Considerations on Outcome-Based Accreditation for Students Receiving Special Education Services* (prepared by University of Kansas School of Education for Kansas Board of Education).

COLLABORATION

Common to all recent approaches to how best meet the needs of students with disabilities is a growing need for collaboration among educators. As districts have incorporated mainstreaming or REI, or have experimented with inclusion, the need for collaboration at various levels has become apparent.

Collaboration is not new in special education. Many school districts initiated the role of consulting teacher in the early 1970s. At that time, however, the consulting teacher role was more circumscribed, largely making a designated teacher serve as a problem solver, staff development specialist, and advisor to other teachers. Further, specialists such as school psychologists and speech pathologists traditionally have used their consulting skills to assist teachers in working with students. For the most part, this emphasis on consultation was inherent in their role as a specialist with a set of skills and expertise.

Today circumstances have changed dramatically. *Everybody* who has expertise has to share it. To enhance and facilitate this universal sharing process, significant progress has been made in isolating consultation skills and in training professionals to use their skills effectively. Robinson (1991) defined collaboration consultation as follows,

> Collaboration consultation is a term used to describe an interactive and ongoing process where individuals with different expertise, knowledge, or experience voluntarily work together to create solutions to mutually agreed upon problems. It is characterized by mutual trust and respect and open communication. Underlying assumptions and beliefs of collaborative consultation include an assumption of parity among participants, belief that all educators can learn better ways to teach all students, and belief that educators should be actively involved in creating, as well as delivering, instructional innovations. The goal of collaborative consultation is to better meet the needs of diverse students, both handicapped and nonhandicapped, in as integrated an educational setting as possible. (p. 441)

Whereas the consulting teacher's role in the 1970s was cast as a delivery model, collaborative consultation today represents an approach characterized by how professionals share information and assist each other. Because students with disabilities often present instructional challenges, particularly in settings where the teacher is responsible for students with varied instructional needs, it is not reasonable to assume that one teacher will have all the necessary skills or knowledge. Therefore, colleagues must have the collaborative skills to effectively share their expertise and to create the climate that allows collaboration to prevail.

Although the need for collaboration is acknowledged and teacher education programs are beginning to prepare teachers with collaboration consultation skills, districts are faced with having to assist teachers in acquiring the needed skills and behaviors. West and Commons (1988) identified 47 skills that were subjected to review by a jury of experts. Table 3.3 reports the essential consultation skills judged to be most important.

Central to educational reform today is a concern for restructuring of schools. West (1990) presented collaboration as one of the keys to successful restructuring of schools.

● *TABLE 3.3*

Essential skills for the process of consultation

<table>
<tr>
<td>Consultation
Theory Models</td>
<td>

1. Practice reciprocity of roles between consultant and consultee in facilitating the consultation process.
2. Demonstrate knowledge of various stages/phases of the consultation process.
3. Assume joint responsibility for identifying each stage of the consultation process and adjusting behavior accordingly.
4. Match consultation approach(es) to specific consultation situation(s), setting(s), and need(s).

</td>
</tr>
<tr>
<td>Research on
Consultation
Theory, Training,
and Practice</td>
<td>

5. Translate relevant consultation research findings into effective school-based consultation practice.
6. Exhibit ability to be caring, respectful, empathic, congruent, and open in consultation interactions.
7. Establish and maintain rapport with all persons involved in the consultation process, in both formal and informal interactions.
8. Identify and implement appropriate responses to stages of professional development of all persons involved in the consultation process.
9. Maintain positive self-concept and enthusiastic attitude through the consultation process.
10. Demonstrate willingness to learn from others throughout the consultation process.
11. Facilitate progress in consultation situations by managing personal stress, maintaining calm in time of crisis, taking risks, and remaining flexible and resilient.
12. Respect divergent points of view, acknowledging the right to hold different views and to act in accordance with convictions.

</td>
</tr>
<tr>
<td>Interactive
Communication</td>
<td>

13. Communicate clearly and effectively in oral and written form.
14. Utilize active, ongoing listening and responding skills to facilitate the consultation process (e.g., acknowledging, paraphrasing, reflecting, clarifying, elaboration, summarizing).
15. Determine own and others' willingness to enter consultative relationship.
16. Adjust consultation approach to the learning stage of individuals involved in the consultation process.
17. Exhibit ability to grasp and validate overt/covert meaning and affect in communications (perceptive).
18. Interpret nonverbal communications of self and others (e.g., eye contact, body language, personal boundaries in space) in

</td>
</tr>
</table>

appropriate context.

19. Interview effectively to elicit information, share information, explore problems, and set goals and objectives.
20. Pursue issues with appropriate persistence once they arise in the consultation process.
21. Give and solicit continuous feedback that is specific, immediate, and objective.
22. Give credit to others for their ideas and accomplishments.
23. Manage conflict and confrontation skillfully throughout the consultation process to maintain collaborative relationships.
24. Manage timing of consultation activities to facilitate mutual decision making at each stage of the consultation process.
25. Apply the principle of positive reinforcement to one another in the collaborative team situation.
26. Be willing and safe enough to say "I don't know...let's find out."

Collaborative Problem Solving

27. Recognize that successful and lasting solutions require commonality of goals and collaboration throughout all phases of the problem-solving process.
28. Develop a variety of data-collection techniques for problem identification and clarification.
29. Generate viable alternatives through brainstorming techniques characterized by active listening, nonjudgmental responding, and appropriate reframing.
30. Evaluate alternatives to anticipate possible consequences, narrow and combine choices, and assign priorities.
31. Integrate solutions into a flexible, feasible, and easily implemented plan of action relevant to all persons affected by the problem.
32. Adopt a "pilot problem-solving" attitude, recognizing that adjustments to the plan of action are to be expected.
33. Remain available throughout implementation for support, modeling, and/or assistance in modification.
34. Redesign, maintain, or discontinue interventions using data-based evaluation.
35. Utilize observation, feedback, and interviewing skills to increase objectivity and mutuality throughout the problem-solving process.

Systems Change

36. Develop role as a change agent (e.g., implementing strategies for gaining support, overcoming resistance).
37. Identify benefits and negative effects that could result from change efforts.

Equity Issues and Values/Beliefs Systems	38. Facilitate equal learning opportunities by showing respect for individual differences in physical appearance, race, sex, handicap, ethnicity, religion, socioeconomic status, or ability.

Equity Issues and Values/Beliefs Systems

38. Facilitate equal learning opportunities by showing respect for individual differences in physical appearance, race, sex, handicap, ethnicity, religion, socioeconomic status, or ability.
39. Advocate for services that accommodate the educational, social, and vocational needs of all students, handicapped and nonhandicapped.
40. Encourage implementation of laws and regulations designed to provide appropriate education for all handicapped students.
41. Utilize principles of the least restrictive environment in all decisions regarding handicapped students.
42. Modify myths, beliefs, and attitudes that impede successful social and educational integration of handicapped students into the least restrictive environment.
43. Recognize, respect, and respond appropriately to the effects of personal values and belief systems of self and others in the consultation process.

Evaluation of Consultation Effectiveness

44. Ensure that persons involved in planning and implementing the consultation process are also involved in its evaluation.
45. Establish criteria for evaluation, input, process, and outcome variables affected by the consultation process.
46. Engage in self-evaluation of strengths and weaknesses to modify personal behaviors influencing the consultation process.
47. Utilize continuous evaluative feedback to maintain, revise, or terminate consultation activities.

Source: Excerpted from J. F. West and G. Commons, "Essential Collaborative Consultation Strategies for Regular and Special Educators," 1988, *Journal of Learning Disabilities, 21,* 56–64.

As professionals develop collaboration consultative skills, schools gain an enlarged instructional resource; each teacher becomes a potential resource to others for helping to resolve a specific instructional problem.

Special education has a history of relying on specialists to assume rather structured roles. Therefore, implementation of collaboration models will require some rethinking of traditional roles, as well as the way special education professionals are prepared. In discussing collaboration and restructuring, Friend and Cook (1990) stated:

> The special education REI proposals for restructured schools are as subject to the conditions for collaboration as other school reform recommendations. In fact, because of the traditional separation between classroom teachers and special service providers, collaboration is, if anything, more essential if proposed restructuring is to be attempted. For example, voluntariness is a condition for collaboration which has not been adequately considered by many REI proponents, and as a result, implementation may be problematic. (p. 81)

Probably no area causes more concern for special educators than that of determining how professionals can work together in the future as schools go through restructuring. As more and more students with disabilities receive their education in regular classrooms, the need for collaboration in sharing expertise as standard professional behavior becomes essential. If one term can appropriately describe students in classrooms today, it is *diversity*. Diversity requires diverse responses from teachers responsible for creating effective instructional environments. For this to occur, teachers need the benefit of the best talent among their colleagues. Collaboration currently may be the most promising solution to this challenge.

SUMMARY

The purpose of special education is to ensure appropriate and effective instruction for students with disabilities. Yet, the energies of the profession frequently have been diverted to issues that are related more to where students with disabilities should be served and who is responsible. The development of instructional resources and intervention has only sporadically received the attention it warrants, leaving to teachers the responsibility for primary decisions on what and how to teach.

Introduction of the IEP through PL 94–142 was a major step toward refocusing attention on instruction. To its proponents, in the beginning of the 1970s, the IEP represented a form of instructional accountability. Unfortunately, during the early years of implementation, the IEP was treated more as an administrative procedure than an instructional planning tool. For that reason, it has not achieved its potential. The IEP, however, continues to represent a sound approach to ensuring an appropriate education for students with disabilities.

Given the history of instructional planning in special education, professionals understandably hold different views of the IEP. Simply as a procedure, however, the IEP may not survive. Or perhaps it will survive, but merely as some sort of administrative ritual. Only as an instructional planning mechanism incorporating accountability can it be nurtured to maturity. Instructional processes evolve; they are not invented. Viewed in the larger historical context, the IEP is evolving. As a political tool, the IEP has served its purpose; it has been institutionalized in public education. The challenge now is to transform it into an instructional tool that can aid teachers in making instructional decisions targeted at ensuring an appropriate education for students with disabilities.

Initiatives such as outcomes-based education and collaboration—both of which are directed toward improving instruction—must receive the support they need in order to mature. The danger is that the profession will become preoccupied with philosophical issues surrounding REI and inclusion and, once again, ignore the substance of special education instructional practices. The extent to which the potential of these practices, as well as the IEP, is realized depends largely on the beliefs and values of new professionals entering the field and their ability to influence others.

REFERENCES

Chambers, J. G., & Hartman, W. J. (1983). *Special education policies: Their history, implementation, and finance*. Philadelphia: Temple University Press.

Cincinnati Public Schools. (1964). *The slow learning program in the elementary and secondary schools.* Curriculum Bulletin No. 119.

Decoeudres, A. (1928). *The education of mentally defective children.* (E. Row, Trans.). Boston: D. C. Heath.

Doll, E. (1962). The mentally deficient. In E. P. Trapp & P. Himelstein (Eds.), *The exceptional child: Research and theory*. New York: Appleton-Century-Crofts.

Duncan, J. (1943). *The education of the ordinary child*. New York: Ronald Press.

Featherstone, W. B. (1951). *Teaching the slow learner*. New York: Columbia University, Teachers College.

Friend, M., & Cook, J. (1990). Collaboration as a predictor for success in school reform. *Journal of Educational and Psychological Consultation, 1*(1), 69–86.

Halpern, A. S., & Nelson D. J. (1990). *Secondary special education and transition teams: Procedures manual.* Eugene: University of Oregon.

Hudson, F. G., et al. (1989). *Hudson education skills inventory: HESI–Writing (Composition, Spelling, Handwriting)*. Austin, TX: Pro–Ed.

Ingram, C. P. (1935). *Education of the slow-learning child*. Yonkers, NY: World Book.

Inskeep, A. D. (1928). *Teaching dull and retarded children*. New York: Macmillan.

Kansas, State of. (1992). *Kansas quality performance accreditation: A plan for living, learning and working in a global society*. Topeka: Kansas State Board of Education.

Kirk, S. A., & Johnson, G. O. (1951). *Educating the retarded child*. Boston: Houghton Mifflin.

Lynch, W. W. (1967). *Instructional objectives and the mentally retarded child*. Bloomington: Indiana University, Bureau of Educational Studies and Testing.

Meyen, E. L. (1968). *Demonstration of dissemination practices in special class instruction for the mentally retarded: Utilizing master teachers as in-service educators* (Final Report, Project No. 6–2883). Iowa City: University of Iowa.

Meyen, E. L., et al. (1991). *Policy considerations on outcomes-based accreditation for students receiving special education services*. Prepared by the University of Kansas School of Education as an informational document at the request of the Kansas Board of Education.

Pheeney, J., & Prehm, H. (1985). *An examination of individualized instruction*. Unpublished manuscript. Council for Exceptional Children, Reston, VA.

Robinson, S. M. (1991). Collaborative consultation. In B. Wong (Ed.), *Learning about learning disabilities*. San Diego: Academic Press.

Skrtic, T. M., Guba, E. G., & Knowlton, H. E. (1985). *Interorganizational special education programming in rural areas* (Technical report on the Multisite Naturalistic Field Study). Washington, DC: National Institute of Education.

Spady, W. G., & Marshall, K. J. (1991). Beyond traditional outcome-based education. *Educational Leadership, 67–72.*

State of Illinois. (1958). A cooperative project of the Office of Public Instruction, Division for Exceptional Children, and the Institute for Research on Exceptional Children at the University of Illinois. "A curriculum guide for teachers of the educable mentally handicapped." *The Illinois Plan for Special Education of Exceptional Children*. Curricular Series B-3, 12. Chicago: Illinois Council for Mentally Retarded Children.

Thorsell, M. (1969). *Kansas plan: Conceptual models for development and implementation of curriculum content structures*. New York: Simon & Schuster.

Turnbull, A. P., Turnbull, H. R., Summers, J. A., Brotherson, M. J., & Benson, H. A. (1986). *Families, professionals and exceptionality: A special partnership*. Columbus, OH: Charles E. Merrill.

Wallin, J. W. (1955). *Education of mentally handicapped children*. New York: Harper & Brothers.

West, J. F. (1990). Educational Collaboration in the Restructuring of Schools. *Journal of Educational and Psychological Consultation, 1*(1), 23–40.

NNNNNNNNNNNNNNNNNNNNNNNNNNNNNNNNNNNN

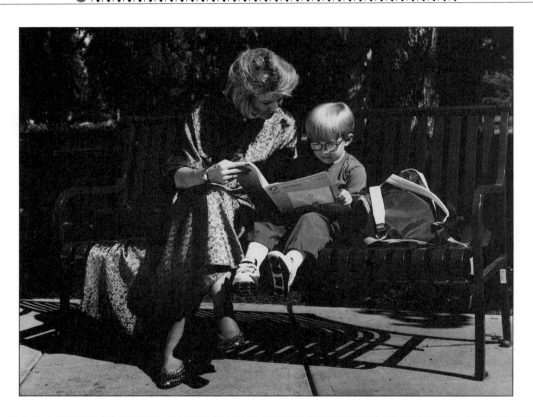

NNNNNNNNNNNNNNNNNNNNNNNNNNNNNNNNNNNN

THE FAMILY OF CHILDREN

AND YOUTH WITH

EXCEPTIONALITIES

*A*NN *P. T*URNBULL, *P*ATRICIA *B*ARBER,
*G*EORGIA *M. K*ERNS, *S*HIRLEY *K. B*EHR

*T*he family, the oldest and most fundamental social institution, is the major source of individual beliefs, values, and codes of behavior. The pivotal role of the family in the nurturing, socialization, education, and career development of its individual members has far-reaching implications for the field of education in general and special education in particular.

The field of special education evolved with a primary focus on the child with the exceptionality. The family, its nature, and the ways in which its members influence one another, were little understood. Research now emphasizes the need for professionals to broaden their concern to the entire family system of which the child with an exceptionality is a member.

FAMILY RESOURCES

A systems perspective recognizes that family members are interrelated to the extent that experiences affecting one member affect all members (Minuchin, 1974). It also highlights the contributions families can make in partnership with professionals and the role professionals play in supporting the integrity of the family. Figure 4.1 provides a framework for organizing the family systems concepts discussed within this chapter. The four major components are:

1. *Family characteristics:* the variables involved in the family's ability to address the individual and collective needs of its members. A major assumption of a systems perspective is that each family is unique and the uniqueness influences how it copes with the child's exceptionality.
2. *Family interactions:* the relationships that occur between individuals and subsystems within the family system. The needs of family members must be addressed constantly. These needs compete with each other for the time and resources of the family unit.
3. *Family functions:* the different categories of needs for which the family is responsible. Because these needs are comprehensive and multiple, families are extremely busy trying to attend to all of their tasks and responsibilities.
4. *Family life cycle:* the sequence of changes that affects families as they pass through various stages in time. These changes include both developmental and nondevelopmental (such as divorce) transitions.

● *FIGURE 4.1*

Family systems conceptual framework

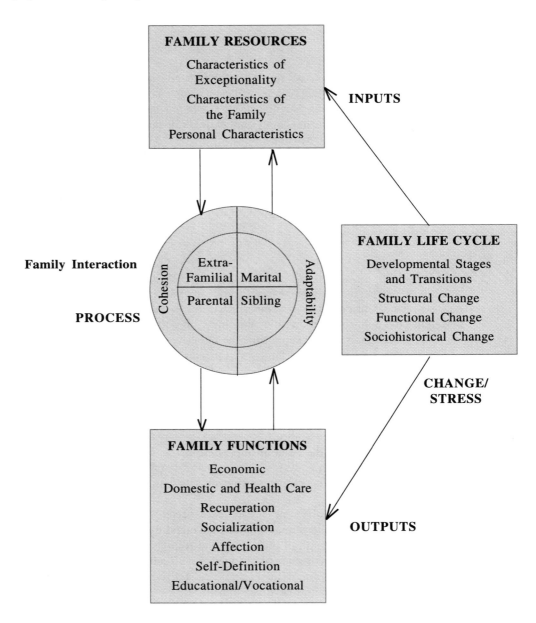

Sandra and Elvin Diehl have five children: Mary, 8; Ralph, 7; Kara, 5; Timmy, 3; and Bobbie, 1. Elvin works as a clerk in a grocery store, and Sandra is a full-time homemaker. Elvin dropped out of high school in the ninth grade. He was in a special education program for students with mild mental retardation. Sandra finished high school by going to night school after Mary was born. Sandra and Elvin are always on the edge of poverty. They rely on their faith in God as an assurance that life will surely get better for them.

School has been a struggle for Mary and Ralph. Both have needed remedial help. Now Kara has been identified, during her kindergarten year, as having a moderate hearing loss. Sandra and Elvin have just been told that their daughter needs a hearing aid and special instruction to learn language. Sandra is depressed about Kara's problems and about the many needs her family is facing. She wonders how in the world they will be able to afford a hearing aid. Elvin reassures her that "the Lord always provides." Sandra's three sisters and Elvin's mother and father always come through. They provide hope and encouragement for Sandra.

Irving and Marsha Greenstein are accustomed to people commenting on the "twins," their two 12-year-old sons, Todd and Sam. But Todd and Sam are not twins; Todd is Marsha's son, and Sam is Irving's son, both from previous marriages. Irving and Marsha at one time saw their life together as a fairy tale come true. Once married, and all living together as a family, however, the problems have been intense. For example, Todd is a gifted student, always performing at the very top of his sixth-grade class, whereas Sam struggles to keep up with below-grade-level work.

Sam is hurt when he sees his stepbrother getting all the glory. He figured out that he could get at least some attention in class by clowning around and generally being a troublemaker. He prides himself on the streak of four-letter words he can put together to make the other students and teachers take notice of him. One morning on the playground he threw a brick, seriously injuring a second-grader. Sam is currently being evaluated for emotional problems as well as for some learning deficits.

At the same time, Todd stacks up award after award—"Mr. Wonderful" from everyone's perspective—except Sam's and Irving's, that is. A new baby is now requiring a lot of time and attention of the family. Meanwhile, between night feedings and other demanding caregiving responsibilities, Todd and Sam both need support and understanding if they are to carry out their own responsibilities as family members and students.

All families differ in how they address both the individual and the collective needs of their members. This is obvious when comparing and contrasting the family characteristics of the Diehls and Greensteins. As no two students are exactly alike, the need to individualize instruction as much as possible has long been recognized.

These two concepts—the *uniqueness of the individual* and the *need to individualize* instruction—apply to the families as well. Because no two families are exactly alike, a beginning point in understanding is to recognize the many different ways families react to exceptionality. Three major variables are: (a) characteristics of the exceptionality itself; (b) characteristics of the family, including its cultural background and structure; and (c) the collective personal values and coping styles of the family members.

CHARACTERISTICS OF THE EXCEPTIONALITY

How does the type of exceptionality influence a family's reaction to it? Different types of exceptionalities influence different families in different ways. For example, a family with high achievement goals is likely to react positively when a child is identified as gifted. On the other hand, families that do not place great value on achievement or education, or are not gifted themselves, may perceive giftedness as a threat. The child is going to have needs that they may not be able to meet.

Elvin Diehl was identified as having mild retardation when he was in school. Probably he would not react to the identification of one of his children as gifted in the same way as a father with a record of outstanding scholastic achievement would. The family's reaction to the type of exceptionality is influenced by the family's values and general lifestyle.

Different exceptionalities pose different kinds of challenges for a family. A child with a language impairment possibly could create problems for the family in trying to establish meaningful, constructive communication. A child with health problems may require extended hospitalizations and expensive medications. A child who is blind needs special adaptations to be able to learn self-care and leisure skills. A family may do quite well with one exceptionality but not with another. Recall the situation of the Greenstein family, which can handle Todd's giftedness better than Sam's learning and emotional problems. No two children, even with the same exceptionality, have exactly the same impact on their families. The unique needs of each create different problems for different families.

How does the degree of exceptionality influence a family's reaction to it? The common assumption is that families experience more stress when the child has a severe disability than when the child has a mild disability, but the issue is not that simple. Severe disabilities typically are identified shortly after birth or during the preschool years. The disability is obvious, and the diagnosis is certain. With less ambiguity, the family can proceed to access community services and plan for the future, all in line with the definitive information they have (Turnbull & Turnbull, 1990).

A milder disability, in contrast, often is not identified until the child has problems in school, and frequently the diagnosis is less certain. In the case of learning disabilities, the child may do quite well in some academic areas; in others, he or she may experience some major problems. Because of this uneven performance, family expectations can be confused. The family might think the child could perform much more successfully if only he or she were motivated or more conscientious. Thus, the child becomes the scapegoat for refusing to try, and the family does not recognize the reality of a learning problem.

FAMILY CHARACTERISTICS AND CULTURAL BACKGROUND

How does the family's cultural background influence its reaction to exceptionality? Cultural background, particularly ethnicity, plays a major role. McGoldrick (1982) described the influences of ethnicity as follows:

> Ethnicity patterns our thinking, feeling, and behavior in both obvious and subtle ways. It plays a major role in determining what we eat, how we work, how we relax, how we celebrate holidays and rituals, and how we feel about life, death, and illness. (p. 4)

The United States frequently is called a melting pot; perhaps "exotic stew" would be more accurate. Although we should not stereotype various ethnic groups, family theorists identified some ethnic characteristics as influencing family adaptation to exceptionality. For example, the values of Anglo-Saxon protestants emphasize self-reliance, self-control, achievement, and self-determination. These are contrasted with identified values of Hispanics: cooperation, interdependence, collectivism, and cohesiveness (McGoldrick, 1982). Different values greatly influence a family's priorities and goals.

Consider the issue of independence for young adults with disabilities. Currently, young adults with disabilities are strongly encouraged to live independently from the family and to work in competitive employment in their communities. This emphasis on independence is more closely aligned to Anglo-Saxon, protestant values than to Hispanic values. A mother with a Hispanic background commented:

> I would be horrified if my son who has Down syndrome moved away from my home and out on his own. That is just not done in my culture. My family and friends would say, "How did she fail so miserably, and what did she do to run her poor son out of the home?" We don't place such great importance on living by yourself, but we do care a lot about attending to the needs of our own children. As long as he's got mama, he's all taken care of.

Ethnic traditions do apply, and professionals, in working with the families of children with exceptionalities, must recognize the role ethnic traditions play in shaping the family's impact on the child (Slonim, 1991). At the same time, professionals must take care to avoid overgeneralizing and stereotyping a particular ethnic group.

How does a family's size and form influence its reaction to exceptionality? Family structure varies in many ways. Families differ in how many children they have, the number of parents, the presence and number of stepparents, extensiveness of the extended family network, and preferences and extensiveness of live-in members of the family who are unrelated by blood or marriage. The parents may be married, divorced, or reestablished, or they may have some other type of arrangement. The notion of two parents living in the home, the father working and the mother devoting full-time care and attention to two children and their collie dog, is a myth of modern society.

Here are some highlights of current family trends:

Positive adaptation to a child's exceptionality appears to be better in two-parent families as compared to one-parent families (Trute & Hauch, 1988).

- Remarried families represent about 17% of all households of children under age 18 (Glick, 1984).
- From 1987 to 1988, 21.9% of all births were to unmarried women (Bureau of the Census, 1990).
- Based on 1988 statistics, 18.9% of children who are white, 54.1% of children who are black, and 32.2% of children who are Hispanic reside in single-parent homes (Bureau of the Census, 1990).

The implications are obvious: The family—its size and form—has a major impact on the special needs of children and youth with exceptionalities.

One aspect of family size is the number and birth order of the children in the family. A larger number of children appears to be related to a greater atmosphere of normalcy in a family (Trevino, 1979). Also, more children means less parental caregiving time because siblings can share this role. More children provide a greater sense of help and support and a greater likelihood that parental expectations for achievement will be realized. On the other hand, more children in the family can split parenting time; competing responsibilities interfere substantially with the amount of attention that can be diverted to one child. Sandra Diehl commented:

> We could afford a hearing aid if we only had Kara. What about Mary, Ralph, Timmy, and Bobbie? How do we make the money stretch across all of them? Kids tease them now because they wear ragged clothes. If we spend all of our money on the hearing aid, they probably won't have any clothes at all.

PERSONAL CHARACTERISTICS

How do values influence a family's reaction to exceptionality? Individual and collective values within a family influence how members perceive the impact of the characteristics of the exceptionality. Family values affect family needs and priorities such as a comfortable life, equality, happiness, independence, security, social recognition, and accomplishment. Also, a family often has more than just one set of values. Mothers and fathers have differing values for themselves and for childrearing, and siblings' values differ as well.

Thus, competing and conflicting values within a family can create more stress as it tries to work through its members' reactions to the exceptionality. Irving Greenstein places great emphasis on ensuring that his son Sam is secure and not ridiculed or excluded by his peers in school. Marsha Greenstein places a much greater value on living in the "real world" and on taking the hard knocks as they come along. These two different value sets can substantially influence educational decisions such as placement and instructional goals, as well as social interactions in the neighborhood. A good beginning point is to be aware of how their own values operate in their identifying and relating to the values of family members.

What different coping styles do families use in reacting to exceptionality? Families vary greatly in how they cope with special needs associated with the exceptionality. One way to categorize family coping styles is by the strategies of passive appraisal, reframing, spiritual support, social support, and formal support (Olson et al., 1983; Turnbull & Turnbull, 1990).

Passive appraisal means ignoring a problem or setting it aside, either temporarily or permanently, rather than working through it directly. Parents use passive appraisal when they decide not to worry about their child's developmental delays in the hope that eventually the child will catch up.

Reframing, a more active approach, involves the family's ability to redefine a situation acceptably to solve problems (Summers, Behr, & Turnbull, 1989). In redefining a situation, parents take a stressful circumstance, such as a child's inability to walk, and reframe it so, for example, they are thankful he won't wreck the house. The ability to make positive comparisons in a situation, to look on the bright side, is a helpful reframing strategy. Another is to use problem-solving skills to alter the course of events. Families learn to identify needs, prioritize needs, generate workable alternatives, select the most appropriate alternative, take action, and evaluate the consequences of the action (Goldfarb, Brotherson, Summers, & Turnbull, 1986; Shank, 1991).

Spiritual support helps some families cope. Fewell (1986) surveyed mothers of children with Down syndrome. Of those mothers, 37% reported that they would seek help and guidance from members of their church or clergy for problems associated with their child, and 66% responded that religion has helped them to understand and accept their child. Other parents, too, have reported this pattern of religious support. It typically involves much more reliance on religious or spiritual interpretation of the exceptionality than on actual support and assistance from organized religion.

Elvin Diehl relies on spiritual support to maintain a sense of hope that things will be better in the future. He fervently believes "the Lord always provides," and that reassurance is crucial in how he handles the daily stress and worries of his family.

Social support is the assistance a family gets from extended family members, friends, neighbors, and co-workers. Social support can be in the form of direct help to the child, such as extending friendship to the child or including the child in special activities, or it can involve indirect support to the family as it works through its reactions and plans for the future. It depends upon how willing and able the family is to reciprocate. The expression is, "What goes around, comes around." This is a key to understanding the nature and continuity of social support.

Formal support is assistance provided by professionals such as teachers, related service providers, physicians, therapists, and rehabilitation counselors. Families have raised some common issues concerning the helpfulness of professional support: the extent to which professionals listen to the respective families; professionals' willingness to try different alternatives when the first is unsuccessful; the importance of informal and frequent communication; and the necessity of providing relevant help rather than generalized and esoteric advice for practical problems (Turnbull & Turnbull, 1990; Walker, 1989).

In considering how families cope, we have to realize that some families just cope better than others, regardless of their style. Generally, families that cope successfully are able to use a variety of styles; their choice of style depends upon the nature of the problem they are facing.

SPECIAL CHALLENGES

How does poverty influence a family's reaction to exceptionality? Harsh statistics define the startling frequency of poverty in the United States. Based on 1989 data when a family was considered poor if its total income was $9,885 for a family of three and $12,675 for a family of four, one in five American children is poor (Johnson, Miranda, Sherman, & Weill, 1991). Three of the specific findings are:

- Hispanics are the fastest growing group of poor children.
- Almost two thirds of all poor families with children have only one or two children.
- The fastest growing poverty problem is in the suburbs rather than in urban areas.

Obviously, when a family is facing challenges posed by poverty, including adequate nutrition, housing, and medical care, its emphasis on education will be limited, compared to the priority on meeting basic needs. Consider the situation in the Diehl family. Although Kara needs a hearing aid, the family also must have food to eat and clothes to wear. If there is not money to go around, Sandra and Elvin have to maintain survival as their top priority.

How does living in a rural area influence a family's reaction to exceptionality? An estimated 11 to 15 million people with disabilities live in rural areas (Seekins, Offner, & Jackson, 1991). They may face special challenges associated with isolation, lack of services, and inadequate transportation. With advances in distance learning, in which technology enables hook-ups of various kinds between instructional centers and schools or homes, some of the barriers associated with living in rural areas are being overcome. Still, comprehensive services will not be available to rural areas to the same degree as in metropolitan areas. Rural families often have to come up with their own resources and get the support they need from indigenous groups such as their churches and farm associations.

FAMILY INTERACTIONS

Dorothy Wilcox is a divorced mother of two children, Ruby, 5, and Harry, 3. Ruby, a bright inquisitive little girl, has been enrolled in kindergarten since the beginning of the school year. Harry was born with cerebral palsy, which affects his motor and language abilities. He has been classified as "severely multiply handicapped" and attends an early intervention program five mornings a week. Dorothy works full-time as an insurance claims adjuster and struggles to meet the ever increasing cost of rearing two small children, one of whom has an exceptionality that requires ongoing medical attention.

Joyce and Kenny Olson always have been considered the "ideal" couple. They both come from well-educated, financially successful families that are proud of Joyce and Kenny and their three children—Bruce, 16; Wanda, 12; and Mathew, 8. Joyce and Kenny are both physicians. Kenny's speciality is internal medicine; he has a large practice in the suburban village where they live. Joyce, a pediatrician, recently received a long sought-after appointment as chair of pediatric medicine at the university medical school in a nearby city.

But things are not as ideal as they appear to those outside the family. Wanda, identified as a gifted child at age 5, has been enrolled in a special program for gifted children. In addition to her emerging academic brilliance, Wanda has musical talent. Her exceptionality requires a great deal of the family's time, attention, and resources. Joyce and Kenny want to make sure she has enough enrichment opportunities. Joyce has spent the past 16 years playing "super mom." She has met the needs of each family member, as well as her own. Bruce is going through a turbulent adolescence; Matthew seems to be doing adequately in school, but he has few outside interests and spends most of his time alone in his room or watching television.

Joyce struggles with conflicting roles: as Kenny's wife, as a professional, and as a mother, particularly Wanda's. Teachers and counselors have advised the Olsons to make certain that Wanda has every opportunity to achieve her full potential. Kenny has been uncommunicative lately, of very little help to Joyce in making her decision about whether to accept the appointment at the medical school. Both sets of grandparents advise Joyce to spend more time at home, especially with Wanda, whom they consider to be the "family genius."

Family interaction refers to the *network* of relationships that exists within families and the ways in which those relationships influence and are influenced by the family member with the exceptionality. In the past, professionals focused primarily on the child with the exceptionality, with the assumption that what was in the child's best interest also was in the family's best interest (Simeonsson & Simeonsson, 1981). Current research and practice, however, examine the child's exceptionality within the *context* of the family, recognizing that any educational or therapeutic intervention affects all family members. Thus, teachers can significantly affect the family and its interactions (Turnbull & Turnbull, 1990).

To address the individual and collective needs of their members, families look to a variety of resources. They also have many ways of interacting and communicating with one another. Families are made up of coexisting subsystems that form the network through which the subsystems interact and carry out their functions. The extent to which each subsystem affects the family unit depends upon the family's characteristics, and the same concepts of uniqueness and individualization apply. The family has four subsystems: marital, parental, sibling, and extrafamilial or extended.

MARITAL SUBSYSTEM

What are the characteristics of the marital subsystem? The marital subsystem is the relationship between a husband and a wife, through which they meet their individual needs for love and affection, physical intimacy, socialization, companionship, and self-identity. The marital subsystem usually describes a traditional family, such as Joyce and Kenny Olson's. Many different types of family arrangements are found today, including single parents who have never been married, or who are divorced or widowed and rear their children alone. Some single parents live with companions or friends of the same or opposite sex, as Dorothy Wilcox does. Many of the needs of single parents, living in less traditional lifestyles, may be met through a central relationship with another adult who is not related to the child or children.

How is the marital subsystem affected by a child with an exceptionality? One must understand the characteristics of the exceptionality and the personal characteristics of the husband and wife, such as the coping strategies they use. In general, the effect is difficult to predict, because individuals respond in unique ways. Past research on families of children with disabilities has stressed the negative impact of the child on the marital subsystem, reporting higher rates of divorce and marital discord (Farber, 1959; Gath, 1977; Reed & Reed, 1965). What past research did not identify was the quality of the marriage prior to the child's birth.

Children with exceptionalities who require a great deal of physical care and medical supervision also demand disproportionate amounts of time and energy from their parents. Often, the needs of the husband and wife as marriage partners are set aside to meet their child's needs. Diverting attention away from the marriage has a long-term effect that depends, once again, on the family characteristics.

Let's consider the marriage of Joyce and Kenny Olson. Their marital relationship is definitely strained by the number and intensity of conflicting roles. Joyce thinks she has spread herself around so thinly that she simply doesn't have much left for her marriage or for herself. Balancing the time she invests in her children, particularly her daughter who is extremely gifted, and in her job seems to constantly preempt the time and energy she would like to put into ensuring a quality marriage.

Some parents report that their marriages have been strengthened by having a child with an exceptionality. They have drawn closer as a couple, learning to love and appreciate one another even more deeply. For example, a research study compared the marital stress of couples with children with spina bifida and couples whose children do not have an exceptionality. Although no differences were revealed between the two groups in marital satisfaction, the couples with children with spina bifida actually reported experiencing higher levels of marital satisfaction (Kazak & Marvin, 1984).

Gordon (1975) drew up a Bill of Rights for parents of children with exceptionalities. It includes getting away together without the children, having "dates" to celebrate birthdays and anniversaries, and not feeling guilty if they do not want to devote time to organizations for children with exceptionalities.

The impact a child with an exceptionality has on the marital subsystem cannot be predicted, and professionals should not assume that it will be negative. Rather, they should recognize the parents have needs as individuals and as a couple, and parents should be encouraged to meet those needs, to devote time to one another, and to create opportunities to enhance their marriage. Professionals should be sensitive to how their expectations for parent participation in a child's program are going to affect the time and energy parents have for one another and their marriage.

PARENTAL SUBSYSTEM

What are the characteristics of the parental subsystem? The parental subsystem refers to the relationships between parents and their children, whether biological, adoptive, or foster arrangements. Parents have certain images of the physical, intellectual, and emotional characteristics their unborn children will have. These images become even more well defined during pregnancy as the fetus begins to move about, the heartbeat becomes detectable, and an anticipated arrival date is set. Normally, parents wish for a "perfect" child, one who is physically fit, attractive, liked by other people, intelligent, and alert. Gabel, McDowell, and Cerreto (1983) suggested that these expectations serve two important functions: (a) the child reflects the parents' desire for a second chance at life and the child will have the opportunity to realize the goals and ambitions they did not achieve; and (b) the child gives parents a sense of immortality.

   How is the parental subsystem affected by a child with an exceptionality? In answering this question, the type and degree of the exceptionality, the parents' social and cultural values, and the strategies they use to cope with problems must all be considered. When parents expect a "perfect" child and the child turns out to have an obvious disability, parents react with shock, disbelief, disappointment, and fear of the future. They may not have had any previous experiences with disabilities; they may be uncertain about what to do or how to behave; and they may be unprepared.

   An initial service that many parents identify as extremely helpful is Parent-to-Parent support. This approach involves matching a veteran parent who has had experience in dealing with these feelings and in reaching meaningful resolutions to provide informational and emotional support to a parent who is brand new to the experience. More than 300 local programs and approximately 12 state networks provide Parent-to-Parent services. Step-by-step guidelines are available for people who are interested in starting new programs (Santelli, 1990).

SIBLING SUBSYSTEM

What are the characteristics of the sibling subsystem? The sibling subsystem refers to the relationships among children in the family. These relationships are influenced by each child's personality and the family's characteristics. In some families siblings compete for parental attention and quarrel frequently. In other families the siblings support one another and develop close friendships with each other. The children's gender and the difference in their ages also affect how they interact.

   How does a child with an exceptionality affect the sibling subsystem? The brothers and sisters of children who have exceptionalities have special concerns. Bruce and Matthew Olson are the brothers of a gifted sister whose exceptionality places extra demands on the family's resources. Although both are good students, Wanda outshines them academically and musically. The relationships in the Olson family sibling subsystem depend, to a large extent, on each child's personal characteristics, the stability of the married subsystem, and the ways in which Joyce and Kenny Olson approach their roles as parents.

When the exceptionality is a disability, as in the case of Dorothy Wilcox's son Harry, other types of concerns arise. Although children often are sensitive to the special needs of their sibling who has a disability, they are in danger of being overextended with extra responsibilities or of having their emotional needs neglected. Research indicates that, as a result, siblings may be at risk for emotional problems (Vadasy, Fewell, Meyer, & Schell, 1984). Research also indicates that benefits may accrue as well: better understanding of other people, more tolerance and compassion, and more appreciation of good health and intelligence (Grossman, 1972).

The needs of the child with the exceptionality may have higher priority than children without exceptionalities. Professionals can play an important role by including them, along with the parents and the child with the exceptionality, as a focus of concern and consideration.

EXTENDED OR EXTRAFAMILIAL SUBSYSTEM

What are the characteristics of the extended family subsystem? The extended family consists of the many different people who may be involved with individual families: relatives, friends, neighbors, co-workers, members of religious and community organizations, and professionals. The nature of the extended family subsystem and the extent to which it is involved in a family's life depend upon the characteristics of the family and of its individual members. This subsystem can play an extremely important role in providing emotional, social, financial, and practical support.

By providing valuable resources, the extended family subsystem can assist families in carrying out their various functions. For example, if the teachers and therapists who work with Harry Wilcox were to expand their concerns to include Dorothy, and Ruby, they would recognize that Dorothy's participation in the early intervention program, although of benefit to Harry, might place additional burdens on an already overburdened family. Instead, they might help Dorothy identify members of her extended family who could assist her with child care, household chores, and financial and emotional support. The entire family would benefit from these new resources. Dorothy could attend to her own personal needs and to Ruby's needs.

Like parents, grandparents often have expectations of the "perfect" child. They, too, may experience grief and disappointment when their grandchild has a disability. The grandparents' grief or rejection of the grandchild can add to the parents' frustrations. Conversely, their love and support can be a source of strength (Vadasy, Fewell, & Meyer, 1986). Grandparents can help the parents carry out their functions in many ways. They can assist with errands, shopping, child care, and transportation. One of their greatest potential areas of contribution is in emotional support, sharing parental concerns and encouraging them to maintain a hopeful outlook (Seligman & Darling, 1989).

FAMILY FUNCTIONS

FUNCTIONAL CATEGORIES

Carl Engel has been rearing his two sons, Marty, 13, and Joe, 9, alone ever since his wife passed away 2 years ago. Joe has always been a slow learner; his learning disabilities were identified when he was 7. Since that time he has been making steady progress with his schoolwork. Joe is socially immature for his age, and extremely uncoordinated and clumsy. Because of these problems, Joe is often rejected by his peers.

Steve and Andrea Syzmanski have an 8-year-old daughter, Jean, who was born with spina bifida, a condition affecting her spinal cord. Paralyzed from the waist down, she uses crutches and a wheelchair for mobility. The spinal damage also has left her without natural control of her bowel and bladder; but with the help of a special diet and a procedure called intermittent catheterization, she is beginning to control elimination and accidents are becoming less frequent. Although some children with spina bifida have mental retardation or learning disabilities, Jean shows no such signs. Steve and Andrea are thankful for that. Jean has a special device, called a shunt, implanted in her brain to eliminate the unnatural buildup of brain fluid—a condition that often accompanies spina bifida.

What are the economic needs of a family? Families are financially responsible for their own survival. They decide how the family budget will be managed. Any family could face economic hardship at one time or another. Illness, loss of employment, a child entering college—all add stress to finite financial resources. In some cases a child with an exceptionality creates either a temporary or a long-term economic demand. Andrea Syzmanski said:

> We had no idea that Jean's care would be so expensive. Our medical insurance has covered some but not all of the costs for surgeries, medication, and many visits to the pediatrician, neurosurgeon, and other specialists. Then there's the wheelchair, braces, diapers, special diets, and other expenses too numerous to list. We've really had to rethink our financial situation to stay one step ahead of the next emergency.

Added to the outright costs for care are the less obvious financial strains the Syzmanskis experience: loss of time from work for various medical appointments and the move to a new house to accommodate Jean's wheelchair. For some families, the child's care requirements force one parent, usually the mother, to withdraw from the workforce, reducing the total family income (Hobbs, Perrin, & Ireys, 1985).

The economic impact differs for each family. Although Jean's medical needs may have a long-term economic impact on the Syzmanskis, the Engels are affected in other ways:

> I've hired a tutor to help Joe with his learning problems, and it has been worth every penny. At the same time, I realized we no longer could get by without some housekeeping help. I also needed to get serious about Marty's college fund. We've had smooth sailing up to now, but the expenses are beginning to add up.

Educators need to be sensitive to these economic considerations, particularly when recommendations for additional services and supports for the child require family financing.

What are the domestic and health-care needs of a family? Families engage in numerous daily tasks to meet the domestic and health-care needs of their members: cooking, cleaning, shopping, transportation, obtaining medical care, and so on. Jean's care places extra demands on her family for time and energy:

> We spend many hours in doctors' offices, hospital rooms, and clinics. Even Jean's daily care routine—dressing, leg braces, bladder control—can be time-consuming. Of course, there are the usual daily chores and our jobs. Steve and I have developed a fairly tight schedule to get everything done, but there are days and sometimes weeks when housework, errands, and even paying bills must be set aside.

Patterson (1991) noted that families do best when they are able to balance the needs of the child with exceptionalities with other family-related needs. Developing a normal family routine is important to maintaining this balance. This means that care-related activities should be incorporated into the family's daily schedule but not take precedence over the other activities that are important for a normal round of life. Professional recommendations requiring families to spend more time and energy on their child with special needs can affect this healthy balance negatively and upset normal routines and activities.

What are the recreational needs of a family? Family members need time to rest, relax, and engage in hobbies and other activities that take them away from their daily demands. In some families recreational needs take a back seat to the other needs of the child with the exceptionality. Carl and Joe talked about the effect of Joe's educational problems on family recreation:

> I set aside about an hour each night to help Joe with his studies, and time on weekends to teach him how to play ball and ride a bike. His teacher suggested that I spend more time on his motor activities, so we've added a little time after dinner during the week. I know it's helping Joe, but we're scheduled all the way up until bedtime. When do we get time to rest or fool around or just talk?

> I really liked playing ball with Dad for just a while, but it's not fun anymore. Dad gets real mad when I don't do it right, and I'd rather play with my trains or build airplanes with Dad or Marty.

Families such as the Syzmanskis may hesitate to engage in recreational activities, either because of the child's inability to participate or because family members feel guilty about leaving the child with caregivers as they pursue their own interests. Andrea expressed these feelings:

> Jean's illnesses and her mobility problems restrict a lot of activities. Steve is always insisting that we take a trip together, but I know it will be disastrous. We occasionally leave Jean with a sitter for a night out with our friends, but I always leave the house with a mental list of all the reasons why I should be home.

What are the socialization needs of a family? The family unit provides both the context and the guidance for socialization. Children acquire social skills initially by interacting with family members. Eventually they broaden their skills through interactions with individuals who are external to the immediate family.

As with recreation, the child with an exceptionality may restrict the social opportunities for family members. In turn, the exceptionality may interfere with the child's ability to interact with others. Families may have to assist the child in developing appropriate social skills or provide opportunities for interaction with people outside of the home.

Carl, for example, recognized his son's social problems early on. By becoming a Boy Scout leader, he was able to help Joe interact with other boys his age. Steve and Andrea, however, failed to recognize Jean's loneliness:

> I really got mad one day. I didn't want to play with my toys, and I didn't want to play with Mom or Dad. I used to hear my friends at school talk about playing at each other's house. Mom and Dad wouldn't ever let me get to know the kids down the street because they made fun of me.

Once Jean's parents understood how she felt, they began to organize birthday, Halloween, and Valentine's Day parties with school and neighborhood children. Not all of the children came, and not all came back, but Jean was happy to make a few close friends. Their extra efforts to provide opportunities for Jean not only fulfilled her socialization needs but also helped the family address a parallel problem they had continually avoided:

> Taking Jean out in public was an uncomfortable venture for all of us. Some people were curious, nosy, rejecting, and at times downright rude. At first I reacted by getting angry, but this only made Jean cry. Finally we made a game of pretending it never happened, although the topic was never actually discussed. Now that Jean has learned she can make new friends, she has become a real charmer with strangers. Even when people hurt her feelings, and ours, we can share our feelings with each other—get the hurt out—and move on.

What are the family's needs for affection? Providing unconditional love and support to its members is an important family function. Many families report that their child with an exceptionality has brought the family closer together, given new meaning to their lives, and enhanced their happiness and sense of fulfillment (Behr & Murphy, 1993; Hunt, 1967). Conversely, an exceptionality at times may generate negative feelings about the child and the family situation in general. Marty Engel reflected on his earlier feelings about his brother Joe:

> Joe was a real pain when he was younger. He was always acting out and getting into things that were off-limits. Joe just couldn't seem to sit still for more than two minutes. I remember Mom and Dad always yelling at him, or trying to bribe him to behave. Eventually they would wind up getting mad at each other. I know I shouldn't have, but I often wished he would just go away. I really hated him. He's much better now, and I guess I understand more than I used to. We're pretty close, but sometimes, well, I just need to get away from him.

Alternating feelings of love/acceptance and anger/rejection are common in all families. When family members and professionals overemphasize the disability, they may fail to recognize the child's strengths and the positive contributions they make to the family.

> When I think of Jean, I've been known to break into tears right in my office. She's a beautiful, smart, happy, friendly child—everything Steve and I would want from a daughter. Yet, I can get so mad at her for being disabled, for changing our lives. I know I'm not really angry at *her*, just the disability. Once I get over that, I can see her for what she really is.

What are the self-identity needs of a family? Although no clear evidence exists that children with exceptionalities have low self-esteem or negative feelings of self-worth, they may need support in dealing with the often negative and stigmatizing societal attitudes toward people with disabilities (Darling & Darling, 1982).

The self-identity of other family members also may be affected. For example, parents' self-identities are closely tied to those of their children. If parental competence is measured in terms of the child's achievement and healthy adjustment to life, disabilities that inhibit these goals can provoke parental feelings of failure. The manner in which the entire family unit defines itself should be considered. As Steve described their situation:

> I often get tired of being the parent of a special child. I just want to be a father, a husband— just myself. Andrea and I work hard at being good professionals, good neighbors and friends, and a part of the community. If we don't, people will continue to see us as a "special" family, and all three of us will begin to define ourselves as disabled.

What are the educational/vocational needs of a family? The family's educational function encompasses all of the other functions. Families provide children both formal and informal instruction in various areas of academic learning. In addition, they guide and train children in leisure time, domestic and health care, and economic concerns. They serve as models of socialization, affection, and self-identity. As a family meets the needs of its children, they, in turn, learn how to meet their own needs, as well as others' needs.

In light of all their other responsibilities, families usually place less emphasis on the child's educational and vocational needs than professionals do. This sometimes strains relations between home and school. It need not be a problem, however, if professionals remember that each family is unique. Each family has different types of needs to address, different resources to work with, and different ways of prioritizing and responding to needs. Therefore, each family responds to professional ideas and suggestions in its own way.

Educational specialists need to maintain close communication with families of children with exceptionalities to understand how family preferences, abilities, and constraints relate to the child's educational and vocational needs. Only then can professionals help families recognize and build on their child's abilities as they plan for the child's future needs.

FUNCTIONAL PRIORITIES

How do families perform multiple functions? Families do not perform functions individually; they perform multiple functions simultaneously. For example, Andrea's job meets a number of family needs. First, it provides economic support. Second, it allows Andrea to socialize with peers and meet new people. Third, it gives Andrea a healthy perception of her personal abilities and worthiness. Finally, her employment serves an educational function, both for her, as she continually learns new ideas and skills, and for her family. Steve and Jean benefit from Andrea's new experience and expanding knowledge.

Families address multiple needs by emphasizing some functions over others. For example, Carl places a high priority on doing things with children:

> My wife and I always felt that the most enjoyable times of our lives were those we spent together as a family. Now that I'm a single parent, my time with the kids is even more important. I may be overreacting, but I've been spending less time on Joe's schoolwork and taking on fewer accounts at work so I can start getting home at a decent hour. The three of us have begun renovating a small boat in our garage. It will give us something special that we can all share. Sometimes you have to take charge and do what you think is best for everybody.

Steve and Andrea, on the other hand, believe the greatest thing they can give to their daughter, besides love and support, is a college education.

Families prioritize different functions differently. They also use different means to meet family needs. In some families the primary affection-giver is the mother; in others, hugging and kissing may be spontaneous among all the members. Moreover, within a family, different members may be responsible for different functions. In addition, some families call upon the immediate and extended family. Other families turn to community service providers when their personal resources are exhausted. Some never do so, regardless of how desperate they may be.

Finally, as they move through the life cycle, families reexamine their priorities. Education may be an important priority for Jean's parents now, but it may be supplanted by a greater concern for her socialization and sexuality as she reaches adolescence. Carl, on the other hand, may begin to stress educational accomplishments for Joe as Joe begins to reach the age of independence. The transitions between the various stages in the life cycle are stressful for all parents, and particularly for parents like the Syzmanskis, who have difficulty accepting their children's adolescent and adult needs because these children still require some of the physical care they needed as children.

FAMILY LIFE CYCLE

Juan Ortiz is 2 . Recently he was identified as having an emotional and behavioral disturbance. He is the second of three children who live with their mother, Carmen. Carmen is 17 and unmarried. Living in a large city, she subsists on welfare, food stamps, and Aid to Families with Dependent Children. The Ortiz family lives in two rooms, sharing a kitchen and bath with three other families.

Carmen is unable to control Juan, who screams and throws tantrums frequently. Her screaming back at him and spanking him only increase the intensity of his outbursts. The teachers and therapists in Juan's early intervention program are trying to help Carmen with child care so she will have some time for herself. They also are attempting to provide her with some training in behavioral techniques so she will be able to control Juan's outbursts.

Carmen has no family nearby to help. Therefore, it is important that she provide stability and guidance for her children in their early childhood. Carmen understands that, but she is barely out of childhood herself. She says, "Juan is my little boy, but I can't help but smack him sometimes when he keeps crying. If it weren't for Peggy, Juan's teacher down at his program, I think I would hurt him bad. I have no one else to turn to. I'm so glad Juan can go to his program. It's helping me teach the other kids, too!"

Sylvia Harris is a 20-year-old woman who has moderate mental retardation. She lives at home with her parents, Andrew and Marge, both professionals and both in their 50s. An only child, she is enrolled in a classroom for high school students with moderate mental retardation and works each morning in a local industrial plant as part of her school program. Her parents have begun looking for apartments or other residential options in their town while considering Sylvia's likes and dislikes. Sylvia participates in several community programs—a music club, an aerobics class sponsored by the recreation department, and a video exchange.

Andrew and Marge have many friends who invite Sylvia over when her parents need time for themselves. Because they are anxious for her to become more independent, they have taught her to do the family grocery shopping and have left her at home alone for short periods. Although Andrew and Marge look forward to Sylvia's independence, it will leave a big hole in the family when she moves out. Sylvia's mother says, "We've struggled for years to make sure Sylvia would be independent. We've tried not to overprotect her, so she could live on her own, but I dread letting go!"

Families grow and change over the life cycle. Their resources, interaction patterns, and functional priorities change with each stage. Carmen Ortiz is trying to provide her children with security and basic needs during the early years, whereas the Harrises are attempting to develop and accept their daughter's independence as she moves into adulthood. A family is like a kaleidoscope. A change in one member influences all the other members and changes the view for everyone in the system. Growth means changing needs. It is normal and natural, but it also is stressful, especially for families who have members with exceptionalities. They may experience changes that are different from those of other families, or they may fail to experience an expected change. Moreover, the change may be of a different nature.

STAGES IN THE LIFE CYCLE

The family life cycle may be categorized in many different ways. One describes seven stages: couple, birth and early childhood, school-age, adolescence, young adult, postparental and aging (Turnbull & Turnbull, 1990).

What may happen during the couple stage? Traditionally, the initial stage is just the couple; however, in reestablished families a husband and wife may bring children from previous marriages into the new relationship. During this stage the values, goals, and expectations of the two families of origin are blended. The couple attempts to establish new priorities and traditions as a nuclear family. They also begin to develop the characteristics that will make their family unique, to form the values that will shape their roles as parents, and to develop expectations concerning their yet-to-be-born children.

What may happen during the birth and early childhood stage? During this stage the family expands to include one or more infants who depend on the parents to meet their physical and emotional needs. The birth of any child is stressful enough and even more so if the child has a disability (Bailey & Simeonsson, 1988). Informal information networks of other young parents or extended family members may not be available. Families with infants who have exceptionalities use professional networks more frequently to provide them with initial information or time for relaxation (Bailey & Simeonsson, 1988). Families with preschoolers may be in contact with a program designed to enhance the child's skills. These programs require parents to attend meetings, reinforce skills taught in school, and search for or attempt to establish other needed services. Carmen Ortiz is receiving training offered through such a program. She stated:

> I have no one else to help me with the kids. Juan's teachers really have become my friends. There's always coffee and someone to talk to when I have a problem with any of the kids.

What may happen during the school-age stage? During this stage, in which the family focuses on the education and socialization aspects of childrearing, the family and the educational professionals usually have more contact. Families with members who have exceptionalities often are involved in their child's instructional program. This may include requesting and searching for needed services such as counseling or vocational training. While Sylvia was in junior high school, Andrew Harris served on several committees to assess the vocational and residential living services available in their community for children with mental retardation. He and Marge realized that planning for Sylvia's adult future had to begin early. Marge remarked:

> It took a lot of time for Andrew to go to meetings and to visit programs, but it was important for all the families who may need those programs to know what's available.

What may happen during the stage of adolescence? Families at this stage in the life cycle typically are involved in preparing their adolescent for independent living. Adolescents with exceptionalities may not participate in certain activities, such as passing a driving test, that other adolescents do. Parents at this stage also need to acknowledge their child's sexuality, a stressful experience for some parents. Gifted children often are ostracized from their peer group; they have unusual skills, and they may have more pronounced difficulties adjusting (Perino & Perino, 1981). Their parents begin to search for appropriate programs and financial aid for their child's further education. Parents like the Harrises begin to plan for their child's future in legal and financial matters such as estates and trust funds. Andrew commented:

> Sylvia won't have to worry financially. We've appointed a guardian in our will, and there's a trust fund set up, too. Sylvia's guardian knows we want her to have as much independence as she can handle. That's clearly set out in our will.

What may happen during the young adult stage? During this stage the membership patterns of families shift. Older children leave home to establish independent identities and become self-supporting to the greatest extent possible. Andrew and Marge Harris admit that, when Sylvia leaves home, it will be stressful for them, even though they have been planning this for several years. They see it as accepting some risk for the future. Some people with disabilities find this a frustrating time, when scarce services must be sought in the adult service system (Haring, Lovett, & Saren, 1991). Some parents get discouraged watching their own friends become freed from childrearing tasks while they must go on caring for their adult child. Children who are gifted or talented, but whose talents have not been enhanced through the school system, may have problems.

The same is true if an exceptional child has not been guided in the right direction as the parents decide on future goals. Marge commented:

> We're concerned about where Sylvia will live once she leaves school. Her IEP has had vocational as well as daily living skill goals for several years. Finding the resources to allow her to live in an apartment with a roommate is difficult. We want her to live nearby, but we also want her to be as independent as possible.

What is involved in the post-parental stage? At this stage parents once again become a couple, without children in the home. The couple is the focus of the family. Families that have a son or a daughter with a severe disability may never go through this stage, because of the lack of residential options for that member (Seltzer, 1985; Zetlin & Turner, 1985). This stage also may involve the family in providing for elderly parents who need care and support. Andrew responded:

> We're really beginning to feel like the "sandwich" generation! We worry about Sylvia— where she'll live and with whom, will she have meaningful work, and so on. At the same time, our parents are becoming more frail. The possibility that our parents may need to move in with us is becoming more real as time passes.

What may be involved at the aging stage? Families at this point usually have completed the task of rearing the children. Now they prepare to enjoy grandchildren and other social relationships. At this final stage families with a member who has a disability worry about the future. Who will care for the member when the parents die? (Russell, 1983).

LIFE CYCLE TRANSITIONS

Everyone goes through shifts from one life stage to another. People also experience change within a given life stage. Changes or transitions between stages are considered developmental; those that may occur at any time within any stage are nondevelopmental.

What are developmental transitions? Developmental transitions are changes that are to be expected in moving from one life stage to another. Change may be sociohistorical, occurring over the span, or structural, such as the change in family size and form when a baby is born. It involves changes in relationships among members and in tasks to be performed. Functions, values, and coping styles may change. The transition from early childhood to school-age is another expected change. Children in our society are expected to enter the public school system at or about age 5. This often is a stressful time for parents, who must accept their child's growth and maturation, but it also is a satisfying time and a positive sign in the child's development.

Parents of preschoolers with exceptionalities may be involved in an early special education program. These programs may be a part of the public school system or a community program. These families, now in contact with the public schools, are making the school-age transition earlier than most. Greater demands may be placed on the family to become involved in the child's program, through follow-up of skill training or practice of the tasks introduced in school. These families must expend far greater effort and time with a child who has an exceptionality, often to the detriment of the other members. The parental subsystem may be emphasized at this time as well, rather than being balanced among all the subsystems. Carmen responded:

> Juan will soon be a big boy and go to school. It's hard because he seems to be such a baby at times, but it will be nice to have some time with the two other kids. Maybe with him in school I can work on my GED.

One father said of his son's entry into the public school system:

> His adjustment was hard on us, too! We hated to see him feel lost in the kindergarten class. We went through the adjustment right along with him.

The transition as children move out of the home and into adult life can be stressful, too. Families that have adolescents and young adults with disabilities face stresses. Will employment opportunities be accessible? Are supported living arrangements available? How will the young adult access transportation? What options are open for leisure-time activities? Can the young adult obtain post-secondary education (Fairweather & Shaver, 1991; Haring, Lovett, & Saren, 1991; Mithaug, Martin, & Agran, 1987).

Andrew described his and Marge's feelings:

> There are so many things our friends take for granted about their children. They'll go to college, find an apartment, get a job, and be successful. We can't feel that way about

Sylvia's adulthood. She'll need help all her life to do those things. We're planning and preparing, but the services aren't guaranteed, so we need to have back-up plans just in case.

What are nondevelopmental transitions? A developmental transition is expected and age-related; a nondevelopmental transition is not. It can happen any time. A diagnosis of exceptionality is an example of a particularly stressful nondevelopmental transition. Parents whose infants are born with obvious disabilities frequently receive the diagnosis during the first few days of the infant's life. One mother stated:

When I was first told by the pediatrician that he wanted to test my daughter for Down syndrome, I was stunned. He even asked me to inform my husband!

When this happens, the parents' expectations of a healthy baby are shattered, and often they grieve for the loss of the expected healthy child (Pueschel, Bernier, & Weidenman, 1988). To grieve is natural. A child born with an obvious disability presents unknown difficulties and future problems that parents may find difficult to accept. Not only must parents mourn their loss of a healthy child, but they also must accept—begin to acknowledge—that their infant has special needs. At the same time, they begin to interact with the myriad of professionals who can provide their child with life-giving and life-enhancing services. They need information and support so they can make informed decisions about services and interventions. Marge described Sylvia's early years:

Very early we knew that Sylvia was not developing like other children. We have never had a specific diagnosis from the hundreds (or so it seems) of professionals we've seen over the years. There wasn't much available when she was little, not like the supports around now. Or the information. We did the best we could.

Not all children with exceptionalities are identified at birth or soon after. Some problems are not evident until the preschool or school years. Parents may be aware of discrepancies between their child's development and that of other children. They often are told, "She'll grow out of it" or "it's all in your imagination." The child does not grow out of it, however, and the problem is real. Carmen described her concerns:

Juan was a pain from the time I got pregnant. I was so sick! His birth was hard. I had no one to help me. He didn't sleep. He threw up all the time. I was so glad when the doctor finally agreed he was hard to handle and had Peggy come to visit. Now at least I know I wasn't such a bad mother like my neighbors made me feel.

A father related:

I'm much more relaxed with Jamie now that there is a label for his unusual behavior.

Some parents may be accused of "shopping around." They are the ones who take their child to several professionals in search of the answers they want. Andrew said:

We tried so hard to find out what Sylvia's problem was. I guess we did go from doctor to doctor. All we really wanted was a term to describe her disability. We finally gave up and decided we'd focus on what she needed and not try to fix her.

Geographic relocation is another stressful transition. It often severely strains family resources. Families move because of job transfers, health factors, or a search for services. If the child has a problem with mobility, a family may need to look for specialized housing. If the child has medical needs, adequate hospitals and physicians must be found. Parents of gifted children need to consider whether challenging programs are available in the community. All families with children who have special needs and are of school age may have to consider programs available through the public schools and whether they meet their child's needs. All of these problems compound the original stress of having to relocate. Carmen described her desire to return home:

> I'd love to go back home. Mama and all my aunts and uncles are there. I've been trying to save, but the rent and food and clothes cost so much. Even if I did go home, the schools are bad and Juan needs help. I only came here because my father was here and he's gone now. It's hard.

In relocating, family functions may shift as well, as economic and domestic needs take priority. Although Sylvia was very young when Andrew and Marge moved to their present home, the couple had spent several months deciding whether to move from the city where they both grew up. Marge stated:

> Andrew received a great job offer and I knew I could get work nearby, but it meant leaving our family and friends a thousand miles behind. We had to decide if the financial security was worth the stress of having to make new friends. We made the right decision but, oh, it meant a lot of sleepless nights! Sylvia has more services here than she would have had, and we have made many wonderful friends.

Divorce is another nondevelopmental transition many families go through. It can cause stress in all of the other three components of the family system: characteristics, interactions, and functions. More demands are placed on one parent to continue therapies and physical caregiving. Financial support may decrease, straining the budget even more. The extrafamilial support network usually shrinks if the separation is accompanied by bitterness or uncertainty. Carmen said:

> It would be nice to have a husband to help with Margarita, Juan, and Carlos, but I see what happens in some families in Juan's program. Fight over money; fight over custody; fight over everything! It's hard when your child isn't right, and it seems that divorce is even harder. That's why I never got married yet. Maybe someday.

Last, but certainly not the least stressful, is the reestablishment, or blending, of families through remarriage. Reestablished families must develop their own styles of interaction and communication. Step-siblings need extra support in understanding and accepting the child with an exceptionality, especially when they see that child getting a lot of what seems to be extra attention. Parents may need time to establish the new marital subsystem, which often is missing when one child requires extensive caregiving.

*S*UMMARY

How a family reacts to and copes with an exceptionality depends on certain characteristics: characteristics of the exceptionality itself, characteristics of the family, personal characteristics, and special challenges, including those posed in rural areas. All families, however, have certain strengths to draw on. The characteristics of a family shape the interactions of its members both within the family and relating to the world outside.

The family has four subsystems that form the network for interactions among family members: the marital, parental, sibling, and extended or extrafamilial subsystems. Through the interactions among the subsystems, families carry out their various functions. Any change, critical event, or intervention in one subsystem affects all the other subsystems within the family system. A child with an exceptionality affects all the subsystems. Professionals should recognize the benefit of addressing all the family subsystems in intervention.

Families have a variety of responsibilities that relate to the needs of all the family members. Education is only one. The child with an exceptionality affects all family functions in different ways. Family functioning depends on the child's unique needs in relation to the needs of the other family members, to the family's use of existing resources, and to members' interactions with each other and with others outside the family unit. Family functioning also depends on the life cycle stage the family is in and on other transitional changes that take place.

Families progress through expected life cycle stages. Each stage of development has its own goals and expectations. Families with members who have exceptionalities may or may not experience the transition from one stage to another at the expected time. Or they may not experience some of the transitions that other families do experience, such as the child's living independently or driving the family car. Assessing each family for its own uniqueness is important, considering its characteristics, interaction patterns, and functional priorities. These, too, differ over the life cycle. Families change and grow, and with change comes often stressful, nondevelopmental transitions, such as divorce. A shift in any aspect of these family systems affects all the other parts as well throughout the life cycle.

*R*EFERENCES

Bailey, D. B., & Simeonsson, R. J. (1988). *Family assessment in early intervention*. Columbus, OH: Merrill Publishing.

Behr, S. K., & Murphy, D. L. (1993). Research progress and promise: The role of perceptions in cognitive adaptation to disability. In A. P. Turnbull, J. M. Patterson, S. K. Behr, D. L. Murphy, J. G. Marquis, and M. Blue-Banning (Eds.), *Cognitive coping, families, and disability* (pp. 151–164). Baltimore, MD: Paul H. Brookes Publishing Company.

Bureau of the Census. (1990). *Statistical abstract of the United States, 1990* (110th ed.). Washington, DC: U.S. Government Printing Office.

Darling, R. B., & Darling, J. (1982). *Children who are different: Meeting the challenges of birth defects in society.* St. Louis, MO: C. V. Mosby.

Fairweather, J. S., & Shaver, D. M. (1991). Making the transition to postsecondary education and training. *Exceptional Children, 57*(3), 264–270.

Farber, B. (1959). Effects of a severely mentally retarded child on family integration. *Monographs of Society for Research in Child Development, 24*(2).

Fewell, R. R. (1986). Support from religious organizations and personal beliefs. In R. R. Fewell (Ed.), *Families of handicapped children: Needs and supports across the life span.* Austin, TX: Pro-Ed Publishers.

Gabel, H., McDowell, J., & Cerreto, M. D. (1983). Family adaptation to the handicapped infant. In S. G. Garwood & R. R. Fewell (Eds.), *Educating handicapped infants* (pp. 455–486). Rockville, MD: Aspen.

Gath, A. (1977). The impact of an abnormal child upon the parents. *British Journal of Psychiatry, 130,* 405–410.

Glick, P. C. (1984). American household structure in transition. *Family Planning Perspectives, 16*(5), 205–211.

Goldfarb, L., Brotherson, M. J., Summers, J. A., & Turnbull, A. P. (1986). *Tapping the wellsprings: A problem-solving guide for families with disabled or chronically ill members.* Baltimore: Paul H. Brookes Publishing.

Gordon, A. (1975). *Living fully: A guide for young people with a handicap, their parents, their teachers and professionals.* New York: John Day.

Grossman, F. K. (1972). *Brothers and sisters of retarded children: An exploratory study.* Syracuse, NY: Syracuse University Press.

Haring, K. A., Lovett, D. L., & Saren, D. (1991). Parent perceptions of their adult offspring with disabilities. *Teaching Exceptional Children, 23*(2), 6–10.

Hobbs, N., Perrin, J. M., & Ireys, H. T. (1985). *Chronically ill children and their families.* San Francisco: Jossey-Bass.

Hunt, N. (1967). *The world of Nigel Hunt: The diary of a mongoloid youth.* New York: Garrett Publications.

Johnson, C. M., Miranda, L., Sherman, A., & Weill, J. D. (1991). *Child poverty in America.* Washington, DC: Children's Defense Fund.

Kazak, A. E., & Marvin, R. S. (1984). Differences, difficulties and adaptation: Stress and social networks in families with a handicapped child. *Family Relations, 33,* 67–77.

Masnick, G., & Bane, M. J. (undated). *The nation's families: 1960–1990: A summary.* Cambridge, MA: Joint Center for Urban Studies of MIT and Harvard University.

McGoldrick, M. (1982). Ethnicity and family therapy: An overview. In M. McGoldrick, J. K. Pearce, & J. Giordano (Eds.), *Ethnicity and family therapy* (pp. 3–30). New York: Guilford Press.

Minuchin, S. (1974). *Families and family therapy.* Cambridge, MA: Harvard University Press.

Mithaug, D. E., Martin, J. E., & Agran, M. (1987). Adaptability instruction: The goal of transitional programming. *Exceptional Children, 53*(6), 500–505.

Olson, D. H., McCubbin, H. I., Barnes, H., Larsen, A., Muxen, M., & Wilson, M. (1983). *Families: What makes them work.* Beverly Hills, CA: Sage Publications.

Patterson, J. M. (1991). Family resilience to the challenge of a child's disability. *Pediatric Annals, 20*(9), 491–499.

Perino, S. C., & Perino, J. (1981). *Parenting the gifted: Developing the promise.* New York: R. R. Bowker.

Pueschel, S. M., Bernier, J. C., & Weidenman, L. E. (1988). *The special child: A source book for parents of children with developmental disabilities.* Baltimore: Paul H. Brookes Publishing.

Reed, E. W., & Reed, S. C. (1965). *Mental retardation: A family study.* Philadelphia: Saunders.

Russell, L. M. (1983). *Alternatives: A family guide to legal and financial planning for the disabled.* Evanston, IL: First Publications.

Santelli, B. (1990). *Parent to parent information packet.* Lawrence: Beach Center on Families and Disability, University of Kansas.

Seekins, T., Offner, R., & Jackson, K. (1991, September). *Demography of rural disability.* Missoula: Montana University Affiliated Rural Institute on Disabilities.

Seligman, M., & Darling, R. B. (1989). *Ordinary families, special children: A systems approach to childhood disability.* New York: Guilford Press.

Seltzer, M. M. (1985). Informal supports for aging mentally retarded persons. *American Journal of Mental Deficiency, 90*(3), 259–265.

Shank, M. S. (1991). *Cooperative family problem solving: An intervention for single-parent families with a child who has a disability.* Ph.D. dissertation, University of Kansas, Lawrence.

Simeonsson, R. J., & Simeonsson, N. E. (1981). Parenting handicapped children: Psychological aspects. In J. L. Paul (Ed.), *Understanding and working with parents of children with special needs.* New York: Holt, Rinehart & Winston.

Slonim, M. B. (1991). *Children, culture, and ethnicity: Evaluating and understanding the impact.* New York & London: Garland Publishing.

Summers, J. A., Behr, S. K., & Turnbull, A. P. (1989). Positive adaptation and coping strengths of families who have children with disabilities. In G. H. S. Singer & L. K. Irvin (Eds.), *Support for caregiving families: Enabling positive adaptation to disability* (pp. 27–40). Baltimore: Paul H. Brookes Publishing.

Trevino, F. (1979). Siblings of handicapped children: Identifying those at risk. *Social Casework: The Journal of Contemporary Social Work, 60,* 488–492.

True, B., & Hauch, C. (1988). Building on family strength: A study of families with positive adjustment to the birth of a developmentally disabled child. *Journal of Marital and Family Therapy, 14*(2), 185–193.

Turnbull, A. P., Summers, J. A., & Brotherson, M. J. (1984). *Working with families with disabled members: A family systems approach.* Lawrence: University of Kansas, Kansas University Affiliated Facility.

Turnbull, A. P., & Turnbull, H. R. (1990). *Families, professionals, and exceptionality: A special partnership.* Columbus, OH: Merrill Publishing.

Vadasy, P. F., Fewell, R. R., & Meyer, D. J. (1986). Supporting extended family members' roles: Integrational supports provided by grandparents. *Journal of the Division for Early Childhood, 10*(1), 36–44.

Vadasy, P. F., Fewell, R. R., Meyer, D. J., & Schell, G. (1984). Siblings of handicapped children: A developmental perspective on family interactions. *Family Relations, 30,* 281–288.

Walker, B. (1989). Strategies for improving parent-professional cooperation. In G. H. S. Singer & L. K. Irvin (Eds.), *Support for caregiving families* (103–120). Baltimore: Paul H. Brookes Publishing.

Zetlin, A. G., & Turner, J. L. (1985). Transition from adolescence to adulthood: Perspectives of mentally retarded individuals and their families. *American Journal of Mental Deficiency, 89*(6), 570–579.

5

LEARNING

DISABLED

SUZANNE ROBINSON AND DONALD D. DESHLER

*T*oday a significant number of children and adolescents are not learning in school as expected. Many of them have a learning disability (LD). Samuel Kirk coined the term *learning disabilities* in 1963, in an attempt to describe a heterogeneous group of youngsters who were labeled in various ways but were similar to one another in that they largely had normal intelligence but learned differently and not as efficiently as their nonhandicapped peers. Some of the labels referred to the presumed cause of specific learning problems (e.g., brain injury, minimal brain damage, psychoneurological disorder). Other labels referred to behavioral manifestations of presumed brain injury (e.g., perceptual disorder, dyslexia, hyperkinetic behavior, Strauss syndrome). In all cases, however, their learning problems seemed not attributable primarily to sensory handicaps, general mental retardation, emotional, family, or social disturbances, or lack of instruction and school experience. Thus, the needs of these children were deemed different from those of children in the other existing categories of learning problems (such as mental retardation or emotional disturbance) in focusing on specific problems of academic achievement caused by presumed neurological abnormalities.

Debate has persisted over the validity of this belief, given that similar educational practices are used to address the learning and behavioral problems of children regardless of label (Ysseldyke, Algozzine, & Thurlow, 1992), and that children with learning disabilities often have educational needs similar to the needs of other low-achieving students. Furthermore, subtle neurological abnormalities are not clearly evident in most children labeled as learning disabled. Yet, this category of exceptional learner is the largest, accounting for 49% of all students served in public school special education programs (U.S. Department of Education, 1991). This confirms that, despite the uncertainty about causes, many children are not learning in school and need special assistance.

The field of learning disabilities had growing pains during the last 30 years. With such unprecedented growth (700,000 students served in 1976–77 to almost 2 million students during 1988–89), the questions of researchers and practitioners have managed to outdistance the current state of knowledge about this relatively new category of exceptional learner. Is the definition accurate? (What are learning disabilities?) Are assessment practices valid? (Can a youngster with learning disabilities be identified reliably by evaluation methods currently available?) How effective are interventions? (Are special education practices really special?) Are all children served in learning disabilities programs truly learning disabled? (Are children with learning disabilities more like than unlike other children with learning problems?) Researchers and practitioners alike heatedly discuss these and other issues.

Debates over the validity of our knowledge base and the effectiveness of our current practices could dismay novices. It need not. This dialogue and constant examination is a necessary step in improving our educational programs for students for whom learning is difficult. It serves to redirect research on children with learning disabilities to areas of importance and instigates evaluation of the validity and effectiveness of our practices. Within this context of examination, transition, and change, learning disabilities, as discussed in this chapter, is organized around three themes: existing practices and current status of knowledge; concerns and confounding data; and future trends or considerations. These themes will guide the discussion.

CURRENT PRACTICES

Work with the population now referred to as learning disabled began long before that term was adopted in 1963. The field's origins lie in studies of the brain and how it functions by neurologists such as Gall, Broca, Wernicke, Head, and Jackson in the late 19th and early 20th centuries. Researchers in the area of spoken language disorders then picked up this thread in the mid-1900s. They wanted to apply existing theory to educational practices for children with learning problems. During a comparable time (from the early to mid-1900s) other medical researchers (for example, Hinshelwood and Orton) developed theories about reading disorders from which other educational practices developed (for example, those of Monroe, Gillingham, Fernald, and Kirk). During the 1930s and 1940s, Alfred Strauss, a psychiatrist, and Heinz Werner, a psychologist, examined the behavior of brain-injured children and developed their theory of perceptual dysfunction and brain injury, from which another set of educational procedures evolved (Lehtinen, Kephart, Frostig, Getman). The disparate knowledge of these early researchers is now subsumed, in terms of etiology and education, under the single label, "learning disabilities." Within this historical context, then, the heterogeneous nature of the LD population, and the diversity of the condition, can be seen as a reasonable outgrowth of the past.

Since the passage of PL 94–142 in 1975, the concept of learning disability has proved useful in promoting differentiated instruction for some youngsters (many youngsters failing in school need alternative or specialized education to learn what their peers learn more easily) and as a way to understand why some children do not learn and are hard to teach. The large number of youngsters labeled learning disabled attests to its conceptual usefulness; yet many questions remain to be answered. This exceptionality is puzzling to individuals with this handicap, their parents, their teachers, and researchers. Youngsters with learning disabilities are very different from one another. For most individuals, learning disabilities are chronic; they persist, in various manifestations, over the life span.

Some evidence indicates that, with parental support and involvement, when individual strengths are developed, and with intensive, systematic educational efforts, the prognosis for both academic achievement and vocational success in adulthood is good (Kavale, 1987). We also know, however, that many individuals with learning disabilities are unemployed or underemployed as adults and, as a group, have a higher than average high school drop-out rate (Edgar, 1987). Simply put, good special education under good environmental conditions seems to be effective in helping youngsters with learning disabilities learn and become productive citizens. For those in less than optimal situations, the prognosis is not favorable.

DEFINITION AND CLASSIFICATION

What are learning disabilities? What causes them? These questions are difficult to answer.

DEFINING LEARNING DISABILITIES

The definition of learning disabilities has been under scrutiny ever since the field's inception. Questioned are the theoretical precepts that underlie any definition, how well the definition describes a unique population, and how it is then operationalized.

According to the definition adopted by the federal government:

> "Specific learning disability" means a disorder in one or more of the basic psychological processes involved in understanding or in using language, spoken or written, which may manifest itself in an imperfect ability to listen, think, speak, read, write, or do mathematical calculations. The term includes such conditions as perceptual handicaps, brain injury, minimal brain dysfunction, dyslexia and developmental aphasia. The term does not include children who have learning problems which are primarily the result of visual, hearing or motor handicaps, of mental retardation, or emotional disturbance, or of environmental, cultural or economic disadvantage. (U.S. Office of Education, 1977, p. 65083)

This federal definition, as worded or with some slight variations, is in common use. It is significant for a variety of reasons. It emphasizes academic behavior over neurological factors. In earlier definitions phrases such as "minimal brain dysfunction" and "minimal brain injury" focused attention on an assumed neurological basis for a learning disorder. But diagnosis of learning disability was based, in most cases, on observed similarities between youngsters labeled "learning disabled" because of learning or behavioral problems and youngsters with relatively well-established brain lesions (e.g., head injury patients). Because little solid evidence of actual tissue damage existed (and still is difficult to produce), "neurological disorder" became a descriptor of theoretical interest but was of little help in identifying individuals with learning disabilities (Hallahan & Bryan, 1981; Hammill, 1990).

Of course, to separate the definition from the theory or the basic assumptions that have guided the development and direction of the field is impossible. Torgesen (1986) described two fundamental assumptions concerning learning disabilities. They are evident in the federal definition. The first assumption is that:

Learning disabilities are caused by limitations or deficiencies in basic psychological processes that are not adequately measured by standard intelligence tests, but that are required to successfully perform academic tasks. A second broad assumption is that these cognitive limitations are caused by naturally occurring variation in the neurological substrate that supports all intellectual activity, or by damage to this substrate caused by accident and disease. (p. 2)

Thus, the federal definition does include "disorder in...the basic psychological processes," which alludes to the belief that learning disabilities are intrinsic to the individual. In addition, including these words differentiates between intrinsic learning disabilities and learning problems caused by environmental influences—for example, poor teaching, a poor home environment, or social and economic disadvantage.

Debate over whether to include references to either neurological dysfunction or psychological processes in the definition is fueled by differing professional opinions as to the etiology, or cause, of learning disabilities and by our inability to describe or measure psychological processes or minimal brain dysfunction in a reliable and valid manner (Hammill, Leigh, McNutt, & Larsen, 1981; Cruickshank, 1983; Tucker, Stevens, & Ysseldyke, 1983). Thus, attempts to define learning disabilities in a way that both reflects the theoretical assumptions about their cause and states these assumptions in descriptive and measurable terms have been stymied.

Another important component of the federal definition is the exclusion clause. This defines learning disabled youngsters by identifying other potential causes of learning problems and stating that learning disabilities cannot coexist with other disabilities. Youngsters with learning disabilities are not those whose learning problems can be attributed to sensory handicaps, mental retardation, emotional disturbance, or environmental, cultural, or economic disadvantage. The idea of excluding youngsters from the learning disabilities category because they have other disabling conditions has many critics (Adelman & Taylor, 1983; Hallahan & Cruickshank, 1973; Hallahan & Kauffman, 1976; Hammill et al., 1981), who say that these excluded individuals are at even greater risk of having or developing learning problems. With criticism leveled at the federal definition, alternative definitions have been proposed.

Most recently, the National Joint Committee for Learning Disabilities (proposed initially in 1981 and revised in 1988) attempted to formulate a more appropriate definition than the federal one. The Committee, made up of representatives from the American Speech-Language-Hearing Association (ASHA), the Association for Children with Learning Disabilities (ACLD) now known as the Learning Disabilities Association (LDA), the Council for Learning Disabilities (CLD), the Division for Children with Communication Disorders (DCCD), the International Reading Association (IRA), and the Orton Dyslexia Society, reached unanimous agreement on the following:

Learning disabilities is a generic term that refers to a heterogeneous group of disorders manifested by significant difficulties in the acquisition and use of listening, speaking, reading, writing, reasoning or mathematical abilities. These disorders are intrinsic to the individual, presumed to be due to central nervous system dysfunction, and may occur across the life span. Problems in self-regulatory behaviors, social perception, and social interaction may exist with learning disabilities but do not by themselves constitute a learning disability. Although learning disabilities may occur concomitantly with other handicapping conditions (for example, sensory impairment, mental retardation, social and emotional disturbance) or with extrinsic influences (such as cultural differences or insufficient or inappropriate instruction), they are not the direct result of those conditions or influences. (National Joint Committee on Learning Disabilities, 1988, p. 1)

This definition represents the broadest consensus in the field to date. Debate will continue, however, until data supporting existing theories of causation become more conclusive. A more pressing practical concern is how to operationalize one's use of the definition to differentiate between those with and those without learning disabilities. Why is that so?

A definition serves a variety of purposes. From a scientific perspective it must be precise. It must clearly describe the unique population under study. To do so, it must be specific and limiting (Keogh, 1987), thus responding to the principle of *exclusivity*. It also should respond to the principle of *universality*, identifying characteristics not unique to learning disabled youngsters but common to all within the condition. Then, research can take place with a clearly described sample of the population and assure generalizability of results. Or, if universal characteristics cannot be found, at least the indicators of learning disability that are used to define the population being studied should be clearly and completely described. Therefore, operationalizing the definition for research purposes is a necessity for research results to be useful.

From a *sociopolitical perspective* the purpose of the definition is for advocacy and policy making. In this case, clear and specific criteria are not as critical because they must bend with the sociopolitical wind. For example, during times of economic prosperity, when self-realization is highly valued, an operationalized definition might identify many more youngsters than during times of fiscal restraint and curtailed social responsibility, when criteria for inclusion might be narrowed to limit those served. This phenomenon is evident in the numbers of learning disabled as analyzed across time and geography (see the section on incidence and prevalence). An undesirable outcome of operationalizing definitions for political reasons is that a youngster could be found to have a learning disability at one place and time and not at another place and time.

Finally, from an *educational perspective* an operationalized definition should describe individual learner characteristics in a way that assists educators in identifying the best treatment. By finding that a child has a learning disability, educators want that identification procedure to describe what the child can and cannot do in a way that will help them plan an effective educational program.

Given the myriad reasons for, and ways of, defining youngsters with learning disabilities, the heterogeneous nature of this population, and the theoretical validation yet to be done, the debate understandably continues. As Kavale, Forness, and Lorsbach (1991) stated, rather than discussing whether a definition is "good" or "bad," the current discussion should focus on usefulness of the definition. Keogh (1987) suggested that the discipline could adopt, instead of one definition, a definitional system, a classification or taxonomy of learning disabilities that orders the array of groups

included within our understanding of "learning disabilities." Then, different definitions could be selected, depending on one's purpose.

SUBGROUPS OF LEARNING DISABILITIES

The current LD label encompasses a heterogeneous group of individuals. This has been
the case historically, with broad agreement among professionals in the field. To
substantiate categorical validity, however, researchers face a dilemma. How does one
prove that these heterogeneous individuals have something in common with one
another that no one outside of the categorical area has?

Differentiating between learning disabilities and boundary conditions such as
underachievement, mental retardation, emotional disturbance, and even average academic performance is difficult. According to a number of researchers (Algozzine &
Ysseldyke, 1983; Schumaker, Deshler, Alley, & Warner, 1980; Shepard & Smith,
1983; Warner, Alley, Deshler, & Schumaker, 1980), considerable overlap exists in the
cognitive, academic, and social characteristics of youngsters with LD and those of
children with boundary conditions. Classification depends on the extent to which a
characteristic is present rather than on the characteristics themselves. Degree of
underachievement, degree of difficulty to teach, and degree of discrepancy between
aptitude and achievement in comparison to school peers are all used to make classification decisions. Finding what characteristic or characteristics are unique to learning
disabilities has eluded researchers.

Another line of research attempts to describe homogeneous subgroups within those
classified under the generic LD label. Lyon and his colleagues (Lyon, 1983, 1985;
Lyon & Watson, 1981; Watson, 1983) identified six subtypes of LD children who
manifest severe reading deficits. Children in subtype 1 had global language and
perceptual deficits, with the most deficient being in reading and spelling skills.
Subtype 2 youngsters also exhibited mixed deficits, but much milder than those of
subtype 1. Subtype 3 members manifested specific language problems, with reading
disorders related to auditory reception and sound blending. Those in subtype 4 had
significant visual-motor integration deficits. Subtype 5 children had global language
deficits including extreme difficulty with auditory sequencing and memory tasks.
Members of subtype 6 evidenced normal profiles; their underachievement could be
attributed to other than intrinsic causes. Other researchers (McKinney, 1984, 1990;
Satz & Morris, 1981; Speece, McKinney, & Applebaum, 1984; Torgesen, 1982)
identified similar and other subtypes, depending of what characteristics were used to
group the children.

Any classification system, or refinement of operational definitions of learning
disabilities, is useful to educators only if the subgroups respond to teaching techniques
differentially. If a subgroup responds uniformly and positively to one type of remediation
strategy, instructional planning can be made more efficient and effective. This premise
is called *aptitude-treatment interaction* (ATI), and research to validate it is preliminary
at this time. Identification of subgroups also would assist researchers in describing

research subjects and informing consumers of that research of its generalizability. The need for a more complex classification system than currently exists is evident.

INCIDENCE AND PREVALENCE

Careful examination of the incidence and prevalence of a condition allows profession-als to plan, evaluate, and develop rational policies (Keogh, 1987). Because of their interrelated use, the terms require defining. Quoting the World Health Organization's definitions, Keogh defined incidence as "the number of instances of an illness commencing...during a given period." Prevalence is "the number of instances of a given disease or other condition in a given population at a given time" (p. 5).

The National Advisory Committee on Handicapped Children (1968) recommended to Congress that 1% to 3% of the school population be served in learning disabilities programs. Members believed this to be a conservative estimate of the number of children with learning disabilities. They stated that more research was needed to determine which underachieving students were to be considered learning disabled before adopting a higher prevalence figure. Implementation guidelines of PL 94–142 then recommended identification of no more than approximately 2% of the school-aged population as learning disabled. Data collected by the U.S. Department of Education show that, beginning in 1977–78, this 2% figure kept steadily rising, reaching 4.71% in the school year 1989–90 (U.S. Department of Education, 1991) (see Table 5.1). The National Association of State Directors of Special Education (NASDSE), as reported in Lerner (1985), offered five reasons for the increasing prevalence and incidence figures in learning disabilities.

1. Improved identification and assessment procedures, including public awareness and pressure to serve these youngsters adequately.
2. Liberal eligibility criteria for learning disabilities in some states and districts.
3. Social acceptance for the learning disabled classification and a preference for it over the other mildly handicapped classifications (mental retardation and emotional disturbance). During this period, a decrease in the percentage of children labeled mentally retarded was reported.
4. Cutbacks in general education alternatives for underachievers or youngsters experi-encing difficulty in regular classes.
5. Court orders requiring the reevaluation of some minority children classified as mentally retarded.

In addition to the total child count data, other information is available through analysis of the prevalence figures. First, the fact that the number of youngsters identified as learning disabled is increasing could be interpreted to mean that learning disabilities is a persistent and long-term condition. If fewer children exit learning disabilities programs than enter, the numbers logically would increase. Second, the variability between states in percentages of children classified as learning disabled indicates that states operationalize the definition differently. For example, Keogh (1987) reported that, for 1982–83, Hawaii labeled 64% and Rhode Island 63% of their

● **TABLE 5.1**

Students receiving special education services, ages 3–21, school year 1989–90

Handicapping Condition	Percentage of Total School Enrollment
Learning disabilities	3.62
Speech or language impairment	1.72
Mental retardation	0.97
Emotional disturbance	0.67
Multihandicaps	0.15
Other health impaired	0.09
Hearing impairment	0.10
Orthopedic impairment	0.08
Visual handicap	0.04
Deaf-blind	0.01
Total	7.44

Source: U. S. Department of Education, 1991, *Thirteenth Annual Report to Congress on the Implementation of the Education of the Handicapped Act* (Washington, DC: U. S. Government Printing Office).

handicapped populations as learning disabled, whereas Alabama reported 26% and Indiana and Kentucky 27%. In 1990, Hawaii identified 3.81% of its school children as learning disabled, and Rhode Island identified 8.66% of its school children as learning disabled (Ysseldyke, Algozzine, & Thurlow, 1992). Although these figures are the extremes, they do suggest that identification as learning disabled, influenced as it is by local policies and pressures, is going to vary.

ETIOLOGY

Four models have been proposed to describe possible causes of learning disabilities: (a) the disordered individual, or medical, model, (b) the maturational lag model, (c) the inadequate environment model, and (d) the ecological model. The first two locate the cause of the problem within the individual; the last two center on the interaction between the learner and his or her environment (Adelman & Taylor, 1983). All represent different theoretical points of view held by professionals in the field of learning disabilities.

The Disordered Individual, or Medical, Model. This is the most prevalent etiological model in learning disabilities. It localizes the cause of the disability within the individual. Within this model many theories assuming neurological damage or dysfunction have been proposed. These theories incorporate the term *central nervous* *system disorder* (or *dysfunction*). Proposed causes of central nervous system dysfunction include (a) acquired brain damage resulting from pre-, peri- or postnatal trauma (Rabinovich, 1959), (b) genetics (Decker & DeFries, 1980; DeFries & Decker, 1982; Smith, 1978), (c) biochemical factors (Kornetsky, 1975), (d) nutritional factors, such as protein, vitamin, and mineral deficiencies, or ingested substances, such as food dye (Crook, 1980; Feingold, 1976), (e) neuropsychological dysfunction of unknown origin (Cruickshank, 1983; Hallahan & Cruickshank, 1973; Orton, 1937), and (f) cognitive processing deficits of unknown origin (Swanson, 1982; Torgesen, 1977; Torgesen & Greenstein, 1982; Vellutino, 1977; Wong, 1980b). The last two theories have attracted the most attention and thus warrant further discussion.

The *neuropsychological explanation* of learning disabilities suggests that we can understand intellectual behavior by understanding the different brain systems that support it. These systems are thought to be localized in different areas of the brain and then organized in different ways. Therefore, deficient performance in certain tasks can be explained in terms of damage to, or dysfunction of, specific areas of the brain. Indeed, early labels of LD ("minimal brain dysfunction," "neurologically impaired," "mixed dominance") reflect these assumptions.

Early means of testing these theories were limited methodologically, and validation through intervention planned according to these theories failed completely. In subsequent years, advances in the field of child neuropsychology have increased the means by which researchers could test these theories. They include:

1. Electrophysiological recording of brain activity during various tasks.
2. Dichotic listening and visual half-field studies to determine hemispheric specialization.
3. Computerized axial tomography and position emission tomography to examine the brains of individuals with abnormal behaviors.
4. Examination of test performances of individuals with known brain damage.

Neurological dysfunction is a plausible way to explain the confusing learning behavior of the group of individuals known as the learning disabled. Moreover, neuropsychological researchers tentatively agree on a model that characterizes differences between those who have learning disabilities and those who do not in terms of their sequential linguistic and visiospatial processing (Hartladge & Telzrow, 1983). Not enough data are available to conclude that the field should adopt this or any other theory of neurological difference. Nor is enough known about brain-behavior relationships for the model to be of practical value in terms of what and how to teach. This is an important area of etiological research that evolving technologies are allowing researchers to explore (see Lyon, Newby, Recht, and Caldwell, 1991, for reviews of these studies), but proponents of the model must supply much more evidence before making the statement that "the learning disabled are neurologically different."

Beliefs about the cause of learning disabilities are rooted in each decade's understanding of how learning occurs. Early models were based on the belief that learning occurs through perceptual and language processing (Frostig & Horne, 1964; Kephart, 1971; Kirk & Kirk, 1971; Osgood, 1957; Wepman, 1964). These models, however, have not explained sufficiently how learning occurs and therefore have not been of much help in guiding the development of effective teaching practices. Extensive reviews of perceptual and language process training have found such training to be ineffective in improving academic skills significantly (Hallahan & Cruickshank, 1973; Hammill & Wiederholt, 1973).

Current thinking on how individuals learn is based on a *cognitive processing* model, which has had a substantial impact on our understanding of learning disabilities. With the development of the information-processing paradigm, attention again is directed at examining possible cognitive processing differences as the cause of learning disabilities. *Information-processing* is a term from cognitive psychology. It is used to describe the way in which individuals acquire, retain, and transform knowledge. This is a conceptualization of the mind as a limited-capacity symbol manipulator analogous to the modern computer (Torgesen, 1986).

Since the late 1970s, more books and articles on the information-processing differences seen in youngsters with LD have been published (Swanson, 1982; Swanson & Cooney, 1991; Torgesen, 1977; 1989; Torgesen & Greenstein, 1982; Vellutino, 1977; Wong, 1980b; 1991). Those researchers reported that many students with LD do not approach learning situations strategically. Instead, they are passive, unaware that they must interact with information to be able to organize, store, or retrieve it. When students with LD are taught appropriate task strategies (for example, cumulative verbal rehearsal or associative clustering), however, they perform at levels comparable to their nondisabled peers (Hallahan & Bryan, 1981; Pressley, 1990; Robinson, 1983). This cognitive processing theory of learning disabilities has been demonstrated to be educationally relevant and thus holds promise as a conceptually useful explanation of some learning problems.

The Maturational Lag Model. This model also locates the cause of learning disability within the individual. It hypothesizes that someone whose neurological development lags behind that of peers might develop a learning disability. Proponents of this point of view state that slower development might cause an individual to be unprepared cognitively for the academic tasks asked for in school at any given time.

Research supports the maturational lag theory in specific cases. In a study of children diagnosed and treated for reading disabilities, Silver and Hagen (1966) found that those exhibiting difficulties in spatial orientation, auditory discrimination, or left-right discrimination had no such difficulties when they were retested many years later as young adults. Other researchers found younger children (most susceptible to maturational lag) in the early grades more likely to have learning problems than their older peers (Diamond, 1983; DiPasquale, Moule, & Flewelling, 1980). An early study by deHirsch, Jansky, and Langford (1966) supports this point of view. They found that the tests that best predicted reading and spelling achievement in the second grade were the tests most sensitive to maturational variables. Their study seemed to relate lack of readiness to learn (in terms of neurological development) to learning disabilities.

In the United States, curriculum and learning environments traditionally have been organized by year. All first graders (aged 6 or 7) are expected to learn the same things at the same rate. The movement toward ungraded primary programs and outcomes-based educational systems possibly would eliminate learning disabilities caused by maturational differences among children.

The Inadequate Environment Model. This model locates the cause not within the individual but, rather, in the interaction between the individual and his or her environment. Often, proponents of environmental explanations of learning problems endorse the behaviorist point of view. They reject the assumptions of neurological processing deficiency on the basis that deviant mental processes cannot be observed; they only can be inferred and may not actually exist. Behavior analysts are aware that youngsters have cognitive differences, but they say learning failure results not from deficiencies within the individual but, instead, from inappropriate instruction (for example, not including instruction in prerequisite skills, not breaking down a learning task into smaller parts), or lack of reinforced practice (for example, not continuing practice until mastery, not giving immediate corrective feedback on performance). The focus is not on the youngster's disability but, rather, on the teaching procedures and environmental variables that affect individual learning.

The behavioral orientation has a long history in learning disabilities. Since the 1960s, a significant amount of research has demonstrated that manipulation of the antecedents and consequences of a desired academic behavior is effective in increasing the academic and behavioral skills of youngsters labeled LD. This research, successful as it has been, challenges the neurological and cognitive explanations of LD. It implies that identifying or considering cognitive process variables is not necessary to provide appropriate education to youngsters having learning difficulties. Torgesen (1986), however, cautioned against wholesale adoption of this theoretical perspective in learning disabilities. While acknowledging its contributions to teaching technology used with LD youngsters, he stated that its application has limitations.

First, intervention studies by behavior analysts typically address only a narrow band of skills. Thus, one study may demonstrate an increase in math computation accuracy, another in computation rate. But long-term improvement in complex math skills, necessary in real-world settings, may go untested. This is not to fault the researchers but, rather, to point out that any true test of the effectiveness of intervention can come only after long-term studies (over many years) with large and carefully described samples of children and youth. *Second,* the behavioral orientation does not provide a conceptual framework for understanding individual differences. To prevent school failure, or to quickly select an appropriate treatment program, individual differences in learning must be understood.

The Ecological Model. Other researchers (Adelman, 1992; Adelman and Taylor, 1983; Keogh and Sears, 1991) argued that the interactional model of learning and learning problems is the one that most accurately describes the learning problems of youngsters with learning disabilities. Although still a minority point of view, it nonetheless is convincing. Simply put, an ecological model demonstrates that behavior is a function of person-environment interaction. Bandura (1978) stated:

It is true that behavior is influenced by the environment, but the environment is partly of a person's own making. By their actions, people play a role in creating the social milieu and other circumstances that arise in their daily transactions. Thus, from the social learning perspective, psychological functioning involves a continuous reciprocal interaction between behavioral, cognitive and environmental influences. (p. 345)

From this position, Adelman and Taylor (1983) posited a series of hypotheses about school success and failure that might describe observed phenomena in the learning disabilities population:

la. The more optimal the match between a student's assimilated adaptive schemata and the pattern of stimulation in the classroom program in which he or she is required to perform, the greater the likelihood of school success.

1b. Conversely, the less optimal the match between the student's schemata and the stimulation experienced in the program, the greater the likelihood of poor school performance. (It should be emphasized that these hypotheses do not indicate why the match is a poor one. The following secondary hypotheses do address this matter.)

2a. The greater a disorder and handicap the individual brings to the situation, the more difficult it is likely to be to establish an appropriate match to facilitate learning and appropriate behavior.

2b. The greater the teacher's ability and school's resources in personalizing instruction and thus facilitating appropriate matches, the fewer will be the number of students who exhibit learning or behavior problems or both.

2c. Conversely, the poorer the teacher's and school's ability in personalizing instruction, the greater will be the number of students with learning or behavior problems. (p. 40)

According to the ecological model, three types of LD youngsters are identified, based on the preceding hypotheses:

1. Those with no intrinsic disorders; their learning problems result from deficiencies in the learning environment.

2. Those who exhibit mild learning problems that result from both individual and environmental deficiencies.

3. Those who have severe disorders caused both by the inability of the environment to respond appropriately and by the severity of the intrinsic individual handicaps.

The ecological model acknowledges the complexity of learning. It encompasses all of the many factors that influence learning success and learning failure. Furthermore, it suggests that a continuum of instructional needs requires a more personalized approach to teaching. Its usefulness is based on these ideas.

What causes a child to be learning disabled? Clearly, a variety of perspectives exists among professionals, reflecting the heterogeneous nature of this population and the various disciplines that have tackled the task of responding to that question. We all want a straightforward, unequivocal answer to the question of etiology, but unfortunately the current state of knowledge precludes our getting one. The only responsible answer at this time is that, whatever the primary, instigating cause of learning disability, it can only be inferred. Future research must confirm or disconfirm existing beliefs.

DESCRIPTION OF LEARNING DISABILITIES

Logically, a group of youngsters labeled learning disabled would share some common characteristics. This assumption, however, has not been confirmed by any well-designed, large-scale studies. Instead, given the inconsistencies in definition and classification, no set of descriptive characteristics, beyond the general "learning problems," has been agreed upon. Take any list of characteristics. Few youngsters with learning disabilities will manifest all of them, and those describing different individuals will vary widely; the description of one LD youngster might not resemble at all that of another. In fact, researchers (Algozzine & Ysseldyke, 1983; Schumaker et al., 1980; Shepard & Smith, 1983) have observed that many descriptive characteristics of a learning disabled population are found to the same extent in the "normal" population.

Therefore, one must regard "LD characteristics" with caution. At this time they must be viewed as correlates of learning problems, maybe unique to learning disabilities but possibly common to youngsters with any type of learning problem. Whether any stated characteristic represents a particular stage of development (age), is of more concern in certain situations (school, home, social), or is unique to specific subgroups of LD youngsters is still unclear.

The most widely reported specification of characteristics was generated by a government-sponsored task force (Clements, 1966). Through analysis of the literature available at that time, the task force grouped the cited characteristics and arrived at 10 most frequently found symptoms:

1. Hyperactivity
2. Perceptual-motor impairment
3. Emotional lability (frequent shifts in emotional mood)
4. General coordination deficits
5. Disorders of attention
6. Impulsivity
7. Disorders of memory and thinking
8. Specific academic problems (reading, writing, arithmetic, spelling)
9. Disorders of speech and hearing
10. Equivocal neurological signs and electroencephalographic (EEG) irregularities

Kaluger and Kaluger (reported in Adelman & Taylor, 1983) made a more recent attempt to describe the characteristics of learning disabled individuals. They divided 52 characteristics among five general categories. These characteristics were derived from a sample of 300 children identified as learning disabled. The five general categories and specific characteristics are:

1. *Difficulties in academic learning*—achievement in reading one or more years below mental age level; poor oral reading fluency; poor reading comprehension; poor ability in phonetic analysis of new words; reversal of letters, words, sounds of syllables in reading; reversal of letters and numbers in writing; spelled words that show little relationship to the sounds they contain; achievement in arithmetic below mental age level; little or no application of skills learned in reading and arithmetic.

2. *Perceptual and perceptual-motor difficulties*—poor auditory perception awareness, discrimination, memory, sequence, etc.; poor visual perception (discrimination, memory, sequence, etc.); confusion about left and right and directional orientation; no consistent use of preferred hand or preferred foot (cerebral dominance); preferred hand and foot not on same side of body (laterality); gross motor awkwardness or clumsiness; uncoordinated use of hands or feet or both (e.g., inability to skip); poor visual-motor coordination (fine motor); illegible or distorted handwriting; mild tremor upon exertion of hands, fingers, or feet; uses only one hand (or side of body) with no assistance from the other; cannot pull main visionary or auditory stimulus from background stimuli (figure-ground); cannot discriminate among different phonetic sounds; impaired form perception, space conception, and/or poor recall of form or space; ocular imbalance or poor adjustment.

3. *Language and speech disorders*—speech defect beyond immature articulation; distinct or distorted speech (omits or adds sounds); distortion in repeating sounds; poor ability in blending sounds; long, rambling conversation or storytelling; poor word or sentence structure; halting, stumbling, or very slow oral delivery; miscalls words, but gives appropriate substitute (e.g., "dad" for "man").

4. *Difficulties with thought processes*—memory and thinking—takes a long time to organize thoughts before responding; capable of concrete thinking, but poor at abstractions; unable to pay attention or respond in an orderly fashion (poor ego control); unable to shift attention or to change behavior, ideas, or words (preservation); pays too little attention to details or to the internal construction of words; pays too much attention to details; cannot see the total pattern of form, thought, or idea; poor organization of work time and work space; cannot follow or remember directions; cannot understand or remember gestures or words; cannot transfer learning from isolated skills to application.

5. *Behavior and affective characteristics*—excessive body or verbal activity (hyperactive or hyperkinetic); rather lethargic and nonactive (hypoactive); easily distracted by sound; short attention or concentration span; works better when someone is standing by, but not when the person moves away; takes much more time than others to do work; one day capable and remembers, but the next day does not (variability of performance); unplanned, impulsive, or "forced" motor responses which appear meaningless or inappropriate (impulsivity or disinhibition); overreaction or overflow of an emotional response (emotional lability). (Adelman & Taylor, 1983, pp. 10–11)

Another way to view the learning characteristics of individuals with learning disabilities is how they remain or change throughout one's life. Table 5.2 gives a breakdown over the life span.

A brief review of findings on each of the major categories of characteristics follows. Kaluger and Kaluger's general categories are used to organize the discussion.

DIFFICULTIES IN ACADEMIC LEARNING

Professionals agree that difficulty in academic subjects is the primary indicator of a learning disability. Subjects include reading, math, writing, and listening comprehension, with reading the most frequently reported academic problem (Deshler, Schumaker, Lenz, & Ellis, 1984; Lewis, 1983). Mercer (1987) noted that 85 % to 90 % of all

● **TABLE 5.2**

Life-span view of learning disabilities

	Preschool	Grades K–1	Grades 2–6	Grades 7–12	Adult
Problem Areas	Delay in developmental milestones (e.g., walking) Receptive language Expressive language Visual perception Auditory perception Short attention span Hyperactivity	Academic readiness skills (e.g., alphabet knowledge, quantitative concepts, directional concepts, etc.) Receptive language Expressive language Visual perception Auditory perception Gross and fine motor Attention Hyperactivity Social skills	Reading skills Arithmetic skills Written expression Verbal expression Receptive language Attention span Hyperactivity Social-emotional	Reading skills Arithmetic skills Written expression Verbal expression Listening skills Study skills (metacognition) Social-emotional-delinquency	Reading skills Arithmetic skills Written expression Verbal expression Listening skills Study skills Social-emotional
Assessment	Prediction of high risk for later learning problems	Prediction of high risk for later learning problems	Identification of learning disabilities	Identification of learning disabilities	Identification of learning disabilities
Treatment Types	Preventive	Preventive	Remedial Corrective	Remedial Corrective Compensatory Learning strategies	Remedial Corrective Compensatory Learning strategies
Treatments with Most Research and/or Expert Support	Direct instruction in language skills Behavioral management Parent training	Direct instruction in academic and language areas Behavioral management Parent training	Direct instruction in academic areas Behavioral management Self-control training Parent training	Direct instruction in academic areas Tutoring in subject areas Direct instruction in learning strategies (study skills) Self-control training Curriculum alternatives	Direct instruction in academic areas Tutoring in subject (college) or job area Compensatory instruction (i.e., using aids such as tape recorder, calculator, computer, dictionary) Direct instruction in learning strategies

Source: Students with Learning Disabilities, 3rd ed., by C. Mercer, 1987 (Columbus, OH: Merrill Publishing, p. 44). Reprinted by permission.

youngsters identified as learning disabled have reading deficits. Common are word recognition difficulties including reversals, transposition of letters within words or words within sentences, substitutions, and mispronunciations. Reading comprehension is also difficult for many students with LD.

Research suggests that youngsters with LD recall fewer main ideas and are less sensitive to the degree of importance of information in reading material, regardless of readability, than are their nondisabled peers (Garner, Alexander, & Hare, 1991; Hansen, 1978; Pflaum, 1979; Smiley, Oaken, Worthen, Campione, & Brown, 1977). Thus, these youngsters are poorer at acquiring information through reading than their cohorts are.

Mathematics gets less attention than reading. Nevertheless, it is a problem for many students with learning disabilities. Skrtic (1980) found many LD adolescents to be deficient in a basic, conceptual understanding of addition, subtraction, multiplication, and division. Rote memorization of math facts and operations is also difficult for many LD students (Bley & Thornton, 1981; Mercer & Miller, 1992). Problems in math may come from other problems in reading. Reading difficulties often interfere with an LD youngster's ability to understand the math text; and the syntactic complexity of many word problems inhibits understanding, even when the text is readable (Larsen, Parker, & Trenholme, 1978). Cawley and Miller (1989) noted that problems of memory, perception, motor function, reasoning, and language also affect math performance.

Written language deficits are characteristic of many LD youngsters. Children who have trouble recognizing words when they read typically have trouble spelling them (Mercer, 1983). Composition, too, can be difficult. Writing examples are shorter and deficient in syntax and words with abstract meanings. LD youngsters also are deficient in monitoring their errors (Deshler, Ferrell, & Kass, 1978); they are unable to find errors so they can correct them.

LD children and youth further exhibit deficits in listening comprehension. Kotsonis and Patterson (1980) found that LD children were poorer than their normal peers in understanding directions. In addition, they did not ask for clarification when they needed it. Others (Bryan, Donahue, & Pearl, 1981; Spekman, 1981) found LD youngsters to be less effective listeners than their peers when listening to information lectures and directions.

Clearly, the academic deficiencies of students classified as learning disabled are well documented. Current intervention efforts focus primarily on these characteristic difficulties.

PERCEPTUAL AND PERCEPTUAL-MOTOR DIFFICULTIES

During the 1930s and 1940s, Heinz Werner and Alfred Strauss found in clinical studies that youngsters believed to be brain-injured had perceptual abnormalities. These researchers and those associated with them (Newell Kephart and Laura Lehtinen, among others) popularized the notion that learning disabled youngsters are deficient in perceptual and perceptual-motor skills. This early tenet of learning disabilities has been the source of much controversy. Training in perceptual and perceptual-motor skills has not proved to demonstrably change reading, math, writing, or listening performance (Hallahan & Cruickshank, 1973; Hammill & Wiederholt, 1973), so it received considerably less attention during the 1980s.

Nevertheless, perceptual and perceptual-motor difficulties still are commonly noted characteristics of learning disability. Hallahan (1982) noted, in a brief review of both visual and auditory perception research, that, although many studies of these characteristics are criticized on methodological grounds, enough evidence exists to conclude that learning disabled youngsters do perform poorly on tasks designed to measure visual and auditory perception abilities and perceptual-motor and general coordination skills. But not all youngsters with reading problems have perceptual and perceptual-motor deficits, and some who do poorly on measures of perception read adequately. Therefore, the credibility of these deficiencies as characteristic of learning disabilities is questioned.

LANGUAGE AND SPEECH DISORDERS

Many students classified as learning disabled have difficulty with phonology, syntax, semantics, or pragmatics, in any combination.

Phonology. Phonology is the study of how sounds are made and the rules that govern how the sounds are ordered into words. Little research has been done specifically on LD youngsters. Researchers, however, have successfully compared the phonological skills of good and poor readers, supporting the hypothesis that poor readers have more difficulty coding information phonemically than do good readers (Mark, Shankweiler, Liberman, & Fowler, 1977; Shankweiler & Liberman, 1972; Vellutino, 1977). They cannot discriminate among sounds; they are not aware of the component parts of words and thus have difficulty making associations between spoken and written language.

Syntax. Syntax refers to the rule system by which words are put together into sentences. Researchers (Vogel, 1974; Wiig & Semel, 1975; Wiig, Semel, & Crouse, 1973) characterized the speech of LD youngsters as having limited vocabulary, shorter sentences, and less complex syntax. Bryan and Pflaum (1978) found deficits in the language development of LD youngsters that might have a negative impact not only on the acquisition of academic skills but also on the development of interpersonal skills. The disabled students in the study had trouble communicating some instructions to other children about how to play.

Semantics. Semantics refers to the meaning of language. Data on the semantic skills of youngsters with LD support the notion that they have less well-developed meaning systems and poorer language comprehension than their nondisabled peers (Perfetti & Goldman, 1976; Perfetti & Lesgold, 1978; Wiig & Semel, 1975). Poor readers are consistently slower at generating words and more apt to make naming errors. Youngsters with LD also are less able to provide definitions for words.

Pragmatics. Pragmatics, or communicative competence, refers to how one uses language. Functional usage is addressed separately from the child's knowledge of the formal grammatical system. Research findings suggest that LD youngsters have difficulty in communicating in social situations (Bryan, 1991). Bryan and colleagues (Bryan, Donahue, & Pearl, 1981) found that their LD subjects uttered more requests for additional information. Also, they were less likely to be asked by others to do something. Their style of communication reflected their lower social status within the group. LD females, more than LD males, did not seem to comprehend language in the social context. Others (Bryan et al., 1981; Kotsonis & Patterson, 1980) found that LD students had difficulty in communicating clearly and in sustaining verbal interactions.

DIFFICULTIES WITH THOUGHT PROCESSES: MEMORY AND THINKING

The memory and thinking skills of LD youngsters dominated research on characteristics during the late 1970s and 1980s. Stimulated by growing acceptance of the information-processing paradigm discussed earlier, researchers have devoted substantial effort toward describing the memory and thinking processes of learning disabled youngsters (Bauer, 1977; Perfetti & Goldman, 1976; Swanson, 1982; Swanson & Cooney, 1991; Torgesen, 1977; Torgesen & Goldman, 1977; Torgesen & Greenstein, 1982; Torgesen & Houck, 1980; Wong, 1991). From the research on memory abilities of learning disabled children, three general conclusions follow:

1. Children with LD have problems with a number of information-processing components. Problems seem to exist in short-term memory, working memory, long-term memory, and executive processes.
2. Many children with LD do not use task-appropriate strategies to help themselves remember in situations in which nondisabled peers typically do. For example, verbal rehearsal and clustering are strategies that efficient learners automatically use to help themselves remember information.
3. After they have been trained in memory strategies, youngsters with memory problems perform like their nondisabled peers on memory tasks. This leads to the conclusion that the memory deficits of LD youngsters can be considered a production deficit, or mediation deficit (they do not produce appropriate strategies but can learn to do so), rather than a capacity deficit (they have limited memory capacity in comparison to average peers).

Researchers have extended their examination of information-processing skills into other areas of thinking. Their preliminary investigations lead one to believe that many LD children and youth may lack metacognitive skills. *Metacognition* refers to both knowledge about cognition and the regulation of one's own cognition. With reference to memory, Flavell and Wellman (1977) delineated the knowledge one must have about cognition. They identified three classes of variables:

1. Memory-relevant characteristics of the person.
2. Memory-relevant characteristics of the task.
3. Potentially employable strategies.

Cognitive strategies are conscious plans to enhance retention or comprehension. A memory or cognitive strategy is not essential for performing a task. It is a *voluntary plan* individuals adopt for cognitive economy. Effective metacognitive skills require that one have the preceding knowledge and use it to regulate independent learning successfully.

Researchers have found evidence that many LD youngsters have metacognitive deficits in a variety of areas. Torgesen (1979) discovered that children with learning disabilities are unable to generate useful strategies to solve a range of problems. Deshler and his associates (Deshler, Ferrell, & Kass, 1978) discovered that LD adolescents are unable to monitor their errors in written products. Others (Hansen, 1978; Pflaum, 1979; Wong, 1991a) found ample evidence that many LD youngsters do not monitor their comprehension adequately when reading. Substantial data, however, demonstrate that training youngsters to use cognitive strategies is an effective intervention approach. These findings support the conclusion that a characteristic common to many LD youngsters is a deficiency in strategic learning behavior (Bauer, 1977; Brown & Palinscar, 1982; Deshler & Schumaker, 1988; Hallahan & Reeve, 1980; Schumaker, Deshler, Alley, & Warner, 1983; Wong, 1991; Wong & Jones, 1982).

BEHAVIOR AND AFFECTIVE CHARACTERISTICS

Professionals in the field of learning disabilities always have been concerned with the ability of children to focus their attention and control their motor activity. In the 1940s, Strauss and Werner established that a characteristic of many learning disabled youngsters is selective attention deficit, the inability to attend to relevant, as opposed to irrelevant, features of a task. Substantial research since then has demonstrated that many youngsters with learning disabilities have this characteristic (see Hallahan & Bryan, 1981, for a review). When given tasks to measure central and incidental learning, LD subjects remembered fewer "central" items (those on which their attention had focused) but just as many, or more, incidental pieces of information than their normal peers. The performance patterns of the LD students actually were similar to those of children 2 to 3 years younger. Hallahan and his colleagues (Hallahan, Gajar, Cohen, & Tarver, 1978; Hallahan & Reeve, 1980; Tarver, Hallahan, Kauffman, & Ball, 1976) found that LD youngsters with selective attention deficits improved when they were trained to use the strategy of *cumulative verbal rehearsal*. Like poor memory performance, poor selective attention seems to be related to a lack of strategic learning behaviors.

Attention disorders are characteristics often ascribed to children with learning disabilities, though this is a condition that can exist separate from learning disabilities. (See Ysseldyke, Algozzine, and Thurlow, 1992, for information about special education services for children with ADHD and ADD under IDEA amendments of 1990.)

The *Diagnostic and Statistical Manual of Mental Disorders–Revised* (American Psychiatric Association, 1987) differentiates between two types of attention disorder: ADD with hyperactivity and ADD without hyperactivity. The attentional aspects of these conditions include inattention and impulsivity; the hyperactivity aspect addresses excessive movement. For both, onset occurs before age 7 and lasts longer than 6 months. The proposed definition of attention deficit disorders for *DSM-IV* (due out in 1994) arranges the attention deficit symptoms into two groups: an attention problems group (primarily inattentive) and a hyperactivity-impulsivity group (primarily hyperactive). The diagnosis of ADHD will be made as one or the other, or as a combined subtype. This expands the potential diagnostic categories of ADHD from two to three and reflects the growing clinical experience with children with attention deficits.

Although the presence of attention disorders in children with learning disabilities never has been questioned, its treatment with stimulant medications (Ritalin, Dexadrine, Cyclert) has been the subject of debate. The effectiveness of drug therapy for many youngsters is not questioned. Drugs do produce side effects, however, (Levine, Brooks, & Shonkoff, 1980; Levy, 1983), so guidelines have been developed to help educators and parents make appropriate treatment decisions (Lerner, 1985). Other treatment programs, such as behavior modification, also have proved effective.

The social skills of youngsters with learning disabilities have undergone intense scrutiny recently. Clinical observation and documentation reveal that LD youngsters often have problems making friends and functioning appropriately in social situations (Bryan, 1991; Bryan & Bryan, 1978; Schumaker, Hazel, Sherman, & Sheldon, 1982; White, Schumaker, Warner, Alley, & Deshler, 1980). Studies by Bryan and colleagues (Bryan & Bryan, 1978; Bryan & Pflaum, 1978; Bryan, Wheeler, Felcan, & Henek, 1976) found significant difficulties in interpersonal exchange and understanding others' affective states because of an inability to interpret nonverbal and verbal communications. Their studies also found that teachers, peers, and strangers, upon observing or interacting with these children, evaluated them negatively. In light of these findings and the importance of social skills to life adjustment and happiness, further attention to this area of functioning is warranted.

The characteristic behaviors of learning disabilities are many. Their number, severity, and interactions with the environment vary from individual to individual.

PREVENTION AND INTERVENTION

Most research regarding learning disabilities has been with children of elementary school age. In the more recent past, however, awareness has been increasing that learning disabilities might vary according to age. Today, many more infants survive a traumatic birth (for example, extremely premature infants and those with health problems). In addition, we have a strong social awareness of the consequences of school failure. These factors, in part, have fueled current interest among educators in early detection and prevention of later learning problems. Early intervention programs for handicapped or "at risk" youngsters have been effective (Karnes, Linnemeyer, & Schwedel, 1981; Keogh & Sears, 1991; Ramey & Bryant, 1982), but identifying potential problems has negative implications, too. Early identification, with diagnostic instruments acknowledged to be of questionable validity, could impose limits on teacher and parental expectations of the identified child, creating a self-fulfilling prophecy.

Furthermore, correctly categorizing the presenting behavior of very young children as "a learning disability," "mental retardation," or "emotional disturbance" often is difficult. The current federal support of research on early diagnosis and intervention should shed light on the important issue of prevention. The University of Kansas Institute for Research in Learning Disabilities has done much to arrive at a description of adolescents and adults considered to have learning disabilities. Epidemiological research suggests the following (the results of many studies are summarized in Schumaker, Deshler, Alley, & Warner, 1983):

1. Academic and cognitive factors differentiated youngsters labeled learning disabled from other low-achieving students. In these studies LD students typically were the lowest of the low achievers, and most LD adolescents exhibited low performance in all achievement areas.
2. LD adolescents seemed to plateau in their development of basic skills. Average achievement in reading and written language for LD youth in seventh grade was high third grade, plateauing at the fifth-grade level in high school. Mathematics performance was at the fifth-grade level in seventh grade, and it plateaued at the sixth-grade level in senior high.
3. LD adolescents were significantly deficient in the study skills and in learning strategies such as test taking, note taking, scanning, studying, and listening.
4. LD adolescents demonstrated significantly poorer social skills than their nondisabled peers.

The data from these studies suggest that intervention for LD adolescents should be substantially different from intervention for younger children.

For young adults with learning disabilities, characteristics relate to their ability to function independently. LD young adults are significantly less satisfied with their jobs than their nondisabled peers are, and the jobs they hold are of a lower social status (White et al. 1980). Significantly more LD young adults (55%) than non-LD young adults (29%) live with family (Vetter, 1983). The reason subjects gave for this was their lack of funds because of low-paying jobs. Even so, few LD young adults planned, nor were they willing to engage in, postsecondary education to increase their job skills (Edgar, 1987). Awareness of the unique special education needs of the adult LD population has increased at the postsecondary level (Adelman & Vogel, 1991; Mangrum & Strichart, 1984; Vogel, 1982).

IDENTIFICATION AND ASSESSMENT

Concern about inappropriate identification of learning disabilities is reflected in the regulations issued by the U.S. Office of Education. The excerpts below are from the sections that refer to the procedures to follow in assessing an individual for learning disabilities.

300.540 Additional team members.

In evaluating a child suspected of having a specific learning disability, in addition to the requirements of 300.532, each public agency shall include on the multidisciplinary evaluation team:

(a) (I) The child's regular teacher; or (2) If the child does not have a regular teacher, a regular classroom teacher qualified to teach a child of his or her age; or (3) For a child of less than school age, an individual qualified by the State educational agency to teach a child of his or her age; and

(b) At least one person qualified to conduct individual diagnostic examinations of children, such as a school psychologist, speech-language pathologist, or remedial reading teacher.

300.541 Criteria for determining the existence of a specific learning disability:

(a) A team may determine that a child has a specific learning disability if

(1) The child does not achieve commensurate with his or her age and ability levels in one or more of the areas listed in paragraph (a) (2) of this section, when provided with learning experiences appropriate for the child's age and ability levels; and

(2) The team finds that a child has a severe discrepancy between achievement and intellectual ability in one or more of the following areas:

(i) Oral expression;

(ii) Listening comprehension;

(iii) Written expression;

(iv) Basic reading skill;

(v) Reading comprehension;

(vi) Mathematics calculation; or

(vii) Mathematics reasoning.

(b) The team may not identify a child as having a specific learning disability if the severe discrepancy between ability and achievement is primarily the result of:

(1) A visual, hearing, or motor handicap;

(2) Mental retardation;

(3) Emotional disturbance; or

(4) Environmental, cultural, or economic disadvantage.

300.542 Observation.

(a) At least one team member other than the child's regular teacher shall observe the child's academic performance in the regular classroom setting.

(b) In the case of a child of less than school age or out of school, a team member shall observe the child in an environment appropriate for a child of that age.

300.543 Written report.

(a) The team shall prepare a written report of the results of the evaluation.

(b) The report must include a statement of:

(1) When the child has a specific learning disability;

(2) The basis for making the determination;

(3) The relevant behavior noted during the observation of the child;

(4) The relationship of that behavior to the child's academic functioning;

(5) The educationally relevant medical findings, if any;

(6) Whether there is a severe discrepancy between achievement and ability which is not correctable without special education and related services; and

(7) The determination of the team concerning the effects of environmental, cultural, or economic disadvantage.

(c) Each team member shall certify in writing whether the report reflects his or her conclusion. If it does not reflect his or her conclusion, the team member must submit a separate statement presenting his or her conclusions. (*Code of Federal Regulations*, revised as of July 1, 1985, pp. 49, 50)

GENERAL ELIGIBILITY REQUIREMENTS

From reading the regulations, many factors clearly have to be taken into account in determining whether a learning disability exists. Three, however, are essential:

1. Low achievement.

2. A severe discrepancy between achievement levels and intellectual ability.

3. Clarification of whether the learning problems are the result of another cause (mental retardation, sensory handicap, emotional disturbance, or cultural or economical disadvantage).

In practice, these eligibility criteria are determined in a variety of ways—among them, examination of test data, observation of student behavior, and teacher and parent reports. The outcome has been more youngsters identified as learning disabled (refer to the earlier section on incidence and prevalence). Therefore, practitioners have focused on how to determine the severity of an achievement discrepancy with more precision and how to improve clinical judgment.

Measuring Achievement Discrepancy. Measurement specialists (Cone & Wilson, 1981; Forness, Sinclair, & Guthrie, 1983) have noted four methods to determine the discrepancy between an individual's potential and actual academic achievement. All of the methods have their advantages and their disadvantages. The first is the *deviation from grade level* method. It identifies youngsters whose achievement scores are below grade placement. Deviation may be 1 year below grade level across all grades, or it may vary, increasing in the higher grades. For example, a second grader, to be eligible for services, may have to show achievement scores at least 1 year below grade level. On the other hand, a fifth grader would have to evidence achievement scores at least 2 years below grade level. Both youngsters would be described as exhibiting a severe achievement discrepancy. Often an IQ cutoff score is used in conjunction with the deviation from grade level method to differentiate a learning disability from mental retardation. (If the test results were to show an IQ of 68 or below, the child might be considered as having mental retardation rather than learning disabilities.) This method is easy for teachers to use, but it has many shortcomings—for example, overidentification of low achievers and variation across states as to cutoff scores (Cone & Wilson, 1981).

A second method of determining discrepancy relies on *formula-based procedures based on age-level scores.* Cone and Wilson (1981) found these to be the procedures most commonly used for determining discrepancy between actual potential and achievement. Harris (1961), Bond, Tinker, Wasson, and Wasson (1984), and Myklebust (1968) all have developed such formulas. They have some statistical shortcomings, though. The test's errors of measurement are not taken into account, and the test norms vary; therefore, tests used are not always comparable.

To address the statistical shortcomings, two other methods have been suggested: *standard score comparisons* and *regression analysis* (Cone & Wilson, 1981). Both require that any test scores used (achievement or intelligence) be converted to standard scores so they may be compared. Regression analysis is the most sophisticated way to measure discrepancy. It takes into account the statistical phenomenon of regression toward the mean. Shepard (1980) noted, however, that although these last methods are statistically accurate, they are still inherently weak. Many commonly used tests have low reliability and validity and therefore do not meet acceptable psychometric standards (Salvia & Ysseldyke, 1981). Thus, sometimes a sophisticated mathematical technique is used on an imprecise and questionable measure of behavior.

Clinical Judgment. Finding a discrepancy between achievement and potential is not the only way to determine learning disability. Many other factors (e.g., disadvantage, sensory handicaps) could be the cause of extreme underachievement. These factors can be determined only through clinical judgment. Clinical judgment involves examining both quantitative and qualitative information about an individual to ascertain whether the evidence confirms or disconfirms the hypothesis that a learning disability is present. Practitioners believe clinical judgment is essential to the diagnostic process,

Test data, assessment, and clinical judgment are important factors for proper instruction of children with disabilities.

but unreliable tests, lack of knowledge about the psychometric properties of tests, unfamiliarity with discrepancy measurement procedures, and failure to understand hypothesis testing to ensure validity of decisions seriously jeopardize the validity of many clinical judgments (Davis & Shepard, 1983; Shepard & Smith, 1983; Ysseldyke, Algozzine, Regan, & Potter, 1979; Ysseldyke & Algozzine, 1990).

Algozzine (1991) recommended using curriculum-based assessment (CBA) to improve the decision-making and educational planning process. CBA includes:

1. Direct observation and analysis of the learning environment.
2. Analysis of the processes students use in approaching tasks.
3. Examination of student products.
4. Control and arrangement of student tasks.

ASSESSMENT OUTCOMES OF CONCERN

Assessment concerns receive extensive attention. Through the assessment process, beliefs about etiology (what causes learning disabilities) manifest themselves. Some argue that the emphasis on assessment for identification is asking the wrong question; the focus should be on assessment for teaching (Algozzine, 1991). When subjected to analysis, assessment procedures for identification have come up short in many cases.

1. Some school-identified LD youngsters meet set criteria for learning disabilities, and others so labeled do not (Algozzine & Ysseldyke, 1983).
2. Other low-achieving students, never classified as LD, meet the eligibility criteria (Algozzine & Ysseldyke, 1983; Epps, Ysseldyke, & Algozzine, 1983).
3. Overlap in scores and behavioral profiles between students with and without learning disabilities often is great (Algozzine & Ysseldyke, 1983; Ysseldyke, Algozzine, Shinn, & McGue, 1982).
4. Placement decisions are not always consistent with the data presented but, rather, seem to be influenced by the referral and by other naturally occurring characteristics of youngsters (Ysseldyke, Algozzine, Richey, & Graden, 1982).
5. The skill of those doing the testing and their knowledge of the psychometric properties of the tests they use are questionable in many cases (Davis & Shepard, 1983; Shepard & Smith, 1983; Ysseldyke et al., 1979).
6. The number of students with learning disabilities has risen consistently since 1977 (Algozzine, 1991).

In summary, assessment practices in the field of learning disabilities are pose problems. A person found to have learning disabilities in one school may or may not have learning disabilities in another school. Growing evidence suggests that CBA procedures are effective when making screening, referral, and classification decisions (Marston, 1989; Shinn, 1989). They are also more helpful in planning instructional intervention. Maybe the time has come to change the questions we ask. Rather than investing resources in identification, the focus should shift to assessment for planning instruction and measuring learning.

*E*DUCATIONAL INTERVENTIONS

Learning disabilities can surface during the preschool years and continue into adulthood. Still, most intervention efforts occur during the school years and consequently are educational in nature. Some interventions, however, are designed and delivered by professionals in noneducational areas (e.g., medicine, nutrition), which are not covered here. For a review of types of interventions, see Adelman and Compas (1977), Whalen and Henker (1976), Kavale (1982), and Kavale and Forness (1983).

During the formative years of the LD field, educational interventions were directed primarily at LD children in elementary schools. Younger students were the target of most intervention efforts, with the reasoning that early intervention, prior to adolescence, would "cure," or significantly reduce, the effects of the learning disability (Alley & Deshler, 1979). During the past two decades, however, services for LD students during the secondary and postsecondary school years have been made available as well. Thus, most school systems provide services to LD students across the complete grade continuum.

A basic premise underlying most educational interventions is that LD students can and should function in mainstream settings. Consequently, LD interventions have been designed to support the student's accommodation in the mainstreamed curriculum rather than to provide an alternative curriculum independent of mainstream offerings. This is why most services are provided to LD students in a resource room setting. These students learn skills that will help them cope with the requirements in their mainstream classes.

Of the numerous interventions developed, many have good face validity, and educators have embraced them. The obvious challenge to teachers, researchers, and developers alike, then, is to validate these interventions. To capture the essence of the broad array of interventions currently used with LD students, their salient features are discussed under the topics of what to teach, discussing the content of the intervention approach, and how to teach, describing the specific approaches used to promote mastery of the targeted skill.

WHAT TO TEACH

As discussed earlier, the poor academic performance of LD students seems to be related to a variety of deficits in acquiring, remembering, organizing, and expressing information. During the course of intervention, a teacher addresses these deficits according to his or her own theoretical orientation. The approach to intervention may be indirect or direct. In an indirect approach teachers improve the student's academic performance by addressing some underlying deficit (e.g., visual perception). In a direct approach teachers address the major presenting problem (e.g., an inability to comprehend grade-level materials). They do not attempt to educate or train any underlying skills that may be related to it.

Indirect Approaches. Indirect approaches prevailed during the field's formative years. They represented an educational departure from traditional remedial practices, and they did much to distinguish LD as a unique educational concept. Among the more popular were perceptual and perceptual-motor interventions and psycholinguistic interventions.

The perceptual and perceptual-motor interventions reflect the work of pioneers in the field such as Alfred Strauss and Heinz Werner. In turn, many early authorities incorporated a strong perceptual and perceptual-motor orientation. Included among them were Raymond Barsch, William Cruickshank, Marianne Frostig, Gerald Getman, and Newell Kephart. Frostig required students to complete worksheets designed to improve their visual perception, arguing that it was prerequisite to successful reading performance. Figure-ground and visual matching exercises were a major part of the intervention program. The efficacy of perceptual and perceptual-motor approaches has been the subject of study of many researchers (e.g., Hallahan & Cruickshank, 1973; Hammill & Wiederholt, 1973; Kavale & Mattson, 1983). Without exception, these investigators reported little evidence to support their use. These interventions do not, they say, impact the academic performance of LD students.

During the 1960s and 1970s, the work of Samuel Kirk and his colleagues strongly affected assessment and intervention practices. The Illinois Test of Psycholinguistic Abilities (ITPA) (Kirk, McCarthy, & Kirk, 1968), a diagnostic test designed to assess psycholinguistic abilities believed necessary for understanding and using spoken language, included a battery of subtests. These assessed things such as verbal and motor expression and visual and auditory reception, association, memory, and closure. The ITPA led to a number of remedial programs designed to improve perceptual and other developmental abilities. Most notable are the Peabody Language Development Kits (Dunn, Dunn, & Smith, 1981; Dunn, Horton, & Smith, 1981; Dunn, Smith, & Dunn, 1981; Dunn, Smith, & Smith, 1981); the Program for Developing Language Abilities by Minskoff, Wiseman, and Minskoff (1972); and the GOAL Language Development Kits by Karnes (1972). The efficacy of this indirect approach also has been the subject of extensive review (e.g., Hammill & Larsen, 1974; Kavale, 1981; Larsen, Parker, & Hammill, 1982; Lund, Foster, & McCall-Perez, 1978). Regardless of the extent to which psycholinguistic training affected ITPA post-test scores, these reviewers disagreed significantly on whether this intervention successfully impacts the academic performance of LD students in the classroom.

In short, the tack that indirect intervention approaches take is to address the underlying deficit through remedial instruction. If a student's functioning in an underlying deficit area (e.g., auditory closure) improves, the assumption is that his or her performance in related academic areas (e.g., listening comprehension in a classroom lecture) also will improve. The logic is sound, but the empirical data either do not support it or are equivocal at this time.

Direct Approaches. A direct approach teaches academic skills to enhance the performance of students in listening, speaking, reading, writing, spelling, and mathematical calculations, in all areas outlined by the definition included in the 1975 Education for

All Handicapped Children Act. Direct intervention, which has been gaining in popularity since the mid-1970s, provides students with skills that will enable them to meet the demands of the mainstream curriculum. To provide instruction directly to an area of academic skill deficiency, not an underlying psychological or perceptual area, is the more efficient, effective method of intervention. Examples are embodied in the works of Siegfried Engelmann, Doug Carnine, Wes Becker, Carl Bereiter, and Tom Lovitt. They emphasized that teachers themselves could bring control to the teaching situation by carefully presenting the content and by increasing opportunities for students to respond and receive feedback and reinforcement.

An example of another direct approach that emphasizes more complex learning tasks is the learning strategies approach (Deshler & Schumaker, 1984; Lloyd, Saltzman, & Kauffman, 1981). Learning strategies are defined as "techniques, principles or rules which facilitate the acquisition, storage, manipulation, retrieval and expression of information across different situations and settings" (Alley & Deshler, 1979; Pressley, 1990). Task-specific learning strategies are designed to enable students to deal strategically with complex curricular demands. For example, the paraphrasing strategy (Schumaker, Denton, & Deshler, 1984) teaches a student how to identify the main ideas and details in a reading passage and then to put the ideas into his or her own words. Similar strategies enable students to retrieve information successfully from textbooks, to listen to lectures and take notes, and to write effective paragraphs and themes (Deshler & Schumaker, 1988; Schumaker, Deshler, Alley, & Warner, 1983). Clearly, students have benefited much in the specific skill areas targeted by the intervention, but only in the training situation. No one knows how well they would do in designing and using their own learning strategies in another situation.

The targets of most direct interventions, regardless of type, have been reading, mathematics, written expression, and spelling. Significantly less attention has been given to deficits in listening, speaking, and thinking. This is an alarming realization, because heavy demands are placed on students in these areas, especially in the middle and secondary grades.

HOW TO TEACH

To benefit successfully from instruction offered in mainstream classes, most learning disabled students must acquire, in a relatively short time, skills and strategies that are significant in both number and amount. Meyen and Lehr (1980a) called it "intensity of instruction." Regardless of what is being taught (i.e., by an indirect or a direct approach), it must be taught with maximum effectiveness and efficiency. Otherwise these students will fall even further behind than they already are. Because the time available for remedial interventions is limited, teachers must make the most of it by increasing the number and amount of skills taught in any one session. According to Meyen and Lehr (1980a), the amount of progress made in a remedial situation must be significantly greater than that made in the standard developmental situation. To do this, more attention must be given to just how a remedial intervention should be carried out.

A host of procedures has been designed to ensure that remedial instruction is highly targeted and specific. Lovitt (1982), for example, delineated the advantages of direct and daily measurement. This instructional approach has five major elements:

1. Direct measurement of the targeted behavior.
2. Daily measurement of student progress toward the end goal.
3. Replicable teaching procedures, preferably daily.
4. Individual analysis.
5. Experimental control through precise record keeping.

Closely aligned with these procedures is a reliance on certain self-management procedures—self-regulation, self-evaluation, and self-reinforcement. Students thus become actively involved in much of the instructional process. This is particularly important for "passive" learners (Torgesen, 1977; Wong, 1980a, 1991b). Self-regulation allows them to have a voice in scheduling certain segments of the academic day. Self-evaluation refers to a broad array of activities that require students to check the correctness of their responses and to record the results on a chart or form (e.g., Kneedler & Hallahan, 1981). In self-reinforcement students are responsible for choosing and delivering reinforcers to themselves once they have successfully completed an established task. Each of these three kinds of self-management can be used individually, although researchers (e.g., Deshler & Schumaker, 1988; Nelson & Hayes, 1981; Seabaugh & Schumaker, 1981) suggest that all three be used as a total system for more effective student gains.

Smith (1981, 1989) has argued strongly for the importance of carefully considering the learner's stage of learning. A learner's entry level into instruction has a lot to do with how efficient the learning process is going to be. Five broad stages of learning—acquisition, proficiency, maintenance, generalization, and adaptation—are applicable for remedial interventions:

1. *Acquisition.* The student is taught how to execute the task. Smith and Robinson (1986) suggested two parts to this stage: initial and advanced. In the *initial* part, modeling and shaping are emphasized heavily. The advanced stage stresses feedback and rewards for accuracy.
2. *Proficiency.* The teacher's role is to help the learner become proficient, or fluent, in performing the targeted skills. Both rate and accuracy are emphasized.
3. *Maintenance.* To aid retention, the reliance is on overlearning the skill—to ensure maintenance over time.
4. *Generalization.* The learned behavior should occur in all appropriate situations. Generalization is a major problem for many LD students. Thus, a significant proportion of instructional time must be spent in this stage.
5. *Adaptation.* Students are encouraged to apply and modify the targeted skills to a broad array of novel but related situations. All too frequently, instructional practices fail to carefully take students through each of these phases of instruction.

Deshler, Alley, Warner, and Schumaker (1981) specified a set of instructional procedures that have proven effective in teaching learning strategies to older students. The acquisition procedure includes the following six steps:

1. The student is tested to determine his or her current learning habits with regard to a specific task, then is informed of his or her strengths and weaknesses and asked to commit to learning a new strategy to remedy a weakness.
2. The new strategy is described to the student. It is broken into component steps: rationales for learning the strategy, the types of results the student can expect to achieve, and situations in which the learning strategy can be used. Students write their own goals regarding how fast they will learn the new strategy.
3. The teacher models new learning strategy for the student from start to finish while "thinking aloud." The student is involved in subsequent demonstrations of the strategy.
4. The student practices the new strategy to a specified criterion performance in controlled materials (i.e., materials reduced in complexity, length, and difficulty level).
5. The student practices the skill to a mastery criterion (both speed and accuracy are emphasized) in materials and situations that closely approximate tasks they encounter in regular classes. Reinforcement and corrective feedback are given after each practice attempt in both steps 4 and 5.
6. The teacher administers a post-test to determine if the student's performance has progressed to a point that will allow him or her to cope with curricular demands in the targeted skill area.

As stated before, the goal is for LD students to gain maximum instructional benefits in the shortest time. To meet this goal, teachers must regularly apply *critical teaching behaviors* in their instruction. These are defined as behaviors a teacher engages in to enhance the intensity, or quality, of instruction in a classroom. Obviously, there is a broad array of teaching behaviors. The following are critical for best instruction:

1. Provide appropriate, positive, and corrective feedback.
2. Use organizers throughout the instructional session.
3. Institute high levels of active academic responding.
4. Program youth involvement in discussions.
5. Provide regular reviews of key instructional points and checks of comprehension.
6. Monitor student performance.
7. Require mastery learning.
8. Communicate high expectations to students.
9. Communicate rationales for instructional activities.
10. Facilitate independence.

SERVICE DELIVERY SYSTEMS

Traditionally, LD students have been "pulled out" of the regular classroom for a segment of the school day (e.g., 20 minutes to 1 hour) to receive special instruction in a resource room from a teacher trained to work with students who have learning disabilities. Although this basic service delivery model is still used a great deal, it has been significantly expanded and modified in recent years. Some authorities question the efficacy of the resource room model, basing their criticism on *evaluation* grounds (students fail to make sufficient gains in such a brief instructional exposure). Others do so on *curricular* grounds (in practice, what is taught in the resource room is not significantly different from what is taught in the general education classroom or is so discrepant that it is not useful in helping the student learn in the general education classroom). Still others do so for *ethical* reasons (separating students into a resource room is a subtle form of discrimination, and transferring them from the resource room placement is not done often enough).

As a result of these concerns, and of a simple desire to design more effective service delivery systems, we see a number of variations of the basic resource room format of service delivery and a movement toward more fully including students with LD in the general education classroom. Nevertheless, the professional organizations in the field (Council for Exceptional Children, Council for Learning Disabilities, CEC's Division for Learning Disabilities) all caution that full inclusion in the general education classroom is not necessarily the best educational environment for all children with learning disabilities; a child's needs and the IEP process should determine how to best serve the individual.

As one of the many examples of inclusionary programs, Wang and Birch (1984) designed a program that meets the needs of general and special education students alike in the regular classroom. It does so by modifying conditions in the school learning environment. Individualized instruction in the basic skills is integrated systematically with a classroom management system that provides a flexible organizational structure for adapting instruction to student differences. Under this system LD teachers are moved into the mainstream along with their students. In other programs LD teachers provide diagnostic services, offer the especially intensive instruction some students require, consult with general education teachers and parents as needed, and are full participants in delivering the standard curriculum to all students (Hudson, 1990; Robinson, 1991). Under these models students with LD are maintained in the regular classroom at all times, supported by the LD teacher.

At times someone other than the LD teacher delivers remedial instruction to students with LD. Several systems utilize other students as instructors. For example, Jenkins and Jenkins (1985) designed a peer tutoring system in which successful students, carefully trained in appropriate interpersonal and instructional behaviors, provide a major portion of the one-on-one instruction to the students with LD. The LD teacher supervises and monitors their work. Johnson and Johnson (1984, 1986) suggested a cooperative group structure in which students with LD are placed in instructional groupings of five to seven students, in a deliberate attempt to maximize heterogeneity. Students are taught how to function as a group; each student is responsible for cooperating with the entire group. In this way everyone masters the assigned tasks. In other service delivery systems the parent is the key agent. In recent years the computer is seen as a potentially reliable instructional agent. In short, however, professionals and practitioners in the LD field are still searching for the most effective way to deliver instructional services to students with LD.

SUMMARY

Learning disabilities constitutes a viable category of exceptionality. Since the passage of PL 94–142, it has been the fastest growing segment of the population of students with special needs and accounts for the greatest proportion of exceptional youngsters. Many students are not learning in school as expected, and the cause of their difficulties cannot be explained easily by environmental factors.

Many theories have been postulated about the possible causes of learning disabilities. Proponents of the *neuropsychological* model suggest a difference in, or dysfunction of, brain systems. Research to confirm this theory is becoming increasingly sophisticated as evolving scientific technologies are used to test beliefs on how the brain functions. Conclusive testing of these hypotheses, however, will take time, so a defensible brain-based explanation of learning disabilities will not occur in the near future. The *information-processing* paradigm of brain behavior has proven to be useful in understanding and addressing learning disabilities. Researchers from this philosophical perspective are contributing much to our understanding of how youngsters might think and how they might be taught more effectively. The *maturational* model, *inadequate environment* model, and *ecological* model all contribute to our understanding of how factors external to youngsters' innate abilities can contribute to learning problems. Much remains to be explained, however, before our understanding of why learning disabilities occur is complete.

Because our conceptual understanding of why youngsters have learning disabilities is incomplete, some assessment and intervention practices are questioned as to their appropriateness or effectiveness. This is unavoidable when the need for answers cannot wait for the necessary research to provide them. Students need help now, and the science of learning disabilities necessarily moves at a slower pace than the demands of youngsters who currently are having difficulty in schools. Therefore, practitioners have adopted practices on the basis of "knowledge to date," recognizing that the questions are still under examination. Without a precise understanding of what learning disabilities are, the definition of learning disabilities comes under question, as do identification practices.

Low achievement is the characteristic most commonly found in the LD population. A significant difference between ability and achievement is the single most accepted criterion for possible diagnosis of learning disabilities. The range of other characteristics is broad. We know that LD individuals are heterogeneous; there is no single prototypic LD youngster. Low achievement is also characteristic of many youngsters who are not learning disabled. Without defining characteristics exclusive of, and universal to, the learning disabled population, disagreement about who does and who does not have learning disabilities will continue. Research must clarify the classification issues in the field of learning disabilities and boundary conditions.

Many interventions have been effective in assisting LD youngsters to learn. Researchers have described precisely how to use those procedures. Policymakers and practitioners have developed a variety of service delivery options that respond to various community, state, and federal needs. Yet, questions remain regarding the long-term effectiveness of these intervention efforts. Longitudinal research is necessary to answer those questions.

The learning disabilities field is in transition. The search for better answers to pressing questions will continue as we examine the effectiveness of existing practices. The most important question is how to structure the learning environment better so all children learn. If we keep that question in sight, we will constantly improve the opportunities for individuals with learning disabilities.

*R*EFERENCES

Adelman, H. S. (1992). The classification problem. In W. Stainback & S. Stainback, (Eds.), *Controversial issues confronting special education*. Boston: Allyn and Bacon.

Adelman, H. S., & Compas, B. E. (1977). Stimulant drugs and learning problems. *Journal of Special Education, 11,* 377–416.

Adelman, H. S., & Taylor, L. (1983). *Learning disabilities in perspective*. Glenview, IL: Scott, Foresman.

Adelman, P. B., & Vogel, S. A. (1991). The learning-disabled adult. In B. Y. L. Wong, (Ed.), *Learning about learning disabilities*. San Diego: Academic Press.

Algozzine, B. (1991). Observations to accompany analyses of the Tenth Annual Report to Congress. *Exceptional Children, 57,* 217–275.

Algozzine, B., & Ysseldyke, J. E. (1983). Learning disabilities as a subset of school failure: The oversophistication of a concept. *Exceptional Children, 50,* 242–246.

Alley, G., & Deshler, D. D. (1979). *Teaching the learning disabled adolescent: Strategies and methods*. Denver: Love Publishing.

American Psychiatric Association. (1987). *Diagnostic and statistical manual of mental disorders* (3rd ed., rev., DSM-III-R). Washington, DC: Author.

Bandura, A. (1978). The self system in reciprocal determinism. *American Psychologist, 33,* 334–358.

Bauer, R. H. (1977). Memory processes in children with learning disabilities: Evidence for deficient rehearsal. *Journal of Experimental Child Psychology, 24,* 415–430.

Bley, N. S., & Thornton, C. A. (1981). *Teaching mathematics to the learning disabled*. Rockville, MD: Aspen Systems.

Bond, G., Tinker, M., Wasson, B., & Wasson, J. (1984). *Reading difficulties: Their diagnosis and correction*. Englewood Cliffs, NJ: Prentice Hall.

Brown, A. L., & Palinscar, A. S. (1982). Inducing strategy learning from tests by means of informed, self-control training. *Topics in Learning & Learning Disabilities, 2,* 1–17.

Bryan, T. (1991). Social problems and learning disabilities. In B. Y. L. Wong (Ed.), *Learning about learning disabilities*. San Diego: Academic Press.

Bryan, T., & Bryan, J. (1978). *Understanding disabilities* (2nd ed.). Sherman Oaks, CA: Alfred Publishing.

Bryan, T., Donahue, M., & Pearl, R. (1981). Learning disabled children's peer interactions during a small group problem-solving task. *Learning Disability Quarterly, 4,* 13–22.

Bryan, T., & Pflaum, S. (1978). Social interactions of learning disabled children: A linguistic, social and cognitive analysis. *Learning Disability Quarterly, 1,* 70–79.

Bryan, T., Wheeler, R., Felcan, J., & Henek, T. (1976). Come on dummy: An observational study of children's communication. *Journal of Learning Disabilities, 9,* 661–669.

Cawley, J. F., & Miller, J. H. (1989). Cross-sectional comparisons of the mathematical performance of children with learning disabilities: Are we on the right track toward comprehensive programming? *Journal of*

Learning Disabilities, 23, 250–254.

Clements, S. (1966). M.B.D. in children. *Terminology and identification* (NINDW Monograph No. 3). Washington, DC: U.S. Department of Health, Education & Welfare.

Cone, T., & Wilson, L. (1981). Quantifying a severe discrepancy: A critical analysis. *Learning Disability Quarterly, 4*, 359–372.

Crook, W. G. (1980). Can what a child eats make him dull, stupid, or hyperactive? *Journal of Learning Disabilities, 13*, 281–286.

Cruickshank, W. M. (1983). Learning disabilities: A neurophysiological dysfunction. *Journal of Learning Disabilities, 16*, 27–29.

Davis, W. A., & Shepard, L. A. (1983). Specialists' use of tests and clinical judgment in the diagnosis of learning disabilities. *Learning Disability Quarterly, 6*, 128–138.

Decker, S. N., & DeFries, J. C. (1980). Cognitive abilities in families of reading disabled children. *Journal of Learning Disabilities, 13*, 517–522.

DeFries, J. C., & Decker, S. N. (1982). Genetic aspects of reading disability: A family study. In R. N. Malatesha & P. G. Aaron (Eds.), *Reading disorders: Varieties and treatments*. New York: Academic Press.

DeHirsch, I., Jansky, J., & Langford, W. (1966). *Predicting reading failure*. New York: Harper & Row.

Deshler, D. D., Alley, G. R., Warner, M. M., & Schumaker, J. B. (1981). Instructional practices for promoting skill acquisition in generalization in severely learning disabled adolescents. *Learning Disability Quarterly, 4*, 415–421.

Deshler, D. D., Ferrell, W. K., & Kass, C. E. (1978). Error monitoring of schoolwork by learning disabled adolescents. *Journal of Learning Disabilities, 11*, 401–414.

Deshler, D. D., & Schumaker, J. B. (1984). *Learning strategies: A new way to teach*. Salt Lake City: Worldwide Media.

Deshler, D. D., & Schumaker, J. B. (1988). An instructional model for teaching students how to learn. In J. L. Graden, J. E. Zins, & M. J. Curtis, (Eds), *Alternative educational delivery systems: Enhancing instructional options for all students*. Washington, DC: National Association of School Psychologists.

Deshler, D., Schumaker, J., Lenz, B., & Ellis, E. (1984). Academic and cognitive intervention for learning disabled adolescents. Part 2. *Journal of Learning Disabilities, 17*, 170–187.

Diamond, G. (1983). The birthday effect–A maturational effect? *Journal of Learning Disabilities, 16*, 161–164.

DiPasquale, G., Moule, A., & Flewelling, R. (1980). The birthdate effect. *Journal of Learning Disabilities, 13*, 234–238.

Dunn, L. M., Dunn, L. M., & Smith, J. O. (1981). *Peabody language development kit: Level #2–Revised*. Circle Pines, MN: American Guidance Service.

Dunn, L. M., Horton, K. B., & Smith, J. O. (1981). *Peabody language development kit: Level #P–Revised*. Circle Pines, MN: American Guidance Service.

Dunn, L. M., Smith, J. O., & Dunn, L. M. (1981). *Peabody language development kit: Level #1–Revised*. Circle Pines, MN: American Guidance Service.

Dunn, L. M., Smith, J. O., & Smith, D. D. (1981). *Peabody language development kit: Level #3–Revised*. Circle Pines, MN: American Guidance Service.

Edgar, E. (1987). Secondary programs in special education: Are many of them justifiable? *Exceptional Children, 53*(6), 555–561.

Epps, S., Ysseldyke, J. E., & Algozzine, B. (1983). Importance of different definitions of learning disabilities on the number of students identified. *Journal of Psychoeducational Assessment, 1*, 341–352.

Feingold, B. F. (1976). Hyperkineses and learning disabilities linked to the ingestion of artificial food colors and flavors. *Journal of Learning Disabilities, 9*, 551–559.

Flavell, J. H., & Wellman, H. M. (1977). Metamemory. In R. V. Karl & J. W. Hagen (Eds.), *Perspectives on the development of memory and cognition*. Hillsdale, NJ: Lawrence Erlbaum.

Forness, S., Sinclair, E., & Guthrie, D. (1983). Learning disability discrepancy formulas: Their use in actual practice. *Learning Disability Quarterly, 6*, 107–114.

Frostig, M., & Horne, D. (1964). *The Frostig program for the development of visual perception*. Chicago: Follett.

Garner, R., Alexander, P. A., & Hare, V. C. (1991). Reading comprehension failure in children. In B. Y. L. Wong (Ed.), *Learning about learning disabilities*. San Diego: Academic Press.

Hallahan, D. P. (1982). Learning disabilities. In D. P. Hallahan & H. M. Kauffman (Eds.), *Exceptional children: Introduction to special education*. Englewood Cliffs, NJ: Prentice Hall.

Hallahan, D. P., & Bryan, T. H. (1981). Learning disabilities. In J. M. Kauffman & D. P. Hallahan (Eds.), *Handbook: Special education*. Englewood Cliffs, NJ: Prentice Hall.

Hallahan, D. P., & Cruickshank, W. M. (1973). *Psycho-educational foundations of learning disabilities*. Englewood Cliffs, NJ: Prentice Hall.

Hallahan, D. P., Gajar, A. H., Cohen, S. B., & Tarver, S. G. (1978). Selective attention and locus of control in learning disabled and normal children. *Journal of Learning Disabilities, 11*, 231–236.

Hallahan, D. P., & Kauffman, J. M. (1976). *Introduction to learning disabilities*. Englewood Cliffs, NJ: Prentice Hall.

Hallahan, D. P., & Reeve, R. E. (1980). Selective attention and distractability. In B. K. Keogh (Ed.), *Advances in special education: Vol. 1. Basic constructs and theoretical orientations*. Greenwich, CT: JAI Press.

Hammill, D. D. (1990). On defining learning disabilities: An emerging consensus. *Journal of Learning Disabilities, 23*, 74–84.

Hammill, D. D., & Larsen, S. C. (1974). The effectiveness of psycholinguistic training. *Exceptional Children, 41*, 5–14.

Hammill, D. D., Leigh, J. E., McNutt, G., & Larsen, S. C. (1981). A new definition of LD. *Learning Disabilities Quarterly, 4*, 336–342.

Hammill, D. D., & Wiederholt, L. (1973). Review of the Frostig visual perception test and the related training program. In L. Mann & D. Sabatino (Eds.), *The first review of special education* (Vol. 1). New York: Grune & Stratton.

Hansen, C. L. (1978). Story retelling used with average and learning disabled readers as a measure of reading comprehension. *Learning Disability Quarterly, 1*, 62–69.

Harris, A. (1961). How to improve reading ability. New York: David McKay.

Hartladge, L. C., & Telzrow, C. F. (1983). The neuropsychological basis of educational intervention. *Journal of Learning Disabilities, 16*, 521–528.

Hudson, F. (1990). *CWC: Class within a class*. Kansas City: University of Kansas, Department of Special Education.

Jenkins, J., & Jenkins, L. (1985). Peer tutoring in elementary and secondary programs. *Focus on Exceptional Children, 17*(6), 1–12.

Johnson, D. W., & Johnson, R. T. (1986). Mainstreaming and cooperative learning strategies. *Exceptional Children, 52*, 553–561.

Johnson, R. T., & Johnson, D. W. (1984). *Structuring cooperative learning: Lesson plans for teachers*. New Brighton, MN: Interaction Book Co.

Karnes, M. (1972). *GOAL: Language development*. Springfield, MA: Milton Bradley.

Karnes, M., Linnemeyer, S., & Schwedel, A. (1981). A survey of federally funded model programs for handicapped infants: Implications for research and practice. *Journal of the Division for Early Childhood, 5*, 25–39.

Kavale, K. (1981). Functions of the Illinois Test of Psycholinguistic Abilities (ITPA): Are they trainable? *Exceptional Children, 47*, 496–510.

Kavale, K. (1982). Meta-analysis of the relationship between visual perceptual skills and reading achievement. *Journal of Learning Disabilities, 15*, 42–51.

Kavale, K. A. (1987). The long term consequences of learning disabilities. In M. C. Wang, M. C. Reynolds, & H. J. Walberg (Eds.), *Handbook of special education: Research and practice* (Vol. 2). Elmsford, NY: Pergamon Press.

Kavale, K. A., & Forness, S. R. (1983). Hyperactivity and diet treatment: A meta-analysis of the Feingold hypothesis. *Journal of Learning Disabilities, 16*, 165–173.

Kavale, K. A., & Mattson, P. D. (1983). "One jumped off the balance beam": Meta-analysis of perceptual-motor training. *Journal of Learning Disabilities, 16*, 165–173.

Kavale K. K., Forness, S. R., & Lorsbach, T. C. (1991). Definition for definitions of learning disabilities. *Learning Disability Quarterly, 14*, 257–268.

Keogh, B. K. (1987). Learning disabilities: Diversity in search of order. In M. C. Wang, M. C. Reynolds, & H.

J. Walberg (Eds.), *Handbook of special education: Research and practice* (Vol. 2). Elmsford, NY: Pergamon Press.

Keogh, B. K., & Sears, S. (1991). Learning disabilities from a developmental perspective. Early identification and prediction. In B. Y. L. Wong (Ed.), *Learning about learning disabilities*. San Diego: Academic Press.

Kephart, N. C. (1971). *The slow learner in the classroom*. Columbus, OH: Charles E. Merrill.

Kirk, S. A., & Kirk, W. D. (1971). *Psycholinguistic learning disabilities diagnosis and remediation*. Urbana: University of Illinois Press.

Kirk, S. A., McCarthy, J. J., & Kirk, W. D. (1968). *The Illinois Test of Psycholinguistic Abilities* (rev. ed.). Urbana: University of Illinois Press.

Kneedler, R. D., & Hallahan, D. P. (1981). Self-monitoring on-task behavior with learning disabled children: Current studies and directions. *Exceptional Education Quarterly, 2*, 73–82.

Kornetsky, C. (1975). Minimal brain dysfunction and drugs. In W. M. Cruickshank & D. P. Hallahan (Eds.), *Psychoeducational practices: Perceptual and learning disabilities in children: Vol. 2. Research and theory*. Syracuse, NY: Syracuse University Press.

Kotsonis, M. E., & Patterson, C. J. (1980). Comprehension monitoring skills in learning disabled children. *Developmental Psychology, 16*, 541–542.

Larsen, S. C., Parker, R. M., & Hammill, D. D. (1982). Effectiveness of psycholinguistic training: A response to Kavale. *Exceptional Children, 49*, 60–66.

Larsen, S. C., Parker, R. M., & Trenholm, B. (1978). The effects of syntactic complexity upon arithmetic performance. *Learning Disability Quarterly, 1*, 80–85.

Lerner, J. (1985). *Learning disabilities*. Boston: Houghton Mifflin.

Levine, M., Brooks, R., & Shonkoff, J. (1980). *A pediatric approach to learning disorders*. New York: John Wiley.

Levy, H. (1983). Developmental dyslexia: A pediatrician's perspective. *Schumpert's Medical Quarterly, 1*, 200–207.

Lewis, R. (1983). Learning disabilities and reading: Instructional recommendations from current research. *Exceptional Children, 50*, 230–240.

Lloyd, J., Saltzman, N. J., & Kauffman, J. M. (1981). Predictable generalization in academic learning as a result of preskill and strategy training. *Learning Disability Quarterly, 4*, 203–216.

Lovitt, T. C. (1982). *Because of my persistence, I've learned from children*. Columbus, OH: Charles E. Merrill.

Lund, K., Foster, G. E., & McCall-Perez, F. C. (1978). The effectiveness of psycholinguistic training: A reevaluation. *Exceptional Children, 44*, 310–319.

Lyon, G. R. (1983). Subgroups of learning disabled readers: Clinical and empirical identification. In H. Myklebust (Ed.), *Progress in learning disabilities* (Vol. 5). New York: Grune and Stratton.

Lyon, G. R. (1985). Identification and remediation of learning disabilities subtypes: Preliminary findings. *Learning Disabilities Focus, 1*, 21–35.

Lyon, G. R., & Watson, B. (1981). Empirically derived subgroups of learning disabled readers: Diagnostic characteristics. *Journal of Learning Disabilities, 14*, 256–261.

Lyon, G. R., Newby, R. E., Recht, D., & Caldwell, J. (1991). Neuropsychology and learning disabilities. In B. Y. L. Wong (Ed.), *Learning about learning disabilities*. San Diego: Academic Press.

Mangrum, C. T., & Strichart, S. S. (1984). *College and the learning disabled student*. New York: Grune & Stratton.

Mark, L. S., Shankweiler, D., Liberman, L. Y., & Fowler, C. A. (1977). Phonetic recoding and reading difficulties in beginning readers. *Memory & Cognition, 5*, 623–629.

Marston, D. (1989). Measuring progress on IEPs: A comparison of graphing approaches. *Exceptional Children, 53*, 423–431.

McKinney, J. D. (1984). The search for subtypes of specific learning disability. *Annual Review of Learning Disabilities, 2*, 19–26.

McKinney, J. D. (1990). Longitudinal research on the behavioral characteristics of children with learning disabilities. In J. Torgeson (Ed.), *Cognitive and behavioral characteristics of children with learning disabilities* (pp. 115–138). Austin, TX: PRO–ED.

Mercer, C. (1987). *Students with learning disabilities* (3rd ed.). Columbus, OH: Merrill Publishing.

Mercer, C. D. (1983). *Students with learning disabilities*. Columbus, OH: Charles E. Merrill.

Mercer, C. D., & Miller, S. P. (1992). Teaching students with learning problems in math to acquire, understand, and apply basic math facts. *Remedial and special education, 13,* 19–35.

Meyen, E. L., & Lehr, D. H. (1980a). Evolving practices in assessment and intervention for mildly handicapped adolescents: The case for intensive instruction. *Exceptional Education Quarterly, 1*(2), 19–26.

Minskoff, E. H., Wiseman, D., & Minskoff, J. G. (1972). *The MWM program for developing language abilities.* Ridgefield, NJ: Educational Performance Assoc.

Myklebust, H. (1968). Learning disabilities: Definitions and overview. In H. Myklebust (Ed.), *Progress in learning disabilities* (Vol. 1). New York: Grune & Stratton.

National Advisory Committee on Handicapped Children. (1968). *Subcommittee on education of the committee on labor and public welfare* (First annual report). Washington, DC: U.S. Government Printing Office.

National Joint Committee on Learning Disabilities. (1988). Letter to NJCLD member organizations.

Nelson, R. O., & Hayes, S. C. (1981). Theoretical explanations for reactivity in self-monitoring. *Behavior Modification, 5,* 3–14.

Orton, S. (1937). *Reading, writing and speech problems in children.* New York: W. W. Norton.

Osgood, C. E. (1957). Motivational dynamics of language behavior. In M. Jones (Ed.), *Nebraska symposium on motivation.* Lincoln: University of Nebraska Press.

Perfetti, C. A., & Goldman, S. R. (1976). Discourse memory and reading comprehension skill. *Journal of Verbal Learning & Verbal Behavior, 14,* 33–42.

Perfetti, C. A., & Lesgold, A. M. (1978). Discourse-comprehension and sources of individual differences. In M. A. Just & P. A. Carpenter (Eds.), *Cognitive processes in comprehension.* Hillsdale, NJ: Lawrence Erlbaum.

Pflaum, S. (1979). *Oral reading in the learning disabled.* Paper presented at the conference of the Association for Children with Learning Disabilities, San Francisco.

Pressley, M. P. (1990). *Cognitive strategy instruction that really improves children's academic performance.* Cambridge, MA: Brookline Books.

Rabinovich, R. D. (1959). Reading and learning disabilities. In S. Arieti (Ed.), *American handbook of psychiatry* (Vol. 1). New York: Basic Books.

Ramey, C., & Bryant, D. (1982). Evidence for prevention of developmental retardation during infancy. *Journal of the Division for Early Childhood, 5,* 73–78.

Robinson, S. M. (1983). *A study of the efficacy of instruction in two strategies—rehersal and self-testing to increase listening skills of learning disabled students.* Unpublished doctoral dissertation, University of New Mexico, Albuquerque.

Robinson, S. M. (1991). Collaborative consultation. In B. Y. L. Wong (Ed.), *Learning about learning disabilities.* San Diego: Academic Press.

Salvia, J., & Ysseldyke, J. E. (1981). *Assessment in special and remedial education* (2nd ed.). Boston: Houghton Mifflin.

Satz, P., & Morris, R. (1981). Learning disability subtypes: A review. In F. J. Pirozzolo & M. C. Wittrock (Eds.), *Neuropsychological and cognitive processes in reading.* New York: Academic Press.

Schumaker, J. B., Denton, P. H., Deshler, D. D. (1984). *Learning strategies curriculum: The paraphrasing strategy.* Lawrence: University of Kansas.

Schumaker, J. B., Deshler, D. D., Alley, G. R., & Warner, M. M. (1980). *An epidemiological study of learning disabled adolescents in secondary schools* (Research Rep. No. 12). Lawrence: University of Kansas, Institute of Research in Learning Disabilities.

Schumaker, J. B., Deshler, D. D., Alley, G. R., & Warner, M. M. (1983). Toward the development of an intervention model for learning disabled adolescents. *Exceptional Education Quarterly, 4*(1), 45–74.

Schumaker, J. B., Hazel, J. S., Sherman, J. A., & Sheldon, J. (1982). Social skill performances of learning disabled, non-learning disabled, and delinquent adolescents. *Learning Disability Quarterly, 5,* 378–392.

Seabaugh, G. O., & Schumaker, J. B. (1981). *Effects of three conferencing procedures on the academic productivity of LD and NLD adolescents.* (Research Rep. No. 36). Lawrence: University of Kansas, Institute for Research in Learning Disabilities.

Shankweiler, D., & Liberman, A. M. (1972). Misreading: A search for causes. In J. F. Kavanaugh & I. G. Mattingly (Eds.), *Language by ear and by eye.* Cambridge, MA: MIT Press.

Shepard, L. (1980). An evaluation of the regression discrepancy method for identifying children with learning disabilities. *Journal of Special Education, 14*, 79–80.

Shepard, L. A., & Smith, M. L. (1983). An evaluation of the identification of learning disabled students in Colorado. *Learning Disability Quarterly, 6*, 115–127.

Shinn, M. R. (1989). Identifying and defining academic problems: CBM screening and eligibility procedures. In M. Shinn (Ed.), *Curriculum-based measurement: Assessing special children* (pp. 90–129). New York: Guilford Press.

Silver, A., & Hagen, R. (1966). Maturation of perceptual functions in children with specific reading disabilities. *Reading Teacher, 19*, 253–259.

Skrtic, T. M. (1980). *Formal reasoning abilities of learning disabled adolescents: Implications for mathematics instruction.* (Research Rep. No. 7). University of Kansas, Institute for Research in Learning Disabilities, Lawrence.

Smiley, S. S., Oaken, D. D., Worthen, D., Campione, J. C., & Brown, A. L. (1977). Recall of thematically relevant material by adolescent good and poor readers as a function of written versus oral presentation. *Journal of Educational Psychology, 69*, 381–387.

Smith, D. D. (1981). *Teaching the learning disabled.* Englewood Cliffs, NJ: Prentice Hall.

Smith, D. D. (1989). *Teaching students with learning and behavior problems* (2nd ed.). Englewood Cliffs, NJ: Prentice Hall.

Smith, D. D., & Robinson, S. M. (1986). Educating the learning disabled. In R. I. Morris & B. Blah (Eds.), *Special education research and trends.* Elmsford, NY: Pergamon Press.

Smith, S. (1978). *Genetics studies and linkage analysis of specific dyslexia: Evaluation of inheritance in kindreds selected for the parents' autosomal dominant transmission.* Unpublished doctoral dissertation, Indiana University, Bloomington.

Speece, D. L., McKinney, J. D., & Applebaum, M. I. (1984). Classification and validation of behavioral subtypes of learning disabled children: *Journal of Educational Psychology, 77*(1), 66–77.

Spekman, N. (1981). Dyadic verbal communication abilities of learning disabled and normally achieving fourth grade and fifth grade boys. *Learning Disability Quarterly, 4*, 139–151.

Swanson, H. L. (1982). Strategies and constraints—A commentary. *Topics in Learning & Learning Disabilities, 2*, 79–81.

Swanson, H. L., & Cooney, J. B. (1991). Learning disabilities and memory. In B. Y. L. Wong (Ed.), *Learning about learning disabilities.* San Diego: Academic Press.

Tarver, S. G., Hallahan, D. P., Kauffman, J. M., & Ball, D. W. (1976). Verbal rehearsal and selective attention in children with learning disabilities. A developmental lag. *Journal of Experimental Child Psychology, 22*, 375–385.

Torgesen, J. K. (1977). The role of nonspecific factors in the task performance of learning disabled children: A theoretical assessment. *Journal of Learning Disabilities, 10*, 27–34.

Torgesen, J. K. (1979). Factors related to poor performance on memory tasks in reading disabled children. *Learning Disability Quarterly, 2*, 17–23.

Torgesen, J. K. (1982). The use of rationally defined subgroups in research on learning disabilities. In J. P. Das, R. F. Mulcahy, & A. E. Wall (Eds.), *Theory and research in learning disabilities.* New York: Plenum Press.

Torgesen, J. K. (1986). Learning disabilities theory: Its current state and future prospects. *Journal of Learning Disabilities, 19*, 399–407.

Torgesen, J. K. (1989). Studies of children with learning disabilities who perform poorly on memory span tasks. *Journal of Learning Disabilities, 21*, 605–612.

Torgesen, J. K., & Goldman, T. (1977). Verbal rehearsal and short-term memory in reading-disabled children. *Child Development, 48*, 56–60.

Torgesen, J. K., & Greenstein, J. J. (1982). Why do some learing disabled children have problems remembering? Does it make a difference? *Topics in Learning & Learning Disabilities, 2*(2), 54–61.

Torgesen, J. K., & Houck, D. G. (1980). Processing deficiencies of LD children who perform poorly on the digit span test. *Journal of Educational Psychology, 12*, 141–160.

Tucker, J., Stevens, L. J., & Ysseldyke, J. E. (1983). Learning disabilities: The experts speak out. *Journal of Learning Disabilities, 10*, 6–14.

U.S. Department of Education. (1991). *Thirteenth annual report to Congress on the implementation of the Individuals with Disabilities Education Act.* Washington, DC: Government Printing Office.

U.S. Office of Education. (1977). Assistance to states for education of handicapped children: Procedures for evaluating specific learning disabilities. *Federal Register, 42,* 65082–65085.

Vellutino, F. R. (1977). Alternative conceptualizations of dyslexia: Evidence in support of a verbal-deficit hypothesis. *Harvard Educational Review, 47,* 334–354.

Vetter, H. (1983). *A comparison of the characteristics of learning disabled and non-learning disabled young adults.* Unpublished doctoral dissertation, University of Kansas, Lawrence.

Vogel, S. A. (1974). Syntactic abilities in normal and dyslexic children. *Journal of Learning Disabilities, 7,* 103–109.

Vogel, S. (1982). On developing LD college programs. *Journal of Learning Disabilities, 15,* 518–528.

Wang, M. C., & Birch, T. W. (1984). Effective special education in regular classes. *Exceptional Children, 50,* 391–398.

Warner, M. M., Alley, G. R., Deshler, D. D., & Schumaker, J. (1980). Learning disabled adolescents in the public schools: Are they different from other low achievers? *Exceptional Education Quarterly, 1*(2), 27–56.

Watson, B. (1983). *Analyses of the responses of empirically derived subgroups of learning disabled readers to different methods of reading instruction.* Research grant application submitted to Special Education Programs.

Wepman, J. M. (1964). Modalities and learning. In H. A. Robinson (Ed.), *Meeting individual differences in reading* (Supplementary Educational Monograph 94). Chicago: University of Chicago Press.

Whalen, C. K., & Henker, B. (1976). Psychostimulants and children: A review and analysis. *Psychological Bulletin, 83,* 1113–1130.

White, W. J., Schumaker, J., Warner, M. M., Alley, G. R., & Deshler, D. D. (1980). *The current status of young adults identified as learning disabled during their school career* (Research Rep. No. 21). Lawrence: University of Kansas Medical Institute.

Wiig, E. H., & Semel, E. M. (1975). Productive language abilities in learning-disabled adolescents. *Journal of Learning Disabilities, 8,* 578–488.

Wiig, E. H., Semel, E. M., & Crouse, M. A. B. (1973). The use of English morphology by high-risk and learning disabled children. *Journal of Learning Disabilities, 6,* 457–465.

Wong, B. Y. L. (1980a). Activating the inactive learner: Use of questions/prompts to enhance comprehension and retention of implied information in learning disabled children. *Learning Disability Quarterly, 1,* 29–37.

Wong, B. Y. L. (1980b). Increasing retention of main ideas through questioning strategies. *Learning Disability Quarterly, 2,* 42–47.

Wong, B. Y. L. (1991a). Assessment of metacognitive research in learning disabilities: Theory, research, and practice. In L. Swanson & B. Keogh (Eds.), *Handbook on the assessment of learning disabilities: Theory, research, and practice.* College Hill Press.

Wong, B. Y. L. (1991b). The relevance of metacognition to learning disabilities. In B. Y. L. Wong (Ed.), *Learning about learning disabilities* (pp. 232–261). San Diego: Academic Press.

Wong, B. Y. L., & Jones, S. W. (1982). Increasing metacomprehension in learning disabled and normally achieving students through self-questioning training. *Learning Disability Quarterly, 5,* 228–240.

Ysseldyke, J. E., & Algozzine, B. (1990). *Introduction to special education* (2nd ed.). Boston: Houghton Mifflin.

Ysseldyke, J. E., Algozzine, B., Regan, R., & Potter, M. (1979). *Technical adequacy of tests used by professionals in simulated decision making* (Research Rep. No. 9). Minneapolis: University of Minnesota, Institute for Research on Learning Disabilities.

Ysseldyke, J. E., Algozzine, B., Richey, L., & Graden, J. (1982). Declaring students eligible for learning disability services: Why bother with the data? *Learning Disability Quarterly, 5,* 37–44.

Ysseldyke, J. E., Algozzine, B., Shinn, M., & McGue, M. (1982). Similarities and differences between underachievers and students classified learning disabled. *Journal of Special Education, 16,* 73–85.

Ysselydke, J. E., Algozzine, B., & Thurlow, M. L. (1992). *Critical issues in special education.* Boston: Houghton Mifflin.

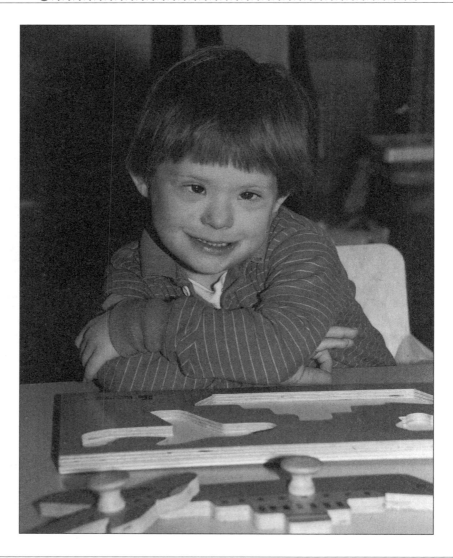

MENTAL

RETARDATION

GALE M. MORRISON
AND EDWARD A. POLLOWAY

*M*ental retardation is a concept largely controlled by our society; it derives its meaning from societal norms and expectations. The concept of mild retardation, in particular, was for many years virtually nonexistent simply because society in general did not perceive it as a problem. The vast majority more or less successfully blended into pre-industrial society. As industry supplanted agriculture as the focus of our economic system, however, people with mental retardation gained greater notice and ultimately were perceived as a problem. From these early perceptions evolved modern conceptualizations of mental retardation that created often inaccurate and occasionally brutal stereotypes of people with retardation (Philips, 1992).

*H*ISTORICAL BACKGROUND

Throughout history the definition and treatment of individuals with mental retardation always have been swayed by the sociopolitical trends of the times, as well as by the current knowledge base. As a group, people with mental retardation have had their ups and downs, from the static ignorance of antiquity to the leaps and bounds of knowledge and humane care in the late 1700s and the early 1800s. In the late 1800s and early 1900s the climate of optimism changed, unfortunately, to one of pessimism and fear. At that time the eugenics movement aimed to restrict the growth of this population and the legal rights of people with mental retardation. The aura of this period impacted the first half of the 20th century. In the 1950s the winds shifted once again, bringing renewed interest in educating children with mental retardation. Parents demanded it, and national policy supported it.

The picture was not as rosy as it seemed, however. Children identified as having mild mental retardation often were segregated within the public schools. Intelligence tests were used oversimplistically to indicate level of retardation and became the target of heated controversy. Some argued that the tests were being used as a cultural sanction against minority children who did not perform well.

A wave of litigation aimed at the rights and treatment of people with retardation welcomed the 1970s. A number of court cases highlighted their constitutional rights: their right to treatment (Wyatt v. Stickney, 1971), their right to education (Pennsylvania Association for Retarded Children [PARC] v. Commonwealth of Pennsylvania, 1972), and their right not to be excluded from appropriate education based on discriminatory assessment procedures and violations of due process (Diana v. State Board of Education, 1970; Larry P. v. Riles, 1972).

These legal reviews culminated in passage of PL 94–142, the Education for All Handicapped Children Act of 1975. In the wake of 94–142, numerous changes have occurred. Previously unserved children, especially those with severe disabilities, were identified and provided services. Assessment for identification and placement became more broad-based, considering multiple areas of child functioning. More options for placement programming were created. Parents and their children were increasingly accorded their rights to due process in education.

To consider progress in the nearly two decades since passage of PL 94–142, the field of mental retardation has undergone a series of paradigm shifts. These trends reflect the reality that our society has increasingly learned to accept persons with mental retardation and acknowledge that, as citizens, they are entitled to a place in our society. The paradigm shifts have become apparent in a variety of areas, perhaps most noticeably in the media. Characters such as Benny Stulwicz on "L. A. Law" and Corky on "Life Goes On" are brought into American living rooms every week. Most significantly, these characters are regular members of series. Before that, on the rare occasions when individuals with retardation were portrayed on television or in the movies, their disability, rather than their humanness, was the focus of the show.

Terms themselves reflect changes. Not too long ago "retardate" was a common referent in journal articles, confirming that those individuals were primarily research subjects. Since that time we have moved from "the retarded" to "persons who are mentally retarded," and finally, in some circles, to terms such as "intellectually challenged."

Assessment practices reflect paradigm changes as well. Historically, tests of measured intelligence were the core of this field. Individuals commonly were referred to by specific IQ scores. We might say, for example, "Johnnie is a 53." More recently, however, assessment focuses on functionality within an individual's environment.

Current educational programs for individuals identified as having mental retardation reflect a commitment to integration. Few special day schools remain as service delivery options for persons with mental retardation. The full-time, self-contained special class is becoming a dinosaur in the educational system. "Full inclusion," in which an individual spends the majority of the, if not the entire, academic day in the regular class, has become the buzzword for public schools.

In some ways, services for adults who have mental retardation provide an apt view of the changes. Traditional state residential facilities for people with mental retardation, which at their peak housed close to 200,000 individuals, typified the idea of *facility-based* programs. The emphasis was largely on the structure itself, and programs were designed to be consistent with the institutional concept. Eventually this attitude gave way to a *services-based* approach and its greater emphasis on individual needs; services were designed to enhance the likelihood that an individual would move into a less restrictive setting. Most recently, programs can be typified as *supports-based*. The assumption is that individuals should be in integrated settings and that programs should be designed to maintain and promote development of an individual within that integrated setting. Thus, the paradigm shifted from retention in segregated settings, to preparation for movement to integrated settings, to the commitment of initial placement within integrated settings.

The discussion in this chapter focuses on key information in the field of mental retardation to provide a basis for understanding individuals who have been identified as having mental retardation. The themes mentioned above recur throughout this discussion.

EDUCATIONAL DEFINITIONS OF MENTAL RETARDATION

Because of the interdisciplinary nature of the care and treatment of people who have mental retardation, reaching agreement on a definition has proved to be a difficult and lengthy process. To appreciate its complexity, one must consider previous attempts to define mental retardation.

HISTORICAL TRADITIONS IN DEFINITIONS

The earliest major contributions were made by physicians who defined mental retardation according to its physical and organic defects. Thus, Seguin (1866/1971) defined what was then referred to as idiocy, "a specific infirmity of the cranio-spinal axis, produced by deficiency of nutrition in utero and neo-nati" (p. 39). Tredgold (1908) also referred to incomplete cerebral development but added the criterion of social adaptability, recognizing the importance of how individuals perform within their sociocultural environment. The psychological measurement of intelligence, spearheaded by Binet and Simon, was another criterion to consider. This one was particularly attractive, because measurement is objective and fits with the theory of "normal" distribution of human characteristics.

In recognition of the multidisciplinary nature of the mental retardation concept, Doll (1941) set forth the following definition:

> Mental deficiency is a state of social incompetence obtaining at maturity, or likely to obtain at maturity, resulting from developmental arrest of constitutional (heredity or acquired) origin; the condition is essentially incurable through treatment and unremediable through training. (p. 215)

This definition recognizes the developmental, intellectual, and social aspects of mental retardation. It also suggests a biological origin while unfortunately pointing to an assumption of incurability. The suggestion of multiplicity of criteria was in contrast to earlier reliance on a single criterion.

AAMR DEFINITIONS

To arrive at some kind of mutually acceptable definition across disciplines and associated professional groups, the American Association on Mental Retardation (AAMR) (formerly American Association on Mental Deficiency [AAMD]) proposed the following:

Mental retardation refers to significantly subaverage general intellectual functioning resulting in or associated with concurrent impairments in adaptive behavior and manifested during the developmental period. (Grossman, 1983, p. 11)

This 1983 definition reflects changes inherent in a series of revisions by this organization (Grossman, 1973, 1977, 1983; Heber, 1961). It is currently the most widely accepted. Three major components consistently (with certain revisions) have appeared in all of the AAMR definitions: subaverage general intellectual functioning, impairments in adaptive behavior, and manifestation during the developmental period.

Subaverage General Intellectual Functioning. Intellectual functioning is determined by performance on an individually administered, standardized intelligence test. Based on the properties of a normal curve, an individual's performance is compared to a specified mean and standard deviation. In Heber's (1961) definition, "subaverage general intellectual functioning" referred to 1 standard deviation below the mean. In the later Grossman definitions, "significantly subaverage general intellectual functioning," or 2 standard deviations below the mean, determined mild mental retardation. Grossman recognized the social-political problems in accurately measuring intelligence in borderline cases that involved members of minority cultures; hence the more conservative cutoff for the intellectual functioning criterion. The major concern was that children from minority cultures were being segregated in schools (and therefore sanctioned) on the basis of an intelligence test score that many considered to be culturally biased.

Impairments in Adaptive Behavior. The adaptive behavior component refers to an individual's failure to effectively adjust to environmental demands. Adaptive behavior is defined and measured less precisely; however, the later Grossman definitions provided more extensive guidelines for definition and measurement, which reflected greater emphasis on the importance of adaptive behavior. One purpose of the adaptive behavior requirement was to help eliminate false identification in borderline cases in which lowered performance on an intelligence test might not have concomitant consequences on the person's functioning in home and school environments. The poor performance of a culturally different child, for example, may reflect learning difficulties only in academic-related school environments.

Manifestation During the Developmental Period. The Grossman (1983) definition identified the developmental period as being birth to 18 years. This was seen as a time of critical development and changes. The onset of any condition after age 18 would not be considered mental retardation.

Between 1959 and 1983, special educators began to rely more on clinical judgment to diagnose mental retardation. The rationale was the same as that of the Grossman revisions: Decisions on borderline cases should be tempered by judgments about a child's functioning in critical environments and the actual need for some kind of treatment or services. For example, a child may score below the cutoff point for mild mental retardation on an intelligence test and appear borderline on adaptive behavior measures; upon further observation, however, the child apparently functions adequately both in school and at home. A clinician's judgment in this case might be to avoid labeling such a child until services are demonstrated to be necessary.

Development of the AAMR definition over time reflects the state of our knowledge about the nature of mental retardation and its role in society. The Grossman (1983) manual expressed the need to continually reconsider this definition:

> The 1983 definition...is intended to represent the current status of scientific knowledge in the field and the current thinking about social issues associated with mental retardation. One may anticipate that as both knowledge and philosophy change, there will be modifications reflecting such changes in future manuals. (p. 10)

LUCKASSON ET AL. REVISION

The comments of Grossman (1983) about the need for periodic review is reflected in the development of the 1992 (Luckasson et al.) revision. The AAMR approved the following revised definition in May 1992:

> Mental retardation refers to substantial limitations in present functioning. It is characterized by significantly subaverage intellectual functioning, existing concurrently with related limitations in two or more of the following applicable adaptive skill areas: communication, self-care, home living, social skills, community use, self-direction, health and safety, functional academics, leisure, and work. Mental retardation manifests before age 18.
>
> The following four assumptions are essential to the application of this definition: (1) Valid assessments consider cultural and linguistic diversity, and differences in communication and behavioral factors; (2) The existence of limitations in adaptive skills occurs within the context of community environments typical of the individual's age peers and is indexed to the person's individualized needs for support; (3) Specific adaptive limitations often coexist with strengths in other adaptive skills or other personal capabilities; and (4) With appropriate supports over a sustained period, the life functioning of the person with mental retardation will generally improve.

Several similar themes are continued from the earlier AAMR definitions. It retains the focus on the two key dimensions of intelligence and adaptation as well as the modifier of age of onset. The conceptual basis, however, varies from those earlier efforts. Based generally on the conceptualizations of mental retardation developed by Greenspan (e.g., 1979, 1990), the 1992 definition reflects a more *functional* approach. Selected descriptors from the AAMR manual describe in more detail certain phrasing within the Luckasson et al. (1992) definition, as follows:

Mental retardation refers to substantial limitations in present functioning: Mental retardation is defined as a fundamental difficulty in learning and performing certain daily life skills. The personal capabilities that must be substantially limited are conceptual, practical, and social intelligence. These three areas are affected specifically in mental retardation, whereas other personal capabilities (e.g., health and temperament) may not be.

Characterized by significantly subaverage intellectual functioning: This is defined as an IQ standard score of approximately 70–75 or lower, based on assessment that includes one or more individually administered general intelligence tests developed for the purpose of assessing intellectual functioning. These data should be reviewed by a multidisciplinary team and validated with additional test scores or evaluative information.

Existing concurrently: The intellectual limitations occur at the same time as the limitations in adaptive skills.

With related limitations: The limitations in adaptive skills are more closely related to the intellectual limitation than to some other circumstances such as cultural or linguistic diversity or sensory limitation.

In two or more of the following applicable adaptive skill areas: Evidence of disabilities in adaptive skills is necessary because intellectual functioning alone is insufficient for a diagnosis of mental retardation. The impact on functioning of these disabilities must be sufficiently comprehensive to encompass at least two adaptive skill areas, thus showing a generalized limitation and reducing the probability of error in measurement.

Communication, self-care, home living, social skills, community use, self-direction, health and safety, functional academics, leisure, and work: These skill areas are central to successful life functioning and frequently are related to the need for supports for persons with mental retardation. Because the relevant skills within each adaptive skill area may vary with chronological age, assessment of functioning must be referenced to the individual's chronological age.

Although the previous Grossman definitions (e.g., 1973, 1977, 1983) have been widely cited and implemented to varying degrees in educational practice (i.e., the words frequently were used in regulations, even though the underlying intent was not always retained; see Frankenberger & Harper, 1988), it remains to be seen if the 1992 definition also will become the basis for state and federal statutes. Deliberations are ongoing at this time.

ALTERNATIVE CONCEPTUALIZATIONS

Though the AAMR definitions frequently have served as the basis for educational regulations, other conceptualizations are noteworthy:

1. A *social system perspective* was taken by Mercer (1973a). She suggested that the AAMR statistical/pathological approach leads to misidentification of individuals from cultural minorities. Mental retardation is a sociological phenomenon, "an achieved status in a social system and the role played by persons holding that status" (p. 36).

2. A *service delivery perspective* addresses more practical concerns: how people with mental retardation function and what types of services they need. For example, the Developmental Disabilities Assistance and Bill of Rights Act of 1978 (PL 95–602) defined developmental disability as:

   ...a severe chronic disability of a person which: (a) is attributable to a mental or physical impairment or combination of mental or physical impairment; (b) is manifested before the person attains age twenty-two; (c) is likely to continue indefinitely; (d) results in substantial functional limitations in three or more of the following areas of major life activity: self-care, receptive and expressive language, learning, mobility, self-direction, capacity of independent living, economic self-sufficiency; and (e) reflects the person's need for a combination and sequence of special, interdisciplinary, or generic care, treatment, or other services which are of lifelong or extended duration and are individually planned and coordinated.

3. A *behavioral perspective* has more tangible implications for intervention. Bijou (1966) suggested that:

> ...developmental retardation be treated as observable, objectively defined stimulus-response relationships without recourse to hypothetical mental concepts such as "defective intelligence" and hypothetical biological abnormalities such as "clinically inferred brain injury." From this point of view a retarded individual is one who has a limited repertoire of behavior shaped by events that constitute his history. (p. 2)

Defining mental retardation, then, depends on the perspective of the professionals involved. It is an interdisciplinary process, and professionals who view it from their various perspectives will emphasize one component over another.

CLASSIFICATION

A classification system is essentially a conceptual scheme for describing a group of individuals and their characteristics. Classification is the natural way to achieve economy of description, especially with a group so diverse as those with mental retardation. These individuals share the three components of the definition, but they are likely to vary a great deal in severity of retardation, etiology, functioning levels, and needs for education and treatment. Classification provides a common communication system considering these variables. It helps determine government funding on the one hand and contributes to scientific inquiry on the other.

Classification systems often have been attacked, particularly in regard to their association with labeling practices, as they may tend to (a) restrict opportunity for schooling, housing, and working; (b) elicit stereotypical negative attitudes and expectations by parents, teachers, and peers; and (c) result in restrictions in certain civil and social rights. Labels continually change throughout history as old ones take on negative associations. For example, "feebleminded," "moron," "imbecile," and "idiot" were terms used in one of the first classification systems in the United States and Great Britain. The term "mental retardation" has begun to be viewed in a similar negative light by some professionals who prefer the concept of "intellectually disabled" or "intellectually challenged."

CLASSIFICATION ACCORDING TO DEGREE OF RETARDATION

The most commonly referenced classification system based on degree of retardation is the one outlined by the AAMD manual (Grossman, 1983). The IQ ranges for this system were intended to be flexible. Based on IQ scores, the levels were:

mild	56–70
moderate	41–55
severe	26–40
profound	25 and below

Although the 1983 manual cautioned that the classification level should be based on both IQ and adaptive behavior, intellectual functioning predominated in classification decisions and IQ ranges often did become the sole basis for labeling. The inherent problems with using IQ scores to designate levels led to alternative systems.

In reaction to the imprecision of the above system, levels of retardation were reduced to two: mild and severe. With these two levels of disability, the focus is more on a functional orientation. The distinctions rely on common conventions in the field and generalized needs for individuals rather than on IQ ranges. The descriptions Dever (1990) provided are consistent with this attempt to define levels consistent with functioning and coincidentally relevant for instruction:

> It is not IQ that determines level of retardation but, rather, the amount and intensity of instruction required to move a person out of the category of "retarded." Thus, persons with mild retardation are those who know a great deal about living in the community without supervision and who require some instruction that could be provided under relatively nonintensive conditions. On the other hand, persons with severe [or profound] retardation are those who have acquired very few of the skills that are required for living in the community unsupervised and who require an enormous amount of instruction that may have to be provided under very intense conditions. (p. 150)

Mental Retardation: A Century of Terminology

simpleton	mongol	educable mentally retarded
fool	mentally deficient	trainable
dumb	mentally subnormal	trainable mentally retarded
stupid	familial	mentally disabled
dull	cultural-familial	the retarded
idiot	garden variety	retardate
imbecile	organic	general learning disability
mentally defective	mentally retarded	cognitively impaired
feebleminded	custodial	cognitively disabled
moron	high grade	developmentally delayed
incompetent	low grade	developmentally disabled
mental orthopedic	congenital idiot	intellectually disabled
amentia	mentally impaired	intellectually challenged
oligophrenic	exogenously mentally retarded	differently abled
mongolian idiot	mentally handicapped	
cretin	educable	

AAMR 1992 CLASSIFICATION SYSTEM

The recently revised AAMR manual (Luckasson et al., 1992) reflects a conceptual change in the classification scheme for mental retardation. Three points are particularly apt:

1. *Eliminating levels of disability.* Among the rationales are the attempt to move away from stereotyped images that unfortunately are often paired to levels, and the goal of refocusing attention on an individual's needs rather than deficits.
2. *Multidimensional system.* In addition to intellectual functioning and adaptive skills, other axes include emotional and psychological, etiological (causal), and related health factors.
3. *Need for supports.* For planning purposes, classification would designate whether an individual had needs for intermittent, limited, extensive, or pervasive levels of supports across the specific adaptive skills areas and the other dimensions noted. Table 6.1 outlines these four levels of support, reflecting the increasing intensity inherent in these concepts.

● **TABLE 6.1**

Definitions and examples of intensity of supports

Support	Definitions	Examples
Intermittent:	Supports on an as-needed, episodic basis. Person does not always need the support(s), or the person needs short-term supports during life-span transitions. When provided, intermittent supports may be high- or low-intensity.	Job loss Acute medical crisis
Limited:	Supports characterized by consistency over time, time-limited but not intermittent; may require less staff and less cost than more intense levels of support.	Employment training Transitional during the school-to-adult provider period
Extensive:	Supports characterized by regular involvement (e.g., daily) in at least some environments (such as work or home), and not time-limited.	Long-term home living
Pervasive:	Supports characterized by their constancy and high intensity, across environments and potentially life-sustaining. Pervasive supports typically involve more staff and intrusiveness than extensive or limited supports.	Chronic medical condition

Source: From R. Luckasson et al. (1992), *Definition and Classification in Mental Retardation* (9th ed.), Washington, DC: AAMR.

INCIDENCE AND PREVALENCE

To plan and implement programs, we need to know how many individuals need special services. Two types of estimates—incidence and prevalence—are used (and often confused) to describe the numbers individuals with mental retardation.

Incidence is the number of individuals who, at some time in their life, have been identified as having mental retardation. Incidence also is described as the number of new cases identified at some point in time (Morton & Hebel, 1979). This might include cases diagnosed at birth or cases diagnosed during preschool or some time after entering school. Estimates of the incidence of mentally retarded individuals historically have approximated the 3% level given by the President's Committee on Mental Retardation (1969).

Prevalence reflects the current or existing numbers of individuals with mental retardation at a given point in time. Tarjan, Wright, Eyman, and Keeran (1973) and Mercer (1973b) estimated prevalence to be closer to 1% because of the difficulty in determining who is mentally retarded at any point in time. McLaren and Bryson's (1987) review of epidemiological studies suggests that the prevalence of severe mental retardation is about 3 to 4 per 1,000 and the prevalence of mild mental retardation ranges from 3.7 to 5.9 per 1,000.

The rates of mental retardation have dropped significantly since passage of PL 94–142, a reduction of 38% as of 1989–90 (U.S. Department of Education, 1991). This is assumed to be largely a result of fewer children with mild retardation being identified, for a number of reasons: (a) reluctance to identify (or misidentification of) minority children as having mild mental retardation, (b) increased placement of children with mild handicaps in the learning disability category (MacMillan, 1989), and (c) lack of documentation for learning disability and no placement when a discrepancy exists between achievement and potential (Forness, 1985). Children who do get identified as having mild retardation are likely to comprise a lower functioning group. This explains why they are staying in segregated special education settings. In fact, what is now the population of children identified with mild retardation and what used to be the population with moderate retardation probably overlap a good deal.

According to MacMillan (1989), estimates of prevalence vary according to:

- Which definition is used. For example, the emphasis on adaptive behavior tends to reduce prevalence.
- The methodology used. Different methodologies produce different results.
- The individual's age. For example, children who have mild mental retardation generally are identified during the school years; before and after these years they may not be formally identified or serviced.
- The community. For example, lower socioeconomic urban and rural areas are likely to identify larger numbers of people as mentally retarded.
- The state. Different states have vastly different rates of identification.
- Sociopolitical factors. These factors have become more salient in recent years. For example, as a result of recent litigation regarding testing and placement of minority children, far fewer children are being serviced under the rubric of mild retardation.

CAUSES AND PREVENTION

In most cases of mental retardation, determining cause is an uncertain process. Only about 50% of the time is a cause known, most frequently of biological derivation. In cases attributed to psychological and social influences, we can refer only to possible correlates and associations. When IQ is below 50, cause can be specified in up to 75% of the cases. This figure, however, drops to 25–40% of the cases above IQ 50 (McLaren & Bryson, 1987).

GENETIC CAUSES

Genes are the basic biological unit of inheritance. They direct the biochemical processes of the body that are critical to the development of basic physical and mental characteristics. An individual's genetic make-up consists of 23 pairs of chromosomes. The mother contributes one chromosome from each pair; the father contributes the other. The female has two X chromosomes; the male has one X and one Y chromosome. This configuration determines the individual's gender. Two X's produce a female; an X and a Y, a male.

Each pair of chromosomes carries a series of gene pairs consisting of a dominant and a recessive gene. Certain disorders result from the way in which dominant and recessive defective genes are recombined. The dominant gene determines whether a specific characteristic will be expressed in the offspring, as it will be manifest whether it is paired with another dominant gene or with a recessive gene. A characteristic associated with a recessive gene will be expressed in the offspring only if the recessive gene of one parent is paired with a recessive gene of the other parent. Thus, both parents may have a certain abnormal recessive characteristic that is not apparent in either of them (they are called *carriers* of the trait or disorder) but could produce a child who bears the abnormal characteristic in question. The most common types of genetic and chromosomal disorders are discussed next.

Single-Gene Disorders. Manifestations of single-gene disorders depend on whether the gene is dominant, recessive, or X-linked.

Dominant Disorders. In this category the disorder is carried on the dominant gene, and structural problems (problems in the body's organs) are common. These disorders are rare, in part because the affected individuals are unlikely to reproduce. Examples are *neurofibromatosis, tuberous sclerosis*, and *Huntington's chorea*. These disorders sometimes result in severe brain damage, although these disorders may be expressed in various ways. In some cases the symptoms are mild; in other instances the full range of symptoms is expressed. The classic example is John Merrick, the "Elephant Man," thought to have had neurofibromatosis, which dramatically affected his physical appearance but not his cognitive development.

Recessive Disorders. The presence of two abnormal recessive genes often is associated with defects in metabolism, the body's inability to process certain food products.

Several recessive disorders have been associated with mental retardation.

Phenylketonuria (PKU) is the faulty metabolism of phenylalanine. The buildup of phenylalanine in the liver is toxic to the developing brain and results in marked mental retardation, seizures, and behavioral abnormalities, if not checked in the early stages. Diet can reduce its severity; in fact, if treatment begins within 3 weeks, the child can be expected to follow typical development milestones and may not have disabilities in intellectual functioning (Koch et al., 1988; Fishler, Azen, Henderson, Friedman, & Koch, 1987; Williamson, Koch, Azen, & Chang, 1981), although this may be compromised by a return to unrestricted diets (Clarke, Gates, Hogan, Barrett, & MacDonald, 1987). Recently, concern for women whose PKU was controlled during childhood has arisen when these women have become pregnant. At this time the diet must be reinstated to prevent negative effects on the fetus (Schultz, 1983; Koch et al., 1988). Designations on grocery items such as diet soda and low-fat yogurt ("caution: contains phenylalanine") are clear indicators of this concern.

Tay-Sachs disease is a defect in the metabolism of fats. It occurs more frequently in families of Ashkenazic (European) Jewish origin, in whom the frequency of carriers is approximately 1 in 30. Late in the first year of the child's life, a progression of blindness, paralysis, convulsions, and mental retardation begins. The life expectancy of these children is not beyond 4 years.

Galactosemia is an inborn error in the metabolism of carbohydrates. Symptoms beginning in early infancy are failure to thrive, jaundice, enlarged liver, and susceptibility to fatal neonatal infection, and those who survive infancy may have mental retardation. If the condition is diagnosed early, however, a milk-free diet can lessen or virtually eliminate the developmental delay (Abuelo, 1983; Koch et al., 1988; Schultz, 1983).

X-linked Genetic Disorders. In this type of disorder, the abnormal gene is located on the X chromosome. Males are affected primarily because they have only one X chromosome and the Y chromosome has no comparable genetic material, increasing the risk for expressing a recessive gene. As only one recessive gene has to be present for the disorder, it represents a special case of recessive inheritance.

The *Lesch-Nyhan syndrome* is X-linked, caused by an inborn error in the metabolism of purine. The condition is characterized by mental retardation, spasticity, and self-mutilation. Drug treatment along with behavioral interventions have had varying degrees of effectiveness in lessening the behavioral problems associated with this syndrome (Polloway & Patton, 1990).

CHROMOSOMAL ABNORMALITIES

The most common genetic disorder is *Down syndrome*. In its most typical form the 21st chromosome has extra genetic material—hence the term *trisomy 21*. Individuals who have Down syndrome often have a distinct appearance, which may include small stature, short hands and neck, almond-shaped eyes, large protruding tongue, broad nose, and a shortened fifth finger. This population often has associated cardiac and respiratory problems. Intellectual capability varies but usually remains within the moderate-to-severe range, although the positive effects of early intervention are radically changing this assumption (Rynders & Horrobin, 1990; Rynders, Spiker, & Horrobin, 1978). Consequently, children with Down syndrome often have mild retardation or may function above the cutoff score (IQ 70–75) for mental retardation. The character of Corky on "Life Goes On" underscores this potential, previously thought to be implausible.

The birth of a Down syndrome child is strongly associated with the mother's age. The rate of risk is 1 in 1,200 between maternal ages 20 and 30; it increases to 1 in 30 after 40 years of age. The relatively high prevalence of Down syndrome assures it significant research attention. Some current avenues of inquiry include plastic surgery, aging and relationship with Alzheimer's disease, and educational and biomedical treatments.

The *Fragile-X syndrome* is a relatively recently identified condition associated with mental retardation. It involves a weakened "arm" on the X chromosome. Detection has been possible only since 1977, so the realization that this syndrome may account for a high proportion of males with mental retardation (second overall to Down syndrome) is a fairly recent development (Gerald, 1980). Characteristics associated with this syndrome are mental retardation, enlarged testes after puberty, long, low-set ears, normal to enlarged head circumference, and a long, narrow face (De la Cruz, 1985; Rogers & Simensen, 1987). Because the X chromosome is affected, males are much more likely to be affected, as they lack a "normal" X chromosome pair to compensate. Women typically are carriers, although up to one third may be affected and have mild retardation or learning disabilities (Rogers & Simensen, 1987).

OTHER RELATED CAUSES

Literally thousands of other causes may be rooted in genetic processes. Only three examples are given here. *Microcephaly* is a cranial disorder in which head size is significantly smaller than the mean and in which severe retardation often is associated. *Hydrocephalus* refers to a series of disorders associated with interference in the flow of cerebrospinal fluid. Shunts are used successfully to drain off fluid, decrease cranial pressure, and prevent severe effects. Both of these two conditions can have a genetic cause, although they are seen most commonly in their secondary form as an effect of physical or environmental factors (e.g., fetal alcohol syndrome).

Prader-Willi syndrome is an endocrine disorder that has been associated with chromosomal imbalance. It has become best known for its association with overeating; individuals with Prader-Willi syndrome have been characterized as constantly foraging for food (Goldman, 1988).

PHYSICAL/ENVIRONMENTAL CAUSES

Development of the human organism from conception to full growth is a highly complex process, vulnerable at all times to assaults from the surrounding physical environment. A number of these—before, during, and after birth—have been identified as the cause of, or at least related to, mental retardation. McLaren and Bryson (1987) estimated that up to half of the cases of mental retardation are associated with *more than one* causal factor.

Prenatal Problems. Proper nutrition is critical to normal development of the growing fetus. Although no clear evidence exists of a direct link between malnutrition and delays in mental development (Susser & Stein, 1981), researchers propose that a relationship, albeit a complex one, does exist. Health, nutrition, social setting, and biological factors all interact to contribute to mental development (Kugel, 1976).

An association between alcohol and delayed mental development has been clearly documented. Called *fetal alcohol syndrome (FAS)*, it has been found consistently in children of mothers who are chronic alcoholics (Jones, Smith, Ulleland, & Streissguth, 1973; Stark, Menolascino, & Goldsbury, 1988). These children often have mild to moderate retardation, with associated motor dysfunctions and distorted craniofacial features. Scientists are uncertain how much alcohol will cause damage, but they suspect that consumption of even mild to moderate amounts (up to 2 ounces) may put the fetus at risk for developing FAS (Hanson, Streissguth, & Smith, 1978) or at least fetal alcohol effects (FAE), a less serious, though nevertheless problematic, condition (Griesbach & Polloway, 1991).

Maternal infections and diseases may injure the fetus. Maternal contraction of rubella (German measles) during the first trimester of pregnancy is commonly associated with deafness, and it also has been associated with mental retardation in a large number of cases. *Syphilis* also has severe consequences for the developing fetus. Chronic maternal illnesses such as *diabetes, kidney disease, thyroid deficiency*, and *hypertension* may affect the nutritional environment of the fetus or cause premature delivery. Blood type *Rh compatibility* between fetus and mother in pregnancies after the first may cause maternal antibodies to damage the fetus. The immune system of an Rh negative mother who has been previously sensitized to Rh positive blood through a previous pregnancy or blood transfusion may produce antibodies that destroy the Rh positive blood cells of the fetus. Maternal *acquired immune deficiency syndrome (AIDS)* has been identified as a possible cause of mental retardation. As many as 93% of infants infected with HIV have associated central nervous system problems (Diamond & Cohen, 1989).

Pregnant women exposed to *toxic pollutants* such as mercury, lead-based paint, asbestos, and radiation risk the health of the developing fetus. Furthermore, drugs, both prescribed and recreational, and cigarettes may significantly affect the fetus. Currently research is focusing in particular on the possible effects of prenatal exposure to cocaine (Dixon, 1989).

Problems at Birth. Premature delivery (gestation age of fewer than 37 weeks) places the newborn at risk for developmental problems. Like prenatal nutrition, the association between prematurity and mental retardation is complex and critical aspects of this association are difficult to isolate. For example, prematurity often occurs in association with poor socioeconomic conditions that are harmful to the health of mother and child alike. Figure 6.1 depicts the physical/environmental factors in prematurity and low birth weight.

Hypoxia, or *anoxia* (oxygen deprivation), another common perinatal cause of mental retardation, is associated with more than 18% of births with mental retardation (McLaren & Bryson, 1987). Oxygen deprivation may occur during the birth process for any number of reasons, including prolonged labor, damage to the umbilical cord, or the use of certain analgesics.

Postnatal Problems. Mental retardation may result from damage to the infant's developing brain, as in head injuries (e.g., auto accidents, child abuse), brain tumors, infection (meningitis, encephalitis), malnutrition, environmental pollutants, or drugs. Any one of the biological "risk" factors at the pre-, peri-, and postnatal stages does not necessarily have a direct relationship with intellectual functioning. A combination of factors may have to be present for a perceptible disorder (Kalverboer, 1988). Further, biological factors likely interact with conditions in the newborn's environment, such as parental mental health and capability and conditions associated with low socioeconomic status (Werner, 1986).

PREVENTION OF GENETIC AND PHYSICAL/ENVIRONMENTAL DISORDERS

Despite the indirect relationship between some of the genetic and physical correlates of mental retardation, preventive approaches can be pursued with varying degrees of success. Intervention with infants at risk for prenatal, perinatal, and postnatal compli-

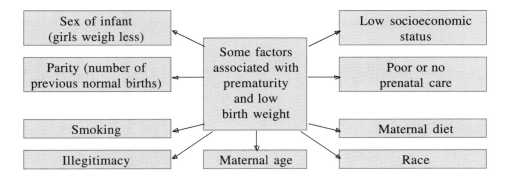

● **FIGURE 6.1**

Physical/environmental factors in prematurity and low birth weight

Source: From President's Committee on Mental Retardation, 1976, *Mental Retardation: The Known and the Unknown*, p. 31, Washington, DC: U.S. Government Printing Office.

cations can take the form of *primary intervention* (before the insult occurs), *secondary intervention* (while the incident is occurring), and *tertiary intervention* (after the disorder has occurred) (Korner, 1987).

An example of primary intervention is genetic counseling, which has come about as a result of our increasing knowledge of the workings of the genetic system. In genetic counseling, couples are advised about the probability of having offspring with specific disorders, based on family history and personal screening. For example, Tay-Sachs screening is easy and inexpensive. It allows couples to make informed decisions based on the risk of having an affected child.

Screening techniques also can identify the presence of genetic disorders after conception. *Amniocentesis*, drawing a sample of amniotic fluid for analysis, is done during the 14th to 16th week of pregnancy. *Chorionic villi sampling* is a more recent screening procedure (Cowart, 1983). It can be done earlier (between the 8th and 10th week) at less risk to the fetus, because the sample is taken from tissues of the chorion, the precursor of the placenta, therefore not requiring puncturing of the womb. *Ultrasound* and *sonography* are other medical techniques that assist in understanding the prenatal environment.

After the child is born, measures can be taken to prevent retardation based on genetics. Successful intervention may depend, however, on early diagnosis. For example, as noted, diet is helpful in cases of PKU or galactosemia diagnosed at birth or shortly after. Early diagnosis of hydrocephaly allows for implantation of a shunt that can alleviate the potentially problematic conditions associated with the condition.

To prevent physical/environmental problems, treatment of the precondition is often enough. For example, vaccination for rubella is encouraged for women in their childbearing years. Blood transfusions are given when there is evidence of blood incompatibility. Pregnant women can be educated about proper nutrition and prenatal care as well as about the dangers of alcohol, drugs, and exposure to environmental pollutants.

Numerous preventive methods exist, and their number is increasing constantly. The challenge that remains, however, is one of communication. How can these available methods be taught to the population of women who need them?

PSYCHOSOCIAL FACTORS AND PREVENTION OF MENTAL RETARDATION

In approximately half of the cases of mental retardation, most of which occur in the mild range, no obvious organic or genetic cause is found for the retardation. Professionals must hypothesize. Without evidence, they can think only in terms of correlates and possible associations.

A strong association has been established between mental retardation and an environment of poverty. Specific risk factors include poor prenatal care, malnutrition, exposure to unhealthy lifestyles, and crowded and disorganized physical environments. The significance of these conditions associated with poverty is underscored by the estimate that 23% of all American preschoolers are in families with incomes below poverty level (Committee on Minority Participation in Education and American Life, 1988).

Psychological factors associated with lower socioeconomic status may deter the child's maximal development. For example, the home environment and childrearing practices may not encourage learning and thinking. Differences in the facilitation of language development have been found between families of lower and of middle social class (Hess & Shipman, 1965). In contrast to low-income mothers, middle-income mothers were more interactive, more verbal, more play-oriented, and more responsive to their babies' verbalizations (Tulkin & Kagan, 1972). These parenting practices associated with developmental retardation have been referred to as the "continuum of caretaking casualty" (Sameroff & Chandler, 1975).

Paralleling the notion that the child's living environment moderates genetic and physical causal conditions, most professionals agree that psychosocial retardation is a result of interaction between environmental and genetic and other biological factors. For example, Ramey, MacPhee, and Yeates (1982) suggested that to assume that only the environment or only heredity influences mental retardation is simplistic. Rather, they suggested "(a) that development involves the action of complex regulatory processes (environmental and constitutional); and (b) that later outcomes have multiple causes such that there are few isomorphic continuities in development" (p. 15). These assumptions led them to adopt Sameroff and Chandler's (1975) transactional model, which proposes that the child not only is modified by the environment but acts on and modifies it as well. Any model of causation that separates psychosocial from biological factors is bound to be simplistic and to overlook the interactive nature of these factors.

Preventing mental retardation depends on the known, or suspected, etiology. With psychosocial mental retardation, when the association between suspected causes and the ultimate outcome is not direct but, rather, multidimensional and interactional, *risk models* such as those presented by Ramey et al. (1982) and Sameroff and Chandler (1975) are instructive. The model proposed by Ramey et al. identified risk factors at the child, caregiver, household, school, neighborhood, and societal levels that are involved in transactional processes and eventually associated with negative developmental outcomes. Risk factors identified in this model can assist in targeting prevention efforts.

These models also acknowledge the importance of resiliency or protective factors in connecting risk to outcome. Balancing risks within the child and his or her environment is the natural "self-righting" tendency (Rutter, 1984). For the child, these factors may include coping strategies or positive social skills. In the environment, a stable, positive adult or a language-rich, stimulating environment may contribute to more positive child outcomes. The mediating role of adults in helping the child to understand his or her world is particularly critical. These relationships provide further guidance in our efforts to prevent mental retardation.

Prevention of psychosocial mental retardation assumes that (a) the environment can have an effect on a child's intellectual functioning, and (b) the effects are likely to be greater if intervention is attempted in the first few years of life (Bloom, 1964).

Given these two major assumptions, a number of early intervention projects have been attempted. In general, they each hearken back to the Skeels and Dye (1939) study, which set the tone for the concept of early intervention. The purpose is to deter developmental delays in lower socioeconomic children through intensive infant and preschool programs (e.g., Bereiter & Engelmann, 1966; Karnes & Zehrbach, 1977; Weikart, 1981). The aim of Head Start, for example, is to provide early educational stimulation to impoverished children. Other programs have attempted to provide assistance both in school and at home (e.g., Garber, 1988; Ramey & Campbell, 1984).

Evaluating these kinds of programs is a challenge because of differences in program philosophy and difficulties in isolating and measuring significant outcomes. The general pattern, however, suggests that, at least initially, the children enrolled in intensive early intervention programs achieve significant gains in intellectual functioning (Nevin & Thousand, 1988; Polloway, 1987). Although the children may not maintain these early intellectual gains, follow-up studies indicate that they are maintaining achievement performance, are avoiding placement in special education settings, and have enhanced adult outcomes (Schweinhart & Weikart, 1981; Schweinhart, Berreuta-Clement, Barrett, Epstein, & Weikart, 1985).

COGNITION

By definition, individuals with mental retardation have delayed intellectual functioning. Of interest to those working with these individuals is not the delayed intellectual functioning itself but, rather, the impact it has on the way the children learn and on their ability to perform the skills necessary to function in real-life situations.

Investigations into cognitive functioning tend to concentrate on specific parts of the process, such as attention or memory. The complexity of the total learning process, how the subprocesses come together, has not yet been understood fully. We cannot discover the "integrated whole," partly because of the variability in the population. Each individual brings to the learning situation a different pattern of abilities and disabilities, so generalizations are difficult to make. Nevertheless, some of the generalizations about the subprocesses of cognitive functioning are relevant to understanding individuals with mental retardation, and we describe them next.

ATTENTION

Attention, a multifaceted concept, is critical to the learning process (Keogh & Margolis, 1976). Two functions are particularly pertinent: temporal and selective. The *temporal* function relates to short-term versus sustained attention (Krupski, 1980). Individuals with mild or moderate retardation have few problems with "orienting responses" (short-term attention); problems surface during "vigilance tasks," activities that require their attention for an extended time (Kirby, Nettelbeck, & Bullock, 1978). The temporal function also relates to the amount of active versus passive responding the task requires. Individuals with mental retardation are less efficient on tasks requiring active manipulation of information and task components (Spitz, 1979).

The *selective* function, like the temporal, requires some degree of active involvement and thinking. Selective attention may mean scanning an array of stimuli in a systematic, goal-directed way (Keogh & Margolis, 1976). It also may mean the ability to focus on relevant stimuli among an array of distractors while ignoring irrelevant stimuli (Hallahan & Reeve, 1980).

Discrimination learning, the ability to differentiate relevant cues and dimensions, has been researched extensively by Zeaman and colleagues (Fisher & Zeaman, 1973; Zeaman & House, 1963). Their theory suggests that discrimination learning occurs in two stages. Stage I is the attention phase. It involves searching for and attending to the relevant dimension of the stimulus. For example, the task Zeaman and House typically used involves discriminating between objects that vary in the dimensions of color and shape. To solve the task, subjects first choose the correct dimension (color or shape), then the correct cue (which color or shape). Stage II is the learning that takes place after attending to the relevant dimension. Their findings indicate that the subjects with retardation differed from the other subjects mainly in Stage I; the former took more trials to attend to the relevant dimension. Once the dimension was discovered, however, the learning curve approximated that of the other subjects.

Recent research on attention (Merrill, 1990) views attention from a perspective of *resource allocation*; attention is one aspect of cognitive processing that can be allocated to specific tasks in a flexible and continuous manner. Because the available resources are limited, it is beneficial when some of these processes become automatic, thereby leaving room for the use of other resources to complete the task. Individuals with mental retardation are less likely to achieve automaticity in their attentional processes, so they are limited in the number of other resources they can utilize in solving complex tasks.

Krupski (1980) noted the importance of analyzing the attention process in the context of task and situation. For example, a child's attention to a task may be affected by (a) the extent of active involvement required, (b) the degree of structure in the task, (c) the amount of attending time expected, (d) the task difficulty, and (e) the nature of feedback and reinforcement offered.

MEMORY

The ability to remember is critical to cognitive functioning. As a result, it always has been an area of intensive study. Studies that include the memory process of persons with mental retardation reveal that these individuals are deficient in certain components of the memory process: attention, very short-term memory, short-term memory, and the strategies necessary to facilitate short-term memory. Figure 6.2 illustrates these components.

To be remembered, information first must be attended to (attention). It then enters *very short-term memory* (VSTM), which serves a brief (milliseconds) storage function. Researchers who study memory processes in people with mental retardation have

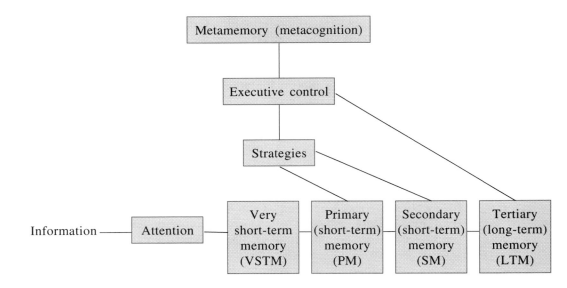

The major components of memory

Source: Adapted from J. G. Borkowski, V. A. Peck, and P. R. Damberg, 1983, "Attention, Memory, and Cognition," in J. L. Matson and J. A. Mulick (Eds.), *Handbook of Mental Retardation*, p. 480, New York: Pergamon Press. Used by permission.

found deficiencies in their very short-term memory; others claim that the major deficiencies are associated with the attention process. The next level of memory, *primary memory* (PM), is the first stage of short-term memory. Information is stored here until the individual can actively integrate it into *secondary memory* (SM), where it is stored for a longer time (Ellis, 1970). Although some researchers maintain that the memory of individuals with mental retardation is limited by structural deficits (Winters & Semchuck, 1986), most researchers and theorists agree that the major deficiency occurs in transferring information from primary to secondary memory. This is because, as research has demonstrated, individuals who have mental retardation fail to spontaneously use memory strategies that facilitate transfer.

Spitz (1966) discussed differences between individuals with and without mental retardation in the ability to cluster or organize the information being memorized. Failure to "chunk" information reduces the capacity for remembering; however, when individuals with mental retardation are instructed to do so, their performance approximates that of their peers without retardation (Gerjuoy & Spitz, 1966). Deficiencies in the use of *rehearsal strategies* also have been described (Bray & Turner, 1986). In recalling a series of digits presented consecutively, individuals with mental retardation have poor recall of the first digits but better recall of the more recently presented digits, indicating that they had difficulty using strategies to retain those presented first. Researchers have been successful in training these individuals to use rehearsal strategies (Belmont & Butterfield, 1971).

Mediation is another useful strategy to promote learning pedagogically. It involves linking two elements through some meaningful association. For example, two words may be associated (paired associates) in such a way that one word brings to mind the other; they are related in some meaningful way (Meyers & MacMillan, 1976).

Once information is acted on in short-term memory and transferred to *tertiary memory* (long-term memory, or LTM), retention is fairly stable. The question about whether individuals with mental retardation have deficits in long-term memory has been difficult to answer because of methodological problems in research studies. Borkowski, Peck, and Damberg (1983) wondered if conclusive answers regarding long-term memory are even possible, given the many deficits existing earlier in the memory chain.

Two other, more complex, processes act on long-term memory: metamemory and executive control (see Figure 6.2). *Metamemory*, or *metacognition*, refers to the individual's awareness and control of his or her own memory processes (Brown, 1975; Campione, Brown, & Ferrara, 1982). Learners with mental retardation are characterized in general as passive learners who do not spontaneously use appropriate strategies (Loper, 1980). Attempts to train them have met with some success; however, generalization of this training has been limited (Spitz, 1988).

Executive control was described by Butterfield and Belmont (1977): "The subject spontaneously changes a control process or sequence of control processes as a reasonable response to an objective change in an information task" (p. 284). Different kinds of tasks necessitate different processing approaches; executive control operates to coordinate these processes. Borkowski et al. (1983) noted that children with intellectual delays can be taught to change their control processes appropriately in multiple training sessions. Some even seem able to analyze a task and choose a strategy. To discover just how they acquire, maintain, and generalize these processes, however, is going to require some further research.

PROBLEM-SOLVING

Recognizing the importance of metamemory and executive control leads naturally to more complex and integrative models of the learning process. According to Spitz (1988), in addition to spontaneously using strategies, a critical difference between learners who have retardation and those who do not is the ability to reason (plan ahead, have foresight, and understand relations). His studies revealed that, in this ability, individuals who have mental retardation are behind both their chronological-age and mental-age cohorts.

Brown (1978) set forth a four-step process of problem-solving involving metacognitive abilities:

1. Analyze and characterize the pertinent problem.

2. Reflect upon what knowledge one has or needs to have to solve the problem.
3. Devise a plan for solving the problem.
4. Check and monitor one's progress toward the solution.

Brown then supplemented Spitz's list with some "if-then" hypothesis testing, to predict the consequences connected with various methods of solving problems.

SPEECH AND LANGUAGE

Language development and cognitive development have a strong connection, and delayed language development is commonly associated with mental retardation. This association has been documented in a number of language areas: vocabulary development, auditory discrimination, receptive language, grammatical structure, and sentence length (Rosenberg, 1982; Spradlin, 1968; Spreen, 1965). The language delays are cognitive, not developmental (Bowerman, 1976); similar patterns of language development might be found in younger children of equal mental age. Children with mental retardation simply acquire language at a slower rate. On the other hand, articulation and voice disorders, of which populations with mental retardation have a higher incidence, probably result from marked delays in motor development (Edwards & Edwards, 1970). Because of the changing nature of children identified with mild mental retardation, we are seeing a higher percentage of speech and language problems in this population (Epstein, Polloway, Patton, & Foley, 1989).

Development of individual language processes is related to development of language as a tool to mediate cognitive processes. In work stemming from Russian psychologist Luria's (1961) finding that people with mental retardation are verbally deficient in the ability to control their motor behavior, Denny (1964) reported that they are less likely to verbalize their actions in discrimination tasks. Also, they use linguistically less sophisticated strategies to organize and relate verbal material (Sitko & Semmel, 1973); they use a sequential-associative strategy to associate words (e.g., dog—bark, red—apple). This tendency negatively affects performance on cognitive tasks. A more efficient strategy would be a hierarchical one associating words according to class membership (e.g., dog—cat, red—black).

Researchers and practitioners now view speech and language within a much broader context of communication. Yoder and Calculator (1981) stated, "Language development is viewed as inextricably intertwined with social and cognitive development, all representing the outgrowth of a child's general interactions with his environment" (p. 108). This approach highlights the pragmatic aspects of language, or "when to speak, when not, and as to what to talk about with whom, when, where, in what manner" (Hymes, 1972). Children with mental retardation are delayed in this area of functioning (Longhurst & Berry, 1975). Dealing with language in this context has a distinct advantage: it is more relevant to the child's life (Caro & Snell, 1989; Peck & Schuler, 1983).

PERSONAL-SOCIAL DEVELOPMENT

Personal and social competencies are critical to a child's functioning. Social behavior, for example, is a major factor in referral, identification, and placement (Morrison, MacMillan, & Kavale, 1985). Similarly, problems that individuals with mental retardation have with personal-social skills often are cited as a major reason for their failure to maintain jobs (Foss & Peterson, 1981). Adaptive behavior is included in the AAMR definition of mental retardation in recognition of the importance of noncognitive characteristics in describing and identifying individuals who have mental retardation. Although adaptive behavior, as currently used in the definition of mental retardation, should be distinguished from social competence per se (Greenspan & Granfield, 1992), Siperstein (1992) argued that social competence is an integral part of adaptive behavior and deserves continued, focused attention.

To facilitate the description of personal and social characteristics, these two concepts often are defined separately. As with the cognitive processes discussed previously, however, personal and social characteristics operate in concert and depend on one another. An individual's personal-social status is affected by his or her own competencies and by significant others' reactions to those competencies.

SELF-CONCEPT

Positive regard for oneself is crucial to overall adjustment in life. Self-esteem is the evaluative component of self-concept (Germain, 1978). The common assumption is that, given their lower competency, individuals with mental retardation have low self-esteem. Evidence as to the validity of this assumption is extremely difficult to gather, however, given the heterogeneity of the population, the variety of environments in which these individuals spend their time, and the difficulty involved in getting valid measurements. As a result, research does not present consistent findings (Widaman, MacMillan, Hemsley, Little, & Balow, 1992).

For example, Meyerowitz (1962) found that children with mild retardation placed in segregated special education classrooms had more negative self-concepts than did a similar group placed in regular classrooms. Other researchers have found that children with mild handicaps have higher self-esteem if they are placed in segregated classrooms (Morrison, 1985; Schurr, Towne, & Joiner, 1972). Carroll (1967) and Strang, Smith, and Rogers (1978) found that partially integrating these students enhanced their self-esteem. Silon and Harter (1985) found that mainstreamed and special day class students with mild mental retardation had similar levels of "perceived competence" when comparing themselves to their respective classmates.

One key to understanding patterns of self-concept seems to be the social context in which the measurements are taken. Variations in the findings of these studies are likely attributable to variations in classroom placement, extent of contact with mainstreamed peers, comparisons available to the students when making their self-evaluations, and the methodology used to measure self-concept. In particular, the aspect of self-concept measured (academic versus personal, physical, social) is likely to contribute to different levels of self-concept (Widaman et al., 1992). Clearly, more tightly controlled investigations are needed. In the meantime, level of self-esteem remains an important consideration in teaching children with developmental delays, given the vulnerable status of their competencies in relation to others in their environments.

MOTIVATION

Motivation, a critical concept in understanding individuals with mental retardation, has received scant attention given its importance. Motivation plays a role in employment success, academic achievement, personal adjustment, and general task performance (Kreitler & Kreitler, 1988). Zigler (1966) described a number of motivational characteristics that cause individuals with mental retardation to perform lower than expected on specific tasks (e.g., positive and negative reaction tendencies and wariness of social contact). Another important concept is expectancy for failure. Given a history of failure, individuals with mental retardation are likely to begin to expect to fail. Therefore, they are less willing to approach tasks, and they expend less effort in performing according to their capabilities.

Harter's (1978) model of effectance motivation encompasses a number of important relationships. She hypothesized that an individual is propelled to achieve competence. Any increase or decrease in this motivation is a result of the socialization history of that individual. Harter's model presents several important dimensions of motivation in addition to those already discussed. For example, a history of failure is likely to lead to dependence on external sources of reinforcement, such as tangible rewards, rather than internal sources, such as self-approval. After repeated failure, individuals also are likely to perceive that events are controlled by external events and people rather than by efforts of their own (external locus of control). These characteristics lead to less motivation, which decreases the likelihood of future success, a vicious cycle. The obvious intervention is somehow to break into this cycle to ensure successful experiences and positive interpretation of them.

SOCIAL COMPETENCE

Social competence refers to a number of dimensions such as "appropriateness of social behavior vis a vis norms of the social setting, the presence or absence of peer relationships, evidence of specific prosocial behaviors, adult or peer judgments of behavior, and even individuals' perceptions of their own self-competence" (Siperstein, 1992, p. iv). Greenspan and Granfield (1992) argued for the use of the term social intelligence, which "refers to a person's ability to understand and to deal effectively with social and interpersonal objects and events. Included in this construct are such variables as role-taking, empathic judgment, person perception, moral judgment, referential communication, and interpersonal tactics" (Greenspan, 1979, p. 483). Zigler & Trickett (1978) suggested a two-dimensional schema for conceptualizing social competence; one aspect reflects the individual's success in meeting societal expectations, and the other reflects the individual's personal development or skills.

Considering both personally based skills and the context in which they develop, we focus here on three aspects of social competence: social skills, social interaction, and social acceptance.

Social Skills. Social skills can be defined as goal-oriented, rule-governed, learned behaviors designed to elicit positive responses from others. These skills are situation-specific and vary according to social context (Cartledge & Milburn, 1983). Many individuals with mental retardation lack the necessary social skills to gain and maintain friendship and working relationships (Chadsey-Rusch, 1992). Healey and Masterpasqua (1992) found that interpersonal cognitive problem-solving skills could distinguish adjusted from nonadjusted classroom behavior among children with mild mental retardation. Positive adjustment was related to the ability to generate a high number of solutions to a problem situation.

Areas in which individuals with mental retardation have been found to be deficient in work settings include following instructions, conversational skills, dealing with criticism, and resolving conflicts and disagreements (Sherman, Sheldon, Harchik, Edwards, & Quinn, 1992). As individuals with mental retardation are being given more opportunities to live and work in integrated settings, a major problem has been in their acquiring and using appropriate social skills to negotiate these settings. Although the research literature indicates that social skills can be taught successfully, more work has to be done in generalizing skills from the teaching situation to real-life applications (Davies & Rogers, 1985).

Social Interaction. Much of the examination of social interactions between persons with and without intellectual delays has taken place in preschool mainstreamed situations. Research on the extent of interaction suggests that the amount decreases as the developmental level of the child with a disability decreases (Guralnick, 1980; Peterson & Haralick, 1977). Children with severe retardation interact with peers who have no retardation at a lower frequency than do those who have less severe retardation. Guralnick and Weinhouse (1984) noted that the social repertoire of young children who are severely delayed is extremely fragmented and limited, consisting primarily of unoccupied and solitary activities. Although less delayed children demonstrated a higher frequency and quality of interactions, levels of solitary play and limited interchanges were still dominant.

Kopp, Baker, and Brown (1992) studied the social interactions of preschool children with mild delays. They found that children with developmental delays did not differ from their agemates in terms of communication behaviors that maintained play or in negative affect. The children with developmental delays, however, evidenced more disruptive entry, more regressive behavior, and less positive affect. Thus, at this early age, limited social interchange is apparent in children with delays in development.

Social Acceptance. Although they may or may not interact socially, children form impressions and perceptions of each other. Research on school-age children with mental retardation has concentrated on the patterns of acceptance and rejection between them and their peers without retardation. The evidence has been fairly consistent: Children with mild or moderate levels of retardation are less accepted and more rejected than their peers who have no retardation (Polloway, Epstein, Patton, Cullinan, & Luebke, 1986).

The reasons for this reduced social status seem to reside in a complex interaction of the characteristics of children with mental retardation (e.g., cognitive competence and behavior) and the nature of the educational setting in which they are situated (Gottlieb, Semmel, & Veldman, 1978; MacMillan & Morrison, 1980a). For example, MacMillan and Morrison suggested that, although the student's lack of competence and misbehavior may be especially salient to that of peers in a mainstreamed setting, these differences may not be as salient to classmates in a special education classroom. When interpreting the social relationships of students with intellectual delays, then, characteristics and setting both must be considered.

IDENTIFICATION AND ASSESSMENT

Whether a child actually is identified and served depends on how the social system (the school) is structured to deal effectively with individuals who deviate from the norm. Mercer (1973a) called this phenomenon "the social system perspective of mental retardation." That is, a social system such as a school or a society allows an individual to maintain a status of normal as long as that individual fulfills society's expectations of his or her role in society. A child who has mild retardation (according to definitional standards) may remain unidentified if he or she does not fail according to the school situational standards.

SYSTEM IDENTIFICATION

System identification has been defined and described as the social process in schools that identifies children for special education services (MacMillan, Meyers, & Morrison, 1980; Morrison, MacMillan, & Kavale, 1985). The process of identification comprises a number of steps, all of which involve potential variations in implementation that can affect whether a child actually is identified as having a disability. Figure 6.3 illustrates these steps, which also are discussed briefly here.

Problem Surfaces. Children experiencing mild delays in development often are not identified until they have problems during their school years when the curriculum becomes more verbal and abstract. Whether a student is considered deviant enough to be referred for special help is determined partially by the teacher's tolerance level (Morrison, MacMillan, & Kavale, 1985); teachers may be more or less tolerant of variability in student characteristics. Behavior problems often determine who actually gets referred (Craig, Kasowitz, & Malgoire, 1978). Apparently, slowness in academics can be tolerated better if the child has no concomitant behavior problems. As the

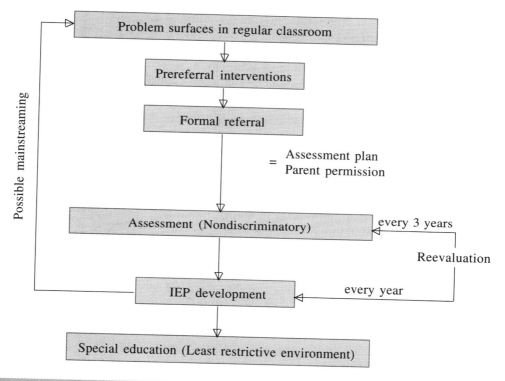

● **FIGURE 6.3**

System identification of the special education student

population of students with mild retardation has changed, however, the likelihood of earlier identification (prior to kindergarten) is increasing.

Prereferral Interventions. Prior to formal referral, a student study team may intervene. This step was added to the procedures of many school systems across the country to avoid placing students in special education services unnecessarily. The team functions by working on the problem within the context of the regular classroom. Team meetings provide the teacher with support and information about alternative interventions. This practice has been found to decrease the rate of referrals to special education (Chalfant & Pysh, 1990; Chalfant, VanDusen, Pysh, & Moultrie, 1979). Questions are being raised, however, about the effectiveness of these prereferral interventions (Reschly & Wilson, 1990). A child in one setting may be identified as disabled; in another setting he or she may not.

Referral. Sometimes problems are not solved at the prereferral stage. Then the child is formally referred for assessment and consideration for eligibility for special services. At this point, referral depends on whether services are available at a given school. Referrals of minority children also may be discouraged because of efforts to reduce their disproportionately high representation in special education classes.

Assessment. To initiate assessment, parental permission is sought. Due process must be considered. The nondiscriminatory assessment component of federal law requires that assessment be multidisciplinary, rely on more than one procedure for determining the child's educational program, and be free of cultural, racial, and sexual discrimination. Within these general guidelines lies a good deal of latitude for choosing measures. The type of test could influence the decisions, giving a good deal of weight to professional orientation and competence.

The AAMR definition of mental retardation specifically refers to two types of assessments that should be included for children suspected of having significant developmental delays: intelligence and adaptive behavior. Despite the guidelines presented by the AAMR definition, intelligence and adaptive behavior criteria vary wildly across the states (Frankenberger & Harper, 1988; Reschly, 1990). Some states use just one criterion, some use the other, and some use both. Also, levels of performance that are considered delayed differ from state to state.

Nondiscriminatory assessment emphasizes that assessment should go beyond a single procedure. It should consist of multiple assessments as necessary to describe and document the specific problems a child might have. Thus, assessment for a child with mild mental retardation might include (in addition to intelligence and adaptive behavior) a series of informal observations to document behavior in different settings and criterion-referenced achievement tests to specify which skills require remediation. Beyond gathering data to determine eligibility for special education services, assessment should be geared to provide information for maximizing instructional environments.

Individualized Education Programs (IEPs). Once the assessment information has been gathered, the IEP meeting is held to determine the child's level of functioning and the goals and objectives for instruction and programming. At this meeting decisions about eligibility and placement are made, based on the goals and objectives. As in any group meeting, decisions regarding children with similar characteristics will vary. For example, Ysseldyke and Algozzine (1982) noted that eligibility and placement decisions often had little relationship to the assessment information presented at IEP meetings. Program availability and parental wishes often are overriding factors in final decisions. Of the overall IEP process, Smith (1990) suggested that compliance rather than individualized programming had become the focus.

Reevaluation. Due process and least restrictive environment provisions have emphasized the importance of reevaluating eligibility and placement decisions periodically (once a year; total reevaluation once every 3 years). Students may enter and exit the ranks of children with disabilities depending on whether they are determined to need specialized services. Their success in regular education programs depends, in part, on how well they learn the survival skills of regular school environments and on how well teachers and peers tolerate their differences.

The process just described may vary according to local interpretation of the legal guidelines. In the case of the child with mild mental retardation, identification and education depend on the nature of the variations in the immediate educational system. Therefore, although personal characteristics determine definition, the social system ultimately determines the diagnosis.

ASSESSMENT OF INTELLIGENCE

In defining and describing mental retardation, intelligence traditionally has received the most attention. Central themes repeatedly cited are (a) the capacity to learn, (b) the total amount of knowledge acquired, and (c) the ability to adapt and adjust to new situations (Robinson & Robinson, 1976). There is little agreement on definitions, but measurement plays a major role in describing intelligence in a practical manner, leading to the notion that intelligence is what an intelligence test measures.

Two tests have been the primary tools used to measure intelligence: the Stanford-Binet and the Wechsler scales.[1] The *Stanford-Binet* (the most recent revision is the Stanford-Binet IV) consists of items that progress in difficulty from manipulative skills to verbal and abstract skills, tapping abilities such as memory, perception, information, and logical reasoning. The *WISC–III* (the most recent revision) consists of two major

---

[1.] Wechsler Intelligence Scale for Children–III (WISC–III); Wechsler Preschool and Primary Scale of Intelligence–Revised (WPPSI–R); and Wechsler Adult Intelligence Scale–Revised (WAIS–R).

Verbal and performance skills are part of assessing intelligence.

areas, verbal and performance. The *verbal* subtests measure abilities related to verbal reasoning and comprehension; the *performance* subtests tap into nonverbal abilities such as visual organization, planning, and coordination. These tests yield an IQ, which originally was based on the relationship between the individual's chronological age (CA) and mental age (MA, the developmental age at which the individual is function-ing). The following formula represents this relationship: MA/CA ∞ 100 = IQ. For example, a child who is the chronological age of 10, but who functions like other children who are age 5, has a ratio IQ of 50. Although the Stanford-Binet was the test that used this formula originally, both it and the Wechsler scales now use deviation IQs (standard scores) derived from tables in their manuals.

The quantification of intelligence in these two tests is based on the assumption that, if measurements of intelligence were to be taken from a large population, the distribution of scores would approximate a normal curve. Figure 6.4 shows the percent of cases under portions of the normal curve. Most of the scores cluster around an average score and vary from this average (the mean) in a predictable way (the standard deviation). The means and standard deviations (SD) for the Stanford-Binet IV and WISC–III are 100 and 16 and 100 and 15, respectively. Because these distributions have the properties of the normal curve, we can compare individuals in a standard way.

Although these tests have been used widely, and have been developed to the point at which they have a high degree of stability, their use has been the subject of much controversy. The major issues surround the use of intelligence tests for identification and classification of individuals in the mild retardation range. Mercer (1973a) noted

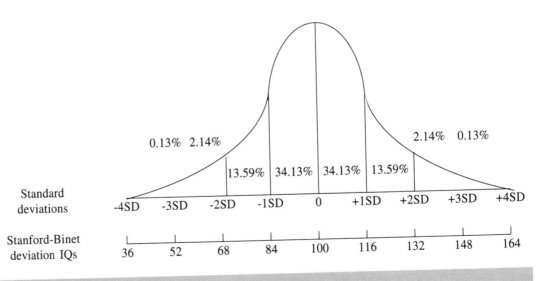

● **FIGURE 6.4**

The normal curve

that minority children so identified were represented in higher proportions than in the population at large, even though they were not considered retarded in their home and neighborhood environments. Charges of bias and discrimination include:

1. Content validity: Will test-takers who have been exposed to a different set of cultural experiences answer the questions correctly?
2. Predictive validity: Do these tests equally predict the performance of different groups of individuals?
3. Inadequacy of norm groups: Do the standardization groups, on which the norms are based, adequately represent minority groups?

The arguments are as complex as they are controversial. Certainly the use of intelligence tests with minority children is of concern in terms of validity of results. Therefore, the tests should be used with caution and should be accompanied by other forms of assessment. Criticism, however, might focus more appropriately on improper administration and interpretation of these tests, as well as on the results of their use— the placement of children in special education settings as a way of handling diversity of educational characteristics (Morrison, 1978).

Given the concern and potential limitations of traditional assessment of intelligence, several viable alternatives have been developed. For example, dynamic assessment attempts to measure the ability of a child to learn, given efficient teaching processes (Haywood, Brown, & Wingenfeld, 1990). Through a "test-teach-test" procedure, a child's cognitive modifiability is assessed and a determination is made about the nature and extent of intervention needed to facilitate learning. Although measuring dynamic rather than static processes in learning has great appeal, the diagnostic and interpretive utilities of these procedures are still in need of refinement.

Assessment of cognitive processing skills also has received recent attention and has led to some promising developments in the assessment of intellectual functioning. Theorists in this area have attempted to explain how abilities such as speed of processing, short-term memory, long-term memory, problem-solving strategies, and metacognitive skills contribute to intellectual functioning. The Cognitive Assessment System (CAS) (Das & Naglieri, in press) is an example of a recently developed test that attempts to measure some of these processes, specifically: planning, attention, and simultaneous and successive processing.

ASSESSMENT OF ADAPTIVE BEHAVIOR

Grossman (1983) defined adaptive behavior as "the effectiveness or degree to which an individual meets the standards of personal independence and social responsibility expected for age and cultural group" (p. 157). Measurement of adaptive behavior has not reached the level of sophistication, in terms of statistical properties, that intelligence testing has. This is attributable in part to the more elusive nature of the construct of adaptive behavior. Its major determiner is the extent to which the adaptation is appropriate to societal expectations. Expectations of subenvironments of a society are likely to change, making standards for these expectations difficult to isolate. Nevertheless, the Luckasson et al. (1992) definition places even more emphasis on adaptive skills, calling for further attention to development of suitable instruments.

Four domains of adaptive behaviors that seem to be measured consistently across a variety of instruments are described by Reschly (1990):

1. *Independent functioning*: Competencies that contribute to personal independence, such as basic toileting, feeding, dressing, community travel, consumer skills, and use of leisure time.
2. *Social functioning*: Skills related to the ability to establish and maintain social relationships; these may include communication skills, sharing, expressing feelings, and avoiding socially inappropriate behavior.
3. *Functional academic competencies*: Knowledge and application of academic skills in daily life, including literacy skills, concepts of time and number, and other skills that are necessary in daily living.
4. *Vocational/occupational competencies*: Knowledge, skills, and attitudes about work and career.

Although various adaptive behavior instruments are available, choice should be based on the functioning level of the target population, the setting of interest (school versus home and community), the method of assessment desired (observation or interview), and the source of information (parent, teacher, peer, child/adult). Reschly (1990) cited three instruments with recent norms and standardizations that are particularly good in terms of technical characteristics: (a) the Comprehensive Test of Adaptive Behavior (CTAB), (b) the Scales of Independent Behavior (SIB), and (c) the Vineland Adaptive Behavior Scales (VABS).

ASSESSMENT FOR TREATMENT

Assessment practices must include tests and procedures that tie into education and treatment efforts that will follow diagnosis. Traditional methods of assessing intelligence have been criticized for having little relevance to education and treatment, that is, poor treatment validity (Witt & Gresham, 1985).

As the focus of assessment turns from determining diagnosis and eligibility for special services, a variety of domain-specific assessment (sometimes called *functional assessment*) procedures are available. For example, observational methods and rating scales are available to gain more detailed information on social behavior and vocational competencies. Tests are available to assess the level of academic functioning. Recent emphasis has been placed on the educational utility of *curriculum-based assessment*, a system for determining the instructional needs of a student based upon the student's ongoing performance within existing course content (Rosenfield & Kuralt, 1990). Test development efforts in the area of cognitive ability measure more relevant aspects of *cognitive functioning*, although the ultimate utility of these instruments in educational settings has yet to be proven (Reshly & Wilson, 1990).

EDUCATIONAL PROGRAMMING

Educational programming for students who have mental retardation requires integration of a number of interrelated variables. Decisions about these variables are made in the context of the system identification process addressed previously (see Figure 6.3). The three major variables entering into educational programs are curriculum, instruction, and administrative arrangements. These include early childhood education and transitional programming as well.

CURRICULUM

Curriculum refers to planned learning experiences that have intended outcomes such as to change or develop behaviors or insights (Armstrong, 1990; Hoover, 1988; Wood & Hurley, 1977). The content (and skill) areas that Reynolds and Birch (1982, p. 101) consider imperative for the meaningful participation of individuals with mental retardation in society are:

1. *Language*: speaking, listening, comprehending, reading, and writing for everyday personal and social needs.
2. *Mathematics*: at least the basic skills required in the marketplace and for daily life.
3. *Health and safety*: knowledge of self-care, health, and protection for community living, if possible.
4. *Social skills*: for acceptable behavior in citizenship and in group life (nondestructive, cooperative, etc.).
5. *Career education*: preparation for employment, an economically useful life, and other life roles.

The instructional emphasis placed on these various areas increases as the educational level advances. An important trend has been to maximize the extent to which the skills and content taught are to be functional, referred to as the "criterion of ultimate functioning" (Brown, Nietupski, & Hamre-Nietupski, 1976). To meet this criterion, educators ask the following questions:

1. Is this activity necessary to prepare students to ultimately function in complex heterogeneous community settings?
2. Can students function as adults if they do not acquire the skill?
3. Would a different activity allow students to realize the criterion of ultimate functioning more quickly and more efficiently?
4. Will this activity impede, restrict, or reduce the probability that students will ultimately function in community settings?
5. Are the skills, materials, tasks, and criteria of concern similar to those encountered in adult life?

This concept is consistent with what Polloway, Patton, Smith, and Roderique (1991) referred to as basing programs on "subsequent environments as an attitude":

Special education should be guided by the reality that each student is in school on a time-limited basis; since we do not have them very long, the real test of what has been taught is how helpful it is after students leave the program. As a consequence, we need to look at what will happen in the future; that requires an approach with our students that is sensitive to the subsequent environments in which they will need to adapt and function.

An approach that clearly reflects a top-down view of curriculum is an orientation toward career education. For example, Brolin (1982) described the life-centered career education (LCCE) model, which combines the goals of special and career education. LCCE was designed to promote three major competencies (daily, personal-social, and occupational) throughout four stages of career development (awareness, exploration, preparation, and placement/follow-up/continuing education), starting early in elementary school and spanning a student's educational career. Brolin indicated that "career education is not intended to replace traditional education but, rather, to redirect it to be more relevant and meaningful for the student and to result in the acquisition of attitudes, knowledges, and skills one needs for successful community living and working" (p. 3).

The emphasis of approaches such as these to curriculum becomes clear when considering the realities of postschool adjustment for students with mental retardation. For example, Edgar and his colleagues (1987, 1988, 1990; Affleck, Edgar, Levine, & Kortering, 1990) reported that students who have gone through mild retardation programs have not fared well after school. Only approximately half or less of this population is working or involved in training programs. Even though relatively few dropped out of school, unfortunately this additional time in school has not paid dividends for them in terms of employment outcomes (Edgar, 1987). Finally, only 21% were living independently 30 months after completing secondary school, a figure that compares poorly to data on individuals without disabilities (Affleck et al., 1990). Although the case can be made that the postschool period in general is a time of floundering (Edgar, 1988), nevertheless, this clearly is more so for students with mild retardation. "Productive adulthood" apparently is an elusive goal for these individuals (Edgar, 1990). Thus, design of the curriculum is crucial for these students.

INSTRUCTION

In contrast to curriculum, which refers to *what* to teach, or content, instruction refers to *how* to teach. Of course, the two are intimately interwoven and in reality cannot be separated. Several selected strategies that have been useful in effectively instructing children with mental retardation are behavior modification, cognitive training, direct instruction, and the unit method.

Behavior Modification. Operant conditioning has had a great impact on the delivery of content in the classroom (MacMillan & Morrison, 1980b). Teachers can (a) decrease disruptive and inappropriate behavior, (b) bring the child's attention to the task at hand, (c) maintain that attention to the task, and (d) shape new behaviors through the systematic application of consequences. Several applications have become popular:

1. A *token economy* can be set up to provide immediate, tangible reinforcement for a desired behavior. Tokens (e.g., checkmarks, poker chips) are given out to reward desired behaviors; these can be traded later for some tangible reward.
2. A *response-cost* system involves removing some of these tokens as a consequence of some behavior targeted for reduction.
3. *Time-out* from reinforcement, a punishment technique, involves physically removing a child from conditions in the classroom that are reinforcing negative behavior.
4. *Shaping* is useful in developing new or more complex behavior, by reinforcing successively greater approximations of the desired behavior.

Although procedures such as these have demonstrated effectiveness when they are employed systematically (MacMillan & Morrison, 1980b), their use should be tempered by certain considerations: Can the teacher apply them consistently? Have they been demonstrated to be effective for a specific child or group of children? Effectiveness should be documented first through observation.

Cognitive Training. Cognitive approaches have met with success with children who have disabilities (Keogh & Glover, 1980; Meichenbaum, 1977). Cognitive training involves the use of reinforcement techniques to facilitate the cognitive process of thinking. The following steps are commonly included:

1. The teacher models the task while describing the procedure outloud.
2. The student performs the task while the teacher repeats the directions.
3. The student repeats the instructions subvocally while performing the task.
4. The student silently repeats the instructions while performing the task.

The content of the speech modeled by the adult, and repeated by the child, can consist of (a) defining the problem (What is it I have to do?), (b) focusing attention (be careful, keep alert), (c) self-reinforcement (Good job, keep it up), and (d) self-evaluation and correction (Let's not make that mistake again, let's try again).

The strength of this approach lies in its use of a number of proven facilitators to learning: modeling, reinforcement, verbal mediation, and, above all, the student's active involvement in reinforcing, evaluating, and controlling his or her own behavior and thinking.

Direct Instruction. Systematic, or direct, instruction is characterized by extensive assessment and monitoring, individualized sequences of content, and immediate and continuous feedback and reinforcement (Haring & Bateman, 1977; Lovitt & Curtiss, 1972). Haring and Bateman (1977, p. 266) described the following components of this approach:

1. Providing specific attention to each child in the classroom.
2. Measuring initial performance directly.
3. Specifying instructional aims individually.
4. Arranging a specific program of instruction.
5. Measuring the child's performance directly and daily.
6. Making decisions on the basis of the child's performance.

7. At the end of specified periods of time, evaluating the child's performance on the basis of stated criteria.

This approach relies heavily on behavioral techniques of presenting reinforcement, as well as observational techniques of evaluation. Arrangement of instructional cues and materials is highly individualized, but within a group setting. Strategies for reinforcing concepts, for example, might include drill, practice, and general application of the information or skills. The strength of this approach lies in its systematic delineation of steps in the learning process, applied in an individualized manner.

Unit Method. The unit method for presenting content and skills (Ingram, 1935; Meyen, 1972) involves teaching life-experience units such as transportation or healthy eating, and, within each, specific skills: arithmetic, communication, social, safety, health, and vocational. The unit method allows students to see that the material is relevant to their everyday experiences.

A concept similar to the unit approach is the integrated curriculum (Kataoka & Patton, 1989). An integrated curriculum draws together content from various academic areas and enables students to apply the academic skills they have been learning across these areas, often in areas such as science and social studies. Furthermore, this type of programming links academic skills and life skills and can accommodate a career education focus. Using a matrix format for organizing the curriculum, the interrelationships can be developed by tying together reading, math skills, and language skills as well as other subject and skill areas.

Finally, an integrated curriculum is advantageous in promoting generalization, a critical concern in programming for students with mental retardation. Although generalization is a concern far larger than its relationship to integrated curriculum (Liberty, Haring, White, & Billingsley, 1988), this approach does provide one way to promote it. The important concern is to promote generalization in varied ways and avoid the "train and hope" philosophy (Stokes & Bear, 1977).

ADMINISTRATIVE ARRANGEMENTS

Appropriateness of administrative arrangements is a subject of controversy in policy-making and research alike. The free and appropriate public education and least restrictive components of PL 94–142 reflect the philosophy that no child should be excluded from school settings and placements should be the result of a concerted effort to integrate them as much as possible into the educational mainstream.

Characteristics of Educational Environments. Classroom settings typically are described in terms of their restrictiveness. Restrictiveness in this sense refers to the extent to which the children in these classrooms are removed from the mainstream. Other variables contribute to classroom appropriateness as well:

1. *Teachers*: may vary in training, attitude toward students with mental retardation, and number of years of experience.
2. *Peers*: may vary in kind (those with and without handicaps) and in number.

3. *Goals and objectives*: IEP requires individual goals and objectives, but programs often have group goals and objectives as well.
4. *Curriculum*: may vary in its nature and balance (academic, social, or vocational).
5. *Instructional strategies*: may vary in appropriateness for individuals and groups.
6. *Expectations*: teacher, parental, and peer expectations vary for academic performance and social behavior.

Regular Classroom. The regular classroom is the most common placement for children with mental retardation in the younger age ranges (preschool to primary). Although placement data to date do not confirm a strong trend toward integration, the near future likely will reflect more involvement of students with mental retardation in regular classes because of the increasing popularity of the regular education initiative and the full inclusion movements. Goals in regular programs are likely to be oriented toward achievement, or readiness, in academic areas, calling upon a wide variety of instructional strategies oriented largely to groups. To accommodate learners who have mental retardation, modifications could include (a) individualized attention from teacher, aide, or peers; (b) alternative materials geared toward lower levels; (c) different expectations according to amount and accuracy of performance on tasks; and (d) a motivational and behavioral system designed to keep students directed and on task.

One of the harshest things that can happen to a student in a mainstreamed setting is not being accepted by peers (Morrison & MacMillan, 1984). Self-esteem suffers because of social rejection and problems in learning (Morrison, 1985). To accommodate these personal and social, as well as academic, difficulties is a challenge to teachers in the regular classroom. Peer-mediated strategies such as cooperative learning can be particularly effective toward this end.

Resource Room. With this alternative arrangement, students remain in the regular classroom most of the school day. The resource room teacher typically pulls students out of the classroom for specific types of remedial help. The resource room affords a lower teacher-pupil ratio, the extent of which is flexible according to how the teacher's time is arranged.

The content delivered in the resource room typically is individualized for each student rather than reflecting an overall, balanced curriculum for a group as a whole. Instructional strategies are geared specifically toward individual children and their specific needs. The emphasis often is on tutorial and remedial learning, and social and affective needs are less likely to be addressed.

Self-Contained Special Class. In the self-contained special class students are in a segregated classroom for half or more of the school day. The mainstreaming portion typically integrates these children for nonacademic subjects only, such as recess, lunch, physical education, music, and art. Teachers of special classes are specially trained, and teacher-student ratios usually are about 1:12. The self-contained classroom may be less academically oriented than other settings. Given the full-day placement, a well rounded curriculum can be presented, incorporating content and skills that are relevant to the real world. The lack of integration, however, may preclude a true sense of what that work world is like.

Perspective on Integration. Data from Illinois (Polloway et al., 1986) indicated that relatively few students with mild retardation were integrated into regular education for more than half the school day; the vast majority were either integrated for less than half the time or not at all, a particularly disturbing finding. Many of these students spent virtually all their time in special classes.

Although these data are somewhat more dramatic than data from other sources, annual reports to Congress suggest a similar phenomenon. Between the time of implementation of PL 94–142 and the 1988–1989 academic year, a decreasing percentage of students with mental retardation apparently are receiving most of their programming in regular classes while an increasing number are receiving instruction in special class-based programs. For example, the ninth annual report to Congress indicated that 53% of students were receiving their programs in special class-based programs, which increased to 58.9% four years later (1988–1989), and only 28.3% of students were receiving their programs in regular class-based programs (regular classes or resource room) (U.S. Department of Education, 1987, 1991). From these data, one might conclude that many of these students could not be integrated successfully. A more plausible rationale, however, is that a commitment to integration has been lacking. The federal data clearly are influenced by the trends in prevalence, as the students who would have been most easily mainstreamed typically are no longer labeled mentally retarded. More precisely, children who might have been seen as "adaptive EMR" students now are rarely classified as having retardation (MacMillan & Borthwick, 1980; Polloway & Smith, 1988; MacMillan, 1989). Thus, those who remain in programs may require significant support to be successful in regular education. Rather than serving as an excuse or an impenetrable barrier, this represents a challenge to what should be considered in terms of planning for social integration. With the movement toward full inclusion, such a change should be evident.

POLICIES AND SERVICES, BIRTH TO AGE 5

Passage of the 1986 Amendment to the Education for All Handicapped Children Act (Part H, Early Intervention Program for Handicapped Infants and Toddlers), Public Law 99–457, signaled exciting developments in treating children with disabilities from birth to age 5. Before this time, most states mandated services to at least a portion of children with disabilities within this age span. PL 99–457 directs states "to develop and implement a statewide, comprehensive, coordinated, multidisciplinary, interagency program of early intervention services for handicapped infants and toddlers and their families" (Section 671(b)). Some important themes in these provisions are especially pertinent to children with mental retardation.

Definitions. Each state is allowed to define "developmental delay" for itself. Delay may be in one or more of the following areas: cognitive development, physical development, including vision and hearing, language and speech development, psychosocial development, or self-help skills. In most states the term "mental retardation" is avoided as a referent for preschool children.

Pertinent to the definition of developmental delay in the birth to age 3 period are the concepts of risk. Two major categories of risk, as defined by Tjossem (1976), are relevant here. Children at *established risk* are those who develop delays related to some known medical etiology. These children are most often in the severe range of mental retardation and often are diagnosed at birth or soon after. Cases of environmental risk have no obvious biological complications, but the children live in environments that may contribute to developmental delays, probably in the mild range. Certainly, children with severe retardation, or those with established risk, are likely to be covered in state definitions. States, however, are given the choice about whether to include children at environmental risk. Most children who have mild disabilities are not likely to exhibit major disabilities during these early years; however, they are likely to have experienced environmental risks. Thus, depending on state decisions in this matter, children with mild retardation may escape identification and services at this early age.

Family Focus. The most pervasive theme in PL 99–457 is the intent to provide services that are family-focused. This theme recognizes that one of the greatest needs of children during these early years is a family that can effectively attend to their needs. The quality of home environment greatly influences the developmental outcomes of children with developmental disabilities (Nihira, Meyers, & Mink, 1980). The extent to which a child with a disability impacts the family's social, emotional, and financial resources differs from family to family. The impact varies according to the status of the family system (Benson & Turnbull, 1986)—how it is structured (its membership and cultural orientation), how it has organized the tasks of living (economic, physical, social), the stage of development of the member with a disability (infant/school-age), and how effectively the family communicates about and adapts to new situations. Families' expectations vary, too. For example, one family may have difficulty accepting the reality that its newborn child has mental retardation, and another family may adjust to the situation much more readily.

To cope with the additional stresses of rearing a child with disabilities, families may need a constellation of services based on the child's individual needs as well as their needs as a family in attempting to support the child's development. Thus, public policy (a) provides a mechanism for coordinating services, and (b) assures that service provision is based on the differential needs of the families involved.

One requirement of the law intended to enhance family functioning is interagency collaboration in providing services. Families with children who have mental retardation tend to need a variety of services from the various disciplines of medicine, social services, health, and education. At this critical time in their child's life, case coordination can avoid the nightmare of dealing with multiple agencies.

The individualized family service plan (IFSP) is the written plan that documents agreements between the family and the service providers. This plan is intended to be family-driven or family-focused. The service recipient is defined as the family, family participation in the process is mandated, and decisions about services to be provided are based on documentation of the family's needs and strengths (Krauss, 1990).

PL 99–457 has provided a scaffolding for service provision for children with disabilities in their early years. These provisions might include respite services for families, support groups for parents, case coordination, assessment, parent training, in-home services, counseling, crisis placement (Herman & Hazel, 1991).

Early Intervention. Given the importance of early stimulation and education, training before school-age is critical. Programs for infants and toddlers at either established or environmental risk typically involve a home-based or a center-based approach to programming, or both. The home-based approach assumes that maximum impact on development will occur when parents and families are involved in training or are at least provided with some kind of support. For example, professionals (or paraprofessionals) are sent into the home to train parents in techniques of behavior modification and systems of direct instruction (Karnes & Zehrbach, 1977), or to improve the quality of the mother's interactions with the infant (Garber, 1988).

An example of support for families of environmentally at-risk children is the Carolina Abecedarian Project (Ramey & Campbell, 1984), which provides social work services, nutritional supplements, medical care, and transportation to and from the day-care center. The Milwaukee Project (Garber, 1988) provided training in vocational skills and rehabilitation for mothers of environmentally at-risk children. Including and considering these families is the key to a successful program in this age range (Bronfenbrenner, 1974).

The center-based approach, by contrast, brings young children to a centralized facility. Here trained personnel provide services such as physical or occupational therapy, in addition to services related to developmental and educational needs. It utilizes various curricular approaches.

These programs fall under three broad kinds of curriculum approaches: (a) a cognitive approach, based on Piaget's theory, emphasizing mental growth through active exploration and manipulation of the environment; (b) a structured approach, based on the work of Bereiter and Engelmann (1966), which teaches children specific preacademic skills in an atmosphere of high structure and positive reinforcement; and (c) a traditional developmental approach, focused on readiness for academic learning and on the child's social and emotional growth. The most effective programs emphasize cognitive or academic instruction, have detailed outcome objectives and a specified plan of learning sequences, are of longer duration, and are followed up by primary school programs that reinforce the successes achieved during preschool (Patton, Payne, & Beirne-Smith, 1990).

SECONDARY AND POSTSECONDARY PROGRAMS

Services to secondary- and postsecondary-age students with disabilities have expanded noticeably, in part, because of (a) increased recognition of the importance of a successful transition from school to work and community life, and (b) the need to preserve education gains from earlier education. An important component of transition from school to community is collaborative planning among the student, parents, school professionals, adult service providers, employers, and postsecondary education staff. Following the tradition of the IEP, an ITP (individualized transition plan) is developed by these individuals. Emphasis on content in the later secondary and postsecondary years should be two-pronged: community living skills and vocational skills (Schalock & Harper, 1981). Community living skills might include food preparation, personal maintenance, social behavior, and home maintenance. Vocational skills might consist of job-getting strategies (making occupational choices, getting and filling out applications, interviewing), job maintenance skills (working with others, following directions, accepting responsibility), and specific job-related skills (e.g., clerical, mechanical). The dual emphasis is affirmed by Brolin (1982), who suggested that these skills can be taught throughout the school career of students with mental retardation.

The focus on vocational and community living skills is intended to enhance the community adjustment of these individuals in their adult years. Although strides have been made toward the community functioning of these individuals, research that follows up high school graduation presents a varied picture. Studies of students with mild retardation indicate that they have been able to adapt to community living with some success when they have the appropriate supports. These individuals, however, were employed in unskilled or semiskilled positions, earned low incomes, and had limited independence. More recent studies with individuals with mild retardation who graduated from special education placements suggest that many of these individuals are struggling to maintain employment and many still live with their families (Haring & Lovett, 1990). The relative failure of secondary high school programs to prepare students for independent living points to the need for continuing services throughout adulthood.

A major push in recent years has been for career and community living training to take place in integrated settings where individuals with mental retardation can participate in normalized activities to the greatest extent possible. Thus integrated participation has led to broader goals of vocational and community training to include skills for residential, social, and leisure activities (Halpern, 1985). For example, many adults with mental retardation currently do not have satisfying leisure activities (Dattilo & St. Peter, 1991).

The success of transitional programming for individuals with mental retardation led to refinements and shifts of emphases in the late 1980s and early 1990s. Beyond teaching the basics of career and community living skills, emphasis has been placed on (a) reforming secondary curriculum to increase its relevance to community and vocational skills, (b) encouraging and facilitating student choice in the vocational area, (c) emphasis on job placement before the student leaves high school, and (d) supporting postsecondary education for students with disabilities (Wehman, 1992).

C<u>OMMUNITY ADJUSTMENT</u>

Two major considerations in community adjustment are employment and place of living.

EMPLOYMENT

Employment options include work-study programs, vocational rehabilitation, sheltered industries, work enclaves, and supported employment.

Work-Study Programs. The teaching of vocational skills is combined with actual on-the-job experience in community work situations. Mercer and Payne (1975) described five phases: (a) vocational exploration, in which the student is exposed to information about a variety of occupations; (b) vocational evaluation, which involves experiences with various job skills and assessment of the student's preferences and abilities; (c) vocational training, to extensively develop specific job skills; (d) vocational placement, or locating and placing the student in a job; and (e) follow-up, which includes providing support as the student encounters difficulties.

Vocational Rehabilitation. An interagency, interdisciplinary approach is employed to provide vocational assessment, counseling, and placement assistance (Patton et al., 1990). Those involved might be medical personnel, psychologists, occupational therapists, teachers, social workers, rehabilitation counselors, and employers. This type of team is especially useful during the transition years between secondary and postsecondary activities, when individuals with mental retardation are establishing themselves as semi-independent or independent community members. Haller, Dyke, and Groeneweg (1990), however, noted that this approach has been criticized in terms of its effectiveness and its ability to achieve the goals of integration.

Sheltered Industries. Training and actual employment are provided in sheltered industries. Mercer and Payne (1975) defined a sheltered workshop as "a structured environment which enables retarded people to learn necessary work habits, receive training in particular skills, and eventually gain salaried employment either within the workshop itself or through placement in the community" (p. 121). Gold (1973) listed three types of sheltered workshops:

1. *Transitional*: temporary placement for an individual to learn skills for a competitive community job.
2. *Extended care*: long-term placement for an individual who is unlikely to achieve the skills necessary to compete in the marketplace.
3. *Comprehensive*: combination of both types of placement.

Sheltered workshops do not offer a wide range of job skills. Moreover, they are plagued by limited funding. Perhaps of greatest concern is that they represent a segregated environment from which many individuals do not progress.

Work Enclaves. The work enclave is an extension of the workshop concept. These work-training programs operate within specific community job settings that enable actual job experience through the help of job coaches who instruct and monitor work performance. The obvious advantage of enclaves is the greater integration into the real world of work.

Supported Employment. Supported employment is defined as the opportunity for paid productive work in socially integrated environments supported by ongoing training to ensure continued employment. In evaluating the effectiveness of this approach, improvement in quality of life is considered (Sinnott-Oswald et al., 1991).

Although most individuals with mental retardation work in sheltered employment environments, Schalock, McGaughey, and Kiernan (1989) found that more are beginning to move into nonsheltered work situations. They found also that disability level was related to employment success and monetary level.

The goal of any work-training program is for the student to gain and maintain "real employment." Successful work adjustment is strongly related to tenure and social/interpersonal skills (Auty, Goodman, & Foss, 1987). Problem behaviors occur in handling criticism from the supervisor, requesting assistance, following instructions, cooperating with co-workers, handling teasing, and resolving personal concerns (Cheney & Foss, 1984).

RESIDENTIAL ARRANGEMENTS

Historically, society often dealt with mental retardation by placing individuals in large residential institutions. In the past several decades, however, criticism of institutional care for the mentally retarded peaked. Institutions were described as "warehouses" (Blatt & Kaplan, 1966; Wolfensberger, 1971), with "dehumanizing" effects (Goffman, 1957). The call for deinstitutionalization was exemplified by the principle of normalization, originally defined by Nirje (1969) as "making available to the mentally retarded patterns and conditions of everyday life which are as close as possible to the norms and patterns of the mainstream of society."

Deinstitutionalization included (a) preventing initial placements in institutions by providing alternative community placements, and (b) returning to the community residents who had been properly habilitated and trained to function in community settings. As a result, the numbers residing in large public residential facilities have decreased dramatically since 1970. At the same time, the number of facilities with fewer residents (community residential facilities) has increased (Bruininks, Hauber, & Kudla, 1980; Scheerenberger, 1982). Significant numbers of individuals who would have been institutionalized in the past now remain in the community (Hauber et al., 1984).

During the past decade, the vision of life in communities for people with mental retardation has changed dramatically. Once individuals with mental retardation were placed in the community, the major issues became access to integrated education, employment housing, transportation, and recreation. As integrated activities increase, the challenge has become one of ensuring that the integrated participation is meaningful and adds to the quality of life for individuals with mental retardation (Taylor & Bogdan, 1990).

Community-based residential facilities provide services to a small group of people with disabilities who are presently or potentially capable of functioning in a community setting with some degree of independence (Janicki, 1981).

The following are examples of the kinds of community-based facilities that accommodate residents with mental retardation. Even though they are based in the community, however, they may not all provide integrated living opportunities.

1. *Foster family-care homes* provide single-family care for one or more children or adults. These families must be licensed by the state, but more often than not, they have no formal training. They generally are reimbursed for their expenses.
2. *Supervised apartment living* is one of the least restrictive types of community residential facilities. Several individuals occupy an apartment or a complex of several apartments. They are supervised by staff members who live nearby, or they are supported by caseworkers. Training in independent living skills is provided for the residents. The supervisory role is reduced as the residents become more capable and more able to live independently.
3. *Group residences* are large facilities where six to 12 individuals live, supervised around the clock by live-in staff members. Residents share in household responsibilities. Work and recreational activities usually are community-based.
4. *Board and care* and *personal care facilities* are superficially similar to group homes except that daytime activities are not supervised. These adult homes may or may not provide habilitation or nursing care. These facilities typically also house elderly individuals with other disabilities.
5. *Convalescent* or *nursing homes* provide full-time care and nursing services and usually serve elderly individuals with mental retardation. These homes were designed to meet the health needs of elderly people in general but have been used increasingly with adults who have mental retardation.

Although the number of community-based facilities has increased rapidly in the last 10 to 20 years, as has their clientele, a variety of types of residential programs is needed to accommodate all people with mental retardation (Janicki, Krauss, & Seltzer, 1988). The success of these programs depends on some of the following factors reviewed by Haney (1988):

1. *Individual characteristics*: Maladaptive behavior is the most salient factor in determining nonsuccess or reinstitutionalization.
2. *Small-group characteristics*: Successful programs are related to the careprovider's mental health and aspects of the treatment program such as freedom of movement, household responsibilities, social integration, and low staff-to-resident ratios.
3. *Organizational characteristics*: Normalized facility design, well trained staff, and high parental involvement are associated with success.
4. *Community characteristics*: An array of community services facilitates success.

Though judgments about the success of community living options are based on criteria such as growth in independence, living in a normalized environment, and community integration, more recent attention is being directed to the importance of social aspects of adjustment. Also, program effectiveness is being evaluated from the point of view of those receiving the services rather than an a value system based upon service delivery policy (Burchard, Gordon, & Pine, 1990). This type of evaluation is based on personal satisfaction rather than on personal competence or independence (Edgerton, Bollinger, & Herr, 1984).

This change in judgments about success reflects much more interest in defining quality of life for people with mental retardation. In quality-of-life discussions, Schalock (1990) suggested that social indicators (environmentally based conditions such as education, housing, friendships, social welfare, and leisure) and psychological indicators (subjective reactions to life experiences) are important to consider when making judgments about quality of life of those with mental retardation.

CURRENT AND FUTURE TRENDS

As we look to the future, our challenge is to go beyond basic services to quality services. Along with refinements to achieve these quality services, the changes must be based on a shared vision or ideology. Bruininks (1991) proposed the following minimal aspects of quality of life: "(1) physical presence in the community, (2) opportunity for personal growth and development, (3) social relationships, (4) valued community participation, (5) personal autonomy and choice, and (6) health, safety and basic comfort" (cited in Bruininks, 1991, p. 244).

Two critical themes arising from quality-of-life conceptualizations are *full participation* and *personal autonomy and choice*. In terms of full participation, we see efforts in the schooling area such as the regular education initiative (Will, 1986), which provides the backdrop for efforts within the schools to fully include students with disabilities in regular educational activities. State-of-the-art practices are being developed and implemented in supported employment opportunities (Wehman, 1992). Bruininks (1991) further argues for expanding access to generic services in other service areas such as health, housing, and social services.

Personal autonomy and choice as a central theme in providing quality services often is referred to as empowerment or "the opportunity to exert control over one's environment, to make decisions, and to pursue choices" (Schalock, Bartnik, Wu, Konig, Lee, & Reiter, 1990, p. 10). Bruininks (1991) maintains that individuals with mental retardation and their families currently have few opportunities to exercise meaningful choices in their interactions with services and service providers. Therefore, the theme of empowerment is seen as a major philosophical guide for family services (e.g., family-focused assessment, family-driven individualized family service plan).

This continuing expansion and refinement of support services for children and adults with mental retardation naturally is placing financial strain on chronically strapped government systems. Part of the challenge of the future will be to obtain continued funding for quality services. A central theme in restructuring and reform in the schools and other agencies is the need for *collaboration* and *cooperation* between human services personnel and agencies. This theme is explicit, for example, in PL 99–457, which requires multidisciplinary and interagency coordination in providing early intervention services. Developing collaborative consultation relationships within schools is a key strategy for providing quality services to children with disabilities (Thousand & Villa, 1991).

Collaboration is especially critical in the transitions throughout the lives of individuals who have disabilities—for example, from early childhood to school age, and from school age to independent living. Transitions also might be seen between environments within the same time frame, such as school, workplace, and home. The point is that, to make these transitions smoothly, the mentally retarded child or adult needs the collaborative help of parents and professionals from all orientations.

SUMMARY

We have emerged from a period of tremendous growth in getting basic services in place for individuals with mental retardation and their families. Through the Education for All Handicapped Children Act (PL 94–142), now called the Individuals with Disabilities Education Act (PL 101–476), we have seen the establishment of procedures to support the basic rights of individualized education, nondiscriminatory assessment, least restrictive environment, and due process. Through PL 99–457 we are seeing these rights extended to infants and toddlers with disabilities and their families.

Definitions of mental retardation have changed throughout the years, reflecting societal and educational expectations for this population. The current definition stresses both intellectual and adaptive limitations during the developmental period. Estimates of prevalence vary according to which definition is used and other factors; the category of "mild" is most prevalent.

Mental retardation can have either genetic or environmental causes, and the level of functioning may be related to both. Genetic causes can be classified as dominant-gene disorders, recessive-gene disorders, X-linked genetic disorders, and chromosomal abnormalities. Physical/environmental causes can be differentiated according to prenatal problems, problems at birth, and postnatal problems. Modern screening procedures are now able to detect some disorders associated with mental retardation, the most common of which is Down syndrome.

In cognitive functioning, those with mental retardation tend to have difficulties with attention, memory, speech and language. In the affective area, they face problems with self-concept, motivation, and social skills.

Identification and assessment follow a procedure that leads from first indications of the problem through prereferral interventions, to referral, to assessment, to IEP development, and finally to reevaluation. The two measures most commonly used to measure intelligence are the Stanford-Binet and the Wechsler scales. Adaptive behavior can be measured through instruments such as the CTAB, the SIB, and the Vineland.

Areas targeted for curricular programming are usually language, mathematics, health and safety, social skills, and career education. In instruction, some strategies that have proved to be constructive are behavior modification, cognitive training, direct instruction, and the unit method. Administrative arrangements include total inclusion in the regular classroom, the resource room, and the self-contained special class.

Programming should extend from preschool through the transition into community life and the working world. Vocational alternatives include work-study programs, vocational rehabilitation, sheltered industries, work enclaves, and supported employment. Residential options range from foster family-care homes to supervised apartment living, to group residences, to board and care and convalescent or nursing homes.

R*EFERENCES*

Abuelo, D. N. (1983). Genetic disorders. In J. L. Matson & J. A. Mulick (Eds.), *Handbook of mental retardation*. New York: Pergamon Press.

Affleck, J. Q., Edgar, E., Levine, P., & Kortering, L. (1990). Postschool status of students classified as mildly mentally retarded, learning disabled, or non-handicapped: Does it get better with time? *Education and Training in Mental Retardation, 25*, 315–324.

Armstrong, D. C. (1990). *Developing and documenting the curriculum*. Boston: Allyn & Bacon.

Auty, W., Goodman, J., & Foss, G. (1987). The relationship between interpersonal competence and work adjustment. *Vocational Evaluation and Work Assessment Bulletin, 2*, 49–52.

Belmont, J. M., & Butterfield, E. C. (1971). Learning strategies as determinants of memory deficiencies. *Cognitive Psychology, 2*, 411–420.

Benson, H., & Turnbull, A. (1986). Approaching families from an individualized perspective. In R. H. Horner, L. M. Voeltz, & H. D. B. Fredericks (Eds.), *Education of learners with severe handicaps. Exemplary service strategies*. Baltimore: Paul H. Brookes.

Bereiter, C., & Engelmann, S. (1966). *Teaching disadvantaged children in the preschool*. Englewood Cliffs, NJ: Prentice Hall.

Bijou, S. W. (1966). A functional analysis of retarded development. In N. R. Ellis (Ed.), *International review of research in mental retardation* (Vol. 1, pp. 1–17). New York: Academic Press.

Blatt, B., & Kaplan, F. (1966). *Christmas in purgatory*. Boston: Allyn & Bacon.

Bloom, B. S. (1964). *Stability and change in human characteristics*. New York: Wiley.

Borkowski, J. G., Peck, V. A., & Damberg, P. R. (1983). Attention, memory, and cognition. In J. L. Matson & J. A. Mulick (Eds.), *Handbook of mental retardation*. New York: Pergamon Press.

Bowerman, M. (1976). Semantic factors in the acquisition of rules for word use and sentence construction. In D. Morehead & A. Morehead (Eds.), *Directions in normal and deficient child language*. Baltimore: University Park Press.

Bray, N. W., & Turner, L. A. (1986). The rehearsal deficit hypothesis. In N. R. Ellis (Ed.), *International review of research in mental retardation* (Vol. 14, pp. 47–71). New York: Academic Press.

Brolin, D. E. (1982). Life-centered career education for exceptional children. *Focus on Exceptional Children, 14*, 1–15.

Bronfenbrenner, U. (1974). *A report on longitudinal evaluations of preschool programs: Vol. 2. Is early intervention effective?* Washington, DC: Department of Health, Education & Welfare.

Brown, A. L. (1975). The development of memory: Knowing, knowing about knowing, and knowing how to know. In H. W. Reese (Ed.), *Advances in child development and behavior* (Vol. 1). New York: Academic Press.

Brown, L., Nietupski, J., & Hamre-Nietupski, S. (1976). Criterion of ultimate functioning. In M. A. Thomas (Ed.), *Hey, don't forget about me!* (pp. 2–15). Reston, VA: Council for Exceptional Children.

Brown, R. H. (1978). Bureaucracy as praxis: Toward a political phenomenology of formal organizations.

Administrative Science Quarterly, 23, 365–382.

Bruininks, R. H. (1991). Presidential address 1991, Mental retardation: New realities, new challenges. *Mental Retardation, 29*, 239–251.

Bruininks, R. H., Hauber, F. A., & Kudla, M. J. (1980). National survey of community residential facilities: A profile of facilities and residents in 1977. *American Journal of Mental Deficiency, 84*, 470–478.

Burchard, S. N., Gordon, L. R., & Pine, J. (1990). Manager competence, program normalization and client satisfaction in group homes. *Education and Training in Mental Retardation, 25*, 277–285.

Butterfield, E. C., & Belmont, J. M. (1977). Assessing and improving the executive cognitive functions of mentally retarded people. In J. Bialer & M. Sternlicht (Eds.), *The psychology of mental retardation* (pp. 277–318). New York: Psychological Dimensions.

Campione, J. C., Brown, A. L., & Ferrara, R. A. (1982). Mental retardation and intelligence. In R. J. Sternberg (Ed.), *Handbook of human intelligence* (pp. 392–490). New York: Cambridge University Press.

Caro, P., & Snell, M. E. (1989). Characteristics of teaching communication to people with moderate and severe disabilities. *Education and Training of the Mentally Retarded, 24*, 63–77.

Carroll, A. W. (1967). The effects of segregated and partially integrated school programs on self-concept and academic achievement of educable mental retardates. *Exceptional Children, 34*, 94–99.

Cartledge, G., & Milburn, J. F. (1983). Social skill assessment and teaching in the schools. In T. Kratochwill (Ed.), *Advances in school psychology* (pp. 175–235). Hillsdale, NJ: Erlbaum.

Chadsey-Rusch, J. (1992). Toward defining and measuring social skills in employment settings. *American Journal on Mental Retardation, 96*, 405–418.

Chalfant, J. C., & Pysh, M. (1990). Teacher assistance teams: Five descriptive studies on 96 teams. *Remedial and Special Education, 10*, 49–58.

Chalfant, J. C., VanDusen, M., Pysh, M., & Moultrie, R. (1979). Teacher assistance teams: A model for within-building problem solving. *Learning Disability Quarterly, 3*, 84–96.

Cheney, D., & Foss, G. (1984). An examination of the social behavior of mentally retarded workers. *Education and Training in Mental Retardation, 19*, 216–221.

Clarke, J. T. R., Gates, R. D., Hogan, S. E., Barrett, M., & MacDonald, G. W. (1987). Neuropsychological studies on adolescents with phenylketonuria returned to phenylalnine-restricted diets. *American Journal of Mental Retardation, 92*, 255–262.

Committee on Minority Participation in Education and American Life. (1988). *One-third of a nation.* Washington, DC: American Council of Education.

Cowart, V. (1983). First-trimester prenatal diagnostic method becoming available in U.S. *Journal of the American Medical Association, 250*, 1249–1250.

Craig, P. A., Kasowitz, D. H., & Malgoire, M. A. (1978). *Teacher identification of handicapped pupils (ages 6–11) compared with identification using other indicators* (Research Rep. EPC 4537–11). Menlo Park, CA: Stanford Research Institute.

Das, J. P., & Naglieri, J. A. (in press). *Das-Naglieri: Cognitive Assessment System.*

Dattilo, J., & St. Peter, S. (1991). A model for including leisure education in transition services for young adults with mental retardation. *Education and Training in Mental Retardation, 26*, 420–432.

Davies, R. R., & Rogers, E. S. (1985). Social skills training with persons who are mentally retarded. *Mental Retardation, 23*, 186–196.

De la Cruz, F. F. (1985). Fragile X syndrome. *American Journal of Mental Deficiency, 90*, 119–123.

Denny, M. R. (1964). Research in learning and performance. In H. A. Stevens & R. Herber (Eds.), *Mental retardation: A review of research* (pp. 100–142). Chicago: University of Chicago Press.

Dever, R. N. (1990). Defining mental retardation from an instructional perspective. *Mental Retardation, 28*, 147–153.

Diamond, G. W., & Cohen, H. J. (1989). *Technical report on developmental disabilities and HIV infection: HIV infection in children: Medical and neurological aspects.* Silver Spring, MD: American Association of University Affiliated Programs.

Diana v. State Board of Education, Civil Action No. C-70-37 (N.D. Cal., January 7, 1970 & June 18, 1973).

Dixon, S. (1989). Effects of transplacental exposure to cocaine and methamphetamine on the neonate (Specialty Conference). *Western Journal of Medicine, 150*, 436–442.

Doll, E. (1941). The essentials of an inclusive concept of mental deficiency. *American Journal of Mental*

Deficiency, 46, 214–219.

Edgar, E. (1987). Secondary programs in special education: Are many of them justifiable? *Exceptional Children, 53*, 556–561.

Edgar, E. (1988). Employment as an outcome for mildly handicapped students: Current status and future directions. *Focus on Exceptional Children, 21*(1), 1–8.

Edgar, G. (Winter, 1990). Is it time to change our view of the world? *Beyond Behavior*, 9–13.

Edgerton, R. B., Bollinger, M., & Herr, B. (1984). The cloak of competence: After two decades. *American Journal of Mental Deficiency, 88*, 345–351.

Edwards, J. S., & Edwards, D. (1970). Rate of behavior development: Direct and continuous measurement. *Perceptual & Motor Skills, 31*, 633–634.

Ellis, N. R. (1970). Memory processes in retardates and normals. In N. R. Ellis (Ed.), *International review of research in mental retardation* (Vol. 4, pp. 1–32). New York: Academic Press.

Epstein, M. H., Polloway, E. A., Patton, J. R., & Foley, R. (1989). Mild retardation: Student characteristics and services. *Education and Training in Mental Retardation, 24*, 7–16.

Fisher, M. A., & Zeaman, D. (1973). An attention-retention theory of retardate discrimination learning. In N. R. Ellis (Ed.), *International review of research in mental retardation* (Vol. 6). New York: Academic Press.

Fishler, K., Azen, C. G., Henderson, R., Friedman, E. G., & Koch, R. (1987). Psychoeducational findings among children treated for phenylketonuria. *American Journal of Mental Retardation, 92*, 65–73.

Forness, S. R. (1985). Effects of public policy at the state level: California's impact on MR, LD, and ED categories. *Remedial & Special Education, 6*(3), 36–43.

Foss, G., & Peterson, S. L. (1981). Social-interpersonal skills relevant to job tenure for mentally retarded adults. *Mental Retardation, 19*, 103–106.

Frankenberger, W., & Harper, J. (1988). States' definitions and procedures for identifying children with mental retardation: Comparison of 1981–82 and 1985–86 guidelines. *Mental Retardation, 26*, 133–136.

Garber, H. L. (1988). *The Milwaukee project: Preventing mental retardation in children at risk*. Washington, DC: American Association on Mental Retardation.

Gerald, P. S. (1980). X-linked mental retardation and an x-chromosome marker. *New England Journal of Medicine, 303*, 696–697.

Gerjuoy, I. R., & Spitz, H. H. (1966). Associative clustering in free recall: Intellectual and developmental variables. *American Journal of Mental Deficiency, 70*, 918–927.

Germain, R. B. (1978). Self-concept and self-esteem reexamined. *Psychology in the Schools, 15*, 386–390.

Goffman, E. (1957). On the characteristics of total institutions. In *Symposium on preventive and social psychiatry*. Washington, DC: U.S. Government Printing Office.

Gold, M. W. (1973). Research on the vocational habilitation of the retarded: The present, the future. In N. R. Ellis (Ed.), *International review of research in mental retardation* (Vol. 6). New York: Academic Press.

Goldman, J. J. (1988). Prader-Willi syndrome in two institutionalized older adults. *Mental Retardation, 26*, 97–102.

Gottlieb, J., Semmel, M. I., & Veldman, D. J. (1978). Correlates of social status among mainstreamed mentally retarded children. *Journal of Educational Psychology, 70*, 396–405.

Greenspan, S. (1979). Social intelligence in the retarded. In N. R. Ellis (Ed.), *Handbook of mental deficiency: Psychological theory and research* (2nd ed.). Hillsdale, NJ: Erlbaum.

Greenspan, S. (1990). A redefinition of mental retardation based on a revised model of social competence. Paper presented to the American Association on Mental Retardation, Atlanta, GA.

Greenspan, S., & Granfield, J. M. (1992). Reconsidering the construct of mental retardation: Implications of a model of social competence. *American Journal on Mental Retardation, 96*, 442–453.

Griesbach, L. S., & Polloway, E. A. (1990). *Fetal alcohol syndrome: Research, review, and implications*. ERIC microfiche report ED326035 (ERIC Document Reproduction Service No. ED 232650).

Grossman, H. J. (Ed.). (1973). *Manual on terminology and classification in mental retardation*. Washington, DC: American Association on Mental Deficiency.

Grossman, H. J. (Ed.). (1977). *Manual on terminology and classification in mental retardation* (rev. ed.). Washington, DC: American Association on Mental Deficiency.

Grossman, H. J. (Ed.). (1983). *Classification in mental retardation*. Washington, DC: American Association on Mental Deficiency.

Guralnick, M. J. (1980). Social interactions among preschool children. *Exceptional Children, 46,* 248–253.

Guralnick, M. J., & Weinhouse, E. (1984). Peer related social interactions of developmentally delayed young children: Their development and characteristics. *Developmental Psychology, 20*(5), 815–827.

Hallahan, D. P., & Reeve, R. E. (1980). Selective attention and distractibility. In B. K. Keogh (Ed.), *Advances in special education: Vol. 1. Basic constructs and theoretical orientations.* Greenwich, CT: JAI Press.

Haller, O., Dyke, C., & Groeneweg, G. (1990). Effectiveness of rehabilitation programs on a remainder population: A retrospective analysis. *Mental Retardation, 28,* 373–380.

Halpern, A. S. (1985). Transition: A look at the foundations. *Exceptional Children, 51,* 479–486.

Haney, J. I. (1988). Empirical support for deinstitutionalization. In L. W. Heal, J. I. Haney, & A. R. Novak Amado (Eds.), *Integration of developmentally disabled individuals into the community* (2nd ed., pp. 59–68). Baltimore, MD: Brookes Publishing Co.

Hanson, J. W., Streissguth, A. P., & Smith, D. W. (1978). The effects of moderate alcohol consumption during pregnancy on fetal growth and morphogenesis. *Journal of Pediatrics, 92,* 457–460.

Haring, K., & Lovett, D. (1990). A study of the social and vocational adjustment of young adults with mental retardation. *Education and Training in Mental Retardation, 25,* 52–61.

Haring, N. G., & Bateman, B. (1977). *Teaching the learning disabled child.* Englewood Cliffs, NJ: Prentice Hall.

Harter, S. (1978). Effectance motivation reconsidered: Toward a developmental model. *Human Development, 21,* 34–64.

Hauber, F. A., Bruininks, R. H., Hill, B. K., Lakin, C., Scheerenberger, R., & White, C. C. (1984). National census of residential facilities: A profile of facilities and residents. *American Journal of Mental Deficiency, 89,* 236–245.

Haywood, H. C., Brown, A. L., & Wingenfeld, S. (1990). Dynamic approaches to psychoeducational assessment. *School Psychology Review, 19,* 411–422.

Healey, K. N., & Masterpasqua, F. (1992). Interpersonal cognitive problem-solving among children with mild mental retardation. *American Journal on Mental Retardation, 96,* 367–372.

Heber, R. F. (1961). A manual on terminology and classification in mental retardation (rev. ed.). *Journal of Mental Deficiency* (suppl. 64).

Herman, S. E., & Hazel, K. L. (1991). Evaluation of family support services: Changes in availability and accessibility. *Mental Retardation, 29,* 351–357.

Hess, R. D., & Shipman, V. C. (1965). Early experience and the socialization of cognitive modes in children. *Child Development, 36,* 869–886.

Hoover, J. J. (1988). *Curriculum adaptation for students with learning and behavior problems: Principles and practices.* Lindale, TX: Hamilton Publications.

Hymes, D. (1972). On communicative competence. In J. B. Pride & J. Holmes (Eds.), *Sociolinguistics.* Baltimore: Penguin Books.

Ingram, C. P. (1935). *Education of the slow-learning child.* Yonkers, NY: World Book.

Janicki, M. P. (1981). Personal growth and community residence environments: A review. In H. C. Haywood (Ed.), *Living environments for developmentally retarded persons* (pp. 59–101). Baltimore: University Park Press.

Janicki, M. P., Krauss, M. W., & Seltzer, M. M. (1988). Agenda for service policy and research. In M. P. Janicki, M. W. Krauss, & M. M. Seltzer (Eds.), *Community residences for persons with developmental disabilities: Here to stay* (pp. 365–372). Baltimore: Brookes.

Jones, K. L., Smith, D. W., Ulleland, C. N., & Streissguth, A. P. (1973). Pattern of malformation in offspring of chronic alcoholic mothers. *Lancet, 1,* 1267–1271.

Kalverboer, A. (1988). Follow-up of biological high-risk groups. In M. Rutter (Ed.), *Studies of psychological risk: The power of logitudinal data* (pp. 114–137). Cambridge, England: Cambridge University Press.

Karnes, M. B., & Zehrbach, R. R. (1977). Alternative models for delivering services to young handicapped children. In J. Jordan, A. H. Hayden, M. B. Karnes, & M. M. Wood (Eds.), *Early childhood education for exceptional children.* Reston, VA: Council for Exceptional Children.

Kataoka, J. C., & Patton, J. R. (1989). Integrated curriculum. *Science and Children, 16,* 52–58.

Keogh, B. K., & Glover, A. T. (1980). The generality and durability of cognitive training. *Exceptional Education Quarterly, 1,* 75–81.

Keogh, B. K., & Margolis, J. (1976). Learn to labor and to wait: Attentional problems of children with learning disorders. *Journal of Learning Disabilities, 9*, 276–286.

Kirby, N. H., Nettelbeck, T., & Bullock, J. (1978). Vigilance performance of mildly mentally retarded adults. *American Journal of Mental Deficiency, 82*, 394–397.

Koch, R., Friedman, E. C., Azen, C., Wenz, E., Parton, P., Ledue, X., & Fishler, K. (1988). Inborn errors of metabolism and the prevention of mental retardation. In F. J. Menolascino & J. A. Stark (Eds.), *Preventive and curative intervention in mental retardation* (pp. 61–90). Baltimore: Paul H. Brookes.

Kopp, C. B., Baker, B. L., & Brown, K. W. (1992). Social skills and their correlates: Preschoolers with developmental delays. *American Journal on Mental Retardation, 96*, 357–366.

Korner, A. F. (1987). Preventive intervention with high-risk newborns: Theoretical, conceptual, and methodological perspectives. In J. D. Osofsky (Ed.), *Handbook of Infant Development* (2nd ed., pp. 1006–1036). New York: Wiley and Sons.

Krauss, M. W. (1990). New precedent in family policy: Individualized family service plan. *Exceptional Children, 56*, 388–395.

Kreitler, H., & Kreitler, S. (1988). The cognitive approach to motivation in retarded individuals. In N. W. Bray (Ed.), *International review of research in mental retardation* (Vol. 15, pp. 81–123). New York: Academic Press.

Krupski, A. (1980). Attention processes: Research, theory and implications for special education. In B. K. Keogh (Ed.), *Advances in special education* (Vol. 1, pp. 101–140). Greenwich, CT: JAI Press.

Kugel, T. B. (1976). Familial mental retardation: Fact or fancy? In J. Hellmuth (Ed.), *The disadvantaged child* (Vol. 1). New York: Brunner/Mazel.

Larry P. v. Riles, 343 F. Supp. 1306, C-71-2270 (N.D. Ca., 1972).

Liberty, K. A., Haring, N. G., White, D., & Billingsley, F. (1988). A technology for the future: Decision rules for generalization. *Education and Training in Mental Retardation, 23*, 315–326.

Longhurst, T. M., & Berry, G. W. (1975). Communication in retarded adolescents: Response to listener feedback. *American Journal of Mental Deficiency, 80*, 158–164.

Loper, A. B. (1980). Metacognitive development: Implications for cognitive training. *Exceptional Education Quarterly, 1*, 1–8.

Lovitt, T. C., & Curtiss, K. (1972). A contingency management classroom: Basis for systematic replication (four studies). In N. G. Haring & A. H. Hayden (Eds.), *The improvement of instruction*. Seattle: Special Child Publications.

Luckasson, R., et al. (1992). *Definition and classification in mental retardation* (9th ed.). Washington, DC: AAMR.

Luria, A. R. (1961). *The role of speech in the regulation of normal and abnormal behavior*. New York: Liveright.

MacMillan, D. L. (1989). Mild mental retardation: Emerging issues. In G. Robinson, J. R. Patton, E. A. Polloway, & L. R. Sargent (Eds.), *Best practices in mild mental retardation* (pp. 1–20). Reston, VA: CEC-MR.

MacMillan, D. L., & Borthwick, S. A. (1980). The new EMR population: Can they be mainstreamed? *Mental Retardation, 18*, 155–158.

MacMillan, D. L., Meyers, C. E., & Morrison, G. M. (1980). System identification of mildly retarded children: Implications for conducting and interpreting research. *American Journal of Mental Deficiency, 85*, 108–115.

MacMillan, D. L., & Morrison, G. M. (1980a). Correlates of social status among mildly handicapped learners in self-contained special classes. *Journal of Educational Psychology, 72*, 437–444.

MacMillan, D. L., & Morrison, G. M. (1980b). Evolution of behaviorism from the laboratory to special education settings. In B. K. Keogh (Ed.), *Advances in special education* (Vol. 1, pp. 101–140). Greenwich, CT: JAI Press.

McLaren, J., & Bryson, S. E. (1987). Review of recent epidemiological studies of mental retardation: Prevalence, associated disorders, and etiology. *American Journal of Mental Retardation, 92*, 243–254.

Meichenbaum, D. (1977). *Cognitive-behavior modification: An integrative approach*. New York: Plenum Press.

Mercer, C. D., & Payne, J. S. (1975). Learning theories and their implications. In J. M. Kauffman & J. S. Payne

(Eds.), *Mental retardation: Introduction and personal perspectives*. Columbus, OH: Charles E. Merrill.

Mercer, J. R. (1973a). *Labeling the mentally retarded*. Berkeley: University of California Press.

Mercer, J. R. (1973b). The myth of 3% prevalence. In R. K. Eyman, C. E. Meyers, & G. Tarjan (Eds.), Sociobehavioral studies in mental retardation. *Monographs of the American Association on Mental Deficiency* (No. 1).

Merrill, E. C. (1990). Attentional resource allocation and mental retardation. In N. W. Bray (Ed.), *International review of research in mental retardation* (Vol. 16, pp. 51–88). New York: Academic Press.

Meyen, E. L. (1972). *Developing units of instruction for the mentally retarded and other children with learning problems*. Dubuque, IA: W. C. Brown.

Meyerowitz, J. H. (1962). Self-derogations in young retardates and special class placement. *Child Development, 33*, 443–451.

Meyers, C. E., & MacMillan, D. L. (1976). Utilization of learning principles in retardation. In R. Koch & J. Dobson (Eds.), *The mentally retarded child and his family: A multidisciplinary handbook* (2nd ed., pp. 339–367). New York: Brunner/Mazel.

Morrison, G. M. (1978). *Nondiscriminatory assessment*. Paper presented at annual meeting of American Association on Mental Deficiency, Denver.

Morrison, G. M. (1985). Differences in teacher perceptions and students' self-perceptions for nonhandicapped and learning disabled students in regular and special education settings. *Learning Disability Research, 1*, 32–41.

Morrison, G. M., & MacMillan, D. L. (1984). Defining, describing and explaining the social status of mildly handicapped children: A discussion of methodological problems. In J. M. Berg (Ed.), *Perspectives and progress in mental retardation: Vol. 1. Social, psychological, and educational aspects*. Baltimore: University Park Press.

Morrison, G. M., MacMillan, D. L., & Kavale, K. (1985). System identification of learning disabled children: Implications for research sampling. *Learning Disability Quarterly, 8*, 2–10.

Morton, R. F., & Hebel, J. R. (1979). *A study guide to epidemiology and biostatistics*. Baltimore: University Park Press.

Nevin, A., & Thousand, J. (1988). Avoiding/limiting special education referrals: Changes and challenges. In M. C. Wang, M. C. Reynolds, & H. Wahlberg (Eds.), *Handbook of special education: Research and practice*. Oxford: Pergamon.

Nihira, K., Meyers, E., & Mink, I. (1980). Home environment, family adjustment and the development of mentally retarded children. *Applied Research in Mental Retardation, 1*, 5–24.

Nirje, B. (1969). The normalization principle and its human management implications. In R. B. Kugel & W. Wolfensberger (Eds.), *Changing patterns in residential services for the mentally retarded* (pp. 179–188). Washington, DC: President's Committee on Mental Retardation.

Patton, J. R., Payne, J. S., & Beirne-Smith, M. (1990). *Mental retardation* (3rd ed.). Columbus, OH: Merrill Publishing Company.

Peck, C. A., & Schuler, A. L. (1983). Classroom-based language intervention for children with autism: Theoretical and practical considerations for the speech and language specialist. *Seminars in Speech & Language, 4*, 93–103.

Pennsylvania Association for Retarded Children (PARC) v. Commonwealth of Pennsylvania, 343 F. Supp. 279 (E. D., PA., 1972).

Peterson, N. L., & Haralick, J. G. (1977). Integration of handicapped and nonhandicapped preschoolers: An analysis of play behavior and social interaction. *Education & Training of the Mentally Retarded, 12*, 235–245.

Philips, P. (1992). Societal conceptualization of mental retardation: A contrived darkness. Unpublished manuscript, Lynchburg College, Lynchburg, VA.

Polloway, E. A. (1987). Early age transition services for mildly mentally retarded individuals. In R. Ianoacone & R. Stodden (Eds.), *Transitional issues and directions for individuals who are mentally retarded* (pp. 11–24). Reston, VA: Council for Exceptional Children.

Polloway, E. A., Epstein, M. H., Patton, J. R., Cullinan, D., & Luebke, J. (1986). Demographic, social and behavioral characteristics of students with educable mental retardation. *Education and Training in Mental Retardation, 21*, 27–34.

Polloway, E. A., & Patton, J. R. (1990). Biological causes. In J. R. Patton, M. Beirne-Smith, & J. S. Payne (Eds.), *Mental retardation*. Columbus, OH: Charles Merrill.

Polloway, E. A., Patton, J. R., Smith, J. D., & Roderique, T. W. (1991). Issues in program design for elementary students with mild retardation: Emphasis on curriculum development. *Education and Training in Mental Retardation, 26,* 142–150.

Polloway, E. A., & Smith, J. D. (1988). Current status of the mild mental retardation construct: Identification, placement and programs. In M. C. Wang, M. C. Reynolds, & H. J. Walberg (Eds.), *The Handbook of special education: Research and practice* (Vol. 2, pp. 7–22). Oxford, England: Pergamon Press.

President's Committee on Mental Retardation (PCMR). (1978, March). Washington, DC: PCMR Newsclipping Service.

President's Committee on Mental Retardation and Bureau of Education of the Handicapped. (1969). *The six-hour retarded child.* Washington, DC: U.S. Government Printing Office.

Ramey, C. T., & Campbell, F. A. (1984). Preventive education for high-risk children: Cognitive consequences of the Carolina Abecedarian Project. *American Journal of Mental Deficiency, 88,* 515–523.

Ramey, C. T., MacPhee, D., & Yeates, K. O. (1982). Preventing developmental retardation: A general systems model. In L. Bond & J. Joffe (Eds.), *Facilitating infant and early childhood development.* Hanover, NH: University Press of New England.

Reschly, D. J. (1990). Adaptive behavior. In A. Thomas & J. Grimes (Eds.), *Best practices in school psychology* (2nd ed., pp. 29–42). Washington, DC: National Association of School Psychologists.

Reschly, D. J., & Wilson, M. (1990). Cognitive processing v. traditional intelligence: Diagnostic utility, intervention implications, and treatment validity. *School Psychology Review, 19,* 443–458.

Reynolds, M. C., & Birch, J. W. (1982). *Teaching exceptional children in all America's schools.* Reston, VA: Council for Exceptional Children.

Robinson, N. K., & Robinson, H. B. (1976). *The mentally retarded child* (2nd ed.). New York: McGraw-Hill.

Rogers, C. R., & Simensen, R. J. (1987). Fragile X syndrome: A common etiology of mental retardation. *American Journal of Mental Deficiency, 91,* 445–449.

Rosenberg, S. (1982). The language of the mentally retarded: Development, processes, and intervention. In S. Rosenberg (Ed.), *Handbook of applied psycholinguistics: Major thrusts of research and theory* (pp. 329–392). Hillsdale, NJ: Erlbaum.

Rosenfield, S., & Kuralt, S. K. (1990). *Best practices in school psychology* (2nd ed., pp. 29–42). Washington, DC: National Association of School Psychologists.

Rutter, M. (1984). Continuities and discontinuities in socioemotional development. In R. N. Emde & R. J. Harmons (Eds.), *Continuities and discontinuities in development.* New York: Plenum Press.

Rynders, J. E., & Horrobin, J. M. (1990). Always trainable? Never educable? Updating educational expectations concerning children with Down syndrome. *American Journal of Mental Retardation, 95,* 77–83.

Rynders, J. E., Spiker, D., & Horrobin, J. M. (1978). Underestimating the educability of Down's syndrome children: Examination of methodological problems in recent literature. *American Journal of Mental Deficiency, 82,* 440–448.

Sameroff, A., & Chandler, M. (1975). Reproductive risks and the continuum of caretaking casualty. In F. D. Horowitz, M. Hetherington, S. Scarr-Salapatek, & I. Siegel (Eds.), *Review of child development research* (Vol. 4). Chicago: University of Chicago Press.

Schalock, R. L. (1990). Attempts to conceptualize and measure quality of life. In R. L. Schalock (Ed.), *Quality of life: Perspectives and issues* (pp. 141–148). Washington, DC: American Association on Mental Retardation.

Schalock, R. L., Bartnik, E., Wu, F., Konig, A., Lee, C. S., & Reiter, S. (1990). *An international perspective on quality of life: Measurement and use.* Paper presented at the annual convention of the American Association on Mental Retardation, Atlanta.

Schalock, R. L., & Harper, R. S. (1981). A systems approach to community living skills development. In R. H. Bruininks, C. E. Meyers, B. B. Sigford, & K. C. Lakin (Eds.), *Deinstitutionalization and community adjustment of mentally retarded people* (pp. 316–337). Washington, DC: American Association on Mental Deficiency.

Schalock, R. L., McGaughey, M. J., & Kiernan, W. E. (1989). Placement into nonsheltered employment: Findings from national employment surveys. *American Journal on Mental Retardation, 94,* 80–87.

Scheerenberger, R. C. (1982). Public residential services, 1981: Status and trends. *Mental Retardation, 20,* 210–215.

Schultz, F. R. (1983). Phenylketonuria and other metabolic diseases. In J. A. Blackman (Ed.), *Medical aspects of developmental disabilities in children birth to three.* Iowa City: University of Iowa Press.

Schurr, K. T., Towne, R. C., & Joiner, L. M. (1972). Trends in self-concept of ability over 2 years of special class placement. *Journal of Special Education, 6,* 161–166.

Schweinhart, L. J., Berreuta-Clement, J. R., Barrett, W. S., Epstein, A. S., & Weikart, D. P. (1985). Effects of the Perry preschool programs on youths through age 19: A summary. *Topics in Early Childhood Special Education, 5*(2), 26–35.

Schweinhart, L. J., & Weikart, D. P. (1981). Effects of the Perry Preschool programs on youths through age 15. *Journal of the Division for Early Childhood, 4,* 29–39.

Seguin, E. (1971). *Idiocy and its treatment by the physiological method.* New York: Augustus M. Kelley. (Original work published 1866)

Sherman, J. A., Sheldon, J. B., Harchik, A. E., Edwards, K., & Quinn, J. M. (1992). Social evaluation of behaviors comprising three social skills and a comparison of the performance of people with and without mental retardation. *American Journal on Mental Retardation, 94,* 419–431.

Silon, E. L., & Harter, S. (1985). Assessment of perceived competence, motivational orientation, and anxiety in segregated and mainstreamed educable mentally retarded children. *Journal of Educational Psychology, 77,* 217–230.

Sinnott-Oswald, M., Gliner, J. A., & Spencer, K. C. (1991). Supported and sheltered employment: Quality of life issues among workers with disabilities. *Education and Training in Mental Retardation, 26,* 388–397.

Siperstein, G. (1992). Social competence: An important construct in mental retardation. *American Journal on Mental Retardation, 96,* iii–vi.

Sitko, M. C., & Semmel, M. I. (1973). Language and language behavior of the mentally retarded. In L. Mann & D. A. Sabatino (Eds.), *The first review of special education* (Vol. 1, pp. 203–259). Philadelphia: Journal of Special Education Press.

Skeels, H. M., & Dye, H. B. (1939). A study of the effects of differential stimulation on mentally retarded children. *Convention Proceedings: American Association on Mental Deficiency, 44,* 114–136.

Smith, S. W. (1990). Individualized education programs (IEP's) in special education—From intent to acquiescence. *Exceptional Children, 57,* 6–15.

Spitz, H. H. (1966). The role of input organizations in the learning and memory of mental retardates. In N. R. Ellis (Ed.), *International review of research in mental retardation* (Vol. 2, pp. 29–56). New York: Academic Press.

Spitz, H. H. (1979). Toward a relative psychology of mental retardation, with special emphasis on evolution. In N. R. Ellis (Ed.), *International review of research on mental retardation.* New York: Academic Press.

Spitz, H. H. (1988). Mental retardation as a thinking disorder: The rationalist alternative to empiricism. In N. W. Bray (Ed.), *International review of research in mental retardation* (Vol. 15, pp. 1–32). New York: Academic Press.

Spradlin, J. E. (1968). Environmental factors and the language development of retarded children. In S. Rosenberg & J. H. Koplin (Eds.), *Developments in applied psycholinguistic research.* New York: Macmillan.

Spreen, O. (1965). Language functions in mental retardation: A review. *American Journal of Mental Deficiency, 69,* 482–492.

Stark, J. A., Menolascino, F. J., & Goldsbury, T. L. (1988). An updated search for the prevention of mental retardation. In F. J. Menolascino & J. A. Stark (Eds.), *Preventive and curative intervention in mental retardation* (pp. 3–25). Baltimore: Paul H. Brookes.

Stokes, T., & Baer, D. M. (1977). An implicit technology of generalization. *Journal of Applied Behavior Analysis, 10,* 341–367.

Strang, L., Smith, M. D., & Rogers, G. M. (1978). Social comparison, multiple reference groups, and the self-concepts of academically handicapped children before and after mainstreaming. *Journal of Educational Psychology, 70,* 487–497.

Susser, M., & Stein, Z. A. (1981). Human development and prenatal nutrition: An overview of epidemiological experiments, quasi-experiments, and natural experiments in the past decade. In P. Mittler & J. M. de Jong

(Eds.), *Frontiers of knowledge in mental retardation: Vol. 2. Biomedical aspects* (pp. 107–118). Baltimore: University Park Press.

Tarjan, G., Wright, S. W., Eyman, R. K., & Keeran, D. V. (1973). Natural history of mental retardation: Some aspects of epidemiology. *American Journal of Mental Deficiency, 77,* 369–379.

Taylor, S. J., & Bogdan, R. (1990). Quality of life and the individual's perspective. In R. L. Schalock (Ed.), *Quality of life: Perspectives and issues* (pp. 27–40). Washington, DC: American Association on Mental Retardation.

Thousand, J., & Villa, R. (1990). Sharing expertise and responsibilities through teaching teams. In W. Stainback & S. Stainback (Eds.), *Support networks for inclusive schooling: Interdependent integrated education* (pp. 151–166). Baltimore: Paul H. Brookes.

Tjossem, T. D. (1976). Early intervention: Issues and approaches. In T. D. Tjossem (Ed.), *Intervention strategies for high risk infants and young children* (pp. 3–33). Baltimore: University Park Press.

Tredgold, A. F. (1908). *Mental deficiency.* London: Bailliera, Tindall, & Fox.

Tulkin, S. R., & Kagan, J. (1972). Mother-child interaction in the first year of life. *Child Development, 43,* 31–41.

U.S. Department of Education. (1987). *Ninth annual report to Congress on the implementation of the Education of the Handicapped Act.* Washington, DC: U.S. Government Printing Office.

U.S. Department of Education. (1991). *Thirteenth annual report to Congress on the implementation of the Education of All Handicapped Children Act.* Washington, DC: U.S. Government Printing Office.

Wehman, P. (1992). Transition for young people with disabilities: Challenges for the 1990's. *Education and Training in Mental Retardation, 27,* 112–118.

Weikart, D. P. (1981). Effects of different curricula in early childhood intervention. *Educational Evaluation & Policy Analysis, 3,* 25–35.

Werner, E. E. (1986). A longitudinal study of perinatal risk. In D. C. Farran & J. D. McKinney (Eds.), *Risk and intellectual and psychosocial development.* Orlando, FL: Academic Press.

Widaman, K. F., MacMillan, D. L., Hemsley, R. E., Little, T. D., & Balow, I. H. (1992). Differences in adolescents' self-concept as a function of academic level, ethnicity, and gender. *American Journal on Mental Retardation, 96,* 387–404.

Will, M. (1986). *Educating students with learning problems: A shared responsibility.* Washington, DC: U.S. Department of Education, Office of Special Education and Rehabilitative Services.

Williamson, M. L., Koch, R., Azen, C., & Chang, C. (1981). Correlates of intelligence test results in treated phenylketonuria children. *Pediatrics, 68,* 161–167.

Winters, J. J., & Semchuck, M. T. (1986). Retrieval from long-term store as a function of mental age and intelligence. *American Journal of Mental Deficiency, 90,* 440–448.

Witt, J. C., & Gresham, F. M. (1985). Review of the Wechsler Intelligence Scale for Children—Revised. In J. Mitchell (Ed.), *Ninth mental measurements yearbook.* Lincoln, NE: Buros Institute.

Wolfensberger, W. (1971). Will there always be an institution? Vol. 2. The impact of new service models. *Mental Retardation, 9,* 31–38.

Wood, M. M., & Hurley, O. L. (1977). Curriculum and instruction. In J. B. Jordan, A. H. Hayden, M. B. Karnes, & M. M. Wood (Eds.), *Early childhood education for exceptional children: A handbook of ideas and exemplary practices.* Reston, VA: Council for Exceptional Children.

Wyatt v. Stickney, 344 F. Supp. 373, 387, 396 (M. D., Ala., 1971).

Yoder, D. E., & Calculator, S. (1981). Some perspectives on intervention. *Journal of Autism & Developmental Disorders, 11,* 107–123.

Ysseldyke, J. E., & Algozzine, B. (1982). *Critical issues in special education.* Boston: Houghton Mifflin.

Zeaman, D., & House, B. J. (1963). The role of attention in retardate discrimination learning. In N. R. Ellis (Ed.), *Handbook of mental deficiency* (pp. 159–223). New York: McGraw-Hill.

Zigler, E. (1966). Research on personality structure in the retardate. In N. R. Ellis (Ed.), *International review of research in mental retardation* (Vol. 1, pp. 77–108). New York: Academic Press.

Zigler, E., & Trickett, P. (1978). IQ, social competence, and evaluation of early childhood intervention programs. *American Psychologist, 33,* 789–798.

EMOTIONAL

DISTURBANCE

RICHARD J. WHELAN

What is the risk of developing an emotional disturbance? Is it one out of 100, one out of 20, one out of 10? No. It is one out of one. This is a frightening thought, but it simply means that, given a particular pattern of stress or a certain combination of internal and external stressors, a person's ability to cope with the environment and the people in it could be hopelessly shattered. And it will remain shattered until the person at risk restores it by rearranging the environment, with or without assistance from others.

This chapter is about children and youth who, for a variety of reasons, have succumbed to the one-out-of-one-risk. It is also about how caring people, competent in professional practice, can help young people regain the dignity that comes with charting a course—sometimes rocky, sometimes smooth—for successful participation in a complex world.

Children who are troubled—and who cause trouble for their parents, brothers, sisters, teachers, and peers—are often diagnosed "emotionally disturbed." They are in conflict with self and others. The diagnosis is a description of their behavior, whose variance exceeds the tolerance and understanding of others. It is also a label, although there are other labels—"educably handicapped," "behavior disordered," "behavior disabled," "mentally disordered." The terms depend on the region or the state and are almost always used interchangeably, although "behavior disorder" is the term educators use most frequently.

Emotional disturbance in children does not discriminate; it occurs in the rich and the poor, the gifted and the retarded, the majority and the minority. It is the second member of each pair, however, who is especially at risk for developing patterns of behavior that are eventually classified as *deviant* (Jones, 1976; Kauffman, 1981; Morse, 1977). Although emotional disturbance is thought to be an entity separate from other conditions of pain, individuals with emotional anguish transcend all other categories.

This chapter first describes current practices in special education and related services for pupils[1] identified as emotionally disturbed, with emphasis on the years since passage of the Education for All Handicapped Children Act (PL 94–142) in 1975, and amended by the Individuals with Disabilities Education Act of 1990 (PL 101–476). Subsequent sections define and classify behaviors that constitute emotional disturbance, identify characteristic styles of coping, discuss procedures for identifying emotional disturbance, and enumerate the types of intervention to assist pupils in

---

[1]The word "pupils" is used to indicate children and youth typically served by educational systems (i.e., ages 3–21).

273

learning effective patterns of behavior. The final section focuses on projections about issues that will require solutions in the near future.

CURRENT PRACTICES

Although PL 94–142 as amended already has established its own historical niche as a model for public policy and educational reform, it clearly bestows no guarantee of quality instructional practice. It mandates specific procedural and substantive safeguards that, when put into practice by competent professionals, provide for a free and appropriate public education. It requires that state, school districts, and other educational agencies comply with regulations for identifying pupils with handicapping conditions and for planning educational evaluations. It does not address issues focused on quality of instruction and related services. When the law was initially passed, the nation clearly needed a strong policy on compliance. Now, however, compliance must serve as the foundation upon which quality educational programs are constructed.

RETROSPECTIVE ON NUMBERS

PL 94–142 has made a substantial difference in, if not the quality, the quantity of special education and related services available to the nation's pupils with various types of disabilities. Table 7.1 shows the increase in numbers of pupils with emotional disturbance served from 1976–77 through 1989–90 (Bureau of the Census, 1991). About 102,000 more pupils were in programs in 1989–90 than in 1976–77.

Yet, to celebrate the increase would be misleading. In 1989–90, 52% *were not served*, although states and school districts were under a mandate to serve *all* pupils with handicapping conditions. Why, after 15 years, is the population of pupils with emotional disturbance largely unserved? One might speculate that the U.S. Office of Special Education Programs' 2% predicted prevalence is wrong. In fact, most surveys indicate that 10% to 20% of the school-age population requires some type of special education intervention because of emotional problems. Clearly, although federal and state laws require special education or related services for all pupils with emotional disturbance, this important goal has not been reached.

● *TABLE 7.1*

Comparison of served and unserved emotionally disturbed pupils as percentages of the 2% prediction for selected school years

	Predicted	Served	Unserved
1976–77	887,740	280,592 (32%)	607,148 (68%)
1989–90	805,240	382,570 (48%)	422,670 (52%)

Another way to look at quantitative indices of progress is to compare enrollments of school-age pupils with the actual numbers in the general population. Table 7.2 compares the actual school-age general population and the recorded numbers who are enrolled in school programs. The important numbers are the percentages of pupils with emotional disturbance served when compared to the population and reported school enrollment. Also, all four percentages are less than 1% and, therefore, are not close to the conservative 2% predicted prevalence. That is, in 1989–90, about 88% of the school-age population was actually enrolled. Can anyone doubt that the 12% not enrolled are a higher risk for developing emotional problems than the 88% in school? Just using the conservative 2% prevalence estimate and applying it to the difference between the 1989–90 population and enrollment columns would mean that an additional 105,400 pupils would require special education and related services if indeed they were in school. Clearly, the mandate for a free appropriate public education for all pupils who are emotionally troubled has not been met.

RETROSPECTIVE ON PLACEMENTS

Federal regulations to implement the intent of PL 94–142 require that a continuum of alternative placements (Office of the Federal Register, 1991, Section 300.551, p. 54) be available to meet pupil needs for special education and related services. Varied instructional placements are necessary to comply with the least restrictive environment (LRE) requirement of PL 94–142. In brief, the LRE concept requires that pupils in need of special education and related services receive them, to the extent appropriate, in environments where pupils who are not handicapped are educated. An eligible pupil cannot be removed from a regular classroom until a determination is made that such placement cannot be maintained by additional professional services.

Table 7.3 shows the percent of pupils served in four types of placements for school years 1976–77, 1982–83, and 1989–90. It reveals little change over the years in placement distribution except for a 3% drop for special schools and a 7% increase for other placements from 1982–83 to 1989–90. Other placements refer to residential treatment centers and other types of hospital settings, or homebound instruction. They

● **TABLE 7.2**

Comparison of emotionally disturbed pupils served as percentages of actual and enrolled school-age populations for selected school years

	School-Age Population	% Served	School-Age Enrollment	% Served
1976–77	50,635,000	.55%	44,387,000	.63%
1989–90	45,388,000	.84%	40,262,000	.95%

are the most restrictive in that they are the most removed from a regular education environment (U.S. Department of Education, 1985, 1991).

Special schools serve only pupils identified as eligible for special education and related services. They do not provide instruction for pupils without disabilities. These schools have (a) highly specialized forms of instruction and other types of intervention, (b) modified facilities and equipment, and (c) interdisciplinary services to support the instructional program. They are not as restrictive as hospitals or residential centers because the pupils are there for only part of the day; they return home when school is dismissed. Yet, because special schools do not include regular education pupils, they are considered very restrictive.

Special classes are in a regular education building. Pupils assigned to them typically receive most, if not all, of their instruction with one teacher and a paraprofessional assigned to the classroom. Once pupils acquire new academic and social behavior skills in the special classroom, however, they may be eligible to receive more academic instruction in regular education classes.

Pupils are enrolled in *regular classes* for half a day or longer and may receive special education and related services from a resource room teacher for 2 or 3 hours a day. Resource room teachers work closely with regular teachers in areas such as academic planning and behavior management. As pupils progress, their time in the regular classroom can be increased. When that occurs, the special teacher's time in direct instruction decreases while time spent in consulting with regular class teachers increases. Resource rooms and consultation services are the least restrictive.

Although pupils with emotional problems seem to be receiving special education and related services in accordance with the requirement for a continuum of alternative placements (i.e., the LRE), there is cause for concern. For example, the federal label is "seriously emotionally disturbed," and it is the reason for the 2% prevalence rather than the 10% estimate some mental health professionals use. Can seriously emotionally disturbed pupils be adequately educated and treated in a regular classroom setting? The answer is a resounding "no!" By definition, those who have serious emotional disturbance require intensive forms of instruction and other services that are not provided in regular education environments.

● **TABLE 7.3**

Comparison of placements of emotionally disturbed pupils for selected school years

	Regular Classes	Special Classes	Special Schools	Other
1976–77	43%	38%	14%	5%
1982–83	43%	38%	16%	3%
1989–90	44%	36%	13%	7%

The conclusion, then, is that more than 40% of the pupils served (that is, the ones in regular classes) do not have serious emotional disturbance. This is not to deny that mildly or moderately affected pupils need specialized services. Indeed, they richly deserve them and should have access to them. Still, given the quantitative data reviewed, the question is: Are seriously involved pupils being displaced by those who have real but fewer needs? Unfortunately, data to address the issue are not readily available or retrievable. Again, either the 2% prevalence estimate is grossly in error or substantial numbers of pupils with serious emotional disturbance have not yet benefited from programs mandated by the federal laws.

RETROSPECTIVE ON PROGRESS

Though present educational programs are not sufficient in either quantity of quality to adequately serve pupils with emotional disturbance, substantial progress has been made. That progress is functionally related to passage of PL 94–142 in 1975.

Schools now take a much more active role in identifying emotional disturbance. Regular classroom teachers receive inservice training to look for behavior patterns that indicate that all is not well with a pupil. They also participate as members of, or contributors to, the comprehensive evaluation process, observing and recording academic and social behaviors, completing behavior checklists, and trying out different instructional approaches.

Regular and special educators are beginning to realize that they have much to contribute to the treatment of pupils with emotional disturbance. Educators are experts in changing behavior through instruction and pupil-teacher relationships. Also, because school is often a 6-hour-a-day experience, what better opportunity is there to provide programs that benefit pupils with emotional disturbance? Educators will not displace mental health professionals, but they are beginning to fully participate in the intervention process.

There are now more options for placement. Residential centers, special schools, and special classes are still used, but the flow of information among and between these administrative arrangements has improved. A youngster should have the opportunity to move through programs according to their progress in adjustment. Resource rooms are effective for children and youth who are not too aggressive and whose emotional problems are manifested by problems in academic or social performance.

For many years, programs for children with emotional disturbance were concentrated almost exclusively in intermediate elementary grades (4 through 6). The new laws, however, emphasize preschool and secondary programs, and attention focuses on these areas. Early intervention and prevention of more serious problems are goals of preschool services. Educators are beginning to realize that emotional disturbance is a concern at the secondary level as well. To exclude pupils because of emotional disturbance is no longer appropriate or legal. Not only has the continuum of service been expanded to include more placement opportunities, but it also has included a wider range of ages.

PREVENTION

It is a truism that it is cheaper (in dollars) to prevent than it is to treat emotional disturbance in children. For example, if $100 per child is spent in a year for a group of 500 first-graders, the yearly cost for a prevention program is $50,000. That is a great deal of money, but is the outcome worth it? Do future benefits exceed initial costs? Assume that in the absence of a prevention program, five (1%) of the 500 pupils will require residential treatment within a year, and that the treatment will last about 3 years at a cost of $30,000 per year. At $90,000 per pupil times 5, the total cost to society (parents, insurance companies, etc.) to treat the five pupils is $450,000. Now assume that a prevention program will inoculate four of the projected five pupils; they will not become emotionally disturbed. Clearly, a monetary savings, $360,000 (4 ∞ $90,000), will be realized. Spending $50,000 early will save $360,000 later, a cost-benefit ratio of about 1:7.

Closely associated with preventing emotional disturbance is, of course, developing optimal mental health. If children can develop mental health and, by so doing, are protected from developing an emotional disturbance, certain conditions must be present. Some years ago the Joint Commission on Mental Health of Children (1970, pp. 3–4) described those developmental and protective conditions as "rights":

1. The right to be wanted.
2. The right to be born healthy.
3. The right to a healthy environment.
4. The right to a satisfaction of basic needs.
5. The right to continuous loving care.
6. The right to acquire the intellectual and emotional skills necessary to achieve individual aspirations and to cope effectively in our society.

When these conditions are present, most infants and children develop competence and eventually become functioning and productive adults. The six basic conditions, however, represent ideal circumstances. Few children are exposed to the ideal each and every day and in every type of environment to which they must respond. Yet, most children experience the six conditions with enough intensity and continuity to ensure relative success in school and to prepare them for the demands of life after formal education ends.

Most programs to promote mental health approach prevention in three ways (Caplan, 1961; Clarizio & McCoy, 1983). One is the *primary* approach. It attempts to ensure that resources are available to help children acquire the six basic rights. Resources include adequate prenatal care, access to nutritious foods, prompt health care, pollution-free living conditions, protection from abuse (programs that teach parents functional parenting skills), and so on. Primary prevention focuses on groups of people; its intent is to keep problems from occurring by keeping children mentally, socially, and physically healthy. Head Start is an example of a primary program. It attempts to counter the impact of poverty by arranging developmental and skill-enhancing experiences for young children and their parents.

The *secondary* approach attempts to identify high-risk children so intervention can occur before minor problems become major ones. For example, a school district may screen all entering first-graders for behavior or learning problems. Screening data may indicate that 5% of the pupils have behavioral patterns (e.g., poor attention, tendency to tantrum, aggressive behavior) that preclude a successful experience in the first grade. The district can initiate a special, but brief, intervention program to teach the children better ways to solve problems. The program may involve direct instruction of the children, specialized inservice training for teachers, or both.

Another approach, called *tertiary* (literally, a third level of action), is basically remedial or rehabilitative, assisting children to progress from a low level to a higher level of functioning. An example is full-time placement of a seriously emotionally disturbed child in a residential center that provides special instruction and other types of therapeutic experiences.

Some interesting primary and secondary approaches are occurring in school environments. Prevention measures should start early, even before birth, but school is the logical place to implement them. Children are required to attend schools. School is where children learn knowledge and skills that enable them to solve problems, plan ahead, and function satisfactorily in a complex world.

School, or curriculum-based (secondary), approaches to preventing emotional disturbance concentrate on teaching pupils how to solve problems (i.e., how to identify alternative solutions), how to accurately predict the consequences of behavior, how to find causes (antecedent events) of behavior, how to find information, how to set goals, and so on. When children learn problem-solving skills, they apply them in interpersonal situations, and they apparently retain their skills for a substantial time (Winett, Stefanek, & Riley, 1983). Some secondary approaches teach children to recognize the relationship between feelings and behavior and to use that understanding, in tandem with problem-solving skills, to increase competence in interpersonal encounters and other learning situations. Still others change school or classroom environments. Classrooms that are task-oriented, yet provide warm, supportive relationships, seem to produce higher pupil achievement and social growth than other arrangements do (Moos, 1979).

Though primary prevention programs apparently result in positive outcomes for children, no coordinated system currently is in place to ensure that every child has access to resources that produce physical and emotional competence. Public and private agencies do provide a variety of services or resources related to acquiring and maintaining mental health, but children, unlike some adults, cannot identify or get to them, simply because they do not have the knowledge to access a complex system. Unless a school's responsibility as a public and social agency is extended to include new programs for physical and mental health, primary prevention efforts likely will remain fragmented or nonexistent.

CATEGORY DEMOGRAPHICS

How do children who are labeled emotionally disturbed behave? Behavior patterns range from almost total withdrawal to extreme aggression or hostility. A child may exhibit behaviors that fall predominantly at one end of the spectrum or the other, or both withdrawal and aggressive behaviors may be observed in the same child at different times, depending on the circumstances.

In what context does emotionally disturbed behavior occur? In some cases, a child's behavior that is considered deviant or reflective of emotional damage may occur only in a specific classroom, not at home, on the playground, at the community center, or even in another classroom. At the other extreme, the child's deviant behavior may be observed in all environments where the child functions.

How do environmental expectations contribute to emotionally disturbed behavior? Consider two children with emotional problems. The first, who has always lived in the same community, develops behavior patterns that are incompatible with community standards. One may assume that the child has been exposed to experiences that evoke acceptable behaviors but, for reasons unknown, has not really acquired them. The second child, although he performs and relates well in a familiar environment, when placed in a new situation with unfamiliar requirements, repeatedly fails to cope. The first is disturbed; the second is not. His behaviors are realistic attempts to cope with expectations of the new environment. They do not show emotional disturbance, even though they are similar to those of the first child. Behavior that appears to be "emotionally disturbed" may actually be a normal response to the stress of an unfamiliar environment.

It is a simple matter of adjustment. An analogy is when one is unable to speak or comprehend the language of a new location and so requires a period of learning, often accompanied by stress and anxiety. Unless the newcomer is accepted with patience, understanding, empathy, and support in the new setting, unusual, even deviant, behavior may be adopted as a coping mechanism.

Educators must give precise and consistent attention to children from family cultures that are different from the majority represented in the school. By attention, I mean perception, understanding, acceptance, and even celebration of differences. The circumstances surrounding these cultural considerations are unique to the United States and pertain to the "melting pot" concept of strength through diversity. Unfortunately, the stew in the melting pot is more of a mush, in which differences are discouraged and conformity is encouraged. The result is equivalent to the scientific term *entropy*, a condition that associates sameness with chaos. This is contrasted to the strength found in differentiation and distinctiveness (Wiener, 1954).

Ideally, the melting pot concept should have been translated into a stew in which all of the various ingredients are compatible and relished, not only for their uniqueness and individual worth but for their value in contributing to the goodness of the whole. In reality, however, attempts to sustain cultural integrity (while not entirely unsuccessful) have not been without cost to communities, schools, and individuals. Indeed, many (white European) cultures have lost—or conceal— their past in order to acquire economic and political power. Others have not been so successful. For them—Native Americans, Hispanics, and African Americans—the path to success has been strewn with obstacles, some only recently removed by humane litigation and progressive legislation. Now, new thinking must follow their lead if the historical melting pot concept, the intrinsic strength of the nation, is to be realized.

Problems arise when one group seeks to impose its standards on another, a situation that usually stems from the first group's fear of the differences of the second group. In a related problem, various groups must interact but the interaction is strained by mutual fear, distrust, and bias. This results from failing to understand and accept individuals as individuals and seeing them rather as stereotypes. This tendency to generalize is why disproportionately more children from minority groups are placed in special education settings.

Teachers often fail to realize that children need different experiences to learn different skills. Discrepancies between a child's experiences and a teacher's expectations often go unrecognized—leading to both learning and instructional failure. A child's failure to learn, moreover, often is misinterpreted and aggravated through labels such as "mentally retarded" or "emotionally disturbed," which are covering up instructional failure. This pattern occurs more often with minority children who, for a variety of reasons, bring to school different competencies from those that are expected and deemed necessary to learn reading, writing, and ciphering. Educators fail to recognize the intrinsic strengths in differences and to use these differences effectively in planning learning experiences. Cultural differences can benefit learning. As Johnson (1976) stressed, the goal of academic and social competence is viable for all children, regardless of whether they are different from the majority. If educators really believe in the value of individual differences and individualized instruction, they can translate their belief into successful child learning.

Any child may be identified as having a disability. Hearing loss, for example, occurs without regard to cultural background. The same is true for any other handicapping condition. Hearing loss is a disability. The disability label, however, must reflect a truly disabling condition, attributed to the presence of the handicapping condition.

Identification of a disability, moreover, should not (although it often does) imply inferior status. Its only intent is to meet the needs of children so they may contribute fully to society. Traditionally, however, certain individuals within a group structure have been shunned because their behaviors have exceeded the bounds of their group's criteria for normality. Some behaviors may lead to a child's total exclusion from a group. Rhodes (1977) and Szasz (1974) discussed exclusion as a reflection of the inner turmoil of the so-called normal group, often so intense that it is too painful to confront. Being too distressful, it is displaced onto those who show deviation, a process known as projection (Freud, 1913/1950). The group is thus justified in purging or extruding the different from the undifferent.

Educators who are aware of these powerful, intrapersonal processes in themselves are better able to help children deal with their own painful realities. At any point in time, we can have an emotional disturbance, and no one is normal 100% of the time (Rhodes, 1977). All individuals encounter adjustment problems to some extent as they cope with both their own and others' needs. Recognition of their own reality, as well as the reality of those needing help, should enable educators to better plan programs that will help pupils help themselves to become more satisfied and competent participants in society.

EDUCATIONAL DEFINITIONS

Definitions do not solve problems, nor do they necessarily predict the precise instructional strategy that is best for a given child. The word *autistic*, as used by Kanner (1943), is a definitional descriptor or label that refers to a rather specific set of behaviors that must be observed before it is applied. Rather than describe the entire set of behaviors, a single descriptor or label is used. As long as there is agreement on the label's meaning, it can function as a brief communication.

Educators should be careful not to use labels to explain behavior. Asked why a child's behavior is peculiar, an educator says, "Because the child is autistic." That response is an "explanation" that explains nothing. Educators often use descriptive labels this way to rationalize instructional failure: "I can't teach this pupil because he is autistic." The proper statement should be, "Under the conditions I have arranged, this pupil has not acquired the skills important for academic and social progress." This positive approach assumes that the problems exhibited do not reside wholly within the pupil but, rather, in the interrelationship between pupil and environment. Indeed, the environment may not provide the support necessary to enable the pupil to progress in adaptive development.

In view of the problems associated with definitions, a behavior description approach is more feasible. One way to describe behavior disorders or emotional disturbance from an educational perspective is to include its effects on others as well as its effects on the pupil. This is accomplished by asking three questions (Pate, 1963):

1. Does the pupil's behavior place disproportionate demands on the teacher and other school personnel?
2. Does the pupil's behavior interfere with the educational progress of the peer group?
3. Does the pupil's behavior become more disorganized and irrational over time?

If the answer to all three questions is *yes*, a rationale for changes in instructional procedures has been established. The three questions cannot be used to diagnose emotional disturbance. A diagnosis is not necessary, however, for educational changes to be made. If the pupil is emotionally disturbed, the answer to all three questions will be *yes*, but three *yes* answers are not sufficient to diagnose emotional disturbance; other conditions may elicit *yes* answers, too.

Further investigation may or may not confirm the presence of emotional disturbance. Even if such a diagnosis is made, its usefulness is only in assigning extra resources consistent with and contingent upon proper identification of the handicapping condition. The fact remains that developing, implementing, and evaluating an instructional program is by far the most important and difficult activity.

In response to the first two questions above, a child's behavior, whether destructive, withdrawn, or both, can take a great amount of teacher time, and, if a child exhibits two or three temper tantrums each day, other children are deprived of time needed with the teacher. The most significant question is the third. If progress is not observed, conditions impinging upon the child obviously must be modified.

A more precise educational description of behaviors is provided by Bower (1969), based on his extensive research in identifying children with emotional or behavioral disorders. According to Bower, emotionally disturbed children exhibit certain behavior patterns that deviate markedly from expectations and are consistently displayed over a substantial period of time:

1. Absence of knowledge and skill acquisition in academics and social behaviors not attributed to intellectual capacity, hearing and visual status, or physical health anomalies.
2. Absence of positive, satisfying interpersonal relationships with adults and peers.
3. Frequent instances of inappropriate behavior episodes that are surprising or unexpected for the conditions in which they occur.
4. Observable periods of diminished verbal and other motor activity (e.g., moods of depression or unhappiness).
5. Frequent complaints of a physical nature, such as stomachaches, soreness in the arm, or general fatigue.

Of the five criteria, the first is often the initial indication that a pupil may be troubled. It is a sign teachers can easily observe. A pupil struggling to cope with inner and external turmoil has little energy left for acquiring successful coping skills. The second criterion is also readily observable. Social behaviors directed at others typically are harsh and unkind or may be marked by avoidance of others. Regarding the third, a teacher may be baffled when a pupil launches a physical and verbal attack upon another pupil or adult for no apparent reason or precipitating cause. Fourth, even the most consistent, overtly hostile pupil will have periods of low behavioral output. This may be observed in slowness of walk and other movements, a look of sadness, speaking without affect, and the content of assigned schoolwork. When the veneer of toughness is dropped, a frightened, confused pupil—one vainly reaching out for help—appears.

Along with teachers, school nurses often are involved in circumstances related to the fifth criterion. In a study designed to check the accuracy of this statement, I asked a school nurse to count the frequency of visits by pupils to the school's infirmary. Independently, the teachers in the same building were asked to rank pupils in overall adjustment. The pupils who ranked lowest predictably visited the school nurse most often. Physical complaints always should be checked; a complaint may have a valid medical basis and, if neglected, could lead to more serious problems.

Teachers can use Bower's five-point educational description of emotionally disturbed pupils to identify children who may need program modifications. These points also are useful in evaluating the effectiveness of a modified program. If skills are acquired, relationships improve, behavior outbursts recede, depression diminishes, and physical complaints are real rather than contrived, an instructional program may be judged as appropriate and effective.

One other aspect of Bower's criteria should be emphasized. The last three criteria may reflect strategies for avoiding and escaping from the lack of competencies associated with achieving success in the first two criteria (R. L. McDowell, personal communication, July, 1969). Failure in skill acquisition, plus not being able to relate to others in a positive fashion, is a painful state of affairs that may lead to avoidance behavior. To avoid a reading lesson that invariably leads to failure, a pupil may have a temper tantrum, withdraw from interaction, or complain about a headache. Avoidance behaviors signal a teacher to review instructional procedures. Are expectations for reading compatible with the pupil's level of competence? Does the student have the necessary skills to relate to others? If not, the pupil's program must be changed.

Bower's five criteria for defining pupils with emotional disturbance have been included in the federal regulations (Office of the Federal Register, 1985, 1991). Section 300.5 (b)(8) defines seriously emotionally disturbed in Bower's terms, but it adds an important statement. One or a combination of the five behavior patterns must be displayed, and it must be demonstrated that an observed pattern *adversely affects educational performance*. The educational implications of this added statement or criterion are obvious. A pupil could exhibit behavior patterns 2 through 4, but if they do not interfere with educational performance, the condition of serious emotional disturbance does not exist. And if it does not exist, the pupil is not eligible for special education and related services. How, then, can school district personnel determine which pupils do or do not have a serious emotional disturbance? The criteria do not address this question.

Others (Bower, 1982; Kauffman, 1980) have raised additional issues regarding the words in the regulations that were added to Bower's original definition. First, Bower's five criteria apply to 8% or 10% of the school-age population, not the 2% estimate used by the federal government. Second, seriously emotionally disturbed children cannot be served appropriately in regular education environments; by definition they typically need more structured, intensive intervention than can be provided in regular classrooms. If pupils now being served in regular education placements are making academic and social behavior progress, the word "serious" should be removed from the definition. This not only would bring the federal definition into agreement with Bower's, but it may enable school districts to serve more troubled and troublesome pupils by removing a restriction. On the other hand, if national policy is to provide excess cost dollars for educating seriously emotionally disturbed pupils (that is, the 2% prevalence estimate), a new definition should be developed.

After comprehensively reviewing many educational descriptions, Kauffman (1977) suggested a brief description of pupils with emotional disorders:

> "Children with behavior disorders are those who chronically and markedly respond to their environment in socially unacceptable and/or personally unsatisfying ways but who can be taught more socially acceptable and personally gratifying behavior." (p. 23)

This description focuses on behaviors that are not consistent with current societal standards. It implies that pupils may be aware that all is not well internal and external to themselves. Most important, it conveys the positive expectation that pupils with emotional disturbance can be helped through appropriate instructional practices. Kauffman's expanded description also presents information regarding the settings in which emotionally disturbed pupils, depending on the seriousness of their condition, can be served (e.g., regular classroom, resource room, special class, residential treatment).

When all of the educational descriptions are analyzed, it becomes apparent that the emotionally disturbed pupils' behavior display is characterized by excesses and deficits (Whelan & Gallagher, 1972). Behavior excesses are actions the pupil displays to an inordinate degree—too many tantrums, too many fights. Deficits are behaviors the pupil does not exhibit or does so to a much lesser extent than the norm—too few appropriate social contacts, too few assignments completed. A listing of behavior excesses and deficits observed in a pupil can illuminate and provide targets or objectives for instructional activities.

Educational descriptions are useful for circumscribing problems that require solutions. They form the foundation for subsequent development of instructional programs. They also contribute to the criteria used to evaluate effects of instructional procedures and programs—that is, does the description change in a positive direction as a function of what is done to, with, and for a pupil with emotional disturbance?

A NEW DEFINITION

Describing or defining pupils with serious emotional disturbance is a continuing problem in search of a solution. There is ferment among professionals about the criteria that should be used to determine if a pupil has emotional or behavioral problems. This resulted in a proposal submitted to the U.S. Congress for a new definition of pupils with serious emotional disturbance to replace the one now contained in the federal regulations in support of the Individuals with Disabilities Education Act (IDEA).

In addition to the previously described criticisms of the current definition, advocates for a new definition stress other failings with the criteria that school districts throughout the country must follow in determining whether a pupil is eligible under the label *seriously emotionally disturbed* (SED). One part of the current definition states that "the term [SED] does not include children who are socially maladjusted." In professional practice, the label *socially maladjusted* often is translated into conduct disorders. The label describes pupils who act out or otherwise visibly show by their conduct problems of adjusting to school rules and other demands imposed by society at large. Their behavior draws the attention of others who perceive the behavior to be far removed from the norm in terms of social expectations for interactions and relationships with others, be they peers or adults.

The difficulty with excluding children who show social maladjustment or conduct disorders is that it is inconsistent with the rest of the federal definition. At least two of the five parts of the current definition—namely, the inability to build or maintain satisfactory interpersonal relationships with peers and teachers, and inappropriate behavior or feelings under normal circumstances—clearly describe behaviors that are characteristic of social maladjustment or conduct disorders. Therefore, professionals are faced with the dilemma of a definition that includes conduct disorders in one of its parts, yet excludes it in a subsequent part.

Forness (1992), a leading proponent in getting the current definition changed to a new one, has pointed out other problems with the present definition in regulations that support IDEA. For example, the first criterion in the current definition, an inability to learn that cannot be explained by intellectual, sensory, or health factors, overlaps a great deal with the definition of learning disabilities.

Another problem is that the phrase "adversely affects educational performance" often is interpreted narrowly in practice to mean performance in academic subjects. Therefore, the identification process tends to overlook consideration of how a pupil deals with interpersonal an social relationships. In attempting to determine whether a pupil meets the definition of seriously emotionally disturbed, the pupil's performance, an area that is extremely important in adjusting to the demands of school and society in general, often is excluded. Finally, Forness pointed out that the current definition is not closely related to diagnostic criteria mental health professionals use, nor does it accurately describe the students predominantly found in special education programs for pupils with serious emotional disturbance.

The Council for Children with Behavior Disorders (CCBD) has joined with a group of professional associations concerned with appropriate services for children with emotional problems. This joint advocacy group is called the National Mental Health and Special Education Coalition. The Coalition has been working for a number of years to strike the present definition of seriously emotionally disturbed from the regulations in support of IDEA (formerly PL 94–142), and to substitute a definition that more clearly describes student characteristics that require special education and related services. The proposed definition now before the U.S. Congress for consideration is:

> (i) The term *emotional* or *behavioral disorder* means a disability characterized by behavioral or emotional responses in school programs so different from appropriate age, culture, or ethnic norms that they adversely affect educational performance. Educational performance includes academic, social, vocational, or personal skills. Such a disability is more than a temporary expected response to stressful events in the environment; is consistently exhibited in two different settings, at least one of which is school-related; and is unresponsive to direct intervention applied in the general education setting, or the child's condition is such that general education intervention would be insufficient.
>
> (ii) Emotional or behavioral disorders can co-exist with other disabilities.
>
> (iii) This category may include children or youth with schizophrenic disorders, affective disorders, anxiety disorders or other sustained disorders of conduct or adjustment when they adversely affect educational performance in accordance with section (i).

Clearly the new definition is more inclusive than the old one. It takes into account not only the affective component of emotional adjustment but also the social and academic performances that are affected when a pupil has emotional or behavioral disorders. If adopted, this definition will set to rest the disputes about whether conduct disorders actually are part of the definition of seriously emotionally disturbed. A key phrase in the definition that will exclude pupils with mild disabilities and those with short-term problems, such as response to a stressful event, is the last phrase in (i). That phrase states "and is unresponsive to direct intervention applied in a general education setting, or the child's condition is such that general education intervention would be insufficient." What this phrase means is that before a pupil can be identified as having an emotional or behavior disorder (EBD), it first must be determined whether modifications in the general education environment produce changes in the pupil's behavior or emotional profile. This phrase in and of itself should preclude inordinate numbers of pupils being referred for special education and related services under the new definition.

Even though the proposed definition fits the actual nature and characteristics of the pupils served by special education programs in the schools, definitions do not solve problems. At best, they provide professionals with guidelines that can be used to improve services to pupils who have so many affective, social, and academic needs. I hope that the proposed definition will be adopted and that professionals can move beyond the controversy of defining pupils under this category into areas of research that will produce instructional and behavioral interventions that are both humanistic and effective.

CLASSIFICATION SYSTEMS

Imagine a child sitting in front of many objects of various colors and size. The child tries various arrangements. The blue objects go in one pile, the reds in another, the greens in another. Not satisfied with classification by color, she tries it by size: small, medium, large. The child is behaving as a classifier, one who sorts or arranges objects, events, or observations into groups that share features in common. This classifier is not yet satisfied, however; the system considers only one variable at a time—size or color. Is there another way to sort, one that will use all of the available information? Indeed there is; she now sorts all small blue objects, medium reds, and so on. Instead of three piles, she now has nine. But has she considered every variable? Several objects are wood, others are plastic, and some are even made of glass. By now, our classifier gives up in frustration, puts all of the objects into one pile, and comes up with a name, a single classification if you will, of all objects that have six sides: BLOCKS.

Like scientists historically, particularly those who must classify emotional disturbance, our little girl acted upon an obligation to bring order out of chaos (Menninger, Mayman, & Pruyser, 1963). In doing so, her classification system became so complex that it was neither clear nor useful (Cromwell, Blashfield & Strauss, 1975). In returning from the specific to the general, she unified a chaotic multitude into a single concept. We who classify emotional disturbance also move from general to specific and back to general, seeking a balance between each experience as new and searching for a perfect system, one that is simple and consistent. For example, when three people independently observe a person, they can arrange the observed behavior patterns into a category (pile, if you will), and that category (lycanthropy[2]) will be the same for all three.

Binary System. Even though the binary approach to classification has no theoretical or philosophical foundation, educational agencies use it widely. It is based on the federal definition of seriously emotionally disturbed. The binary model applies a *yes–no* decision process: Either disturbance exists (yes), or it does not (no). A pupil is or isn't. The binary system does not allow for variations or degree of emotional disturbance (mild, moderate, severe).

Behavior Analysis System. The behavior analysis system is an outgrowth of disenchantment with diagnostic categories or labels. Essentially, its proponents believe labels are not functional. They are not related to differential intervention, are not used reliably across pupils, and add little to predicting length or success of intervention. A behavior analysis system does not label individuals. Instead, it describes or classifies behavior as excessive (needing to be eliminated or reduced in frequency) or deficient (needing to be replaced or increased) in frequency (Kanfer & Saslow, 1967; Phillips, Draguns, & Bartlett, 1975).

The process used to determine if a behavior is beyond the boundaries of societal norms includes several procedures. In a question format:

1. How often does the behavior occur? How long does it last when it does occur? Example: Temper tantrums occur 3 times a day in the classroom; the average time per tantrum is 12 minutes.
2. What elicits and maintains the behavior? Example: Tantrums occur prior to request to read aloud; tantrums seem to be maintained by peer attention and escape from oral reading requests.
3. What is the developmental history of the behavior? Example: Tantrums have been and are used in other situations (e.g., getting a toy that initially was denied).
4. Are there any instances of the behavior not occurring in situations that usually elicit it? Example: Tantrums do not occur when child is asked to read directions for constructing a car model.

The information collected for each question is used to establish if a problem even exists. Just as important, information related to an intervention plan also is collected. Using the simple examples for each question, several important points are apparent. First, tantrums area a problem in the classroom. Second, they happen when the pupil is asked to read orally, and they enable the pupil to escape from the task. Third, tantrums are used to get objects as well as to avoid stressful situations. Fourth, the pupil does have the ability to use self-control in some situations (e.g., read directions aloud before getting parts for a model car).

An intervention plan to reduce or eliminate tantrums could use several concurrent

---

[2]False belief of being transformed into a wolf during the month of February (Menninger et al., 1963, p. 424). Although the observers may agree on the category, it is not a guarantee that the category is useful unless one has a treatment for wolf transformations.

procedures. For example, intervention could include an analysis of reading skills. Are the directions for the model car easier to read than a story? If so, changing the difficulty level of the story book is a first step. If the pupil has a tantrum to avoid revealing an inability to pronounce a word, easier passages may ensure a successful reading response. At the same time, control of consequences may be essential. What would happen if the tantrums were ignored, if they did not provide an escape route from a task that could be accomplished? Further, would *possible* consequences (the car model) decrease tantrum behavior? And last, intervention could emphasize teaching an alternative response to tantrums when confronted with a difficult situation: "Mr. Jones, these words are too hard. Would you help me?"

The advantages of this system are twofold. The first, and most obvious, is that it describes behaviors rather than labels pupils. At the same time, the analysis process provides information that can be used in developing and carrying out an intervention plan. Disadvantages can be noted, too. There is no nationally accepted format for classifying types of problem behaviors or degrees of their seriousness. One tantrum a day may be considered serious in one place but considered a developmental stage in another. Another problem relates to the criteria for determining if observed problems reflect emotional disturbance—no trivial point when the label means dollars and other resources for special education programs. Should a pupil exhibit three, four, or five deviant behaviors at a specific frequency before the label is applied?

Medical System. Although not typically used by special educators or educational agencies, DSM-III-R has by far the best known system for classifying behaviors. The full title of this book of diagnostic categories developed by the American Psychiatric Association (APA, 1987) is *Diagnostic and Statistical Manual of Mental Disorders.* Most mental health professionals (for example, psychiatrists, clinical psychologists, and psychiatric social workers) use DSM-III-R guidelines to classify patterns of behavior.

The roots of DSM-III-R can be traced back to the work of a European psychiatrist named Emil Kraeplin (1856–1926). Kraeplin believed that emotional disturbance or mental disorder meant diseases with traceable, organic causes (Achenbach & Edelbrock, 1983; Menninger et al., 1963). Just as bacteria cause infection, some as yet unknown agent causes mental disorder (the brain becomes diseased).

Not all mental health professionals believe this. Many, for example, believe that internal conflicts produce observable bizarre or nonfunctional behaviors or symptoms (e.g., hearing voices from afar). In any event, be it internal conflict or germ, the cause must be found and corrected if deviant symptoms are to be decreased or eliminated.

Until recently, medical classification systems rarely included children or adolescents. Classification was for adults. Young people, if classified at all, were placed in one of a variety of categories for adult mental disorders. DSM-III-R has 11 major diagnostic categories under "Disorders Usually First Evident in Infancy, Childhood or Adolescence." These 11 can be grouped into five functional areas. Table 7.4 provides a summary only, and the examples in parentheses are illustrations. DSM-III-R offers a complete description of the 11 diagnostic categories.

The DSM-III-R *Manual* has, under each diagnostic category, two sections, entitled "Differential Diagnosis" and "Diagnostic Criteria." The differential diagnosis section lists other disorders to consider before selecting a specific category as the focus of intervention or treatment. The diagnostic criteria include a rather detailed description of the behaviors as well as a required minimum duration for each. Table 7.5 is an adaptation of a typical diagnostic category from DSM-III-R.

Cluster System. The cluster system is based upon complex statistical procedures applied to responses to items on various behavior rating scales. Quay (1965) reviewed the pioneering work conducted by Hewin and Jenkins in the mid-1940s. This was before the introduction of high-speed computers, so by today's standards it is considered simplistic. A cluster system (sometimes referred to as "factorial," or "dimensional") typically correlates the items from the scales. If several items correlate highly with each other, they are said to form a cluster. For example, Hewitt and Jenkins identified a cluster of items they called "unsocialized aggressive." The items or, more

---

● **TABLE 7.4**

Adaptation of DSM-III-R 11 categories of childhood mental disorders into five major areas

    A. Intellectual
        1. mental retardation
    B. Developmental
        2. pervasive (autistic-like behaviors)
        3. specific (disorders in academic subjects, speech, language, motor coordination)
        4. gender (distress about being a boy or girl, plus intense desire to be of the opposite sex)
    C. Behavioral
        5. attention deficit (inattentive, impulsive, fidgets)
           conduct (violates rights of others and societal norms, steal, lies, cruel)
        6. other (loss of interest in others or activities; refusal to talk; uncertainty regarding goals, morals, friends; repetitive, useless behaviors such as body rocking, hand waving)
    D. Affective
        7. anxiety (pervasive worry about separation from parents, meeting new people, past and future events)
           avoidant (excessive withdrawal from contact with people other than family)
    E. Physical
        8. eating (includes anorexia nervosa, bulimia, pica, rumination)
        9. tics (repetitive movements with no apparent purpose, twitches, grimaces, vocalizations)
       10. elimination (loss of bladder or bowel control not from organic causes; passing feces or urinating in inappropriate places, e.g., clothes, floor)
       11. speech (fluency disorder in speech rate and rhythm that produces unintelligibility; unrelated groups of words)

accurately, behavior descriptions associated with this cluster were (a) assaultive behavior, (b) starting fights, (c) cruelty, (d) defiance of authority, (e) destruction of property, and (f) lack of guilt for inappropriate behaviors.

Following up the original work of Hewitt and Jenkins, Quay (1975, 1979) produced four clusters of behaviors considered to be more reliable and valid. These are shown in Table 7.6. Each cluster has several items that are closely associated with each other. When a pupil scores high, for example, on the four sample items listed under

● **TABLE 7.5**

Adaptation of DSM-III-R diagnostic category of oppositional disorder

A. Differential diagnosis
   1. Not due to presence of (a) conduct disorder, (b) psychotic disorder, (c) depression. Also, behavior is much more frequent than in most people of the same mental age.
B. Diagnostic criteria
   1. Behavior pattern observed for at least 6 months.
   2. Displays at least five of the following behaviors:
      a. loses temper
      b. argumentative with adults
      c. defies rules, requests
      d. annoys other people
      e. blames others for his/her mistakes
      f. easily bothered by others
      g. angry and resentful
      h. vindictive and seeks revenge
      i. obscene language

● **TABLE 7.6**

Adaptation of Quay's behavioral clusters

A. Conduct Disorder
   1. verbal and physical aggression
   2. disruptive
   3. negative
   4. defies authority
B. Anxiety–Withdrawal
   1. fearful
   2. few social contacts
   3. isolation
   4. shyness

C. Immaturity
   1. preoccupied
   2. attention deficit
   3. passive
   4. daydreaming
   5. slowness
D. Socialized Aggression
   1. gang activity
   2. stealing
   3. truancy

"conduct disorder," a classification can be made. Quay and his colleagues pointed out that this classification system has implications for differential use of classroom structure, instructional activities, and effective use of reinforcers (Von Isser, Quay, & Love, 1980). For instance, pupils classified under "conduct disorder" or "socialized aggression" may require much concrete reinforcement to change their behavior, as compared with pupils who are fearful or immature.

Other researchers (Achenbach & Edelbrock, 1983) also use a cluster approach to classify types of emotional disturbance. For example, according to some, pupils may be classified as *internalizers*. These pupils show behaviors that are described as depressed or withdrawn, and they often are overly concerned about bodily pains or functions. In contrast, others are classified as *externalizers*. Their behavior pattern typically is described as aggressive, overly active, and cruel.

To a classroom teacher, classification issues may hold little importance. After all, the teacher's role is to help pupils learn academic material, gain understanding about self and others, and develop functional self-control and independence. What does it matter if a pupil has one label or another? Does the label tell the teacher how or what to teach? Unfortunately, the answer to both questions is *no*. In fact, a specific classification is no more likely to predict educational procedures than is the academic assessment information educators typically gather (Sinclair, Forness, & Axleson, 1985). Yet, research on classification should continue. Cluster systems seem to have some application to differential teaching, especially in selecting consequences for behavior and in planning learning environments.

At the present time, classification systems, because they are descriptive, at least show a pupil's behavior profile in a manner that can be used to further a pool of information, which teachers can translate (albeit primitively) into instructional planning. That is no small contribution. Meanwhile, the profession can continue to seek a system that prescribes type, length, and probability of successful intervention.

*E*TIOLOGY

Behaviors that deviate substantially from the norm do not occur in a vacuum. Etiology of emotional disturbance usually involves the interaction of multiple factors. It is not a one-to-one relationship between a single cause and a single effect. Behaviors of emotionally disturbed children typically are chronic (persist over time) and acute (deviate to the point of attracting attention from others).

Search for cause involves identifying two general kinds of factors: predisposing and precipitating. *Predisposing* factors are conditions that may increase the probability of developing behavior disorders. A child who has never been allowed to develop skills for independent functioning may be predisposed to problems when placed in a classroom in which expectations to plan and work alone are high. *Precipitating* factors are the immediate stressors or incidents that trigger maladaptive behaviors. Using the example of an overly dependent child, if the mother suddenly dies, the child is left with little support—a condition that may elicit a panic reaction of withdrawal from or attacks upon the environment. Predisposing and precipitating factors usually operate in tandem. If given sufficient support, most children can manage the grief of a parent's death; they eventually adjust and continue to progress.

The causes of emotional disturbance may be divided into two major categories: biogenic and psychogenic. *Biogenic* refers to the physical, biological, and hereditary insults that diminish an individual's capability to cope with environmental demands. Psychogenic describes internal conflicts raging within a child and the relationship of these conflicts to external, complex, environmental events.

Biogenic factors usually are more evident in the severe types of emotional disturbance. The presence of a genetic correlation has been noted for years; the risk of becoming psychotic is greater for those who are genetically related to a person diagnosed as psychotic. Shields and Slater (1961) and Kauffman (1981) described this relationship in some detail.

A note of caution is necessary here to forestall erroneous conclusions. If one identical twin is schizophrenic, the other's risk of becoming schizophrenic is high. It is about 90% if the twins are not environmentally separated; the risk drops to about 75% if they are separated. This difference may be attributed to environmental influences. The caution is that the risk estimates are correlational, not causal. If schizophrenia were postulated to be caused by a recessive gene, for example, it would follow that all children of two schizophrenic parents would be schizophrenic. This does not occur. The risk, while high, is about 39% (Shields & Slater, 1961).

Clearly, especially for severe forms of emotional disturbance, heredity and a predisposition to become maladjusted are related. For example, the risk of developing schizophrenia for the general population is about 1% or less. If a child's parents are "normal" and other aspects of the environment, such as normal siblings, are supportive, and if few health or psychological risks are present, the probability of developing schizophrenia for that child is quite small. But, if a child of one schizophrenic parent is adopted by normal parents, the risk for that child developing schizophrenia is about 10%—6% less than being reared by the biological parent (Cullinan, Epstein, & Lloyd, 1983; Shields & Slater, 1961). Apparently, other factors, including family situations and childrearing practices, operate along with genetic factors in determining outcomes. If two schizophrenic parents provide a highly pathological environment, why do not more than 39% of their children develop schizophrenia?

Psychogenic factors are associated with the relationship between child and environment over time. The search for psychogenic causation of emotional disturbance involves careful study by mental health professionals for the full range of emotional disorders, mild through severe, and covers an individuals's infancy, early childhood, late childhood, and adolescence. These time periods are designated only for convenience in developing an interpersonal history; the periods overlap and are interwoven. The study ranges from comprehensive analysis of events occurring over years, to intensive study of immediate situations. If a child suddenly exhibits maladaptive behaviors, the search for cause may be confined to the present or immediate past; if troublesome behavior has developed gradually to the point that it increasingly attracts the attention of others, the search may probe for traumatic experiences in both the distant and recent past.

Etiology is as varied as the behavior of children diagnosed as emotionally disturbed. In analyzing the many factors associated with causes of emotional disturbance, Rhodes (1972) reviewed the various theories or approaches to determining etiology. Educators realistically concerned with understanding the causes of behavior must realize that, whatever the etiology, their responsibility for arranging productive learning environments remains constant. A child with biological insults must be taught just as responsibly as one who has experienced psychological trauma. Better understanding of these conditions can lead to learning strategies that are related directly to correcting the factors that evoked the maladaptive behavior patterns in the first place. Understanding is a foundation, a rationale, for approaching solutions to problems that children present to educators.

Two divergent approaches to understanding the origins of emotional disturbance have been selected for illustration, as shown in Figure 7.1. This schematic is vastly simplified here. The two selected approaches are highly complex and require extensive study for complete understanding. Nevertheless, the figure is designed to point out some contrasts and similarities.

An *intrapsychic* (at times referred to as *psychoanalytic*) *approach* seeks to understand etiology through an intense examination of the inner turmoil reflected by the observable behaviors. The *behavioral approach*, an accumulation of several learning theories, searches for the understanding of cause by observing the relationship among the complex environmental events that elicit and maintain deviant behavior. The commonality between the two approaches is the *chaotic environment*. Chaotic environ-

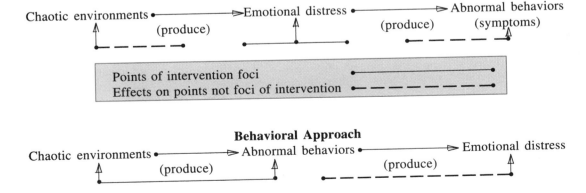

● **FIGURE 7.1**

Simplified schematic of two approaches for explaining origins of emotional disturbance

ments are characterized by (a) incorrect and inconsistent behavior expectations and (b) incorrect and inconsistent application of behavior events.

Incorrect and inconsistent behavior expectations are those that are too high or too low and too variable in the manner presented. For example, a child may be expected to perform considerably beyond capability at one time, yet, at another, be kept from performing by being forced into a dependency relationship. Behavior events refer to the consequences that follow behavior. A child may be punished severely for the same act that is praised at another time. The child is confronted by confusion and chaos, a situation of uncertainty in which sustained, adaptive growth potential is diminished seriously.

In the intrapsychic approach, chaotic environments are believed to produce emotional distress (anxiety); the child's inner life is so disorganized that accurate perceptions and functional cognitive strengths are absent. The emotional distress logically produces or is reflected by the resulting abnormal behaviors (symptoms). Abnormal behavior, thus, is a reflection and functional result of emotional distress. It also provides a tactic to relieve the distress or anxiety caused by chaotic environments. One way to manage the fear of uncertainty, for instance, is to become extremely compulsive and "busy" via bizarre actions of counting, pointing, and chanting. This activity keeps anxiety at a tolerable level but does so at the expense of adequate solutions to daily tasks of living.

Intervention or therapeutic efforts concentrate on changing the inner turmoil or emotional distress. If the inner self can be strengthened, a predictable environment can be built from the chaos. And, because the symptoms reflect emotional distress, they will disappear when intervention is successful in reducing the distress or anxiety.

Contrasted to the intrapsychic approach, the behavioral approach focuses intervention efforts on both the abnormal behaviors and the chaotic environment that is producing them. If individuals can learn abnormal behavior, they can learn adaptive behavior through rearrangement of the environment. A child who behaves in ways that bring on negative attention from others is assumed to feel emotional distress or pain. At some level, the child realizes that deviant behavior is neither gratifying nor helpful. Emotional distress reflects evaluation of experiences. A child who fails a reading lesson feels less worthy as a result of that experience, despite bravado—the external display of not caring—to cover up the pain.

Emotional distress also provides a negative anticipatory set for entry into future interaction. If learning interactions are associated with failure, motivation to exhibit behavior that avoids interaction is strengthened. If the child and those who assist in changing environments and behaviors are successful, emotional distress is changed to emotional happiness (a condition reflecting positive evaluations of experience) and an eagerness to approach future positive interactions (Whelan, 1977).

Whatever etiological understanding and associated intervention strategies professionals prefer, they must realize that children are not interested in theories. The theory that most successfully leads to alleviation of pain and to personal and interpersonal feelings of accomplishment is the ultimate validation. One approach may work better in dealing with inner turmoil. Another may work better with a child in conflict with the environment. The child, not the theory, must be the winner. Only when children win can professionals win, too. The search for etiology leads to classification of children and their behaviors and thus has a profound influence on children, resulting in either proper assistance or victimization through error (Hobbs, 1975).

*P*REVALENCE

When a school district starts new or expanded instructional services for pupils with emotional disturbance, it must determine the number of pupils who are in need of and will benefit from them. For example, suppose a school district has 10,000 pupils in grades 1 through 12. How many of the 10,000 are troubled or troublesome (emotionally disturbed) to the extent that they need special education services? If the district's screening and identification program finds that 200 need services, the prevalence is 2%. If 800 pupils are identified as emotionally disturbed, the prevalence is 8%. Actual prevalence of emotional disturbance within a defined school-age population varies from district to district because of differences in definitions, identification procedures used, and how district personnel apply evaluation data to arrive at the decision to use the label of emotional disturbance.

The Office of Special Education programs in the U.S. Department of Education uses a conservative 2% national estimate of prevalence of seriously emotionally disturbed children and youth. The Joint Commission on Mental Health of Children (1970) has estimated that about 2.6% to 3.6% of the school-age population is severely disturbed. This estimate is quite consistent with the one used by the federal government and most state education agencies. The Joint Commission, however, also states that an additional 10% above the 2.6% of pupils are moderately emotionally disturbed. Further, it asserts that yet another 20% of the school-age population experiences temporary or aperiodic emotional reactions to various types of stress and therefore needs some type of mental health services to prevent problems from becoming acute or chronic. Based on the Joint Commission's estimates, approximately 34% of the school-age population may be considered to have some form of emotional disturbance ranging from severe (3.6%), to moderate (10%), to mild (20%). How a school district defines emotional disturbance clearly affects prevalence. Obviously, the federal office is concerned mainly with the severely involved segment—at least in terms of how federal dollars are used to provide special education programs. As noted elsewhere in this chapter, however, the moderate and mild segments seem to be recipients of services at local district levels.

To illustrate the bouncing percentages of prevalences reported by various agencies, a comparison should be made between single-survey studies (cross-sectional) and longitudinal studies. One significant survey (Kelly, Bullock, & Dykes, 1977) found that teachers perceived 20.4% of pupils in kindergarten through grade 12 as having emotional problems. Of the 20.4%, 2.2% were considered to fall into the severe range, a percentage consistent with those of the Office of Special Education Programs and the

Joint Commission. The remaining 18.2% fell into the mild or moderate ranges, a percentage lower than the Joint Commission's estimates.

An advantage of a longitudinal study over a survey is that a known population of children can be tracked over time. Rubin and Balow (1978) followed more than 1,500 children from kindergarten through sixth grade to determine yearly prevalence of emotional problems and the persistence of problems from one year to the next. Teacher questionnaires revealed that, among the children who received six teacher ratings, 60% were considered at one point in time to have a behavior problem. That is, at least one teacher in six rating the same child believed the child had an emotional problem. Only 40% of the children were never identified by a teacher as having problems. The 60% cumulative figure contrasted sharply with the yearly prevalence for each grade of about 24%–31%.

What about the children who were consistently identified as having problems? For children with three or more teacher ratings, 7.5% fell into the persistent categories. When six teacher ratings were used, 3% were consistently classified as having emotional problems. The 3% to 7.5% prevalence figures are similar to both the Office of Special Education Programs and the Joint Commission's estimates for severe and moderate problems. The yearly 24% to 31% is also analogous to the survey study results.

Prevalence findings, whether achieved through surveys or longitudinal study, yield similar results, indicating that about 2% to 3% of school-age children probably need intensive special education services or other intervention programs. Another 6% to 8% need some supportive special educational services. Yet another 10% to 15% may require less intensive service aperiodically or only once during their school years.

PL 94–142 and the rules and regulations pursuant to it require that all children and youth identified as emotionally disturbed receive a free and appropriate public education—special education and related services. Yet the federal definition refers to the seriously emotionally disturbed, a group that, according to prevalence studies and estimates, represents about 2% to 3% of the school-age population. Obviously, if a school district is to comply with federal and state laws, it must provide special education and related services to the seriously emotionally disturbed. It can do that only if it uses a precise definition, clearly specifies identification procedures to be implemented, and relies on data from comprehensive evaluations to arrive at numbers of children and youth needing specialized instruction and intervention. The value of prevalence data is in providing school districts with accurate information that can be used to plan a budget for personnel and other resources to be used in programs for children with serious emotional disturbances.

LEARNING AND BEHAVIOR

The ways children cope with internal and external chaos are as varied as the children who display them. Kauffman (1981) delineated four coping styles or behavior patterns. The first covers the common dimensions of undifferentiated responses to stimuli:

distraction, hyperactivity, and impulsive behaviors. The second is aggression directed against self and others. A third describes children who withdraw from interaction and regress to immature styles (e.g., tantrums and extreme dependence). The fourth represents behavior that violates a code prescribing the differences between right and wrong.

As indicated previously, behavior coping styles are usually of two types, excesses and deficits. Excesses are the behaviors that parents, teachers, and peers would like to reduce or eliminate. Deficits are behaviors that children fail to display or do not have in their repertoire at a level commensurate with expectations or capabilities. Deficit and excessive behaviors are ways of avoiding circumstances associated with pain and failure, of coping with problems from within and without, problems with which they very much need assistance.

Excessive and deficit behaviors can be further delineated into academic and social behaviors. In a study completed at a mental health workshop (Whelan & Gallagher, 1972), school teachers were asked to list specific behaviors they believed to interfere with children's adjustment. As anticipated, boys exceeded girls by a ratio of 4 to 1 for the behaviors the teachers listed. More than half of the behaviors listed were social, usually excessive, and 37% were academic, usually deficit.

Examples of social behaviors were disruptive talking without permission, being out of seat, touching, hitting, pushing, tripping, squirming, thumb sucking, and low frequency of social interaction (deficit). Academic behaviors involved incomplete work, late completion of work, inaccurate work, slowness, and sloppiness. Of the behaviors listed, 57% were targeted for decreasing (excesses) and 43% for increasing (deficits). Thus, teachers readily recognize behaviors children display as coping devices that require special instructional strategies and tactics.

The coping styles children adopt usually are identified as one of three types. Type 1 is demonstrated by the child who can succeed but will not invest energy in task completion. The teacher's expectations for performance are realistic, but the child's avoidance behaviors are so well established that discrimination between realistic and unrealistic requests to become involved with a task is not operational. The probability of pain through failure poses too high a risk.

The Type 2 child accepts an assigned task but either does not complete it or makes many errors. Again, this coping style functions to avoid personal investment. To invest and still fail is a proposition too devastating to risk. This coping style is not characterized by the verbal and physical hostility inherent in refusal to try, as is the case with Type 1. Rather, the Type 2 child can avoid the painful consequences of inappropriate aggression by placidly using up allotted task time in a nonproductive fashion. For both types, though, the result is the same—another failure.

The Type 3 child is described as having given up, characterized by the absence of behavior, withdrawal from fighting expectations, or even the semblance of attempting to meet requests for performance. The child is described as having resigned from the environment. All three types demand considerable teaching expertise to change the pattern of failure to one of success, but the Type 3 child presents the greatest challenge to those who hope to help children.

Children's ways of managing or coping with internal and external conflicts may not be consistent. For one situation the style may be aggression. In another circumstance the style may be withdrawal. In yet another situation the child may feign compliance but remain unproductive as far as improving competencies for dealing with expectations. Their past history is laced with many failures, all resulting from the inability of the environment to sustain acquisition and maintenance of increasingly complex styles needed for successful coping. Until it is changed, the chaotic environment functions to strengthen the very behaviors that interfere with the child's developing personally gratifying coping styles.

Although the description of coping styles is generally applicable to all children and youth with behavior disorders, specific academic and social behavioral characteristics should be noted. Academic and social problems are described separately, even though a pupil tends to have both. Rarely are social problems observed in the absence of serious academic deficits.

ACADEMIC ACHIEVEMENT

Pupils in the age range of 5 through 17 spend more time in classrooms than in any situation other than the home environment. Signs of emotional disturbance, whatever the cause, often show up in class. Problems rarely are confined to one aspect of a child's life. If a child has problems at home, they will show up at school. Conversely, if the child has problems at school, parents often see problems in family interactions as well.

A reliable and valid score (IQ) for intelligence in generally acknowledged to be the best *single* predictor of academic achievement. A high IQ usually is associated with relatively high achievement. How then do children with emotional disturbance or behavior disorders fare in relation to measures of intelligence?

Bower's (1969) extensive research on children with emotional disabilities addressed the issue of IQ in addition to several other variables. The average IQ for normal pupils was 103; for pupils with emotional disorders, the mean IQ was 93. The intelligence scores, however, were derived from pencil-and-paper group tests. When using individually administered tests, the emotionally disturbed sample was not significantly different from the nondisturbed group.

Other studies have found that, as a group, children with emotional disturbance fall below the average on measures of intellectual ability. For example, a longitudinal study conducted by Rubin and Balow (1978) included data on IQ obtained by individually administered tests. The average IQ of children consistently identified as having behavior problems was about 93, compared to about 108 for children not so identified. Further, Kauffman (1981) reported that the average IQ of 120 children with emotional disturbance in a public school setting was 91. Of interest, though, was the range of scores—62 to 137. This indicates that some children with emotional problems function as having retardation, and some actually may fall into the gifted range of intelligence.

A number of researchers (Bower, 1969; Cullinan, Epstein, & Lloyd, 1983; Kauffman,

1981; Rubin & Balow, 1978) have reported that pupils with emotional disturbance are behind their nondisturbed peers in reading and arithmetic. Further, academic retardation increases with age or grade level. For example, a 1-year discrepancy in reading in grade 4 may grow to 5 years by grade 10 or 11. The amount of academic retardation cannot be attributed solely to intellectual scores. Those mean scores still tend to be within the low-average range (93) and are not discrepant enough from the average (100) to predict the large observed achievement deficits. Stated another way, pupils who have emotional disturbance achieve below expectations, even when mental age is used for comparison purposes. For example, a pupil with a chronological age (CA) of 12 has an IQ of about 92, or a mental age (MA) of 11. At CA 12, the pupil should be in about the seventh grade, but with an MA of 11, the expected achievement level should be about sixth grade. Yet, even using MA as a base measure, many pupils may be delayed 2 or more years in academic subjects; our example pupil may be achieving at the fourth- rather than the expected sixth-grade level.

Clearly a relationship exists among emotional problems, academic achievement, and intellectual ability. To specify any of the three variables as cause or effect, however, is difficult, if not impossible. A low IQ puts a child at risk for developing adjustment problems, simply because the lower the IQ, the longer the child takes to master the complex coping skills needed to function successfully in a complex world. Also, a low IQ usually is predictive of academic achievement that is lower than CA expectations. A pupil's perception of not achieving as well as CA peers can cause a negative self-image, and a negative self-image may lead to behaviors that others may view as deviant or reflective of emotional disturbance. At this point, a reciprocal or self-sustaining process is operating. Behavior problems lead to academic problems, and increased failure in academic subjects produces even more deviant intra- and interpersonal problems.

SOCIAL ADJUSTMENT

The first of the categories of inappropriate social behaviors, developed by Kauffman (1981), is a cluster of three types of behaviors frequently observed in children who have emotional problems. The cluster encompasses (a) frequent episodes of apparently nonpurposeful motor activity (e.g., chair bouncing, fidgeting), (b) difficulty in attending to a task (e.g., switching attention to task-irrelevant items such as a paper clip), and (c) a tendency to respond quickly and without prior planning (e.g., quickly selecting a response from several alternatives without regard to all of the elements in a problem— grabbing a toy from another child, thus losing the chance to share several toys).

A second category is aggression, behaviors that produce emotional or physical harm to another person. Aggressive behaviors also may lead to the destruction of property. Aggressive behaviors usually are of the excessive type; the behaviors occur often and with great intensity. For example, a child who starts a verbal or physical fight with a peer on the average of one time per hour is behaving in a way that fits the description of aggression. Many pupils who exhibit high rates of aggressive behaviors probably would be placed in the conduct disorder category of DSM-III-R. They repeatedly violate the rights of others and socially accepted norms for appropriate ways of behaving.

The third category focuses on behaviors described as withdrawn and immature. The two descriptions, however, may not always be observed in the same child. For instance, a child may initiate or respond to few social encounters, but the few that do happen can be age-appropriate and adequate for the situation. On the other hand, a child may express a high rate of immature or inadequate behaviors such as crying, helplessness, and tantrums; consequently, observers probably would not label the child as withdrawn. Nevertheless, many children who have difficulty coping with their environment because their behaviors are inadequate in relation to demands, withdraw or avoid situations in which their lack of competence will be exposed.

The fourth category has to do with behavior "that is considered to be morally 'wrong' in the eyes of the child's social group or the law" (Kauffman, 1981, p. 265). Essentially, this category describes behaviors that are morally wrong (unfair), when compared to a social or legal standard, rather than right (fair). Many children in this category behave in ways that violate legal codes. If they are caught and adjudicated, they are labeled as juvenile delinquents.

Several factors account for the development of behavior patterns that violate moral and legal codes. They include chaotic environments with all of their inconsistencies about expectations and consequences for behaviors, outright abuse, lack of family cohesiveness, and clear rewards by significant adults for taking unfair advantage of another person. These factors often produce a person who feels no guilt or remorse for acting immorally, thus making the condition difficult to change by interventions in school, courts, or other agencies.

IDENTIFICATION

Failure to recognize behavioral differences as welcome and positive elements that should be encouraged and enjoyed may lead to errors in identifying children as having a disability. Children who are thought to have a handicapping condition, but are merely different from some arbitrary standard, may suffer by being placed in learning situations that are totally unsuitable to their real needs. They may need only recognition and acceptance of their differences, plus changes in instructional strategies, to achieve success. Errors in placement decisions are difficult to reverse—a primary reason why corrective action by the legal system has become necessary (Whelan & Jackson, 1971).

If children with disabilities are to obtain needed educational resources, both human and material diagnostic or identification procedures must be accurate. Identification of obvious physical disabilities (e.g., vision or hearing impairment), while by no means easy, can be accurately accomplished by competent professional examiners. When diagnostic efforts are directed at establishing the presence or absence of emotional disturbance, the processes are less clear. The confusion between physical illness and mental illness, and the tendency to treat both as the same when they are not, is responsible for the difficulty (Szasz, 1974).

THE DIAGNOSTIC DILEMMA

Historically, educational experiences for children with emotional problems has followed the lead of mental health professionals who usually use terms associated with psychiatry (e.g., neurotic, psychotic). Because psychiatry is a branch of medicine rather than of education, educators often misinterpret the meanings of psychiatric terms. If the labels derive from the medical discipline, observed deviance must be symptomatic of an unobservable cause, just as a high temperature is a symptom of an inflamed appendix. When educators are informed that a child is "neurotic," and that the recalcitrant behaviors observed are caused by trauma during infancy, they still are left with the task of helping the child learn more appropriate behavior patterns in a classroom. Labels rarely help educators do this.

Educators react to this frustration, blaming the medical model for not providing explicit formulas for classroom-based intervention. The culprit is not medicine or the medical model, though. Rather—to paraphrase a popular quotation—we have met the culprit, and it is us. The medical model simply applies the scientific method, a process most children learn during their elementary school years. That method requires accurate observation of behavior and application of knowledge to relate it to antecedent and subsequent events. It is applicable to educators along with physicians and psychiatrists.

The problem, then, is not the medical model but, instead, the failure of educators to differentiate diagnostic issues unique to medicine and those unique to education. In medicine, *positive* indicates the presence of a disease; in education, it indicates a disability of academic or social behaviors. In a *false positive* diagnosis, the individual diagnosed as diseased or disabled really is not. *Negative* denotes the absence of disease or disability. A *false negative* diagnosis represents a situation in which an individual considered to be free of disease or disability really has the condition.

For medicine, the false positive does not present a significant issue. If, for example, a tuberculin skin test shows a reaction, additional tests can be administered to confirm or disconfirm the diagnosis. On the other hand, false negatives are a serious problem. If a skin test produces no reaction but the individual really does have tuberculosis, the needed treatment may be delayed until it is too late.

The opposite is true for education. False positives represent the most potentially serious problems for educators. The problem arises when, for example, a child is educationally diagnosed as having an emotional disturbance because observed behaviors are not perceived correctly as an inability to comprehend standard English. Other false positives occur when an examiner does not understand a child's cultural background. For example, a child's failure to establish eye contact with an adult may seem symptomatic of autism. If the child is a Native American from a certain tribe, however, casting the eyes downward when addressed by an adult is a sign of respect. The child is responding adaptively, but the examiner is not, and the child is misdiagnosed. Enough of these situations have occurred that some parents and child advocacy groups have begun to push for the three Ls—leverage, litigation, and legislation—on behalf of appropriate educational diagnoses and placement of children with handicapping conditions (Whelan & Sontag, 1974).

Finally, false negative rarely are a problem for educators. Children who truly have a disability are not often diagnosed as nondisabled. Educators have the professional knowledge and skill to formulate precise diagnoses and to construct instructional programs based on them. They need not blame medicine for problems unique to education. Reducing the frequency of false positives will enable educators to devote scarce resources to those who are definitely in need.

EVALUATION PROCEDURES

Individuals with emotional disturbance behave in a manner that attracts attention from others. Attention may take the form of fear, avoidance, anger, curiosity, empathy, sympathy, and so on. In any event, the attention usually leads to referral for formal identification procedures. In schools, the person who usually does this is the classroom teacher.

Among the more useful devices for identifying emotional disturbance, either before or after teachers or parents express concerns, are *behavior rating scales*. These can be completed by teachers, parents, peers, and the child under observation. Many scales and checklists compare favorably with intensive diagnostic evaluations (Shea, 1978). Rating scales differ in the number of items and in the range of scores for each item. An example of an item is "gets into fights." This is rated on a scale such as "frequently, sometimes, infrequently." Because most of these instruments are standardized, a cutoff score indicates whether a problem does or does not exist.

Even though teacher ratings and observations have been extremely accurate (Bower, 1969) in identifying pupils with emotional disturbance, these scales are not sufficient for a complete assessment. PL 94–142 requires that identification must include several sources of data. Some of the more typical areas evaluated are academic achievement, intellectual ability, self-concept, personality, adaptive behavior, motor skills, and perceptual abilities. When all of the data from identification and diagnostic efforts are examined, a profile of emotional disturbance may emerge.

For example, Rubin and Balow (1978) reported that when a group of children with emotional disturbance was compared with a group of peers without emotional disturbance, the emotionally disturbed group scored significantly lower on measures of intelligence, language age, and academic achievement, especially in reading. A profile of unsuccessful academic performance, in combination with inadequate social coping behaviors, portrays a typical child or youth with emotional disturbance. Not all emotionally disturbed children fit a group profile, however. Not all underachievers have an emotional disturbance. Other factors, such as hearing loss, may be a primary problem. Therefore, every suspected pupil should receive a complete and individual evaluation before being identified as having an emotional disturbance.

In any event, state and federal laws require school districts to follow a rather prescriptive set of procedures for determining if a child is eligible for special education and related services because of emotional disturbance. The first step is known as *screening*. Screening usually includes a quick assessment of hearing and visual functions. In addition, measurement devices such as group intelligence tests, formal and informal achievement tests, daily work samples, and behavior checklists may be used. The screening process selects pupils who are of concern to teachers, support staff, and parents. More than one person always is included in screening, which protects a pupil's rights and makes the process more accurate. If only one teacher in four views a pupil as having an emotional disturbance, to label the pupil would be grossly unfair. Perhaps the teacher and the pupil have a relationship problem that might be dealt with best by placing the pupil with another teacher.

If staff members and parents essentially agree that a pupil is having intra- and interpersonal adjustment problems, a *comprehensive evaluation* will be conducted. The outcomes of a comprehensive evaluation are used to decide if a pupil needs or does not need special education and related services.

Comprehensive presentations of evaluation, or assessment, strategies have been provided by Ollendick and Hersen (1984) and by Kerr and Nelson (1983). The list is quite lengthy, and not all of them may be used for all pupils; the evaluation team usually selects procedures and instruments based upon information produced by screening. Some of the strategies are:

1. *Interviewing:* A member of the evaluation team may interview the pupil, parents, and teacher to pinpoint major problem areas and to obtain an idea of goals for the pupil to attain.
2. *Behavior characteristics:* An informant (teacher, parent, peers) is asked to complete a behavior rating scale. A scale typically contains a number of statements that are adaptive ("relates well to peers") or maladaptive ("threatens peers") in content. An informant then marks a numerical scale for each item. For example, the scale may range from "frequently" to "seldom."
3. *Pupil report scales:* The pupil who is being evaluated responds to an instrument, which may measure (a) level of anxiety, (b) self-concept, (c) reaction to anger-inducing events, and (d) how the pupil attributes outcomes of behavior (luck versus self-determination).
4. *Direct observation:* Evaluation team members may visit a pupil's classroom and record behavior episodes. For example, a pupil may be described as having frequent temper tantrums. A visit to the classroom may confirm that the pupil has from four to six tantrums per day. Direct observations also include a pupil's performance on daily schoolwork (e.g., arithmetic worksheets).
5. *Intellectual and achievement tests:* A school psychologist probably will administer an individual test of intelligence. The obtained score then can be compared to the pupil's score on a group test to determine any significant difference. In addition, achievement test scores are reviewed. Patterns of intellectual and academic performances may indicate that a pupil is having emotional problems.

A useful behavior checklist is called the Behavior Evaluation Scale (BES) (McCarney, Leigh, & Cornbleet, 1983). The BES is unique in that it has items for each of the categories used in the federal definition of emotionally disturbed. A pupil is rated for each of the categories in the definition, and not those that may not be associated with establishing eligibility for special education and related services.

Another scale is the Behavior Rating Profile (BRP) (Brown & Hammill, 1983). The BRP includes (a) a self-rating scale completed by the pupil, (b) a scale for the teacher, (c) a scale for the parent, and (d) a sociogram that obtains peer perceptions of the pupil. The sociogram indicates peer acceptance or rejection of the pupil being evaluated. A question such as, "Whom would you most like as a partner or a friend?" followed by a "least like" question, may reveal that our target pupil is not included in "most like" and is listed in "least like" by 80% of the peer group. The sociogram adds one more important piece of information in the evaluation process.

Identification is a complex process, one that requires a great deal of skill and dedication to accuracy from those who administer and interpret assessment devices. The results from various tests are used to make special education placement decisions about children and youth. A placement requires a label (e.g., seriously emotionally disturbed). That label can carry a load of stigma, even in this modern age, because adults still have fixed, mostly erroneous, notions about how people with emotional disturbance should behave. These notions often are associated with negative attitudes and lower expectations for appropriate child performance.

In contrast, if an evaluation does not detect problems that require intervention, pupils may be denied much-needed assistance. Salvia and Ysseldyke (1978) identified three sources or errors associated with making decisions from evaluation data. These potential errors should be ever present in the minds of professionals who do assessments and make placement decisions based upon the results. The first error is using the wrong test. A wrong test may be (a) improperly constructed in terms of item selection, reliability, and validity, (b) used for a purpose other than that for which it was designed (e.g., a vocabulary test as a substitute for a test of intellectual ability), and (c) inappropriate for the child (e.g., using a highly verbal test with a pupil who has severe hearing loss). Another error is making faulty decisions about test results. At best, tests give a measure of a pupil's responses, correct or incorrect, to test items; they do not provide a cause for what is observed. A third source of error is making mistakes such as adding incorrectly, not following testing procedures, or simply assuming that a test measures more of an attribute (e.g., intelligence) than it really does.

Identification procedures require educators to be the best professionals they can be. Evaluation has to be a serious business because the future of children and youth is at stake. Mistakes that function to deny specialized instruction to pupils who need it must be avoided. At the same time, placing a pupil in a special education program when a different type of arrangement in regular education is more appropriate is clearly not a supportable action.

INCLUSION VERSUS EXCLUSION

Identification, or determining eligibility for special education and related services, is a way of deciding who will be included and who will be excluded from receiving special education and related services mandated by federal and state laws. This ongoing debate about identification among professionals in special education has profound implications for pupils with emotional and behavior problems. Two areas of concern are especially worrisome to special educators today. The first is whether pupils with conduct disorders should be included under the federal definition of seriously emotionally disturbed. The second concern has to do with providing a free and appropriate public education for pupils with emotional disorders who in many respects continuously act out those disorders in ways that are contrary to school policies on conduct. Their behavior reflects patterns that lead to temporary suspension or exclusion for a number of days from the opportunity to attend the school and participate in special education services as described in their individualized education programs (IEPs).

Kelly (1992) has taken the position that pupils with conduct problems do not fit under the federal definition of seriously emotionally disturbed. He believes that conduct problems and serious emotional disturbance are not part of the same continuum. Each group of students who exhibit one of these disorders do so along a parallel but entirely different continuum of severity ranging from mild to very, very complex and severe. He believes that by mixing these two groups in programs for the seriously emotionally disturbed, students with true mental disorders, as described in the DSM-III-R (American Psychiatric Association, 1987), do not receive their fair share of the teacher's time because so much of it is devoted to dealing with management problems exhibited by pupils with conduct disorders. He further believes that pupils who exhibit conduct problems do so while recognizing the consequences their behaviors may bring. He therefore believes these pupils are really the problem of general or regular education professionals and should not be considered a part of special education. In so doing, he is not denying that pupils with conduct disorders need specialized programs, but he believes strongly that these programs must be provided by professionals other than those in special education and certainly in programs separate from those that serve the clinically identified needs of pupils with serous emotional problems or mental disorders.

Kelly (1990) has developed a test to separate students with conduct problems from those with emotional problems, called the Differential Test of Conduct and Emotional Problems. The test itself has 63 items that give descriptions of behavior. The respondent is to mark "true" or "false" for each statement. For example, item 4 on the test states "constantly fighting or beating up others." That item is weighted in favor of the conduct problem dimension, whereas another item, such as "withdrawn, aloof, or unresponsive" is weighted toward the emotional disturbance dimension. In validating the test, Kelly developed norms by ethnic group and by school level in terms of pupils' age. In a small pilot test of the instrument, the author found that approximately 30% of the students currently served in programs for the severely emotionally disturbed would fall totally under the dimension of conduct disorders and therefore, in Kelly's view, would not be eligible for special education and related services for pupils designated seriously emotionally disturbed. The rest of the pupils in the small pilot study either met the criteria for emotional disturbance or qualified under both dimensions; that is, they were seriously emotionally disturbed and also exhibited conduct disorders. How Kelly would determine exact responsibility or placement for these pupils is unclear because they apparently fit under both dimensions. One would hope they would be eligible for services under the label or category of seriously emotionally disturbed.

Obviously the debate about who should be included or excluded under the category of seriously emotionally disturbed has led to increased efforts to change the federal definition of seriously emotionally disturbed. One hopes the debate of who should be included or excluded under the definition of seriously emotionally disturbed does not overshadow the other, equally important message of Kelly's position. The concern is that students with severe conduct disorders will simply overwhelm the children with more clinical characteristics of mental disorders and the teachers who must spend significant time with them. If teachers have to devote much of their time to controlling pupils with conduct disorders, they have little time left for those who have many needs for positive interaction with adults. Kelly's message and position on this matter have important implications for how students are grouped for the purpose of providing special education instruction and related services. Professionals in this field are well advised to attend to this part of his message rather than concentrating solely upon whether he wants to exclude students in need of services, which clearly he does not.

A second area of concern surrounding inclusion versus exclusion in serving children with severe emotional disturbance is associated with a U.S. Supreme Court case entitled *Honig v. Doe* (1988). Basically the Supreme Court determined that the stay-put provision of PL 94–142 prohibits local school district personnel from excluding pupils with disabilities indefinitely from opportunities to participate in the educational program described in their IEP. The stay-put provision (34 C.F.R. 300.513, 1991) describes a child's status during the proceedings of any due process action. Specifically, the regulation states that the child involved in the complaint or proceeding must remain in his or her educational placement unless the educational agency and the parents agree otherwise.

The issue in the Honig case revolved around the question of whether the stay-put provision applies to pupils with serous emotional disturbance whose behavior endangers themselves or other students. Also related to the Court's decision in this case was the determination of whether a student's behavior results from the disabling condition of seriously emotionally disturbance itself. If the behavior does not, the school's rules about suspension and expulsion can be followed. In the case of students with serious emotional disturbance, however, dangerous behavior cannot be separated from the condition itself. Therefore, the Court had to determine whether a school, using the rationale that a student's behavior is dangerous to self and others, could logically exclude him or her from special education and related services for a cumulative period exceeding 10 days.

The Court decided the district could not unilaterally exclude such children because it was the U.S. Congress' intent that the stay-put provision definitely prohibited such exclusion. Further, the Court declared that if the Congress, in writing PL 94–142, intended to make an exception to the stay-put provision, it would have done so at that time. The Court, however, did not leave the schools without some relief in this matter. It noted that school personnel or administrators can seek injunctive relief when it can show a court of jurisdiction that it has exhausted all of the administrative processes or remedies available to it and to the parents in such a situation. Some of these remedies would require (a) reconvening the IEP or staffing team, (b) attempting alternative placements, some of which may be more restrictive in nature, and (c) working closely with the parents to determine what changes are needed in the current IEP to accommodate the pupil's needs while at the same time not endangering other pupils in the school setting.

The *Honig v. Doe* decision has several implications for school administrators in public schools:

1. They will have to develop programs that will serve a wide continuum of severity for pupils identified as seriously emotionally disturbed.
2. They will have to develop policies for dealing with pupils whose behavior is dangerous to themselves and others. This will require a substantial amount of professional development for staff members involved in identification and program planning for these pupils.
3. They will have to be careful in the identification process to avoid accusations that they are not identifying pupils who need special education and related services in an attempt to avoid serving students whose behaviors deviate considerably from the school's regular behavior standards for conduct.

The debate on inclusion versus exclusion is taking place on two fronts. One is in the professional domain of determining the characteristics of the students who will be served under the categorical label of seriously emotionally disturbed. The second area of conflict among professionals is in the legal arena. Obviously special educators would like wide latitude in making professional decisions about pupils who do or do not require specialized instructional services, but clearly the federal and state laws for students with disabilities convey an expectation that there will be no exclusions based upon a school district's inability or lack of commitment to provide free and appropriate public education to all children, including those with the most severe and complex of emotional disorders.

EDUCATIONAL PRACTICES

Educators must deal with the coping styles of children who have emotional disturbance. Patterns of failure must be changed to patterns of success. When adults intervene to help, they must convince children that the intervention is not another form of rejection (Long, 1974), a pain they have experienced many times during their lives.

Years ago, the field of educational planning, implementation, and evaluation for children with emotional disturbances was rife with theoretical ferment, unchanging positions, and failure to address the real issue—ensuring that children become winners (Morse, Cutler, & Fink, 1964). In retrospect, that ferment was desirable to the extent that the issues were defined and therefore could be resolved. As Morse (1977) pointed out, advocates of supposedly divergent theoretical positions began dialogues leading to mutual understanding. Children's needs no longer are sacrificed for the protection of theoretical turf.

This is not to imply that all is well in the education of troubled and troublesome children. There is much to be done and much to learn from the best teachers of all—the children. Their responses to what professionals say and do are the best guide to evaluating the success or failure of educational strategies.

The instructional procedures described here are being used by competent teachers of emotionally disturbed children and youth. They are descriptive rather than prescriptive. Their functional use requires intensive study and supervised practice and should be applied only when those circumstances prevail.

EDUCATIONAL ENVIRONMENTS

Not many years ago schools routinely excluded pupils with problems. Children and youth with emotional disturbances were the responsibility of agencies other than schools. They either remained at home or were placed in residential centers for custodial purposes. If education and other therapeutic services were provided, they were the exception rather than the rule. As educators became more involved in and responsible for the emotional well-being of children, the public schools gradually initiated programs. At first these programs consisted of special day schools and isolated special classes. This seemed like a giant step at the time, but one that seems small from our current frame of reference.

Progress has been slow, but steady—a pattern of "advance two steps and retreat one." Educators finally are starting to match "say" with "do" behaviors. They realize that children come to school as individuals and therefore require individualized planning. This concept is paramount to pupils with emotional problems, who present variable quantities and qualities of diverse needs, all requiring differently planned educational environments.

Figure 7.2 displays an administrative design for providing educational services directly related to children's needs. The services are called *facilitative education programs* (Whelan, 1972) to emphasize the goal of progress—every child a winner. These programs are designed to provide functional assistance and services to children who have not progressed as anticipated in areas of academic and social behavior development within their current learning environments. The programs provide facilitative learning experiences for children whose progress in academic and social behavior has been limited by the nature of past and present learning environments. They attempt to change that history by facilitating acquisition of academic and social behaviors necessary for realistic and desirable progress.

Facilitative learning environments offer many options for children to experience opportunities for learning and growth, both academically and socially. Placement according to individual needs is a critical factor. Another critical element is the freedom of movement among placements, again based upon the unique requirements that pupils bring to instructional organizations.

Coordinated and concerted use of community resources is vital for the successful operation of facilitative education programs. Children with emotional disturbance, perhaps more than any other handicapped group, require the best efforts of a multidisciplinary team if they are to be the beneficiaries rather than the victims of the caring professions. Psychiatrists, social workers, and clinical psychologists comprise the staffs of mental health and guidance centers. These are community resources that educators who plan assistance for children and their parents must call upon. Unless services are coordinated through effective communication, parents and children will be caught in unnecessary professional conflict, a burden they should not be expected to carry.

Development and operation of administrative program arrangements, though important, represent the beginning rather than the end. What goes on within these arrangements is the most important consideration. Unless child-helper interactions are filled with warmth, understanding, and supportive firmness when children's internal controls fail, goals will not be accomplished. Establishing ends is not enough; means must be arranged to reach them.

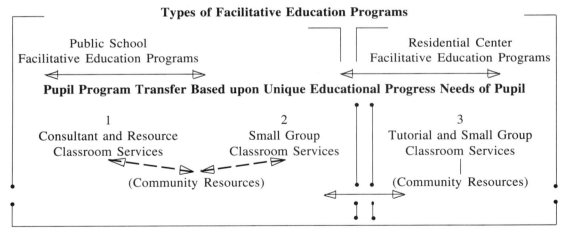

Schematic of facilitative education program services

POSITIVE PUPIL-TEACHER RELATIONSHIPS

Rothman's (1977) soul-searching and emotionally wrenching book should be required reading for all teachers, and especially for teachers of children and youth with emotional disturbance. Rothman makes the point that teachers should not aspire to win status by dominating children. Teacher status is enhanced when children's learning styles are recognized and responded to by differential teaching. Teachers win when children win. Rothman pleads the case for inner examination of motivation, as well as scrutiny of the external trappings of professional identification. If teachers have experienced past hurt and are unaware, they all too easily transfer that hurt to children under the guise of instruction. This phenomenon is known as *negative environmental practices* (Long, 1974; Long & Duffner, 1980), the tendency to respond in like manner to responses from others directed at self (e.g., aggression is met with aggression).

Few would challenge the assertion that a teacher is effective only after mastering how and what to teach. Like administrators, teachers must be adept at arranging means to ends. They must know how to involve children in establishing ends and the means to reach them. They must establish a child-teacher relationship that enhances academic and social growth in the children for whom they are responsible. Role and relationship are intertwined, mutually interdependent; one cannot exist without the other. Children

Teachers need to be sensitive and have empathic skills to work with children who have behavior disorders.

with emotional disturbance are extremely perceptive, a skill they learned from their devastating experiences with supposedly helpful adults. They can "smell out" incompetence, absence of caring, and the true motivations of their professional helpers. An ineffective teacher does not establish positive relationships with children, and desirable learning does not occur.

What are the requirements for building positive relationships with children who have emotional disturbance? Morse (1980) believes that two affective elements are essential: differential acceptance and empathic relationship.

Differential Acceptance. Differential acceptance is the ability of teachers to receive large doses of hate, aggression, and hostility without reacting in kind to the children who transmit them. These behaviors should be accepted for what they are—expressions of pain and anguish from the many hurts previously inflicted upon them. Accepting behavior should not be confused with condoning it, a disservice to children. Differential acceptance means understanding the act without condemning the child. A child who destroys property in angry frustration can be understood, but the teacher need not approve of the destructive act.

I once said to a child who was tearing up a book, "You know, it's okay to be angry, but I will not let you destroy the book. We can work together to deal with your anger." The child responded, wide-eyed, "I didn't know that. I thought that being angry was bad." From that point on, the child did not destroy any instructional materials and gradually, through modeling, learned to manage and express anger in productive ways, a step toward achieving the goal of self-control. To allow a child to act out every impulse in a destructive manner is to fail the child, and when that happens, the teacher fails, too. After all, children with emotional disturbance, by their very label, are unable to set a viable self-structure. They must depend for a while on the external structure others provide for support in dealing with inner feelings and expressions of them.

Empathic Relationship. The empathic relationship requires teachers to develop the ability to discover clues, other than verbal ones, that children provide as mirrors to their inner states of being. During a therapeutic camping experience, I responded to the nonverbal cues (e.g., pacing, hand-wringing, and other anxiety reactions) of a child who did not want to camp overnight. The child said, "It's baby stuff to camp. Who needs it?" This particular child, however, really was afraid of being assaulted by other children during the night and wanted to avoid this incorrectly perceived risk. To argue logically about issues of safety, the benefits of camping, and so forth would have been futile. Instead, this child was told that an assistant was needed to pitch tents and build a good campfire. The child responded to this approach, discovered that assaults did not occur, and, just to make sure, kept the fire roaring all night. With each subsequent camping experience the reluctance to participate diminished, and the child soon began to enjoy camping. Anxiety was displaced by joy and the anticipation of aversive events by anticipation of pleasurable events, by using the empathic relationship.

Goals. Once teachers learn to use differential acceptance and empathic relationship skills, positive interpersonal interactions with these pupils can be established. Brendtro

(Trieschman, Whittaker, & Brendtro, 1969) further described the goals of developing a positive interpersonal relationship. Table 7.7 shows the structural components intrinsic to the relationship-building process. The process includes children's needs and teachers' roles in meeting them. Because of their failure-oriented history, children with emotional disturbance are not responsive to teachers' requests for certain behaviors and do not seek out their approval. In fact, approval often has the opposite effect; the responding ceases when a teacher approves it.

By building trust and supporting children's efforts, teachers gradually become valued sources of expectations and corrective feedback. Whenever possible, teachers should encourage children to talk about their feelings, a more appropriate mode than destructive acting out of feelings and impulses. Talking leads to insight and often to changes in behaviors: "Yes, there's a better way to express anger than by tearing up a book. Here are some alternatives." This is analogous to the "light bulb" over a cartoon character's head: "Now I understand. I see it all now."

The teacher also must be a functional model source. The word *functional* is stressed because, if what the teacher models does not work for the child, the relationship is impaired. A child will respond in kind to the teacher's modeling of an appropriate response to frustration if it functions to enhance adaptive behaviors and leads to satisfaction.

Describing child-teacher positive relationships, of course, is much easier than establishing them. Hard, dedicated work is required by teachers and children alike. Many ups and downs will occur along the way, but progress will become apparent with sustained effort.

Establishment of relationships usually passes through several stages (Haring & Whelan, 1965):

1. *Orientation* or, as some describe it, the honeymoon. This stage is in evidence when children first enter a placement. They try to appear controlled, although obviously this is done at great cost, a veneer. This stage may last several weeks.
2. *Shaping* or *reality testing*. As children become more comfortable and discern that the teacher will not destroy them, they start to display the behaviors that originally

● TABLE 7.7

Structural components of a facilitative interpersonal relationship

Pupil Needs	Teacher Role
1. Develop responsiveness to instructions and consequences	1. Expectations and corrective feedback source
2. Develop analytic and synthetic insight	2. Communication facilitation source
3. Develop identification and imitation adaptive behavior styles	3. Functional model source

led to their placement. They test limits and teacher patience frequently. Will the teacher's "say" and "do" behaviors match? If the match is consistent, the third stage is reached.

3. During *cognition*, children begin to internalize the external environmental supports. They can verbalize them but cannot always match their behavior with the acquired insights.

4. *Integration* is characterized by consistent matching of insights with observable behaviors. Children have put them together in a truly functional style of coping with daily living, including its joys and hurts. Now, though, the joys are much more frequent than the hurts. Based on guaranteed success provided by teachers, children become motivated to approach and solve problems by the pleasure intrinsic to achievement. They become motivated by the opportunity to attain rather than by the avoidance of failure. Changed motivation is reflected in changed coping styles.

EDUCATIONAL INTERVENTIONS

Rather than describe intervention approaches as disconnected parts, they are presented in relationship to situations pupils with emotional problems encounter during one school day. A sequence of school situations is shown in Figure 7.3. The outer six boxes of the cycle are situations that occur many times during a school day. All pupils, with

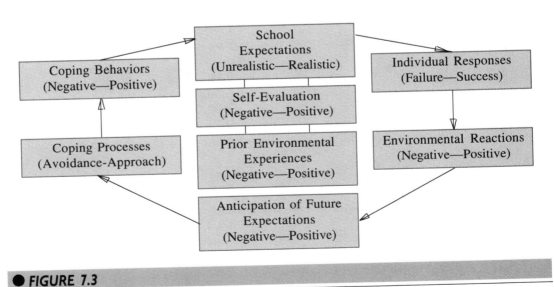

● **FIGURE 7.3**

School behavior cycle

Source: From R. J. Whelan, 1977, "Human Understanding of Human Behavior," in A. J. Pappanikou and J. L. Paul (Eds.), *Mainstreaming Emotionally Disturbed Children*, pp. 64–79, Syracuse, NY: Syracuse University Press. Copyright 1972 by the Syracuse University Press. Reprinted by permission of the publisher.

or without significant problems, experience them. The two inner boxes represent the developmental level (e.g., previous home, community, and school experiences) that pupils bring to a school setting. The school behavioral cycle is somewhat similar to the stress or conflict cycle developed by Long and Duffner (1980) except that it goes beyond an understanding of how maladaptive behaviors are learned to include the acquisition of adaptive and functional behaviors.

The cycle provides a visual display of how positive-negative or successful-unsuccessful behavior patterns are learned. Just as important, critical points in the cycle can be selected for introducing a specific type of intervention or behavior change process. The following parts of this section describe each box in the cycle and the point at which interventions can be implemented.

Prior Environmental Experiences and Self-Evaluation. Children begin their long years of schooling with a variety of experiences that have occurred over a 5-year period. For many children, these experiences are mostly positive. They live with nurturing parents or other adults who provide their basic needs and the support to learn and trust. Early experiences, however, can be more negative than positive. If these experiences are chaotic, inconsistent, and characterized by neglect or rigid control, children do not develop a sense of their place in relation to others. They do not learn the skills and knowledge necessary to perform successfully when confronted with reality-based expectations. Negative experiences typically produce behavior patterns that are not functional. The behaviors are contrary to societal norms (excessive), or they are not adequate to complete necessary tasks (deficits).

Clearly, the history children bring to school for the first time, and carry with them from school year to school year, has a profound influence upon their ability to cope with the demands of learning new knowledge and skills. If the experiential history has been largely negative in terms of more failure than success encounter, it is reflected by self-evaluation feelings of worthlessness. Conversely, successful experiences usually build positive self-evaluation or self-esteem.

Children with more negative than positive encounters have a great deal of emotional distress (anxiety) that is either the cause or the result of abnormal behaviors (see Figure 7.1), and they, of course, exhibit behaviors that others view as deviant. These children are confronted by internal and external conflicts (and the resulting anxiety) so complex and pervasive that they overpower the limited competence available to resolve them. The problems are just too large for the children to solve. Faced with these situations, children in conflict resort to primitive, often ineffective, behaviors to reduce or avoid conflict-produced anxiety. Because these behaviors do tend to reduce anxiety, children repeat them again and again to the extent that learning new skills is seriously impaired.

In addition, the behaviors may lead to distortion of reality. For example, a child may be terribly angry at a parent for taking action that the child perceives as unfair or harsh. At the same time, this child has learned that expressing anger is not tolerated or is punished severely by the parent. The angry affect associated with the parent is still present in the child, but if the child acknowledges it, intolerable anxiety results. One way the child can deal with the anger is to express it to someone other than the parent (e.g., a neighbor child). Another way is to deny the anger and assign it to another person (e.g., "I'm not angry at you. You're mad at me."). By denying real feelings and taking unrealistic positions to keep anxiety in check, the child has distorted reality. The neighbor child did not do anything to provoke the anger. The other person is not angry at the child.

If this pattern of dealing with anger is repeated again and again, and if it is brought into school situations, as it surely will be, the child will encounter difficulty in learning. With so much effort going into primitive methods of controlling anxiety, little effort can be devoted to building positive peer and teacher relationships and learning new knowledge and skills. And our example child is not even aware of the processes used to deal with anger and the anxiety it produces.

As indicated, the child in the example may bring to school a lengthy history of inefficient behavior patterns. The question naturally arises as to how the child can be taught to recognize and manage anger appropriately and that to be angry is not to be bad. What intervention could be introduced to help the child acquire more effective ways of dealing with anger? One obvious choice is *psychotherapy* or *counseling*. The goal of psychotherapy is for a child to understand the sources, or causes, of anxiety to be able to deal with them realistically. Understanding is achieved by interactions between therapist and child over weeks or months of therapy sessions. In time, the child gains insights into the connection between feelings and behaviors (Tuma & Sabotka, 1983) through the therapeutic process of interpretation. An example of an interpretation is the following statement to a child: "It appears that when you are mad at your Dad, you take it out on your friend, who then avoids you." Another example might be: "You seem to believe that many people are mad at you, but you haven't said what you did to get them mad." In any event, when the child gains insights or makes connections, he or she begins to understand the relationship between feelings (affects) and behavior of self in relation to others.

Psychotherapy is an intervention that can help a child learn how past events, even though apparently long forgotten, profoundly influence present behaviors and relationships. Insights are gained only after many hours of hard work by child and therapist. Even then, there is no guarantee that more understanding of causes for deviant actions will lead to more productive or positive behaviors. It may, and often does, but a child with insight may not have the ability to construct new behavior patterns; new skills must be taught and learned.

School Expectations. Every moment of every day in school, children are confronted with expectations for specified behaviors: walk, don't run; pay attention; work carefully; complete your work on time; no fighting on the playground; be ready to recite; and so on. The expectations are realistic for many pupils. They are within individual capabilities to respond successfully. Pupils who bring to school a history of negative prior environmental experiences and a negative self-evaluation, however, may find many school expectations completely unrealistic. Some pupils may not have had the developmental experiences necessary for them to perform up to expectations. Other sources of unrealistic expectations, of course, can be attributed to educators' errors in instructional planning. They overestimate some pupils' abilities and set expectations based upon the estimation error; pupils are exposed to overexpectations.

At this point an obvious intervention, used too infrequently, is a *modified curricular approach* (Edwards, 1983). A simple change is to find material that is at a lower reading level but that still covers the content to be learned. Other possible changes include provision of audiotapes of the content, instruction in study skills (Deshler & Graham, 1980), and simplification of the pages on which responses are required. Of course, curricular modifications do require accurate assessment of pupil abilities in a variety of performance areas. Instructional changes and realistic expectations are mutually dependent; one cannot reasonably occur without the other. In comparison to regular content, modified content (a) increased correct responding by 10%, (b) increased attention to task by 30%, and (c) reduced disruptive behaviors by about 67% for a group of pupils with behavior disorders (Edwards, 1983).

Individual Responses. This part of the cycle involves pupil responses to expectations. Again, there are two alternatives; the response can be right or wrong. A pupil either responds successfully or fails to do so. A failure response may be 50% correct on an arithmetic worksheet, whereas a successful one may by 80% or higher.

A failure response clearly may be caused by unrealistic expectations. Such expectations produce failure, and if the pattern is frequent, it can add to or evoke negative self-evaluation. Though one can learn from mistakes, making too many mistakes only teaches failure, not competence.

Environmental Reactions. Skinner (1953) long ago determined that human responses operate on the environment so it reacts in a negative or positive manner. It also may be neutral, in that a response is seemingly ignored; in this instance a response eventually declines in frequency. In school settings, however, failure responses usually bring negative reactions from the environment in the form of low grades, teacher reprimands, scapegoating by peers, and so on. In contrast, successful responses usually elicit positive environmental reactions, such as passing grades, teacher approval, high peer status, and other forms of recognition. And, of course, successful responding in and of itself is a powerful motivation to continue the same pattern of behavior (Skinner, 1974).

A powerful intervention that can be used at this part of the cycle is the consequence aspect of a *behavior analysis* approach. Assume that expectations are realistic but a pupil does not respond successfully—can, but won't try. This pupil's history of failure has not provided opportunities for success; he or she has not experienced the intrinsic motivational features of success. Assume again that this pupil will respond successfully for a tangible environmental reaction (consequence), such as an opportunity to run the photocopy machine in the office. This environmental event occurs upon successful responding to realistic expectations; it does not occur after failure responding. Two key teacher observations have to be made here. First, if the opportunity to run the copy machine doesn't function to improve the pupil's performance, other arrangements should be made (changing the consequence). The second observation, really an action, is a plan to remove the tangible reaction once motivation for success begins to take over.

Anticipation of Future Expectations. This part of the cycle deals with internal feelings produced by the sequences of (a) expectations, (b) responses, and (c) environmental reactions. If the sequence has been positive, internal feelings will reflect the experiences; they will be positive, joyful, pleasing, and satisfying. In contrast, a negative sequence results in internal feelings of anxiety (fear), sadness, incompetence, and despair.

Educators have to be acutely aware of pupils' internal feeling states and use this awareness to make needed changes in the preceding parts of the cycle. When pupils feel good about themselves, they usually do well in school. And how they do in school influences internal feelings. Teachers can get some indication of internal feelings through pupil self-reports. They can use these reports to plan expectations and reactions to assist pupils in attaining school success. In a research study by Whelan, deSaman, and Fortmeyer (1984), feelings and achievement were found to have a strong relationship. One relationship pattern emerging from the study was that, when pupils felt low, then did well on tasks, the feelings became more positive. Another pattern was feeling good, doing tasks poorly, and then feeling bad. A third pattern was feeling good, doing well, and still feeling good.

Although teacher awareness of pupil feelings is not an intervention per se, it is essential in planning interventions. The empathic relationship plays an important role in accurately identifying pupil feelings. Also, teacher "withitness"—teacher awareness of what is going on in a classroom—is essential (Kounin, 1977).

Coping Processes. Based upon internal feeling states, pupils' coping processes facilitate approach or avoidance behaviors. The intrapsychic model of understanding deviant behavior usually identifies these processes as *defense mechanisms* (Kessler, 1966). Negative anticipation of future expectations typically produces an avoidance tendency. Failure experiences are painful, instill anxiety, and are to be avoided. Therefore, a pupil who experiences failure sequences in the cycle will attempt to avoid expectation for performance in school. Conversely, successful experiences tend to evoke approach tendencies: "If this school thing is so good, then I want to have more of it."

One aspect of the *psychoeducational approach* (Fagen, 1979) to intervention that could be used at this part of the cycle is the *life-space interview* (LSI) (Morse, 1980; Redl, 1980). The psychoeducational approach emphasizes the reciprocal nature of the relationship between emotional and cognitive experiences. It supports the position that how a pupil performs on a task influences internal feelings, and internal feelings (anxiety) may have an adverse effect upon task performance. An LSI procedure, in which the teacher helps the child work out responses to situations, requires supervised training and practice on the part of the teacher or other helping professional if it is to be accomplished correctly and with sensitivity.

The procedure itself helps a pupil work through an incident (e.g., destroying a book while in a rage) by carefully eliciting comments regarding perceptions of the incident, the feelings attached to it, and some planning for how a similar incident might be managed in the future. For example, assume that the pupil tore up a book because he was asked to read orally. This pupil makes many oral reading errors, and when they occur, peers laugh. An empathic teacher would go beyond the torn book part of the incident and explore with the pupil his feelings at that moment in time: anger at self for being incompetent, anger at peers for making fun, and anger at the teacher for expecting too much in front of the group. The teacher and the pupil can use the incident for a teaching-learning encounter. For the future, they might arrange a signal from the pupil that the reading material is too hard; the signal would cue the teacher to call on someone else, precluding another torn book incident. In the way of prevention, the teacher could assure the pupil that the two of them would practice together on any material that might have to be read orally before a group.

Coping Behaviors. The last part of the cycle consists of the behavior patterns that lead back to the expectations. These patterns are the products of all that has transpired previously in the cycle, and they feed into the process that keeps the cycle going. Coping behaviors are the natural outcomes of coping processes. An avoidance process evokes avoidance behaviors. If unrealistic expectations lead to response failures that cause anxiety, these expectations are to be avoided at all costs. Unfortunately, others view a pupil's coping/avoidance behaviors as deviant or disturbing. And they are: tantrums, throwing up, noncompliance, withdrawal. In contrast, if the cycle has been mostly positive, the coping behaviors will reflect that process: motivation to learn new skills, willingness to try new tasks, increased attention to task, high task involvement, interest in problem solving. School experiences are viewed as satisfying rather than painful.

In many ways, coping behaviors are the sum of experiences or history a pupil brings to and accumulates during the formal schooling years. In that way they are like prior experiences, except for recency of occurrences. Coping behaviors are the result of history, a history recorded minute by minute during each school day.

Coping behaviors can be differentiated from individual responses. They reflect a set or attitude for entry into a situation, whereas responses occur after stimuli have been presented in the situation. For example, prior to an academic test, coping behaviors might include sweating, pacing, and nervous gestures because of fear (anxiety) about what is going to take place. Individual responses are made to the test items. If all goes well with the test (e.g., test results are very good), the coping behaviors prior to a similar test experience may be less aversive. A pupil's entry behaviors may be described as relaxed or self-confident.

To apply intervention techniques at the coping behavior portion of the cycle does very little good. All of the behavior analysis, psychotherapy, and LSI procedures together will not change coping behaviors. Coping behaviors change as a function of changes in other parts of the cycle. Stated simply, bushels of M & M candies and complete insight into behavior to change a negative coping behavior will not work if (a) expectations are unrealistic, (b) responses are inadequate, (c) environmental responses are punitive, (d) anxiety is high, and (e) there is a high probability of avoiding a situation. Coping behaviors are the outcome of both failure and success portions of the total cycle. As such, they can be used to evaluate the effects of an intervention. What better evaluation is there than evidence that pupils come to school early and eagerly rather than late or not al all?

CLASSROOM APPLICATIONS

Building relationships is concurrent with providing successful learning experiences, in both the academic and the social behavior areas. The concept of structure (Haring & Phillips, 1962; Hewett, 1968) provides the philosophical milieu in which relationship and instruction are combined to help emotionally disturbed children enjoy success. The concept is based on the assertion that, when a child succeeds in a task in an environment that facilitates success, progress in academic and social behavior occurs. More specifically, *structure* is defined as behavior-change procedures, designed to specify and clarify the interactions between environmental events and behaviors, combined with the arrangement of environmental events to promote those specified behavior changes (Whelan & Gallagher, 1972).

In addition to its use as an intervention method, structure includes the precise use of behavior analysis as a measurement tool. The effectiveness of LSI (Morse, 1980) can be determined by applying the measurement procedures of behavior analysis. It is neutral and adaptable to intervention procedures.

Scientific validation of an intervention program requires both specification of the behavior to be changed and observation of the behavior before, during, and after intervention. This procedures can be used with both intrapsychic and behavioral intervention through precise, though not complex, measurement procedures.

An example of this validation procedure is displayed in Figure 7.4. The behavioral descriptions—distractions (excitement) and group contagions—are associated with an intrapsychic orientation (Redl & Wineman, 1957). "Hurdle help" is just one of the many intervention techniques Redl and Wineman suggested for teachers to use in instructional environments for emotionally disturbed children. Hurdle help is an external support from a teacher, designed to aid children in overcoming frustration before it culminates in a tantrum or other wise prevents completion of a task, an obstacle to problem solving (completing an assignment). When one child becomes excited or distracted, other children may respond in the same manner; one child's behavior is contagious to other children. As shown in the figure, a one-to-one relationship between the number of distractions and the number of contagions is not the case, but the two are correlated.

Hurdle help was applied only to the child with distractions; during intervention the other children did not receive hurdle help. In the figure, the behavior of the child receiving hurdle help with a task is indicated by empty circles. Total number of group contagions is illustrated by filled-in circles. Clearly the intervention helped to decrease both individual distractions and group contagions. When hurdle help was terminated, distractions and contagions began to increase again, a sign that it was removed too soon. The natural or intrinsic consequences of completing a task successfully were not

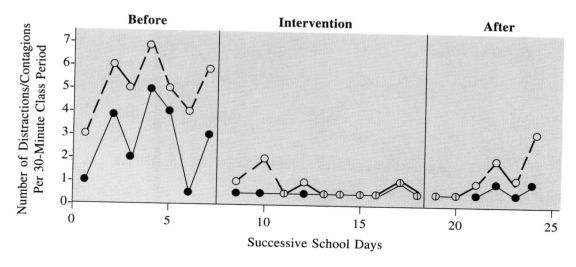

● **FIGURE 7.4**

Hurdle help as intervention to decrease individual distractions and group contagions

internalized sufficiently to justify the removal of external support.

The figure also verifies the "ripple effect" (Kounin, 1977). The ripple effect describes what happens to children as they observe what happens to another child. Even though the group was not involved in the prescribed intervention, the number of contagions diminished.

Thus, structure and behavior analysis provide a match between children's needs and the procedure used to meet them. By measuring the effects of hurdle help, for example, a teacher can determine if it works. If it does not, a match is not made and other procedures should be applied.

The concept of structure and measurement can be applied to academic behaviors as well as social ones. Figure 7.5 displays the result of one brief intervention in which the subject, a 13-year-old emotionally disturbed male, was rewarded with model car parts for successful word recognition of at least 95%. After the car was assembled, word recognition scores remained high. The internal gratification associated with successful task completion became strong enough to maintain the behavior.

Earlier, we discussed the three types of coping styles. A Type 1 child can succeed

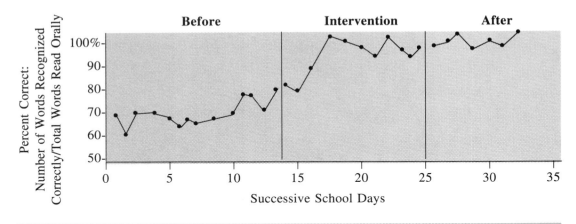

● FIGURE 7.5

Effects of an intervention to increase word recognition in oral reading

but will not take on the task. This study is one example of how a teacher might relate to a Type 1 child through the precise use of motivation. It is also an example of how a teacher can become a source of expectations and consequences—one component of establishing a positive child-teacher relationship (see Table 7.7). A Type 2 child, who accepts the task but does not complete it, requires intensive materials-presentation arrangements and brief tasks to achieve success. External motivation, although important, may be of only secondary importance to the Type 2 child. The Type 3 child has given up. He or she requires precise planning of task presentation and careful, consistent use of appropriate environmental consequences. Whatever the child's coping style, the three most critical factors are *effective use of instructional materials, external and internal motivation,* and *strength of interpersonal relationships.*

The intervention results of Figure 7.5 also can be described in relation to the school behavior cycle displayed earlier, in Figure 7.3. For example, during the intervention phase the individual responses to the oral reading task were completely inadequate. The error rate was so high that is was doubtful the pupil was comprehending the meaning of the material he was reading. At this juncture, the teacher had to make a decision. Was the material too difficult? Was the expectation unrealistic? Obviously environmental reactions were negative because the responses were in the failure category. Also, this pupil wanted to avoid reading because he attained little satisfaction from it. He avoided it through noncompliant behaviors such as complaining, refusing to open the book, and so forth.

What was the teacher's decision? First, it was decided that this pupil was Type 1— can, but won't. Second, it was decided that the reading material was at the pupil's instructional level, so no changes were made. Finally, a behavior analysis intervention was decided on. The toy car was introduced as part of the environmental reaction for correct responses. The intervention's success moved the pupil from an avoidance set to one of approach. He finally learned that he could succeed and that doing well brought satisfaction, as illustrated by high correct response rates after the model car was constructed.

An applied intervention need not be of only a single type or associated with only one specific theory. A teacher can use a variety of means to help pupils grow and change (to learn and use self-control). For example, a teacher can use LSI and behavior analysis with a child who is also in psychotherapy. Understanding the connection between feelings and behaviors, including the reality that behaviors produce feelings, is important for pupils if they are to learn. Teachers have the knowledge and skills to help pupils with their many important learning experiences.

Presenting an overview of all the educational interventions available to teachers and other helping professionals is not possible. For example, LSI is just one procedure from the *psychoeducational approach.* Others also can be used—for example, signal interference and proximity control (Long & Newman, 1980; Redl & Wineman, 1957). A teacher uses *signal interference* with a pupil who is about to exceed the boundary of acceptable behavior. If a pupil starts to get loud, the teacher may arch an eyebrow. This signal is arranged ahead of time by the pupil and the teacher. The teacher's gesture reminds the pupil that the behavior is not acceptable or that it may lead to loss of self-control. Until the pupil can internalize the signal (self-control), the teacher provides an external support for the self-control process. *Proximity control* is the support a trusted teacher gives to a pupil who is having difficulty with tasks or social behaviors. The teacher may have to stand by a pupil's desk to provide that external support, possibly extending a friendly hand on the shoulder. Knowing that an adult is close may give the pupil the support to cope with a perplexing or painful situation.

Cognitive behavior modification (CBM) (Meichenbaum, 1977, 1980; Wallace & Kauffman, 1986) frequently is used to train social and academic skills. Pupils are taught to self-monitor their behavior before, during, and after they attempt to complete a social or academic task. Self-monitoring instruction begins with a teacher doing a task while verbalizing the steps necessary to complete it: "I'll do this next. Did I put that number in the right place?" The pupil then imitates, or models, the teacher's motor and verbal performance. Upon completing the self-monitoring training, the pupil completes tasks through covert (silent) instructions. Much like psychotherapy and LSI, which also assist pupils in gaining insight into their behaviors, CBM helps them become aware of how their cognitive and affective processes are related to environmental reactions. In addition, CBM teaches them how to influence or cope with those reactions.

The classroom applications described here are not necessarily unique to special education classrooms or to professionals who serve emotionally disturbed children and youth. These and many other types (see Algozzine, 1982; Kerr & Nelson, 1983) can be used in regular education settings. For example, Blankenship and Lilly (1981) described several procedures for changing disruptive behaviors in regular classrooms. They explained how teachers can use consequences to assist pupils in developing successful responses and in decreasing inappropriate ones. *The most significant contribution a regular classroom teacher can make is to plan the classroom so behavior problems will not develop.*

1. Place pupils at the curricular level consistent with their skills; have realistic expectations.
2. Let pupils know what rules to follow. Concentrate on rules that emphasize positive behaviors; stress "do," not "don't." Follow the rules consistently.
3. If possible, ignore minor inappropriate behaviors. Give attention and praise for appropriate behaviors; praise attention to work assignments.
4. Identify and correct situations in which behavior problems are likely to occur. For example, transition from a group activity to individual seatwork may be troublesome because the pupils are not engaged in a task. As another example, when the teacher is working with a group and other pupils have completed their individual tasks, arrange a pupil-selected enjoyable activity for those who have completed their work.
5. Acknowledge improvement in academic and social skills. Recognition for a job well done goes a long way in teaching appropriate behaviors.

Gallagher (1970, 1979) developed specific ways of applying the structured approach to classroom settings.

1. Focus initial instruction upon the individual child; introduce group instruction as children are ready.
2. Expand classroom physical arrangements from individual task areas to include cooperative group problem-solving areas.
3. Change prescribed times for completing tasks to flexible time periods for completing long-term individual and group projects.
4. Gradually introduce student participation in planning tasks.
5. Partially replace teacher supervision of classroom activities with children's self-supervision.
6. Replace extrinsic consequences for task completion with intrinsic feelings of self-worth that accompany success. Achievement and self-esteem go together.
7. Make initial placement of a child for special educational services on a full-time basis. As he or she progresses, phase him or her into activities with peers in regular classrooms.

These seven guidelines are selected examples of the elaboration Gallagher proposed to make the structured approach even more useful to teachers. The approach has been used to teach positive, creative behavior coping styles (Gallagher, 1972). Implementing the guidelines is much more difficult than verbalizing them. It requires many teacher hours of individual and group planning. The guidelines closely follow the notion that *children and youth who have emotional disturbances need experiences with external structure before they can develop internal strengths* for functioning successfully in a variety of environments.

PERSPECTIVES ON CURRENT PRACTICES

Comparing practices for educating pupils with emotional and behavior disorders today with those that were described almost 30 years ago can be instructive. Table 7.8 compares characteristics of students in public school programs serving the educational needs of pupils with emotional disabilities then and now. The first column represents an analysis of programs in a Council for Exceptional Children project completed by Morse, Cutler, and Fink. (1964). The second column synopsizes a Bank Street College of Education study reported by Knitzer, Steinberg, and Fleisch (1990). An analysis of the 12 findings from the two studies reveals both positive and negative results. Some program practices have improved in the nearly three decades that separate the two studies. On the other hand, some results can only be described as saddening to professional special educators and to parents of children with emotional and behavior disorders.

In the study conducted in 1964, the majority of children served were between ages 7 and 11, reflecting the availability of programs at that time. Most programs were at the elementary level, and few were available to students in secondary schools. In 1990, most of the children served in programs were between ages 12 and 16. Again this reflects more program options for students as they progress through the educational system. It probably also reflects current federal and state laws that mandate a full range of services for children of all ages. Clearly apparent, though, is the failure of professionals in this component of special education to expend time and efforts at early identification and intervention. Significant numbers of programs designed to serve preschool and primary age children should be available by now, but they are not.

A particularly distressing finding is the comparison of curricula in 1964 and 1990. In 1964, the curriculum was described as remedial in emphasis. This can be construed as positive in that teachers were presenting instructions in multiple ways to overcome pupils' academic and affective deficits. In 1990, however, the curriculum was characterized mostly by simple worksheets and independent seatwork. If this finding holds up under subsequent investigations, it represents several steps backward in providing appropriate education for these pupils with so many needs. Especially distressing is that the profession has not adopted the principles of effective teaching that are being implemented largely by colleagues in general education programs. This is even more distressing in that most of the procedures involved in effective teaching were developed by educators who serve students with special needs.

Whether teacher education programs have not caught up with the need for teachers to be well qualified professionals or whether they simply are not teaching the components of effective instruction cannot be clearly determined at this time. This result might reflect the use of provisional teachers, those not fully certified in the area of emotional disorders. Because all students eligible for special education must be served as mandated by federal and state laws, school districts may be placing less than fully prepared educators in classrooms for these students. I hope this condition, if true, will not last long, because of all students in special education, those with emotional and

● **TABLE 7.8**

Characteristics of students in programs: Then and now

Public School Classes for the Emotionally Handicapped: A Research Analysis (Morse, Cutler, and Fink, 1964)	**At the Schoolhouse Door** (Knitzer, Steinberg, & Fleisch, 1990)
1. Majority served were between ages 7 and 11.	1. Majority served are between ages 12 and 16.
2. Boys outnumbered girls 5 to 1. Ethnic data were not reported.	2. Asian and Hispanic pupils are underrepresented; African Americans are underrepresented. Gender data are not reported.
3. Curriculum was remedial in emphasis.	3. Curriculum is defined largely by dittoed worksheets and seatwork.
4. About 70% of pupils were in program for 18 or fewer months.	4. Not reported, but drop-out rates are reported at 42% or higher, indicating low percentages of pupils returning to regular education status.
5. About 83% of pupils had IQs within normal range.	5. About 86% of pupils have IQs within normal range.
6. Approximately 55% of the pupils performed below expected levels in reading.	6. About 70% of the pupils perform below grade level in reading.
7. Home environments were moderate to severely dysfunctional.	7. Family problems compound pupils' problems.
8. About 25% of pupils were in therapy outside of classroom.	8. In-school mental health services are increasing.
9. About 88% of the pupils were in special classrooms 4 to 6 hours per day.	9. About 37% of the pupils are in special classrooms. Others are in a continuum mandated by federal law.
10. About 70% of the observed programs were judged to be successful.	10. New reforms in general education are not being incorporated into current programs.
11. Teachers cited lack of parent cooperation as major problem.	11. Parental/family involvement occurs in isolation; not consistently planned, even though valued as necessary.
12. Teacher management of pupils' inappropriate behavior was stressed in order of frequency: (a) life-space interviewing, (b) learning self-control, (c) high expectations for performance, and (d) positive consequences for meeting academic and social performance goals.	12. Behavior management to the point of classroom silence is stressed over pupil learning.

behavior problems require the best of professional education practices and educators.

The profile of students served does not seem to vary much over the last 30 years. For example, a little over 80% had intellectual ability within the normal range. More than half of the students performed below their expected grade level in academic areas. Both studies reinforced the importance of parental and family participation in programs.

Teachers in 1964 seem to have used a much broader variety of behavior management procedures, as compared to what teachers were using in 1990. In 1990, token systems seemed to be the predominant mode for ensuring that classrooms were silent and that students performed via simple response modes, largely paper and pencil. Related to this point is the finding in 1964 that about 70% of the observed programs were judged to be successful in meeting the needs of students, whereas in 1990 the new reforms in general education were not being incorporated into current programming for students with emotional and behavior disorders.

Part of the good news is that children with emotional and behavior problems are being served in a continuum of placements, whereas in 1964 only two options or so were available besides the regular classroom. Those options were special classes or special schools, including day schools and residential treatment centers. Table 7.8 clearly shows that much has to be done in this area of special education, especially in providing appropriate curriculum and instructional practices for this group of students who have so many needs in academic and social performance areas. I hope a study done within the next five or ten years will show improvements in the finding reported by the authors of *At the Schoolhouse Door.*

SUMMATION AND PROJECTIONS

Among the many millions of school-age pupils in this nation, why should a few hundred thousand children and youth who do not fit into the normal mold receive services from already strained resources of professional staff and materials? This is a difficult question, but the answer is really quite simple. As a nation founded on democratic principles and the dignity and value of individuals, we have no other choice. The reality that children and youth with emotional problems require extensive resources if they are to learn new ways of living is not an excuse for evasion or neglect. These pupils may be few in number, but their needs are many. And, if an argument for services based upon humanistic and moral principles is not persuasive, there is, of course, the economic argument. Intervention during the early years of life is less costly than providing institutional placement for most of a person's adult years. In fact, spending for early intervention may provide a return of more than 200% when compared to the impact of waiting too long to provide services (Schweinhart & Weikart, 1981).

Let's revisit the children and youth discussed in this chapter, children with emotional disturbance. Who are they? How does their behavior or coping style set them apart from others in school environments? The following description tells the story:

> Children whose school progress is erratic and puzzling, whose behavior is perplexing, or whose personalities manifest traits that give cause for concern, are to be found in every school. Sometimes these children are unresponsive, repressed or unhappy, sometimes they are serious discipline cases—the trouble frequently constituting more of a challenge to school or parental management than a fault of the child. Whatever the type of difficulty, the past few years have seen a significant change in attitude toward these problems of childhood. Better methods, based upon efforts to understand the child's nature and the factors in his environment which are causing his difficulties, are gradually replacing the older forms of repressive discipline and blind compulsion. It is often found that the problems are due to unsuspected factors for which the home, the school, or neighborhood influences, rather than the child himself, are responsible. Ways are being sought and followed, in the light of this understanding, to give early attention to the difficulties with which such children struggle and to prevent serious problems of scholarship and conduct from developing. (Sayles, 1925, p. 7)

It is truly remarkable that this historical description of pupils with emotional problems is still very much germane to present-day definitions of emotional disturbance. The similarity to Bower's (1969) definition is apparent. The first characteristic mentioned is an academic problem (erratic and puzzling responses to academic tasks). A second one is the perplexing behavior of withdrawal (unresponsive, repressed, unhappy) and aggressions (serious discipline cases).

The description also is preeminent because it identifies the interaction between person and environment. This is an enlightened view when even today so many people are inclined to believe that emotional difficulties reflect a deficit within a child or other young person. It also points out that better ways of helping children are possible instead of repressive discipline and blind compulsion. Finally, it makes the case for prevention and early intervention—indeed, a modern concept.

A question that could be raised by the description is about the better methods that were replacing repressive discipline. What were the better methods, and who used them? The "who" were Visiting Teachers (VTs), educators professionally prepared as teachers and social workers. The better methods included the following types of interventions:

1. Child-focused
   a. Counsels directly with the child to provide insight into the cause of problems.
   b. Provides instruction for improved academic and social skills.
   c. Clearly points out the relationship between behavior and its consequences.
2. School-focused
   a. Arranges classroom transfer to ensure a positive pupil-teacher relationship.
   b. Assists teachers in developing new instructional approaches.
   c. Provides modified or simplified curricular materials.
3. Home-focused
   a. Instructs parents directly about discipline, expectations, and the importance of positive role models.
   b. Acts as a case manager for the family if it needs extra support from community resources.

The interventions advocated in 1925 are much like the ones used today in many school districts and mental health agencies. The VT is now known in many agencies as a *consulting teacher* (CT). A CT's role includes many of the functions described for the VT. Most CTs, however, do not have formal preparation in social work knowledge and skills even though much of their work requires that competence.

One might question why the VT concept did not thrive and grow and become standard procedure in today's schools. There are several reasons, mostly based on speculation. Yet, these reasons often are given today for failure to increase the quality of special education the related services for pupils with behavior disorders. First, the VT was an added expense to a school district that already employed support personnel such as nurses, psychologists, and attendance officers. Second, the VT was a new role in the schools. This required solutions to problems of turf and coordination of services. Third, the VT was an experimental program that was supported largely from outside the school system. When the dollars were not available and a school district could not add them to its budget, the VT position was lost. Lastly, the nation entered 20 years of severe depression and worldwide war. Resources that otherwise might have gone to unique educational services were diverted to address problems of basic educational services for all pupils.

At present, many of the functions envisioned for the VT program are being carried out in many school districts. A wide range of services is available for pupils with emotional problems—far more than in 1925, or even 1975 for that matter. Nevertheless, the teacher is the one who must provide most of the direct instruction, and that is no easy task. No matter what the diversity of service models is, teachers of children and youth with emotional disturbance must continually question their approaches to relationships and instruction and work diligently to find answers. The questions and procedures listed in Table 7.9 represent processes for solving the problems that arise. They are not solutions but can lead to them. They include diagnosis, program planning, implementation, and evaluation.

Besides the basic instructional competencies involved in teaching subject matter, teachers must know how to measure behavior, evaluate instructional effectiveness, prepare and organize learning environments, instruct with media, use differential instructional procedures based on children's needs, and apply principles of behavior in wise and productive ways. These skills and knowledge are not learned quickly or easily. They must be refined constantly as teachers learn from and with children. Teachers also must learn how to help children develop self-control over their lives (Fagen, Long, & Stevens, 1975), the ultimate goal of what we do for, to, and with them. Teachers must learn the techniques of smoothly changing classroom activities to reduce frustration encountered by children with emotional problems during periods of little external support. The list of skills and understandings is endless, but important if these children are to change their life pattern from one of predominant failure to one of earned success.

Emotional planning and programming for children with emotional disturbance have improved considerably over the years. Cultural, minority, and economic backgrounds now are recognized as valued differences rather than as undesirable deviance.

● *TABLE 7.9*

Behaviors designated for application of behavior change processes

Questions	Procedures
1. What behavior excesses and deficits are observed in the present learning environment, and prior to entry into a changed learning environment?	1. Identification and analysis of behavior excesses and deficits observed in specific learning environments.
2. What specific terminal or target behaviors will be acquired within, and upon departure from, a changed learning environment?	2. Specification of terminal behaviors that should be acquired to decrease the extent of excesses and deficits.
3. What systematic environment transaction experiences will be implemented to reduce discrepancies between behavior excesses/deficits and specified terminal behaviors?	3. Implementation of environmental transaction experiences in learning environments designed to reduce the discrepancies between behavior excesses/deficits and specified terminal behaviors.
4. What measurement and evaluation procedures can be applied to determine effectiveness of environmental transaction experiences implemented to reduce discrepancies between observed entry and departure behaviors?	4. Application of simultaneous measurement and evaluation procedures to assess the effectiveness of environmental transaction experiences in attaining specified terminal behaviors.
5. What measurement procedures can be utilized to assess maintenance and generalization of acquired terminal behaviors after departure from a changed learning environment?	5. Initiation of systematic aperiodic measurement to ascertain extent of maintenance and generalization of terminal behaviors in learning environments different from the one in which acquisition occurred.

Descriptions and definitions are becoming more educationally relevant, rather than medically based. Various approaches to understanding child development have been combined, in some instances, to form a foundation for planning academic and social behavior instructional strategies. Educators are becoming more aware of the role children's language plays in self-instruction procedures, a cognitive approach to behavior change. They also are learning to enlist the assistance of other children to help children in need (Graubard & Rosenberg, 1974).

Much progress in educational programming has been made, but more remains to be accomplished. Additional evaluation-research studies must be done to assess the effectiveness of educational efforts. Appropriately applying what is known is another challenge, for merely knowing what to do does not ensure that conditions will support the actual doing. Often, conditions are not present to sustain dedicated, professional educators, and as a result they become discouraged and leave the field (Knoblock & Goldstein, 1971). Yet, we have reason for optimism, especially from an historical perspective. Today schools are serving more children and youth with emotional problems than ever before. Educators seem to have a new willingness to place scarce resources in programs of prevention and early intervention. At the same time, programs are expanding for adolescents in secondary schools, a long neglected population. All in all, programs of instruction and related services for pupils with emotional disturbance have improved over the years. Although complacency is not in order, special educators can be justifiably proud of their accomplishments.

ISSUES

Even though emotional disturbance is listed as a separate category of exceptionality, this condition obviously can and does occur within every other category, from severe retardation through the gifted and talented classification. Emotional disturbance still represents one of the most unserved groups of school-age children and youth. Public Law 94–142, as amended, has reduced the numbers of unserved children, but several concerns must still be addressed:

1. How will schools serve the 15% to 18% who have been consistently identified beyond the 2% with serious emotional disturbance? Do we need renewed emphasis on a mental health curriculum? Should schools initiate, with the cooperation of mental health professionals, brief counseling and therapy sessions?
2. Why are 60% of school-age pupils identified as having behavior problems at least once over a 6-year period? Are children responding to infrequent stress? Do teachers view normalcy as a narrow or restrictive range of behavior?
3. Do children behave deviantly in response to a curriculum they can neither understand nor master? If so, what curricular changes can be made to provide successful learning experiences?
4. How can regular classroom teachers be helped to modify content and instructional practices for pupils who fail to progress satisfactorily? Could a visiting teacher (VT) be employed effectively to assist in a regular classroom (e.g., provide teacher release time for interaction with fewer children; model adapted instructional methods)?
5. Can technology such as the microcomputer be used effectively as an instructional mode? Or will it increase the alienation that many pupils with emotional disturbance exhibit?
6. If troubled pupils can be taught cognitive approaches to self-monitoring in special programs, will they be able to transfer and use the skills effectively in regular education programs?
7. Can general and special educators collaborate to ensure that pupils who display

severe conduct disorders are served well, that they do not fall between the two service systems of general and regular education?

These seven issues are representative samples at best. Many more can be raised from the information in the chapter and from additional study. Though the issues listed are specific, they do relate to a larger concern that professionals in the area must address.

One important concern is programmatic. Special education and related service programs should incorporate several program elements before they may be considered to be acceptable or to reflect quality of operation. Elements include the specific program aspects of (a) philosophy, (b) goals, (c) population to be served, (d) program entry criteria, (e) instructional content and procedure, (f) program exit criteria, and (g) a program evaluation system (Grosenick & Huntze, 1983) An additional element is related to physical plant or facilities, funding, and administrative arrangements. Grosenick and Huntze selected 81 programs from literature descriptions that addressed the seven elements listed in (a) through (g). They wanted to determine the number and percent of programs that focused upon each element in an acceptable manner. The elements and percents are:

1. Philosophy	46%	5. Instructional	69%
2. Goals	37%	6. Exit criteria	20%
3. Population served	54%	7. Evaluation	52%
4. Entry criteria	41%		

If these seven elements are critical for program success, a great deal of work clearly must be accomplished with the population of youngsters who have emotional problems. Even more alarming is that 365 program descriptions had to be reviewed to identify 81 that even included the elements in their write-ups. School districts and agencies that operate special education and related services programs should be able to document policy and procedures for all of the elements. If they cannot or do not, how can they know the why, how, and what effect they have on the who they are mandated to serve?

A BRIEF POSTSCRIPT

This chapter provides a spot check, a still photograph, of a dynamic topic and field. Educators of children and youth with emotional disturbance still search for more precise child behavior descriptions, better understanding of how behavior develops and changes, more functional approaches to help children acquire self-control, and more efficient and effective ways to ensure that the children for whom they are responsible experience the joys of successful learning. The ferment is still present but now is targeted toward helping children help themselves to become winners. What happens when these children become winners? The children know best what it is all about:

- Yep! She told me I did good work today.
- Why can't I stay after school to finish this? It's fun.
- I like to be in your class.

- That tantrum is really crazy. Doesn't he know that won't get him any place?
- I'm tired of being so happy.

What better validation is there than these statements from the children themselves? Indeed, children are the best evaluators of program effectiveness. Responsible educators must ensure that the evaluations reflect positive and successful, rather than negative and unsuccessful, programs for this country's most important resource—our children and youth.

R*EFERENCES*

Achenbach, T. M., & Edelbrock, G. S. (1983). Taxonomic issues in child psychopathology. In T. H. Ollendick & M. Hersen (Eds.), *Handbook of child psychopathology* (pp. 65–93). New York: Plenum Press.

Algozzine, B. (1982). *Problem behavior management.* Rockville, MD: Aspen Systems.

American Psychiatric Association. (1987). *Diagnostic and statistical manual of mental disorders* (3rd ed. rev.). Washington, DC: Author.

Blankenship, C., & Lilly, M. S. (1981). *Mainstreaming students with learning and behavior problems.* New York: Holt, Rinehart & Winston.

Bower, E. M. (1969). *Early identification of emotionally handicapped children in school* (2nd ed.) Springfield, IL: Charles C Thomas.

Bower, E. M. (1982). Defining emotional disturbance: Public policy and research. *Psychology in the Schools, 19,* 55–60.

Brown, L. L., & Hammill, D. D. (1983). *The behavior rating profile.* Austin, TX: Pro-Ed.

Bureau of the Census. (1991). *Statistical abstract of the United States* (111th ed.) Washington, DC: U.S. Government Printing Office.

Caplan, G. (Ed.). (1961). *Prevention of mental disorders in children.* New York: Basic Books.

Clarizio, H. F., & McCoy, G. F. (1983). *Behavioral disorders in children* (3rd ed.). New York: Harper & Row.

Cromwell, R. L., Blashfield, R. K., & Strauss, J. S. (1975). Criteria for classification systems. In N. Hobbs (Ed.), *Issues in the classification of children* (Vol. 1, pp. 4–25). San Francisco: Jossey-Bass.

Cullinan, D., Epstein, M. H., & Lloyd, J. W. (1983). *Behavior disorders of children and adolescents.* Englewood Cliffs, NJ: Prentice Hall.

Deshler, D. D., & Graham, S. (1980). Tape recording educational materials for secondary handicapped students. *Teaching Exceptional Children, 12,* 52–54.

Edwards, L. (1983). Curriculum modification as a strategy for helping regular classroom behavior disordered students. In E. Meyen, G. Vergason, & R. Whelan (Eds.), *Promising practices for exceptional children: Curriculum implications* (pp. 87–104). Denver: Love Publishing.

Fagen, S. A. (1979). Psychoeducational management and self-control. In D. Cullinan & M. H. Epstein (Eds.), *Special education for adolescents: Issues and perspectives* (pp. 235–271). Columbus, OH: Charles E. Merrill.

Fagen, S., Long, N. J., & Stevens, D. J. (1975). *Teaching children self-control.* Columbus, OH: Charles E. Merrill.

Forness, S. (1992, February). Proposed EBD definition update. *CCBD Newsletter,* p. 4.

Freud, S. (1950). *Totem and taboo* (J. Strachey, Trans.). New York: W. W. Norton & Company. (Original work published 1913)

Gallagher, P. A. (1970). A synthesis of classroom scheduling techniques for emotionally disturbed children. *Focus on Exceptional Children, 2*(5), 1–10.

Gallagher, P. A. (1972). Procedures for developing creativity in emotionally disturbed children. *Focus on Exceptional Children, 4*(6), 1–9.

Gallagher, P. A. (1979). *Teaching students with behavior disorders: Techniques for classroom instruction.* Denver: Love Publishing.

Graubard, P., & Rosenberg, H. (1974). *Classrooms that work*. New York: E. P. Dutton & Co.

Grosenick, J. K., & Huntze, S. L. (1983). *More questions than answers: Review and analysis of programs for behaviorally disordered children and youth*. Columbia: University of Missouri-Columbia, Department of Special Education.

Haring, N. G., & Phillips, E. L. (1962). *Educating emotionally disturbed children*. New York: McGraw-Hill

Haring, N. G., & Whelan, R. J. (1965). Experimental methods in education and management. In N. Long, W. Morse, & R. Newman (Eds.), *Conflict in the classroom* (1st ed.) (pp. 389–405). Belmont, CA: Wadsworth.

Hewett, F. M. (1968). *The emotionally disturbed child in the classroom*. Boston: Allyn & Bacon.

Hobbs, N. (1975). *The futures of children: Categories, labels, and their consequences*. San Francisco: Jossey-Bass.

Honing v. Doe, U.S. Supp. Ct. 1988, reported in *Education for the Handicapped Law Report*, January 29, 1988.

Johnson, J. L. (1976). Mainstreaming black children. In R. L. Jones (Ed.), *Mainstreaming and the minority child* (pp. 159–180). Reston, VA: Council for Exceptional Children.

Joint Commission on Mental Health of Children. (1970). *Crisis in child mental health: Challenge for the 1970's*. New York: Harper & Row.

Jones, R. L. (Ed.). (1976). *Mainstreaming and the minority child*. Reston, VA: Council for Exceptional Children.

Kanfer, F. H., & Saslow, G. (1967). Behavioral analysis: An alternative to diagnostic classification. In T. Millon (Ed.), *Theories of psychopathology* (pp. 375–387). Philadelphia: W. B. Saunders.

Kanner, L. (1943). Autistic disturbances of affective contact. *Nervous Child, 2*, 217–250.

Kauffman, J. M. (1977). *Characteristics of children's behaviors*. Columbus, OH: Charles E. Merrill.

Kauffman, J. M. (1980). Where special education for disturbed children is going: A personal view. *Exceptional Children, 46*, 522–527.

Kauffman, J. M. (1981). *Characteristics of children's behavior disorders* (2nd ed.). Columbus, OH: Charles E. Merrill.

Kelly, E. (1992). *Conduct problem/emotional problem interventions: A holistic perspective*. East Aurora, NY: Slosson Educational Publications.

Kelly, E. (1990). *Differential list of conduct and emotional problems*. East Aurora, NY: Slosson Educational Publications.

Kelly, T. J., Bullock, L. M., & Dykes, M. K. (1977). Behavior disorders: Teachers' perceptions. *Exceptional Children, 43*, 316–318.

Kerr, M. M., & Nelson, C. M. (1983). *Strategies for managing behavior problems in the classroom*. Columbus, OH: Charles E. Merrill.

Kessler, J. W. (1966). *Psychopathology of childhood*. Englewood Cliffs, NJ: Prentice Hall.

Knitzer, J., Steinberg, Z., & Fleisch, B. (1990). *At the schoolhouse door*. New York: Bank Street College of Education.

Knoblock, P., & Goldstein, A. (1971). *The lonely teacher*. Boston: Allyn & Bacon.

Kounin, J. S. (1977). *Discipline and group management in classrooms*. Huntington, NY: R. E. Krieger Publishing.

Long, N. J. (1974). In J. M. Kauffman & C. D. Lewis (Eds.), *Teaching children with behavior disorders: Personal perspectives* (pp. 168–196). Columbus, OH: Charles E. Merrill.

Long, N. J., & Duffner, B. (1980). The stress cycle or the coping cycle? The impact of home and school stresses on pupils' classroom behavior. In N. Long, W. Morse, & R. Newman (Eds.), *Conflict in the classroom* (4th ed.) (pp. 218–228). Belmont, CA: Wadsworth.

Long, N. J., & Newman, R. G. (1980). Managing surface behavior of children in school. In N. Long, W. Morse, & R. Newman (Eds.), *Conflict in the classroom* (4th ed., pp. 233–241). Belmont, CA: Wadsworth.

McCarney, S. B., Leigh, J. E., & Cornbleet, J. (1983). *Behavior evaluation scale*. Columbia, MO: Educational Services.

Meichenbaum, D. (1977). *Cognitive-behavior modification: An integrative approach*. New York: Plenum Press.

Meichenbaum, D. (1980). Cognitive behavior modification: A promise yet unfilled. *Exceptional Education Quarterly, 1*(1), 83–88.

Menninger, K., Mayman, M., & Pruyser, P. (1963). *The vital balance: The life process in mental health and illness*. New York: Viking Press.

Moos, R. H. (1979). *Evaluating educational environments*. San Francisco: Jossey-Bass.

Morse, W. C. (1977). Serving the needs of children with behavior disorders. *Exceptional Children, 44*, 158–164.

Morse, W. C. (1980). Worksheet on life-space interviewing for teachers. In N. Long, W. Morse, & R. Newman (Eds.), *Conflict in the classroom* (4th ed.) (pp. 267–271). Belmont, CA: Wadsworth.

Morse, W. C., Cutler, R. L., & Fink, A. H. (1964) *Public school classes for the emotionally handicapped: A research analysis*. Reston, VA: Council for Exceptional Children.

Office of the Federal Register. (1985). *Code of federal regulations* (Title 34; Pts. 300–399). Washington, DC: U.S. Government Printing Office.

Office of the Federal Register. (1991). *Code of federal regulations* (Title 34; Pts. 300–399). Washington, DC: U.S. Government Printing Office.

Ollendick, T. H., & Hersen, M. (Eds.). (1984). *Child behavioral assessment: Principles and procedures*. New York: Pergamon Press.

Pate, J. E. (1963). Emotionally disturbed and socially maladjusted children. In L. Dunn (Ed.), *Exceptional children in the schools* (pp. 239–283). New York: Holt, Rinehart & Winston.

Phillips, L., Draguns, J. G., & Bartlett, D. P. (1975). Classification of behavior disorders. In N. Hobbs (Ed.), *Issues in the classification of children* (Vol. 1, pp. 26–55). San Francisco: Jossey-Bass.

Quay, H. C. (1965). Personality and delinquency. In H. C. Quay (Ed.), *Juvenile delinquency* (pp. 139–169). New York: D. Van Nostrand.

Quay, H. C. (1975). Classification in the treatment of delinquency and antisocial behavior. In N. Hobbs (Ed.), *Issues in the classification of children* (Vol. 1, pp. 377–392). San Francisco: Jossey-Bass.

Quay, H. C. (1979). Classification. In H. C. Quay & J. S. Werry (Eds.), *Psychopathological disorders of childhood* (2nd ed.) (pp. 1–42). New York: John Wiley.

Redl, F. (1980). The concept of the life space interview. In N. Long, W. Morse, & R. Newman (Eds.), *Conflict in the classroom* (4th ed., pp. 257–266). Belmont, CA: Wadsworth.

Redl, F., & Wineman, D. (1957). *The aggressive child*. New York: Free Press.

Rhodes, W. C. (Ed.). (1972). *A study of child variance* (Vol. 1). Ann Arbor: University of Michigan Press.

Rhodes, W. C. (1977). The illusion of normality. *Behavioral Disorders, 2*, 122–129.

Rothman, E. P. (1977). *Troubled teachers*. New York: David McKay.

Rubin, R. A., & Balow, B. (1978). Prevalence of teacher identified behavior problems: A longitudinal study. *Exceptional Children, 45*, 102–111.

Salvia, J., & Ysseldyke, J. E. (1978). *Assessment in special and remedial education*. Boston: Houghton Mifflin.

Sayles, M. B. (1925). *The problem child in school*. New York: Joint Committee of Methods of Preventing Delinquency.

Schweinhart, L. J., & Weikart, D. P. (1981). Perry Preschool effects nine years later: What do they mean? In M. J. Begab, H. C. Haywood, & H. L. Garber (Eds.), *Psychosocial influences in retarded performance: Vol. 2. Strategies for improving competence*. Baltimore: University Park Press.

Shea, T. M. (1978). *Teaching children and youth with behavior disorders*. St. Louis: C. V. Mosby.

Shields, J., & Slater, E. (1961). Heredity and psychological abnormality. In H. J. Eysenck (Ed.), *Handbook of abnormal psychology* (pp. 298–344). New York: Basic Books.

Sinclair, E., Forness, S. R., & Axleson, J. (1985). Psychiatric diagnosis: A study of its relationship to school needs. *Journal of Special Education, 19*, 333–334.

Skinner, B. F. (1953). *Science and human behavior*. New York: Macmillan.

Skinner, B. F. (1974). *About behaviorism*. New York: Knopf.

Szasz, T. S. (1974). *The myth of mental illness* (rev. ed.). New York: Harper & Row.

Trieschman, A. E. Whittaker. J. K., & Brendtro, L. K. (1969). *The other 23 hours*. Chicago: Aldine.

Tuma, J. M., & Sabotka, K. R. (1983). Traditional therapies with children. In T. H. Ollendick & M. Hersen (Eds.), *Handbook of child psychopathology* (pp. 391–426). New York: Plenum Press.

U.S. Department of Education. (1985). *Seventh annual report to Congress on the implementation of the Education of the Handicapped Act*. Washington, DC: U.S. Government Printing Office.

U.S. Department of Education. (1991). *Thirteenth annual report to Congress on the implementation of the Individuals with Disabilities Education Act.* Washington, DC: Author.

Von Isser, A., Quay, H. C., & Love, G. T. (1980). Interrelationships among three measures of deviant behavior. *Exceptional Children, 46,* 272–276.

Wallace, G., & Kauffman, J. M. (1986). *Teaching students with learning and behavior problems* (3rd ed.). Columbus, OH: Charles E. Merrill.

Whelan, R. J. (1972). What's in a label? A hell of a lot! In R. Harth, E. Meyen, & G. S. Nelson (Eds.), *The legal and educational consequences of the intelligence testing movement: Handicapped children and minority group children* (pp. 34–58). Columbia: University of Missouri Extension Division.

Whelan, R. J. (1977) Human understanding of human behavior. In A. J. Pappanikou & J. L. Paul (Eds.), *Mainstreaming emotionally disturbed children* (pp. 64–79). Syracuse, NY: Syracuse University Press.

Whelan, R. J., deSaman, L. M., & Fortmeyer, D. J. (1984). Oh! Those wonderful feelings: The relationship between pupil and achievement. *Focus on Exceptional Children, 16*(8), 1–8.

Whelan, R. J., & Gallagher, P. A. (1972). Effective teaching of children with behavior disorders. In N. G. Haring & A. H. Hayden (Eds.), *The improvement of instruction* (pp. 183–218). Seattle: Special child Publications.

Whelan, R. J., & Jackson, F. S. (1971). Labeling. In J. Cohen (Ed.), *Confronting and change: Community problems of mental retardation and developmental disabilities* (pp. 45–78). Ann Arbor: University of Michigan Press.

Wiener, N. (1954). *The human use of human beings* (2nd ed.). New York: Doubleday.

Winett, R. A., Stefanek, M., & Riley, A. W. (1983). Preventive strategies with children and families: Small groups, organizations, communities. In T. H. Ollendick & M. Hersen (Eds.), *Handbook of child psychopathology* (pp. 485–521). New York: Plenum Press.

8

SPEECH AND LANGUAGE IMPAIRMENTS

MABEL L. RICE
AND C. MELANIE SCHUELE

*O*ur society places a high value on oral communication. We are surrounded daily by talking—people conversing, giving lectures, engaging in one-to-one interactions, radio dialogues, television programs, and reporting play-by-play action in athletic events. We are highly aware of the manner of speech, how appropriate it is to the occasion, and how effective. We want our children to be fluent, clever speakers, able to express their wants and needs in a winning manner.

Early facility with words and language often is equated with general intelligence. Children and youth who cannot speak and use language in the same way as their peers are noticeably different. They struggle to learn, but their efforts to communicate are in marked contrast to the effortless mastery of most of their normally developing peers. In conversation their attention gets shifted away from what they have to say to how they try to say it. Somewhere around late second grade, peers begin to notice and ridicule their efforts to talk. Furthermore, children with limited language are at risk for academic failure, particularly in reading. In short, school is a frustrating experience for students with communicative handicaps.

Social adaptation demands that all children learn to talk the "right" way; hence, there are formalized remediation programs. The professionals primarily responsible for these programs are speech-language pathologists (SLPs), who work in schools, clinics, hospitals, and residential treatment programs, as well as in private practice. This chapter concerns the most extensive service setting, the public school. Schools employ 53% of the speech-language pathologists affiliated with the American Speech-Language-Hearing Association (ASHA) (Blake & Shewan, 1992). ASHA is the professional certifying organization for speech-language pathologists and audiologists. Although most school SLPs are ASHA-affiliated, this level of professional certification is not a uniform requirement, so the full number of school SLPs exceeds the ASHA membership estimates.

SLPs work with children whose only handicapping condition may be a problem in speech, language, or hearing. They also work with children whose speech-language or hearing problem occurs as either a primary or a secondary problem with another condition, such as mental retardation, emotional disturbance, or learning disabilities. Some speech-language problems are severe; others are less disabling. In all cases, the life of a child with a speech-language impairment can be enriched by improved communicative competence. This is the job of the school SLP, to determine the most effective way to enhance the child's communicative skills and then to implement a treatment program.

CURRENT PRACTICES

Public school speech-language pathologists are influenced by: (a) the traditional service model worked out in the 1920s when speech therapy was first introduced into the public schools, (b) the medical models of speech-language pathology practiced in noneducational settings, (c) contemporary knowledge describing how normal children acquire speech and language, and (d) developments in related areas of special education services and the interpretations and service demands of the Education for All Handicapped Children Act (PL 94–142) and its amendments. The service delivery models, the contemporary knowledge base, and the new developments and interpretations are not independent of each other. They interact, overlapping in ways that encourage development of some new kinds of services, maintenance of some traditional activities and roles, and elimination of some familiar but ineffective approaches.

Speech and language services to children in the public schools in many respects continue to be influenced by traditional models of therapy. Traditionally, children have been seen in small groups or individually in a setting separate from their classroom. SLPs have worked with children on specific goals and objectives designed to remediate identified speech and language deficits. The medical model of speech-language pathology has greatly influenced approaches to diagnosing speech and language disorders. Clinicians evaluate children to identify a disorder, and a course of treatment is prescribed. The treatment is expected to resolve the speech or language problems.

The current state of knowledge of speech and language development suggests that these traditional practices may not be appropriate for all children. For example, we now realize that language impairments can have a profound and long-lasting effect not only on an individual's communicative skills but also on social, academic, and vocational competencies. Thus, language impairment can be a long-standing area of difficulty, with symptoms that change as an individual matures and faces more sophisticated social and academic demands. Further, we now recognize that the influence of the sociocultural context on language acquisition and use is quite powerful. Thus, SLPs have to focus on communication development in the context of meaningful activities. SLPs increasingly are providing speech-language services in nonsegregated settings; communication skills are learned and practiced in real-life situations. Consultation and collaboration with teachers are means to ensure that therapy plans address children's primary communicative needs. Increased recognition of the impact of language abilities on children's academic performance has led SLPs to focus on language-based academic tasks and to use classroom curricular materials with children who are speech and language impaired.

Contemporary theories of speech and language development emphasize that children acquire communication competencies in a social context. Language is closely associated with other aspects of a child's functioning, especially cognitive and social abilities. Limited language skills impact on academic achievement and social development, areas of ever increasing concern in the field today. Thus, therapy programs implemented by SLPs must address the interaction of speech and language with other developmental domains. Goals must address the interaction of speech and language with social and academic abilities and, ultimately, progress in communicative abilities must include consideration of these other areas.

Speech and language services are continually undergoing redefinition and transition as a consequence of legislation and public policy. PL 99–457 mandated that school districts provide special education services to preschool children. Many school SLPs have limited experience providing services to 3- to 5-year-old children. Speech and language therapy with preschool children can be quite different from therapy with school-age children. The push toward inclusion and the provision of services in the least restrictive environment is seen as SLPs are called upon to serve children in the context of their regular classroom. Whereas most speech-language services previously were provided in separate therapy rooms, SLPs are working more often in classrooms (e.g., providing language enrichment in kindergarten classrooms) and consulting with teachers.

MAJOR CHANGES SINCE PL 94–142 AND 99–457

Prior to the enactment of PL 94–142, school clinicians focused primarily on remediating articulation errors, and speech-language therapy services were viewed as quite separate from a child's educational programs. Now, nearly 20 years later and with the passage of PL 99–457, school SLPs are in a much different position. The requirements of special education legislation and advances within the field of speech-language pathology have combined to create a multifaceted role for school SLPs.

Speech and language therapy services are only one aspect of a broad range of special education services. The SLP is a member of a team of professionals who collaborate to meet the needs of children with special needs. The SLP has two roles on this team: (a) to evaluate children to determine whether they qualify for services, and (b) to design and implement individualized education programs (IEPs) to meet children's communicative needs. With these two roles come a range of responsibilities for the SLP:

- Evaluate speech and language skills.
- Set goals and objectives to improve speech and language skills.
- Design and implement an instructional program to meet the individual needs of each child qualifying for speech and language therapy.
- Evaluate progress on goals and objectives.
- Determine when and if services are no longer needed.
- Collaborate with teachers and parents to ensure that communicative needs in the classroom and home are addressed in the IEP.
- Consult with teachers and parents on ways to ensure that communicative limitations are overcome or addressed in the child's daily activities.

Most SLPs provide these services to a large group of children with vastly different speech and language problems who range in age from preschool to high school—a most challenging task!

STATUS OF OUR EFFECTIVENESS

Overall, impression of the effectiveness of PL 94–142 have been mixed. In a survey of ASHA members who had 5 or more years of experience with children in school settings (Hyman, 1985; Mansour & Lingwall, 1985), more than 70% agreed that the law has improved the quality of speech, language, and hearing services for children with impairments. Of this group, 80% believed that, in particular, the law had enhanced access to services and had contributed to parental involvement in the educational process. Furthermore, more than two thirds of this group believed the law had improved communication among the various types of professionals in the schools.

On the other hand, "only 27% of these experienced school personnel felt that the law had helped to increase the amount of services that they were able to provide to clients, and almost one half agreed that communicatively handicapped children are still not receiving all the services that they need" (Hyman, 1985, p. 37). In addition, "63% of the clinicians in schools reported that state and local government requirements often frustrate the purposes of PL 94–142. Many members expressed concern over the paperwork and 'red tape' involved in providing services to children" (Mansour & Lingwall, 1985, p. 38). In sum, SLPs seem to endorse the spirit of PL 94–142 and believe it has increased access to services and cross-disciplinary communication but are frustrated by the additional paperwork demands and consequent redirection in time available for working with children.

*E*DUCATIONAL DEFINITIONS

In ancient times some children had difficulty learning to speak despite normal hearing and intelligence. This was known and studied in the 19th century (Weiner, 1984). In modern times the earliest therapy program, including elementary instruction in basic school subjects, was proposed in 1888 by a Viennese scholar, Rafael Coen (as described in Weiner, 1984). Public school programs for children with communication handicaps began to appear in the United States in the 1920s, but they were not widespread until the infusion of federal monies during the 1960s. Coen's scholarly definition of speech and language handicaps was a product of his environment, as were the definitions of the 1960s a product of those times.

Early on, these definitions centered only on speech (articulation, voice, and fluency) and hearing disorders. Articulation (speech sound production) was the disorder seen most often in public school therapy. Only within the last 20 years have new studies of children's language development led us to recognize the centrality of language and symbolic processing in communicative disorders. Our current definition of communication disorders, adopted by ASHA (1993), reflects this. The definition includes language disorders, speech disorders, hearing disorders, and communication variations (dialect, augmentative/alternative communication). Table 8.1 is an adaptation of part of the ASHA definition.

Children receiving speech and language therapy in the public schools represent a

● *TABLE 8.1*

Communication disorders and their variations

Communication Disorder	Speech Disorder	Language Disorder	Hearing Disorder
A *communication disorder* is an impairment in the ability to receive, send, process, and comprehend concepts or verbal, nonverbal, and graphic symbol systems. A communication disorder may be evident in the processes of hearing, language, and/or speech. A communication disorder may range in severity from mild to profound. It may be developmental or acquired. Individuals may demonstrate one or any combination of communication disorders. A communication disorder may result in a primary disability or it may be secondary to other disabilities.	A *speech disorder* is an impairment of the articulation of speech sounds, fluency, and/or voice. 1. An *articulation disorder* is the atypical production of speech sounds characterized by substitutions, omissions, additions, or distortions that may interfere with intelligibility. 2. A *fluency disorder* is an interruption in the flow of speaking characterized by atypical rate, rhythm, and repetitions in sounds, syllables, words, and phrases. This may be accompanied by excessive tension, struggle behavior, and secondary mannerisms. 3. A *voice disorder* is characterized by the abnormal production and/or absences of vocal quality, pitch, loudness, resonance, and/or du-	A *language disorder* is impaired comprehension and/or use of spoken, written, and/or other symbol systems. The disorder may involve (1) the form of language (phonology, morphology, syntax), (2) the content of language (semantics), and/or (3) the function of language in communication (pragmatics) in any combination. 1. Form of Language 　a. *Phonology* is the sound system of a language and rules that govern the sound combinations. 　b. *Morphology* is the system that governs the structure of words and the construction of word forms. 　c. *Syntax* is the system governing the order and combination of words to form sentences, and the relationships among the	A *hearing disorder* is the result of impaired auditory sensitivity of the physiological auditory system. A hearing disorder may limit the development, comprehension, production, and/or maintenance of speech and/or language. Hearing disorders are classified according to difficulties in detection, recognition, discrimination, comprehension, and perception of auditory information. Individuals with hearing impairments frequently may be described as deaf or hard of hearing. 1. *Deaf* is defined as a hearing disorder which limits an individual's aural/oral communication performance to the extent that the primary sensory input for communication may be other than the auditory channel. 2. *Hard of hearing* is defined as a hearing

● **TABLE 8.I (CONTINUED)**

Communication disorders and their variations

Speech Disorder	Language Disorder	Hearing Disorder

ration, which is inappropriate for an individual's age and/or sex.	elements within a sentence.
	2. Content of Language
	  a. *Semantics* is the system that governs the meanings of words and sentences
	3. Function of Language
	  a. *Pragmatics* is the system that combines the above language components in functional and socially appropriate communication.
		disorder whether fluctuating or permanent, which adversely affects an individual's communication performance. The hard of hearing individual relies upon the auditory channel as the primary sensory input for communication.

Communication Variations

Communication difference/dialect is a variation of a symbol system used by a group of individuals that reflects and is determined by shared regional, social, or cultural/ethnic factors. A regional, social, or cultural/ethnic variation of a symbol system should not be considered a disorder of speech or language.

Augmentative/alternative communication systems attempt to compensate and facilitate, temporarily or permanently, for the impairment and disability patterns of individuals with severe expressive and/or language comprehension disorders. Augmentative/alternative communication may be required for individuals demonstrating impairments in gestural, spoken, and/or written modalities.

Source: Adapted from "Definitions of Communication Disorders and Variations" prepared by the Ad Hoc Committee on Service Delivery in the Schools, American Speech-Language-Hearing Association (1993a). *ASHA, 35* (Suppl. 10), pp. 40–41. They are not intended to address issues of eligibility and compensation.

heterogeneous group. Communicative difficulties are primary handicapping conditions for some children. For other children, communicative impairments are secondary to a handicapping condition such as mental retardation or hearing impairment. The definition or characterization of communicative impairments can be approached from two perspectives: (a) classification of children for purposes of providing special education in accordance with federal guidelines, and (b) a description of speech and language abilities for purposes of identification of areas in need of remediation. The following paragraphs address the first purpose. The next section discusses distinctions that SLPs use to describe communicative deficits.

Children receiving speech and language therapy as their only special education service are classified as "speech impaired." The definition of speech impairment, as set forth by the U.S. Department of Education, is: "a communication disorder such as stuttering, impaired articulation, a language impairment, or a voice impairment, which adversely affects a child's educational performance." Typically these children receive all of their other educational programming in a regular classroom.

Children with other primary handicapping conditions (e.g., mental retardation, hearing impairment) may receive speech and language therapy as a related service in which the speech impairment is the secondary handicapping condition. For these children communicative impairments are related to another disability. Children with mental retardation typically are late in learning to talk. Communication deficits are central to the problems of children with autism. Language impairment is a substantial component of many learning disabilities.

The guidelines for PL 99–457 allow states to opt to serve 3- to 5-year-old children in noncategorical placements. Thus, many states do not require school districts to classify preschool children under specific handicapping conditions. Rather, a generic term, such as "developmental delay," is applied to all preschool children in need of special education.

Special education categorical labels as defined by the federal government are for placement purposes. A child must qualify for special education services in one or more categories (handicapping conditions). These categories reveal little about the nature of a child's communicative abilities. SLPs also define communicative impairments in terms of the aspects of speech and language that pose problems for a given child.

LANGUAGE IMPAIRMENTS

Language impairments involve difficulty in comprehending and/or using spoken or written language. Language commonly is subdivided into several component yet interrelated parts: phonology, syntax, morphology, semantics, and pragmatics. Individuals with language impairments can have difficulties involving one or more aspects of language.

Children who have a language disability yet whose other developmental milestones are within the normative range are referred to in the literature as having a *specific language impairment* (SLI). Much research in the field of speech-language pathology in recent years has focused on this subgroup of people with communicative impairments. The findings suggest that the initial identifying characteristic of children with SLI is a late onset of talking. These children often do not speak their first words until age 2 and do not combine words until age 3 (e.g., Rescorla & Schwartz, 1990). Some children with SLI have deficits in using and comprehending language, whereas other children with SLI may exhibit comprehension abilities within normal limits yet have substantial expressive difficulties. Children with SLI as a group show deficits in all areas of language (see subsections below), though individual children with SLI may not have difficulties in all areas of language.

In many ways a language disability in the face of normal intelligence is a significant disability. Preschool children with SLI typically do not "outgrow" their language problems. Rather, the symptoms of their language impairments change over time and manifest themselves in different ways over the school years and into adulthood. Children with SLI are likely to have substantial academic difficulties, and indeed, after receiving services as "speech impaired," often are relabeled "learning disabled" in the early school years because of significant academic problems (Snyder, 1984a). These children commonly continue to receive speech and language services as well as learning disability services throughout their school years. Further, they are likely to experience social consequences resulting from their language limitations (Rice, 1993). Early on, their language limitations may cause teachers and other adults to perceive them as less socially competent than their normally developing peers. The following sections describe each aspect of language along with difficulties children may display in each of these areas.

PHONOLOGY

Each language has its own sound system consisting of *phonemes*, or sound categories, that are meaningful contrasts. For example, we know that in English the words "bat" and "pat" are different, because we recognize the contrast between /b/ and /p/ as phonological (a sound difference that relates to a meaning difference). English has 46 phonemes, composed of 25 consonants, 16 vowels, and 5 diphthongs. Children learning language must learn to produce all these sounds and use them correctly when saying words.

Problems with phonology traditionally have been described as *articulation disorders*. In the past decade, SLPs have begun to describe some articulation disorders as *phonological disorders*. This term usually is used to describe children who have many speech errors, rendering their speech unintelligible; however, their speech errors are not entirely attributable to an inability to make specific speech sounds. Their speech problems are better described by patterns that prevail in their speech rather than specific sounds they have difficulty producing. (See section on articulation disorders for more information.)

MORPHOLOGY

Morphemes traditionally are defined linguistically as the smallest units of language that have meaning. A unit consists of a sequence of phonemes. The two kinds of morphemes are:

1. *Free morphemes* can stand alone as words. For example, "bat" is a free morpheme.
2. *Bound morphemes* are attached to words, as prefixes or suffixes. For example, the "un" in "unhappy" is a bound morpheme, as is the "s" in "bats." Bound morphemes can serve as inflections to indicate grammatical concepts such as tense, number, gender, and case.

The changes in the verb in the sentences below reflect the role of inflectional morphemes:

> I like the idea.
> He likes the idea.
> He liked the idea.
> He has liked the idea.
> He is liking the idea.

Morphology and phonology are intimately linked. A child having problems with one can be mistakenly regarded as having difficulty with the other. For example, the problem of the child who inconsistently omits final /s/, /z/, and /d/ may be one of articulation or of morphology. The context of omission must be considered carefully.

Difficulties with morphology often are a component of a young child's language difficulties. Children with SLI may learn to use morphological markers later than their peers do. For example, past tense may not be marked with -ed ("Yesterday I play with my friend" instead of "Yesterday I played with my friend").

SYNTAX

Syntax refers to our ability to put words together to form sentences and to judge which strings of words are not grammatical. It involves knowledge of word order, morphology, and the meanings of words. For example, we know that "Mary saw Bill in the morning" is grammatical and equivalent to "In the morning Mary saw Bill," but it does not mean the same as "Bill saw Mary in the morning." Likewise, we know that "In Bill morning the saw Mary" is not grammatical.

Children's ability to comprehend and produce grammatical sentences is based on their knowledge of the grammatical rules of their native language. Some English grammatical constructions are notoriously difficult for children with SLI or younger, normally developing children. Passives and embedded clauses, for example, are tricky. Children with immature syntax are likely to interpret "The cow was hit by the horse" as "The cow hit the horse," and "The cow who liked the horse died" as "The cow and the horse died." They may have trouble forming sentences with embedded clauses, saying for example, "The man owns it said that" rather than "The man *who* owns it said that."

SEMANTICS

Semantics concerns word and morpheme meanings, as well as the meanings of word combinations. Children's knowledge of the meanings of words is evident in their ability to perform a variety of tasks: identifying synonyms and word opposites, providing multiple meanings for the same word, creating sentences with different structures to relate the same idea; understanding and using idioms, metaphors, and other forms of nonliteral language. Children with SLI often perform poorly on formal tests of vocabulary development. Experienced teachers are familiar with their problems with the abstract word lists that accompany textbooks of history, social studies, and English. Furthermore, children with SLI often are unable to appreciate puns and other forms of humor based on multiple meanings of words.

PRAGMATICS

To communicate effectively, children must learn more than how to produce well-formed sentences. They must learn how to use their language in socially appropriate ways. Pragmatics involves (a) the rules speakers call on to adjust their speech to their listener, the social context, and their communicative intent; and (b) their ability to use language in units bigger than the individual sentence, such as in carrying on a conversation.

One can say the same thing in many ways and speakers must be able to select the way that is best in a given situation. Suppose you are not feeling well and you want to tell someone. You might put it one way to your mate, another to your physician, and another to your boss. For each, you likely will change the words you use, your manner of speaking, and even the preciseness of your pronunciation. Speakers match their communicative intent with the situation. They also must choose among linguistic alternatives. Many different combinations of words express the same intent. If you are ill and want a drink of water, you could say "Get me some water," or you could say "A drink of water sure helps a cold." Conversely, the same words can express different intents. In some contexts "A drink of water sure helps a cold" is a request; in others it is a simple statement.

Pragmatic skills pose problems for many children with SLI. Pragmatic competence is, of course, related closely to the other dimensions of language such as sentence structure. For example, a child whose sentence structure is rudimentary will have limited pragmatic ability. He or she may be unable to formulate a hint such as "I wish I had a cookie" because of the complex grammar involved. Instead, the youngster probably resorts to a less charming form of request, such as "Gimme cookie." Because of deficient pragmatic skills, children with SLI may have difficulty interacting with peers.

MODE OF LANGUAGE IMPAIRMENT: COMPREHENSION AND PRODUCTION

Knowledge of language is evident in two performance modes: comprehension and production. In comprehension, listeners must be able to understand what speakers say; in production, speakers must be able to formulate and produce grammatical utterances. Generally, young children learn how to comprehend language before they learn to speak correctly. Generally we understand more language than we produce; we understand the meanings of some words we do not use in verbal expression.

Children with SLI in some cases demonstrate considerable discrepancy between comprehension and production skills. The most frequent pattern is one of reasonably good comprehension and impaired production, although other patterns involve both limited comprehension and production, or better production than comprehension. The youngster who understands language but who does not know how to formulate it has different therapy needs than the child who neither comprehends nor produces language. To fully describe language competencies, communication assessment must include both modalities.

METALINGUISTIC AWARENESS

Children with SLI have difficulties not only in using language to communicate but also in their ability to focus on language as an object of thought, or metalinguistic awareness. Their difficulties with metalinguistic tasks are consequential because much of the schoolwork children do expects them to have metalinguistic awareness. Language arts and reading tasks such as correcting ungrammatical sentences, sound-blending activities, and choosing the correct verb form in a sentence require a child to examine the form as well as the meaning of the word or sentence. Thus, many of the problems children with SLI demonstrate in reading and writing tasks are attributable to their lack of metalinguistic awareness. For example, in kindergarten children with SLI may have difficulty with early reading tasks such as rhyming or identifying the initial sounds of words. Both of these tasks require the child to focus on the sound structure of words to the exclusion of the meaning of the words. This shift, moving from communicative use of language to examining the form of language, is particularly difficult for children with SLI.

ETIOLOGY OF LANGUAGE IMPAIRMENTS

Language difficulties can be manifestations of mental retardation, hearing loss, some form of emotional disturbance, and some kinds of brain dysfunction. When none of these is present, the etiology is difficult to determine. This is the case with most children with SLI.

Researchers have explored possible causes of SLI with few conclusive findings. One possible cause is the amount of (or lack of) language stimulation in a child's home.

Cultural or linguistic practices in the immediate home may vary from those of the dominant culture. Studies document that normally developing children manage to acquire language readily in widely variable home circumstances. From this and other evidence, current models of SLI do not attribute children's language delay to "faulty" parental input. Instead, it is recognized that some children may need a more enriched language environment than other children, perhaps even more than their peers. Recent studies document the tendency for language impairments to cluster in families, suggesting the possibility of a genetic factor (Tomblin, 1989; Tallal, Ross, & Curtiss, 1989).

SPEECH DISORDERS

Speech disorders involve the faulty production of sound and the sound system itself. Disorders are of three kinds: articulation, fluency, and voice. All involve movement of the muscles of the speech production mechanism, muscular movements that are not under our conscious control as we are speaking.

ARTICULATION

Sometimes children have difficulty producing certain speech sounds. They are said to have an articulation disorder. Articulation disorders range from mild (difficulty with a few sounds) to severe (many sound errors, making what the child says difficult to understand). Children with many sound errors frequently are described as having a phonological disorder. In making articulation errors, children substitute one sound for another, or distort or omit a sound. An example of a *substitution* is "wabbit" for "rabbit." In sound *distortion*, the sound is produced in a nonstandard manner, such as a "mushy" or "slushy" sounding /s/, referred to as a lisp. *Omissions* often appear at the end of words, such as "ca" for "cat," but also can appear at the beginning or middle of words. Omissions can lead to limited intelligibility. For example, "I ee ca" is not likely to be understood as "I see the cat" unless the listener is familiar with the child and the situation.

Children learn to pronounce sounds as they learn to talk. Pioneering studies in the 1950s by Mildred Templin (1957) demonstrated that certain sounds are learned at certain ages and that most children follow the same sequence of mastery of sounds. Some sounds are easier than others and are learned earlier, such as /b/, /p/, /m/, /n/, and most of the vowels. Other sounds are much more difficult, such as /l/, /r/, /s/, "sh," and "ch." Many children will not have mastered these sounds before entering kindergarten. A child should be able to produce all sounds correctly by age 7 or 8, though. Most school-age children with mild articulation disorders have difficulty with these later developing, more difficult sounds. The Templin study and subsequent similar studies established the normative standards by which to judge if a child has an articulation disorder.

Children with phonological disorders have limited intelligibility. Their speech errors are better described by patterns that are prevalent in their speech than by specific sound errors. This is true because they may produce and use a sound in some words but not others, or in one position of words (e.g., beginning) but not others. Their speech errors are often more complex than simple sound substitutions, omissions, or distortions. Several patterns, called phonological processes, are observed quite frequently in the speech of children with phonological disorders. In *final consonant deletion* the ends of words are left off, so "cap" sounds like "ca" and "puppet" sounds like "puppuh." In *cluster reduction* sound blends are reduced to a single sound—"top" for "stop," "gas" for "glass." Sometimes entire groups of sounds are in error. For example, *velar sounds* /k/ and /g/, produced in the back of the mouth, may be substituted by *alveolar sounds* /t/ and /d/, made in the front of the mouth. Thus, the child says "titty" for "kitty" and "dod" for "dog." Children with phonological disorders often have difficulty with other aspects of language. Whereas children with mild articulation disorders are not likely to have difficulties in academic subjects, children with phonological disorders are apt to have language problems in other areas (e.g., syntax), which may lead to academic difficulties.

Correction of faulty articulation was at one time the primary focus of SLPs. With better understanding of language development, clinicians are focusing less on articulation. The interface between aspects of language such as phonology and morphology has led to intervention practices that better address children's difficulties. Nevertheless, the difficult task of correcting articulation disorders and phonological disorders confronts school SLPs. The child's incorrect productions often represent learned behavior that can be changed only with extensive practice.

The etiology of articulation disorders sometimes is linked to a physical or structural cause. Hearing problems can lead to articulation difficulties, as can problems with motor control or coordination, which often are evident in children with cerebral palsy and mental retardation. Some structural problems, such as cleft palate, can cause articulation difficulties. Other structural components, such as dental misalignments or malformations of the tongue, seldom are implicated. In fact, many people with severe structural problems, such as missing much of the tongue, nevertheless have normal speech. People seem to be able to adapt the speech production mechanism in many ways to produce normal speech sounds.

The large majority of children's articulation problems is functional (having no apparent physiological or structural cause). For unknown reasons, some children learn to produce sounds in a nonstandard fashion. Sometimes they can hear the differences in others' speech but not their own. Usually children do not recognize when they have mispronounced a word, because as speakers we tend to focus on what we are saying (the message) rather than how we are saying it (the articulation of words). Studies of families of children with severe phonological disorders suggest that these speech impairments are likely to run in families (Lewis, Ekelman, & Aram, 1989; Parlour, 1990).

FLUENCY AND DYSFLUENCY

The lay term for fluency disorders is *stuttering*, which involves disruption in the timing of speaking. Problems with fluency include repetitions or prolongations of sounds, words, or phrases; hesitations or long pauses; and struggle behaviors, such as contortions of the lips and mouth, facial grimaces, eye blinks, and other extraneous body movements that accompany the effort to speak. It is interesting that even severe stutterers often do not stutter when singing or talking to their pets or young children.

Children in the preschool or early school years sometimes go through a period of dysfluency, characterized by easy repetitions, hesitations, false starts, and a general appearance of fumbling around in their attempts to talk. Because the phenomenon is widely reported, and because most children seem to outgrow the stage if the adults around them do not draw attention to it, most clinicians regard these dysfluencies as normal. Symptoms of muscle tension, struggle behavior, or avoidance of speaking, however, suggest a serious fluency problem, even if the youngster is a preschooler.

The search for an explanation of dysfluency has occupied some of the best scholars in speech pathology for decades, yet we are nowhere near consensus. Various explanations are based on competing etiologies. Organic problems, psychological differences, linguistic difficulties, inappropriate learning—all have been proposed. Recently, the linguistic abilities of stutterers and the possible neuromotor components of nonfluencies have generated considerable interest. Clearly, dysfluencies are affected by how the speaker feels about the speaking situation and about the listeners, as well as the speaker's general physical condition (for example, the likelihood of dysfluencies is greater when the speaker is fatigued). Counseling with parents and other family members is an important component of therapy for children who stutter. In addition, collaborative arrangements with teachers and other significant adults are necessary. For example, decreasing the speaking demands, at least temporarily, may be desirable until the child establishes more fluent speech.

Therapy with children who stutter can vary quite a bit depending on the child's age. Typically with preschool and early school-age children, the SLP provides the child with a model of easy, relaxed fluent speech to imitate. The child's attention generally is *not* drawn to the dysfluent nature of the speech. In contrast, with older elementary and high school age children, therapy may focus on identifying dysfluencies in one's own speech, factors contributing to dysfluency, and learning ways to produce fluent speech.

VOICE

Voice refers to the suprasegmental dimension of sound production: pitch, loudness, resonance, vocal quality (e.g., hoarseness, breathiness, stridency), and duration. The effective vocal performance of singers, politicians, news broadcasters, and the like depends on these features.

To produce a normal sounding voice, a speaker must coordinate the air flow in the lungs, the vibration of the vocal folds in the larynx, and the two resonance chambers in the oral (mouth) and nasal (nose) cavities. Problems can arise in any of these areas, but the most common are in the larynx and in the resonance chambers.

Problems seldom are a result of improper breathing (e.g., a low intensity). Our lungs must supply adequate air for the basic processes of living, and the amount of air required for speech is relatively small, well within the capacity of healthy individuals. Children with breath support problems almost always have a serious associated condition, such as cerebral palsy, or other multiple handicaps. In these cases, proper posture and support are essential for adequate vocal production. Lungs squeezed in a slumping position increase the child's problems.

Hoarseness. A number of problems appear at the level of the larynx: excessive breathiness (inability to close the vocal folds properly); unusual quality (excessively harsh, hoarse, or guttural—all related to uneven vibration of the vocal folds); and inappropriate pitch levels. The most prevalent voice problem in school children is marked chronic hoarseness, as with a cold or a sore throat, that persists without any sign of infection or other symptoms. The hoarseness often is accompanied by taut muscles in the throat area during speech. The most common etiology is a history of vocal abuse, such as frequent yelling (cheerleaders, for example, often are affected). The vocal tissues, which are extremely delicate, develop callous-like thickenings (vocal nodules) in response to chronic abuse. Allergies and other upper respiratory infections that cause swelling and friction can aggravate the condition. To treat hoarseness, the vocal abuse first must be reduced. If that proves to be unsuccessful alone, surgical removal of the nodules may be necessary.

Hoarseness can be related to other changes in the larynx, such as polyps and other growths. Change in vocal quality is the first sign of a serious problem, such as malignancy. In that case, the hoarseness appears before the pain of swallowing or talking. Any time hoarseness persists for longer than 2 weeks, a specialist, such as an otolaryngologist, should be consulted for a medical diagnosis.

Pitch. In some adolescent males, pitch remains high when other males of the same age have shifted to a lower pitch. This is the most frequent pitch problem. Prior to adolescence, pitch levels do not differ according to gender. The hormonal and growth changes of adolescence produce a larger larynx in males, resulting in lower pitch. The notion of appropriate pitch levels does not apply to females, because a wider range of pitch in a female's voice is acceptable in our society. Pitch problems usually are functional (having no organic or structural origins), although some unusual exceptions always exist.

Resonance. Resonance problems result from too much nasality (hypernasality) or too little nasality (denasality), as with a cold when the nose is stuffed up. Attached to the back of the roof of the mouth is a flap of tissue. When we produce nasal sounds, such as /m/ and /n/, the flap is open, but it is closed in the production of non-nasal sounds. If the flap does not close properly at the appropriate time, excessive nasality distorts sounds, such as making /b/ sound like /m/. If the flap stays closed, or if the opening is blocked, the sounds are denasal, making /n/ sound like /d/, for example.

Several factors are associated with resonance problems. Some are attributable to *physiological* problems such as neuromotor dysfunctions (e.g., cerebral palsy) and some to *structural* deficiencies (e.g., cleft palate, in which the roof of the mouth may be partially open or the back flap missing). Others have an apparent *functional* (learned) etiology, as in the case of dialectal differences in the desired amount of nasality. Resonance problems may require full evaluation by a medical team to identify or rule out physiological or structural causes. Resonance problems are difficult to change through practice or exercise, though medical intervention (surgery to alter the speech mechanism) sometimes is successful.

Deafness or hearing loss can affect voice functioning. It may be associated with inappropriate pitch (too high or too low), inappropriate intensity (too loud or too soft), denasality, and a general lack of inflectional variety (monotone). Voice differences of deaf people usually are regarded as secondary to the more serious problems of speech and language acquisition. Therapy with hearing impaired persons can focus on improving vocal quality.

*P*REVALENCE

No accurate figures for prevalence of childhood communicative handicaps are available for the population at large. Although the best indicators are the child counts reported by the Division of Education Services (Special Education Programs) of the U.S. Department of Education, these, too, are unreliable; each child is counted only once, based on his or her *primary* handicap. Therefore, a child whose primary handicap is mental retardation but who also has a communication handicap is counted only among the number of children with mental retardation receiving services. When the number of children with *secondary* speech-language impairments is included in the count of the communicatively handicapped, the prevalence increases (McDermott, 1981). According to an ASHA study (Dublinske, 1981), 42.4% of all handicapped children served by speech-language pathologists have other primary handicaps, such as mental retardation, a hearing impairment, or a learning disability.

By adding up the counts for all primary handicaps that include a secondary communication handicap, we come up with an overall figure of 5% (based on the ASHA figures reported by Dublinske). Of those children, 46.7% have a language disorder (47% articulation, 2.4% voice, and 3.9% fluency). Of course—and this is something not evident in the percentages above—some of these children have more than one communication problem. For example, many young children with language impairment also have articulation disorders (and vice versa); young stutterers sometimes have language difficulties.

There are also age-related differences. Of the preschool children who received special education services in 1986, 69% were categorized as speech impaired, according to the Office of Special Education Programs' (OSEP) Report to Congress (1988). The percentages of children with articulation and language problems are greater in the preschool and early elementary grades, declining by late elementary grades. Some authors (e.g., Snyder, 1984b) argue that the decline is apparently because the communication problem is redefined from one of speech and language to one of academic achievement (learning disability). Other authors (e.g., Prather, 1984) say it is because we lack the normative evaluation instruments necessary to identify certain problems of communication, such as difficulties in the social uses of language evident in adolescence.

PREVENTION

The ASHA Committee on Prevention of Speech, Language, and Hearing Problems defined prevention as "the elimination of factors which interfere with the normal acquisition and development of communication skills" (American Speech-Language-Hearing Association, 1982; see also American Speech-Language-Hearing Association, 1988). Prevention was defined as encompassing three phases:

1. Primary prevention is the elimination of or inhibition of the onset and development of a communicative disorder by altering susceptibility or reducing exposure for susceptible individuals. Example: Cigarette smoking is eliminated to prevent future laryngeal and breathing anomalies. (p. 425)
2. Secondary prevention is the early detection and treatment of communicative disorders. Early detection may lead to the elimination of the disorder or the retardation of the disorder's progress, thereby preventing further complications. One of the major practices of secondary prevention is mass screening of persons without symptoms. Example: The institution of a school auditory screening program which systematically tests the hearing of all children on a periodic basis and after certain illness, such as infectious diseases of the ear. (p. 425)
3. Tertiary prevention is the reduction of a disability by attempting to restore effective functioning. The major approach is rehabilitation of the disabled individual who has realized some residual problems as a result of the disorder. Example: The institution of a program of rehabilitation for an aphasic patient as soon as possible after the onset of the neuropathology in order to prevent more serious communicative and behavioral problems. (p. 431)

Marge (1984) identified some examples of preventable and nonpreventable causes of speech and language problems, listed in Table 8.2, along with 13 prevention strategies: immunization, genetic counseling, prenatal care, mass screening and early identification, early intervention programs, family planning, proper medical care, public education, child and youth education, environmental quality control, quality-of-life programs (such as stress management), governmental action, and elimination of poverty. Of these, public school SLPs do mass screening, early identification and early intervention programs, and parent and teacher education programs. When time and opportunity are available, they also talk with interested community groups about speech and language problems and how to prevent them. Clinicians, of course, spend much time consulting with colleagues as well.

● **TABLE 8.2**

Examples of preventable and nonpreventable causes of communicative disorders

Disorder	Preventable Causes	Nonpreventable Causes
Articulation	Hearing loss Dental abnormalities Chronic infections, especially upper respiratory infections Most types of mental retardation Injuries Infectious diseases (mumps, measles, encephalitis)	Developmental immaturity Neuromuscular disorders associated with unknown etiologies Some types of genetic disorders
Voice	Vocal abuse Upper respiratory infections Allergies Airborne irritants Smoking Hearing loss Trauma and injury Faulty respiration attributable to allergies, infections, and emphysema Drug and alcohol abuse Some genetic disorders	Constitutional factors Some cancers Viral infections Some genetic disorders
Language	Familial factors Cultural factors Some types of mental retardation Some types of hearing loss Some genetic disorders Brain damage because of prematurity, anoxia, physical trauma, Rh blood factor, infections Malnutrition Low birth weight Fetal alcohol syndrome Prenatal drugs and smoking Strokes Environmental pollutants (lead poisoning)	Some types of hearing loss Some genetic disorders Developmental immaturity Autism Progressive neurological deficits Suspected constitutional factors resulting in psychosis (schizophrenia) Some types of mental retardation

Fluency (Stuttering)	Environmental factors:
	   General Stress
	   Communicative stress
	Adverse reactions by others
	Cultural factors
		Suspected genetic factors
		Suspected neurophysiological problems

Source: From M. Marge, 1984, August, "The Prevention of Communication Disorders, *ASHA, 26,* 29–37. Used by permission.

LEARNING AND BEHAVIOR

Speech and language disorders appear in such a wide variety of individuals, as either a primary or a secondary problem, that generalizations about learning and behavioral characteristics are difficult, if not impossible, to make. The children may be exceptionally bright, or they may have severe cognitive deficits. They can be shy and passive or gregarious and even boisterous. They may be athletically gifted or physically handicapped. A child with a speech or language disorder may be a class leader or have severe emotional problems. What has become clearer in recent years is that speech and language deficits are likely to influence other developmental domains, such as social skills and academic achievement. For example, a child with mental retardation who has an impairment in articulation may be hindered in becoming independent because others cannot understand her verbally expressed needs.

Evidence for academic risk is widespread. For example, an ASHA survey (Dublinske, 1981) reported that over half (56%) of the children whose primary handicapping condition was communication and who were enrolled in speech services had academic problems. Communicative competency is crucial to social, academic, and vocational adjustment.

IDENTIFICATION AND ASSESSMENT

ELIGIBILITY

Children whose speech and language is not commensurate with that of their peers are eligible for intervention services. The notion of "peers" assumes that children are of the same chronological age and that they demonstrate the same level of communicative competence. If a child's mental age is lower than chronological age (mental retardation), mental age is used as the developmental index. Peers also includes the cultural group to which a child belongs, the ethnic or cultural subgroup within the general, mainstream American cultural group. Therefore, eligibility must be defined within the context of local cultural, as well as age-related, expectations. Some children speak a nonstandard dialect of English, or a non-English language. Their total communicative repertoire must be considered in determining if their abilities are commensurate with developmental expectations (see the position paper, "Clinical Management of Communicatively Handicapped Minority Language Populations," ASHA, 1985.)

IDENTIFICATION

Speech-language pathologists are interested in assuring that all children with communication impairments receive the services they need. Some children have received services prior to school entry and are referred to the school SLP by previous service providers. Other children suspected of speech-language impairments must be identified and referred for a complete speech-language evaluation. Several avenues of identification are apparent.

For some time mass screening of children was conducted in certain grades. This is no longer widespread. Screening has many difficulties that perhaps have contributed to its unpopularity. Some children are reluctant to talk to the examiner, an unfamiliar adult. Only a brief time (at most 10–15 minutes) is allotted for screening each child, which may not allow the SLP to gain an accurate perception of the child. Most important, others who are most familiar with the child—for example, parents and teachers—may be best able to make a judgment as to whether concerns about speech and language warrant further assessment. Thus, SLPs often prefer to consult with parents and teachers on the indicators of speech and language impairments. In turn, teachers and parents can refer children suspected of having a communication problem for a complete evaluation.

SLPs conduct inservice training for teachers on the characteristics of speech-language problems and when to refer children for assessment. Some speech and language errors are normal for young children, and teachers should be aware that these errors are not considered a problem at a young age. Teachers might be given checklists listing the communication skills children should demonstrate at different ages and grade levels. Because teachers and parents are most familiar with children's communication skills, they can be excellent referral sources.

In addition, educational diagnosticians and school psychologists are in the position of referring children for speech-language assessment. As they evaluate children referred for other special education services (e.g., because of a diagnosis of cerebral palsy or suspected learning disabilities), diagnosticians and psychologists may suspect that communication deficits are present and warrant further assessment by the SLP. Thus, the SLP frequently is a member of the team of professionals assessing the child.

Screening of children at kindergarten entry is still a fairly common practice. When parents register their child for kindergarten, they may be asked if they have any concerns about their child's speech and language skills. Further, clinicians may complete some brief speech-language screening tasks with the child, to indicate whether further assessment is warranted. These tasks might include following directions, telling a story, and labeling pictures.

With the implementation of PL 99–457 (and the subsequent amendments in PL 102–119, Individuals with Disabilities Education Act), identification of preschoolers needing services has become a great concern. The SLP is likely to be quite involved with this process, as most preschoolers eligible for special education programs have communicative impairments (OSEP, 1988). Part of the legislation requires providers of special education services to ensure that transition between service providers is accomplished. That is, children from birth to age 3 may be provided special education services through the health department but at age 3 these same services may be available only through the local school district. Professionals must work together to assure that children and families receiving services continue receiving needed services at the next level.

Because the availability of services for birth to age 3 is not mandatory in all states, many children will not receive services until age 3. Beginning in 1991, all public school districts were required to provide special education services to eligible children from 3 to 5 years of age. These children are identified to the school district through referrals from other professionals such as social workers, physicians, and SLPs practicing in hospital and community-based services. Parents also can refer their child to the school for services.

In sum, children may be identified as needing a speech and language evaluation through referrals from parents, teachers, and other school personnel, as well as professionals outside of the schools (e.g., physicians). Further, children may be referred for services because they received speech-language therapy in another program prior to school entry. Occasionally, mass screening is a means of identifying children with suspected speech-language impairments.

AREAS OF ASSESSMENT

The SLP's initial task is to determine whether a child demonstrates a significant deficit in speech and language skills. To make this determination, the SLP benefits from having some information about a child's cognitive abilities. Information on the child's intellectual abilities is helpful to the SLP for a number of reasons. If the child has substantial cognitive impairment, the SLP may use this information to adjust expectations regarding the child's demonstrated communicative abilities. One expects the language skills of a 5-year-old child with mental retardation to be substantially different from those of a 5-year-old child with age-appropriate cognitive skills. In addition, standard intelligence tests such as the Wechsler Intelligence Scale for Children-Third Edition (Wechsler, 1991) and the Stanford-Binet Intelligence Scale (Thorndike, Hugen, & Suttler, 1986) rely heavily on verbal items or on verbal instructions. Thus, for a child with communicative limitations, performance on verbal intelligence tests may not accurately reflect the child's general cognitive abilities.

SLPs may be interested in differences between verbal and nonverbal intellectual abilities. Further, nonverbal intelligence measures, such as the Leiter Performance International Scale (Arthur, 1952) or the Hiskey-Nebraska Test of Learning Aptitude (Hiskey, 1966), may provide a better picture of the intellectual abilities of a language-impaired individual. As a general rule, verbal and nonverbal intellectual functioning is tested by an educational diagnostician or a school psychologist.

The goals of assessment are twofold. First, the SLP is interested in making a diagnosis, a determination of whether the child has or does not have a communication disorder. This aspect of assessment basically answers the question of whether the child qualifies for special education services, in this case speech and language therapy. Second, a complete assessment enables the clinician to describe the child's abilities in all areas of communication. This aspect of the assessment enables the SLP to describe the child's strengths and needs and, thus, set appropriate goals and objectives for therapy.

Assessment of communication includes evaluation of abilities in all areas: speech (articulation), voice, fluency, syntax and morphology, vocabulary, and pragmatics. If children are very young or have limited communication skills, evaluation includes nonverbal indications of communication, such as gestures and eye contact, and communicative intents (the reasons one communicates), such as commenting and protesting. Children with multiple handicaps may be evaluated for their ability to use augmentative communication devices, such as computer-assisted communication.

Various aspects of speech production are assessed. Speech, voice, and fluency evaluations focus on the child's ability to *produce* sounds in connected speech (conversational speech). A clinician also evaluates how well a child can *imitate* problem sounds, or how well a child can modify targeted aspects of voice or fluency in different speaking circumstances, such as when whispering or pretending to be another speaker. The ability to improve in different circumstances is called a child's *stimulability* for targeted speech or voice behaviors.

Language skills are assessed in *production* and *comprehension* formats. Production items require the child to name or describe something, such as "Tell me about the picture" or "Here the man runs. Yesterday the man _____." Comprehension tasks require the child to process language and respond nonverbally; for example, "Point to _____" or "Make the horse bite the cow" or "Listen to the story and then I will ask you to answer some questions by pointing to pictures."

Two dimensions of language production are *elicited* versus *spontaneous* uses. The SLP may seek to elicit specific utterances from the child in structured situations. In these situations clinicians usually are interested in children's ability to verbally use specific grammatical structures, such as marking verbs with "-ed" to indicate past tense. Spontaneous utterances are gathered by engaging children in conversation activities such as talking while playing, or telling about a favorite TV show. SLPs generally audiorecord a child's spontaneous conversation and later transcribe the child's utterances. This provides a record of the child's conversational language skills and can be analyzed to answer questions about the child's production of speech sounds, specific grammatical structures, ability to engage in conversation, and so on.

SLPs increasingly are recognizing that a complete picture of a child's speech and language skills must include the child's performance in his or her daily environment. Thus, assessment has to include gathering information from others concerning the child's communication strengths and needs. If a child is in the regular classroom, this might include observing the child during reading instruction, as well as obtaining the teachers' and parents' impressions regarding the child's communication needs. If a child has multiple handicaps, the SLP may consult with the child's teachers and parents to determine the communication demands of the classroom and home (e.g., What does the child need to "talk" about? In what ways does the child use communication, and for what purposes?). Information of this nature is crucial to planning therapy goals appropriate for the child and establishing links between the SLP, teachers, and parents.

FULL EVALUATION AND DIAGNOSIS

All children referred for assessment must receive a complete evaluation of speech and language skills. The SLP evaluates children suspected of having only a speech or language problem as well as children for whom communication impairments are secondary to other handicaps. A full evaluation requires a considerable amount of time—at least 1 to 2 hours with the child, and additional time for analyzing the results and writing reports. The goals of assessment are twofold: (a) diagnosis of a problem, and (b) description of communication skills. Specifically, full evaluation of an individual child's speech and language competencies is conducted for the following purposes:

1. To determine whether a speech-language disorder is or is not present.
2. To describe speech-language competencies.
3. To describe areas of speech-language in need of remediation.
4. To arrive at a judgment of overall severity.
5. To document any possible causal factors or associated conditions (e.g., history of mild hearing loss).
6. To determine management alternatives and recommendations.
7. To identify any relevant factors that may influence intervention.

Assessment with most children involves the administration of standardized, norm-referenced tests. In norm-referenced tests a child's performance is compared to the normative sample—scores of children tested during standardization of the test—to derive numerical scores such as standard scores, percentile ranks, and age-equivalent scores. Scores on these tests enable SLPs to judge whether a child's language skills are commensurate with those of peers. If a child's score falls significantly below expectations for his or her age or cognitive ability, a speech-language impairment is diagnosed.

A wide variety of standardized tests is available. Each test is administered to all children in a like manner; all children are asked the same questions in the same way. Among the more popular tests are the Peabody Picture Vocabulary Test–Revised (Dunn & Dunn, 1981), the Test of Language Development Primary, Second Edition (Newcomer & Hammill, 1988), the Goldman-Fristoe Articulation Test (Goldman & Fristoe, 1986), the Fisher-Logemann Articulation Test (Fisher & Logemann, 1971), and the Test for Auditory Comprehension of Language–Revised (Carrow-Woolfolk, 1985).

Beyond obtaining numerical scores on tests, clinicians must describe children's communication abilities, a purpose for which standardized tests are not designed. Standardized tests, however, may indicate areas of language in need of further description. Standardized tests are not appropriate with some groups of children (e.g., children with multiple handicaps or very limited cognitive ability; children from ethnic or cultural minorities; children whose dominant language is not English). With these children, the goal of assessment is not to document a discrepancy between the child's chronological age and language ability. Rather, SLPs seek to describe how the child presently communicates and what communication skills should be learned next for the child to gain greater independence in school and the home environment. To describe a child's speech-language skills or communication abilities, the SLP is likely to engage the child in a series of structured or semistructured tasks.

Descriptive testing can be adapted to the individual child's competencies. SLPs further explore only those areas that present problems for a child. Therefore, clinicians must be prepared to explore in depth a range of communication problems: fluency, voice, articulation, language. The kinds of evaluation tasks and the time required for evaluation vary widely, depending on the child's age and the kinds of speech-language problems suspected. The result of descriptive testing is a behavioral description the SLP can interpret by comparing it to what is known about speech and language development in other children. Sometimes children's competencies cannot be described fully in one session. Children with complex speech and language problems often are scheduled for multiple evaluation sessions. Moreover, to fully describe a child's competencies may not be possible within the constraints of evaluation timelines. In these cases the SLP is likely to continue to do assessment during the first therapy sessions with the child.

Assessment is an ongoing process. A large component of an effective therapy plan is to continually evaluate, albeit on a small scale, the child's communicative competencies. As the child makes progress in one area of communication, problems in other areas of communication sometimes may become evident.

To obtain a description of the child's speech and language abilities, the SLP can engage the child in a range of activities. Most often SLPs want to elicit a spontaneous language sample. With young children this usually consists of getting the child to talk while he or she is engaged in play activities. Older children may be more talkative in conversations that center on friends or activities with friends and family after school. If children are nonverbal or have limited communication skills, the clinician elicits a communication sample. Generally, the SLP engages the child in activities appropriate to his or her abilities and notes the child's means of communication in accomplishing goals within the activity (e.g., How does the child indicate the need for help?).

Input from other members of the educational team and from parents is valuable in arriving at a description of the child's communication abilities. Teachers and parents can provide information on how and when the child's communicative limitations interfere with the child's interactions with others. For example, a child who stutters may have great difficulty when answering aloud in front of the class but rarely stutters when talking individually with parents or teacher. A child with language expression problems may have great difficulty answering open-ended questions about a reading story but less of a problem answering multiple-choice questions. Information of this nature is crucial to determining the extent of a child's communication problem and the appropriate goals and plan of therapy designed for that child. Children from minority ethnic or linguistic communities that are different from the clinician's require special consideration: The SLP has to consult with members of the group, or refer to the appropriate descriptive literature, to determine if the child's performance differs from the group's standards.

Before arriving at a final determination of whether a speech or language disorder exists, the clinician should compare his or her judgment with the standards of both the school (classroom teachers) and the home (parents or caregivers). For example, the SLP may decide a problem exists; the teachers think not. Or the parents may be concerned about some aspect of their child's performance that the SLP regards as normal. The discrepancy can go either way, but if it is significant, the clinician must consider carefully the potential value of therapy. The traditional model of assessment is based on the interaction between clinician and child. Today, however, with our growing awareness of the social dimensions of speech and language, as well as the impact of communication problems on academic achievement, we have to collect information from a number of other sources, such as other school personnel and people in the child's home environment (see Rice, 1985). An experienced school SLP can learn much about a child's communication in one or two diagnostic sessions. These working hypotheses, however, must be validated by observations of the child in other settings and by reports from other people with whom the child interacts. In short, evaluation means far more than a test score derived in only one kind of situation.

EDUCATIONAL INTERVENTION

Public school SLPs are responsible for assessing and treating children with communicative disorders. They also are responsible for maintaining the general instructional program of speech and language services. Clinicians further must coordinate the child's communication services with other instructional programs and establish prevention programs. Part of managing the general instructional program is administrative (maintaining records, completing reports). In addition, professional skills must be updated at meetings, conferences, and conventions. Finally, a growing number of school SLPs are conducting research and must spend time submitting grant proposals for financial support.

Once a child is identified as needing speech-language therapy, the SLP and other members of the IEP team develop an IEP. This IEP specifies the goals the child will be working on and the extent of speech-language services the child will receive (i.e., the amount of time in therapy services). The SLP then is usually responsible for determining the nature of the services each child receives. Because intervention needs of communicatively impaired children vary, SLPs employ a range of service delivery options. The options discussed next are not mutually exclusive, and SLPs must be free to use their professional judgment in designing intervention programs that best meet each child's needs. In some school districts an SLP is assigned to provide services to more than one school, and this influences which options are used.

Like all special education services, speech-language therapy services are to be given in the least restrictive environment. Traditionally, nearly all therapy has been provided in a context separate from the child's educational setting (i.e., outside the classroom), but continued emphasis on least restrictive environment has created the opportunity for more varied service delivery options in recent years (also see ASHA, 1993b).

TRADITIONAL, OR "PULLOUT," THERAPY

The most common intervention option has been, and continues to be, therapy provided individually or to small groups of children for a relatively brief period each week. Children leave their usual classroom and receive therapy in a room separate from their classrooms; they are pulled out of their classroom for therapy. Children typically receive therapy in 30-minute sessions twice a week, though more or less therapy can be scheduled depending on the child's needs. Whether a child is seen individually by the SLP or in a small group, usually two to four children, should be based on the child's communicative needs. The nature of the problems of other children receiving therapy is apt to influence the decision. Therapy in small groups is best provided when the children in the group have similar problems.

Several advantages and disadvantages of this intervention model are apparent. Perhaps the primary advantage of individual pullout therapy is the amount of one-to-one attention and instruction a child receives. This situation can provide the child with many opportunities for practicing new communication skills, and the SLP can manipulate the learning environment to meet the needs of that child. For the distractible child, this intervention situation can easily be structured to minimize distractions so as to maximize learning. The primary disadvantage of this therapy model, SLPs argue, is that the context of therapy is too different from the real-life situations in which children must use their new communication skills. Therapy in small groups of children addresses this disadvantage to some extent. In group therapy, children have opportunities to practice their communication skills in interactions with peers, a situation favorable to learning.

Another disadvantage of pullout therapy is that when children leave their classroom for therapy they miss vital instruction and must catch up on missed work when they return to the classroom. Because children with speech-language impairments often have academic difficulties, they cannot afford to miss instruction. Without adequate speech-language intervention, however, they are not likely to benefit from their academic instruction. In addition, the content of the therapy sessions frequently is different from what the child is learning in the classroom. Thus, the child must master skills targeted in therapy in addition to his or her classwork. Some concern arises, too, that pulling a child out of the classroom for therapy can make the child feel ostracized; this is more of a concern with children in middle school or high school. Also, some goals and objectives (for example, social interaction skills) may not be addressed adequately in a pullout program. Last, an exclusive program of pullout therapy may violate the intent of providing services in the least restrictive environment.

CLASSROOM-BASED THERAPY

The concerns with pullout therapy models led SLPs to design alternative service delivery models. Miller (1989) discussed classroom-based language intervention and specified five major classroom-based formats: self-contained language class; team teaching; one-to-one intervention; inservice/curriculum development; and consultation (discussed in the next section).

Self-contained classes for children with communication impairments have been developed for children with severe communication difficulties whose needs cannot be met in other self-contained classrooms. The SLP is responsible for teaching communication skills as well as academic content. In the preschool and early elementary grades a self-contained classroom has the benefit of structuring the entire curriculum so it is language-based. With high school students, self-contained language classes usually are planned for one period a day (Ehren & Lenz, 1989). Students are able to get credits for therapy as they do for other academic classes.

Team teaching, on the other hand, involves the SLP working alongside another teacher, in either a regular education or a special education classroom. Both professionals bring their expertise to creating a language-learning situation that maximally benefits children. The SLP teaches speech-language skills using the child's usual curricular materials. For example, the SLP may work on vocabulary development using the reading story or science unit. This intervention approach, as well as the pullout one, often is used with preschool children because nearly all preschool children with handicaps require communication intervention.

Children need to be encouraged to communicate. Games and activities should include both sending and receiving.

One-to-one classroom-based intervention is similar to pullout therapy. The SLP, however, does not introduce new content in therapy sessions but, rather, uses the child's curricular materials to teach specific language objectives. The teacher and the SLP can collaboratively decide on what will be taught in the therapy sessions. This option is becoming more and more popular with SLPs and teachers alike. Not only does the child get the needed language intervention, but it avoids the problems of missing class work as well.

Another means of intervention—which benefits all children, not just those with communication impairments—is for the SLP to conduct inservice workshops on the importance of language skills to academic and social success. SLPs also can participate in curriculum development, choosing textbooks, and so forth. In this way the SLP can provide information on how language development can be fostered in the regular academic curriculum, as well as further understanding of the language demands of different curricular materials.

CONSULTATION

In the past, consultation was seen as an indirect service usually to monitor students who seemed to have accomplished their goals and were awaiting final dismissal from therapy. In recent years the value of consultation and collaboration with teachers has been more widely recognized. It is a model of a service delivery that can be used alone or, increasingly, in combination with other intervention options. Consultation, rather than direct service, can be more beneficial than individual pullout therapy for some children, particularly those with severe impairment.

For children with multiple disabilities, communication intervention should be intense and incorporated into all aspects of daily living. SLPs can collaborate with teachers, parents, and paraprofessionals on implementing strategies to develop a child's communicative skills. Although the SLP is responsible for overall management of the communication intervention program, parents, teachers, and paraprofessionals in daily contact with the child are responsible for daily implementation of the program.

SLPs are finding that consultation with teachers is critical in implementing successful therapy. Not only can SLPs provide teachers with suggestions on how to facilitate speech and language development in the classroom, but teachers can provide insights into how the child's speech-language limitations are affecting the child's daily performance in the classroom. This enables the SLP to structure therapy to better meet the child's needs.

CASELOAD SIZE

A recurring dilemma for SLPs is the large number of children needing speech and language therapy. Some states and school districts have caseload limitations on the maximum number of children an SLP can serve; others do not. When limits exist, they often are so high as to be unhelpful. Certainly the number of children an SLP can serve adequately depends on the nature and severity of the children's communication problems (see ASHA, 1993b). As we have come to better understand the impact of speech and language on academic, social, and vocational adjustment, the SLP's role has broadened, increasing the time needed to design and implement effective intervention. This obviously reduces the number of children an SLP can realistically serve.

In Dublinske's (1981) survey, SLPs reported an average caseload of 43 children in a given week; 67% of the children were seen in groups, with an average size of three; 26% were seen individually; 3% were served on a consultation basis; and 4% were in self-contained or resource classrooms. Dublinske characterized the typical caseload:

> Forty-three moderate-to-severe language and articulation cases were seen twice per week in a group of three for 20–30 minutes per session. Of these cases, 43% have handicaps other than speech impairment. Of the 57% "speech-impaired only" cases, 56% have academic problems. Of the total caseload, 31% receive less than the needed service. (p. 196)

GENERALIZATION

Ultimately, the goal of intervention with all children is for them to be able to apply newly learned communication skills in all daily living environments. The generalization or carry-over of new skills from intervention contexts to daily living has always been of concern to SLPs. Clinicians have recognized the need for intervention activities to be similar to real life activities and have sought to substitute drill work with socially appropriate and meaningful activities. Communication intervention with preschool children, for example, can take place in the context of age-appropriate play activities. Collaboration and consultation with teachers ensure that they are aware of children's newly developed skills and can assist them in using these skills. A high school student who stutters, for example, may have improved his ability to speak in groups and, thus, would benefit from giving a class presentation. When speech and language intervention takes place in isolated therapy contexts, children will not use their new skills automatically in other situations. Generalization and carry-over must be programmed into all stages of therapy.

CLASSROOM IMPLICATIONS

Verbal communication is automatic, a means to an end, a way for children to express their wants, ideas, personality, and social standing. It is integral to their total psychological functioning. Perhaps because of its subconscious, habitual nature, verbal communication is hard to change. Speech-language clinicians can give a child a strong foundation on which to begin, but usually they cannot effect complete retraining within the constraints of therapy sessions that are relatively brief.

A successful program depends on close collaboration between the classroom teacher, specialized teachers, parents, and the clinician. The collaboration begins by identifying problems and establishing goals and continues throughout the course of therapy. Many children with speech and language impairments, for instance, have problems with reading. SLPs can include academic content in therapy activities, such as using social studies textbooks as a source of vocabulary items. If an oral presentation is required in class, SLPs can help prepare children for the task. Collaboration is enhanced when SLPs visit classrooms and teachers visit therapy sessions.

Teachers can help the child master new communication skills in a number of ways:

- Adjust language to the child's comprehension levels.
- Identify and report problem areas to the SLP.
- Encourage the child to use new skills in the classroom.
- Paraphrase the child's statements in ways that model targeted language forms and rules.
- Give quiet, unobtrusive praise for successful use of new language skills, as well as statements that emphasize individual differences in acceptable communication.

By establishing an overall climate in which verbal communication is a positive experience for the child, teachers can foster successful intervention.

ISSUES OF CONCERN FOR THE FUTURE

An issue that continues to concern educators is the substantial increase over the last decade in the number of children for whom English is not their first language. A second issue concerns the changes taking place in special education relative to providing services to preschool children with impairments. Both of these issues are likely to affect the work of speech-language clinicians in the schools.

NON-NATIVE ENGLISH SPEAKERS

Today, large numbers of immigrant children who do not speak English as a native language attend our schools. Immigrants are arriving in the United States from Mexico and Southeast Asia every day. The parents of these children often do not speak English; yet English is the language we teach their children. An estimated 34.6 million people, or 15% of the U.S. population, do not speak English as their primary language. Approximately 3.5 million of these non-native English speakers have speech, language, or hearing disorders unrelated to their own language (ASHA, 1985). Moreover, in 1979, "about 3.6 million school-age children in the United States were limited in English proficiency" (Grosjean, 1982, p. 78).

The largest and fastest growing minority language group in the United States is Spanish-speaking. Many other languages are evident as well. In the public schools in Fairfax County, Virginia, for example, more than 70 different languages are spoken (Cordes, 1985). The concern for English as a second language is not limited to one area of the country or to the coasts; it is evident throughout, especially in the Southwest, Northeast, and Upper Midwest.

Educational management is complex and controversial. Speech and language therapy has traditionally avoided teaching English as a second language. The topic is not a required part of the curriculum for certification. Less than 1% of the members of the American Speech-Language-Hearing Association are fluent in a foreign language (National Colloquium on Underserved Populations Report, 1985). This situation is becoming more difficult to avoid, however, as responsibilities increase. The pressure on schools to provide language services for these growing numbers of non-native speakers of English often exceeds the available resources. As SLPs have special expertise in communication, they may be asked to assist with planning services for children who are not competent in English.

Some children have speech and language problems in their native language as well as in English; they require special instruction to master any language. Furthermore, some of them have general learning problems that interact with their acquisition of languages and their academic achievements. SLPs will be asked to participate in evaluations in an attempt to unravel these interlocking dimensions of children's speech and language problems.

As part of the new concern with language development, particularly its socially situated uses, recent emphasis has been placed on home and cultural influences on language development. The basic literature on children's language development is showing an increased interest in bilingual and bicultural language acquisition, reflecting in part our increased desire to understand how children manage to learn language. The most interesting observation is that most people in the world grow up learning more than one language. The United States is unusual in its strong monolingualism.

Many questions arise. How do we provide speech and language services to this group of children? How can a clinician who does not know the native language of a child evaluate the speech and language of that child? Not only is the language structure different, but the sound system, voice quality, and even the rhythms and intonational patterns are likely to be different. Should the clinician learn the language? If so, how can he or she grasp all of the many different non-English languages spoken in the schools? How can a clinician determine if the child's non-English language is developing normally? Most languages other than English have no reported norms.

Suppose a child has difficulty acquiring the home language. What language should be taught, English or the child's home language? Which language is dominant? Should intervention be in the dominant language? Should intervention focus on the development of communication skills for the home or for the school? How can the clinician utilize interpreters or translators in evaluation and intervention? How can the clinician work with parents who do not speak English or are ambivalent about their child receiving special services?

These questions have no clear answers. Our professional organization has grappled with these problems and formulated a position paper for some initial guidelines on how to proceed (ASHA, 1985). For the immediate future, clinicians, with the help of these guidelines, will have to develop creative solutions of their own, ones that will work for individual children within the context of the specific school system.

PRESCHOOLERS WITH COMMUNICATION IMPAIRMENTS

Although some states have provided special education for 3- to 5-year-olds for many years, PL 99–457 has made these services mandatory entitlements in all states. In addition, services to infants and toddlers are discretionary (optional and reimbursable if provided). Many speech-language pathologists are having to broaden their skills to serve these young children. Infants, toddlers, and preschoolers provide challenges that are different in many respects from the challenges of working with school-age children.

Assessment instruments for young children are fewer in number and often less psychometrically valid and reliable. Getting an accurate measure of a preschooler's ability in testing sessions conducted at the school is difficult in many cases, as school is a strange, unfamiliar place to the young child. Assessment must be approached from a developmental rather than an educational perspective. Including families in the assessment and intervention processes is even more vital for young children and is, in fact, required by PL 99–457 for services to infants and toddlers.

Traditional models of therapy are less suitable for young children and their families, so creative alternatives must be devised. Among the new alternatives are demonstration preschool classrooms designed to facilitate language acquisition in naturalistic social interactions. One of these is the Language Acquisition Preschool (LAP), established in 1984 at the University of Kansas (Rice & Wilcox, in press). Distinctive features of this program include:

- A least restrictive environment in which children with SLI, normally developing children, and children learning English as a second language are equally represented.
- Classroom-based language facilitation activities with no individual pullout therapy.
- Intensive parent support services.
- Development of detailed curricular plans for classroom activities (Bunce, in press).
- A cross-disciplinary team of service providers.

Evidence collected from the children in LAP demonstrates the viability of this classroom-based program. LAP is but one of many new service delivery options for young children now under development across the country. If we are to meet the challenges of the new legislation, we will need a variety of new options from which to choose, as well as careful evaluation of the effectiveness of these options.

SUMMARY AND CONCLUSION

Children with speech and language impairments are a diverse lot, but they share a common challenge: the need to improve their communication skills to a level that matches as closely as possible the expectations of the educational setting, where the ability to communicate one's thoughts, ideas, preferences, state of mind, and emotions is absolutely essential. Without these abilities an individual is at risk for educational and social difficulties.

Providing appropriate programming for these youngsters requires the technical knowledge of SLPs, who are trained to identify and describe speech and language impairments, and to design, implement, and evaluate plans of intervention. At the same time, speech and language intervention is, at best, not an isolated activity. It must be well coordinated with a child's overall educational plan to ensure that communication activities are grounded in meaningful cognitive and social contexts.

Children bring their full identity to their communication competencies, including ethnic background, previous school experiences, and what they (and others around them) perceive to be the "right way to talk." Parents of young children bring all these things, and also their own versions of why their children may not communicate as well as other children. Thus, a child does not have a "speech and language part" to be "fixed up." Instead, children have a fundamental capacity for speech and language acquisition and use, a capacity manifest in circumstances that are meaningful to a child, parents, and professionals. The professional challenge is to devise an individual program of intervention that maximizes this capacity, in ways that are useful to a child's immediate communication needs.

*R*EFERENCES

American Speech-Language-Hearing Association, Committee on Prevention of Speech, Language, and Hearing Problems. (1982). Definitions of the word "prevention" as it relates to communicative disorders. *ASHA, 24,* 425, 431.

American Speech-Language-Hearing Association. (1985). Clinical management of communicatively handicapped minority language populations. *ASHA, 27,* 29–32.

American Speech-Language-Hearing Association (1988, March). Position statement: Prevention of communication disorders. *ASHA, 30,* 90.

American Speech-Language-Hearing Association. (1993a). Definitions of communication disorders and variations. *ASHA, 35,* (Suppl. 10), 40–41.

American Speech-Language-Hearing Association. (1993b). Guidelines for caseload size and speech-language service delivery in the schools. *ASHA, 35,* (Suppl. 10), 33–39.

Arthur, G. (1952). *Leiter performance international scale.* Chicago: Stoelting.

Blake, A., & Shewan, C. (1992). ASHA data: An update on PL 94–142. *ASHA, 34,* 52.

Bunce, B. H. (in press). *The language acquisition preschool: Classroom curriculum.* Baltimore, MD: Paul H. Brookes.

Carrow-Woolfolk, E. (1985). *Test of auditory comprehension of language–Revised.* Allen, TX: DLM Teaching Resources.

Cordes, C. (1985). Studies dispute Bennett's attack on bilingualism. *APA Monitor, 16,* 6.

Dublinske, S. (1981). Action: School services. *Language, Speech, & Hearing Services in Schools, 12,* 192–200.

Dunn, L., & Dunn, L. (1981). *Peabody picture vocabulary test–Revised* (PPVT–R). Circle Pines, MN: American Guidance Services.

Ehren, B. J., & Lenz, B. K. (1989). Adolescents with language disorders: Special considerations in providing academically relevant language intervention. *Seminars in Speech and Language, 10,* 192–204.

Fisher, H., & Logemann, J. (1971). *The Fisher-Logemann test of articulation competence.* Boston: Houghton Mifflin.

Goldman, R., & Fristoe, M. (1986). *Goldman-Fristoe test of articulation.* Circle Pines, MN: American Guidance Services.

Grosjean, F. (1982). *Life with two languages: An introduction to bilingualism.* Cambridge, MA: Harvard University Press.

Hiskey, M. S. (1966). *Hiskey-Nebraska test of learning aptitude.* Lincoln, NE: Union College Press.

Hyman, C. S. (1985). PL 94–142 in review. *ASHA, 27,* 37.

Lewis, B., Ekelman, B., & Aram, D. (1989). A familial study of severe phonological disorders. *Journal of Speech and Hearing Research, 32,* 713–724.

Mansour, S. L., & Lingwall, J. B. (1985). ASHA omnibus survey 1984. *ASHA, 27,* 37–40.

Marge, M. (1984). The prevention of communication disorders. *ASHA, 26,* 29–37.

McDermott, L. D. (1981). The effect of duplicated and unduplicated child count on prevalence of speech-impaired children. *Language, Speech, & Hearing Services in Schools, 12,* 115–119.

Miller, L. (1989). Classroom-based language intervention. *Language, Speech, & Hearing Services in Schools, 20,* 153–169.

National Colloquium on Underserved Populations Report. (1985). *ASHA, 27,* 31–35.

Newcomer, P., & Hammill, D. (1988). *Test of language development primary, Second edition* (TOLD–P:2). Austin, TX: ProEd.

Office of Special Education Programs (OSEP). (1988). *Tenth Annual Report to Congress.* Washington, DC: Government Printing Office.

Parlour, S. (1990). *Familial risk for articulation disorder: A 28-year follow-up.* Unpublished dissertation, University of Minnesota, Minneapolis.

Prather, E. M. (1984). Developmental language disorders: Adolescents. In A. Holland (Ed.), *Language disorders in children* (pp. 159–172). San Diego: College-Hill.

Rescorla, L., & Schwartz, E. (1990). Outcome of toddlers with specific expressive language delay. *Applied Psycholinguistics, 11,* 393–407.

Rice, M. L. (1985, November). *Television and children's talk: Clinical implications.* Mini-seminar presented at the Annual National Convention of American Speech-Language-Hearing Association, Washington, DC.

Rice, M. L. (1993). "Don't talk to him: He's weird": A social consequences account of language and social interactions. In A. Kaiser & D. Gray (Eds.), *Enhancing children's communication: Research foundations for intervention.* Baltimore, MD: Paul H. Brookes.

Rice, M. L., & Wilcox, K. (Eds.). (in press). *The Language Acquisition Preschool: A classroom program for language facilitation.* Baltimore, MD: Paul H. Brookes.

Snyder. L. S. (1984a). Communicative competence in children with delayed language development. In R. L. Schiefelbusch & J. Pickar (Eds.), *The acquisition of communicative competence* (pp. 423–478). Baltimore, MD: University Park Press.

Snyder, L. S. (1984b). Developmental language disorders: Elementary school age. In A. Holland (Ed.), *Language disorders in children* (pp. 129–158). San Diego: College-Hill.

Tallal, P., Ross. R., & Curtiss, S. (1989). Familial aggregation in specific language impairment. *Journal of Speech and Hearing Disorders, 54,* 167–173.

Templin, M. C. (1957). *Certain language skills in children.* Minneapolis: University of Minnesota Press.

Thorndike, R. L., Hugen, E. P., & Suttler, T. M. (1986). *Stanford-Binet intelligence scale: Fourth edition.* Chicago. Riverside Publishing.

Tomblin, B. (1989). Familial concentration of developmental language impairment. *Journal of Speech and Hearing Disorders, 54,* 287–295.

Wechsler, D. (1991). *Wechsler intelligence scale for children-Third edition.* New York: Psychological Corp.

Weiner, P. S. (1984). The study of childhood language disorders in the nineteenth century. *ASHA, 26,* 35–38.

GIFTED AND TALENTED

STUDENTS

LINDA KREGER SILVERMAN

At 2 weeks old, Jessica smiled on cue. At 14 months, she spoke in sentences and had a vocabulary of more than 250 words. By the age of 2, she could do a 60-piece puzzle. She was so far beyond the other children in her day care that she became the teacher's helper. At 3, Jessie taught herself to read.

What happens when children like Jessie enter school? Are schools prepared to allow her to progress at her own rate? Unfortunately, too often the answer to this question is *no*. Jessie is expected to wait patiently while other children learn skills and knowledge she has already mastered. She is implicitly taught to slow down her natural rate of learning to make the teacher and the other students more comfortable. But Jessie pays a price for her social adaptation. She learns to be less than she can be, to slide by without stretching herself, to deny her talents, and, eventually, to trade her dreams for simpler, less demanding goals. This tragic waste of Jessie's potential affects not only her, but also society, for we have all lost whatever gifts she might have contributed. Instead of teaching to the lowest common denominator, the schools should become a place where individual differences are appreciated and where talents are recognized and nurtured.

CURRENT PRACTICES

Attitudes toward the gifted and talented in the United States have been on a perpetual roller coaster. This group has been alternately applauded, attacked, "mined" as a natural resource, and abandoned. Programs for the gifted currently are perceived as politically incorrect or as unnecessary frills to be discarded when budgets are tight. These attitudes are costly for the children involved and for society in general.

In the first half of this century, efforts to serve the gifted and talented were sporadic and short-lived, with a few notable exceptions, such as the Cleveland Major Work Program and the Bronx High School of Science. National interest in the gifted was sparked in 1957 with the launching of Sputnik, the Russian space satellite. Programs for the gifted suddenly seemed necessary for our national defense. By the early 1960s, 21 states had such programs, but by the late 1960s, most of them were gone. Interest in the gifted was reignited in the 1970s by a congressional study instituted by Commissioner Marland (1972), resulting in Public Law 93–380, the first federal recognition of gifted children. Federal support, however, has been unstable—as evidenced by the appearance, disappearance and reappearance of the national Office of Gifted and Talented over the last two decades—leaving the burden of responsibility to the states.

In the 1980s there were steady gains in state appropriations, state mandates, administrative personnel, teacher certification requirements, individual educational plans for students, and graduate training programs. By 1990, 26 states had mandatory services for the gifted and talented (K–12 in 21 states), 21 states had due process rights for the identification of gifted students, 25 states allowed early entrance to school, 39 states had at least one full-time state coordinator, 18 states had certification or endorsement requirements for teachers, and 12 states required individualized education programs for gifted students (Council of State Directors of Programs for the Gifted, 1991).

The 1990s ushered in the school reform movement, which called for an end to tracking and ability grouping and brought with it a wholesale attack on gifted education. Tracking and ability grouping have been used as interchangeable terms, and the distinction between gifted and high-achieving students has been equally blurred. The rhetoric against programs for the gifted assumes that they are extra privileges for the privileged.

Currently, the field is so enshrouded by myths and misinformation that many exemplary programs throughout the country are being discontinued (Benbow, 1992). These myths must be dispelled if the needs of gifted children are to be met within the school system. The myths are:

1. Tracking and ability grouping are synonymous.
2. Gifted students are all high achievers.
3. Gifted students are all economically advantaged.
4. Provisions for the gifted are undemocratic.
5. Special attention to the gifted fosters elitism.
6. Gifted children can make it on their own; they don't need assistance.

First, the difference between tracking and ability grouping requires clarification. Tracking involves the permanent placement of students into low-, average-, and high-achieving groups. It is an organizational plan designed for students in the mid-range of abilities, and it has been questioned for years. Ability grouping at both extremes, however, has been found to be beneficial (Kulik & Kulik, 1991; Rogers, 1991). As far back as the 1920s, Hollingworth distinguished between these two very different concepts:

> Professor Hollingworth was convinced that homogeneous grouping offers the most effective type of education in populous centers...large enough for the organization of special classes. It is important to emphasize that Hollingworth did not interpret homogeneous grouping as advocating the sectioning of all students in the educational system on an ability basis. She repeatedly stated that in the distribution of intelligence, only the extremes are so far removed from the average that regular school cannot meet their needs. (Pritchard, 1951, p. 53)

Part of the problem lies in the confusion about the meaning of giftedness. The research on cooperative learning that undergirds the attack against ability grouping is all based upon the division of students into high-, average-, and low-achieving groups. When the gifted are defined as the top third of the school population, a notion meant to democratize the concept, the anti–ability-grouping arguments apply. When the gifted are defined as a special education population, constituting a small portion of the school population (2–5%), however, the existing research base is *not appropriate*. "The research base for applications of cooperative learning to the truly gifted is weak. Knowing this area well, I'd characterize it as virtually non-existent" (Slavin, 1990, p. 28).

Perhaps the most pernicious belief is that gifted students are economically advantaged. The gifted come from all social classes (Dickinson, 1970), and poor children have less opportunity to achieve academic success. While the percentage of gifted students among the upper classes may be higher, there is a much greater number of gifted children among the lower classes (Zigler & Farber, 1985), because the poor far outnumber the rich. If we abandon gifted programs, gifted children from culturally diverse groups and low socioeconomic circumstances will be the ones to suffer most. Affluent parents can send their children to private schools, and some two-parent families can opt to homeschool their children. But the majority of gifted children will not have those options. These children are prevented from fulfilling their potential when public school provisions for the gifted are eliminated. Instead, greater efforts must be made to include bright children from all socioeconomic classes in gifted programs.

Provisions for the gifted are as democratic as provisions for any other exceptional child. A gifted child is a child with special needs. Because giftedness occurs on a continuum, the more the child's abilities vary from the norm, the greater is the need for an individually tailored program and accompanying support services. A child whose IQ is 3 standard deviations above the norm (145) has learning needs as unique as those of a child whose IQ is 3 standard deviations below the norm (55). Figure 9.1 illustrates this concept. There are profoundly gifted children, just as there are profoundly retarded children. Most gifted children, however, are found in regular classrooms without the benefit of special provisions or teachers with special training.

The claim that special services for gifted students create elitism also is unsupported by research (Newland, 1976). Elitism is a function of *socioeconomic* differences, not intellectual ones. In teaching and counseling gifted students, I have found that feelings of inferiority in the gifted are much more prevalent than feelings of superiority. Children who act superior usually feel isolated and use their verbal abilities as a defense against the rejection of their agemates. Separating gifted students and ignoring their needs actually fosters elitism to a greater extent than congregating them for advanced instruction. Students who are the smartest in their class for 12 years, never crack a book or take home homework, and ace all the tests without studying can get a ballooned sense of their own importance and place in the universe. When gifted students are placed in classes together, they do not come to the conclusion that they are "better than everyone else." Rather, they are *humbled* by finding peers who know more than they do. "Conceit was corrected, rather than fostered, by the experience of daily contact with a large number of equals" (Hollingworth, 1930, p. 445).

Much of the fear of elitism is based on the assumption that if individuals discover that they are unusually able, they will develop aristocratic values, caring little for the plight of others. Research, however, indicates that exactly the opposite is true. Giftedness often is accompanied by a strong sense of responsibility, empathy, moral concern, and compassion (Dabrowski, 1972; Hollingworth, 1942; Marland, 1972; Passow, 1988; Terman, 1925; Ward, 1985). The gifted in our country are the backbone of social reform and egalitarianism. They care desperately about injustice (Roeper, 1988). Programming for gifted students enhances these higher values rather than creating an aristocracy.

Many gifted children do *not* make it on their own. Some become drop-outs (Marland, 1972), delinquents (Seeley & Mahoney, 1981), underachievers (Supplee, 1990; Whitmore, 1989), depressed (Kerr, 1991) and victims of suicide (Delisle, 1990). For every child with recognized gifts, still another goes unrecognized (Dickinson, 1970). Gifted children may have learning disabilities or other handicaps, and these dual exceptionalities tend to mask each other so the child appears average (Silverman, 1989). Unrecognized and undeveloped talents may be lost permanently (Borland, 1986).

There is growing national concern with America's loss of standing globally. Numerous research studies reveal that America's top students rank close to the bottom in all subject areas in international comparisons (Stevenson & Stigler, 1992). The situation has been attributed to public education's neglect of gifted students (U.S. Department of Education, 1993). A report released in November of 1993, *Excellence: A Case for Developing America's Talents* (U.S. Department of Education, 1993), described the "quiet crisis" in educating talented students:

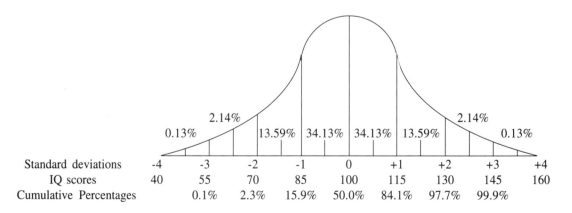

Standard deviations	-4	-3	-2	-1	0	+1	+2	+3	+4
IQ scores	40	55	70	85	100	115	130	145	160
Cumulative Percentages		0.1%	2.3%	15.9%	50.0%	84.1%	97.7%	99.9%	

● FIGURE 9.1

Percent of cases under portions of normal curve

The United States is squandering one of its most precious resources—the gifts, talents, and high interests of many of its students. In a broad range of intellectual and artistic endeavors, these youngsters are not challenged to do their best work. This problem is especially severe among economically disadvantaged and minority students, who have access to fewer advanced educational opportunities and whose talents often go unnoticed....

Compared with top students in other industrialized countries, American students perform poorly on international tests, are offered a less rigorous curriculum, read fewer demanding books, do less homework, and enter the work force or postsecondary education less well prepared. (p. 1)

Research studies show that gifted and talented elementary school students have mastered from 35 to 50 percent of the curriculum to be offered in five basic subjects before they begin the school year. (p. 2)

Negative stereotypes of high-achieving students have created an atmosphere in which students do not want to be identified as very smart. (p. 13)

Despite myths to the contrary, giftedness does not develop in a vacuum. We have romanticized the "self-made man," but research indicates that talent requires considerable cultivation to develop fully (Bloom, 1985; Feldman, 1986). The potential concert violinist must have a violin and continuous nurturing of this ability to fulfill its potential. We cannot know how much talent has been lost for lack of discovery and development; nor can we assess the magnitude of that loss to our society—the music that was never composed, the medical cure that was never discovered, the political strategy that might have averted a war.

*C*URRENT DEFINITIONS

One of the greatest obstacles to establishing programs is lack of agreement about who may be considered gifted. Giftedness was originally defined as performance 2 standard deviations above the norm on a standardized intelligence test (Terman, 1925). This simple, operational definition left out many capable children who, for a variety of reasons, did not perform well on intelligence tests. Newer ideas about intelligence consider multiple abilities, which has led to the concept of multiple types of giftedness (Gardner, 1983; Guilford, 1956; Sternberg, 1986). Guilford's (1975) *Structure-of-intellect* model postulated 150 kinds of intelligence. A definition including all of these specific abilities naturally would be impossible to implement.

In the Gifted and Talented Children's Education Act (1978) (PL 95–561), "gifted and talented" was defined as follows:

"Gifted and talented" means children, and whenever applicable, youth, who are identified at the preschool, elementary, or secondary level as possessing demonstrated or potential abilities that give evidence of high performance capability in areas such as intellectual, creative, specific academic, or leadership ability, or in the performing and visual arts, and who, by reason thereof, require services or activities not ordinarily provided by the school. (Sec. 902)

Although many states have adopted this definition (or its predecessor, which appeared in the Marland report), the emphasis in most programs has been on general academic achievement. Identification usually involves group achievement tests, grades, and teacher recommendations (Gillespie, 1982).

Another popular definition was proposed by Renzulli (1978), who contends that a gifted student must have equal portions of above average abilities, creativity, and task commitment applied to any performance area. Renzulli (1980) advocates a "revolving door" approach to gifted education that would allow as many as one third of the student body to have access to special services when engaging actively in special projects. This view has been particularly appealing to administrators because it appears more democratic than traditional approaches, but it is difficult to orchestrate and often provides insufficient stimulation to the most capable students in the school.

I define giftedness as *advanced development*—precocity that can be observed early in life as rapid advancement through developmental milestones, and demonstrated ability to reason like a much older child. Individual intelligence tests can detect this precocity in preschool and primary-aged children; therefore, high scores on intelligence tests are positive indications of giftedness. Low scores, however, are not as trustworthy. If a child demonstrates advanced ability to conceptualize but does not attain a score in the gifted range on an IQ test, he or she may still be gifted and other methods of identification should be used.

A new definition of giftedness acknowledges the differentiated inner experience of the gifted by virtue of the unevenness of their development:

> Giftedness is *asynchronous development* in which advanced cognitive abilities and heightened intensity combine to create inner experiences and awareness that are qualitatively different from the norm. This asynchrony increases with higher intellectual capacity. The uniqueness of the gifted renders them particularly vulnerable and requires modifications in parenting, teaching and counseling in order for them to develop optimally. (Columbus Group, 1991)

This definition places the emphasis on the child being out of sync both internally, in terms of varying rates of cognitive, social/emotional and physical development, and externally, in relation to group norms. It also suggests that cognitive complexity gives rise to emotional intensity. An individual intelligence test provides an estimate of the degree of asynchrony, as well as vulnerability, of the child.

The net result of this plethora of definitions is that each state, school district, and, in some cases, school arrives at its own definition of giftedness according to the population it chooses to serve. In one school giftedness is confined to 1% of the school population, whereas in another school 25% of the students are considered gifted. Needless to say, this lack of standardization causes considerable confusion. A child might be defined as gifted in one school and not gifted in another school, even within the same district. When identification criteria lack consistency, children come to think of their giftedness as unreal—something that is easily taken away when they move from one school to another. In no other field of exceptionality are placement decisions made in such an arbitrary manner.

*L*EARNING AND BEHAVIORS

The list of characteristics below applies to gifted children in general. Those considered gifted in one domain, such as the visual or performing arts, usually exhibit a number of these traits in addition to those relating to their main area of competence. The traits may be used as a teacher checklist to locate potentially gifted children, keeping in mind that no child exhibits all of them. The child may show unusual leadership ability, outstanding artistic, musical, or dramatic talent, precocity in mathematics or reading, specific psychomotor abilities, inventiveness, intense responses to social injustice, or a combination of these special abilities. Gifted children:

1. Are developmentally advanced; they usually learn to walk, talk, read, write, earlier than others.
2. Often have a unique learning style, grasping ideas all at once rather than step-by-step.
3. Learn at a faster pace and solve problems rapidly.
4. Have unusually good memory.
5. Tend to have a high degree of energy and sometimes need less sleep than others their age.
6. Have a vivid imagination and may have imaginary companions.
7. Are very curious and tend to ask complex questions.
8. Give complicated answers; their detailed explanations often show great depth of understanding of topics.
9. Are quick to recognize relationships, even relationships that others don't see.
10. Organize information in new ways, creating new perspectives; often see many solutions to a problem.
11. Often see ambiguity in what appears to be "factual" information.
12. Have a large vocabulary and tend to express themselves well.
13. Have a sophisticated sense of humor for their age.
14. Usually have a wide range of interests.
15. Have a long attention span and usually persevere in their areas of interest.
16. Think more abstractly than their classmates, imagining what could be instead of what it is.
17. Are highly sensitive and tend to be compassionate toward others.
18. Are often perfectionists (except with their bedrooms!); they can become very upset if things don't turn out as they had hoped.
19. Seem mature for their age at times and may prefer the company of older children and adults.
20. May be leaders or loners (preferring to watch others before joining in an activity).
21. May be avid readers or great mathematicians but are not necessarily gifted in all areas.

LEARNING CHARACTERISTICS

Gifted children learn faster, earlier, and in a different manner than average children do. The first signs of giftedness are unusual alertness and long attention span in infancy. This alertness may lead to keen powers of observation and extraordinary feats of memory. Advanced language development is the most frequently mentioned characteristic in young gifted children. Many of the children we have assessed at The Gifted Development Center spoke their first word at 6 months and were talking in sentences by 18 months. But we have also found many gifted children who did not communicate early. In these cases, the children understood language but did not speak until much later, and their first "word" was usually a complex sentence, such as, "Charlie, will you please pass the salt?"

Regardless of whether they are early or late talkers, gifted children usually have a remarkable vocabulary. They pick up language rapidly, and their communication is unusually complex and sophisticated. They develop an intense interest in books at an early age and often begin to read before they reach school age. Half of the children we assessed taught themselves to read before age 5.

Vocabulary development and reading ability are not isolated skills but instead reflect an advanced cognitive organization that is the primary quality of giftedness. Gifted children think more abstractly than their agemates, and they understand complex concepts. They are extremely curious, and this questioning attitude remains throughout life, enabling them to become good problem finders as well as problem solvers.

The complex mental organization of the gifted child can be likened to a new, high-powered computer. It has a greater memory capacity than older models. It takes in information at a faster rate and stores it more efficiently. It can also retrieve the information more quickly and link it with other stored information. In this way, it accumulates much more information at a much faster rate than other models. In addition, the human mind can generate new concepts and applications of the stored information, and the gifted child demonstrates these proficiencies. With each passing year, gifted children's storehouse of information and ability to manipulate concepts diverge more and more from those of their agemates.

Methods designed for the average child are inadequate for instructing the gifted. An average child needs a certain amount or repetition to understand concepts (albeit not as much as most textbooks and teachers provide). A child who is below average needs much more drill to comprehend a concept. As intelligence increases, the amount of needed drill decreases. Much of the time gifted children spend in school is wasted on needless review of already mastered concepts.

Gifted children often learn in conceptual leaps rather than step by step. They can see the whole picture and the complex interrelationship of the parts. They are quick to see patterns and principles in what appear to others as unrelated events. They can learn classes and systems while others are learning units. They can envision many possibilities while others their age can relate only to concrete experiences. They organize information in new ways, creating new perspectives. They need opportunities to develop these strengths instead of being asked to learn in the same manner as others their age.

PERSONALITY CHARACTERISTICS

The emotional lives of the gifted are complex, mirroring their cognitive complexity. Three key personality characteristics associated with giftedness are perfectionism, sensitivity, and intensity. These critical elements of the gifted personality must be understood and accepted; attempts to "cure" them are not only ineffective, but they are actually damaging to the child's self-esteem. Perfectionism enables the gifted individual to strive toward excellence and moral integrity in adult life. Sensitivity is the root of compassion and humanitarian values. Intensity evolves into the passion found in superb art, music, theater, poetry; it undergirds the determination to fight injustice and create a better society. These qualities are difficult for the child and others to cope with, but it helps to know that their presence serves to further the evolution of society.

Uneven development leads to high levels of frustration. For example, the gifted kindergartner with a 7-year-old mind in a 5-year-old body sets standards for herself more appropriate for an older child. She sees the horse with the clarity of a 7-year-old, but her 5-year-old hands cannot form the clay to match her vision, so she gives up in despair and throws the clay across the room. It is useless to tell her not to feel the way she does; instead, one should validate her feelings of frustration and urge her to keep trying. If she doesn't give up, each attempt will more closely resemble the horse she envisions.

In our studies, more than 90% of the gifted children we tested were found to be extremely sensitive (Silverman, 1983). This sensitivity makes the gifted child particularly vulnerable (Roedell, 1984). Gifted kindergarten boys, for example, often cry on the playground and are scapegoated by other little boys who have less sensitivity. To teach these boys to "toughen up" would be unwise; instead, they need to know that there are safe places for them to show their feelings—at home, or with an understanding teacher—and unsafe places, like the playground.

The intensity observed in gifted children is a function of a highly responsive nervous system (Piechowski, 1979, 1991). As infants, gifted children tend to have a high degree of energy, less need for sleep, and allergic reactions, such as colic. They are sometimes prone to asthma in childhood. They react intensely to a wide variety of stimuli—intellectual, emotional, imaginational, sensual, and psychomotor (Dabrowski, 1972). Intense reactions may be more evident in firstborn children than in younger siblings (Silverman, 1986b), but they are likely to be seen in all gifted children in response to injustice.

Another characteristic of gifted children is a well-developed sense of humor, which manifests itself early in life. A highly gifted 2-year-old boy was playing under his mother's bed while she was trying to take a nap. He asked, "Mommy, are you resting?" She said, *"yes."* He responded, "Does that mean I'm under arrest?" Many times a child's sense of humor may be the only obvious sign of his or her giftedness, particularly among underachievers, culturally diverse, or gifted children with learning disabilities.

Introversion is another personality characteristic often seen in highly gifted children. We have found that the brighter the child, the more likely he or she is to be introverted (Silverman, 1986b). Introverted children are often overlooked in public school settings because they tend to be quiet in large groups. In small-group activities, however, they may be surprisingly talkative. They will not be the first to raise their hands or jump into new activities; they need time to observe first. But when they do respond, they are thoughtful and reflective, often demonstrating profound insights and exemplary performance.

Gifted children often prefer older companions or adults. If at age 5 they have 7-year-old minds, when they are 10 they will have 14-year-old minds. They need the mental stimulation and emotional depth of other children their *mental age*. If they cannot find gifted peers, they crave the attention of adults in their environment. When they have only children their own chronological age to relate to, they tend to develop maladaptive behaviors, such as isolating themselves, hiding their abilities to fit in with the group, or becoming the big brother or big sister, taking care of the other children but not developing true friendships.

Other characteristics of the gifted include high degrees of creativity, active imaginations—including the creation of imaginary companions—wide ranges of interests, perseverance in areas of interest, intense curiosity, and compassion for those less fortunate. Not all gifted children demonstrate all of the characteristics of giftedness, and some have them but hide them because they have been punished for being gifted. Gifted junior high school girls, in particular, often experience depression and lowered self-esteem if they choose to be high achievers (Petersen, 1988).

The list of learning and personality characteristics does not include excellent performance in all academic subjects. No one can be equally gifted in every area. The expectations—and disparagement—that result from this assumption are truly unfair to the child. Teachers who say, "If you're so gifted, how come you're running down the hall?" are scapegoating gifted children, and this should not be tolerated. Any gifted child who is the top student in all subjects probably is not challenged sufficiently to show his or her pattern of strengths or weaknesses. When gifted children are placed with others like themselves, they soon find that if they are the best mathematicians, there are others whose reading ability far surpasses their own. This is an important lesson to learn.

IDENTIFICATION AND ASSESSMENT

Early identification of the gifted is essential to prevent later underachievement (Martinson, 1974). As with other exceptionalities, the earlier the recognition, the greater is the opportunity to help the child reach his or her potential. Unfortunately, many school districts delay identification of the gifted until the middle grades. The rationale for this delay usually involves a belief that intelligence tests cannot accurately identify young gifted children and that many children will be misidentified as gifted in the early grades and later have to be "ungifted" or removed from gifted programs. In actuality, the tests are quite capable of identifying preschool and primary-aged gifted children (Silverman, 1986a). Gifted 4-year-olds can be accurately assessed because they have the mental powers and concentration of first-graders.

Many people believe that early signs of developmental precocity are inconsequential and that slower children eventually will "catch up" to an advanced child. But because the gifted child learns more, at an accelerated pace, and has better retrieval and application of information than his or her agemates, the only way other children could "catch up" is if the gifted child were to suddenly regress. If we go back to the computer analogy, the older model can never have the power of the newer model unless the new machine uses only a fraction of its capacity. When advanced children no longer appear gifted, something in the environment is preventing them from learning at their full capacity. There is much greater danger of older gifted children's regressing than of overidentifying young gifted children.

Many gifted children go into hiding by the third grade, when peer pressure to conform becomes strong. If being gifted—and therefore different—becomes socially unacceptable, these children may choose to hide their abilities. Children who make this choice must be found early in their school careers or they may never again be recognized as gifted. The problem seems to be particularly acute for girls, who by third grade learn that it is "smart not to be smart" (Silverman, 1986c). Educators may assume that these early bloomers are not really gifted after all. But we do not know how many of them have simply *chosen* underachievement.

ASSESSMENT CONCERNS UNIQUE TO GIFTEDNESS

Identification and assessment are not differentiated as clearly in gifted education as in other branches of special education. Assessment, in the usual sense of the term, is conspicuously absent in gifted education, except in the few states that apply PL 94–142 to the education of gifted students. The potential exists within the identification process for assessing specific needs of these students, but unfortunately the information gathered in the identification process is commonly ignored in future programming. The diagnostic-prescriptive approach is rare in programs for the gifted.

The situation is not corrected easily because clarity in answer to the question "Who is gifted?" is lacking. Adopting the definition in PL 95-561 does not solve the problem, as no single school program can meet all of the diversified needs of children who have talents in various areas. Most school districts choose which segment of the gifted population to serve, and they develop identification procedures accordingly. The reality that not all gifted children can be served leads to some special issues in their identification.

The foremost issue is whether to identify the children and then fit the program to their needs or to determine the program first and then find the children likely to benefit most from it. The former approach is used consistently throughout special education, but the small budgets commonly available for gifted programs reduce its feasibility. The latter approach limits the target population to those who can be served by the available resources. Its major drawback is that it fails to serve many gifted children. It also introduces the possibility that the program devised will bear no relationship to the actual needs of gifted students.

Another critical issue revolves around the underachieving gifted child. This student seems to need a gifted program most but also may be least likely to benefit from one. A great deal of research has been done on the underachieving gifted child, most of which indicates that our educational solutions to date are insufficient (Gallagher, 1985; Tannenbaum, 1983; Whitmore, 1980). Renzulli (1978) suggested that gifted programs should be geared to the highly motivated student, because this student is most likely to contribute to society. However, many gifted underachievers are able to reverse the pattern of underachievement when they are placed in classes for the gifted (Emerick, 1992).

One other problem that must be solved is whether a program should serve a broad or a narrow spectrum of giftedness. Broad definitions attempt to include potentially gifted students, culturally diverse students, and students with special abilities in only one area. They may comprise as much as 33% of the school population. The broad view minimizes the number of false negatives—the number of truly gifted students who might be missed if more stringent guidelines were followed. On the other hand, the narrow approach minimizes the number of false positives—the number of misidentified children who cannot perform as well as others in a gifted program. A narrow scope emphasizes serving a small number of exceptional students in a qualitatively different way. Advocates of the narrow approach fear that the needs of the brightest students may not be served in a more inclusive program. They recommend that programs serve only the top 1–5% of the school population. Some school districts have resolved this dilemma by creating two types of gifted programs: one that is broadly inclusive and another for the highly gifted.

These issues are compounded by the fact that IQ scores in the gifted range are more variable than scores in any other range. This is because of *ceiling effects* of the tests—the lack of items of sufficient difficulty to allow students to demonstrate the full range of their abilities. The problem is particularly acute for the highly gifted. Comparisons of IQ scores generated on various instruments reveal discrepancies greater than 50 points!

> One child was found who scored 182 on the Stanford-Binet (Form L–M) and 127 on the Stanford-Binet: Fourth Edition. Another scored 187 on the L–M and 139 on the WISC–III. The most remarkable difference was a child who scored 137 on the WISC–R, and a year later tested 229+ on the Stanford-Binet (Form L–M), at the age of 9, missing only two items on the entire test! (Silverman & Kearney, 1992, p. 9)

Depressions in IQ scores occur across all ages and affect the moderately as well as the highly gifted. According to the test manuals for the Stanford-Binet IV, the WPPSI–R and the WISC–III, children who previously tested in the gifted range (130+) are now testing in the superior range (120–130). These differences are usually explained as an artifact of the general population gaining in intelligence over time. The gain is about one-fourth to one-third of an IQ point per year (Flynn, 1984). Therefore, a score of 100 obtained on 1960 norms would be comparable to a score of approximately 92 on 1991 norms. In the same period, however, scores in the gifted range have dropped **one point per year**, generating a loss of 31 IQ points in 31 years (Silverman & Kearney, 1992). Only eight of those points can be attributed to the increase in intelligence of the general population. The rest of the depression seems to have been a result of force-fitting the gifted population into the normal curve of distribution.

Newer tests also place undue emphasis on speed of performance, depressing scores for introverted, reflective thinkers and children who have motoric delays of any kind.

> The biggest negatives for gifted assessment are the new emphasis on problem-solving speed on the WPPSI–R [and] the substantially increased stress on performance time in the WISC–III compared to the WISC–R.... The speed factor will penalize gifted children who are as reflective as they are bright, or who tend to go slow for other non-cognitive reasons such as a mild coordination problem. (Kaufman, 1992, p. 158)

Kaufman (1992) goes on to say that if a child of 12 solved all Performance items correctly but received no bonus points for speed, he or she would score **below average** on every subtest. This makes it extremely difficult to gain accurate information on gifted children with learning disabilities.

Given the difficulties with current instruments, it is recommended that (a) entrance requirements for gifted programs be lowered to 120 to take into account the lower norms on newer instruments; (b) children who obtain 3 or more subtests in the ceiling range of any current instrument (e.g., 17, 18, or 19 on the WISC or WPPSI subtests) be retested on the Stanford-Binet (Form L–M), which has a higher range (Silverman & Kearney, 1992); and (c) children who have difficulties with motor speed or processing speed be allowed take the Stanford-Binet (Form L–M), which is an untimed test.

THE ASSESSMENT PROCESS

An ideal assessment process determines who should be placed in a gifted program and the specific needs of those individuals. It involves (a) search, (b) screening, (c) identification, (d) selection, and (e) case study.

The *search* entails informing the community about the program. It should include inservice education for teachers and parents about the characteristics of gifted children and their special needs. This is necessary because untrained teachers tend to nominate high achievers rather than gifted students (Martinson, 1974). Nomination forms are made available to parents, teachers, counselors, students (for themselves and each other), and community members. *All* children must have equal access to the nomination process. The purpose of the search is to create as large a pool of potentially gifted children as possible so no one who could benefit from the program will be overlooked.

The *screening* attempts to narrow the pool to a reasonable size for detailed individual evaluation. Screening procedures tend to be group-oriented, quantitative, and easy to administer and score. The purposes are to sift through the nominees quickly and to provide access to unnominated children. Screening procedures usually include teacher rating scales, parent rating scales, group achievement scores, and group intelligence tests. School districts have found the *Cognitive Abilities Test* to be a useful means of screening gifted students (Silverman, 1986a).

The rating scales may be composite lists of characteristics, such as the one presented earlier in this chapter, or they may be separate lists of characteristics for each type of giftedness. The Renzulli-Hartman Rating Scales (1971) can be used if individual lists are desired. A combination of group achievement and intelligence tests is useful in screening but should *not* be used for final selection because of low ceilings. These tests maximize both false positives and false negatives; that is, they increase the likelihood of misidentifying children and missing truly gifted children. Any district that employs only screening procedures risks attack for unfair selection processes.

Identification refers to a detailed, individual assessment of students' strengths, weaknesses, interests, needs, and desires to be placed in the program. Several procedures are appropriate; the choice of method depends on the type of program, grade level, program philosophy, time, and cost factors. These procedures consist of:

1. Individual intelligence tests.
2. Interview (group or individual).
3. Assessment of student products or portfolios.
4. Creativity tests.
5. Essay on why student wishes to be in the program.
6. Developmental history/parental biography.
7. Autobiography.
8. Piagetian conservation tasks.
9. Student interest survey.
10. Independent study proposal.

Final *selection* should be made by a committee consisting of the program coordinator, classroom teacher, parent representative, student representative, counselor, and administrator. Quite commonly, school districts construct matrices in which subjective evaluations are converted into a numerical scoring system. Each part of the identification process is arbitrarily weighted according to the philosophy of the program. Borland (1986) cautions against the use of matrices because they create the impression of a "gifted index" and mask essential diagnostic information. Richert (1982) recommends that, after the number of students that can be accommodated within the program is determined, the students should be ranked *according to greatest need*. She also urges school districts to provide additional modifications in the regular program for gifted students who cannot be served within the gifted program. A probationary period is recommended as part of the selection process for all students or for students about whom there are questions.

A *case study* follows the selection process. All information gleaned from this study should be considered in designing the student's program and determining objectives. To gauge the child's progress toward those objectives and to permit needed changes, periodic reassessment is essential.

An *appeal process* should be available to all families who think their children have been unjustly disqualified. If individual intelligence tests have not been used, they may be introduced in the appeal process. The child may be allowed to participate in the gifted program on a "guest" basis to determine if he or she is actually capable of performing at the level of those selected; final judgment should rest with the teacher.

INFORMAL METHODS OF IDENTIFICATION

Today, gifted children tend to be identified by informal means. Many programs use screening procedures only, failing to appraise each student's unique educational needs. When formal assessment is not feasible, other ways of determining membership in a gifted program protect the rights of students better than does group screening. Student self-selection can be used successfully when the gifted program is confined to specific subject areas (Silverman, 1976). Students who have adequate research skills may submit proposals for independent study. The revolving-door approach Renzulli (1980) described enables any child needing assistance on an individual project to receive services without elaborate identification.

Another way to shorten the process is to automatically include children with the most obvious needs and to reserve evaluation for others with less obvious needs. The former group would consist of highly gifted students, those who received repeated nominations and high group test scores, those who scored in the gifted range on previously administered individual intelligence tests, those who attain high SAT scores in junior high school talent searches, and those who have been enrolled in other gifted programs. Individual full-scale assessment still is needed in all cases in which there is some question about the extent of the child's abilities.

Three general guidelines should be considered in any identification plan:

1. Both objective and subjective means should be used.
2. Culturally diverse children should be assessed according to cultural norms.
3. A program should be provided for each child identified.

INTERVENTION

INSTRUCTIONAL MODELS

Several models may be consulted for instructional strategies for the gifted and talented. The most popular of these is Bloom's (1956) *Taxonomy of Educational Objectives*. This model describes six levels of teaching strategies, as depicted in Figure 9.2. Most teaching involves the lower three levels: knowledge, comprehension, and application. In teaching gifted students, the emphasis is placed on the three higher levels: analysis, synthesis, and evaluation.

Guilford's (1956) *structure-of-intellect* also has been used as an instructional base

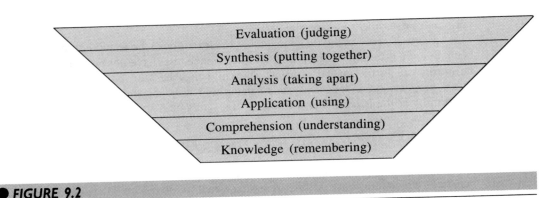

● **FIGURE 9.2**

Bloom's taxonomy of educational objectives

in gifted education. The concepts of *divergent production* (generating many solutions) and *convergent production* (seeking one right answer) have had a marked effect on programming. Open-ended divergent questions are the cornerstone of gifted methodology. The four factors of divergent production—fluency, flexibility, originality, and elaboration—provide a basis for the study of creativity.

1. *Fluency* is the ability to generate many responses.
2. *Flexibility* is the ability to change the form, modify information, or shift perspectives.
3. *Originality* is the ability to generate novel responses.
4. *Elaboration* is the ability to embellish an idea with details.

Another useful part of Guilford's system is his "products": units, classes, relations, systems, transformations, and implications. While regular students are learning units, gifted students can be concentrating on classes. When others are learning about classes, gifted students can be learning about relationships between classes. Learning about systems, transformations, and implications can be correlated with the higher-level thinking skills of analysis, synthesis, and evaluation. Understanding systems requires analysis; creating transformations requires synthesis; and grasping implications requires evaluation. These and other facets of Guilford's model are shown in Figure 9.3.

Williams' (1970) model incorporates Guilford's four cognitive factors of creativity and four affective factors: curiosity, risk taking, complexity, and imagination. Also included are instructional strategies, such as teaching paradoxes and attributes, and various subject areas. Williams suggests that all of these factors should be considered in developing the curriculum for the gifted. This model is illustrated in Figure 9.4.

Williams developed his teaching strategies from his own observation of teachers of the gifted rather than from a theoretical model. These strategies can develop critical thinking skills in gifted students:

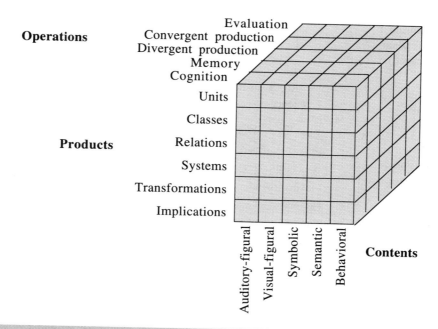

Guilford's structure-of-intellect model

Source: From J. P. Guilford, 1956, "The Structure of Intellect," *Psychological Bulletin, 53*, pp. 267–293.

1. Paradoxes.
2. Attributes.
3. Analogies.
4. Discrepancies.
5. Provocative questions.
6. Examples of change.
7. Examples of habit.
8. Organized random search.
9. Skills of search.
10. Tolerance for ambiguity.
11. Intuitive expression.
12. Adjustment to development.
13. Study of creative people and processes.
14. Evaluation of situations.
15. Creative reading skills.
16. Creative listening skills.
17. Creative writing skills.
18. Visualization skills.

For specific examples of activities that fit these categories, see Williams (1970).

Taba's teaching strategies (Institute for Staff Development, 1971) are also helpful in developing analysis and verbal reasoning abilities.

Renzulli (1977) proposed a three-stage enrichment model, shown in Figure 9.5 with the following elements:

Type I: General exploratory activities.

Type II: Group training activities.

Type III: Individual and small-group investigations of real problems.

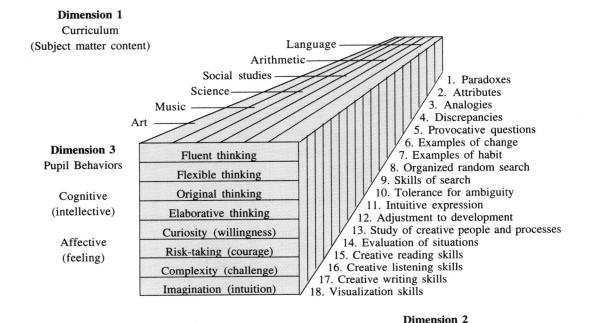

Dimension 1
Curriculum
(Subject matter content)

Language
Arithmetic
Social studies
Science
Music
Art

Dimension 3
Pupil Behaviors

Cognitive
(intellective)

Affective
(feeling)

Fluent thinking
Flexible thinking
Original thinking
Elaborative thinking
Curiosity (willingness)
Risk-taking (courage)
Complexity (challenge)
Imagination (intuition)

1. Paradoxes
2. Attributes
3. Analogies
4. Discrepancies
5. Provocative questions
6. Examples of change
7. Examples of habit
8. Organized random search
9. Skills of search
10. Tolerance for ambiguity
11. Intuitive expression
12. Adjustment to development
13. Study of creative people and processes
14. Evaluation of situations
15. Creative reading skills
16. Creative listening skills
17. Creative writing skills
18. Visualization skills

Dimension 2
Teacher Behavior
(Strategies or modes of teaching)

● *FIGURE 9.4*

A model for implementing cognitive-affective behavior in the classroom

Source: From F. E. Williams, 1970, *Classroom Ideas for Encouraging Thinking and Feeling*, East Aurora, NY: DOK Publishers. Used by permission of the publisher.

He believes that only Type III activities provide qualitatively different experiences for the gifted, because all children are capable of taking part in Type I and Type II enrichment. Renzulli's model is quite popular in programs for the gifted.

Maker (1982) provides a critique of all of these models and a discussion of their applications.

INSTRUCTIONAL VARIABLES

Programming can be modified in a number of ways to meet the needs of gifted learners, both in the regular classroom and in special placements. The following instructional variables can be used as a basis for providing qualitatively differentiated educational opportunities for the gifted.

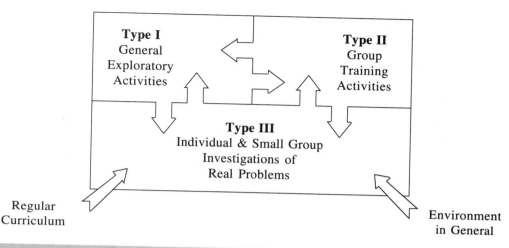

Renzulli's enrichment triad model

Source: From J. S. Renzulli, 1977, *The Enrichment Triad Model: A Guide for Developing Defensible Programs for the Gifted and Talented.* Wethersfield, CT: Creative Learning Press. Used by permission.

Continuous Assessment. Ongoing assessment, routine in other areas of special education, often is forgotten in programming for the gifted. Students who achieve several years above grade level on standardized achievement tests usually are taught the regular curriculum with no adjustments. This practice must change. Gifted students can be given final examinations at the beginning of the year to determine the content they have already mastered. Unit tests also should be given in advance. When a student scores very well on a standardized measure, an above-level test should be administered to ascertain the full extent of his or her capabilities. For example, elementary students scoring at or above the 95th percentile on a group achievement test should be given high school achievement tests.

Telescoping. Covering the same amount of material in less than the usual amount of time is called telescoping or compacting. The assessment process reveals areas in which students can spend less time learning the basic curriculum. Because they require less repetition to master concepts, gifted students should be able to skip most drill exercises. Instead they can be asked to answer only the most difficult questions on each page of exercises. Telescoping gives gifted students more time for enrichment activities suited to their needs or enables them to accelerate, covering advanced content.

Pacing. The most critical element in differentiated programming for the gifted is the pace at which material is presented. Instruction for gifted students should be paced rapidly to suit their learning style. When the tempo of instruction is increased, students become more alert and responsive, and they are able to learn the material in far less time than it takes to teach it to the others. Self-paced individualized instruction is less effective than fast-paced group instruction. Most individualized materials are written for average students, and their repetitious presentation format often bores gifted students.

Level of Abstraction. Gifted students can engage in hypothetical reasoning, discuss complex issues, make abstract inferences, and utilize systematic procedures in their quest for knowledge. Teaching strategies that involve the higher-level thinking skills—analysis, synthesis, and evaluation—enhance these abilities. Many average students cannot process abstract information well; their thinking processes require more concrete experiences. They tend to view situations as having one right answer and have difficulty understanding different perspectives. Material containing several levels of meaning, such as metaphor, analogy, and paradox, may be too difficult for them, whereas this type of material is ideal for the gifted.

Type of Subject Matter. Interdisciplinary studies are well suited to the complex minds and synthesizing abilities of the gifted. These students can wrestle with social and ethical issues too complicated for other students to grasp. They can search for solutions to real problems and assimilate accelerated content several grade levels above their placement.

Depth of Study. For gifted students, depth is preferable to breadth. Many brief studies are *not* recommended, because the information explosion may make obsolete whatever superficial knowledge a student is able to obtain. The process of studying a topic in depth serves gifted students better. Most enrichment programs include opportunities for independent study.

Range of Resources. Gifted students should have access to a greater variety of and more advanced-level resources than average students. Junior high school students, for example, may be given college library cards and taught to use university resources. Human resources also should be used to a greater extent. Mentorships have been found to be critical to the development of high-level talent.

Independence. The gifted are capable of greater independence of thought and action than are most students. This attribute should be encouraged through independent study. Opportunities to learn research skills that will facilitate high-level performance should be made available.

Time Allotment. Gifted students take less time to cover required material and can benefit from using the time saved to pursue independent study or enrichment activities. They need extra time to study topics in depth or to explore some of the numerous tangents that often emerge from a given enrichment activity or topic.

Sophistication of Products. Gifted students generate higher-level products than do their agemates, even for regular assignments. The quality of student products is the most remarkable result of programming for the gifted.

Level of Evaluation. Evaluation presupposes high levels of reflective judgment. Gifted students should be asked to formulate criteria based upon which to base their judgments. For example, they may be asked to determine the bases for grading independent study projects.

Dissemination. High-quality student products should be shared with the community in some way—through science fairs, editorials, speeches to parents, learning centers for other classes, publications, and so on. Gifted classes in various schools may wish to share their projects with each other. These dissemination activities increase the level of student evaluation.

Risk Taking. Risk taking is important to achievement. Gifted and creative children occasionally have unpopular ideas, but this unpopularity should not be a deterrent. Gifted students also must learn to accept occasional failure as part of the learning process. Girls in particular need encouragement to take risks.

DELIVERY SYSTEMS

Many programming alternatives may be used with gifted students, several of which are often delivered simultaneously within a school district. These programs are categorized into five basic types: acceleration, enrichment, special classes, before-/after-school options, and off-campus instruction.

Acceleration. Of the available options, acceleration has received the most research attention. Although resistance to acceleration has been considerable, research overwhelmingly supports it as a viable approach to educating gifted students (Feldhusen, 1992; Feldhusen & Moon, 1992; Robinson & Noble, 1991). Stanley (1979), at Johns Hopkins University, has studied "radical accelerates" extensively, and finds that children who *choose* to accelerate make good social adjustments. Acceleration can take a variety of forms:

1. *Subject-matter acceleration*—remaining at grade level while advancing in specific subject areas (e.g., Advanced Placement classes).
2. *Telescoping*—covering more than a full year's work in a given year (e.g., multi-age grouping).
3. *Grade skipping*—bypassing at least one year of instruction (e.g., early graduation).
4. *Early entrance*—entering school at least one year younger than the norm (e.g., early admission to kindergarten or college).

Although subject-matter acceleration is the most common option, it is also the most risky. If a child completes the third-grade math book while in second grade, all future teachers must accommodate his or her advancement. If one teacher refuses, the student must repeat an entire year's work and lose what he or she has gained. Combining two years of study in one is much easier administratively than is subject-matter acceleration, because no curriculum adjustment need be made after the child is placed in the higher grade.

Grade skipping was once much more prevalent than it is now although it is gradually regaining popularity (Wernick, 1992). Much of the skepticism surrounding grade skipping pertains to the student's social adjustment. Because gifted children are advanced developmentally and prefer the company of older children, much of this fear is unjustified. Highly gifted students can be skipped two or more years with no ill effects (Robinson & Noble, 1991; Stanley, 1979). Skipping the last year of elementary school and entering junior high a year early has been found to reduce adjustment problems.

Early entrance is a particularly useful option for girls (Kerr, 1991). Gifted girls are often ready for school earlier than boys because girls mature more rapidly. Before school the peer group is of mixed age. Establishing an older peer group from the beginning makes the child's adjustment easier than does grade skipping. Because girls seem more vulnerable to social pressures than boys, they are less willing to be accelerated (Fox, 1976); therefore, accelerating them between third and ninth grade is considered unwise. Early entrance to kindergarten and to college are more appropriate alternatives for them. Research indicates that early entrance is beneficial in most cases (Daurio, 1979; George, Cohn, & Stanley, 1979; Robinson & Weimer, 1991).

Enrichment in the Regular Classroom. Enrichment is the most popular alternative used with gifted children. Enrichment strategies include:

1. Individualized programming.
2. Independent study.
3. Ability grouping.
4. Cluster grouping. All gifted students at a grade level are placed with one teacher to facilitate differentiated instruction.
5. Flexible scheduling. Students attend class less often than peers, perhaps only four days each week.
6. Faster-paced, higher-level materials.
7. Field trips.
8. Community resource persons at school.

Much of what passes for enrichment is actually MOTS (more of the same). For example, a child might be asked to do 20 more division problems if he or she finishes the first 20 before the others. *Busywork is not enrichment.* The lack of regular classroom teacher training regarding the needs and methods of teaching gifted students reduces the possibility that true enrichment will occur in the regular classroom.

Special Classes. Various kinds of special classes are:

1. Honors classes and seminars.
2. Extra coursework.
3. Special course offerings (e.g., Junior Great Books).
4. Use of a resource room or itinerant teacher on a weekly basis.
5. Segregated "pullout" program for part of the day or week.
6. Full-time placement in a special class.
7. Special study centers.

8. Magnet schools (one may specialize in science, another in language arts; students choose to enroll in a school that will serve them best).
9. School within a school (a portion of the school is reserved for gifted students in specialized classes).
10. Specialized schools for the gifted (e.g., Bronx High School of Science).

Special classes enable the gifted to gather for instructional and social purposes. Gifted children need contact with each other to develop optimally. Special schools for the gifted may be established at low cost by converting a school with declining enrollment into a magnet school or a school within a school. Magnet schools are gaining popularity as part of the schools-of-choice movement.

Before-/After-School Options. Offerings before and after school and during lunch periods, weekends, and summers can provide other alternatives.

1. Extracurricular clubs.
2. Early-bird classes (special classes held before school).
3. Extended day.
4. Extended school year.
5. Saturday or after-school workshops, classes, excursions.
6. Summer courses.
7. Evening courses.

This student is both intelligent and highly creative.

Off-Campus Options. Gifted students can receive some of their instruction in the community through:

1. Mentorships.
2. Individual study with a community member.
3. Internships (working in the field with a specialist).
4. Outreach activities (programs developed for the gifted at local museums, colleges, businesses, etc.).
5. Residential summer institutes and Governor's Schools.
6. Community-based career education.
7. Student exchange programs.
8. Credit for educational experiences outside school (e.g., travel).

Mentoring is particularly important to the development of gifted children. The mentor acts as role model, counselor, tutor, friend, and guide to advanced experiences and insights in a field. Mentorships with local college professors, businesspeople, honors students, and other community members can be developed.

TEACHER CHARACTERISTICS AND STRATEGIES

A teacher need not be gifted to teach the gifted and talented, but he or she must have a certain level of intellectual power to follow the gifted child's thought processes. Renzulli's (1978) essential characteristics for giftedness—above-average intelligence, creativity, and task commitment—are more appropriate criteria for selecting teachers of the gifted.

Teaching gifted children is exciting. Their quick minds and creativity often carry lessons in unexpected directions. Teachers must be flexible enough to leave lesson plans behind and travel some uncharted paths with these students. Gifted children need teachers with high self-esteem; teachers must not be threatened by students who may surpass them intellectually. Teachers of the gifted cannot possibly answer all their questions accurately; it is far more important that they learn with their students. Teachers need enthusiasm and love of learning to inspire these qualities in their students. A good sense of humor also is essential to appreciate the students' sophisticated wit.

To deal with the high energy levels of the students and the increased demands of the position, teachers of the gifted have to be highly energetic. They have to be facilitators rather than directors of learning. Finally, they must be willing to devote extra time and effort to their teaching (Maker, 1975). Teaching the gifted is exhilarating, but it isn't easy.

In supervising teachers of the gifted, special educators, early childhood educators, and elementary school teachers, I find some rather consistent differences between the teaching strategies master teachers of the gifted and talented employ and those other teachers use.

Methods of providing information are highly similar among all groups, but teachers of the gifted devote less time to "instruction" and more to *questioning*. Questioning patterns are markedly different. Teachers of the gifted tend to ask many divergent questions (questions with many answers), whereas other teachers ask almost exclusively convergent questions (questions with only one right answer). Teachers of the gifted use questions to stimulate discussion, clarify the meaning of student responses, expand students' thoughts, or increase student involvement. They also attempt to understand thought processes by asking questions such as, "What made you think that?"

Feedback techniques are also quite different. Most teachers rely heavily on feedback. They respond verbally and nonverbally to every student response. Some teachers of the gifted, however, intentionally avoid giving feedback to students. Their behavior is like that of counselors: attentive and interested but nonjudgmental. This strategy usually increases interaction between students, stimulates student self-evaluation, and reduces dependency on teacher reinforcement.

When teachers of the gifted make use of feedback, it is not in the form of stereotyped response patterns. Discussions resemble adult conversations instead of question-and-answer periods. These teachers also control the classroom differently, using humor, nonverbal cues, and unobtrusive ways to refocus students' attention on the task at hand. They tend to include themselves among the culprits with statements such as, "*We* had better get back to the subject or we won't finish with this section today," rather than "*You* had better get back to work."

Teachers of the gifted seem to enjoy their students as interesting people. This is evident in the conversations that occur before and after class and at transition periods. They often discuss issues unrelated to school, freely exchanging viewpoints. These teachers also reveal personal information about themselves to their students. Often, a high level of mutual trust develops. Teachers of the gifted are willing to change roles with their students, to be taught by them, especially when computers are involved (Silverman, 1980).

Gifted students perform their best when they are presented with questions and situations that have many correct answers and many paths to a solution. They respond exceptionally well to discovery techniques that provide them with the opportunity to be detectives, hypothesis testers, and problem solvers. In the *discovery method*, an intriguing problem is presented to the students; they then must discover the means by which to solve the problem. This usually involves discovering a pattern or a relationship, a natural ability for the gifted.

Guided discovery is an inductive approach to learning; the student is presented with several illustrations of a rule and is asked to infer the underlying principle. In *deductive learning*, the principle is presented first, and the student is asked to apply the rule to several specific examples. Mathematics books that show a model of the solution followed by 50 similar problems represent the deductive approach. Exercises that require the student to "guess the rule" utilize the *inductive approach*. Figure 9.6 shows examples of the inductive approach to learning.

The difficulty of the task must not exceed the child's confidence level. A series of problems should be arranged from simplest to most difficult. The child learns how to succeed at the task by solving the simpler problems. The same method then can be applied to the more difficult problems. Discovery learning heightens the child's ability

	□	△		□	△
$5 \infty 8 = 8 \infty 5$	3	9		3	2
$4 \infty 6 = 6 \infty 4$	4	12		6	4
$5 \infty 9 = 9 \infty 5$					
What is the principle here?	What is the rule?			What is the rule?	

● **FIGURE 9.6**

Examples of inductive exercises

to perceive and express abstract relationships, to analyze, to hypothesize, and to verify hypotheses.

INSTRUCTIONAL MATERIALS

Basic textbooks and workbooks are designed with the average learner in mind. The pace of the materials, types of questions asked, and level of difficulty are usually inappropriate for the gifted child. Nevertheless, materials stressing higher-level thinking skills can be located, adapted, or created. Numerous curricular materials in all subject areas employ the discovery or inquiry approach to learning. Inquiry training materials in science, discovery lessons in mathematics, critical thinking exercises in social studies, Orff and Suzuki techniques in music, and Junior Great Books' questioning patterns in reading and language arts are all possibilities. Regular, deductive materials can be converted into inductive learning experiences simply by presenting the illustrations first, then asking students to discover the principle. The following verbs (in italics) indicate the types of questions that produce higher-level thinking in children:

1. Analysis (taking apart): *analyze, compare, contrast, classify, categorize, examine.*
2. Synthesis (putting together): *create, invent, compose, predict, construct, design, imagine, improve, produce, propose.*
3. Evaluation (judging): *judge, select, decide, critique, justify, verify, debate, assess, recommend, argue, evaluate.*

Another way to modify instructional materials is to present a model and have the students create their own versions of it. In this way they have the opportunity to be creative, to produce something original, to apply what they have learned, and to create curricular activities for others (e.g., puzzles, learning centers).

Materials are not as important as is information about how to obtain materials when they are needed. A teacher of the gifted should be a good librarian, able to help students locate information on any topic of their interest. The teacher should also be a "people collector." Human resources are just as necessary as material resources. One helpful idea is to keep file cards on the talents and interests of parents and other family members who are willing to help.

In brief, materials should have the following characteristics:

1. *Open-ended*, allowing the student to pursue knowledge in his or her own way.
2. *Intrinsically interesting* to the student.
3. Focus on *active learning*, encouraging the student to construct and create.
4. *Motivational*, increasing the student's desire to pursue the subject area further.
5. *Thought-provoking*, rather than primarily factual, in its questions and experiences.
6. *Discovery-oriented*, allowing the student to find relationships.
7. *Nonstereotyped* in sex roles.

The two examples of teacher-made materials in mathematics in Exercise A can be used for both assessment and programming. When administered to students at the beginning of the math program, they can give evidence of the creativity and analytical ability a student brings to the program. As ideas are shared in the group in response to Exercise A, the opportunities for instruction are limitless.

THE STATE OF THE ART

In some ways gifted education is similar to where handicapped education was in the mid-1960s. A groundswell of concern for the gifted is mounting nationwide. In recent years, considerable media coverage has been bringing attention to this neglected group.

Parents are beginning to realize they can ask the schools for more individual attention to the needs of their gifted children. Where schools have been unresponsive, there have been some appeals to litigation. Following the models set by parents of children with handicaps, parents of the gifted are banding together in advocacy groups to help schools provide services to their children and to exert pressure on school boards and state legislators to upgrade programs. In some districts, individual schools have taken the initiative to provide fast-paced, accelerated coursework for gifted students. Other districts have responded to the needs of these students only when state mandates require it. The need is evident for mandated special services for the gifted in every state.

There is still a large gap between research findings on giftedness and practices employed in the schools. Gifted children develop and learn at an accelerated pace. We know they are capable of learning a great deal more—and more rapidly—than they currently are learning in most school settings. We know that we can accurately identify gifted children early in life, and that this early intervention is as essential to their development as it is to the development of children with disabilities. We know that gifted children learn best and have better emotional and social adjustment when they are grouped, at least part of the time, with other gifted children. We know that, in the vast majority of cases, acceleration has proven helpful rather than harmful to them. Yet, these research findings rarely are acted upon in the public schools.

Exercise A

Have students write down all the unusual ways they can think of, within 2 minutes, to arrive at the number 12. At the end of that time, find out the following:

1. Who had the most answers (fluency)?
2. Who had the answer with the greatest number of operations (elaboration)?
3. Who had an answer that no one else in the group thought of (originality)?
4. How many different operations, systems, and ideas were used to depict the number (flexibility)? (Some students use only addition. Some use the basic four operations, plus bases, exponents, Roman numerals, pictures, etc.)

Exercise B

Can you find the pattern? Strategy: Ask yourself what you did to the first number to get the second one. Write that above the line *in between* the two numbers.

1, $^{+2}$ 3, $^{+2}$ 5, $^{+2}$ _____, $^{+2}$ 9, $^{+2}$ _____, $^{+2}$ _____

Look at the pattern above the line. What would you call that kind of pattern? What other patterns occur in these number sequences?

1, 3, 5, _____, 9, _____, _____, _____

17, 14, _____, 8, _____, _____, _____, _____

5, 1, 5, 2, _____, 3, _____, _____, _____

0, 1, 3, 6, 10, _____, _____, _____, _____

4, 10, 16, _____, 28, _____, _____, _____

5, 10, _____, 40, _____, 160, _____

42, 35, _____, 21, _____, _____, 0, _____, _____

3, _____, 27, 81, _____, _____, _____

_____, 4, _____, 16, _____, 64, _____, _____

8, 4, 9, 5, _____, _____, 11, _____, _____, _____

2, 4, _____, 5, _____, 6, 5, _____, _____, _____

1, 4, 9, 16, _____, _____, _____, _____

8, 12, 11, 15, _____, 17, _____, _____, 14, _____

6, 7, 2, 5, _____, 5, 0, 7, 2 *Bonus (must show pattern above line for points)

8, 12, 12, 16, _____, 12, 4, 8, 2 *Bonus (must show pattern above line for points)

Can you make up a pattern?

_____, _____, _____, _____, _____, _____, _____

Perhaps in time the combined efforts of parents and educators to stimulate greater awareness of the needs of the gifted will result in improved programming. Legislation, litigation, and concern for national defense likely will play major roles in shifting attitudes toward the gifted. Just as federal and state mandates to serve those with handicaps led to special funding, training, certification, and programming, mandates will be needed if we hope to reach the majority of gifted children. Where mandates exist, parents can resort to litigation if a school is not in compliance with the law. As it becomes apparent that our global ranking is tied to the education of our brightest students, national attention may once more focus on the gifted, and major educational reforms are likely to follow.

ISSUES AND PROJECTIONS FOR THE FUTURE

A continuing controversy in the field of gifted education concerns the nature of giftedness itself and the methods by which it should be assessed. The current trend is toward the concept of multiple intelligences. This focus suggests abandoning ability testing in favor of assessments of performance, such as portfolios. The term "giftedness" is replaced with "talent," as talent can be developed in the environment, whereas giftedness implies innate qualities.

Although this view of giftedness sounds more egalitarian and inclusive, and certainly is more palatable in today's political climate, it raises certain questions. For example, how will the highly gifted child who simply cannot perform meaningless, redundant assignments be identified? Or the culturally diverse child whose cultural values are not represented in the curriculum? Or the gifted child with learning disabilities who has difficulty performing simple, sequential tasks? Or the underachiever who learns material differently from the way it is traditionally taught? Or the gifted girl who purposely gets B's to keep her friends? Or the creative child in the uncreative classroom? Or the introvert who does not perform in large groups? None of these children is likely to reveal outstanding performance scholastically or in a talent domain but could be recognized on an ability measure as having extraordinary abstract reasoning abilities. Ironically, IQ tests are opposed on the grounds of cultural bias, yet performance criteria are even more culturally biased because they depend more upon environmental exposure.

As the field matures, interest likely will increase in special populations of gifted learners who may not excel academically. Underachievers, gifted children with learning disabilities, gifted girls, the exceptionally gifted, and gifted students from culturally diverse backgrounds need more attention in identification procedures (Richert, 1982) and program planning.

UNDERACHIEVERS

Tannenbaum (1983) likened underachievement to a skin rash, as both have multiple causes. A skin rash can signify anything from an encounter with poison ivy to a brain tumor; therefore, a specialist has to be called upon to diagnose it properly. Under-achievement also requires comprehensive diagnosis. The specialist has to determine the onset and duration of the problem. Were motivational problems apparent before the child entered school, or do they occur only in relation to school? If this child was always difficult, family counseling may be indicated. If the problems began when the child was enrolled in a specific class, a different placement may resolve the problem. Long-term underachievement is more difficult to reverse than short-term motivational problems; therefore, early intervention should be stressed. Many underachievers actu-ally have hidden learning disabilities that can be detected only through professional assessment.

GIFTED/LEARNING DISABLED

About one-sixth of the children brought to the Gifted Development Center for assess-ment of giftedness have hidden learning disabilities. Recognizing learning disabilities in gifted children is difficult because their abstract reasoning abilities enable them to compensate for and mask their weaknesses. Their learning disabilities may depress their IQ scores so they do not qualify for gifted programs. Discrepancies in perfor-mance can reveal hidden learning disabilities: Verbal/Performance differences in excess of 14 points; 7-point discrepancies between high and low subtest scores; 25-point differences between ability and achievement scores.

Many gifted/learning disabled children are visual-spatial learners who have diffi-culty processing auditory sequential material, such as phonics, spelling, and phone numbers. Through extensive interviews, we discovered that the majority of these children had a history of chronic early ear infections or a parent who had similar learning difficulties in childhood (Silverman, Chitwood, & Waters, 1986). Some of the interventions that seem helpful include using computers for instruction as well as to complete assignments; visualization techniques; a sight approach to reading; advanced conceptual material; and de-emphasis on rote memorization and timed tests (Silverman, 1989).

GIFTED GIRLS

Gifted girls and boys begin life in equal numbers, but by junior high school, two-thirds of the identified gifted students are male and one-third are female (Silverman, 1986c). Why do gifted girls gradually disappear? The main culprit seems to be the socialization process. From early childhood on, gifted boys are called "leaders," whereas girls with similar leadership abilities are labeled "bossy." The most vulnerable period for girls seems to be adolescence. Girls' confidence in their abilities is particularly fragile during the teen years; they often attribute their successes to hard work, luck, or teachers liking them, rather than to high abilities. Unfortunately, teachers tend to reinforce this view, using the term "overachiever" to describe high-achieving girls who put effort into their schoolwork. The term "overachiever" is actually meaningless, as no one can achieve more than she is capable of achieving! But the put-down leaves a lasting impression on girls, undermining their belief in their talents.

Gifted girls should be identified in the preschool and primary years, before they go underground. They should be considered for early entrance to school; grouped with other gifted girls for support; strongly encouraged to take a challenging program of coursework in high school, including 4 years of mathematics; exposed to gifted women who have made various life and career choices; and provided opportunities to work with mentors. Other suggestions for preserving giftedness in girls are presented in Kerr (1985, 1991) and Silverman (1986c, 1991, 1993).

EXCEPTIONALLY GIFTED

The child's special needs increase in direct proportion to the extent of exceptionality. A child in the 120–130 IQ range fits into the school system decidedly better than a child in the 180–190 IQ range (Hollingworth, 1942). The highly gifted range has been variously defined as IQ scores in excess of 140, 145, or 150. Given the problems in gaining accurate assessment in this range, however, 140+ seems sufficient. Actually, many more exceptionally gifted children are in the population than would be predicted by the normal curve of distribution. At the Gifted Development Center, we have located more than 175 children with Binet IQs above 170. We have established a support group for families with children with IQs above 160 to keep the children from becoming socially isolated.

A research study currently is under way to learn as much as possible about this population. Families of these children are exploring various educational alternatives, including radical acceleration (2 or more years), simultaneous enrollment in several grade levels, private schools for the gifted, homeschooling, partial homeschooling and partial placement with agemates, and mentoring. An individualized program is essential for extraordinarily gifted students.

CULTURALLY DIVERSE

Gifted programs should be representative of the racial and ethnic composition of the school district. Students who score 2 standard deviations above cultural norms on *either* verbal or nonverbal measures should qualify for placement in programs, since some cultures stress verbal abilities whereas others emphasize spatial abilities. Peer nominations also are important in locating culturally diverse gifted students. Community leaders should be consulted to determine which gifts and talents are most valued in the community and which young people demonstrate these abilities. They may include leadership, responsibility, ingenuity, and resourcefulness; bilingual proficiency; excellent memory; rapid learning; keen sense of humor; emotional responsiveness; and creativity. Special considerations should be given to abilities demonstrated outside of school, such as assisting with a family business or helping to rear several siblings.

When auditions are part of the selection process (as in a fine arts program), they should be held in local churches or community centers. Gifted programs have to be responsive to the cultural values of the children selected and to celebrate the cultural diversity of the participants. Individual attention should be given to assure that the participants are successful. The richness of a culturally diverse milieu can have lasting benefits for all of the students (Hollingworth, 1930; Harris, 1992).

CONCLUSION AND SUMMARY

The field of gifted education has many unresolved issues. There is little agreement on who is gifted, which leads to confusion for the child. Children have been known to say, "I used to be gifted, but my school district doesn't have a program anymore." Giftedness is as real as retardation, but the methods used to identify and serve the gifted are shallow in comparison to those employed in every other field of exceptionality. No parent of a developmentally delayed child would agree to have a child placed in a program on the basis of group achievement tests, teacher recommendations, or grades, nor would it be feasible for a school to determine arbitrarily that 2% or 10% of the population will be labeled "retarded." These labels have a permanent impact on children's lives. Identifying a child as gifted implies a commitment to serve that child's needs, even during periods of budget cuts.

Those who educate the gifted must look to the rest of special education for guidance on appropriate methods of identification, educational delivery systems, and teacher certification. For the gifted to be served appropriately, more parents of gifted children must follow the lead of parents of children with disabilities in attaining national awareness, funding, and regulation of services. Parents and educators of children with disabilities and gifted children should form cooperative networks. Many children with disabilities have special gifts, and many gifted children have hidden handicaps that must be recognized and served. It is time for education of the gifted to become a national priority.

Whenever a society has chosen to nurture its most gifted individuals, it has realized its dreams. Today we have record-breaking athletes. We did this by nurturing the finest athletic talent in the country. Tomorrow we could solve many pressing social issues if we put the same investment into other abilities.

REFERENCES

Benbow, C. P. (1992). Everywhere but here! *The Gifted Child Today, 15*(2), 2–8.

Bloom, B. S. (Ed.). (1956). *Taxonomy of educational objectives: Handbook 1. Cognitive domain.* New York: David McKay.

Bloom, B. S. (Ed.). (1985). *Developing talent in young people.* New York: Ballantine Books.

Borland, J. H. (1986). IQ tests: Throwing out the bathwater, saving the baby. *Roeper Review, 8,* 163–167.

Columbus Group. (1991, July). Unpublished transcript of meeting of Columbus Group. Columbus, OH.

Council of State Directors of Programs for the Gifted. (1991). *The 1990 state of the states gifted and talented education report.* Augusta, ME: Maine Department of Education.

Dabrowski, K. (1972). *Psychoneurosis is not an illness.* London: Gryf.

Daurio, S. P. (1979). Educational enrichment versus acceleration: A review of the literature. In W. C. George, S. J. Cohn, and J. C. Stanley (Eds.), *Educating the gifted: Acceleration and enrichment* (pp. 13–63). Baltimore: Johns Hopkins University Press.

Delisle, J. R. (1990). The gifted adolescent at risk: Strategies and resources for suicide prevention among gifted youth. *Journal for the Education of the Gifted, 13,* 212–228.

Dickinson, R. M. (1970). *Caring for the gifted.* Boston: Christopher.

Emerick, L. J. (1992). Academic underachievement among the gifted: Students' perceptions of factors that reverse the pattern. *Gifted Child Quarterly, 36,* 140–146.

Feldhusen, J. F. (1992). Early admission and grade advancement for young gifted learners. *The Gifted Child Today, 15*(2), 45–49.

Feldhusen, J. F., & Moon, S. M. (1992). Grouping gifted students: Issues and concerns. *Gifted Child Quarterly, 36,* 62–66.

Feldman, D. H., with L. T. Goldsmith. (1986). *Nature's gambit: Child prodigies and the development of human potential.* New York: Basic Books.

Flynn, J. R. (1984). The mean IQ of Americans: Massive gains 1932 to 1978. *Psychological Bulletin, 95,* 29–51.

Fox, L. H. (1976). Sex differences in mathematical precocity: Bridging the gap. In D. P. Keating (Ed.), *Intellectual talent: Research and development* (pp. 183–214). Baltimore: Johns Hopkins University Press.

Gallagher, J. J. (1985). *Teaching the gifted child* (3rd ed.). Needham Heights, MA: Allyn & Bacon.

Gardner, H. (1983). *Frames of mind: The theory of multiple intelligences.* New York: Basic Books.

George, W. C., Cohn, S. J., & Stanley, J. C. (1979). *Educating the gifted: Acceleration and enrichment.* Baltimore: Johns Hopkins University Press.

Gillespie, W. J. (1982). *A national survey of urban gifted educational programs.* Unpublished doctoral dissertation, University of Denver.

Guilford, J. P. (1956). The structure of intellect. *Psychological Bulletin, 53,* 267–293.

Guilford, J. P. (1975). Varieties of creative giftedness, their measurement and development. *Gifted Child Quarterly, 19,* 107–121.

Harris, C. R. (1992). The fruits of early intervention: The Hollingworth group today. *Advanced Development, 4,* 91–104.

Hollingworth, L. S. (1930). Personality development of special class children. *University of Pennsylvania Bulletin. Seventeenth Annual Schoolmen's Week Proceedings, 30,* 442–446.

Hollingworth, L. S. (1942). *Children above 180 IQ Stanford-Binet: Origin and development.* Yonkers-on-Hudson, NY: World Book.

Institute for Staff Development. (1971). *Hilda Taba teaching strategies program.* Miami: Author.

Kaufman, A. S. (1992). Evaluation of the WISC–III and WPPSI–R for gifted children. *Roeper Review, 14,* 154–158.

Kerr, B. A. (1985). *Smart girls, gifted women.* Columbus, OH: Ohio Psychology.

Kerr, B. A. (1991). *A handbook for counseling the gifted and talented.* Alexandria, VA: American Counseling Association.

Kulik, J. A., & Kulik, C-L. C. (1991). Ability grouping and gifted students. In N. Colangelo & G. A. Davis (Eds.), *Handbook of gifted education* (pp. 178–196). Needham Heights, MA: Allyn & Bacon.

Maker, C. J. (1975). *Training teachers for the gifted and talented: A comparison of models.* Reston, VA: Council for Exceptional Children.

Maker, C. J. (1982). *Teaching models in education of the gifted.* Rockville, MD: Aspen.

Marland, S., Jr. (1972). *Education of the gifted and talented* (Report to the Congress of the United States by the U.S. Commissioner of Education). Washington, DC: U.S. Government Printing Office.

Martinson, R. A. (1974). *The identification of the gifted and talented.* Ventura, CA: Office of the Ventura County Superintendent of Schools.

Newland, T. E. (1976). *The gifted in socio-educational perspective.* Englewood Cliffs, NJ: Prentice Hall.

Passow, A. H. (1988). Educating gifted persons who are caring and concerned. *Roeper Review, 11,* 13–15,

Petersen, A. (1988). Adolescent development. *Annual Review of Psychology, 39,* 583–607.

Piechowski, M. M. (1979). Developmental potential. In N. Colangelo & R. Zaffrann (Eds.), *New voices in counseling the gifted* (pp. 25–67). Dubuque, IA: Kendall/Hunt.

Piechowski, M. M. (1991). Emotional development and emotional giftedness. In N. Colangelo & G. Davis (Eds.), *A handbook of gifted education* (pp. 285–306). Needham Heights, MA: Allyn & Bacon.

Pritchard, M. C. (1951). The contributions of Leta S. Hollingworth to the study of gifted children. In P. Witty (Ed.), *The gifted child* (pp. 47–85) (American Association for Gifted Children). Boston: D. C. Heath.

Renzulli, J. S. (1977). *The enrichment triad model: A guide for developing defensible programs for the gifted and talented.* Wethersfield, CT: Creative Learning Press.

Renzulli, J. S. (1978). What makes giftedness? Reexamining a definition. *Phi Delta Kappan, 184,* 180–185.

Renzulli, J. S. (1980). Will the gifted child movement be alive and well in 1990? *Gifted Child Quarterly, 24,* 3–9.

Renzulli, J. S., & Hartman, R. (1971). Scale for rating behavioral characteristics of superior students. *Exceptional Children, 38,* 243–248.

Richert, E. S. (1982). *National report on identification: Assessment and recommendations for comprehensive identification of gifted and talented youth.* Sewell, NJ: Educational Improvement Center–South.

Robinson, N. M., & Noble, K. D. (1991). Social-emotional development and adjustment of gifted children. In M. C. Wang, M. C. Reynolds, & H. J. Walberg (Eds.), *Handbook of special education: Research and practice, Vol. 4: Emerging programs* (pp. 57–76). New York: Pergamon Press.

Robinson, N. M., & Weimer, L. J. (1991). Selection of candidates for early admission to kindergarten and first grade. In W. T. Southern & E. D. Jones (Eds.), *The academic acceleration of gifted children* (pp. 29–50). New York: Teachers College Press.

Roedell, W. C. (1984). Vulnerabilities of highly gifted children. *Roeper Review, 6,* 127–130.

Roeper, A. (1988). Should educators of the gifted and talented be more concerned with world issues? *Roeper Review, 11,* 12–13.

Rogers, K. B. (1991). *The relationship of grouping practices to the education of the gifted and talented learner: Executive summary* (Report No. 1). Storrs, CT: National Research Center on the Gifted and Talented.

Seeley, K. R., & Mahoney, A. R. (1981). Giftedness and delinquency: A small beginning toward some answers. In R. E. Clasen et al., *Programming for the gifted, talented and creative: Models and methods* (2nd ed., pp. 247–258). Madison: University of Wisconsin Extension.

Silverman, L. K. (1976). The gifted: The next frontier for inservice education. *Inservice Consultor, 3,* 1–7.

Silverman, L. K. (1980, October). *How are gifted teachers different from other teachers?* Proceedings of the 27th Annual Convention of the National Association for Gifted Children, Minneapolis.

Silverman, L. K. (1983). Personality development: The pursuit of excellence. *Journal for the Education of the Gifted, 6*(1), 5–19.

Silverman, L. K. (1986a). The IQ controversy: Conceptions and misconceptions. *Roeper Review, 8,* 136–140.

Silverman, L. K. (1986b). Parenting young gifted children. In J. R. Whitmore (Ed.), *Intellectual giftedness in young children: Recognition and development* (pp. 73–87). New York: Haworth Press.

Silverman, L. K. (1986c). What happens to the gifted girl? In C. J. Maker (Ed.), *Critical issues in gifted education: Vol. 1. Defensible programs for the gifted* (pp. 43–89). Rockville, MD: Aspen.

Silverman, L. K. (1989). Invisible gifts, invisible handicaps. *Roeper Review, 22,* 37–42.

Silverman, L. K. (1991). Helping gifted girls reach their potential. *Roeper Review, 13,* 122–123.

Silverman, L. K. (1993). Social development, leadership, and gender issues. In L. K. Silverman (Ed.), *Counseling the gifted and talented* (pp. 291–327). Denver: Love.

Silverman, L. K., Chitwood, D. G., & Waters, J. L. (1986). Parents as identifiers of the gifted. *Topics in Early Childhood Special Education, 6*(1), 23–38.

Silverman, L. K., & Kearney, K. (1992). Don't throw away the old Binet. *Understanding Our Gifted, 4*(4), 1, 8–10.

Slavin, R. E. (1990). Cooperative learning and the gifted: Who benefits? *Journal for the Education of the Gifted, 14,* 28–30.

Stanley, J. C. (1979). The case for extreme educational acceleration of intellectually brilliant youths. In J. C. Gowan, J. Khatena, & E. P. Torrance (Eds.), *Educating the ablest: A book of readings* (pp. 93–102). Itasca, IL: F. E. Peacock.

Sternberg, R. J. (1986). Identifying the gifted through IQ: Why a little bit of knowledge is a dangerous thing. *Roeper Review, 8,* 143–147.

Stevenson, H. W., & Stigler, J. W. (1992). *The learning gap: Why our schools are failing and what we can learn from Japanese and Chinese education.* New York: Summit.

Supplee, P. L. (1990). *Reaching the gifted underachiever: Program strategy and design.* New York: Teachers College Press.

Tannenbaum, A. J. (1983). *Gifted children: Psychological and educational perspectives.* New York: Macmillan.

Terman, L. M. (Ed.). (1925). *Genetic studies of genius: Vol. 1. Mental and physical traits of a thousand gifted children.* Stanford, CA: Stanford University Press.

U. S. Department of Education. (1978). *Gifted and Talented Children's Education Act of 1978, Title IX-A of the Elementary and Secondary Education Act of 1965* (PL 95–961). Washington, DC: U.S. Government Printing Office.

U. S. Department of Education. Office of Educational Research and Improvement. (1993). *National excellence: A case for developing America's talent.* Washington, DC: U.S. Government Printing Office.

Ward, V. S. (1985). Giftedness and personal development: Theoretical considerations. *Roeper Review, 8,* 6–10.

Wernick, S. (1992, July 8). Interest renewed in grade skipping as inexpensive way to aid the gifted. *The New York Times,* p. 17.

Whitmore, J. R. (1980). *Giftedness, conflict and underachievement.* Needham Heights, MA: Allyn & Bacon.

Whitmore, J. R. (1989). Re-examining the concept of underachievement. *Understanding Our Gifted, 2*(1), 1, 7–9.

Williams, F. E. (1970). *Classroom ideas for encouraging thinking and feeling.* Buffalo, NY: D.O.K. Publications.

Zigler, E., & Farber, E. A. (1985). Commonalities between the intellectual extremes: Giftedness and mental retardation. In F. D. Horowitz & M. O'Brien (Eds.), *The gifted and the talented: Developmental perspectives* (pp. 387–408). Washington, DC: American Psychological Association.

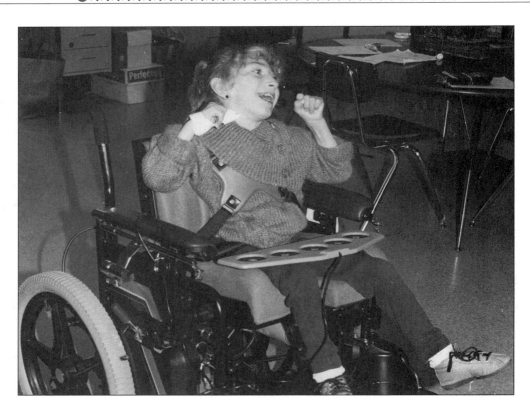

10

SEVERE AND MULTIPLE

DISABILITIES

ELLIN SIEGEL-CAUSEY,
BARBARA GUY, AND DOUG GUESS

Joe, who is 15, lives in the inner city of a large metropolis. Each morning, after boarding the bus, Joe travels 18 blocks to his local high school, located in the middle of a busy, commercial area. There he attends homeroom, freshman speech, and physical education with students his age. Joe looks forward to school each day. He has friends in his classes, and he also enjoys the company of some "special friends," who sit with him during lunchtime in the large, often noisy, cafeteria.

Joe's friends are, indeed, special. They realize Joe has difficulty doing things they take for granted. Joe, who is considered to have severe and multiple disabilities, has limited use of his arms and legs. He requires a special lift to get his wheelchair onto the bus each morning, and someone to push it. Joe uses a specially designed board with pictures on it to communicate to others, because motor impairments prevent him from speaking clearly. He needs assistance in learning and in remembering things.

Radiating a warm smile, he laughs a lot at the things most people his age consider funny. He really enjoys being around others and works hard in school. Joe is learning to be as independent as possible and has the help of those around him to achieve this goal. A teacher, specially trained to assist Joe, helps Joe's regular education teachers adapt their lessons to meet his needs. For example, in homeroom, Joe is responsible for passing out the daily minutes and taking attendance. This gives him practice in reaching and grasping and applying the mathematical concept of one-to-one correspondence (one person to each desk). The special education teacher or a paraprofessional accompanies Joe each day to a nearby factory where he works. He also spends some of his school day in the community, learning how to buy things in stores, order meals at a fast-food restaurant, and take part in other enjoyable activities like his nondisabled peers.

During some parts of the day, an occupational therapist works with Joe in class, the community, or at work. This therapist, in conjunction with Joe's teachers, designs better ways for Joe to use his arms and hands. For example, she designed a wide handle for silverware, to help Joe grasp his eating utensils. A speech therapist visits Joe's classes three times each week to assist Joe's special education teacher in selecting pictures for his communication board and provide suggestions for helping Joe and the people he interacts with to use the board to communicate with each other. The teachers and the therapists all work together with Joe's parents to design the best possible program for Joe, one that will help him function more independently not only in the school but at home and in the community as well.

J oe's case is not unique. Children like him—those with severe and multiple disabilities, who live in both urban and rural areas throughout the country—are now attending special classes in regular community schools and attending regular classrooms in their neighborhood school. In these classes a variety of professions and disciplines provide them special services. These children need many opportunities to interact daily with their age peers who do not have disabilities.

Prior to enactment of PL 94–142 and PL 99–457, the Education for All Handicapped Children Act and a later act covering early intervention, Joe's life would have been quite different. He might have stayed at home all day cared for by his parents or some other caregiver. More likely, however, he would have been placed in a large state institution for the mentally retarded, or perhaps a special, self-contained private school, if his parents could afford it. In either case, the chance to live at home and go to the regular school would have been quite slim, if not nonexistent. He would not have had "special friends," nor would he have the opportunity to experience work and daily life in the community.

PL 94–142 likely has had the greatest impact on children who, like Joe, have severe and multiply disabling conditions. This law, accompanied by an extensive investment of federal funds and programs (cf. Noel, Burke, & Valdivieso, 1985), provided for several major national policy changes in the education and treatment of school-age children with severe and multiple disabilities.

First, it guaranteed the rights of all school-age children, regardless of the severity of their disability, to a *free and appropriate education* extending throughout the regular school day. Thus, Joe's severely disabling condition could not be used as a reason to exclude him from public school.

Second, PL 94–142 specified that such education should take place in the *least restrictive educational environment*. For Joe, the least restrictive educational placement is a regular elementary school where he has the opportunity to interact with nondisabled peers.

Third, this federal legislation extended to each child with a disability the right to any *special services* needed to help him or her develop to the maximum extent possible. In Joe's case, the services of an occupational therapist and a speech therapist were essential to his total educational and training program.

Other facets of PL 94–142 are important to Joe's educational program. These include participation of his parents in the IEP process, provision for transportation to and from school, and identification and monitoring of educational goals and objectives to meet Joe's special needs.

PL 99–457, Part H, enacted in 1986, added to PL 94–142 by establishing a new program to encourage each state to establish a comprehensive, multidisciplinary system of early intervention services. The Part H program provides for children from birth through age 2 who meet eligibility criteria as having developmental delays, diagnosed conditions, or, at the option of the state, at risk of substantial delay. Therefore, today, Joe and other children like him are eligible for family-focused, multidisciplinary, comprehensive services beginning at birth. PL 99–457, Part B, provides mandatory services at age 3.

CURRENT PRACTICES

Today, educational practices for students with severe and multiple disabling conditions are oriented heavily toward preparing them to function to the maximum extent possible in home, school, and community settings. The emphasis for these students in particular is on preparing them to participate in as many postschool community settings as possible. These practices imply several components that did not exist in the past and are not always emphasized by the general field of special education for other types of disability areas.

First, the *instructional content* of programs for students with severe and multiple disabilities now emphasizes teaching life skills that will be needed to function in future environments. This includes basic instruction in areas such as feeding, dressing, communicating, and interacting socially with others. As the student gets older, instruction expands to include community living skills, such as shopping, leisure-time activities, riding a bus, ordering food in restaurants, taking care of personal needs, and, especially, work opportunities. Academic areas such as reading and writing, or their adaptations, are taught in the context of the community living skill. For example, some students may be taught to recognize signs such as "walk–don't walk" and "men–women" in the community and "office" or "restroom" in the school building. Other students might be taught to recognize pictures or symbols rather than the words.

A second area of difference from previous educational practices is the *method of instruction*. In the past, instruction was delivered largely in *massed trials* within the classroom, using materials matched to students' *mental ages* rather than chronological age. An older adolescent, for example, learned how to place rings on a peg and practice this repeatedly (massed trials), rather than a more age-appropriate, useful skill such as inserting money into a soft-drink machine to obtain a drink. Today, direct teaching of life skills in the community is an important component of the educational process. The need for this type of instruction becomes clear when considering the learning characteristics common in this population of exceptional learners (to be discussed later). Educational practices today, in essence, stress the teaching of chronologically age-appropriate skills in the context of natural environments (including the community). Instruction takes place at precisely those times when the behaviors typically occur for anyone.

HISTORICAL EDUCATIONAL AND LEGISLATIVE CHANGES

Several positive things have happened since enactment of PL 94–142 in 1975 and the more recent enactment of 99–457, Part H. Today, far more students with severe and multiple disabilities are being provided with educational services in classrooms all across the country, and many of the services begin at birth in hospitals and homes. Although school-aged children still may be in classrooms that are in segregated settings, such as state institutions and self-contained schools in communities, the increase in number of students now being provided with extensive education opportunities is impressive.

The 1990 passage of the Americans with Disabilities Act (ADA), PL 101–336, extends the principles introduced in PL 94–142 by providing civil rights protection for *all* individuals with disabilities. ADA specifies that private employers, telecommunication carriers, and public services, accommodations, and transportation systems cannot refuse or exclude service to people because of their disability. In this act the term *disability* is defined to include: (a) people who have a life disability, (b) people who no longer have a physical or mental impairment but who are discriminated against because they have a record of the condition, and (c) people who are regarded as having an impairment but the perceived impairment does not limit any major life activity. Enactment of this act in 1992 should assist graduates of special education to make a successful transition to community life.

Other changes that will affect the lives of students with severe disabilities include the development of teacher training programs and advocacy groups specific to the needs of these students. The increase in number of educational institutions that now provide teacher certification programs has grown from around six in the early 1970s to programs in almost every state. In addition, the number of states that now require approved credentials for teachers of students with severe and multiple disabilities has increased. According to a survey reported by Geiger and Justen (1983), 21 states now have established certification requirements.

The Association for Persons with Severe Handicaps (TASH), established in 1974, is a major positive addition to the field. Approximately 7,000 teachers, parents, administrators, and related service providers function as a major advocacy organization. TASH now has 37 state chapters, holds a yearly national conference, and disseminates a quarterly professional journal containing research reports, theoretical discussions, and best-practice approaches to education and treatment. In addition, TASH is actively involved in court actions and legal suits supporting the rights and humane treatment of persons with severe and multiple disabilities.

On the less positive side, their integration and acceptance is far from complete. A proportionately high percentage of residents in state institutions have severe and multiple disabilities. Segregated schools for students with severe and multiple disabilities are still being built, and considerable resistance still is found among public school administrators, and even among some special educators, to accept students with severely disabling conditions into the regular schools. Finally, many special education programs throughout the country do not offer quality instruction for these students. This, coupled with a chronic teacher shortage in many states, and especially in rural areas, illustrates a field of special education in need of change even today.

STATUS OF OUR EFFECTIVENESS

Both the technology and the pedagogy involved in educating and treating students with severely disabling conditions have improved immensely since enactment of PL 94–142. Yet, we are short of effectively meeting the complex educational needs of these students.

In many respects, our expectations have not been met. The kinds of educational outcomes we are seeing do not match the equal educational opportunities we are committed to for these students. The rate of substantive improvement in their overall growth and development has remained exceedingly slow, even in programs that utilize fully current, best-practice educational approaches. This is evident especially in students with the most pronounced disabling conditions.

In spite of the educational shortcomings, a sense of optimism remains. New treatment and education approaches will be discovered and developed. Our attempts to improve educational interventions are still relatively new for this population of exceptional children. Also, we are now trying to educate and train individuals who in past years were ignored, considered in many respects to be hopelessly disabled.

EDUCATIONAL DEFINITIONS AND TERMINOLOGY

Problems in definition have existed ever since this population was first recognized in the field of special education in 1974. Various terms are commonly found in the literature, including severely handicapped, profoundly retarded, severely retarded, and multiply handicapped. As Sailor and Guess (1983) noted, this "has the troublesome distinction of being 'everybody who is not someone else' " (p. 5). These exceptional children have been defined according to disability characteristics, service needs, and the extent of their functional retardation.

In 1974, an early definition of persons with severe and multiple disabilities was provided by the Bureau of Education for the Handicapped (U.S. Office of Education, 1975), now the Office of Special Education Programs. This definition was based on a detailed description of *disability characteristics* commonly associated with this group of exceptional children. Sailor and Haring (1977) provided a definition based upon the types of special education *service needs* of students with severe and multiple disabling conditions; it focused on the areas of instruction the student needs, especially in basic skills such as communicating and self-help. A third attempt to define this population was based on the concept of *functional retardation* (Guess & Mulligan, 1982). Functional retardation was not intended as a descriptor for categorizing students; rather, it acknowledged the heterogeneity of this group of students and the need for programmatic instruction with environmental modification.

At present, no generally agreed-upon educational definition exists for students with severe and multiple disabilities. Indeed, definitions vary considerably among states, and likely among school districts within states as well. A survey by Geiger and Justen (1983) showed that 70% of the states did, however, define these students in some way, and their teacher certification requirements were based upon these definitions.

PREVALENCE AND INCIDENCE

The challenges involved in defining this group of students make it difficult to estimate prevalence and incidence figures. The U.S. Office of Education (1975) determined that about 2.3% of the school-aged population was mentally retarded. Of this number, an estimated 0.6% was "deaf/blind and other multihandicapped." Gast and Berkler (1981) maintain that one in 1,000 of the total population can be categorized as having severe and multiple disabilities. Thus, in a city of 100,000, the incidence of individuals with severe and multiple disabilities (those born with the disability) might be approximately 100.

ETIOLOGY

Conditions that produce severe and multiple disabilities necessarily have complex and extensive sources. In this book we can cover only some general, and certainly not complete, medical factors. Further information can be found in Batshaw and Perret (1981, 1986), Blackman (1990), Bleck and Nagel (1982), and Ensher and Clark (1986). These books, intended for the nonmedical service provider, discuss causative factors, specific syndromes, and related medical conditions and treatment for a variety of disabling conditions that occur among children. After reviewing the etiologies of the population of the severely and multiply disabled, Snell (1982) discovered that approximately 75% of cases had some type of organic cause, 21% were of unknown cause, and the remaining 5% were attributed to other conditions. Most of these conditions occur prior to or during birth.

PRENATAL CAUSES

Severe and multiple disabilities have two major prenatal causes: (a) various types of genetic abnormalities, and (b) teratogens (agents that cause malformations in developing embryos).

Genetic Abnormalities. First, genetic abnormalities can be differentiated by three *chromosomal deviancies* during cell division: (a) nondisjunction, (b) deletion, and (c) translocation. *Nondisjunction* occurs when the chromosomes divide unequally, exemplified by one form of Down syndrome caused by an extra #21 chromosome. Children born with Down syndrome as a result of nondisjunction have 47 chromosomes rather than the normal 46. *Deletion* occurs when segments of chromosomes are pulled off and lost during cell division. The Cri-du-chat syndrome is an example of deletion; a portion of the #5 chromosome is lost during cell division. This condition can produce severe mental retardation, accompanied by microcephaly (small head circumference), delayed physical growth, and a cat-like cry during infancy. *Translocation* occurs when segments of chromosomes are pulled off but transfer to another chromosome. Batshaw and Perret (1981) reported that about 2 in 500 newborns have a chromosomal abnormality associated with nondisjunction, deletion, or translocation, and that at least one syndrome is associated with each of the 23 pairs of chromosomes. Most of these syndromes, however, do not result in severe and multiple disabilities.

A second major type of chromosomal abnormality that causes genetic defects results from *chance*, or from *external causes* such as drugs and radiation. In these errors the DNA (deoxyribonucleic acid) of a single gene might lead to production of a malfunctioning enzyme. The mutations become part of the genetic code and are transmitted from parent(s) to child across generations. Batshaw and Perret (1981) reported more than 2,000 single-gene inherited diseases and conditions. Again, however, only a relatively small number of these genetic defects results in severe and multiple disabilities. In one type, termed *autosomal recessive*, both parents must carry the abnormal gene for the child to be affected. An associated syndrome is phenylketonuria (PKU), an enzyme deficiency that may result in profound mental retardation if not treated early in life. Fortunately, a mandatory newborn screening procedure can detect PKU at birth and, with appropriate dietary treatment, mental retardation can be prevented. In another type, *autosomal dominant*, just one parent can have the abnormal gene for the disorder to be manifested in offspring. Crouzon's disease and Apert's syndrome are the result of autosomal dominant genetic disorders and may, in some cases, produce severe mental retardation.

A third type of genetic disorder affects the *sex-linked chromosomes* and usually does not involve mental retardation. One exception is the Lesch-Nyhan syndrome, a degenerative disorder of the nervous system that results in profound mental retardation, self-injurious behavior, and progressive cerebral palsy.

Teratogens. Outside agents or conditions that cause malformations in developing embryos include radiation, virus-related infections, and drugs. Among the viral infections, congenital rubella often leads to severe and multiple disabilities. Rubella syndrome is associated with women who contract German measles during pregnancy, especially, the first trimester. Children born with this disorder often have visual and hearing impairments, mental retardation, and congenital heart disease. At present, vaccination is provided routinely, even though sporadic cases still might be expected to occur (Bleck, 1982b). Other viral infections include syphilis, herpes virus, toxoplasmosis, and cytomegalovirus. Drugs and other chemical substances such as alcohol and anticonvulsant medicine also can cause severely disabling conditions in the fetus if the pregnant mother ingests them.

PERINATAL CAUSES

Conditions during birth can affect the mother or the child. Maternal factors during birth include toxemia (a condition characterized by high blood pressure, abnormal amount of fluid in body tissues, and protein in the urine), premature detachment of the placenta, and structural abnormalities of the uterus or pelvis (Batshaw & Perret, 1981). In some cases the baby's head is too big to pass through the mother's pelvis, depriving the baby of oxygen during prolonged labor. Cesarean delivery can prevent oxygen deprivation.

POSTNATAL CAUSES

Several conditions following birth also can result in severe and multiple disabilities. They include childhood infections such as meningitis and encephalitis, and environmental agents such as severe head trauma, lack of oxygen (e.g., near drowning), and lead poisoning. Cerebral palsy is not a cause for severe, multiple disabilities but it is commonly associated with these impairments.

SEVERE CEREBRAL PALSY

A discussion of etiology in relation to severe and multiple disabilities has to take into account the condition of cerebral palsy, which is commonly associated with severe and multiple disabilities. By definition and common usage, cerebral palsy is a nonprogressive disorder of movement or posture that begins in childhood and is caused by a malfunctioning of, or damage to, the brain (cerebral dysfunction) (Bleck, 1982a. p. 59).

Cerebral palsy usually is acquired either prior to or during birth. Prenatal factors that can result in damage to the brain include metabolic disorders, lack of oxygen to the unborn child, maternal infections, and Rh incompatibility. Perinatal causes include birth trauma and lack of oxygen during delivery. Head injuries, brain hemorrhages, and brain infections may produce cerebral palsy after birth. Whatever the etiology, the result is various disabling conditions that occur singly or in combination, including perceptual and motor impairments, vision and hearing losses, convulsive disorders, and problems with speech. In addition, approximately 75% of children with cerebral palsy manifest some degree of mental retardation, including its severe and profound levels (Bleck, 1982a). Children with severe forms of cerebral palsy are commonly seen in classrooms that serve students with severe and multiply disabling conditions.

PREVENTION

Recent advances in prenatal diagnoses of potentially disabling conditions, as well as some emerging in-utero surgery techniques, offer a measure of optimism for the amelioration, if not the prevention, of some severely disabling conditions. At present, however, the possibility of preventing most disorders is far into the future. Procedures will depend on scientific advances in genetics, disease epidemiology, biochemistry, and numerous other related sciences and disciplines. Recent understanding of the causes, early detection, and prevention of PKU is a good example of how one condition causing severe disabilities can be virtually eliminated. Most etiologies, however—genetic, disease, and environmental—are less clearly understood. Unlike more common medical problems, many syndromes producing severe disabilities are relatively rare and so do not have high priority among medical researchers.

IDENTIFICATION AND ASSESSMENT

The outcome of federal legislation and litigation since the 1970s has been the development of educational services for individuals with severe and multiple disabilities. All children, regardless of the severity of their disabling condition, are guaranteed a free, public education in environments best suited to their rights and needs. Public Law 94–142 extends these rights to receiving educational programs in the least restrictive environment (LRE). As Brown et al. (1977) interpreted the LRE mandate: "The educational service delivery models used for severely handicapped students must closely approximate the best available educational service delivery models used for nonhandicapped students" (p. 93). To provide the most appropriate educational services, individuals with special needs must be identified through various assessment procedures.

ASSESSMENT FOR CHILDREN FROM BIRTH TO AGE 3

PL 99–457, Part H, specifies new assessment procedures for finding eligible children and identifying special needs. The law requires states to establish a Child Find system to ensure that families know that early intervention services are available and how to obtain them. Coordination of Child Find programs across many state agencies and programs is required. In addition, each state must have a central directory or toll-free 800 number to access available information and referral about early intervention.

Each child must be given a timely, comprehensive, multidisciplinary evaluation to determine whether he or she is eligible for early intervention services. This evaluation must cover specific content, such as the five developmental areas specified in the regulations.

An eligible child must be given a multidisciplinary assessment to identify the child's unique needs, the family's strengths and concerns related to the child's development, and the needed early intervention services for the child and the child's family.

Congenital severe and multiple impairments usually are identified at birth by physicians, nurses, and family members. Recent advances in medical technology save the lives of many infants with severe medical conditions. Thus, the number of infants who need services for their severe and multiple disabilities has increased. At birth, the parents of infants like Joe likely would be referred to the Child Find network in their state to find out where evaluation and assessment services are available in their community.

At Joe's birth his physician was aware of medical problems (respiratory distress and increased bilirubin levels) coupled with possible neurological impairments (high muscle tone and low Apgar scores). He referred Joe for an assessment with the Brazelton *Neonatal Behavioral Assessment Scale* (1973) and a physical therapy examination to further ascertain the issues. The physical therapist determined that Joe displayed many neurological and motor patterns indicating possible severe spastic cerebral palsy involving his entire body (quadriplegia). The therapist referred Joe for an overall evaluation conducted every 2 months at the local church.

Joe's evaluation determined that he was eligible for early intervention services and revealed his needs to be physical, motor, communication, and self-help. The next step was the multidisciplinary assessment, which involved further testing of Joe and meeting with his parents. His parents relayed that Joe had difficulty swallowing and often had his mouth wide open. The assessment revealed that Joe's oral musculature was impaired because he had limited tongue movements and restricted lip closure resulting from tight muscle tone and reflexive oral patterns. In addition, Joe's parents relayed that he vocalized infrequently. His hearing and vision assessment showed normal hearing and vision skills.

The combination of severe cerebral palsy and delay in speech production, coupled with oral-motor deficits, allowed Joe to be referred to an early intervention program for children with severe/multiple disabilities. In this special setting Joe and his parents gained access to educational and therapeutic specialists with expertise in combined disabling conditions. Ongoing assessment procedures continued as Joe got older, through a variety of means as described next.

ASSESSMENT FOR PRESCHOOL AND SCHOOL-AGED STUDENTS

Prior to a student's being placed into preschool or school-aged special education programs with services in the area of severe disabilities, educational personnel conduct a variety of assessments. After the placement has been determined, an ongoing process of assessment is conducted. Assessment for students with severe disabilities, a complicated process, begins with the selection of instruments that are appropriate for specific purposes. Selecting an appropriate one considers the type of instrument available, purpose of the assessment, and the student's skills.

Types of Assessments. Assessment instruments can be norm-referenced, criterion-referenced, or standardized. *Norm-referenced* assessments compare the individual's performance with that of other individuals the same age. *Criterion-referenced* assessments focus on differences in the student's skill attainment, centering on the individual's mastery of skills, which is helpful in educational programming. *Standardized assessments* use instruments that have norms and are administered following specific directions such as stimuli presentation and time allotted for student responses.

Assessments for Identification and Placement. Diagnostic assessments usually are standardized. Individuals with severe and multiple disabilities typically produce low scores (e.g., slow responses, nonverbal communication) which may not reflect their actual abilities. These assessments may not benefit diagnosis but, rather, may identify weaknesses and point out what the individual *cannot* do. Therefore, the tool may require two scoring methods: (a) the standardized administration, and (b) an adapted administration. If significant differences in scores result, another instrument, more appropriate for diagnosing the student's abilities, should be used.

Placement and diagnosis of students with severe and multiple disabilities may be aided by administering more than one assessment. *Intelligence tests* must be given by certified psychologists or psychometrists who have specialized training. The test formats and their uses are limited for people with severe and multiple disabilities because of the reliance on intact neurological and sensory functioning as well as receptive language skills. Tests of *adaptive behavior* tend to target behaviors important to an individual's adjustment to cultural and age standards of performance. These tools may help to define the problems but not the severity or the cause of the delays. Also, they generally are not adequately standardized.

Many assessment tools are available for determining developmental problems, educational diagnosis, and programming. Some representative diagnostic instruments are: the AAMD Adaptive Behavior Scale: Public School Version (Lambert, Windmiller, Cole, & Figueroa, 1975); the TARC Assessment Inventory for Severely Handicapped Children (Sailor & Mix, 1976); and the 1985 revision of the Wisconsin Behavior Rating Scale (Song & Jones, 1979).

Assessment to Identify Educational Needs. The importance of individualized instruction is linked to the adequacy of educational assessment. "The first and possibly most important steps in teaching are determining the student's needs, what content to teach, and what strategies will be useful to convey that content" (Gaylord-Ross & Holvoet, 1985, p. 2).

Service personnel working with individuals who have severe and multiple disabilities are faced with the challenge of determining appropriate goals and objectives that promote independent functioning. These special students need a variety of skills. Thus, educational decision making must determine essential skills to teach and the manner of implementation that utilizes instructional time efficiently. Lehr (1982) suggested that successful assessment procedures will: (a) identify instructional targets in all areas that aid independent functioning, (b) provide instructional targets essential to the student's functioning, and (c) detect emerging skills. Assessments that may aid educational decision making include: the Behavior Rating Instrument for Autistic and Atypical Children (BRIAAC) (Ruttenberg, Kalish, Wenar, & Wolf, 1978), the Callier-Azusa Scale (Stillman, 1982), and A Manual for the Assessment of a Deaf-Blind Multiply Handicapped Child (Collins & Rudolph. 1975).

The assessment process also must determine how to teach skills to the individual student. The most effective and efficient ways of acquiring information, as well as individual preferences, should be taken into consideration. Assessment must be comprehensive. Programming may be aided by instruments focusing on sensory (auditory, visual, tactile) and motor components. These assessment tools may have to be administered by specialists.

Most instructional programs for children with severe and multiple disabilities center on remediation of behaviors and development of skills found to be limited during the assessment process. The educational team (e.g., teacher, parents, speech clinician, physical therapist) together determines what each student should learn and provides instruction to promote the specific skills that enhance independent functioning. Traditionally, teachers seldom have allowed the *student* to choose what skills to learn, what materials to use, or what people to work with. Recently, however, researchers and educators are beginning to question this exclusion of the individual's preferences. Everyone should be able to indicate preference.

The opportunity to choose is crucial to those with severe and multiple disabilities because they often are dependent on others to move them and attend to their physical needs. Some students are able to indicate whether they prefer to learn a certain skill by their enthusiasm and alertness, by more correct responses, or by their positive affective behavior. Skills they do not prefer are indicated by off-task behaviors, fussing, aggression, not responding, or waiting for physical assistance. Most skills selected for instruction can be broad-based. Tasks can be learned using various materials or events in diverse contexts and with various personnel.

Assessment of the various environments and activities with which the individual is currently involved is important, as is assessment of future environments and their corresponding necessary skills. Ecological inventories provide:

—detection of relevant environments.
—delineation of physical and subenvironments.
—determination of age-appropriate activities as typically occurring within the identified subenvironments.
—detection of skill sequences of activities for instruction.

Determining educational needs means inventorying work, leisure, school, residence, community, and related present and future environments. In addition, environmental assessment includes interviews with people in the environments (e.g., group home or apartment supervisors, potential employers, parents, trainers) and observations of individuals in these settings. From these environmental assessments one can better determine what skills to teach, what functional materials to use, what natural cues and consequences work best, appropriate location, and the sequence of the skills to be taught.

SERVICE DELIVERY: THE TEAM APPROACH

Students with severe and multiple disabilities have a wide range of special needs. To plan, manage, and deliver special services requires coordinating an array of personnel: a team encompassing the teacher, paraprofessionals, parents, and ancillary staff. The involvement of ancillary staff depends on individual needs and often requires physical and occupational therapists, speech and language clinicians, vision specialists, and audiologists. The three team approaches most commonly utilized are multidisciplinary, interdisciplinary, and transdisciplinary.

The Multidisciplinary Team. The multidisciplinary team approach evolved from the typical medical model involving various individual disciplines all performing separate evaluations and formulating separate treatment recommendations. It is frequently used in the initial identification of children with disabilities.

Evaluation of students usually takes place in locations and at times separate from the classroom or home environment (Haring, 1977; Hart, 1977). Assessment information derived from the individual team members is implemented in individual therapy sessions in the school building. Therapy programs follow the same practice of removing the student from the classroom, utilizing an isolated therapy model (Perske & Smith, 1977; Sternat, Nietupski, Lyon, Messina, & Brown, 1976).

The Interdisciplinary Team. The interdisciplinary team also evaluates and makes treatment recommendations outside the classroom or home, but it does not do so separately. Instead, it promotes (a) the establishment of formal communication channels between disciplines and (b) the assignment of a care manager to coordinate services (McCormick & Goldman, 1979). Members of the team meet to exchange evaluation outcomes, make recommendations, and develop a single overall educational plan (Hart, 1977).

The Transdisciplinary Team. In the transdisciplinary approach each discipline works cooperatively from the start in designing and implementing educational programs (Lyon & Lyon, 1981). Team members exchange information and skills. A vital part of this approach is *role release*, which means training and authorizing other team members to implement specialized programs. All members are accountable, however. Team members (parent, teacher, paraprofessional) who have an ongoing, daily relationship with the student deliver the educational and therapeutic services with support of and training by the other transdisciplinary team members. Programs are implemented within the classroom and home environments, unlike the other two approaches in special therapy rooms or other isolated settings.

Students with severe and multiple disabilities require services from many different disciplines. Coordinated and integrated service delivery assures that the expertise of multiple disciplines is provided throughout the school day, not just once or twice a week with an individual therapist. According to York (1985), this approach has a number of advantages:

- An orientation viewing a student as a whole person rather than looking at separate problem areas.
- Functional activities in natural contexts.
- Consistent expectations and management by team members.
- Shared responsibility for educational programming.
- Integration of each discipline's expertise.
- Cooperative team relationships.

The trandisciplinary approach to service delivery was initiated in Joe's case. The difference from the other two models is in the determination of instructional goals. Rather than each member of the team independently choosing instructional programming priorities for Joe, the transdisciplinary team as a whole meets to determine all of Joe's educational needs at once and prioritizes all the suggested goals. (In the other two models each team member likely would determine top priorities within his or her own professional domain.) Instructional time is prioritized, and appropriate personnel are picked for specific instructional activities to provide Joe with a program that meets his current and future needs in an integrated manner.

Joe's team views him as a whole person, providing him with physical therapy, occupational therapy, and speech therapy within the context of natural routines. An example is lunchtime. A member from each discipline trains the classroom staff to instruct Joe. Joe learns to:

—signal to the staff that he has finished his work and is ready for lunch.
—wheel himself to the bathroom.
—position the wheelchair under the sink.
—turn on the warm water.
—obtain soap from the soap dish.
—lather and rinse his hands.
—turn off the water.
—wheel over to the paper towel dispenser.
—signal to a peer that he needs help reaching a paper towel.
—dry his hands and throw the towel in the trash can.
—wait for his special friend from homeroom to wheel him to the lunchroom.
—wait in the lunch line.
—obtain silverware, napkin, and tray,
—wait for his friend to wheel him to the lunch table.

S*KILLS AND CHARACTERISTICS*

Students with severe and multiple disabilities cannot be easily grouped in regard to learning and behavioral characteristics. Just as these individuals have many different etiological correlates, their social and academic behaviors also vary. Noonan and Siegel-Causey (1990) suggest, however, that a number of learning attributes of students with severe disabilities can be grouped into three general characteristics:

1. They learn slowly and often fail to notice relevant features of what is being taught.
2. They do not demonstrate learned skills spontaneously.
3. They often do not generalize learned skills to new situations. (pp. 384–385)

Although each individual may have any combination of these characteristics, as a group these students do demonstrate severe lags in social, intellectual, and physical development. Many of the delays are caused in part by observable damage to the child's motor and sensory systems. In other cases, reasons for severe delayed development are less obvious. Some students who do not display easily identified physical differences may show profound delays in intellectual, social, and language skills.

Current educational strategies include the identification of general skills in the social, cognitive, motor, and language areas, based in some part on comparing the differences between development of these skills in people with severe disabilities and their development in people with no disabilities. The major emphasis, however, is on identifying the specific skill level an individual has, or needs, to complete specific tasks. Given the differences in these two approaches, the discussion here centers on typical social, cognitive, physical, and communicative skill levels of students with severe disabilities.

SOCIAL DEVELOPMENT AND ADAPTIVE BEHAVIOR

Behaviors and deficiencies in social skills development consist of social interactions with others and deviant behaviors or mannerisms. Adaptive behavior refers to development of self-help skills, or behaviors fundamental to the individual's ability to care for his or her basic needs.

Self-Help Skills. The ability to feed oneself, to dress and undress, to brush one's teeth, wipe one's nose, comb one's hair, and so on are all skills that people without a disability often take for granted. People with severe disabilities, however, may have to exert enormous energy and practice repeatedly to learn these basic skills. In some cases, people with severe disabilities may never be able to complete one or all of these tasks independently. Teaching emphasizes identifying skills the student has and increasing the student's level of participation in the tasks.

Many people with severe disabilities are not toilet trained and others only partially so. In some cases, physical and neurological damage precludes the development of normal sphincter control. Spina bifida is one example of a neurological impairment in which bowel and bladder control may not be possible. In most cases, however, incontinence is indicative of the profound developmental delay typical in individuals with severe disabilities, especially younger children.

Interactions with Others. The opportunities for interaction between individuals with and without disabilities are ever increasing. As those opportunities continue to expand, appropriate and inappropriate social behaviors of the person with severe disabilities receive more attention. Although some behaviors, such as masturbating in public, are always deemed inappropriate, others are not so easily defined. For example, cussing and chewing tobacco are not acceptable behaviors in a fine restaurant, yet they are acceptable in many service stations. This, of course, is an extreme example, and most teachers would not choose to teach cussing and chewing tobacco as a social behavior. It does, however, underline the importance of defining why (or where) a behavior is inappropriate.

At times interactions with others goes beyond appropriate behaviors to the social characteristics of people with severe disabilities. For example, some students appear to be oblivious to others. They neither initiate interaction nor respond to environmental stimulation. This type of behavior may be associated either with profound mental retardation or with a withdrawal pattern, as frequently is found in cases of severe emotional disturbance. Differentiating between the two is often difficult.

Stereotyped Behaviors. This most common of type of behavior that is usually deemed inappropriate is stereotyped behavior, seemingly purposeless motor responses, repetitive movements, or unusual body posturing. These type of behaviors are common in everyone. Look around your college lecture room or a physician's waiting room. The girl in front of you is chewing on her pencil, the guy next to you is flicking a rubber band again and again, and you are moving your leg back and forth. Some students with severe disabilities show these same types of behaviors. Common stereotyped behaviors include rocking, waving their hands in front of their face, rolling their head back and forth, flicking their fingers, grinding their teeth, and twirling or spinning objects. These types of behaviors are common among children with severe emotional disturbances, children with profound retardation, and children with retardation who are partially or totally blind as well.

Various theories try to explain why stereotyped behaviors occur. Some researchers (e.g., Berkson & Mason, 1964) maintain that it happens when the child is aroused or overstimulated. This theory is supported by studies that report increased body rocking in retarded children before meals (Kaufman & Levitt, 1965). Some propose that stereotyped behaviors provide a means for these children to respond to frustrating situations (Baumeister & Forehand, 1971). Others suggest that it is a form of self-stimulation. According to the latter theory, children engage in stereotyped behaviors because they are not stimulated by the environment. This interpretation is supported by findings that two thirds of institutionalized residents engage in some form of stereotyped behavior. Moreover, the longer an individual remains in an institution, the more likely he or she is to develop the behaviors (Berkson & Davenport, 1962).

Still other researchers suggest that stereotyped acts are learned behaviors, rewarded by the attention the children receive from other people (Spradlin & Girardeau, 1966). This explanation is supported by studies showing an increase in stereotyped acts when rewards (reinforcers) follow them and a decrease when reinforcers are removed (Hollis, 1976).

The high occurrence rate of stereotyped behaviors in students with severe disabilities is likely attributable to more than one cause. One model (Guess & Carr, 1991) combines the theories mentioned previously to describe the emergence of stereotypic behavior. This model suggests that some behaviors emerge as a result of internal conditions, other behaviors arise as adaptive responses to the environment, and still other behaviors are learned behavior to control others. In this model, a behavior first might appear at one level and then change to another mode. For example, a young child with severe disabilities may begin waving his hands in front of his eyes as a result of internal conditions but then may begin to do it purposefully as a result of low environmental stimulation.

At present, all of the above theories have some research and theoretical support. Again, stereotyped behavior is not unique to individuals with severe disabilities, nor is it always an inappropriate behavior that should be eliminated.

Self-Injurious Behavior. The most difficult kind of behavior to understand is the self-injurious act when an individual does physical damage to himself or herself. Fortunately, this is not common in students with severe disabilities. Corbett (1975) has reported that some form of self-injurious behavior occurs in 5–15% of individuals with severe retardation. He also stated that it occurs more frequently at younger ages and is observed most often in children with profound retardation and severe emotional disturbance.

Self-injurious behavior may take a variety of forms, including banging the head or body against hard objects, hitting, pinching, biting or scratching oneself, eye-poking, and self-induced vomiting. As with stereotyped behavior, several theories are offered. Psychoanalytical theory interprets this type of behavior in various ways—as a reduction of guilt through self-inflicted pain, as inverted aggression, as an attempt to establish body reality, and as a form of autoerotic activity.

This form of behavior is characteristic of a number of somewhat rare clinical syndromes. In fact, self-injury occurs most frequently in association with conditions such as *Cornelia de Lange* syndrome. It also is accompanied by profound mental retardation and distinctive facial and body features. The *Lesch-Nyhan* syndrome, mentioned earlier, is another; this is an organic condition associated with mental retardation, athetoid cerebral palsy, and an enzyme deficiency.

Other research findings have shown that self-injurious behavior occurs more frequently in children with motor impairments and those who are both blind and retarded or deaf and retarded. Children with multiple disabilities have been observed to engage in more stereotyped behaviors as well. These observations support both "arousal" and "self-stimulation" interpretations, similar to those of stereotyped behavior.

Other theories propose that the child learns self-injurious behavior. In one explanation (Frankel & Simmons, 1976), the child is thought to engage in self-injurious behavior to reduce adult contact in high-demand situations; the child purposely engages in this kind of behavior to avoid an unpleasant task or situation. Another learning theory explanation maintains that the child purposely hurts himself or herself to gain attention from adults. Results of investigation show that adult attention increases self-injurious behavior in children who are severely disturbed and that the removal of adult attention decreases the behavior (Lovaas, Frietag, Gold, & Kassorla, 1965). Many factors are recognized as potential causes of self-injurious behavior in children with severe disabilities. As in stereotyped and other behaviors, brief episodes of self-injurious behavior are common in normal infants.

PHYSICAL DEVELOPMENT

Many students with severe disabilities show pronounced delays in sensory and motor development, and multiple disabilities are common. Delayed and abnormal motor and sensory skills are discussed next.

Delayed Motor Skills. Because Chapter 13, Physical Disabilities, focuses on students with orthopedic impairments and other conditions, we will not provide an extensive description here of severe orthopedic conditions or their causes. Severe delays in motor development in combination with profound mental retardation, however, do represent a common severely disabling condition. Many of these people cannot move independently and require mechanical assistance in the form of wheelchairs, walkers, braces, or support canes. For these students, the teaching emphasis is on increasing independent mobility, whether through an electric wheelchair or by assisting in transfers from one position to another.

Others with more severe disabilities do not achieve the basic milestones of motor development. They often have difficulty rolling over, holding up their heads, or grasping objects. Voluntary movement of any type may be limited. Often their muscles are contracted, flaccid, or underdeveloped. Abnormal body postures and reflexes caused by brain damage are common. The extent of motor involvement varies widely, ranging from virtual immobility to no apparent motor skill impairment.

Impaired Sensory Skills. Accurate assessment of hearing and vision among children with severe disabilities is difficult in many cases. Recent advances in techniques and procedures, however, are aiding the assessment of hearing abilities, and innovative approaches are being developed for more accurate testing of visual skills. Vision and hearing impairments are common in people with severe and multiple disabilities. Many have extensive sensory impairments, either alone or in combination.

Other Physical Conditions and Complications. Severe disabilities frequently are accompanied by physical problems that affect the person with the disability and caregivers. One common complication is seizures, ranging in severity from brief loss of contact with the outside world to major motor convulsions. In some seizure disorders the student may briefly stare off in space. Students with grand mal seizures may fall to the floor, and the body jerks in pronounced movements. During this latter type of seizure, the person may lose bowel or bladder control, and saliva may bubble around the mouth. Many types of seizures result from abnormal electrical brain discharges. Seizure activity is especially prevalent in children with cerebral palsy. The severity and frequency of most seizures can be reduced significantly through appropriate medication. Undesirable side effects from medication, however, may include drowsiness and swelling of gums around the teeth. Respiratory infections and ear infections also are common in students with severe disabilities. Some students have oral motor difficulties that may affect students' ability to chew and swallow and thus affect the person's nutritional status. Skin rashes also can result from braces, immobility, or incontinence.

COGNITIVE SKILLS

Students with severe disabilities typically have cognitive skills identified as being at Piaget's early childhood sensorimotor stages of development. Even though these skills frequently are considered "precursors" to learning academic skills, some students (with early and intensive education) learn to read, write, and perform other academic skills. In this developmental area, perhaps more than any other, students with severe disabilities vary widely. For example, though some students can recognize or match colors, shapes, or objects, others cannot remember that an object exists after it is removed from their sight. Some students may learn to follow one-, two-, or even three-step directions. Others learn that they have some control over their environment.

COMMUNICATION SKILLS AND LANGUAGE

Without exception, students with severe disabilities have some type of communication and language impairment. This area of disability, the topic of Chapter 8, historically has focused on speech and language, the ability to understand and express language by talking. Current practice now includes enhancing communication skills and augmentative/alternative communication systems. Service providers (including speech-language clinicians) must look beyond speaking as the only skill training area.

This change evolved because of the diversity of communication and language competencies across students with severe disabilities. Some learn to speak; some speak but their talking is not clear; some have unusual speaking patterns; some seem to understand what is said to them but do not speak. The main purpose of communication and language intervention for students with severe disabilities is to provide them with an effective means to control their environment and influence the people who interact with them.

Communication. An important assumption of this chapter and of others in the field (McCormick & Noonan, 1984; Falvey, 1986; Noonan & Siegel-Causey, 1990) is that all students, including students with severe disabilities, communicate in some way. For example, Joe smiles when his friend admires the new bookbag that holds his picture board, Rachel vocalizes "ah" when the teacher asks her if she is ready to go to recess, and Samuel screams when he is put on the bus to leave home in the morning.

Individuals who do not speak use alternative modes of communication such as vocal sounds, gestures, body movements, facial expressions, and eye contact. All young children learn to communicate before they learn a formal language system of symbols such as speech or sign language. Developing and implementing a communication or language program for students with severe disabilities involves a series of decisions based on the individual needs of each student. These decisions involve determining the student's current communication abilities and selecting a combination of systems that promote the individual's independence and meet needs across home, school, and communities activities.

At both home and school Joe answers direct questions by looking up to convey yes and looking down to convey *no*. He expresses himself by looking at what he wants. For example, his teacher holds up a juice pitcher and a milk carton and asks him which drink he wants at snacktime; Joe looks at the juice pitcher. Or Joe is asked, "Is 4 + 5 = 9 or 8?" Joe looks at the flashcard 9 in reply. Joe also uses his communication board of pictures by pointing to pictures that compose his message. For example, he points to a picture of himself, one of his friend, Bill, and one of the tire swing. Joe has used his board to convey "I want to swing with Bill."

Speech and Language Delay. Although some students learn to speak, delay in speech and language development remains a major problem for many students who have severe disabilities. Clearly, lack of communication skills is an ongoing concern of teachers and therapists. Many intervention techniques for facilitating speech are presented in Chapter 8. These intervention strategies should be considered, taking into account some of the speech and language characteristics of students with severe disabilities. Some students with severe disabilities have unusual speech patterns. What they say may be out of context or inappropriate to the situation. They may repetitiously recite phrases or commercials they hear on television. Their articulation may be quite clear, but the content is not meaningful. These unusual speech patterns also are found often in children with severe emotional disturbances.

Another speech pattern observed commonly in students with profound retardation or emotional disturbance is called *echolalia*. As the term suggests, students with this speech pattern repeat, or echo, what is said to them. Techniques and procedures are available for intervening with echolalic speech. The prognosis for developing appropriate speech is more optimistic than for students who are totally without speech.

Technology. Technology has expanded the horizons of communication and language. Complete assessment of the student's communication needs and the technology available to enhance those needs is necessary. Electronic devices include displays wherein the student's selected item lights up or the message is conveyed by programmed speech. Other devices produce a printout of each message. If students cannot use their hands accurately because of physical impairments, interface switches can be positioned to allow the student to access the device by using the movement he or she has. Sarah uses her forearm to lean on a switch mounted to her wheelchair tray. Amy uses her head to touch the switch mounted to the back of her wheelchair headrest. When the switch is activated, a light moves across the boards until Amy takes her hand off the switch to indicate the selected message. Joe taps a switch that starts his tape recorder, and his teacher hears his message of "I need help."

This child activates a switch with her chin to operate a tape recorder.

EDUCATIONAL PRACTICES

Often student with severe motor, mental, and sensory impairments cannot learn *all* of the skills necessary in current and future environments. Educational personnel are responsible, therefore, for designing curricula that meet each student's individual needs. Teachers routinely face decisions concerning which instructional procedures, arrangements, and materials are appropriate. Because the nature and intensity of different disabling conditions vary greatly within a single classroom, classroom instructional models and the specific skills to be taught also must vary. Teaching techniques might incorporate, for example, physical management to accommodate motor needs, placement and adaptation of materials and stimuli to accommodate sensory needs, and attention to medical and health needs. Whatever the need, the student's unique characteristics must guide the teacher in developing an individualized education program.

Joe requires assistance in getting to the cafeteria and then to his lunch table. The staff would have less work if Joe were to eat in the classroom, but that would exclude him from interacting with nondisabled peers and preclude the independence involved in getting his own meal. Therefore, *partial participation* is best for Joe. Joe does the tasks he can do (with and without adaptation) and gets help with the skills he has not yet acquired (e.g., moving his wheelchair distances of more than 5 feet).

INSTRUCTIONAL PROCEDURES

The educational team must design intervention that will meet each student's unique needs. Regardless of the targeted intervention areas, all personnel must follow instructional procedures including systematic instruction, varied learning trial approaches, and task analysis.

Systematic Instruction. To accommodate the unique learning characteristics of these students, they should be taught systematically. The teaching "uses performance data (both probe and instructional) to make modifications, and includes acquisition, proficiency, maintenance, and generalization learning" (Snell & Zirpoli, 1987). This type of instruction must be conducted while using natural cues and across a variety of environments rather than in a rote manner or in sterile settings.

Massed, Distributed, or Spaced Trial Learning. Historically, *massed trial* instruction focused on a specified time slot to teach a specific program such as counting, and the task was practiced repetitively for a 15–30 minute period daily (massed trials). This approach has been discarded except for skills in which learning time is critical or repeating a task is natural, such as putting away clean silverware or buttoning a shirt.

Group instruction, when students rotate taking turns, creates a *spaced trial* instruction. When skills are chained, as most skills are, performance of the skills is *distributed* rather than practiced again and again *(massed training)*. Most functional skills are distributed; for example, a person reaches for the doorknob, turns it, pushes the door open, and greets the people inside. This task lends itself to distributed trials, but some instructors who take a massed trial approach might inappropriately separate the skills and have the student practice greeting people again and again or reach for items out of the context of needing to use them.

Task Analysis. Task analysis is a common instructional method for individuals with severe and multiple disabilities. This format can be applied effectively in many skill areas—for example, self-help, vocational, motor, communication, leisure, and social. Essentially, subskills and parts of a complex skill or set of skills are analyzed sequentially, and each subtask is specified and defined objectively. The skill being analyzed is divided into its component behaviors, each of which promotes the next. Task analysis allows educators and therapists to determine what components of an activity or task the student can perform. In this way, the steps not yet learned can be taught more readily within the ordered sequence of steps that accomplishes a task.

INSTRUCTIONAL ARRANGEMENTS AND MATERIALS

Various instructional arrangements and adaptations of materials can further a quality educational program. For students with severe, multiple disabilities, considerations of group versus one-to-one instruction, instruction in natural settings, adaptive materials, and inclusion in regular settings are all crucial to providing a sound educational program.

Instructional Arrangements. *One-to-one instruction* is commonly assumed to be the most beneficial mode of instruction for learners with severe disabilities. Research, however, has shown that these students acquire a variety of skills in group instruction formats at rates better than or comparable to one-to-one instruction. In addition, group situations can motivate the individual, provide natural opportunities to use skills, and promote peer interaction. A combination of group and one-to-one instruction is thought to be the best approach, given the limited research available to determine which skills might be facilitated best using one approach over the other.

Settings and Materials. To help learners spontaneously use their skills in a variety of places, the skills must be done in *natural settings*.

Joe needs to learn to use signals when he needs help during the daily routine in the natural setting of the classroom. Taking him to a "clinic" or "therapy room" to practice asking for help by passing the staff member a card printed with the word "help" will not aid his understanding of how to use this skill when he really needs help in a variety of situations. Instead, Joe should learn to use a switch to activate a tape recorder that says "I need help" when he needs help getting his coat on the hook or opening his milk carton as this occurs during his school day.

Intervention utilizes the natural setting and materials to provide instruction. Simulated materials such as pictures, pretend foods, or paper clocks would be replaced with learning in the grocery or convenience store, lunchroom, or coat closet.

Learners should have opportunities to interact with peers with and without disabilities. Integrated educational settings allow many opportunities for these interactions. Students with disabilities can benefit from age-appropriate social skills and more skill generalization. Students without disabilities learn to see these students as unique individuals with positive attributes, and friendships may form in systematic peer programs.

Adaptation of Environment and Materials. *Adaptive devices* and materials are often found in special education classrooms. In some situations, with only one set of standard materials, a student with severe and multiple disabilities may not be able to participate in certain activities. Adapting the materials extends the range of settings and activities the student can participate in.

Having severe cerebral palsy, Joe cannot grasp the small, metal handles of the silverware at school. The occupational therapist made some soft, wide handles to encase the utensils. Joe carries these special handles in his bookbag and brings them with him to the cafeteria. One of Joe's friends holds the utensil, and Joe pushes the handle onto it. Joe also has difficulty scooping from the flat, plastic lunch trays. The occupational therapist has provided a plateguard that is clipped around the side of the lunch tray so Joe has a surface to scoop against.

In addition, *alternative response forms* often are provided to students who are unable to talk, so they can communicate to others their needs, wants, and preferences.

Joe can make only a few sounds. It has been this way ever since he was about a year old. He always has been a social boy, anxious to interact with people. During his preschool program, Joe was taught to vocalize an "ah" sound and smile to indicate *yes* and vocalize an "nn" sound and turn his head away for *no*. This alternative response form allowed him to control immediate situations and activities, but he had no way to initiate communication. Often unable to guess his message, adults could not ask him a *yes/no* question to determine his need.

During his elementary program Joe used a picture communication board to express himself. His teacher and speech therapist taught Joe to match pictures to objects, indicate items by pointing, differentiate smaller and smaller sized pictures, and so on. This enabled Joe to learn to construct full sentences: "I want go bathroom," and "I am finished with my work." By pointing to the appropriate picture with the word underneath, Joe is able to communicate to others.

Inclusive Activities. Although integrated settings provide opportunities for more interaction between students with and without disabilities, structured activities often are needed to promote *inclusion* of the student with disabilities within the school setting. This term implies integration with those who have no disability but stresses the active participation of students with severe disabilities in the school and community activities that surround them. Currently its meanings range from full placement in a regular classroom to a few structured activities. Regular classroom interactions, peer tutoring, special friends, and student-centered interactions are all ways to further inclusion.

Regular Classroom Interactions. For students with severe and multiple disabilities, social interaction tends to be limited to a one-way exchange with a care-providing adult. In the past, students were not encouraged to initiate communication, to make choices, or to interact with peers, disabled or not. Current practice advocates extending the typical one-way adult-to-child interaction to include interactions between peers. Training programs have been developed to teach students, nondisabled and disabled alike, to interact with one another. Table 10.1 outlines the advantages and disadvantages of the three approaches introduced below.

Peer Tutoring. In peer tutoring, a nondisabled student instructs the student with disabilities. The former serves as instructor trained by the classroom teacher.

Student-centered. The student-centered interaction is structured by two peers rather

● **TABLE 10.1**

Advantages and disadvantages of three interaction approaches

Advantages	Disadvantages
Peer Tutoring	
provides structured interaction	little interaction during free-play or nonstructured activities
organizes the flow of communication and interactions in a reciprocal manner	may hinder development of friendships
increases ratio of instructors to students, more one-to-one instruction	promotes student as needy and helpless
Student-Centered Interaction	
enables peers to interact in normalized environments resulting in student finding peers important, pleasurable people, and vice versa	possibly requires student to initially train with adult
encourages better social behaviors through role modeling and imitation	
Special Friends	
builds true reciprocal relationships	may require adult prompting and reinforcement
develops social-leisure skills	
extends peers' understanding of the *whole* person; precludes judgments based on stereotypes or physical appearance	

than by the teacher. Usually no adult is present. Settings include recess, breaktime, home, the park, and so forth.

Special Friends. Special friends facilitate social interaction. For a designated time (weeks to months), pairs of students are named as special friends. The student pairs meet regularly to participate in recreational/leisure activities. The interactions may take place at recess, in special or regular classrooms, or off campus.

INSTRUCTIONAL MODELS

Two ecological approaches have been proposed to accommodate the learning characteristics of students with severe disabilities and incorporate the "best" instructional practices just described: (a) a *community-referenced model* (Brown, Nietupski, & Hamre-Nietupski, 1976b; Brown et al., 1985), and (b) an *individualized curriculum sequence model* (Brown, Holvoet, Guess, & Mulligan, 1980; Holvoet, Guess, Mulligan, & Brown, 1980; Helmstetter, Murphy-Herd, Roberts, & Guess, 1984). Both include curricular implementation that stresses the interrelationship between environment and skills. These are functional approaches, and they depend on analysis of the individual's present repertoire of skills compared with the actual demands of the environment. Assessment takes place in the natural environment the individual is functioning in currently and considers environments that will come into play in the future.

Community-Referenced Model. This curriculum model, developed by Lou Brown and colleagues in Madison, Wisconsin, has been implemented widely in the areas of both severe and moderate disabilities. Although predominantly oriented toward the latter, the model's underlying philosophy has had a tremendous influence in both areas of disability.

Curriculum is based on normalization. Its thrust is to enable students to learn a myriad of skills they will need to function within the community. Decisions on what to teach are based on the *criterion of ultimate functioning*. Ecological assessments help teachers select functional, chronological, age-appropriate skills to teach.

Prior to implementing an instructional program, teachers should ask:

- What is the purpose of the activity?
- Is the activity or skill necessary for the child to function in the community?
- Could he or she function as an adult without the skill?
- Would another skill facilitate the criterion of ultimate functioning faster and more efficiently?
- Might the activity in fact impede, restrict, or reduce the probability that the student will function in community settings (e.g., teaching students to always walk in a line when going from place to place)?
- Are the skills, materials, tasks, and criteria really similar to those encountered in adult life?

This model takes a top-down assessment approach. It begins by identifying the requirements of independent adult functioning in four skill categories: domestic, vocational, leisure/recreation, and community living. In developing the curriculum, the six phases are:

1. Identify the curricular domains.
2. Identify and survey current and future natural environments.
3. Divide relevant environments into subenvironments.
4. Inventory these subenvironments for the relevant activities performed there.
5. Examine the activities to isolate the skills required to perform them.
6. Design and use instructional programs to teach the identified skills.

Individualized Curriculum Sequencing (ICS) Approach. Part of the remedial logic inherent in this approach is that the individual with severe and multiple disabilities must be taught many basic skills of development much later in life than the typical child. Thus, the focus is on (a) which skills, and (b) in what order they are acquired most quickly to accomplish some improvement in the learner's immediate interactions with the environment. This pragmatic approach further takes into account the differences between the normally developing child and the child with severe and multiple disabilities.

Instructional objectives may be drawn from developmental data, but, unlike the developmental approach, the normal sequence of development does not necessarily describe the most logical ordering of objectives for intervention. An objective from a developmental curriculum may be of little relevance, or just not particularly useful to the individual. Thus, objectives should be functional—of practical use to the student in a specific environment. Two requirements of the ICS approach are: (a) teaching skills in clusters, and (b) sequencing skills in a natural manner.

Teaching skills in clusters recognizes and therefore promotes the interdependence of some naturally occurring behaviors. Environments are complex. They require one to perform a number of different actions, either concurrently or in rapid succession. Skills that readily form sequential clusters often are those that are useful and meaningful to the learner. Generally, *functional* skills are those that are demanded frequently, promote independent performance, produce immediate motivational effects, and are natural to current and future environments.

The other requirement of the ICS approach, *sequencing skills in a natural manner*, also may be thought of as functional task sequencing. Skills are arranged so progressing through the sequence is logical and meaningful to the student. In addition, any sequence of skills is arranged to closely approximate a similar sequence of events as would occur naturally in the environment.

The two requirements combine to create appropriate skill cluster sequences that teach skills from typical content domains (e.g., self-help, communication, vocational, socialization, sensory, motor) and also form an interdependent, meaningful series of events. A skill cluster sequence for a preschool child may be (1) roll to play area (motor), (2) bear weight on forearms (motor), (3) visually fixate on toy of preference (sensory), (4) produce a sound to request the toy (communication), (5) interact with the toy appropriately (motor and cognitive). The format for the ICS model consists of:

—teaching learners a cluster of skills in functional ways.

—arranging instruction so skills are taught using two or more materials, activities, instructors, responses, and locations.

—giving learners opportunities to make choices.

—using functional materials and activities that occur in natural environments and are used by similarly aged peers without disabilities.

—teaching skills that promote independence and increase opportunities for being with peers without disabilities.

—providing training, using natural cues and consequences, that is scheduled at appropriate times in natural routines and incorporates learner-initiated behavior.

Joe's teachers, speech therapist, and occupational therapist used an ICS approach to intervention. Joe's treatment first entailed formal and informal assessment, student preferences inventory, and environmental inventories. The team then determined these priority goals for Joe:

- To strengthen his arms.
- To learn to signal for his needs.
- To learn to wait his turn.
- To increase the range of motion of his shoulders, arms, ankles, hips, and legs.
- To express past and future events.

These skills then were integrated into various sequences across the range of typical classroom activities. For example:

Activity	Skill
At arrival time:	
Wheels 3 feet to locker.	Strengthens arms.
Signals with loud voice and bell that he needs help with jacket.	Signals needs.
Pulls jacket off his right arm.	Increases range of motion of shoulders/arms.
Waits for peer to come and help him hang up jacket.	Waits turn.
Does last step himself by putting jacket on hook.	Increases range of motion.
Wheels 3 feet to homeroom.	Strengthens arms.
On a community trip to the store:	
Wheels 3 feet to bus stop.	Strengthens arms.
Waits for driver to put him on wheelchair lift.	Waits turn.
Signals that his wheelchair seatbelt is not buckled.	Signals needs.
Wheels last 3 feet to store entry.	Strengthens arms.
Reaches for items on grocery shelf.	Increases range of motion of arms/shoulders.
Uses communication board to ask clerk for items.	Signals needs.

STATE-OF-THE-ART PRACTICES

Our efforts to educate students with severe and multiple disabilities are relatively recent. In the last decade these students have received extensive educational opportunities in regular school settings. Given the severity of their learning problems, substantive gains have been made in a relatively short time. Over the past 10 years we have recognized that these students can learn a variety of skills if appropriate instructional programs are implemented. These programs vary in quality, but they have certain common components, or objectives, that reflect what are now considered optimal practices, four of which are:

1. A variety of *functional skills* that are chronologically age-appropriate to the student are taught. The skills are consistent with those of their nondisabled peers and enable the students to interact better in their home, school, and community environments.
2. Teaching takes place in *natural environments* as much as possible. This means teaching real-life skills in settings where they normally occur, such as restaurants, buses, grocery stores, and so on.
3. Best practices emphasize a coordinated *team approach* involving a variety of professional disciplines (e.g., occupational therapists, speech clinicians, dieticians) and parents. Team members work together closely to assess educational and treatment needs of students and to implement programs.
4. Opportunities for interactions and building of personal relationships are the aims of *inclusive* activities between students with disabilities and their peers in regular education. Activities may have to be implemented to facilitate integration and inclusion.

Finally, state-of-the-art practices incorporate new *technology*, especially computer equipment. As a result, communication skills in these students are vastly improved.

ISSUES AND CONCERNS ABOUT THE FUTURE

Several important issues relate to the education and treatment of students with severe and multiple disabilities. First, many school districts are continually trying to cut back on educational services for this population. Administrators, even special education directors, do not always perceive public schools as the appropriate setting for these students. They base their argument on the increased cost to the schools. Theirs is the traditional view of schools as institutions for academic instruction only, and they clearly have the old negative attitudes toward persons who are perceived as deviating substantially from the norm. These stereotypes are still shared by many members of the community at large, who would rather see people with severe disabilities placed in special, segregated schools or even in institutions. In many respects, students with disabling conditions still suffer from the prejudice and discrimination that have existed for so long for other minority groups. Their full acceptance into schools and communities requires some basic value changes. Until then, the educational opportunities they have gained will have to be defended for the foreseeable future. We will have to use, to the fullest extent possible, the right-to-education guarantees that have resulted from litigation and legislated mandates, especially those of PL 94–142.

Another related area of concern pertains to our own instructional procedures and the methods we commonly use to educate and treat persons with severe and multiple disabilities. Over the years, our best-practice recommendations for classroom instruction have become increasingly narrower. They reflect, in large part, the learning principles that evolved from a Skinnerian behavioral psychology. Without argument, many of these learning principles and procedures are of immense practical value. On the other hand, their application has not proved to be entirely successful with all students, or even with many targeted skill areas within individual students. For example, students with severe disabilities often fail to generalize the behaviors taught them; moreover, they are unable to maintain the learned behavior over time.

In addition, behavioral psychology uses aversive procedures with students who have severe and multiple disabilities, including a wide variety of stimuli such as electric shock, ammonia spray, noxious substances in the mouth, pinching, forced body movements, and so on. Unfortunately, this type of punishment has spread to regular classrooms, to "control" a variety of behaviors that are not all that "deviant." In many instances, punishment has been used to "teach" new skills (see Guess, Helmstetter, Turnbull, & Knowlton, 1986, 1987, for a historical review of aversive procedures with persons with disabilities). The effectiveness of these measures is certainly questionable, and so is the message to society. This sort of action contributes nothing to the positive attitude we want to create toward this population. It exemplifies an attitude that is not advanced when educators themselves use extreme behavior-control procedures that most of society neither uses nor accepts.

Many professionals in the field now see a need to explore other theoretical approaches. Some new perceptions are called for—to see the student more totally as a whole person, to regard him or her as someone who has preferences, and to look at some intervention alternatives that do not attend so intensely to identifying and changing "deviant" behavior.

A HOLISTIC VIEW

Current practice follows a mechanistic model of behaviorism, perceiving behavior as a collection of stimulus-response units conditioned by reinforcers in our environment. In the study and modification of human behavior, feelings, emotions, and other subjective states are relatively unimportant, unscientific.

We hope that, in the future, the approach to education and treatment of students with severe and multiple disabilities will be different, in that the student will be recognized as a whole person, a totality, not just a responder to stimuli. We need to consider all of the internal motivating factors and conditions, emotions, complex cognitive processes, and other physiological and psychological parameters that interact with the environment to produce human behavior.

CHOICE AND PREFERENCE

Generally, the orientation of special education, particularly in the area of severe and multiple disabilities, is to impose instruction on learners rather than to involve them in making any choices of their own or expressing preferences. The prevailing attitude is that people with severe and multiple disabilities are not interested in making choices, they do not have the skills necessary to make choices or exert preferences, and the choices they make might not concur with what service providers perceive as in their best interests. Interest in incorporating choices and preferences into educational programs is increasing. Preliminary research indicates that choice making may foster independence, improve skill maintenance, increase learner involvement, and provide more individualized programming.

A POSITIVE FOCUS

Guess (1984) pointed out that current educational practices, which are of a behavioral orientation, follow a "let's fix it" model. The emphasis is on perceived deviant behavior, a preoccupation with what a child with a disability *cannot* do. This, of course, is important to know for remedial education and treatment and necessarily constitutes a primary purpose for special education. The effect, however, is that, by viewing the child only as a collection of deficits, one tends to see little else. This serves in the long term to perpetuate the negative societal perceptions of people with severe disabilities, a tendency to always view the child in relation to how we would like him or her to be in accordance with our standards of what is good or appropriate. Educational and treatment success, then, is measured by the extent to which the child's behavior can be modified to be more like societal expectations.

This orientation, along with related educational practices, causes one to overlook the many positive behaviors of people with severe disabilities and to fail to appreciate the things they can do. Lost also is an appreciation for how people with disabling conditions can impact positively on others. We hope future approaches to the education and treatment of students with severe and multiple disabilities will better acknowledge the positive influences they have on others and attend more closely to the skills they already have that are similar to our own behaviors. Until we do this, our perceptions of individuals with severe disabilities will continue to focus on their differences and behaviors that are not consistent with the expectations of those who are trying to change them.

The need to explore alternative educational theories and approaches offers us a new direction and a new commitment to our field. It means fresh research, exciting discovery, other ways to look at human behavior, better instructional procedures and techniques, and, we hope, a more positive attitude toward people with severe and multiple disabilities, one that perceives and appreciates more extensively their unique human and personal qualities.

*R*EFERENCES

Batshaw, M. L., & Perret, Y. M. (1981). *Children with handicaps: A medical primer.* Baltimore: Paul H. Brookes.

Batshaw, M. L., & Perret, Y. M. (1986). *Children with handicaps: A medical primer* (2nd ed.). Baltimore: Paul H. Brookes.

Baumeister, A. A., & Forehand, R. (1971). Effects of extinction of an instrumental response on stereotyped body rocking in severe retardates. *Psychological Record, 21,* 235–240.

Berkson, G., & Davenport, R. K. (1962). Stereotyped movements in mental defectives: Initial survey. *American Journal of Mental Deficiency, 66,* 849–852.

Berkson, G., & Mason, W. (1964). Stereotyped behaviors of chimpanzees: Relation to general arousal and alternative activities. *Perceptual & Motor Skills, 19,* 635–652.

Blackman, J. A. (1990). *Medical aspects of developmental disabilities in children birth to three.* Rockville, MD: Aspen Systems.

Bleck, E. (1982a) Cerebral palsy. In E. Bleck & D. Nagel (Eds.), *Physically handicapped children: A medical atlas for teachers* (2nd ed.) (pp. 59–132). New York: Grune & Stratton.

Bleck, E. (1982b). Rubella syndrome. In E. Bleck & D. Nagel (Eds.), *Physically handicapped children: A medical atlas for teachers* (2nd ed.) (pp. 431–432). New York: Grune & Stratton.

Bleck, E., & Nagel, D. (Eds.). (1982). *Physically handicapped children: A medical atlas for teachers* (2nd ed.) (pp. 431–432). New York: Grune & Stratton.

Brazelton, T. B. (1973). *Neonatal behavioral assessment scale.* Philadelphia: Lippincott.

Brown, L., Branston-McClean, M. B., Baumgart, D., Vincent, L., Falvey, M., & Schroeder, J. (1985). Using the characteristics of current and subsequent least restrictive environment in the development of curricular content for severely handicapped students. In *Innovative strategies for life long planning* (pp. 1–34) (Conference monograph). Washington, DC: U.S. Department of Education.

Brown, L., Holvoet, J., Guess, D., & Mulligan, M. (1980). The individualized curriculum sequencing model: 3. Small group interaction. *Journal of the Association for the Severely Handicapped, 7,* 19–28.

Brown, L., Nietupski, J., & Hamre-Nietupski, S. (1976). The criterion of ultimate functioning and public school services for severely handicapped students. In L. Brown, N. Certo, & T. Crowner (Eds.) *Papers and programs related to public school services for secondary-age severely handicapped students* (Vol. 6, Part 1). Madison, WI: Madison Metropolitan School District.

Brown, L., Wilcox, B. L., Sontag, E., Vincent, E., Dodd, N., & Gruenewald, L. (1977). Toward the realization of the least restrictive educational environments for severely handicapped students. *AAESPH Review, 2,* 195–201.

Collins, M. T., & Rudolph, J. M. (1975). *A manual for the assessment of a deaf-blind multiply handicapped child* (rev. ed.). Denver: Mountain Plains Regional Center for Deaf-Blind.

Corbett, J. (1975). Aversion for the treatment of self-injurious behavior. *Journal of Mental Deficiency Research, 19,* 79–95.

Ensher, G. L., & Clark, D. A. (1986). *Newborns at risk: Medical care and psychoeducational intervention.* Rockville, MD: Aspen Publications.

Falvey, M. A. (1986). *Community-based curriculum instructional strategies for students with severe handicaps.* Baltimore: Paul H. Brookes.

Frankel, F., & Simmons, J. (1976). Self-injurious behavior in schizophrenic and retarded children. *American Journal of Mental Deficiency, 80,* 512–522.

Gast, D., & Berkler, M. (1981). Severe and profound handicaps. In E. Blackhurst & W. Berdine (Eds.), *An introduction to special education* (pp. 431–461). Boston: Little, Brown.

Gaylord-Ross, R. J., & Holvoet, J. F. (1985). *Strategies for educating students with severe handicaps.* Boston: Little, Brown.

Geiger, W., & Justen, J. (1983). Definitions of severely handicapped and requirements for teacher certification. *Journal of the Association for the Severely Handicapped, 8*(1), 25–29.

Guess, D. (1984, April). *Allowing the child greater participation in the educational process.* Keynote Address presented at Fifth Annual Montana Symposium, Early Education and the Exceptional Child, Billings, MT.

Guess, D., & Carr, E. (1991). Emergence and maintenance of stereotypy and self-injury. *American Journal on Mental Retardation, 96,* 299–319.

Guess, D., Helmstetter, E., Turnbull, H. R., III, & Knowlton, S. (1986). *Use of aversive procedures with persons who are disabled: A historical review and critical analysis* (TASH Monograph Series, No. 2). Seattle: The Association for Persons with Severe Handicaps.

Guess, D., Helmstetter, E., Turnbull, H. R., & Knowlton, S. (1987). *Use of aversive procedures with persons who are disabled: An historical review and critical analysis.* Unpublished paper, University of Kansas, Lawrence.

Guess, P. D., & Mulligan, M. (1982). The severely and profoundly handicapped. In E.L. Meyen (Ed.), *Exceptional children and youth* (2nd ed.). Denver: Love Publishing.

Haring, M. G. (1977). Measurement and evaluation procedure for programming with the severely and profoundly handicapped. In E. Sontag, N. Certo, & J. Smith (Eds.), *Educational programming for the severely and profoundly handicapped.* Reston, VA: Council for Exceptional Children.

Hart, V. (1977). The use of many disciplines with the severely and profoundly handicapped. In E. Sontag, N. Certo, & J. Smith (Eds.), *Educational programming for the severely and profoundly handicapped.* Reston, VA: Council for Exceptional Children.

Helmstetter, E., Murphy-Herd, M. C., Roberts, S., & Guess, D. (1984). *Individualized curriculum sequence and extended classroom models for learners who are deaf and blind.* Unpublished manuscript, University of Kansas, Lawrence.

Hollis, J. (1976). Steady and transition rates: Effects of alternate activity on body-rocking in retarded children. *Psychological Reports, 39,* 91–104.

Holvoet, J., Guess, D., Mulligan, M., & Brown, F. (1980). The individualized curriculum sequencing model: 2. A teaching strategy for severely handicapped students. *Journal of the Association for the Severely Handicapped, 5,* 337–351.

Kaufman, M. E., & Levitt, H. A. (1965). A study of three stereotyped behaviors in institutionalized mental defectives. *American Journal of Mental Deficiency, 69,* 467–473.

Lambert, N., Windmiller, M., Cole, L., & Figueroa, R. (1975). *AAMD adaptive behavior scale: Public school version.* Washington, DC: American Association of Mental Deficiency.

Lehr, D. H. (1982). Severe multiple handicaps. In E.L. Meyen (Ed.), *Exceptional children in today's schools: An alternative resource book* (pp. 453–484). Denver: Love Publishing.

Lovaas, O. I., Frietag, G., Gold, V. J., & Kassorla, I. C. (1965). Experimental studies in childhood schizophrenia: Analysis of self-destructive behavior. *Journal of Experimental Child Psychology, 2,* 67–84.

Lyon, S., & Lyon, G. (1981). Roles and responsibilities of the transdisciplinary team members. In D. Guess, C. Jones, & S. Lyon (Eds.), *Combining a transdisciplinary team approach with an individualized curriculum sequencing model for severely/multiply handicapped children.* Lawrence: University of Kansas.

McCormick, L., & Goldman, R. (1979). The transdisciplinary model: Implications for service delivery and personnel preparation for the severely and profoundly handicapped. *AAESPH Review, 4*(2), 152–161

McCormick, L., & Noonan, M. J. (1984). A responsive curriculum for severely handicapped preschoolers. *Topics in Early Childhood Special Education, 4*(3), 79–96.

Noel, M. M., Burke, P. J., & Valdivieso, C. (1985). Educational policy and severe mental retardation. In D. Bricker & J. Filler (Eds.), *Severe mental retardation: From theory to practice* (pp. 12–35). Reston, VA: Council for Exceptional Children, Division on Mental Retardation.

Noonan, M., & Siegel-Causey, E. (1990). Special needs of students with severe handicaps. In L. McCormick & R. L. Schiefelbusch (Eds.), *Early language intervention, An introduction.* (2d ed.) (pp. 383–425). Columbus, OH: Charles E. Merrill.

Perske, R., & Smith, J. (Eds.). (1977). *Beyond the ordinary.* Seattle: American Association for the Education of the Severely/Profoundly Handicapped.

Ruttenberg, B. A., Kalish, B. I., Wenar, C., & Wolf, E. G. (1978). *Behavior rating instrument for atypical children* (BRIAC). Chicago: Stoelting.

Sailor, W., & Guess, D. (1983). *Severely handicapped students. An instructional design.* Boston: Houghton Mifflin.

Sailor, W., & Haring, N. (1977). some current directions in education of the severely/multiply handicapped. *AAESPH Review, 2*, 3–23.

Sailor, W., & Mix, B. J. (1976). *TARC assessment system.* Lawrence, KS: H & H Enterprises.

Snell, M. (1982). Characteristics, education, and habilitation of the profoundly mentally retarded. In P. Cegelka & H. Prehm (Eds.), *Mental retardation: From categories to people* (pp. 291–342). Columbus, OH: Charles E. Merrill.

Snell, M. & Zirpoli, T. J. (1987). Intervention strategies. In M. Snell (Ed.), *Systematic instruction of persons with severe handicaps* (3rd ed.) (pp. 110–149). Columbus, OH: Charles E. Merrill.

Song, A., & Jones, S. (1979). *Wisconsin behavior rating scale.* Madison: Central Wisconsin Center for Developmentally Disabled.

Spradlin, J. E., & Girardeau, F. L. (1966). The behavior of moderately and severely retarded persons. In N. R. Ellis (Ed.), *International review of research in mental retardation* (Vol. 1). New York: Academic Press.

Sternat, J., Nietupski, J., Lyon, S., Messina, R., & Brown, L. (1976). Integrated vs. isolate therapy models. In L. Brown, N. Scheuerman, & T. Crowner (Eds.), *Madison's alternative zero exclusion: Toward an integrated therapy model for teaching motor, tracking, and scanning skills to severely handicapped students* (Vol. 6, Pt. 3). Madison, WI: Madison Metropolitan School District.

Stillman, R. (1982). *Callier-Azusa scale-G.* Dallas: Callier Center for Communication Disorders.

U.S. Office of Education. (1975). *Estimated number of handicapped children in the United States, 1974–75.* (RFP 74:10). Washington, DC: U.S. Bureau of Education for the Handicapped.

York, J. L. (1985). A transdisciplinary model of service delivery for educational teams who serve students with severe and multiple handicaps: Implications for developmental therapists. In *Innovative strategies for life long planning* (pp. 104–130) (Conference monograph). Washington, DC: U.S. Department of Education.

HEARING

IMPAIRMENT

SHEILA LOWENBRAUN

E ducation for children who have a hearing impairment has changed substantially in the last 15 years. This is a result in part of the provisions of the Education for All Handicapped Children Act (PL 94–142) and the subsequent regular education initiative; in part to a fundamental change in the hearing impaired population brought about by the end of rubella epidemics (which had led to periodic increases in the number of hearing impaired); in part to new and improved technologies such as computer networking, better hearing aids, and closed captioning; and, to a great extent, to the change in educational philosophy of those charged with educating students who have hearing loss. The changes have been so fundamental and so widespread that some researchers warn that educational, social, and psychological studies of hearing impaired children and youth done before the 1970s may not be valid for today's population because of the differences in student cohort groups.

Hearing impaired children always have been a low-prevalence group within the special education, school-age population with disabilities. The *Twelfth Annual Report to Congress* (U.S. Department of Education, 1990) lists 3,955,184 students as being served as disabled during the 1988–89 school year. Of these, only 52,783 were served as deaf or hard-of-hearing. (The vast majority of children and youth receiving special education services are classified as learning disabled, mentally retarded, speech and language impaired, and seriously emotionally disturbed.) PL 94–142 and subsequent laws such as Individuals with Disabilities Education Act (IDEA) were not written primarily to improve services to children with hearing impairment. Most hearing impaired children already were receiving services from trained and certified teachers, and most had access to related services as well.

Some educators believe, as do many deaf adults, that at least one provision of PL 94–142, the least restrictive environment (LRE) mandate, has had an *adverse* impact on this student cohort. What has happened is that more small school districts are running programs for students with hearing impairment. Some of these "programs" have only two students; many have one multigraded class. The students in these programs do not have a readily available hearing impaired peer group to identify with, and they lack older children and adult role models. They may have no opportunity to become acquainted with the deaf culture.

On the positive side, more multihandicapped, hearing impaired children are being identified and served. Children with hearing impairment are being educated with their nondisabled peers, and educational interpreters to facilitate integration have become increasingly prevalent. Because of the IEP provision, some of the age-old debates on oral versus sign language education have become less strident and slowly are being replaced by discourse on how individual children's needs might best be met. This represents a profound change in the profession—from treating children with hearing impairment as a group for whom appropriate methodologies and outcomes can be determined, to focusing on the needs of individual students and their families.

CURRENT PRACTICES

Today, children with hearing impairment are being educated in a variety of placements using a variety of educational practices. Placement options range from relatively large center schools with diversified staffs and graded classes where, traditionally, some students reside during the school term, to small one- or two-student local school district programs with varying degrees of mainstreaming. Less severely impaired children, those who might be classified as hard of hearing, usually receive much of their education in regular classes, with support services from audiologists, speech and hearing therapists, and teacher/tutors. In a major philosophical and methodological switch, most programs for children with more severe hearing impairment now use some form of *total communication.* Total communication (discussed more fully in succeeding sections) may be loosely defined as the use of some form of sign language, along with speech, speechreading, and audition and nonlinguistic communication modes, for sending and receiving communication. Moreover, recent successes in some new methods of teaching language (see Chapter 8) are beginning to make an impression on service providers, who now realize the importance of attending to the semantic and pragmatic aspects of human communication in their instruction.

Children with hearing impairment are being identified earlier. They also are being fitted with amplification devices (hearing aids) sooner. The miniaturization of hearing aid components allows even infants under 1 year of age to wear binaural ear-level hearing aids. Early intervention programs permit children under age 3 to begin language, speech, and auditory training soon after initial diagnosis. This is the critical period for language acquisition.

MAJOR CHANGES SINCE PL 94–142

Although the education of children with hearing impairment has changed dramatically within the past two decades we do not know how much of it is a direct result of PL 94–142. Two changes, however, might be attributable to the least restrictive environment provision: (a) the decrease in enrollment in residential schools, and (b) an increase in the number of students who are partially or totally mainstreamed. The *American Annals of the Deaf* publishes a yearly summary of enrollments in schools and classes for the deaf. A comparison between data collected just before implementation of PL 94–142 and data collected 10 years later (*American Annals of the Deaf*, 1974, 1985) shows a drop in students served in residential schools, from approximately 40% of the reporting population to 32%. The most precipitous decline was in the number of students served in private residential schools, from 1,387 to 465, a decrease of more than 65% in 10 years! This might best be attributed to the increase in the number of local school district programs (stemming from PL 94–142 and the LRE mandate) and a disinclination on the part of states and school districts to assume the higher residential school tuition costs that now are the responsibility of public schools.

In 1974, no numbers were published on fully or partially mainstreamed hearing impaired children. We can safely assume, however, that mainstreaming was not prevalent. In 1984, however, approximately 67% of hearing impaired students who were attending day class programs were reported as being fully or partially mainstreamed, and only 8% of those attending residential schools were similarly integrated (*American Annals of the Deaf*, 1985). Although residential schools tend to serve more students who have multiple handicaps or severe hearing impairment than do day classes, this does not fully account for the huge difference between the two percentages. The *Twelfth Annual Report to Congress* (1990) has data that are not comparable to those in the *Annals*, as the former reports the categories of hard-of-hearing and deaf together. The reported figures for the 1987–88 school year indicated that only 8.6% of the deaf and hard of hearing population ages 6 through 21 were reported as served in residential schools. An additional 10.8% were served in separate day schools. By contrast 24.5 % were reported as spending at least 80% of their school day in regular classes, and an additional 20.9% were reported as served in resource room-regular class configurations. (p. 23) These figures represent a dramatic shift in programming and have enormous significance for the future of the deaf and hard of hearing culture in the United States.

STATUS OF OUR EFFECTIVENESS

For the past several decades—indeed, throughout much of the history of the education of children with hearing impairment—the field has been preoccupied with determining which communication mode to use—oral, manual, or some combination of both—and the most efficient way to tackle the major deficit area, language acquisition. Only recently have we attended to improving social and decision-making skills, content area knowledge, and reading instruction. Our research in meeting the needs of hearing impaired students, particularly multiply handicapped hearing impaired children, is still in its infancy. Even so, we have every reason to expect that education of hearing impaired children and youth will improve still more in the next few decades.

EDUCATIONAL DEFINITIONS

Hearing loss can be thought of in two basic ways. One involves using the psychometric measurement of hearing acuity at various frequencies (audiometric data) to assess the degree and type of physical impairment. The other takes into consideration the effects of the physical loss on speech and language development and on socialization and acculturation.

PHYSICAL PARAMETERS OF HEARING LOSS

Sound is produced by the periodic vibration of molecules set in motion by some force, such as the movement of a bow against the strings of a violin, the striking of a hammer on a nail, or the vibration of human vocal cords on a column of air. The number of periodic vibrations per second determines the *frequency* of the sound. The higher the frequency, the higher the perceived *pitch*. Each doubling of frequency is perceived as a pitch change of one octave. Frequency is measured in *Hertz* (Hz). A sound of 250 Hz is approximately the fundamental frequency of middle C on the piano; 500 Hz, therefore, is one octave above middle C, 1000 Hz two octaves above, and so on. The normal human ear is sensitive to sounds in the frequency range of approximately 20 to 20000 Hz. It is most sensitive to frequencies in the middle of the range, which is where most speech sound frequencies are located.

The *intensity*, or degree of force used in producing the sound, is measured in logarithmic units called *decibels* (dB). An increase in the number of decibels is perceived as increased loudness. Normal range of hearing is defined as the ability to hear sound at each measured frequency when it is presented at between zero and 20 dB. Hearing levels usually are measured between the frequencies of 125 and 8000 Hz at octave intervals. A person's *hearing threshold* is the decibel level at which that person can hear the sound half of the time it is presented at a given frequency. The degree of impairment can be estimated by averaging the results obtained for each ear at the frequencies of 500, 1000, and 2000 Hz. Normal thresholds are generally set at 20 dB. Losses from 20 dB to 60 dB are considered mild to moderate. Losses from 60 to 90 dB are severe. A 90 dB or greater threshold signals a profound loss.

In defining hearing loss, the site in the ear at which the impediment occurs is also important. The ear is divided into three main parts. The *outer ear*, composed of the auricle and external auditory canal, ends at the eardrum, or *tympanic membrane*. Soundwaves pass through the auditory canal and strike the tympanic membrane, causing it to vibrate. This in turn sets up a chain or vibration in the three tiny bones in the *middle ear*. The chain starts with the *malleus*, or hammer, which is connected to the tympanic membrane, then goes to the *incus*, or anvil, and last, to the *stapes*, or stirrup, the smallest bone in the human body. The footplate of the stapes rests in the *oval window*, the entrance to the *inner ear*. Figure 11.1 illustrates the parts of the ear.

Impairment in the outer or middle ear interferes with the mechanical conduct of the soundwaves to the inner ear. Hearing losses caused by these impairments are called *conductive hearing losses* and generally do not exceed 60 dB. A person with a conductive hearing loss perceives sounds to be softer than normal, but usually not as distorted. If a sound can be made loud enough it usually is heard clearly. Often the underlying cause of a conductive hearing loss (such as a middle ear infection or a malformed ossicle) can be treated medically or surgically.

The inner ear serves two functions: the *semicircular canals* aid in balance control; and the *cochlea*, a snail-shaped tube, is the organ of hearing. By a complicated mechanism, mechanical soundwaves are transformed into neural impulses. The *eighth cranial nerve* takes these impulses and transmits them to the temporal lobes of the

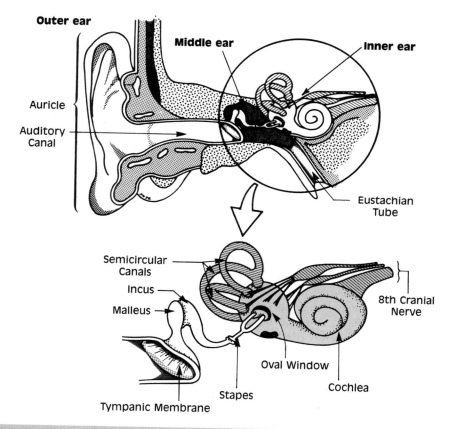

● FIGURE 11.1

Parts of the ear

brain. Impairment in the cochlea or the auditory nerve gives rise to *sensorineural hearing loss*. Sensorineural losses usually are not amenable to surgical or medical treatment, although some promising work is being done with multichannel cochlear implants that electronically bypass the defective cochlea. Sensorineural losses, like conductive losses, cause sound to be heard as less loud but, unlike a conductive loss, sound distortion also frequently occurs. Even with appropriate amplification, a person with sensorineural loss may not perceive sounds clearly. Configuration of the loss—the *degree* of loss at various frequencies—also affects sound perception.

PSYCHOLOGICAL PARAMETERS OF HEARING LOSS

The extent to which an individual is affected by his or her hearing loss is especially critical in the areas of speech and language acquisition. Several factors are involved: Some of the most important, listed below, contribute to the educational definition of hearing impairment.

1. *Age of onset.* A hearing loss that is present at birth or acquired prior to language and speech is termed a *prelingual* hearing loss. Its effects are far more drastic than those of a *postlingual*, or *adventitious*, loss, a loss acquired after language and speech have been established. The later a child acquires a hearing loss, the less drastic are its effects on speech and language. The associated psychological problems, however, may be severe.

2. *Age at amplification and intervention.* For a child with a prelingual hearing loss, the earlier the diagnosis is made, appropriate hearing aids prescribed, and educational intervention started, the better are the child's chances of developing language and speech skills. Parent education, including training in sign language if appropriate, is an essential part of early intervention.

3. *Type of communication input.* A series of retrospective studies compared the school achievement of deaf children whose parents are deaf with the achievement of deaf children of hearing parents. The studies indicate that the early use of sign language by deaf parents leads to increased achievement in the deaf child (see review in Moores, 1982). Some of the studies are flawed methodologically, but the evidence does seem to support early manual communication as an aid to English language acquisition.

4. *Presence or absence of multiple handicaps.* As might be expected, hearing impaired children who are multihandicapped have more difficulty acquiring speech and language than do those who are otherwise normal.

The Conference of Executives of American Schools for the Deaf (CEASD) in 1975 adopted educational definitions that emphasize the impact of physical hearing impairment on language processing.

- *Hearing impairment* is a generic term that indicates a hearing disability and does not indicate the degree of severity. It includes the subsets of deaf and hard of hearing.
- A *deaf* person is someone whose hearing disability is so severe that it precludes successful processing of linguistic information through audition, with or without a hearing aid.
- A *hard of hearing* person, generally with the use of a hearing aid, has sufficient residual hearing to successfully process linguistic information through audition.

The CEASD definitions encompass far more than the physical parameters of hearing loss. Given two people with the same audiometric data, one may be functioning as hard of hearing and the other may be deaf. Furthermore, the boundary between hard of hearing and deaf depends, at least in part, on the sophistication of hearing aid technology. Many people who would have functioned as deaf 20 years ago now are properly regarded as hard of hearing.

*I*NCIDENCE AND PREVALENCE

Incidence and prevalence figures for hearing loss are hard to estimate because different states define hearing impairment differently and set different eligibility criteria. As an example, Kirk and Gallagher (1983) quoted a 1979 publication of the National Center for Education Statistics as estimating the prevalence of hearing handicaps at 0.3–0.5%, or 140,700 to 230,450 school-age children. The *Twelfth Annual Report to Congress* (U.S. Department of Education, 1990) gave a figure of 52,783 hard of hearing and deaf children between the ages of 6 and 21 served in 1988–89 (the report does not distinguish between the two categories). This figure would put the deaf and hard of hearing children at 1.33% of the population of all children with disabilities age 6–21 served during these school years. Hearing impairment is truly a low-incidence condition.

A large number of children with hearing impairment have special needs in addition to those resulting from the impairment alone. Many (some estimate up to 20%) are multihandicapped and need special curricular and instructional modifications because of their additional disabilities. Delgado (1985) reported that some large cities such as "Houston, Miami, and New York are at or approaching 50% Hispanic enrollments in their schools for the deaf" and that the upward trend does not seem to be leveling off. Educators of hearing impaired students will have to devote much more effort toward providing appropriate services to those whose home language is neither English nor American Sign Language (ASL).

*E*TIOLOGY

Hearing losses acquired before, during, or after birth result from a variety of causes. Conductive hearing loss is caused postnatally most often by *otitis media*, inflammation of the middle ear. This condition usually can be attenuated by administering antibiotics medically. In some cases, a tube is inserted surgically into the middle ear through the tympanic membrane after the fluid has been drained from the middle ear. This allows for equalization of pressure between the external and the middle ear. Children with short-term impairment from otitis media do have some degree of hearing loss so are at a disadvantage in a large classroom, but they seldom require special education. If the condition is chronic, however, students may require special services, including help in speech and speechreading. Conductive hearing loss also may occur prenatally as part of syndromes such as the *Treacher-Collins syndrome*.

Most children enrolled in schools and classes for hearing impaired students have a sensorineural hearing loss. Unlike a conductive hearing loss, a sensorineural loss cannot at present be "cured" either medically or surgically. The origin may be genetic, or this type of loss may result from disease or injury before, during, or after birth.

Genetic hearing loss sometimes can be traced to abnormalities in dominant or recessive genes. *Autosomal (non-sex-linked) dominant gene deafness* appears in successive generations of a family. If one parent has an affected dominant gene, each offspring has a 50% probability of acquiring the abnormal trait.

A small percentage (about 5%) of hearing impaired school-age children have one or two deaf parents. If the parents are members of the American Deaf culture, these children learn the language of that culture, American Sign Language, in a natural fashion. Their acculturation into the deaf culture proceeds normally by transmitting the culture from parent to child during the formative period.

Another kind of inherited hearing loss is *autosomal recessive gene deafness*. In this case, each parent, although not deaf, carries the abnormal recessive gene. If two abnormal recessive genes are passed from each of the hearing parents to an offspring, that offspring will have a hearing impairment. Statistically, each offspring has a 25% chance of being affected. A family with two or more hearing impaired siblings is not a rarity even though both parents hear normally.

Genetic deafness also may occur as part of a syndrome, such as *Waardenberg's syndrome*, which may include other features: a white forelock of hair, two different-colored eyes, and abnormal pigmentation. Not all genetically caused hearing loss is present at birth. In some cases the effect of the abnormal gene is not evident until late childhood or adulthood.

Hearing impairment also may occur as part of a chromosomal defect syndrome, most notably *Down syndrome*. A significant proportion of children with Down syndrome has congenital hearing loss.

Prenatal and perinatal sensorineural hearing losses can be caused by *maternal viral infections*, such as rubella; the use of *drugs* that are toxic to the ear (some antibiotics); and *maternal illness during pregnancy*, from conditions such as diabetes and toxemia. *Premature birth* and *low birth weight* are associated with a higher than normal incidence of hearing loss. *Anoxia* (lack of sufficient oxygen during the birth process) is another cause. *Fetal alcohol syndrome* also is implicated in some cases.

Many of these causes also precipitate conditions such as cerebral palsy and mental retardation. Therefore, the high incidence of multiple handicapping conditions in the deaf population is not surprising.

Postnatal hearing losses may be caused by infections, such as measles, mumps, and meningitis. Hearing loss also may result from trauma, or injury, including the battered child syndrome, in which physical abuse to the head may cause permanent damage of the ear structures or the brain.

A growing cause for concern is hearing loss from *acoustic trauma*, repeated exposure to extremely loud sounds, including amplified music. We are seeing an increased incidence of permanent sensorineural loss in teenagers who listen to very loud music, either live or over headphones. Although usually not sufficient to warrant special education, the losses are severe enough to reduce the overall quality of life for these individuals. For further information on causes of hearing loss, see Roeser and Downs (1981).

PREVENTION

Because hearing loss has so many different causes, prevention requires a multifaceted approach. Among the techniques that may be applied to decrease the incidence of hearing loss in children are *genetic counseling, better prenatal and perinatal care, increased immunization against childhood diseases*, and *reduced exposure to overly loud sounds*. These approaches are briefly discussed below. A checklist for parents and educators to use in determining the need for further evaluation also is presented. Although early identification does not, of course, prevent hearing loss, early appropriate treatment can greatly mitigate the effects of a loss.

Genetic-based hearing loss usually cannot be prevented by medical or surgical techniques. It can, however, be prevented in succeeding generations by genetic counseling provided to parents of newly diagnosed hearing impaired children, as well as hearing impaired adolescents and young adults. This allows affected individuals to make personally appropriate choices about marriage and childbearing. Even a vigorous program of counseling, however, can never eliminate all genetic hearing loss, because recessive genes for deafness are not presently identifiable in the heterozygous or carrier form.

Hearing impairment caused by maternal infection during pregnancy can best be prevented by a program of immunization, such as that now available for rubella. This procedure alone has massively reduced the incidence of congenital hearing loss during the past 25 years. Other prenatal and perinatal causes of hearing loss can best be controlled by excellent care during pregnancy and the birth process.

Postnatally, hearing loss caused by infectious diseases such as measles and mumps can be prevented by routine immunization. Conductive hearing losses resulting from ear infections can be prevented or minimized by prompt medical intervention.

To prevent hearing loss from acoustic trauma (exposure to loud noises), public education and awareness are the best tools we have. Much more should be done, though, to alert the public to the dangers of overly loud environmental sounds and amplified music.

Minimizing the effects of an existing hearing loss requires prompt diagnosis, audiological assessment, and fitting the person with appropriate amplification devices. To this end, physicians and nurses must recognize the normal stages of language development so they can refer children who are not progressing normally for specialized evaluation. Schools, including preschools, should require auditory screening for new admissions and periodic screening during the school years. Children who fail the screening test should be referred promptly for further evaluation. Some signs parents, teachers, and other caregivers can look for are listed in Table 11.1.

LEARNING AND DEVELOPMENT

Children with hearing impairment vary at least as much in their academic, social, and emotional development as their non-hearing-impaired counterparts. Thus, to general-

● *TABLE 11.1*

Symptoms of ear problems: A checklist for parents and teachers

Middle Ear Problems

Does the child

☐ display runny ears?

☐ display inflamed or red-looking ears?

☐ frequently pull on earlobes?

☐ complain of earaches?

☐ have frequent colds?

☐ talk in an inappropriately quiet voice?

☐ have poor articulation?

☐ have trouble attending during storytime or other large-group activities?

☐ have trouble following oral directions?

Inner Ear Problems

Does the child

☐ have delayed speech?

☐ have multiple articulation problems, especially with high-pitched sounds such as /f/, /s/, and /sh/?

☐ cock or turn the head to one side while listening?

☐ display inappropriate pitch patterns for age and gender (for example, talk in a monotone, have a voice that is too high or too low)?

☐ talk in an inappropriately loud voice?

☐ have an impoverished vocabulary?

☐ have trouble attending during storytime or other listening activities?

☐ have trouble following directions?

ize about their learning and development is difficult. Some students with hearing impairment attend colleges and universities, attain advanced degrees, and have successful careers in the professions or in technology. At the other end of the scale, some people with hearing impairment are functionally illiterate and fail to attain competence in either English or ASL. Many hard of hearing people have normal or near normal speech. Many people with more profound hearing losses have speech that is unintelligible to naive listeners, but even within this group some have attained near normal speech. The discussion here, then, should be taken with caution because individuals within this diverse population may differ radically from the norm.

INTELLIGENCE

To characterize the intelligence of people with severe hearing impairments is difficult because many of the traditional standardized tests require an oral response or rely on verbal directions, so they do not provide valid measures of intelligence for this population. Vernon's (1968) review of 50 studies indicated that, when using performance (nonverbal) tests, the intelligence distribution of deaf and hearing populations is essentially the same. Genetically deaf individuals score higher on WISC–R performance subtests than do either deaf children of hearing parents who are not genetically deaf or the normally hearing standardization population (Kusche, Greenberg, & Garfield, 1983). Thus, deafness per se appears to have no limiting effect on intellectual potential as measured by nonverbal tests.

EDUCATIONAL ACHIEVEMENT

Hearing impaired students differ widely in academic achievement. According to achievement test results over the past 50 years, however, they lag approximately 4–6 years relative to normally hearing peers. The area of greatest deficit is language, including reading.

Students with less impairment, those whose parents who are also hearing impaired, and those who received early intervention all perform better than average. Minority group status and multiple handicaps are correlated negatively with achievement.

In general, the achievement of hearing impaired students seems to be not in accord with their intellectual potential. As expected, they have the most difficulty in areas in which language knowledge is most critical.

LANGUAGE

On the average, the use and comprehension of standard English by hearing impaired students is below that of their normally hearing peers, and their competence in English is correlated negatively with increased hearing loss. Because of the difficulty in comprehending the speech of many deaf people, investigations of language throughout this century often have used written rather than oral samples. These investigations have concluded that deaf individuals tend to write shorter sentences and their productions are less complex, less flexible, more stereotyped, more inclined to include fixed, repetitive phrases, and less grammatically correct than those of hearing peers. Deaf students use a greater proportion of nouns and verbs in their writing, with a paucity of pronouns, prepositions, adverbs, adjectives, and conjunctions.

In Figure 11.2 are two actual compositions of 15-year-old profoundly deaf students who are not multihandicapped. These were written in response to the same picture series. Note the many typical errors in the two samples. How much of the deficit stems from inadequate hearing and how much from inadequate education is a matter of debate.

First Day of Fishing

Many people were fishing on the brigde [sic] rather than boat. A man name is Peter Stephan. He has been fishing for sixty three years every summer. When many people fishing south side of brigde and Stephen move to other side of brigde.

For few minute a man caught fish. Many people saw him and rush to other side of brigde.

He caught fish few second ago.

Then he moved to other side of brigde and cought [six] big fish again.

People Goes to Fishing

The boy's name is John.

John went to fishing on the pier on the left side. People went fishing on the right side. The boy caught one big fish.

The people saw that the boy caught a fish and they ran over the left side. The boy was angry he wanted alone to fishing so he walked over the left side.

● *FIGURE 11.2*

Two samples written by profoundly deaf students in response to a picture series

One area in which students with hearing loss are particularly weak is their mastery of English idioms and multiple meanings. Many common words in English assume radically different meanings depending on context. The word *right*, for example, can mean the opposite of left (He is *right*-handed), the opposite of wrong (That's the *right* answer), and straight ahead (Walk *right* up the street). The *Oxford Dictionary* devotes more than 27 column inches to the definitions of *right* and many more to idioms such as right about, right angle, and right away.

SPEECH

The speech of the average prelingually hearing impaired child with a prelingual hearing loss is significantly impaired relative to the norm. Speech intelligibility correlates negatively with increased hearing loss; most profoundly hearing impaired children do not develop intelligible speech. A review by Ling (1976) suggests that speech intelligibility of students with severe or profound hearing losses did not change markedly in the five decades before the review, despite advances in hearing aid technology, acoustic phonetics, and speech science. Their speech, then and now, is characterized by multiple articulatory errors, including neutralization of vowels, nasalization of vowels, and omissions, distortions, and substitution of consonants. It also is marked by distortion of prosodic elements, including prolongation of syllables, inappropriate fundamental pitch, inappropriate pitch variation, and hypo- or hypernasality.

Again, even profoundly deaf children can, and some do, acquire intelligible, fairly natural-sounding speech. This takes an exceptionally well-structured program of speech development (such as that proposed by Ling), a supportive environment, and maximum use of available hearing aid technology to maximize any residual hearing. Extraordinary schools devoted to aural-oral education have produced a much greater proportion of students with intelligible speech than might be expected on the basis of hearing loss.

IDENTIFICATION AND ASSESSMENT

In general, for a hearing impaired child to receive services under IDEA and the various state laws, documentation of significant hearing loss must be provided through medical and audiological assessment. These data must indicate that the loss is causing, or will cause, significant problems in language development, speech skills, and educational achievement. A typical assessment battery for a hearing impaired child begins with audiological testing (assessment of hearing), followed by language assessment, speech assessment, developmental scales, achievement tests, and cognitive assessment.

AUDIOLOGICAL TESTING

The primary area of assessment is the evaluation of hearing. Following a complete medical examination and any appropriate medical correction, the child is referred to an audiologist for audiological testing. This testing is designed to reveal the extent of the loss at specific frequencies, to explicate the type of loss and the site at which it occurs, to discover the effect of the loss on speech detection and speech discrimination, and to allow the fitting of appropriate amplification devices.

Medical evaluation of ear function is the province of an otologist (sometimes an otolaryngologist or otorhinolaryngologist). Otologists prescribe medications (e.g., antibiotics to combat middle ear infections) and perform needed medical and surgical interventions. Precise measurement of hearing is done by an *audiologist*, a person with an advanced degree in speech and hearing science. Audiologists are certified by the American Speech-Language-Hearing Association (ASHLA).

Measurement of hearing is accomplished in two ways: behaviorally and objectively. In *behavioral audiometry* the individual voluntarily responds to a sound stimulus. The response is appropriate to the individual's stage of development. *Objective audiometry* does not require a behavioral response. Using *tympanometry*, a form of objective audiometry, the audiologist can reliably assess the status of the middle ear and determine whether hearing loss is attributable to middle ear dysfunction (conductive loss) or to sensorineural damage. Another form of objective audiometry is the *auditory brainstem response* (ABR). Electrodes placed on the scalp record neural responses to sound stimuli. ABR is used with children who are very young, have retardation, or have developmental delays who are unable to respond behaviorally.

Behavioral Audiometry. During the first few months of life, some infants are at high risk for hearing loss because of factors such as family history, prematurity, and maternal infection. Their hearing can be evaluated in a sound-attenuated room, where sounds of specific frequencies and intensities are introduced through loudspeakers. Upon hearing the sound, an infant may show a range of responses, such as startle reflexes, quieting, or crying. Because infant responses are difficult to observe and judge reliably, great skill and training are required on the part of the audiologist.

Children approximately 6 months to 2 years old are evaluated the same way. In addition, the extent to which the child *localizes*, turning his or her head toward the sound source, can be evaluated. Localization responses can be reinforced after a correct response by presenting attractive visual reinforcers, such as animated puppets. ABR and tympanometry also are used with this age group.

Testing with Preschoolers. After age 2, developmentally normal children can be trained to respond voluntarily to sounds introduced through earphones or through a bone conduction receiver placed behind the ear. Earphones enable the audiologist to evaluate the function of each ear separately. The bone conduction receiver allows sound to bypass the outer and middle ear and go directly to the inner ear via the bones of the skull. If earphone presentation (air conduction) testing reveals a loss but bone conduction is normal, the loss is *conductive*.

Stimuli are generated by an *audiometer*, a machine that produces sounds of precise frequencies and intensities. In pure-tone testing, sounds are presented through the earphones at frequencies of 125, 250, 500, 1000, 2000, 4000, and 8000 Hz. By presenting the sounds at different intensity levels, the threshold for each measured frequency can be determined. The hearing threshold is that point at which the individual responds to the stimulus half the time it is presented. The results are plotted on a graph called an *audiogram*. Preschoolers respond through some developmentally appropriate playlike activity—stacking a block or a ring, placing a puzzle piece, putting a peg in a pegboard—each time a sound is presented.

To determine how effective a hearing aid is in enhancing the auditory function, sounds are introduced through loudspeakers while the child is wearing the aid. The various responses described above then can be used to obtain the *aided threshold*. In addition to determining the relative effectiveness of various hearing aids, aided thresholds are useful in deciding on techniques for teaching language and speech and in selecting optimum communication modes.

Procedures used in evaluating the hearing of school-age children and adults are similar to those used with preschoolers, but the expected responses are age-appropriate, usually a finger or a hand raised in response to the stimulus. Again, tympanometry is used to determine the status of middle ear function and to help differentiate conductive and sensorineural problems.

Speech Audiometry. Speech audiometry, conducted with preschool and older children and adults, tests speech reception and speech discrimination. To determine the *speech reception* threshold, the audiologist presents speech at different intensity levels until the person indicates that he or she can just barely hear the words. To determine *speech* *discrimination*—the ability to discriminate among speech sounds—the audiologist reads aloud a phonetically balanced set of one-syllable words at a comfortable listening level. The individual being tested is asked to repeat the words he or she has heard. The percentage of words correctly repeated represents that person's speech discrimination score. Speech audiometry also is done with augmentation by a hearing aid to determine the aid's effectiveness in enhancing speech perception.

Bill, age 11, was born with Treacher-Collins syndrome. One of the symptoms of this syndrome is missing or malformed external ears and middle ear anomalies. Bill has no left ear canal, and his right auricle is a small, round bump with no external auditory canal opening. His middle ears are malformed and not functional. Because Bill cannot receive airborne sounds through his outer and middle ears, he relies on bone conduction hearing aids fitted to the mastoid bone behind his ears. His moderate conductive hearing loss is corrected with amplification so he can hear normally with hearing aids, but he needs special help in speech and language. Bill attends regular classes most of the day and is achieving at grade level. As illustrated in Figure 11.3, he seems to have a slight sensorineural loss at 1000 and 2000 Hz in his right ear.

Mary, whose audiogram at age 5 is presented in Figure 11.4, has sensorineural hearing loss, probably caused by ototoxic drugs administered during her first week of life to combat an infection. Her hearing loss is in the moderate-to-severe range and shows a characteristic slope. She hears much better at the lower frequencies than she does at higher pitches, typical of sensorineural losses. Mary derives considerable benefit from her ear-level hearing aids, which put most speech within her range, but she still does not perceive sounds normally. Both her speech and her language are affected.

At the time of her initial evaluation, at age 3.5, Mary had no intelligible speech and could speechread only a few words, but she was reported to be exceptionally compliant, highly communicative in nonverbal ways, and highly stimulable. Mary spent six years, from age 3.5 to 9.5, in a highly structured special class where total communication is used and where heavy emphasis is placed on auditory training and speech development. Her parents and grandparents took courses in manual English and use it routinely. Mary made rapid progress in that enriched atmosphere. Three years after her initial diagnosis, her speech was rated as 75%–90% intelligible to a naive listener. Her average sentence length was seven words. She routinely produced sentences such as "May I put the eraser in my bag?" "I washed the mirror because it was dirty" and " He is drying off." When Mary was in the fourth grade her family moved to a small town. Mary now attends a regular sixth-grade class with a full-time interpreter. She receives no other academic support and is performing in the top quartile of her class.

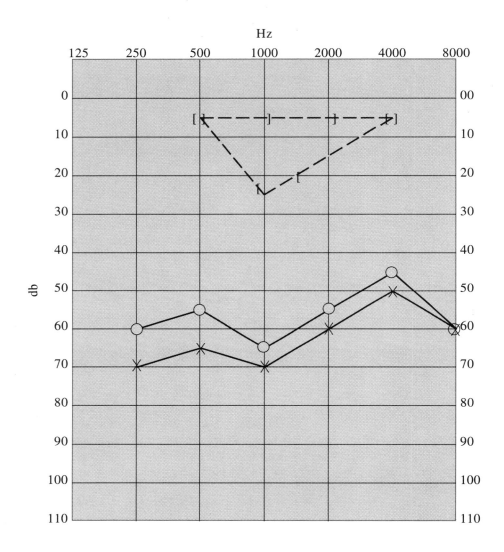

Audiogram Key

	Right	Left
Air Conduction	○	X
Bone Conduction	[	]

● *FIGURE 11.3*

Audiogram: Bill H., age 11

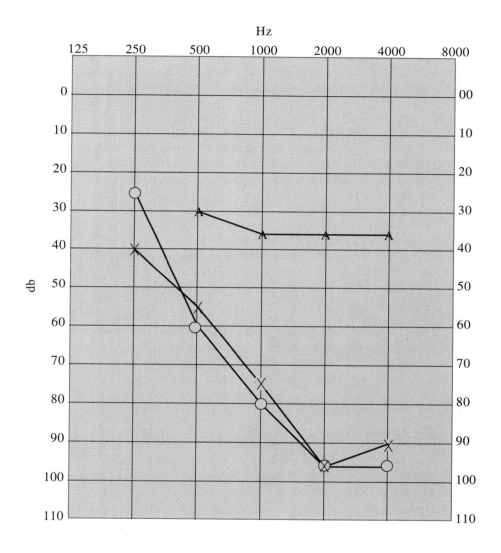

Audiogram Key		
	Right	Left
Air Conduction	O	X
Aided	A	A

● FIGURE 11.4

Audiogram: Mary H., age 5

INTELLIGENCE TESTS

Formal, normed, verbal tests of intelligence, such as the Stanford-Binet or full-scale WISC, usually are inappropriate for testing children with hearing impairment because they assume exposure to a normal language environment, obviously a condition people with prelingual hearing loss do not meet. Therefore, the intelligence testing of hearing impaired children is limited to adaptations of behavior or developmental scales to eliminate verbal items, and to nonverbal (performance) tests of intelligence.

With very young hearing impaired children, scales such as the Bayley Scales of Infant Development (Bayley, 1984) can be adapted by eliminating items that require hearing or a language response. School-age children are tested most frequently with the revised edition of the Wechsler Intelligence Scale for Children (WISC–R) Performance Scale (Wechsler, 1974). The performance scale in its original form consists of various subtests, such as block design and picture arrangement, which do not require verbal responses. The directions, however, are presented in standard oral form. Anderson and Sisco (1977) standardized the scale on a hearing impaired sample, using directions that were variously oral, pantomime, and signed. Also used with this population are other nonverbal tests such as the Hiskey-Nebraska (Hiskey, 1966), which has been normed on both hearing impaired and normally hearing students; Raven's (1948) Progressive Matrices; and Arthur's revision of the Leiter International Performance Scale (Arthur, 1952). The results obtained with hearing impaired students on nonverbal IQ tests, however, do not predict future academic achievement very well and so are of limited value.

LANGUAGE ASSESSMENT

The assessment of language with children who have hearing impairment is an extremely complex process, because so many aspects of language, and of preverbal or nonverbal communicative behavior, must be assessed before appropriate interventions can be selected and their efficacy evaluated. At least the following aspects must be assessed:

1. The expressive and receptive vocabulary available to the child through various modalities (signs, fingerspelling, audition, speechreading, and reading/writing).
2. The child's syntax or grammatical ability—his or her ability to string words together to form English sentences or, in some cases, to use grammatically correct ASL.
3. The child's ability to use and understand language as well as nonlanguage communication, such as gestures, posture, and facial expression, in socially and situationally appropriate ways.

The language of children with hearing impairment is evaluated using a battery of standardized and informal (nonstandardized) tests. Thompson, Biro, Vethivelu, and Hatfield (1986) exhaustively described the tests available for this population. An essential part of any language evaluation is to elicit an expressive language sample. These samples of oral or sign communication, or both, are analyzed in many ways to determine how language development is progressing. Sequential samples yield information on vocabulary and concept growth, inflection markers (-ed, -s, -ing), length of utterances, syntactic complexity and pragmatic usage.

SPEECH ASSESSMENT

The speech of children with hearing impairment can be evaluated in several ways. For most hard of hearing children, *articulation tests* suitable for normally hearing children may be used. These tests generally require the child to pronounce words or syllables with the phoneme of interest in the initial, medial, or final position. The word *bone*, for example, could be used to test articulation of the initial /b/, the medial vowel /o/, and the final /n/. Errors are categorized as omissions, distortions, substitutions, or additions (see Chapter 8).

For more severely hearing impaired children, or those with limited speech skills, population-specific, in-depth tests, such as the phonological and phonetic-level evaluations of Ling (1976), are available. The *phonological evaluation* tests for the presence of the various speech features in the child's spontaneous speech. At the phonetic evaluation level, the Ling test begins with the evaluation of nonsegmental aspects of speech, including loudness, fundamental pitch, and pitch variation and duration. Each vowel and diphthong then is tested separately, and each consonant and consonant blend is evaluated in several vowel contexts as well as in prevocalic and postvocalic positions, both alone and alternated with other consonants. Once the child has been tested, teaching targets, teaching strategies, and modalities can be selected. Can the sound(s) be taught through audition alone or must they be taught through audition supplemented by visual and tactual input?

INTERVENTION

The major area of special education for students with a hearing impairment is language acquisition and use. Controversy always has surrounded the modalities and methodologies involved in presenting language, and even the desired outcomes of language/communication training for deaf individuals. The controversies continue, supplemented and sometimes exacerbated by the requirements of IDEA for pragmatic assessment of the needs of individual students and a need to consider the wishes of their parents in regard to both placement and instruction.

A brief, and necessarily simplistic, review of the language development of normally hearing children can help us understand the modality options possible in educating children with hearing impairment. Normally hearing children, from birth, and perhaps even in-utero, are exposed to the language of their environment. Because language, with the notable exception of the sign languages, is an auditory-oral phenomenon, and because audition cannot be shut off voluntarily, a baby is exposed to all of the linguistic information present in the immediate environment, whether speech is addressed to the infant or to other people.

Communication directed to infants usually is repeated many times, accompanied by appropriate activity. Thus, babies learn to associate phrases such as "Here's Mommy" with the appearance of a familiar face, and "Wave bye-bye" with the manipulation of their arms and hands. Babies learn to recognize the intonational patterns and words that constitute their linguistic environment. At the same time, they begin, in a fixed developmental sequence, to control their own breathing patterns, lips, tongue, and other musculature to produce differentiated sounds. Infants are reinforced by the auditory feedback of others and by listening to self-produced oral stimuli. Eventually they learn to modify the range of their productions to conform more closely to the sounds and rhythms of the language environment. Thus, the baby actively takes in thousands and thousands of models of linguistic units, then processes these models using capabilities thought to be unique to the human species.

At about 1 year of age, the baby begins to speak in the language of the environment. Babies who hear German speak German; babies who hear Japanese speak Japanese. Babies who hear imperfectly speak imperfectly and are delayed in speech production; those who do not hear at all within the range of intensity and frequency of speech sounds do not develop language spontaneously and therefore do not speak.

By the time a developmentally normal child enters school, he or she has mastered most of the grammatical complexity of the language, is well on the way to developing skill in the social uses of language, and has an oral vocabulary of several thousand words. Other children and adults in the language community readily understand the child's speech. Schooling then teaches children to code their auditory-oral language into written form. As a consequence their language also can be received visually, through reading, and expressed motorically by writing. And both reading and writing, are superimposed on the auditory-oral language base. At the same time, children learn to receive and send nonlinguistic communication, through means such as gesture, posture, facial expression, art, music, dance, and pantomime.

For infants with hearing impairment, auditory-oral language reception is diminished quantitatively, commensurate with their degree of loss. The absolute number of language models they receive is reduced, because they are unable to overhear others' conversations at a distance. The quality of any auditory signal that does get in also may be reduced, because of the distortion accompanying sensorineural losses.

OPTIONS FOR COMMUNICATION

The job of educators of children with hearing impairment is to find ways of getting language to the child despite the defective auditory apparatus, to give the child the model he or she needs to establish a communication system. Options for expressive and receptive language modalities are presented below. Selecting any one, or any combination of these modalities for language input, carries far-reaching psychological, sociological, and educational implications for the child and the community alike.

Manual Options. The two best known methods of manual communication are American Sign Language (ASL) and manually coded English (MCE).

American Sign Language (ASL). The deaf community in the United States developed a visual gestural language, American Sign Language (ASL, or Ameslan), which bypasses the auditory channel and allows visual reception of complex communication. ASL is a complete language with its own vocabulary and complex syntactic, semantic, and pragmatic structures that are radically different from those of English or any other auditory-oral language. ASL does not have a widely utilized written form (though some experimental prototypes have been developed). It is the native language of deaf children whose parents are deaf. These children learn ASL in a fashion remarkably similar to the language learning of normally hearing children whose parents speak. Many educators of the deaf, however, believe that ASL is not suitable as a teaching language because it is not English and is not readily transferable to speaking, reading and writing skills in English.

A growing minority of educators believes that deaf children have the right to be educated, at least initially, in the language of the deaf community, ASL, and that English as a second language (ESL), in manual or oral or written form, should be taught as part of a bilingual-bicultural program. This implies that normally hearing people in the deaf child's environment should learn ASL as quickly as possible and that the deaf child and his or her family should be integrated into the deaf community, to ensure the availability of adult linguistic models.

This view has enormous sociological implications. It calls into question the very purpose of education for this population. Even though proponents liken their approach to that of other bilingual–bicultural approaches for linguistic minority groups, the two populations have a real difference. For linguistic minority groups the family structure would support the initial acquisition of a language other than English; for deaf children of hearing parents, ASL is not the language of their family or community and would have to be taught simultaneously to all parties.

Manually Coded English (MCE). All MCE systems have a base of ASL vocabulary and superimpose upon this base, to a greater or lesser extent, the syntactic, semantic, and pragmatic structures of English. In some forms of MCE, the semantic boundaries of the ASL signs are changed greatly to conform to English multiple meanings. The root word "run" in ASL, for example, is signed in the sentences "She has a run in her stocking" and "The water is running," with two very different semi-iconic signs. The word "fall" also has many signs. Two different ones represent the two concepts of snow falling and a person falling. In some forms of MCE, if the English root word is spelled the same and sounds the same (as in the two cases above) it is represented by one ASL sign even if the meanings are quite different. This may lead to some odd iconic misrepresentations. Some forms of MCE use invented (non-ASL) signs for inflections such as -ing and -ed and English prefixes and suffixes (un-, pre-, -ment, -ness). Others string ASL signs together in English word order without grammatical inflections to form a Pidgin Signed English.

All MCE systems use fingerspelling to supplement the signs. Fingerspelling is a visual representation of the letters of the English language. Each letter and numeral is represented by a different hand configuration. English letters are spelled sequentially to produce a temporal representation of a word, phrase, or sentence. When no ASL sign exists, fingerspelling may be used, for example, for technical words and proper nouns. The manual alphabet is shown in Figure 11.5.

MCE as part of total communication allows the child to receive and send communication quickly and easily though the visual channel, as well as to receive and send auditory-oral messages. With all its inherent limitations, MCE enhances the opportunity for children with hearing impairment to learn a language system in a way that may be natural to them.

The Auditory-Oral Option.

The philosophy of oral education is that hearing impaired children should be given the opportunity to learn to speak and to understand speech, learn through spoken language in

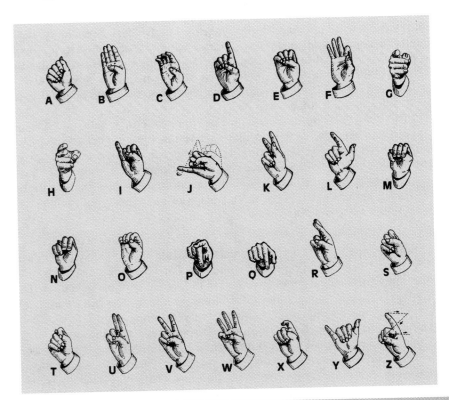

● FIGURE 11.5

The manual alphabet

Source: Gallaudet University Division of Public Services, Kendall Green, Washington, DC 20002.

school, and later function as independent adults in a world in which people's primary mode of communication is speech. (Ling, 1984, p. 9)

The auditory-oral option excludes the use of any form of language that is not used in the general population, including American Sign Language, fingerspelling, and manually coded English of any variety. Instead, appropriate amplification devices are fitted and residual hearing is trained to the maximum extent possible so oral language can be received "naturally," through the auditory mechanism.

When necessary, because of the nature or severity of the hearing loss, the auditory system is supplemented by the visual reception of speech through speechreading (lipreading). Speech production is taught insofar as possible through audition, supplemented as necessary by visual and tactile stimulation. Components of the auditory-oral approach are described briefly.

Amplification. As soon as possible after diagnosis, children are fitted with appropriate personal hearing aids. Personal aids are of different types, including the body aid (a microphone-amplified box worn on the chest, connected to a receiver in the ear by a cord), ear-level aids, and all-in-the-ear aids. All contain a *microphone*, which picks up sound from the environment, an *amplifier*, which electronically increases the loudness of the sound, and a *receiver*, which converts the electronic impulses back into amplified soundwaves that enter the ear. To prevent leakage of sound, the receiver is connected to the ear through a custom-made earmold that seals off the auditory canal. Most children are appropriately fitted with binaural, ear-level hearing aids so they can hear sound as normally as possible in both ears and localize the sound source. Amplification devices are illustrated in Figure 11.6.

In some schools children switch from their own personal aids to a group amplification system during instruction. In the most commonly used system the teacher wears a cordless microphone that broadcasts his or her voice over an FM radio frequency. The children wear boxes on their chests, which act as FM radios tuned to the teacher's frequency. These are connected by cords to special ear-level receivers, or to the child's personal hearing aid. The advantage of this system is that the teacher's voice is amplified selectively and the loudness of the signal is constant no matter what the physical distance between teacher and student. Hearing aids cannot totally restore to normal the hearing of a person with sensorineural loss, but they can be of significant aid in bringing speech sounds into the range of audibility.

Auditory training. Because hearing aids do not restore hearing to normal, students using amplification need explicit training in perceiving, discriminating, and identifying both environmental and speech sounds through their hearing aids. The auditory-oral approach stresses the primacy of the auditory system in receiving language. Parents and teachers are encouraged to talk to their children from behind them or while the face is occluded so the children get used to relying on audition to detect and identify speech.

Speechreading. As a supplement to audition, speech can be received visually, by "reading" movements of the lips, tongue, jaw, and other musculature that accompanies normal speech production. The functionality of speechreading is limited in that many phonemes share the same place of production and therefore look the same on the lips (e.g., /p, b, m/; /t, d, n/; and /f, v/), whereas others are invisible because they are produced near the back of the mouth (/k, g,-ng, h/). Thus, even under ideal conditions a good speechreader receives less than half the information a normally hearing person gets—and ideal conditions are hard to come by.

Among the factors that limit speechreading are visual fatigue, adverse lighting conditions or low light, excess facial hair of the speaker (as many oral deaf children have discovered, Santa Claus is *impossible* to speechread), excessive distance between speaker and speechreader (as, for example, in a theater or a lecture hall), group conversation, lecturers who move around as they speak, and people who do not move their lips much while speaking. Good adult speechreaders use their own knowledge of English vocabulary and structure to fill in the gaps. For example, in the sentence, "Please pass the corn," the speechread word "corn" is indistinguishable from the words "court" "horn," and "gourd" but a proficient English speaker can determine, through contextual or situational cues, which is meant. As a vehicle for initially learning a language, however, speechreading has obvious limitations.

Speech training. Because of the limitations of auditory and speechread language input, speech does not develop spontaneously in most severely and profoundly prelingually hearing impaired children. Although speech does develop spontaneously in less severely impaired children, it often is characterized by multiple articulation errors as well as problems with rhythm and intonation. Speech is taught to deaf children through a structured curricular sequence. One program (Ling, 1976) begins with instruction in the production of nonsegmental aspects of speech, sounds of varied duration, sounds of varied pitch, and sounds of varied intensity. The sequence then proceeds to each vowel sound in order of difficulty. Then each consonant sound is taught in vowel contexts, in a specific sequence that varies according to manner of production and place of production in the mouth. As the student masters each sound, he or she is required to use the sound appropriately in spontaneous speech throughout the day.

The auditory-oral approach emphasizes that deaf children are entitled to the opportunity to learn to use the prevailing (oral) language of the community. If the children are allowed to use sign language, which is initially easier to acquire, auditory-oral advocates believe that children may not have the motivation or the intensity of effort necessary to become fluent in the oral language of the normally hearing community. Only if a child fails to achieve oral language by perhaps the mid-elementary or middle school years would auditory-oral advocates suggest that the child be placed in an educational program that utilizes sign language. Of course, by then the child is far behind his or her peers in language skills and in academic subjects that depend on language and has missed the prime time for language learning.

The Total Communication Option.

Total communication is a philosophy incorporating appropriate aural, manual, and oral modes of communication in order to ensure effective communication with and among hearing impaired persons. (Conference of Executives of American Schools for the Deaf, quoted in Arnold, 1984)

For some children with severe and profound sensorineural hearing losses, attaining intelligible speech may be an unreachable goal. Karchmer, Milone, and Wolk (1979) reported that, of children with severe (71–90 dB losses), 24.8% had unintelligible speech or would not speak, and an additional 20.2% had barely intelligible speech. Of students with hearing losses of 90 dB or more, 48.6% had unintelligible speech or would not speak, and the speech of 28.2% was rated as barely intelligible. Thus, a large proportion of severely and profoundly hearing impaired students will not attain the goal of full social integration into a speaking society. Even students who eventually do acquire intelligible speech find the language learning process and the speech learning process slow and laborious, hardly the seemingly effortless, natural learning of young hearing children.

In the late 1960s a deaf educator and parent, Roy Holcomb, came up with the concept of total communication. It combines the components of the auditory-oral approach with a signed representation of English. The rationale underlying total communication is that every child with a hearing impairment has the right to receive language under the most favorable conditions possible. By making both oral and sign language available as early in life as possible, the child can utilize whatever channels are accessible to comprehend and send messages. An additional benefit is that the child is learning the communication modalities necessary to integrate socially into the deaf community as well as into the normally hearing world. A good total communication program stresses all components of a good auditory-oral program—amplification, auditory training, speechreading, and speech development—and adds one of the several variants of manually coded English (MCE) along with active encouragement of nonverbal communication behaviors.

The efficacy of total communication depends on the willingness and ability of the child's parents, extended family, and school contacts to learn and consistently use it in the child's presence. Ideally, TC should be used not just when directly addressing the child but whenever the child is present. The child will learn through normal eavesdropping on the conversation of others. Advocates of total communication stress that it is not a second-rate option to be applied only when the oral approach has failed. Instead, from the earliest possible time, deaf children have the right to multichannel information.

EDUCATIONAL DELIVERY SYSTEMS

Early intervention is essential in minimizing the handicaps imposed by hearing loss. Infant and preschool training for hearing impaired children and their parents is prevalent throughout the United States. Two types of programs are: (a) *center-based*, wherein preschoolers and their parents go to a special facility for training; and (b) *home-based*, wherein the parent/infant trainer goes to the home. In both types the goals are the same:

1. To provide parents with support and information as they adjust to the reality of

rearing a child with a hearing impairment.

2. To provide the child with the best possible amplification and to initiate a program of auditory training.

3. To teach the parents how to communicate with their child and how to use everyday situations—such as bathing, cooking, shopping, and dressing—to promote language development. Parents who choose total communication are taught Manually Coded English. Those who choose ASL must learn that language to fluency.

School-age children are educated in a variety of placements ranging from segregated, special residential or centralized schools to regular classes with support services. Less severely impaired children are likely to be enrolled in mainstream classes with itinerant support, but they also may be found in more restrictive placements. More severely impaired children and those with multiple handicaps are likely to be enrolled in self-contained classes or residential schools.

Residential Schools. Residential schools, also called centralized schools, can be either public or private. These schools usually have a sufficient population base to allow for graded classes, subject matter specialists, and a variety of extracurricular activities. They also have the resources to employ specialists such as audiologists, psychologists, speech and hearing personnel, and computer programmers. Residential schools often hire hearing impaired adults as teachers, aides, and counselors, and for other positions. These personnel serve as role models, as well as in their professional capacities. The negative side is that contact with non-hearing-impaired peers usually is minimal or nonexistent; and the students may become strangers in their own homes. Parents cannot keep up with their child's growing sign language vocabulary, so communication becomes increasingly difficult.

Day Schools. Some larger metropolitan school districts have special schools called day schools. These resemble residential schools, but all students commute daily.

Day Classes. Day classes are self-contained classes located on or adjacent to the campus of a regular elementary, middle, or secondary school. In general, day classes are integrated administratively and share support staff and special facilities such as learning resource center, cafeteria, and gym. Day class students often are mainstreamed with or without an interpreter for some academic or nonacademic subjects.

Resource Rooms and Itinerant Services. Children with less severe impairments and those functioning near grade level may be placed primarily in regular classes. For help in areas such as auditory training and speech, they go to a resource room or a special teacher. In the regular class an interpreter may accompany them.

Postsecondary Education. Students with hearing impairment have a variety of postsecondary educational options. Gallaudet University, in Washington, DC, is a 4-year liberal arts college that enrolls primarily hearing impaired students as undergraduates. All courses are taught in simultaneous communication. Gallaudet's offerings approximate those of other small liberal arts colleges. At the graduate level, Gallaudet enrolls both hearing impaired and normally hearing students in areas such as teacher education, administration, and counseling. Gallaudet is a major research and policy center for all matters concerned with hearing impairment.

The National Technical Institute for the Deaf (NTID) is affiliated with the Rochester Institute of Technology, in Rochester, New York. It offers programs in business, technology, and computer sciences, as an alternative to the more traditional liberal arts orientation of Gallaudet. At NTID, students take the more technical courses at Rochester Institute, with the aid of note-takers and interpreters. NTID is also a major research center, focusing on the postsecondary education of people with hearing impairment.

Some regular 4-year colleges have made an outstanding effort to accommodate students with hearing impairments. One example is California State University at Northridge. Through its Center on Deafness, the university provides a number of support services: interpreters, tutoring, note-takers, and counselors.

Many community colleges offer special services for students with hearing impairment. Seattle Central Community College in Washington is a pioneer in this area. A staff of counselors and educators works with each student to determine his or her needs in basic skill areas and vocational training. Once a program has been agreed upon, interpreter services and other support enable the student to complete vocational training and enter the competitive job market.

EDUCATIONAL TECHNOLOGIES

Captioned Films/Videos for the Deaf, funded by the U.S. Department of Education, provides funds to caption a variety of educational and recreational films so people with hearing impairment can access a film medium similar to that of hearing peers. Captioned Films sponsors many other special projects: teacher guides, visuals for use with overhead projectors, and programmed instruction sequences.

Telecommunication Devices for the Deaf (TDDs) allow deaf people to communicate written messages via telephone lines to others who have the device. TDDs have become much more portable and easy to use. In part because of Section 504, most hospitals, police stations, emergency centers, and fire stations now have TDDs. More schools and businesses are now acquiring them, allowing deaf people direct access to services without having to depend on a hearing intermediary.

Closed caption television allows individuals with hearing impairment to see captioned programs on major television networks and over the Public Broadcasting System. The captions are visible only to television owners who have a special decoder. This device allows hearing impaired people access to at least part of the information and entertainment available to the hearing public.

The *computer* is an exciting device for educating hearing impaired children. Because computers are basically a visual medium and are interactive, they present an ideal tool for individualizing instruction in areas such as written language, reading, math, and the physical and biological sciences. The combination of computers and videodiscs allows programming in sign language and instruction in social and occupational skills. Computer networks also allow deaf and hearing people to communicate through bulletin boards and electronic mail systems.

REGULAR CLASSROOM IMPLICATIONS

Children and youth with hearing impairments may be mainstreamed with or without the support of an interpreter. The interpreter is a professional who is trained to enhance communication between hearing and hearing impaired people. Interpreters operate under a code of ethics that takes into account the sensitive nature of their work. They serve in a variety of areas—medical, legal, counseling, vocational, academic—as an interface between the hearing and deaf cultures. Some interpreting is "oral"; the interpreter sits near a hearing impaired person in large lecture halls or group discussions and mouths the words being said to provide a clearer signal for speechreading. Hard-to-speechread words may be replaced by more perceptually salient words as well. Most interpreting is "manual"; however, the interpreters either transliterate oral English into manually coded English or translate oral English into ASL. Interpreters also reverse-interpret clients' signs into oral English if the client cannot speak intelligibly or chooses not to do so. The following guidelines will be useful for regular class teachers who have students with hearing impairment in their classrooms.

Physical Arrangements
- Allow the student to choose his or her own seat. If an interpreter is present, allow the pair to seat themselves in the manner most conducive to communication.
- Allow the student to move freely about the room in response to various communication situations.
- When speaking without an interpreter, do not turn your back on the class or move around the room. Stand in one place when communicating. Use an overhead projector rather than a chalkboard so you do not lose eye contact with the class.
- Women: do not wear distracting jewelry or make-up that interferes with speechreading. Men: avoid excessive facial hair.
- Make sure that lighting does not put the speaker's face into shadow.

Instructional Considerations
- Speak in complete sentences. Do not overarticulate or speak more loudly or more slowly than normal.
- To check for comprehension, ask the student to repeat what you have said, or ask a specific question. Do not ask, "Did you understand?" Many hearing impaired children have learned to nod *yes*, even when they do not understand at all.
- Assign a normally hearing "buddy" to make sure the hearing impaired student gets orally presented assignments.
- In lecture situations assign a hearing student to take notes with carbon copies. The student cannot watch an interpreter or speechread and take notes at the same time.
- Try to alternate oral activities with independent seatwork or motor activities. This lessens the visual fatigue that comes from speechreading or watching the interpreter.

Social Considerations
- Explain hearing loss to the class. Demonstrate hearing aids, interpreting, speechreading, and other special materials and techniques. Invite the special teacher, the parents, and

the child new to the classroom, if he or she is old enough and wishes to be part of the discussion.

■ Have the student assume the same responsibilities and privileges as any other student in the class with regard to such things such as disciplinary procedures, holding class offices, running errands, and cleaning the room.

■ Encourage cooperative projects that enable the hearing impaired child to work in small groups with hearing peers.

Working with an Interpreter. Unless special arrangements are made explicitly, the interpreter's sole function in the classroom is to facilitate communication. Teachers should not expect the interpreter to function as a disciplinarian, a tutor, an aide, or a counselor. By way of etiquette for working with an interpreter:

■ Always look directly at the student when addressing him or her; never face the interpreter.

■ Talk directly to the student. Do not address the interpreter or ask the interpreter if the student understands. The interpreter's only task is to interpret your exact words to the student.

■ Vary class activities so direct discourse does not go on for a long time. Interpreters need frequent breaks.

■ Call upon interpreters, by special arrangement, to teach sign language to the class or the staff. This greatly facilitates the social integration of hearing impaired students.

■ Expect the interpreter to relate not only the formal discourse of the lesson, but your and the others students' side comments and social chatter as well. The student who has a hearing impairment has the same rights as everyone else to "eavesdrop" on informal communications. Of course be sure not to discuss students "behind their backs."

For the interpreter to discuss or report to anyone about things that may have happened in your classroom is a breach of ethics unless you have given permission.

S*UMMARY AND PROJECTIONS*

Individuals with *hearing impairment* are those who are designated as either deaf or hard of hearing. *Deaf* people cannot use hearing, with or without amplification, as their primary mode for acquiring or receiving language. *Hard of hearing* individuals can use their hearing as a primary language reception channel, but they require special modifications in instructional programs to learn most efficiently. The extent to which an individual is impacted by his or her hearing loss depends on many factors, including physical site of the loss, configuration of the loss, age of onset, presence or absence of additional handicapping conditions, age at initial diagnosis, availability of appropriate amplification devices, and age of exposure to a language system through early intervention programs.

Hearing loss may occur before birth (prenatal), during the birth process (perinatal), or any time after birth (postnatal). Sometimes hearing loss is inherited, through either dominant or recessive genes. Genetic loss can be part of a larger medical syndrome. Other causes of hearing loss are prenatal maternal viral infections, trauma during the birth process, ototoxic drugs, accidents and injuries, prolonged exposure to loud noise, and illnesses such as meningitis and encephalitis.

The primary effect of a *prelingual* hearing loss (before approximately 18 months of age) is on initial development of a language system. Because of the loss, both the quantity and the quality of linguistic information the child receives are reduced. This lack of clear linguistic input impacts all aspects of the language development process: phonology, morphology, syntax, semantics, and pragmatics. Education of children with hearing impairment in the United States attempts to compensate for language deprivation in various ways. *Aural-oral approaches* stress the development of auditory-based language through training in the use of residual hearing with amplification, supplemented if necessary by speechreading, to give the hearing impaired child access to the spoken language of his or her culture. The *total communication* approach combines auditory-oral training with a visual signed English system. This approach is designed to allow the child access to all communication modes that can aid in the acquisition of language and in cognitive development. In a third option, the child initially acquires *American Sign Language* (ASL), a unique visual language used by the American adult deaf culture, and the subsequent introduction of English as a second language (ESL).

Children and youth with hearing impairment are served in a variety of placements, from residential schools to mainstreamed classrooms. Mainstreaming may be facilitated by an interpreter who transliterates oral or manual English or translates from ASL to English and back.

Major challenges to educators and parents of hearing impaired children in the next decades include:

- Providing services to hearing impaired children in small school district-based programs while still allowing them access to all necessary support services, appropriate role models, and a hearing impaired peer group.
- Improving the academic achievement of children with hearing impairment to more closely match their intellectual potential.
- Incorporating the results of new findings in normal language development, cognitive psychology, and reading theory into coherent educational programs.
- Providing appropriate education for children with hearing impairment from low-English-proficient and culturally diverse families, and those who are multihandicapped.

The next few decades should both challenge and reward all those who work with people with hearing impairment and their families.

REFERENCES

American Annals of the Deaf. (1974). *Directory issue, 119*(2).
American Annals of the Deaf. (1985). *Directory issue, 130*(2).
Anderson, R. J., & Sisco, F. Y. (1977). *Standardization of the WISC–R performance scale for deaf children.*

Washington, DC: Gallaudet College, Office of Demographic Studies.

Arnold, P. (1984, February). The education of the deaf child: For integration or autonomy. *American Annals of the Deaf, 129*(1), 29–37.

Arthur, G. (1952). *Leiter performance international scale.* Chicago: Stoelting.

Bayley, N. (1984). *Bayley scales of infant development.* Cleveland: Psychological Corp.

Conference of Executives of American Schools for the Deaf. (1975). Report of the ad hoc committee to define deaf and hard of hearing. *American Annals of the Deaf, 120*, 509–512.

Delgado, G. (1985). *Advocate for Education of the Deaf, 2*(4).

Hiskey, M. (1966). *Nebraska test of learning aptitude.* Lincoln, NE: Union College Press.

Karchmer, M. A., Milone, M. N., & Wolk, S. (1979). Educational significance of hearing loss at three levels of severity. *American Annals of the Deaf, 124*, 97–109.

Kirk, S. A., & Gallagher, J. J. (1983). *Educating exceptional children* (4th ed.). Boston: Houghton Mifflin.

Kusche, C., Greenberg, M., & Garfield, T. (1983). Nonverbal intelligence and verbal achievement in deaf adolescents: An examination of heredity and environment. *American Annals of the Deaf, 128*(4), 458–466.

Ling, D. (1976). *Speech and the hearing-impaired child: Theory and practice.* Washington, DC: Alexander Graham Bell Association for the Deaf.

Ling, D. (Ed.). (1984). *Early intervention for hearing-impaired children: Oral options.* San Diego: College-Hill Press.

Moores, D. F. (1982). *Educating the deaf: Psychology, principles, and practices* (2nd ed.). Boston: Houghton Mifflin.

Raven, J. (1948). *Progressive matrices.* New York: Psychological Corp.

Roeser, R. J., & Downs, M. P. (1981). *Auditory disorders in school children.* New York: Thieme-Stratton.

Thompson, M., Biro, P., Vethivelu, S., & Hatfield, N. (1986). *Language assessment of hearing impaired school age children.* Seattle: University of Washington Press.

U.S. Department of Education. (1990). *Twelfth annual report to Congress on the implementation of the Education of the Handicapped Act.* Washington, DC: U.S. Government Printing Office.

Vernon, M. (1968). Fifty years of research on the intelligence of deaf and hard of hearing children: A review of literature and discussion of implications. *Journal of Rehabilitation of the Deaf,* pp. 4–7.

Wechsler, D. (1974). *Wechsler intelligence scale for children—Revised.* New York: Psychological Corp.

*V*ISUAL

*I*MPAIRMENT

*D*EAN *W*. *T*UTTLE
AND *K*AY *A*LICYN *F*ERRELL

*T*he philosophy undergirding the education of children and youth with visual impairment is the same as that for any other special education area. Simply stated, every person who has a visual impairment has the right to a complete and satisfying life as a fully participating member of society. For the school setting, this philosophical position translates into the right to equal opportunity and equal access to all parts of the educational program, both curricular and extracurricular.

To put this philosophy into practice, two conditions must exist. First, the attitudinal climate among administrative staff, teachers, and students must be accepting and positive, as demonstrated through their expectations, standards of evaluation, and value systems. The second has to do with the skills and abilities of the child with visual impairment that demonstrate his or her effectiveness for full inclusion in school and community life. The same is true of any child in school.

Schools and related agencies are in the business of helping all students become fully functioning, competent individuals. Basic competence in life can be defined in terms of the ability to love, to work, and to play (Bower, 1966). The concept of love involves having enough of self to be able to, and willing to, share it with another. Work refers to effort that contributes to another's welfare. And play is the ability to relax and renew oneself through a variety of recreational outlets. The exercise of these abilities is based on good decision-making skills couched in an appropriate value or belief system. The education of children with visual impairments has these same goals. Children who happen to have visual loss have the same needs and desires as all children and youth do. Equal opportunity to achieve these goals through the schools has been guaranteed by the U.S. Congress through passage of the Individuals with Disabilities Education Act (IDEA), the Americans with Disabilities Act (ADA), and Section 504 of the Vocational Rehabilitation Act of 1973.

Although the concept of mainstreaming exceptional children in the regular classroom seems to be associated with passage of PL 94–142, the Education for All Handicapped Children Act, which was the precursor to the Individuals with Disabilities Education Act (IDEA), students who have visual impairments have been successfully integrated into the regular classroom since the early 1900s. Before that, all children with visual impairments had been educated in residential schools where children attended classes during the school day and lived in dormitories the rest of the time. As early as 1871, Samuel Gridley Howe, who founded one of the first residential schools for children with visual disabilities in Boston, advocated integrating students with visual disabilities into public day programs in the parents' home communities. In an address to the American Association of Instructors of the Blind, Howe said, "I would have the blind attend common schools in all cases where it is feasible" (Lowenfeld, 1982, p. 72). The percentage of children with visual impairments attending public day school programs rose from 10% in the 1940s to 87% in the 1990s (American Printing House for the Blind, 1992; U.S. Department of Education, 1992).

Hubbard (1983) identified some advantages of mainstreaming students with visual impairments into regular education classrooms:

1. Children who are visually impaired are able to remain in the family home and attend local schools with siblings and peers from the neighborhood.
2. The variety of curricular and extracurricular offerings usually is much broader.
3. Opportunities for social interaction and competition between children with and without visual disabilities are greater, as is the opportunity for sighted children to role-model appropriate or acceptable behavior.
4. To survive, students with visual impairments must be more self-reliant within a mainstreamed setting, even while continuing to receive support services from a qualified teacher of students with visual disabilities.
5. Some of the strategies, techniques, and materials available for students with visual impairments can benefit all children.
6. School staff and sighted children tend to become more knowledgeable about, and more accepting of, individuals who are blind, and more aware of, and sensitive to, problems visually impaired students encounter.

Although the advantages of mainstreaming may seem to make residential schools obsolete or unnecessary, Silverstein (1985) outlined the legal basis for maintaining residential schools. IDEA requires that a full continuum of services be made available to meet the wide spectrum of needs found in the school-age population of individuals with visual disabilities. In the 1990s, residential schools continue to have a strong role in the education of these children and youth (Council of Executives of American Residential Schools for the Visually Handicapped, 1991; Huebner & Koenig, 1991).

In residential schools, specialized staff, materials, and equipment are extensive throughout the campus, whereas some local school districts simply cannot provide all services required to appropriately serve children with visual impairments. Residential schools are available for either short-term instruction or long-term intervention in a wide range of areas—for example, academics, adaptive skills, orientation and mobility, independent living skills, recreation, technology, and career education. They have the capacity for 24-hour-a-day treatment programs for students who need a very controlled environment. Residential schools for students with visual impairments will continue to serve a vital role in the future.

CURRENT PRACTICES

The education of children and youth with visual impairments is a cooperative effort shared between regular education and special education. Although their overall curricular needs are the same, access to that curriculum is achieved by providing some specialized services. The intent of IDEA was to maximize the participation of children with disabilities in the regular classroom. Therefore, special education services are provided when students with visual impairments need some modification or alteration of the regular education program to equalize educational opportunities for participation and growth. These students may need one or more of the following types of modifications:

1. Curriculum (partial or total adaptation).
2. Learning strategies (compensatory or adaptive skills).
3. Materials and devices (texts, educational aids, adapted equipment).
4. Classroom management (teaching techniques).
5. Environment (lighting, work space, storage).

A student whose disability is interfering with or disrupting adequate educational progress requires at least one, and frequently more than one, of these modifications. The more severe the disability, or the more severe the multiplicity of disabilities, the greater is the number of modifications required to meet that student's educational needs.

Five key participants are involved in providing the required modifications to students with visual impairments:

1. The students' families.
2. The federal government.
3. The state department of education.
4. The local education agency or residential school.
5. The national, state, and local agencies and organizations serving individuals with visual disabilities.

Families are crucial to implementation of students' educational plans. As one of the few constants in the life of a child who has a visual impairment, parents often make the difference in how well students achieve independence (Ferrell, 1986b). They also are responsible for helping children learn social skills and other aspects of daily living. Perhaps most important, parents play an integral role in developing and monitoring the individualized education program (IEP) by participating in meetings, contributing objectives, assuring carry-over of adaptive skills at home, and discussing long-range plans for their children's future.

Within the federal government, the legislative branch has enacted, the executive branch has implemented, and the judicial branch has interpreted many laws designed to support and equalize educational opportunities for all children and youth with disabilities, which, of course, includes students with visual impairments. The federal government has a responsibility to monitor and enforce state and local compliance with federal regulations, to assure that basic essential services are provided appropriately. Some state departments of education employ a full-time consultant for students with visual impairments; others designate someone to fulfill this function as part of other responsibilities. The state vision consultant is the state's primary advocate for and facilitator of appropriate, quality education for all its students who have visual impairments, as well as the state's primary monitor of local compliance with state and federal regulations.

At the local level, the teacher of students with visual disabilities is the primary advocate for and facilitator of appropriate, quality education for all children and youth with visual impairments within the district or education unit. The administrator is responsible for securing the services of a qualified and certified teacher of students with visual disabilities, to obtain and manage the necessary fiscal resources to make available related services as required, to provide the structure and guidelines for efficient implementation of the program, and to periodically evaluate its effectiveness. The state residential school for students with visual disabilities is actually an extension of each local school district, assuring the availability of a full continuum of services to every visually impaired student in the state.

Many public and private agencies and organizations offer support services or provide specialized materials and equipment for individuals who have visual impairments. For example, the *American Printing House for the Blind* in Louisville, Kentucky, produces and distributes educational texts, materials, and equipment in a variety of media. The *American Foundation for the Blind* in New York City publishes professional literature and films, provides consultative services, and sells adaptive devices (such as braille watches, kitchen equipment, and tactile measuring devices) for all ages of people with visual impairments. Volunteers with *Recordings for the Blind*, in Princeton, New Jersey, record books on tape. For recreational reading, the *National Library Service for the Blind and Physically Handicapped* of the Library of Congress in Washington, DC, distributes braille, large type, and talking books.

Effectively utilizing these resources enhances the quality of the educational experience for students who have visual impairments. When all the key participants work together toward the common goal of quality educational services for these children and youth, all children benefit. If any of the participants begins working at cross-purposes to the others, the students with visual impairments are the ones who suffer.

Special education services must span the full spectrum from infancy and preschool intervention (e.g., Ferrell, 1985, 1986a; Pogrund, Fazzi, & Lampert, 1992) to prevocational, vocational, and transitional programs (Simpson, 1986). Intensive services at the infant and preschool level, along with a strong family-centered program, can minimize many of the problems that arise later in school. Moore (1984) expressed the conviction that early special education can ameliorate or eliminate later handicapping conditions, and that failure to provide early developmentally appropriate stimulation to infants with visual disabilities may actually contribute to the onset of secondary disabilities. Infant and preschool children who have visual impairments are served by one of the following types of programs:

1. A teacher-counselor who works with child and family in the home.
2. A regular nursery or preschool program supported by the services of an itinerant specialist for children with visual disabilities.
3. A preschool program for children with disabilities, with or without the support of a vision specialist.
4. A center-based program serving only children with visual impairments in self-contained classes.

During the school years, regular classroom teachers play a primary role in educating most children with visual impairments.

Children with visual limitations, like all school-age children, are first and foremost the responsibility of general education. Only when it is clear that the regular education provisions provided for all children are inadequate to meet the needs of children who are blind or partially seeing should special programming be sought. (Ashcroft & Zambone-Ashley, 1980, p. 29)

The role of the regular classroom teacher is to provide for the general curricular needs of all children in his or her classroom, including children with visual impairments. Therefore, "the overall curriculum and standards should not be different for the child who is visually impaired" (p. 33).

The vision specialist's role is to support the efforts of the regular classroom teacher who has a student with a visual impairment in his or her class. To equalize the educational opportunities, the vision specialist provides academic remediation when the visual impairment causes the lag, instruction in compensatory or adaptive skills, informational counseling relative to blindness issues, and other administrative support. The vision specialist is a special educator who has been trained to work specifically with children who have visual impairments.

MAJOR CHANGES SINCE PL 94–142 AND IDEA

Because large numbers of children with visual impairments already had been mainstreamed prior to 1975, one might surmise that PL 94–142 had minimal impact on their education. Yet, some significant changes have taken place, though not all are necessarily attributable directly to passage of the laws. More attention has been directed to services for and curricular needs of infant and preschool children with visual impairments. Assessment tools and techniques have improved. Parents and the children themselves have become more involved in identifying goals and objectives and in making placement decisions, with the result that parents are more active advocates for their children.

Two national parents' groups, the National Association for Parents of the Visually Impaired in Watertown, Massachusetts, and the Parents of Blind Children, Division of the National Federation of the Blind, in Baltimore, have become eloquent advocates for the needs of children with visual disabilities. As computers have been integrated into the schools, more attention has been paid to adapting technology to meet the needs of students with visual problems and their concomitant skills in language arts areas. In recent years, debate also has centered on the meaning of least restrictive environment and the alternative concept of appropriate and enabling educational environments (Curry & Hatlen, 1988; Huebner, 1989; Huebner & Koenig, 1991).

Changing Roles. The role of the specialized teacher of children and youth with visual impairments in public day school programs has been expanding in recent years. During the early years of mainstreaming, vision specialists tended to focus on the academic needs of their students who had visual impairments and, as a result, served primarily as academic tutors. Unfortunately, some students began to leave school with adequate academic skills but poor life skills (Tuttle, 1981). The ability of high school graduates with visual impairments to function competently and independently in the community was not demonstrated consistently. The vision specialist's role now has expanded to include nonacademic areas such as daily living skills, personal and home management skills, social and recreational skills, and affective and career education. Unfortunately, some administrators resist this shift in role as unnecessary or beyond the scope of school function.

The vision specialist's role also has expanded to using and maintaining technological aids and devices and teaching their use to students with visual impairments. Technology has produced new products for them at an ever increasing rate (Jackson & Busset, 1991; Schreier, 1990). People with visual impairments now have access to printed or typed materials through an optical character recognition device that converts print symbols to auditory, tactual, or large-print displays (Converso & Hocek, 1990). Synthetic speech devices enable a person who is blind to use computers, calculators, clocks, watches, and microwave ovens. Computer monitors and printers may have displays or output in braille, large print, or synthesized speech. Adapted technology has enabled a person who is blind to use portable computerized note-takers in classes, to use phone modems for telecommunications, and to obtain entire books on disk. Electronic mobility devices provide information about the environment to assist the blind traveler. These are but a few examples of the ways in which technology has positively impacted the lives of children and youth with visual impairments.

Large urban and suburban school districts usually have enough children and youth with visual impairments to employ several qualified specialists representing various disciplines: the educator of preschool children with visual disabilities and their parents, the orientation and mobility instructor, the teacher of children with visual and multiple disabilities, and the traditional teacher of students with visual disabilities who supports the standard curriculum. Rural, sparsely populated regions, through cooperative arrangements with neighboring districts, may have enough students with visual impairments to employ one teacher but not three or four different specialists. As a result, some critical needs of these students in rural areas have not been met. To address the problem, some colleges and universities have begun preparing multicompetent teachers with full qualifications in two or more of the specialized disciplines (Gates & Kappan, 1985; Head, 1989).

Other rural communities with small, widely scattered populations have developed an interdisciplinary team approach to service delivery for their low-prevalence students. New Hampshire's Multidisciplinary Interagency Core Evaluation (MICE) project has demonstrated how a comprehensive care plan can be developed, using the general and specialized services already existing within the student's community. The team's job is to:

1. review information [from and] about the child and family,
2. reach a consensus on impressions and diagnosis,
3. recommend a complete child and family care plan,
4. develop a system for implementing the plan based on funding and transportation needs, and
5. plan a coordinated system of services for each case. (Morse, 1983, p. 54)

To be successful, the interdisciplinary approach requires organization, cooperation, and coordination.

An unfortunate trend of recent years in some districts is to employ a generic special educator (one trained to work generally with all disabilities) to serve students with visual impairments (Head, 1989). Admittedly, a generic special educator can work with children who have visual impairments to the extent that children with disabilities share common problems and solutions. The extent to which generic special educators cannot meet the specialized, unique needs of children with visual disabilities, however, is the extent to which they will do more harm than good (Long, 1984). Children with visual impairments must acquire the specialized, unique coping skills and adaptive behaviors that enable them to be competent, fully assimilated members of society (Hazekamp & Huebner, 1989).

The role of the residential school for the visually impaired has been undergoing some change during the past 20 years (Scholl, 1986). Although some residential schools continue to provide a comprehensive academic curriculum for kindergarten through 12th grade, many are serving a greater number of children with visual impairments who are also severely multihandicapped. In light of the many needs of children with such severe disabilities, the residential school is not necessarily more restrictive than public day school programs, nor is it necessarily a restrictive setting for children without multiple disabilities. Least restrictive environment "must not be construed as the physical boundaries to an educational institution but rather as that setting in which the child will be least restricted in attaining his or her potential for educational growth" (Spungin, 1982, p. 229). The Division for Visual Handicaps of the Council for Exceptional Children believes that:

> The least restrictive environment for a student with a visual disability is the most enabling and most appropriate educational environment—the environment in which specialized services are provided by qualified staff with the intensity and frequency needed by each student commensurate with all of his or her specific needs as appropriately identified in the IEP. (Huebner & Koenig, 1991, p. 14)

According to Silverstein (1985), residential schools are able to provide nonacademic programs for the development of self-help, social, interpersonal, independent living, orientation and mobility, and play and recreational skills, as well as concentrated compensatory academic skills. In addition to the regular 10-month school program, some residential schools are providing short-term special skills coursework and special summer programs, to address both academic and nonacademic needs. In some states the residential school is becoming a statewide resource to all the local education agencies in areas such as assessments, specialized coursework, instructional materials and devices, parent education, and consultation pertaining to the education of children with visual impairments.

At different points in his or her educational career, the student with a visual disability may find the need for greater support than the local school district is able to offer, economically or otherwise. Then an array of service options must be available. No one pattern of service delivery is appropriate for all students with visual disabilities.

The promise of IDEA is that education will be individualized to the student's needs, not limited to what the school has to offer.

Instructional Materials Centers (IMCs). Another change of the past few years is the emergence of many centralized, statewide instructional materials centers for students with visual impairments. In an attempt to reduce costly duplication, they coordinate the procurement and distribution of educational materials in braille, enlarged print, or recorded formats through APH-CARL et al., the American Printing House for the Blind's automated database of all reading materials produced in the United States for visually impaired people, and through other electronic bulletin boards, such as SpecialNet and ForSights.

If the educational materials are not available from any of the national agencies, the IMC staff coordinates or cooperates with volunteer groups who produce the required adapted books by hand. With the tremendous technological boom of the past quarter century, IMCs also purchase, evaluate, and distribute adapted devices and technology for the visually impaired population. Instructional materials centers have had an impact in at least three ways:

1. They have relieved teachers of students with visual disabilities of the time-consuming burden of tracking down adapted materials so the teacher is able to spend more time with students.
2. Coordination of materials intra- and interstate has reduced duplication from district to district and state to state by facilitating the sharing of unused materials among schools; this has reduced the costs of adapted materials.
3. Most important, students with visual impairments have had access to more adapted materials, and the time required to obtain them has been reduced, increasing the ability of these students to utilize and learn from the regular curriculum.

STATUS OF OUR EFFECTIVENESS

Under IDEA, states are required to monitor all special education programs within the state. According to the Annual Reports to Congress, most of the programs for children and youth with visual impairments have met minimum guidelines as outlined in IDEA. Unfortunately, these guidelines address procedural rather than qualitative issues (Hatlen, 1990; Scholl, Long, & Tuttle, 1980).

With respect to evaluating the effectiveness of programs for students with visual impairments, few studies are reported in the literature. Hodges (1983) evaluated 245 public-school-day and 63 residential-school students with visual impairments throughout Kansas. With respect to academic achievement, 64% in reading, 57% in mathematics, and 57% in spelling were at or above grade level. Roughly two-thirds of the goals and objectives pertaining to social integration had been achieved. Overall, 90% of the parents and 90% of the students expressed satisfaction with their educational programs and services, and 63% indicated that there was no other more appropriate placement. The conclusion to be drawn from the Hodges study is that programs for students who are visually impaired in Kansas are reasonably effective.

Nationally, the data are more obscure. The Office of Special Education Programs (SEP) began examining student outcomes and reported that in the 1989–90 school year, 60.5% of students with visual disabilities and 61.4% of students with deaf-blindness graduated with a high school diploma (compared to 44.8% of all children with disabilities), and only 12.3% and 7.8%, respectively, dropped out of school (compared to 27.0% of all children with disabilities) (U.S. Department of Education, 1992).

The U.S. Department of Education (1992) also reported that, during the 1989–90 school year, 63% of students with visual impairments nationwide spent almost all of their time in regular education classes, whereas 37% spent no time in regular education. Physical presence in the regular education classroom, however, does not assure that the social and emotional needs of students with visual disabilities are being met. Hoben and Lindstrom (1980) found that mainstreamed children with visual impairments were more socially isolated than their sighted peers. Ten years later, the social integration of students with visual disabilities does not seem to have made much progress (Kekelis & Sacks, 1992; MacCuspie, 1992).

Frequently a mainstreamed student with visual disabilities is the only person who is visually impaired in the school, and he or she spends the entire school career with little or no opportunity to learn self-attitudes, adaptive behaviors, and coping skills from other individuals with visual impairments. If one accepts that special education involves cognitive, behavioral, and affective components, the cognitive element seems to be dealt with reasonably well, the behavioral is dealt with acceptably, but the affective frequently is served inappropriately (Tuttle, 1984).

Although the general picture looks fairly healthy, many students with visual impairments still have unmet needs or are served inappropriately, because small districts seldom have the concentration of students with visual disabilities to warrant a full-time qualified vision specialist. Sometimes a district avoids, either intentionally or unintentionally, identifying a child with visual impairment, and thus avoids the requirement to provide a qualified special education program (Huebner & Ferrell, 1989; Kirchner, 1989). Some districts band together into cooperatives and jointly hire a qualified teacher to serve their students with visual impairments. Yet this teacher frequently serves a large geographic region and spends more time traveling than working with students. Other districts serve their students with visual impairments through generically trained special educators who simply are unable to meet the specialized, unique needs of visually impaired students. Finally, some students in residential schools would be better served in a public-school day program mainstreamed with sighted peers. More effective statewide procedures are needed for making placement decisions more appropriate to the needs of students who have visual impairments.

Three topics receiving a great deal of attention recently are technology, effective and accurate braille instruction, and postsecondary transition needs.

Technology. Through technology, access is much more readily available to a variety of visual information, such as identification of paper currency, location of specific buildings, map of the campus, and print textbooks. As useful as the technological aids and devices are, however, they tend to be complex to operate, expensive to purchase, and costly to repair (Parker, et al., 1990). Effective systems for training professionals, purchasing and repairing the equipment for schools and individual blind students, and developing curriculum for teaching their use to the students are just now emerging.

Braille Instruction. Although many students are acquiring excellent braille skills through the prescribed IEP process, too many students are failing to develop their braille skills. Some students are being served by special education teachers who do not know braille. Some vision specialists who learned braille during their university preparation program have become less proficient year by year because most case loads are predominantly students with low vision who use print as their primary learning medium. Some students and parents resist braille because they reject or deny what it represents, blindness. To address these concerns, some states already have passed or are considering passing a "braille bill" mandating that braille instruction and materials be provided for students who meet specific criteria and that those providing the instruction must have passed a braille proficiency test.

Citing statistics of the low number of students who read braille (approximately 13%, according to the American Printing House for the Blind, 1992), many critics have suggested that these data reveal not only poor literacy skills in students, but also the failure of IDEA to address the specialized needs of students with visual disabilities (Schroeder, 1989; Spungin, 1989). In mainstreamed education, students are thought to be given too little instruction by teachers who have too little time and who have even less interest or competency in teaching braille (Rex, 1989). These arguments fail to account for the large numbers of children with visual impairments who are able to read print (27%), who prefer auditory reading modes (10%), or whose reading mode has not yet been determined (22%). The 31% of students with legal blindness who are nonreaders may be indicative of the growing number of children with handicapping conditions in addition to blindness. Teacher competency and attitudes towards teaching braille, though heavily criticized as responsible for the suspected decline in literacy levels (Mullen, 1990), has not been supported by subsequent research (Wittenstein, 1992).

Postsecondary Transition. With the current push from the federal government, attention has been directed to the problems of students with visual impairments in making the transition from school to the world of work and independent living. Supported by a federal grant, the American Foundation for the Blind helped each state develop a transition plan to aid in solving some of the current problems. Today, educators and rehabilitation specialists work with parents to assure a smooth transition from one system to the other, usually beginning when the student is 14 years old.

EDUCATIONAL DEFINITIONS

Children and youth with visual impairments vary considerably with respect to type of visual disorder, degree of visual limitation, and extent to which the reduced visual capacity interferes with daily functioning. Some children are born with a visual impairment; others acquire it later. Some students' vision is static from day to day or from setting to setting; other students' vision fluctuates. Some eye conditions are stable; some deteriorate either suddenly or gradually; and some improve with treatment. Some children and youth with visual impairments require high levels of illumination; others prefer low levels. Some are able to distinguish colors; others are color-deficient, either partially or fully. Optical devices and corrective lenses have no effect on some students; they improve the vision of others. Central visual acuity may be restricted, or peripheral fields may be restricted, or both.

A visual impairment is an anomaly or disorder of the eye and/or its related structures that results in less-than-normal vision and may necessitate modifications in a person's approach to daily tasks. Three other terms are used more or less synonymously in the literature—visual handicap, visual disability, and low vision—but they have some subtle differences. *Visual impairment* often refers to the physiological anomaly that results in seeing less well. *Visual handicap* is used most often by educators (Barraga & Erin, 1992), because it is the term the Office of Special Education Programs uses in the regulations implementing IDEA. It is defined as a "visual impairment which, even with correction, adversely affects a child's educational performance. The term includes both partially seeing and blind children" (34 C.F.R. § 300.5(b)(10)). *Disability* means "a physical or mental impairment that substantially limits one or more of the major life activities" (Americans with Disabilities Act, § 12102(2)(A)). Corn (1989) defined low vision as

> A level of vision which, with standard correction, hinders an individual in the planning and/ or execution of a task, but which permits enhancement of the functional vision through the use of optical or nonoptical devices, environmental modifications and/or techniques. (p. 28)

Blind and *low vision* are used to differentiate persons without sight from those who can use vision.

Differentiating between visual acuity and visual efficiency is important. *Visual acuity* is the clinical measurement obtained in the eye doctor's office and usually ranges from 20/20 for normal vision to 20/800 or less for a severe visual impairment. A person with 20/200 vision must be within 20 feet to see what the normally sighted person sees at 200 feet. Nevertheless, because the ability to use one's vision is learned, and because students vary considerably in the range and variety of visual experiences as well as in their rate of learning, children with the same measured visual acuity do not necessarily respond to their visual environment in the same way. Of two students with identical visual acuity of 20/400, one may operate efficiently with residual vision and read print, and the other may rely primarily on tactile and auditory information and read braille. The former usually is called a *visual learner,* and the latter a braille or *tactile learner.* From an educational point of view, understanding the child's visual efficiency is more important than simply knowing a visual acuity score.

CLASSIFICATION

One way to classify children and youth with visual impairments is by the *age of onset* of the disability. Children who are born with the disorder are said to be *congenitally visually impaired.* Other students, who acquire a visual loss later in life, are *adventitiously blinded.* In reality, any child who loses vision before age 2 will not keep clear visual memories for long and will function as though congenitally visually impaired.

Another way to classify students with visual impairments is with respect to the types and number of *additional disabilities.* Approximately half to two-thirds of school-age individuals who are visually impaired have additional disabilities (Gates, 1985; Packer & Kirchner, 1985). Some classify these students by the type of additional disability—for example, deaf-blind, retarded visually impaired, emotionally disturbed visually handicapped. When a child has one additional disability, there is a greater likelihood that he or she will have even more. Therefore, some believe that classifying these children by the number and severity of additional disabilities is advantageous.

The classification of "legally blind" has its roots in passage and implementation of the Social Security Act of 1935. Having declared that blind people would be eligible for certain benefits, the federal government had to define what was meant by "blind." The conclusion was that anyone with 10% of normal vision or worse would be considered blind. More specifically, the term *legally blind* refers to anyone with a visual acuity of 20/200 or worse in the better eye with best correction, or a peripheral field loss restricted to 20° or less. Some state and federal programs still use this definition to determine eligibility for services.

Another classification frequently found in past literature is "partially seeing" or "partially sighted." These terms usually referred to individuals with visual acuity ranging from 20/70 to 20/200. They were not "legally blind," but their visual impairment may have been severe enough to interfere with daily functioning. The term *low vision* is replacing the former terms, and it includes those classified as legally blind who have useful residual vision. A student with low vision has sufficient residual vision to be able to use it as a primary learning channel.

THE STRUCTURE AND FUNCTION OF THE EYE

The external shell of the eye is called the *sclera,* which, at the front of the eye, is the clear window, the *cornea.* A person "sees" when light from an object passes through the cornea, pupil, lens, and on to the *retina,* where it is transformed into neurological impulses that are transmitted to the brain through the optic nerve. Figure 12.1 is a simplified diagram of the parts of the eye. The *lens* assists in the refraction or bending of light rays so they come to focus at the retina. This permits a person to accommodate or adjust from viewing objects at a distance to looking at something close and then back again.

Two types of light receptors in the retina—cones and rods—transform light rays into neurological impulses. *Cones* are concentrated in the macular or central part of the retina and serve two functions: (a) fine detailed discrimination and (b) color detection. The cones permit reading, threading a needle, and differentiating red from green. *Rods,* scattered throughout the periphery of the retina, have two other functions: (a) night vision and (b) movement detection. Entering a dark movie theater requires an adaptation provided by a chemical change in the rods.

DISORDERS OF THE EYE

Myopia, hyperopia, and astigmatism are three common eye disorders that usually are correctable through prescription eyeglasses or contact lenses. Therefore, these conditions do not, as a general rule, result in a visual disability by themselves but, in conjunction with other eye disorders, have a compounding effect. *Myopia,* or near-sightedness, occurs when the refractive power of the eye system is too great, or when the eyeball is too big, causing the light rays to come to focus in front of the retina. Figure 12.2 illustrates myopia. Without correction, near-sighted people can focus on close objects but cannot focus on distant objects. A person with high myopia has vision that can be corrected only partially, enabling him or her to see up close but not at a distance. If the eye's refractive power is not strong enough, or if the eyeball is too small, the light rays focus behind the retina, a condition known as *hyperopia,* or far-sightedness. Figure 12.3 illustrates hyperopia. Without correction, far-sighted people have no trouble focusing on distant objects but are unable to focus up close. *Astigmatism* produces an irregularly focused image on the retina, with parts of the image more in focus than others.

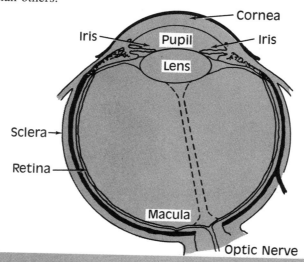

● **FIGURE 12.1**

Anatomy of the eye

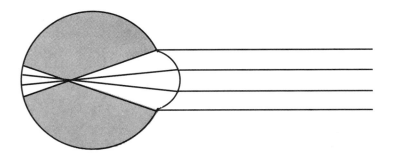

● FIGURE 12.2

Myopia

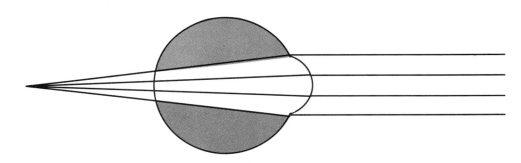

● FIGURE 12.3

Hyperopia

Some of the more common conditions or disorders that result in visual impairments are discussed next.

DISORDERS OF THE EYE MUSCLES

If the sets of muscles of the two eyes are not aligned properly, the eyes have trouble looking in the same direction at the same target, resulting in a condition known as *strabismus.* When the brain is unable to fuse the two different images, it suppresses one of the images. If the suppression continues over a long time, *amblyopia ex anopsia,* or blindness through disuse, results. Remedial techniques include patching the good eye, prism eyeglasses, or surgery.

Nystagmus, involuntary rapid movements of the eye, occurs with many eye conditions. It may slow down reading because the student has difficulty maintaining focus, and it frequently creates fatigue during visual tasks. When the student is concentrating hard or is tired or tense, eye movements tend to increase.

DISORDERS OF THE CORNEA, IRIS, AND LENS

Corneal injuries and diseases are serious because, if untreated, they may result in permanent visual impairment ranging from blurred vision to total blindness. Even if the loss is not great when visual acuity is checked, the opacity may interfere with some activities, such as playing ball. Corneal transplants frequently improve vision significantly.

Congenital or acquired *glaucoma* is caused by a restriction in the outflow of fluid within the eye, causing intraocular pressure to build. As a result of this pressure, cells of the retina are damaged, and there is progressive, irreversible loss of visual field, visual acuity, or both. For many, the high intraocular pressure can be remedied through surgery, eyedrops, or both.

Aniridia, failure of the iris to develop fully, and *albinism,* lack of pigment in hair, skin, and eyes, both result in *photophobia,* extreme sensitivity to light. Glaucoma may be a secondary problem. Sunglasses, low vision devices, or dim illumination sometimes help.

Cataracts, a condition in which the lens becomes cloudy or opaque, can be congenital (present at birth) or adventitious (acquired later in life). Effects on vision range from blurred vision to perception of light only. Most students with congenital cataracts have had surgery to remove the lens, and they wear corrective eyeglasses or contact lenses.

DISORDERS OF THE RETINA

Diabetic retinopathy, resulting from diabetes, causes changes in the blood vessels of the eye. Visual impairment may be insignificant, or total blindness may result from hemorrhaging and retinal detachment. Although some new medical procedures retard the deterioration process, no effective treatment for advanced retinopathy has been found.

Degeneration of the macula, the small area near the center of the retina responsible for detailed vision, causes absence of fine central vision. The peripheral vision is useful for seeing large objects and colors but not for reading. Magnification may help enlarge the image sufficiently to stimulate the portion of the retina that is intact.

Leber's congenital amaurosis is a genetic retinal dystrophy characterized by nystagmus and varying degrees of visual loss.

Retinopathy of prematurity (ROP), previously known as *retrolental fibroplasia,* is associated with low birthweight and preterm birth. As medical technology becomes better able to sustain life in vulnerable infants, the number of children with ROP seems to be increasing (Hatton, 1991). One study suggests that it may be the leading cause of visual impairment in young children nationally (Ferrell, Deitz, Trief, & Faye, 1992). ROP can regress spontaneously, resulting in only mild visual impairment, or it can progress to total retinal detachment. Recent surgical advances have successfully limited the number of cases that progress to retinal detachment, but they seldom succeed in correcting the visual problem entirely.

In *retinal detachment* the retina becomes separated from its supporting structures, leaving a blind area in the field of vision. Laser treatment or surgery may be successful in restoring some or all vision.

Retinitis pigmentosa is a genetic eye condition that leads to a progressive decrease in peripheral visual field and, in later life, possibly total blindness. Night blindness is often a first symptom. *Usher's syndrome* is a condition in some congenitally deaf children who later lose some or all of their vision through retinitis pigmentosa. No specific treatment is known.

Retinoblastoma is a malignant tumor of the posterior retina that may spread along the optic nerve to the brain. Immediate enucleation (surgical removal) of the affected eye is the treatment of choice in almost all cases, and the child is fitted with a prosthesis, an artificial eye.

DISORDERS OF THE OPTIC NERVE

Leber's disease affects individuals, usually males, in late adolescence, and leads to rapid, sometimes total, loss of vision. The quick progression of the disease often necessitates psychological counseling and intense training in compensatory skills.

Optic nerve atrophy can be caused by many diseases. Loss of visual field can range from being barely noticeable to total blindness. Treatment is based on the underlying cause of the atrophy.

Optic nerve hypoplasia can affect one or both eyes and varies in severity. It is manifested by an underdeveloped optic nerve and can be accompanied by severe central nervous system anomalies and endocrine disorders.

DISORDERS OF THE CENTRAL NERVOUS SYSTEM

Children with *cortical visual impairments* or *cortical blindness* often do not seem to be visually impaired because the structures of the eye are intact. The visual loss is caused by damage to the visual pathways in the brain leading from the retina to the occipital cortex, the area of the brain responsible for interpreting visual images, or by damage to the occipital cortex itself. Many children with cortical visual impairments are not totally blind, and providing tactile and kinesthetic strategies often assists them to utilize their vision. Some authors believe the prevalence of cortical visual impairment is increasing (Groenveld, Jan, & Leader, 1990; Morse, 1990).

*I*NCIDENCE AND PREVALENCE

To obtain current, accurate, incidence ratios for children with visual impairments is almost impossible. Apparently, no statistics provide the rate of occurrence or the number of new cases per year (Kirchner, 1989). From the annual count (kept by the American Printing House for the Blind, Louisville, Kentucky) of legally blind students receiving educational services, we have seen an average of 1,700 new cases each year for the past 15 years, a rise of 62% since PL 94–142 was passed. These figures do not take into account all the children who have visual impairments but are not classified as legally blind.

The U.S. government does not keep a register of all individuals with visual impairments. There are two major statistical sources, but they are incomplete and therefore insufficient (Kirchner, 1989). The American Printing House for the Blind receives a federal appropriation each year to help defray the high cost of producing educational books and materials for children and youth with legal blindness. To qualify for a share, each state is required, once a year, to submit a report on the number and characteristics of the students with legal blindness it serves. Any student in the state, therefore, is eligible for materials and equipment at federal expense, as long as he or she is classified as legally blind. The most recent count reports approximately 51,813 children and young adults with legal blindness in the United States (American Printing House for the Blind, 1992).

The Annual Report to Congress on IDEA (U.S. Department of Education, 1992) identified 25,125 children who were visually impaired and deaf-blind during the 1990–91 school year, less than half the number of children reported to the American Printing House for the Blind (APH), even though APH requires the stricter eligibility criterion of legal blindness. This is probably because of the estimated 50% of visually impaired children who are multihandicapped, so that many children with visual impairments are reported to the U.S. Department of Education under categories other than "visually handicapped" or "deaf-blind," even though they are served by vision specialists.

To illustrate the depth of this counting problem, the Colorado Department of Education recently reported 314 children with visual disabilities being served under IDEA but a total of 734 students with visual disabilities actually receiving special education services from either a teacher of students with visual impairments or an orientation and mobility specialist (Colorado Instructional Materials Center, 1992). This means that funding and other decisions based on the federal count do not begin to address the needs of all students with visual disabilities in Colorado. We have every reason to believe the same situation exists in other states.

The prevalence figure for the school-age population of students with legal blindness is estimated at .5%, or 5 legally blind students in 1,000 school children (Hatfield, 1975; Scholl, 1986). A number of children who are visually impaired, however, do not qualify as "legally blind." Kirchner (1989) reviewed data that placed the prevalence rate in a range from .42 per 1,000 children to 170, depending on the data source and the definition of visual impairment used. Scott (1982) suggested that .2%, or 2 visually impaired children per 1,000 school-age population, better reflects all children with visual impairments, including, of course, those with legal blindness.

*P*REVENTION

The National Society to Prevent Blindness (NSPB) in New York City, together with its respective state chapters, has developed an active prevention program. NSPB assists communities to establish vision screening programs for the purpose of early detection and referral for possible treatment. NSPB also is concerned about the number of needless eye injuries. In one year alone 175,000 school-age children suffered eye injuries, 90% of which could have been prevented (Benton & Truelove, 1978). Some special eye care and safety materials have been developed for school use, and young elementary-age children have the option of establishing Wise Owl Clubs sponsored by NSPB (Poirier, 1984). NSPB has done extensive work in business and industry to reduce job-related hazards to the eye. In addition, medical researchers continue to investigate the causes of eye disorders and to look for more effective treatment. Through genetic counseling, individuals with visual impairments can ascertain the likelihood that their children also will have visual impairments.

*V*ISUAL IMPAIRMENT, LEARNING, AND BEHAVIOR

Several misconceptions, or myths, about blindness and individuals with visual disabilities should be dispelled. Individuals with visual impairments are not endowed automatically with better hearing or touch as compensation for their lack of vision. If hearing and touch seem better than normal, this is because of training and their greater reliance on these other sensory modalities. Contrary to popular opinion, individuals who are blind do not live in a world of darkness or blackness. They are not all gifted with special musical abilities. Individuals with visual impairments are not social misfits or dependent parasites.

Instead, children who are visually impaired are, first of all, children, with the same needs and drives we find in all children. They are more like than unlike other children. The methods or approaches used to meet some of their needs, however, may be different. Observing someone doing things differently ought not to carry with it a value judgment of that person. Unfortunately, differentness is suspect in society.

A visual impairment impacts upon a child's learning and behavior in several ways: conceptualization and cognitive development, personal and home management, orientation and mobility, reading and writing, psychosocial development, and vocational and avocational potential. If the individual with visual impairment has additional impairments, these impacts are compounded. In addition, the person interacts with negative or devaluating attitudes and societal stereotypes. The following paragraphs discuss the implications directly attributed to limited or no vision and the natural deprivations of a visual environment.

CONCEPTUALIZATION AND COGNITIVE DEVELOPMENT

A visual limitation by itself does not impair the brain's ability to process information, but it has somewhat less information upon which to operate, a condition that may result in incomplete or distorted ideas about objects and events in one's environment. The three primary learning channels are *visual* (limited though it may be), *tactile/kinesthetic*, and *auditory*.

Visual, tactile, and auditory skills are learned through a developmental sequence. To optimize their development, structured learning experiences must be provided from earliest infancy. To utilize sensory information effectively, a person must respond to visual, tactile, and auditory stimuli according to five developmental levels:

1. Awareness of and attending to the stimulus.
2. Identification and recognition of the stimulus.
3. Comprehension and understanding of the meaning of the stimulus.
4. Evaluation and interpretation of the significance of the stimulus.
5. Analysis and synthesis of new and old information.

Barraga and Erin (1992) estimated that 80% of the student population who are legally blind have sufficient residual vision to use it as a primary learning channel. When all students with low vision are included, nine of ten students with visual impairments use vision for reading, writing, and other activities. According to Corn (1983), three distinct components contribute to seeing: (a) the physiological, optical functions of the eye, including acuity, fields, fixation, tracking, and accommodation; (b) individual personal abilities such as intelligence, cognition, perception, sensory integration, and psychological and physical makeups; and (c) environmental conditions including color, contrasts, illumination, viewing time, and viewing distances. Intervention in any of these three components can help a student with visual impairment learn to use and respond to visual stimuli.

For most individuals, vision plays a primary role in learning and conceptualization. In comparison to the other senses, vision is more efficient; of all the senses, vision organizes information the most effectively. A visual impairment, then, "handicaps the child simply by giving him less total information about the world" (Warren, 1984, p. 34). The more severe the visual impairment is, the less the child can rely on the accuracy and efficiency of the organizational function of vision, and without appropriate intervention, the more significant are the potential lags or gaps in conceptualization. Barraga and Erin (1992) proposed that "for children who are blind or who have low vision, movement may be the most accurate replacement for vision in clarifying information about the world" (p. 45).

In a study of mental imagery among congenitally blind children, Anderson (1984) suggested that "blind children develop their mental images or concepts of objects from their unique experience with the world, and that the language they use reflects that experience and their form of mental representation rather than their knowledge of the language of sighted people" (p. 209). With adequate supportive nonvisual experiences, the concepts or mental images developed by children with congenital blindness were not significantly different from those acquired by sighted children. These findings underscore the necessity of providing children who are blind with activity-oriented programs, to give them ample opportunities for hands-on exploration of and experimentation with objects.

The extent to which the conceptualization process is fully developed is the extent to which cognitive skills will be adequate. In a study of the Piagetian reasoning abilities of congenitally blind children, Stephens and Simpkins (1974) found that some blind children were significantly behind their sighted peers. Based on these findings, an extensive training program was initiated to ameliorate these deficits by providing reasoning activities geared to the needs of individual students. Stephens and Grube (1982) reported that "after provision of developmentally appropriate experiences in reasoning, the performance of the blind subjects was equivalent to that of the sighted subjects" (p. 133).

PERSONAL AND HOME MANAGEMENT

Most individuals learn personal and home management skills by observing and imitating others. Children with visual impairments have more difficulty acquiring these skills without direct intervention and instruction. Personal and home management skills are the very foundation for acquiring the critical life skills to successfully assimilate into society, either during the school years or later in life.

During the preschool and early school years, children with visual impairments are acquiring the basic self-care skills of eating, dressing, toileting, washing, grooming, and so on. A strong parent education program will provide parents with realistic goals, objectives, strategies, and special materials to facilitate the child's developing these skills in the home. Without this support many parents are at a loss.

As a child approaches and moves through the adolescent years, other home management skills become important. The development of organization, shopping, cooking, sewing, and elementary home repair skills all contribute to an individual's independence and sense of competence and confidence. The extent to which the young adult who has visual impairment masters these skills has a greater impact on quality of life than does knowing trigonometry or ancient history (Tuttle, 1981).

Mastery over and responsibility for personal and home management skills permit an individual with visual impairment to assume his or her share of the home chores and thus to contribute to the welfare of the home. Until a child who has visual impairment masters a skill to the point of its being routine, he or she will take longer to do it, and it probably will require more physical and mental energy. Parents, teachers, and others are tempted to take over for the child, to save time, or to get it done "right." The child with visual impairment, though, has the right to practice skills free of unnecessary interference, to fail, or to accomplish the task incompletely.

ORIENTATION AND MOBILITY

Visual impairment carries with it reduced or restricted ability to travel through one's physical and social environment until adequate orientation and mobility skills have been established. Because observational skills are more limited, self-control within the immediate surroundings is limited. The individual who has visual impairment is less able to anticipate hazardous situations or obstacles to avoid.

Orientation refers to the mental map one has of one's surroundings and to the relationship between self and that environment. The mental map is best generated by moving through the environment and piecing together relationships, object by object, in an organized approach. With little or no visual feedback to reinforce this mental map, an individual who has visual impairment must rely on memory for key landmarks and other clues. Landmarks and clues enable these individuals to affirm their position in space.

Mobility is the ability to travel safely and efficiently from one point to another within one's physical and social environment. Good orientation skills are prerequisite to good mobility skills. Once students with visual impairments learn to travel safely as pedestrians, they also need to learn to use public transportation to become as independent as possible.

To meet the expanding needs and demands of individuals who have visual impairment, a sequence of instruction begins during the preschool years and may continue after high school. Many children with visual impairments lack adequate concepts regarding time and space or objects and events in their environment. During the early years much attention focuses on developing some fundamental concepts, such as inside and outside, in front and behind, fast and slow, movement of traffic, the variety of intersections, elevators and escalators, and so forth. These concepts are essential to safe, efficient travel through familiar and unfamiliar settings, first within buildings, then in residential neighborhoods, and finally in business communities. The five basic modes of travel are discussed briefly in the following paragraphs. Students may use one or another, depending on the situation, or they may use a combination of several.

With or Without a Low-Vision Device. Some individuals have sufficient residual vision to be safe and efficient travelers without a low-vision device. Lighting conditions, contrast between object and background, intensity and variety of colors, distance from an object, stationary or moving objects, and previous experiences with an object or event—all are factors that contribute to the ability of a person with low vision to recognize clues and landmarks during travel. Some students with low vision find telescopes useful, to read signs or to recognize distant landmarks. Blind students traveling through a familiar setting such as the classroom, hall, or home find that trailing and other safety techniques are sufficient. Unfortunately, some choose to travel without a low-vision device, even when this is unsafe, because they reject the symbol of blindness the device represents.

Sighted Guide. Some individuals who have visual impairment choose to walk with a sighted companion, lightly holding the companion's arm just above the elbow and following the companion by half a step. By the clues he or she gets from the companion's body movements and supplementary comments, the individual with visual impairment is able to anticipate and manage curbs, stairs, doorways, and congested areas. This method allows the person to carry on a conversation without being preoccupied with efficiently using a mobility aid. If a sighted guide is a person's sole means of travel, however, the person with visual impairment is extremely dependent.

The Cane. The most popular mobility aid is the long cane, which is typically white. Through its proper use, a person can detect step-ups, step-downs, and other obstacles. The cane also can provide information about the texture of approaching terrain. Sounds of the cane echo back from the environment and provide additional information. The comprehensive sequence of instruction in how to use the cane properly may begin in the primary grades, and it must be taught by a specialist qualified in orientation and mobility.

Dog Guide. This country has fewer than 10 dog guide schools, the oldest of which is Seeing Eye in Morristown, New Jersey. Only about 4% of the population with legal blindness both desires and qualifies for training to use a dog. The schooling and the dog are provided at minimal or no cost to the individual who is blind. Dog guide schools are reluctant to accept students under 16 years of age because of maturity and responsibility factors, so few school-age children use dog guides.

Electronic Aids. Some technological developments, especially in navigational devices for defense, have specific application to mobility aids for individuals who are blind. Most are not sufficiently refined to be used as a sole aid but can supplement either the cane or the dog guide. Most of these devices use ultrasonic energy to scan the environment. The reflected energy is transformed into tactual or auditory signals, which, if interpreted properly, provide clues about size, distance, and surface texture of an object. Electronic aids, however, are still too expensive to be in common use.

READING AND WRITING

Most students with visual impairments use their residual vision for reading and writing tasks. A *low-vision person* has four possible ways to access print materials:

1. Some students are able to attain sufficient magnification of the image on the retina simply by holding the reading material closer to their eyes; holding materials at 4" instead of the standard 16" actually quadruples the image on the retina.
2. Another way to enlarge the image on the retina is to enlarge the stimulus, or size of print; the capital letters in large-print or large-type books range from " to " tall.
3. Low-vision devices and magnifiers can be handheld or stand magnifiers, microscopic or telescopic devices, monocular or binocular.
4. Electronic reading aids magnify printed materials; closed-circuit television readers, for example, can enlarge an image up to 80 times its original size.

Students with low vision who can read regular-print books have access to a greater variety of materials, because the availability of large print is much more limited. The ability to read print is affected by lighting, texture of paper, contrast, and size and simplicity of type. Large-print books may increase the low-vision person's reading comfort, but they do not necessarily increase reading speed or comprehension. Some students find that large-print books, which are awkward to handle, draw unwanted attention to themselves. The Division for Visual Handicaps of the Council for Exceptional Children has taken the position that regular print and low-vision devices are preferable to large print (Gardner & Corn, 1991).

Students who have limited vision must be taught how to use low-vision devices effectively. Each magnifier has a specific focal distance that determines the distance the magnifier should be held from the reading material. The stronger the magnifier is, the smaller is the viewing field. With some powerful low-vision devices, the student may be reading only one or two letters at a time. As in the case of large-print books, some students feel self-conscious about using low-vision devices.

The tactile learner accesses educational materials primarily through the medium of braille. Figure 12.4 depicts the braille alphabet. Although braille is bulky and the average reading rate is slow (approximately 100 words per minute), it is the best system devised thus far for tactual reading and writing. Braille is composed of a series of six-dot cells, two columns of three dots each. Different combinations of these six dots represent different letters, groups of letters (contractions), numbers, and punctuation. To illustrate contractions, a single cell in braille might represent a whole word such as "more," or part of a word such as "-ble," and two cells might represent a whole word such as "mother," or part of a word such as "-ation."

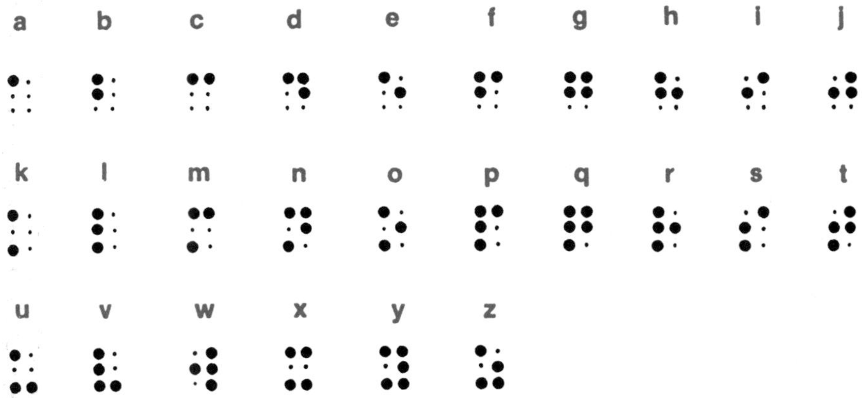

● **FIGURE I2.4**

Braille alphabet

Another reading aid for tactile learners is the Optacon. The name is derived from its function: optic-to-tactual converter. Through an optical scanner, it transforms the shapes of the print symbols into tactual images composed of combinations of tiny vibrating pins. Rather than reading braille, the blind person actually is feeling the shape of the print symbol. Unfortunately, the reading rate via Optacon is rarely even half that of braille. Although braille reading readiness usually begins in kindergarten and follows a sequence similar to teaching print reading, reading with the Optacon may not begin until first grade or later.

Visual and tactile learners alike may supplement their reading with audio materials, or talking books on disk or cassette. Developing good listening skills is essential to effectively using audio reading. Recorded books can be accelerated, either mechanically with faster but higher pitched speech, or electronically, to produce compressed speech without the "Donald Duck" effect. Reading comprehension by listening to either normal or compressed speech is the same as reading comprehension by braille or large-type materials, but it is two to three times faster (Tuttle, 1972). Even though audio is more efficient, not all students are comfortable with it. Furthermore, studying from recorded tapes is not feasible for highly technical materials.

Many individuals with visual impairments must rely on a human reader for materials that are not available in the adapted media of braille, recordings, or large type. A reader might be needed to assist with correspondence, current events, shopping advertisements, library research, and taking tests. The use of a reader, of course, deprives the individual who has visual impairment of a certain amount of privacy.

Computer technology has greatly enhanced the reading and writing capabilities of students with visual impairments (Dixon & Mandelbaum, 1990). Microcomputers have been adapted in three ways: enlarged monitors and enlarged letters on the monitors, speech synthesizers to read the print on the screens, and braille display units to substitute for the screens. Scanners attached to these adapted computers permit students to read a variety of printed texts and typed materials. Portable, lightweight, laptop computers and electronic note-takers provide a fast, quiet, and efficient method for taking notes in class.

Software has been developed that makes the production of hard-copy braille materials much quicker and easier. Some of this software permits the production of a standard-print version, a large-print version, and a braille version from the same file. Production of braille materials is being automated increasingly through the use of scanners, computers, software that translates text into braille, and braille printers. More and more books are being made available to students on computer disk, and the students can then choose to read them in their medium of choice (braille, synthetic voice, or large print) via their adapted computers.

PSYCHOSOCIAL ASPECTS

Blindness denotes no unique psychology, and visual impairment bestows no distinct personality (Kirtley, 1975; Lowenfeld, 1981; Schulz, 1980; Tuttle, 1984). The general psychological principles that explain the behaviors of all people also explain the behaviors of children and youth with visual impairments. Nevertheless, some psychosocial implications are directly linked to visual limitation. These emerge as tendencies rather than absolutes.

Children and youth who have visual impairments tend to remain egocentric longer, to be more socially immature, and to be more self-conscious than their sighted peers. With a visual restriction, they have more difficulty viewing events from another person's vantage point. Social maturity comes with social experiences, and children with visual impairments often have fewer social contacts with peers. The self-consciousness results from feeling different and from using adaptive aids and devices.

An isolating factor is inherent in restricted vision. The individual who has visual impairment may not be able to locate a friend in a crowded room, determine who is talking to whom in a small group, or receive complete or correct messages, because the availability of nonverbal communication is limited. Social interactions are more energy-consuming than for sighted peers and, as a result, some individuals with visual impairments prefer to withdraw into secure comfort zones.

Children and youth with visual impairments tend to be more passive and more dependent than their sighted peers. Far too often they are rewarded for being docile and compliant. Too many decisions are made for them rather than their being involved in exploring alternative courses of action and making choices. More times than not, others do things for these children that they could have done for themselves. Unfortunately, some people inadvertently cultivate the traits of passivity and dependence. Children with visual disabilities do have obvious dependency needs, but these must be kept in proper perspective. All children and adults are mutually interdependent to some extent.

The exposure of children and youth with visual impairments to appropriate social role models is more limited than that of their sighted peers. All children learn by modeling others' behaviors, but students with visual impairments do not have as much ability to observe, and therefore to model, desired behaviors. As a consequence, blind children tend to exhibit mannerisms or behaviors that are socially inappropriate—for example, eye poking, rocking from the hips, and rolling the head. These self-stimulating behaviors seem to disappear when the child becomes involved actively in a project of interest. To be socially accepted, children with visual impairments must learn socially acceptable behaviors.

VOCATIONAL AND AVOCATIONAL POTENTIAL

A visual impairment does not restrict vocational and avocational possibilities as much as one might think at first. With a few exceptions, individuals who have visual impairments have been involved successfully in almost every type of employment and recreation. Jobs that involve driving are, of course, not possible, but many individuals who are blind have taken related jobs in the transportation industry. Individuals who have visual impairments are at a disadvantage in team sports or in games such as badminton or tennis, which involve following a moving object. With the 20th-century technological advances and the abundance of adaptive aids and devices, however, individuals with visual impairments can accomplish almost anything.

The problem is not so much with the limited range of vocational and avocational pursuits as with the limited learning opportunities and the failings of the educational process. Children and youth who have visual impairments often are unaware of the number and variety of jobs and recreational outlets available to them. They are less able to observe a variety of adults engaged in occupations. During the exploration phase, children with visual impairments are most restricted in the opportunities to learn about the requirements and demands of various endeavors. Unfortunately, they are not afforded the same opportunities that sighted children have to work at part-time jobs or to try extracurricular activities. By the time the young adult with visual impairment is ready to choose a vocation or an avocation, the choices already have been made from a narrow range of experiences based on a superficial body of knowledge.

When he was executive director of the President's Committee on Employment of the Handicapped, Rochlin (1985) stated his belief that economic freedom, not charity, is what most people with disabilities are seeking: "Business owes no one a living, but it does owe people the right and opportunity to earn a living.... Part of the solution to career mobility is for people with disabilities to take charge of their own lives" (pp. 10, 13).

Much of what sighted children learn in the vocational and avocational arenas is accidental and incidental. For children with visual impairments, this cannot be left to chance. The schools must provide a comprehensive recreation and career education program spanning all the grades from kindergarten through high school.

EFFECTS OF MULTIPLE IMPAIRMENTS

As a result of advanced medical knowledge and treatment, more and more children who formerly would have died at birth or from accident or disease now survive. Schools are required to develop programs for children with multiple disabilities. In the school-age population of children with visual impairments, more than half have additional impairments. A child with visual impairments is likely to have more than one additional disability simultaneously. Additional disabilities may be hearing impairment, neurological impairment, a physical or chronic health problem, mental retardation, emotional disturbance, or learning disabilities.

The overall effect of two or more disabilities is not just a simple arithmetic sum of several independent, specific effects but, instead, a compounding of one effect upon the other. For example, a child who is blind has difficulty with mobility, but a child who is deaf does not; a child who is deaf has difficulty with language development, whereas the child who is blind does not. A child who is blind uses auditory clues to help in mobility; a child who is deaf utilizes vision to assist with language development. Therefore, the mobility and language development of a child who is deaf-blind are even more restricted because the effects of one disability compound the effects of the other.

Some special educators believe that children with multiple disabilities mature through the same developmental stages as all other children, but at a slower rate and with more delays in some areas than in others. Their developmental needs center on self-care, gross and fine motor abilities, social, language, and adaptive behavior skills. Other special educators feel strongly that children and youth with multiple disabilities must be challenged with age-appropriate skills and tasks to prepare them more fully for the demands of living. Traditionally, most students with visual and multiple disabilities have been served either in residential schools or in self-contained classes in public day school programs, but growing numbers are being served in regular classrooms under a philosophy of full inclusion. Inclusion means that, regardless of the severity of a student's disability, he or she is entitled to attend the same school and classroom the neighbors attend. Inclusion does not mean that students do not receive special assistance; rather, their special education and related services are delivered in the classroom. An aide or intervenor might be assigned to facilitate interaction with peers. Chapter 10 covers children with multiple disabilities in more depth.

A SSESSMENT

IDEA and the corresponding state provisions do not adhere to a medical definition of a visual impairment to determine eligibility for special education services. Instead, they use a more functional definition: The child's visual impairment must be severe enough to interfere with his or her ability to benefit fully from the regular education program without one or more of the special modifications described earlier in this chapter. Consequently, a child whose visual impairment does not interfere with school functioning is not eligible for special education services. Eligibility and placement decisions are determined by a comprehensive assessment.

AREAS OF ASSESSMENT

Four broad areas of assessment must be considered before making any program or placement decisions: *medical and related services, psychological, social, and educational.* Medical and related services assessments glean information regarding general health, status of visual and auditory abilities, and extent of any additional physical disabilities. A psychologist addresses the student's intellectual abilities and learning characteristics. A social worker summarizes the family history as it relates to social and emotional development. Educational assessment is the responsibility of special education and regular education teachers.

The discussion here is based on the Colorado Needs Assessment Model developed by the special education staff within the Colorado Department of Education to ensure that all educational needs are addressed (Schrotberger & Tuttle, 1978). These needs parallel those described in Hazekamp and Huebner's (1989) *Program Planning and Evaluation for Blind and Visually Impaired Students: National Guidelines for Educa-*

tional Excellence. Unfortunately, some needs of some children have been overlooked as educational services for students with visual disabilities have become decentralized. For example, special educators who saw themselves as primarily academic tutors focused on curricular needs. Special educators who believed their role was mainly to provide emotional support and counseling emphasized social-emotional needs. Vision specialists who saw their role primarily as assisting the student to develop adaptive behavior and coping skills tended to minimize needs in other areas.

The educational assessment battery encompasses functional vision and seven other areas. The functional vision assessment, done by the vision specialist, determines how well the child is using his or her residual vision in the educational setting (Barraga & Morris, 1980). This information is compared with medical reports from the eye specialists. Results of this functional visual assessment can guide decisions about classroom management strategies and appropriateness of educational materials and devices. The seven other areas are:

1. *Curricular needs.* Needs with respect to the standard regular education curriculum are assessed. Previous school records and results from adapted academic achievement tests are the primary tools.

2. *Adaptive or compensatory skills assessment.* Adaptive or compensatory skills are the specialized coping behaviors a child with a disability needs so he or she can compensate for the disability. For the student with visual impairment, braille, abacus, orientation and mobility, slate and stylus, visual efficiency, handwriting, typing, computers, listening, social, self-care, use of low-vision devices, and other skills might be considered. The teacher of students with visual disabilities has the primary responsibility for assessing this area.

3. *Social-emotional needs.* This assessment covers topics such as school problems, emotional growth, peer relationships, self-concept and self-esteem, and attitudes toward a visual impairment. The psychologist, social worker, regular classroom teacher, vision specialist, and parent all play a role.

4. *Classroom management needs.* Strategies are identified to enable the child who has visual impairment to function most effectively in the classroom. Assessment addresses the medium the child needs to benefit from textbooks and other materials, types of educational aids and devices, how to handle tests, chalkboard work, movies, overheads, and so forth.

5. *Physical/environmental needs.* The orientation and mobility specialist evaluates the school setting to determine any architectural barriers or potential hazards. Lighting, workspace, outlets, and storage space are some other critical factors for the classroom.

6. *Home/community needs.* The two components of this assessment are: (a) parent, sibling, and peer relationships in the home and neighborhood, and (b) community agencies and organizations—church or synagogue, Boy Scouts or Girl Scouts, city recreation, county mental health agencies—which are evaluated in terms of their capabilities to serve the child with a disability.

7. *Vocational and avocational needs.* Vocational education, vocational rehabilitation,

physical education, therapeutic recreation, and other services may be required for a student to be fully served.

Results of the comprehensive educational assessment battery, together with the medical, psychological, and social assessments, provide the basis for delineating the goals, objectives, and service requirements of the child's individualized education program. If the parents disagree with the findings of the assessment, they have the right to request a second opinion at no cost to themselves. According to IDEA, the whole assessment must be completed at least once every 3 years, and the IEP must be reviewed at least annually.

For children under 3 years of age, an individualized family service plan (IFSP) is developed annually and reviewed every 6 months. Although it is similar to the IEP for older students in terms of its required components, the IFSP is designed to help families meet the needs of their baby who is visually impaired. The emphasis is less on direct instruction of the infant than it is on collaborative problem solving among family members and professionals.

SCREENING, IDENTIFICATION, AND DIAGNOSIS

IDEA requires every school district to develop and implement community child-find procedures. The intent is to let parents of children with disabilities know that special education services are available in the district. Many districts use television and radio announcements, newspaper articles, posters, and billboards.

Vision screening can be conducted at both the preschool level and during the school years. Screening for visual acuity problems in 3- to 5-year-old children usually is accomplished with a Snellen tumbling E chart (for distance visual acuity), the Allen Picture Card Test using seven pictures, or the Faye Symbol Chart with the apple, house, and umbrella for near visual acuity) (Hatfield, 1979). Careful inspection of the eyes and observation of seeing behaviors also may reveal potential problems: red or crusty eyes, excessive tearing, squinting, rubbing the eyes, unusual eye movements, and the like. Observation of the eyes, distance acuity, near acuity, and a test for eye muscle balance are components of preschool screening recommended by the National Society to Prevent Blindness, the American Academy of Ophthalmology, the American Academy of Pediatrics, and the American Optometric Association (Trief & Morse, 1987). Radke and Blackhurst (1978) described an extensive preschool vision screening program in which 81% of the children referred to eye specialists were found to have significant eye defects.

Responsibility for school vision screening usually rests with the school nurse. Most districts have policies to screen extensively in the primary grades, and then every two or three years, on the condition that all transfer students are screened the year they enroll. The nurse commonly utilizes volunteers along with the vision specialist to do the screening. Good school vision screening programs check for distant visual acuity, hyperopia, near-point reading acuity, strabismus or fusion, and color discrimination (Rathgaber, 1981). Those who do not pass the initial screening receive a follow-up rescreening. Parents of the children who do not pass then are advised to take their child to an eye specialist for a thorough check.

Diagnosis and treatment are done by two types of eye specialists: the ophthalmologist and the optometrist. The *ophthalmologist* is a medical doctor, specializing in eye disorders, who can conduct examinations, prescribe corrective lenses, and perform surgeries and other medical interventions. The *optometrist* is an expert in optometry who can measure vision and prescribe corrective lenses but cannot perform surgery. If medical problems are suspected, the optometrist will refer the patient to an ophthalmologist.

*I*NTERVENTION

The education of children with visual impairments is a joint effort of general education and special education. As the number of additional disabilities increases, so does the proportional share that special education usually must assume for educating children with visual and multiple disabilities. As a rule, general education is primarily responsible for planning and implementing elements of the standard school curriculum. Special education provides the instructional support needed to help maintain children who have visual impairments in as normal an educational setting as possible.

According to IDEA, the local education agency (LEA) is responsible for planning and implementing free and appropriate public education for children with disabilities residing within its boundaries. Many of the smaller school districts do not have enough children with visual impairments to warrant employing a full-time vision specialist. In these cases, they usually establish cooperative agreements with other small neighboring districts to hire a full-time teacher of students with visual disabilities to serve their joint needs.

Within the LEA, the teacher of students with visual disabilities is the person mainly responsible for developing and implementing the special education program for students with visual impairments. He or she has multiple roles: teacher-counselor, advocate, parent educator, manager, and coordinator of resources and services. Each individualized education program (IEP) is based on the seven common characteristics and the findings from the needs assessment described earlier. In addition to identifying goals and objectives, the IEP specifies the extent to which the student who has visual impairment can function in the regular classroom, the service deliverers, and the expected duration of special services. The vision specialist's role is to fulfill the following functions and responsibilities (Spungin & Ferrell, 1990):

1. Direct instruction for the student who is visually impaired
   a. *Academics.* Except for residential schools and self-contained special education classes, regular education has the primary responsibility for academic instruction.
   b. *Academic remediation.* The teacher of students with visual disabilities is responsible for academic remediation only when the deficit or lag is attributable directly to the visual loss.

c. *Compensatory or adaptive skills.* The teacher of students with visual disabilities is responsible for providing instruction in the specialized or unique skills required by the child who has visual impairment to function effectively in school and society. For each child, the vision specialist considers instructional areas such as reading and writing braille, visual efficiency, print adaptations and low-vision devices, handwriting, typewriting and keyboarding, use of technology, listening skills, study skills, motor development, reasoning, tactual skills, subject-area adaptations, orientation and mobility, concept development, physical education, human sexuality, leisure and recreation, activities of daily living, and career and affective education.

d. *Guidance and counseling.* The teacher of students with visual disabilities must provide emotional support and informational counseling, particularly with respect to issues stemming from the visual impairment.

2. Indirect support services

a. *Referral follow-up.* The teacher of students with visual disabilities evaluates all children who are referred for possible consideration for the program for children with visual disabilities.

b. *Educational assessment.* The teacher of students with visual disabilities does many of the vision-related initial assessments and subsequent periodic reassessments.

c. *Preparation, procurement, and distribution of educational materials and equipment.* The teacher of students with visual disabilities uses national, state, and local resources to obtain the necessary braille, recorded, and large-print texts, as well as other specialized equipment and devices.

d. *Consultation with staff.* The teacher of students with visual disabilities is available to administrators, teachers, and other staff to discuss methods of working with children who are visually impaired.

e. *Consultation with and counseling for parents.* To enhance the student's climate for growth and development, the teacher of students with visual disabilities provides information, support, and encouragement to parents and other family members.

f. *Monitoring student progress.* The teacher of students with visual disabilities is responsible for keeping in touch with students who have visual impairments and their classroom teachers to monitor their progress, discuss potential problems, and anticipate future needs.

g. *Inservice training for staff.* The teacher of students with visual disabilities must provide periodic inservice training regarding the nature, needs, and intervention strategies appropriate for students who have visual impairments.

h. *Informational counseling for sighted peers.* The teacher of students with visual disabilities assists the student's sighted peers in developing an awareness of and a sensitivity to some of the differences imposed by a visual impairment.

i. *Coordination and training of volunteers.* The teacher of students with visual disabilities uses volunteers to supplement classroom instruction and to assist in the preparation of braille, recorded, or large-print materials.

j. *School vision screening efforts.* The teacher of students with visual disabilities is involved in the vision screening program as a potential source of referrals.

  k. *Advocacy role.* The teacher of students with visual disabilities speaks on behalf of and acts in support of the child's best interests.

3. Administrative and other duties

  a. *Professional meetings, including staffings.* The teacher of students with visual disabilities keeps in contact with a number of different schools, each having its own teachers' meetings, parent meetings, committees, and so on, in addition to the special education meetings.

  b. *Child-find efforts.* The teacher of students with visual disabilities has a responsibility to assist with the district's child-find policies and procedures.

  c. *Eye reports.* The teacher of students with visual disabilities reads and interprets eye reports from the ophthalmologist or optometrist and maintains contact for any needed clarification.

  d. *The IEP.* The teacher of students with visual disabilities plays a critical role in developing and implementing the child's IEP.

  e. *Office preparation time.* The teacher of students with visual disabilities needs preparation time for planning, scheduling, record keeping, and report writing.

  f. *Coordination of national, state, and local resources.* The teacher of students with visual disabilities maintains a file of the resources and services available to students with visual impairments and their parents.

  g. *Maintenance of equipment.* The teacher of students with visual disabilities must make sure that all specialized devices and equipment are maintained in good working order.

  h. *Travel.* The teacher of students with visual disabilities usually serves students in several different schools, requiring time to travel from school to school.

  i. *Professional growth and maintenance.* The teacher of students with visual disabilities is responsible for keeping current and certified in a rapidly changing profession.

  j. *Program evaluation.* The teacher of students with visual disabilities periodically evaluates the effectiveness of the special education program for students who have visual disabilities for the purpose of improving the quality of services.

  k. *Relations with the community and media.* The teacher of students with visual disabilities serves a public relations function to improve the understanding of people within the community and attitudes toward individuals with visual impairments.

EDUCATIONAL DELIVERY SYSTEMS

IDEA requires that a full continuum of special education services, ranging from least restrictive to most intensive, be available. The intent of the law is to place the child with visual impairment in the regular education classroom as much of the day as possible without compromising the quality of that child's educational program. Six basic types of service delivery models are described here, presented in the order they appeared historically—and, coincidentally, in the order from most intensive to least restrictive (Scholl, 1986).

Residential School. The first residential schools in the United States were founded in Boston, New York, and Philadelphia during the 1830s. With a few exceptions, every state has its own residential school, but fewer than 15% of the current school-age population of children with visual disabilities attend residential schools. These are comprehensive, total-care settings with qualified staff, fully equipped classrooms, dormitory or cottage living quarters, gymnasium and other recreational facilities, and a health center. Arrangements are made for the students to return home frequently on weekends, holidays, and summer vacations.

Self-Contained Classroom. Self-contained classrooms for students who have visual impairments, though not used commonly today, began to appear in the Chicago public schools soon after the turn of the 20th century. Usually, the average-sized school district had only one self-contained classroom, typically located in a central school building. Students lived at home but, for some, it meant long hours being transported to and from school. Opportunities to associate with sighted peers occurred during recesses and lunch breaks.

Cooperative Program. Some teachers of self-contained classes began to seek ways to selectively integrate some of their students with visual impairments into a few regular education classrooms for specified subjects. This model is contingent upon the cooperation and willingness of the regular classroom teacher to accept a student who has visual impairment for a portion of the day. The primary responsibility for the child's program still rests with the vision specialist.

Resource Room. As more and more students with visual impairments were integrated successfully into the regular classroom, it became apparent that many of them could spend most of their day in the regular classroom, attending the special education classroom for instruction only in compensatory or adaptive skills. At any time during the school day, the resource room is available for specialized intervention, and it is available to the classroom teacher for consultation with respect to classroom strategies or special materials. Usually the student who has visual impairment is scheduled into the resource room for a specific time during the day for specialized instruction.

A fundamental concept is that the student with visual impairment identifies himself or herself as a member of the regular classroom along with sighted peers. That is where attendance is taken and where the child's lunch, jacket, and books are left for the day. The regular education teacher has primary responsibility for planning and implementing the academic curriculum for all students in the classroom, including those with visual impairments.

Itinerant Teacher. Some students who have visual impairments who did not need daily contact with the vision specialist began attending their own neighborhood schools with their siblings and neighborhood friends. The itinerant teacher of students with visual disabilities travels to the school where the student is enrolled, to provide specialized materials and instruction. The frequency of visits ranges from three times a week to once every 2 weeks or so. The vision specialist must carry the necessary instructional materials for each visit, and the instructional lesson sometimes is offered at the back of the regular classroom, in the hall, in a corner of the library or cafeteria, or in a janitor's closet—wherever space is available. Because the vision specialist is not present daily or immediately, the student with visual impairment is expected to function more independently and more resourcefully. Despite these restraints, most children who have visual impairments are served by itinerant teachers.

Teacher-Consultant Program. As the student with visual impairment mastered the personal and academic skills necessary for school and home success, the vision specialist no longer had to provide direct instruction. Instead, the student was maintained through consultative services provided to the classroom teacher by the vision specialist. The philosophy of the teacher-consultant model maintains that the general and specialized needs of the child with visual impairment can be met best by equipping the classroom teacher and other school staff with management strategies and skills, reducing the amount of time the vision specialist has to spend with the child. The teacher-consultant model is more common in rural, sparsely populated regions, where students with visual impairments are scattered among many school districts and even several counties. As a result, the teacher-consultant frequently spends more than half the workday on the road.

The number of children and youth served by the teacher of students with visual disabilities varies from three to 24 students, depending on the intensity of their needs and the program model. In actual practice, a district usually does not restrict itself to only one program model. Some residential schools have developed agreements with the local public school district to integrate some of their students into a neighboring school for part or all of the school day. Some vision specialists serve a few in a resource room at one school for part of the day and spend the remainder of the day as itinerant teachers in several other schools. The intensity of needs of the student with visual impairment should be the determining factor as to which program model to employ at any given time during the child's school career. Flexibility, creativity, and resourcefulness are critical ingredients of good programming for children with visual impairment.

TYPICAL INSTRUCTIONAL MATERIALS

The instructional materials used in educating children and youth with visual impairments are extensive and diverse. Some of the materials are relatively inexpensive; others, such as complex electronic devices, are very expensive. Depending on the students' needs, a school district needs many of the materials listed below; and, depending on the parents' resources, some of the materials are used in the home for homework and personal use. The materials listed are only a sample of the possible range available:

1. *Reading and writing aids*: standard and large-type typewriters, braille writer, slate and stylus, talking book disk and cassette players, magnifiers, closed-circuit televi-

For low vision children the light box stimulates awareness of light and color. It assists in a variety of visual-perceptual skills. (Photo courtesy of American Printing House for the Blind)

sion reader, Optacon, electronic braille note-taker, adapted microcomputer.

2. *Mathematical aids*: abacus, talking calculator, graph and geometric aids, instructional kits.
3. *Geographic aids*: braille and large-print atlases, tactile globe, take-apart puzzle maps, relief or boldline outline map, map-making kit, instructional kits.
4. *Science aids*: adapted ruler, weights, scales, light probe, audible circuit analyzer, instructional kits.
5. *Orientation and mobility aids*: Chang mobility kit, maps, variety of canes and electronic aids.
6. *Recreational aids*: wooden or plastic puzzles, adapted table games, audible goal locater, beeper balls, bowling guide rail, tandem bicycle.
7. *Personal and home aids*: braille or talking watch or clock, kitchen timers, bathroom scales, adapted medical supplies, braille labels for appliances.

The technological boom of the 20th century has done much to enhance the quality of life for individuals with visual impairments. Depending on special aids, however, has some disadvantages. Most are not available locally and must be ordered by mail. Most of the complex electronic devices are costly in both initial purchase and subsequent maintenance. The advantages of these aids, however, far outweigh the disadvantages.

RESEARCH APPLICATIONS

The transition from research to practice seems to be a long-standing problem in education and is particularly so in the education of children with visual disabilities (Scholl, 1983). In the first place, the design and methodological difficulties of conducting research in a low-incidence population that is so varied and diverse are quite apparent when reviewing the literature (Warren, 1984). Also, the high cost of developing, demonstrating, and disseminating research projects has been prohibitive. Finally, the time delay between research findings and educational practice is discouraging, possibly attributable in part to the conservative nature of teachers and their reluctance to change. Despite these difficulties, some research projects over the past 20 years have impacted significantly on the education of children with visual impairments.

Utilization of Low Vision. Barraga's initial research on utilization of low vision has revolutionized the strategies employed with children who have residual vision. Formerly, it was believed that their residual vision could be damaged by using the eyes improperly or too much. Consequently, schools had sight-saving or sight-conservation classes. Barraga (1964), however, demonstrated that seeing is a learned behavior and can be enhanced through instructional activities designed to stimulate the use of residual vision. During the 1970s an extensive project was undertaken to teach vision specialists the new philosophy and strategies. The most recent revision of these materials has been published by the American Printing House for the Blind under the title *Program to Develop Efficiency in Visual Functioning* (Barraga & Morris, 1980).

Science Activities for the Visually Impaired (SAVI). Science instruction in the elementary grades depends on visual observation of demonstrated activities or projects. Some hands-on materials were needed for children with visual impairments. The Adapted Science Materials for the Blind was the first set of materials produced by the Lawrence Hall of Science, Berkeley, California. From this earlier work a new set of materials emerged as Science Activities for the Visually Impaired, and again a nationwide dissemination project was undertaken to teach teachers how to use the materials (Lawrence Hall of Science, 1981).

Piagetian Approach to Visually Handicapped Education (PAVE). Stephens and Simpkins (1974) found that congenitally blind children fell behind their sighted peers in Piagetian reasoning abilities but that these lags could be remediated through specifically designed instructional activities. Special workshops were conducted throughout the entire United States to train vision specialists in using the assessment instrument properly and in designing appropriate intervention strategies (Stephens & Grube, 1982).

Materials Adaptation for the Visually Impaired in Social Studies (MAVIS). Another curriculum adaptation project, undertaken by the Social Science Education Consortium, Boulder, Colorado, looked at how an elementary school social studies curriculum could be adapted to accommodate children with visual impairments in the regular classroom. A series of monographs provides the essential background for the actual adapted social studies curriculum (Social Science Education Consortium, 1981).

Adapted Microcomputers. With microcomputers becoming so common in the schools, teachers of students with visual disabilities have to learn about the hardware and software adaptations that make the microcomputer accessible to students who have visual impairments. Applications of microcomputer research to the education of students with visual impairments have taken place rapidly (Ashcroft, 1984; Goodrich, 1984) because of extensive dissemination activities involving teachers of students with visual disabilities across the United States. The federal government funded many of the dissemination projects to offset the high cost of working with this low-incidence population. Other dissemination activities included journal articles, conference presentations, marketing efforts, and inservice workshops for teachers of students with visual disabilities. Finally, many of the dissemination efforts targeted college and university faculty in the education of students with visual disabilities, with immediate revisions in the teacher preparation curriculum.

IMPLICATIONS FOR THE REGULAR CLASSROOM

For a number of years, children and youth with visual impairments have been mainstreamed successfully into regular classrooms. When students have the appropriate books, adaptive aids, and special equipment and have acquired, or are in the process of acquiring, the requisite adaptive skills and coping behaviors, they should be able to participate fully in most classroom and related school activities. The classroom teacher does not need to know braille, how to use the abacus, or how to administer any other specialized services, because instruction in these areas is the vision specialist's responsibility. Many classroom teachers never have encountered a child with a visual impairment and understandably are apprehensive. Perhaps the following principles would be helpful as a guide to the classroom teacher (Tuttle, 1984).

1. Children who have visual impairments are, first of all, children with the same needs, drives, and desires as sighted children. They are more like than unlike all other children.
2. As a general rule, the classroom teacher should include the student with visual impairment in most school activities. If any question arises regarding appropriate strategies, the vision specialist should be consulted.
3. The child's perception of the world without vision is a valid experience. The classroom teacher should not unnecessarily impose a visual frame of reference.
4. A positive attitude of encouragement, and a healthy emphasis on the student's abilities rather than on his or her disabilities, fosters a sense of acceptance and cultivates the freedom to try. The right to try and fail must be honored.
5. Classroom instructions must be articulated clearly without relying on gestures or facial expressions. Sometimes, with the student's permission, his or her body parts may have to be manipulated to a desired posture or motion.
6. The student with visual impairment must be encouraged to accomplish tasks independently even though it may take more time.
7. Praise for tasks well done is essential, but false praise for routine or ordinary tasks is detrimental.
8. Students who have visual impairments should meet the same behavior standards expected of all children. Blindness should never be used as an excuse for unacceptable behavior.
9. Children with visual impairments rely on candid, honest feedback from others to determine the social acceptability of their appearance and behaviors.
10. Conversations with students who have visual impairments should be natural, with no need to shout or to avoid visually oriented words.

11. When uncertain about what assistance, if any, is needed, the best practice is to simply ask the student with visual impairment.
12. The teacher's own attitude toward blindness is communicated, either consciously or unconsciously, to students with visual impairments. Negative or devaluating attitudes must be recognized and dispelled.

The classroom teacher should not feel reluctant or embarrassed about interacting with the student who has visual impairment. Teachers should call these students by name so the student knows when he or she is being addressed. A little common sense usually is the best approach to an apparently awkward situation. The individual with visual impairment probably will be happy to offer his or her own suggestions or preferences regarding appropriate strategies.

Torres and Corn (1990) have written a guide for the regular classroom teacher entitled *When You Have a Visually Handicapped Child in Your Classroom,* available from the American Foundation for the Blind. It offers many specific, concrete suggestions the classroom teacher will find helpful. The student who has visual impairment has greater access to information on the chalkboard when the teacher verbalizes aloud everything written on the board. When arranging classroom seating, the classroom teacher should consider the student's preferences for lighting conditions and distances from the chalkboard. Because students with low vision tend to have a great deal of difficulty with purple dittos, the teacher may want to provide black copies. Or a sheet of yellow acetate over a purple ditto may improve the contrast sufficiently for readability.

Concrete objects and experiences enable students with visual impairments to profit from picture-related activities in worksheets and workbooks—for example, real money to replace pictures of money. For some classroom activities or field trips, a partner or buddy system for the entire class allows the student with visual impairment more immediate assistance without being singled out for special attention. As suggested earlier, the practical, commonsense approach usually provides adequate solutions to many questions about classroom procedures.

ISSUES AND CONCERNS

The needs of children and youth who have visual impairments are generally the same as those of all children and youth, though the strategies for meeting some of them may differ. The consequences directly attributable to a visual impairment that require some remediation or modified techniques include issues related to conceptualization, personal and home management, orientation and mobility, reading and writing, psychosocial development, vocational and avocational skills, and multiplicity of disabilities.

Once the full spectrum of needs of the student with visual impairment has been assessed and identified, general education and special education share the responsibility for meeting those needs. With the support of special education, students who have visual impairments can participate in every aspect of the regular education curriculum. The support or modifications offered by special education may include one or more of the following: curricular adaptations and remediation, instruction in compensatory or adaptive skills, specialized materials and equipment, consultations on strategies for classroom management, and suggestions related to physical/environmental factors.

Children and youth with visual impairments have been mainstreamed successfully since the first decade of this century. Currently, 87% of students with legal blindness are being served in public day schools, either in self-contained classes or in regular education classes with the support of a resource room teacher, an itinerant teacher, or a teacher-consultant. The residential school, however, continues to play a critical and vital role. Some significant research findings of the past 20 years, particularly in curricular adaptation and technology, have greatly influenced today's education of children and youth with visual impairments.

THE FUTURE

Programs for a low-prevalence population always struggle to maintain quality services in the face of economic pressures and limited resources. Some children who have visual impairments are not being identified for special education services, and others are being served inappropriately. Some districts serve these students through a generically trained special educator who is unable to meet the specialized, unique needs of blind students. Districts in rural, sparsely populated parts of the country employ teacher-consultants who tend to burn out quickly because of the time spent traveling from one student to the next. Perhaps a new, more satisfactory service delivery model will have to be created to meet the educational needs of these children and youth in the future.

Technological advances of recent years certainly have enhanced the quality of life and expanded the opportunities available to individuals with visual impairments. Learning to use the new technological devices, however, puts a strain on an already overloaded educational program. Students who have visual impairments are expected to keep up with the general education curriculum, the adapted curriculum, the special instruction in compensatory skills, and now the new technological aids and devices. The high cost of these aids and devices will require some form of subsidy if the children are to continue using them as adults.

A PERSONAL PERSPECTIVE

Individuals who have visual impairments have not been assimilated into the society to the fullest extent possible (Lowenfeld, 1975). The two major reasons are: (a) the continued devaluating misconceptions and negative attitudes of society, and (b) insufficient numbers of blind adults who have acquired the essential skills and traits to permit them to achieve a full, satisfying life. Because little can be done about the former problem, it would be better to focus efforts on the latter.

Young adults with visual impairments are graduating from school with adequate academic skills but inadequate life skills essential to survival in society (Tuttle, 1984).

Corn and Bishop (1984), who studied the acquisition of practical knowledge in 116 students with visual impairments from both residential and public day programs, found that, though both groups did more poorly than sighted norms, the students with visual disabilities had more difficulty than the students who were totally blind. The vision specialist's role must expand to encompass the teaching of life skills, and a curriculum specifically designed for students with visual impairments must be developed soon. This type of curriculum could be taught during after-school hours, weekends, or summer school.

Many young adults who have visual impairments have a poorly developed self-concept and inadequate self-esteem (Mangold, 1982; Tuttle, 1984). The problem is not inherent in the visual impairment but, rather, results from interaction of the student with visual disabilities with significant others in his or her environment. A child's self-concept and self-esteem are rooted in the reflections he or she receives from others. These reflections are full of negative messages and devaluating attitudes—people who are blind are pitiable, miserable, helpless, incompetent, immoral, sexually maladjusted, unapproachable, unemployable. The negative reflections outweigh the positive by a ratio of six to one.

Adequate self-esteem, on the other hand, is derived from a sense of competence, of being in control. Before acquiring good coping skills, the individual with visual impairment is at a disadvantage, because he or she is less able to exercise control over events within the physical and social environment. Even after acquiring good coping skills, individuals who have visual impairments are at a disadvantage, because others frequently do not permit them to exercise any control. Children and youth with visual impairments are frequently told what to do, problems tend to be solved for them, and decisions often are made on their behalf. The vision specialist's role must expand to include the functions of a teacher-counselor in implementing activities that foster the student's self-concept and self-esteem.

REFERENCES

American Printing House for the Blind. (1992). *Distribution of federal quota based on the registration of eligible students.* Louisville, KY: Author.

Anderson, D. (1984). Mental imagery in congenitally blind children. *Journal of Visual Impairment & Blindness, 78*(5), 206–210.

Ashcroft, S. (1984). Research on multimedia access to microcomputers for visually impaired youth. *Education of the Visually Handicapped, 15*(4), 108–118.

Ashcroft, S., & Zambone-Ashley, A. (1980). Mainstreaming children with visual impairments. *Journal of Research & Development in Education, 13*(4), 22–36.

Barraga, N. (1964). *Increased visual behavior in low vision children* (Research Series No. 13). New York: American Foundation for the Blind.

Barraga, N. C., & Erin, J. N. (1992). *Visual handicaps & learning* (3rd ed.). Austin, TX: Pro-Ed.

Barraga, N., & Morris, J. (1980). *Program to develop efficiency in visual functioning.* Louisville, KY: American Printing House for the Blind.

Benton, V., & Truelove, N. (1978). "Adopt a school"—A program of eye care for children. *Sight Seeing Review, 48*(2), 77–80.

Bower, E. M. (1966). The achievement of competency. In *Mental health and learning*. Washington, DC: Association for Supervision and Curriculum Development.

Colorado Instructional Materials Center. (1992). *Visually impaired registration: Preliminary statistics 1992*. Colorado Springs, CO: Department of Education.

Converso, L., & Hocek, S. (1990). Optical character recognition. *Journal of Visual Impairment & Blindness, 84*, 507–509.

Corn, A. (1983). Visual functioning: A theoretical model for individuals with low vision. *Journal of Visual Impairment & Blindness, 77*(8), 373–376.

Corn, A. (1989). Instruction in the use of vision for children and adults with low vision: A proposed program model. *RE:view, 21*, 26–38.

Corn, A., & Bishop, V. (1984). Acquisition of practical knowledge by blind and visually impaired students in grades 8–12. *Journal of Visual Impairment & Blindness, 79*(2), 352–355.

Council of Executives of American Residential Schools for the Visually Handicapped (CEARSVH). (1991). Least restrictive environment and appropriate educational setting. *RE:view, 23*(3), 119–121.

Curry, S. A., & Hatlen, P. H. (1988). Meeting the unique educational needs of visually impaired pupils through appropriate placement. *Journal of Visual Impairment & Blindness, 82*, 417–424.

Dixon, J. M., & Mandelbaum, J. B. (1990). Reading through technology: Evolving methods and opportunities for print-handicapped individuals. *Journal of Visual Impairment & Blindness, 84*, 493–496.

Ferrell, K. A. (1985). *Reach out and teach*. New York: American Foundation for the Blind.

Ferrell, K. A. (1986a). Infancy and early childhood. In G. T. Scholl (Ed.), *Foundations of education for blind and visually handicapped children and youth: Theory and practice* (pp. 119–135). New York: American Foundation for the Blind.

Ferrell, K. A. (1986b). Working with parents. In G. T. Scholl (Ed.), *Foundations of education for blind and visually handicapped children and youth: Theory and practice* (pp. 265–273). New York: American Foundation for the Blind.

Ferrell, K. A., Deitz, S. J., Trief, E., & Faye, E. (1992). *Developmental risk in young children with retinopathy of prematurity*. Manuscript submitted for publication.

Gardner, L. R., & Corn, A. L. (1991). Low vision: Access to print. *Division for the Visually Handicapped: Statements of position* (pp. 6–8). Reston, VA: Council for Exceptional Children.

Gates, C. (1985). Survey of multiply handicapped visually impaired children in the Rocky Mountain Great Plains region. *Journal of Visual Impairment & Blindness, 79*(9), 385–391.

Gates, C., & Kappan, D. (1985). Triple competency training of teachers of the visually impaired in rural areas. *Journal of Visual Impairment & Blindness, 79*(7), 306–307.

Goodrich, G. (1984). Applications of microcomputers by visually impaired persons. *Journal of Visual Impairment & Blindness, 78*(9), 408–413.

Groenveld, M., Jan, J. E., & Leader, P. (1990). Observations on the habilitation of children with cortical visual impairment. *Journal of Visual Impairment & Blindness, 84*, 11–15.

Hatfield, E. (1975). Why are they blind? *Sight Saving Review, 45*(1), 3–22.

Hatfield, E. (1979). Methods and standards for screening preschool children. *Sight Saving Review, 49*(2), 71–83.

Hatlen, P. (1990). Meeting the unique needs of pupils with visual impairments. *RE:view, 22*(2), 79–82.

Hatton, D. (1991). Leading causes of blindness in the infant-preschool population. *Journal of Visual Impairment & Blindness, 85*, 99–101.

Hazekamp, J., & Huebner, K. M. (1989). *Program planning and evaluation for blind and visually impaired students: National guidelines for educational excellence*. New York: American Foundation for the Blind.

Head, D. (1989). The future of low incidence programs: A national problem. *RE:view, 21*, 145–152.

Hoben, M., & Lindstrom, V. (1980). Evidence of isolation in the mainstream. *Journal of Visual Impairment & Blindness, 74*(8), 289–292.

Hodges, H. (1983). Evaluating the effectiveness of programs for the visually impaired: One state's approach. *Journal of Visual Impairment & Blindness, 77*(3), 97–99.

Hubbard, C. (1983). Reversing mainstreaming sighted children into a visually impaired special day class. *Journal of Visual Impairment & Blindness, 77*(5), 193–194.

Huebner, K. M. (1989). *The education of students with disabilities: Where do we stand?* Unpublished

Congressional testimony, American Foundation for the Blind, New York.

Huebner, K. M., & Ferrell, K. A. (1989). Ethical practice in the provision of services to blind and visually impaired infants, children, and youth. In J. Hazekamp & K. M. Huebner (Eds.), *Program planning and evaluation for blind and visually impaired students: National guidelines for educational excellence* (pp. 82–96). New York: American Foundation for the Blind.

Huebner, K. M., & Koenig, A. J. (1991). Student-centered educational placement decisions: The meaning, interpretation, and application of least restrictive environment. *Division for the Visually Handicapped: Statements of position* (pp. 12–15). Reston, VA: Council for Exceptional Children.

Jackson, D., & Busset, P. (1991). Making information accessible to blind and visually impaired mainstreamed students. *Journal of Visual Impairment & Blindness, 85,* 228–229.

Kekelis, L. S., & Sacks, S. Z. (1992). The effects of visual impairment on children's social interactions in regular education programs. In S. Z. Sacks, L. S. Kekelis, & R. J. Gaylord-Ross (Eds.), *The development of social skills by blind and visually impaired students: Exploratory studies and strategies* (pp. 59–82). New York: American Foundation for the Blind.

Kirchner, C. (1989). National estimates of prevalence and demographics of children with visual impairments. In M. C. Wang, M. C. Reynolds, & H. J. Walberg (Eds.), *Handbook of special education research and practice, volume 3: Low incidence conditions* (pp. 135–153). Oxford: Pergamon Press.

Kirtley, D. (1975). *The psychology of blindness.* Chicago: Nelson-Hall.

Lawrence Hall of Science. (1981). *Science activities for the visually impaired.* Berkeley: University of California.

Long, E. (1984). Funding. In G. T. Scholl (Ed.), *Quality services for blind and visually handicapped learners: Statements of position* (pp. 26–28). Reston, VA: ERIC Clearinghouse on Handicapped and Gifted Children.

Lowenfeld, B. (1975). *The changing status of the blind.* Springfield, IL: Charles C Thomas.

Lowenfeld, B. (1981). *Berthold Lowenfeld on blindness and blind people: Selected papers.* New York: American Foundation for the Blind.

Lowenfeld, B. (1982). In search of better ways. *Education of the Visually Handicapped, 14*(3), 69–77.

MacCuspie, P. A. (1992). The social acceptance and interaction of visually impaired children in integrated settings. In S. Z. Sacks, L. S. Kekelis, & R. J. Gaylord-Ross (Eds.), *The development of social skills by blind and visually impaired students: Exploratory studies and strategies* (pp. 83–102). New York: American Foundation for the Blind.

Mangold, S. S. (1982). Nurturing high self-esteem in visually handicapped children. In S. S. Mangold (Ed.), *A teacher's guide to the special educational needs of blind and visually handicapped children.* New York: American Foundation for the Blind.

Moore, S. (1984). The need for programs and services for visually impaired infants. *Education of the Visually Handicapped, 16*(2), 48–57.

Morse, M. (1983). The MICE project, an innovative service delivery system for visually handicapped children. *Journal of Visual Impairment & Blindness, 77*(2), 52–56.

Morse, M. T. (1990). Cortical visual impairment in young children with multiple disabilities. *Journal of Visual Impairment & Blindness, 84,* 200–203.

Mullen, E. A. (1990). Decreased braille literacy: A symptom of a system in need of reassessment. *RE:view, 22,* 164–169.

Packer, J., & Kirchner, C. (1985). State-level counts of blind and visually handicapped school children. *Journal of Visual Impairment & Blindness, 79,* 257–261.

Parker, S., Buckley, W., Truesdell, A., Riggio, M., Collins, M., & Boardman, B. (1990). Barriers to the use of assistive technology with children: A survey. *Journal of Visual Impairment & Blindness, 84,* 532–533.

Pogrund, R. L., Fazzi, D. L., & Lampert, J. S. (Eds.). (1992). *Early focus: Working with young blind and visually impaired children and their families.* New York: American Foundation for the Blind.

Poirier, R. (1984). Scorecard: An update on NSPB's planning system. *Sight Saving, 53*(2), 18–21.

Radke, E., & Blackhurst, R. (1978). Preschool screening of vision: The Michigan experience. *Sight Saving Review, 48*(3), 99–106.

Rathgaber, A. (1981). Manitoba vision screening study. *Journal of Visual Impairments and Blindness, 75*(6), 239–243.

Rex, E. J. (1989). Issues related to literacy of legally blind learners. *Journal of Visual Impairment & Blindness*, *83*, 306–307, 310–313.

Rochlin, J. (1985). The future isn't what it used to be. *Braille Forum, 6*, 127–130.

Scholl, G. (1983). Bridges from research to practice in education of visually handicapped people. *Journal of Visual Impairment & Blindness, 77*(7), 340–344.

Scholl, G. (Ed.). (1986). *Foundation of education for blind and visually handicapped children and youth: Theory and practice.* New York: American Foundation for the Blind.

Scholl, G., Long, E., & Tuttle, D. (1980). Monitoring program quality: Who and how should it be done? *Division for the Visually Handicapped Newsletter, 25*(1), 12–18.

Schreier, E. M. (1990). The future of access technology for blind and visually impaired people. *Journal of Visual Impairment & Blindness, 84*, 520–523.

Schroeder, F. (1989). Literacy: The key to opportunity. *Journal of Visual Impairment & Blindness, 83*, 290–293.

Schrotberger, W., & Tuttle, D. (1978). *Educational assessment of visually handicapped children.* Greeley: University of Northern Colorado.

Schulz, P. (1980). *How does it feel to be blind?* Van Nuys, CA: Muse-Ed.

Scott, E. P. (1982). *Your visually impaired student.* Baltimore: University Park Press.

Scott, R. (1969). *The making of blind men.* New York: Russell Sage Foundation.

Silverstein, R. (1985). The legal necessity for residential schools serving deaf, blind, and multi-impaired children. *Journal of Visual Impairment & Blindness, 79*(4), 145–149.

Simpson, F. (1986). Transition to adulthood. In G. T. Scholl (Ed.), *Foundations of education for blind and visually handicapped children and youth: Theory and practice* (pp. 405–422). New York: American Foundation for the Blind.

Social Science Education Consortium. (1981). *Social studies materials adaptations for visually handicapped elementary students* (Final Report, Grant No. G007701353). Boulder, CO: Author.

Spungin, S. J. (1982). The future role of residential school for the handicapped. *Journal of Visual Impairment & Blindness, 76*(6), 229–233.

Spungin, S. J. (1989). *Braille literacy: Issues for blind persons, families, professionals, and producers of braille.* New York: American Foundation for the Blind.

Spungin, S. J., & Ferrell, K. A. (1990). The role and function of the teacher of students with visual handicaps (rev. ed.). *DVH Quarterly, 36*(2), 20–23.

Stephens, W. B., & Grube, C. (1982). Development of Piagetian reasoning in congenitally blind children. *Journal of Visual Impairment & Blindness, 76*(4), 133–143.

Stephens, W. B., & Simpkins, K. (1974). *The reasoning, moral judgment, and moral conduct of the congenitally blind.* Washington, DC: U.S. Department of Health, Education and Welfare.

Torres, I., & Corn, A. (1990). *When you have a visually handicapped child in your classroom: Suggestions for teachers.* New York: American Foundation for the Blind.

Trief, E., & Morse, A. R. (1987). An overview of preschool vision screening. *Journal of Visual Impairment & Blindness, 81*(5), 197–200.

Tuttle, D. (1972). A comparison of three reading media for the blind. *Education of the Visually Handicapped, 4*(2), 40–44.

Tuttle, D. (1981). Academics are not enough. In G. D. Napier, D. L. Kappan, D. W. Tuttle, W. L. Schrotberger, A. L. Dennison, & C. W. Lappin (Eds.), *Handbook for teachers of the visually handicapped* (rev. ed.) (pp. 38–44). Louisville, KY: American Printing House for the Blind.

Tuttle, D. (1984). *Self-esteem and adjusting with blindness.* Springfield, IL: Charles C Thomas.

U.S. Department of Education. (1992). *To assure the free appropriate public education of all children with disabilities: Fourteenth annual report to Congress on the implementation of the individuals with disabilities education act.* Washington, DC: Office of Special Education Programs.

Warren, D. (1984). *Blindness and early childhood development* (2nd ed.). New York: American Foundation for the Blind.

Wittenstein, S. (1992). *The relationship between pre-service braille training experiences and teacher attitudes towards braille as a learning medium.* Unpublished doctoral dissertation, Teachers College, Columbia University, New York.

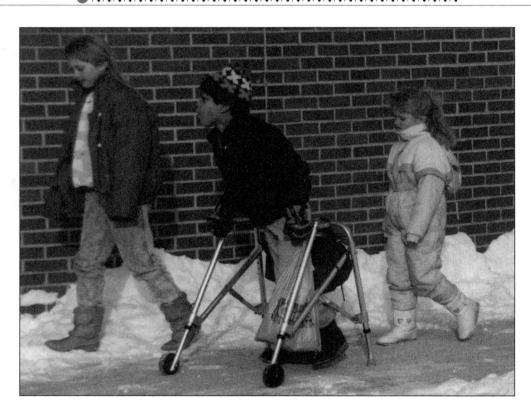

PHYSICAL DISABILITIES AND

CHRONIC HEALTH

IMPAIRMENTS

BARBARA P. SIRVIS
AND TERRY HEINTZ CALDWELL

*H*istorically, the education of students with physical disabilities evolved from a medical model. Most children with orthopedic or health impairments were treated in hospitals or state institutions. Health and physical problems were attended to, but little attention was paid to a person's long-term needs, including that of education. The "whole person" was essentially ignored. Gradually, however, special classes and home and hospital instruction developed. As the importance and relevance of education for special students generally came to be realized, children with more severe physical problems—for example, cerebral palsy, muscular dystrophy, spina bifida—were allowed access to education. Interdisciplinary teams began to work with these students in a conscious effort to maximize their educational potential.

CURRENT PRACTICES

PL 94–142, the Education for all Handicapped Children Act, created greater support for the concept of interdisciplinary programming and for educational programs in less restrictive environments. Previously isolated, students with physical disabilities now have more opportunities for full inclusion in regular classrooms. Students who need special assistance receive related or supplemental services, often available on an itinerant or resource room basis in the regular school setting. Students benefit from the regular curriculum through adaptations such as alternative response methods to demonstrate mastery of material, extra time, and extra assistance. Despite the law, however, some schools are still inaccessible as the result of architectural or attitudinal barriers, and professionals, parents, and advocates continue to work toward inclusion and acceptance. The composition of special education classrooms also has changed, primarily as a result of inclusionary practices. Twenty years ago, a class for students with physical disabilities was composed primarily of academically able students who happened to use wheelchairs. Now most students in special education classrooms have multiple disabilities that require unique educational programs to serve their combined physical and cognitive disabilities.

Other changes in educational programs for students with physical disabilities and health impairments resulted from significant increases in life expectancy, the use of medical and communicative technology, changes in teacher training programs, and greater need for intra- and interagency coordination. In 1955, the life expectancy for a child who had leukemia was less than a year. By 1964, life expectancy had risen to almost 5 years (Steinherz, 1991), and now 85% of children diagnosed with leukemia live more than 5 years (American Cancer Society, 1988). Early diagnosis and better treatments of children who have Duchenne muscular dystrophy also have resulted in an increased life expectancy to approximately 20 years (Synoground & Kelsey, 1990). Improved medical and communicative technologies are providing new challenges for educators. Children with significant pulmonary problems can now live in the community and require an array of portable technology such as oxygen systems and ventilators (breathing machines) in school. Children who have spina bifida stand and walk much sooner using standing parapodiums and reciprocating braces. Children with cerebral palsy who have impaired communicative skills use an array of communication equipment for "talking" and "printing" copies of class work. These technologies can be complex and require the teacher to have a general understanding of the applications and mechanics of technology as well as specific training in the use of a student's specific piece of equipment.

Categorical preparation of teachers to teach students with physical disabilities is much less frequent than it was even 10 years ago. Many states now require generic certification in special education, and preparation programs focus on the most common types of disabilities (learning disabilities, emotional and behavioral problems, and mental retardation). As a result, few teachers have received the comprehensive training necessary to manage the complex physical and technological problems accompanying a physical disability. With fewer self-contained classes for students with physical disabilities, many of the teachers who are specifically trained now are functioning in consultant roles, assisting regular education teachers to accommodate complex equipment and health and self-care routines.

Intra- and interagency collaboration have become essential components of education of children with physical disabilities and health conditions. Collaboration between regular and special education teachers gives each student the opportunity to progress in a regular class. In addition, many children with physical disabilities receive related services such as physical and occupational therapy to assist them in achieving their educational goals. School districts throughout the United States are struggling to provide appropriate related services. Previously, finances, difficulty with separating educational and medical needs, differences in educational and medical reimbursement schedules, and the complexities of supervising medical/nonteaching personnel did not allow students to access appropriate related services.

Recent legislation offers new hope. As a result of expanded medicaid funding in some states, the school systems and medicaid have entered into partnerships to provide related services to students. In addition, as a result of Part H of PL 99–457, which addresses services for students birth through age 5, interagency coordinating councils have been formed at state and regional levels. Federal, state, and local education, health, and mental health agencies are forging working relationships to provide unique arrangements for providing related services, paving the way for blending fiscal resources and expertise to best serve children. This blending prescribes a new role for teachers, who often act in concert with parents as service coordinators (case managers) to assist their students in accessing an array of appropriate services.

DEFINITIONS

To provide a categorical definition of students with physical disabilities is difficult because the range of disabilities is so broad. A disability may be characterized by limited function affecting mobility, activities of daily living, and participation in gross motor and fine motor activities. A student may have additional handicaps associated with emotional, social, or educational needs. These problems may relate to learning, social-emotional adjustment, developmental lag, speech and language development, or a visual or hearing impairment. The terminology used to label this population—*physically handicapped, crippled and other health impaired (COHI), physically limited*—still lacks uniformity. The guidelines for PL 94–142 define students with *orthopedic impairments* as those having

> ...a severe orthopedic impairment which adversely affects a child's educational performance. The term includes impairment caused by congenital anomaly (e.g., clubfoot, absence of some member, etc.), impairments caused by disease (e.g., poliomyelitis, bone tuberculosis, etc.), and impairments from other causes (e.g., cerebral palsy, amputations, and fractures or burns which cause contractures). (*Federal Register*, p. 42478)

Also identified are those with *health impairments*:

> ...limited strength, vitality, or alertness, due to chronic or acute health problems such as a heart condition, tuberculosis, rheumatic fever, nephritis, asthma, sickle cell anemia, hemophilia, epilepsy, lead poisoning, leukemia, or diabetes, which adversely affect a child's educational performance. (*Federal Register*, p. 42478)

PREVALENCE

Prevalence figures are difficult, if not impossible, to determine, in part because of problems in defining the population—whether to include those with multiple handicaps or sensory (hearing or vision) impairments, for instance. The data collected by the federal government on children and youth served under PL 94–142 and PL 89–313, however, give some indication. In the *Thirteenth Annual Report to Congress*, 91,008 students were classified as having orthopedic or health impairments during 1989–90 (U.S. Department of Education, 1991). This does not account for a percentage of the students classified as multiply handicapped who likely also have a physical disability.

CAUSES AND PREVENTION

The causes of physical disabilities and health impairments are as diverse as the actual disabilities. Moreover, causes of many conditions are unknown. Etiology is not prerequisite to teaching; however, it is helpful to understand some general factors, any one of which may influence the development of a physical disability in a given child.

Prenatal factors may be *genetic* or *environmental*. A disability, although not evident in the parents, may appear in one or more of the children. *Muscular dystrophy* is an example of a genetic (hereditary) disorder. It usually is caused by a sex-linked recessive gene that is transmitted from unaffected mothers to their sons. Another example is *cystic fibrosis*, a genetic disorder commonly found among caucasian populations. Environmental factors are external influences (*teratogens*) on a developing fetus. Inadequate prenatal medical care, poor maternal diet, and abuse of substances (alcohol, cigarettes, drugs) all may cause a physical disability. Also, injury to the fetus as a result of injury to the mother may produce prenatal trauma (Crain, 1984).

The *perinatal* period is the birth process, from the first labor pain to the infant's first breath. The greatest risk here is related to *trauma* or *anoxia* (lack of oxygen), either of which may occur if the doctor has to change the position of the fetus during the birth process or if the oxygen supply is obstructed during delivery. The most common disability occurring during this period is *cerebral palsy*.

The *postnatal* period is generally considered to be from birth to 2 years of age. Physical disabilities that appear during this time are commonly the result of bicycle or automobile accidents. In addition, infections, such as encephalitis and meningitis, may cause permanent damage to the central nervous system. The result may be brain damage or paralysis or both .

Many physical disabilities remain *idiopathic* (cause unknown). For those known to be hereditary, research continues to try to determine the actual genetic makeup. In some cases, research has identified the cause but failed to effect a cure; in other cases, interim treatment procedures have been identified. There is a need to continue considerable investment in both medical and genetic research in the interests of prevention and intervention. Some environmentally based causes are open to prevention and intervention. Adequate prenatal care focuses on educating expectant mothers about diet, environment, and negative substances that likely cause disabilities. Trauma, infection, and accidents are sometimes, but not always, preventable. Environmental awareness, adequate supervision of young children, and health promotion and disease prevention programs are all potentially effective intervention and prevention strategies.

*O*RTHOPEDIC AND NEUROLOGICAL IMPAIRMENTS

Orthopedic and neurological impairments often are categorized in accordance with the part of the body affected. If the paralysis is complete, the root of the following terms is "plegia." If the body area is not totally paralyzed but muscle groups are difficult to control or are partially paralyzed, the root of the word is "paresis." For instance, most children who have cerebral palsy have "paresis," whereas those with spinal cord injury usually have paralysis. The following descriptors are stated in terms of total paralysis, but the root can be changed to paresis.

monoplegia: paralysis of one limb
paraplegia: paralysis of both lower extremities

> *hemiplegia:*   paralysis of both extremities on the same side
> *quadriplegia:*   paralysis of all four extremities
> *diplegia:*   paralysis of all four extremities; greater involvement in the lower limbs.

CEREBRAL PALSY

Of students with physical impairments who need special education services, those with cerebral palsy comprise the largest number. The term generally refers to a category of motor disabilities that entails impairment of muscle coordination and abnormal motor patterns and skills (Bobath, 1980). It is the result of damage to, or maldevelopment of, the motor coordination area of the brain before, during, or after birth. Causes of this disorder—anoxia (lack of oxygen), trauma, maternal infection, childhood trauma—are as varied as the effects of the brain damage itself (Bleck, 1982).

Each of several types of cerebral palsy manifests itself in a slightly different pattern. *Hypertonia* refers to either spasticity or stiffness with increasing limitations of movement because of muscle contractures (Bigge, 1991); motor activities often result in muscular resistance to movement and slow, uncoordinated responses. *Hypotonia* refers to muscle weakness. Most infants born with cerebral palsy are hypotonic; their balance is poor, and their level of activity is slow (Bigge, 1991). *Athetosis* (extrapyramidal involvement) refers to uncontrolled, jerky, irregular movements caused by fluctuating muscle tone. Extraneous, uncontrolled movements make gross motor tasks difficult and fine motor tasks all but impossible. *Ataxia* refers to a lack of coordination related to balance. Fine motor tasks are difficult, and ambulation is possible but unsteady. *Mixed cerebral palsy* is common because brain damage is most often diffuse (Bigge, 1991); it includes various combinations of the above types.

The extent of physical ability in cases of cerebral palsy varies greatly, as does its overall impact. Some students have only fine motor coordination problems; others have difficulty walking without the aid of orthoses (braces) and crutches. Many use a wheelchair, and others cannot maneuver one independently, requiring assistance for any movement even within the smallest space. In the most involved cases, cerebral palsy interferes with head control, arm use, normal sitting positions, balance and posture, and independent mobility (Connor, Williamson, & Siepp, 1978). Stress and fatigue often contribute; even simple motor coordination tasks are more difficult to perform under stress. Whenever possible, the stress of situations such as timed tests should be reduced and students taught stress management techniques.

Cerebral palsy is the physical disability most likely to have associated problems related to learning, social-emotional growth, perception, vision, hearing, and intellectual functioning. These associated disabilities are discussed in other chapters. In any event, assessment often is difficult because traditional standardized tests do not allow for the variance caused by limited hand use and nonoral communication. Treatment of children with cerebral palsy focuses on "the maintenance of proper body alignment, [the provision of] adequate nutrition, [the development of] communication skills [and] fostering independence and self-care" (Synoground & Kelsey, 1990, pp. 40–41).

All students who have cerebral palsy are not multiply disabled. Teachers should not label a child with limited hand use or no oral speech as mentally retarded before the child has had a chance to attempt academic tasks. In many instances, criterion-referenced tests, task analysis, and behavioral observations are necessary to provide an initial assessment and to monitor progress. Class placement and educational expectations cannot be based on traditional data collection methods.

MUSCULAR DYSTROPHY

Muscular dystrophy has several forms, the most common of which is *Duchenne* muscular dystrophy. Characterized by increasing weakness of skeletal muscles, its initial symptoms may hamper a child when running or climbing stairs. Progressive muscle weakness, awkwardness, and slowness in movement eventually become so pronounced that the child must use a wheelchair. Shoulder and arm weakness may appear concurrently with lower extremity involvement or somewhat later. Duchenne muscular dystrophy is a hereditary disorder usually caused by a sex-linked recessive gene transmitted from mother to son. Consequently, Duchenne rarely is found in female children. The progression of muscular dystrophy is relatively rapid, and in the early 1980s, life expectancy was in the early teens (Chutorian & Engel, 1982). Currently, life expectancy is adolescence or young adulthood (Grove, Cusick, & Bigge, 1991).

As the disease progresses, students with muscular dystrophy become increasingly weak, and they fatigue more easily. Although they may be ambulatory in a typical school setting, they often need a wheelchair for field trips and other excursions. Even while ambulatory, they may have difficulty maintaining balance, getting up after they fall, and opening heavy doors. Some need to rest out of their wheelchair to avoid becoming excessively fatigued. To acknowledge the physical impact of the disability is important, but perhaps more important is to focus on appropriate levels of academic and social participation in and out of the school setting.

SPINA BIFIDA

Spina bifida is a congenital defect in the development of the vertebral column, which damages the spinal cord and nerve roots. It takes several forms including *myelomeningocele*. The form and position of the defect affects the extent of neurological deficits. The effects vary from minor sensory and ambulation problems in the milder form, to paraplegia, lack of sensation, and incontinence (lack of bladder control) in the more severe form. Urinary tract, orthopedic, and skin sensitivity problems often are present. In addition, children with spina bifida are more susceptible to developing hydrocephalus, an abnormal retention of cerebrospinal fluid in the cranial cavity. If not surgically corrected, hydrocephalus can cause mental retardation and related learning problems (Anderson & Spain, 1977).

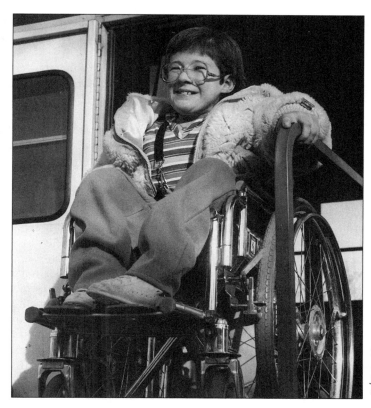

This young student has spina bifida and is in a full inclusion classroom each day.

To meet their physical and academic goals, students with spina bifida usually need related and support services from a number of disciplines. These include health services to accommodate urinary and bowel function and develop good personal hygiene; physical therapy for development of gait (walking) patterns or wheelchair use; and academic programs appropriate to their learning ability, with adaptations for those with potential learning problems that result from hydrocephalus or developmental delays stemming from motor impairments. The outlook for these students has improved tremendously in the past 10 years because of early identification of hydrocephalus and the shunting technique. (Nadell, 1990).

OSTEOGENESIS IMPERFECTA

Frequently called brittle bone disease, osteogenesis imperfecta involves defective development of both the quality and the quantity of bone tissue. Collagen, found in the connective tissues of bone, is not produced. As a result, bones do not grow normally in length and thickness, resulting in their brittle composition. The impact of this disability varies from mild to severe, and some students will be wheelchair users and require adaptive equipment. Dwarfism, caused by multiple fractures, and deafness may be secondary in severe cases (Molnar, 1983).

Academic potential is not directly affected, although students may be absent frequently because of fractures and hence fall behind in their work. Students with osteogenesis imperfecta should be encouraged to develop a self-protective attitude and to recognize that some fractures are inevitable. They should be encouraged to participate in more sedentary activities. Teachers should be aware of the nature of the disability, keeping a distant but watchful eye over the students while refraining from overprotective reactions.

LIMB DEFORMITIES

Absence of a limb may be congenital or acquired. Early intervention by rehabilitation personnel is crucial in most instances. The location and severity of limb deficiency determines the extent and potential of the rehabilitation process. For example, loss of a leg below the knee allows nearly normal function, including participation in sports and games, but loss of a leg above the knee is more disabling and requires more extensive adaptation. Prosthetic devices (artificial limbs) can be important to both the physical and psychological well-being of some students. Others choose to rely on the remaining portion of the deficient limb. For example, those who have lost a hand may prefer to learn to adapt their daily activities to one-handed action, using no prosthesis at all or a nonfunctional cosmetic replacement rather than a more functional hook. Students need to understand fully the potential usefulness of a prosthesis before they decide, especially because its successful use depends on their motivation (Marquardt, 1983).

Initially, teachers may have to adapt educational activities for students learning to use upper extremity prostheses. They also should be aware of functional skills training programs and facilitate practice in the classroom. Most important, teachers should allow students to be as independent as possible so that they will learn new ways of accomplishing motor tasks.

SPINAL CORD INJURY

Accidents (usually involving automobiles and bicycles), sports injuries, and falls are the most common causes of spinal cord injury in the school-age child (Synoground & Kelsey, 1990). The extent of the disability varies according to the level and type of lesion or injury and whether it is a complete or an incomplete lesion. Generally, paralysis and lack of sensation occur below the level of the lesion. Urinary and bowel systems are usually affected, and the respiratory system is seriously affected if the injury is above cervical level 3 on the spinal cord. In general, cervical injuries affect upper and lower extremities, whereas thoracic and lumbar injuries affect the lower extremities. Treatment involves extensive medical and psychological rehabilitation with an emphasis on daily living, vocational, and leisure activities (Corbet, 1980).

JUVENILE RHEUMATOID ARTHRITIS

All of the several forms of juvenile rheumatoid arthritis develop in early childhood. This chronic, painful inflammation of the joints and surrounding tissues has a number of associated symptoms including fever spikes (quick, abnormal, extreme increases in temperature), rash, and morning stiffness. Medical intervention is necessary for independent functioning, and casts, splints, or orthoses may be prescribed. Improvement or remission of major symptoms often occurs by age 18. Residual orthopedic effects vary among individuals (Hanson, 1983).

Chronic attacks, pain, and related treatment indirectly affect academic performance. During the chronic phase of this disability, teachers should provide students with some freedom to move in the classroom, to avoid "gelling" or stiffness in the joints, and an extra set of books at home so the student does not have to carry heavy books. Contact sports or activities such as jump rope, which stress the joints, are usually not recommended. Specific activity recommendations should be secured from the student's family and physicians.

OTHER HEALTH IMPAIRMENTS

Children with health impairments who attend school present unique problems within the school setting. Their educational needs may be the same as their peers; yet, they may require special health interventions in school. Typical problems of this nature are described briefly here.

CHRONIC CONDITIONS

Children in this category have conditions such as asthma, diabetes, cancer, sickle cell anemia, hemophilia, and cystic fibrosis. The conditions frequently are invisible (Kleinberg, 1986), and, as a result, children can have difficulty securing the resources they require. Ongoing communication with medical personnel and the family is essential, as is an emergency plan describing the parameters of an emergency and the intervention required (Caldwell, Todaro, & Gates, 1989; Caldwell & Sirvis, 1991). Children with chronic conditions frequently experience school failure because of the cumulative effect of school absences. Supplemental services including tutoring, home instruction, and an extended school year can provide the opportunity to reach yearly educational goals (Bigge, 1991). A few of the most common conditions illustrate specific educational needs.

Asthma is a common obstructive pulmonary condition characterized by difficulty with breathing because of narrowed or blocked air passages (Synoground & Kelsey, 1990). Asthma attacks differ in severity and are triggered by many sources including infections, allergens, strenuous exercise, and changes in climate (Silkworth & Jones, 1986). Treatment focuses on reducing the symptoms by avoiding allergens and using medications and immunotherapy (allergy shots). Teachers require information about allergens, exercise tolerance, treatments, medications and side effects, warning signs and symptoms, and interventions in the case of emergencies. Educational personnel must be prepared to help students relax during an attack. All personnel also should be trained to provide CPR (Caldwell, Todaro, & Gates, 1989). School absence is common, and intervention to avoid school failure can be essential.

Insulin dependent diabetes mellitus, or Type I diabetes, is a metabolic disorder that renders the body unable to produce or use insulin, which is needed to burn sugars and starches to create energy. Educational personnel who work with children with diabetes need information about the student's treatment, medications, diet, ability to tolerate exercise, signs and symptoms of hypoglycemia and hyperglycemia, and corresponding interventions. The care plans of students center on their management of diet and exercise routines.

Epilepsy is a seizure disorder that occurs as a single problem or in association with other physically disabling conditions. Epilepsy occurs in approximately .4% of the childhood population and in 3% of children with mild mental retardation (Corbett, 1985). Seizures usually are characterized by abnormal, excessive, electrical brain discharges, and not all seizures are readily visible, nor do they necessarily involve loss of consciousness. Seizures are of two basic categories: generalized and partial. *Generalized seizures* include tonic-clonic (grand mal), absence (petit mal), myoclonic and infantile spasms, atonic and akinetic (Wong & Whaley, 1990). They are characterized by loss of consciousness.

Tonic clonic seizures involve bodily tension followed by extraneous, uncontrolled movement of the entire body with increased salivation and possible loss of bladder and bowel control. Teachers should act calmly and quickly, setting a good example for other students. Furniture and other objects should be moved out of the way. If possible, the student's head should be turned gently to the side, allowing saliva to drain and to prevent choking and tongue-biting. (Epileptics do not "swallow their tongue" as is commonly believed.) After a seizure the student probably will be tired and should be allowed to sleep.

Absence seizures are less noticeable because behavior changes are minimal. The only clue may be that the student is mildly disoriented, resulting from a short lapse of attention. If not controlled, however, this type of seizure may significantly affect learning. For example, the student, pausing briefly in the middle of listening to oral instructions, misses a direction and therefore does not complete the assignment correctly.

Myoclonic seizures involve an upward, or myoclonic, jerk of the arms, as well as trunk flexion (bending) which may cause the student to fall.

Atonic and akinetic seizures involve sudden loss of muscle tone and postural control. In both of these situations, the students cannot protect themselves as they fall and may wear a helmet to prevent head injury (Low, 1982).

Partial seizures include simple partial seizures, special sensory seizures, and complex partial seizures (psychomotor seizures), and they may affect motor function, sensations, and behavior. Patterns vary, ranging from brief loss of consciousness to extended periods of unconsciousness. Complex partial seizures can include purposeless activity, and the student may not be aware that he or she is behaving unusually, such as running around the room (Wong & Whaley, 1990). The behavior may appear to uninformed observers as an "acting out" pattern.

Seizure disorders need not disrupt the classroom. Properly prescribed medication controls most seizures, but multiple medications may affect classroom performance. Teachers should monitor behavior changes (especially drowsiness and inattentiveness) and report them to medical personnel. Teachers need information about the type of seizure a child has, as well as precautions, activity restrictions, medications and their side effects (Caldwell, Todaro, & Gates, 1989). Most children should not go home after a seizure, but they may need rest and redirection so they can pick up material missed during the seizure. As with other chronic conditions, ongoing communication, individualized emergency plans, and mechanisms to make up missed work are essential. "The majority of children with seizure disorders do well, . . . both intellectually and in tending to 'grow out of' their epilepsy" (Verity & Ross, 1985, p. 133).

BODY AND SKIN DEFORMITIES

Children with chronic conditions face many complexities because of the invisibility of their conditions in contrast to children with body and skin deformities, who face complexities because of their visibility. About Face, an international organization representing individuals with body and skin deformities, and several of the Shriner's Burn Centers provide technical assistance to schools regarding the entry or reentry of students with these visible deformities. Classmates and school personnel need preparation, and the student requires preparation and ongoing support, particularly during transitions, i.e., movement to high school. With the exception of children with burns, many of these children do not require any type of health care in school. (Bigge, 1991; Caldwell & Sirvis, 1991; Caldwell, Sirvis, Todaro, & Alcouloumre, 1991).

MEDICALLY FRAGILE CHILDREN

In the last 20 years the term *medically fragile* has been used in several ways to define children with special health conditions. For a number of years, all children with special health needs were considered medically fragile. The term later was used to describe students with more "complex" health needs, such as students with spina bifida and those supported by technology. The term connotes the image of a child who is easily broken, a connotation important for educators. Some children are fragile because they are in the final, fatal stages of their disease process. Other children are fragile because they have catastrophic emergencies that are difficult to predict and difficult to intervene with consistent results. Educators must identify those children to be able to provide appropriate and safe educational programs. Medically fragile is a status, not a condition, and no one group (e.g., technology-assisted children) fits that status, but anyone from any of the categories could be fragile at some point in their disease progression.

Because determining which children are medically fragile can be difficult, a team is required to diagnose a student's status. The team should include educational and medical personnel and the family. Together, team members find the appropriate balance between risk and benefit for the child. Children can move in and out of the fragile status, so placement must be reviewed frequently. Finally, teachers who work with medically fragile children require information about loss, death, and dying so they can deal with their own feelings and support the child and the child's classmates (Bigge, 1991; Caldwell & Sirvis, 1991; Caldwell, Sirvis, Todaro, & Alcouloumre, 1991).

INFECTIOUS CONDITIONS

Infectious conditions of childhood can affect a number of systems, including the nose and throat and the respiratory, neurologic, and skin systems. Children are more susceptible to infectious conditions and will have more serious reactions to them for a number of reasons. Children do not have the immunologic defenses of adults since exposure is often to new infections, which have not been introduced to their systems. In addition, their physiology, including small respiratory passages and young cells, makes them more vulnerable (Moffet, 1991). It is important to identify children with infectious conditions that are fairly common in childhood, such as measles and mumps. These infectious conditions can be fatal to children who have compromised immune systems, such as children receiving chemotherapy treatments for cancer.

Other infectious conditions such as *hepatitis* and *HIV infection* pose another set of challenges for educators. The first cases of the previously unrecognized immunodeficiency disorder in children were reported in 1981 at the same time as this new immunologic disorder was being described in adults. The most striking aspect of the pediatric syndrome (unlike other syndromes) was that the patients' mothers were similarly affected (Novick, 1989). By the end of June, 1990, the Centers for Disease Control reported that 1,266 children under age 13 had died from AIDS (Kaiser, 1990). "Approximately 30,000 cases of hepatitis A are reported each year; they represent a small proportion of actual cases" (Betz & Poster, 1989, p. 168). Unlike measles and mumps, HIV Infection and hepatitis can be invisible, and they require appropriate universal precautions with every child. Universal precautions involve appropriate hand-washing, disposal of waste, management of emergencies, and cleaning of toys and equipment. The school nurse or principal prescribes individual school procedures. Training in appropriate universal precautions and emergency management is a minimum for all teachers.

Also unlike measles and mumps, HIV infection and sometimes hepatitis can last for long periods, sometimes throughout the child's life. This makes decisions regarding school placement difficult because one may not expect the condition to end. School placement is best determined by a team consisting of medical and educational personnel and the family (Bigge, 1991; Caldwell, Todaro, & Gates, 1991). Confidentiality and the child's rights to an appropriate education can be protected through the team process. Each state and local system has guidelines regarding who should receive information regarding a student's infectious condition. Education personnel should practice appropriate universal precautions with every child, as children with infectious conditions such as HIV infection may not be diagnosed or identified.

NEUROLOGICAL CONDITIONS

Acquired neurologic conditions result from a number of factors including trauma and infection. Accidents are the single highest cause of death of children between ages 5 and 19, and 90% of pediatric *head injuries* are closed head injuries. "Physical forces act on the head through acceleration, deceleration, or deformation...[and the] brain is injured through compression, tearing and/or shearing (Menkes & Batzdork, 1985, p. 471). When the injury is mild, the child loses consciousness briefly. Major closed head injuries involve interruption for longer periods of time. The prognosis for children under age 2 is poor. In the case of major injuries, 15% of children will be free of both neurologic and behavior abnormalities (Menkes & Batzdork, 1985).

Meningitis is an infection of the nervous system. The progress of this neurological condition is dependent on the "nature of the infectious agent and severity of the initial process, age of the patient, duration of symptoms before diagnosis and institution of intensive antibiotic therapy...and the type and amount of antibiotic used" (Weil, 1985, p. 327). About 29% of the patients have significant handicaps, and 48% are free of sequelae but function at a lower level. (Weil, 1985).

Students who have neurological conditions require specialized evaluations and placement to accommodate their behavioral, cognitive, and social problems. No one classroom is appropriate. They also require curricula building on their strengths while teaching them to utilize and develop appropriate systems for cueing, to compensate for deficits (Alcouloumre & Caldwell, 1991).

TECHNOLOGY SUPPORT

Students who are supported by technology "require the routine use of a medical device to compensate for the loss of a life-sustaining body function and require daily and ongoing care and/or monitoring by trained personnel" (Office of Technology Assessment, 1987, p. xiii). These students "may be dependent on mechanical ventilators or other device-based respiratory or nutritional support such as tracheostomy tubes, oxygen support, or intravenous and/or enteral (tube) feeding" (Task Force on Technology-Dependent Children, 1988, p. 7). Ironically, the major medical support in the school setting, the school nurse, is declining in numbers at the same time the number of students who require health care is increasing.

Students supported by technology require a comprehensive transition plan before they may begin or return to school (Caldwell, Todaro, & Gates, 1991). Preparation should involve school system administrators, the school health care coordinator (often the school nurse), the family, and community medical personnel (Haynie, Porter, &

Palfrey, 1989). "Preplanning provides for the...completion of a nursing assessment,...the development of a health care and emergency plan...[development of a] coordination plan for the student's in-school health care plan,...[and the provision of] general staff training [and]...child specific technical training" (Haynie, Porter, & Palfrey, 1989, pp. 14–15).

Since 1983, students supported by technology have successfully participated in their neighborhood schools in regular classrooms or educationally appropriate classrooms in several states (Anguzza, 1991). The ability of the school system to provide adequate services depends on its ability to access the resources necessary to provide care in school and its ability to access staff training from specialists in the care of technology-assisted students. Issues such as fiscal responsibility and least restrictive environment (LRE) are still a problem in many states.

IDENTIFICATION AND ASSESSMENT

Initial identification of students with physical disabilities is primarily through a medical diagnosis. Appropriate class placement is more complicated because many students with physical disabilities have no related academic or psychosocial difficulties in the classroom. For some students, appropriate educational services are found in schools that are accessible to wheelchair users, and no further adaptations are necessary. Nevertheless, a large percentage may need special education and related services. Especially for those who have multiple handicaps, educational placement is complicated by difficulties in obtaining accurate assessment information.

In many cases, assessment should provide information about how a student can best participate in the regular classroom (logistical considerations, adaptations, and individualized learning requirements). If a student has severe physical limitations or multiple handicaps, a comprehensive assessment requires interdisciplinary involvement. If a student has no upper-extremity involvement, standardized tests may be appropriate. Consider, however, the pitfalls of giving an IQ test such as the Wechsler Intelligence Scale for Children (WISC) to a student with severe athetoid cerebral palsy who lacks motor coordination. Obviously, test results will be affected because the test has sections requiring completion within a specified time. Thus, the test will not produce a fair assessment.

Many instruments assume that a student has adequate use of the hands for manipulative tasks. Also, they often require communication ability beyond a yes/no response. Some tests create a cultural or experiential disadvantage because a physical disability may limit students' opportunities to leave home or school to explore the world as their nondisabled peers have done since early childhood. This is analogous to testing the standard English language skills of a child from a cultural minority group.

Criterion-referenced assessments are suggested for students with physical disabilities. These instruments allow measurement of students' progress as compared only to their own earlier performance and does not force them into a standardized test framework. This enables more accurate determination of skills and progress. Task analysis and behavioral observation also are valuable tools for collecting nonstandardized assessment data. They aid in identifying of abilities, disabilities, and potential areas for adapting techniques and equipment. In addition, these tools facilitate differentiation of learning problems caused by physical disability and those caused by behavioral reactions to other problems.

MULTIDISCIPLINARY INVOLVEMENT IN ASSESSMENT AND PROGRAMMING

Assessment of students with physical disabilities requires the participation of a variety of professional personnel. The multidisciplinary approach—based on the premise that professionals exchange assessment data *and* programmatic implications and strategies for maximum efficiency and effectiveness—facilitates maximum communication among professionals. As many personnel as possible know and implement the student's program goals. For example, if a teacher is introducing color concepts in an early intervention program, a physical therapist could use colors in developing a gait training program. At the same time, the regular classroom teacher could learn to use the specific body position recommended by the therapist to facilitate achievement of trunk control (Sirvis, 1978).

Medical personnel usually are involved in initial diagnosis and medical follow-up of all students with physical disabilities. This includes prescription of needed surgery, special therapy, and equipment, as well as continued monitoring of medication and other interventions. Physical and occupational therapists evaluate the quality of an individual's movement and physical characteristics, then suggest adaptive equipment and techniques that may facilitate independent function. Speech therapists work with students on communication skills, and they also may be involved in feeding programs. Adapted equipment and techniques recommended during this phase should be implemented *before* academic assessment. Otherwise students may not perform at their optimum level during assessment.

Psychologists, social workers, special education teachers, and resource personnel should all participate actively on the assessment team, evaluating students' academic and educational potential and then suggesting methods and materials for curricular implementation. When working with regular education personnel, they also should be able to suggest alternatives for classroom participation—for example, other ways for a student who cannot write to complete an examination.

AREAS OF ASSESSMENT AND PROGRAMMING

An appropriate individualized education program should focus on several major areas of assessment. If students are in a regular education curriculum, this information is essential to determine what accommodations they will need in the regular classroom.

Physical Abilities and Limitations. Given the diverse nature of physical disabilities, body positions and postures should be identified and adaptive equipment and techniques to facilitate independent functioning introduced. Education, employment, leisure, and independent living should all be assessed in regard to both present ability and future potential.

Mobility. How students move from place to place, their potential for independence, and their need for assistance in moving about should be assessed, and physical therapists should take an active role in this assessment. Recommendations should focus on both current and subsequent potential for independence. Equipment includes a variety of assistive devices ranging from adapted toys for young children, which allow them to move about on the floor with other children to sophisticated, breath-controlled electric wheelchairs that climb curbs (Blossom & Ford, 1991).

Psychosocial Development. People with physical disabilities have the same social and emotional needs as their nondisabled peers do. Primarily and specifically, they need to communicate with and relate to others. Like their peers, they have adjustment and coping problems. Often, however, societal and attitudinal barriers hinder their emotional development. In examining concepts of ability and disability, assessment should integrate these with concepts of self-image, body image, social relationships, emotions, and intellectual performance.

Communication. In recent years, new mechanisms have been developed to assist with speech impairments and writing impairments. *Augmentative communication* "refers to supplemental communication techniques that are used in addition to whatever natural speech and vocalization may be present" (Bigge, 1991, p. 199). The technology can be simple and handmade or complex electronic equipment. The emphasis for all equipment is access to communication through play, socialization, and developmental or academic interaction in the school setting. Because no one piece of equipment can fit every child's needs or abilities, assessment of needs for augmentative communication must be individualized. The teacher is one of a team including language and movement therapists as well as the family. This team determines equipment needs and recommends implementation practices. The team also looks to the child's future social and developmental/academic needs and makes sure the child has continuing access to the types of communication required.

Activities of Daily Living. Current skills and potential skill development should be assessed in all areas related to self-help and daily living. This includes basic skills such as eating, drinking, dressing, toileting, and personal hygiene, as well as more advanced skills such as cooking, housecleaning, and using public transportation. Ultimately, all of these lifetime skills will facilitate maximum independent functioning throughout the individual's life span.

Academic Potential. The academic potential of students with physical disabilities and health impairments varies. Most students are able to benefit from the regular education curricula. A few students may have neurologically based emotional problems as the result of trauma, disease, or treatment. These problems can interfere with cognitive function. For example, *some* children who experience brain radiation at a young age may have permanent neurological damage. Other children with physical and health impairments may experience temporary deficits including problems with adjustment, attention, concentration, initiation, and fatigue.

Adaptations for Learning. There is a need to identify specific physical and academic strategies, techniques, and adaptations that enhance the potential for independent learning of many students. This includes a range of intervention options, from how to manage classroom tools such as pencils and paper to behavior management techniques and assessment of preferred learning style.

Transition Skills. Transition is a major focus of PL 101–476, Individuals with Disabilities Education Act (IDEA), the 1990 amendments to EHA. Transition plans are required for major movements between preschool and elementary services and often high school placements. Successful transitions from school to postschool living and employment situations are far more diverse, especially for this population. Success beyond school means independent living and participation in leisure activities as well as employment. This does not deny the importance of assessing vocational potential but, rather, it stresses the necessity of examining all factors that might affect a student's life satisfaction following school (Sirvis, 1980).

EDUCATIONAL INTERVENTION

The interdisciplinary team identifies and develops short- and long-term goals related to skill development in five basic developmental areas: (a) physical independence, including mastery of daily living skills; (b) self-awareness and social maturation; (c) communication; (d) academic growth; and (e) life skills training.

PHYSICAL INDEPENDENCE

Physical and occupational therapists provide valuable help in designing programs for the development of maximum physical independence. This includes skills related to physical function (e.g., mobility) and self-help skills (e.g., eating, drinking, toileting, bathing). It also covers activities of daily living such as cooking, grooming, and home maintenance. Adaptive equipment and methods are crucial in this area. *Task analysis* is an effective evaluative and curricular planning tool, not only in determining skills that have potential but also in developing intervention strategies (Bigge, 1991). In task analysis a task is broken down into its subskills or components to determine what tasks and subtasks a disabled person can and cannot do; then adaptive means are devised for independent completion. Systematic instruction should be used in both motor and academic programs. Potential types of adaptations and equipment considerations are discussed later in this chapter.

In addition to these areas of independence, a sense of overall independence can be facilitated by an accessible environment. The Americans with Disabilities Act (ADA) requires that community facilities, public schools, and transportation be accessible to promote independence in mobility and function. Baker (1980) and Somerton-Fair (1980) have suggested some guidelines and specific modifications. Guidelines for public buildings are available through the American Institute of Architects, New York.

SELF-AWARENESS AND SOCIAL MATURATION

The psychological problems of individuals with physical disabilities are not necessarily unique to them, but differences in etiology, onset, and functional effect do create some associated problems, especially in psychosocial development and adjustment. Although gross generalizations are to be avoided, two categories of personal reaction to one's physical disability have been suggested. Neff and Weiss (1965) proposed that individuals with *acquired* disabilities experience a *sense of loss*; those with *congenital* disabilities experience a *sense of differentness*. Wright (1983) suggested that a range of social, psychological, and environmental factors may affect the psychosocial development of individuals with physical disabilities. Some individuals may have developed coping mechanisms and strategies for accepting their disability and adjustment; others may have had such negative experiences that the disability seriously affects them. These psychosocial factors affect socialization and decision-making situations for those who need to vent their anger, frustration, and fear before they can begin to think about solving problems and entering into social situations with their nondisabled peers. These are global generalizations, however. Each individual has his or her own ways of coping.

Opportunities should be provided for social maturation, a positive and healthy self-concept, appropriate self-expression, the ability to love and feel secure, and a sense of belonging. The classroom may give students the encouragement they need to begin to explore their own attitudes toward themselves, as well as their social, sexual, academic, and vocational possibilities. Students with disabilities need to know that to experience, and then to express, a wide range of feelings is normal and acceptable. They need to learn to recognize and express their feelings including happiness, sadness, and anger, without fear of repercussions, and they should have opportunities to do so. Dealing with constructive criticism enables them to meet frustration and disappointment head-on without fatal blows to their egos. They also need to learn to evaluate each experience and use the information from these self-evaluations for future planning. This also points up the important role for the teacher to facilitate this exploration of feelings, including those related to family life, sexuality, and death, in a safe environment (Carpignano, Sirvis, & Bigge, 1991).

Family Life and Sexuality. Personal development, independence, and family life education should be part of academic, social, and life skills training. Some people with physical disabilities have neither the socialization experiences nor the information about social and sexual development they need to interact with their peers in school.

Yet, their physiological needs are the same, including their sexuality. Knowledge of sexuality should be integrated into the curriculum as a continuous process, not as a single unit of instruction.

Death. Loss and death education should be a part of personal development. Students with physical disabilities often think about death more than others do, and they also tend to be ill prepared to deal with it. Basic information about the role of death in the natural life cycle leads to understanding. This developmental process requires professionals to understand the development of children's concepts of death (Bluebond-Langner, 1978). Educators should be willing to discuss death honestly and to express their own concerns, fears, and discomfort. This provides opportunities for discussion, to answer questions and correct misconceptions, and to support students who are confronting the idea of death—their own, a family member's, or a friend's.

Families. Families of children with physical disabilities and chronic health conditions have their own unique difficulties in coping with their child's condition. Parents often are responsible for therapy programs and health care. Their time and finances are strained, as is their ability to provide attention to all family members. They also must deal with the uncertainty of care and outcome (Caldwell, Sirvis, Todaro, & Alcouloumre, 1991). In addition, the child and family have difficult transition points, including the transitions to school and to adolescence (Moses, 1989), and difficult points in the family life cycle such as changes in jobs (Trivette, 1988). These factors combine to add to "normal" family stresses. Organized efforts to provide support can be helpful. Support can be gained through parent-to-parent encounters and professional help. Parents also can be empowered to be part of all decision making. Information about specific support groups can be secured through the National Information Center for Handicapped, Washington, DC.

As parents grow older and their child continues to need physical care, they begin to focus more and more on the reality that they are less able to provide this care. The child resents it, and so do the parents. It is a time when most children are leaving home. Teachers and other professionals can help parents develop realistic attitudes that will foster their child's maximum physical and emotional independence. A non-home residential setting (e.g., group home, supervised living, independent attendant care) may be a workable solution. Assisting child and parents alike in planning such a move is important to the transition.

COMMUNICATION

Students with physical disabilities often have trouble interacting communicatively with their environment. For a major segment of this population, severity of the problem warrants its identification as a separate goal area. Students with cerebral palsy or other brain trauma, for example, may have deficient speech musculature control that makes talking difficult or impossible to understand. Other students have trouble with written communication because of motor control problems in their upper extremities. Several options are available for them, and all should be explored to find the best, most efficient solution. A typewriter or a microcomputer keyboard is one possibility. Some may need a headwand (a pointer fastened to a headband or helmet) to hit the keys, or other adaptive pointing device, perhaps something as simple as the eraser on the end of a pencil held in their fist.

Those with oral communication difficulties may need an augmentative communication system. Initially, the challenge is to find the most efficient and effective means of expression. Even a simple way to say *yes* and *no* can open up a whole new world to a previously noncommunicating student. Instruction in the concepts of affirmation and negation introduces the student to choices and expression of desires. By developing an ability to communicate *yes* and *no*, students may be motivated to expand their communication through more complex systems. Selection of an augmentative system is a complex process requiring many considerations and the input of many people, including professionals, parents, and most important, the potential user (Bigge, 1991). The cause, current communication system, communication needs, and status of language-processing skills (inner, receptive, and expressive) must all be considered. With this information, available communication systems can be examined and the optimal system chosen. Picture boards often are effective with younger or multiply handicapped students. Some develop only an ability to respond with *yes* or *no*. Others use word communication boards, permitting their vocabulary to grow with their communication ability. Still others are able to use sophisticated electronic devices. Even after the proper device is chosen, however, a student may have trouble communicating with others who are not familiar with the augmented system. Nondisabled classmates should be instructed in its use and encouraged to communicate with nonvocal students.

ACADEMIC GROWTH

Academic curricula for students with physical disabilities may be as varied as the students themselves. As much as possible, students should receive the same academic instruction as their nondisabled peers. When they have learning problems, curricula should be modified accordingly. Every effort should be made to introduce basic and survival skills that have lifetime application. In addition, teachers should treat these students as normally as possible. For example, special considerations in grading create false expectations on the part of the student and the parent alike; thus, grading should be the same for all students, regardless of ability or disability. Students should be encouraged to evaluate themselves and their work realistically, including their strengths and limitations, and the areas in which they would benefit from improvement. Major curriculum adaptations may not be found in the content but, rather, in the method of presentation and response.

LIFE SKILLS TRAINING

Educational goals for students with physical disabilities must incorporate activities and experiences to make possible future success in employment, social relationships, and recreation and leisure. Bigge (1982) suggested some goals critical to a successful transition from school to post-school environments:

1. Ability to obtain meaningful employment (whether it be homebound, sheltered workshop, or competitive).
2. Capacity for independent living appropriate to physical and mental capabilities.
3. Capacity for community involvement (including a variety of daily living skills).
4. Skills for participation in meaningful leisure-time activities (a well-defined free-time management system).
   a. recreational experiences
   b. making and retaining friends.
5. Development of reliable transportation.
6. Mastery of self-care skills.
7. Ability to maintain residence away from parents, convalescent hospitals, or state institutions.
8. Development of a healthy self-concept. (pp. 314–315)

Although many of these goals are discussed elsewhere in relation to other education goals, two—career education and recreation and leisure education—warrant further discussion here.

Career Education. Generically defined, career education means all skills an individual needs after completing school. It includes the basic survival skills previously mentioned in relation to growth and transition. Academic instruction often provides the means for the students to learn these skills, including those necessary for job preparation, such as reading and interpreting want ads, using the telephone book, and completing job application forms. Arithmetic involves skills related to money management, such as making change and managing the checkbook. Social studies and science instruction can instill citizenship and hygiene skills. Adaptive techniques and equipment should be developed so students can learn how to complete these tasks independently or with minimal assistance.

The primary benefits and goals of a career education curriculum vary according to individual needs and abilities (Sirvis, 1980). Traditionally, options for employment for individuals with physical disabilities have been limited. The usual choice has been a sheltered workshop. More recently, however, transition programs and vocational education are enhancing opportunities for their being trained and finding employment in a variety of occupations in education, science, and business. Those who are receptive to adaptive methods and equipment will be accepted in the world of work. For some, the microcomputer has been a boon. Private firms are investing research and development dollars in adapting computers and work stations so more companies will consider employing individuals with physical and sensory impairments. Not all people with physical disabilities are easily employable, but all options should be explored. Even with considerable adaptation, individuals with severe disabilities will have difficulty gaining employment. Vocational programs must focus on specific job skills as well as motor skills.

Transition programs and career education curricula can help foster decision-making skills in students. The choice may be between vocational training and some other constructive, satisfying use of time. The puritan work ethic is strongly ingrained in our society, and statements that challenge it may bother families and professionals alike. *Quality of life* is an important consideration. A severe physical disability should not automatically limit or suggest boundaries to a person's quality of life. Different individuals, however, interpret this quality differently. Unproductive days in front of TV sets are inappropriate and nonrewarding. Leisure education can teach students how to make satisfying use of their time. Students' judgment of their own personal satisfaction is the key to their individual quality of life.

Recreation and Leisure Education. Leisure is essential to life satisfaction (Sirvis, Musante, & Bigge, 1991; Caldwell, Adolph, & Gilbert, 1989) for individuals with disabilities. Transition from student life to adult life should include, as part of the educational outcome process: employment (including nonpaid work experiences and volunteer positions), independent living skills (Wehman, Moon, Everson, Wood, & Barcues, 1988) and satisfying leisure lifestyle (Sirvis et al., 1991). In IDEA (1990), legislators recognized the schools' obligation for providing leisure education by including therapeutic recreation to the list of related services. Students facing barriers in establishing and maintaining social and work-related relationships, planning and implementing recreation activities, developing lifetime leisure skills, or utilizing community resources require educational interventions. Leisure education goals, included in the individualized education program (IEP), can help students develop leisure-related skills, attitudes, and knowledge (Sirvis et al., 1991). Leisure education interventions may include social skills training, development of lifetime leisure skills, utilizing cognitive processes such as planning, choosing and implementing, and community skills such as safety, money management, transportation and resource utilization. Leisure education enhances the students' ability to achieve educational and vocational successes as it facilitates their move toward integration and inclusion in their community and school (Collard, 1981).

Recreation and leisure enhance physical, intellectual, social, and emotional growth. Opportunities for social interaction and development of lifetime skills should be provided through leisure education programs. In developing curricula, the importance of student participation and choice must be recognized. Leisure programs allow students to choose, make decisions, and interact with peers. In addition, recreation activities enhance the learning of other skills—for example, money management for transportation and a movie, or reading the newspaper to find recreational outlets in the community.

Leisure education, including recreation skill development, should begin at the preschool level. Mundy and Odom (1979) suggested a continuum of developmental skills, beginning with leisure awareness and progressing through social and recreation skills to awareness, exploration, and use of community resources. Bender, Brannan, and Verhoven (1984) suggested several curriculum areas and related goals and activities that can be modified to meet students' unique learning and leisure needs. Community recreation programs and public agencies should not be overlooked as excellent resources. Many have greatly expanded their programs for individuals with physical disabilities.

ADAPTIVE EQUIPMENT, METHODS, AND INSTRUCTIONAL MATERIALS

Students with physical disabilities have such a variety of educational needs that curricula must integrate adaptive techniques with a variety of educational materials. Some of these students have learning disabilities, mental retardation, and sensory impairment. Some are gifted. Techniques and materials must be adapted accordingly. Whenever possible, adapting existing materials is better than creating new materials to meet the needs of individual students. The crux of program modification lies in adapting tasks to encourage maximum independence. Often a student can achieve independence with slight adaptation of regular techniques or with an adaptive device. For example, a student may be able to use a writing implement inserted through a rubber ball or lump of clay to increase the grasping surface. Another who is unable to use a pen or pencil may successfully type on a typewriter or computer keyboard. Students with limited arm or hand control can use a headwand to hit typewriter keys. Still others may need to tape-record assignments or dictate them to a note-taker.

Some students also need to adapt their physical position to complete an assignment. A traditional desk may or may not be appropriate. Some students perform better with an adapted seating device placed in their wheelchair. Others do best lying over a bolster on the floor. Some need to lie prone on a board that leans against a desk or table, leaving their arms and hands free. Others need to stand; specially designed standing tables with a desk attached in front are useful here. (For more examples, see Bigge, 1991; Blossom & Ford, 1991; Fraser and Hensinger, 1983.)

Daily living skills also may require adaptive methods and devices. A special cup may help a youngster with cerebral palsy who has poor motor control keep from spilling a drink. Another child may need a spoon with an oversized handle that permits easy grasping. Yet another may need to use a plateguard to get food onto a spoon. Some students use buttonhooks to help them dress, and others use special fasteners instead of zippers and buttons (Hale, 1979).

Research and development in the field of rehabilitation engineering have produced tremendous technological advances in systems and equipment. This field has expanded to address the complex functional needs of individuals with physical disabilities, from feeding themselves to communicating by means of sophisticated computers. The emphasis is on mobility, seating, prosthetics, orthotics (braces), communication, and computer usage at the various rehabilitation engineering centers (*Rehabilitation R & D*, 1984).

The environment must be adapted as well. The Americans with Disabilities Act now mandates that any barriers denying equal access to individuals with disabilities must be removed. Classroom doors should be wide enough, and desks and tables high enough, for students in wheelchairs and those with any other unique positioning needs.

Bathroom stalls may have to be widened and deepened; sinks and water fountains may have to be higher so wheelchairs can fit under them. Bruck (1978) and others have provided guides to environmental access, including housing, transportation and travel, consumer resources, and recreation services.

EDUCATIONAL PROGRAMMING AND DELIVERY SYSTEMS

Any number of professions must be involved in developing and implementing educational programs for students with physical disabilities: educational programs; special education, regular education, physical and occupational therapy, social work, nursing, psychology, speech-language therapy, rehabilitation counseling, and therapeutic recreation. In a hospital setting a medical team is there to provide a full range of services. Educational programs are necessarily diverse to meet the needs of this population. The advent of PL 94–142 decreased significantly the number of segregated special schools and increased the number of special classes and resource room programs in regular schools. Some students may need home or hospital instruction during periods of extensive medical treatment. In general, however, instruction should be classroom-based whenever possible and appropriate.

Early Intervention. Early intervention is vital for infants and young children with physical impairment. The positive effects of early intervention programs that emphasize developmental skills in gross and fine motor coordination, daily living, and social interaction have been well documented (Hanson, 1984). Physical and occupational therapists play a major role in program development because physical skills are important for young children. Development of physical skills coordination should include environmental exploration and movement experiences. Wheelchairs can be restrictive, so children should be free of them as much as possible. Basic self-help skills and communication should be developed during this period, as should readiness for academic work and for inclusion in general education programs.

Many early intervention programs have been developed by nonprofit agencies such as the United Cerebral Palsy Association; these emphasize parent involvement and include home visits in addition to structured intervention. In addition, as a result of PL 99–457, most states provide preschool services for children between ages 3 and 5, and many other states provide services for children from birth to 3.

Elementary School. Elementary school is the first introduction to general education for many students. Motor development, and the physical independence it provides, is still important, but its importance diminishes because the focus of intervention now is on academics. Basic skills in reading, arithmetic, language arts, science, and social studies are introduced to all students. Some need to continue the readiness activities. Some students with severe multiple handicaps will continue in special classes, although the classroom itself may be located in a regular school. All students, including those with severe and multiple disabilities, should be integrated as much as possible into the regular activities going on at the school. Whether services are in special or general education classes, most school-age students with physical impairment still require supplementary instruction and physical, occupational, or speech therapy.

Secondary School. Programs in high school are getting more attention now as a result of the increased federal support for *transition*. IDEA requires the development of transition plans. By the time they reach adolescence, students need to understand the relationship between academic skills and basic survival skills. For example, reading includes basic skills for information seeking, and math involves simple computation and money management skills. These are basic to independent function, but they should not be considered the limit. Many students with physical disabilities exceed these basic survival skills as they complete the regular academic high school program. Others focus on preparing for jobs outside school or some other adult life situation. The interdisciplinary team for transition programs is somewhat different from the team for professionals who serve younger students. It may include rehabilitation counselors, group home personnel, and vocational education instructors in addition to special educators and therapists.

Postsecondary Education. Students who have the requisite academic abilities and who persevere should be encouraged to prepare for education or training following high school. Community colleges, universities, and professional and other training programs are available for adults with physical disabilities. Methods and equipment may have to be adapted extensively, but this ought not stop students who want to achieve in postsecondary education. Vocational rehabilitation often provides a variety of support services for students with severe disabilities. As a result of federal legislation, most colleges and universities now offer resource services for students with disabilities. Students in higher education now can get help from readers, note-takers, attendants, and counselors. In addition, specific social and recreational programs have been established to serve these adult students with physical disabilities.

IMPLICATIONS FOR THE REGULAR CLASSROOM

Successful participation in general education depends on several factors:

1. Interdisciplinary cooperation and communication.
2. Availability of support and related services.
3. Transportation.
4. Architectural accessibility.

Success is contingent upon the ability of personnel to facilitate the transition. Once a student is enrolled in a general education program, continued adaptation may be necessary and may require the assistance of special education personnel. Several guidelines facilitate initial success for students and teachers.

Physical and Health Management. Teachers need to understand the characteristics of, as well as the physical and health management needs involved in, each disability. Consultation should be with the appropriate allied health personnel (physical, occupational, and speech therapists; nurse) when teachers need information (e.g., appropriate physical positions for optimal independent learning; how to manage wheelchairs and other adaptive equipment; how to develop self-help skills). In addition, teachers need to know about medications and limits on a student's activities.

Health-related information that may affect successful inclusion in a regular class should be communicated to all the students in the class. For example, if a student with muscular dystrophy is ambulatory but still has some difficulty walking, the other students need to understand that the student's balance is precarious. At the same time, students with physical disabilities and health impairments must assume partial or full responsibility for their own health and disability management as soon as possible. If not, nondisabled classmates may choose simply to avoid the student rather than try to establish a relationship. The school nurse and health aides can provide for health care, help the student learn successful independent care, and supervise the student once he or she is independent.

Psychosocial Development. Social skills and emotional growth can best be developed if students are given enough opportunities to communicate and otherwise interact with peers, both nondisabled and disabled. Augmentative communication aids are helpful in socialization as well as academics. Peers should be instructed in the various systems so they can initiate interaction without the teacher having to intervene. To promote a healthy attitude, teachers can provide a student's peers with activities that build awareness; set a good example; and consult with parents, physicians, and when appropriate, the student, about how much and what kind of information about the specific disability to share.

Academic Planning. In planning curriculum, teachers should be aware of adaptive techniques, materials, and equipment that facilitate learning for these students. Special considerations in grading should be avoided. They need realistic information about their progress if they are to develop appropriate self-expectations. Nonvocal students need many opportunities to participate in class discussion and complete assigned tasks.

As in other areas of instruction and health management, a transition program requires regular classroom teachers to encourage students with disabilities to assess their own abilities realistically, noting that all people, regardless of disability, have both strengths and limitations. All students should be provided with information on careers, and encouraged to develop maximum independence in all activities including leisure and recreation.

SUMMARY AND PROJECTIONS

Emerging from a traditional medical model, educational services for students with physical disabilities and chronic health impairments now address the spectrum of student needs relating to physical management and health concerns, education and academic potential, social-emotional development, and career potential. Whether enrolled in special or general education, students have educational, social, and developmental needs that are as diverse as this population itself. For the best educational program, individualized instructional strategies always will be necessary.

Students who have physical disabilities can have a multiplicity of additional disabilities. Curricula from other areas often apply to, and often are necessary for the development of an effective instructional program. The essence of planning lies in an interdisciplinary approach to assessment and program implementation. Learning objectives should not be determined on the basis of the physical diagnosis but, instead, on the basis of each student's unique educational needs. Ultimately, the goal is for each student to participate in the educational process and perform all tasks as independently as possible.

Cooperation and communication among members of the interdisciplinary team are vital to the program's success. Their involvement in its development may be direct or indirect. For example, physical and occupational therapists teach appropriate motor skills and suggest adaptive equipment and techniques to promote independent completion of assignments and activities. Specialists in communication disorders play a major role in assessing and developing appropriate communication modes, especially for students with cerebral palsy. Social workers and school psychologists, trained in administering adaptive tests that do not hinder student responses, lend valuable support to teacher, student, and family during both assessment and intervention.

Progress in education has been significant, reflecting the major advances now occurring in medicine, genetics, and rehabilitation engineering. Medical and technological innovations should continue to augment treatment, intervention, and educational programming. Medical research, for example, is now examining procedures for spinal cord regeneration, microcomputer technology to stimulate walking in individuals with paraplegia resulting from spinal cord injury, and the genetic and neurophysiological aspects of various disabilities. Research in rehabilitation engineering searches for more effective ways to communicate and move about, some involving diverse applications of the microcomputer to enhance independent functioning.

Invention of the microprocessor chip has had a major effect on quality of life for many people with physical disabilities. Others still face environmental barriers to independent functioning, including social and attitudinal in addition to the architectural ones. All three pose problems for students entering general education classes. Nondisabled peers may ridicule or discriminate. To help these peers become aware of and explore such unhealthy attitudes, teachers need to explore their own attitudes and concerns. Management and planning strategies must be developed carefully to find a realistic way of ensuring that students who have physical impairment are accepted in regular classrooms. Although considerable efforts have been made, the problem still is far from being totally resolved.

Part of the resolution will be found in the development of adequate support and related service provision systems. When fiscal support is limited, related service personnel often are the first to go. This puts a burden on special and general education personnel. Administrators and funding agencies need to know what a central role related service personnel and the interdisciplinary team have in the overall educational program and the continued development of quality educational services.

The current emphasis is on transition programming. In some instances, teachers may have to abandon traditional curricula in favor of adequate transition programming. Faced at times with parental and administrative objections, they may find this decision difficult to make—and to enforce. The student's quality of life must be considered, however, along with the factors that are going to affect it. Deciding on an educational program, whether traditional or transitional, should be done with as much objectivity and student input as possible, to assure that it is appropriate and flexible.

Federal legislation has had a major impact. Passage of PL 94–142, PL 99–457, the Americans with Disabilities Act (ADA), and the Individuals with Disabilities Education Act (IDEA) have provided significant direction. Of concern at this moment is the regulatory and fiscal support needed to develop and continue to provide quality educational services. It is a critical time, and we need to maintain perspective, focusing squarely on inclusionary programs with adaptations only to the extent necessary. The mandate for reduced overprotection and increased independent life participation continues to be clear.

REFERENCES

Alcouloumre, D. & Caldwell, T. H. (1991). *Neurological conditions: Traumatic brain injury.* In Caldwell, T., Sirvis, B., Todaro, A., & Alcouloumre, D. Special Health Care in the School. (pp. 5–13). Reston, VA: The Council for Exceptional Children.

American Cancer Society. (1988). *Back to school: A handbook for teachers of children with cancer.* New York: Author.

Anderson, E. M., & Spain, B. (1977). *The child with spina bifida.* London: Methuen.

Auguzza, R. (1990, September). *Care of a child who is ventilator-assisted.* Paper presented at the Conference on School Services for Children Who Are Technology Assisted, Mobile, AL.

Baker, D. B. (1980). Guidelines for evaluating and modifying the physical environment. In J. Umbreit & P. J. Cardullias (Eds.), *Educating the severely physically handicapped: Modifying the learning environment* (Vol. 3) (pp. 1–14). Columbus, OH: Special Press.

Bender, M., Brannan, S. A., & Verhoven, P. J. (1984). *Leisure education for the handicapped: Curriculum goals, activities, and resources.* San Diego: College-Hill Press.

Betz, C., & Poster, E. (1989). Hepatitis (pp.167–173.) *Mosby's pediatric nursing reference.* St. Louis: C. V. Mosby.

Bigge, J. L. (1982). *Teaching individuals with physical and multiple disabilities* (2nd ed.). Columbus, OH: Charles E. Merrill.

Bigge, J. L. (1991). *Teaching individuals with physical and multiple disabilities* (3rd ed.). Columbus, OH: Charles E. Merrill.

Bleck, E. (1982). Cerebral palsy. In E. Bleck & D. Nagel (Eds.), *Physically handicapped children: A medical atlas for teachers* (2nd ed., pp. 431–432). New York: Grune & Stratton.

Blossom, B., & Ford, F. (1991). *Physical therapy in public schools: A related service, Vol. I.* Roswell, GA: Rehabilitation Publications and Therapies.

Bluebond-Langner, M. (1978). *The private world of dying children.* Princeton, NJ: Princeton University Press.

Bobath, K. (1980). *A neurophysiological basis for the treatment of cerebral palsy* (Clinics in Developmental Medicine No. 75). Philadelphia: Lippincott.

Bruck, L. (1978). *Access: The guide to a better life for disabled Americans.* New York: David Obst Books/ Random House.

Caldwell, R., Adolph, S., & Gilbert, A. (1989). Caution! Leisure counselors at work: Long-term effects of leisure counseling. *Therapeutic Recreation Journal, 23*(3), 41–49.

Caldwell, T. H., & Sirvis, B. (1991). Students with special health conditions: An emerging population presents new challenges. *Preventing School Failure, 35,* 13–18.

Caldwell, T. H., Sirvis, B., Todaro, A., & Alcouloumre, D. (1991). *Special health care in school.* Reston, VA: Council for Exceptional Children.

Caldwell, T. H., Todaro, A., & Gates, A. J., (1989). *The community provider's guide: An information outline for community providers working with children with special health care needs.* New Orleans: Children's Hospital.

Caldwell, T. H., Todaro, A., & Gates, A. J., (1991). *The community provider's guide: An information outline for community providers working with children with special health care needs.* New Orleans: Childrens's Hospital.

Carpignano, J. L., Sirvis, B., & Bigge, J. L. (1991). Psychosocial aspects of physical disability. In J. L. Bigge (Ed.), *Teaching individuals with physical and multiple disabilities* (2nd ed.) (pp. 110–137). Columbus, OH: Charles E. Merrill.

Chutorian, A. M., & Engel, M. (1982). Diseases of the muscle. In J. A. Downey & N. L. Low (Eds.), *The child with disabling illness: Principles of rehabilitation* (2nd ed.) (pp. 291–347). New York: Raven Press.

Collard, K. (1981). Leisure education in the schools: Why, who, and the need for advocacy. *Therapeutic Recreation Journal, 15*(4), 8–16.

Connor, F. P., Williamson, G. G., & Siepp, J. M. (Eds.). (1978). *Program guide for infants and toddlers with neuromotor and other developmental disabilities.* New York: Teachers College Press.

Corbet, B. (1980). *Options: Spinal cord injury and the future* (2nd ed.). Newton Upper Falls, MA: National Spinal Cord Injury Foundation.

Corbett, J. (1985). Epilepsy as part of a handicapping condition. In E. Ross and E. Reynolds, *Pediatric perspectives on epilepsy.* New York: John Wiley & Sons.

Crain, L. S. (1984). Prenatal causes of atypical development. In M. J. Hanson (Ed.), *Atypical infant development* (pp. 27–55). Baltimore: University Park Press.

Federal Register. (1977, August 23) 42 (163), 42474–42518.

Fraser, B. A., & Hensinger, R. N. (1983). *Managing physical handicaps.* Baltimore: Paul H. Brookes.

Grove, N., Cusick, B., & Bigge, J. (1991). Conditions resulting in physical disabilities. In J. Bigge, *Teaching individuals with physical and multiple disabilities* (3rd ed., pp. 1–15). Columbus, OH: Merrill.

Hale, G. (Ed.). (1979). *The sourcebook for the disabled.* New York: Paddington Press.

Hanson, M. J. (Ed.) (1984). *Atypical infant development.* Baltimore: University Park Press.

Hanson, V. (1983). Juvenile rheumatoid arthritis. In J. Umbreit (Ed.) *Physical disabilities and health impairments: An introduction* (pp. 240–249). Columbus, OH: Charles E. Merrill.

Haynie, M., Porter, S., & Palfrey, J. (1989). *Children assisted by medical technology in educational settings: Guidelines for care.* Boston: Project School Care, Children's Hospital.

Kaiser, M. (1990, Spring). Young patients find help through pediatric AIDS program. *Small World,* pp. 4–8.

Kleinberg, S. (1986). *Educating the chronically ill child.* Rockville, MD: Aspen.

Low, N. J. (1982). Seizure disorders in children. In J. A. Downey & N. L. Low (Eds.), *The child with disabling illness: Principles of rehabilitation (2nd ed.)* (pp. 121–144). New York: Raven Press.

Marquardt, E. G. (1983). A holistic approach to rehabilitation for the limb-deficient child. *Archives of Physical Medicine & Rehabilitation, 64*(6), 237–242.

Menkes, J., & Batzdork, S. (1985). Postnatal trauma & injuries by physical agents. In Menkes, J., *Textbook of child neurology* (3rd ed). Philadelphia: Lea & Febiger.

Moffett, H. (1991). *Pediatric infectious conditions: A problem-oriented approach* (3rd ed.) Philadelphia: J. B. Lippincott.

Molnar, G. E. (1983). Musculoskeletal disorders. In J. Umbreit (Ed.), *Physical disabilities and health impairments: An introduction* (pp. 108–116). Columbus, OH: Charles E. Merrill.

Moses, K. (1989, March). Conference presentation, New Orleans.

Mundy, J., & Odom, L. (1979). *Leisure education: Theory and practice.* New York: John Wiley.

Nadell, J. (1990, March). *The neurological sequaelae of head injury.* Paper presented at Head Injury Conference, Jefferson Parish Schools.

Neff, W. S., & Weiss, S. A. (1965). Psychological aspects of disability. In B. B. Wolberg (Ed.), *Handbook of clinical psychology.* New York: McGraw-Hill.

Novick, B. (1989). Pediatric AIDS: A medical overview. In J. Seibert and R. Olson (Eds.), *Children, adolescents, & AIDS.* Lincoln: University of Nebraska Press.

Office of Technology Assessment, U.S. Congress. (1987). *Technology dependent children: Hospital vs. home care* [Technical memorandum, OTA–TM–H–38]. Washington, DC: U.S. Government Printing Office.

Rehabilitation R & D Progress Reports—1984. (1984). Washington, DC: Veterans Administration, Office of Technology Transfer.

Silkworth, C., & Jones, D. (1988). In G. Larson (Ed.), *Managing the school age child with a chronic health condition.* Wayzata, MN: DCI Publishing.

Sirvis, B. (1978). Developing IEPs for physically handicapped students: An interdisciplinary approach. *Teaching Exceptional Children, 10(3)*, 78–82.

Sirvis, B. (1980). Career education for the severely handicapped. In G. M. Clark & W. J. White (Eds.), *Career education for the handicapped: Current perspectives for teachers.* Boothwyn, PA: Educational Resources Center.

Sirvis, B., Musante, P., & Bigge, J. (1991). Leisure education and adapted physical education. In J. Bigge (Ed.), *Teaching individuals with physical and multiple disabilities* (3rd ed., pp. 428–459). New York: Macmillan.

Somerton-Fair, E. (1980). Physical modifications in the classroom. In J. Umbreit & P. J. Cardullias (Eds.), *Educating the severely physically handicapped: Modifying the learning environment* (Vol. 3, pp. 15–26). Columbus, OH: Special Press.

Steinherz, P. (1991, October). *Overview of childhood cancer.* Paper presented at conference on The Student With Cancer: A Workshop for School Personnel, Memorial Sloan-Kettering Cancer Center, New, York.

Synoground, S. G., & Kelsey, M. C. (1990). *Health care problems in the classroom: A reference manual for school personnel emphasizing teacher classroom observations and management techniques.* Springfield, IL: Charles C Thomas.

Task Force on Technology-Dependent Children. (1988). *Fostering home and community-based care for technology-dependent children*: Report of the Task Force on Technology-Dependent Children (Vols. 1–2). Washington, DC: U.S. Government Printing Office.

Trivette, C. (1988). Family life cycles. Paper presented at Early Intervention Institute, New Orleans, August.

U.S. Department of Education. (1991). *To assure the free appropriate public education of all children: Individuals with Disabilities Education Act.* (Thirteenth Annual Report to Congress.) Washington, DC: U.S. Government Printing Office.

Verity, S., & Ross, E. (1985). Longitudinal studies of children's epilepsy. In E. Ross & E. Reynolds (1984), *Paediatric perspectives on epilepsy.* New York: John Wiley & Sons.

Wehman, P., Moon, M. S., Everson, J. M., Wood, W., & Barcues, J. M. (1988). *Transition from school to work.* Baltimore: Brookes.

Weil, M. (1985). Infections of the nervous system. In J. Menkes, *Textbook of child neurology* (3rd ed). Philadelphia: Lea & Febiger.

Wong, D., & Whaley, L. (1990). *Clinical manual of pediatric nursing* (3rd ed.). St. Louis: C. V. Mosby.

Wright, B. (1983). *Physical disability—A psychological approach* (2nd ed.). New York: Harper & Row.

INTRODUCTION TO PART TWO
ALTERNATIVE PERSPECTIVES

T he material in Part One addressed the field's established (and emerging) way of seeing itself, its knowledge and practices, and its clients. Part Two addresses the book's second purpose: to introduce readers to the idea that special education and the very notion of student disability can and should be viewed from alternative perspectives—perspectives that challenge the field's traditional way of viewing itself, its knowledge and practices, and those who consume its professional services.

Chapter 14 considers the nature of the professions and professional knowledge and explains why today it is possible, and indeed morally and politically essential, for professions such as special education to view their knowledge, practices, and consumers from alternative perspectives. Chapter 15 extends this discussion to the field of special education specifically, first by considering the theoretical grounding of its knowledge and practices, and then by showing how the current debate over inclusive education undermines those grounds and thus the legitimacy of special education as a professional practice.

The remaining chapters in Part Two present three alternative ways of interpreting the nature and implications of special education and the notion of student disability—specifically, a sociological perspective (Chapter 16), an anthropological perspective (Chapter 17), and an organizational perspective (Chapter 18). In addition, Chapter 18 offers an alternative perspective on the knowledge and practices of general education. Because this view undermines the legitimacy of the institution of public education itself, it opens up the possibility of reconceptualizing public education in a way that not only resolves the current crisis in general and special education but also addresses the unprecedented social, political, and economic problems noted in Chapter 1.

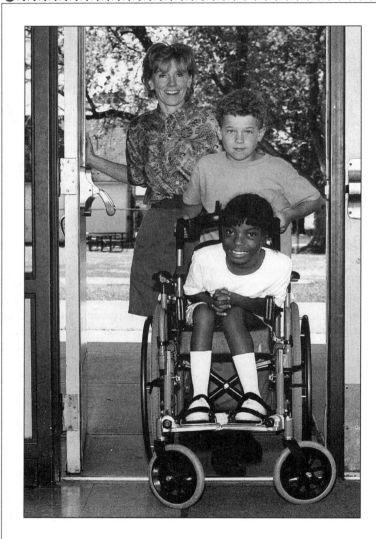

THE CRISIS IN

PROFESSIONAL

KNOWLEDGE

THOMAS M. SKRTIC

*T*he knowledge that grounds and legitimizes a profession's practices (what its members do) and its discourses (what its members think, say, read, and write about what they do) is premised on a network of anonymous, historically situated assumptions that organize and give meaning to perception, thought, communication, and activity (Kuhn, 1970b). The assumptions are anonymous because they are grounded in layers of largely unquestioned presuppositions. They are historically situated, rather than universal or context-free, because they are the social products of a specific place and time.

There is a crisis in professional knowledge because fundamental questions have been raised about the legitimacy of the knowledge that underwrites and justifies the professions and their practices and discourses, including the professions of education and special education. The crisis in professional knowledge stems from an unprecedented crisis in knowledge *per se*, a fundamental questioning of the knowledge that grounds the modern world and legitimizes its institutions, including the institution of the professions. In the late 20th century, the very meaning of knowledge has changed, and this has created both a crisis and an opportunity for professional fields such as education and special education—a crisis because it calls into question the legitimacy of their knowledge, practices, and discourses; an opportunity because, as we will see, a crisis in knowledge is a necessary precondition for growth of knowledge and progress in the professions and in society.

THE PROFESSIONS AND PROFESSIONAL KNOWLEDGE

Understanding the significance of a crisis in professional knowledge requires us to understand the larger crisis in modern knowledge, as well as the nature of the professions and professional knowledge itself. We will set the stage by considering the traditional view of the professions and professional knowledge. The most straightforward way to begin the discussion is to consider the nature of professional work, which we will do by first considering the distinction between simple and complex work and then differentiating two types of complex work, one of which is professional work.

Simple work is work that can be rationalized—that is, broken down or task-analyzed into a series of simple subtasks, each of which can be completely prespecified and done by a separate worker (Mintzberg, 1979). The obvious example of simple work is the automobile assembly line. Although building an automobile is a complex undertaking, reducing the total enterprise to a sequence of thousands of separate, relatively simple, routine subtasks makes automobile assembly simple work. People who do this type of work do not need extensive knowledge of automotive engineering or a set of complex associated skills. By design, simple work is done by "unskilled" workers who can be trained in a matter of days or even hours (Braverman, 1974).

Conversely, *complex work* is work that cannot be rationalized because it is not understood well enough to be completely prespecified and thus requires judgment on the worker's part. Ordinarily this type of work requires that the entire undertaking be done by a single worker who, to make the necessary judgments, must have a relatively extensive knowledge base and an associated set of skills that take an extended period of time to learn (Schein, 1972). *Craft work* is complex work for which the required knowledge and skills have not been codified, or systematically identified, arranged, and recorded. Although people learn to do craft work over a long time, they learn to do it as an apprentice under the guidance of a master who learned it in the same way. The specialized knowledge and skills of a craft are the conventions and customs of a craft culture, conveyed from person to person as a tradition of experienced practice (Mintzberg, 1979). *Professional work* also is complex work. Like craft work, it requires the people who do it to have an extensive knowledge base and an associated set of complex skills that take an extended period to learn. The difference is that the knowledge and skills necessary to do professional work have been codified; they exist as a curriculum of specialized knowledge and skills (Schein, 1972). Whereas people gain access to craft knowledge on the job in the role of an apprentice, access to professional knowledge occurs in professional schools, repositories of the codified knowledge and skills necessary to do professional work.

Although considering the nature of professional work provides some insight into the nature of the professions, a great deal of confusion abounds as to which occupations actually qualify as professions. This is so because the nature of work itself has not remained constant. Earlier in this century the distinctions were relatively clear, but as new technologies have emerged and new knowledge has been developed, much of what was craft work has been transformed into simple work through rationalization, or into professional work through codification (Braverman, 1974). Thus, in a knowledge-based and increasingly technological society such as ours, understanding the professions and professional knowledge requires consideration of the broader concept of professionalism.

PROFESSIONALISM

Professionalism is an important concept in the social sciences and humanities (hereafter, social sciences or disciplines) because the professions have a special relationship with society (see Haskell, 1984; Hughes, 1963; Parsons, 1968; Wilensky, 1964). The key element in this relationship is that society allows the professions greater autonomy than it does other social groups. Professions set their own standards, regulate entry into their ranks, discipline their members, and, in general, operate with fewer restraints than the arts, trades, or business. In return, professionals are expected to serve the public good and to set and enforce higher standards of conduct and discipline than these other groups (Bledstein, 1976). The argument for allowing the members of professions to govern themselves is based on two claims:

> The first is that the knowledge that members of the professions control is specialized, useful to society, and not easily mastered by the layman. The second is that the members of the professions set higher standards for themselves than society requires for its citizens, workers, and business men and women. (DeGeorge, 1982, p. 226)

Thus, professionalism is premised on a logic of confidence. Society gives the professions greater autonomy than other social groups on the assumption that their specialized knowledge and skills are valid and useful, and that they will use their professional knowledge to solve problems on behalf of the public good.

Although the concept of professionalism sheds some light on the nature of the professions and professional knowledge, identifying the professions is still difficult today because the growth of specialization in our society has increased the prestige, wealth, and autonomy of professionals. Because being identified as a professional has considerable advantage in such a context, many occupational groups claim to be professions. Thus, in our complex, specialized society, specifying additional criteria for identifying the professions has become necessary.

Although social scientists rarely agree on the specific criteria for identifying the professions, most agree on the necessity of a multiple-criterion definition. Schein (1972) developed such a definition by synthesizing the work of a number of social scientists. According to Schein, his criteria fit best the traditional or "learned" professions of medicine, law, and divinity, and fit in varying degrees other professions such as architecture, engineering, social work, and teaching.

1. The professional, as distinct from the amateur, is engaged in a *full-time occupation* that comprises his principal source of income.
2. The professional is assumed to have a *strong motivation* or calling as a basis for his choice of a professional career and is assumed to have a stable lifetime commitment to that career.
3. The professional possesses a *specialized body of knowledge and skills* that are acquired during a *prolonged period of education and training*.
4. The professional makes his decisions on behalf of a client in terms of *general principles, theories, or propositions*, which he applies to the particular case under consideration....
5. At the same time, the professional is assumed to have a *service orientation*, which means that he uses his expertise on behalf of the particular needs of his client....
6. The professional's service to the client is assumed to be based on the *objective needs of the client* and independent of the particular sentiments that the professional may have about the client.... [T]he professional relationship rests on a kind of *mutual trust between the professional and client*.
7. The professional is assumed to know better what is good for the client than the client himself.... [T]he professional demands *autonomy of judgment of his own performance*. Even if the client is not satisfied, the professional will, in principle, permit only his colleagues to judge his performance. Because of this demand for professional au-

tonomy, the client is in a potentially vulnerable position.... The profession deals with this potential vulnerability by developing strong ethical and professional standards [of conduct] for its members...usually enforced by colleagues through professional associations....

8. Professionals form *professional associations which define criteria of admission, educational standards, licensing or other formal entry examinations, career lines within the profession, and areas of jurisdiction* for the profession. Ultimately, the professional association's function is to protect the autonomy of the profession....

9. Professionals have great power and status in the area of their expertise, but their *knowledge is assumed to be specific*. A professional does not have a license to be a "wise man" outside the area defined by his training.

10. Professionals make their service available but ordinarily *are not allowed to advertise or to seek out clients*. Clients are expected to initiate the contact and then accept the advice and service recommended, without appeal to outside authority. (Schein, 1972, pp. 8–9)

Given these criteria, a professional is someone who is highly motivated and committed to a lifelong career of full-time employment in a professional occupation. Professionals are prepared for service during a prolonged period of education in which they are given access to professional knowledge in the form of general principles or theories that are applied to the needs of clients. Professionals adopt a posture in which expert services—in a particular area of expertise—are made available to clients who accept the services on trust, without appeal to an outside authority.

As in the relationship between the professions and society, we see that confidence also plays a key role in professionalism—here, in the relationship between the professional and the client. On the basis of access to professional knowledge, the professional is assumed to know best what is good for the client. Client vulnerability is recognized and accounted for by virtue of the development and enforcement of professional standards. But these standards are developed and enforced by the professionals themselves, through the collective action of their professional associations. The circularity of this proposition stems from the argument that only the professions can judge the adequacy of their performance because they alone have access to the specialized knowledge and skills upon which it is based. Thus, when we consider the nature of professional work and the concept of professionalism, two central elements emerge: professional autonomy and professional knowledge.

PROFESSIONAL AUTONOMY

Most social scientists consider professional autonomy to be the ultimate criterion of professionalism. As we have seen, professional autonomy implies that professionals know best what is good for their clients because of exclusive access to the specialized knowledge and skills of the profession. It also implies that the professionals themselves make all decisions as to the adequacy of this knowledge and skill. Given these two characteristics, the various professions can be understood as "professional communities" in which members are bound by "a common sense of identity, self-regulation, lifetime membership, shared values, a common language, clear social boundaries, and strong socialization of new members" (Schein, 1972, p. 10).

A key point to grasp about professional autonomy is its relationship to the concept of professional knowledge. Society allows the professions greater autonomy than it does other groups because they possess and control a body of specialized knowledge that society needs. Moreover, virtually all decisions about the adequacy of this knowledge are left to the professionals themselves. Thus, a profession is an insulated, self-regulating community whose members share an image of the world, their work and their clients, and their profession and themselves—an image based on strong socialization and common exposure to the profession's communally accepted specialized knowledge. The special relationship between the professions and society yields professional autonomy. The circular relationship between professional autonomy and professional knowledge means that a profession is the sole judge of the adequacy of its knowledge and skills, an important point that will be expanded upon after considering the nature of professional knowledge in more depth.

PROFESSIONAL KNOWLEDGE

The legitimacy of the professions' claims about the adequacy of their knowledge is premised on *positivism*, the positivist epistemology or theory of knowledge. Put simply, positivism is an "extremely positive evaluation of science and scientific method" (Reese, 1980, p. 450). It is the conviction that the knowledge produced through the scientific method is cumulative, convergent, and objective, and thus that science is the only source of correct knowledge about reality.

The scientific method is a process of logical inference and empirical experimentation aimed at finding general causes, or the ultimate true laws of nature, for the purpose of prediction and control (Hesse, 1980; Wolf, 1981). Although positivists recognize other forms of knowledge, they believe the highest form is scientific or "positive" knowledge—knowledge based on mathematics, logic, and empirical observation of controlled experiments (Angeles, 1981; Bernstein, 1976). Positive knowledge is thought to be objective because it is assumed that, by using the scientific method, observers can separate themselves from what they observe, thus protecting the knowledge they produce from the influence of any value system (Harre, 1981; Lincoln & Guba, 1985). The growth of knowledge, then, is understood simply to be "a cumulative process in which new insights are added to the existing stock of knowledge and false hypotheses eliminated" (Burrell & Morgan, 1979, p. 5). As such, the positivist assumes that the scientific method can be used to systematically accumulate objective knowledge about reality, a process that ultimately will converge upon the truth about the world.

Although the positivist epistemology is only one theory of knowledge, it has been so pervasive that, until recently, it was viewed as the only theory of knowledge. Although vanguard thinkers in virtually every discipline have discredited it (see Bernstein, 1976; Harre, 1981; Hesse, 1980; Rorty, 1979), positivism is the theory of knowledge upon which the modern university is premised (Shils, 1978). As such, positivism is built into the very structure and culture of universities and their associated professional schools, where it serves as the model for professional knowledge (Schön, 1983; Schein, 1972; Glazer, 1974).

The positivist theory of knowledge yields a threefold model of professional knowledge, described by Schein (1972) as:

1. An *underlying discipline* or *basic science* component upon which the [profession's] practice rests or from which it is developed.
2. An *applied science* or *"engineering"* component from which many of the [profession's] day-to-day diagnostic procedures and problem-solutions are derived.
3. A *skills and attitudinal* component that concerns the actual performance of [professional] services to the client, using the underlying basic and applied knowledge (p. 43).

Thus, professional knowledge can be understood as the interdependent hierarchical relationship among three types of knowledge: disciplinary, basic, or *theoretical knowledge*; engineering or *applied knowledge*; and knowledge based on skills and attitudes, or *practical knowledge*.

The positivist model of professional knowledge legitimizes professional practice as the use of theoretically grounded applied knowledge to solve practical problems. The actual performance of professional services to clients rests on applied knowledge, which itself rests on a foundation of basic or theoretical knowledge. Basic or disciplinary science yields theoretical knowledge, which, according to the positivist theory of knowledge, is assumed to be cumulative, convergent, and objective (Schön, 1983). Applied scientists in professional schools receive theoretical knowledge from the basic or disciplinary sciences and engineer it into the models, procedures, and techniques to be used in everyday professional practice. The professional practitioner receives this applied knowledge from applied scientists and uses it in the performance of services to clients. Thus, rigorous professional practice depends on applied scientists' developing models, practices, and tools that, given their grounding in the theoretical knowledge of the basic or disciplinary sciences, are themselves assumed to be cumulative, convergent, and objective (Glazer, 1974; Greenwood, 1981).

The distinction between "received" knowledge and "objective" knowledge is important. Both the applied researcher and the professional practitioner are assumed to operate on the basis of received knowledge, the knowledge each receives on faith from the next higher level in the hierarchy of professional knowledge (Greenwood, 1981; Schein, 1972). According to the model, however, the basic or disciplinary scientist does not "receive" knowledge. The assumption is that he or she "discovers" it through the scientific method, and that, as such, it is cumulative, convergent, and objective, according to the positivist theory of knowledge (Glazer, 1974; Schön, 1983).

PROFESSIONAL INDUCTION

Individuals are inducted into a profession—admitted as a member of a professional community—through a formal program of professional *education* in which the inductee is given access to professional knowledge and skills. The curriculum of professional education follows the hierarchy of professional knowledge presented in the preceding section. First, students are given some exposure to the theoretical knowledge of the relevant basic or disciplinary science in colleges of liberal arts and sciences, then more extensive exposure to the applied knowledge of the profession in the relevant professional school, and finally to a practicum or internship in which, under the guidance of an experienced practitioner, they learn to apply the profession's theoretically grounded applied knowledge to problems of professional practice (Greenwood, 1981; Schön, 1983). For example, those preparing for professional roles in education ordinarily are exposed to the theoretical knowledge of the discipline of psychology (among others); then to the applied knowledge of educational psychology in professional schools of education; and finally to a practicum in which they apply the profession's knowledge and practice its skills in actual classrooms under the supervision of an experienced teacher.

Students are on their way to becoming full-fledged professionals when they can demonstrate that they have internalized the theoretical, applied, and practical knowledge and skills of their profession. Becoming a professional entails more than internalizing knowledge and skills, however. The would-be professional also must be socialized. *Socialization* is the process by which a new member internalizes the value system, norms, and established behavior patterns of the group he or she is entering (Etzioni, 1961). Professional socialization inculcates inductees with the standards for how members of the profession ought to behave (Schein, 1968). It is a vital part of professional induction because it is the mechanism by which the professions regulate and discipline the professional behavior of their members, according to the special relationship between the professions and society (DeGeorge, 1982; Mintzberg, 1979). When students can demonstrate that they have internalized the profession's knowledge, skills, norms, and values—how to think and act as professionals—they are duly certified as professionally competent by the professional school, admitted to the professional community by the relevant professional association, and licensed by the state to practice the profession.

In sum, then, a profession is an autonomous community of members who, through strong socialization and common exposure to a body of specialized knowledge and skills, share a perspective on the world, their work, their clients, and themselves. Professional practices and discourses are shaped by this communally shared outlook. Professionals are certain that they know and do what is best for their clients because, given the positivist model of professional knowledge, they implicitly assume their practices and discourses ultimately are derived from a body of theoretical knowledge that is cumulative, convergent, and, above all, objective.

THE CRISIS IN SCIENTIFIC KNOWLEDGE

The crisis in professional knowledge stems from a more fundamental crisis in the dominant conceptualization of knowledge that underwrites the legitimacy of the modern world and its institutions. At this point, we can identify that conceptualization of knowledge as the positivist theory of knowledge, which has been called into question recently because of a revision in the traditional understanding of science and scientific knowledge. Thus, to understand the crisis in professional knowledge, we first must consider the more fundamental crisis in scientific knowledge, central to which are the notions of paradigms and paradigm shifts.

PARADIGMS AND PARADIGM SHIFTS

Although the positivist theory of knowledge has been under attack for more than a century (Phillips, 1987), the most devastating and accessible critiques have appeared over the past 30 years. Without question, the most significant critique has been that of Thomas Kuhn. In his influential book, *The Structure of Scientific Revolutions* (1962, 1970b), Kuhn used the concepts of paradigm and paradigm shift to reconceptualize the common understanding of scientific knowledge, practice, and progress in the physical sciences—in scientific fields such as physics, chemistry, and biology. Although Kuhn limited his analysis to the physical sciences, his work has had its most profound effect on the social sciences and, by implication, on what I will call the social professions, those that draw their theoretical knowledge, in whole or in part, from one or more of the social disciplines.

Paradigms, Scientific Knowledge, and Scientific Practice. Although the concept of a paradigm was the central element in Kuhn's analysis, he was neither clear nor consistent about what he meant by it. Masterman (1970) noted a number of different uses of the term in Kuhn's original work, which she reduced to a hierarchy of three basic types of paradigms, ranging from most to least abstract. She called Kuhn's most abstract use of the term the *metaphysical paradigm*, which is the broadest unit of consensus within a given science, a total world view or gestalt that subsumes and defines the other two types of paradigms (see Ritzer, 1980). Kuhn used "paradigm" in this sense to refer to a way of seeing, a perceptual organizer or mental map that yields a corresponding set of theories and guiding assumptions that define for scientists which entities exist (and which do not) and how they behave.

At the next lower level of abstraction, Masterman placed the *sociological paradigm*, what Kuhn referred to as a concrete set of habits or practices (1962) based on universally accepted models or exemplars (1970b). Thus, the sociological paradigm is a set of habitual practices based on exemplary models which themselves are grounded in the theories and guiding assumptions derived from the metaphysical paradigm. Finally, Masterman called Kuhn's narrowest and most concrete use of the term paradigm the *construct paradigm*. Kuhn used "paradigm" in this sense to refer to the specific research tools and instruments that scientists use to produce and collect data, given the logic of their sociological paradigm's models and practices and, ultimately, their metaphysical paradigm's theories and assumptions.

Broadly construed, then, a metaphysical paradigm is a set of implicit basic beliefs or presuppositions that unrandomize complexity and thus provide scientists with a general picture of the world and how it works. In turn, these presuppositions yield a corresponding set of theories that scientists use to explain and act upon actual phenomena. These presuppositions can be thought of as *meta*theories—as something more basic or fundamental than theories—because, although theories are grounded in scientific observations (Feigl, 1970), the observations themselves are shaped by the scientists' prior conceptual system of metatheoretical presuppositions (see Mulkay, 1979; Shimony, 1977).

Below metatheories and theories in the hierarchy are implicit guiding assumptions, which are derived from the logic of the theories and, in turn, yield a corresponding set of models that define and subsume an associated set of research practices and tools. Thus, a scientific community can be understood as operating on the basis of the hierarchy depicted in Figure 14.1, a hierarchy that, from its most to least abstract elements, includes metatheories, theories, assumptions, models, practices, and tools. Each level of the hierarchy is defined and subsumed by the higher levels, and all levels ultimately are defined and subsumed by the metatheoretical presuppositions of the metaphysical paradigm.

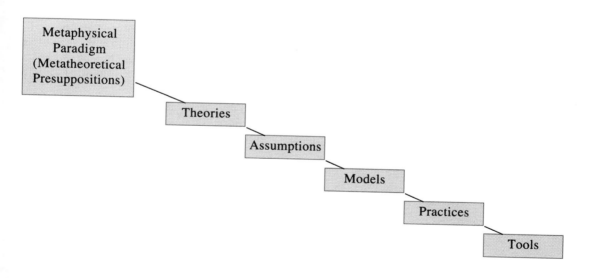

● **FIGURE 14. 1**

Hierarchy of presuppositions: Physical sciences

Source: Adapted from G. Ritzer, 1980, *Sociology: A Multiple Paradigm Science*, p. 239, Boston: Allyn & Bacon; and T. Skrtic (1991), *Behind Special Education: A Critical Analysis of Professional Culture and School Organization*, p. 14, Denver: Love Publishing.

Paradigm Shifts and Scientific Progress. Given this paradigm-based characterization of scientific knowledge and practice, Kuhn used the notion of paradigm shift to reconceptualize the growth of knowledge or progress in scientific fields. His key insight in this regard was to distinguish between "continuous" and "discontinuous" scientific progress. Continuous scientific progress, or what Kuhn called *normal science*, progresses by gradual additions to a knowledge base; a highly cumulative and convergent enterprise that articulates an already existing paradigm. An accepted metatheoretical paradigm is essential for scientific work because it unrandomizes the inherent complexity of nature and gives scientists the theories, assumptions, models, practices, and tools necessary to recognize, retrieve, and interpret data (Kuhn, 1970b). Although this is the traditional image of scientific progress, Kuhn argued that normal science is merely a necessary prelude to *revolutionary science*, which he described as a discontinuous and divergent breakthrough that demands an entirely new paradigm for recognizing, collecting, and understanding data.

Revolutionary science uncovers new and previously unsuspected phenomena and invents radical new theories, assumptions, practices, and tools to describe and explain them. It begins with the recognition and extended exploration of an anomaly—a violation of the paradigm-induced expectations of normal science. When the anomaly comes to be seen as more than just another normal science problem, the scientific community enters a state of paradigm crisis in which the rules of normal science are blurred. The blurring of the paradigm's rules gives rise to extraordinary research and theoretical speculation, which further loosen the paradigm's stereotypes and begin to expose the parameters of a new metatheoretical paradigm. Although in some cases this foreshadows the shape of the new paradigm, more often the new paradigm emerges all at once, "sometimes in the middle of the night, in the mind of a [scientist] deeply immersed in crisis" (Kuhn, 1970b, p. 90).

In any event, the shift to a new paradigm is revolutionary science. Whereas normal science requires mutual acceptance of a given metatheoretical paradigm among a community of scientists, revolutionary science requires a paradigm shift, a shift in allegiance to a new paradigm by the entire scientific community. After the paradigm shift, normal science begins anew under the guiding framework of the new paradigm, setting the stage for new anomalies, another paradigm crisis, and eventually the emergence of a new metatheoretical paradigm and its associated theories, assumptions, models, practices, and tools.

THE SUBJECTIVIST VIEW OF SCIENCE

A key element in Kuhn's reconceptualization of science was the idea that, rather than an objective, *rational-technical* process, paradigm replacement is a social-political phenomenon, a *nonrational-cultural* process of persuasion and conversion in which the victorious paradigm is the one that wins the most converts (Barnes, 1985; Ritzer, 1980). Thus, subjective or nonrational-cultural factors affect and largely determine the emergence of a new paradigm. In the face of criticism that he overemphasized non-rationality in scientific work (Lakatos & Musgrave, 1970), Kuhn softened his position somewhat (Kuhn, 1970a). Others who have used and expanded upon Kuhn's thesis to frame their work, however, have argued that paradigms in the physical sciences indeed rise and fall as a result of subjective rather than objective factors (Bloor, 1976; Law, 1975; Phillips, 1973; Knorr, Krohn & Whitley, 1981). For example, Krohn (1981) summarized the findings of the first body of detailed ethnographic and historical research on actual scientific activity by saying that physical scientists are "literally constructing their world rather than merely describing it" (p. xi).

Kuhn's work was important for what it had to say about the role of culture, convention, and tradition in the production of knowledge. His analysis of the conventional nature of knowledge, and the nature of convention itself, contradicted the common perception that science and knowledge are objective and advanced the idea that both depend on their cultural context for meaning and interpretation. Barnes (1982) noted the significance of culture in science when he said that "the culture is far more than the setting for scientific research; it is the research itself" (p. 10). The image of scientists as objective and impersonal observers who *discover* objective knowledge that is free from time and context has been replaced by the image of scientists as craftspersons who, bound by the culture of a particular place and time, *construct* historically situated knowledge that is of temporary validity and utility (Ravetz, 1971). This revised image of science and scientific progress necessarily has undercut the positivist theory of knowledge. Scientific knowledge, once conceived as the product of "a separate verbal and symbolic high culture [with] the power to reveal, order and enlighten...is being brought down to earth, demystified as a human construction" (Krohn, 1981, p. xii).

This subjectivist view of science rejects the traditional positivist or, what we can call "objectivist," image of science as a neutral, rational-technical undertaking that discovers objective knowledge. Rather, it recognizes science as an inherently nonrational-cultural endeavor, a paradigm-bound, communal act of knowledge construction that yields subjective knowledge. From this perspective, science is a form of engagement between an object of study and a community of observers conditioned to see the object in a certain way by their paradigm. As Morgan (1983) noted in this regard:

> Scientists engage a subject of study by interacting with it through means of a particular frame of reference.... Moreover, since it is possible to engage an object of study in different ways—just as we might engage an apple by looking at it, feeling it, or eating it—we can see that the same object is capable of yielding many different kinds of knowledge. This leads us to see knowledge as a potentiality resting in an object of investigation and to see science as being concerned with the realization of potentialities—of possible knowledges. (p. 13)

Kuhn's subjectivist reconceptualization of science is not a critique of science or the scientific method; it is a critique of the traditional objectivist *view of* science (Barnes, 1985). As such, the Kuhnian view of science leaves the legitimacy of the physical sciences intact; it merely provides a different way of understanding the nature of scientific knowledge, practice, and progress. Kuhn and those who have extended his work called into question the traditional objectivist conceptualization of science and the positivist notion that scientific knowledge is cumulative, convergent, and objective. They replaced the traditional view with one in which science, scientific knowledge, and scientific progress are discontinuous, divergent, and inherently subjective.

THE CRISIS IN PROFESSIONAL KNOWLEDGE

The idea that science produces subjective knowledge rather than objective knowledge has profound implications for the professions. Given the special relationship between society and the professions, and the circular relationship between professional autonomy and professional knowledge, the most obvious implication is the question of the validity of professional knowledge, which in turn raises serious questions about the claim that the professions know and do what is best for their clients and society. To set the stage for a discussion with respect to the professions of education and special education, we first consider the implications of the subjectivist view of science for the professions generally. The subjectivist view of science is used to reconceptualize the distinction noted earlier between objective knowledge and received knowledge and then, given this reconceptualization, to reconsider the process of professional induction.

SUBJECTIVIST VIEW OF PROFESSIONAL KNOWLEDGE

According to the positivist model of professional knowledge, the knowledge of applied scientists and professional practitioners is merely received knowledge—knowledge accepted on faith from the basic or disciplinary science level of the hierarchy of professional knowledge. Thus, the legitimacy of a profession's claim to know and do what is best for its clients ultimately rests on the assumption that basic scientists discover objective knowledge about reality. Given the subjectivist view of science and scientific knowledge, however, we can begin to see the parallels between the work of the basic scientist and that of applied scientists and professional practitioners.

The key point to grasp in this regard is that, like applied scientists and professional practitioners, basic scientists also operate on the basis of received knowledge. The theoretical knowledge of the basic or disciplinary sciences is not objective knowledge about reality. Rather, it is knowledge received by looking at the world through a particular metatheoretical paradigm, a process that yields subjective knowledge that ultimately is of temporary validity and utility. Like the objectivist image of science and the positivist theory of knowledge, the role of basic scientist has been demystified and brought down to earth as a subjective act of knowledge construction.

SUBJECTIVIST VIEW OF PROFESSIONAL INDUCTION

Although the need to standardize the thought and behavior of professionals through education and socialization is generally understood (see Kuhn, 1970b, 1977; Mintzberg,

1979; Chapter 18), the actual process of professional induction has received little critical attention. This is true in all professions (Barnes, 1982; Schön, 1983), including education (Champion, 1984; Haberman, 1983; Koehler, 1985; Zeichner & Tabachnick, 1981) and special education (Skrtic, 1986, 1988), because the objectivist conceptualization of the professions largely takes induction for granted. The general assumption has been that the two components of professional induction—education and socialization—are merely different means for accomplishing different ends. Professional education is assumed to be a rational-technical process for conveying an objective body of knowledge and its associated skills, according to the positivist model of professional knowledge (Schön, 1983). Professional socialization is assumed to be a nonrational-cultural process for inculcating a subjective value system and its associated behavior norms, according to the self-regulatory responsibility of the professions (DeGeorge, 1982; Greenwood, 1981).

Beyond these general assumptions about the nature and aims of professional education and socialization, little is known about the actual process through which professionals are inducted into professional communities. Nevertheless, we can shed some light on it by turning once again to Kuhn (1970b, 1977). Kuhn's work is important in this regard because a central feature in his reconceptualization of science was an analysis of scientific education, which for him is a matter of inducting would-be scientists into the established knowledge tradition—that is, the accepted metatheoretical paradigm and corresponding theories, assumptions, models, practices, and tools—of a scientific community (also see Barnes, 1982). According to Kuhn, scientific education is a process whereby a student is inducted into a culture of customs and conventions, much like the induction of an apprentice into a craft culture. From this perspective, a scientific community's knowledge tradition is the time-honored, mutually agreed-upon conventions and customs of its members. Kuhn's analysis is relevant to the induction process in the professions because, in all its essential dimensions, it is virtually identical to that of professional induction (see Cherryholmes, 1988; Popper, 1970).

Of the two objectivist assumptions about professional induction—internalization of objective knowledge through education and inculcation of subjective norms through socialization—there is no argument about the subjectivity of values and norms, or of socialization itself. Kuhn's conceptualization of the relationship between scientific knowledge and scientific culture, however, characterizes the internalization of knowledge and skills as a subjective process of socialization as well (Barnes, 1982; Popper, 1970). According to this interpretation, professional education, like scientific education, is a process whereby a student is inducted into a culture of customs and conventions, not unlike the induction of an apprentice into a craft culture. The implication, of course, is that professional knowledge is not objective, in the sense that it represents an objective reality existing apart from and prior to its definition by the profession. Instead, a profession's knowledge tradition and associated skills are the time-honored, mutually agreed-upon customs and conventions of its members. In this sense, a profession's knowledge and skills are as subjective as its values and norms. At this point, let us reconsider the process of professional induction, using the Kuhnian conceptualization as a frame of reference.

Professional induction requires the inductee to submit to the authority of the teacher (who ordinarily is also an applied scientist) and the institutional legitimacy of the profession. The information the teacher conveys is taken on trust by the student because of the context in which it appears. As such, professional education tends to be dogmatic and authoritarian, as well it might be, given its institutional context and the fact that the inductee initially lacks enough of the profession's specialized knowledge to be able to evaluate it on its own terms (Barnes, 1982). This applies to the professional education of both the applied scientist and the practitioner of the profession as well. Although the applied scientist learns to apply theories and the practitioner learns to apply techniques and procedures, both are taught in a dogmatic spirit. Each receives knowledge from a higher authority in the status hierarchy of professional knowledge, and each accepts it on faith (Popper, 1970). Each is regarded as a novice whose very perception must be guided and shaped to conform to the profession's conventional knowledge, to its established way of structuring the world and seeing itself, its clients, and its work (Barnes, 1982; Greenwood, 1981). The process corresponds to Kuhn's characterization of the induction of physical scientists:

> Looking at a contour map, the student sees lines on paper, the cartographer a picture of a terrain. Looking at a bubble-chamber photograph, the student sees confused and broken lines, the physicist a record of familiar subnuclear events. Only after a number of such transformations of vision does the student become an inhabitant of the scientist's world, seeing what the scientist sees and responding as the scientist does. (Kuhn, 1970b, p. 111)

As in the induction of scientists into scientific cultures, teaching textbooks play a key role in the "transformations of vision" necessary for an inductee to become an inhabitant of the world of a professional culture. The textbook conveys to the inductee the profession's mutually agreed-upon substantive domain, and its models, practices, and tools; and it conveys by implication the profession's grounding assumptions, theories, and metatheoretical presuppositions. In the hands of the teacher, who personifies for the student the authority and legitimacy of the profession, the teaching textbook becomes the principal vehicle for maximizing the authority and credibility of the profession's knowledge tradition (see Barnes, 1982; Kuhn, 1977). The authority implied by the teaching textbook is essential because professional induction demands complete acceptance of the profession's received knowledge on faith. Anything that might question or offer an alternative to the profession's established knowledge tradition is avoided. Past and current but unorthodox perspectives tend to be overlooked in training and rarely find their way into teaching textbooks (Kuhn, 1970b). This sort of textbook education demands complete concentration on one knowledge tradition to the exclusion of all others. Its goal is to inculcate in the would-be professional a deep commitment to a particular way of viewing the world and operating in it.

As in the case of Kuhn's reconceptualization of science, his description of scientific induction is not a critique of scientific education; it is merely a critique of the traditional objectivist *view of* the induction process. Indeed, Kuhn offered his subjectivist interpretation of the process as an account of an extremely effective system of education (Kuhn, 1970b, 1977). If we can conceive of a field of endeavor—whether in the sciences or the professions—as a collective enterprise grounded in conventionally based, communal judgment, then an authoritarian textbook-based education is a productive preparation for it. As Barnes (1982) noted with regard to the induction of physical scientists into scientific communities:

> Standardization of perception and cognition facilitates communication, organization, interdependence and division of labor: the more dogmatic their training, the more scientists are bound together into a communal enterprise with all the familiar gains in efficiency which that entails.... The consequence of the commitment encouraged by dogmatic training is that investigation is narrowed and focused, and is thus made more productive. (p. 19)

Like scientific work, professional work is too complex to be approached in a random, unsystematic manner. As in the case of scientific knowledge and skills, professional knowledge and skills are premised on a commitment to view the world in a particular way. The advantage of dogmatic commitment to a particular way of seeing is that it unrandomizes complexity and thus narrows and focuses activity, making it more productive. In this sense, one would expect the same benefits that Kuhn and Barnes noted for the physical sciences to accrue for the professions. We will see, however, that, even though an authoritarian education and a dogmatic commitment to a particular knowledge tradition is an advantage for a physical science, it can become a severe disadvantage for a profession, particularly for social professions such as education and special education, which ground their professional knowledge, practices, and discourses in the theoretical knowledge of one or more of the social sciences.

The crisis in professional knowledge turns on the contradictions between the traditional positivist or objectivist conceptualization of the professions and the newer subjectivist understanding of science and scientific knowledge. To address the significance of these contradictions for social professions such as education and special education, however, we first must consider the implications of the subjectivist view of science for the social sciences and the knowledge they produce. As we have seen, Kuhn's work is not a critique of science; it is a devastating critique of the traditional objectivist view of science. As we will see below, this has profound implications for the social sciences because, historically, the social disciplines have modeled themselves after the very objectivist image of science that has been called into question. Moreover, implications of the subjectivist view of science for the social sciences apply with even greater force to social professions such as education and special education, given that the legitimacy of their professional knowledge, practices, and discourses is premised on the presumed objectivity of their grounding social scientific knowledge.

THE CRISIS IN MODERN SOCIAL KNOWLEDGE

Modern social knowledge is the theoretical knowledge developed by the social disciplines during the modern era—knowledge of the social world produced over roughly the past 200 years. What is so ironic about this knowledge, however, is that over the last half of the modern era, a period in which the objectivist understanding of science was losing its relevance, the social disciplines fought to gain recognition as genuine sciences by adopting the very objectivist image that was falling out of favor (Bergner, 1981; Bernstein, 1983; Foucault, 1973b). As we know, the subjectivist notion that science is a paradigm-bound, communal activity that progresses by constructing a series of temporarily valid possible knowledges is not a critique of science; it is a devastating critique of the objectivist conceptualization of science. The problem for the social sciences is that, given that they are modeled on the objectivist conceptualization of science, the subjectivist view undermines the very claim to legitimacy upon which they are premised. The problem for the social professions, then, is that, by delegitimizing the social sciences, the subjectivist view of science calls into question the professional knowledge, practices, and discourses of fields that draw their knowledge claims from them.

PARADIGMATIC STATUS OF THE SOCIAL SCIENCES

Although Kuhn reserved his conception of paradigms and paradigm shifts exclusively for the physical sciences, others have used his work to reconceptualize the traditional understanding of the social sciences and the knowledge they produce (e.g., Barnes, 1982, 1985; Bernstein, 1976, 1983; Ritzer, 1980, 1983, 1990; Rorty, 1979, 1982). Masterman (1970) made an important contribution in this regard by using Kuhn's paradigm concept to differentiate four types of sciences: paradigmatic, nonparadigmatic, dual paradigmatic, and multiple paradigmatic.

According to Masterman, a *paradigmatic* science is one in which there is broad consensus on a single paradigm within the scientific community (e.g., physics after Newton); whereas a *nonparadigmatic* science is one in which there is no such consensus (e.g., "physics" before Newton). A *dual paradigmatic* state exists immediately before a Kuhnian scientific revolution, when an older, crisis-ridden paradigm and a new, emerging paradigm are vying for the dominance that only one of them ultimately will achieve. For example, the Newtonian paradigm dominated physics until irreconcilable anomalies set it up for defeat by the Einsteinian paradigm (Clark, 1971). During the period when both paradigms were competing for dominance, however, physics was a dual paradigm science. Finally, Masterman characterized *multiple-paradigm* sciences as those in which several viable paradigms compete unsuccessfully for dominance within a scientific community. The multiple-paradigm state is particularly important for present purposes because it permits one to differentiate between the physical and social sciences on the basis of their paradigmatic status.

The various physical sciences are paradigmatic or single-paradigm sciences, more or less. The birth of a particular physical science can be thought of as the point at which it emerged from a nonparadigmatic state by achieving paradigmatic consensus. From there, its history is a series of discontinuous progressions in which normal science—now possible because of paradigmatic consensus—produces enough anomalies to create a crisis of sufficient scope and duration to yield a scientific revolution and thus a new paradigm. The social sciences, on the other hand, are multiple-paradigm sciences.

Unlike the physical sciences, in which one paradigm dominates until crisis and revolution replace it with another one, in the social sciences multiple paradigms co-exist. This has created two fundamental problems for social scientists.

First, the multiple-paradigm status of the social sciences has made normal science more difficult. This is because, as Ritzer (1980) noted, social scientists are forced to spend most of their energy engaged in the politics of winning converts and defending themselves against attacks from rival paradigms.

Second, and more important, in principle, Kuhnian scientific revolutions are impossible in the social disciplines because there is simply no single, mutually agreed upon paradigm to be overthrown. This has retarded the advances of the social sciences (relative to the physical sciences) because, as Kuhn (1977) noted, although "one can practice [social] science...without a firm consensus, this more flexible practice will not produce the pattern of rapid consequential scientific advance [of the physical sciences, in which]...development occurs from one consensus to another" (p. 232). Although members of a social scientific community can shift paradigms, paradigm shifts in multiple-paradigm sciences have a fundamentally different meaning than those in single-paradigm sciences.

PARADIGMS OF MODERN SOCIAL SCIENTIFIC KNOWLEDGE

Burrell and Morgan (1979) conceptualized the multiple paradigms of the social sciences in terms of the relationship between two dimensions of metatheoretical presuppositions about the nature of social science: one dimension about the nature of science, and one about the nature of society. Drawing from the field of philosophy of science, they formulated the nature of science or *subjective-objective* dimension of their analysis by using four areas of disagreement among philosophers that have shaped the debate over the nature of social science throughout the modern era: (a) ontology (the nature of reality), (b) epistemology (the nature of knowledge), (c) human nature (the nature of human action), and (d) methodology (the nature of inquiry). Table 14.1 presents the extreme positions of each of the four areas of disagreement.

● *TABLE 14.1*

The subjective-objective dimension of social scientific thought

Subjectivist		Objectivist
Nominalism	ontology	Realism
Anti-positivism	epistemology	Positivism
Voluntarism	human nature	Determinism
Idiographic	methodology	Nomothetic

Source: Adapted from G. Burrell and G. Morgan, 1979, *Sociological Paradigms and Organizational Analysis,* p. 3, London: Heinemann Educational Books.

According to Burrell and Morgan (also see Morgan & Smircich, 1980), the *realist* assumes the social world exists "out there," independent of an individual's appreciation of it, and that it is virtually as hard and concrete as the physical world. The *nominalist*, in contrast, assumes that the social world external to individual cognition is made up of names, concepts, and labels that serve as tools for describing, making sense of, and negotiating the external world. The *positivist*, as we know, seeks to explain and predict social events by searching for regularities and determinate causal relationships. Growth of knowledge is seen as a cumulative process in which new information is added to an existing knowledge base and false hypotheses are eliminated. The *anti-positivist*, conversely, assumes the social world to be essentially relativistic—understandable, but only from the point of view of the individuals directly involved in the activities to be investigated. Anti-positivists reject the notion of objective observer as a valid vantage point for understanding human activities (also see Bernstein, 1976, 1983; Harre, 1981).

Burrell and Morgan characterized *determinists* as social scientists who assume that humans respond mechanistically or even deterministically to the situations they encounter in the external world. *Voluntarists*, on the other hand, give human beings a much more creative role. They ascribe free will and autonomy to humans and see them as creating or constructing their environments rather than being controlled by them. Social scientists who see the social world as an objective, external reality favor *nomothetic* methodologies—systematic protocols, standardized instruments, and quantitative analysis. They use these methodologies to search for universal laws that explain and govern the one, concrete, objective social reality that is presumed to exist. Conversely, *idiographic* methodologies (emergent protocols, nonstandardized instruments, qualitative analysis) are adopted by those who assume the importance of individuals' subjective experience in constructing their social world. The principal concern for social scientists using idiographic methodologies is to understand the ways in which humans construct and interpret their social world (also see Guba, 1990; Lincoln & Guba, 1985).

Taken together, the extreme positions on ontology, epistemology, human nature, and methodology at each end of Burrell and Morgan's subjective-objective dimension form the two philosophies of social science that have influenced social inquiry during the modern era: logical positivism, or *objectivism*; and German idealism, or *subjectivism*. Objectivism has been the dominant philosophy of social science in the West during the modern period. It represents:

> ...the attempt to apply the models and methods of the natural [or physical] sciences to the study of human affairs. It treats the social world as if it were the natural world, adopting a "realist" approach to ontology...backed up by a "positivist" epistemology, relatively "deterministic" views of human nature and the use of "nomothetic" methodologies. (Burrell & Morgan, 1979, p. 7)

Although subjectivism was the favored philosophy of social science in some parts of Europe during the 19th century, it has been virtually ignored in the West until recently (see below). Subjectivism stands in complete opposition to objectivism in that, rather than treating the social world as if it were as hard and concrete as the natural world, it presupposes that:

> ...the ultimate reality of the [social world] lies in "spirit" or "idea" rather than in the data of [empirical observation]. It is essentially "nominalist" in its approach to social reality..."antipositivist" in epistemology, "voluntarist" with regard to human nature and it favours idiographic methods as a foundation for social analysis. (Burrell & Morgan, 1979, p. 7)

The nature-of-society dimension of the Burrell and Morgan framework can be considered in at least two ways: sociologically or analytically. Burrell and Morgan (1979) approached it sociologically by using the concepts "sociology of regulation" and "sociology of radical change" to describe the extreme positions on their nature-of-society or *order-conflict* dimension. Table 14.2 differentiates the two positions in terms of the issues with which each are concerned.

The sociology of regulation or *order* perspective is the dominant position in the West. It reflects the value position of theorists who are concerned about explaining society's underlying unity, order, and cohesion. Conversely, theorists of the sociology of radical change or *conflict* perspective characterize modern society in terms of inherent contradictions, conflict, and modes of domination. They are concerned with emancipating people from existing social structures.

In his conceptualization of the multiple paradigms of the social sciences, Ritzer (1980, 1983) used the same subjective-objective dimension, but approached the nature of society dimension analytically by making a "levels of social analysis" or *microscopic-macroscopic* distinction. Instead of Burrell and Morgan's order-conflict distinction, he used social scientists' presuppositions about the appropriate target of social analysis to differentiate several metatheoretical positions. Ritzer's levels of social analysis range from the micro level of individual thought and action, human interac-

● **TABLE 14.2**

The order-conflict dimension of social scientific thought

Sociology of regulation (order) is concerned with:	Sociology of radical change (conflict) is concerned with:
the status quo	radical change
social order	structural conflict
consensus	modes of domination
social integration	contradiction
solidarity	emancipation
need satisfaction	deprivation
actuality	potentiality

Source: Adapted from G. Burrell and G. Morgan, 1979, *Sociological Paradigms and Organizational Analysis,* p. 18, London: Heinemann Educational Books.

tion, and groups to the macro level of organizations, whole societies, and total world systems.

As used here, the microscopic and macroscopic levels of Ritzer's interpretation correspond, respectively, to the order and conflict positions of the Burrell and Morgan scheme, with the microscopic perspective being the dominant level of analysis in the West. In either case, when the nature of science and the nature of society dimensions are related as in Figure 14.2, they produce four paradigms of modern social scientific thought: the *functionalist* (micro-objective), *interpretivist* (micro-subjective), *radical humanist* (macro-subjective), and *radical structuralist* (macro-objective) paradigms.

Each of the four paradigms is premised on a fundamentally different set of metatheoretical presuppositions about the nature of science and of society, and thus a fundamentally different conceptualization of the nature of social science itself. In turn, each metatheoretical paradigm defines and subsumes a corresponding set of social scientific theories, assumptions, models, practices, and research tools, as noted previously relative to the physical sciences, and as illustrated in Figure 14.3 for the functionalist paradigm.

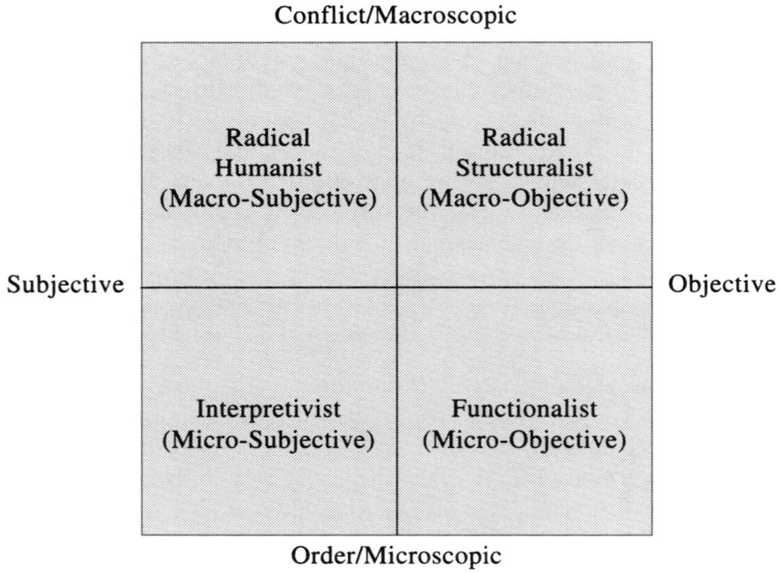

Conflict/Macroscopic

Radical Humanist (Macro-Subjective)	Radical Structuralist (Macro-Objective)
Interpretivist (Micro-Subjective)	Functionalist (Micro-Objective)

Subjective — Objective

Order/Microscopic

● **FIGURE 14.2**

Four paradigms of modern social scientific thought

Source: Adapted from G. Burrell and G. Morgan, 1979, *Sociological Paradigms and Organizational Analysis*, p. 29, London: Heinemann Educational Books; and G. Ritzer, 1980, *Sociology: A Multiple Paradigm Science* (rev. ed.), p. 239, Boston: Allyn & Bacon.

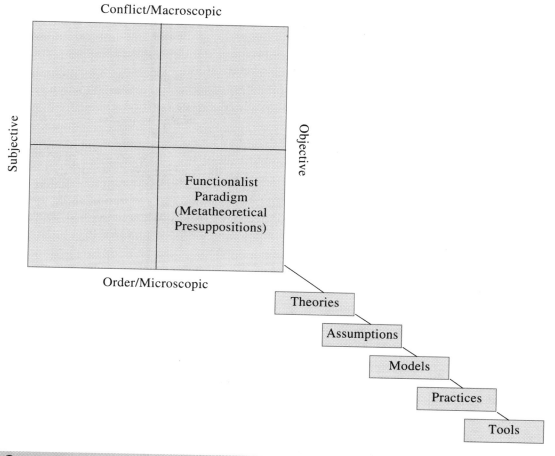

● *FIGURE 14.3*

Hierarchy of presuppositions: Social sciences

Source: Adapted from G. Burrell and G. Morgan, 1979, *Sociological Paradigms and Organizational Analysis*, p. 29, London: Heinemann Educational Books; G. Ritzer, 1980, *Sociology: A Multiple Paradigm Science* (rev. ed.), p. 239, Boston: Allyn & Bacon; and T. Skrtic, 1991, *Behind Special Education: A Critical Analysis of Professional Culture and School Organization*, p. 14, Denver: Love Publishing.

Functionalist Paradigm. Given the dominance of the objectivist image of science and the microscopic/order view of society, the functionalist paradigm has been the dominant framework for social science during the modern era, particularly in France, Great Britain, and the United States (Bernstein, 1976; Burrell & Morgan, 1979; Foucault, 1973b; Ritzer, 1980). Functionalist social science is grounded firmly in the sociology of regulation, takes a more or less microscopic view of social reality, and studies its subject matter from an objectivist point of view. Following an approach to science premised in the tradition of logical positivism, it seeks to provide rational explanations of social action for the purpose of prediction and control. As such, functionalism represents:

> ...the attempt, *par excellence*, to apply the models and methods of the natural sciences to the study of human affairs.... The functionalist approach to social science tends to assume that the social world is composed of relatively concrete empirical artifacts and relationships which can be identified, studied and measured through approaches derived from the natural sciences. (Burrell & Morgan, 1979, p. 26)

The functionalist paradigm is equivalent to Ritzer's micro-objective approach to social science. Social scientists operating from this vantage point use positivist methodologies to study microscopic social phenomena—patterns of behavior, action, and interaction—in an attempt to predict and thus control various aspects of social life. As Ritzer (1980, 1983) noted, the functionalist views society as a social system composed of interrelated parts, each of which contributes to maintenance of the others. As such, the parts of society are:

> ...believed to be in a kind of balance with a change in one part necessitating changes in the other parts. The equilibrium of the social system is not static, but a moving equilibrium. Parts of society are always changing, and these changes lead to sympathetic changes in other parts of the system. Thus, change is basically orderly, rather than cataclysmic. (1980, p. 48)

At the extreme, functionalists argue that all events and structures in society are functional because, if they were not, they would not exist. This leads to the conservative bias that all current aspects of society are indispensable to the system and that, as such, "all structures that exist should continue to exist...[which] holds out little possibility of meaningful change within a social system" (Ritzer, 1980, p. 49).

Interpretivist Paradigm. Burrell and Morgan characterized interpretivist social scientists as being committed only implicitly to regulation and order. Although they assume the social world is cohesive, orderly, and integrated, interpretivists (unlike functionalists) are oriented toward understanding the ongoing processes through which humans subjectively construct their social world (see Berger & Luckmann, 1967). The interpretivist paradigm addresses the same social issues as the functionalist paradigm, but it is concerned with understanding the essence of the everyday world as an emergent social process. When a social world outside the consciousness of the human is recognized, it is regarded as a network of assumptions and intersubjectively shared meanings. Burrell and Morgan's interpretivist paradigm corresponds to Ritzer's micro-subjective perspective. Social scientists of this persuasion are concerned with understanding the social construction of reality, with the way humans construct and share meaning (also see Dallmayr & McCarthy, 1977; Lincoln & Guba, 1985).

Radical Humanist Paradigm. Although radical humanists share a view of social science with the interpretivist paradigm, their frame of reference is the sociology of radical change. According to Burrell and Morgan, their view of society emphasizes the importance of transcending the limitations of existing ideological structures, which they view as distorting true human consciousness. Thus, society is viewed as being anti-human, as inhibiting human development and fulfillment. Humanist theorizing centers on a critique of the status quo from Ritzer's macro-subjective paradigm. As such, radical humanists focus their analyses on ideational structures such as culture, norms, and values, and are concerned with the role these structures play in shaping human thought and action (also see Bernstein, 1983; Habermas, 1971).

Radical Structuralist Paradigm. Like radical humanism, the radical structuralist paradigm mounts a critique of the status quo and advocates change. It takes this stance from the objectivist perspective, however, thus sharing a conceptualization of social science with the functionalist paradigm. Working from Ritzer's macro-objective frame of reference, radical structuralists characterize contemporary society in terms of fundamental conflicts that generate change through political and economic crises. As Burrell and Morgan (1979) noted, whereas radical humanists are concerned with ideological structures, radical structuralists focus their critique upon material structures such as language, law, bureaucracy, technology, and economy (also see Giddens, 1981).

Each paradigm of modern social scientific thought represents a mutually exclusive view of the social world and how it might be investigated because each rests on an incommensurable set of metatheoretical presuppositions about the nature of social science. Each of the four modern paradigms produces a particular type of social knowledge because it is a unique, historically situated way of seeing. As such, each paradigm explicitly or, most often, implicitly defines the metatheoretical frame of reference—and thus the theories, assumptions, models, practices, and research tools—of the social scientists who work within it (Burrell & Morgan, 1979; Ritzer, 1980, 1983).

Ultimately, the type of theoretical knowledge a community of social scientists produces depends on whether functionalism, interpretivism, radical humanism, or radical structuralism serves as its metatheoretical frame of reference. This has profound implications for the social professions because, given the traditional model of the professions, the nature of their applied and practical knowledge—and, more important, the effects of this knowledge on individuals and society—depends on the paradigmatic grounding of the social science discipline or disciplines from which they draw their theoretical knowledge. I will return to these implications later. First, though, let's consider the nature and effects of several paradigm shifts in the social sciences since the 1960s.

PARADIGM SHIFTS IN THE SOCIAL SCIENCES

Although in principle the multiple-paradigm status of the social sciences precludes the kind of paradigm shifts Kuhn described for the physical sciences, paradigm shifts do occur in the social disciplines. As we know, a paradigm shift in a physical science means abandoning an older, crisis-ridden paradigm and adopting a new one by (more or less) the entire scientific community. A paradigm shift in a social science, however, is merely a change in paradigmatic commitment for some members of the scientific community. The difference is that a paradigm shift in a social science affects only those who have changed their paradigmatic allegiance; it does not overthrow the other paradigms or change the outlook of members of the scientific community who remain loyal to them.

In principle, each modern social science paradigm is a conceptually viable and intellectually honest way to view and study the social world. Although allegiances to particular paradigmatic perspectives have shifted throughout the modern era—and particularly since the 1960s—all four paradigms of modern social scientific thought continue to exist. Paradigm shifts notwithstanding, each of the modern social scientific paradigms serves as the guiding framework for the portion of the social scientific community that subscribes to it (Bernstein, 1976, 1991; Burrell & Morgan, 1979; Ritzer, 1980, 1990).

Describing the paradigm shifts in the social sciences is a difficult undertaking. It requires tracing a complex series of interrelated and mutually shaping developments in philosophy and the social sciences, developments that have followed different paths and have had different consequences in and across different disciplines and national contexts (see Bernstein, 1971, 1976, 1983; Burrell & Morgan, 1979; Giddens & Turner, 1987; Rorty, 1979, 1991). Thus, although what follows is necessarily an oversimplification of the paradigm shifts in the social sciences over the past 30 years, my aim is simply to outline the broad parameters of the changes in paradigmatic commitment.

Because the functionalist paradigm has been the dominant framework for social science in the West, most modern social theorizing has been premised on the metatheoretical presuppositions of the functionalist or micro-objective perspective. Nevertheless, over the past 30 years there have been several significant paradigm shifts away from functionalism (Bernstein, 1976, 1983, 1991; Rorty, 1979, 1982, 1991), three of which are important for present purposes. The first of these shifts occurred in the 1960s on the objectivist side of the four-paradigm scheme developed above (refer to Figure 14.2). It reflects a shift in allegiance for a portion of the social scientific community from the micro-objective to the macro-objective perspective—from the functionalist to the radical structuralist paradigm. This shift was associated with the emergence and refinement of various forms of macro-objective or structuralist social analysis (e.g., Chomsky, 1959; Lévi-Strauss, 1963; Saussure, 1966), as well as a corresponding rise of interest in the social and political philosophy of the mature Marx (e.g., Althusser, 1969; Marcuse, 1964).

Two parallel shifts occurred during the 1970s and 1980s, both of which were associated with the questioning of positivism and, following Kuhn, what became a general trend away from the traditional objectivist conceptualization of social science and toward the subjectivist perspective (Outhwaite, 1987). One of these shifts occurred at the microscopic (order) level of social analysis, from the functionalist to the interpretivist paradigm. Given the apparent eclipse of positivism, this shift was associated with the reemergence of interest in various forms of micro-subjective or interpretivist social analysis, such as phenomenology, ethnography, and hermeneutics (see Bernstein, 1976; Geertz, 1983).

The other shift associated with the general trend toward subjectivism occurred at the macroscopic level of social analysis, from the macro-objective or radical structuralist paradigm to the macro-subjective or radical humanist paradigm. This shift was associated with a revival of interest in the social and political philosophy of Hegel and the young Marx, as well as the emergence and refinement of various forms of radical humanist social inquiry, such as critical theory (see Held, 1980; Jay, 1973), radical ethnography (e.g., B. Bernstein, 1971; Bourdieu, 1977), and radical hermeneutics (see Bernstein, 1976; Caputo, 1987).

Here again, a comprehensive treatment of the implications of these paradigm shifts for the social sciences is beyond the scope of this chapter (see Bernstein, 1971, 1976, 1983; Outhwaite, 1987; Rorty, 1979, 1991). Nevertheless, for present purposes we can identify two key sets of implications of these paradigmatic realignments and assess their impact on the social sciences and—as a prelude to a more extensive discussion in the final section—on the social professions. The first set of implications is related to the general shift in commitment among social scientists from objectivism to subjectivism. The second, and more important, set of implications is related to the emergence of a perspective on social knowledge that falls outside the four-paradigm matrix of modern social thought altogether.

The Rise of Subjectivism. As we have seen, each of the paradigm shifts in the social sciences over the past 30 years has been away from functionalism as a framework for social inquiry (see Giddens, 1977; Ritzer, 1990). This is important in a negative sense because, given its dominance in the modern era, the general abandonment of functionalism as a framework for social theorizing has undermined the legitimacy of most modern social theory. This is critically important for present purposes because, as we will see, it necessarily calls into question the substantive and methodological legitimacy of the social professions, virtually all of which—including education and special education—have relied explicitly or implicitly on functionalist theory to ground their knowledge, practices, and discourses (see Chapter 15).

Another important consequence of the paradigm shifts in the social sciences has been the substantive and methodological development of the interpretivist, radical structuralist, and radical humanist paradigms. Relative to functionalism, these paradigms previously had been underdeveloped, particularly in the United States (Bernstein, 1976; Burrell & Morgan, 1979). This is important in a positive sense because it has provided new (or previously underutilized) modes of theorizing in the social disciplines, which in turn has produced new forms of social scientific knowledge (Bernstein, 1976, 1983; Ritzer, 1990; Rorty, 1979). This is critically important for the social professions because the availability of new forms of disciplinary knowledge has allowed fields such as education (see Soltis, 1984) and special education (see Skrtic, 1986, 1991, 1993; Chapter 15) to consider the possibility of grounding their professional knowledge, practices, and discourses in paradigmatic perspectives other than functionalism.

Finally, the paradigm shifts of the 1970s and 1980s have elevated subjectivism to a position of increasing prominence within the social scientific community and, to a lesser extent, within the social professions. This has had both positive and negative effects. One positive effect of the rise of subjectivism has been an increase in the perceived legitimacy of the interpretivist and radical humanist paradigms (see Bernstein, 1976; Ritzer, 1990), the two subjectivist perspectives that, because of the dominance of objectivism prior to the 1970s, had been neglected in the social sciences and social professions. As noted, the advantage of this development has been the production and broader utilization of subjectivist forms of knowledge in the social disciplines and, to a lesser extent, in the social professions.

On the negative side, however, the rise of subjectivism has led some longstanding and newly converted interpretivists and radical humanists to the faulty conclusion that their particular paradigm provides the only correct way of comprehending the social world. This has been true in the social sciences (Bernstein, 1983; Ritzer, 1990; Rorty, 1991) and in social professions such as education and special education (see Skrtic, 1990; Chapters 15), because the implications of the rise of subjectivism have been interpreted too narrowly as simply a vindication of subjectivist over objectivist modes of social theorizing. This is understandable, of course, because, whether we think of total paradigm replacement in the physical sciences, or the competitive coexistence among multiple paradigms in the social sciences, the very idea that paradigms exist in the minds of humans who operate under their received meaning supports the subjectivist philosophy of science, and thus the interpretivist and radical humanist frames of reference.

The problem with this narrow interpretation, however, is that it has tended merely to intensify the historical pattern of political competition among advocates of different paradigms, the primary difference being a tilt in the balance of power away from the once impregnable objectivist perspective. Fortunately, however, this new wave of paradigmatic conflict began to subside somewhat in the social sciences during the 1980s, giving rise to what seems to be an unprecedented sense of paradigmatic and theoretical diversity, if not pluralism (see Ritzer, 1990).

The Emergence of Antifoundationalism. Whereas the paradigm shifts in the social disciplines represent realignments of commitment to various forms of modern knowledge, the most revolutionary development associated with these shifts and the general trend toward subjectivism has been the formulation of a frame of reference for social analysis that falls outside the four-paradigm matrix of modern social knowledge itself. This new *post*modern view of knowledge represents a fundamental reconceptualization of the very nature of social knowledge (see Bernstein, 1983; Lyotard, 1984; Rorty, 1979).

During the modern period, the general conceptualization of knowledge was *foundational*, the idea that there is a fixed set of foundational criteria against which all knowledge claims can be judged. Thus, the modern perspective is *monological*; it regards knowledge or truth as a monologue spoken in the voice of a single paradigm or theoretical frame of reference. The postmodern conceptualization of knowledge, in contrast, is *antifoundational*; it is based on the *dialogical* idea that there are no independent foundational criteria for judging knowledge claims, and thus that the truth about the social world is better understood as an ongoing conversation or dialogue among many paradigmatic voices and theoretical perspectives (Bernstein, 1983, 1991).

Moreover, the postmodern notion of antifoundational knowledge has begun to blur the traditional distinctions among the various social disciplines themselves (Geertz, 1983). Given a conceptualization of knowledge as interpretation with no independent criteria for choosing among interpretations, there is no meaningful way to establish the cognitive authority of one social discipline over another. Social inquiry premised on the foundational view of knowledge has led to a monological quest for the single best method, theory, paradigm, or discipline for social analysis. Today, however, scholars in the social disciplines are calling for dialogical social analysis—an antifoundational discourse premised on an appreciation of the utility of multiple methodological, theoretical, disciplinary, and paradigmatic perspectives for interpreting and acting upon social life (Bernstein, 1983, 1991; Ricoeur, 1981; Rorty, 1979, 1991).

Although at present postmodernism is a relatively vague and controversial conception in the social sciences, Antonio (1989) identified two predominant forms. First, there is the more radical or Continental form of postmodernism (e.g., Baudrillard, 1983; Derrida, 1982; Foucault, 1980a; Lyotard, 1984), which rejects modern social knowledge outright. It is incredulous toward paradigms *per se*, regarding them simply as historically situated meta-narratives about the social world written in the genre of philosophy (Lyotard, 1984). The second form of postmodernism is the progressive liberal or American version (e.g., Bernstein, 1983; Rorty, 1979), which is a reappropriation of American pragmatism and thus primarily a reappropriation of the work of John Dewey (e.g., 1982, 1988), William James (1975), George Herbert Mead (1934), and Charles Sanders Peirce (1931–35).

The difference between the antifoundationalism of the Continental and American postmoderns is that, whereas the former reject modern social knowledge as oppressive and attempt to deconstruct it, the latter accept modern knowledge conditionally as a starting point for reconstructing new forms of emancipatory knowledge through a critical and democratized form of dialogical social inquiry (see Antonio, 1989; Kloppenberg, 1986). Like the original pragmatist philosophers, the American postmoderns or neo-pragmatists propose that we use modern knowledge pragmatically by forging a *via media* or way between its traditional subjective-objective and micro-macro/order-conflict dichotomies (Kloppenberg, 1986). They propose a radically open and partici-patory form of social discourse in which all forms of knowledge are accepted or rejected, in whole or part, on the basis of their contribution to the realization of social ideals, rather than on whether they are true in a foundational sense (Bernstein, 1991; Rorty, 1979, 1989, 1991).

In essence, the progressive liberal form of postmodernism, like the earlier philo-sophical pragmatism of Dewey, is a method for deconstructing and reconstructing social knowledge, practices, discourses, and institutions under conditions of uncertainty—conditions in which it is recognized that there are no independent, cognitive criteria for choosing among interpretations of the social world. Whereas the aim of modern social inquiry is to justify social practices and institutions by showing that they are based on an accurate *representation* of the social world, the goal of philosophical pragmatism is to change social practices and institutions by *reconciling* them with our moral ideals (Bernstein, 1971, 1991; Rorty, 1982, 1989; Chapter 15).

Now we will consider in greater depth the implications of subjectivism and antifoundationalism for the social professions, and particularly for the social professions of education and special education.

CRISIS AND OPPORTUNITY IN THE SOCIAL PROFESSIONS

As we know, social professions ground their applied and practical knowledge in the theoretical knowledge of one or more of the social disciplines. Thus, the legitimacy of a social profession's knowledge, practices, and discourses rests on the adequacy of the theoretical knowledge in which they are grounded. As such, the rise of subjectivism and the emergence of antifoundationalism in the social sciences have created both a crisis and an opportunity in the social professions. The crisis stems from subjectivism and antifoundationalism calling the legitimacy of the social professions' knowledge, practices, and discourses into question. The opportunity arises from two sources. On one hand, a crisis in knowledge is a precondition for the growth of knowledge and progress in the social professions. On the other hand, antifoundationalism provides the social professions with methods for deconstructing and, more important, reconstructing their knowledge, practices, and discourses. The crisis and opportunity in the social professions is considered next in terms of three related postmodern critiques: a philosophical critique of professional knowledge, a cultural critique of professional induction, and a political critique of professional power.

PHILOSOPHICAL CRITIQUE OF PROFESSIONAL KNOWLEDGE

The philosophical critique of the social professions turns on the epistemological implications of the rise of subjectivism and the emergence of antifoundationalism in the social sciences. Inherent in the subjectivist philosophy of science, of course, is a critique of positivism and the objectivist view of social science. Social professions such as education and special education are implicated in this critique because they are premised on the positivist epistemology of knowledge, and thus on the assumption that the social sciences produce objective knowledge about social reality. As such, the professional knowledge required for performing services to students in these social professions is presumed to be grounded in a foundation of objective scientific knowledge about social reality.

Subjectivism, in contrast, rejects the traditional image of science as a purely technical undertaking that yields objective knowledge. As we have seen, the subjectivist view is that, rather than a neutral, rational-technical activity, science is a nonrational-cultural undertaking, a form of engagement that yields different kinds of possible knowledges, depending on which social science paradigm serves as the observers' metatheoretical frame of reference. This means the theoretical knowledge that grounds the professional knowledge, practices, and discourses of the fields of education and special education—and thus the knowledge that shapes educators' thought and action toward their students—is not objective knowledge about social reality. It is subjective knowledge based on a particular, historically situated frame of reference. Given the implications of subjectivism, the social professions of education and special education must confront the fact that nothing is inherently true or correct about their professional knowledge, practices, and discourses.

Two epistemological implications of antifoundationalism apply to the social professions. The first relates to the multiple-paradigm status of their grounding disciplines. Given that these professions are grounded in the social sciences, each of which is a multiple-paradigm science, social professions such as education and special education can be thought of as *multiple-paradigm professions*. As such, antifoundationalism means that these professions have no independent, foundational criteria for determining which of the paradigms of any given social discipline is the correct one for grounding their professional knowledge, practices, and discourses. The second implication is related to way antifoundationalism has blurred the distinctions among the various social disciplines. Given the antifoundational conceptualization of knowledge as interpretation with no independent criteria for choosing among interpretations, there is no meaningful way to establish the cognitive authority of one social discipline over another. Together, the epistemological implications of antifoundationalism mean the social professions of education and special education have no way to establish the cognitive authority of any one social science paradigm *or* disciplinary orientation as a grounding for their professional knowledge, practices, and discourses.

Philosophically, then, the rise of subjectivism in the social sciences means educators must face the reality that nothing is inherently true or correct about their current knowledge, practices, and discourses. Moreover, the emergence of antifoundationalism means they must confront the more disturbing realization that there is no cognitively certain way to choose an alternative theoretical grounding from among the various modern paradigmatic perspectives or disciplinary orientations.

CULTURAL CRITIQUE OF PROFESSIONAL INDUCTION

According to the objectivist view, professional induction entails two processes: socialization, an admittedly nonrational-cultural process for inculcating subjective values and norms; and education, which is assumed to be a rational-technical process for conveying objective knowledge and skills. The subjectivist view of professional induction, however, challenges this characterization on the grounds that neither the knowledge conveyed through professional education nor the process itself is objective. As we have seen, the professional knowledge of any given social profession is subjective; it is one of many possible knowledge traditions premised on the particular paradigmatic perspective and disciplinary orientation of its grounding social science. Moreover, the education component of professional induction is not a rational-technical process. Like professional socialization, it too is a nonrational-cultural process, a mechanism for inducting students into an established knowledge tradition of time-honored, mutually agreed-upon customs and conventions.

As a means of inculcating professionals with a deep commitment to a particular way of viewing the world and operating in it, professional induction, like scientific induction, is necessarily dogmatic and authoritarian. Professional induction requires inductees to submit to the institutional legitimacy and authority of the profession, the teacher, and the textbook. Students must accept the profession's established knowledge tradition on faith as the only correct way of unrandomizing the world and seeing the profession, its work, and its clients. In itself, however, this is not a criticism of the induction process, for as Kuhn (1970b, 1977) and Barnes (1982) noted relative to scientific induction, such a transformation of vision is essential if the inductee is to become an inhabitant of the world of a professional culture. In principle, preparation for any collective enterprise that relies on conventional knowledge and communal judgment requires a dogmatic, authoritarian education. This is as necessary for the social professions of education and special education as it is for the physical and social sciences, because the work in all of these fields is too complex to be approached in a random, unsystematic manner. By encouraging commitment to a particular way of unrandomizing complexity, a dogmatic, authoritarian education narrows and focuses activity, making it more productive (Barnes, 1982).

Although we would expect the same benefits that Kuhn and Barnes noted for the physical sciences to apply to the social sciences and social professions, what begins as an advantage for all three groups, and remains so for the physical sciences, can become a disadvantage for the social sciences, and particularly for social professions such as education and special education. Ultimately, the extent to which a narrow, dogmatic focus remains an advantage rather than becomes a disadvantage depends on the paradigmatic status of the communal enterprise and the conditions under which its work is performed. Paradigmatic status is a key factor because it relates to the degree to which the members of a scientific or professional culture are prepared to recognize anomalies. As Barnes (1985) noted in regard to the physical or single paradigm sciences:

> A group of scientists engaged in normal science is a very sensitive detector of anomaly. Precisely because the group is so committed to its paradigm and so convinced of its correctness, any...residue of recalcitrant anomalies...may eventually prompt the suspicion that something is amiss with the currently accepted paradigm, and set the stage for its demise. (pp. 90–91)

Given their multiple-paradigm status, however, the inherent dogmatism associated with the induction process has been a disadvantage for the social sciences throughout their history.

As we have seen, normal science is more difficult for a multiple-paradigm science because of the inherent political infighting over the correct paradigm (Ritzer, 1980). More important, however, the multiple-paradigm status of the social sciences also makes revolutionary science more difficult because the lack of commitment to a particular paradigm within a scientific culture renders anomalies more difficult to detect. As Kuhn (1970b, 1977) noted, advancement of the social sciences has been retarded relative to that of the physical sciences because, although a science can be practiced without a firm consensus on a paradigm, it will not produce the pattern of rapid advancement in which development occurs from consensus to consensus. Indeed, this is what makes the emergence of postmodernism in the social sciences so significant. If we think of the four-paradigm matrix of modern social scientific knowledge as a single paradigm composed of four different types of foundational knowledge, the emergence of postmodernism and the notion of antifoundational knowledge in the social sciences is equivalent in magnitude, if not in form, to an episode of Kuhnian revolutionary science.

The narrow, dogmatic focus of the induction process has been particularly disadvantageous for social professions such as education and special education. First of all, because they are grounded in the multiple-paradigm sciences, they suffer the same disadvantages as the social sciences relative to the detection of anomalies. Moreover, as we will see in Chapter 18, the organizational conditions under which the social professions work tend to distort anomalies, which further reduces their effect as a source of uncertainty and thus as a mechanism of change. Without the uncertainty caused by anomalies, there is nothing to prompt suspicion in the professional culture that something is amiss with the currently accepted paradigm. The lack of suspicion in a professional community reinforces conventional thinking, which ultimately retards the growth of knowledge and progress (see Skrtic, 1991).

As we have seen, the professions' special relationship with society yields professional autonomy, which leaves determination of the adequacy of professional knowledge, practices, and discourses to the professionals themselves. As we know from the philosophical critique of the professions, however, there is no way to establish the adequacy of a professional knowledge tradition because there is no way to establish the cognitive authority of the theoretical knowledge in which it is, or possibly could be, grounded. Moreover, professional induction is designed to produce professionals with a deep commitment to their particular knowledge tradition. The problem is that, whereas the focused vision of physical scientists uncovers anomalies that force them to question the adequacy of their knowledge tradition and eventually to replace it with a different one, professional cultures such as those of education and special education are far less sensitive to anomalies because of the multiple-paradigm status of their grounding disciplines and the organizational conditions under which they work.

The result is that the effectiveness of professional induction in fields such as education and special education produces professionals who rarely question the adequacy of their knowledge tradition. Instead, they tend to remain committed to their practices and discourses because, lacking a residue of recalcitrant anomalies, they understandably assume that their knowledge tradition is valid and objective, and thus that their practices and discourses serve the best interests of their students and of society.

POLITICAL CRITIQUE OF PROFESSIONAL POWER

The political critique of the social professions is based on the political and moral implications of antifoundationalism. Given a conceptualization of knowledge as interpretation, a distinctly human and historically situated process in which no single interpretation ever has enough cognitive authority to privilege it over another, the act of choosing an interpretation of social reality upon which to premise professional knowledge is far from the neutral, technical undertaking it is assumed to be. Ultimately, choosing a theoretical grounding in social professions such as education and special education is a political and moral act with profound implications for ethical practice and a just society (Derrida, 1982; Feyerabend, 1975; Foucault, 1980a).

Moreover, this assumes that the social professions consciously choose the interpretation that grounds their knowledge, practices, and discourses. As we have seen, however, professionals rarely recognize the metatheoretical paradigm that stands behind their field's knowledge tradition. Indeed, the traditional objectivist model of professional knowledge is premised on the assumption that there is nothing behind theory except reality.

Another major outcome of the rise of subjectivism and the emergence of antifoundationalism in the social sciences has been a series of revisions in the metaphor for social life—first, from an organism to a game; then, from a game to a drama; and, finally, from a drama to a text (Geertz, 1983). The text metaphor implies a mode of social analysis that views human and institutional practices as discursive formations that can be read or interpreted in many ways, none of which is correct in a foundational sense but all of which carry with them particular political and moral implications.

Social analysis under the text metaphor is the study of that which conditions, limits, and institutionalizes discursive formations. Ultimately, it asks how power comes to be concentrated in the hands of those who have the right to order, classify, exclude, and generally affirm or deny the truth of propositions. Social analysis under the text metaphor asks how power comes to be concentrated in the hands of those who have the authority to interpret reality for others (Dreyfus & Rabinow, 1983).

No aspect of social life has received more critical attention under the text analogy than the social professions, for this is the group in modern societies that has the authority to interpret normality, and thus the power to define and classify others as abnormal and to treat their bodies and their minds. The principal figure behind this line of criticism is the French moral and political philosopher Michel Foucault (e.g., 1980a). Foucault turned social analysis on itself by studying the knowledge, practices, and discourses of what he called the "human sciences," an inclusive term for what I am calling the social sciences and social professions. Foucault was interested primarily in the various modes by which modern societies turn human beings into subjects for investigation, surveillance, and treatment, practices that, he noted, regularly involve various forms of medicalization, exclusion, and confinement. His critiques of the knowledge, practices, and discourses of the social sciences and particular social professions, such as medicine (1975), criminology (1979), and psychiatry (1973a), are attempts to reveal the nature and effects of the power of the social sciences and social professions to interpret normality.

Although in some ways Foucault's work is indistinguishable from that of an historian, the key difference is that he was far less interested in the events of history than in the modes of understanding that produced them. Ultimately, he wanted to know what, in a particular time and place, leads people to believe in what they are doing.

Foucault's primary substantive contribution to social analysis has been a critique of "the way modern societies control and discipline their populations by sanctioning the knowledge-claims and practices of the [social sciences and professions, such as] medicine, psychiatry, psychology, criminology, sociology, and so on" (Philp, 1985, p. 67). In this regard, he argued that the classical notion of political rule based on sovereignty and rights has been subverted by the social sciences and social professions. He called this new type of non-sovereign power "disciplinary power" (Foucault, 1980b, p. 105), a form of power exercised through the knowledge, practices, and discourses of the social sciences and social professions, which together establish the norms for human behavior in modern societies. Although Foucault did not extend his notion of disciplinary power directly to the field of education, others have applied it to the social professions of education (e.g., Cherryholmes, 1988) and special education (Skrtic, 1991). The broader implications of the notion of disciplinary power for modern societies are apparent in Philp's (1985) summary of Foucault's work:

> In workplaces, schoolrooms, hospitals and welfare offices; in the family and the community; and in prisons, mental institutions, courtrooms and tribunals, the human sciences have established their standards of "normality." The normal child, the healthy body, the stable mind...such concepts haunt our ideas about ourselves, and are reproduced and legitimated through the practices of teachers, social workers, doctors, judges, policemen and administrators. The human sciences attempt to define normality; and by establishing this normality as a rule of life for us all, they simultaneously manufacture—for investigation, surveillance and treatment—the vast area of our deviation from this standard. (p. 67)

Foucault provided several methodological guidelines for those who would apply his unique understanding of the human sciences as a form of disciplinary power, two of which are important for present purposes. First, analysts should not focus on the traditional notion of power—the centralized and juridical power of the State, with its various apparati and associated ideologies. Rather, the analyst of disciplinary power should be "concerned with power at its extremities, in its ultimate destinations...that is, in its more regional and local forms and institutions...at the extreme points of its exercise, where it is always less legal in character" (Foucault, 1980b, pp. 96–97). This means that analysts of disciplinary power should be concerned with the nature and effects of the application of human science knowledge, practices, and discourses in particular institutional contexts. They should analyze that which conditions, limits, and institutionalizes the way human science professionals such as teachers, social workers, doctors, psychologists, judges, criminologists, and social scientists actually practice their professions in schools, welfare offices, hospitals, mental institutions, courtrooms, prisons, and universities.

Foucault's second guideline is that the analyst of disciplinary power should understand power as a form of domination associated with subjugation. Foucault, however, did not use subjugation in the sense of an intentional desire of certain people to dominate others. Rather, he used it in the unintentional or unconscious sense of well meaning professionals who, operating under the taken-for-granted conventions and customs of their knowledge tradition, have the effect of turning others into subjects for investigation, surveillance, and treatment. In this regard, the analyst of disciplinary power ultimately should be concerned with the ways in which "subjects are gradually, progressively, really and materially constituted" (Foucault, 1980b, p. 97). For Foucault, these practices are the micro-mechanisms of power modern societies use to control and discipline their populations.

DECONSTRUCTING AND RECONSTRUCTING EDUCATIONAL PRACTICES AND DISCOURSES

Applied to the field of education, a Foucauldian analysis of disciplinary power would be concerned with the nature and effects of the practices and discourses educators and special educators employ both to define normality in schools and, after establishing this standard, to constitute as subjects those students who deviate from it. Such an analysis would begin by considering the nature and effects of the various techniques, procedures, and apparati of investigation, surveillance, treatment, exclusion, confinement, and medicalization these professions have developed and refined. Then, in the interest of determining what led educators and special educators to believe in the legitimacy of their practices and discourses, one would consider that which has conditioned, limited, and institutionalized the knowledge tradition that stands behind these particular practices and discourses (see Cherryholmes, 1988; Skrtic, 1991).

The goal of such an analysis is to delegitimize or deconstruct these practices and discourses by exposing the inconsistencies, contradictions, and silences contained in the knowledge tradition that both underwrites and sustains them. Ultimately, however, the purpose of deconstructing the practices and discourses of educators and special educators is to clear the path for reconstructing them in a way that recognizes and avoids their unintentional negative consequences.

Because the world is ambiguous and complex, to be productive, a field of endeavor—be it a physical science, a social science, or a social profession—must have a way of unrandomizing complexity. Thus, like a scientific culture, a professional culture must have a paradigm or knowledge tradition, an accepted way of interpreting the world and acting upon it. Although professionals never can escape the need for an accepted paradigm, they can be reflexive about their knowledge tradition and its implications for individuals and society. Professional autonomy and the objectivist view of professional knowledge, however, mean that, without a paradigm crisis, nothing compels a profession to question its knowledge tradition. As in the physical and social sciences, a crisis in knowledge is a precondition for growth of knowledge and progress in the professions of education and special education.

As we know, progress and the growth of knowledge in the physical or single-paradigm sciences begins with the recognition of anomalies that, because the scientific community is so committed to the correctness of its accepted paradigm, are exposed as a matter of course during normal science. Because their multiple-paradigm status and bureaucratic working conditions conceal and distort anomalies, however, professions such as education and special education need a way to bring their knowledge tradition's inconsistencies, contradictions, and silences to the surface. They need something like deconstruction to register these inconsistencies, contradictions, and silences in the consciousness of the professional culture—register them, that is, as a residue of recalcitrant anomalies that eventually may prompt the suspicion that something is amiss with their accepted knowledge tradition, thus setting the stage for its demise.

Whether such a crisis leads to positive growth and renewal in a profession depends upon the manner in which the professional community reconstructs its professional practices. In the final analysis, reconstruction always involves making pragmatic choices among alternative theories and practices, a process that can take one of two general forms: *naive pragmatism* or *critical pragmatism*. Naive pragmatism values functional efficiency; pure utility or expediency. Although naive pragmatism questions professional practices, it unreflectively accepts the assumptions, theories, and metatheories that stand behind them. As such, it "is socially reproductive, instrumentally and functionally reproducing accepted meanings and conventional organizations, institutions, and ways of doing things for good or ill" (Cherryholmes, 1988, p. 151). Critical pragmatism approaches decision-making in a way that recognizes and treats as problematic the assumptions, theories, and metatheories that ground professional practices; it accepts the fact that our assumptions, theories, and metatheories themselves require evaluation and reappraisal (Skrtic, 1991).

Critical pragmatism is a method for evaluating and reappraising professional practices and discourses by critically evaluating the assumptions, theories, and metatheories in which they are grounded (see Cherryholmes, 1988; Skrtic, 1991). The goal of critical pragmatism, however, is not certainty; it does not seek objective knowledge or monological truth. Rather, the goal is education, or self-formation; it is a pedagogical process of remaking ourselves as we redefine our practices and discourses in alternative theoretical and metatheoretical languages (Gadamer, 1975). As such, critical pragmatism is premised on a continual search for "new and more interesting [ways] of expressing ourselves, and thus of coping with the world. From [this] educational...point of view, the way things are said is more important than the possession of truths" (Rorty, 1979, p. 359). Rorty referred to this project of finding new and better ways of describing ourselves as *edification*. Applied to the professions, edification is a mode of inquiry that, by constantly forcing professionals to face the fact that what they think, do, say, write, and read as professionals is shaped by convention, helps them avoid the delusion that they can know themselves, their profession, their clients, "or anything else, except under optional descriptions" (Rorty, 1979, p. 379). For Rorty (1989) edification is:

> ...the same as the "method" of utopian politics or revolutionary science (as opposed to parliamentary politics or normal science). The method is to redescribe lots and lots of

things in new ways, until you...tempt the rising generation to...look for...new scientific equipment or new social institutions. This sort of philosophy...works holistically and pragmatically. It says things like "try thinking of it this way"—or more specifically, "try to ignore the apparently futile traditional questions by substituting the following new and possibly interesting questions." (p. 9)

SUMMARY

This chapter begins the process of deconstructing the special education knowledge tradition by deconstructing the traditional objectivist view of the professions and professional knowledge. My intent has been to raise doubts in the reader's mind about the legitimacy of the process of professionalization itself. In the next chapter I continue the process of deconstruction by focusing specifically on the inconsistencies, contradictions, and silences contained in the special education knowledge tradition. The purpose of deconstructing the special education knowledge tradition is to clear the path for reconstructing it in a way that recognizes and avoids its unintentional negative consequences.

REFERENCES

Althusser, L. (1969). *For Marx*. Hamondsworth, England: Penguin.

Angeles, P. A. (1981). *Dictionary of philosophy*. New York: Barnes & Noble Books.

Antonio, R. J. (1989). The normative foundations of emancipatory theory: Evolutionary versus pragmatic perspectives. *American Journal of Sociology, 94*(4), pp. 721–748.

Barnes, B. (1982). *T. S. Kuhn and social science*. New York: Columbia University Press.

Barnes, B. (1985). Thomas Kuhn. In Q. Skinner (Ed.), *The return of grand theory in the human sciences* (pp. 83–101). Cambridge, England: Cambridge University Press.

Baudrillard, J. (1983). *Simulations*. P. Foss, P. Patton and P. Beitchman (Trans.). New York: Semiotext(e), Inc.

Berger, P. L., & Luckmann, L. (1967). *The social construction of reality*. New York: Doubleday.

Bergner, J. T. (1981). *The origin of formalism in social science*. Chicago: University of Chicago Press.

Bernstein, B. (1971). *Class, codes and control, volume 1: Theoretical studies towards a sociology of language*. London: Routledge & Kegan Paul.

Bernstein, R. J. (1971). *Praxis and action: Contemporary philosophies of human activity*. Philadelphia: University of Pennsylvania Press.

Bernstein, R. J. (1976). *The restructuring of social and political theory*. Philadelphia: University of Pennsylvania Press.

Bernstein, R. J. (1983). *Beyond objectivism and relativism: Science, hermeneutics, and praxis*. Philadelphia: University of Pennsylvania Press.

Bernstein, R. J. (1991). *The new constellation*. Cambridge, England: Polity Press.

Bledstein, B. J. (1976). *The culture of professionalism: The middle class and the development of higher education in America*. New York: W. W. Norton and Company.

Bloor, D. C. (1976). *Knowledge and social imagery*. London: Routledge & Kegan Paul.

Bourdieu, P. (1977). *Outline of a theory of practice*. R. Nice (Trans.). Cambridge, England: Cambridge University Press.

Braverman, H. (1974). *Labor and monopoly capital: The degradation of work in the twentieth century*. New York: Monthly Review.

Burrell, G., & Morgan, G. (1979). *Sociological paradigms and organizational analysis.* London: Heinemann Educational Books.

Caputo, J. D. (1987). *Radical hermeneutics: Repetition, deconstruction, and the hermeneutic project.* Bloomington, IN: Indiana University Press.

Champion, R. H. (1984). Faculty reported use of research in teacher preparation courses: Six instructional scenarios. *Journal of Teacher Education, 35*(5), 9–12.

Cherryholmes, C. H. (1988). *Power and criticism: Poststructuralist investigations in education.* New York: Teachers College Press.

Chomsky, N. (1959). Review of Skinner's "Verbal Behavior." *Language, 35,* 26–58.

Clark, R. (1971). *Einstein: The life and times.* New York: Avon Books.

Dallmayr, F. R., & McCarthy, T. A. (1977). *Understanding and social inquiry.* Notre Dame, IN: University of Notre Dame Press.

DeGeorge, R. T. (1982). *Business ethics.* New York: Macmillan.

Derrida, J. (1982). *Margins of philosophy.* A. Bass (Trans.). Chicago: The University of Chicago Press.

Dewey, J. (1982). Reconstruction in philosophy. In J. A. Boydston (Ed.), *John Dewey: The middle works, 1899–1924* (Vol. 12, pp. 77–201). Carbondale: Southern Illinois University Press. (Original work published 1920)

Dewey, J. (1988). The quest for certainty. In J. A. Boydston (Ed.), *John Dewey: The later works, 1925–1953* (Vol. 4, pp. 1–250). Carbondale: Southern Illinois University Press. (Original work published 1929)

Dreyfus, H. L., & Rabinow, P. (1983). *Michel Foucault: Beyond structualism and hermeneutics.* Chicago: University of Chicago Press.

Etzioni, A. (1961). *A comparative analysis of complex organizations.* New York: Free Press.

Feigl, H. (1970). The "orthodox" view of theories: Remarks in defense as well as critique. In M. Radner & S. Winokur (Eds.), *Minnesota studies in the philosophy of science* (Vol. 4). Minneapolis: University of Minnesota Press.

Feyerabend, P. (1975). *Against method.* London: Verso.

Foucault, M. (1973a). *Madness and civilization: A history of insanity in the age of reason.* R. Howard (Trans.). New York: Vintage/Random House. (Original work published 1961)

Foucault, M. (1973b). *The order of things: An archaeology of the human sciences.* New York: Vintage/Random House. (Original work published 1966)

Foucault, M. (1975). *The birth of the clinic: An archeology of medical perception.* A. M. Sheridan Smith (Trans.). New York: Vintage/Random House. (Original work published 1963)

Foucault, M. (1979). *Discipline and punish: The birth of the prison.* New York: Vintage/Random House. (Original work published 1975)

Foucault, M. (1980a). *Power/knowledge: Selected interviews and other writings, 1972–1977.* C. Gordon (Ed.); C. Gordon, L. Marshall, J. Meplam & K. Soper (Trans.). New York: Pantheon Books.

Foucault, M. (1980b). Two lectures. In M. Foucault, *Power/knowledge: Selected interviews and other writings, 1972–1977* (C. Gordon, Ed.; C. Gordon, L. Marshall, J. Mepham & K. Soper, Trans.) (pp. 78–108). New York: Pantheon Books.

Gadamer, H. G. (1975). *Truth and method.* G. Barden and J. Cumming (Eds. and Trans.). New York: Seabury Press.

Geertz, C. (1983). *Local knowledge: Further essays in interpretive anthropology.* New York: Basic Books.

Giddens, A. (1977). *Studies in social and political theory.* London: Hutchinson.

Giddens, A. (1981). A contemporary critique of historical materialism. London: Macmillan.

Giddens, A., & Turner, J. (Eds.). (1987). *Social theory today.* Stanford, CA: Stanford University Press.

Glazer, N. (1974). The schools of the minor professions. *Minerva, 12*(3), 246–364.

Greenwood, E. (1981). Attributes of a profession. In N. Gilbert and H. Specht (Eds.), *The emergence of social work and social welfare* (pp. 241–255). Itasca, IL: F. E. Peacock.

Guba, E. G. (1990). *The paradigm dialog.* Newbury Park, CA: Sage Publications.

Haberman, M. (1983). Research on preservice laboratory and clinical experiences: Implications for teacher education. In K. R. Howey & W. Gardner (Eds.), *The education of teachers: A look ahead* (pp. 98–117). New York: Longman.

Habermas, J. (1971). *Knowledge and human interests.* J. J. Shapiro (Trans.). Boston: Beacon Press. (Original work published 1968)

Harre, R. (1981). The positivist-empiricist approach and its alternative. In P. Reason & J. Rowan (Eds.), *Human inquiry: A sourcebook of new paradigm research* (pp. 3–17). New York: Wiley.

Haskell, T. L. (1984). *The authority of experts: Studies in history and theory.* Bloomington, IN: Indiana University Press.

Held, D. (1980). *Introduction to Critical Theory.* Berkeley and Los Angeles: University of California Press.

Hesse, M. (1980). *Revolutions and reconstructions in the philosophy of science.* Bloomington: Indiana University Press.

Hughes, E. C. (1963). Professions. *Daedalus, 92,* 655–668.

James, W. (1975). Pragmatism. In F. Burkhardt, F. Bowers & I. K. Skrupskelis (Eds.), *William James: Pragmatism and the meaning of truth* (pp. 1–166). Cambridge, MA: Harvard University Press. (Original work published 1907)

Jay, M. (1973). *The dialectical imagination.* Boston: Little, Brown.

Kloppenberg, J. T. (1986). *Uncertain victory: Social Democracy and Progressivism in European and American thought, 1870–1920.* New York: Oxford University Press.

Knorr, K. D., Krohn, R., & Whitley, R. (Eds.). (1981). *The social process of scientific investigation.* Boston: D. Reidel Publishing.

Koehler, V. (1985). Research on preservice teacher education. *Journal of Teacher Education, 36*(1), 23–30.

Krohn, R. (1981). Introduction: Toward the empirical study of scientific practice. In K. D. Knorr, R. Krohn, & R. Whitley (Eds.), *The social process of scientific investigation* (pp. 7–25). Boston: D. Reidel Publishing.

Kuhn, T. S. (Ed.). (1962). *The structure of scientific revolutions.* Chicago: University of Chicago Press.

Kuhn, T. S. (1970a). Reflections on my critics. In I. Lakatos & A. Musgrave (Eds.), *Criticism and the growth of knowledge* (pp. 231–278). Cambridge, England: Cambridge University Press.

Kuhn, T. S. (1970b). *The structure of scientific revolutions* (2nd ed.). Chicago: University of Chicago Press.

Kuhn, T. S. (1977). The essential tension: Tradition and innovation in scientific research. In T. S. Kuhn (Ed.), *The essential tension: Selected studies in scientific tradition and change* (pp. 225–239). Chicago: University of Chicago Press.

Lakatos, I., & Musgrave, A. (Eds.). (1970). *Criticism and the growth of knowledge.* Cambridge, England: Cambridge University Press.

Law, J. (1975). Is epistemology redundant? *Philosophy of the Social Sciences, 5,* 317–337.

Lévi-Strauss, C. (1963). *Totemism.* Boston: Beacon Press.

Lincoln, Y. S., & Guba, E. G. (1985). *Naturalistic inquiry.* Beverly Hills, CA: Sage.

Lyotard, J. (1984). *The postmodern condition: A report on knowledge.* Minneapolis: University of Minnesota Press. (Original work published 1979)

Marcuse, H. (1964). *One-dimensional man.* Boston: Beacon Press.

Masterman, M. (1970). The nature of a paradigm. In I. Lakatos & A. Musgrave (Eds.), *Criticism and the growth of knowledge* (pp. 59–89). Cambridge, England: Cambridge University Press.

Mead, G. H. (1934). *Mind, self, and society: From the standpoint of a social behaviorist.* C. W. Morris (Ed.). Chicago: University of Chicago Press.

Mintzberg, H. (1979). *The structuring of organizations.* Englewood Cliffs, NJ: Prentice Hall.

Morgan, G. (Ed.). (1983). *Beyond method: Strategies for social research.* Beverly Hills, CA: Sage.

Morgan, G., & Smircich, L. (1980). The case of qualitative research. *Academy of Management Review, 5,* 491–500.

Mulkay, M. J. (1979). *Science and the sociology of knowledge.* London: Allen & Unwin.

Outhwaite, W. (1987). *New philosophies of social science: Realism, hermeneutics and Critical Theory.* London: Macmillan.

Parsons, T. (1968). Professions. *International encyclopedia of the social sciences.* New York: Macmillan.

Peirce, C. S. (1931–35). C. Hartshorne and P. Weiss (Eds.), *Collected papers of Charles Sanders Peirce.* Cambridge, MA: Harvard University Press.

Phillips, D. C. (1987). *Philosophy, science, and social inquiry: Contemporary methodological controversies in social science and related applied fields of research.* Oxford, England: Pergamon Press.

Phillips, D. (1973). Paradigms, falsifications and sociology. *Acta Sociologica, 16*, 13–31.

Philp, M. (1985). Michel Foucault. In Q. Skinner (Ed.), *The return of grand theory in the human sciences* (pp. 65–81). Cambridge, England: Cambridge University Press.

Popper, K. R. (1970). Normal science and its dangers. In I. Lakatos & A. Musgrave (Eds.), *Criticism and the growth of knowledge* (pp. 51–58). Cambridge, England: Cambridge University Press.

Ravetz, J. R. (1971). *Scientific knowledge and its social problems.* Oxford, England: Clarendon Press.

Reese, W. L. (1980). *Dictionary of philosophy and religion.* Atlantic Highlands, NJ: Humanities.

Ricoeur, P. (1981). *Paul Ricoeur: Hermeneutics and the human sciences.* J. B. Thompson (Ed. and Trans.). Cambridge, England: Cambridge University Press.

Ritzer, G. (1980). *Sociology: A multiple paradigm science* (rev. ed.). Boston: Allyn & Bacon.

Ritzer, G. (1983). *Sociological theory.* New York: Knopf.

Ritzer, G. (1990). *Frontiers of social theory: The new syntheses.* New York: Columbia University Press.

Rorty, R. (1979). *Philosophy and the mirror of nature.* Princeton, NJ: Princeton University Press.

Rorty, R. (1982). *Consequences of pragmatism.* Minneapolis: University of Minnesota Press.

Rorty, R. (1989). *Contingency, irony, and solidarity.* Cambridge, England: Cambridge University Press.

Rorty, R. (1991). *Objectivity, relativism, and truth: Philosophical papers, volume 1.* Cambridge, England: Cambridge University Press.

Saussure, F. (1966). *Course in general linguistics.* New York: McGraw-Hill.

Schein, E. H. (1968). Organizational socialization and the profession of management. *Industrial Management Review, 9*(2), 1–16.

Schein, E. H. (1972). *Professional education.* New York: McGraw-Hill.

Schön, D. A. (1983). *The reflective practitioner: How professionals think in action.* New York: Basic Books.

Shils, E. (1978). The order of learning in the United States from 1865 to 1920: The ascendancy of the universities. *Minerva, 16*(2), 159–195.

Shimony, A. (1977). Is observation theory-laden? A problem in naturalistic epistemology. In R. G. Colodny (Ed.), *Logic, laws and life.* Pittsburgh: University of Pittsburgh Press.

Skrtic, T. M. (1986). The crisis in special education knowledge: A perspective on perspective. *Focus on Exceptional Children, 18*(7), 1–16.

Skrtic, T. M. (1988). The crisis in special education knowledge. In E. L. Meyen & T. M. Skrtic (Eds.), *Exceptional children and youth: An introduction* (pp. 415–447). Denver: Love Publishing.

Skrtic, T. M. (1990). Social accommodation: Toward a dialogical discourse in educational inquiry. In E. Guba (Ed.), *The paradigm dialog* (pp. 125–135). Newbury Park, CA: Sage Publications.

Skrtic, T. M. (1991). *Behind special education: A critical analysis of professional culture and school organization.* Denver: Love Publishing.

Skrtic, T. M. (1993). The crisis in special education knowledge: A perspective on perspective. In E. Meyen, G. Vergason & R. Whelan (Eds.), *Challenges facing special education* (pp. 165–192). Denver: Love Publishing.

Soltis, J. F. (1984). On the nature of educational research. *Educational Researcher, 13*(9), 5–10.

Wilensky, H. L. (1964). The professionalization of everyone? *American Journal of Sociology, 70*, 137–148.

Wolf, F. A. (1981). *Taking the quantum leap.* San Francisco: Harper & Row.

Zeichner, K. M., & Tabachnick, B. R. (1981). Are the effects of university teacher education washed out by school experience? *Journal of Teacher Education, 32*, 7–11.

THE SPECIAL EDUCATION

KNOWLEDGE TRADITION:

CRISIS AND OPPORTUNITY

THOMAS M. SKRTIC

*I*n this chapter I continue the process of deconstructing the special education knowledge tradition by focusing specifically on its inconsistencies, contradictions, and silences. As the chapter title suggests, the deconstruction or delegitimization of the traditional objectivist view of professional knowledge creates both a crisis and an opportunity for the field of special education—a crisis in that it calls the special education knowledge tradition into question; an opportunity in that a crisis in knowledge is a precondition for growth of knowledge and progress in the field. Thus, although I want to deconstruct the special education knowledge tradition, my ultimate goal is to clear the path for reconstructing it in a way that avoids its unintentional negative consequences, thus reconciling the field's professional knowledge, practices, and discourses with its ethical ideal of serving the best interests of its clients and of society.

A knowledge tradition is the hierarchy of presuppositions that guides and justifies the practices and discourses of communal enterprises such as the physical sciences (Kuhn, 1970; Masterman, 1970), the social sciences (Barnes, 1982; Bernstein, 1983), and the social professions (Schön, 1983; Skrtic, 1986; Chapter 14). The hierarchy of presuppositions that constitutes the special education knowledge tradition includes the metatheories, theories, assumptions, models, practices, and tools that guide and justify what the field's practitioners think, do, say, read, and write as professionals. Each level of the hierarchy is defined and subsumed by the higher levels and, as we know from Chapter 14, all levels ultimately are defined and subsumed by the metatheoretical presuppositions of the functionalist paradigm, the dominant mode of social theorizing during the modern era.

Deconstructing the special education knowledge tradition is complicated by several factors. First, the profession of special education is composed of several subfields organized around categories of exceptionality or disability. This poses a problem because each subfield has a somewhat unique body of professional knowledge (and associated practices and discourses) that reflects the presumed differences among the traditional categories of exceptionality. Nevertheless, behind these surface differences, each subfield subscribes to a more or less common foundation of basic special education professional knowledge. My aim in this chapter is to deconstruct this common foundation of professional knowledge, which is what I am referring to as the special education knowledge tradition.

A second challenge in deconstructing the special education knowledge tradition is deciding whose interpretation of it to accept as the genuine article. To draw a crude analogy, asking special education professionals about the nature of their knowledge tradition is like asking a school of fish about the nature of water. Professionals ordinarily have difficulty specifying their knowledge tradition because it is so basic to them that they take it for granted. Thus, considering a variety of interpretations of the special education knowledge tradition will be helpful, and I do so later in the chapter by presenting key examples of criticism of special education theory and practice that have been put forth by social scientists, as well as by special education professionals and advocates themselves.

Finally, the most significant complication in considering special education's knowledge tradition is the field's relationship to the broader profession of education, as well as the role special education has played historically as an institutional practice of public education. In this regard, we will see that the profession and institutional practice of special education are products of the functionalist conceptualization of education that has been dominant in the 20th century, and particularly the functionalist understanding of the phenomenon of school failure (see also Skrtic, 1986, 1987b, 1988b, 1991a, 1991b; Chapter 18). Thus, I begin deconstructing the special education knowledge tradition by considering the way functionalism has shaped both the institution of public education and the knowledge, practices, and discourses of the various subfields of the profession of education, central among which are the fields of general education and educational administration.

FUNCTIONALIST EDUCATION

TWO DISCOURSES ON SCHOOL FAILURE

As the dominant mode of social theorizing in the modern era, functionalism is the interpretation of social reality that grounds the knowledge, practices, and discourses of the social professions (Glazer, 1974; Schön, 1983). This includes the social profession of education, of course, and thus the various professional fields within it, including general education (Bowles & Gintis, 1976; Feinberg & Soltis, 1985; Giroux, 1981), educational administration (Griffiths, 1983, 1988), and special education (Heshusius, 1982; Iano, 1986; Skrtic, 1986). We know from Chapter 14 that the functionalist or micro-objective paradigm is grounded in the sociology of regulation, takes a more or less microscopic view of social reality, and approaches social science from an objectivist point of view.

Given its realist ontology and deterministic view of human nature, functionalism assumes a single social reality to which humans merely react mechanistically. Moreover, given its positivist epistemology and preference for nomothetic methodologies, it assumes that, by employing the methods of the physical sciences, social science can discover objective truth about this reality and thus predict and control the way humans react to it. Together, the metatheoretical presuppositions of functionalism yield a view of social reality in which the current arrangement of society is assumed to be functional and thus indispensable, if not inherently correct (Ritzer, 1980; Chapter 14).

Because functionalism presupposes that social reality is objective, inherently orderly, and rational, it assumes that social and human problems are pathological (Foucault, 1976; Ritzer, 1980). As such, the dominance of the functionalist world view institutionalized the mutually reinforcing theories of *organizational rationality* and *human pathology* in society and in public education. As a result, when industrialization, immigration, and compulsory school attendance converged to produce large numbers of students who were difficult to teach in traditional classrooms, school failure was reframed as two interrelated problems: inefficient (nonrational) organizations and defective (pathological) students. This distorted the problem of school failure by largely removing it from the general education discourse and compartmentalizing it into two separate but mutually reinforcing discourses on school failure.

The first discourse on school failure was in the developing field of educational administration, which, in the interest of maximizing the efficiency of school organizations, was compelled to rationalize its practices and discourses according to the precepts of "scientific management," an approach to administration specifically designed to increase the efficiency of industrial organizations or factories (see Callahan, 1962; Chapter 18). The second discourse on school failure was in the new field of special education, which emerged as a means to remove and contain the most recalcitrant students, in the interest of maintaining order in the new rationalized school plant (Lazerson, 1983; Sarason & Doris, 1979).

As we know from Chapter 14, the practices and discourses of all social professions are shaped by a hierarchy of presuppositions that are grounded in their respective foundations of disciplinary knowledge. At this point I can add that the practices and discourses of the social professions also are shaped by other presuppositions that are grounded in prevailing social norms. That is, as members of a professional community, the practices and discourses of individuals who have been educated and socialized as professionals are shaped by the presuppositions contained in a body of disciplinary knowledge. Because professionals are members of society as well, however, their practices and discourses also are shaped by the common beliefs and assumptions contained in social norms.

For present purposes, we can think of disciplinary presuppositions as *explicit* presuppositions and normative presuppositions as *implicit* presuppositions. Moreover, the two types of presuppositions are mutually shaping. Disciplinary knowledge informs and changes social norms and, when the resulting changes in social practices and discourses are represented in the empirical descriptions and theoretical constructions of the social disciplines, they inform and thus change disciplinary knowledge (Giddens, 1990).

Given the dominance of functionalism in the social sciences, the most significant social norms relative to the social professions of general education, educational administration, and special education are the functionalist theories of human pathology and organizational rationality. In this sense, human pathology and organizational rationality are more than social science theories; in the modern world they have become social norms.

Because its professional knowledge tradition is grounded in scientific management, the field of educational administration explicitly presupposes that school organizations are rational (Clark, 1985; Griffiths, 1983), and, given the social norm of human pathology, it implicitly presupposes that school failure is pathological (see Skrtic, 1991a, 1991b; below). Conversely, special education's professional grounding in psychology and biology (medicine) means that it explicitly presupposes that school failure is pathological (see Mercer, 1973; Skrtic, 1986; below), and, given the social norm of organizational rationality, implicitly presupposes that school organizations are rational (Skrtic, 1987b, 1988b, 1991a; Chapter 18). Moreover, the knowledge tradition of general education is grounded in psychology *and* scientific management (Cherryholmes, 1988; Spring, 1980), which means that its practices and discourses explicitly presuppose that school organizations are rational and that school failure is a pathological condition (Oakes, 1985; Skrtic, 1991a).

Taken together, these theoretical and normative presuppositions yield four mutually reinforcing assumptions that shape and guide the practices and discourses of all three fields and thus of the institution of public education as a whole. Synthesizing the work of a number of authors (Bogdan & Kugelmass, 1984; Cherryholmes, 1988; McNeil, 1986; Oakes, 1985; Sirotnik & Oakes, 1986; Skrtic, 1986, 1991a, 1991b; Spring, 1980), these assumptions are that:

1. School failure is a (psychologically or sociologically) pathological condition that students have.
2. Differential diagnosis (i.e., homogeneous classification by ability, need, or interest) is an objective and useful practice.
3. Special programming (e.g., in-class ability grouping, curricular tracking, and segregated and pull-out special needs programs) is a rationally conceived and coordinated system of services that benefits diagnosed students.
4. Progress in education (i.e., greater academic achievement and efficiency) is a rational-technical process of incremental improvements in existing diagnostic and instructional practices.

The four guiding assumptions are derived directly from the two functionalist theories; the first two from the theory of human pathology, and the last two from the theory of organizational rationality. Moreover, inquiry in general education (Cherryholmes, 1988; Giroux, 1981), educational administration (Griffiths, 1983, 1988; Lincoln, 1985), and special education (Poplin, 1987; Skrtic, 1986) is dominated by functionalist methodologies, which favor data over theory and thus assume that empirical data are objective and self-evident (Churchman, 1971; Mitroff & Pondy, 1974). Thus, research in these fields produces and interprets empirical data on student outcomes and school effects intuitively, according to the four guiding assumptions and, ultimately, the two functionalist theories in which they are grounded. This reproduces the status quo in all three fields, which reinforces the four assumptions and, ultimately, reaffirms the functionalist theories of organizational rationality and human pathology in the profession of education, the institution of public education, and society at large.

The implication for the field of special education is that the institutional practice of special education is an artifact or byproduct of the functionalist quest for rationality, order, and certainty in the profession and institution of education, a quest that is both intensified and legitimized by the institutional practice of educational administration (see Chapter 18). In this sense, the institutional practices of special education and educational administration distort the problem of school failure, which ultimately prevents the profession of education from entering into a productive confrontation with uncertainty. And, because uncertainty is a necessary precondition for progress in communal activities such as the physical sciences (Kuhn, 1970), social sciences (Barnes, 1982), and social professions (Schön, 1983; Skrtic, 1991a; Chapter 14), the objectification and legitimization of school failure as student disability prevents public education from moving beyond its functionalist knowledge tradition.

The problem in special education and educational administration has been that, although both fields have experienced enough uncertainty to call their knowledge, practices, and discourses into question (see Chapter 18; below), they have lacked a method for addressing their problems in a critical manner (Bates, 1980, 1987; Foster, 1986; Skrtic, 1986, 1991a; Tomlinson, 1982).

The problem in general education is more fundamental. Not only has it lacked a method of critical discourse (Cherryholmes, 1988; Giroux, 1981, 1983; Sirotnik & Oakes, 1986), but it largely has been prevented from having to confront uncertainty altogether, precisely because of the objectification of school failure as student disability.

As we will see in Chapter 18, the problem in the profession of education is that the functionalist distortion of school failure as student disability eliminates it as an anomaly and thus as an opportunity to call the prevailing knowledge tradition into question. Ultimately, this prevents the institution of public education from seeing that its practices are inconsistent with the democratic ideal of providing every citizen with an education that is both excellent and equitable. At this point, however, let us consider the actual practices of general education and educational administration, which will permit us to see how their functionalist orientation gives rise to the need for an institutional practice such as special education.

FUNCTIONALIST EDUCATION PRACTICES

As the dominant framework for social theorizing in the modern era, functionalism has had differing manifestations in the various social science disciplines, two of which are particularly important for present purposes: functionalist sociology and functionalist psychology. Functionalist sociology is important because, more than any other approach to social inquiry, it embodies the functionalist theory of organizational rationality applied to society and social institutions such as education. As we know from Chapter 14, the sociological functionalist views society as being composed of interrelated parts, each of which is functional because it contributes to the maintenance of the other parts and thus of the system as a whole. Because the parts of society are always changing, and these changes lead to sympathetic changes in other parts of the system, change from the functionalist perspective is essentially an orderly, continuous, and integrated process rather than a disorderly, discontinuous, and disintegrative one (Burrell & Morgan, 1979).

In the extreme, functionalists argue that all parts of society are functional and thus indispensable to the system. This outlook leads to the conservative bias that all current aspects of society should continue to exist, which has the effect of limiting the possibility of fundamental change (Ritzer, 1980).

Functionalist psychology is important because psychology is the explicit disciplinary grounding of the profession of education. Two branches of functionalist psychology are especially relevant in this regard: *psychological behaviorism*, which in the 20th century has dominated education's conceptualization of curriculum and instruction (Giroux, 1981; Resnick & Klopfer, 1989); and *experimental psychology*, which underwrites education's psychometric approach to assessment and evaluation (Cherryholmes, 1988).

The manifestation of functionalism in education is largely a product of both psychological and sociological functionalism, which of course are themselves shaped by the metatheoretical presuppositions of the functionalist paradigm, and thus by the theories of human pathology and organizational rationality. These presuppositions have shaped virtually every aspect of public education in this century, including the accepted view of knowledge itself, which in turn has influenced the common conceptualization of curriculum, instruction, and learning (see Cherryholmes, 1988; Feinberg & Soltis, 1985; Freire, 1970, 1973; Giroux, 1981).

Given functionalism's objectivist ontology and epistemology, knowledge is viewed as certain, objective, and monological—as a body of objective facts about a single reality that exists apart from and prior to humans' appreciation of it. As such, curriculum from the functionalist perspective is the codification of this knowledge into a rationalized or task-analyzed hierarchy of higher- and lower-order facts and skills (Cherryholmes, 1988). Combining this view of knowledge with the functionalist conceptualization of human nature as a deterministic reaction to the environmental contingencies posed by an objective reality, instruction is defined as the application of a systematic technology of behavioral procedures for knowledge and skill acquisition.

Given the functionalist interpretation of knowledge, curriculum, and instruction, the teacher's role is conceptualized as that of a technician who organizes the codified knowledge for efficient presentation and arranges the environmental contingencies to reward and punish desirable and undesirable responses. As such, the learner's role is that of a passive receiver of the factual material and skill training under the conditions imposed by the environmental contingencies (Giroux, 1981; Heshusius, 1986). Learning, then, is understood as "an accumulation of pieces of knowledge and bits of skill...[that are] placed in learners' heads through practice and appropriate rewards" (Resnick & Klopfer, 1989, p. 2).

The same functionalist assumptions underwrite the approach to evaluation in schools, as well as the view of the function of schooling itself (see Feinberg & Soltis, 1985; Giroux, 1981; Skrtic, 1988a). The positivist orientation of functionalist educational psychology yields psychometrics, a quantitative approach to evaluation that serves two functions. On one hand, standardized ability testing is used to group students into relatively homogeneous tracks for efficient delivery of instruction. On the other hand, standardized achievement tests are used to evaluate students' acquisition of the knowledge and skills contained in the rationalized curriculum. Ability testing is assumed to serve the interest of organizational efficiency by reducing student variability within tracks (Oakes, 1985); achievement testing is assumed to serve the interest of economic efficiency by providing a means of credentialing graduates for efficient assignment to occupational roles in business and industry (Meyer & Rowan, 1978). Thus, from the functionalist outlook the function of schooling in society is similar to that of industrial psychology in business and industry: the efficient slotting of workers into occupational roles in the economy (Spring, 1980).

The way schools are organized and managed conforms to the functionalist outlook as well. That is, given the functionalist view of the nature and function of schooling, the formal structure of such a system takes on the configuration of a "machine bureaucracy," the pyramid-shaped, top-down structure of control relations that is common to mass-production firms in business and industry (Callahan, 1962; Haber, 1964; Mintzberg, 1979).

Although I will have much more to say about the nature and implications of this organizational configuration in Chapter 18, at this point we can understand it as a centralized hierarchy of formal authority relations which, in conjunction with scientific management, is assumed to be the most efficient way of organizing and managing schools relative to their primary functions: codifying objective knowledge, implementing behavioral technologies, and awarding credentials. Applied to schools, the goal of scientific management is to assure teacher-proof and learner-proof instruction through standardization of curricular content, instructional procedures, personnel roles, and student classifications, as well as the enforcement of these standards through direct supervision and competency testing of students and, more recently, of teachers (Callahan, 1962; Mintzberg, 1979; Chapter 18).

Managing planned change in such a system follows the procedures that are used to change industrial machine bureaucracies. The assumption is that school organizations are like machines that can be fine-tuned in a rational-technical manner through more standardization of work processes and outcomes, further specification of professional roles and student classifications, and closer supervision of personnel and clients (House, 1979; Wolcott, 1977; Wise, 1979). As such, change is viewed as a matter of fine-tuning the existing system rather than changing it in more fundamental ways or replacing it altogether. From this perspective, change is simply a matter of creating a more efficient machine bureaucracy (Skrtic, 1988b, 1991a; Chapter 18).

Educational accountability from the functionalist perspective amounts to the legal-bureaucratic control of personnel, work processes, and student classifications and outcomes (Martin, Overholt, & Urban, 1976; Skrtic, 1991a; Wise, 1979, 1988). This mode of accountability is based on standardization of services and outcomes and is aimed at efficiency of operation and equal treatment of clients. Accountability premised on equality of treatment through standardization of services and outcomes, however, tends to produce a routinized system that, given the inevitability of client variability, is too rigid to accommodate students whose needs do not correspond to the standardized routines. This, in turn, creates the need for various "special needs" programs—those designed to serve students whose needs are "special" by virtue of the fact that they do not fall within the scope of the organization's conventional instructional models, practices, and tools.

As we will see below and in Chapter 18, although these programs are intended to and, in a sense, actually do serve the interests of students with special educational needs, they largely act to protect the legitimacy of the system by deflecting the problem of school failure onto society, parents, or the students themselves (see Skrtic, 1987b, 1991a, 1991b; Chapter 18). This is accomplished administratively by formally identifying recalcitrant students as economically disadvantaged, culturally or linguistically different, or educationally handicapped or gifted, and subsequently removing them from the system, for all or part of the school day, by assigning them to one of several categorical special needs programs such as Chapter 1, bilingual education, migrant education, and special education.

FUNCTIONALIST SPECIAL EDUCATION

Given the presuppositions of functionalism, we can understand special education as a more extreme version of functionalist education—more extreme in both an objectivist and a microscopic sense. Special education's disciplinary grounding in psychology and biology (see below) yields an approach to diagnosis and intervention premised on diagnostic-prescriptive teaching and behavioristic theory (Bogdan & Knoll, 1988; Skrtic, 1986; Chapter 16). Diagnostic-prescriptive teaching is the attempt to design instructional programs on the basis of test performance, using one of two approaches: ability training or task analysis. Given the lack of a psychometric technology for actualizing the ability training model, however, the preference in special education has been for the task analysis approach (Salvia & Ysseldyke, 1981).

The task analysis version of diagnostic-prescriptive teaching is based on the application of behavioristic theory to instruction in specific knowledge and skills. Relatively complex instructional goals are selected from the rationalized general education curriculum and task analyzed further into subskills, which are taught using an even more systematic application of behavioral procedures for skill acquisition. This more advanced application of behavioral technology is commonly referred to as "systematic instruction," an approach that conceptualizes the special education teacher as even more of a technician than the general education teacher (see, for example, Haring, 1978; White & Haring, 1976).

According to special education applied researchers, systematic instruction is premised on the science of applied behavior analysis, and thus ultimately on the psychological behaviorism of B. F. Skinner (1953, 1957, 1971). According to Haring (1978), systematic instruction is a valid approach because it is grounded in:

> ...the experimental analysis of behavior, which, as a scientific discipline, sought to find a systematic interpretation of human behavior based on generalized principles, or laws, of behavior. The goal of this search for laws of behavior was much the same as in any other branch of science—to make reliable predictions. The development of behavior analysis has been rigorously scientific, beginning with basic laboratory research and slowly generalizing the results to social situations. (p. 21)

Metatheoretically, the form of psychological behaviorism that underwrites systematic instruction and special education's task analysis approach to diagnostic-prescriptive teaching is located in the extreme objectivist region of the functionalist paradigm. Referring to their four-paradigm matrix of modern social scientific knowledge (presented in Chapter 14 and reproduced below as Figure 15.1), Burrell and Morgan (1979) noted that:

> Skinner's perspective is a highly coherent and consistent one in terms of the four strands of the subjective-objective dimension of our analytical scheme. Ontologically, his view is firmly realist; epistemologically, his work is the archetype of positivism; his view of human nature reflects a determinism of an extreme form; [and] the highly nomothetic methodology reflected in his experimental approach is congruent with these other assumptions. (p. 103)

Thus, special education's grounding in the psychometrics and behavioral technology of functionalist psychology locates its knowledge tradition in the most extreme objectivist region of the functionalist paradigm (also see Heshusius, 1982; Iano, 1987; Poplin, 1987; Skrtic, 1986; Tomlinson, 1982), as indicated in Figure 15.1.

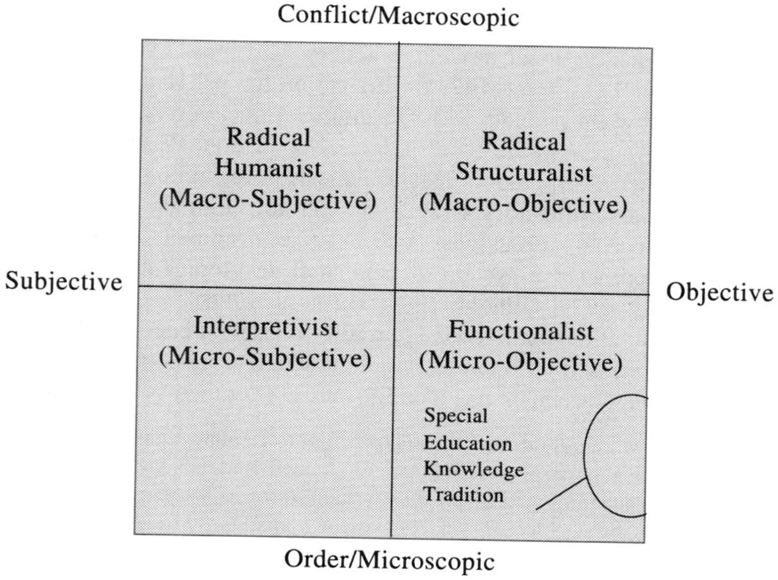

Conflict/Macroscopic

Radical Humanist (Macro-Subjective)	Radical Structuralist (Macro-Objective)
Interpretivist (Micro-Subjective)	Functionalist (Micro-Objective) Special Education Knowledge Tradition

Subjective — Objective

Order/Microscopic

● **FIGURE 15.1**

Paradigmatic status of the special education knowledge tradition

Source: Adapted from T. Skrtic, 1991a, *Behind Special Education: A Critical Analysis of Professional Culture and School Organization*, p. 107, Denver: Love Publishing.

As in the case of the profession of education generally, special education's extreme functionalist outlook means that the assumptions that shape and guide its professional models, practices, and tools are premised on the functionalist theories of human pathology and organizational rationality. Drawing on the work of a number of authors (Bogdan & Kugelmass, 1984; Bogdan & Knoll, 1988; Heshusius, 1982; Iano, 1987; Poplin, 1987; Rist & Harrell, 1982; Skrtic, 1986; Tomlinson, 1982), and restating the assumptions presented above in special education terms, special education's professional practices and discourses are premised on four assumptions, the first two of which are derived from the theory of human pathology and the last two of which are derived from the theory of organizational rationality. The assumptions are that:

1. Disability is a pathological condition that students have.
2. Differential diagnosis is an objective and useful practice.
3. Special education is a rationally conceived and coordinated system of services that benefits diagnosed students.
4. Progress in special education is a rational-technical process of incremental improvements in existing diagnostic and instructional practices.

Given these assumptions, and the functionalist theories and metatheories upon which they are premised, progress in the field of special education is conceptualized in terms of using positivistic methodologies to improve and extend its technology of diagnostic and instructional models, practices, and tools. As we will see below (and again in Chapter 18), PL 94–142, the Education for All Handicapped Children Act of 1975 (EHA) (now Individuals with Disabilities Education Act), is the actualization of this notion of progress in the field of special education. When it was enacted, the law was perceived as an improved special education technology, an advanced model of diagnostic (nondiscriminatory evaluation, multidisciplinary assessment) and instructional (parent participation, least restrictive environment, individualized education programs, comprehensive system of personnel development) practices and tools (see Abeson & Zettel, 1977; Gilhool, 1989; Turnbull, 1986).

Given its functionalist knowledge tradition, special education's sense of itself as a profession is premised on an implicitly functionalist version of the liberal ideology of benevolent humanitarianism. As Tomlinson (1982) noted in this regard:

> The way in which children are categorized out of...mainstream education and into special education is generally regarded as enlightened and advanced, and an instance of the obligation placed upon civilized society to care for its weaker members. Special education is permeated by an ideology of benevolent humanitarianism, which provides [the] moral framework within which professionals...work. (p. 5)

True to both the functionalist and liberal ideologies, special educators' traditional conceptualization of an effective and equitable system of education is based on implicitly accepting the inevitability of the status quo in public education, while at the same time seeking progress in the form of quantitative and bureaucratic solutions to educational inequities (see Skrtic, 1991a; Chapter 18). In effect, the field of special education calculates progress toward an effective and just educational system in terms of identifying more students as disabled and securing for them and their parents more rights, resources, and participation within the general education system. Ultimately these outcomes are to be achieved bureaucratically through procedural compliance with EHA rules and regulations and administrative adherence to the logic of mainstreaming.

To this point in the discussion, we have seen that the institutional practice of special education is a product of the functionalist view of education that has been dominant in the 20th century, and particularly the functionalist conceptualization of the problem of school failure. We also have seen that the need for a professional field such as special education within the institution of public education emerged directly from the unintentional negative effects of the functionalist practices and discourses of the fields of general education and educational administration. By relating special education to the functionalist theories and practices of the broader profession of education, and establishing its historical role within the institution of public education, my intent has been to show that, far from being a rational and just response to the problem of school failure, special education is merely an historically situated, social construction of the 20th century profession and institution of education.

There is nothing inherently correct or true about special education. Had the profession of education been grounded in a different discipline or in one of the other paradigms of modern social knowledge, special education would be something other than what it is today. Indeed, had the profession of education been grounded in a different discipline or paradigm, the need for an institutional practice such as special education may not have emerged at all.

PRACTICAL CRITICISM OF SPECIAL EDUCATION

Like all social professions, the knowledge tradition of the field of special education is based on the positivist model of professional knowledge described in Chapter 14 (see Schein, 1972; Skrtic, 1986). As the reader will recall, the positivist model is premised on a threefold hierarchy of knowledge, at the top of which is the theoretical knowledge of one or more underlying discipline or basic science, which is assumed to be objective knowledge about social reality. This is the knowledge upon which the legitimacy of the profession's knowledge tradition ultimately rest. At the next lower level of the hierarchy is applied knowledge, the knowledge that applied scientists develop by engineering the profession's grounding theoretical knowledge into the models, practices, and tools necessary to solve the field's problems relative to diagnosis and intervention. Finally, at the lowest level of the hierarchy is the practical knowledge of the professional practitioner. Practical knowledge is premised on the field's underlying theoretical and applied knowledge and takes the form of the professional knowledge, skills, attitudes, and norms necessary for actually performing services to clients.

According to the model, the special education knowledge tradition is grounded in and thus legitimized by the theoretical knowledge of one or more underlying social disciplines. At the applied science level of the field, this theoretical knowledge is transformed into applied knowledge, which takes the form of the models, practices, and tools needed to solve the day-to-day problems of special education practice. Finally, through an extended program of professional education and socialization, special education's theoretically grounded applied knowledge is transmitted to the special education practitioner in the form of the knowledge, skills, attitudes, and norms necessary to apply the models, practices, and tools of the profession. The performance of special education professional services to students is based on practical knowledge, conceptualized as the result of a rational process in which objective theoretical knowledge is engineered into the applied knowledge needed to solve the diagnostic and instructional problems of special education practice.

Historically, there have been two types of criticism of special education theory and practice: *practical* criticism, which focuses exclusively on special education models, practices, and tools; and *theoretical* criticism, which also criticizes the field's models, practices, and tools but, more important, does so by criticizing the implicit theories and guiding assumptions upon which they are premised. Whereas practical criticism has been mounted by parents, special education consumers and advocates, and special education professionals themselves, until recently theoretical criticism has come largely from the social sciences. As we will see, however, an important development in the 1980s has been the emergence of a critical theoretical discourse within the field of special education.

Of the two types of criticism of special education, practical criticism has been more apparent to the special education professional community and thus has had a greater impact on the way special education actually is practiced in public education. We can think of the way special education currently is practiced in schools as a response to criticism of the field's previous models, practices, and tools. Although this dialectical relationship between practical criticism and changes in practice can be traced over the entire history of the field, two episodes of criticism and change are particularly important for present purposes.

The first episode, which I will refer to as the "mainstreaming debate," occurred in the 1960s and 1970s, a period in which special education's traditional model of segregated special classrooms and schools was criticized and subsequently replaced with the mainstreaming model. A second episode of criticism and change is under way today. It began in earnest in the 1980s with sharp criticism of the EHA and the mainstreaming model and several proposals for a more integrated or inclusive approach to special education. I will refer to this current episode of criticism and change as the "inclusion debate."

THE MAINSTREAMING DEBATE

At the height of the political ferment of the 1960s, parents, special education consumers and advocates, and special education applied scientists and practitioners used the period's increased sensitivity to human and civil rights to mount a case against the ethics and efficacy of special education as it was practiced at that time. The argument against the traditional segregated model of special education was that it and its associated practices and tools were racially biased, instructionally ineffective, and psychologically and socially damaging (Blatt & Kaplan, 1966; Dunn, 1968; Johnson, 1962). This particular round of practical criticism led to victories in courtrooms and statehouses across the country and eventually in the U.S. Congress, which ultimately redefined special education practice through the statutory mandate of the EHA.

The EHA mandated a free, appropriate public education for all students with disabilities in the least restrictive environment (LRE) possible. Although the law did not mandate mainstreaming per se (Abeson & Zettel, 1977), the mainstreaming or "cascade of services" model (Deno, 1970; Dunn, 1973; Reynolds, 1962; Chapter 2) became the "legal preference" for complying with the LRE principle (Turnbull & Turnbull, 1978, p. 149). As such, implementation of the EHA and the mainstreaming model changed special education practice by changing the field's structural relationship to general education and by extending to students and their parents certain constitutional rights and procedural safeguards including, among others, the right to education or treatment in the most integrated setting possible, participation in decision making, and recourse through due process of law.

Of course, the EHA did not end critical commentary on special education practice. Public debate and legal action over the precise meaning of concepts such as appropriate education and least restrictive environment have continued until today (see Turnbull, 1993). The point is that, although practical criticism resulted in changes in special education practice, the changes brought about by the EHA did not result from theoretical criticism. The law and the changes in practice it introduced were the product of practical criticism—moral, legal, and political arguments against the ethics and efficacy of special education models, practices, and tools (Ballard-Campbell & Semmel, 1981; Biklen, 1985) and not arguments against the theoretical knowledge and guiding assumptions in which these models, practices, and tools were grounded (Skrtic, 1986, 1988a).

THE INCLUSION DEBATE

The first round of practical criticism of special education subsided somewhat in 1975 with enactment of the EHA and broad adoption of the mainstreaming model, both of which were assumed to be solutions to the problems associated with the segregated special classroom model (Abeson & Zettel, 1977; Dunn, 1968). Over the past decade, however, a new episode of practical criticism has emerged. The debate over what originally was known as the "regular education initiative" (see, for example, Davis, 1989; Fuchs & Fuchs, 1991; Skrtic, 1987b, 1988b, 1991a) and, more recently, as the "inclusion" or "inclusive education" movement (see, for example, Goetz & Sailor, 1990; Stainback & Stainback, 1992) grew out of recognition among some of the leading figures in the field (see below) that the practices associated with the EHA and mainstreaming had created virtually the same problems as the special classroom model: racial, cultural, and linguistic bias; instructional ineffectiveness; and psychological and social damage to students (see Heller, Holtzman, & Messick, 1982; Wang, Reynolds & Walberg, 1987).

No one in the special education community disputes that some positive changes have occurred since 1975, at least for some students (see Will, 1984, 1986). Nevertheless, the implication is that, rather than resolving the special education problems of the 1960s and 1970s, the EHA and mainstreaming merely reproduced them in the 1980s and 1990s (see Skrtic, 1987b, 1988b). Although the inclusion model has opposition, even those who oppose it agree that the EHA and mainstreaming have problems that should be addressed (see Fuchs & Fuchs, 1991; Skrtic, 1991a, 1991b). Critics of the inclusive education reform proposals are concerned, however, that the proposed changes could result in a loss of hard-won rights and resources and, in the worst case, a full-circle return to the unacceptable conditions that existed before the EHA (Kauffman, 1988, 1989, 1991; Kauffman, Gerber, & Semmel, 1988).

Practical criticism of the assessment and classification practices of the EHA began to appear in the early 1970s (Hobbs, 1975; Kirp, 1973), as the law was being formulated. But the first practical criticism of the mainstreaming model, in the language of what was to become the inclusion debate, appeared in November 1976, barely a year after the EHA had been enacted. In this criticism, Reynolds (1976; cf. Reynolds & Birch, 1977) rejected the mainstreaming or cascade of services model as being too "place"-oriented and proposed instead an approach to special education premised on making "regular classrooms...more diverse educational environments, which would diminish the need to develop and use separate specialized educational environments" (1976, p. 8). According to Reynolds, this was to be accomplished "through the redistribution of resources and energies, through training, and, finally, through the redistribution of students" (p. 18).

Although in effect Reynolds started the inclusion debate in 1976, the push for inclusive education did not emerge as a full-scale reform movement until the early 1980s. Since then, a substantial body of literature supporting the inclusion concept has been produced by a number of authors (e.g., Biklen, 1985; Biklen & Zollers, 1986; Goetz & Sailor, 1990; Sailor, 1989; Snell, 1991), but primarily by four teams of inclusion proponents whose names have become synonymous with the concept. The four teams are: (a) Maynard Reynolds and Margaret Wang (Reynolds, 1988, 1991; Reynolds & Wang, 1983; Reynolds, Wang, & Walberg, 1987; Wang, 1981, 1988, 1989a, 1989b; Wang & Reynolds, 1985, 1986; Wang, Reynolds, & Walberg, 1985, 1986, 1987, 1988, 1989; Wang & Walberg, 1988); (b) M. Stephen Lilly and Marleen Pugach (Lilly, 1986, 1987, 1989; Pugach & Lilly, 1984); (c) Susan Stainback and William Stainback (Stainback & Stainback, 1984b, 1985a, 1985b, 1987a, 1987b, 1989, 1991, 1992; Stainback, Stainback, Courtnage, & Jaben, 1985; Stainback, Stainback, & Forest, 1989; Villa, Thousand, Stainback, & Stainback, 1992); and (d) Alan Gartner and Dorothy Kerzner Lipsky (Gartner, 1986; Gartner & Lipsky, 1987, 1989; Lipsky & Gartner, 1987, 1989a, 1989b, 1991).

In this literature the proponents of inclusion present two lines of argument. The first criticizes the ethics and efficacy of the current special education system, and the second argues for certain reforms in general and special education intended to correct the current situation by restructuring the separate general and special education systems into a more flexible, unitary system of public education and, depending on the specific inclusive education reform proposal, integrating some, most, or all students with special educational needs into it full-time (see Chapter 18). Referring more or less to a common body of EHA implementation research (for reviews, see Wang et al., 1987; Gartner & Lipsky, 1987; Lipsky & Gartner, 1989a), the inclusion proponents' arguments against the current system of special education point to a number of problems related to the diagnostic practices and tools associated with the elaborate student classification model established by the EHA, as well as problems related to the instructional practices and tools associated with the pull-out approach of mainstreaming.

Although each of the inclusive education reform proposals is somewhat unique (see Chapter 18), all of the inclusion proponents agree that the diagnostic and instructional models, practices, and tools associated with the EHA and mainstreaming are fundamentally flawed, particularly for students considered to have mild to moderate disabilities, a group that, depending on how it is characterized, represents from 68% to 90% of the students served under the EHA (see Algozzine & Korinek, 1985; Reynolds & Lakin, 1987; Shepard, 1987; Wang et al., 1989).

The first published reactions to the inclusion concept (Lieberman, 1985; Mesinger, 1985) were decidedly negative but focused exclusively on one inclusive education position paper (i.e., Stainback & Stainback, 1984b). These were followed by reactions from three formal or informal subgroups within the field, which, although sensitive to current problems and generally supportive of reform, merely called for more information about the new reform proposals (Teacher Education Division, 1987), specified a set of preconditions of reform (Heller & Schilit, 1987), or proposed a mechanism for interpreting information and building a consensus within the special education professional and advocacy community (Skrtic, 1987a).

At that point in the development of the debate, neither these reactions nor those of others who commented on the implications of the inclusion concept (e.g., Davis, 1989; Davis & McCaul, 1988; Lieberman, 1988; Sapon-Shevin, 1988; Skrtic, 1987b) had much of an impact on the course of events. A full-blown controversy began to emerge in 1988, however, when the *Journal of Learning Disabilities* (*JLD*) published a *tour de force* response to the inclusion concept by several of the leading figures in the three mild disability subfields of mental retardation, emotional disturbance, and learning disabilities, who, to one degree or another, opposed the inclusive education reform proposals (Bryan, Bay, & Donahue, 1988; Hallahan, Kauffman, Lloyd, & McKinney, 1988; Hallahan, Keller, McKinney, Lloyd, & Bryan, 1988; Kauffman et al., 1988; Keogh, 1988; Lloyd, Crowley, Kohler, & Strain, 1988; McKinney & Hocutt, 1988; Schumaker & Deshler, 1988).

Since publication of these reaction papers, the controversy over inclusive education has been fueled largely by a series of publications by the proponents that promote and expand upon the concept (see above) and a number of rebuttals and counterproposals written by some of the authors of the *JLD* papers and others (e.g., Anderegg & Vergason, 1988; Braaten, Kauffman, Braaten, Polsgrove, & Nelson, 1988; Bryan, Bay, Lopez-Reyna, & Donahue, 1991; Council for Children with Behavioral Disorders, 1989; Gerber, 1988a, 1988b; Kauffman, 1988, 1989, 1991; Vergason & Anderegg, 1989; Walker & Bullis, 1991).

The controversial nature of the debate and the extent to which it has divided the field are abundantly clear in the inclusion literature. For example, the inclusion advocates have characterized the opponents as segregationists (Wang & Walberg, 1988) and have compared the current system of special education to slavery (Stainback & Stainback, 1987b) and apartheid (Lipsky & Gartner, 1987). The inclusion opponents have responded by characterizing the proponents as misguided "abolitionists" (Fuchs & Fuchs, 1991, p. 241) and politically naive liberals who are playing into the hands of political conservatives who wish to continue the Reagan-Bush policy of "decreasing federal support for education, including the education of vulnerable children and youth" (Kauffman, 1989, p. 7). When one cuts through this rhetoric, however, the inclusion debate turns on two sets of issues: the ethics and efficacy of the diagnostic and instructional models, practices, and tools associated with the EHA and mainstreaming on one hand, and the wisdom and feasibility of the inclusive education reform proposals on the other.

I will present an in-depth analysis of the arguments put forth in the inclusion debate in a subsequent section of this chapter (also see Chapter 18). At this point, however, I want to note the similarities and differences between the mainstreaming and inclusion debates, both as a way of illustrating the fundamental inadequacy of practical criticism for resolving problems of special education practice and as a way of introducing my discussion of theoretical criticism of the special education knowledge tradition.

COMPARING THE MAINSTREAMING AND INCLUSION DEBATES

The inclusion debate parallels the mainstreaming debate in several important ways. First, in both cases the ethics and efficacy of special education practices are criticized and a new approach is proposed. In the 1960s, the target of criticism was the special classroom model, and mainstreaming emerged as the solution. Today, mainstreaming is under attack and the inclusive education approach is being advocated as the solution.

Second, in both cases the new approach draws opposition and the field is divided. Although mainstreaming had some opposition (e.g., Keogh & Levitt, 1976; MacMillan & Semmel, 1977), that debate was far less divisive than the inclusion debate because, although mainstreaming was radical for its time, it was far less ambitious than inclusion and, moreover, there was far less to lose in the 1960s in terms of hard-won special education rights, resources, and recognition. In fact, we will see below that the inclusion debate not only has divided the field of special education into two camps, inclusion proponents and opponents, but more recently it has divided the inclusion proponents themselves into two camps over the issue of which students are to be integrated into the general education classrooms of the new unitary system.

The third parallel between the mainstreaming and inclusion debates is that both of them take place during a period of apparent reform in general education. In the 1960s, Dunn (1968) argued that mainstreaming was a real possibility because it was consistent with what he called the "American Revolution in Education" (p. 10), his term for a number of apparent reforms in general education. These included the introduction of more powerful instructional technologies, such as individualized instruction, teaching machines, computers, and educational television, as well as attempts to restructure school organizations to accommodate more flexible instructional practices such as team teaching, ungraded primary and open classrooms, and the broader use of ancillary personnel. Dunn believed these reforms held the promise of making the general education system "better able to deal with individual differences in pupils" (p. 10). And even though he recognized that reform was "still more an ideal than a reality," he argued that the field of "special education should begin moving now to fit into a changing general education program and to assist in achieving the program's goals" (p. 10).

In the current debate, proponents of inclusion are making the same arguments. Although inclusion proponents recognized the push for higher standardized text scores in the first wave of the excellence movement as a threat to both the inclusion concept and mainstreaming (Pugach & Sapon-Shevin, 1987; Sapon-Shevin, 1987; Shepard, 1987), they believe the more recent school restructuring wave of general education reform is consistent with the inclusion concept (e.g., Pugach & Lilly, 1984; Wang et al., 1985, 1986; Lipsky & Gartner, 1989a). Moreover, like Dunn, they are arguing that the availability of more powerful instructional (e.g., cooperative learning, peer-mediated instruction, adaptive learning, effective teaching, collaborative consultation) and diagnostic (e.g., curriculum-based assessment, prereferral assessment) technologies make inclusive education a real possibility in today's schools (see Lipsky & Gartner, 1989a; Pugach & Lilly, 1984; Stainback et al., 1989; Wang 1989a, 1989b).

The fourth and, for present purposes, most important parallel between the mainstreaming and inclusion debates explains the first three parallels: Both debates are forms of naive pragmatism. As we know from Chapter 14, the problem with naive pragmatism as a method for analyzing and resolving problems of professional practice is that, although it questions professional models, practices, and tools, it unreflectively accepts the assumptions, theories, and metatheories that stand behind them. As such, naive pragmatism is socially reproductive; rather than resolving problems of professional practice, it merely reproduces them in a new form (Cherryholmes, 1988; Skrtic 1991a, 1991b).

The EHA and mainstreaming reproduced the special education problems of the 1960s and 1970s in the 1980s and 1990s because the practical criticism of the mainstreaming debate stopped at the level of the special classroom model and its associated practices and tools; it did not question the assumptions, theories, and metatheories in which the model and its practices and tools are grounded. As a result, the new models, practices, and tools introduced under the EHA and mainstreaming were premised on the same functionalist theories of human pathology and organizational rationality, and thus on the same set of traditional assumptions about the nature of disability, diagnosis, special education, and progress (Skrtic, 1986, 1988a).

Figure 15.2 depicts the hierarchy of presuppositions that constitute the special education knowledge tradition. As we know from Chapter 14, everything professionals think, do, say, read, and write as professionals is shaped ultimately by a metatheoretical paradigm that subsumes and defines a corresponding set of theories and guiding assumptions upon which the profession's models, practices, and tools are premised. To understand the problem with using naive pragmatism as a means to identify and resolve problems of professional practice, imagine that Figure 15.2 illustrated the hierarchy of special education presuppositions *before* the introduction of the EHA and mainstreaming, and then ask what would be different. The answer of course is that, although the models, practices, and tools would be different, the assumptions, theories, and metatheories would be exactly the same. This is why the diagnostic and instructional practices and tools associated with the EHA and mainstreaming have reproduced the problems associated with the special classroom model; they are premised on the same functionalist theories and guiding assumptions.

What is so troubling today is that the inclusion debate is largely following the same pattern (see Skrtic 1991a, 1991b; Chapter 18). The debate over inclusive education is also a form of naive pragmatism; it criticizes current special education models, practices, and tools without explicitly criticizing the theories and assumptions that stand behind them. As a form of naive pragmatism, the danger is that, rather than resolving the special education problems of the 1980s and 1990s, the inclusion debate will simply reproduce them in the 21st century.

Fortunately, however, the mainstreaming and inclusion debates are different in two important ways. If capitalized upon, these differences may mitigate against the possibility of yet another episode of criticism and change that merely reproduces old problems in a new form. First, the proponents of inclusion have implicated school organization in the problem of school failure, a position with which even the most strident opponents of inclusion agree (see Skrtic, 1991a, 1991b; below). By arguing that the problem lies largely outside the student, in the organizational context of schooling, the inclusion debate is an implicit critique of special education's grounding assumptions and thus ultimately an implicit critique of the functionalist theories of human pathology and organizational rationality. The participants in the debate, however, do not explicitly recognize the connection between practices, assumptions, and theories. As a result, neither the reform proposals of the inclusion proponents nor the counter-proposals of the opponents resolve the problems identified in the debate (see Skrtic, 1988b, 1991a; Chapter 18).

The second difference arose because participants in the mainstreaming debate had no meaningful way to interpret the negative empirical evidence on the ethics and efficacy of the special classroom model and its associated practices and tools. As such, the field of special education had no way to conceptualize the sources of the problems associated with the special classroom model or how to resolve them, other than defaulting implicitly to its traditional grounding theories and assumptions. In the end, mainstreaming emerged as the solution to these problems, not because it was conceptually sound but because, morally, legally, and politically, it was the right thing to do (Ballard-Campbell & Semmel, 1981; Biklen, 1985; Skrtic, 1986).

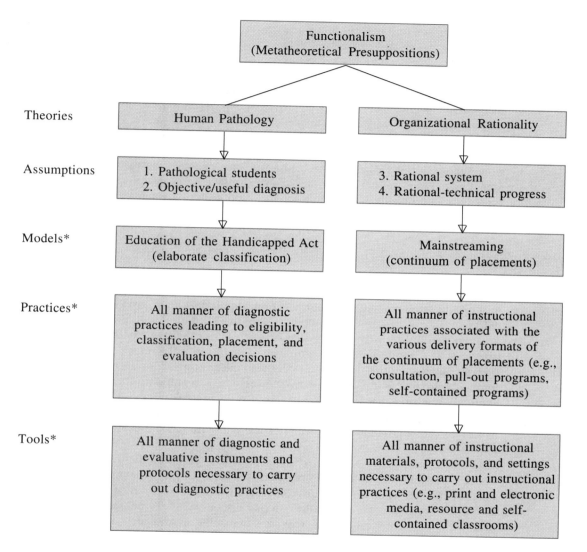

*The models, practices, and tools illustrated here are those that emerged after 1975. If the figure depicted the hierarchy of presuppositions before 1975, the models, practices, and tools would be (more or less) different, but the assumptions, theories, and metatheories would be the same.

● **FIGURE 15.2**

The special education knowledge tradition: Hierarchy of presuppositions

Source: Adapted from T. Skrtic, 1991a, *Behind Special Education: A Critical Analysis of Professional Culture and School Organization*, p. 55, Denver: Love Publishing.

The difference today is that an array of conceptual resources is available for interpreting the negative empirical evidence on the ethics and efficacy of the special education practices and tools associated with the EHA and the mainstreaming model. As we will see in the section to follow, this is so because an alternative, theoretical discourse has emerged within the field of special education, one that appropriates theoretical insights from the social sciences and applies them to past and current problems of special education practice.

The inclusion debate questions special education's current diagnostic and instructional models, practices, and tools, in the same way the mainstreaming debate questioned those of the 1960s. The problem, of course, is that simply questioning professional practices is not enough. If the field of special education is to resolve rather than reproduce its problems, it must question the legitimacy of the theoretical knowledge in which its practices are grounded.

THEORETICAL CRITICISM OF SPECIAL EDUCATION

Like practical criticism, theoretical criticism questions the ethics and efficacy of special education models, practices, and tools, but it does so by criticizing the theoretical knowledge and guiding assumptions upon which the models, practices, and tools are premised. Whereas practical criticism is an empirical critique of the field's models, practices, and tools, theoretical criticism is a theoretical critique of its grounding theories and assumptions. As such, rather than interpreting empirical data by defaulting implicitly to the field's traditional theories and assumptions, theoretical criticism explicitly questions the legitimacy of the theories (and assumptions) themselves, and on this basis proposes alternative theories, both as a way to interpret empirical data and as an alternative grounding for special education's professional models, practices, and tools.

Prior to emergence of the theoretical discourse within the field of special education, theoretical criticism came from external sources, largely from the social sciences. Because the new internal theoretical discourse is more or less a reappropriation of the theoretical insights contained in the external discourse, it will be helpful to begin the discussion of theoretical criticism by reviewing the case against special education theory and practice made by social scientists.

THE EXTERNAL THEORETICAL DISCOURSE

The arguments that social scientists have made against the profession and institutional practice of special education are based on one or more of three interrelated claims. The three claims are that special education is atheoretical; that it confounds theory; and that it is premised on the wrong theory.

The Atheoretical Claim. The first type of theoretical criticism is based on the claim that the field of special education operates in the absence of a guiding theory. The argument here is that, rather than being grounded in the theoretical knowledge of one or more the social disciplines, special education practices and discourses are guided simply by the narrow set of implicit assumptions noted above, that (a) disabilities are pathological conditions, (b) diagnosis is objective and useful, (c) special education is a rational system that benefits diagnosed students, and (d) progress in the field is a rational-technical process of incremental improvements in conventional diagnostic and instructional models, practices, and tools (see, for example, Bogdan & Kugelmass, 1984; Bogdan & Knoll, 1988; Rist & Harrell, 1982; Tomlinson, 1982).

Important to note, however, is that the atheoretical claim does not mean there are no theories behind special education's guiding assumptions. Indeed, as we have seen, the four assumptions are grounded in the mutually reinforcing functionalist theories of human pathology and organizational rationality. Moreover, given the positivist theory of knowledge that underwrites the objectivist model of professional knowledge, all professional fields assume that their knowledge tradition is the end product of a rational system of knowledge production, and thus that their profession is a rational system that serves the interests of its clients. As we will see below, the real problem for special education is the unconscious—and thus acritical—nature of these assumptions, and not whether they are grounded in theory.

The Confounded Theory Claim. The second type of theoretical criticism is based on the claim that the special education knowledge tradition confounds theories. The most notable example of this type of criticism is Mercer's (1973) explanation of the way biological and psychological theories of deviance are confounded within the clinical perspective of mental retardation (also see Foucault, 1976). Derived from medicine and psychology, the clinical perspective is the familiar frame of reference that guides research and practice in all of the helping professions, including special education. It contains two contrasting theories of normal/abnormal: the pathological model from medicine (biology) and the statistical model from psychology.

According to Mercer, the *pathological model* defines normal/abnormal according to the presence or absence of observable biological symptoms. Biological processes that interfere with system preservation are "bad," or pathological; those that enhance the life of the organism are "good," or healthy. Thus, the pathological model is bipolar. At one pole is normal, or the absence of pathological symptoms and health; at the other pole is abnormal, or the presence of pathological symptoms and illness. As such, the pathological model is evaluative: To be abnormal is to be unhealthy; this is bad and should be prevented or alleviated.

The *statistical model* is based on the concept of the normal curve, the idea that an individual's attributes can be described by his or her relative position in a frequency distribution of other persons measured on those attributes. Whereas the pathological model defines abnormality as the presence of observable pathological symptoms, the statistical model defines abnormality according to the extent to which an individual varies from the average of a population on a particular attribute. Unlike the bipolar pathological model, which defines only one type of abnormality, the statistical model defines two types of abnormality: abnormally large and abnormally small amounts of the measured characteristic. Whereas the pathological model is evaluative (pathological signs are always bad), the statistical model is evaluatively neutral; whether large or small amounts of an attribute are good or bad depends on the attribute being measured. And whether large or small amounts of a particular attribute are good or bad is defined by society.

According to Mercer, both models are used to define mental retardation—the pathological model for assessing biological manifestations and the statistical model for assessing behavioral manifestations, which are not comprehensible within the pathological model. Although instances of moderate to severe/profound mental retardation are associated with observable patterns of biological symptoms (syndromes) and thus are comprehensible under the pathological model, the vast majority of individuals labeled mentally retarded are regarded as mildly mentally retarded, a condition that in most cases does not show any biological signs. In these instances, the statistical model is used and a low score on an intelligence (IQ) test is accepted as a symptom of pathology. The problem is that when the models are used in conjunction with one another, the tendency is to transpose them, turning behavioral patterns into pathological signs. Mercer (1973) explained the confusion by saying:

> The implicit logic that underlies this transformation is as follows: Low IQ = "bad" in American society: a social evaluation. "Bad" = pathology in the pathological model. Therefore, low IQ = pathology. Thus, IQ, which is not a biological manifestation but is a behavioral score based on responses to a series of questions, becomes conceptually transposed into a pathological sign carrying all of the implications of the pathological model. (pp. 5–6)

Although Mercer identified a number of negative implications of the conceptual transposition, the primary implication is that, given the logic of the clinical perspective, mental retardation is regarded as a pathological condition, an objective attribute of the individual. Although Mercer limited her criticism to the special education category of mental retardation, the same type of criticism has been leveled against the field's knowledge, practices, and discourses relative to the categories of learning disabilities (Rist & Harrell, 1982; Schrag & Divorky, 1975) and emotional disturbance (Algozzine, 1976, 1977; Apter, 1982; Hobbs, 1975; Rhodes, 1970; Ross, 1980; Swap, 1978). And, of course, the students who make up these three categories of exceptionality represent the majority of all students identified as disabled in public education.

The Wrong Theory Claim. The third type of theoretical criticism rests on the claim that the special education knowledge tradition is based on the wrong theory, or that it relies too narrowly on some theories to the exclusion of others. The social scientists who have mounted this type of criticism argue that social professions such as special education rely too narrowly on theory derived from the disciplines of psychology and biology (e.g., Farber, 1968; Goffman, 1961, 1963; Gould, 1982; Lemert, 1967; Scott, 1969; Szasz, 1961). The argument is that, by their very nature, these disciplines place the root cause of deviance within the person and exclude from consideration causal factors that lie in the larger social and political processes external to the individual. In addition, social scientists who make this claim view diagnostic and instructional models based solely on theories derived from the behavioral and biological sciences as superficial because they do nothing to assess, alter, or circumvent the social-political-cultural context of "disability."

Whereas the behavioral and biological sciences study organisms and consider disability to be an objective condition that people have, the social sciences study social and political systems and processes and consider deviance to be a subjective condition that is socially constructed and maintained (Biklen, 1977; Bogdan, 1974; Braginsky & Braginsky, 1971; Davis, 1963; Goffman, 1961, 1963; Gould, 1982; Gubrium, 1975; Lemert, 1967; Scheff, 1966; Scott, 1969; Szasz, 1961; Taylor & Bogdan, 1977; Wiseman, 1970). This is more than an academic argument. Many of the social scientists who raise the issue are concerned ultimately with the impact of social and political processes on people and society. From their perspective, special education in industrialized societies is largely an arm of education that not only creates powerless groups but ultimately works against their social, political, and economic interests (see Barton & Tomlinson, 1984; Farber, 1968; Sarason & Doris, 1979; Smith, 1985; Tomlinson, 1982, 1988).

Although theoretical criticism of special education from outside the field has been leveled since the 1960s, it has had virtually no effect on the field's practices and discourses or on its guiding assumptions and theories (Bogdan & Kugelmass, 1984; Skrtic, 1986, 1988a). One problem, of course, is that unorthodox perspectives such as these tend to be overlooked in professional education and rarely find their way into teaching textbooks. As we know from Kuhn (1970; Chapter 14), professional induction demands complete acceptance of the profession's received knowledge on faith. Anything that might question or offer an alternative to the profession's established knowledge tradition is avoided. Professional education demands complete concentration on one knowledge tradition to the exclusion of all others. Its goal is to inculcate in the would-be professional a deep commitment to a certain way of viewing the world and operating in it.

Moreover, we will see below that, even when special education professionals are confronted with theoretical criticism, they ordinarily have difficulty accepting and using its critical insights. These insights are difficult for special educators to accept because, by their very nature, they question the field's taken-for-granted assumptions about itself, its clients, and its practices and discourses. They are difficult for special educators to use because they are presented in theoretical languages that fall outside the logic of the special education knowledge tradition, and thus are largely incomprehensible to members of the professional community. Although special educators cannot deny that theoretical criticism is scientific, they tend to ignore it because, given their commitment to the field's established knowledge tradition, it seems to be irrelevant or, at best, ill informed.

INTERNAL THEORETICAL DISCOURSE

As noted above, the critical theoretical discourse that has emerged within the field of special education (e.g., Bogdan & Knoll, 1988; Bogdan & Kugelmass, 1984; Carrier, 1983; Ferguson, 1987; Heshusius, 1982, 1986; Iano, 1986, 1987; Janesick, 1988;

Poplin, 1984, 1987; Sigmon, 1987; Skrtic, 1986, 1988a, 1991a; Sleeter, 1986; Tomlinson, 1982, 1988) is largely a reappropriation of the theoretical insights contained in the external discourse of the social sciences. For example, by their very nature, all of the internal theoretical critiques make the case, implicitly or explicitly, that the field of special education is atheoretical, or acritical, in the sense noted above.

In addition, most of the internal theoretical critiques draw on the confounded theory argument to make a case against what is characterized as special education's overreliance on biological theories of deviance (the "medical model") and its inappropriate use of functionalist or "reductionist" approaches to curriculum, instruction, assessment, and research (see, particularly, Bogdan & Kugelmass, 1984; Heshusius, 1982, 1986; Iano, 1986, 1987; Poplin, 1984, 1987; Sigmon, 1987).

Finally, each of the internal theoretical critiques represents a version of the wrong theory claim. Implicitly or explicitly, each one argues against special education's traditional theoretical and disciplinary grounding in what I have called functionalist psychology and makes a case for an alternative theoretical grounding in a different paradigm and in one or more different or additional disciplines, as illustrated in Figure 15.3.

The emergence of an internal theoretical discourse creates several potential advantages for the field of special education. First, as illustrated in Figure 15.3, the general trend in the special education theoretical discourse is away from functionalism and toward the other three paradigms, which parallels the paradigm shifts in the social sciences over the past 30 years (see Chapter 14). The advantage here is that the field of special education now has available to it theoretical interpretations of the nature and effects of its practices and discourses from all four paradigms of modern social scientific thought (see Skrtic, 1990a, in press). A second potential advantage of the internal theoretical discourse is that it makes available to special educators a number of alternative disciplinary interpretations of the field's practices and discourses and their effects on clients and society.

In principle, the availability of these alternative paradigmatic and disciplinary interpretations provides the field of special education with an array of conceptual resources for mounting a critical reconstruction of its professional knowledge, practices, and discourses. I will consider this possibility in more depth below, but at this point we should note some of the problems with the internal theoretical discourse, problems that stand in the way of critical reconstruction.

Because the internal theoretical discourse is being carried out by special educators, it has been more difficult for the special education professional community to ignore. Nevertheless, its impact on the field has been minimal because, like the external theoretical discourse, it questions taken-for-granted assumptions and is carried out in unfamiliar theoretical languages. The difference is that, because the internal theoretical discourse comes from within the field and thus cannot be ignored as irrelevant or ill informed, the special education community has condemned it as unscientific and misleading at best (e.g., Lloyd, 1987; Simpson & Eaves, 1985; Ulman & Rosenberg, 1986) and rude, ideological, and dangerous at worst (Carnine, 1987; Forness & Kavale, 1987; Kavale & Forness, 1987).

For example, the field reacted to Heshusius' (1982) argument for grounding special education practices and discourses in the holistic orientation of the interpretivist paradigm (rather than the mechanistic world view of the functionalist paradigm) by dismissing it entirely as unscientific superstition (Ulman & Rosenberg, 1986). This was to be expected, of course, because, given their grounding in the functionalist paradigm, Heshusius' critics naturally evaluated her proposal exclusively on the basis of functionalist presuppositions about the nature of reality, knowledge, and inquiry, which, given the foundational logic of the functionalist perspective, they took to be the only criteria that exist.

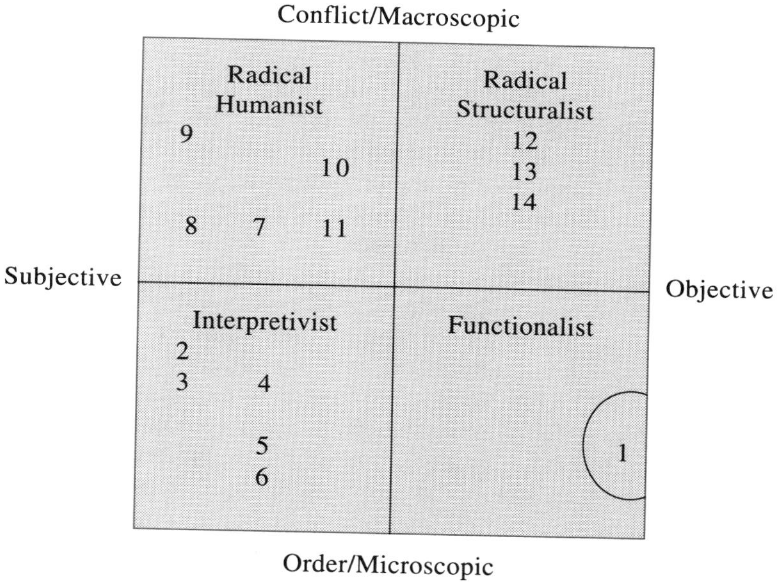

Conflict/Macroscopic

	Radical Humanist 9 10 8 7 11	Radical Structuralist 12 13 14
Subjective	Interpretivist 2 3 4 5 6	Functionalist 1	Objective

Order/Microscopic

1 = Special education knowledge tradition
2 = Heshusius (1982, 1986)
3 = Poplin (1984, 1987)
4 = Ferguson (1987)
5 = Bogdan and Knoll (1988)
6 = Biklen (1985)
7 = Janesick (1988)

8 = Iano (1986, 1987)
9 = Kiel (in press)
10 = Tomlinson (1988)
11 = Sigmon (1987)
12 = Carrier (1983)
13 = Tomlinson (1982)
14 = Sleeter (1986)

● **FIGURE 15.3**

The theoretical discourse in special education

Source: Adapted from T. Skrtic, 1991a, *Behind Special Education: A Critical Analysis of Professional Culture and School Organization*, p. 120, Denver: Love Publishing.

Another example is the way the special education community characterized Sleeter's (1986) radical structuralist critique of the learning disabilities construct as "ideological rhetoric...a distorted account of history" (Kavale & Forness, 1987, p. 7), an account that her critics considered dangerous in that it "may be taken seriously because of its...ready appeal to egalitarian 'instincts' and [its] warping of reality" (Kavale & Forness, 1987, p. 7). Here again, given their metatheoretical grounding in the functionalist paradigm, and thus their presupposition of a rational, objective social reality, Sleeter's critics naturally read her unconventional interpretation as a dangerous distortion of reality.

The inclusion debate is important because it is empirical; it questions the legitimacy of special education's models, practices, and tools in the language of the field and in terms of its own standards, which makes it comprehensible to the members of the special education community. However, because empirical data can be interpreted in a variety of ways depending on the interpreter's explicit or implicit presuppositions (Lincoln & Guba, 1985), the field's atheoretical (acritical) orientation means that special educators must default conceptually to their traditional implicit theories and taken-for-granted assumptions to interpret the meaning of the empirical evidence put forth in the inclusion debate. This is naive pragmatism. Rather than resolving problems of special education practice, it reproduces them in a new form (see Chapter 18).

The theoretical discourse is important because it is critical. It questions the field's implicit theories and assumptions and proposes a number of alternative theories (and associated assumptions) for grounding the field's practices and discourses. The advantage of a theoretical discourse is that it recognizes that altering practices and discourses in a way that does not reproduce old problems requires altering the theories and assumptions upon which they are based. A major problem with the theoretical discourse, however, is that it is carried out in alternative theoretical languages that are not immediately comprehensible to members of the special education community. This minimizes its impact on the field because, given their incomprehensibility, its theoretical insights tend to be ignored when they come from outsiders or condemned when they come from insiders.

Thus, in its current confrontation with uncertainty, the special education community is faced with three problems. As we know from Chapter 14 and the discussion above, the first problem is *naive pragmatism*, the problem of special educators reproducing rather than resolving their problems of practice because they lack a way to question the theories behind their conventional models, practices, and tools. The second problem is the *incomprehensibility* of the theoretical insights contained in the internal and external theoretical discourses. Together, the problems of naive pragmatism and theoretical incomprehensibility create a situation in which the practical criticism of the inclusion debate is *comprehensible but acritical*, whereas the theoretical discourse that is necessary to avoid reproducing current problems is *critical but incomprehensible* to the field.

One way to respond to this situation is to combine the field's empirical evidence on the ethics and efficacy of its practices with the critical insights of the theoretical discourses, creating the potential for an expanded discourse in special education that is both critical *and* comprehensible to the field. The significance of such a discourse is that it would make available for theoretical and critical analysis the empirical evidence produced by the field itself, according to its conventional assumptions and in its traditional language.

Although an expanded discourse of this sort is necessary, it is not sufficient to understand and resolve past and current problems of special education practice. This is so because, although the theoretical discourse is *critical*, it is not *pragmatic*. It is critical because it questions the field's traditional theoretical grounding and provides alternative theories for interpreting data and conceptualizing solutions, but it is not pragmatic because it does not solve the problem of choosing among the various theories put forth in the theoretical discourse. To be critical *and* pragmatic, the expanded discourse must not only look behind special education practices to expose the unquestioned theories and assumptions in which they are grounded, but it also must look behind the various theories themselves to expose the metatheoretical presuppositions in which they are grounded. To be critical and pragmatic at the metatheoretical level, the expanded discourse must be antifoundational. Thus, the third problem that the special education community faces today is that the theoretical discourse it needs to carry out the expanded discourse is *foundational*.

The remaining sections of the chapter are devoted to the problems of incomprehensibility and foundationalism. I address the incomprehensibility problem by conducting a critical reading of the empirical arguments put forth in the inclusion debate, a reading that interprets these arguments about special education's current models, practices, and tools in terms of their implications for the legitimacy of the assumptions, theories, and metatheories in which they are grounded.

I have two purposes for reading the inclusion debate in this way. First, I want to provide a methodological example of how the special education community can combine its empirical evidence on the ethics and efficacy of its current models, practices, and tools with critical theoretical and metatheoretical insights, providing a prototype of an expanded discourse on the legitimacy of the special education knowledge tradition that is both critical and comprehensible to the field. My second purpose is to use this prototypical example of an expanded discourse to provide a substantive deconstruction of the field's knowledge tradition, one that draws on and combines empirical evidence and critical insights.

In the concluding section I address the problem of foundationalism. Given my argument that, to be comprehensible, the expanded discourse must be both empirical and critical, here I will substantiate my claim that, to be useful, such a discourse must be both critical and pragmatic. It must provide a way to choose among alternative theoretical interpretations of empirical evidence. Whereas one of my aims in the first section below is to deconstruct the special education knowledge tradition, my aim in the concluding section is to provide metatheoretical guidelines for reconstructing it in a way that permits special education professionals, advocates, and consumers to reconcile the field's practices with what they believe is right.

CRITICAL IMPLICATIONS OF THE INCLUSION DEBATE

In this section I deconstruct the special education knowledge tradition by considering the empirical arguments put forth in the inclusion debate in terms of their implications for the legitimacy of the assumptions, theories, and metatheories that underwrite special education knowledge, practices, and discourses.

As we know, the inclusion debate has two lines of argument. One concerns the adequacy of the current special education system. The other questions the feasibility of the inclusive education reform proposals. I begin my critical reading with the first line of argument, with the empirical arguments on both sides of the inclusion debate about the adequacy of the current special education system. Then, turning to the second line of argument, I provide a critical reading of the inclusion opponents' claims against the feasibility of the inclusive education reform proposals. Although to do this I must present the major inclusive education reform proposals, I do not provide a critical reading of the proposals in this chapter because doing so requires a critical understanding of schools as organizations and the manner in which they change. And because this is the topic of Chapter 18, I will reserve my critical analysis of the inclusive education reform proposals until then.

My use of the qualifiers "explicit" and "implicit" in this section requires some clarification because, as we will see, I use three different types or levels of explicitness and implicitness. The first type refers to the nature of agreement between the inclusion proponents' and opponents' assessments of various aspects of the current system of special education. In these cases I simply use the terms explicit and implicit in the customary way.

I use the second type when discussing the implications of the inclusion proponents' and opponents' empirical arguments for special education's grounding assumptions, theories, and metatheories. Clearly, participants in the inclusion debate are not speaking explicitly to the field's assumptions, theories, and metatheories. Indeed, that is the problem with the inclusion debate, what I referred to above as the problem of naive pragmatism. In these cases I at times omit the qualifiers "explicit" and "implicit," particularly when including them is cumbersome. In any event, when I say, for example, that inclusion proponents or opponents "reject" or "retain" an assumption, theory, or metatheory, it should be understood that they do so implicitly.

Finally, at the end of the section, I use a third type of explicitness and implicitness in reference to the source of special education's grounding assumptions, theories, and metatheories—in reference to whether they are explicit (derived from the field's disciplinary grounding in psychology and biology) or implicit (derived from a social norm), as explained in a previous section.

CRITICISM OF THE CURRENT SYSTEM

The debate over the adequacy of the current system of special education is important because, given a critical reading, it becomes a debate over the legitimacy of the field's grounding assumptions, theories, and metatheories. Thus, the value of a critical reading is that, given the empirical arguments for and against special education's current models, practices, and tools, and the implications of these arguments for the field's assumptions, theories, and metatheories, it deconstructs the entire hierarchy of presuppositions that constitutes the special education knowledge tradition. And, of course, the value of deconstructing the special education knowledge tradition is that it clears the path for reconstructing it in a way that avoids its unintentional negative consequences, a matter addressed in the concluding section of the chapter.

Are disabilities pathological?

No one would argue that most low-incidence disabilities (those in the severe to profound range of exceptionality) are associated with observable patterns of biological symptoms (or syndromes) and thus are comprehensible under the pathological model (see above). The concern with regard to these students is whether they are being served adequately and ethically under the current system and whether the pathological distinction is of any use in designing effective instructional interventions (see Stainback & Stainback, 1984b). Thus, the question of whether disabilities are pathological refers primarily to the high-incidence disability classifications of learning disabilities, emotional disturbance, and mild mental retardation, which in most cases do not show biological signs of pathology (see Algozzine, 1976, 1977; Apter, 1982; Hobbs, 1975; Mercer, 1973; Rhodes, 1970).

Although the inclusion debate has been quite heated, virtually no disagreement exists on this question relative to the high-incidence classifications. Both the proponents (see Gartner & Lipsky, 1987; Pugach & Lilly, 1984; Stainback & Stainback, 1984b; Wang et al., 1986, 1988) and the opponents (see Bryan et al., 1988; Braaten et al., 1988; CCBD, 1989; Kauffman et al., 1988; Keogh, 1988) of inclusion agree that the EHA's handicapped designation is a pathological distinction for some students in the high-incidence classifications, but, because of a number of definitional and measurement problems, as well as problems related to the will or capacity of teachers and schools to accommodate student diversity, most of these students are not disabled in a pathological sense, a situation that is particularly true for students identified as learning disabled. Moreover, both sides in the debate agree that additional students in school remain unidentified and thus unserved, some who have pathological disabilities and others who do not but nonetheless require assistance (see, e.g., Bryan et al., 1988; Braaten et al., 1988; CCBD, 1989; Stainback & Stainback, 1984b; Wang et al., 1986, 1988; Keogh, 1988).

Although the inclusion proponents recognize that many students with special educational needs present difficult problems for classroom teachers, their point is simply that neither the general education system nor the special education system is sufficiently adaptable to accommodate their individual needs (e.g., Gartner & Lipsky, 1987; Pugach & Lilly, 1984; Wang et al., 1985, 1986), a point with which most inclusion opponents agree, implicitly or explicitly (see Bryan et al., 1988; Kauffman, 1988; Kauffman et al., 1988; Keogh, 1988). On the related matter of the attribution of student failure, the inclusion opponents and proponents agree that an exclusively "student-deficit" orientation is inappropriate. Although some of the inclusion opponents argue that the proponents lean too far toward an exclusively "teacher-deficit" orientation (Kauffman et al., 1988; Keogh, 1988), the inclusion proponents clearly recognize the student's responsibility in the learning process (e.g., Gartner, 1986; Wang, 1989b; Wang & Peverly, 1987).

Is diagnosis objective and useful?

The inclusion proponents argue that differential diagnosis does not result in objective distinctions, either between the disabled and nondisabled designations or among the three high-incidence disability classifications (Wang et al., 1986, 1987; Stainback & Stainback, 1984b; Gartner & Lipsky, 1987). As noted, the inclusion opponents generally agree that the disabled-nondisabled distinction is not objective. Moreover, they agree that distinctions among the three high-incidence disability classifications are not objective because, in addition to measurement and definitional problems, the process for making these decisions in schools is "embedded in a powerful economic, political, and philosophical network" (Keogh, 1988, p. 20; see also CCBD, 1989; Gerber & Semmel, 1984; Hallahan & Kauffman, 1977; Kauffman, 1988).

On the matter of the utility of differential diagnosis, the inclusion proponents argue that there are no instructionally relevant reasons for making the disabled-nondisabled distinction or for distinguishing among the three high-incidence classifications. Their point is that all students have unique learning needs and, further, that students in the high-incidence disability classifications, as well as those in the other special needs classifications (e.g., Chapter 1, bilingual education, migrant education), can be taught using similar instructional methods (e.g., Lipsky & Gartner, 1989a; Reynolds et al., 1987; Stainback & Stainback, 1984b, 1989; Wang et al., 1986, 1987; Wang, 1989a, 1989b). Here, too, most of the inclusion opponents agree, admitting that "effective instructional and management procedures will be substantially the same for nonhandicapped and most mildly handicapped students" (Kauffman et al., 1988, p. 8; Gerber, 1987; Hallahan & Kauffman, 1977).

The only inclusion opponent who makes a case for the potential instructional relevance of differential diagnosis considers it to be an empirical question, which, if answered in the negative, should signal the discontinuance of the practice of differential diagnosis and the categorical approach to special education (Keogh, 1988). Although Bryan et al. (1988, p. 25) do not make an explicit argument for the instructional relevance of differential diagnosis, by arguing that "one cannot assume that any two learning disabled children would be any more similar than a learning disabled child and a normally achieving child, or a normally achieving child and an underachieving child," they actually make an implicit argument against the instructional utility of differential diagnosis, and thus implicitly agree with the inclusion proponents' position that all students have unique learning needs and interests, even those within the traditional high-incidence disability classifications.

Is special education a rational system?

The inclusion proponents argue that the only rational justification for the special education system is that it confers instructional benefit on students who are designated handicapped (e.g., Lilly, 1986; Lipsky & Gartner, 1987; Reynolds, 1988; Reynolds et al., 1987; Stainback & Stainback, 1984b; Wang et al., 1987), a position with which the inclusion opponents generally agree (see Kauffman et al., 1988; Keogh, 1988). On this basis, the inclusion proponents believe that, given the weak effects of special education instructional practices and the social and psychological costs of labeling, the current system of special education is at best no more justifiable than simply permitting most students to remain unidentified in regular classrooms, and at worst far less justifiable than regular classroom placement in conjunction with appropriate in-class support services (e.g., Lipsky & Gartner, 1987, 1989a; Pugach & Lilly, 1984; Stainback & Stainback, 1984b; Wang et al., 1987). Thus, the inclusion proponents reject the idea that special education is a rational system.

Although some inclusion opponents argue that the handicapped designation is beneficial, none of them argues that it has been shown to lead to direct instructional benefit. For example, neither Keogh (1988) nor Hallahan, Keller, McKinney, Lloyd, and Bryan (1988) believes that the instructional effectiveness of special education interventions has been demonstrated. Furthermore, although Bryan et al. (1988) and Hallahan, Keller, McKinney, Lloyd, and Bryan (1988) present arguments in favor of instruction delivered in special education settings, neither argument is based on the claim that current special education instructional interventions have been shown to be effective. Bryan et al. argue in favor of special education interventions purely on the basis of what they perceive to be the inability of classroom teachers to meet the diverse needs of students with learning disabilities, and the argument put forth by Hallahan and his colleagues rests completely on the speculation that more powerful instructional techniques might be implemented more easily in separate special education settings than in general education classrooms (cf. Hallahan & Keller, 1986).

Although none of the inclusion opponents argues that special education has been shown to lead to direct instructional benefit, some of them argue that it nevertheless is beneficial in a political sense because it targets otherwise unavailable resources and personnel to designated students. Thus, they believe the current special education system is justifiable because targeting is essential if these students are to receive instructional assistance in the context of the resource allocation process in schools (CCBD, 1989; Kauffman, 1988, 1989; Kauffman et al., 1988). Given their recognition that the special education system has not been shown to confer instructional benefit on designated students, the inclusion opponents in effect agree with the proponents that special education is not an *instructionally* rational system. On the weight of the important argument that the current system is *politically* rational, however, let us say for present purposes that the inclusion opponents' position is that special education is a rational system, politically and ethically if not instructionally.

As we will see below, in response to the question of the nature of progress, the inclusion opponents argue that progress in special education is possible through rational-technical means. In effect, given their position on the third and fourth assumptions, the inclusion opponents who argue for the political rationality of special education are saying that, although special education has not been shown to be an instructionally rational system *at present*, it is politically rational at present and can be rendered instructionally rational (or, at least, more instructionally rational) *in the future*. Thus, their position on the assumption about the rationality of special education cannot be separated from their position on the nature of progress. This is so because, although arguing for retaining an instructionally ineffective but politically essential system may be politically justifiable *if* that system will be rendered instructionally effective in the future, arguing for an instructionally ineffective but politically essential system that will not be rendered instructionally effective in the future is not justifiable, politically or ethically. This is an important point I will return to below in my discussion of the inclusive education reform proposals and the opponents' reaction to them.

Finally, as for the question of whether special education is a rationally coordinated system of services, the inclusion proponents argue that it is coordinated neither with the general education system nor with the other special needs programs. Rather than a rationally coordinated system, they characterize the entire special needs enterprise, including the special education system, in terms of disjointed incrementalism, a collection of disjointed programs, each with its own clients, personnel, administrators, budget, and regulations, which have been added to schools incrementally over time (Reynolds & Birch, 1977; Reynolds & Wang, 1983; Reynolds et al., 1987; Wang et al., 1985, 1986). Although the inclusion opponents are generally silent on the issue of lack of coordination among special education, general education, and the other special needs programs, those who recognize lack of coordination as a problem consider it to be an inevitable and unavoidable consequence of the targeting strategy required to make special education a politically rational system (Kauffman et al., 1988).

Is progress rational and technical?

This question asks whether progress can be made under the current system through incremental improvements in the diagnostic practices required by the EHA and the various instructional and support services technologies associated with mainstreaming. The inclusion proponents argue that the diagnostic and instructional models and practices of the current system are fundamentally flawed and thus cannot and should not be salvaged. They believe these models and practices (and thus the entire system of special education) must be replaced through fundamental restructuring of the current special and general education systems (Lilly, 1986; Lipsky & Gartner, 1987, 1989a; Pugach & Lilly, 1984; Reynolds et al., 1987; Stainback & Stainback, 1984b; Stainback et al., 1989). This, then, is an argument against the possibility of rational-technical change.

Like the inclusion proponents, the opponents recognize that the current special education system has serious problems that should be corrected. They believe, however, that incremental progress is possible through additional research and development aimed at improving special education diagnostic and instructional models and practices while maintaining the current system, including the pull-out approach of mainstreaming (see Braaten et al., 1988; Bryan et al., 1988; CCBD, 1989; Hallahan, Keller, McKinney, Lloyd, & Bryan, 1988; Kauffman et al., 1988, Kauffman, 1988; Keogh, 1988; Lloyd et al., 1988). This, of course, is an argument for the possibility of rational-technical change.

At this point in my critical reading of the empirical arguments put forth in the inclusion debate, the proponents and opponents reject special education's first two guiding assumptions: (a) that student disabilities are pathological conditions, and (b) that differential diagnosis is objective and useful. As such, both sides in the debate reject the functionalist theory of human pathology, the explicit disciplinary grounding of special education professional knowledge, practices, and discourses. Moreover, the inclusion proponents reject the assumptions that special education is a rational system and that it can be improved in a rational-technical manner, which means that they also reject the functionalist theory of organizational rationality, the implicit normative grounding of special education professional knowledge, practices, and discourses.

By rejecting all four assumptions and both functionalist theories, the inclusion proponents reject functionalism itself, calling into question the legitimacy of the entire hierarchy of presuppositions that guides and justifies special education as a professional practice. Although the inclusion opponents reject special education's first two guiding assumptions and thus the explicit disciplinary theory of human pathology, by arguing that the special education system is politically (if not instructionally) rational, and that it can be improved in a rational-technical manner, they retain the third and fourth assumptions and thus the field's implicit normative theory of organizational rationality.

Although the inclusion proponents and opponents agree (implicitly) that special education's guiding assumptions and theories about the nature of disability and diagnosis are inadequate, their disagreement over the nature of special education and progress has resulted in virtual total disagreement over an appropriate course of ameliorative action. On one hand, the inclusion proponents believe that, given the negative empirical evidence on the ethics and efficacy of special education models and practices *and* the nonadaptability of the general education system, a completely new system should be formed by restructuring the current special and general education systems into a single adaptable one. On the other hand, the inclusion opponents believe that negative evidence on the instructional adequacy of special education models and practices notwithstanding, the current system and its associated practices should be retained for political purposes, *given* the nonadaptability of the general education system and the fact that special education practices can be improved incrementally.

In practical terms, then, the key issue that separates the inclusion proponents and opponents is the question of the nature of schools as organizations and their capacity for change. As such, the inclusion debate turns on the question of whether school organizations can and will be restructured into the adaptable system the inclusion advocates envision, a matter I will consider in some depth in Chapter 18.

THE INCLUSION REFORM PROPOSALS

In this section I review the actual reform proposals of the four teams of inclusion proponents in terms of the students who are to be integrated into the new, restructured system, as well as the manner in which the new system is to be created. This is followed by a review of the inclusion opponents' reactions to the proposals. As above, my intent is to read these reactions in terms of what they say about the legitimacy of the hierarchy of presuppositions that guides and justifies special education practices and discourses.

Whom to integrate?

To one degree or another, each of the four inclusion reform proposals calls for eliminating the EHA classification system and the pull-out approach associated with the mainstreaming model. Each also proposes restructuring the separate general and special education systems into a new system in which students who need help in school are provided with in-class assistance. Although the four teams of inclusion proponents generally agree that this restructured system should be "flexible, supple, and responsive" (Lipsky & Gartner, 1987, p. 72), a "totally adaptive system" (Reynolds & Wang, 1983, p. 199) in which professionals personalize instruction through "group problem solving...shared responsibility, and...negotiation" (Pugach & Lilly, 1984, p. 52), they disagree on which students should be integrated into the new system on a full-time basis. In fact, this issue is what has separated the four teams of inclusion proponents into two camps of "inclusion" (Reynolds/Wang and Lilly/Pugach) and "full inclusion" (Lipsky/Gartner and Stainback/Stainback) advocates.

Although I will not use this distinction here, we should recognize that the Lipsky/Gartner and Stainback/Stainback teams have distanced themselves from the others, noting that, although the inclusion concept has resulted in some positive momentum for reform, ultimately it is lacking. For Gartner and Lipsky (1989), it is merely "blending at the margin" (p. 271), because ultimately it maintains two separate systems. For Stainback and Stainback (1989), it is too exclusive because it "does not address the need to include in regular classrooms and regular education those students labeled severely and profoundly handicapped" (p. 43).

Each of the four teams of inclusion proponents believes that all students currently served in compensatory and remedial education programs, as well as every other student who needs help in school but is not currently targeted for it, should remain in the regular classrooms of the restructured system full-time and receive whatever assistance they need in those classrooms. Where they differ, however, is with respect to which students currently classified as handicapped under the EHA should be served in this manner.

The Lilly/Pugach proposal is the least inclusive. In addition to the students noted above, it includes only "the vast majority of students [currently] served as 'mildly handicapped' " (Pugach & Lilly, 1984, p. 53). This not only excludes students with moderate, severe, and profound disabilities, who, according to the proposal, would be taught by special educators in separate settings within regular school buildings, but also excludes some students classified as mildly handicapped, such as those who have "developmental learning disabilities" (cf. Kirk & Chalfant, 1983).

The Reynolds/Wang proposal is somewhat more inclusive in that it maintains "most students with special learning needs" (Wang et al., 1985, p. 13; Reynolds & Wang, 1983) in general education classrooms full-time, while reserving the option of separate settings for some students, presumably those with severe and profound disabilities (see Reynolds & Wang, 1983). Wang et al. (1985) reserve the option of separate settings for some students because they believe that "surely there will be occasions to remove some students for instruction in special settings" (p. 13).

The Gartner/Lipsky proposal includes all students currently served under each EHA disability classification except those with the most severely and profoundly disabling conditions. These students would receive their primary instruction in separate classrooms located in regular, age-appropriate school buildings, following an inclusive education proposal for students with severe and profound disabilities put forth by Sailor (1989; Sailor et al., 1986).

Finally, in what is the most inclusive proposal, Stainback and Stainback (1984b) argue for the integration of all students, including those with the most severely and profoundly disabling conditions. They do recognize the need to group students, "in some instances, into specific courses and classes according to their instructional needs" (p. 108; Stainback et al., 1989).

What is to be merged?

Although the strategy for creating the adaptable system necessary to implement the inclusive education proposals is characterized most often as a merger of the general and special education systems, only the Stainback/Stainback and Gartner/Lipsky proposals actually call for what can be considered a merger of the two systems at the classroom level. The other two teams propose what amounts to a merger of instructional support personnel above the classroom level. For example, Reynolds and Wang (1983) propose eliminating all categorical special needs pull-out programs through a two-step merger. The first merger is within special education, among the programs serving students in the three high-incidence disability classifications, forming "a 'generic' or noncategorical base" (p. 206). The second is between this merged or noncategorical special education program and the other "compensatory services that are provided for disadvantaged, bilingual, migrant, low-English proficiency, or other children with special needs" (p. 206). Supported by paraprofessionals, these generic specialists form a school-based support team that works "mostly in the regular classrooms...to supply technical and administrative support to regular classroom teachers" (p. 206). Above the regular classroom teachers and generic specialists, they propose a merger of district-level consultants who would provide the classroom teachers and generic specialists with consultation and training on generic topics (see also Wang et al., 1985).

The Lilly/Pugach proposal merges the special education resource and support programs that currently provide services "for the mildly handicapped, and primarily for the learning disabled" (Pugach & Lilly, 1984, p. 54), with the traditional general education support service of remedial education. They recognize the need for support services but propose a single, coordinated system of services based in general educa-tion and provided largely in general education classrooms. They argue for this ap-proach over the current array of special pull-out programs on the grounds that such an arrangement will be less stigmatizing and will respond more quickly and efficiently to the needs of students and teachers (Lilly, 1986; Pugach & Lilly, 1984).

Although the Reynolds/Wang and the Lilly/Pugach proposals modify the current notion of instructional support services by replacing the categorical pull-out approach with a noncategorical or remedial model of in-class support services, both of them retain the traditional notion of a classroom, in the sense of one teacher with primary responsibility for a group of students. Beyond the recommended use of what are characterized as more powerful instructional technologies (e.g., cooperative learning, curriculum-based assessment, peer tutoring, adaptive learning), the primary difference between the current approach and these proposals at the classroom level is that some (Lilly/Pugach) or most (Reynolds/Wang) students who would have been removed under the current system remain in the general education classroom full-time and they, their classroom teacher, and any other students who need assistance are provided with noncategorical in-class support services.

Stainback and Stainback (1984b) argue for a merger of general and special education as a means of forming a "unified system" to replace the current "dual system" (p. 102), which they characterize as ineffective, inefficient, and unnecessary. Although their reform proposal calls for merger at the classroom level, it actually merges general and special education subject areas, not special education and general instructional programs or personnel. It calls for disbanding special education programs and integrating the residual personnel into the general education system according to an instructional specialization. Each teacher in this system would have "a strong base in the teaching/learning process" (Stainback & Stainback, 1984b, p. 107) and special-ization in a traditional general education subject (e.g., science, reading) or a special education subject (e.g., alternative communication systems, supported employment), and each would work individually in a separate subject-area classroom (see Stainback & Stainback, 1987a; Stainback et al., 1989).

As with the first two proposals, this one provides support services above the classroom level. Here, however, the support personnel are organized as subject-area specialists rather than generic specialists, which modifies the current categorical pull-out approach by replacing it with in-class subject-area support services. As in the case of the other two support services models, this one retains the traditional notion of a classroom, in the sense of one teacher with primary responsibility for a group of students (see Stainback & Stainback, 1984b, 1987a).

The Gartner/Lipsky proposal calls for a merged or unitary system in which education is "both one and special for all students" (Lipsky & Gartner, 1987, p. 73), which means completely abandoning a separate special education system for all students except those with the most severely and profoundly disabling conditions. Although originally their reform proposal also emphasized the support services level (see Gartner & Lipsky, 1987), in a more recent version (Lipsky & Gartner, 1989a) they stress the classroom level by linking their proposal for a restructured system to the excellence movement in general education, which for them is the effective schools movement (see Edmonds, 1979; Lezotte, 1989; Chapter 18). As such, their basic assertion is that, through broad adoption of the principles and practices identified in the effective schools research, "the education of students labeled as handicapped can be made effective" (Lipsky & Gartner, 1989a, p. 281).

They build their case for the effective schools approach by combining Edmonds' (1979) assertion that if some schools are effective, all schools can be effective, with Gilhool's (1976) parallel assertion that if some schools can effectively integrate students with disabilities, all schools can do so. They conclude that achieving effective schools, and thus effective education for students labeled handicapped, is a matter of will and commitment on the part of teachers and schools to adopt the principles and practices contained in the effective schools literature.

Finally, and somewhat ironically given their assertion about will and commitment, Gartner and Lipsky call for a new legal mandate, one "that requires a unitary system, that is 'special' for all students" (Lipsky & Gartner, 1989a, p. 282). In effect, they propose "an effective schools act for all students" (p. 282) as a successor to the EHA.

REACTIONS TO THE INCLUSIVE EDUCATION PROPOSALS

The inclusion opponents argue against the possibility of achieving the type of adaptable system proposed by the inclusion proponents on historical, logical, and political grounds. On the basis of these arguments, they conclude that special educational needs have not, are not, and simply cannot be accommodated in general education classrooms. For example, Kauffman (1988, 1989) and others (CCBD, 1989) argue that, historically, the separate special education system emerged to serve students who were forced out of a single system "in which most mildly handicapped students were not identified as such, one in which nearly all general educators were expected to teach nearly all students regardless of their characteristics" (Kauffman, 1988, p. 493). And, arguing that nothing has happened to change the general education system or its classrooms, Kauffman predicts that abandoning the special education system to create a single general education system most likely will result in rediscovering the need for a separate special education system (see also CCBD, 1989).

Keogh (1988) presents a logical argument against the inclusion proponents' reform proposals. Given her reading of these proposals, her position is that expecting the general education system "to take over the educational responsibility for pupils it has already demonstrated it has failed," is illogical, particularly because it currently serves "regular" students inadequately (p. 20). For her, something must change in the general education classroom before inclusion is a real possibility; major reforms are required if general education is to serve a broader range of students.

Although both of these arguments are important, they are not arguments against the inclusive education proposals; they are implicit arguments against the 20th-century notion of a classroom. Kauffman's historical argument is silent about the fact that the inclusion proponents are arguing for a restructured general education system in which classrooms are adaptable, and not a return to the traditional system. And, though Keogh's logical argument at least recognizes that accommodating students with special needs in general education classrooms will require major reform of the contemporary general education system, it is silent about the fact that this is precisely what the inclusion advocates are proposing.

In their political or microeconomic critique of the inclusive education reform proposals, Kauffman et al. (1988; cf. Gerber, 1988b; Gerber & Semmel, 1985) argue that "teachers, whether in regular or special class environments, cannot escape the necessary choice between higher means [i.e., maximizing mean performance by concentrating resources on the most able learners] and narrower variances [i.e., minimizing group variance by concentrating resources on the least able learners] as long as resources are scarce and students differ" (Gerber & Semmel, 1985, p. 19, cited in Kauffman et al., 1988, p. 10). This is true, they say, "whenever a teacher instructs a group of students...[except] when new resources are made available or more powerful instructional technologies are employed" (Kauffman et al., 1988, p. 10). Although this is a compelling argument, it is silent about the fact that the inclusive education reform proposals call for creating a system of adaptable classrooms by making new human resources available and introducing more powerful instructional technologies, the exact conditions that can narrow group variances without negatively affecting class means, according to the microeconomic argument itself.

Like the historical and logical arguments, the microeconomic critique is not an argument against the inclusive education reform proposals; it is a compelling argument against the traditional notion of a classroom. Actually, by arguing that both general and special education classrooms are nonadaptable in a microeconomic sense, Kauffman et al. make a stronger case against the current system of special education than the inclusion proponents do. Moreover, by arguing that the general education classroom has not changed historically, and that neither it nor the special education classroom can change politically, the inclusion opponents contradict their position on the possibility of rational-technical change, and thus their implicit support of special education's fourth guiding assumption. And, given that, politically and ethically, their position on the fourth assumption cannot be separated from their position on the third assumption, the inclusion opponents contradict their position on the rationality of the current system of special education as well.

THE INCLUSION DEBATE AND THE SPECIAL EDUCATION KNOWLEDGE TRADITION

In practical terms, the inclusion proponents argue that, instructionally, the current system of special education is a nonrational system that cannot be changed incrementally and so must be replaced entirely with a new system. In their defense of the current system, the inclusion opponents argue that it is a politically rational system that can be improved (i.e., rendered instructionally rational in the future) incrementally through research and development (Braaten et al., 1988; Bryan et al., 1988; CCBD, 1989;

Hallahan, Keller, McKinney, Lloyd, & Bryan, 1988; Kauffman et al., 1988; Kauffman, 1988, 1989; Keogh, 1988; Lloyd et al., 1988). In their criticism of the inclusion proponents' reform proposals, however, the inclusion opponents contradict their implicit positions on both assumptions by arguing against the possibility of incremental change, and thus against the current political rationality and future instructional rationality of the special education system.

In critical terms, this means that, on the question of adequacy of the current system of special education, the inclusion proponents reject all four of the field's guiding assumptions, whereas the opponents reject the two about the nature of disability and diagnosis but retain the two about the nature of special education and progress. In their criticism of the inclusive education proposals, however, the inclusion opponents reverse their position on the third and fourth assumptions and, thus, like the inclusion proponents, reject all four of the field's guiding assumptions. At this point in my critical reading of inclusion debate, then, the empirical arguments for and against the current system of special education and those against the inclusive education reform proposals reject all four guiding assumptions, which means they also reject the functionalist theories of human pathology and organizational rationality and thus the metatheoretical paradigm of functionalism itself. Given a critical reading of its inconsistencies, contradictions, and silences, the inclusion debate deconstructs or delegitimizes the hierarchy of presuppositions that constitutes the special education knowledge tradition, and thus delegitimizes the knowledge that guides and justifies special education as a professional practice.

Although the inclusion debate is replete with inconsistencies, contradictions, and silences, another contradiction deserves our attention. In this chapter I have conducted a critical reading of the inclusion proponents' arguments against the current system of special education, the opponents' arguments for the current system, and the opponents' arguments against the proponents' inclusive education reform proposals. Although I presented the proponents' reform proposals, I did not read them critically. When their reform proposals are read critically (see Skrtic, 1988b, 1991a, 1991b; Chapter 18), however, the inclusion proponents reverse their position on the third and fourth assumptions as well. That is, although in their criticism of the current system, they argue against the rationality of special and general education and against the possibility of rational-technical change, we will see in Chapter 18 that their reform proposals actually call for a rational-technical approach to change that reproduces and extends the current systems of special and general education and thus the traditional organization of schools.

What is so troubling about this confusion over the third and fourth assumptions is that the inclusion debate, and thus the legitimacy of special education as a professional practice in the 1990s and beyond, hangs on the question of the nature of school organization and change, the very question about which so much uncertainty abounds in the special education community.

RECONSTRUCTING THE SPECIAL EDUCATION KNOWLEDGE TRADITION

To this point in Part Two, my aim has been to deconstruct the special education knowledge tradition and thus to raise doubts in the reader's mind about the legitimacy of special education as a professional practice. Now I want to comment on the process of reconstructing the special education knowledge tradition by expanding upon my earlier argument that the process must be premised on a discourse that is empirical, critical, and pragmatic. In the interest of demonstrating that, on its own, theoretical criticism is inadequate for carrying out the type of critical reconstruction necessary, I first extend my argument about the problem of foundationalism. Then, in the interest of making the important methodological and political point that a critical reconstruction of the special education knowledge tradition must include in the discourse the voices of special education clients and advocates, I expand upon what I mean by "empirical" and redefine the traditional notion of "client." Finally, in the interest of providing some methodological guidelines for reconstructing the special education knowledge tradition, I reconsider the method of critical pragmatism, the antifoundational approach to social analysis that I introduced in Chapter 14. Here I argue that the field of special education can mount a critical reconstruction of its knowledge tradition by adopting the method of critical pragmatism as a mode of professional practice and discourse.

THE PROBLEM OF FOUNDATIONALISM

In the previous section I illustrated my first point about the type of expanded discourse that is necessary to reconstruct the special education knowledge tradition—to be comprehensible to the field and yet avoid reproducing its problems of practice, such a discourse must be both empirical and critical. Here I want to substantiate my claim that, to be useful, this discourse also must be pragmatic; it must provide a way to choose among alternative theoretical interpretations of special education and disability under conditions in which the truth of any given interpretation cannot be established.

As we know from Chapter 14, the subjectivist view of science is that, rather than a rational-technical process that produces objective knowledge, science is a nonrational-cultural undertaking that yields different kinds of knowledges, depending on the observer's frame of reference. Given the relationship between the social sciences and the social professions, this means that, far from being objective knowledge about social reality, the theoretical knowledge that guides and justifies special education's professional practices and discourse is subjective knowledge based on a historically situated and, at best, temporarily valid frame of reference.

Although the subjectivist view of science means that nothing is inherently true about the special education knowledge tradition, the antifoundational view of knowledge means that nothing is inherently false about it either. Indeed, the question of the adequacy of the special education knowledge tradition is not whether it is true or false but whether it serves the best interests of the field's clients and of society. As such, the problem the field of special education faces today is that the professional models, practices, and tools that flow from its assumptions, theories, and metatheories have been shown to be largely ineffective at best and harmful at worst, first during the mainstreaming debate and again during the inclusion debate.

Given that its knowledge tradition is neither true nor effective, the field of special education is compelled intellectually and ethically to reconstruct its professional knowledge, practices, and discourses in a way that serves the best interests of its clients and society. Of course, antifoundationalism means the field has no way to establish the cognitive authority of any other theoretical perspective or disciplinary orientation as a grounding for its knowledge tradition. Here again, however, the question is not whether any specific theoretical or disciplinary grounding is true or false but whether the professional practices and discourses that flow from it promote the best interests of special education clients and of society.

Thus, if special educators are to reconstruct their knowledge tradition in a way that avoids its past and current inadequacies, they must have a method of discourse that is empirical, critical, and pragmatic. I will expand upon what I mean by "empirical" and "client." At this point, however, I want to consider the reasons why the method of discourse must be critical and pragmatic.

The theoretical discourse on special education is critical because it questions the field's traditional theoretical grounding and provides an array of alternative theories for conceptualizing new practices and guiding and interpreting research on their effects. As noted above, however, the problem with the theoretical discourse is that it is foundational. Although it provides the field with an array of optional descriptions of special education and disability, and thus a variety of possible knowledges for grounding the field's practices and guiding its research, each theoretical critique is a version of the wrong theory claim. Implicitly or explicitly, each alternative theoretical perspective argues against special education's traditional theoretical (and disciplinary) grounding in the functionalist paradigm and makes a case for an alternative theoretical grounding in one of the other paradigms of modern social scientific thought (refer to Figure 15.3). Thus, although the theoretical discourse is critical, it is not pragmatic because it does not solve the problem of choosing among the various theories and disciplinary orientations it puts forth.

To be critical and pragmatic, the method of discourse that special educators need to reconstruct their knowledge tradition must be critical on two levels. It must be critical with respect to the *theories* that ground its practices and critical with respect to the *metatheoretical paradigms* that ground the various theoretical interpretations proposed as alternatives. And, of course, to be critical and pragmatic at the metatheoretical level, the method of discourse special educators need to reconstruct their knowledge tradition must be antifoundational.

THE PROBLEM OF VOICE

The field of special education can address the problems of naive pragmatism and theoretical incomprehensibility by combining its empirical evidence on the effects of its practices with the critical insights of the theoretical discourse, thus creating an expanded discourse that is both critical and comprehensible to the field. Although such a discourse is necessary for critically reconstructing the special education knowledge tradition, it is insufficient for two reasons. One reason, of course, is that the theoretical discourse is foundational and thus not pragmatic, as noted above. The second reason is that empirical research itself is inadequate.

As a nomothetic methodology grounded in the functionalist paradigm, empirical research seeks objective truth by using systematic protocols, standardized instruments, and various forms of quantitative data analysis (see Chapter 14). With the rise of subjectivism, however, the legitimacy of empirical research has been called into question, and, at the same time, the perceived legitimacy of idiographic methodologies associated with the interpretivist paradigm has increased. Interpretivist methods, such as ethnography (Erickson, 1973) and naturalistic inquiry (Lincoln & Guba, 1985; Skrtic, 1985; Skrtic, Guba, & Knowlton, 1985), generally use emergent protocols, nonstandardized instruments, and various forms of qualitative analysis. They are concerned with subjective truth, with the way humans construct meaning and thus interpret and act upon the social contexts in which they find themselves.

In the field of educational inquiry, the difference between functionalist and interpretivist methods was cast initially in terms of the type of data favored by each approach, which gave rise to the "quantitative-qualitative debate" (Smith & Heshusius, 1986, p. 4; Firestone, 1990; Howe, 1988) of the 1970s and early 1980s. The quantitative-qualitative distinction, however, is superficial because, by emphasizing type of data used at the expense of type of knowledge produced, it glosses over the fact that both types of research produce knowledge by using both quantitative and qualitative data (see, e.g., Lincoln & Guba, 1985; Yin, 1984).

Thus, the distinction between functionalist and interpretivist methods is better cast as the difference between types of knowledge produced, which is a difference between empirical knowledge—*etic*, outsider- or researcher-driven—and phenomenological knowledge—*emic*, insider- or participant-driven. As such, empiricists conceive of truth as objective knowledge based on a consensus among researchers on the meaning of a particular data set, whereas interpretivists define it as subjective knowledge based on a consensus among research participants on the meaning of a particular social context (see Skrtic, 1990b).

In the 1970s the quantitative-qualitative debate centered on the question of whether the functionalist or interpretivist paradigm is the "best" paradigm for grounding educational research. But perceptions began to change in the 1980s, and today the educational research community generally recognizes that both types of research are useful and, indeed, essential in educational decision making (see Firestone, 1990; Howe, 1988; Sirotnik & Oakes, 1986; Skrtic, 1990b, 1991a). The historical dominance of functionalist methodologies in educational inquiry has meant that, for most of this century, the decision-making process in public education has been dominated by educational researchers, by the applied science level of the profession of education (see Chapter 14).

Calls for greater use of interpretivist methodologies began in the 1960s (see Bogdan & Biklen, 1982) and have continued with increasing intensity throughout the quantitative-qualitative debate, in both general education (e.g., Lincoln & Guba, 1985; Sirotnik & Oakes, 1986) and special education (e.g., Poplin, 1987; Stainback & Stainback, 1984a). The perceived value of these methods is that they consider the nature and effects of educational practices from the multiple perspectives of research participants, which include the perspectives of education clients (students, parents, advocates) and educational practitioners, giving them a voice in the decision-making process. And, although questions have been raised about the capacity of interpretivist methodologies to actually represent the interests of research participants (Lather, 1991), these methods at least hold out the possibility of achieving a better balance among the interests of applied scientists, practitioners, and clients in educational decision making (see Chapter 18).

I raised the issue of the inadequacy of a solely empirical approach to educational inquiry to extend my argument that, to be comprehensible to special educators, the expanded discourse for critically reconstructing the special education knowledge tradition must be empirical (as well as critical and pragmatic). Given this discussion, I can say at this point that the discourse must be comprehensible to special education professionals at both the applied science and the practitioner levels of the field, as well as to special education clients and advocates, and thus, methodologically and politically, it must be based on empirical *and* phenomenological knowledge of the nature and effects of special education practices. I will have more to say about the voice of professional practitioners. For now, however, I want to note that expanding the critical discourse to include the voice of special education clients necessarily requires redefining them as special education "consumers."

According to Schein (1972), *consumer* is an economic construct that implies that individuals know best what is good for them. Conversely, the notion of a *client* is an artifact of the traditional objectivist view of the professions. It implies that professionals "know better what is good for the client than the client himself" (Schein, 1972, p. 9; Chapter 14). The objectivist view of the professions has meant that the relationship between professionals and their clients in this century has taken the form of a monologue, the familiar one-way conversation in which professionals diagnose and prescribe and clients simply accept their pronouncements on faith (Bledstein, 1976; Schein, 1972). By calling this view into question, however, subjectivism and antifoundationalism have given currency to the idea that the traditional professional-*client monologue* should be transformed into a professional-*consumer dialogue*, a more democratic process in which professionals share decision-making power with those who consume their services (Collins, 1979; Freidson, 1970, 1986; Schein, 1972; Chapter 18).

CRITICAL PRAGMATISM AS A MODE OF PROFESSIONAL PRACTICE AND DISCOURSE

As we know from Chapter 14, critical pragmatism is the progressive liberal form of postmodernism espoused by John Dewey and the other American pragmatists, as well as by contemporary philosophical pragmatists such as Bernstein (1983) and Rorty (1979). As an antifoundational approach to social inquiry, critical pragmatism seeks edification rather than objective knowledge or monological truth. It is a pedagogical process for deconstructing and reconstructing social and institutional practices and discourses by redescribing them in alternative theoretical and metatheoretical languages, a dialogical process in which "the way things are said is more important than the possession of truths" (Rorty, 1979, p. 359; Gadamer, 1975). As such, critical pragmatism is a radically democratic and participatory form of social inquiry in which all forms of knowledge are accepted or rejected on the basis of their contribution to the realization of social ideals, rather than on whether they are true in a foundational sense (Bernstein, 1983, 1991; Rorty, 1979, 1989, 1991).

Whereas the aim of modern social inquiry is to justify social practices and institutions by showing that they are based on a true representation of the social world, the goal of critical or philosophical pragmatism is to change social practices and institutions by reconciling them with our moral ideals (Bernstein, 1971, 1991; Rorty, 1982, 1989). According to William James (1975), philosophical pragmatism is:

> ...a method of settling metaphysical disputes that otherwise might be interminable. Is the world one or many?—fated or free?—material or spiritual?—here are notions either of which may or may not hold good of the world; and disputes over such notions are unending. The pragmatic method in such cases is to try to interpret each notion by tracing its respective practical consequences. What difference would it practically make to anyone if this notion rather than that notion were true?...Whenever a dispute is serious, we ought to be able to show some practical difference that must follow from one side or the other's being right. (p. 28)

In Chapter 14 I used critical pragmatism as a method of social analysis to deconstruct the objectivist view of the professions, and in this chapter to deconstruct special education as a professional practice. Critical pragmatism, however, is more than a method of social analysis; it also can be used as a mode of professional practice and discourse, one premised on continually evaluating and reappraising the practical consequences of a profession's knowledge, practices, and discourses by critically assessing them and the assumptions, theories, and metatheories in which they are grounded (see Cherryholmes, 1988; Skrtic, 1991a; Chapter 14). As such, I am suggesting that the profession of special education reconstitute itself as a community of critical inquiry, and that the mode of inquiry should be critical pragmatism, an example of which is provided by the methods I used in this chapter and the previous one and will use again in Chapter 18 (also see Cherryholmes, 1988; Maxcy, 1991; Skrtic, 1991a, 1991b; Stanley, 1992).

As a mode of professional practice and discourse, critical pragmatism entails two ongoing and interrelated critical activities:

1. *Critical practice*, "continual movement between construction of a practice, which justifies why things are designed as they are, and deconstruction of that practice, which shows its incompleteness and contradictions" (Cherryholmes, 1988, pp. 96–97).

2. *Critical discourse*, "continual movement between the constitution of a methodology designed to [carry out the construction and deconstruction of practices] and subsequent criticism of that approach" (Cherryholmes, 1988, p. 97).

Applied to the profession of special education, critical pragmatism is both a way for special educators to continually evaluate and reappraise the practical consequences of what they do (critical practice), and a way to continually evaluate and reappraise how they carry out such critical appraisals of their practices (critical discourse) (see Skrtic, 1991a). And, of course, the goal of critical pragmatism is not to justify special education practices by showing that they are based on a true representation of the world. It is to change those practices by reconciling them with what special education professionals and consumers believe is right. The value of this approach to professional practice and discourse is that it provides a way for special educators to avoid the delusion that they can know themselves, their practices, or the interests of their consumers, "except under optional descriptions" (Rorty, 1979, p. 379).

As we saw in Chapter 14, subjectivism and antifoundationalism have recast social inquiry as a distinctively human process in which potential knowledges, alternative interpretations, or optional descriptions are constructed. This has resulted in the production or rediscovery of several methods that are well suited for conducting critical pragmatic analyses. Although other methods can be used for this purpose (see Cherryholmes, 1988; Maxcy, 1991; Stanley, 1992), in the following sections I will describe the four I have used in this chapter and in Chapters 14 and 18 (also see Skrtic, 1991a). These are the methods I am recommending for applying critical pragmatism as a mode of professional practice and discourse in the field of special education. They are: *immanent critique* (see Antonio, 1981; Benhabib, 1986; Taylor, 1977), *ideal types* (Weber, 1949; Mommsen, 1974), *deconstruction* (Derrida, 1982a, 1982b), and *genealogy* (Foucault, 1980a, 1983).

Immanent Critique and Ideal Types. Immanent critique is more than a method of analysis. Historically, it has been understood as the driving force behind social progress and change. For example, Hegel (1977) described the history of Western civilization as the progressive development of human consciousness, a process driven by the affinity of self-conscious humans to reconcile their claims about themselves (ideals) with their actual social conditions (reality) (see Benhabib, 1986; Kojeve, 1969; Taylor, 1977). As a method of social analysis, immanent critique is a means of exposing the contradictions between our claims and our conditions. Moreover, as a form of critical analysis, an immanent critique seeks to transform the real into the ideal by describing "what a social totality holds itself to be, and then confronting it with what it is in fact becoming" (Schroyer, 1973, pp. 30–31), that is, by confronting social actors with the fact that they are not living up to their own standards.

In Chapter 14 I used the method of immanent critique to expose the contradictions between the claims and condition of the social professions, and in this chapter to expose those between the ideals and actual practices of the field of special education. Chapters 16 and 17 also can be read as immanent critiques because, as alternative theoretical interpretations of special education and disability, they implicitly confront the reader with contradictions between the ideal and the real in the field of special education. Finally, Chapter 18 is an explicit immanent critique of special education as an institutional practice of public education and, as we will see, of the institution of public education itself.

Although immanent critique is a powerful form of criticism, it does not on its own provide a way of identifying either the ideals or the actual conditions associated with a given social phenomenon. This requires something like Max Weber's (1949) method of ideal types, an analytic device for characterizing actual social phenomena in terms of the cultural ideals that shape and sustain them. Weber (1949) argued that the meaning of a social phenomenon derives from the value orientation upon which it is premised, and thus that, properly construed, the social sciences are cultural sciences, disciplines that "analyze the phenomena of life in terms of their cultural significance" (Dallmayr & McCarthy, 1977, p. 20). As such, he proposed the formulation of mental constructs, or ideal types, as a means for grasping the cultural significance or value orientation that gives particular social phenomena their unique character.

According to Weber (1949), an ideal type is an exaggerated mental construct "formed by the one-sided *accentuation* of one or more points of view.... In its conceptual purity, this mental construct...cannot be found empirically anywhere in reality. It is a *utopia*" (p. 90). Thus, ideal types are not true in an objectivist sense. They are mental constructions, the value of which stems from their utility as conceptual tools for analyzing the nature and practical implications of particular social and institutional practices (Dallmayr & McCarthy, 1977; Mommsen, 1974; Ritzer, 1983). Nor is a single ideal type ever sufficient for characterizing a social phenomenon. The more complex the phenomena of interest, and thus "the more many-sided their cultural *significance*" (Weber, 1949, p. 97), the more difficult it is to characterize them in terms of a single ideal type. "In such situations," Weber noted, "the frequently repeated attempts to discover ever *new* aspects of significance by the construction of new ideal-typical concepts is all the more natural and unavoidable" (p. 97).

Ideal types always are predicated on subjective presuppositions because "knowledge of cultural reality...is always knowledge from *particular points of view*" (Weber, 1949, p. 81), which is a conceptualization of social inquiry completely consistent with subjectivist and antifoundationalist views of science and knowledge. Writing before these views held much sway in the social disciplines, Weber anticipated the reactions of his objectivist critics by arguing that even their ostensibly "presuppositionless" theoretical constructions and empirical descriptions "*must* use concepts which are precisely and unambiguously definable only in the form of ideal types" (Weber, 1949, p. 92). For Weber the problem in the social sciences is not their inherent subjectivity but, rather, objectivists' tendency to think that their theoretical constructions and empirical descriptions actually portray "the 'true' content and the essence of historical reality" (p. 94), that they are something more than one-sided accentuations of certain paradigm-bound points of view.

In Chapter 14 I used ideal types to characterize the objectivist and subjectivist versions of modern social science in terms of their respective value assumptions regarding the nature of reality, human agency, knowledge, and methodology. I also used them to characterize the objectivist and subjectivist conceptualizations of the professions in terms of their respective value assumptions regarding the nature and effects of professional knowledge and the process of professionalization. In this chapter I used ideal types to characterize the special education knowledge tradition in terms of the four value assumptions that guide and justify it, as well as to characterize the arguments put forth in the inclusion debate relative to those assumptions and the functionalist theories and metatheories in which they are grounded. In addition, I will use my own and others' ideal types in my analysis of the organizational context of special education in Chapter 18. Finally, although Chapters 16 and 17 were not expressly written as ideal types, they can and should be read that way.

Deconstruction and Genealogy. As we know from Chapter 14, under subjectivist and antifoundationalist conceptions of social science the metaphor for social life has been recast as a text that can be interpreted in many ways, none of which can be correct in a foundational sense but each of which, if acted upon, carries with it profound moral and political consequences for individuals and society (Derrida, 1982a; Foucault, 1972, 1983; Geertz, 1983). Social analysis under the text metaphor is the study of that which conditions, limits, and institutionalizes social knowledge, practices, and discourses. Ultimately, such an analysis is concerned with the moral and political implications of a process in which certain individuals or groups are given the authority to interpret reality for others (Dreyfus & Rabinow, 1983). And, of course, the social professions have become a key target of criticism because in modern societies they have the authority to interpret normality, and thus the power to define others as abnormal and to treat their bodies and minds.

Given that critical pragmatism is concerned with deconstructing and reconstructing professional knowledge, practices, and discourses, Foucault's method of genealogy and certain aspects of Derrida's method of deconstruction are particularly useful. Deconstruction and genealogy are both antifoundational methods associated with the radical Continental version of postmodernism (see Chapter 14). As such, Derrida and Foucault reject modern knowledge outright, and thus the metatheoretical grounding of philosophy and, either explicitly (Foucault) or implicitly (Derrida), the social sciences and social professions. In this sense, they are both "end-of-philosophy" *meta*philosophers. They argue that philosophy has come to an end and that philosophers must do something different, something beyond philosophy. The difference between the two metaphilosophers is in what they choose to do now that philosophy is over. Whereas Derrida has elected to "write metaphilosophical deconstructions of the history of philosophy," Foucault "writes concrete histories of practical attempts to gather social and psychological knowledge" (Hoy, 1985, p. 59), concrete genealogies of the development of the knowledge, practices, and discourses of the social sciences and social professions.

In his reading of Western philosophy, Derrida (1982b) does not focus on the central ideas or arguments of philosophical texts. Instead, he is concerned with the margins of these texts, with what is not said, as well as with the various rhetorical devices that are used to gloss over their contradictions, inconsistencies, and incompleteness. Whereas traditional analyses purport to enable us to read these texts, Derrida's objective is to demonstrate that they are unreadable. Rather than "assuming the text succeeds in establishing its message, Derrida's strategy is to get us to see that it does not work. In short, he does not reconstruct the text's meaning, but instead deconstructs it" (Hoy, 1985, p. 44).

For Derrida, a philosophical work would succeed if it were to represent a reality external to itself. Deconstructing these texts "shows the failure of a work's attempt at representation and, by implication, the possibility of comparable failure by any such work, or by any text whatsoever" (Hoy, 1985, p. 44). And, of course, this failure to represent the world refers to the texts of the social sciences and social professions (Ryan, 1982), including this one.

Epistemologically, deconstruction is more radical than modern subjectivism because it means that there are no limits whatsoever on how a text can be read and thus that a text cannot refer beyond itself to an independent reality. Derrida emphasized the "undecidability" of texts because deconstruction is meant to be a criticism of objectivism and foundationalism, a critique of:

> ...the assumption in philosophy that a set of formal logical axioms can be constructed which provides a complete account of the truth or meaning of the world, as well as the related assumption that a single foundation...could be posited...into which everything in the world ultimately resolves itself. (Ryan, 1982, p. 16)

Given the undecidability of texts, and thus the futility of seeking true interpretations under conditions in which there is never enough cognitive authority to place one interpretation over another, Derrida (1982a) argued that philosophers should abandon the traditional project of interpretation and instead take up "dissemination," the project of continuously illustrating, through alternative interpretations or optional descriptions, the fundamental illegibility of texts.

In Chapter 14 I used deconstruction to expose the inconsistencies, contradictions, and silences in modern social knowledge and the objectivist view of the professions. And I used it in this chapter to expose those contained in the functionalist knowledge tradition of special education by, among other things, rereading the inclusion debate in terms of its implications for the assumptions, theories, and metatheories behind special education's professional models, practices, and tools. In addition, I will use deconstruction in Chapter 18 to raise doubts about special education as an institutional practice of public education, as well as to deconstruct the institution of public education itself.

Although Derrida's approach is useful for deconstructing professional knowledge and discourses, it does not on its own provide a means to reconstruct them. Actually, Derrida seems to be ambivalent about the implications of deconstruction for the social sciences and social professions, a posture for which Foucault (1983) has criticized him. Moreover, I have argued elsewhere that Derrida's radical attacks on interpretation are overstated and that they assume a lack of communication that philosophical pragmatism makes possible (see Skrtic, 1991a).

Although Foucault also was a metaphilosopher, his work emphasizes the moral and political implications of antifoundationalism for the social sciences and social professions. As we know from Chapter 14, Foucault was concerned about "disciplinary power" (1980b, p. 105, 1980a, 1983), about the way modern societies control and discipline their populations by sanctioning the knowledge claims and practices of the social sciences and social professions, a phenomenon that has subverted the classical notion of political rule based on sovereignty and rights. By establishing norms for human behavior, the social sciences and social professions "simultaneously manufacture—for investigation, surveillance and treatment—the vast area of our deviation from this standard" (Philp, 1985, p. 67).

For Foucault (1980b), disciplinary power "never ceases its interrogation, its inquisition, its registration of truth: it institutionalizes, professionalizes and rewards its pursuit" (p. 93). "In the end," he argued, "we are judged, condemned, classified, determined in our undertakings, destined to a certain mode of living or dying, as a function of the [knowledge traditions of the social sciences and social professions] which are the bearers of the specific effects of power" (p. 94).

Given his concern with the moral and political implications of disciplinary power, Foucault focused his genealogical analyses on the knowledge traditions that guide and justify professional practices and discourses in fields such as medicine (1975), criminology (1979), and psychiatry (1973). Ultimately, he was interested in the "norms, constraints, conditions, conventions, and so on" (Dreyfus & Rabinow, 1983, p. 108) that lead members of professional communities to believe in the legitimacy of their practices and discourses. As such, his genealogies of the nature and effects of professional practices and discourses trace the development of the historically situated knowledge traditions upon which they are premised. This is what Foucault meant by "an *ascending* analysis of power, starting, that is, from its infinitesimal mechanisms, which each have their own history, their own trajectory, their own techniques and tactics" (Foucault, 1980b, p. 99).

In his genealogical analyses, Foucault (1980b) searched for two kinds of knowledge. First is the theoretical and metatheoretical knowledge that has been "buried and disguised in a functionalist coherence or formal systemisation" (p. 81). These are the possible knowledges, alternative interpretations, or optional descriptions of the interpretivist, radical humanist, and radical structuralist paradigms, forms of knowledge that have been distorted and hidden from the social sciences and social professions because of the dominance of functionalism during the modern era. For the field of special education, this is the type of knowledge contained in the theoretical discourse on special education theory and practice—possible knowledges that have been hidden from special educators because of their field's historical grounding in the functionalist paradigm.

The second type of knowledge is what Foucault (1980b) called "disqualified knowledge (such as that of the psychiatric patient, of the ill person, of the nurse, of the doctor...of the delinquent, etc.)" (p. 82). Here, Foucault is referring to the experiential knowledge of the client *and* the professional practitioner, "a whole set of knowledges that have been disqualified as inadequate...knowledges located low down on the hierarchy, beneath [what is presumed to be] the required level of cognition or scientificity" (p. 82). Given the traditional monological relationship between professionals and clients, Foucault not surprisingly viewed clients' experiential knowledge as a form of disqualified knowledge. Foucault, however, considered the experiential knowledge of professional practitioners to be disqualified as well, because of his unconventional view of power as domination through subjugation (see Chapter 14). In this regard, he argued that, rather than something professional practitioners possess and use on their clients, disciplinary power circulates in a netlike fashion, subjugating professionals as well as clients, though not to the same extent or in the same way (Foucault, 1980b). For Foucault, the experiential knowledge of the client and the practitioner alike is essential to the process of deconstructing and reconstructing professional practices and discourses because it is through "these local popular knowledges, these disqualified knowledges, that criticism performs its work" (p. 82).

I used Foucault's genealogical approach in this chapter to trace the development of the knowledge tradition that guides and justifies special education practices and discourses. I will use it again in Chapter 18 to trace the development of the knowledge tradition that guides and justifies the practices and discourses of the field of educational administration relative to school organization, management, and change. The purpose of these analyses is to show that, far from objective knowledge of reality, the knowledge traditions of both fields are simply historical artifacts of the functionalist discourse of 20th-century social science.

Ultimately I am concerned with the nature and implications of special education practices and discourses. And, because these practices and discourses are grounded in unquestioned assumptions, theories, and metatheories, I am proposing critical pragmatism as a method of exposing and reappraising the layers of presuppositions that have conditioned, limited, and institutionalized them. Considering these presuppositions is important for special educators because it is the first step toward developing the critical posture they need to assess the ethics and efficacy of their traditional and emerging models, practices, and tools, as well as the ethics and efficacy of the institutional practice of special education itself. Until now the determination of a valid grounding for professional practice has been left to the discretion of the professions themselves. On the basis of the objectivist view of science and the positivist model of professional knowledge, it was assumed that the validity of professional knowledge is not problematic and that, with the growth of positive knowledge in the social sciences, incremental refinements are sufficient to revise and extend what is at bottom a solid foundation of objective knowledge about reality.

But subjectivism has undermined this view, creating both a crisis and an opportunity for the social profession of special education: a crisis in that it deconstructs the special education knowledge tradition, an opportunity in that the deconstruction of a knowledge tradition is the precondition for its reconstruction. Moreover, the reemergence of antifoundationalism has led to a rediscovery of philosophical pragmatism and thus some of the methodological insights necessary to carry out the needed deconstruction and reconstruction of knowledge, practices, and discourses.

To be productive, the profession of special education must have a knowledge tradition. To be morally and politically justifiable in a democracy, it must have a method for continuously reappraising its knowledge tradition and its implications for individuals and society. And, though I am recommending critical pragmatism as the method, I do so with the understanding that special educators need more than a method of discourse to deconstruct and reconstruct their knowledge tradition. They need adequate conditions of discourse as well, a topic I will return to in Chapter 18.

PARADIGMATIC OVERVIEW OF REMAINING PART TWO CHAPTERS

Chapters 16 through 18 present three alternative interpretations or optional descriptions of special education and the notion of student disability. They are examples of possible knowledges that have been distorted and hidden from the profession of special education because of its metatheoretical grounding in the functionalist paradigm of modern knowledge. As such, these chapters are meant to serve a dual purpose. First, by redescribing special education and disability from unconventional perspectives, and thus calling the conventional outlook into question, they continue the process of deconstructing the special education knowledge tradition. In addition, by providing the reader with optional descriptions, these chapters contribute substantively to the process of reconstructing the special education knowledge tradition for the future. They have been written to tempt the rising generation of special educators to consider new forms of knowledge for grounding the field's practices and discourses, forms more consistent with the field's ideal of serving the best interests of its consumers and of society at large.

Although they represent only three of many possible knowledges, these chapters show that viewing special education and disability differently is both possible and desirable, and that different perspectives have profoundly different implications for the field of special education and the institution of public education, for society, and, most important, for students labeled disabled and their families.

The most distinctive feature of the alternative perspectives discussed in the remaining chapters is the way they expand the frame of reference for thinking about special education and disability. In Chapter 16 Bob Bogdan and Jim Knoll take the perspective of society at large and argue for the utility of the discipline of sociology as a useful frame of reference for considering the problem of special education and student disability. But they are not simply arguing for a sociology of special education and disability. They are arguing for a largely interpretivist sociology, which grounds their analysis in the interpretivist paradigm of modern social scientific thought. Moreover, in the spirit of the antifoundational approach recommended here, they attempt to blur the lines between modern paradigms and disciplines with a unique blend of insights from interpretivist and radical humanist sociology and ecological psychology, the latter of which can be located in the less objectivist region of the functionalist paradigm.

In Chapter 17 Valerie Janesick reframes the problem of special education and student disability from the perspective of culture. Specifically, she argues for the utility of the discipline of anthropology as a perspective for reconsidering the longstanding problem of the relationship among special education, minority status, and poverty in this country. Although the field of special education confronted this unsettling relationship in the 1960s and is faced with it again today, Janesick approaches it largely from the perspective of humanist anthropology. Here again, however, in the spirit of antifoundationalism, she blurs the lines between paradigms and disciplines by combining anthropological insights from the radical humanist and interpretivist paradigms with economic and political insights from the radical structuralist paradigm. Drawing on this unique blend of modern paradigms and disciplines, she argues that understanding the issues that flow from the interaction of special education, minority status, and poverty requires that we consider the problem in terms of the sociocultural context within which educational inequality exists.

In Chapter 18 I reframe the problem of special education and disability in terms of the nature and effects of the school organizations that society has used in this century to provide for the education of its members. I argue that, methodologically, organization is a particularly fruitful vantage point because organization analysis, the field concerned with the study of organizations, is itself a multidisciplinary, multiparadigmatic endeavor. In my analysis I draw theoretical perspectives on organization and change from all four modern paradigms and use them to construct an ideal-typical characterization of school organization and change. Then, using this characterization as an analytic device, I deconstruct the institutional practice of special education and the institution of public education itself by considering the structural and cultural implications of 20th-century school organizations for educational equity and excellence. Finally, I propose an alternative organizational configuration for schooling and show how it not only eliminates the need for a separate system of special education but also makes possible the kind of educational excellence necessary for the emerging political and economic contingencies of the 21st century.

*R*EFERENCES

Abeson, A., & Zettel, J. (1977). The end of the quiet revolution: The Education for All Handicapped Children Act of 1975. *Exceptional Children, 44*(2), 115–128.

Algozzine, B. (1976). The disturbing child: What you see is what you get? *Alberta Journal of Education Research, 22*, 330–333.

Algozzine, B. (1977). The emotionally disturbed child: Disturbed or disturbing? *Journal of Abnormal Child Psychology, 5*, 205–211.

Algozzine, B., & Korinek, L. (1985). Where is special education for students with high prevalence handicaps going? *Exceptional Children, 51*(5), 388–394.

Anderegg, M. L., & Vergason, G. A. (1988). An analysis of one of the cornerstones of the Regular Education Initiative. *Focus on Exceptional Children, 20*(8), 1–7.

Antonio, R. J. (1981). Immanent critique as the core of critical theory: Its origins and developments in Hegel, Marx, and contemporary thought. *British Journal of Sociology, 32*(3), 330–345.

Apter, S. J. (1982). *Troubled children, troubled systems.* New York: Pergamon Press.

Ballard-Campbell, M., & Semmel, M. (1981). Policy research and special education: Research issues affecting policy formation and implementation. *Exceptional Education Quarterly, 2*(2), 59–68.

Barnes, B. (1982). *T. S. Kuhn and social science.* New York: Columbia University Press.

Barton, L., & Tomlinson, S. (Eds.). (1984). *Special education and social interests.* London: Croom-Helm.

Bates, R. J. (1980). Educational administration, the sociology of science, and the management of knowledge. *Educational Administration Quarterly, 16*(2), 1–20.

Bates, R. J. (1987). Corporate culture, schooling, and educational administration. *Educational Administration Quarterly, 23*(4), 79–115.

Benhabib, S. (1986). *Critique, norm, and utopia: A study of the foundations of critical theory.* New York: Columbia University Press.

Bernstein, R. J. (1971). *Praxis and action: Contemporary philosophies of human activity.* Philadelphia: University of Pennsylvania Press.

Bernstein, R. J. (1983). *Beyond objectivism and relativism: Science, hermeneutics, and praxis.* Philadelphia: University of Pennsylvania Press.

Bernstein, R. J. (1991). *The new constellation.* Cambridge, England: Polity Press.

Biklen, D. (1977). Exclusion. In B. Blatt, D. Biklen, & R. Bogdan (Eds.), *An alternative textbook in special education* (pp. 135–151). Denver: Love Publishing.

Biklen, D. (Ed.). (1985). *Achieving the complete school: Strategies for effective mainstreaming.* New York: Columbia University.

Biklen, D., & Zollers, N. (1986). The focus of advocacy in the LD field. *Journal of Learning Disabilities, 19*(10), 579–586.

Blatt, B., & Kaplan, F. (1966). *Christmas in purgatory.* Boston: Allyn & Bacon.

Bledstein, B. J. (1976). *The culture of professionalism: The middle class and the development of higher education in America.* New York: W. W. Norton & Company.

Bogdan, R. (1974). *Being different: The autobiography of Jane Fry.* New York: Wiley.

Bogdan, R., & Biklen, S. (1982). *Qualitative research for education: An introduction to theory and methods.* Boston: Allyn & Bacon.

Bogdan, R., & Knoll, J. (1988). The sociology of disability. In E. L. Meyen & T. M. Skrtic (Eds.), *Exceptional children and youth: An introduction* (pp. 449–477). Denver: Love Publishing.

Bogdan, R., & Kugelmass, J. (1984). Case studies of mainstreaming: A symbolic interactionist approach to special schooling. In L. Barton & S. Tomlinson (Eds.), *Special education and social interests* (pp. 173–191). New York: Nichols.

Bowles, S. & Gintis, H. (1976). *Schooling in capitalist America.* New York: Basic Books.

Braaten, S. R., Kauffman, J. M., Braaten, B., Polsgrove, L., & Nelson, C. M. (1988). The regular education initiative: Patent medicine for behavioral disorders. *Exceptional Children, 55,* 21–27.

Braginsky, D., & Braginsky, B. (1971). *Hansels and Gretels.* New York: Holt, Rinehart & Winston.

Bryan, T., Bay, M., & Donahue, M. (1988). Implications of the learning disabilities definition for the regular education initiative. *Journal of Learning Disabilities, 21*(1), 23–28.

Bryan, T., Bay, M., Lopez-Reyna, N., & Donahue, M. (1991). Characteristics of students with learning disabilities: The extant database and its implications for educational programs. In J. W. Lloyd, N. N. Singh, & A. C. Repp (Eds.), *The Regular Education Initiative: Alternative perspectives on concepts, issues, and models* (pp. 113–131). Sycamore, IL: Sycamore Publishing Company.

Burrell, G., & Morgan, G. (1979). *Sociological paradigms and organizational analysis.* London: Heinemann Educational Books.

Callahan, R. (1962). *Education and the cult of efficiency.* Chicago: University of Chicago Press.

Carnine, D. (1987). A response to "False standards, a distorting and disintegrating effect on education, turning away from useful purposes, being inevitably unfulfilled, and remaining unrealistic." *Remedial and Special Education, 8*(1), 42–43.

Carrier, J. G. (1983). Masking the social in educational knowledge: The case of learning disability theory. *American Journal of Sociology, 88*(5), 948–974.

Cherryholmes, C. H. (1988). *Power and criticism: Poststructuralist investigations in education.* New York: Teachers College Press.

Churchman, C. W. (1971). *The design of inquiry systems.* New York: Basic Books.

Clark, D. L. (1985). Emerging paradigms in organizational theory and research. In Y. S. Lincoln (Ed.), *Organizational theory and inquiry: The paradigm revolution* (pp. 43–78). Beverly Hills, CA: Sage.

Collins, R. (1979). *The credential society*. New York: Academic Press.

Council for Children with Behavioral Disorders. (1989). Position statement on the regular education initiative. *Behavioral Disorders, 14*, 201–208.

Dallmayr, F. R., & McCarthy, T. A. (1977). *Understanding and social inquiry*. Notre Dame, IN: University of Notre Dame Press.

Davis, F. (1963). *Passage through crisis*. Indianapolis: Bobbs-Merrill.

Davis, W. E. (1989). The regular initiative debate: Its promises and problems. *Exceptional Children, 55*(5), 440–446.

Davis, W. E., & McCaul, E. J. (1988). *New perspectives on education: A review of the issues and implications of the regular education initiative*. Orno, ME: Institute for Research and Policy Analysis on the Education of Students with Learning and Adjustment Problems.

Deno, E. (1970). Special education as developmental capital. *Exceptional Children, 37*(3), 229–237.

Derrida, J. (1982a). *Dissemination*. (B. Johnson, Trans.). London: Athlone Press. (Original work published 1972)

Derrida, J. (1982b). *Margins of philosophy*. (A. Bass, Trans.) Chicago: University of Chicago Press. (Original work published 1972)

Dreyfus, H. L., & Rabinow, P. (1983). *Michel Foucault: Beyond structualism and hermeneutics*. Chicago: University of Chicago Press.

Dunn, L. M. (1968). Special education for the mildly retarded—Is much of it justifiable? *Exceptional Children, 35*(1), 5–22.

Dunn, L. M. (1973). *Exceptional children in the schools: Special education in transition* (2nd ed.). New York: Holt, Rinehart & Winston.

Edmonds, R. (1979). Some schools work and more can. *Social Policy, 9*(5), 26–31.

Erickson, F. (1973). What makes school ethnography "ethnographic?" *Council on Anthropology and Education Newsletter, 4*(2), 10–19.

Farber, B. (1968). *Mental retardation: Its social context and social consequences*. Boston: Houghton Mifflin.

Feinberg, W., & Soltis, J. F. (1985). *School and society*. New York: Teachers College Press.

Ferguson, P. M. (1987). The social construction of mental retardation. *Social Policy, 18*(1), 51–56.

Firestone, W. A. (1990). Accommodation: Toward a paradigm-praxis dialectic. In E. G. Guba (Ed.), *The paradigm dialog* (pp. 105–124). Newbury Park, CA: Sage Publications.

Forness, S. R., & Kavale, K. A. (1987). Holistic inquiry and the scientific challenge in special education: A reply to Iano. *Remedial and Special Education, 8*(1), 47–51.

Foster, W. (1986). *Paradigms and promises: New approaches to educational administration*. Buffalo, NY: Prometheus Books.

Foucault, M. (1972). *The archaeology of knowledge*. (A. M. Sheridan Smith, Trans.). New York: Harper Colophon. (Original work published 1969)

Foucault, M. (1973). *Madness and civilization: A history of insanity in the age of reason*. (R. Howard, Trans.). New York: Vintage/Random House. (Original work published 1961)

Foucault, M. (1975). *The birth of the clinic: An archaeology of medical perception*. (A. M. Sheridan Smith, Trans.). New York: Vintage/Random House. (Original work published 1963)

Foucault, M. (1976). *Mental illness and psychology*. Berkeley, CA: University of California Press. (Original work published 1954)

Foucault, M. (1979). *Discipline and punish: The birth of the prison*. (A. M. Sheridan Smith, Trans.). New York: Vintage/Random House. (Original work published 1975)

Foucault, M. (1980a). *Power/knowledge: Selected interviews and other writings, 1972–1977*. (C. Gordon, Ed.; C. Gordon, L. Marshall, J. Mepham, & K. Soper, Trans.). New York: Pantheon Books.

Foucault, M. (1980b). Two lectures. In M. Foucault, *Power/knowledge: Selected interviews and other writings, 1972–1977* (C. Gordon, Ed.; C. Gordon, L. Marshall, J. Mepham, & K. Soper, Trans.) (pp. 78–108). New York: Pantheon Books.

Foucault, M. (1983). The subject and power. In H. L. Dreyfus & P. Rabinow (Eds.), *Michel Foucault: Beyond structuralism and hermeneutics* (pp. 208–226). Chicago: University of Chicago Press.

Freidson, E. (1970). *Professional dominance: The social structure of medical care*. New York: Atherton.

Freidson, E. (1986). *Professional powers: A study of the institutionalization of formal knowledge.* Chicago: University of Chicago Press.

Freire, P. (1970). *Pedagogy of the oppressed.* New York: Continuum.

Freire, P. (1973). *Education for critical consciousness.* New York: Continuum.

Fuchs, D., & Fuchs, L. (1991). Framing the REI debate: Abolitionists versus conservationists. In J. W. Lloyd, N. N. Singh, & A. C. Repp (Eds.), *The Regular Education Initiative: Alternative perspectives on concepts, issues, and models* (pp. 241–255). Sycamore, IL: Sycamore Publishing Company.

Gadamer, H. G. (1975). *Truth and method.* G. Barden & J. Cumming (Eds. and Trans.). New York: Seabury Press.

Gartner, A. (1986). Disabling help: Special education at the crossroads. *Exceptional Children, 53*(1), 72–79.

Gartner, A., & Lipsky, D. K. (1987). Beyond special education: Toward a quality system for all students. *Harvard Educational Review, 57*(4), 367–390.

Gartner, A., & Lipsky, D. K. (1989). *The yoke of special education: How to break it.* Rochester, NY: National Center on Education and the Economy.

Geertz, C. (1983). *Local knowledge: Further essays in interpretive anthropology.* New York: Basic Books.

Gerber, M. M. (1987). Application of cognitive-behavioral training methods to teach basic skills to mildly handicapped elementary school students. In M. C. Wang, M. C. Reynolds, & H. J. Walberg (Eds.), *Handbook of special education: Research and practice (Vol. I: Learner characteristics and adaptive education)* (pp. 167–186). Oxford, England: Pergamon Press.

Gerber, M. M. (1988a). Tolerance and technology of instruction: Implications for special education reform. *Exceptional Children, 54,* 309–314.

Gerber, M. M. (1988b). Weighing the regular education initiative: Recent calls for change lead to slippery slope. *Education Week, 7*(32), 36, 28.

Gerber, M. M., & Semmel, M. I. (1984). Teacher as imperfect test: Reconceptualizing the referral process. *Educational Psychologist, 19,* 137–148.

Gerber, M. M., & Semmel, M. I. (1985). The microeconomics of referral and reintegration: A paradigm for evaluation of special education. *Studies in Educational Evaluation, 11,* 13–29.

Giddens, A. (1990). *The consequences of modernity.* Cambridge, England: Polity Press.

Gilhool, T. K. (1976). Changing public policies: Roots and forces. In M. C. Reynolds (Ed.), *Mainstreaming: Origins and implications* (pp. 8–13). Reston, VA: Council for Exceptional Children.

Gilhool, T. K. (1989). The right to an effective education: From *Brown* to P. L. 94–142 and beyond. In D. K. Lipsky & A. Gartner (Eds.), *Beyond separate education: Quality education for all* (pp. 243–253). Baltimore, MD: Paul H. Brookes.

Giroux, H. A. (1981). *Ideology, culture, and the process of schooling.* Philadelphia: Temple University Press.

Giroux, H. A. (1983). *Theory and resistance in education.* South Hadley, MA: Bergin & Garvey.

Glazer, N. (1974). The schools of the minor professions. *Minerva, 12*(3), 346–364.

Goetz, L., & Sailor, W. (1990). Much ado about babies, murky bathwater, and trickle-down politics: A reply to Kauffman. *Journal of Special Education, 24*(3), 334–339.

Goffman, E. (1961). *Asylums: Essays on the social situation of mental patients and other inmates.* Garden City, NY: Doubleday/Anchor Books.

Goffman, E. (1963). *Stigma: Notes on the management of spoiled identity.* Englewood Cliffs, NJ: Prentice Hall.

Gould, S. J. (1982). *The mismeasure of man.* New York: W. W. Norton.

Griffiths, D. E. (1983). Evolution in research and theory: A study of prominent researchers. *Educational Administration Quarterly, 19*(3), 201–221.

Griffiths, D. E. (1988). Administrative theory. In N. J. Boyan (Ed.), *Handbook of research on educational administration* (pp. 27–51). New York: Longman.

Gubrium, J. (1975). *Living and dying at Murray Manor.* New York: St. Martin's Press.

Haber, S. (1964). *Efficiency and uplift: Scientific management in the Progressive Era, 1890–1920.* Chicago: University of Chicago Press.

Hallahan, D. P., & Kauffman, J. M. (1977). Categories, labels, behavioral characteristics: ED, LD, and EMR reconsidered. *Journal of Special Education, 11,* 139–149.

Hallahan, D. P., Kauffman, J. M., Lloyd, J. W., & McKinney, J. D. (1988). Introduction to the series: Questions about the regular education initiative. *Journal of Learning Disabilities, 21*(1), 3–5.

Hallahan, D. P., & Keller, C. E. (1986). *Study of studies for learning disabilities: A research review and synthesis.* Charleston: West Virginia Department of Education.

Hallahan, D. P., Keller, C. E., McKinney, J. D., Lloyd, J. W., & Bryan, T. (1988). Examining the research base of the regular education initiative: Efficacy studies and the Adaptive Learning Environments model. *Journal of Learning Disabilities, 21*(1), 29–35, 55.

Haring, N. G. (1978). *Behavior of exceptional children: An introduction to special education.* Columbus, OH: Charles E. Merrill.

Hegel, G. W. F. (1977). *Phenomenology of spirit.* Oxford, England: Clarendon Press. (Original work published 1807)

Heller, K. A., Holtzman, W. H., & Messick, S. (Eds.). (1982). *Placing children in special education: A strategy for equity.* Washington, DC: National Academy Press.

Heller, W. H., & Schilit, J. (1987). The regular education initiative: A concerned response. *Focus on Exceptional Children, 20*(3), 1–6.

Heshusius, L. (1982). At the heart of the advocacy dilemma: A mechanistic world view. *Exceptional Children, 49*(1), 6–13.

Heshusius, L. (1986). Paradigm shifts and special education: A response to Ulman and Rosenberg. *Exceptional Children, 50*(5), 461–465.

Hobbs, N. (1975). *The futures of children: Categories, labels and their consequences.* San Francisco: Jossey-Bass.

House, E. R. (1979). Technology versus craft: A ten year perspective on innovation. *Journal of Curriculum Studies, 11*(1), 1–15.

Howe, K. R. (1988). Against the quantitative-qualitative incompatibility thesis, or dogmas die hard. *Educational Researcher, 17*(8), 10–16.

Hoy, D. (1985). Jacques Derrida. In Q. Skinner (Ed.), *The return of grand theory in the human sciences* (pp. 41–64). Cambridge, England: Cambridge University Press.

Iano, R. P. (1986). The study and development of teaching: With implications for the advancement of special education. *Remedial and Special Education, 7*(5), 50–61.

Iano, R. P. (1987). Rebuttal: Neither the absolute certainty of prescriptive law nor a surrender to mysticism. *Remedial and Special Education, 18*(1), 51–56.

James, W. (1975). Pragmatism. In F. Burkhardt, F. Bowers, & I. K. Skrupskelis (Eds.), *William James: Pragmatism and The Meaning of Truth* (pp. 1–166). Cambridge, MA: Harvard University Press. (Original work published 1907)

Janesick, V. J. (1988). Our multicultural society. In E. L. Meyen & T. M. Skrtic (Eds.), *Exceptional children and youth: An introduction* (pp. 519–535). Denver: Love Publishing.

Johnson, G. O. (1962). Special education for the mentally handicapped—A paradox. *Exceptional Children, 29*(2), 62–69.

Kauffman, J. M. (1988). Revolution can also mean returning to the starting point: Will school psychology help special education complete the circuit? *School Psychology Review, 17*, 490–494.

Kauffman, J. M. (1989). The regular education initiative as Reagan-Bush education policy: A trickle-down theory of education for the hard-to-teach. *Journal of Special Education, 23*(3), 256–278.

Kauffman, J. M. (1991). Restructuring in sociopolitical context: Reservations about the effects of current reform proposals on students with disabilities. In J. W. Lloyd, N. N. Singh, & A. C. Repp (Eds.), *The Regular Education Initiative: Alternative perspectives on concepts, issues, and models* (pp. 57–66). Sycamore, IL: Sycamore Publishing Company.

Kauffman, J. M., Gerber, M. M., & Semmel, M. I. (1988). Arguable assumptions underlying the regular education initiative. *Journal of Learning Disabilities, 21*(1), 6–11.

Kavale, K. A., & Forness, S. R. (1987). History, politics, and the general education initiative: Sleeter's reinterpretation of learning disabilities as a case study. *Remedial and Special Education, 8*(5), 6–12.

Keogh, B. K. (1988). Improving services for problem learners: Rethinking and restructuring. *Journal of Learning Disabilities, 21*(1), 19–22.

Keogh, B. K., & Levitt, M. L. (1976). Special education in the mainstream: A confrontation of limitations? *Focus on Exceptional Children, 8*(1), 1–11.

Kirk, S. A., & Chalfant, J. D. (1983). *Academic and developmental learning disabilities.* Denver: Love Publishing.

Kirp, D. L. (1973). Schools as sorters: The constitutional and policy implications of student classification. *University of Pennsylvania Law Review, 121,* 705–797.

Kojeve, A. (1969). *Introduction to the reading of Hegel.* New York: Basic Books.

Kuhn, T. S. (1970). *The structure of scientific revolutions* (2nd ed.). Chicago: University of Chicago Press.

Lather, P. (1991). Deconstructing/deconstructive inquiry: The politics of knowing and being known. *Educational Theory, 41*(2), 153–173.

Lazerson, M. (1983). The origins of special education. In J. G. Chambers & W. T. Hartman (Eds.), *Special education policies: Their history, implementation, and finance* (pp. 15–47). Philadelphia: Temple University Press.

Lemert, E. (1967). *Human deviance, social problems, and social control.* Englewood Cliffs, NJ: Prentice Hall.

Lezotte, L. W. (1989). School improvement based on the effective schools research. In D. K. Lipsky & A. Gartner (Eds.), *Beyond separate education: Quality education for all* (pp. 25–37). Baltimore, MD: Paul H. Brookes.

Lieberman, L. M. (1985). Special education and regular education: A merger made in heaven? *Exceptional Children, 51*(6), 513–516.

Lieberman, L. M. (1988). *Preserving special education...for those who need it.* Newtonville, MA: GloWorm Publications.

Lilly, M. S. (1986, March). The relationship between general and special education: A new face on an old issue. *Counterpoint,* p. 10.

Lilly, M. S. (1987). Lack of focus on special education in literature on education reform. *Exceptional Children, 53*(4), 325–326.

Lilly, M. S. (1989). Teacher preparation. In D. K. Lipsky & A. Gartner (Eds.), *Beyond separate education: Quality education for all* (pp. 143–157). Baltimore, MD: Paul H. Brookes.

Lincoln, Y. S. (1985). *Organizational theory and inquiry: The paradigm revolution.* Beverly Hills, CA: Sage Publications.

Lincoln, Y. S., & Guba, E. G. (1985). *Naturalistic inquiry.* Beverly Hills, CA: Sage Publications.

Lipsky, D. K., & Gartner, A. (1987). Capable of achievement and worthy of respect: Education for handicapped students as if they were full-fledged human beings. *Exceptional Children, 54*(1), 69–74.

Lipsky, D. K., & Gartner, A. (1989a). *Beyond separate education: Quality education for all.* Baltimore, MD: Paul H. Brookes.

Lipsky, D. K., & Gartner, A. (1989b). School administration and financial arrangements. In S. Stainback, W. Stainback, & M. Forest (Eds.), *Educating all students in the mainstream of regular education* (pp. 105–120). Baltimore, MD: Paul H. Brookes.

Lipsky, D. K., & Gartner, A. (1991). Restructuring for quality. In J. W. Lloyd, N. N. Singh, & A. C. Repp (Eds.), *The Regular Education Initiative: Alternative perspectives on concepts, issues, and models* (pp. 44–56). Sycamore, IL: Sycamore Publishing Company.

Lloyd, J. W. (1987). The art and science of research on teaching. *Remedial and Special Education, 8*(1), 44–46.

Lloyd, J. W., Crowley, E. P., Kohler, F. W., & Strain, P. S. (1988). Redefining the applied research agenda: Cooperative learning, prereferral, teacher consultation, and peer-mediated interventions. *Journal of Learning Disabilities, 21*(1), 43–52.

MacMillan, D. L., & Semmel, M. I. (1977). Evaluation of mainstreaming programs. *Focus on Exceptional Children, 9*(4), 1–14.

Martin, D. T., Overholt, G. E., & Urban, W. J. (1976). *Accountability in American education: A critique.* Princeton, NJ: Princeton Book Company.

Masterman, M. (1970). The nature of a paradigm. In I. Lakatos & A. Musgrave (Eds.), *Criticism and the growth of knowledge* (pp. 59–89). Cambridge, England: Cambridge University Press.

Maxcy, S. J. (1991). *Educational leadership: A critical pragmatic perspective.* New York: Bergin and Garvey.

McKinney, J. D., & Hocutt, A. M. (1988). The need for policy analysis in evaluating the regular education initiative. *Journal of Learning Disabilities, 21*(1), 12–18.

McNeil, L. M. (1986). *Contradictions of control: School structure and school knowledge.* New York: Methuen/ Routledge & Kegan Paul.

Mercer, J. R. (1973). *Labeling the mentally retarded.* Berkeley: University of California Press.

Mesinger, J. F. (1985). Commentary on "A rationale for the merger of special and regular education." *Exceptional Children, 51*(6), 510–512.

Meyer, J. W., & Rowan, B. (1978). The structure of educational organizations. In M. W. Meyer (Ed.), *Environments and organizations* (pp. 78–109). San Francisco: Jossey-Bass.

Mintzberg, H. (1979). *The structuring of organizations.* Englewood Cliffs, NJ: Prentice Hall.

Mitroff, I. I., & Pondy, L. R. (1974). On the organization of inquiry: A comparison of some radically different approaches to policy analysis. *Public Administration Review, 34*(5), 471–479.

Mommsen, W. J. (1974). *The age of bureaucracy: Perspectives on the political sociology of Max Weber.* New York: Harper and Row.

Oakes, J. (1985). *Keeping track: How schools structure inequality.* New Haven, CT: Yale University Press.

Philp, M. (1985). Michel Foucault. In Q. Skinner (Ed.), *The return of grand theory in the human sciences* (pp. 65–81). Cambridge, England: Cambridge University Press.

Poplin, M. S. (1984). Toward an holistic view of persons with learning disabilities. *Learning Disabilities Quarterly, 7*(4), 290–294.

Poplin, M. S. (1987). Self-imposed blindness: The scientific method in education. *Remedial and Special Education, 8*(6), 31–37.

Pugach, M., & Lilly, M. S. (1984). Reconceptualizing support services for classroom teachers: Implications for teacher education. *Journal of Teacher Education, 35*(5), 48–55.

Pugach, M., & Sapon-Shevin, M. (1987). New agendas for special education policy: What the regular education reports haven't said. *Exceptional Children, 53*(4), 295–299.

Resnick, L. B., & Klopfer, L. E. (1989). *Toward the thinking curriculum: Current cognitive research.* Alexandria, VA: Association for Supervision and Curriculum Development.

Reynolds, M. C. (1962). A framework for considering some issues in special education. *Exceptional Children, 28*, 367–370.

Reynolds, M. C. (1976). New perspectives on the instructional cascade. Paper presented at the conference, "The Least Restrictive Alternatives: A Partnership of General and Special Education," sponsored by Minneapolis Public Schools, Special Education Division, November 22–23.

Reynolds, M. C. (1988). A reaction to the JLD special series on the regular education initiative. *Journal of Learning Disabilities, 21*(6), 352–356.

Reynolds, M. C. (1991). Classification and labeling. In J. W. Lloyd, N. N. Singh, & A. C. Repp (Eds.), *The Regular Education Initiative: Alternative perspectives on concepts, issues, and models* (pp. 29–42). Sycamore, IL: Sycamore Publishing Company.

Reynolds, M. C., & Birch, J. W. (1977). *Teaching exceptional children in all America's schools.* Reston, VA: Council for Exceptional Children.

Reynolds, M. C., & Lakin, K. C. (1987). Noncategorical special education: Models for research and practice. In M. Wang, M. Reynolds, & H. Walberg, *Handbook of special education: Research and practice (Vol. I: Learner characteristics and adaptive education)* (pp. 331–356). Oxford, England: Pergamon Press.

Reynolds, M. C., & Wang, M. C. (1983). Restructuring "special" school programs: A position paper. *Policy Studies Review, 2*(1), 189–212.

Reynolds, M. C., Wang, M. C., & Walberg, H. J. (1987). The necessary restructuring of special and regular education. *Exceptional Children, 53*(5), 391–398.

Rhodes, W. C. (1970). A community participation analysis of emotional disturbance. *Exceptional Children, 36*, 306–314.

Rist, R., & Harrell, J. (1982). Labeling and the learning disabled child: The social ecology of educational practice. *American Journal of Orthopsychiatry, 52*(1), 146–160.

Ritzer, G. (1980). *Sociology: A multiple paradigm science* (rev. ed.). Boston: Allyn & Bacon.

Ritzer, G. (1983). *Sociological theory.* New York: Knopf.

Rorty, R. (1979). *Philosophy and the mirror of nature.* Princeton, NJ: Princeton University Press.

Rorty, R. (1982). *Consequences of pragmatism.* Minneapolis: University of Minnesota Press.

Rorty, R. (1989). *Contingency, irony, and solidarity.* Cambridge, England: Cambridge University Press.

Rorty, R. (1991). *Objectivity, relativism, and truth: Philosophical papers, volume 1.* Cambridge, England: Cambridge University Press.

Ross, A. O. (1980). *Psychological disorders of children* (2nd ed.). New York: McGraw-Hill.

Ryan, M. (1982). *Marxism and deconstruction: A critical articulation.* Baltimore, MD: Johns Hopkins University Press.

Sailor, W. (1989). The educational, social, and vocational integration of students with the most severe disabilities. In D. K. Lipsky & A. Gartner (Eds.), *Beyond separate education: Quality education for all* (pp. 53–74). Baltimore, MD: Paul H. Brookes.

Sailor, W., Halvorsen, A., Anderson, J., Goetz, L., Gee, K., Doering, K., & Hunt, P. (1986). Community integrative instruction. In R. Horner, L. Meyer, & H. Fredericks, *Education of learners with severe handicaps* (pp. 251–288). Baltimore, MD: Paul H. Brookes.

Salvia, J., & Ysseldyke, J. E. (1981). *Assessment in special and remedial education* (2nd ed.). Boston: Houghton Mifflin.

Sapon-Shevin, M. (1987). The national education reports and special education: Implications for students. *Exceptional Children, 53*(4), 300–307.

Sapon-Shevin, M. (1988). Working towards merger together: Seeing beyond distrust and fear. *Teacher Education and Special Education, 11*(3), 103–110.

Sarason, S. B., & Doris, J. (1979). *Educational handicap, public policy, and social history.* New York: Free Press.

Scheff, T. J. (1966). *Being mentally ill: A sociological theory.* Chicago: Aldine.

Schein, E. H. (1972). *Professional education.* New York: McGraw-Hill.

Schön, D. A. (1983). *The reflective practitioner: How professionals think in action.* New York: Basic Books.

Schrag, P., & Divorky, D. (1975). *Myth of the hyperactive child.* New York: Pantheon Books.

Schroyer, T. (1973). *The critique of domination.* Boston: Beacon Press.

Schumaker, J. B., & Deshler, D. D. (1988). Implementing the regular education initiative in secondary schools: A different ball game. *Journal of Learning Disabilities, 21*(1), 36–42.

Scott, R. (1969). *The making of blind men.* New York: Russell Sage Foundation.

Shepard, L. A. (1987). The new push for excellence: Widening the schism between regular and special education. *Exceptional Children, 53*(4), 327–329.

Sigmon, S. B. (1987). *Radical analysis of special education: Focus on historical development and learning disabilities.* London: Falmer Press.

Simpson, R. G., & Eaves, R. C. (1985). Do we need more qualitative research or more good research? A reaction to Stainback and Stainback. *Exceptional Children, 51*(4), 325–329.

Sirotnik, K. A., & Oakes, J. (1986). Critical inquiry for school renewal: Liberating theory and practice. In K. Sirotnik & J. Oakes (Eds.), *Critical perspectives on the organization and improvement of schooling* (pp. 3–93). Boston: Kluwer-Nijhoff Publishing.

Skinner, B. F. (1953). *Science and human behavior.* New York: Macmillan.

Skinner, B. F. (1957). *Verbal behavior.* New York: Appleton-Century-Crofts.

Skinner, B. F. (1971). *Beyond freedom and dignity.* New York: Knopf.

Skrtic, T. M. (1985). Doing naturalistic research into educational organizations. In Y. S. Lincoln (Ed.), *Organizational theory and inquiry: The paradigm revolution* (pp. 185–220). Beverly Hills, CA: Sage Publications.

Skrtic, T. M. (1986). The crisis in special education knowledge: A perspective on perspective. *Focus on Exceptional Children, 18*(7), 1–16.

Skrtic, T. M. (1987a). The national inquiry into the future of education for students with special needs. *Counterpoint, 4*(7), 6.

Skrtic, T. M. (1987b). An organizational analysis of special education reform. *Counterpoint, 8*(2), 15–19.

Skrtic, T. M. (1988a). The crisis in special education knowledge. In E. L. Meyen & T. M. Skrtic (Eds.), *Exceptional children and youth: An introduction* (pp. 415–447). Denver: Love Publishing.

Skrtic, T. M. (1988b). The organizational context of special education. In E. L. Meyen & T. M. Skrtic (Eds.), *Exceptional children and youth: An introduction* (pp. 479–517). Denver: Love Publishing.

Skrtic, T. M. (1990a). Counter-hegemony: A radical's attempt to demystify special education ideology. (Review of *Radical analysis of special education: Focus on historical developments and learning disabilities*, by S. Sigmon). *Contemporary Psychology, 35*(1), 54–55.

Skrtic, T. M. (1990b). Social accommodation: Toward a dialogical discourse in educational inquiry. In E. Guba (Ed.), *The paradigm dialog* (pp. 125–135). Newbury Park, CA: Sage Publications.

Skrtic, T. M. (1991a). *Behind special education: A critical analysis of professional culture and school organization.* Denver: Love Publishing.

Skrtic, T. M. (1991b). The special education paradox: Equity as the way to excellence. *Harvard Educational Review, 61*(2), 148–206.

Skrtic, T. M. (Ed.). (in press). *Exploring the theory/practice link in special education: A metatheoretical genealogy.* New York: Teachers College Press.

Skrtic, T. M., Guba, E. G., & Knowlton, H. E. (1985). *Interorganizational special education programming in rural areas: Technical report on the multisite naturalistic field study.* Washington, DC: National Institute of Education.

Sleeter, C. E. (1986). Learning disabilities: The social construction of a special education category. *Exceptional Children, 53*, 46–54.

Smith, D. J. (1985). *Minds made feeble: The myth and legacy of the Kallikaks.* Rockville, MD: Aspen.

Smith, J. K., & Heshusius, L. (1986). Closing down the conversation: The end of the quantitative-qualitative debate among educational inquirers. *Educational Researcher, 15*(1), 4–12.

Snell, M. E. (1991). Schools are for all kids: The importance of integration for students with severe disabilities and their peers. In J. W. Lloyd, N. N. Singh, & A. C. Repp (Eds.), *The Regular Education Initiative: Alternative perspectives on concepts, issues, and models* (pp. 133–148). Sycamore, IL: Sycamore Publishing Company.

Spring, J. (1980). *Educating the worker-citizen: The social, economic, and political foundations of education.* New York: Longman.

Stainback, S., & Stainback. W. (1984a). Broadening the research perspective in special education. *Exceptional Children, 50*, 400–409.

Stainback, W., & Stainback, S. (1984b). A rationale for the merger of special and regular education. *Exceptional Children, 51*(1), 102–111.

Stainback, S., & Stainback, W. (1985a). *Integration of students with severe handicaps into regular schools.* Reston, VA: Council for Exceptional Children.

Stainback, S., & Stainback, W. (1985b). The merger of special and regular education: Can it be done? A response to Lieberman and Mesinger. *Exceptional Children, 51*(6), 517–521.

Stainback, S., & Stainback, W. (1987a). Facilitating merger through personnel preparation. *Teacher Education and Special Education, 10*(4), 185–190.

Stainback, S., & Stainback, W. (1987b). Integration versus cooperation: A commentary on educating children with learning problems: A shared responsibility. *Exceptional Children, 54*(1), 66–68.

Stainback, S., & Stainback, W. (1989). Integration of students with mild and moderate handicaps. In D. K. Lipsky & A. Gartner (Eds.), *Beyond separate education: Quality education for all* (pp. 41–52). Baltimore, MD: Paul H. Brookes.

Stainback, W., & Stainback, S. (1991). Rationale for integration and restructuring: A synopsis. In J. W. Lloyd, N. N. Singh, & A. C. Repp (Eds.), *The Regular Education Initiative: Alternative perspectives on concepts, issues, and models* (pp. 225–240). Sycamore, IL: Sycamore Publishing Company.

Stainback, S., & Stainback, W. (1992). Schools as inclusive communities. In W. Stainback & S. Stainback (Eds.), *Controversial issues confronting special education: Divergent perspectives* (pp. 29–44). Baltimore, MD: Paul H. Brookes.

Stainback, W., Stainback, S., Courtnage, L., & Jaben, T. (1985). Facilitating mainstreaming by modifying the mainstream. *Exceptional Children, 52*, 144–152.

Stainback, S., Stainback, W., & Forest, M. (1989). *Educating all students in the mainstreaming of regular education.* Baltimore, MD: Paul H. Brookes.

Stanley, W. B. (1992). *Curriculum for utopia: Social reconstructionism and critical pedagogy in the postmodern era.* Albany, NY: State University of New York Press.

Swap, S. (1978). The ecological model of emotional disturbance in children: A status report and proposed synthesis. *Behavioral Disorders, 3*(3), 156–186.

Szasz, T. S. (1961). *The myth of mental illness.* New York: Harper & Row.

Taylor, C. (1977). *Hegel.* Cambridge, England: Cambridge University Press.

Taylor, S., & Bogdan, R. (1977). A phenomenological approach to "mental retardation." In B. Blatt, D. Biklen, & R. Bogdan (Eds.), *An alternative textbook in special education* (pp. 193–203). Denver: Love Publishing.

Teacher Education Division of the Council for Exceptional Children. (1987). The regular education initiative: A statement by the Teacher Education Division, Council for Exceptional Children. *Journal of Learning Disabilities, 20*(5), 289–293.

Tomlinson, S. (1982). *A sociology of special education.* Boston: Routledge & Kegan Paul.

Tomlinson, S. (1988). Why Johnny can't read: Critical theory and special education. *European Journal of Special Needs Education, 3*(1), 45–58.

Turnbull, H. R. (1986). *Free appropriate public education: The law and children with disabilities* (2nd ed.). Denver: Love Publishing.

Turnbull, H. R. (1993). *Free appropriate public education: The law and children with disabilities* (4th ed.). Denver: Love Publishing.

Turnbull, H. R., & Turnbull, A. P. (1978). *Free appropriate public education: Law and implementation.* Denver: Love Publishing.

Ulman, J. D., & Rosenberg, M. S. (1986). Science and superstition in special education. *Exceptional Children, 52*(5), 459–460.

Vergason, G. A., & Anderegg, M. L. (1989). Save the baby! A response to "Integrating the Children of the Second System." *Phi Delta Kappan, 71*(1), 61–63.

Villa, R. A., Thousand, J. S., Stainback, W., & Stainback, S. (Eds.). (1992). *Restructuring for caring and effective education: An administrative guide to creating heterogeneous schools.* Baltimore, MD: Paul H. Brookes.

Walker, H. M., & Bullis, M. (1991). Behavior disorders and the social context of regular class integration: A conceptual dilemma? In J. W. Lloyd, N. N. Singh, & A. C. Repp (Eds.), *The Regular Education Initiative: Alternative perspectives on concepts, issues, and models* (pp. 75–93). Sycamore, IL: Sycamore Publishing Company.

Wang, M. C. (1981). Mainstreaming exceptional children: Some instructional design and implementation considerations. *Elementary School Journal, 81,* 195–221.

Wang, M. C. (1988, May 4). A promising approach for reforming special education. *Education Week, 7*(32), 36, 28.

Wang, M. C. (1989a). Accommodating student diversity through adaptive instruction. In S. Stainback, W. Stainback, & M. Forest (Eds.), *Educating all students in the mainstream of regular education* (pp. 183–197). Baltimore, MD: Paul H. Brookes.

Wang, M. C. (1989b). Adaptive instruction: An alternative for accommodating student diversity through the curriculum. In D. K. Lipsky & A. Gartner (Eds.), *Beyond separate education: Quality education for all* (pp. 99–119). Baltimore, MD: Paul H. Brookes.

Wang, M. C., & Peverly, S. T. (1987). The role of the learner: An individual difference variable in school learning and functioning. In M. C. Wang, M. C. Reynolds, & H. J. Walberg (Eds.), *Handbook of special education: Research and practice (Vol. I: Learner characteristics and adaptive education)* (pp. 59–92). Oxford, England: Pergamon Press.

Wang, M. C., & Reynolds, M. C. (1985). Avoiding the "catch-22" in special education reform. *Exceptional Children, 51*(6), 497–502.

Wang, M. C., & Reynolds, M. C. (1986). "Catch 22 and disabling help": A reply to Alan Gartner. *Exceptional Children, 53*(1), 77–79.

Wang, M. C., Reynolds, M. C., & Walberg, H. J. (1985). Rethinking special education. Paper presented at the "Wingspread Conference on the Education of Students with Special Needs: Research Findings and Implications for Policy and Practice," Racine, WI, December 5–7.

Wang, M. C., Reynolds, M. C., & Walberg, H. J. (1986). Rethinking special education. *Educational Leadership, 44*(1), 26–31.

Wang, M. C., Reynolds, M. C., & Walberg, H. J. (1987). *Handbook of special education: Research and practice (Vol. I: Learner characteristics and adaptive education).* Oxford, England: Pergamon Press.

Wang, M. C., Reynolds, M. C., & Walberg, H. J. (1988). Integrating the children of the second system. *Phi Delta Kappan, 70,* 248–251.

Wang, M. C., Reynolds, M. C., & Walberg, H. J. (1989). Who benefits from segregation and murky water? *Phi Delta Kappan, 71*(1), 64–67.

Wang, M. C., & Walberg, H. J. (1988). Four fallacies of segregationism. *Exceptional Children, 55*(2), 128–137.

Weber, M. (1949). "Objectivity" in social science and social policy. In E. A. Shils & H. A. Finch (Eds. & Trans.), *The methodology of the social sciences* (pp. 49–112). New York: Free Press. (Original work published 1904)

White, O. R., & Haring, N. G. (1976). *Exceptional teaching: A multimedia training package.* Columbus, OH: Charles E. Merrill.

Will, M. C. (1984). Let us pause and reflect—But not too long. *Exceptional Children, 51*(1), 11–16.

Will, M. C. (1986). Educating children with learning problems: A shared responsibility. *Exceptional Children, 52*(5), 411–416.

Wise, A. E. (1979). *Legislated learning: The bureaucratization of the American classroom.* Berkeley: University of California Press.

Wise, A. E. (1988). The two conflicting trends in school reform: Legislated learning revisited. *Phi Delta Kappan, 69*(5), 328–333.

Wiseman, J. (1970). *Stations of the lost.* Englewood Cliffs, NJ: Prentice Hall.

Wolcott, H. F. (1977). *Teachers versus technocrats: An educational innovation in anthropological perspective.* Eugene, OR: Center for Educational Policy and Management.

Yin, R. (1984). *Case study research: Design and methods.* Beverly Hills, CA: Sage Publications.

16

THE SOCIOLOGY OF

DISABILITY

ROBERT BOGDAN AND JAMES KNOLL

B y 1900, American schools were required by law to provide an education for all citizens with an implied duty to funnel the children of the waves of immigrants into "the great melting pot." The system's response was to find an efficient way to effectively teach the largest possible number of students the values of a democratic society and the basic skills they would need to stay out of trouble and make a living. When confronted with a growing group of students who did not seem to be profiting from—or were actually disrupting—the lockstep, regimented approach to instruction, however, the schools turned to what they considered their only alternative—excluding them from general education classes (see Chapters 15 and 18).

The Progressive era in the United States (circa 1900–1920, cf. Rothman, 1980) was marked by a pervasive sense of social responsibility, of trust in the power of scientific treatment and control to remedy individual problems. In education it provided the proper environment for the founding and growth of special education. Reformers saw education as the social tool needed to lift immigrant people out of the double morass of poverty and the decadence of Old World cultures. To deal with those who, as they thought, could not make it in general education classes because of apparent individual defects and disabilities, educators turned to the growing science of psychology and new medical technology for models. In addition, the ascendancy of the eugenics movement, with its logic of racial perfectibility, genetic segregation, and mental testing, with its ability to predict scholastic achievement, provided special education with a rationale and a scientific basis for the differential and separate treatment of some students.

Teachers assigned to teach the excluded students in "ungraded" classes were faced with an incredibly diverse group. One room might contain students who had physical handicaps, learning disabilities, emotional disturbances, sensory impairments, mental retardation, seizure disorders, and speech impairments, as well as first-generation immigrants who had difficulties in learning English. (Students with tuberculosis and some with other diseases were placed in other, "health" classes.) The standard teacher training programs emphasized efficient group instruction but did not equip graduates to meet the challenge of the segregated class. To fill the gap, the emerging field of special education, in wholesale fashion, began to borrow clinical methods from medicine and psychology and to implement them in the classroom. What emerged from this process is the diagnostic/prescriptive or clinical teaching method, which has come to characterize special education (see Chapter 15) until today.

On the one hand, this individualistic clinical perspective has, in the long run, systematized special education, thereby giving it professional legitimacy as a field. On the other hand, as Bart (1984) pointed out, part of the price for this legitimacy is a narrow focus that causes some significant presuppositions to become largely invisible to practitioners. Special education, as it was conceived and still practiced, attributes a child's failure in school to some flaw within him or her—most notable, an insufficient intelligence quotient—rather than inadequacy on the part of the educational institution (Bart, 1984, p. 83).

Heshusius (1982) expanded on Bart's critique by pointing out that tacit acceptance of what she called the "mechanistic model of special education" has led to a situation in which the teacher has been reduced to an "educational technician" or "behavioral engineer." In these roles "the teacher cannot act in a professional and intelligent manner, for much is forbidden, much prescribed, and much so rigid that personal initiative is impossible" (p. 11). She ended by calling for a holistic, nonmechanistic approach to education, which prepares teachers to do what is meaningful in the larger personal and academic life of their students.

A central point in both these critiques is that teachers' ability to place their students' life in a broad social context, and to critically evaluate their own performance, largely depends on the theoretical framework or paradigm within which they operate (see Skrtic, 1986; Chapters 14 and 15). We believe the special education teacher's role as a clinician, concerned with providing direct service to specific individuals, requires a basic understanding of the fundamentals of the diagnostic/prescriptive model. Implementation of this instructional technology, however, must be informed by a world view and a professional self-image that sees beyond the narrow confines of the child in the classroom. The behavioral objectives and the annual goals must be geared to the real demands of students' present as well as future lives. And teachers cannot be separated from individual advocacy and collective action for social change.

SOCIOLOGICAL PERSPECTIVES

Sociology provides alternatives to the clinical approach for examining special education and the situation of people with disabilities in the United States. Until recently, sociological perspectives have received little attention in clinical fields, even though contributions from sociologists have been substantial. A growing number of them now are taking special education and disability issues as a research focus, and special educators increasingly are developing and incorporating sociological concepts in their work.

Unfortunately, much of the sociological work dealing with special education suffers from the same limitation as do traditional studies in the field, a failure to seek a different vantage point. Some sociologists assume, along with the special education professional community, that:

- A disability is a condition an individual has.
- The disability/typical distinction is useful and objective.
- Special education is a rationally conceived and coordinated system of services that help "disabled children."

■ Progress in the field is made by improving diagnosis, intervention, and technology (Bogdan & Kugelmass, 1984).

This could be called special education sociology, because it accepts the field of special education's assumptions at face value. By working within the basic premises of the field, it often confirms beliefs rather than providing critical alternatives.

A few people in special education, as well as in sociology (Dexter, 1956; Farber, 1968), have questioned the basic premises of special education and related disciplines and have made a lasting contribution to their field. This group examines its underlying logic and so constitutes a sociology *of* special education (Freidson, 1970). From this vantage point, fundamental questions can be asked, which would be out of place in the special education research tradition in which one of the most important activities is to test the efficacy of various special education interventions. The questions might include: Who are these children? Who judges them to be "special," and in what context does this judgment occur? What do practitioners mean when they talk about the effectiveness of their programs? What really goes on in special education classes? How does special education fit with problems of social structure and social control? How do social class, gender, ethnicity, and race fit within special education?

In a sociology *of* special education/disability, what professionals accept at face value is questioned. Even statements that on the surface seem to be simple and straightforward are subjected to critical examination. For example, someone studying a special education class designated as being "for students with severe emotional disturbance" would not simply ask a teacher what was going on in the room and then fill in a blank on a questionnaire with "reading instruction" or "sex education for the emotionally disturbed." This type of researcher would take a desk in the classroom, observe what was really going on, and try to understand what the terms "reading instruction," "sex education," and "emotionally disturbed" meant in the mind and action of the teacher in that particular classroom.

Precisely by raising the question of how a person becomes transformed into a special education student or a client of human services, some of the pioneers in this emerging sociology of special education/disability have begun to affect clinical practice. A number of authors (e.g., Blatt, 1970; Braginsky & Braginsky, 1971; Goffman, 1961, 1963; Sarason & Doris, 1979; Scheff, 1966; Scott, 1969; Szasz, 1961) pointed out the changeable nature of various client classifications, such as "mentally retarded," "mentally ill," and "hyperactive," and so laid the groundwork for thinking about so-called handicaps as social constructs rather than as objective conditions.

These same authors, and others in the "labeling" school of sociology, pointed to the importance of examining the interaction between labelers and the labeled as a prerequisite for understanding how the creation of clients comes about (cf. Goffman, 1961; Lemert, 1951; Wiseman, 1970). Finally, when researchers have examined the influence of larger social institutions on the process of labeling, they often have concluded that specific disabilities have little to do with officially imposed labels (e.g., Bogdan, 1976; Conrad, 1976; Higgins, 1980).

As a result of this and other sociological work, many special educators have become aware of the arbitrary nature of many clinical labels and, therefore, are sensitive to the potentially deleterious effect of labeling students. Yet, for the most part, they remain largely ignorant of the sources of these ideas, and almost completely unaware of the theoretical perspective that informs this particular approach to scientific inquiry. It is unfortunate because the symbolic interactionist perspective, which undergirds most of the work cited above, has the potential for counterbalancing some of the limitations inherent in the dominant clinical paradigm. It is one scientific paradigm that consciously seeks to nurture the holistic perspective that Heshusius advocates as being crucial to good special education practice. As such, it has the potential to radically transform the field.

SYMBOLIC INTERACTIONISM: THE SEARCH FOR MEANING

Symbolic interaction developed as the conceptual underpinning of an approach to sociology that the University of Chicago's Sociology Department espoused in the 1920s. Sociologists working there at that time were concerned with understanding the range of human behavior both as it occurred in the real world and from the point of view of the actual people they were studying. They told their students to follow their example, and to do their research among the immigrants, hoboes, juvenile delinquents, and other such groups in the city of Chicago.

This stood in sharp contrast to other research traditions in which scholars formulated grand theories that might be partially tested by questionnaires or by testing in quasi-experimental researcher fabricated situations. In the second generation of this tradition, Everett Hughes taught his students to do field work in ordinary places such as local schools, just as anthropologists did in strange lands. Herbert Blumer (1969) coined the term *symbolic interaction*, and in his writing systematized the theory underlying this approach to doing sociology.

The cliche "beauty is in the eye of the beholder" is the simplest way to begin to describe what symbolic interaction means. We all know, but seldom take seriously, that the meaning of objects, people, situations, life, and the world is not communicated to us spontaneously as we experience something. These things have meaning conferred upon them. Meaning is not intrinsic to things and events; rather, the viewer's interpretation or definition gives something meaning. For symbolic interactionists, how people define the world, and the process by which that understanding is constructed and communicated, is a subject for investigation. From this perspective, human beings are seen as primarily interpreting, defining, symbolic creatures whose behavior can be understood only by entering into the defining process.

Conferring meaning is not an autonomous act. Humans are social, and meaning develops only through interaction with others. People, who are in contact with each other, are influenced by one another in how they come to define a given situation. They may see things in a similar way. When trying to understand a new setting, a person may use the definitions and interpretations others have, or may apply meaning previously encountered in other settings. Through the process of feeling out the situation, the individual attempts to make it meaningful (i.e., impose some conceptual order on it).

Only within a complex interaction involving the setting, the others in it, the past, and the larger social present does meaning emerge for the person.

Groups in a particular situation or in similar positions—students in a certain school, for example—often develop common definitions they see as the truth (the only possible meaning of what they are defining). Their constructions of reality are seen as "reality," and the commonality of definition helps them confirm this as the truth. Once this meaning is attached to an object or event, it is seen as being intrinsic to it. The commonly created definition is transformed into the essence of the event or object. This socially created essence, rather than the group members' shared process of definition, henceforth is taken as the explanation for the common understanding that the "insiders" share.

Because the symbolic interactionist theory emphasizes human experience as subjective, not absolute, it shies away from terms such as "truth." At certain historical periods, among certain groups, a specific definition or set of definitions of the world or objects may be dominant, seen as "the truth." This domination of a single meaning is the crux of the issue here. It has more to do with the politics of perspective than with the way a given definition fits the phenomena about which it conveys "the truth."

Despite all this talk of meaning, symbolism, and the relative nature of reality, symbolic interaction should not be seen as an intuitive, or mystical, approach to knowledge. It is fundamentally an empirical approach. Symbolic interactionism is based on the premise that the subjective states of others can be studied. Sociologists accomplish this by systematically piecing together and analyzing the world from the subject's point of view. In the process, they come to understand how meaning develops within a network of relationships. This requires that they get close enough to their subjects to really know them. To reiterate, to use this symbolic interactionist perspective in understanding the meaning of a situation, one has to look at the group that is defining the situation, as well as at the history and nature of the processes of both defining and sharing, rather than narrowly focusing analysis on the object or event in isolation.

In this approach to understanding, the terms *perspective, definition, meaning,* and *interaction* are key to making sense out of behavior. We act toward objects in ways that reflect the meaning we attach to them, not because of our internal drives, personalities, attitudes, conscious motives, or role obligations, or because of any social control mechanisms, or structural, cultural, or demographic variables. All of these concepts, which other social scientists use to discuss, explain, and predict behavior, place meaning and interaction in the background. Other theoretical constructs might be useful in understanding special aspects of behavior, but, from the symbolic interaction perspective, they miss the central element of human behavior: meaning.

For example, a proponent of symbolic interaction would not deny that film projectors show films and that there are certain norms about what, how, and when a teacher should show a film. But, they would say, films and projectors cannot be understood without studying them in terms of how the various people—students, teachers, instructional technologists, administrators—come to define them in the specific situations in which they find themselves (Bogdan, 1972). People experience films differently and exhibit different behaviors when viewing them in different situations. A teacher in one room may come to define the proper time to show films, what to show, and how to show them in a way that is significantly different from that of a teacher in another room. A film can be a way to coast through a Friday, an opportunity to teach content, a way to settle down the class, or a control measure over troublesome students (nor are any of these mutually exclusive). For some teachers, a film may be the central event of the day; for others, something thrown in as a reward. Films have an involved meaning that cannot be understood solely in terms of projectors and titles.

An important facet of the interactionist perspective is how it deals with the concept of the "self." The self is not seen as lying solely within, like an ego, or an organized body of needs and motives and internalized norms and values. Rather, the self lies outside the individual and is a product of the person's self-definition. People become objects to themselves, and the definition they construct of that object is the self. In defining the self, people attempt to see themselves as others see them. By interpreting words, gestures, and actions directed toward them, and by placing themselves in the role of observer, individuals come to construct their own self-image. We see ourselves, in part, as others see us. The self is a social construct resulting from our perceiving ourselves as objects and then developing a self-definition through interaction with others. We use feedback as a source of discovering who we are. This notion is central to the concept of "labeling," which probably has made the most important contribution of the symbolic interaction approach to special education. Classifying, thinking of, and treating students as being disabled has a profound effect on who they are, what they become, and their self-concepts.

QUALITATIVE RESEARCH: THE INSIDERS' POINT OF VIEW

Closely aligned with symbolic interaction is a particular approach to research, one that turns its back on isolating variables, categorizing people, performing carefully controlled laboratory experiments, and getting quantitative measures of discrete behaviors. Called *qualitative research*, it refers to several strategies that share certain characteristics. The data collected are termed "soft": rich in description of people, places, and conversations—the type of information that is not handled readily through statistical procedures.

When researchers use qualitative methods, they do not frame their questions by carefully operationalizing variables; they formulate them to elicit all of the complexity of a situation. People conducting qualitative research may develop a focus as they collect their data, but they do not approach their research with any preconceived questions that must be answered or with any hypotheses to test. They are more concerned with understanding behavior from the subject's own frame of reference. External causes are secondary. They tend to collect their data through sustained contact with people in the settings where they normally spend their time. The best known examples of qualitative research methods are participant (or naturalistic) observation and in-depth interviewing.

A few qualitative researchers have been studying special education settings (e.g., Bercovici, 1983; Bogdan, 1976; Buckholdt & Gubrium, 1979; Heshusius, 1981; Kielhofner, 1983; Taylor, 1982). For the most part, these researchers are trained as sociologists or anthropologists. The value of qualitative research in special education and related fields is becoming more apparent (cf. Stainback & Stainback, 1984), but training in qualitative research has not yet been generally incorporated into the curriculum for advanced degrees at the applied science level in special education. Additional information on this approach to research can be found in Bogdan and Biklen (1982) and Taylor and Bogdan (1984).

Life Histories. Rather than review the variety of qualitative research techniques, we will limit our discussion to one approach that Bogdan became associated with that has not been popular in special education: first-person life histories. In first-person life histories "clients," using their own words, reveal their view of personal experiences, organizations, and other aspects of the world in which they live. They may reflect and describe a certain period of, or a whole, life. They may be spontaneously produced, intended for confidential use only, as in personal diaries, or elicited, as when someone is asked to write or tell his or her own story.

Researchers have advocated this approach throughout the history of the social sciences (Dollard, 1935). It was popular in American sociology in general after the turn of the century, and particularly in the Chicago School (e.g., Thomas & Znaniecki, 1927; Shaw, 1966; Sutherland, 1937). As important as these early studies were, interest in first-person accounts waned when positivist theories and quantitative statistical procedures gained prominence. The pursuit of "facts" and statistical relationships relegated interests in subjective states—"meaning"—to a minor place in the social sciences (see Chapter 14).

The first-person story or autobiography makes available the client's own view of his or her situation, unaltered by professionals' interpretations. It offers a reality generated from a different place within the service delivery system. The approach has political, moral, and research implications and connections with symbolic interactionist theory that will become clear as we discuss the insights gained from first-person documents.

We will draw upon the unstructured life history interviews that Bogdan and Taylor conducted with two "clients": a man, Ed Murphy (Bogdan & Taylor, 1976), and a woman Patty Burt (Bogdan & Taylor, 1982). They were in their late teens and early 20s when they were interviewed; they were labeled "retarded," spent years of their lives in large residential state schools for the mentally retarded, and, at the time of the interviews, were clients of several community service organizations.

Although the two people interviewed were officially classified as "retarded," what we have to say about them is directly relevant to all categories of special education and human service clients. We chose people labeled mentally retarded because they are the clients we seem to listen to the least, and by listening to their voices for purposes of research and understanding, we are saying that the point of view and experiences of all categories of clients need to be heard. By extension, the first-person accounts of parents and others intimately involved in the lives of people with disabilities merit serious attention in our programs of personnel preparation. Fortunately, many sources are available to turn to in these areas (e.g., Asch, 1984; Brightman, 1985; Crossley & McDonald, 1980; Featherstone, 1982; Jones, 1983; Massie & Massie, 1973; Pieper, 1977; Roth, 1981).

Distrust of the Client's Perspective. In the mid-1960s Burton Blatt and Fred Kaplan published their now-famous photographic essay on mental retardation, *Christmas in Purgatory* (Blatt & Kaplan, 1966), depicting the atrocious conditions at five state mental retardation facilities. The pictures on which the essay was based were taken with a camera secured to Kaplan's belt and hidden from view by his sports jacket. On one occasion, a patient in one of the institutions discovered Kaplan's camera and reported it to an administrator whose attention Blatt had monopolized up to that time. The administrator laughed and casually dismissed the report with the remark, "Boy, these retardates have imaginations!" Ironic, but not surprising or unusual.

Those who are labeled "retarded" have a wide range of imperfections imputed to them in addition to their alleged low intelligence (Lorber, 1974). According to the stereotype, they are incompetent, irrational, undependable, dangerous, and unable to analyze their lives and current situations. It is no wonder that, when studying organizations, what "the retarded" have to say is devalued or ignored. As Ed put it, "Once you have been labeled retarded, you can't convince them how smart you are." Similarly, when discussing a friend of his who had Down syndrome, Ed related that the major problem his friend had was that people didn't take him seriously. In Ed's words: "He was a mongoloid. People couldn't see beyond that. He was locked into what other people thought he was."

As a society, and as researchers, we have chosen to devalue the perspectives and understandings of those our society has designated as incompetent. Seldom are those labeled retarded approached with the idea that they have important insights to offer researchers. Their views are almost completely neglected in the professional and organizational literature. We know next to nothing about how these people evaluate the services they receive.

In addition to the negative stereotypes, other factors get in the way of our listening to those labeled retarded. In most encounters with these people, they tend to be less than candid and straightforward in communicating their lives and feelings. Similarly, nonretarded people talking to those so labeled tend to selectively skew the content of the interaction (Goffman, 1959, 1963). In certain relationships, such as that between the professional and the client with mental retardation, the distortion is complicated further because the professional has certain rewards and punishments at his or her disposal, and definite ideas about what he or she will sanction (Braginsky & Braginsky, 1971). Clients who realize this are pressured to give impressions that are in their own best interests.

For example, in one discussion with Pat, she told of the sex lives of residents of the institution in which she was a resident and how the residents systematically kept information about those activities from professionals and the ward staff. Conversely, in a good first-person account, the person is anonymously telling his or her story, no holds barred, because the sanctions have been minimized.

Insiders' Views of Services. First-person accounts of "retarded" persons are valuable because they bring us together in a different relationship with a person we might casually dismiss as less capable or incoherent. In reading and collecting their accounts, the goal is to understand the narrator's point of view; the disposition is to assume that the person has something to say. The listener's responsibility is to abandon assumptions and to work at comprehending the subjective reality of the person's life.

Reading and collecting first-person life histories of people with disabilities help researchers or readers put some distance between themselves and their preconceived notions and prejudices (Becker, 1966). This distance can lead to empathy, to see the world from another's point of view. In accomplishing this freedom from predispositions, personal concerns, and organizational roles, the researcher and the reader are given a unique mirror in which to examine their commonsense assumptions about the kind of person who is sharing his or her life with them.

For example, when Bogdan first began studying organizations in which people labeled as retarded were clients, he assumed that they would not be articulate, that they would not be able to think abstractly, that they did not have much to say that was worth listening to. Clearly, the people he interviewed did not match his preconceived notions. They were anomalies to commonsense understanding. At first he dealt with this dissonance by thinking of these people as exceptions; he assumed that they were misdiagnosed and that they were not really retarded. They were clearly legitimate members of that classification, however; they had been officially diagnosed and were being treated and related to by professionals as being retarded. In the end, this dissonance was resolved, not by treating them as unauthentic cases but, rather, by questioning the value of a system that classified people as either "retarded" or "normal."

The autobiography of the person labeled retarded gives us a view of organizations from the standpoint of persons who have participated in them at levels that we are not used to hearing from (Becker, 1966). By traveling with a person who has been a "retarded" client through his or her encounters with schools, clinics, institutions, and professionals, we can get a new perspective on these facilities. Through clients' stories, it becomes plain that their perspective on the client-professional relationship is very different from the professionals' point of view. Cure and treatment usually dominate the official view, whereas boredom, manipulation, and coercion constitute the client's perspective. From the staff's perspective, behavior modification, seclusion, and tranquilizing medication serve therapeutic ends. For the "retarded," however, these are often methods of punishment and behavior control.

To develop programs with the desired effect, one has to realize that people participating in programs define their own involvement. These definitions, not the ideas and wishes of program planners, determine how participants act toward a program and its effect on them. A young resident, who is seeing a counselor for whom he feels contempt because the counselor represents a facility he hates, knows he has to "lay a good story on him" to get certain privileges in the institution. This is quite a different picture from how professionals would have us view counseling relationships.

Devaluing the client's perspective by viewing it as naive, unsophisticated, immature, or a symptom of pathology, or not taking that perspective into account at all, makes many of the organizations that serve people with special needs indulge in one-sided rituals in the name of science. The life history can help us deal with this problem by educating us with the words of those who know the most about their difficulties.

The Holistic Perspective. The autobiographical account provides us with a holistic view of people in organizations. Case record material found in official folders shows only selected aspects of a person's life and character. People are much more complicated than a profile constructed from a series of IQ tests or a few pages of selected "facts" and anecdotes. Similarly, understanding a family entails a lot more than knowing that its members are on welfare and lack education. That type of record emphasizes the person as a client, obscuring the importance of understanding him or her as a member of a family, a peer group, a neighborhood, a church, and so on. What is in the folder often highlights the person's "pathological" behavior. It lists the strikes against the person and therefore serves more as an indictment than as a balanced picture of the client. The life history allows us to see through these biases; it offsets the often one-sided nature of records by presenting the other side.

As we have already suggested, the life history allows us to view the person in the context of his or her personal history and present relationships. It presents a person from birth to the time of writing. It can lead us to a fuller understanding of the stages and critical periods of development and the role of organizations in those transitions. It also can lead us to understand events that over the short term may seem unimportant. For example, knowing that a child is occasionally teased in class for being "odd looking" or "dumb" may not seem important unless one puts it in the context of a life of teasing and how the person has tested ways of combating it.

Clients are subjects for therapeutic practices that are extensions of theories created by researchers. By experiencing the service delivery world with the client through his or her life history, we can become keenly aware of how discrepancies in interpretation and application of these theories of causation and cure can affect treatment. For example, the current practice is to move state school residents out of institutions into group homes. Residents are placed in menial jobs, and people with similar institutional backgrounds live together. Although Pat and Ed favored these placements over institutions, living in proximity to others with such similar backgrounds created a great strain on them. Through the life history we can experience and begin to understand the web of life the client has to deal with. This should make us more sensitive in designing our service systems.

Standard methodological procedure is to isolate variables to show relationships among them. Even with new statistical procedures, we are unable to deal with the complex interaction of variables and how they relate to each other in the reality of people's lives. The life history allows us to deal with life in all its complexity. It therefore sets before us the interrelationships of all the variables for us to sort out.

Although the life history does not allow us to come up with exact statements of relationships, it does provide the opportunity to wrestle with this complexity in context and from the perspective of the client's system of logic rather than in a system of mathematical logic. It helps us to be careful about believing simple explanations for complex problems and to meet squarely the many unknowns in human behavior.

The personal document and other forms of qualitative research allow us to deal with concepts that are all but impossible to discuss or study in other forms of research. Subjective phenomena such as beauty, faith, pain, suffering, frustration, hope, and love can be dealt with as real people experience them in the real world.

Finally, the life history of a person with a disability is a political document; it gives voice to a disenfranchised minority. Seldom is a forum provided for a confrontation between client and professional. The life history throws into the struggle of diagnosis and theory another voice, which allows us to examine the possibility that we are misrepresenting those whom we say we are presenting. This confrontation with another "reality" is important for the good of research and practice as well as for the liberation of clients.

Often we have studied "the handicapped" as a separate category of human beings, as "deviants," using the commonplace definitions in our society. People with labels are assumed to be fundamentally different from others. By studying this subject in this way, we have reified categorizing people as either "normal" or as "handicapped" and legitimized service organizations as rational instruments for goal attainment. The life history allows us to get to know the client intimately as a person. Through this intimacy, what the subject is to himself or herself, and what he or she has in common with us all, becomes clear. What is different takes on less importance. Through the life history, we are forced to think of clients as people; concepts of pathology become less relevant and actually may be seen as destructive.

ECOLOGICAL THEORY: THE INDIVIDUAL IN CONTEXT

The ecological perspective is a catch phrase for what has become a dominant intellectual current in the second half of this century. Originating in biology, the central thesis of this perspective is that no single organism can be studied properly in isolation from its environment. A major corollary of this, which has been popularized by the environmentalist movement, is that the smallest change in the environment upsets the subtle balance of life and so affects all organisms in the exosphere. Even before these ideas were popularized in the 1960s, researchers and theorists across the whole gamut of behavioral sciences were exploring the implications of these ideas in the realm of human interaction.

The ecological approach to understanding the position of people with a disability in our society is fully congruent with symbolic interaction and qualitative research, but its roots are somewhat different. As we have seen, symbolic interactionism and qualitative research are grounded firmly in sociology and focus on attempting to understand the meaning individuals confer on a situation. Ecological theory is psychology informed by sociology. It is an attempt to develop a theory of human behavior that does not fall prey to the limitations of the traditional approach to psychological research. The focus is on the role people play in their environment, the match between the individual and the demands of the environment, and the complex interplay of forces that influence individual behavior. This stands in sharp contrast to the laboratory approach to psychology, which takes individuals out of their natural environments and subjects them to specific artificial stimuli under researcher controlled circumstances (Bronfenbrenner, 1979, p. 19).

Rather than seeing behavior as caused by some internal drive or as the mechanistic response to an external stimulus, the initial formulators of what has become the ecological perspective took their lead from Kurt Lewin's field theory. In a classic statement, which now seems self-evident, Lewin (1935) defined behavior as being a function of the interaction between a person and the environment, B = (PE).

In the years immediately after World War II, a group of researchers used Lewin's earlier work as their theoretical basis and undertook a social-psychological examination of the lives of people with physical disabilities (Dembo, Leviton, & Wright, 1956). This and other work that merged psychological and sociological approaches, as well as the first comprehensive survey and critique of the research on physical disability, resulted in formulation of the social-psychological concept of somatopsychology as a tool for understanding the meaning of disability in our society (Barker, Wright, & Gonick, 1946; Barker, Wright, Meyerson, & Gonick, 1953; Wright, 1960). This concept views most of the limitations on people with disabilities as being imposed by society rather than being intrinsic to an individual's functional deficit. In this regard, the concept is largely indistinguishable from concepts such as "stigma" (Goffman, 1963), which have their origins exclusively in sociology.

From his work in formulating the concept of somatopsychology, Roger Barker went on to use extensive qualitative research techniques to study the process of growing up in one midwestern town (Barker & Wright, 1955). This intensive long-term involvement provided much of the impetus for his efforts to conceptualize ecological psychology (Barker, 1968). Building on Barker's work, Bronfenbrenner (1979) and his colleagues attempted to articulate the study of human ecology as an independent discipline. They defined this approach as:

> ...the scientific study of the progressive, mutual accommodation between an active, growing human being and the changing properties of the immediate settings in which the developing person lives, as this process is affected by relations between these settings, and by the larger context in which the settings are embedded. (p. 21)

The central point of this definition is that how an individual acts, and how that behavior is defined, is the product of a series of complex interactions. All of the elements contributing to behavior are not immediately present in the specific setting where an event occurs. Bronfenbrenner (1979) conceptualized these interactions as the relationship between four concentrically nested environments:

1. The *microsystem* or behavior setting is the innermost of these environments. It is the place where people engage in face-to-face interaction. It is made up of the indi-

vidual and the activities, roles, and interpersonal relationships available within that setting. Home, classroom, playground, and street corner are all examples of microsystems.

2. The *mesosystem*, the second level in this nested model, is made up of the interactions among the various behavior settings within which a person acts. It is a way of explaining the effect of one part of a person's life on every other aspect of his or her life. It takes into account how home affects school, peers affect the home, and so forth.

3. The *ecosystem* refers to social structures that transcend the world of the individual but formally and informally influence, or are influenced by, what occurs within behavior settings. They include, among others, the community, government agencies, the media, and informal social networks.

4. The *macrosystem* is furthest removed from the individual's immediate experience. It refers to the dominant cultural and subcultural institutions (economic, social, educational, legal, and political systems) of which the other levels are the manifestations. Macrosystems are conceptualized not only as social structures but also as carriers of the dominant value system or ideology. So, in a certain sense, they can be seen as the cultural blueprints that account for the consistencies seen throughout a culture. For example, throughout our culture most classrooms and educational practices are essentially interchangeable.

William Rhodes (1967) was the first to see the value of an ecological perspective for practitioners in special education. Speaking specifically of students labeled emotionally disturbed, he pointed out that educators had come to see disturbance as something residing in the student. Hence, their interventions were geared exclusively toward remedying the flaw within the child. Rhodes saw disturbance as residing in the tension between the child and the demands of the environment and proposed an ecological view focusing on the interactive nature of the problem behavior.

Subsequently, a number of authors have explored the theoretical and programmatic implications of an ecological analysis of people with disabilities in our society (e.g., Algozzine, 1977; Apter, 1982; Hobbs, 1975, 1980; Swap, 1974, 1978). Following Rhodes' lead, most of these authors focused almost exclusively on the need to see what is called "emotional disturbances" as resulting "from a discrepancy between a given child's skills and abilities and the demands or expectations of that child's environment" (Apter, 1982, p. 2). A bit more recently, ecological theory has been used as a model for the most innovative programs for individuals with severe disabilities (Brinker, 1985; Brown et al., 1986). Nonetheless, the basic assumptions of an ecological orientation toward disability are translated easily into terms that apply to any individual—adult or child—who is labeled (Apter, 1982, pp. 69, 71):

1. Every individual is an inseparable part of a small social system.

2. Disability is not viewed as a disease located in the person but, rather, as discordance in the system.

3. Discordance may be defined as a disparity between a person's abilities and the demands of the environment, a failure to match the person and the system.

4. The goal of any intervention is to make the system work, ultimately without the intervention.
5. An improvement in any part of the system can benefit the entire system.
6. From this broader view of disability, three possible areas for intervention are:
   a. Change the person.
   b. Change the environment.
   c. Change attitudes and expectations.
7. Finally, a major implication of an ecological orientation is that we give up searching for a magic answer to the problems of disabled people. Instead, we must begin to think about problems in the system and increase our understanding of the interaction between the individual and the environment.

Symbolic interactions and qualitative research offer us a framework for examining and appreciating the student's perspective. An ecological orientation expands on this focus, providing us with a structure for placing students' points of view in a larger social context. We believe an eclectic theoretical perspective integrating both of these approaches offers a useful conceptual tool. Its intent is to enable practitioners to see beyond the web of terminology that so often surrounds them and obscures the nature of their work. To put it another way, the traditional, purely practical approach to professional preparation allows "the forest to get lost in the trees, and the trees to get lost in the forest." The intent in the ecological approach is to offer practitioners some intellectual tools that will enable them to see both the forest and the trees and appreciate how they are inextricably bound together.

UNDERSTANDING LABELS: THE SOCIAL MEANING OF DISABILITY

Symbolic interactionist and ecological theorists do not deny the need for organizations to develop shared definitions and thereby ease communication. They emphasize, however, that when these arbitrary definitions are used in constant day-to-day interaction, they often become reified as "the truth" about the individuals to whom they are applied. From an interactionist perspective, "disabled students" do not exist in any absolute sense (Bogdan & Kugelmass, 1984). The generic term "disabled" and the specific disability categories are ways of thinking about and categorizing others. Whether people are thought of as disabled and what criteria are used to determine who gets labeled have to do with how the definers think about these things. The mentally retarded, emotionally disturbed, learning disabled, and even the blind appeared only after a way of thinking developed toward them that acknowledged them as existing and important to take note of.

For the symbolic interactionist and ecological theorist, there are no "true" counts of the number of people with disability or "correct" definitions of mental retardation, blindness, and other disability categories (Bogdan & Ksander, 1980). Counts and definitions are reifications of customs and practices. Standardized diagnostic measures and procedures make conventionalized judgments appear to be truths, but they should not be confused with "truth" in any absolute sense. As concepts such as "mentally retarded" and "learning disabled" become reified, the criteria and conceptual base for placement take on a reality that belies their existence as social creations. For example, people come to believe that individuals really have IQs and that grade levels exist.

Although at any given time one definition may be said to be "official" (the one accepted by the most influential professional organizations), a clear consensus never can be found on the meaning of terms such as "disability," or the specific diagnostic categories falling under a given classification. Many social scientists have pointed to the ambiguity of the terminology and the differential application of "standard" terms in different contexts.

Mercer (1973) demonstrated that the reported number of mentally retarded persons in the population is more a function of age than of any "mental" condition, because the overwhelming majority of individuals diagnosed as mentally retarded is not identified until entering school and then "disappears" upon reaching adulthood. Dexter (1964) presented similar arguments. In their study of institutionalized children, Braginsky and Braginsky (1971) presented evidence that even such relatively "hard" and "official" measures of mental capacity as IQ scores are effectively manipulated by the allegedly incompetent children to make themselves "bright" or "dull," given different consequences. In his analysis of the seemingly objective area of blindness, Scott (1969) demonstrated that stereotypic preconceptions and arbitrary operational measures result not only in a widely varying count of the "officially blind" but also in a situation wherein a majority of the people so classified are actually able to see. Szasz (1961) and a host of others have noted the ambiguity and metaphorical terminology in the area of mental illness and emotional disturbance.

Symbolic interactionist and ecological theories suggest that, instead of concentrating on arriving at accurate definitions and true counts, we should understand official definitions and counts as the products of the people, processes, organizations, and societies that compile them. For symbolic interactionists, definitions and counts are artifacts of the process of their production rather than "reliable" or "unreliable" information. While other theoretical approaches assume that definitions and counts are ways of measuring reality, symbolic interactionists suggest that they should be approached as methods of constructing reality.

From the ecological perspective, counts and definitions of concepts such as "mental retardation" are temporal and represent larger political and social forces. Professionals in special education and researchers, as well as government officials and organization leaders, choose one dimension of meaning or develop one set of conventions to arrive at a method of constructing a definition and a real rate of disability. Whatever is arrived at, it is the product of the assumptions used and the concepts employed. To claim to have a true measure and accurate definition is to claim the supremacy of one definition and method over another and should not be confused with "true" in any strict sense.

Interactionists and human ecologists are not radical idealists. They emphasize the subjective, but they do not deny a reality "out there" that stands over and against human beings, capable of resisting action toward it (Blumer, 1980). The physical, behavioral, social, and mental characteristics of children enter the process through which the meaning of the child emerges, but not in the deterministic way commonly believed. The external reality of what is being defined or counted influences the emerging definitions and counts. Nevertheless, a social process of discerning and classifying always lies between the phenomenon and its definition. Things such as not being able to read, or not being able to pass a test, or not being able to walk, or having organic brain damage, set parameters in which definitions develop, but they do not determine how people with these characteristics will be defined or even if they will be taken special note of.

Although they do not deny physical and behavioral realities, symbolic interactionists emphasize that human beings act toward others based on the meaning they assign to these differences. This resulting treatment then can provide the vehicle for transforming the preassigned meaning into a self-fulfilling prophecy. Not being able to perform up to a level in school and acting "funny" does not have to mean that a child will be socially isolated and reacted to in a specific way by others. The slow child's functioning may be dependent upon the definition given to his or her condition by those in positions to influence the circumstances of the child's life as the "reality" of his or her "slowness."

Be it mental retardation, cerebral palsy, deafness, blindness, emotional disturbance, or learning disability, disability is only in the narrowest possible sense something that someone has. Disability is always interactional. This label does not simply symbolize a condition that is already there; it makes possible the existence or the appearance of the condition, for it is part of the mechanism whereby the condition is created (Rose, 1962). Disability is a designation and therefore is embedded in social relations. Disability is a way of thinking about and a way of acting and reacting. The creation of a disability concept and its application in specific settings, the effect it provokes, is derived and sustained in interaction. In one sense, disability changes by changing how we think about it.

The meaning of disability varies at different levels of our society. Hence, disability can be understood only by seeing the process of labeling as a multilayered transactional process. Official definitions are produced high up in bureaucracies, yet practitioners apply them. Clients think about disabilities differently than do officers in professional organizations. Often those collecting the data about disability operate on different assumptions than those who receive the data. Those who issue data requests often are not familiar with the nature of the phenomena to be counted or with the dilemmas and concerns of the counters.

A U.S. congressional mandate in 1973 required that 10% of Head Start enrollments were to consist of handicapped children. When a directive came out of Washington to report the number of handicapped children, there were repercussions up and down the bureaucracy (Bogdan, 1976). People in the programs did not think in terms of the disability categories those in Washington were proposing. Data collection at the program level came to be defined differently when it reached Washington. The meaning and purpose of definitions and counting was viewed differently in Washington, in regional offices, in state-run programs, in local administrative centers, and in Head Start classes. All these levels have to be studied to understand what occurs as the result of such a directive, and to understand the meaning of figures created and who is served.

The reason for defining, and who initiates disability designations, affects the meaning, the process, and the understanding generated. When federal funding is tied to serving certain rates of specific categories of people, the tendency may be for that number to reach the target level independent of what actually changes, who is served, and what is done. For example, in Bogdan's (1976) Head Start study, programs reported doubling the number of handicapped children and reaching 12.1% students with a disability without appreciably altering the individuals being served!

The diagnostic category of learning disability also illustrates the importance of studying professionals and definitions. Some learning disabilities specialists report that up to 40% of all children are afflicted; other professionals not associated with this specialty claim that "learning disability" is a contrived diagnosis (Schrag & Divoky, 1975). Professional specializations grow by enlarging their definition of who they are trained to serve.

Disability, as special education constructs it, is a particular frame of mind by which to organize the world. The salience of special education's way of seeing human differences and influencing how others see them has to be understood as an issue of politics of competing perspectives (Skrtic, 1986; Chapter 15). The development and the politics of special education—how it came to construct disability as it has, whom it fought with in the process, and what its commonsense, unnoticed assumptions are—are important to understanding special education (Conrad & Schneider, 1980). Histories in special education written by people who are special educators should be taken as the data of a symbolic interactionist's history of special education, not the conclusion.

People who develop and apply definitions of disability in schools are subject to social pressures and structural forces similar to those touching other work groups. Studies of factories and other workers have provided useful concepts such as quota restriction, gold bricking, self-aggrandizement, co-optation, and goal displacement to describe the effect of group processes and other structural forces on work production. Understanding the effect of social processes and structural forces on how people come to define and use the concept of disability in their own situations is important.

Disability is situational. Alleged differences have particular meanings in particular settings. Not knowing how to read has a different meaning from one school, or one classroom, to another. The concept of the 6-hour retarded student highlights that a student who may be defined as retarded in school may not be thought of that way in his or her family or neighborhood. Questions about the efficacy of various special education programs have to be approached in terms of the meaning of special education and various disability categories in a wide range of contexts. The culture of the professional work group and the structural constraints teachers and specialists operate under have to be understood in comprehending the situational meaning of disability designations.

Symbolic interactionists can help us understand that when we apply the concept of disability, or any specific designation falling under this generic term, we cast the situation in a certain way. "Disability" can change the meaning of behavior. The word disability, or more specifically its many subcategories, such as mental retardation, emotional disturbance, and deafness, makes us selectively sensitive to certain behaviors and actions. Things that might not have been noticed before jump out and take on meaning within the framework of such ideas. Behavioral and physical characteristics that were noted and interpreted in one way get reinterpreted when defined as a disability.

Disability categories give those who use them a sense of knowing, and therefore a way of relating and programming for those who fall under their headings. Labeling a child suggests that he or she is understood as being like those in the category. A whole set of expectations and assumptions is applied. Thus, the child is liable for behaviors, ways of thinking, and settings that alter his or her circumstances. These alterations may have negative as well as positive consequences for the child.

How an individual defines himself or herself in terms of an alleged disability is a function of, and is constructed through, interaction. People come to see themselves as blind, mentally retarded, or by other epithets, or they reject such concepts. Whether they are ashamed or proud of their condition, or feel neutral about it, is mediated by significant others—parents, teachers, peers, attendants—who enter their lives in social interaction. In attempting to see themselves as others see them, people interpret others' gestures and actions and thereby construct a self-concept. In rehabilitation, the prognosis for recovery has been strongly associated with the individual's self-concept. People with particular disabilities do not have particular personalities or ways of thinking about themselves. For some, "disability" dominates how they see themselves. For others, it is an insignificant part of how and what they think.

The meaning of disability in special education goes far beyond alleged physical, behavioral, and psychological differences. Disability has symbolic meaning that must be looked at in terms of what society honors and what it degrades. Society's thoughts about intelligence, confidence, beauty, and winning must be understood to understand what we mean when we mockingly call someone "retarded" or "blind as a bat." Our society traditionally has been structured to bring shame to people with alleged disabilities. From a symbolic interactionist and an ecological frame of reference, only a small part of problems of discrimination—providing physical access to wheelchairs, building communication systems for nonverbal people—is technical. The problems of disability are much more social, located much deeper in the seams of our society than professionals in special education touch or acknowledge.

HANDICAPISM

The interactionist and ecological perspectives may contribute to improving human services by sensitizing practitioners to the individual's unique point of view and experience. Yet the major strength of these paradigms lies in their ability to look beyond the traditional confines of the clinical endeavor. They enable the special education teacher, the therapist, the school administrator, the social worker, and the residential worker to view their job through lenses focusing on the social and cultural elements that define the lives of people with disabilities. This, in turn, should motivate conscientious practitioners to conceptualize their role as involving as much advocacy and action for social change as in making efforts to change individual behavior.

One effort to coherently apply interactionist and ecological theory to the situation of people with disabilities is contained in the concepts of handicapism. Essentially, handicapism has its roots in the same type of social critique as that carried out by the civil rights and women's liberation movements. Hence, it has direct parallels to the concepts of racism and sexism. In their initial discussion of this concept, Bogdan and Biklen (1977) defined handicapism as "a set of assumptions and practices that promote the differential and unequal treatment of people because of apparent or assumed physical, mental, and behavioral differences" (p. 14). When handicapism is used as the paradigm for understanding our society, a person with a disability is seen not as a client or recipient of special services but, rather, as a member of a traditionally discriminated-against minority. An understanding of three terms—prejudice, stereotype, and discrimination—is essential to the meaning of sexism, racism, or handicapism.

Prejudice is a grossly simplified belief about the characteristics of some group of people, which is uncritically generalized to all members of that group. Prejudice toward people with disabilities takes the form of indicting assumptions such as:

- They are all incompetent and incapable.
- To be disabled is to be naturally inferior ("Thank God, I'm not like that!").
- There are mentally retarded, deaf, blind, physically disabled, or disturbed personalities.
- Their senses and tolerances are different from those of typical people.
- They are so fundamentally different that they have more in common with each other than they do with nondisabled people.
- They really just want to be with their own kind.

These and other beliefs are the essence of handicapism. They provide the rationale for our actions toward people with disabilities.

When a prejudice takes the form of a specific belief regarding a particular group, it is a stereotype. For example, people labeled "mentally retarded" are regarded as childlike individuals who enjoy boring, highly repetitive activities and have a tendency to be oversexed (Wolfensberger, 1975). Individuals characterized as "emotionally disturbed" are seen as erratic, dangerous, and bizarre in their behavior, especially during a full moon (Biklen, 1976; Scheff, 1966). Deaf people are supposed to be fantastic painters (Jernigan, 1975). And, of course, blind people develop unusual compensatory senses that equip them for special occupations, such as tuning pianos, but they do tend to have melancholy personalities (Scott, 1969).

It does not matter that these sets of stereotypes often are mutually contradictory. They continue to be taken seriously and are used to justify certain modes of treatment. Hence, people with mental retardation can be treated like children, individuals who are labeled "mentally ill" can be locked up, and segregated facilities of all types continue to be regarded as "best" for people with a disability.

Regardless of their inaccuracy and contradictory nature, stereotypes are steadfastly maintained. The process that transmits and maintains these fallacious assumptions is itself part of handicapism. First, society, in its institutions, its popular mythology, and its media, supports the transmission of stereotypes and so continually reinforces them. Second, the group that is stereotyped is isolated—in an institution, a ghetto, or any other segregated setting—with little opportunity to interact with the majority of the population, and so has little chance to disprove the stereotype. Finally, and most significantly, members of the victimized group are treated in a manner consistent with the stereotypes and are rewarded for living up to others' images of them (Lemert, 1951). Thus, people with disabilities learn their role and fall victim to self-fulfilling prophecies (Merton, 1957) that conform to society's stereotypes.

Prejudice and stereotype are concepts that capture the cognitive and ideological content of handicapism. The manner in which these concepts become actualized in society's structures and in the behavior of individuals is discrimination. Standards of fairness are highly relative, varying from society to society, and developing over time as a society's criteria for equality or discrimination respond to changing social values. For centuries, slave labor, the total subservence of women to their husbands, and parents' literal right of life and death over their children were seen as in line with the natural order of things; the treatment these ideas fostered was not regarded as unfair or cruel. So it is today that people with a disability are thought to have a high quality of life in this society because of the availability of various categorical social service programs. Based on what our society knows about the condition of people with disabilities (prejudice and stereotypes), these programs and their treatment methods are deemed to be appropriate and deserved.

Regardless of the legal mandate to integrate disabled students (PL 94–142, the Education for All Handicapped Children Act, now the Individuals with Disabilities Education Act), many states continue to segregate a large proportion of their special education students in separate classes or in special schools (Biklen, 1987, 1992). Although some social service agencies have made great strides in providing residential supports for people labeled disabled (Taylor, Bogdan, & Racino, 1991), in many regions of the United States, people with developmental disabilities who need support in their daily lives find that the only residential opportunities available to them are large group homes or mini-institutions (Hauber et al., 1984). Yet no empirical evidence supports any educational or social benefit from segregated facilities that congregate people with similar disabilities together. These policies and practices discriminate against people with disabilities. They represent handicapism in action.

HANDICAPISM IN INTERPERSONAL RELATIONS

Like any other form of prejudice, handicapism manifests itself in the contacts between typical people and those who are members of a discriminated-against minority group, as well as in private conversation when a member of the minority is not present. Several researchers (Davis, 1961; Goffman, 1963; Wright, 1983) have commented on the anxiety and strain evident in the face-to-face interactions between labeled and nonlabeled individuals. On the one hand, "the stigmatized individual may find that he feels unsure of how we normals will identify and receive him" (Goffman, 1963, p. 13). On the other hand, the so-called normals act as if they are walking on egg shells for fear the disabled person will read some unintended meaning into their words or actions.

The self-conscious uneasiness that pervades social contacts sets the stage for many handicapist practices. For example, some people totally avoid contact with anyone they perceive as "non-normal." When interactions are unavoidable, they are characterized by engaging in labored conversation and quickly concluding the contact. There also is a tendency for the disability to become the most significant factor in the nondisabled person's mind. This often results in the nondisabled person's being overly gracious, sympathetic, and patronizing or, alternatively, showing insensitivity and ignoring the person with the disability. Goffman (1963) noted that on some occasions this takes the form of the disabled person's being transformed into what he called a "nonperson."

So, in casual contacts, nondisabled people tend to measure people with a disability against the stereotypes and by this comparison further reinforce the stereotypes. For example, as a number of typical skiers watched a blind skier coming down the hill, they commented on her "amazing feat." From the tone of their comments, they obviously regarded this individual as anything but an ordinary blind person. Hence, they were not led by this experience to question their stereotype of all blind people as physically inept. Instead, they reaffirmed the stereotype by perceiving this person as the exception to the rule. If she were not skiing, but instead sitting in the lodge by the fire, where they would have expected to find her, they undoubtedly would have commented on the tragedy of her disability that causes her to miss so many of life's pleasures.

Handicapism also is exemplified and perpetuated in conversations among nondisabled people. Our daily conversation is replete with examples of handicapist stereotypes and prejudices: "Poor Uncle Bill has never been able to hear without a hearing aid." "If I had a baby that was handicapped, I'd never bring it home; it would be better off dead." Our casual interpersonal conversation and popular "humor" is heavy with handicapism: "Did you hear the one about the moron who threw the clock out the window?" "It's just another case of the blind leading the blind." "What are you, deaf and dumb?" "Don't listen to that babbling idiot." "You're such a retard."

HANDICAPISM AT THE SOCIETAL LEVEL

An understanding of handicapism at the societal level demands an in-depth analysis of the culture and of the basic institutions of society—what an ecologist would call the ecosystem and macrosystem—for manifestations of prejudice, stereotypes, and discrimination. In addition, both the legally sanctioned and the illegal, but tacitly approved, forms of mistreatment to which people with a disability are subjected must be explored. Within the limits of this discussion, we will confine ourselves to an examination of societal-level handicapism as it is manifested in three areas: (a) physical and literacy barriers to participation, (b) discrimination as it appears in and is fostered by some recent court decisions, and (c) the public debate over medical treatment of infants born with disabling conditions.

Physical and Literacy Barriers. Discrimination is easy to spot when it takes the form of totally inaccessible buildings, transportation, and public toilets. Passage of the Americans with Disabilities Act (ADA), the proliferation of ramps leading to public buildings, special "disabled" jitney services, and seemingly omnipresent wheelchair signs marking reserved parking spaces and signs pointing the way to the accessible entrance or the special toilet mitigate the issue somewhat. There is no denying that progress has been made. Yet, as it now stands, people with disabilities have made only the slightest movement in our social consciousness from having their existence denied to becoming visible. The imagery in a photograph from the civil rights movement of the 1950s will shed a little light on this: The scene is the hall of a Southern courthouse. We see two water fountains, one labeled "Whites only," the other marked "Coloreds."

America today assumes that the "separate but equal" approach to many basic services, which was legally unacceptable for African American people, is enough for those who happen to have a disability. In most cases, our society has responded to the demands of people with disabilities and their advocates by adopting short-term, expensive, exceptionalistic solutions. This approach reflects a perspective that sees including people with disabilities as an "add-on" to the rest of society.

This same point of view has led some commentators to decry expenditures for accessibility as well-meaning but fiscally irresponsible (Starr, 1982). Of course, retrofitting the New York City subway system to make it accessible is expensive but, once accomplished, will benefit a wide spectrum of the population. On the other hand, a subsidized special taxi service must have renewed funding every year and, because of restrictions on eligibility, will give limited benefit to a restricted group. When public facilities are constructed with the need for full accessibility figured in from the outset (as in the Washington, DC or San Francisco Bay Area rapid transit systems), the added cost is minimized and is amortized over the life of the project.

Just as architectural barriers deny access to people with a physical disability, our society's dependence on written communication severely restricts the freedom of those who cannot read or write. Many individuals who have moved into the community after years in state mental retardation institutions report that the ability to handle written material is a major barrier to integration. Someone who is unable to learn, or never was taught to read and write, faces a nearly insurmountable wall of forms, signs, and maps in daily life. Because it is generally expected that people can read, it is terribly embarrassing, as well as difficult, for individuals who lack this ability to live independently.

The literacy barrier is mentioned to illustrate just a single area in which the discriminatory and exclusionary assumptions of our society should be explored. These assumptions are so widespread that they often are difficult to recognize. Because nondisabled people do not directly experience the effect of these barriers, their impact on the lives of people with disabilities is seldom understood.

Judicial Discrimination. Just as many of the obvious physical barriers are being corrected, many of the most obvious examples of legalized discrimination have fallen by the wayside under pressure from federal and state legislation (e.g., PL 94–142, Section 504 of the Rehabilitation Act of 1973, New York state's 1974 Disability Amendments to the Human Rights Law, Americans with Disabilities Act), and subsequent court decisions based on these laws (e.g., *Davis* v. *Southeastern Community College*, 1979). This does not mean legal discrimination has vanished from the landscape.

In its new form, discrimination, particularly against those who have severe disabilities, is shaped by failure of the U.S. Supreme Court to unambiguously affirm the full citizenship of people with disabilities. In a series of decisions, the Court has allowed continued discriminatory treatment of individuals with disabilities if these practices can be justified under the broadly define rubric of "a responsible professional decision" or "overriding governmental interest."

- In *Board of Education* v. *Rowley* (1982), the Court defined the right of disabled students to a "basic floor of educational opportunity" (i.e., access and a program with some educational benefit), which minimizes the burden on schools to have their "special" programs conform with measures of the highest quality. Under these guidelines, segregated programs continue to be justifiable and acceptable.
- When asked to affirm the absolute right of the residents of a state institution for the mentally retarded to live in the least restrictive environment, the Court instead declared a minimal right to "reasonably safe conditions of confinement, freedom from unreasonable bodily restraint, and such minimally adequate training as may reasonably be required by these interests." The Court's criteria for reasonability? "The judgment exercised by a qualified professional, whose decision is presumptively valid" (*Youngberg* v. *Romeo*, 1982, p. 4681). Once again, this decision would allow the use of segregated facilities and aversive behavioral controls to continue.
- In another case, the Court found that a community may not enact a zoning ordinance that arbitrarily restricts the opening of a group home for people with developmental disabilities (*City of Cleburne* v. *Cleburne Living Center*, 1985). In the same decision, however, the justices refused to grant special protection to the rights of people labeled mentally retarded because they "have a reduced ability to cope with and function in the everyday world [and] are thus different from other persons" (p. 5022).
- Finally, in *Bothman* v. *Warren B. and Patricia B.* (1979) the Court refused to intervene in a case in which the parents' conscious decision to forego medical treatment for their son with Down syndrome guaranteed the child's premature death.

Commenting on the common thread running through the Supreme Court's decisions regarding children with disabilities, Biklen (1981) drew the following conclusions, reflected in all these cases:

> The Supreme Court is influenced as much by social prejudices as by logic or a concern for fairness. To accede to a child's probable death in one instance and to institutionalization of thousands in another is neither logical nor fair. Both decisions are informed by prejudice (p. 5)

Discriminatory Medical Treatment. No single issue exemplifies the depth of handicapism in our society as much as the national debate over the right of children born with serious disabilities to receive life-sustaining medical treatment (cf. Kosterlitz, 1984). The arguments of those who think criteria should be different in decisions to treat children with potentially severe disabilities reveal some of our society's most deeply seated prejudices regarding people with disabilities. The most frequent position is that these children lack the potential for a "meaningful life" (Duff & Campbell, 1973).

Some authors elaborate on this by contending that the presence of a disabled child adversely affects the family's quality of life by being a constant burden on the parents (Heifetz & Mangel, 1975). For others, the low probability of an individual's being able to function independently is enough reason to be less than aggressive in preserving life (Baldwin, 1982). Another contention is that the high cost of medical care and future services is yet another element to figure in the life or death equation (Duff, 1981).

At the heart of many of these arguments lies the belief that a person with severe disabilities is less than human. In some cases the supposed inability to form relationships is enough to earn an infant the label "subhuman" (Heifetz & Mangel, 1975). Indeed, one philosopher's contribution to this debate is a set of guidelines for determining humanhood (Fletcher, 1972). A major factor weighted here is IQ score.

In their critique of the positions of advocates of "passive euthanasia," Biklen and Ferguson (1984) pointed out the counterintuitive logic of an argument that uses society's failure to provide sufficient services for people with disabilities as a rationale for allowing them to die. As with all the arguments cited, however, logic has little to do with positions informed by prejudice and stereotypes.

HANDICAPISM IN THE ARTS AND MEDIA

Leslie Fielder (1984), one of the nation's leading literary critics, commented that the imagery and mythology of physical difference in our arts is directly connected to the willingness to allow "abnormal" babies to die. His contention is that this desire for a homogeneous world, where "some nostalgic poet, in love with difference for its own sake, would yearn for a world where ugliness is still possible" (p. 42), is inspired by the perpetuation of some of our species' primal myths and not by any "truth" about disabled people.

In a society as pervaded with imagery as ours is, a strong case can be made that the various media have gone a long way toward supplanting the family, the school, and the church as the primary transmitter of the culture's values. Even if this assertion is only partially true, it behooves any social critic to seriously examine the media for the subtle messages it is sending. A thorough analysis of the arts and media from a handicapism perspective would require an extensive examination of the values communicated by the media's emphasis on youth, slimness, body building, and conformity. Within the confines of this chapter, we will limit ourselves to a necessarily brief discussion of the dominant handicapist prejudices communicated by our media.

Literature. In a survey of the portrayal of disabled people in classic literature, Biklen and Bogdan (1977) traced 10 recurring themes that reflect handicapist stereotypes. These same themes are repeated on stage, screen, and television.

1. The disabled person as pitiable and pathetic. Often this role acts as a vehicle for demonstrating some other character's goodness or sensitivity (e.g., Somerset Maugham's *Of Human Bondage*; Tennessee Williams' *The Glass Menagerie*).
2. The disabled person as an object of violence. Usually the disabled victim is a one-dimensional character, a symbol of the helpless and dependent person upon whom evil preys (e.g., Victor Hugo's *The Hunchback of Notre Dame*).
3. The disabled person as sinister or evil. When a disabled person does have a central role in the plot, it usually is as a villain (e.g., Richard III, Captain Ahab, Captain Hook, Long John Silver).
4. The disabled person as atmosphere. The blind musician, the beggar with no legs, the dwarf from a sideshow, and the like frequently are thrown into the plot solely for the purpose of adding a little color (e.g., in the works of Charles Dickens).
5. The disabled person as "Super Crip." This role often is a literary amplification of the notion that all people with disabilities develop uncommon compensatory abilities. A major variation on this theme is the disabled person who overcomes all obstacles and goes on in triumph to become a "credit to the 'race'" (e.g., Kurt Vonnegut's *Slapstick*, Wilfred Sheed's *People Will Always Be Kind*).
6. The disabled person as laughable. This role for a disabled character often takes the form of a comic interlude in the plot. Alternately the role is played out within a tale of poetic justice. In this plot twist, a naive, good-natured disabled person makes fools of the "normal" characters who are exploiting him or her (e.g., Chance, the hero of Jerzy Kosinski's *Being There*).
7. The disabled person as his or her own worst-and-only enemy. This is the stereotype of disabled persons who refuse to help themselves because they are so caught up in feeling bitter about their fate (e.g., part of the message in Carson McCullers' *The Heart Is a Lonely Hunter*).
8. The disabled person as a burden. This theme is generally a reflection of the stereotype that all people with disabilities are helpless and dependent on the care of others. This device often is used to develop the long-suffering endurance of the character who must bear the burden of the disabled person (e.g., Joseph Heller's *Something Happened*, Katherine Ann Porter's *Ship of Fools*).
9. The disabled person as nonsexual or, in its alternative version, sex-starved or degenerate (e.g., Lennie in John Steinbeck's *Of Mice and Men*).
10. The disabled person as incapable of fully participating in everyday life. This is a stereotype by omission. Disabled people almost never are shown as well-adjusted, productive members of society (e.g., Charlie, in Daniel Keyes' *Flowers for Algernon*).

Another significant message interwoven in much of the material surveyed was that "even the most sensitive materials overplay individual solutions to disability problems without referring at all to societal factors that cause disability, or to societal discrimination against disabled people" (Biklen & Bogdan, 1977, pp. 5–6).

Film and Television. In addition to repeating the themes found in literature, film-makers took a lead from the circus freak shows (Bogdan, 1988) of the last century, and, in horror and gangster films, made their own special contribution to the catalogue of handicapist stereotypes (cf. Bogdan, Biklen, Shapiro, & Spelkoman, 1982). By consistently linking physical and mental difference with murder, terror, and violence, *Frankenstein, Phantom of the Opera, The Werewolf, The Bodysnatcher, Mystery of the Wax Museum, Scarface,* and the like have effectively communicated the need to beware of people with disabilities—they may be monsters. In general, television, with its portrayals of the Incredible Hulk and Ironsides, as well as its coverage of events such as the Special Olympics, has replicated all of the major stereotypic treatments of people with a disability.

We do not want to be too negative in regard to television's attempts to change its depictions of people with developmental disabilities. People in wheelchairs can be seen in regular commercials, and programs such as *L. A. Law* and *Life Goes On* have grappled with the challenge of presenting multidimensional portraits of people with disabilities with some success. Even here, though, progress is slow. We think it is a significant sign of change that a person with Down syndrome has a central role on a regularly broadcast television series, but it is significant only in light of the fact that people with these conditions have been virtually invisible until now.

Photography. Since the end of World War II, photography has secured its position as a fine art. A number of major figures in this art form (e.g., Diane Arbus, Bruce Davidson, Danny Lyons, Les Krims, Eugene Meatyard, Garry Winogrand) have adopted as their hallmark images of "the dwarf, the freak, the prostitute, the disenfranchised...the insane, the retarded....Their collective subject matter was the unseemly, the outcast, the dangerous, the forbidden, the exotic, and the bizarre" (Green, 1984, p. 119).

In an analysis of these and other images, Knoll (1984) found that people with disabilities were one-dimensional symbols. The presence of a physical or mental difference made them visually interesting and a ready icon for "blindness," isolation, and existential fears of all people. The entire emphasis in these images is individualistic and internally directed. There is no reflection of the social realities that make these people's situations so "interesting."

Children's Media. Children's stories are full of hunchbacks, trolls, and other deformed, and therefore dangerous, people lying in wait to carry off pretty children. Material produced by Walt Disney is full of handicapist imagery: the hunchbacked, wart-nosed "old witch" who poisons Snow White; the childlike seven dwarfs, including Dopey with his Down syndrome-like features; and, of course, Captain Hook, with his patched-eye pirates. Saturday morning cartoons are saturated with villains who mirror images borrowed directly from horror films. "Stupid idiot," "moron," "dumb," and "crazy" appear regularly in the vocabulary of comic strip characters. Not only do these portrayals convey prejudicial and stereotypic attitudes to children, but they also teach them that everyday terms for describing certain groups are also potent curse words.

Journalism. Handicapist stereotypes surface, too, in news coverage. Print journalism frequently links various disabilities and violent crime (Bogdan et al., 1982). An Associated Press account of an execution described the murderer as "an alcoholic and mentally incompetent psychotic who was mentally retarded" (Bogdan & Biklen, 1977, p. 16). In reporting on especially violent crimes, exploring a suspect's psychiatric background is almost standard practice, as if to equate a mental disability with the capability to be a mass murderer. The demands of broadcast journalism and photojournalism mean that coverage of an event often is limited to one powerful image or a one-minute spot with strong visual content. This lends itself to "heartwarming" images of the poor, dependent disabled people being helped, or yet another story in the "see them overcome their handicap" genre. In general, this also means that coverage of "disability stories" is limited to an agency function or an event such as the Special Olympics.

Even when the event being covered has more substantive content, the media often seek material that meets their preconceived notions. For example, the National Federation of the Blind called a press conference to discuss the group's political agenda for dealing with discrimination. Reporters who attended were not interested in the complexities of the social problems that confronted blind people. Instead, they were interested in pictures of adaptive equipment, seeing eye dogs, and watching blind people compete in various sporting events (Jernigan, 1975). Unfortunately, this approach has not changed noticably.

HANDICAPISM IN HUMAN SERVICES

Unfortunately, much of the imagery of disabled people in America is formed by their association with the agencies and institutions that have an official duty to care for, rehabilitate, and process people designated as disabled. The need of these organizations to continue in existence by obtaining funding and acquiring new clients means they must project a public image of serving the public interest by meeting the real needs of disabled people. The categorical nature of most traditional agencies leads them to use an approach emphasizing the unique needs of "autistic children," "the blind," "crippled children," "the deaf," "the disturbed," "the multihandicapped," "the retarded." This organizational need to survive, linked with the tendency of diagnostic/prescriptive models of service to focus narrowly on discrete clinical interventions, has perpetuated a handicapist orientation within most services.

Segregation. As pointed out, the essence of discrimination is segregation. Although our society has a substantial rhetoric of integration, our service system for people with disabilities, which ranges from categorical services in the community on one extreme to isolated, rural, total institutions on the other, is largely segregated. More than 87,000 people labeled mentally retarded continue to live in large public institutions (Amardo, Lakin, & Menke, 1990, p. 5). Although the most blatant abuses of institutional life appear to be a thing of the past, the reality of segregation remains the same:

> Each resident is served by an individualized program plan in a place where countless residents can be seen aimlessly sitting or standing or lying around....An institution is in

compliance with all sorts of federal standards, though we see barren environments and wasted lives everywhere (Blatt, Ozolins, & McNally, 1979, p. 23).

In the community, segregation continues in many programs that subject people to differential treatment because of some disability. Although most students in America now are served by the public school system, a large percentage—particularly those labeled severely handicapped or emotionally disturbed—attend class in separate "special" facilities (U.S. Department of Education, 1984). The vocational services routinely track thousands of people with all manner of disabilities into sheltered workshops, where they are cut off from interacting with nondisabled peers, the pay usually is well below minimum wage, and everyone has a "goal" of movement to competitive employment, which is realized for almost no one (Whitehead, 1979; see Brown et al., 1986, for an alternative).

Every year sees an increase in the number of community residences for people with developmental disabilities (Hill, Lakin, & Bruininks, 1984); yet most of these group homes stand in sharp contrast to our society's definition of a typical home. Their large size, and the institution-like regulations imposed on them, erects an effective barrier between many of these homes and their surrounding communities (Biklen & Knoll, 1987).

Economics. Providing services to people with disabilities is a big business in America— such a big business that some sociologists (e.g., Scull, 1981) claim the only way to understand how our society treats these people is to look at the economics of the service system. From this perspective, the "right" questions to ask are: Who holds the mortgage on state institutions? Who is making money from group homes? Why is the wheelchair industry a virtual monopoly that artificially maintains high prices (Medsger, 1979)? Why do sheltered workshop employees make less than nondisabled workers who are less productive at the same job (Kwitney & Landauer, 1979)?

One root of the problem is that service to disabled people is viewed as a gift or a privilege bestowed on these "deserving unfortunates" by a benevolent society. We give from our excess to provide them with a safety net of survival. This system degrades those it purports to serve by perpetuating the prejudice that they are inferior people. Charity campaigns distort the image of people with disabilities to play on the public's pity and elicit contributions. All of these perceptions lessen the possibility that people with disabilities will be regarded as individuals with the same basic needs, rights, and aspirations as everyone else.

Federal and state governments are the other leading source of funds for special services. This funding stream also makes a major contribution to handicapism. To obtain most of these governmental funds, public and private services must officially confer "client" status on the people they serve by classifying them according to the appropriate clinical categories. This fosters a system in which people are transformed into commodities and service agencies become headhunters. With such a system, it should come as no surprise that an increase in funding for a given category of client is followed by a dramatic growth in the number of people with that label (cf. Schrag & Divoky, 1975).

Professionalism. Often the individuals responsible for providing service to disabled people contribute to the perpetuation of handicapism. Many professionals uncritically assume that the narrowly focused categorical and specialized approach to clinical practice that they were taught is actually appropriate and beneficial for the people they serve (see Chapter 14). This frequently takes the form of "professional preciousness"—the claim that people with particular disabilities can be properly served only by a duly trained and credentialed professional. The implication is that professional training communicates some specialized knowledge that "un-initiates"—parents, paraprofessionals, and the like—cannot utilize properly. Although this is true to some extent, it is not wholly or perpetually the case. The challenge for professionals is to demystify themselves and join in a creative dialogue in which they can share freely some of their understanding and skills with others who, in turn, can help them to a more holistic awareness of the people they serve.

Overcoming Handicapism. From this discussion, it should be obvious that handicapism is a multidimensional problem that finds expression at many points in our society. It largely defines the social ecology surrounding people with disabilities and their families. One thing is clear: Change is happening. The years since passage of PL 94–142 and Section 504 have seen growing social awareness of the issues introduced here and a slow, gradual movement away from the prejudices, stereotypes, and discrimination of the past. Although we need to be cautious in our optimism and add to the accounting the difficult economic times we are facing, the thousands of homeless sleeping on the streets, as well as our deteriorating health care system, passage of the Americans with Disabilities Act is a hopeful sign of continued progress in certain dimensions of the problems outlined. Segregation still exists, but every year it becomes a little less prevalent. Many "good" laws and court decisions have been passed, recognizing the full citizenship of all people regardless of disability.

The right of self-determination by people with disabilities is affirmed daily by growing self-help and self-advocacy movements. Artists, writers, advertisers, and journalists are becoming increasingly sensitive to the issues confronting people with disabilities. The movement is in the proper direction, but the process of reeducating our society is slow and must continue.

Biklen and Foster (1985) pointed out that service providers cannot hope to eradicate all vestiges of handicapism from society, but they can make sure they and their programs do not contribute to handicapism. They offered 10 specific suggestions for combating handicapism in community programs:

1. Don't ever seek public support based on pity for people with a disability.
2. Eliminate all demeaning language, needless labels, and professional jargon that are not also regularly used when referring to nondisabled people.
3. Treat people in a manner consistent with their chronological age.
4. Always assume that recipients of services are fully aware of what is being said and done around them. To speak in front of people as if they are not there is dehumanizing.
5. Expend maximum effort to obtain any technology that will improve the quality of

life of a person with a disability. The message of the service to the public should be: "Yes, these people are worth the added expense."

6. Operate services in a cost-efficient, fiscally responsible fashion. Cost should not be artificially inflated, nor should seemingly cheaper, short-term solutions to problems be accepted (e.g., one-time capital investments often are more thrifty than "special" adaptations that must constantly have their funding renewed).

7. Encourage and support the active, substantive involvement of recipients of services in all aspects of the programs affecting their lives

8. Pay particular attention to the location and physical characteristics of a service setting. The message should be that people with a disability live in homes, attend schools, and work in businesses alongside everyone else.

9. Avoid special title and program names (e.g., a group home should have a street address, not a sign and a name; students should be taught in room 230 or Ms. Smith's class, not the EMR or the ED room).

10. Avoid grouping people with disabilities in specialized settings. Instead, disabled and nondisabled people should be grouped in "generic" schools, communities, and work sites.

Indeed, by conscious efforts to eliminate handicapism from our agencies and schools, as well as from our own relationships with people who have disabilities, the direct service provider can make a significant contribution to reeducating the rest of society. In the past, the service system reinforced handicapist attitudes. Today, sensitive, self-conscious teachers and service providers must be in the forefront of efforts to transform handicapism from an all-too-present social reality into an historical artifact.

SUMMARY

Humans are social, and meaning develops only through interactions. Our perceptions of self are influenced by how others react to us. This has particular implications for special education, as people with disabilities form impressions of themselves according to how society views people with disabilities. The symbolic interactionist theory emphasizes human experience as subjective, not absolute. Thus, many practices in special education over the years that have been followed as "fact" are in actuality meanings people place on the actions they carry out.

On aspect of the symbolic interaction approach is qualitative research. Life histories, for example, entail studying people in their own environments, using their own words to reveal their views of their world. This approach contrasts with prior research that demonstrated distrust and devaluing of the client's perspective as being naive, unsophisticated, immature, or a symptom of pathology. The life history takes a holistic perspective of people and leads to fuller understanding of the person. People with labels, such as "mentally retarded" are assumed to be fundamentally different from others, and this approach allows us to see the similarities rather than the differences.

Ecological theory, stemming from Lewin's work, is congruent with symbolic interaction and qualitative research. It focuses on the role people play in their environment—in contrast to the traditional laboratory approach. Bronfenbrenner conceptualized behavioral interactions as the relationship between four nested environments: microsystem, mesosystem, ecosystem, and macrosystem.

"Disabled students" do not exist in any absolute sense. The term and the specific disability categories are ways of thinking about and categorizing others. Thus, there is no "true" count of the number of people with disability or "correct" definitions of any disability category. In fact, the numbers of people in each category shrink and expand according to arbitrary variables such as gaining funding to provide services in the various categories, changes in IQ designations, and other factors external to the individual. Within these labels, students are taught differently in different schools and in different classrooms, as educators and service providers interpret the labels differently. Head Start is one example, in which a wide variety of preschool children have been served according to the labels local providers apply.

Handicapism is a set of assumptions and practices that promote the differential and unequal treatment of people because of apparent or assumed physical, mental, and behavioral differences. A person with a disability is seen not as a client or recipient of special services but, rather, as a member of a discriminated-against minority. Prejudice is a grossly simplified belief about the characteristics of some group of people that is generalized to all members of that group. When a prejudice takes the form of a specific belief regarding a group, it becomes a stereotype. When people within a stereotypical group receive differential treatment, it becomes discrimination. People unknowingly engage in a number of discriminatory practices against people with disabilities, including being overly gracious, sympathetic, and patronizing or, in contrast, showing insensitivity or ignoring the person with the disability.

On the societal level, handicapism is manifested in physical and literacy barriers, judicial discrimination, and discriminatory medical treatment, among others. Handicapism also occurs in literature, film and television, photography, children's media, and journalism. Unfortunately, handicapism also occurs in human services, by segregation in institutions or group homes, through economic priorities, and categorical treatment by professionals.

Handicapism can be overcome, and we have made strides in doing so. Direct service providers can make a significant contribution by being in the forefront of efforts to transform the negative practices of the past into the positive directions that are beginning to make inroads.

*R*EFERENCES

Algozzine, B. (1977). The emotionally disturbed child: Disturbed or disturbing? *Journal of Abnormal Child Psychology, 5,* 205–211.

Amardo, A. N., Lakin, K. C., & Menke, J. M. (1990). *1990 chartbook on services for people with developmental disabilities.* Minneapolis: University of Minnesota, Center for Residential and Community Services.

Apter, S. J. (1982). *Troubled children, troubled systems*. New York: Pergamon Press.

Asch, A. (1984). Personal reflections. *American Psychologist, 39*, 551–552.

Baldwin, T. (1982). Life and death in newborn special care nursery. *Connecticut Medicine, 46*, 589–600.

Barker, R. G. (1968). *Ecological psychology*. Stanford, CA: Stanford University Press.

Barker, R. G., Wright, B. A., & Gonick, M. R. (1946). *Adjustment to physical handicap and illness: A survey of the social psychology of physique and disability*. New York: Social Science Research Council.

Barker, R. G., Wright, B. A., Meyerson, L., & Gonick, M. R. (1953). *Adjustment to physical handicap and illness: A survey of the social psychology of physique and disability* (Rev. ed.). New York: Social Science Research Council.

Barker, R. G., & Wright, H. F. (1955). *Midwest and its children*. New York: Harper & Row.

Bart, D. S. (1984). The differential diagnosis of special education: Managing social pathology as individual disability. In L. Barton & S. Tomlinson (Eds.), *Special education and social interests* (pp. 81–121). London: Croom-Helm.

Becker, H. S. (1966). Introduction. In C. Shaw (Ed.), *The jack roller*. Chicago: University of Chicago Press.

Bercovici, S. (1983). *Barriers to normalization*. Baltimore: University Park Press.

Biklen, D. (1976). Behavior modification in a state mental hospital: A participant observer's critique. *American Journal of Orthopsychiatry, 46*, 53–61.

Biklen, D. (1981). The Supreme Court v. retarded children. *Journal of the Association for the Severely Handicapped, 6*(2), 3–5.

Biklen, D. (1987). The integration question: Educational and residential issues. In D. Cohen, A. Donnellan, & R. Paul (Eds.), *Handbook of autism and disorders of atypical development* (pp. 653–667). New York: Wiley.

Biklen, D. (1992). *Schooling without labels*. Philadelphia: Temple University Press.

Biklen, D., & Bogdan, R. (1977). Media portrayals of disabled people: A study in stereotypes. *Interracial Books for Children Bulletin, 8*(6 & 7), 4–9.

Biklen, D., & Ferguson, P. (1984, Summer). In the matter of baby Jane Doe: Does Ronald Reagan really agree with us? *Social Policy*, 5–8.

Biklin, D., & Foster, S. (1985). Principles for integrated community programming. In M. Brady & P. Gunther (Eds.), *Integrating moderately and severely handicapped learners: Strategies that work* (pp. 16–46). Springfield, IL: Charles C Thomas.

Biklen, D., & Knoll, J. (1987). The community imperative revisited. In J. A. Mulick & R. F. Antonak (Eds.), *Transitions in mental retardation* (Vol. 3). Norwood, NJ: Ablex.

Blatt, B. (1970). *Exodus from pandemonium*. Boston: Allyn & Bacon.

Blatt, B., & Kaplan, F. (1966). *Christmas in purgatory*. Boston: Allyn & Bacon.

Blatt, B., Ozolins, A., & McNally, J. (1979). *The family papers: A return to purgatory*. New York: Longman.

Blumer, H. (1969). *Symbolic interactionism: Perspective and method*. Englewood Cliffs, NJ: Prentice Hall.

Blumer, H. (1980). Comment, Mead and Blumer: The convergent methodological perspective of social behaviorism and symbolic interaction. *American Sociological Review, 45*, 409–419.

Board of Education v. *Rowley*, 458 U.S. 176, 102 S. Ct. 3034, 75 L. Ed. 2d 690 (1982, June 29).

Bogdan, R. (1972). *Participant observation in organizational settings*. Syracuse, NY: Syracuse University Press.

Bogdan, R. (1976). National policy and situated meaning: The case of Head Start and the handicapped. *American Journal of Orthopsychiatry, 46*, 229–235.

Bogdan, R. (1988). *Freak show: Exhibiting human oddities for amusement and profit*. Chicago: University of Chicago Press.

Bogdan, R., & Biklen, D. (1977, March/April). Handicapism. *Social Policy*, 14–19.

Bogdan, R., & Biklen, D. (1982). *Qualitative research for education: An introduction to theory and methods*. Boston: Allyn & Bacon.

Bogdan, R., Biklen, D., Shapiro, A., & Spelkoman, D. (1982, Fall). The disabled: Media's monsters. *Social Policy*, 32–35.

Bogdan, R., & Ksander, M. (1980). Policy data as a social process: A qualitative approach to quantitative data. *Human Organization, 39*, 302–309.

Bogdan, R., & Kugelmass, J. (1984). Case studies of mainstreaming: A symbolic interactionist approach to special schooling. In L. Barton & S. Tomlinson (Eds.), *Special education and social interests* (pp. 173–191). New York: Nichols.

Bogdan, R., & Taylor, S. (1976). The judged, not the judges: An insider's view of mental retardation. *American Psychologist, 31*, 47–52.

Bothman v. Warren B. and Patricia B., No. 79-698, U.S. Supreme Court (1979).

Braginsky, D., & Braginsky, B. (1971). *Hansels and Gretels*. New York: Holt, Rinehart & Winston.

Brightman, A. (Ed.). (1985). *Ordinary moments: The disabled experience*. Syracuse, NY: Human Policy Press.

Brinker, R. P. (1985). Curricula without recipes: A challenge to teachers and a promise to severely mentally reatarded students. In D. Bricker and J. Filler (Eds.), *Severe mental retardation: From theory to practice* (pp. 208–229). Reston, VA: Council for Exceptional Children.

Bronfenbrenner, U. (1979). *The ecology of human development*. Cambridge, MA: Harvard University Press.

Brown, L., Shiraga, B., Ford, A., Nisbet, J., Vandeventer, P., Seet, M., York, J., & Loomis, R. (1986). Teaching severely handicapped students to perform meaningful work in nonsheltered vocational environments. In R. J. Morris and B. Blatt, (Eds.), *Special education: Research and trends* (pp. 131–189). New York: Pergamon.

Buckholdt, D. R., & Gubrium, J. F. (1979). *Caretakers: Treating emotionally disturbed children*. Beverly Hills: Sage.

City of Cleburne v. *Cleburne Living Center*, 53 U.S.L.W. 5022 (1985, June 25).

Conrad, P. (1976). *Identifying hyperactive children: The medicalization of deviant behavior*. Lexington, MA: Heath.

Conrad, P., & Schneider, J. (1980). *Deviance and medicalization*. St. Louis: C. V. Mosby.

Crossley, R., & McDonald, A. (1980). *Annie's coming out*. Harmondsworth, England: Penguin Books.

Davis, F. (1961). Deviance disavowal: The management of strained interaction by the visibly handicapped. *Social Problems, 9*, 120–132.

Dembo, T., Leviton, G. L., & Wright, B. A. (1956). Adjustment to misfortune—A problem of social psychological rehabilitation. *Artificial Limbs, 3*, 4–62.

Dexter, L. (1956). Towards a sociology of the mentally defective. *American Journal of Mental Deficiency, 61*, 10–16.

Dexter, L. (1964). *The tyranny of schooling: An inquiry into the problem of "stupidity."* New York: Basic Books.

Dollard, J. (1935). *Criteria for life histories*. New Haven: Yale University Press.

Duff, R. S. (1981). Counseling families and deciding care of severely defective children: A way of coping with "medical Vietnam." *Pediatrics, 67*, 315–320.

Duff. R. S., & Campbell, A. G. M. (1973). Moral and ethical dilemmas in the special-care nursery. *New England Journal of Medicine, 289*, 890–894.

Farber, B. (1968). *Mental retardation: Its social context and social consequences*. Boston: Houghton Mifflin.

Featherstone, H. (1982). A difference in the family. New York: Penguin Books.

Fielder, L. (1984). The tyranny of the normal. *Hasting Center Report, 14*(2), 40–42.

Fletcher, J. (1972). Indications of humanhood: A tentative profile of man. *Hastings Center Report, 2*(5), 1–4.

Freidson, E. (1970). *Professional dominance: The social structure of medical care*. New York: Atherton.

Goffman, E. (1959). *The presentation of the self in everyday life*. Garden City, NY: Doubleday.

Goffman, E. (1961). *Asylums: Essays on the social situation of mental patients and other inmates*. Garden City, NY: Doubleday/Anchor Books.

Goffman, E. (1963). *Stigma: Notes on the management of spoiled identity*. Englewood Cliffs, NJ: Prentice Hall.

Green, J. (1984). *American photography: A critical history, 1945 to the present*. New York: Abrams.

Hauber, F. A., Bruininks, R. H., Hill, B. K., Laken, C., Scheerenberger, R., & White, C. C. (1984). National census of residential facilities: A 1982 profile of facilities and residents. *American Journal of Mental Deficiency, 89*, 236–245.

Heifetz, M. D., & Mangel, C. (1975). *The right to die*. New York: Berkley.

Heshusius, L. (1981). *Meaning in life as experienced by persons labeled retarded in a group home*. Springfield, IL: Charles C Thomas.

Heshusius, L. (1982). At the heart of the advocacy dilemma: A mechanistic world view. *Exceptional Children, 49*(1), 6–13.

Higgins, P. (1980). *Outsiders in a hearing world: A sociology of deafness.* Beverly Hills, CA: Sage.

Hill, B. K., Lakin, K. C., & Bruininks, R. H. (1984). Trends in residential services for people who are mentally retarded: 1977–1982. *Journal of the Association for Persons with Severe Handicaps, 9,* 243–250.

Hobbs, N. (1975). *The futures of children: Categories, labels, and their consequences.* San Francisco: Jossey-Bass.

Hobbs, N. (1980). An ecologically oriented service-based system for the classification of handicapped children. In S. Salzinger, J. Antrobus, & J. Glick (Eds.), *The eco-system of the "sick" child: Implications for classification and interventions for disturbed and mentally retarded children.* New York: Academic Press.

Jernigan, K. (1975, July). *Blindness: Is the public against us?* Address to the annual banquet of the National Federation of the Blind, Chicago.

Jones, R. (1983). *Reflections on growing up disabled.* Reston, VA: Council for Exceptional Children.

Kielhofner, G. (1983). "Teaching" retarded adults: Paradoxical effects of the pedagogical enterprise. *Urban Life, 12,* 307–326.

Knoll, J. (1984, November). *Blurred images: Photography, art, and disability.* Paper presented at the annual convention of the Association for Persons with Severe Handicaps, Chicago.

Kosterlitz, J. (Ed.). (1984, January/February). Talk back: The case of baby Jane Doe. *Common Cause Magazine,* pp. 35–39.

Kwitney, J., & Landauer, J. (1979, October 17). Minimal wage. *Wall Street Journal,* pp. 1, 24.

Lemert, E. (1951). *Social pathology.* New York: McGraw-Hill.

Lewin, K. (1935). *A dynamic theory of personality.* New York: McGraw-Hill.

Lorber, M. (1974). *Consulting the mentally retarded: An approach to the definition of mental retardation by experts.* Unpublished doctoral dissertation, University of Michigan, Ann Arbor.

Massie, R., & Massie, S. (1973). *Journey.* New York: Ballantine.

Medsger, B. (1979, March). The most captive consumers. *The Progressive, 43,* 34–35.

Mercer, J. R. (1973). *Labeling the mentally retarded.* Berkeley: University of California Press.

Mercer, J. R. (1973). The myth of 3% prevalence. In R. K. Eyman, C. E. Meyers, & G. Tarjan (Eds.), Sociobehavioral studies in mental retardation. *Monographs of the American Association on Mental Retardation* (No. 1).

Merton, R. (1957). *Social theory and social structure.* New York: Free Press.

Pieper, E. (1977). *Sticks and stones.* Syracuse, NY: Human Policy Press.

Rhodes, W. C. (1967). The disturbing child: A problem of ecological management. *Exceptional Children, 33,* 449–455.

Rose, A. (1962). *Human behavior and social processes.* Boston: Houghton Mifflin.

Roth, W. (1981). *The handicapped speak.* Jefferson, NC: McFarland.

Rothman, D. J. (1980). *Conscience and convenience: The asylum and its alternative in progressive America.* Boston: Little, Brown.

Sarason, S. B., & Doris, J. (1979). *Educational handicap, public policy, and social history.* New York: Free Press.

Scheff, T. J. (1966). *Being mentally ill: A sociological theory.* Chicago: Aldine.

Schrag, P., & Divoky, D. (1975). *Myth of the hyperactive child.* New York: Pantheon Books.

Scott, R. (1969). *The making of blind men.* New York: Russell Sage Foundation.

Scull, A. (1981). The new trade in lunacy: The recommodification of the mental patient. *American Behavioral Scientist, 24,* 741–754.

Shaw, C. (1966). *The jack roller.* New York: Russell Sage Foundation.

Skrtic, T. M. (1986). The crisis in special education knowledge: A perspective on perspective. *Focus on Exceptional Children, 18*(7), 1–16.

Stainback, S., & Stainback, W. (1984). Broadening the research perspective in special education. *Exceptional Children, 50,* 400–409.

Starr, R. (1982, January). Wheels of misfortune. *Harper's, 264,* pp. 7, 15.

Sutherland, E. (1937). *The professional thief.* Chicago: University of Chicago press.

Swap, S. (1974). Disturbing classroom behavior: A developmental and ecological view. *Exceptional Children, 41*, 162–171.

Swap, S. (1978). The ecological model of emotional disturbance in children: A status report and proposed synthesis. *Behavioral Disorders, 3*(3), 156–186.

Szasz, T. S. (1961). *The myth of mental illness.* New York: Harper & Row.

Taylor, S. (1982). From segregation to integration: Strategies for integrating severely handicapped students in normal school and community settings. *Journal of the Association for the Severely Handicapped, 7*(3), 42–49.

Taylor, S., & Bogdan, R. (1984). *Introduction to qualitative research methods: The search for meanings.* New York: John Wiley.

Taylor, S. J., Bogdan, R., & Racino, J. (1991). *Life in the community.* Baltimore: Paul H. Brookes.

Thomas, W. I., & Znaniecki, F. (1927). *The Polish peasant in Europe and America.* New York: Knopf.

U.S. Department of Education. (1984). Sixth annual report to Congress on the implementation of Public Law 94–142: The Education for All Handicapped Children Act. Washington, DC: U.S. Government Printing Office.

Whitehead, C. (1979). Sheltered workshops—Effective accommodation or exploitation? *Amicus, 4,* 273–276.

Wiseman, J. (1970). *Stations of the lost.* Englewood Cliffs, NJ: Prentice Hall.

Wolfensberger, W. (1975). *The origin and nature of our institutional models.* Syracuse, NY: Human Policy Press.

Wright, B. (1960). *Physical disability—A psychological approach.* New York: Harper & Row.

Wright, B. (1983). *Physical disability—A psychological approach* (2nd ed.). New York: Harper & Row.

Youngberg v. *Romeo,* 457 U.S. 307 (1982).

OUR MULTICULTURAL SOCIETY

SOCIETY

VALERIE J. JANESICK

Alonzo should be in first grade. He is nearly 7 years old and has been absent from his inner-city Baltimore school about 15 days each month this year. His teacher discovered that Alonzo works for a crack house in his neighborhood and earns $125 per week by not coming to school. He has been labeled "learning disabled" (LD) at school. His teacher is trying to work with Alonzo's mother, a single parent, to ask for help in getting Alonzo to come to school daily.

In southern California, Ouan, an 11-year-old Laotian girl, is in fifth grade and is reading at the first-grade level. The teacher of English as a Second Language (ESL) says Ouan has difficulty speaking in English sentences and rarely makes eye contact with the teacher. Ouan is listed as LD and is pulled out of classes twice a day for special education services and ESL classes.

Alonzo and Ouan illustrate some of the issues surrounding minority status, special education, and "disability." To understand these issues, we also must understand their social context, which includes poverty and affluence, social class stratification and educational inequality, and race. For Alonzo and Ouan, and any other minority children who have disabilities, the disadvantage is at least doubled. Besides being classified as "minority"—which automatically brings us into the social context of problems with race, poverty, and educational inequality—the student is classified as disabled. To understand the meaning of disability as a minority, we need to look at some of the data related to our multicultural society.

POVERTY AND AFFLUENCE

Following the 1990 census, the U.S. Bureau of the Census (1991) released its statistical report. The United States, by virtue of two indicators—median annual family income and gross national product—is one of the wealthiest nations on earth. Evidence from the report is solid. The U.S. median annual family income in 1989 was $28,000 and currently is slightly higher. The gross national product (GNP) at the time was $5,200 billion and now is slightly higher. Of course, we are dealing with averages here, so we have to go deeper into the individual statistics themselves to understand the wide disparity between the rich and the poor. The disparity follows from the extremely small number of rich people who control the wealth of this country.

For example, the wealthiest 1% of the population owns more than half of all privately held corporate stock. The richest half of 1% owns nearly half of all corporate stock. The richest 1% also owns:

—10% of all privately owned real estate.
—more than 52% of all federal, state, and local bonds.
—nearly 9% of the nation's cash supply.
—almost 81% of all trust assets.

In contrast, the poorest 20% of all Americans have about 5% of the total national income and almost no assets.

Around 32 million Americans are below the government-defined poverty level, according to the following breakdown by race:

—nearly 20 million whites
—almost 9 million blacks
—nearly 4 million Hispanics

In America, 13% of all American families have incomes below the poverty level, and more than half have incomes below $25,000. In contrast, only 6% have incomes above $50,000, and there are only about 600,000 millionaires. Economist Paul Samuelson vividly described the situation:

> If we made an income pyramid out of a child's blocks, with each layer portraying $1,000 of income, the peak would be far higher than the Eiffel Tower, but almost all of us would be within a yard of the ground. (Blumberg, 1980, p. 34).

What this means quite simply is that the rich own more and earn more. These proportions have remained virtually the same for many years. Besides the fact that so many families live at the poverty level, those who are above that level continue to struggle to make ends meet. Our national emphasis on equality and middle-class norms and values permits us to overlook the contrast of a handful of extremely wealthy people and tens of millions of poor Americans.

MINORITY GROUPS AND POVERTY

When we ask ourselves who are the poor, a startling finding emerges. Well over half of all poor families are headed by women, and this trend is growing steadily. In 1989, more than 70% of poor African American families were headed by women. In contrast, more than 46% of poor white families were headed by women, and 55% of Hispanic families were headed by women. Furthermore, 37% of all poor children live in female-headed households. Males head less than 20% of poor households. As it turns out, about 20% of all children in America live in poverty, and African Americans and other minorities continue to be overrepresented in the ranks of our country's poor. For example, in 1989, 31% of African Americans were living below the poverty level, 26% of Hispanics were below the poverty level, and about 10% of whites lived below the poverty level. The median income for whites in 1989 was $30,406, whereas the median income for African Americans was $18,083 and for Hispanics was $21,921. Only about 40% of African Americans were working at full-time jobs.

Some of the reasons are economic and social. Take, for example, the fact that minorities, particularly African Americans and Hispanics, are more likely to drop out of school than their white counterparts. Currently, the drop-out rate for African Americans is around 11.4%, and it is almost 28% for Hispanic students. Within a subgroup such as minority children of migrant farm workers, the drop-out rate is a devastating 93%. Jobs for high school drop-outs often are dead-end jobs, jobs that pay the minimum wage or less with little hope for advancement. Racial discrimination often is most evident in the employment lines. How can anyone be surprised that more than half of African American workers are blue-collar workers? Even with a college education, African Americans earn only 80% as much as whites. African American, college-educated women earn less than African American college-educated men. In contrast to college-educated whites, African Americans earn only 60% of what their white counterparts earn. Clearly, poverty and race can easily restrict economic advancement for minorities.

Although poverty affects all aspects of social life, we cannot possibly deal here with issues such as housing opportunity, health care, or the criminal justice system. These topics are open for prospective teachers to study through texts in sociology, cultural anthropology, urban studies, law, and criminal justice. Rather, the emphasis in the remainder of this chapter is on education and its relationship to minorities.

EDUCATION FOR EVERYONE

Public schools reflect the values of society. The schools never have been neutral in terms of these values. One of the reasons educational researchers spend time in schools is because they wish to describe and explain what values dominate the schools. One of the stated values of the schools is a strong commitment to the egalitarian ideal. Simply put the egalitarian idea is the belief that each student should have an equal educational opportunity. Presumably, this will translate to social, economic, and political equality. Yet, after studying statistics on the disparity between rich and poor and the difference in levels of poverty among minorities, equality obviously is hard to come by.

Across the board, the poor have less opportunity than those who are not poor. Children of poor people stay in school fewer years, complete high school less often, and consequently are less likely to go to college. If they attend school from kindergarten through 12th grade, chances are high that they will be taught by middle-class teachers with the values and core beliefs of the middle class. These teachers may not have training in or understand what being a disadvantaged child by virtue of poverty means. Furthermore, these teachers are more likely to classify disadvantaged minority children as having a disability. Historically, a disproportionate number of disadvantaged minority students have been found in special education classes (see Dunn, 1968; Mercer, 1970; Sarason & Doris, 1979; Brantlinger & Guskin, 1987). Teachers of disadvantaged students consequently may be reluctant to admit that less educated people in our society receive less income and have greater difficulty in moving out of the poverty cycle. The poor are caught in a cycle that feeds and perpetuates poverty from generation to generation.

LEARNING FROM RESEARCH

EDUCATING MINORITIES FROM GENERATION TO GENERATION

As educators, we need to realize that minorities bear the burden of poverty and that this is connected somehow to educational opportunity and success in school. Why do some children, especially minority children, do so badly in school? This question intrigued the anthropologist John Ogbu (1974). He went to Stockton, California, and spent 21 months studying that community, which had a high proportion of school failure among African Americans and Hispanics. In his now classic book, *The Next Generation: An Ethnography of Education in an Urban Neighborhood*, Ogbu focused on the beliefs, behaviors, and functions of education in that neighborhood, which he called "Burgherside." Originally from Nigeria, Ogbu set out to study:

> ...how the people in Stockton...conceptualize their education system and their place in it and how these conceptualizations influence the way they behave within the institution. I feel that understanding this would throw some light on...why they [minorities] have such a high proportion of failures. (p. 15)

After months of observation, interviewing, and reviewing documents, Ogbu carefully analyzed the data and offered an eloquent and provocative explanation of school failure as a historical adaptation to unequal opportunity. He probed the combination of forces that created, and sustain, the pattern of failure, including:

- Social stratification.
- Myths and stereotypes that support the system.
- Local teachers' and administrators' behaviors and beliefs about school.
- The attitudes of ghetto residents toward competition with members of the dominant whites.
- Exclusion of minorities from the rewards of education.

In the end, he concluded that most remedial programs are not effective because they treat the symptoms rather than the causes of the problem. Worse, he saw this cycle repeating itself in "the next generation."

Ogbu took issue with theories that attempt to explain school failure for minorities through factors such as cultural deprivation, inferiority of schools attended, or genetic inferiority. He took all of these theorists to task for not studying this problem with any sense of history.

> The inadequacy of these theories is their essentially ahistorical approach to a problem that has its roots in history. (p. 254)

A fundamental historical factor in school failure of African Americans and other subordinate minorities, Ogbu explained, is the basis of their association with the dominant group and the adaptation they have made to the institutions of American society because of their real and historical experiences in these institutions. In his final chapter he argued that the initial association of subordinate minorities such as African Americans was not voluntary. Furthermore, it was not motivated by the drive for economic self-improvement, as in the case of other immigrant minorities such as the Japanese and Koreans.

Even more striking is that historically, after emancipation, African Americans were led to believe they would receive equal treatment with whites in education and the benefits of education. In practice, they have systematically been denied this equal treatment. Historically, African Americans have been given both an inferior education and inferior rewards for education. They often have been denied the opportunity of getting good jobs and good wages. Ogbu's argument rests on these historical factors, which ultimately led to African Americans' adapting to these factors by reducing their efforts in school tasks. This, of course, meant they eventually would have fewer rewards in the workplace, perpetuating the cycle that restricts success and advancement. Ogbu supported his detailed analysis with evidence from the statements and actions of the "Burghersiders" in his book. In conclusion, he described three ways in which adaptation to school failure is maintained:

1. There is a "lag" in efforts to achieve stated educational goals. For example, absenteeism is high, and some students do not try to make it academically.
2. Teachers behave in a way that indicates they do not understand subordinate minorities' educational problems.
3. The school system insists on defining educational problems in psychological and clinical terms.

In general, Ogbu's study shows us that the egalitarian ideal, or "equal educational opportunity," refers to (a) equal favorable learning conditions for all children, and (b) equal enjoyment of the benefits or rewards of education by individuals according to their educational achievement. When these two meanings begin to be realized and make sense to minorities, then and only then will some changes take place. This study is powerful and instructive. It leaves the reader with a realistic explanation for the schools' failure with subordinate minority groups.

BLACK AND WHITE ATTITUDES IN SCHOOL

Another long-term ethnographic study has much to say regarding education and race. Janet Ward Schofield (1982), assisted by a team of researchers, spent nearly 7 years researching and writing *Black and White in School: Trust, Tension, or Tolerance.* This book reports the study of Wexler Middle School, situated in a large, industrial, northeastern city. Schofield focused on beliefs and behaviors related to the dynamics of racial interaction. She looked at individual classrooms and the relationship of the classroom to the policies of the school board and the city. This is a careful study of the role of race and social class in a desegregated middle school—a model school created with high hopes, good intentions, superb facilities, and staff and community support. Even so, the school soon was diverted from its stated original goals and objectives. Schofield explained the political trade-offs involved in integration, class politics, and racial politics. The main message of the book is straightforward: Local political realities determined the future of the school.

Through observations and interviews, Schofield studied teachers, administrators, students, and other related personnel. Her findings are grouped by major categories relating to students and teachers. As for the teachers, Schofield found their main orientation to be one of "academics: first, last, and only." In fact, academics were stressed so heavily that other goals, such as social goals, were virtually excluded. At the same time, the school was highly publicized as one fostering positive interracial relations. Other beliefs of teachers included the notion that black and white relations will occur and develop naturally rather than through planned or forced activities. Schofield labeled this the "natural progression assumption."

Teachers also tended toward what Rist (1978) has called "the colorblind view of interracial schooling"—a view that sees interracial education as a vehicle for success in a middle-class world. In this context, to bring up the topic of race is almost inappropriate. If one does so, it implies racism or prejudice, or both. All these beliefs of teachers, along with the belief that the individual classroom is a world in itself, contributed to the development of a strong norm or taboo. This taboo discouraged teachers and students from making direct reference to or even discussing the fact that, in most cases, blacks and whites in this country are distinct social groups (p. 55).

Given this ideology of the teachers, it is not surprising to find black and white students separate and unequal. Schofield is masterful in her analysis of the achievement gap, classroom policies and desegregation, and racial stereotypes in relationship to the achievement gap. She probed into students' social relationships by analyzing the patterns of interaction between male and female groups, and went still further by analyzing race and romance and fears of both groups. Schofield did find that as students progressed through Wexler over a 3-year period, they found ways to work with each other, even though both groups held traditional racial stereotypes of each other. Most of Wexler's staff held a traditional assimilationist perspective (p. 219): Integration will be achieved when African Americans are assimilated into white culture in terms of behavior, economic status, education, and access to the rewards of education and other social institutions. This is a widely held belief, as other researchers have documented (Rist, 1978; Sagar & Schofield, 1982; Willie, 1973). Schofield (1982) concluded by arguing that:

> Rather than creating problems, sensitivity to and careful analysis of underlying racial tensions can help schools to avoid exacerbating such tensions and to better meet the needs of all their constituents. (p. 222)

THE CUSICK STUDIES

Another researcher, Philip Cusick (1983), dealt with some of these issues in his book, *The Egalitarian Ideal and the American High School.*

Cusick undertook three studies that bear upon our understanding of this multicultural society of ours. The data in his book are taken from three high schools, two of them urban and biracial, one all white and suburban. Cusick pointed out that, although differences exist among the three, all share a similar structure as embedded in a strong "commitment to an American version of the egalitarian ideal; that is, to provide each student with an opportunity for social, political, and economic equality" (p. 1). These schools were studied in the early 1970s, a time characterized by white flight from the inner cities and a time of outspoken black militancy. Two of the schools under study were changing from a predominantly white to a predominantly black makeup. In the districts where both schools were located, litigation was underway with the Civil Rights Commission regarding integration.

Cusick identified biracialism as the strongest contributor to conflicts among students. They did not openly riot, but they did fight frequently, and they remained isolated, black from white. He argued that the isolation was a result of the formal structure of the school, which was designed to "keep the lid on":

> The total organization was gearing up to prevent the potential conflict among students from developing into violence. "Keeping the lid on" devoured all the excess energy that might have been used for pursuing other ends. Biracialism...dominated everything else in the school. (p. 23)

Cusick designed his studies of the biracial schools to pursue the question: What do black and white students do together, and how does this affect the school? What he found was that blacks and whites did very little together:

> Biracialism was too sensitive an issue to talk about rationally in either of our urban schools. One could not even publicly discuss its potentially good effects such as increasing racial tolerance and mutual understanding. Its ill effects of increasing tension and occasions for violence were treated, but as part of the general problem of attendance or discipline. (pp. 104–105)

Like Schofield, Cusick found teachers and students unwilling to talk about race. Cusick related this fact to the standards set in the schools regarding attendance and discipline. He found the schools to be obligated to the egalitarian ideal to such an extent that the schools needed to demonstrate they could maintain order. This meant maintaining order among many who "would prefer not to come to school" (p. 109). Cusick argued that the very legitimacy of the schools rests with its obligation to preserve the egalitarian ideal. In fact, black students' chances for political, social, and economic equality are improved by virtue of attending classes and attending those classes in a "disciplined" fashion.

MAKING SENSE OUT OF RESEARCH

What can we as educators learn about our multicultural society through the study of these three research projects? Ogbu, Schofield, and Cusick did studies in the participants' settings. They probed into the participants' real problems in their everyday lives. The researchers became participant observers and interviewers seeking to describe and explain, through the participants' words, what it meant to be a Burghersider, a student, or a teacher at Wexler Middle School, or a student or teacher in a biracial urban high school. These descriptive data allow us to extract what we need to know for our role as educators.

Ogbu, for example, raised many sub-issues relative to his major finding that minorities do poorly in school because they have adapted to unequal opportunity. He forces us to think about the realities of (a) social stratification, (b) myths and stereotypes that support unequal opportunity, (c) the beliefs and attitudes of minorities and their teachers and parents regarding school achievement, and (d) the exclusion of minorities from the rewards of education.

Similarly, Schofield took on these issues in the setting of a desegregated middle school. She analyzed the factors affecting the achievement gap between blacks and whites and the patterns of social interaction between blacks and whites, including fears, romances, and tensions. Adding to our knowledge of beliefs and behaviors in biracial urban high schools, Cusick found race, discipline, and attendance to be critical themes in "keeping the lid on" in these schools. Like Schofield, he found the topic of race nearly unapproachable; if the topic came up at all, it somehow was masqueraded conveniently as part of the general problem of discipline or attendance.

If we go back to the cases of Alonzo and Ouan, we can more clearly understand the difficulties for them and others like them in school. If Ogbu is correct, they already have adapted to unequal opportunity and its lack of reward. If Schofield is correct, they will make it only if they come to believe in the egalitarian ideal. As educators, we must begin the task of working with the Alonzos and Ouans of our multicultural society to help them achieve what they can in terms of an equal education and the rewards that follow from it.

MINORITY STUDENTS IN SPECIAL EDUCATION

The students in our multicultural society are caught up in another major problem: the disproportionate number of minority students in special education. Historically, the number of students in special education classes has grown steadily since World War II. Of the students in special education classes, minority groups unquestionably have been overrepresented. Most recently, Brantlinger and Guskin (1987) brought this disparity to the academic community. In their review of the social-psychological effects of handicapped classification, the writers emphasized findings congruent with the earlier work of Dunn (1968–69), Sarason and Doris (1979), Mercer (1970, 1971, 1973, 1974), and the U.S. Office of Special Education and Rehabilitative Services (OSERS) study

(Applied Management Services 1983). The findings of all of these studies are powerful and include the following points of agreement:

1. There is a relationship between minority status and handicap classification.
2. There are inequities between high- and low-income schools in terms of material and human resources.
3. Being classified as handicapped has a powerful impact on the future of an individual in school and in future careers.
4. Specific handicapped minorities have difficulty in gaining access to and benefiting from appropriate educational interventions and activities.
5. Minority students continue to be overrepresented in special education classes and programs.

What is disturbing about these findings over nearly 30 years is that the problem seems to be getting worse not better. Sleeter (1986) undertook a historical study of learning disabilities from post-Sputnik days to the 1980s. She explained how reading achievement standards were raised after Sputnik, and students were overtested in many respects. Students who could not keep up were classified into one of five categories. Four of the categories were used to describe minority students. One category, "learning disabled," was used most often to describe white middle-class students who were failing, to protect them from the stigma of failure. This held true for about 10 years. Then, after 1972, a major shift occurred, which resulted in the overrepresentation of African Americans in the LD category by 1974 and thereafter. What is striking about this situation is that it has become part of our history in terms of educational practice, and it is a contradiction in terms of our belief in an equal educational opportunity for all students.

Not only have academic researchers dealt with these issues, but the government has been involved in investigation of these charges for some time. Two major sources of information are available on the matter of overrepresentation of minority students in special education since implementation of PL 94–142 (the Education for All Handicapped Children Act of 1975, now Individuals with Disabilities Education Act). The first source is a study commissioned by the Office of Special Education and Rehabilitative Services (OSERS), the office within the Department of Education officially charged with evaluating implementation of PL 94–142. The second is represented by a number of surveys conducted by, and a major study commissioned by, the Office of Civil Rights (OCR), the office charged with monitoring compliance with the equal protection clause of the Fourteenth Amendment and Title VI of the Civil Rights Act of 1964, which "prohibit the classification of persons in such a way that disproportionate harm—including the harm of separateness—accrues to members of a group identified by race, color, or national origin" (Heller, Holtzman, & Messick, 1982, p. 3).

The OSERS study (Applied Management Sciences, 1983) was carried out between 1979 and 1982. It used questionnaire, interview, and case file data drawn from a national sample of 464 elementary and secondary schools in 100 school districts to evaluate the testing and assessment practices used to identify, classify, and diagnose the educational needs of students either suspected of, or ultimately classified as, having a handicap for the purposes of PL 94–142. The aim of the study was to evaluate the procedures schools and school districts used to prevent the erroneous classification of students as handicapped. "A critical aspect of the study was comparing the various assessment practices in each of these three areas—identification, classification, diagnosis of needs—as they affected minority and nonminority students" (p. 1).

The general conclusion of the OSERS study was that "current performance has been improved with respect to the proportionality of minority students classified as mentally retarded, when compared with the historical record reflected by the Office of Civil Rights (OCR) data" (p. 6). The study reported, however, that some problems remained. For example, minority students at the secondary level were referred at a rate somewhat proportionately higher than their prevalence in the public school population; school psychologists classified minority students as "probably mentally retarded"; there was little evidence of the use of culture-fair or adaptive behavior measures in assessing minority students; and minority students were reported to be "potentially eligible but not yet referred" at higher proportionate rates than nonminority students were.

Nevertheless, the OSERS study concluded that, "ultimately...minority students are apparently being placed in special education programs at a current rate that is more clearly proportional to minority student representation in the public school enrollment than has been found in the past" (p. 6). The study did point out, however, that "the variability of the disproportionate distribution of minority student enrollment in EMR and other special education classes is higher in some states than the national percentage of overrepresentation; within those states variability in overrepresentation across school districts is also high" (p. 10).

Quite a different picture of the status of the overrepresentation issue emerged from the OCR data, which derived from two sources. The first is OCR's biannual (since 1968) Elementary and Secondary Civil Rights Survey, which is a routine check on disproportion in special education and other programs nationally. The results of these surveys represent the historical record referred to in the OSERS study. The second source of OCR data on the overrepresentation issue is a commissioned study carried out under the auspices of the National Research Council (Heller et al., 1982). The actual study group—the Panel of Selection and Placement of Students in Programs for the Mentally Retarded—conducted its investigation between 1979 and 1982, essentially concurrent with the OSERS study. Among other things, the study group conducted an extensive quantitative analysis of OCR's 1978 Elementary and Secondary School Civil Rights Survey (see Finn, 1982).

Results from the first data source—OCR's biannual survey of school enrollment carried out since 1968—are clear and consistent: "a persistent disproportion of minority children...in classes for educable mentally retarded (EMR) students" (Heller et al., 1982, p. 4). Actually, OCR's concern over these survey results is what prompted the commissioning of the National Research Council study, and thus the analysis of what then was the most recent OCR survey data (i.e., data for the 1978–79 school year). This particular OCR study sampled 6,040 school districts (about a third of the districts in the United States), which included 54,082 elementary and secondary schools (Heller et al., 1982):

The analysis accomplished three purposes: (1) it verified that the relative disproportions cited by OCR do indeed exist, documenting in the process the magnitude and distribution of minority-white...differences in EMR rates; (2) it identified geographic trends in racial...imbalances in EMR programs; and (3) it provided an examination of possible correlates of disproportion...as well as an appraisal of minority-white...differences for special education programs other than EMR and for individual racial or ethnic categories. (p. 4)

By disaggregating the survey data to the district level, the analysis provided a detailed description of disproportional placements in special education programs. "Most striking in the description is the extreme variability in the magnitude of disproportion; these differences are attributable to ethnic group membership, to geographic region, to specific demographic characteristics of the districts (e.g., size, racial composition, overall preference of EMR classifications, desegregation status) and to handicapping condition."

Although disproportions in minority placements in special education programs other than EMR programs are quite variable—depending on the region of the country and state and district characteristics—"it is clear...that disproportionate EMR placements for minorities are greater and more consistent than differences in other programs" (Finn, 1982, p. 363). The panel concluded that disproportionate EMR placement is a nationwide phenomenon with clear geographic and demographic conditions under which it occurs to a greater extent.

Although the OSERS and OCR data sources disagree on the nature of progress and the scope of the problem of overrepresentation of minority students in special education since PL 94–142, they do agree on the matter of variability. Both data sources reported variability according to the state and school district under consideration. The OSERS study was based on the performance of 100 school districts, which, while variable with respect to correcting the problem of overrepresentation, generally showed progress when compared to OCR's historical record. The OCR studies, based on the performance of a substantially larger number of school districts, also noted great variability but described overrepresentation of minority students in special education programs as a persistent national phenomenon. Short of a critical analysis of the merits of the two data sources, and considering the OSERS and OCR data together, the best that can be said is that overrepresentation of minority students in special education programs, particularly EMR programs, continues to be a problem in certain states and school districts, the Fourteenth Amendment, Title VI of the Civil Rights Act, and PL 94–142 notwithstanding.

SUMMARY

In our multicultural society, the school is a complex institution. It reflects a strong commitment to the egalitarian ideal of providing each and every student an equal educational opportunity. In the long run, this will ensure social, political, and economic equality. At the same time, many contradictions are apparent in its implementation, considering that African Americans and other subordinate minority groups consistently do less well in school than their white counterparts. They also are more likely to drop out of school or to be placed in special education programs. Obviously, race is an issue here. Moreover, poverty and the overall economic inequities minorities experience are related somehow to performance in school.

Minority students and their parents have adapted to unequal opportunity, and, as a result, they achieve less in school. Consequently, they are less successful economically. More African Americans, for example, fall below the poverty level than any other group in our society. Even worse, statistics and ethnographic studies indicate that African Americans and minorities experience fewer rewards in the economic, social, and political arena than do their white counterparts. Still worse, serious and profound problems are associated with overrepresentation of minorities in special education, and even though PL 94–142 was to remedy these problems by eliminating overrepresentation, it remains a serious problem in some states and school districts. At worst, overrepresentation of minority students in special education continues to be a national phenomenon.

Furthermore, educational researchers have begun to study the achievement gap between African Americans and other minorities and whites. This has provided us with data related to the discrepancy between the egalitarian ideal and its real-world implementation, and it has implications not only for racial minorities such as African Americans and Hispanics but also for other ethnic minority groups arising from our immigration flow.

Teachers in general need to understand the economic, political, and social context of minority groups in our schools. Special education teachers in particular need to know about the issues related to overrepresentation of minorities in special education. Until we are aware of the ramifications, we will not be able to restructure and refine the current diagnosis and classification system of special students to benefit those students and meet the challenge of the egalitarian ideal. In sum, these realities and concerns are:

- Educators need to understand the complexities of minority status for children in school, and to what extent this affects their achievement.
- Educators need to realize the significance of the discrepancy between the egalitarian ideal and its real-world implementation.
- Minority students have adapted to unequal opportunity and consequently achieve less in school. They also have the potential of dropping out of school and may never realize the economic rewards that may be available to them.
- Teachers often behave in a manner that indicates they may not understand the educational problems of minority students. Teacher training programs should address this and provide opportunities for teachers in training to redirect their behavior.
- When the egalitarian ideal makes sense to minorities in practice—when they realize both equal education opportunity and equal rewards for their education—we should see change in the status quo.
- Educators need to be aware of the overrepresentation of minorities in special education classes.
- Educators need to be aware that the longer a student is labeled as handicapped, the

further that student falls behind other students and the more difficult it is to return to the general education classroom.

■ The current system of diagnosis and classification in special education should be restructured to benefit students in special education more comprehensively and to meet the challenge of the egalitarian ideal.

*R*EFERENCES

Applied Management Services. (1983). A study to evaluate procedures undertaken to prevent erroneous classification of handicapped children (Contract No. 300-79-0669). Silver Spring, MD: Applied Management Services.

Blumberg, P. (1980). *Inequality in an Age of Decline.* New York: Oxford University Press.

Brantlinger, E. A., & Guskin, S. L. (1987). Ethnocultural and social-psychological effects on learning characteristics of handicapped children. In M. Wang & H. Walberg, *Handbook of special education: Research and Practice: Vol 1. Learner Characteristics and Adaptive Education.* Oxford, England: Pergamon Press.

Cusick, P. A. (1983). *The egalitarian ideal and the American high school.* New York: Longman.

Dunn, L. M. (1968-69). Special education for the mildly retarded—Is much of it justifiable? *Exceptional Children, 35,* 5-22.

Dunn, L. M. (Ed.). (1973). *Exceptional children in the schools: Special education in transition* (2nd ed.). New York: Holt, Rinehart, and Winston.

Finn, J. D. (1982). Patterns in special education placement as revealed by the OCR surveys. In K. A. Heller, W. H. Holtzman, and S. Messick (Eds.). *Placing children in special educations: A strategy for equity* (pp. 322-381). Washington, DC: National Academy Press.

Heller, K. A., Holtzman, W. H., & Messick, S. (Eds.). (1982). *Placing children in special education: A strategy for equity.* Washington, DC: National Academy Press.

Mercer, J. R. (1970). Sociological perspectives on mild mental retardation. In H. C. Haywood (Ed.), *Social-cultural aspects of mental retardation.* New York: Appleton-Century Crofts.

Mercer, J. R. (1971). The meaning of mental retardation. In R. Koch & J. C. Dobson (Eds.), *The mentally retarded child and his family.* New York: Brunner/Mazel, 1971.

Mercer, J. R. (1973). *Labeling the mentally retarded.* Berkeley: University of California Press.

Mercer, J. R. (1974). A policy statement on assessment procedures and the rights of children. *Harvard Educational Review, 44*(1), 125-141.

Ogbu, J. U. (1974). *The next generation: an ethnography of education in an urban neighborhood.* New York: Academic Press.

Rist, R. C. (1978). *The invisible children.* Cambridge, MA: Harvard University Press, 1978.

Sagar, H. A., & Schofield, J. W. (1982). Integrating the desegregated school: Problems and possibilities. In D. E. Bartz & M. L. Maehr, (Eds.), *The effects of school desegregation on motivation and achievement.* Greenwich, CT: JAI Press.

Sarason, S. B., & Doris, J. (1979). *Educational handicap, public policy, and social history: A history broadened perspective on mental retardation.* New York: Free Press.

Schofield, J. W. (1982). *Black and white in school: Trust, tension, or tolerance.* New York: Praeger.

Sleeter, C. E. (1986). Learning disabilities: The social construction of a special education category. *Exceptional Children, 53*(1), 46-54.

U.S. Bureau of the Census, Department of Commerce. *Statistical abstract of the United States* (1991). Washington, DC: U.S. Government Printing Office.

U.S. Department of Education, Office of Special Education and Rehabilitation Services. (1983). *Applied management services study.* Washington, DC: U.S. Government Printing Office.

Willie, C. (1973). *Race mixing in public schools.* New York: Praeger.

THE ORGANIZATIONAL

CONTEXT OF

SPECIAL EDUCATION AND

SCHOOL REFORM

THOMAS M. SKRTIC

Young people today will have to learn organization the way their forefathers learned farming. (Drucker, cited in Scott, 1981, p. 1)

T raditionally, organizations have been viewed as social tools, mechanisms that societies use to achieve goals beyond the reach of individual citizens (Parsons, 1960). But Drucker's comment refers to the reality that organizations are much more than mere tools. In addition to doing things for society, organizations do things to society. Historically, they have been criticized for doing things such as dominating the political process, causing alienation and overconformity, and stunting normal personality development (Argyris, 1957; Galbraith, 1967; Goodman, 1968). More recently, organizations have been recognized as having an even more pernicious effect on society. As Scott (1981) noted, the nature and needs of organizations shape the very goals that societies use them to achieve. Consider the following examples of this organizational phenomenon:

> In his crucial decision on how to react to the installation of Russian missiles in Cuba, President Kennedy had to select from among a naval blockade, a "surgical" air strike, and a massive land invasion, not because these were the only conceivable responses but because these were the principal organizational routines that had been worked out by the Pentagon. (Allison, 1971)

> Although we seek "health" when we visit the clinic or the hospital, what we get is "medical care." Clients are encouraged to view these outputs as synonymous although there may be no relation between them. In some cases, the relation can even be negative: more care can result in poorer health. (Illich, 1976)

> Products manufactured by organizations reflect the manufacturing process. They often reflect the need to subdivide work and to simplify tasks, and the manufacturing pressures toward standardization of parts and personnel....Customization—in the genuine sense, not in the Detroit sense—becomes prohibitively expensive. Metal replaces wood and plastic replaces metal in many products to satisfy organizational, not consumer, needs. (Scott, 1981, p. 6)

Like defense, health, and consumer goods, education is a social goal that is shaped by the medium of an organization. Society wants *education*, but what it gets is a particular kind of *schooling*, one that is shaped by the nature and needs of the organizations that are used to provide it. Although one would expect the organizational context of schooling to be an important topic of study in the field of education, historically it has been neglected. Part of the problem is that, until relatively recently, school organization has been the exclusive domain of the field of educational administration, which historically has avoided research on the effects of school organization on educational outcomes (Bridges, 1982; Erickson, 1979). Moreover, we will see below that even when the field has considered organizational issues, it has taken a narrow view of the nature of school organizations.

TWO DISCOURSES ON SCHOOL ORGANIZATION

Understanding school organization and the way the field of educational administration has conceptualized it requires some understanding of the history of the study of organizations per se. This is so because, for most of this century, the practices and discourses of educational administration have been dominated by this broader discourse on organization, which is actually two discourses: the prescriptive and the scholarly. The prescriptive discourse on organization is dominated by practitioners in business and industry who are concerned primarily with controlling people who work in organizations (Edwards, 1979). The scholarly discourse emerged after World War II, when organization became a legitimate area of academic study in virtually every social and behavioral science (hereafter, social sciences) (Scott, 1981). Since then, social scientists have carried out the scholarly discourse on organization in what has become the multidisciplinary field known as *organization analysis*. Although the prescriptive discourse of business and industry continues to influence organization analysis, it is concerned primarily with understanding the nature and functioning of organizations and their effects on people and society (Pfeffer, 1982).

HISTORICAL PERSPECTIVE

The study of organizations, including schools, can be thought of as progressing over three interrelated and overlapping time periods and corresponding schools of thought. These are: the classical period, the human relations era, and the theory movement.

The Classical Period. During the first quarter of this century, the prescriptive discourse was dominated by two overriding organizational concerns—the division of labor and the coordination or control of work (Mintzberg, 1979). These concerns gave rise to two complementary schools of thought on organization and management. The first was premised on Frederick Taylor's concept of *scientific management* (Taylor, 1947). Originally known by the more descriptive name of "shop management" (Callahan, 1962, p. 245), scientific management amounts to a detailed set of prescriptions for subdividing and standardizing work processes in industrial organizations. The second school of thought, the so-called *principles of management* (Fayol, 1949; Gulick & Urwick, 1937) approach, was concerned with formal authority exercised through direct supervision. It amounts to a set of administrative prescriptions for bringing work under the formal control of managers.

The major accomplishment of the classical period was to synthesize the notion of standardization of work processes with that of formal administrative authority. This became the key organizing principle of the prescriptive discourse and, when it was applied to the mass production process in industry, yielded the basic hierarchical organizational form referred to in Chapter 15 as the "machine bureaucracy." This is the familiar pyramid-shaped, top-down structure of formal control relations depicted in most organization charts (Mintzberg, 1979; below).

The machine metaphor dominated the prescriptive discourse during the classical period. It guided organizational design and shaped the approach to management, which was premised on the notion of man-as-machine (Worthy, 1950). Managers were concerned with the division of labor, the specification of work processes and roles, and the allocation of power. They were virtually oblivious to the social dynamics of people at work as well as to the influence of the environment on organizations (Scott, 1981). The overarching goal was efficiency, and the guiding conceptualization of organizations was that they were rational—that is, purposeful and goal-directed. Organizations were understood as physical entities, as machines whose structures and processes could be rationally fine-tuned to achieve ever higher levels of efficiency (Haber, 1964).

Enthusiasm over scientific management and the machine bureaucracy configuration did not stop on the shop floor. Although they were intended as methods for organizing and managing the mass production process in industrial organizations, some progressive era reformers promoted scientific management and the machine bureaucracy configuration as means to maximize the efficiency of social organizations, including schools (Callahan, 1962; Haber, 1964). According to Callahan, educational administrators were particularly vulnerable to the push for scientific management and the machine bureaucracy structure because of the unfortunate timing of several events:

> First, by 1910 a decade of concern with reform...had produced a public suspicious and ready to be critical of the management of all public institutions. Second, just at this time Taylor's system was brought dramatically before the nation, not with a mundane label such as "shop management" but with the appealing title of "scientific management." By 1912 the full force of public criticism had hit the schools. Third, by 1912 Americans were urging that business methods be introduced into the operation of government and were electing businessmen to serve on their school boards. Fourth, and of basic importance, was the fact that the "profession" of school administration was in 1910 in its formative stage, just being developed. If America had had a tradition of graduate training in administration— genuinely educational, intellectual, and scholarly, if not scientific—such a tradition might have served as a brake or restraining force. As it was, all was in flux. (p. 245)

As a result of these events, the professional grounding of the field of educational administration became the prescriptive discourse of scientific management and machine bureaucracy rather than the theoretical discourse of one or more social science disciplines such as history, philosophy, or psychology. Instead of becoming social, moral, or instructional leaders, school administrators became "experts in how to administrate and control organizations" (Spring, 1980, p. 100). Moreover, rather than a restraining force or a corrective, applied research in the field of educational administration also emphasized efficiency, and toward this end school organization and management were analyzed much like work in the factory (see Ayres, 1909; Bobbitt, 1913). In effect, the machine model and the efficiency mentality reinforced the functionalist view of education discussed in Chapter 15. That is, they reinforced the view of teaching and learning as routinized drill and practice (Getzels & Jackson, 1960), the perceived purpose of schooling as the mass production of a socialized workforce (Bakalis, 1983; Spring, 1980), and the functionalist theories of organizational rationality and human pathology (Skrtic, 1991a; below).

The Human Relations Era. Ironically, the classical period's lack of attention to the social dynamics of the workplace is what ushered in the human relations era. Beginning in the 1920s (Follett, 1924, 1940) and coming to fruition in the 1930s and 1940s (Mayo, 1933; Roethlisberger & Dickson, 1939), the key insight of the human relations orientation was the idea that an informal (social, cultural, or nonrational) structure of unofficial worker relations existed within the formal (rational) structure of organizations. The message for managers was that worker behavior did not conform to the official specifications of the organization but instead was determined by the norms and value orientation of the workers in the informal structure. Proponents of the human relations approach argued against the classical notion of man-as-machine, recommending instead that greater attention be paid to the relations of work groups and worker satisfaction and motivation, to the virtual exclusion of formal (rational) organizational considerations.

In this pure form the human relations approach was short-lived, giving way to the most significant outcome of this period—Chester Barnard's (1938) synthesis of the classical notion of formal administrative authority with the human relations concept of informal worker norms. In this synthesis Barnard (1938; also see Simon, 1947) argued that organizations are essentially cooperative (rational) systems that can become uncooperative (nonrational) in the absence of certain management practices intended to maintain them in a state of equilibrium. To maintain the cooperative state, he urged managers to alter or condition the behavior and attitudes of workers through training, indoctrination, and manipulation of incentives. Ultimately, however, Barnard (1938) considered humans to be inherently cooperative, and he regarded those who were "unfitted for co-operation" (p. 13) to be "pathological cases, insane and not of this world" (Burrell & Morgan, 1979, p. 149).

Appearing roughly a decade before the English publication of Max Weber's treatise on bureaucracy, which was to become the conceptualization of organization that launched the theory movement in organizational studies (see below), Barnard's synthesis was the first academic treatment of organization. As such, it became extremely influential in the history of organizational studies (Perrow, 1972) and subsequently in the development of practices and discourses of the field of educational administration (see Griffiths, 1979).

The impact of the human relations movement in industry was not lost on the field of educational administration. In the 1940s and early 1950s educational administrators translated it into the notion of "democratic practices," an approach to school management emphasizing democracy and participation in virtually all aspects of school organization and administration—democratic teaching, democratic supervision, democratic decision making (see Campbell, 1971). Although on the surface greater attention was paid to the interpersonal aspects of life in schools, democratic practices were more apparent than real. Most often they meant little more than a new set of prescriptions for school administrators to follow (Campbell, 1971). As in the case of business administration, the most significant outcome of the human relations era for educational administration was Barnard's (1938) synthesis of the classical and human relations perspectives. Barnard's theory of administration was imported into the field of educational administration by way of the Getzels–Guba model of administration (Getzels & Guba, 1957), which Griffiths (1979) characterized as "the most successful theory in educational administration" (p. 50).

The Theory Movement in Organization Analysis. Scott (1981) marked the emergence of the study of organizations as a disciplined area of inquiry with the English publication of Max Weber's analysis of bureaucratic organizational structure in the late 1940s (Weber, 1946, 1947). Writing in German during the classical period, Weber chronicled the advance of organizational rationality in the industrialized world by tracing the emergence of the bureaucratic organizational form and the way that its rational-legal type of authority relations were replacing more traditional (nonrational) forms. Of course, today "the terms bureaucracy and bureaucrat are epithets—accusations connoting rule-encumbered inefficiency and mindless overconformity" (Scott, 1981, p. 23), but in the 1940s, when Weber's work was published in English, the bureaucratic form was held in high regard within the prescriptive discourse.

The irony was that, although Weber intended to warn his readers of the negative effects of bureaucracy, his analysis was misinterpreted as an endorsement of bureaucracy as the organizational form that was capable of attaining the highest level of efficiency (see Burrell & Morgan, 1979; Mommsen, 1974). I will return to Weber's warning about bureaucracy, but at this point let us continue the discussion of the theory movement in organization analysis and the impact of Weber's work on the scholarly discourse.

Weber's theory of bureaucracy—in essence, a sociology of organization—launched the theory movement in the academic disciplines because it gave social scientists a theory of organization, which was essential if they were to study organizations *as* organizations. The availability of Weber's treatise spurred interest among social scientists in the work of other relevant intellectual forebearers, including the authors of the classical era and the human relations movement. This body of work became the initial knowledge tradition for the emerging field of organization analysis and the scholarly discourse on organization. Expansion of the scholarly discourse across the social disciplines occurred rapidly. Its first journals and texts, which appeared between the mid-1950s and the early 1960s, began to provide some integration of the rapidly growing volume of theoretical work and empirical research (Scott, 1981).

Forty years of research and theory building in organization analysis have produced what seems to be a bewildering array of competing and contradictory theories of organization (Pfeffer, 1982). One source of variability is the field's multidisciplinary nature. As we might expect from the discussion of the social sciences in Chapter 14, the various disciplinary specializations involved in the study of organizations tend to emphasize different aspects of organization in their research (see Scott, 1981). Another source of variability stems from the fact that, in addition to being a multidisciplinary field, organization analysis is a multiparadigmatic intellectual endeavor. It is multiparadigmatic because each of the social science disciplines involved in the study of organizations is a multiple paradigm science (see Chapter 14). As such, the theories the field of organization analysis produces reflect the various modes of theorizing found in the social disciplines, which can be understood in terms of the four paradigms of modern social scientific thought presented in Chapter 14: the functionalist, interpretivist, structuralist, and humanist paradigms.

As in the case of the social sciences generally, we will see below that the rise of subjectivism and the emergence of antifoundationalism have affected the field of organization analysis in ways that parallel their effects in the social disciplines. For now, however, we need only note that virtually all of the thinking about organization and management contained in the prescriptive discourse, both prior to and after the emergence of the scholarly discourse in the social sciences, is characteristic of the functionalist world view. Although the human relations movement contained the seeds for what were to become nonrational theories of organization, these insights were lost in Barnard's synthesis, which is a purely functionalist formulation (Burrell & Morgan, 1979).

Moreover, because the functionalist paradigm has been the dominant mode of theorizing in the social sciences, most of the work in organization analysis over its entire history has been done from the functionalist perspective. This is particularly true for the initial work done in the late 1940s and early 1950s, including the misinterpretation of Weber's theory of bureaucracy. In fact, although Weber's work is so rich and insightful that in subsequent years all four paradigms have claimed it, its misinterpretation during this period is the result largely of reading it from the functionalist perspective (Burrell & Morgan, 1979; Mommsen, 1974).

The Theory Movement in Educational Administration. In the early 1950s several of the leading professors of educational administration rejected the prescriptive discourse as a grounding for their field. In effect, they argued that the atheoretical nature of the prescriptive discourse had precluded the development of a theoretically grounded research base to guide the practice of educational administration. This, the leading professors believed, was responsible for the intellectual provincialism of their professional education programs and, ultimately, for the inadequate state of the field's administrative models, practice, and tools (see Griffiths, 1983).

Arguing for a more scientific and theoretical basis for educational administration, they urged their colleagues to adopt the emerging field of organization analysis as a disciplinary grounding for the profession, with the hope of drawing from it the growing body of theoretically based research on organizations (Griffiths, 1959, 1983; Hayes &

Pharis, 1967). In addition, the leading professors urged the field of educational administration to adopt positivism, the dominant mode of inquiry in the social sciences and thus in the field of organization analysis at that time, as well as the prevailing conceptualization of organizations as rational, machine bureaucracies (see Griffiths, 1983; Clark, 1985). All of this, of course, meant that what was being adopted from the field of organizational analysis was the functionalist approach to social science.

Between the mid-1950s and mid-1960s the leading professors of educational administration published several textbooks that attempted to integrate the prevailing organizational and methodological insights of the multidisciplinary field of organization analysis into the field of educational administration (e.g., Campbell & Gregg, 1956; Coladarci & Getzels, 1955; Griffiths, 1959, 1964; Halpin, 1958). Although the authors clearly advocated for the prevailing positivist orientation of the social sciences and the notion of theory as a guide to practice, the emphasis in the textbooks was on administration, not organization. In fact, material on schools *as* organizations was noticeably absent in these texts, which is understandable because the first theoretical treatment of schools as organizations in the field of organization analysis (Bidwell, 1965) appeared after the first theory-oriented texts on educational administration had been published.

This was not recognized as a problem, however, because at the time it was assumed that all organizations were rational, machine bureaucracies (Clark, 1985) and that, as such, school organizations were like any other organization (Erickson, 1979). Following this line of thinking, it was assumed that administering a school was much like administering any other type of organization (see Griffiths, 1983).

The theory movement in educational administration has several major problems. First, it was based exclusively on the functionalist perspective on organization, which, given contemporary thinking in organization analysis (see below), is an extremely narrow view of organization. From the mid-1950s to the mid-1960s, a period in which leading professors of educational administration appropriated organizational insights from the scholarly discourse, the field of organization analysis itself had a narrow functionalist view of organization, a perspective that, although still dominant, has been enriched radically over the last 30 years by theoretical insights from the other three paradigms (see Burrell & Morgan, 1979). Although some professors of educational administration (e.g., Bates, 1980, 1987; Boyd & Crowson, 1981; Foster, 1986; Maxcy, 1991) have kept pace with these developments, virtually all of the work on school organization in the field of educational administration has been done from the functionalist perspective (see Griffiths, 1983, 1988; Clark, 1985).

The second problem is that the theory movement in educational administration never really captured the imagination of the professoriate or of practicing administrators, the vast majority of whom remained tied to the prescriptive discourse (Cunningham, Hack, & Nystrand, 1977; Halpin, 1970; Halpin & Hayes, 1977). Finally, given the inability of the theory movement to influence either the applied science or the practitioner levels of the field, the leading professors' ultimate goal of improved administrative practice was not achieved (Campbell & Newell, 1973; Immegart, 1977). Thus, although the field of organization analysis continued to mature in its perspectives on organization from the late 1940s until today, the field of educational administration remains today largely as it was in the mid-1950s, particularly with respect to the field's domination by functionalist conceptualizations of inquiry, school organization, and the practice of school administration (see Bates, 1980; Clark, 1985; Foster, 1986; Griffiths 1988).

The theory movement in educational administration did have at least two effects, however. First, it introduced Weber's theory of bureaucracy to the field, which, given the functionalist misreading it received by social scientists (Mommsen, 1974) and educational administrators (Clark, 1985), further reinforced the functionalist theory of organizational rationality. Second, it appropriated Barnard's theory of administration into the field through the Getzels–Guba model of administration (Getzels & Guba, 1957).

As we know, this model is based on Barnard's theory and thus on his presupposition that organizations are cooperative (rational) entities and those in the organization who are "unfitted for co-operation" are "pathological cases." Given the broad application of the Getzels-Guba model in the field (Griffiths, 1979), this not only further reinforced the theory of organizational rationality in educational administration but introduced the functionalist theory of human pathology as well. Thus, although I noted in Chapter 15 that the field of educational administration is only implicitly committed to the theory of human pathology, as a result of the theory movement, human pathology became an explicit presupposition in its grounding knowledge tradition.

SCHOOL ORGANIZATION AND THE PROBLEM OF CHANGE

The most significant development in the field of education relative to school organization has been the emergence of a research tradition on educational change. Although one can find attempts to study school organization and change throughout most of this century (see, e.g., Miles, 1964; Mort & Cornell, 1941), the most sustained and concentrated effort began in the 1950s, when the National Science Foundation began funding what was to become a series of curriculum development projects (Elmore & McLaughlin, 1988).

Organizationally, the research tradition is largely a loose confederation of applied researchers representing virtually every subfield in the profession of education (see Lehming & Kane, 1981). Although most of the tradition's pioneers were from educational administration, special educators became somewhat involved in organizational studies in the 1960s, relative to assessing the efficacy of the special classroom model of service delivery (see Bruininks & Rynders, 1975), and more earnestly in the 1970s and 1980s, relative to implementation of PL 94–142, the Education for All Handicapped Children Act (EHA) (now Individuals with Disabilities Education Act) (e.g., McDonnell & McLaughlin, 1982; Skrtic, Guba & Knowlton, 1985; Weatherley, 1979; Weatherley & Lipsky, 1977).

The emergence of the educational change research tradition has had both political and methodological implications for organizational studies in education. Politically, it ended the exclusive grip of educational administration on the study of school organization. As we know, questions had been raised about the tendency of educational administration to avoid research topics related to school effects and student outcomes (Bridges, 1982; Erickson, 1979). Of even greater concern, however, were the political implications of a situation in which educational administrators—the group ultimately accountable for the effects of school organizations—also were the primary group evaluating those effects (see Becker, 1983; Erickson, 1977).

The primary methodological advantage is related to the fact that, over the decades since the research tradition emerged, the central issue in education has become the apparent inability of planned change efforts to actually bring about changes in school organizations. For example, Boyd and Crowson (1981) summarized the educational change research of the 1960s and 1970s by saying that:

> One of the great paradoxes of American public education is how little...our schools have changed over the past two decades of systematic efforts at reform.... Indeed, American public schools have become notorious for their ability to resist change and innovation. (p. 311)

The methodological advantage is that the consistent pattern of failed attempts to change schools forced educational change researchers to change their perspective on the nature of educational change itself.

According to House (1979), the first change in perspective was a shift from the narrow objectivist or rational-technical concern for the innovation itself, which had dominated educational change research in the 1960s, to a broader concern in the mid-1970s for understanding the innovation-in-context. The second shift was from the innovation-in-context orientation of the mid-1970s to an even broader subjectivist or nonrational perspective premised on understanding the culture of the implementation context itself. Thus, while the field of educational administration remained tied largely to the functionalist outlook, the research tradition of educational change made the shift from objectivism to subjectivism, paralleling the course of development in the social sciences (see Chapter 14; below).

Although the shift from the rational-technical perspective to the nonrational-cultural perspective provided new ways to understand the nature of educational change, it did not improve efforts to change school organizations. For example, although the insights of the new nonrational-cultural perspective on educational change were available prior to the publication of *A Nation at Risk* (National Commission on Excellence in Education, 1983) and the push for inclusive education in special education, they have had little impact on the change strategies in either reform movement (Elmore & McLaughlin, 1988; Skrtic, 1987, 1988). As noted in Chapter 15, the inclusive education movement continues to follow the rational-technical approach to change (see below). Moreover, the same rational-technical approach was the principal strategy of the first wave of the excellence movement in general education (Cuban, 1989; Skrtic, 1988; Wise, 1988).

Even though emergence of the cultural perspective has not resulted in more successful change efforts, it has registered in the consciousness of educational reformers the previously unrecognized notion that educational change requires changing the professional culture of schools. The problem, however, is that today the pendulum has swung virtually completely toward the nonrational-cultural perspective, and far too little attention is being paid to the material structure of school organizations (see Skrtic, 1991a). Moreover, although the emphasis on culture has produced sophisticated theoretical treatments of schools as cultures (e.g., Sarason, 1982; Sirotnik & Oakes, 1986), it also has led to an increasing sense of despair within the educational change research community. For example, after recognizing the centrality of school culture in the problem of educational change and noting the apparent inability to influence these cultures in any meaningful way, some educational change researchers have begun to recommend abandoning the American system of public education altogether (e.g., Everhart, 1990; Sarason, 1983).

In part, this sense of despair stems from approaching the study of organizational change monologically—that is, from one particular perspective, regardless of which perspective one chooses (see Skrtic, 1991a). Thus, in the analysis to follow, I consider school organization and change dialogically—that is, from multiple perspectives within a single antifoundational analysis. My goal is to construct an ideal-typical characterization of school organization and change by combining several theories of organization and change drawn from each of the four paradigms of modern social scientific thought. After developing my ideal-typical characterization of school organization and change, I will use it as a heuristic to reconsider the empirical criticisms of the current system of special education, as well as to analyze and compare the reform proposals of the proponents of inclusion in special education and the advocates of school restructuring in general education.

TOWARD A POSTMODERN METATHEORY OF SCHOOL ORGANIZATION AND CHANGE

Because the field of organization analysis is grounded in the disciplines of the social sciences, the theories it produces reflect the various modes of theorizing found in the social disciplines, which can be understood in terms of the four paradigms of modern social scientific thought presented in Chapter 14. As we know, the four paradigms are formed by the interaction of two dimensions of metatheoretical presuppositions: an objective-subjective dimension of presuppositions about the nature of science, and a microscopic-macroscopic or order-conflict (hereafter simply microscopic-macroscopic) dimension that reflects various presuppositions about the nature of society. Applying this conceptual framework to theories of organization (see Figure 18.1), the objective-subjective dimension corresponds to metatheoretical presuppositions about the nature of action in and by organizations, ranging from the extremes of *rational action* (prospective and purposeful or goal-directed) to *nonrational action* (emergent within evolving systems of meaning or cultures) (see Pfeffer, 1982; Scott, 1981).

The microscopic-macroscopic dimension corresponds to metatheoretical presuppositions about the level at which organizational activity is analyzed most appropri-

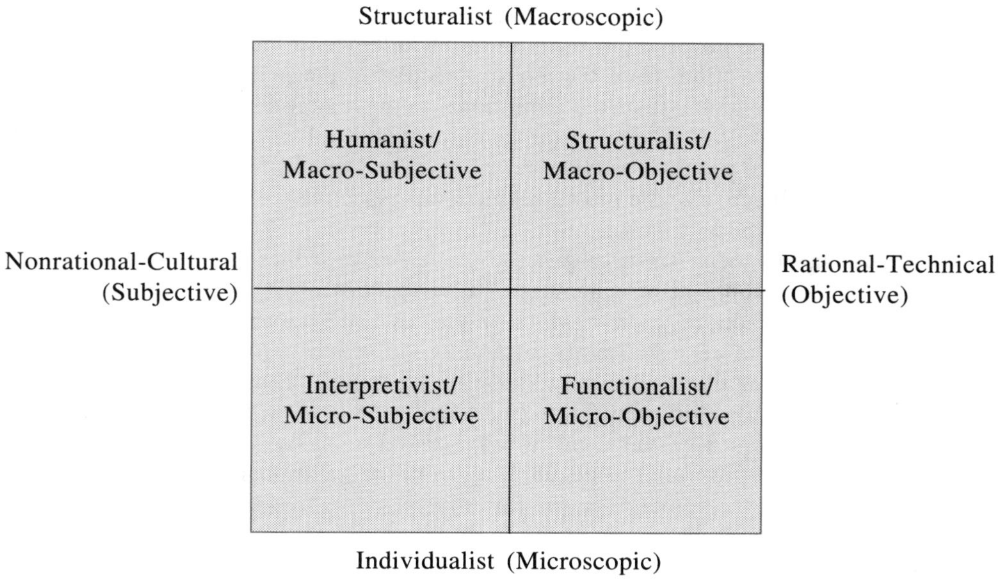

Structuralist (Macroscopic)

Humanist/ Macro-Subjective	Structuralist/ Macro-Objective
Interpretivist/ Micro-Subjective	Functionalist/ Micro-Objective

Nonrational-Cultural (Subjective)

Rational-Technical (Objective)

Individualist (Microscopic)

● *FIGURE 18.1*

Four paradigms of modern organization theory

ately. *Individualist* theories of organization emphasize the micro level of individuals and small groups and are concerned with organizing processes within organizations. *Structuralist* theories emphasize the macro level of total organizations and are concerned primarily with organization structure (Pfeffer, 1982; Scott, 1981). Thus, we can think of all modern theories of organization as being grounded in one of the four paradigms of modern social scientific thought—that is, as being shaped by either the functionalist (micro-objective), interpretivist (micro-subjective), structuralist (macro-objective), or humanist (macro-subjective) modes of social theorizing. Each mode of theorizing produces a fundamentally different way to understand organization and change, because each is premised on a different set of metatheoretical presuppositions about the nature of action in organizations and the appropriate level at which to analyze organizational activity (Burrell & Morgan, 1979; Morgan, 1983).

Because the functionalist paradigm has been the dominant mode of theorizing in the social sciences, most of the theoretical work in the field of organization analysis has been done under the rational perspective on action at the individual level of analysis—that is, under the metatheoretical presuppositions of the functionalist or micro-objective paradigm. As a result, most modern theories of organization are premised on the functionalist world view. Over the past 30 years, however, three shifts in emphasis have occurred that correspond to the paradigm shifts in the social sciences discussed in Chapter 14. The three shifts include one in the 1960s within the rational perspective on action, from the micro-objective to the macro-objective paradigm; as well as two parallel shifts from the rational to the nonrational perspective on action in the 1970s and 1980s—one at the individualist level of analysis, from the micro-objective to the micro-subjective perspective, and one at the structuralist level, from the macro-objective to the macro-subjective perspective (see Burrell & Morgan, 1979; Pfeffer, 1982; Scott, 1981).

As in the social sciences generally, one result of these shifts in perspective has been the development of a number of new theories of organization grounded in the other three paradigms, each of which previously had been underdeveloped in organizational studies. More significantly, beginning in the late 1970s, theories of organization began to appear that bridge paradigms; they combine theoretical insights from more than one paradigmatic perspective (see Skrtic, 1987, 1988; below).

Methodologically, the trend in organization analysis during the 1980s, as in the social sciences generally, has been away from the traditional foundational perspective of one best paradigm or theory for understanding organizations and toward the antifoundational approach of using multiple perspectives in a single analysis. Thus, although discourse in the field of organization analysis had been dominated by the functionalist perspective and premised on the modern or foundational view of knowledge, today it is characterized by theoretical and paradigmatic diversity, if not pluralism (Burrell & Morgan, 1979; Pfeffer, 1982; Scott, 1981), and, at the margins at least, by an antifoundational methodological orientation (see Morgan, 1983). Given these substantiative and methodological developments, today we can study school organization and change dialogically by using multiple theories of organization within a single antifoundational or postmodern analysis (see Skrtic, 1987, 1988, 1991a).

Like each of the social science disciplines of which it is constituted, the field of organization analysis is a multiple paradigm science, which means that, given the antifoundational orientation, no foundational criteria exist for selecting the correct paradigm or theoretical construction (see Chapter 14). Thus, in the antifoundational analysis to follow, I combine a number of theoretical perspectives on organization and change from each of the four paradigms of modern social scientific thought. Drawing on the American pragmatist notion that scientific knowledge is a social product of normatively regulated intersubjective communication within scientific communities (Peirce, 1931–35), I treat the various theories of organization as the ideal-typical constructions of communities of organization theorists, constructions shaped by their value assumptions with respect to the metatheoretical dimensions of the analytic framework described above and illustrated in Figure 18.1 (see Weber, 1949; Chapters 14 and 15).

In the analysis I treat each theory as an ideal type and, by combining them dialogically, attempt to create a multiparadigmatic or metatheoretical heuristic for understanding school organization and change. Of course, I do not expect to discover or create the ultimate, true theory of school organization and change. Rather, I am interested in using what I can from each of the theories, as well as from the growth in understanding that results from being open to multiple perspectives in a single analysis, to create a heuristic for deconstructing special education as an institutional practice of public education. Given the antifoundational epistemology of critical pragmatism, I am interested in developing a theory that is useful for reconciling the institutional practice of special education with the ideal that it serves the best interests of students with special educational needs and of society.

FRAMES OF REFERENCE

For ease of presentation, the theoretical territory in the analysis is divided into two general frames of reference, the *structural* and the *cultural*, each of which includes two theoretical perspectives that bridge two or more of the four paradigms. As illustrated in Figure 18.2, the structural frame of reference includes *configuration theory* (Miller & Mintzberg, 1983; Miller & Friesen, 1984; Mintzberg, 1979, 1983), which bridges the micro-objective and macro-objective paradigms; and *institutional theory* (M. W. Meyer, 1979; Meyer & Rowan, 1977, 1978; Meyer & Scott, 1983), which bridges the macro-objective and macro-subjective paradigms.

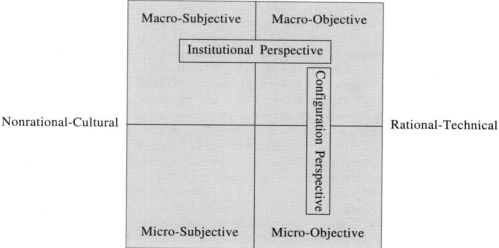

● **FIGURE 18.2**

The structural frame of reference: Configuration and institutional perspectives

Configuration theory is an important theoretical perspective in organization analysis because it synthesizes the individualists' concern for organizing processes with the structuralists' concern for organizational structure, under the analytical concept of organizational structur*ing* (see below). As such, configuration theory is important for analyzing school organization because it provides several ideal-typical organizational configurations, two of which—the *machine bureaucracy* and the *professional bureaucracy*—are particularly helpful for understanding the structure and functioning of traditional school organizations, as well as a third configuration, the *adhocracy*, which is helpful for conceptualizing the organizational structure implied in both the school restructuring movement in general education and the inclusive education movement in special education (see Skrtic, 1987, 1988, 1991a, 1991b, 1991c; Skrtic & Ware, 1992).

Institutional theory is an important theoretical perspective in organization analysis because it synthesizes the macro-subjective concern for *normative* structures and the macro-objective concern for *material* structures. It does this with the analytical notion that organizations maintain two structures—a material structure that conforms to the technical demands of their work, and a normative structure that reflects beliefs and prescriptions that have been institutionalized in society. As such, institutional theory is an important theoretical perspective for understanding the nature and functioning of school organizations and particularly how they respond to change demands (see Skrtic, 1987, 1988). By combining institutional theory and configuration theory in a single analysis, we can understand the traditional school organization as a two-structure bureaucratic configuration that is inherently nonadaptable at both the micro level of professional practice and the macro level of organization structure.

The two theoretical perspectives within the cultural frame of reference are illustrated in Figure 18.3. They are what I will refer to as *paradigmatic theories* of organization (Brown, 1978; Golding, 1980; Jonsson & Lundin, 1977; Rounds, 1979, 1981), which bridge the macro-subjective and micro-subjective paradigms; and *cognitive theories* of organization (Weick, 1979a, 1979b, 1985), which bridge three paradigms—micro-subjective, macro-subjective, and macro-objective.

Paradigmatic theories of organization are important because, by synthesizing certain key theoretical concepts from the macro- and micro-subjective perspectives, they provide a way to understand the ways in which an organizational culture or paradigm orients the thought and action of organizational members, as well as the ways in which, under certain conditions, the activities and perceptions of organizational members result in revisions in the organizational culture. From this perspective, organizational change is similar to a Kuhnian (1970) paradigm revolution (see Chapter 14). Paradigmatic theories are important for understanding school organization as a culture or system of meaning, as well as the ways in which such systems change.

Cognitive theories of organization emphasize the ways in which organizational members create and recreate organizational paradigms. They are important for organization analysis because they bridge the micro-subjective and macro-subjective perspectives by emphasizing how organizational paradigms shape the thought and action of their members (macro perspective) and also are shaped and reshaped by the thought and action of organization members (micro perspective). Cognitive theories are impor-

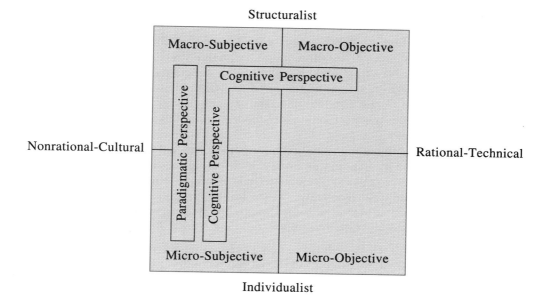

● FIGURE 18.3

The cultural frame of reference: Paradigmatic and cognitive perspectives

tant for an analysis of school organization because they provide a useful way to understand the nature of school organization change. The cultural frame of reference is important for present purposes because it provides a way to understand school organizations as corrigible systems of meaning.

STRUCTURAL FRAME OF REFERENCE

Every organized human activity gives rise to two fundamental and opposing requirements: the "*division of labor* into various tasks to be performed and the *coordination* of these tasks to accomplish the activity" (Mintzberg, 1983, p. 2). As such, the structure of an organization can be defined as "the sum total of the ways in which it divides its labor into distinct tasks and then achieves coordination among them" (Mintzberg, 1979, p. 2). The central idea in configuration theory is that organizations structure themselves into one of several regularly occurring configurations according to, among other things, the particular type of division of labor and means of coordination they employ (Miller & Friesen, 1984; Mintzberg, 1979, 1983). Given the division of labor and means of coordination employed in 20th-century school organizations, they configure themselves as professional bureaucracies (Mintzberg, 1979), even though for most of the century they have been managed and governed as if they were machine bureaucracies (see Callahan, 1962; Weick, 1982a).

According to institutional theory, organizations like schools deal with this contradiction by maintaining two structures: a material structure that conforms to the technical demands of their work, and a normative structure that conforms to the social norms or cultural expectations of their institutionalized environments (Meyer & Rowan, 1977, 1978). By combining the insights of configuration theory and institutional theory, school organization can be understood in terms of two organizations, one inside the other, as it were. On the outside, their normative structure conforms to the machine bureaucracy configuration, the structure that educational administrators strive for because of their professional grounding in scientific management and the machine bureaucracy model, and that society and school boards expect because of the social norm of organizational rationality. On the inside, however, the material structure of schools conforms to the professional bureaucracy configuration, the structure that corresponds to the technical requirements of their work.

Differences Between the Machine and Professional Bureaucracy. Ultimately, the differences between the two organizational configurations stem from the type of work they do and a variety of situational factors such as age, size, and the nature of the social environment in which they operate. Type of work is a key factor because the nature of an organization's work limits the means available to managers for dividing its labor into distinct tasks and then achieving coordination among them, means that together determine the organization's actual structural configuration.

According to Mintzberg (1979, 1983), organizations configure themselves as machine bureaucracies when their work is *simple*—when it is comprehensible or certain enough to be task-analyzed into a series of separate, relatively routine subtasks, each of which can be completely prespecified and done by a different worker (see Chapter 14). This type of division of labor is called *rationalization*, as indicated in Table 18.1. Because simple work can be completely prespecified, it can be coordinated by standardizing the work processes through *formalization*—that is, through the specification of precise rules and regulations for doing each subtask.

● **TABLE 18.1**

Structural differences: Machine vs. professional bureaucracy

	Machine Bureaucracy	**Professional Bureaucracy**
Nature of Work	**SIMPLE**	**COMPLEX**
Divison of Labor	**RATIONALIZATION**	**SPECIALIZATION**
Means of Coordination	**FORMALIZATION**	**PROFESSIONALIZATION**
Form of Interdependence	**TIGHT COUPLING**	**LOOSE COUPLING**

Source: Substantive material drawn from H. Mintzberg, 1979, *The Structuring of Organizations*, pp. 314–379. Englewood Cliffs, NJ: Prentice-Hall.

Perhaps the best example of a machine bureaucracy is the automobile assembly plant, an organizational configuration in which the activity of building an automobile is rationalized into a sequence of thousands of relatively routine subtasks, each of which is done by a separate worker along the assembly line. The total activity is coordinated by standardizing the work processes through formalization, by specifying precise rules and regulations for doing each subtask in the rationalized sequence.

Organizations configure themselves as professional bureaucracies when their work is *complex*—when it is too uncertain to be rationalized and thus formalized. Examples of organizations that configure themselves as professional bureaucracies are hospitals, law and accounting firms, social welfare agencies, and all manner of schools, including universities, colleges of education, and public schools (Mintzberg, 1979). The work of these client-centered organizations is complex not only because it is too uncertain to be rationalized but also because it requires the application of general principles or theories to the particular and often variable needs of individual clients. As we know from Chapter 14, complex work such as this requires judgment on the worker's part, which means it requires that the entire undertaking be done by a single worker who, to make the necessary judgments, must work closely with clients and have a relatively extensive knowledge base and an associated set of skills (Mintzberg, 1979; Schein, 1972).

Because its work is too uncertain to be task-analyzed and distributed among a number workers, division of labor in the professional bureaucracy is achieved through *specialization*, a situation in which clients are distributed among the workers, each of whom specializes in the knowledge and skills necessary to serve a specific type of client, the type of client presumed to have needs that correspond to the worker's specialized knowledge and skills. Given this form of division of labor, complex work is coordinated by standardizing the skills of the workers, accomplished through *professionalization*, or intensive education and socialization carried out in professional schools (Mintzberg, 1979, 1983; Miller & Mintzberg, 1983).

The logic behind rationalization and formalization in the machine bureaucracy is premised on *minimizing discretion* and *separating theory from practice*. The theory behind the work rests with the engineers and technocrats who rationalize and formalize it; they do the thinking, and the workers simply follow the rules. Conversely, specialization and professionalization are meant to *increase discretion* and to *unite theory and practice* in the professional's knowledge and skills. This is necessary because containing the uncertainty of complex work within the role of a particular professional specialization requires the professional to adapt the theory behind the work to the client's particular needs (see Mintzberg, 1979; Schein, 1972; Chapter 14).

Formalization in the machine bureaucracy is meant to serve the consumers' interests by placing a barrier (rules and regulations) between them and the organization's workers. But professionalization is premised on removing the barrier so a close working relationship can develop between the professional and the client, in the interest of making the informed judgments necessary to adapt the theory to the client's particular needs (Mintzberg, 1979).

In principle, professionals know the theory behind their work and have the discretion to adapt it to their clients' actual needs. In practice, however, the standardization of skills is circumscribed in two ways. First, of course, it is circumscribed by the particular metatheoretical paradigm in which the profession's knowledge tradition is grounded. As we know from Chapters 14 and 15, a profession's paradigm defines and subsumes the theories, assumptions, models, practices, and tools upon which its knowledge and skills are premised. In addition, standardization of skills produces professionals with a finite repertoire of standard practices applicable to only a finite set of contingencies or perceived client needs. This is a problem because it turns professional practice into a matter of the professional "pigeonholing" (Mintzberg, 1979, p. 374) a presumed client need into one of the standard practices in his or her repertoire of skills. Given adequate discretionary space (see below), there is room for some adjustment, but when clients have needs that fall on the margins or outside the professional's repertoire of standard practices, they either must be forced artificially into one of the available practices or sent to a different professional specialist, one who presumably has the proper standard practices (Perrow, 1970; Simon, 1977; Weick, 1976).

As we will see in a subsequent section, a fully open-ended process—one that seeks a truly creative solution to each unique need—requires a problem-solving orientation. Professionals, however, are performers, not problem solvers. They *perfect* the standard practices in their repertoires; they do not *invent* new ones for unfamiliar contingencies. Instead of accommodating heterogeneity, professionals screen it out by forcing their clients' needs into one of their standard practices, or by forcing them out of the professional-client relationship altogether (Segal, 1974; Simon, 1977).

Together, the division of labor and means of coordination in an organization shape the nature of the *interdependence* or "coupling" among its workers (March & Olsen, 1976; Thompson, 1967; Weick, 1976, 1982a). Because machine bureaucracies coordinate their work through rationalization and formalization, their workers, like links in a chain, are *tightly coupled* or highly dependent on one another. In a professional bureaucracy, however, the workers are *loosely coupled* (Bidwell, 1965; Weick, 1976). They are only minimally dependent on one another because specialization and professionalization create a form of interdependence in which professional specialists share common facilities and resources but do the entire work activity alone with their assigned clients. Coordination in the professional bureaucracy, which is a loose form of coordination at best, is achieved through everyone knowing roughly what everyone else is doing by way of their common professionalization (Mintzberg, 1979).

Managing Professional Bureaucracies Like Machine Bureaucracies. Given the social norm of organizational rationality and the prescriptive discourse of educational administration, school organizations are managed and governed as if they were machine bureaucracies, even though the technical demands of their work configure them as professional bureaucracies. As such, schools are forced by managers (Weick, 1982a) and their institutionalized environment (Meyer & Rowan, 1978; Mintzberg, 1979) to adopt many of the management practices of the machine bureaucracy configuration, particularly those associated with the rationalization of work and the standardization of work processes through rules and regulations. This is so, of course, even though these practices are ill suited to the technical demands of doing complex work. In principle, the effect is that the professional bureaucracy configuration of schools is driven to be more like the machine bureaucracy. As Weick (1982a) noted in this regard:

> When conventional management theory [i.e., that based on the machine bureaucracy configuration] is applied to organizations that [are not machine bureaucracies], effectiveness declines, people become confused, and work doesn't get done. That seems to be one thing that is wrong with many schools. They are managed with the wrong model in mind. (p. 673)

The most serious outcome of this drive toward the machine bureaucracy configuration is the violation of the discretionary logic of professionalization. Managing and governing schools as if they were machine bureaucracies misconceptualizes teaching as simple work that can be rationalized and formalized. Misguided attempts to rationalize teaching and to coordinate it through rules and regulations reduces the discretion teachers need to adapt their instructional practices to their students' actual needs. This reduces the effectiveness of school organizations because it minimizes the extent to which teachers can personalize their instructional practices to the particular needs of their students. As Mintzberg (1979) noted, complex work cannot be formalized through rules and regulations:

> ...except in misguided ways which program the wrong behaviors and measure the wrong outputs, forcing the professionals to play the machine bureaucratic game—satisfying the standards instead of serving the clients.... The individual needs of the students—slow learners and fast, rural and urban—as well as the individual styles of the teachers have to be subordinated to the neatness of the system. (p. 377)

Fortunately, however, attempts to rationalize and formalize teaching do not work completely in school organizations. This is so because the mechanisms used to rationalize and formalize it exist largely in the formal, machine bureaucracy structure of schools, which, from the institutional perspective, is *decoupled* from the professional bureaucracy structure where the work is done. The outer machine bureaucracy structure of schools is largely a myth, an assortment of symbols and ceremonies that corresponds to the knowledge tradition of educational administrators and the social norm of organizational rationality but has little to do with the way the work actually is done in schools (Meyer & Rowan, 1977, 1978). This decoupled, two-structure arrangement permits schools to do their work according to the localized judgments of teachers—the essence of the logic behind specialization and professionalization—while protecting their legitimacy by giving managers and the public the appearance of the rationalized and formalized machine bureaucracy they expect. As Meyer and Rowan (1977) explained:

> Decoupling enables organizations to maintain standardized, legitimating, formal structures while their activities vary in response to practical considerations. The organizations in an industry [broad sense] tend to be similar in formal structure—reflecting their common institutional origins—but may show much diversity in actual practice. (p. 357)

But decoupling does not work completely either because, from the configuration perspective, no matter how contradictory they may be, misplaced rationalization and formalization require at least overt conformity to their precepts and thus circumscribe professional thought and action (Mintzberg, 1979; cf. Dalton, 1959). Decoupling notwithstanding, managing and governing schools as if they were machine bureaucracies increases rationalization and formalization and thus decreases professional thought and discretion, which reduces the degree to which teachers can personalize their instructional practices even further.

Professional Bureaucracies and Change. Even though they are different in these respects, the machine bureaucracy and professional bureaucracy configurations are similar in one important way: Both are premised on the principle of *standardization,* and thus both are inherently nonadaptable structures at both the micro level of workers and the macro level of organization structure (see Table 18.2). Because bureaucracies coordinate their work through standardization, they are *performance organizations*, structures configured to *perfect* the practices they have been standardized to perform, thus producing *standard products* or *services.*

Of course, the standardization of skills is intended to allow for enough professional thought and discretion to accommodate client variability. Even with adequate discretionary space, however, professionals are limited in the extent to which they can adjust their standard practices, and, moreover, they can adapt only the standard practices that are in their repertoires. In a professional bureaucracy, coordination through standardization of skills itself circumscribes the degree to which the organization can accommodate variability. A fully open-ended process of accommodation requires a problem-solving organization, a configuration premised on inventing new practices for unique client needs (see Table 18.2). But the professional bureaucracy is a performance organization; it screens out heterogeneity by forcing its clients' needs into one of its standard practices, or by forcing them out of the system altogether (see Mintzberg, 1979; Segal, 1974).

● **TABLE 18.2**

Structural similarities: Machine and professional bureaucracy

	Machine Bureaucracy	**Professional Bureaucracy**
Organizing Principle	STANDARDIZATION (of work)	STANDARDIZATION (of skills)
Type of Organization	PERFORMANCE	PERFORMANCE
Goal of Organization	PERFECTION	PERFECTION
Output of Organization	STANDARD PRODUCTS	STANDARD SERVICES
Environment	STABLE	STABLE

Source: Substantive material drawn from H. Mintzberg, 1979, *The Structuring of Organizations*, pp. 314–379. Englewood Cliffs, NJ: Prentice-Hall.

Because bureaucracies are performance organizations, they require a *stable environment* and thus are potentially devastated under dynamic conditions, that is, when their environments require them to do something other than what they were standardized to do (Mintzberg, 1979, 1983). Nevertheless, machine bureaucracies can change by restandardizing their work processes, a more or less rational-technical process of rerationalizing their work and reformalizing worker behavior. When its environment becomes dynamic, however, the professional bureaucracy cannot respond by making rational-technical adjustments in its work because its coordination rests within each professional, not in its work processes. At a minimum, change in a professional bureaucracy requires a change in what each professional does because each professional does virtually all aspects of the work individually and personally with his or her clients.

Nevertheless, because schools are managed and governed as if they were machine bureaucracies, attempts to change them typically follow the rational-technical approach (see Elmore & McLaughlin, 1988; House, 1979), which assumes that changes in, or additions to, the existing rationalization and formalization will result in changes in the way the work gets done. Of course, this fails to bring about the desired changes because the existing rationalization and formalization are located in the decoupled machine bureaucracy structure. Because these changes or additions require at least overt conformity, however, they act to extend the existing rationalization and formalization in schools. This, of course, drives the organization further toward the machine bureaucracy configuration, which reduces teacher thought and discretion even further, leaving students with even less personalization and thus even less effective services.

Managing and governing schools as if they were machine bureaucracies forces them to be more like machine bureaucracies, which reduces teacher discretion and thus leaves students with less effective services. Rational-technical change efforts extend this push, driving schools to be even more like the machine bureaucracy, which reduces teacher discretion even further, thereby leaving students with even less effective services. As in the case of management by rules, the inner professional bureaucracy structure of schools cannot be changed by adding more rules, except in the misguided way of putting even more pressure on teachers to play the machine bureaucracy game of satisfying the standards instead of serving the students.

Even though schools are nonadaptable structures, their status as public organizations means they must respond to public demands for change. From the institutional perspective, schools deal with this problem by using their outer machine bureaucracy structure to deflect and distort change demands. They relieve pressure for change by signaling the environment that a change has occurred, which creates the illusion that they have changed when, in fact, they remain largely the same (see M. W. Meyer, 1979; Rowan, 1980; Zucker, 1981).

One way in which school organizations signal change is by building symbols and ceremonies of change into their outer machine bureaucracy structure, which, of course, is decoupled from the actual work. Another important signal of change is the *decoupled subunit*. Not only are the two structures of schools decoupled, but their units (classrooms and programs) are decoupled from one another as well (Meyer & Rowan, 1978).

As we know from the configuration perspective, this is possible because specialization and professionalization create precisely this sort of loosely coupled interdependence within the organization. Thus, schools can respond to pressure for change simply by adding on separate classrooms or programs—by creating new specializations—to deal with the demand for change. Like symbols and ceremonies of change, this acts to buffer the organization from the change demand because the subunits are decoupled from the rest of the organization, making any substantive reorganization of activity unnecessary (see Meyer & Rowan, 1977; Zucker, 1977, 1981).

CULTURAL FRAME OF REFERENCE

Theories of organization within the cultural frame of reference are premised on the subjectivist idea that humans construct social reality through intersubjective communication (see Berger & Luckmann, 1967). As such, theorists who operate from the cognitive and paradigmatic perspectives think of organizations as bodies of thought, as schemas, cultures, or paradigms. They are concerned with the way people construct meaning and how these processes affect the way thought, action, and interaction unfold over time in organizations. The difference is that, whereas cognitive theories emphasize the micro-processes through which workers construct their organizational schemas, paradigmatic theories emphasize the macro-processes by which existing organizational cultures shape the thought and action of workers. Together, cognitive and paradigmatic theories reflect the interactive character of the cultural frame of reference—people creating culture, culture creating people (Pettigrew, 1979).

Organizations as Paradigms. Paradigmatic theorists conceptualize organizations as paradigms or shared systems of meaning. They are concerned with understanding the ways in which existing socially constructed systems of meaning affect and constrain thought and action in organizations. From Kuhn (1970) we know that a paradigm is a general guide to perception, a conceptual map, or a way of viewing the world (see Chapter 14). Applied to organizations, a paradigm is a system of beliefs about cause-effect relations and standards of practice and behavior. Regardless of whether these beliefs are true, the paradigm guides and justifies action by consolidating the organization's inherent ambiguity into an image of orderliness (Brown, 1978; Clark, 1972).

From this perspective the process of organizational change is similar to a Kuhnian paradigm revolution: long periods of stability maintained by the self-reinforcing nature of the organization's current paradigm (Kuhn's long period of normal science) and occasional periods of change in which irreconcilable anomalies eventually undermine the paradigm's legitimacy (Kuhn's revolutionary shift to a new paradigm) (see Jonsson & Lundin, 1977; Golding, 1980). Change is a slow and traumatic process in an organization because, once in place, the prevailing paradigm self-justifies itself (and thus the thought and action of organizational members) by distorting information about the validity of the paradigm so it supports the conventional view (Golding, 1980). Nevertheless, when sufficient anomalies build up to undermine and eventually overthrow the prevailing paradigm, a new one emerges and action proceeds again under the guidance of the new organizing framework (Jonsson & Lundin, 1977; Golding, 1980).

One way anomalies are introduced into organizational paradigms is when values and preferences change in society. In this case, the paradigm falls into crisis because the social theory underlying it changes. To the extent that the new social values and preferences are inconsistent with the prevailing paradigm, however, resistance emerges in the form of political clashes and an increase in ritualized activity, which together act to reaffirm the paradigm that has been called into question (Rounds, 1979; also see Lipsky, 1976; Perrow, 1978; Zucker, 1977).

Another way that anomalies are introduced is through the availability of technical information that the current paradigm is not working, which can bring about a paradigm shift in one of two ways (Rounds, 1981). The first way is through a confrontation between an individual (or a small constituency group), who rejects the most fundamental assumptions of the current paradigm on the basis of information that the system is not working, and the rest of the organization's members, who are acting in defiance of the negative information to preserve the prevailing paradigm. The second way is when an initially conservative action is taken to correct a generally recognized flaw in what otherwise is assumed to be a viable system. Here, the corrective measure exposes other flaws, which, when addressed, expose more flaws, and so on, until enough of the system is called into question to prepare the way for a radical reconceptualization of the entire organization. In this scenario, what initially were conservative attempts to protect the system act to undermine it and ultimately usher in a new paradigm.

Organizations as Schemas. From the cognitive perspective, an organization is a human schema, "an abridged, generalized, corrigible organization of experience that serves as an initial frame of reference for action and perception" (Weick, 1979a, p. 50). The difference in emphasis between the cognitive and paradigmatic perspectives perhaps is best captured in Weick's (1979a) assertion that "an organization is a body of thought thought by thinking thinkers" (p. 42). Although Weick's assertion recognizes that organizational paradigms orient the thought and action of people who work in organizations, at the same time it accounts for "the important role that people play in creating the environments that impose upon them" (1979b, p. 5).

The cognitive perspective bridges the micro- and macro-subjective perspectives by emphasizing the active and creative role workers play in constructing and reconstructing organizational paradigms. As Weick noted, through activity, selective attention, consensual validation, and luck, people in organizations unrandomize streams of experience enough to form a "sensemaking map" (Weick, 1979a, p. 45), or paradigm of the territory. Of course, the paradigm is not the territory, it is only a *re*presentation of it. For Weick, however, "the map *is* the territory if people treat it as such" (p. 45). The point is that, accurate or not, organizational paradigms structure the territory sufficiently so that members can initiate activity in it, out of which may emerge a workable order.

Organizational members' sampling of the environment, and thus the paradigms they construct, are shaped by prior beliefs and values, which act as filters through which they examine their experiences (Weick, 1979a, 1979b, 1985). Although this assertion is consistent with the paradigmatic perspective, by emphasizing action as the pretext and raw material for sensemaking, Weick actually bridges the structural and cultural frames of reference. According to Weick (1979a, 1985), activity in organizations is shaped by material structures such as rationalization, formalization, specialization, and professionalization. These structural contingencies shape members' construction of reality because they influence the contacts, communication, and commands they experience, which in turn affect the streams of experience, beliefs, values, and actions that constitute their organizational paradigms.

The process works the other way as well: "Maps, beliefs, and thoughts that summarize actions, themselves constrain contacts, communication, and commands. These constraints constitute and shape organizational processes that result in structures" (Weick, 1979a, p. 48). Thus, from the cognitive perspective, organization is a mutually shaping circularity of structure and culture. Depending on where one enters the circle, organization is a continuous, mutually shaping process in which structural contingencies shape the activities of organizational members, which in turn shape their value orientation and thus the nature of the paradigms they construct to make sense of the organization—to interpret the very structural contingencies that shape their activities (see Weick, 1979b, 1985).

Although organization theorists have described schools as chaotic, unorganized, or anarchical systems (Cohen & March, 1974; Cohen, March, & Olsen, 1972), Weick (1985) suggested that "underorganized systems" (p. 106) is a more useful characterization. This is so, he argued, because although school organizations are ambiguous and to an observer may appear to be disorderly systems, they have some order, most of which is supplied by the schemas or paradigms their members use to make sense of the organizations and their experiences in them. This is an important point for Weick because it is the basis of his explanation for the nature of change in school organizations.

From the structural frame of reference, ambiguity in school organizations stems from two sources—the loosely coupled form of interdependence among professionals and the decoupled (or loosely coupled) relationship between their formal and informal structures—both of which minimize the potential for meaningful change (see above). Building on these structural insights, Weick (1979a, 1982b, 1985) noted a third type of loose coupling that pervades school organizations—a loose or indeterminate relationship between cause and effect—and used it to explain change from the cognitive perspective.

For Weick (1985), "a loosely coupled system is a problem in causal inference" (p. 121). Actors in these systems have difficulty predicting and actualizing cause-effect relations because the relations are indeterminate; they are "intermittent, lagged, dampened, slow, abrupt, and mediated" (p. 121). Given these cognitive conditions, the actors in loosely coupled systems:

> ...rely on trust and presumptions, are often isolated, find social comparison difficult, have no one to borrow from, seldom imitate, suffer pluralistic ignorance, maintain discretion, improvise, and have less hubris because they know the universe is not sufficiently connected to make widespread change possible. (Weick, 1985, p. 121)

A loosely coupled system, however, is not a flawed system (Weick, 1982b). It is a social and cognitive response to ambiguity,

> ...a social and cognitive solution to constant environmental change, to the impossibility of knowing another mind, and to limited information-processing capabilities. Loose coupling is to social systems as compartmentalization is to individuals, a means to achieve cognitive economy and a little peace. (Weick, 1985, p. 121)

Given this cognitive interpretation of the nature and effects of loosely coupled systems, Weick (1982b, 1985) used the ideas of superstitious learning (cf. Hedberg, 1981) and self-fulfilling prophecy (cf. Jones, 1977) to explain change in underorganized systems such as schools. Superstitious learning occurs when organizational members mistakenly see a change in the environment as the effect of their action (cause). As a result, they build into their paradigm or "cause map" (Weick, 1985, p. 124) the belief that they are able to change environments. Of course, this is an error in the sense that it is an incorrect interpretation of what actually happened. But Weick argued that when environments are sufficiently malleable, as in underorganized systems, acting on this mistaken belief can set in motion a sequence of activities that allows people to construct a reality in which the belief is true. That is, in ambiguous environments, an apparent efficacy can transform a superstitious conclusion into a correct perception.

> An original prophecy is incorrect and may result from a mistaken perception that an environmental outcome was caused by an individual action. Later, when the person acts as if the prophecy were correct, the prophecy can become correct and the environment becomes responsive to the individual action rather than to some other exogenous factor. Thus, the incorrect theory of action becomes self-correcting. It sets into motion a set of events that validate what was originally an invalid belief. (Weick, 1985, p. 124)

Ambiguity in loosely coupled, underorganized systems is reduced when people can incorporate into their paradigms an inference—rightly or wrongly—about cause and effect. When people act on the stored inference as if it were true, a previously loose relationship between cause and effect becomes tightened and the uncertainty surrounding the effect is reduced. For Weick (1982b, 1985) confident action based on a presumption of efficacy can reinforce the inference about efficacy stored in the paradigm. In short, people in ambiguous, underorganized systems can make things happen.

The inherent structural and cognitive ambiguity in loosely coupled, underorganized systems increases the extent to which action is guided by beliefs, values, and ideology (Weick, 1979a, 1982b, 1985). And when ambiguity is present in an organizational context, the people who can resolve it gain power because the beliefs and values they use to reduce ambiguity affect what the organization is and what it can become. Moreover, when ambiguity in an organization is increased, it sets the stage for ideology and values to be reshuffled; it sets the stage for a paradigm shift. Here again, the people best able to resolve the ambiguity gain power, as does their vision of the world and the organization.

According to Weick (1985), recognition of an important, enduring ambiguity—an unresolvable anomaly in the prevailing paradigm—is an occasion when an organization may redefine itself. Those who resolve the ambiguity for themselves and others can implant a new set of values in the organization, which creates a new set of relevancies and competencies and introduces a source of innovation. Ambiguity sets the occasion for organizations to learn about themselves and their environments and allows them to emerge from their struggle with ambiguity in a different form than when they started the confrontation. But behind it all are people with ideas rooted in their values and vision of what can and should be. For Weick the importance of presumptions, expectations, and commitments cannot be overestimated. Confident, forceful, persistent people can span the breaks in loosely coupled, underorganized systems with their presumptions, expectations, and commitments by encouraging interactions that tighten settings. "The conditions of order and tightness in organizations exist as much in the mind as they do in the field of action" (Weick, 1985, p. 128).

SPECIAL EDUCATION AS AN INSTITUTIONAL PRACTICE

Here I use the ideal-typical characterization of school organization and change developed in the previous section to reconsider the legitimacy of special education from an organizational perspective. In Chapter 15, my goal was to deconstruct special education as a *professional* practice. By exposing the inconsistencies, contradictions, and silences in the special education knowledge tradition, I tried to raise doubts in the reader's mind about the legitimacy of the field's professional knowledge, practices, and discourses. In this section, I want to deconstruct special education as an *institutional* practice of public education. I want to use the organizational insights developed above to raise doubts in the reader's mind about whether the institutional practice of special education is a rational and just response to the problem of school failure.

The analysis to follow is organized according to the assumptions that guide and justify the knowledge, practices, and discourses of both the profession and institutional practice of special education. As we know from Chapter 15, these assumptions are that (a) student disabilities are pathological conditions, (b) diagnosis is objective and useful, (c) special education is a rationally conceived and coordinated system of services that benefits diagnosed students, and (d) progress in the field is a rational-technical process of incremental improvements in conventional diagnostic and instructional practices (see, for example, Bogdan & Kugelmass, 1984; Heshusius, 1982; Iano, 1987; Rist & Harrell, 1982; Skrtic, 1986; Tomlinson, 1982). I will deconstruct special education as an institutional practice of public education by questioning the legitimacy of the models, practices, and tools that flow from these assumptions as well as the functionalist theories and metatheories in which they are grounded.

Deconstructing special education at an institutional level, of course, will permit me to raise further doubts about the legitimacy of special education as a professional practice. Moreover, deconstructing special education as an institutional practice will permit me to also deconstruct the 20th-century discourse on school failure. The broader significance of deconstructing the discourse on school failure is that it will permit me to deconstruct the institution of public education itself, clearing the way for reconstructing it according to the traditional ideal of public education in a democracy.

THE NATURE OF DISABILITY AND DIAGNOSIS

From the structural frame of reference, professional bureaucracies are nonadaptable at the level of the professional because they use professionalization to coordinate their work. In schools this creates a situation in which a teacher's knowledge and skills can be thought of as a finite repertoire of standard instructional practices that are matched to a finite set of predetermined contingencies or presumed student needs. This raises several questions relative to the nature of student disability and diagnosis, questions about the nature and source of these standard practices and the way they are applied in schools.

As we know from Chapter 14, the positivist model of professional knowledge assumes that professional practices are the end result of a rational system of knowledge production, a system in which applied scientists engineer the practices from objective social scientific knowledge. Because this knowledge is subjective, however, professionals' standard practices cannot be considered inherently correct in an objective sense; they are merely social artifacts, the customs and conventions of a professional culture grounded in a particular paradigm-bound knowledge tradition. Nevertheless, assuming, for the sake of argument, that these standard practices are the most effective ones available relative to the contingencies for which they have been engineered, let us consider the question of whether they are the standard practices that teachers actually use.

In Chapters 14 and 15 my argument about the subjective nature of professional knowledge and professional induction stopped at the level of the professional culture. At this point, however, I can extend it by introducing the idea that, rather than one continuous culture, a profession is actually composed of two largely discontinuous or decoupled *subcultures*: the subculture of applied scientists who work in schools of education (or research labs and centers) and the subculture of professional practitioners who work in public schools (see Elliott, 1975; House, 1974; Rudduck, 1977; Schön, 1983).

The implication is that teachers leave their professional education programs with a repertoire of standard practices grounded in the conventions and customs of the applied science subculture, but upon entry into the public schools, they are inducted into the practitioner subculture, which, faced with a different set of contingencies and relevancies, has developed different customs and conventions and thus a different set of standard practices. The result is that the professional practices most teachers use in actual school settings have little to do with what they learned in their professional education programs (Dornbusch & Scott, 1975).

Further evidence for the notion of decoupled subcultures can be found in the educational change literature. Given the objectivist view of the professions, the assumption is that the standard practices teachers use are updated continually as new, research-based procedures become available at the applied science level of the profession. One of the painful lessons of the educational change research tradition, however, is that this rarely occurs (see House, 1974, 1979). In most schools the methods of instruction and the curriculum itself are little different from what they were earlier in the century (Cuban, 1979). Thus, though the structural frame of reference assumes that the standard practices teachers use in schools derive from *professionalization*, we can think of the source of these standard practices as *acculturation*. That is, upon entry into school organizations, during their student teaching internship and later as employees, teachers are inducted into an existing subculture of practicing teachers, a subculture with its own set of norms, customs, and conventions.

From this perspective, professional behavior in schools is governed more by institutionalized cultural norms than by rational, research-based actions designed to improve instructional effectiveness. Things are done in certain ways in schools simply because they always have been done that way. To do anything else in these organizations would not make sense because, from this perspective, teaching is a ritualized activity that takes place in an institutionalized environment (see Zucker, 1977, 1981). Teachers learn to teach by modeling people they have seen teach—people such as their former public school teachers and the cooperating teachers under whom they serve their student teaching internships, professionals who got their standard practices in the same way from previous models (Gehrke & Kay, 1984; Lortie, 1975; Schempp & Graber, 1992). These practices are passed on from one generation of teachers to another within an institutionalized context. There is nothing rational or inherently correct or incorrect about them; they are simply artifacts of a professional subculture. What is important about these practices is whether they serve the best interests of students, a question that can be addressed by asking how they are applied in practice.

From the structural frame of reference, professional practice is a matter of pigeonholing a presumed client need into one of the standard practices in the professional's repertoire of skills. A common problem associated with this pigeonholing process, however, is that "the professional confuses the needs of his clients with the skills he has to offer them" (Mintzberg, 1979, p. 374). Of course, pigeonholing is less of a problem when a student's needs actually match the skills the teacher has to offer. The problem arises when the student's individual learning style and needs do not match any of the standard practices in the teacher's repertoire of skills. In this situation the teacher must either force the student's needs artificially into one of the available standard practices or force the student out of the professional-client relationship and into another one with a different professional specialist presumed to have the necessary standard practice in his or her repertoire of skills.

Professionals are performers, not problem solvers. They perfect the standard practices in their repertoire of skills. They do not invent new practices for each unique need. Thus, the problem of innovation at the level of the professional, what Mintzberg (1979) called the "means-ends inversion" (p. 373), finds its roots "in convergent thinking, in the deductive reasoning of the professional who sees the specific situation in terms of the general concept. In the professional bureaucracy this means that new problems are forced into old pigeonholes" (p. 375). And this is not a dysfunction of the professional bureaucracy structure. It is configured precisely to screen out heterogeneity and uncertainty by forcing its clients' needs into one of the standard practices of one or another of its professional specializations.

> The fact is that great art and innovative problem solving require inductive reasoning, that is, the induction of new general concepts or programs from particular experiences. That kind of thinking is divergent—it breaks away from old routines or standards rather than perfecting existing ones. And that flies in the face of everything the professional bureaucracy is designed to do. (Mintzberg, 1979, p. 375)

We can understand the means-ends inversion from the cultural frame of reference by thinking of a professional's repertoire of skills as a paradigm, a technology of standard practices premised on beliefs about cause-effect relations (Brown, 1978; Weick, 1979a). Regardless of whether the standard practices in these paradigms are effective, they persist because the paradigm guides and justifies professional thought and action (Brown, 1978; Clark, 1972; Pfeffer, 1982). Moreover, once the paradigm is in place, it and its associated practices change very slowly because the self-justifying nature of the paradigm distorts anomalies so as to make them consistent with the prevailing view (Jonsson & Lundin, 1977). Although paradigm shifts can occur, resistance takes the form of political clashes between advocates of a new paradigm and defenders of the old one, conservative attempts to patch up the system incrementally, and an increase in ritualized activity (Rounds, 1979, 1981).

As we know from Chapter 15, the arguments on both sides of the inclusion debate implicitly reject the assumptions that disabilities are pathological conditions and that diagnosis is objective and useful. Rather, proponents and opponents of inclusion alike recognize that many students are identified as handicapped under the EHA simply because they have needs that cannot be accommodated in general education classrooms. This contradiction can be understood from an organizational perspective by reconceptualizing student disability as an *organizational pathology* that results from the inherent structural and cultural characteristics of traditional school organizations.

Structurally, schools are nonadaptable at the classroom level because professionalization ultimately results in convergent thinking. Given a finite repertoire of standard practices, students whose needs fall outside the standard practices must be forced into them, or forced out of general education classrooms and into the special education system (or one of the other special needs programs). The situation is compounded by the rational-technical approach to school management, which, by introducing unwarranted rationalization and formalization, reduces professional thought and discretion. This minimizes the extent to which teachers can personalize their standard practices, thus forcing more students into the special education system than otherwise would be the case.

The same phenomenon can be understood culturally by thinking of teachers' repertoires of skills as a paradigm of practice that persists because anomalies are distorted to preserve its validity. The principle distortion is the institutional practice of special education, which, by removing students from the general education system, prevents teachers from recognizing anomalies in their conventional paradigm of practice. Without anomalies, of course, the professional culture has no way to see that something is amiss with its paradigm and its associated instructional practices. This acts in a mutually reinforcing way to strengthen teachers' belief in both the validity of their conventional practices and the notion that school failure is a human pathology.

Moreover, misplaced rationalization and formalization compound and further mystify the situation because they conflict with the values that ground the paradigm and thus increase ritualized activity (see below). This reduces professional thought and thus the extent to which general education teachers can personalize their practices, which forces more students into the special education system and further reinforces the view that conventional practices are valid and that students who fail to learn from them are pathological.

Whether we think of school organizations from the structural or the cultural frame of reference, the implication is that student disability is neither a pathological condition nor an objective distinction. It is an organizational pathology, a matter of not fitting the standard practices of the prevailing paradigm of a professional culture, the legitimacy of which is maintained and reinforced by the objectification of school failure as student disability through the institutional practice of special education.

THE NATURE OF SPECIAL EDUCATION

As public organizations, schools depend on the public for support and legitimacy and thus must be responsive to what the public wants them to be and do (Mintzberg, 1979). We have seen, for example, that in this century schools have had to adopt many of the trappings of the machine bureaucracy configuration, not because they conform to the technical demands of doing complex, client-centered work but, rather, because, as a social norm the machine bureaucracy is what the public expects all legitimate school organizations to look like (Meyer & Rowan, 1977, 1978). The public is a constant source of pressure on school organizations in this respect. When values and priorities in society change, however, the public makes additional demands on schools, demands that often require them to change what they and their professionals are accustomed to doing (Rounds, 1979).

In some cases school organizations are required to make *incidental*, add-on changes, which they are able to do quite easily because of their loosely coupled internal structure. For example, when the public wanted schools to start teaching high school students to drive, they simply added a new professional specialization—the driver education teacher—and thus a new program to the existing structure. Incidental changes such as this simply require school *organizations* to do something *additional*.

In other cases, however, the public demands that schools make *fundamental* changes, ones that require their *professionals* to do something *different*, something other than what they were standardized (structural perspective) or acculturated (cultural perspective) to do. Structurally, this is a problem for school organizations because of the professionals' convergent thinking and deductive reasoning. Culturally, it is a problem because, by requiring professionals to do something different, the values that underwrite the change demand contradict those of their prevailing paradigm of practice (Rounds, 1979, 1981).

From the institutional perspective we know that school organizations deal with their inability to change through various forms of decoupling. For example, they deal with the contradiction of an inappropriate machine bureaucracy structure by simply decoupling it from their actual work activities, signaling the public that they have adopted the machine bureaucracy structure, while at time same time turning its associated management practices into little more than symbols and ceremonies of compliance.

We also know that the loosely coupled internal structure of schools allows them to make incidental changes by simply adding decoupled programs and specialists. The greater significance of this form of decoupling, however, is that it permits school organizations to respond to demands for fundamental change by converting them into incidental changes. Schools deal with teachers' inability to do something fundamentally different by doing something additional. By adding separate programs and specialists to their existing operation, school organizations can respond to fundamental change demands incidentally, without making any fundamental changes in what their professionals actually do.

The segregated special education classroom is the ideal-typical example of this form of decoupling. Earlier in the century, when society required schools to serve children from working class and immigrant families, the special classroom model emerged to deal with students whose needs could not be accommodated within the standard practices of public education's prevailing paradigm (see Bogdan & Knoll, 1988; Sarason & Doris, 1979; Tweedie, 1983; Chapter 15). From an organizational perspective the segregated special classroom served as a legitimating device, a means for schools to signal the public that they had complied with the demand to serve a broader range of students, while at the same time allowing them to maintain their traditional paradigm of practice.

Once special classrooms were created, they simply were decoupled from the rest of the school organization, buffering schools from the need to change by buffering their teachers from the need to change the way they actually teach. Indeed, this decoupled relationship between the general education system and the special classroom was one of the major criticisms of the special classroom model within the mainstreaming debate of the 1960s and 1970s (see Christophos & Renz, 1969; Deno, 1970; Dunn, 1968; Johnson, 1962).

Another special education example is the overrepresentation of minority students in special classrooms, a problem that emerged in the 1960s (Chandler & Plakos, 1969; Dunn, 1968; Janesick, 1988; MacMillan, 1971; Mercer, 1973; Wright, 1967) following *Brown* v. *Board of Education* in 1954, the Supreme Court decision requiring public education to end its institutional practice of racial segregation. From an organizational perspective the overrepresentation of minority students in special classrooms can be understood as a form of decoupling, a process in which school organizations use an existing decoupling device, the segregated special classroom, to maintain their legitimacy in the face of failing to meet the needs of disproportionate numbers of these students in general education classrooms. This is a process that, in a different form, has been maintained under the EHA and the mainstreaming model (see Cummins, 1989; Harry, 1992; Heller, Holtzman, & Messick, 1982; Rueda, 1989).

Considering the function of special education from an organizational perspective, one hardly can claim that it is a rationally conceived and coordinated system of services. It is not a rationally conceived system because, historically, it has served as a legitimating device for school organizations to cope with the change demands of their institutionalized environments. It is not a rationally coordinated system because, by design, it is decoupled from the general education system, as well as from the other special needs programs (see Reynolds & Wang, 1983; Reynolds, Wang, & Walberg, 1987), each of which has been added to traditional school organizations incidentally as values and priorities have shifted in society. The unintended consequence of using organizations to provide services to society is that the nature and needs of the organizations themselves shape services. From an organizational perspective, student disability and the institutional practice of special education are unintended consequences of the particular kind of schooling that traditional school organizations provide.

As we know from Chapter 15, participants in the inclusion debate disagree over the sense in which special education can be considered a rational system. Proponents of inclusion recognize that, in its current form, special education is not an instructionally rational system, and therefore argue that it must be replaced with a new inclusionary system. Opponents of inclusion also recognize that special education is not an instructionally rational system, but they contend that it nevertheless is a politically rational system because it targets otherwise unavailable educational services to designated students, even though at this point the services do not necessarily benefit them instructionally.

This contradiction can be understood from the structural perspective by conceptualizing the institutional practice of special education as an organizational artifact that emerged to protect the legitimacy of a nonadaptable bureaucratic structure faced with the changing value demands of a dynamic democratic environment. Even though schools are nonadaptable structures, they maintain their legitimacy and support under dynamic social conditions by signaling the public that changes have occurred, including the addition of decoupled subunits such as special education and the other special needs programs. Moreover, from a cultural perspective special education and the other special needs programs distort the anomaly of school failure and thus preserve public education's prevailing paradigm of practice, which ultimately reinforces the theories of organizational rationality and human pathology both in the profession and the institution of education and in society at large.

THE NATURE OF PROGRESS

Participants in the inclusion debate agree that most disabilities are not pathological and that diagnosis is neither objective nor useful. As such, they implicitly reject special education's first two guiding assumptions and thus the functionalist theory of human pathology upon which they are premised. The two sides in the debate, however, are at odds over an appropriate course of ameliorative action because they disagree about the nature of special education and progress, the field's third and fourth guiding assumptions. As I noted in Chapter 15, the disagreement stems from the participants' confusion over the nature of school organization and change, which ultimately stems from the field's implicit grounding in the functionalist theory of organizational rationality.

Confusion among the inclusion opponents was evident in Chapter 15, where we saw that, in their defense of the current system of special education, they retain the assumptions associated with the theory of organizational rationality but, in their criticism of the inclusive education reform proposals, they reject them. At this point I can demonstrate the confusion among the inclusion proponents by considering the current system of special education and their reform proposals from an organizational perspective. To do this, however, I first must introduce a third organizational configuration—what Mintzberg (1979, p. 432) called the "adhocracy."

The Adhocracy. As we know, professional bureaucracies are nonadaptable structures because they are premised on the principle of *standardization*, which configures them as performance organizations that perfect their existing standard practices, not problem-solving organizations that invent new ones. The difference is that adhocracies are premised on the principle of *innovation* rather than standardization and, as such, they are problem solving organizations that invent new practices. An adhocracy is an organizational form that configures itself around work that is so ambiguous and uncertain that initially the knowledge and skills for doing it are completely unknown.

> At the outset, no one can be sure exactly what needs to be done. That knowledge develops as the work unfolds.... [And so] the success of the undertaking depends primarily on the ability of the [workers] to adapt to each other along their uncharted route. (Mintzberg, 1979, p. 3)

This type of organization was recognized first in the 1960s, when organizational analysts began to describe what they called "organic" (Mintzberg, 1979, p. 433) organizational structures (see Pugh et al., 1963). Because they operated in dynamic environments, and thus under extremely uncertain conditions in which innovation and adaptation were necessary for survival, these organizations configured themselves as the inverse of the bureaucratic form (Burns & Stalker, 1966; Woodward, 1965). Mintzberg (1979) called these organic configurations adhocracies, following Alvin Toffler (1970), who popularized the term in his book, *Future Shock*. The structure of an adhocracy "must be flexible, self-renewing, organic...a 'tent' instead of a 'palace' "(Mintzberg, 1979, p. 433).

> An organizational tent actually exploits benefits hidden within properties that designers have generally regarded as liabilities. Ambiguous authority structures, unclear objectives, and contradictory assignments of responsibility can legitimate controversies and challenge traditions.... Incoherence and indecision can foster exploration, self-evaluation, and learning. (Hedberg, Nystrom, & Starbuck, 1976, p. 45)

According to Mintzberg (1979), the best example of the adhocracy configuration is the National Aeronautics and Space Administration (NASA) during its Apollo phase in the 1960s. Given its mission to land an American on the moon by the end of the decade, it configured itself as an adhocracy because at that time no established practices existed for manned space flight. At that point in its history, NASA had to rely on its workers to invent these practices on an *ad hoc* basis, "along their uncharted route" to the moon, as it were.

Moreover, although the Apollo project employed professional workers, it could not use specialization and professionalization to divide and coordinate its work because no professional specializations had developed the knowledge and perfected the practices for doing the type of work assumed to be required. Thus, division of labor and coordination of work within the Apollo project were premised on *collaboration* and *mutual adjustment*, respectively (see Table 18.3).

Under these structural contingencies, division of labor is achieved by deploying professionals from various specializations on multidisciplinary project teams, a situation in which team members work collaboratively on the team's project and assume joint responsibility for its completion. Under mutual adjustment, coordination is achieved through informal communication among team members as they invent (and reinvent) novel problem solutions on an *ad hoc* basis, a process requiring them to adapt, adjust, and revise their conventional theories and practices relative to those of their colleagues and the team's progress on the task at hand (Chandler & Sayles, 1971; Mintzberg, 1979). Together, the structural contingencies of collaboration and mutual adjustment give rise to a *discursive coupling* arrangement premised on reflexive problem solving through communication, and thus on the unification of theory and practice in the team of workers (see Burns & Stalker, 1966).

● **TABLE 18.3**

Structural differences: Professional bureaucracy vs. adhocracy

	Professional Bureaucracy	**Adhocracy**
Nature of Work	COMPLEX	AMBIGUOUS
Division of Labor	SPECIALIZATION	COLLABORATION
Coordination	PROFESSIONALIZATION	MUTUAL ADJUSTMENT
Interdependence	LOOSE COUPLING	DISCURSIVE COUPLING
Type of Organization	PERFORMANCE	PROBLEM SOLVING
Goal of Organization	PERFECTION	INNOVATION
Output of Organization	STANDARD SERVICES	NOVEL SERVICES
Environment	STABLE	DYANMIC

Source: Substantive material drawn from H. Mintzberg, 1979, *The Structuring of Organizations*, pp. 348–379, 431–480. Englewood Cliffs, NJ: Prentice-Hall.

By contrast, during its current Space Shuttle phase, NASA has reconfigured itself as a professional bureaucracy (see Romzek & Dubnick, 1987), a performance organization that perfects a repertoire of standard launch and recovery practices, most of which were invented during its Apollo phase. This transformation from adhocracy to professional bureaucracy is a natural tendency in adhocracies (see Mintzberg, 1979, 1983). It begins when uncertainty is reduced, when the organization's members begin to believe that they have solved all or most of their problems of practice, and thus that the practices they have invented can be standardized as ready-made solutions for future use. The difference between the two configurations is that, faced with a problem, the adhocracy "engages in creative effort to find a novel solution; the professional bureaucracy pigeonholes it into a known contingency to which it can apply a standard [practice]. One engages in divergent thinking aimed at innovation; the other in convergent thinking aimed at perfection" (Mintzberg, 1979, p. 436).

Finally, under the organizational contingencies of collaboration, mutual adjustment, and discursive coupling, accountability in the adhocracy is achieved through a presumed community of interests, a sense among the workers of a shared interest in a common goal. Under this form of accountability, responsibility flows from the workers' common concern for the well-being of the organization with respect to progress toward its mission, rather than from an ideological identification with a professional culture (professional bureaucracy) or a formalized relationship with a hierarchy of authority (machine bureaucracy) (see Burns & Stalker, 1966; Chandler & Sayles, 1971; Romzek & Dubnick, 1987). Thus, rather than the *professional-bureaucratic* mode of accountability that emerges in the professional bureaucracy configuration (Martin, Overholt & Urban, 1976; Meyer & Rowan, 1978; Wise, 1979), the organizational contingencies of the adhocracy give rise to a *professional-political* mode of accountability, a situation in which work is controlled by experts who, although they act with discretion, are subject to sanctions that emerge within a political discourse among professionals and between them and client constituencies (Burns & Stalker, 1966; Chandler & Sayles, 1971; Romzek & Dubnick, 1987).

The EHA and Mainstreaming.[1] From an organizational perspective the problem with the EHA is that it requires professional bureaucracies to act like adhocracies by treating them as if they were machine bureaucracies. The ends of the EHA are adhocratic. Given its procedural requirements of interdisciplinary assessment and programming, parent participation, individualized education programs, and least restrictive placements (see Turnbull & Turnbull, 1978), the EHA requires schools to become problem-solving organizations in which teams of professionals collaborate among themselves and with their clients to invent personalized practices. At the same time, however, the means by which the EHA seeks to achieve this transformation are

---

[1] The bulk of the citations appearing in this section are references to empirical and interpretive research evidence that supports my theoretical claims. In these cases, the authors of the cited research are not making the theoretical claims asserted in the text. The assertations are mine; the research cited simply supports my assertions.

completely consistent with the rational-technical approach to change. The EHA assumes that schools are rational machine bureaucracies, organizations in which worker behavior is controlled through formalization and thus subject to modification through revision and extension of existing rules and regulations (see Elmore & McLaughlin, 1982).

Because the ends of the EHA are adhocratic, they contradict the inner professional bureaucracy structure of traditional school organizations, which has both structural and cultural implications. The structural contradiction arises because, whereas the EHA requires a problem-solving organization in which professionals work together to invent personalized instructional practices, the inner professional bureaucracy of schools configures them as performance organizations in which professionals work alone to perfect the standard practices in their repertoires. In turn, this produces a cultural contradiction, a conflict between the bureaucratic values that ground the prevailing performance-oriented paradigm of the professional culture and those that underwrite the problem-solving or adhocratic orientation of the EHA. This is a problem because the contradiction in values leads to resistance in the form of political clashes that undermine the goal of collaboration, and an increase in ritualized activity that intensifies the problem of professionalization (performance of standardized problem solutions) and thus deflects the goal of personalization (interdisciplinary problem solving) (see Bogdan, 1983; Lortie, 1978; Martin, 1978; Moran, 1984; Patrick & Reschly, 1982; Singer & Butler, 1987; Skrtic et al., 1985; Weatherley, 1979).

Because the means of the EHA are completely consistent with the outer machine bureaucracy structure of traditional school organizations, they extend and elaborate the existing rationalization and formalization in schools. This creates two interrelated structural problems. The first is that more rationalization and formalization reduces professional thought and discretion even further. This intensifies the problem of professionalization and thus reduces the possibility of personalization, which results in even more students whose needs fall outside the standard practices of teachers. And, because many of these students must be forced into the special education system, the bureaucratic means of the EHA ultimately lead to ever greater numbers of students identified as handicapped (see Gerber & Levine-Donnerstein, 1989; U.S. Department of Education, 1988).

The second problem stems from the fact that the outer machine bureaucracy structure of schools is decoupled from their internal professional bureaucracy structure, which means that the additional rationalization and formalization associated with the EHA has little to do with the way teachers actually teach students with special educational needs (see below). Ultimately, then, not only do the bureaucratic means of the EHA produce more students who must be identified as handicapped, but at the same time the two-structure bureaucratic configuration of schools largely deflects the law's adhocratic ends from these and other students identified as handicapped, the very students the law is intended to benefit.

Nevertheless, because the EHA requires at least overt conformity, a number of symbols of compliance have emerged to signal the public that the intent of the law is being achieved. For example, the symbol of compliance for programs that serve students in the EHA's low-incidence classifications is the traditional decoupled subunit, the segregated special classroom. Like the special classrooms of the 1960s, these programs simply are added incidentally to the loosely coupled internal structure of schools and, to one degree or another, decoupled from the general education program and the other special needs programs, including the special education programs serving students in the EHA's high-incidence disability classifications.

Because the needs of students in the low-incidence programs are beyond the standard practices of any single professional specialization and thus require an interdisciplinary approach, their efficacy depends on the will and capacity of local school organizations to provide the team of professionals required (see Biklen, 1985; McDonnell & McLaughlin, 1982; Noel & Fuller, 1985; Skrtic et al., 1985). Beyond this, these programs and the specialists who work in them have very little to do with the other programs and specialists in schools. Indeed, the decoupled nature of these programs is a key point of criticism in the inclusion debate (Gartner & Lipsky, 1987; Stainback & Stainback, 1984, 1987).

The symbol of compliance for most students in the EHA's high-incidence classifications is the special education resource room, a new type of decoupled subunit associated with the mainstreaming model. From an organizational perspective, resource rooms are even more problematic than the traditional special classroom because they violate the logic of the division of labor, means of coordination, and form of interdependence in the professional bureaucracy configuration. Under the mainstreaming model, the responsibility for implementing a student's IEP is divided among one or more general education teachers and a special education resource teacher. This contradicts the specialized division of labor and professionalized means of coordination in schools because it requires that the student's overall instructional program be rationalized and assigned to more than one professional, which is justified implicitly on the assumption that the professionals will work collaboratively to implement the IEP in an integrated manner. The collaboration required to integrate the student's IEP, however, contradicts the logic of specialization and professionalization, and thus the form of interdependence among professionals in schools. In principle, a team of teachers working collaboratively in the interest of a single student for whom they share responsibility violates both the logic of loose coupling and the sensibility of the professional culture and thus should not be expected to occur as a generalized phenomenon in schools (Bidwell, 1965; Mintzberg, 1979; Weick, 1976).

The mainstreaming model requires a collaborative division of labor and a means of coordination premised on mutual adjustment, and thus ultimately on the discursive coupling arrangement associated with the adhocracy configuration. But this is not the type of interdependence that specialization and professionalization produce. By design, schools have no need for collaboration or mutual adjustment because specialization and professionalization locate virtually all of the necessary coordination within the roles of individual specialists. If it occurs at all in schools, collaboration within or across specializations is at best rare, fleeting, and idiosyncratic (see Bishop, 1977; Lortie, 1975, 1978; Skrtic et al., 1985; Tye & Tye, 1984).

Although the EHA requires placements in the general education classroom to the maximum extent possible, students are identified as handicapped under the law precisely because they cannot be accommodated within the existing standard practices in these classrooms (see Skrtic et al., 1985; Walker, 1987). Given the logic of specialization and the deductive reasoning associated with professionalization, mainstreaming for most of these students is largely symbolic and ceremonial (see Biklen, 1985; Skrtic et al., 1985; Wright et al., 1982). Given the adhocratic ends of the EHA, it was intended to decrease the effects of student disability by increasing personalized instruction and general education integration. Given its bureaucratic means and the bureaucratic nature of traditional school organizations, however, the EHA has resulted in more students classified as disabled (Gerber & Levine-Donnerstein, 1989; U.S. Department of Education, 1988), disintegration of instruction (Gartner & Lipsky, 1987; Walker, 1987; Wang, Reynolds, & Walberg, 1986, 1987), and less personalization in general education (Bryan, Bay, & Donahue, 1988; Keogh, 1988) and special education classrooms (Carlberg & Kavale, 1980; Skrtic et al., 1985).

The Inclusive Education Reform Proposals.[2] The problem with the inclusive education reform proposals (reviewed in Chapter 15) is that each of them reproduces the structural and cultural contradictions of the EHA and the mainstreaming model. This is so because even though the inclusion proponents reject the theory of human pathology, ultimately they retain the theory of organizational rationality, and thus the assumptions that school organizations are rational and that changing them is a rational-technical process. In organizational terms, the result is that, although the inclusive education reform proposals require an adhocratic structure for schools, they reproduce their traditional two-structure bureaucratic configuration. Like the EHA and mainstreaming, they reproduce the professional bureaucracy inner structure of schools and extend their outer machine bureaucracy structure.

As we know, the Lilly/Pugach, Reynolds/Wang, and Stainback/Stainback inclusive education reform proposals call for collaborative problem solving between a classroom teacher and a support services staff (see Chapter 15). By retaining the traditional role of classroom teacher, however, each of these proposals retains a specialized division of labor and a professionalized means of coordination, which of course yields a loosely coupled form of interdependence and thus deflects the goal of collaboration. In principle, as long as the work in schools is distributed through specialization and coordinated through professionalization, teachers do not have to collaborate. Collaboration emerges when work is distributed on the basis of a collaborative division of labor and coordinated through mutual adjustment, an arrangement that is premised on shared responsibility and a team approach to problem solving and yields a form of interdependence premised on reflective discourse.

Although the Reynolds/Wang, Lilly/Pugach, and Stainback/Stainback proposals call for collaborative problem solving between a classroom teacher and a support

---

[2] For the most part, citations for the inclusive education reform proposals have been omitted in this section. The proposals of interest here are the four reviewed in Chapter 15. In addition, my use of citations in this section follows the format explained in footnote 1.

services staff, by retaining the notion of a classroom and placing the support services staff above it, they actually extend the rationalization and formalization of the machine bureaucracy configuration and thus undermine the ideals of problem solving and personalized instruction. This is so because placing a support staff above the classroom teacher implies that the *theory* of teaching is at the support level, whereas the mere *practice* of teaching takes place in the classroom, which maintains the misplaced practice of separating theory from practice. Moreover, this politicizes and thus undermines the ideal of collaboration, because placing support personnel above the practice context makes them technocrats rather than support staff (see Mintzberg, 1979).

In an actual machine bureaucracy technocrats are the people with the theory; they control and define the activities of the other workers. This is not collaboration in an organizational sense; it is bureaucratic control and supervision. In professional bureaucracies the notion of a technocracy within the organization violates the logic of professionalization (see Mintzberg, 1979), and thus teachers resist technocrats, particularly change agents and other school improvement personnel (see Wolcott, 1977).

The same problems are inherent in the Gartner/Lipsky proposal (see Lipsky & Gartner, 1989; Chapter 15). This reform proposal retains the general education classroom and proposes to make it effective for all students by implementing the principles of effective schools research through school improvement projects. Here, the assumption is that the theory of effective teaching, which is known by the school improvement and effective schools specialists apart from and prior to the classroom context, is contained in the principles identified in effective schools research, and that implementing these principles in the practice context is simply a matter of the teacher making a commitment to follow them.

In principle, imposing these standards from above, their apparent efficacy in some other context notwithstanding, can only lead to an extension of existing rationalization and formalization, and thus to an increase in professionalization and a corresponding decrease in personalization (see Cuban, 1983, 1989; Slavin, 1989; Stedman, 1987; below). As Cuban (1989) noted in this regard, under the effective schools formula many schools have returned to the traditional practice of standardizing curriculum and instruction and thus are ignoring individual differences.

Although the arguments put forth in the inclusion debate reject the assumption of human pathology and thus represent progress relative to the mainstreaming debate, the outcome is the same. Like the EHA and mainstreaming, the adhocratic ends of the inclusion proponents are distorted by the bureaucratic value orientation of school organization and, because they retain the presupposition of organizational rationality, their adhocratic ends are deflected by the bureaucratic value orientation of their own proposals.

As we know from Chapter 15, participants in the inclusion debate reject the theory of human pathology but are inconsistent and contradictory about the theory of organizational rationality. At this point, however, we have seen that a critical reading of the discourse on school organization and change, in conjunction with an organizational analysis of the EHA and the inclusion reform proposals, rejects the theories of human pathology *and* organizational rationality, which deconstructs special education, both as a professional practice and as an institutional practice of public education. In terms of the adequacy of its grounding theories and assumptions, special education cannot be considered a rational and just response to the problem of school failure.

PUBLIC EDUCATION AND THE DISCOURSE ON SCHOOL FAILURE

To this point in the analysis, we have been concerned with special education, first as a professional practice from the vantage point of the inclusion debate (Chapter 15), then as an institutional practice of public education from the perspective of school organization and change. In this section I want to consider the implications of deconstructing special education for the discourse on school failure and, ultimately, for the legitimacy of the institution of public education itself. Considering these implications requires expanding the analysis to include the voice of the general education professional community and what it has to say (and not say) about school failure from the perspective of educational excellence. If we think of the mainstreaming and inclusion debates in special education as two phases in a *discourse on equity*, and the "effective schools" and "school restructuring" debates in general education as two phases in a *discourse on excellence*, we can begin to see how the two discourses parallel, mirror, and, ultimately, converge upon one another to deconstruct the 20th-century discourse on school failure.

By the effective schools debate I mean the early phase of the excellence movement, which was shaped by the thinking in *A Nation at Risk* (National Commission on Excellence in Education, 1983) and generally sought excellence through means that were quantitative and top-down. They were quantitative in that they simply called for more of existing school practices—more difficult courses, more homework, more time in school, and more rigorous standards. They were top-down in that they were bureaucratic and thus characterized by more "state control, with its emphasis on producing standardized results through regulated teaching" (Wise, 1988, p. 329), which ultimately distorted the goal of higher standards into more standardization (see, e.g., Bacharach, 1990; Cuban, 1983, 1989; Meier, 1984; Resnick & Resnick, 1985). The advocates of the effective schools approach, like the proponents of the EHA and mainstreaming, did not question the traditional bureaucratic structure of schools. As Cuban (1989) noted, "Their passion was (and is) for making those structures more efficient" (p. 784).

By the school restructuring debate I mean the more recent phase of the excellence movement, which was shaped by the thinking in books such as *High School* (Boyer, 1983), *A Place Called School* (Goodlad, 1984), and *Horace's Compromise* (Sizer, 1984). The participants in this debate generally seek excellence through means that are qualitative and bottom-up: qualitative in that they call for fundamental changes in the structure of school organizations; bottom-up in that they call for an increase in professional discretion, adult-adult collaboration, and personalized instruction (see, e.g., Bacharach, 1990; Clark, Lotto, & Astuto, 1984; Cuban, 1983, 1989; Elmore,

1987; Elmore & McLaughlin, 1988; Lieberman & Miller, 1984; McNeil, 1986; Oakes, 1985; Sergiovanni & Moore, 1989; Sirotnik & Oakes, 1986; Wise, 1988).

The first parallel between the equity and excellence discourses is that the initial debate in each discourse is an extreme form of naive pragmatism that merely reproduces and extends the problems it sets out to solve. As in the case of the EHA and mainstreaming, the new practices that emerged out of the effective schools debate largely reproduced and extended the original problems (see Clark & Astuto, 1988; Cuban, 1983, 1989; Meier, 1984; Resnick & Resnick, 1985; Slavin, 1989; Stedman, 1987; Timar & Kirp, 1988; Wise, 1988).

The second parallel is that the failure of the first debate in each discourse gives rise to a second debate, which, although it is less naive, is also a form of naive pragmatism that promises to reproduce and extend current problems. As we will see, although the restructuring debate is less naive than the effective schools debate, it does not explicitly recognize the connection between general education practices and guiding assumptions. Like the inclusion debate in special education, it promises to reproduce and extend the general education problems of the 1980s and 1990s into the next century (see Cuban, 1983, 1989; Skrtic, 1991a; Wise, 1988; below).

Although the restructuring debate parallels the inclusion debate in this second respect, the effects of this pattern in the two debates are mirror images of one another. As we know, the inclusion debate is less naive than the mainstreaming debate because it implicates *school organization* in the problem of *school failure* (Chapter 15). The mirror image of this in the restructuring debate is that, by pointing to the emergence and persistence of homogeneous grouping practices—curricular tracking, in-class ability grouping, and compensatory pull-out programs—as an indication of deep structural flaws in traditional school organization (see Cuban, 1989; Oakes, 1985, 1986a, 1986b; Stedman, 1987; Wise, 1988), participants in the restructuring debate have implicated *school failure* in the problem of *school organization*.

The second way the inclusion and restructuring debates mirror each other is that, although both of them reject two of the four assumptions and question the other two, in the final analysis they retain the assumptions they question. We saw this pattern for the inclusion proponents and opponents relative to the question of the rationality of school organization and change. The mirror image of this contradiction in the restructuring debate is that, although its participants reject the two assumptions about the rationality of school organization and change, they question but ultimately retain the two about the nature of school failure and diagnosis. That is, although restructuring advocates criticize the institutional practices of tracking and compensatory pull-out programs (Goodlad, 1984; Sizer, 1984), and even the overrepresentation of minority students in certain special education programs (Oakes, 1986a, 1986b), they do not criticize special education as an institutional practice (see Skrtic, 1991a, 1991b; Chapter 1). Thus, in the end, the participants in the school restructuring debate retain the assumptions that school failure is pathological and that diagnosis is objective and useful.

The restructuring debate fails to recognize special education as a form of tracking because its criticism of homogeneous grouping practices stops at the point of presumed pathology, which is the third and most important way that the two debates mirror one another. Whereas the inclusion debate rejects the theory of human pathology but retains that of organizational rationality, the restructuring debate rejects the theory of organizational rationality but retains that of human pathology. The significance here, of course, is that the two debates—and thus the discourses on excellence and equity in public education—converge to reject both of the functionalist theories that ground and legitimize the 20th-century discourse on school failure and thus deconstruct it. The broader significance of the deconstruction of the discourse on school failure is that it provides the grounds for an imminent critique of the institution of public education.

As the institution through which America "sought to hold itself together and prepare its citizens for the greatest of all experiments in democracy" (Greer, 1972, p. 17), public education had to be both excellent and equitable. If America were to remain democratic and avoid tyranny, Thomas Jefferson argued, public education had to be excellent; it had to produce intelligent citizens and thoughtful leaders (Ford, 1904). Moreover, he cautioned that if America were to remain a free society, one in which positions of power were open to all on the basis of merit, public education also had to be equitable. It had to ensure "that [persons] of talent might rise whatever their social and economic origins" (Greer, 1972, p. 16). The significance of the convergence of the discourses on excellence and equity is that the institution of public education finally must confront the fact that its professional and institutional practices are neither excellent nor equitable. In organizational terms, public education must confront the fact that in the 20th century it has become more bureaucratic than democratic. Moreover, it must account for this fact without recourse to the distorting and legitimizing effects of the functionalist discourse on school failure. Ultimately, to be able to continue making the claim that it embodies the Jeffersonian ideal of democratic education, the institution of public education must reconstruct itself in a way that is both excellent and equitable.

EXCELLENCE, EQUITY, AND ADHOCRACY

We can begin the process of reconstructing public education by considering the convergence of interests in the reform proposals of the proponents of inclusive education and school restructuring from an organizational perspective. As we know, the inclusion proponents call for eliminating the bureaucratic means of the EHA and mainstreaming. The corresponding argument among the proponents of restructuring is for eliminating scientific management, the bureaucratic approach to administration and change (see, e.g., Boyer, 1983; Cuban, 1983, 1989; Goodlad, 1984; Oakes, 1985, 1986a, 1986b; Sirotnik & Oakes, 1986; Sizer, 1984; Wise, 1988). In organizational terms, the first convergence of interests is that both sets of proponents are arguing for the elimination of rationalization, formalization, and tight coupling, the misplaced structural contingencies of the machine bureaucracy.

The second convergence is between the inclusion proponents' arguments for merging general and special education and those of the restructuring proponents for merging the traditional general education curricular and instructional tracks. Here, both sets of reform proposals are calling for the elimination of specialization, professionalization, and loose coupling, the structural contingencies of the professional bureaucracy configuration. In practical terms, both sets of proponents seek an adaptable system in which teachers collaborate among themselves and with their clients to personalize instructional practices (see Boyer, 1983; Cuban, 1983, 1989; Goodlad, 1984; McNeil, 1986; Oakes, 1985; Sizer, 1984).

Of course, because the restructuring proponents retain the theory of human pathology, the two sets of proposals have differences. But these are differences in degree, not in kind. In organizational terms, both sets of proponents are arguing for the introduction of collaboration, mutual adjustment, and discursive coupling, the structural contingencies of the adhocratic form. In principle, both sets of reform proposals require an adhocratic school organization and a corresponding adhocratic professional culture.

As we know from Chapter 15, the inclusion opponents' position on equity and excellence is that, given the nonadaptability of school organizations and general education classrooms, the targeting function of the EHA and the pull-out logic of mainstreaming must be maintained for political purposes, diagnostic and instructional inadequacies notwithstanding. The moment of truth in this position is the argument that, as long as resources are constant and students differ, no teacher, whether in a general or special education classroom, can escape the necessary choice between higher class means (i.e., excellence) and narrower class variances (i.e., equity), unless additional resources and more powerful instructional technologies are available (Kauffman, Gerber, & Semmel, 1988; Chapter 15).

In organizational terms, this is true because the structural contingencies of rationalization and formalization circumscribe a finite set of resources relative to a prespecified set of activities and outcomes, whereas those of specialization and professionalization circumscribe a finite repertoire of standard practices relative to a corresponding set of presumed client needs. Thus, students whose needs fall on the margins or outside of these standard practices must be either forced into them or forced out of the classroom.

Given the inevitability of human diversity, a professional bureaucracy can do nothing but create students who do not fit the system. In a professional bureaucracy, all forms of tracking—curriculum tracking and in-class ability grouping in general education, as well as self-contained and resource classrooms in special, compensatory, bilingual, and gifted education—are organizational artifacts, the unintended consequences of using specialization and professionalization to divide and coordinate work in schools, consequences that are compounded by the misguided organizational practices of rationalization and formalization. Students are subjected to, and subjugated by, homogeneous grouping practices in public education because, given their structural and cultural contingencies, traditional school organizations cannot accommodate diversity and so must screen it out by first containing it and then decoupling it from their basic operation.

The problem with the inclusion opponents' argument, however, is that it assumes that nonadaptability is inherent to *schooling* rather than to its traditional bureaucratic *organization*. Student diversity is not an inherent problem for school organizations; it is a problem only when schools are premised on standardization and thus configure themselves as performance organizations that perfect standard practices for known contingencies. As we have seen, the adhocratic form is premised on innovation. It configures itself as a problem-solving organization for inventing new practices for unfamiliar contingencies. Regardless of its *causes* and its *extent*, student diversity is not a liability in a problem-solving organization. It is an asset, an enduring uncertainty, and thus a valuable source of innovation.

The problem with the inclusive education and school restructuring proposals in this regard is that, although their ends require the adhocratic configuration, their means reproduce the professional bureaucracy configuration. This is so because, by retaining the notion of a classroom, they retain a specialized division of labor, a professionalized means of coordination, and thus a loosely coupled form of interdependence. Thus, both reform approaches eliminate rationalization and formalization and thus the misplaced machine bureaucracy outer structure of schools, while retaining specialization and professionalization and thus the professional bureaucracy inner structure.

From an organizational perspective the argument for eliminating rationalization and formalization is an argument for uniting theory and practice in the professional. The problem with this move in the inclusive education and school restructuring proposals, however, is that, by retaining the professional bureaucracy configuration, they unite theory and practice in the *individual* professional specialist rather than in a multidisciplinary *team* of professionals.

From a structural perspective innovation is "the building of new knowledge and skills [which] requires the combination of different bodies of existing ones" (Mintzberg, 1979, p. 434). This requires a division of labor and a means of coordination that "break through the boundaries of conventional specialization," creating a situation in which "professionals must amalgamate their efforts...[by joining] forces in multidisciplinary teams, each formed around a specific project of innovation" (pp. 434–435). From a cultural perspective, repertoires or paradigms of practice are *social* constructions; innovation occurs when new paradigms emerge through confrontations over uncertainty within social *groups* (Brown, 1978; Rounds, 1981; Weick, 1979a). From an organizational perspective professional innovation is not a solitary act. When it does occur, it is a social phenomenon that requires a reflexive discourse (see Skrtic & Ware, 1992).

Beyond the problem of innovation, eliminating rationalization and formalization while retaining specialization and professionalization creates a purely professional mode of accountability, which places virtually all decisions about the adequacy of practice in the hands of individual professionals. From an organizational perspective this is a problem in a structural sense because the convergent thinking and deductive reasoning of professionals means they tend to see their clients' needs in terms of the skills they have to offer them (Mintzberg, 1979; Perrow, 1970; Segal, 1974). Moreover, this is a problem in a cultural sense because professionals tend to distort negative information about the effectiveness of their practices to make it consistent with their prevailing paradigm (e.g., Brown, 1978; Rounds, 1979, 1981; Weick, 1985).

From a structural perspective the proponents of inclusion and school restructuring are right about eliminating scientific management and the bureaucratic means of the EHA because they tend to separate theory from practice in school organizations. At a minimum, achieving the adhocratic ends of their reform proposals will require merging theory and practice. If merging theory and practice is to have the adhocratic effects they desire, however, they will have to do more than merge general education tracks and the general and special education systems in the ways they have proposed. Achieving their adhocratic ends will require merging theory and practice *in conjunction with* eliminating specialization and professionalization. This will require *eliminating the traditional classroom*, which, from a structural perspective, is the only way to introduce collaboration, mutual adjustment, and discursive coupling, the structural contingencies of the adhocracy configuration.

Furthermore, from a cultural perspective, achieving their adhocratic ends will require that an adhocratic professional culture emerge and be sustained within public education. To emerge, such a culture will require the structural contingencies of the adhocratic form. To be sustained, it will require an enduring source of uncertainty because, as in the case of NASA, without problems to solve, adhocracies eventually reconfigure themselves as bureaucracies.

In political terms the institution of public education cannot be democratic unless its practices are excellent and equitable. In organizational terms public education's practices cannot be excellent and equitable unless its school organizations are adhocratic. In structural and cultural terms school organizations and the professionals who staff them can neither become nor remain adhocratic without the uncertainty of student diversity. In the adhocratic school, educational equity is a precondition for educational excellence.

*P*UBLIC EDUCATION, DEMOCRACY, AND INDUSTRIALISM

In addition to being excellent and equitable, public education in a democracy also must promote stability and change. When the historical conditions of the late 19th century produced a rapidly expanding economy and an increasingly diverse population, political leaders and educational pioneers argued that public education had to represent a stabilizing force, a mechanism for America to socialize its citizens. At the same time, they understood that public education in a rapidly expanding democracy had to be dynamic enough to change with the spiritual mood of the public and the material needs of society (Cremin, 1961, 1965).

Moreover, when the historical conditions associated with industrialization produced unprecedented changes in the social and material needs of society, early 20th-century political and educational reformers argued for a more proactive role for public education. Not only did public education have to promote excellence and equity and stability and change, but it also had to transform the cultural sensibility of the public when, in the interest of responding to such changes, America had to reconstruct itself and its social institutions (Cremin, 1961; Dworkin, 1959; Kloppenberg, 1986).

The first real test of the idea that public education should transform society occurred during the progressive era, a period in which the notion of a rational democratic society was shaken by industrialization and its associated problems of urbanization and immigration. America's first response to the problem of industrialization was shaped by the idea of "social efficiency" (Haber, 1964, p. 59), which was promoted by progressive reformers who were grounded in the functionalist discourse of scientific management and the machine bureaucracy configuration.

Although the social efficiency phase of the progressive movement was short-lived, its intensity and timing were sufficient to instill the idea in government, business, and education that the problem with democracy is that it is inefficient and, more important, that things could be set right in America if government, and particularly public education, simply were to adopt industry's bureaucratic form and its emerging "science" of efficiency (see Callahan, 1962; Haber, 1964). And, of course, the efficiency approach applied to education gave America the segregated special classroom and the profession of special education, which, in the interest of efficiency, isolated and contained students who violated bureaucratic expectations (see Lazerson, 1983; Sarason & Doris, 1979; Skrtic, 1991a).

The idea of social transformation through education took on new significance in the social disarray following World War I and the stock market crash of 1929. During this period a generation of progressive reformers grounded in philosophical pragmatism contended that the problem with democracy *is* bureaucracy. Drawing on Weber's (1947, 1978) theories of bureaucracy and economy and Dewey's (1965, 1980) philosophy of education, they argued that nothing short of a reconstruction of society was necessary to save democracy from the distorting effects of bureaucracy (Kliebard, 1988; Kloppenberg, 1986). According to Weber (1978), democracy and bureaucracy grow coincidentally because the actualization of an egalitarian democratic government requires development of the bureaucratic administrative form. The problem arises in the contradiction between the democratic ends and the bureaucratic means of government because, although democracy is intended to be dynamic, the bureaucratic form on which it depends resists change.

Weber believed that the contradiction between democracy and bureaucracy is the central and irresolvable fact of the modern state. But the participants in the social reconstructionist phase of the progressive movement tempered his pessimism with Dewey's (1988b) argument that, although industrialization had intensified the very real problem of bureaucracy, it also provided an opportunity for America to recover democracy through a social reconstruction of the modern state itself.

According to Dewey (1976, 1988b), the problem of bureaucracy is intensified by industrialization because it places more of life—particularly work and education—under the bureaucratic form, which, by design, virtually eliminates the need to think reflectively and to solve problems collaboratively through discourse. And because these are the essential skills of democratic citizenship, the extension of bureaucracy under industrialization ultimately undercuts the public's ability to govern itself democratically. Nevertheless, Dewey (1988a, 1988b) argued that industrialization also had created an expanding network of regional, national, and international interdependencies, which in turn had created the need for a new cultural sensibility, a shift from the *possessive* form of individualism that had served America well in the 18th and 19th centuries to a *social* form of individualism that was more suited to democratic life in an inherently interdependent world.

Dewey pointed to the mounting social and political costs of this cultural contradiction and argued that the new conditions of interdependence made possible and begged for a new approach to public education, one premised on developing in the public a new sense of itself as an interdependent community of interests. Moreover, Dewey and the other social reconstructionists believed that the cultural transformation required by industrialization would produce a new American public, one capable of carrying out the reconstruction of society necessary to save democracy from the distorting effects of bureaucracy (see Kloppenberg, 1986).

Before industrialization and urbanization, Dewey (1976) argued, children's daily experiences at home and on the farm provided them with a multitude of problems to solve through their encounters with other children and with adults. When industrialization removed work and education from the home, though, children lost the rich problem-solving context that had provided their parents and grandparents with ample opportunity to develop imagination and intelligence.

Although Dewey was an optimist, he was not a romantic. Instead of arguing for a return to the problem-rich context of the past, he proposed that the goal of public education should be to return problems to the lives of children by turning schools into problem-rich contexts, communities of inquiry in which teachers engage their students' minds with problems rather than simply fill their heads with "facts." Of course, the approach Dewey (1965) recommended was *progressive education,* a pedagogy in which teachers engage their students' native capacities and enthusiasm by linking learning to life through concrete problem solving, or what he called the "concrete logic of action" (Dewey, 1976, p. 69).

Understanding what Dewey meant by progressive education is difficult because, as Kloppenberg (1986) noted, it "has been so distorted by generations of well-meaning but ill-equipped educational administrators that its original significance has been almost entirely lost" (p. 374). Nevertheless, in the space remaining I can note the most distinctive features of progressive education by referring to my previous discussion of critical or philosophical pragmatism, the antifoundational or postmodern theory of knowledge upon which it is premised. As we know from Chapter 14, philosophical pragmatism cuts a *via media* or way between the traditional subjective-objective and order-conflict dimensions of modern social knowledge (Kloppenberg, 1986). Although it recognizes the inadequacies of modern or foundational social knowledge, philosophical pragmatism uses it as a starting point for reconstructing new forms of knowledge through a critical and democratized form of dialogical social discourse (see Antonio, 1989; Kloppenberg, 1986; Chapter 14).

In such a discourse, all forms of knowledge are accepted or rejected on the basis of their contribution to the realization of social ideals rather than whether they are true in a foundational sense (Bernstein, 1991; Rorty, 1979, 1989, 1991). Whereas the aim of modern social inquiry is to justify social knowledge and practices by showing that they accurately represent the social world, the goal of philosophical pragmatism is to change social knowledge and practices by reconciling them with our moral ideals (Bernstein, 1971, 1991; Rorty, 1982, 1989).

Given its grounding in philosophical pragmatism, progressive education is a pedagogy under which students deconstruct and reconstruct their knowledge and experiences under conditions of uncertainty. It conceives of thinking as arising from the activity of solving concrete problems, "from the need of meeting some difficulty, in reflecting upon the best way of overcoming it, and thus leads to planning, to projecting mentally the result to be reached, and deciding upon the steps necessary and their serial order" (Dewey, 1976, p. 69).

Dewey favored experiential problem solving as a pedagogical approach because he believed it is the best means for developing the capacity to think critically. In turn, critical thinking is important because, for Dewey (1976), education ultimately is a dialogical process of critical reflection leading to a "reconstruction...of experience which adds to the meaning of experience, and...increases the ability to direct the course of subsequent experience" (p. 93). As such, the goal of the progressive educator:

> ...is not to train students to perform familiar tasks in time-honored ways, but to help them learn to solve unanticipated problems with imagination, not to impart bodies of knowledge but to develop the capacity to think...without the assistance of inherited methods or the reassurance of knowing that a correct answer always exists. (Kloppenberg, 1986, p. 375)

Moreover, because the purpose of reconstructing knowledge and experience is to reconcile them with ideals, progressive education must be based on a theory of ethics as well as a theory of knowledge. Here again, Dewey (Dewey & Tufts, 1989) premised his conception of progressive education on the theory of ethics contained in philosophical pragmatism. As such, he conceived of ethical activity as he did all activity—in terms of problem solving through dialogical discourse within a community of interests. For Dewey, ethics is "the concrete task of bringing the broadest lessons of experience and the resources of inventiveness to the solution of particular problems, not the application of a fixed and pre-set code of moral universals" (Edel & Flower, 1989, p. xxvii). It is a way of "dealing with reconstruction and resolution of conflicts and problems in particular situations...not the application of rules that simply sum up past experience" (Edel & Flower, 1989, p. xxv).

As such, Dewey considered the traditional conflict in the field of ethics between freedom and responsibility—between individual interests (excellence) and the common good (equity)—to be a pseudo-problem created by the artificial split between the individual and the social in modern knowledge (Kloppenberg, 1986). Thus, the pragmatist theory of ethics, actualized through progressive education, contains the key to Dewey's analysis of freedom and responsibility:

> Freedom is essentially the capacity to learn and to make creative and innovative use of learning in guiding conduct. The pragmatic emphasis is on responsibility as prospective rather than retrospective...on sensitivity, learning, and self-development. (Edel & Flower, 1989, p. xxv)

Drawing on Dewey's philosophy of education, and thus on the pragmatist theories of knowledge and ethics, the social reconstructionists rejected the prevailing idea put forth by advocates of social efficiency that public education should serve as a vehicle for conditioning individuals to restrain themselves and to follow the rules. Instead, they proposed the progressive theory that people should be freed from external restraints and expected to freely choose to be responsible. Ultimately, then, progressive education in a democracy should cultivate in students a *sense of social responsibility* by developing an *awareness of interdependence,* and engender a critical attitude toward received knowledge by promoting an *appreciation of uncertainty* (see Bourgeois, 1912; Croly, 1914, 1965; Dewey, 1897, 1965, 1976, 1980).

Dewey framed the social reconstructionists' concern over the decline of democracy as a twofold problem. Speaking of the new interdependencies that had emerged with industrialization, he said:

> In spite of attained integration, or rather perhaps because of its nature, the Public seems to be lost; it is certainly bewildered.... The social situation has been so changed by the factors of an industrial age that traditional general principles have little practical meaning. They exist as emotional cries rather than as reasoned ideas. (1988b, pp. 308–318)

Thus, the first problem for Dewey (1988b) was a bewildered public that, because of changed social conditions, could no longer express its interests and thus was unfit for participation in democracy. The second problem was "the essential need...[for] improvement of the methods and conditions of debate, discussion and persuasion" (p. 365), which was essential if the public were to develop a sense of itself as a community of interests and thus be able to reconstruct society.

Of course, Dewey and the other reconstructionists (see Kloppenberg, 1986) believed that, once progressive education had been instituted in the public schools, philosophical pragmatism and public education would provide the necessary methods and conditions of debate, discussion, and persuasion. But here the social reconstructionists were confronted with the problem that ultimately blocked their reform efforts. In organizational terms, the problem was the contradiction between the adhocratic value orientation of progressive education and the bureaucratic culture and structure of the institution of public education. As Kloppenberg (1986) noted, the circularity in the social reconstructionists' argument for transforming society through education is that:

> Education inevitably involves institutions as well as the ideas to be communicated, and unshackling students from a false individualism and a false subservience to [received knowledge] must therefore await the unshackling of their teachers.... If the problems facing society can be traced to its individualism, as these thinkers believed, and reform must proceed by means of education, how can reformers get around the awkward fact that the educational system is imbued with precisely the values that they have isolated as the source of the problem? (p. 377)

No one grasped the circularity problem better than Weber (1978). Whereas the problem of an unreflective public could be traced to the contradiction between democracy and bureaucracy in the modern state, he argued that the circularity of trying to solve the problem through education turns on a double contradiction in the logic of modernity itself: the contradiction between democracy and bureaucracy, on one hand, and between education and professionalization on the other.

Weber (1978) explained that the ever increasing push to further bureaucratize the economy and government creates the need for more and more experts and thus continually increases the importance of specialized knowledge. But the logic of expertise contradicts democracy because it creates "the struggle of the 'specialist' type of man against the older type of 'cultivated' man" (p. 1090). And because the progressive project is premised on restoring democracy by educating the cultivated citizen, it is stymied because public education itself becomes increasingly bureaucratized in the interest of training specialized experts for an increasingly bureaucratized economy. Thus, democracy continues to decline, not only because the bureaucratic form resists change but because the cultivated citizen continues to disappear.

Moreover, as more of life comes under the control of the specialization and professionalization of the professional bureaucracy, the need to solve problems and to engage in discourse diminishes even further. This impedes the capacity for critical thought and dialogical discourse in society *and* in the professions, which not only undercuts the ability of the public to govern itself democratically but reduces even further the capacity of the professions to view themselves and their practices critically.

*P*ROSPECTS FOR THE FUTURE

We can assess the significance of the social reconstructionist debate for contemporary society by comparing the emerging historical conditions of the 21st century to those of the early 20th century, the historical conditions in which the debate took shape.

> By 1932...industrialism has moved into overdrive and an urban society is clearly in the making.... A new physics has replaced the Newtonian outlook and a new logic is shaking philosophy.... The social sciences have been staking claims for the study of human life and thrusting different perspectives of method and research into the arena. Ethics is in a particularly precarious position: formerly it had coasted on the comfortable assumption that people agreed about morality but only argued about how it was to be justified.... Now it is startled into the perception that there are fundamental conflicts on moral questions. (Edel & Flower, 1989, pp. viii-ix)

In the late 20th century we have a better understanding of the implications of the "new physics," particularly for the social disciplines, which, on the basis of these implications, are beginning to question some of their earlier objectivist claims about epistemology, methodology, and social life (see Chapter 14). Moreover, we have had more than century to think about antifoundationalism, the new logic of pragmatism that began shaking philosophy in the 1870s and has continued to shake it and social and political theory ever since. As we know, this has produced new and reappropriated old methodologies for addressing fundamental conflicts on moral questions, particularly questions about the relations of power and knowledge in the emerging postmodern world (see Chapter 15). Finally, and most important in terms of determinant possibilities for the future, industrialism has stalled out in the late 20th century and is being overtaken by *postindustrialism.*

The significance of the emergence of postindustrialism is that it is premised on an even greater and more pervasive form of interdependence and social responsibility than industrialism. Whereas the network of social interdependencies industrialization created stopped at the boundaries of industrial organizations themselves, postindustrialization extends the network into the very core of the postindustrial organizational form (see Dertouzos, Lester, & Solow, 1989; Drucker, 1989; Kearns & Doyle, 1988; Naisbitt & Aburdene, 1985; Reich, 1983, 1990). The key difference is that, as performance organizations premised on standardization, industrial firms depend on the machine bureaucracy configuration and thus on the separation of theory and practice and an unreflective, mechanical form of interdependence among workers. The emerging postindustrial firm, however, is a problem-solving organization premised on innovation. It requires the adhocratic form, and thus the structural contingencies of collaboration, mutual adjustment, and discursive coupling, as well as a professional-political mode of accountability premised on a community of interests among workers and managers and, ultimately, among the organization's members, consumers, and host community (Dertouzos et al., 1989; Drucker, 1989; Mintzberg, 1979; Reich, 1983).

Reich (1990) characterized the adhocracies of the postindustrial economy as "environments in which people can identify and solve problems for themselves" (p. 201), as contexts in which:

> Individual skills are integrated into a group.... Over time, as group members work through various problems...they learn about each others' abilities. They learn how they can help one another perform better, what each can contribute to a particular project, and how they can best take advantage of one another's experience. (p. 201)

The system of education needed for the postindustrial economy is one that prepares young people "to take responsibility for their continuing education, and to collaborate with one another so that their combined skills and insights add up to something more than the sum of their individual contributions" (Reich, 1990, p. 202). As such, educational excellence in the postindustrial era is more than basic numeracy and literacy; it is a capacity for working collaboratively with others and for taking responsibility for learning (Dertouzos et al., 1989; Drucker, 1989; Kearns & Doyle, 1988; Naisbitt & Aburdene, 1985; Secretary's Commission on Achieving Necessary Skills, 1991; Reich, 1983, 1990). Moreover, educational equity is the precondition for excellence, growth of knowledge, and progress in the postindustrial era. This is so because collaboration means learning collaboratively with and from individuals with varying interests, abilities, skills, and cultural and linguistic perspectives, and taking responsibility for learning means taking responsibility for one's own learning *and* that of others (Dertouzos et al., 1989; Drucker, 1989; Kearns & Doyle, 1988; Secretary's Commission on Achieving Necessary Skills, 1991). Ability grouping and tracking have no place in such a system because they "reduce young people's capacities to learn from and collaborate with one another" (Reich, 1990, p. 208). Moreover, these practices work against promoting social responsibility in students and developing their capacity for negotiation within a community of interests, outcomes that are unlikely unless public schools become settings where "class unity and cooperation are the norm" (Reich, 1990, p. 208; Dertouzos et al., 1989).

Given the relevancies of the postindustrial era, the successful school in the 21st century will be one that produces cultivated citizens, liberally educated young people who can work responsibly and interdependently under conditions of uncertainty. It will do this by promoting in its students a sense of social responsibility, an awareness of interdependence, and an appreciation of uncertainty. It will achieve these things by developing its students' capacity for experiential learning through collaborative problem solving and reflective discourse within a community of interests. The successful school in the postindustrial era will be one that achieves excellence and equity simultaneously—indeed, one that recognizes equity *as the way to* excellence. The successful school in the postindustrial era will be one that produces cultivated citizens by providing all of its students with a progressive education in an adhocratic setting.

Where do we stand today in relation to the problems Dewey identified at the start of the century? Certainly, the problem of an unreflective public is still with us. One need do little more than consider the state of political and cultural life today to see that the public continues to be bewildered. Nevertheless, the prospects for reflective discourse have improved considerably. As we have seen, developments in the social disciplines are providing new methodological resources, as well as a vindication and reappropriation of those associated with philosophical pragmatism. Not only are these developments finding their way into educational inquiry, but the methods themselves are premised on and aimed at education, edification, and self-formation.

Moreover, beyond providing much useful information about school organization and change, more than three decades of unsuccessful attempts to change the general and special education systems has resulted in enough uncertainty about public education to create a convergence of interests regarding the problem of school failure. And, of course, the most significant development is the emergence of postindustrialism, which, in principle, holds out the possibility of a convergence of interests regarding the problem of public education itself.

In the final analysis, however, cultural transformation and social reconstruction will depend on adequate methods and conditions of discourse. Given the emerging historical conditions of the 21st century, and the fact that democracy *is* collaborative problem solving through reflective discourse within a community of interests, critical pragmatism and the adhocratic school organization provide us with a glimpse of the methods and conditions to resume the critical project of American pragmatism, and thus with a second chance to save ourselves, our children, and our democracy from bureaucracy.

The significance of postindustrialism for the special education advocacy community is that it raises the possibility of the type of reform required to actualize its value orientation in public education, as those values have been expressed in the *spirit* of the EHA and mainstreaming and more recently in the *spirit* of inclusion. Indeed, these are the very values upon which postindustrialism is premised, and, more important, the precise values needed to reconcile the institutional practice of education with its democratic ideals. If the special education community is to play a positive role in reforming public education, however, it must recognize and reconcile the contradiction between its democratic ideals and its bureaucratic practices. To do this, of course, special educators must have the courage and insight to deconstruct and continuously reconstruct their professional knowledge tradition, as well as the commitment and conviction to help other educators do the same. Together, the Part Two chapters have attempted to provide some of the necessary insights. The matter of the necessary courage, commitment, and conviction is up to the rising generation of special educators.

REFERENCES

Allison, G. T. (1971). *Essence of decisions: Explaining the Cuban missile crisis.* Boston: Little, Brown.

Antonio, R. J. (1989). The normative foundations of emancipatory theory: Evolutionary versus pragmatic perspectives. *American Journal of Sociology, 94*(4), 721–748.

Argyris, C. (1957). *Personality and organization.* New York: Harper & Brothers.

Ayres, L. P. (1909). *Laggards in the schools: A study of retardation and elimination in city school systems.* New York: Charities Publication Committee.

Bacharach, S. B. (1990). *Education reform: Making sense of it all.* Boston: Allyn and Bacon.

Bakalis, M. J. (1983). Power and purpose in American education. *Phi Delta Kappan, 63*(1), 7–13.

Barnard, C. I. (1938). *Functions of the executive.* Cambridge, MA: Harvard University Press.

Bates, R. J. (1980). Educational administration, the sociology of science, and the management of knowledge. *Educational Administration Quarterly, 16*(2), 1–20.

Bates, R. J. (1987). Corporate culture, schooling, and educational administration. *Educational Administration Quarterly, 23*(4), 79–115.

Becker, H. S. (1983). Studying urban schools. *Anthropology and Education Quarterly, 31*(2), 99–108.

Berger, P. L., & Luckmann, L. (1967). *The social construction of reality.* New York: Doubleday.

Bernstein, R. J. (1971). *Praxis and action: Contemporary philosophies of human activity.* Philadelphia: University of Pennsylvania Press.

Bernstein, R. J. (1991). *The new constellation.* Cambridge, England: Polity Press.

Bidwell, C. E. (1965). The school as a formal organization. In J. G. March (Ed.), *Handbook of organizations* (pp. 972–1022). Chicago: Rand-McNally.

Biklen, D. (Ed.). (1985). *Achieving the complete school: Strategies for effective mainstreaming.* New York: Teachers College Press.

Bishop, J. M. (1977). Organizational influences on the work orientations of elementary teachers. *Sociology of Work and Occupation, 4,* 171–208.

Bobbitt, F. (1913). Some general principles of management applied to the problems of city school systems. In *The supervision of city schools* (12th Yearbook of the National Society for the Study of Education) (Pt. 1, pp. 137–196). Chicago: University of Chicago Press.

Bogdan, R. (1983). Does mainstreaming work? is a silly question. *Phi Delta Kappan, 64*(6), 425–434.

Bogdan, R., & Knoll, J. (1988). The sociology of disability. In E. L. Meyen & T. M. Skrtic (Eds.), *Exceptional children and youth: An introduction* (pp. 449–477). Denver: Love Publishing.

Bogdan, R., & Kugelmass, J. (1984). Case studies of mainstreaming: A symbolic interactionist approach to special schooling. In L. Barton & S. Tomlinson (Eds.), *Special education and social interests* (pp. 173–191). New York: Nichols.

Bourgeois, L. (1912). *Solidarité* (7th ed.). Paris: Colin. (Original work published 1896)

Boyd, W. L., & Crowson, R. L. (1981). The changing conception and practice of public school administration. In D. C. Berliner (Ed.), *Review of research in education* (pp. 311–373). Itasca, IL: F. E. Peacock.

Boyer, E. L. (1983). *High school.* New York: Harper & Row.

Bridges, E. M. (1982). Research on the school administrator: The state of the art, 1967–1980. *Educational Administration Quarterly, 18*(3), 12–33.

Brown v. Board of Education (1954). 347 U.S. 483, 74 S. Ct. 686, 98 L. Ed. 873.

Brown, R. H. (1978). Bureaucracy as praxis: Toward a political phenomenology of formal organizations. *Administrative Science Quarterly, 23,* 365–382.

Bruininks, R. H., & Rynders, J. E. (1975). Alternatives to special class placement for educable mentally retarded children. In E. Meyen, G. Vergason, & R. Whelan (Eds.), *Alternatives for teaching exceptional children* (pp. 92–111). Denver: Love Publishing.

Bryan, T., Bay, M., & Donahue, M. (1988). Implications of the learning disabilities definition for the regular education initiative. *Journal of Learning Disabilities, 21*(1), 23–28.

Burns, T., & Stalker, G. M. (1966). *The management of innovation* (2nd ed.). London: Tavistock.

Burrell, G., & Morgan, G. (1979). *Sociological paradigms and organizational analysis.* London: Heinemann Educational Books.

Callahan, R. (1962). *Education and the cult of efficiency.* Chicago: University of Chicago Press.

Campbell, R. (1971, August). *NCPEA—Then and now.* Paper presented at National Council of Professors of Educational Administration Meeting, University of Utah.

Campbell, R. F., & Gregg, R. T. (Eds.). (1956). *Administrative behavior in education.* New York: Harper & Brothers.

Campbell, R. F., & Newell, L. J. (1973). *A study of professors of educational administration: Problems and prospects of an applied academic field.* Columbus, OH: University Council for Educational Administration.

Carlberg, C., & Kavale, K. (1980). The efficacy of special versus regular class placement for exceptional children: A meta-analysis. *Journal of Special Education, 14,* 295–309.

Chandler, J. T., & Plakos, J. (1969). *Spanish-speaking pupils classified as educable mentally retarded.* Sacramento: California State Department of Education.

Chandler, M. D., & Sayles, L. R. (1971). *Managing large systems.* New York: Harper and Row.

Christophos, F., & Renz, P. (1969). A critical examination of special education programs. *Journal of Special Education, 3*(4), 371–380.

Clark, B. R. (1972). The organizational saga in higher education. *Administrative Science Quarterly, 17,* 178–184.

Clark, D. L. (1985). Emerging paradigms in organizational theory and research. In Y. S. Lincoln (Ed.), *Organizational theory and inquiry: The paradigm revolution* (pp. 43–73). Beverly Hills, CA: Sage Publications.

Clark, D. L., & Astuto, T. A. (1988). *Education policy after Reagan—What next?* (Occasional paper No. 6). Charlottesville, VA: Policy Studies Center of the University Council for Educational Administration.

Clark, D. L., Lotto, L. S., & Astuto, T. A. (1984). Effective schools and school improvement: A comparative analysis of two lines of inquiry. *Educational Administration Quarterly, 20*(3), 41–68.

Cohen, M. D., & March, J. G. (1974). *Leadership and ambiguity.* New York: McGraw-Hill.

Cohen, M. D., March, J. G., & Olsen, J. P. (1972). A garbage can model or organizational choice. *Administrative Science Quarterly, 17,* 1–25.

Coladarci, A. P., & Getzels, J. W. (1955). *The use of theory in educational administration.* Stanford, CA: Stanford University.

Cremin, L. A. (1961). *The tranformation of the school.* New York: Knopf.

Cremin, L. A. (1965). *The genius of American education.* New York: Vintage.

Croly, H. (1914). *Progressive democracy.* New York: Macmillan.

Croly, H. (1965). The promise of American life. In J. W. Ward (Ed.), *The American heritage series.* Indianapolis: Bobbs-Merrill. (Original work published 1909)

Cuban, L. (1979). Determinants of curriculum change and stability, 1870–1970. In J. Schaffarzick & G. Sykes (Eds.), *Value conflicts and curriculum issues.* Berkeley, CA: McCutchan.

Cuban, L. (1983). Effective schools: A friendly but cautionary note. *Phi Delta Kappan, 64*(10), 695–696.

Cuban, L. (1989). The "at-risk" label and the problem of urban school reform. *Phi Delta Kappan, 70*(10), 780–784, 799–801.

Cummins, J. (1989). A theoretical framework for bilingual special education. *Exceptional Children, 56*(2), 111–119.

Cunningham, L. L., Hack, W. G., & Nystrand, R. O. (Eds.). (1977). *Educational administration: The developing decades.* Berkeley, CA: McCutchan.

Dalton, M. (1959). *Men who manage.* New York: Wiley.

Deno, E. (1970). Special education as developmental capital. *Exceptional Children, 37*(3), 229–237.

Dertouzos, M. L., Lester, R. K., & Solow, R. M. (1989). *Made in America: Regaining the productive edge.* Cambridge, MA: MIT Press.

Dewey, J. (1897). My pedagogic creed. *The School Journal, 54*(3), 77–80.

Dewey, J. (1965). Progressive education and the new science of education. In M. S. Dworkin (Ed.), *Dewey on education* (pp. 113–126). New York: Teachers College Press. (Original work published 1928)

Dewey, J. (1976). The school and society. In J. A. Boydston (Ed.), *John Dewey: The middle works, 1899–1924* (Vol. 1, pp. 1–109). Carbondale, IL: Southern Illinois University Press. (Original work published 1899)

Dewey, J. (1980). Democracy and education. In J. A. Boydston (Ed.), *John Dewey: The middle works, 1899–1924* (Vol. 9, pp. 1–370). Carbondale, IL: Southern Illinois University Press. (Original work published 1916)

Dewey, J. (1988a). Individualism, old and new. In J. A. Boydston (Ed.), *John Dewey: The later works, 1925–1953* (Vol. 5, pp. 41–123). Carbondale, IL: Southern Illinois University Press. (Original work published 1929–1930)

Dewey, J. (1988b). The public and its problems. In J. A. Boydston (Ed.), *John Dewey: The later works, 1925–1953* (Vol. 2, pp. 235–372). Carbondale, IL: Southern Illinois University Press. (Original work published 1927)

Dewey, J., & Tufts, J. H. (1989). Ethics. In J. A. Boydston (Ed.), *John Dewey: The later works, 1925–1953* (Vol. 7, pp. 1–462). Carbondale, IL: Southern Illinois University Press. (Original work published 1932)

Dornbusch, S. M., & Scott, W. R. (1975). *Evaluation and the exercise of authority: A theory of control applied to diverse organizations.* San Francisco: Jossey-Bass.

Drucker, P. F. (1989). *The new realities.* New York: Harper & Row.

Dunn, L. M. (1968). Special education for the mildly retarded—Is much of it justifiable? *Exceptional Children, 35*(1), 5–22.

Dworkin, M. S. (Ed.). (1959). *Dewey on education: A centennial review.* New York: Teachers College Press.

Edel, A., & Flower, E. (1989). Introduction. In J. A. Boydston (Ed.), *John Dewey: The later works, 1925–1953* (Vol. 7, pp. vii-xxxv). Carbondale, IL: Southern Illinois University Press.

Edwards, R. C. (1979). *Contested terrain: The transformation of the workplace in the twentieth century.* New York: Basic Books.

Elliott, J. (1975). *Objectivity, ideology, and teacher participation in educational research.* Norwich, England: University of East Anglia, Centre for Applied Research in Education.

Elmore, R. F. (1987). *Early experiences in restructuring schools: Voices from the field.* Washington, DC: National Governors Association.

Elmore, R. F., & McLaughlin, M. W. (1982). Strategic choice in federal education policy: The compliance-assistance trade-off. In A. Lieberman & M. W. McLaughlin (Eds.), *Policy making in education: Eighty-first yearbook of the National Society for the Study of Education* (pp. 159–194). Chicago: University of Chicago Press.

Elmore, R. F., & McLaughlin, M. W. (1988). *Steady work: Policy, practice, and the reform of American education.* Santa Monica, CA: Rand Corporation.

Erickson, D. A. (1977). An overdue paradigm shift in educational administration, or, how can we get that idiot off the freeway? In L. L. Cunningham, W. G. Hack, & R. O. Nystrand (Eds.), *Educational administration: The developing decades* (pp. 129–143). Berkeley, CA: McCutchan Publishing.

Erickson, D. A. (1979). Research on educational administration: The state-of-the-art. *Educational Researcher, 8*(3), 9–14.

Everhart, R. B. (1990). Disruptive behavior in organizational context. In P. Leone (Ed.), *Understanding troubled and troubling youth: Multidisciplinary perspectives* (pp. 272–289). Beverly Hills, CA: Sage Publications.

Fayol, H. (1949). *General and industrial management.* Marshfield, MA: Pitman. (Original work published 1916)

Follett, M. P. (1924). *Creative experience.* London: Longman & Green.

Follett, M. P. (1940). *Dynamic administration: The collected papers of Mary Parker Follett.* H. C. Metcalf & L. Urwick (Eds.). New York: Harper & Brothers.

Ford, P. L. (Ed.). (1904). *Thomas Jefferson, works.* New York: Knickerbocker Press.

Foster, W. (1986). *Paradigms and promises: New approaches to educational administration.* Buffalo, NY: Prometheus Books.

Galbraith, J. K. (1967). *The new industrial state.* Boston: Houghton Mifflin.

Gartner, A., & Lipsky, D. K. (1987). Beyond special education: Toward a quality system for all students. *Harvard Educational Review, 57*(4), 367–390.

Gehrke, N. J., & Kay, R. S. (1984). The socialization of beginning teachers through mentor-protege relationships. *Journal of Teacher Education, 35,* 21–24.

Gerber, M. M., & Levine-Donnerstein, D. (1989). Educating all children: Ten years later. *Exceptional Children, 56*(1), 17–27.

Getzels, J. W., & Guba, E. G. (1957). Social behavior and the administrative process. *School Review, 65,* 423–441.

Getzels, J. W., & Jackson, P. W. (1960). Research on the variable "teacher": Some comments. *School Review, 68,* 450–462.

Golding, D. (1980). Establishing blissful clarity in organizational life: Managers. *Sociological Review, 28,* 763–782.

Goodlad, J. I. (1984). *A place called school: Prospects for the future.* New York: McGraw-Hill.

Goodman, P. (1968). *People or personnel.* New York: Vintage.

Greer, C. (1972). *The great school legend: A revisionist interpretation of American public education.* New York: Basic Books.

Griffiths, D. E. (1959). *Administrative theory.* New York: Appleton-Century-Crofts.

Griffiths, D. E. (Ed.). (1964). *Behavioral science and educational administration* (63rd yearbook of the National Society for the Study of Education, pt. 2). Chicago: University of Chicago Press.

Griffiths, D. E. (1979). Intellectual turmoil in educational administration. *Educational Administration Quarterly, 15*(3), 43–65.

Griffiths, D. E. (1983). Evolution in research and theory: A study of prominent researchers. *Educational Administration Quarterly, 19*(3), 201–221.

Griffiths, D. E. (1988). Administrative theory. In N. J. Boyan (Ed.), *Handbook of research on educational administration* (pp. 27–51). New York: Longman.

Gulick, L., & Urwick, L. (Eds.). (1937). *Papers on the science of administration.* New York: Columbia University, Institute of Public Administration.

Haber, S. (1964). *Efficiency and uplift: Scientific management in the Progressive Era, 1890–1920.* Chicago: University of Chicago Press.

Halpin, A. W. (Ed.). (1958). *Administrative theory in education.* Chicago: University of Chicago, Midwest Administration Center.

Halpin, A. W. (1970). Administrative theory: The fumbled torch. In A. M. Kroll (Ed.), *Issues in American education.* New York: Oxford University Press.

Halpin, A. W., & Hayes, A. E. (1977). The broken ikon, or what ever happened to theory? In L. L. Cunningham, W. G. Hack, & R. O. Nystrand (Eds.), *Education administration: The developing decades* (pp. 261–297). Berkeley, CA: McCutchan.

Harry, B. (1992). *Cultural diversity, families, and the special education system: Communication and empowerment.* New York: Teachers College Press.

Hayes, D., & Pharis, W. (1967). *National conference of professors of educational administration.* Lincoln: University of Nebraska.

Hedberg, B. (1981). How organizations learn and unlearn. In P. C. Nystrom & W. H. Starbuck (Eds.), *Handbook of organizational design* (Vol. 1, pp. 3–27). New York: Oxford University Press.

Hedberg, B. L. T., Nystrom, P. C., & Starbuck, W. H. (1976). Camping on seesaws: Prescriptions for a self-designing organization. *Administrative Science Quarterly, 21*(1), 41–65.

Heller, K., Holtzman, W., & Messick, S. (1982). *Placing children in special education: A strategy for equity.* Washington, DC: National Academy of Sciences Press.

Heshusius, L. (1982). At the heart of the advocacy dilemma: A mechanistic world view. *Exceptional Children, 49*(1), 6–13.

House, E. R. (1974). *The politics of educational innovation.* Berkeley, CA: McCutchan.

House, E. R. (1979). Technology versus craft: A ten year perspective on innovation. *Journal of Curriculum Studies, 11*(1), 1–15.

Iano, R. P. (1987). Rebuttal: Neither the absolute certainty of prescriptive law nor a surrender to mysticism. *Remedial and Special Education, 18*(1), 51–56.

Illich, I. (1976). *Medical nemesis.* New York: Random House.

Immegart, G. L. (1977). The study of educational administration, 1954–1974. In L. L. Cunningham, W. G. Hack, & R. O. Nystrand (Eds.), *Educational administration: The developing decades.* Berkeley, CA: McCutchan.

Janesick, V. J. (1988). Our multicultural society. In E. L. Meyen & T. M. Skrtic (Eds.), *Exceptional children and youth: An introduction* (pp. 519–538). Denver: Love Publishing.

Johnson, G. O. (1962). Special education for the mentally handicapped—A paradox. *Exceptional Children, 29*(2), 62–69.

Jones, R. A. (1977). *Self-fulfilling prophecies.* Hillsdale, NJ: Lawrence Erlbaum.

Jonsson, S. A., & Lundin, R. A. (1977). Myths and wishful thinking as management tools. In P. C. Nystrom & W. H. Starbuck (Eds.), *Prescriptive models of organizations* (pp. 157–170). New York: Elsevier North-Holland.

Kauffman, J. M., Gerber, M. M., & Semmel, M. I. (1988). Arguable assumptions underlying the regular education initiative. *Journal of Learning Disabilities, 21*(1), 6–11.

Kearns, D. T., & Doyle, D. P. (1988). *Winning the brain race: A bold plan to make our schools competitive.* San Francisco: Institute for Contemporary Studies.

Keogh, B. K. (1988). Improving services for problem learners: Rethinking and restructuring. *Journal of Learning Disabilities, 21*(1), 19–22.

Kliebard, H. M. (1988). The effort to reconstruct the modern American curriculum. In L. E. Beyer & M. W. Apple (Eds.), *The curriculum: Problems, politics, and possibilities* (pp. 19–31). New York: State University of New York Press.

Kloppenberg, J. T. (1986). *Uncertain victory: Social Democracy and Progressivism in European and American thought, 1870–1920.* New York: Oxford University Press.

Kuhn, T. (1970). *The structure of scientific revolutions* (2nd ed.). Chicago: University of Chicago Press.

Lazerson, M. (1983). The origins of special education. In J. G. Chambers & W. T. Hartman (Eds.), *Special education policies: Their history, implementation, and finance* (pp. 15–47). Philadelphia: Temple University Press.

Lehming, R., & Kane, M. (1981). *Improving schools: Using what we know.* Beverly Hills, CA: Sage Publications.

Lieberman, A., & Miller, L. (1984). *Teachers, their world and their work: Implications for school improvement.* Alexandria, VA: Association for Supervision and Curriculum Development.

Lipsky, D. K., & Gartner, A. (1989). *Beyond separate education: Quality education for all.* Baltimore, MD: Paul H. Brookes.

Lipsky, M. (1976). Toward a theory of street-level bureaucracy. In W. D. Hawley, M. Lipsky, S. B. Greenberg, J. D. Greenstone, I. Katznelson, K. Orren, P. E. Peterson, M. Shefter, & D. Yates (Eds.), *Theoretical perspectives on urban politics* (pp. 196–213). Englewood Cliffs, NJ: Prentice Hall.

Lortie, D. C. (1975). *Schoolteacher: A sociological study.* Chicago: University of Chicago Press.

Lortie, D. (1978). Some reflections on renegotiation. In M. Reynolds (Ed.), *Futures of education for exceptional students* (pp. 235–244). Reston, VA: Council for Exceptional Children.

MacMillan, D. L. (1971). Special education for the mildly retarded: Servant or savant? *Focus on Exceptional Children, 2*(9), 1–11.

March, J. G., & Olsen, J. P. (1976). *Ambiguity and choice in organizations.* Bergen, Norway: Universitetsforlaget.

Martin, D. T., Overholt, G. E., & Urban, W. J. (1976). *Accountability in American education: A critique.* Princeton, NJ: Princeton Book Company.

Martin, E. (1978). Preface. In M. C. Reynolds (Ed.), *Futures of education for exceptional students* (pp. iii-vi). Reston, VA: Council for Exceptional Children.

Maxcy, S. J. (1991). *Educational leadership: A critical pragmatic perspective.* New York: Bergin and Garvey.

Mayo, E. (1933). *The human problems of an industrial civilization.* New York: Macmillan.

McDonnell, L. M., & McLaughlin, M. W. (1982). *Education policy and the role of the states* (Rand Report No. R-2755-NIE). Santa Monica, CA: Rand Corporation.

McNeil, L. M. (1986). *Contradictions of control: School structure and school knowledge.* New York: Methuen/ Routledge & Kegan Paul.

Meier, D. (1984). "Getting tough" in the schools. *Dissent, 31*(1), 61–70.

Mercer, J. (1973). *Labeling the mentally retarded: Clinical and social system perspectives on mental retardation.* Berkeley, CA: University of California Press.

Meyer, J. W., & Rowan, B. (1977). Institutionalized organizations: Formal structure as myth and ceremony. *American Journal of Sociology, 83,* 340–363.

Meyer, J. W., & Rowan, B. (1978). The structure of educational organizations. In M. W. Meyer (Ed.), *Environments and organizations* (pp. 78–109). San Francisco: Jossey-Bass.

Meyer, J. W., & Scott, W. R. (1983). *Organizational environments: Ritual and rationality.* Beverly Hills, CA: Sage Publications.

Meyer, M. W. (1979). Organizational structure as signaling. *Pacific Sociological Review, 22*(4), 481–500.

Miles, M. B. (1964). *Innovation in education.* New York: Teachers College, Columbia University.

Miller, D., & Friesen, P. H. (1984). *Organizations: A quantum view.* Englewood Cliffs, NJ: Prentice Hall.

Miller, D., & Mintzberg, H. (1983). The case for configuration. In G. Morgan (Ed.), *Beyond method: Strategies for social research* (pp. 57–73). Beverly Hills, CA: Sage.

Mintzberg, H. (1979). *The structuring of organizations.* Englewood Cliffs, NJ: Prentice Hall.

Mintzberg, H. (1983). *Structure in fives: Designing effective organizations.* Englewood Cliffs, NJ: Prentice Hall.

Mommsen, W. J. (1974). *The age of bureaucracy: Perspectives on the political sociology of Max Weber.* New York: Harper and Row.

Moran, M. (1984). Excellence at the cost of instructional equity? The potential impact of recommended reforms upon low achieving students. *Focus on Exceptional Children, 16*(7), 1–11.

Morgan, G. (Ed.). (1983). *Beyond method: Strategies for social research.* Beverly Hills, CA: Sage Publications.

Mort, P. R., & Cornell, F. G. (1941). *American schools in transition: How our schools adapt their practices to changing needs.* New York: Teachers College, Columbia University.

Naisbitt, J., & Aburdene, P. (1985). *Re-inventing the corporation.* New York: Warner Books.

National Commission on Excellence in Education. (1983). *A nation at risk: The imperative for educational reform.* Washington, DC: U.S. Government Printing Office.

Noel, M. M., & Fuller, B. C. (1985). The social policy construction of special education: The impact of state characteristics on identification and integration of handicapped children. *Remedial & Special Education, 6*(3), 27–35.

Oakes, J. (1985). *Keeping track: How schools structure inequality.* New Haven, CT: Yale University Press.

Oakes, J. (1986a). Keeping track, part 1: The policy and practice of curriculum inequality. *Phi Delta Kappan, 68*(1), 12–17.

Oakes, J. (1986b). Keeping track, part 2: Curriculum inequality and school reform. *Phi Delta Kappan, 68*(2), 148–154.

Parsons, T. (1960). *Structure and process in modern societies.* Glencoe, IL: Free Press.

Patrick, J., & Reschly, D. (1982). Relationship of state educational criteria and demographic variables to school-system prevalence of mental retardation. *American Journal of Mental Retardation, 86,* 351–360.

Peirce, C. S. (1931–35). *Collected papers of Charles Sanders Peirce* (C. Hartshorne & P. Weiss, Eds.).

Cambridge, MA: Harvard University Press.

Perrow, C. (1970). *Organizational analysis: A sociological review*. Belmont, CA: Wadsworth.

Perrow, C. (1972). *Complex organizations: A critical essay*. New York: Scott, Foresman.

Perrow, C. (1978). Demystifying organizations. In R. C. Sarri & Y. Hasenfeld (Eds.), *The management of human services* (pp. 105–120). New York: Columbia University Press.

Pettigrew, A. M. (1979). On studying organizational cultures. *Administrative Science Quarterly, 24*, 570–581.

Pfeffer, J. (1982). *Organizations and organization theory*. Marshfield, MA: Pitman.

Pugh, D. S., Hickson, D. J., Hinnings, C. R., MacDonald, K. M., Turner, C., & Lupton, T. (1963). A conceptual scheme for organizational analysis. *Administrative Science Quarterly, 8*(4), 289–315.

Reich, R. B. (1983). *The next American frontier*. New York: Penguin Books.

Reich, R. B. (1990). Education and the next economy. In S. B. Bacharach (Ed.), *Education reform: Making sense of it all* (pp. 194–212). Boston: Allyn and Bacon.

Resnick, D., & Resnick, L. (1985). Standards, curriculum, and performance: Historical and comparative perspectives. *Educational Researcher, 14*(4), 5–20.

Reynolds, M. C., & Wang, M. C. (1983). Restructuring "special" school programs: A position paper. *Policy Studies Review, 2*(1), 189–212.

Reynolds, M. C., Wang, M. C., & Walberg, H. J. (1987). The necessary restructuring of special and general education. *Exceptional Children, 53*(5), 391–398.

Rist, R., & Harrell, J. (1982). Labeling and the learning disabled child: The social ecology of educational practice. *American Journal of Orthopsychiatry, 52*(1), 146–160.

Roethlisberger, F. J., & Dickson, W. J. (1939). *Management and the worker: An account of a research program conducted by the Western Electric Company, Hawthorne Works, Chicago*. Cambridge, MA: Harvard University Press.

Romzek, B. S., & Dubnick, M. J. (1987). Accountability in the public sector: Lessons from the Challenger tragedy. *Public Administration Review, 47*(3), 227–238.

Rorty, R. (1979). *Philosophy and the mirror of nature*. Princeton, NJ: Princeton University Press.

Rorty, R. (1982). *Consequences of pragmatism*. Minneapolis: University of Minnesota Press.

Rorty, R. (1989). *Contingency, irony, and solidarity*. Cambridge, England: Cambridge University Press.

Rorty, R. (1991). *Objectivity, relativism, and truth: Philosophical papers, volume 1*. Cambridge, England: Cambridge University Press.

Rounds, J. (1979). *Social theory, public policy and social order*. Unpublished Ph.D. Dissertation, University of California, Los Angeles.

Rounds, J. (1981). *Information and ambiguity in organizational change*. Paper presented at the Carnegie-Mellon Symposium on Information Processing in Organizations, Carnegie-Mellon University, Pittsburgh.

Rowan, B. (1980). *Organizational structure and the institutional environment: The case of public schools*. Unpublished manuscript, Texas Christian University, Ft. Worth.

Rudduck, J. (1977). Dissemination as encounter of cultures. *Research Intelligence, 3*, 3–5.

Rueda, R. (1989). Defining mild disabilities with language-minority students. *Exceptional Children, 56*(2), 121–128.

Sarason, S. B. (1982). *The culture of the school and the problem of change* (rev. ed.). Boston: Allyn and Bacon. (1st edition 1971)

Sarason, S. B. (1983). *Schooling in America: Scapegoat or salvation*. New York: Free Press.

Sarason, S. B., & Doris, J. (1979). *Educational handicap, public policy, and social history*. New York: The Free Press.

Schein, E. H. (1972). *Professional education*. New York: McGraw-Hill.

Schempp, P. G., & Graber, K. C. (1992). Teacher socialization from a dialectical perspective: Pretraining through induction. *Journal of Teaching in Physical Education, 11*(4), 329–348.

Schön, D. A. (1983). *The reflective practitioner: How professionals think in action*. New York: Basic Books.

Scott, W. R. (1981). *Organizations: Rational, natural, and open systems*. Englewood Cliffs, NJ: Prentice Hall.

Secretary's Commission on Achieving Necessary Skills (1991). *What work requires of schools: A SCANS report for America 2000*. Washington, DC: U.S. Department of Labor.

Segal, M. (1974). Organization and environment: A typology of adaptability and structure. *Public Administration Review, 34*(3), 210–220.

Sergiovanni, T. J., & Moore, J. H. (1989). *Schooling for tomorrow.* Boston: Allyn & Bacon.

Simon, H. A. (1947). *Administrative behavior.* New York: Macmillan.

Simon, H. A. (1977). *The new science of management decision* (rev. ed.). Englewood Cliffs, NJ: Prentice Hall.

Singer, J. D., & Butler, J. A. (1987). The Education for All Handicapped Children Act: Schools as agents of social reform. *Harvard Educational Review, 57*(2), 125–152.

Sirotnik, K. A., & Oakes, J. (1986). Critical inquiry for school renewal: Liberating theory and practice. In K. Sirotnik & J. Oakes (Eds.), *Critical perspectives on the organization and improvement of schooling* (pp. 3–93). Boston: Kluwer-Nijhoff Publishing.

Sizer, T. R. (1984). *Horace's compromise: The dilemma of the American high school.* Boston: Houghton Mifflin.

Skrtic, T. M. (1986). The crisis in special education knowledge: A perspective on perspective. *Focus on Exceptional Children, 18*(7), 1–16.

Skrtic, T. M. (1987). An organizational analysis of special education reform. *Counterpoint, 8*(2), 15–19.

Skrtic, T. M. (1988). The organizational context of special education. In E. L. Meyen & T. M. Skrtic (Eds.), *Exceptional children and youth: An introduction* (pp. 479–517). Denver: Love Publishing.

Skrtic, T. M. (1991a). *Behind special education: A critical analysis of professional culture and school organization.* Denver: Love Publishing.

Skrtic, T. M. (1991b). The special education paradox: Equity as the way to excellence. *Harvard Educational Review, 61*(2), 148–206.

Skrtic, T. M. (1991c). Students with special educational needs: Artifacts of the traditional curriculum. In M. Ainscow (Ed.), *Effective schools for all* (pp. 20–42). London: David Fulton Publishers.

Skrtic, T. M., Guba, E. G., & Knowlton, H. E. (1985). *Interorganizational special education programming in rural areas: Technical report on the multisite naturalistic field study.* Washington, DC: National Institute of Education.

Skrtic, T. M., & Ware, L. P. (1992). Reflective teaching and the problem of school organization. In E. W. Ross, J. W. Cornett, & G. McCutcheon (Eds.), *Teacher personal theorizing: Connecting curriculum practice, theory, and research* (pp. 207–218, 298–303). Albany, NY: State University of New York Press.

Slavin, R. E. (1989). PET and the pendulum: Faddism in education and how to stop it. *Phi Delta Kappan, 70*(10), 752–758.

Spring, J. (1980). *Educating the worker-citizen: The social, economic, and political foundations of education.* New York: Longman.

Stainback, S., & Stainback, W. (1984). A rationale for the merger of special and regular education. *Exceptional Children, 51*(2), 102–111.

Stainback, S., & Stainback, W. (1987). Integration versus cooperation: A commentary on educating children with learning problems: A shared responsibility. *Exceptional Children, 54*(1), 66–68.

Stedman, L. C. (1987). It's time we changed the effective schools formula. *Phi Delta Kappan, 69*(3), 215–224.

Taylor, F. W. (1947). *Scientific management.* New York: Harper & Row. (Original work published 1911)

Thompson, J. D. (1967). *Organizations in action.* New York: McGraw-Hill.

Timar, T. B., & Kirp, D. L. (1988). *Managing educational excellence.* New York: Falmer Press.

Toffler, A. (1970). *Future shock.* New York: Bantam Books.

Tomlinson, S. (1982). *A sociology of special education.* Boston: Routledge & Kegan Paul.

Turnbull, H. R., & Turnbull, A. P. (1978). *Free appropriate public education: Law and implementation.* Denver: Love Publishing.

Tweedie, J. (1983). The politics of legalization in special education reform. In J. G. Chambers & W. T. Hartman (Eds.), *Special education policies: Their history, implementation, and finance* (pp. 48–73). Philadelphia: Temple University Press.

Tye, K. A., & Tye, B. B. (1984). Teacher isolation and school reform. *Phi Delta Kappan, 65*(5), 319–322.

U.S. Department of Education. (1988). *Annual report to Congress on the implementation of the Education for All Handicapped Children Act.* Washington, DC: Government Printing Office.

Walker, L. J. (1987). Procedural rights in the wrong system: Special education is not enough. In A. Gartner & T. Joe (Eds.), *Images of the disabled/disabling images.* New York: Praeger.

Wang, M. C., Reynolds, M. C., & Walberg, H. J. (1986). Rethinking special education. *Educational Leadership, 44*(1), 26–31.

Wang, M. C., Reynolds, M. C., & Walberg, H. J. (1987). *Handbook of special education: Research and practice (Vol. I: Learner characteristics and adaptive education)*. Oxford, England: Pergamon Press.

Weatherley, R. (1979). *Reforming special education: Policy implementation from state level to street level*. Cambridge, MA: MIT Press.

Weatherley, R., & Lipsky, M. (1977). Street level bureaucrats and institutional innovation: Implementing special education reform. *Harvard Educational Review, 47*(2), 171–203.

Weber, M. (1946). Bureaucracy. In H. H. Gerth & C. W. Mills (Eds. & Trans.), *From Max Weber: Essays in sociology* (pp. 196–244). New York: Oxford University Press. (Orignal work published 1922)

Weber, M. (1947). *The theory of social and economic organization* (A. H. Henderson & T. Parsons, Eds. & Trans.). Glencoe, IL: Free Press. (Original work published 1924)

Weber, M. (1949). "Objectivity" in social sciences and social policy. In E. A. Shils & H. A. Finch (Eds. & Trans.), *The methodology of the social sciences* (pp. 49–112). New York: Free Press. (Original work published 1904)

Weber, M. (1978). *Economy and society*. (G. Roth & C. Wittich, Eds.; E. Fischoff, H. Gerth, A. M. Henderson, F. Kolegar, C. W. Mills, T. Parsons, M. Rheinstein, G. Roth, E. Shils, & C. Wittich, Trans.) (2 vols). Berkeley: University of California Press. (Original work published 1922)

Weick, K. E. (1976). Educational organizations as loosely coupled systems. *Administrative Science Quarterly, 21*(1), 1–19.

Weick, K. E. (1979a). Cognitive processes in organizations. In B. M. Staw (Ed.), *Research in organizational behavior* (Vol. 1, pp. 41–74). Greenwich, CT: JAI Press.

Weick, K. E. (1979b). *The social psychology of organizing* (2nd ed.). Reading, MA: Addison-Wesley.

Weick, K. E. (1982a). Administering education in loosely coupled schools. *Phi Delta Kappan, 63*(10), 673–676.

Weick, K. E. (1982b). Management of organizational change among loosely coupled elements. In P. Goodman (Ed.), *Change in organizations* (pp. 375–408). San Francisco: Jossey-Bass.

Weick, K. E. (1985). Sources of order in underorganized systems: Themes in recent organizational theory. In Y. S. Lincoln (Ed.), *Organization theory and inquiry: The paradigm revolution* (pp. 106–138). Beverly Hills, CA: Sage Publications.

Wise, A. E. (1979). *Legislated learning: The bureaucratization of the American classroom*. Berkeley: University of California Press.

Wise, A. E. (1988). The two conflicting trends in school reform: Legislated learning revisited. *Phi Delta Kappan, 69*(5), 328–333.

Wolcott, H. F. (1977). *Teachers versus technocrats: An educational innovation in anthropological perspective*. Eugene, OR: Center for Educational Policy and Management.

Woodward, J. (1965). *Industrial organization: Theory and practice*. London: Oxford University Press.

Worthy, J. C. (1950). Factors influencing employee morale. *Harvard Business Review, 28*, 61–73.

Wright, A. R., Cooperstein, R. A., Reneker, E. G., & Padilla, C. (1982). *Local implementation of P. L. 94–142: Final report of a longitudinal study*. Menlo Park, CA: SRI International.

Wright, J. S. (1967). *Hobson v. Hansen: Opinion by Honorable J. Skelly Wright, Judge, United States Court of Appeals for the District of Columbia*. Washington, DC: West Publishing.

Zucker, L. G. (1977). The role of institutionalization in cultural persistence. *American Sociological Review, 42*, 726–743.

Zucker, L. G. (1981). Institutional structure and organizational processes: The role of evaluation units in schools. In A. Bank & R. C. Williams (Eds.), *Evaluation and decision making* (CSE Monograph Series, No. 10). Los Angeles: UCLA Center for the Study of Evaluation.

GLOSSARY

ability grouping Combining students in separate instructional arrangements based on their achievement in an area of study (e.g., math or reading).

acceleration An approach in gifted education in which a student completes more than one school grade each year. Practices such as early admission, grade-skipping, advanced placement, telescoping of grade levels in upgraded situations, and credit by examination are some examples.

accommodation, eye Adjustment of the eye by changing the shape of the lens to allow a person to see clearly at different focal lengths.

active listening A technique in which an individual conveys understanding of, and interest in, what a person is saying, through expressions, gestures, reflecting or reiterating statements, and similar means.

adaptive behavior An individual's ability to meet standards set by society and his or her cultural group. The American Association on Mental Deficiency considers three areas of performance in assessing adaptive behavior: maturation, learning, and social adjustment.

adaptive equipment Devices developed to assist in the physical management of individuals with physical disabilities.

adaptive physical education Physical education programs designed to meet the specific needs of disabled children and youth.

adventitious Acquired after birth through accident or illness, as contrasted with congenital (present at birth).

adventitious deafness A condition in which a person born with normal hearing sensitivity loses hearing as a result of accident or disease.

advocacy Efforts by parents and professionals to establish or to improve services for exceptional children and youth.

Self-advocacy describes efforts made by the individual who will benefit from the results of advocacy.

age norms Standards based on the average performance of individuals in specific age groups.

agraphia Inability or loss of ability to write.

AIDS The acronym for the disease complex called acquired immune deficiency syndrome, which affects the body's disease-fighting capacity so that the person is susceptible to a number of diseases that the body otherwise is able to fight off.

air conduction The process whereby sound waves travel through the air to the auditory mechanism.

albinism An inherited condition that results in a deficiency of pigment in the skin, hair, and iris of the eye. The condition causes the eyes to appear pinkish and in most cases is accompanied by sensitive and defective vision.

ambiopia Double vision.

American Sign Language Also known as ASL or Ameslan, a visual-manual or sign language entirely unrelated to English. ASL is the language used most often by the adult deaf population in the United States, where it originated.

amniocentesis A procedure applied during pregnancy to identify certain genetic disorders in the fetus.

anecdotal method A procedure for recording and analyzing observations of child behavior; narrative description.

aniridia Failure of the iris of the eye to develop fully.

annual goals Activities or achievements to be completed or attained within a year. Annual goals for disabled children must be stated in individualized education programs (IEPs), as directed in Public Law 94–142.

anoxia Lack of oxygen. If this occurs, brain damage may result.

aphasia Impairment in the ability to understand or use oral language; often associated with an injury or dysfunction of the brain.

apraxia A condition involving difficulty with voluntary, or purposeful, muscular movement with no evidence of motor impairment.

aqueous humor The fluid that fills the front chamber of the eye, in front of the crystaline lens.

architectural barrier An environmental obstruction that prevents disabled persons from using facilities. Examples include stairs, narrow hallways, and conventional restrooms.

articulation Speech sound production by modification of the stream of voiced and unvoiced breath, usually through movements of the jaws, lips, tongue, and soft palate.

asphyxia Deprivation of oxygen, as in smoke suffocation or drowning. If the deprivation is prolonged, the person may go into a coma, with accompanying brain injury or death.

assistive technology Any technology or tool that can aid a person with a disability in becoming more independent.

Association for Retarded Citizens (ARC) Organization concerned with advocacy and public policy affecting children and adults with mental retardation.

astigmatism An eye condition involving a refractive error in which rays from one point of an object are not brought to a single focus because of a difference in the degree of refraction in the different meridians of the eye; causes blurred visual images.

ataxia A form of cerebral palsy characterized by lack of muscle coordination; contributes to problems in balance and position.

athetosis A form of cerebral palsy characterized by involuntary, jerky movements of the extremities, as a result of fluctuating muscle tone.

atonia Also known as hypotonia; lack of muscle tone.

at risk Often used to describe students with potential for experiencing some problem or deficiency.

attention deficit disorder (ADD) A condition characterized by developmentally inappropriate degrees of inattention, impulsiveness, and hyperactivity.

Attention Deficit Disorder with Hyperactivity (314.01) One of the classifications of the DSM III System; inattention, impulsivity, and hyperactivity are present before age 7. Attention Deficit Hyperactivity Disorder is the same as attention deficit disorder except emphasis is placed on the hyperactivity. Either ADD or ADHD is acceptable language.

audiogram A graph of hearing threshold levels as measured by an audiometer and plotted for different pure tone frequencies for each ear.

audiometer An instrument that measures hearing sensitivity and acuity. The measurement of hearing loss is recorded in terms of decibels, units of hearing loss, or as a percentage of normal hearing sensitivity.

auditory training Systematic training to improve an individual's use of remaining (residual) hearing.

augmentative communication systems Assistive devices and symbol systems that enhance the communication ability of individuals who have limited verbal communication skills.

aural Pertaining to the ears and hearing. Binaural refers to both ears.

autism A severe childhood disturbance characterized by bizarre behavior, developmental delays, and extreme isolation. Although it is now categorized as an exceptionality under "Other Health Impaired," the behavioral features are often appropriate for interventions employed with students who have emotional disturbance.

baseline Beginning observations as a foundation for measurement prior to intervention or treatment; a beginning point for comparison of treatment effects.

behavior analysis The science employing the principles of behavior to facilitate improvement of behavior or learning.

behavior disorder (BD) A condition in which a person's actions are so inappropriate, disruptive, and possibly destructive that they may interfere with education and may require special services. This term has replaced emotionally disturbed in most government programs.

behavior modification Shaping behavior to minimize or eliminate negative behaviors and to emphasize and reinforce positive behaviors, through control of a learning environment with planned and systematic application of the principles of learning.

bilingual Having proficiency in two languages. Frequently used with reference to children who attend schools in which English is the standard language but who speak another language at home.

blind Having only light perception without projection or being totally without the sense of vision. Educationally, the blind child learns through tactile and auditory materials. (See also *legal blindness*.)

bone conduction Transmission of sound through the bones of the skull to the inner ear.

braille A system of six raised dots used to present a code that can be read through the sense of touch.

brain-injured child One who before, during, or after birth has received an injury or suffered an infection to the brain that impedes normal development.

cataract A condition causing opacity of the lens of the eye, resulting in visual limitation or blindness. Surgical removal of the lens is the most frequently used method of restoring or improving sight. Cataracts occur much more often among adults than among children; in children the condition may occur as a result of rubella (one form of measles).

catheter A narrow tube of rubber, plastic, metal, or glass, which can be inserted into the body to empty the bladder or kidneys by a method known as catheterization.

CEC Abbreviation for the Council for Exceptional Children.

central nervous system (CNS) The brain and spinal cord.

cerebral palsy (CP) An abnormal alteration of human movement or motor function arising from a defect, injury, or disease of the tissues of the central nervous system. Three main types are usually described—spastic, athetoid, and ataxic.

Child Find An organized effort to identify all disabled children in need of special services.

class action A legal procedure carried out on behalf of a particular person to benefit all others with similar problems.

class size A factor in many state laws, regulating the number of disabled students to be served by one teacher; also expressed as pupil-teacher ratio.

cleft palate A condition characterized by an opening in the roof of the mouth, involving the hard or soft palate, or both, and often extending through the upper lip. Causes nasal speech, certain articulation problems, and sometimes additional physical problems. Cleft palate usually is treated by surgery and speech therapy.

code-switching A speaker's ability to shift between two or more dialects (Black English to Standard American English) or between formal and informal Standard American English in adjusting to different listeners and settings.

cognition The understanding of information.

collaboration A term used in the late 1980s referring to a need for special education and regular education to work more closely, especially in communicating about children. The term arose out of the regular education initiative and the implied need to bring the two disciplines closer together. Implies teachers, administrators, and parents working together.

communication board Pictorial or symbol representations used in nonoral communication. Individuals with little or no speech are taught to communicate by pointing to symbols on the special board.

communication skills The many ways of transferring thought from one person to another through speech, written words, and bodily gestures.

community-based instruction Teaching the skills necessary for community functioning in the natural community setting.

community-referenced instruction Instructional goals that are prioritized on the basis of their importance relative to a student's functioning in the natural environments found in the community-at-large.

community service program A variety of offerings, including emergency programs, community consultation and education, and counseling and therapy, throughout the locality.

compulsory attendance Federal and state laws requiring children to attend school.

conduct disorder One of the classifications of behavior disorder in Quay's dimensional classification system; describes individuals who have aggressive and other negative behaviors (e.g., boisterous, bullying).

conductive hearing loss A form of hearing loss characterized by obstruction along the sound conduction pathway leading to the inner ear. This form of hearing loss is the most preventable and treatable.

congenital Describes the presence of a condition or characteristics in an individual at birth but not limited to hereditary factors. Examples are congenital deafness and congenital heart defects. In contrast, adventitious conditions are acquired after birth.

consent Permission from parents to evaluate a child or to place a child in a program. PL 94–142 contains specific provisions regarding consent.

consulting teachers Specially trained instructors who consult with teachers and other instructional personnel involved in educational programs for exceptional children. Their roles differ from those of itinerant teachers in that consulting teachers do not provide direct services to disabled children and youth except when demonstrating a technique as part of the consultation.

convergent production Seeking one solution or answer to a problem or question.

cornea The clear, transparent, outer coat of the eyeball forming the covering of the aqueous chamber.

Council for Exceptional Children Professional organization based in Reston, Virginia, and concerned with the education of children with special needs.

Council for Learning Disabilities (CLD) An organization of professionals who work directly or indirectly with persons who have learning disabilities. Formerly the Division of Children with Learning Disabilities of the Council for Exceptional Children.

counseling therapy A structured relationship or process through which an individual is helped to feel and behave in a more satisfying way, gain a better understanding of himself or herself, and take positive steps toward dealing with the environment through information, reactions, and stimulation. A counselor or therapist directs this process.

criterion-referenced test A measure to ascertain an individual's performance compared to a set criterion. The person is evaluated on his or her own performance and not in comparison to others.

cultural-familial Describes a condition in which an individual is diagnosed as having mental retardation without evidence of cerebral pathology, but having a family history of intellectual subnormality and cultural deprivation.

curriculum-based assessment (CBA) Assessment in relation to the curriculum objectives.

curriculum-based measurement (CBM) A system of repeated measurements of achievement with a prescriptive orientation toward remediation. The system involves small samples of subject matter that has previously been taught.

cystic fibrosis (CF) The most common, and usually fatal, hereditary disease of childhood; affects most body organs, particularly the lungs and pancreas. Abnormal mucus secretions obstruct bodily functions, especially the ability to clear the lungs, which results in excessive coughing.

deaf (deafness) A condition in which the sense of hearing is so lacking or drastically reduced as to prohibit normal functioning and the auditory sense is not the primary means by which speech and language are learned.

decibel (db) A unit of hearing or audition; extent of hearing is expressed as the number of decibels necessary for the person to hear pure tones above the baseline used to measure normal hearing.

defense mechanisms An individual's coping processes to facilitate approach or avoidance behaviors.

deficit A level of performance that is less than expected for an individual.

deinstitutionalization The practice of placing disabled persons in community programs rather than large residential facilities. Large numbers of people have been removed from institutions and placed in more appropriate community environments.

denial A defense mechanism operating unconsciously to resolve emotional conflict and anxiety by not recognizing thoughts, feelings, needs, or external reality factors that are consciously unacceptable.

dependence The tendency to rely on someone else for assistance in decision making, personal care, and other areas of need.

deregulation A process employed to reduce the restrictiveness of regulations governing the implementation of laws.

developmental disability A condition that originates in childhood and results in a significant disability for the individual, such as mental retardation, cerebral palsy, epilepsy, and conditions associated with neurological damage.

diabetes A metabolic disorder in which the body is unable to properly utilize carbohydrates in the diet because of failure of the pancreas to secrete an adequate supply of insulin, or failure of the insulin secreted to function properly in the digestive process, resulting in an abnormal concentration of sugar in the blood and urine. Symptoms are excessive thirst, excessive urination, weight loss, slow healing of cuts and bruises, pain in joints, and drowsiness.

dialect Rule-governed sound, form, and content variations in a language as a result of age, race or ethnic group, geography, or other factors that isolate one group of speakers from another; the standard dialect is that used by those of the prevailing group.

differential reinforcement Providing rewards for behavior in the presence of one stimulus situation and not reinforcing in the presence of other stimulus conditions.

diplegia Paralysis of the body in which both sides are affected; a result of injury to both hemispheres of the brain.

disability A functional limitation resulting from a condition (e.g., a paraplegic would have a disability because of the inability to use the lower part of the body).

discrimination learning The ability to differentiate relevant cues and dimensions.

dispute settlement The outcome of methods used to resolve disagreements between parents (or parent surrogates) and school officials. Conferences, mediation, and hearings may be involved.

divergent production Generating many solutions to a problem.

Down syndrome A clinical type of mental retardation resulting from a specific abnormal chromosomal arrangement. Most individuals with Down syndrome have intelligence in the moderate range of retardation.

DSM-III-R *The Diagnostic and Statistical Manual of Mental Disorders* (third edition–revised) published by the American Psychiatric Association; it serves as a manual of mental disorders and criteria used in making psychiatric diagnoses.

due process In an educational context, refers to procedures and policies established to ensure equal educational opportunities for all children. PL 94–142 contains due process procedures specific to disabled children.

dyslexia A serious reading disability in which an individual fails to learn to read despite adequate intelligence and proper classroom instruction; commonly associated with an injury or dysfunction of the brain.

echolalia A speech conditon characterized by involuntary repetition of words, syllables, or sounds spoken by others, as if echoing them; a common characteristic of severe retardation.

ecological assessment The process used to identify the specific skills an individual needs to function in domestic, vocational, recreational, and community environments.

educable mentally retarded (EMR)/educable mentally handicapped (EMH) The term ascribed to the highest level of retardation, including individuals capable of becoming self-sufficient and learning academic skills through upper elementary grades.

electroencephalogram (EEG) A mechanical tracing made by an electroencephalograph that depicts electrical output of brain waves. An EEG is useful in studying seizures accompanying brain injuries, epilepsy, etc.

elegibility Criteria to determine who does and who does not qualify for a specified program.

emotional disorder (disturbance) A term applied to individuals who are not able to control their emotions well enough to maintain behavior within an acceptable range. A comparable term used in many states in behavior disordered.

emotional lability Frequent and unexplainable shifts in a person's mood.

endogenous Originating from within rather than outside of (exogenous) a person.

enrichment An approach in teaching talented or gifted pupils whereby curricular activities or experiences are expanded into greater depth of understanding and application than those of a regular class. May include resource reading, creative projects, community application, special assignments, small group work, and other adaptations of routine school processes.

epilepsy A chronic condition of the central nervous system, characterized by periodic seizures accompanied by convulsions of the muscles and, with the more severe attacks, loss of consciousness.

equal protection The principle set forth in the Fourteenth Amendment that guarantees the same rights and benefits to all citizens with respect to government, unless the withholding of rights and benefits has a justifiable reason—e.g., an epileptic person with regular seizures may not be allowed a driver's license and certain other rights, to protect others.

etiology The cause of a disorder, disease, or disabling condition.

exceptional children Those whose performance in school-related behaviors varies from the norm to the extent that special instruction, assistance, and/or equipment are required. Children may be classified as exceptional because of intellectual, physical, behavioral, or sensory reasons. The term also is used to describe gifted children.

excess costs Extra costs incurred in educating a disabled child. For example, if the average per-pupil cost for educating a nondisabled child is $1,800 per year and the average per-pupil cost for educating a disabled child is $2,800 per year, the excess cost is $1,000.

exogenous Originating from external rather than internal (endogenous) causes.

expressive language The aspect of communication whereby messages are conveyed verbally, symbolically, or in writing.

family dynamics Refers to the structures, interactions, patterns, and responses of individuals within a family unit. With a disabled child, family dynamics may include overcompensation or rejection by some or all members, for example.

fetal alcohol syndrome (FAS) A condition found in some infants of alcoholic women, marked by low birth weight, retardation, cardiac and physical defects.

field of vision The entire area one can see without shifting the gaze; in visually impaired individuals a reduction in field of vision can be considered a disabling condition.

flow-through funds Those that are mandated to local districts by federal laws but are required to be distributed by the state education agency (SEA). Also called pass-through funds.

fluency 1. Uninterrupted smoothness and rapidity, as in reading or speaking. 2. In Guilford's structure of the intellect, the factors in creative thinking that represent the quality and the number of ideas produced.

foster home A living environment other than one with the parents, in which a child may be placed for rearing, usually by a family or welfare agency.

fragile-X syndrome A recently identified chromosomal disorder associated with mental retardation.

free appropriate public education (FAPE) Used in PL 94–142 to mean special education and related services that are provided at public expense, meet requirements of the state education agency, and conform to the individualized education program (IEP) requirement of PL 94–142.

functional Nonorganic; without known organic cause.

functional curriculum The model of curriculum that prioritizes instruction based on skills that are critical to independent functioning in adult integrated community environments.

functional domains The domains in which adults typically live, including domestic, vocational, recreation/leisure, and community.

galactosemia The condition characterized by an inborn error in the metabolism of carbohydrates. Mental retardation is one effect, as is visual impairment.

generalization (of learning) The process of forming a conclusion based on or inferred from a number of specific facts or instances. Lack of ability to generalize learning to situations other than that in which the learning occurred is characteristic of children with reduced intelligence.

grade level The placement of a child in the school program: students typically enter first grade at age 6 and progress one grade per year.

grammar Descriptive or prescriptive rules governing the interactions of word order (syntax) and word form (morphology) in any language.

grand mal A severe form of epileptic seizure involving loss of consciousness and extreme convulsions.

group home A form of alternative living arrangement in which individuals with retardation and multiple disabilities live in a community setting rather than in an institution.

guilt Feelings of being responsible or at fault for an event or circumstance. Some parents of disabled children, for instance, feel they are to blame for their child's disabling condition.

habilitation The process of improving an individual's performance in a broad range of skills and abilities. Often used in reference to services provided to persons with severe disabilities to prepare them for employment opportunities.

handicap The consequence of a disability when it causes an individual to function measurably lower than typical individuals intellectually, emotionally, or physically, to an extent that special programs and services are needed. This term does not include gifted individuals as does the term "exceptionality."

handicapism A term referring to prejudice, stereotyping, and discrimination against persons with disabilities.

hearing loss (impairment) A deficiency in the ability to hear. May range from a mild loss to a total lack of hearing ability (deafness). At the level of severe loss, defined as 70–90 dB, measured on an audiometer, hearing impaired individuals require extensive training in communication methods.

hemiplegia (hemiparesis) Paralysis of the arm and leg on one side of the body. The latter term implies lesser severity.

hertz (Hz) A unit of measurement of frequency, or vibrations per second of sound waves.

heterarchy Vertical orderings on a comparable level; no one entity is on top of everything; in contrast to hierarchy.

hologram An image created by a dynamic process of interaction and differentiation.

homebound instruction Teaching provided by specially trained instructors to students who are unable to attend school. Homebound instruction usually is provided on a short-term basis.

hydrocephalus (hydrocephaly) A condition of excess cerebrospinal fluid accumulation in the cranial cavity, causing undue pressure on the brain and resulting in an enlarged head. Referred to sometimes as "waterhead." Now, surgical procedures such as shunting are used to reduce fluid pressure and head enlargement. If unchecked, the condition usually causes mental retardation.

hyperactive Describes behavior characterized by abnormal, excessive activity or movement that may interfere with a child's learning and cause considerable problems in managing behavior.

hyperopia Farsightedness; poor vision at close range, because of shortened eyeball from back to front so the light rays tend to focus behind the retina. Hyperopia most often is corrected by using convex lenses, which bend the rays so they will focus on the retina.

IEU An abbreviation for intermediate education unit. Several states have educational units that comprise several districts or counties. These units also may be referred to as intermediate districts or cooperative, multicommunity, or county units.

IHE An abbreviation for institutions of higher education. Frequently used in referring to private or public colleges and universities.

immaturity A state of being not as fully developed as normally would be expected in physical, mental, or emotional capacities. Opposite of maturity.

impulsivity The act of making quick and often erroneous responses without considering the consequences of the action.

incidence As applied to exceptional children, incidence refers to the number of individuals who at some time in their lives might be considered exceptional.

inclusion Term used to describe the integration of students with disabilities into the regular classroom. Full inclusion refers to the inclusion of students with severe disabilities.

individual family service plan (IFSP) A feature of PL 99–457; an expanded individualized education program (IEP) for preschool children with disabilities and their whole family. The plan outlines the family's strengths and needs related to enhancing the child's development.

individualized curriculum sequencing (ICS) approach A remedial intervention used with students who have severe and multiple disabilities, following the most logical order of learning for a given child.

individualized education program (IEP) A requirement of PL 94–142 stipulating that a written education plan must be developed and maintained for each disabled child. The IEP must include a statement of the child's current level of educational performance, annual goals, short-term instructional objectives, specific services to be provided, dates services are to be provided, and criteria for evaluation.

Individuals with Disabilities Education Act (IDEA) This law (PL 101–476) was passed in 1990 to revise and update the Education for All Handicapped Children Act (EHA), which was passed in 1975 as PL 94–142. Autism and traumatic brain injuries are two of the disabilities added in 1990.

inner ear Made up of the cochlea and the semicircular canals, the innermost part of the hearing mechanism.

integrated therapy The delivery of related services such as occupational therapy, physical therapy, and speech therapy by incorporating therapeutic interventions into students' usual daily activities. Contrasted with the isolated therapy model, in which students receive specific therapy in one area.

integration In the context of special education, refers to the placement of disabled children in educational programs also serving nondisabled children.

interdisciplinary The collective efforts of individuals from several disciplines in assessing and/or planning a program for an individual. An interdisciplinary team might include, for example, a teacher, psychologist, physician, and social worker.

interpreter A professional who facilitates communication between hearing and deaf individuals, usually by translating between voiced information and sign language. Oral interpreters mouth the speaker's verbal information to enable the hearing disabled individual to speechread the message.

intrapsychic approach Also termed "psychoanalytic approach"; seeks to understand etiology through examining inner turmoil reflected by observable behaviors.

iris The colored portion of the eye, which contracts or expands involuntarily depending upon the amount of light entering it. The iris functions similarly to the shutter of a camera.

itinerant teachers Those who are trained to provide direct services to disabled children and youth. They do not operate a classroom but visit disabled children and youth assigned to regular classes. They also consult with regular classroom teachers.

language A system of words or symbols and the rules for putting them together to form a method of communication among a group of individuals.

LD An acronym for learning disabilities.

LEA An abbreviation for local education agency.

least restrictive environment (LRE) The educational milieu that is as much as possible like that of students in the "mainstream" school environment, without detracting from the learning and growth of the student with a disability.

legal blindness The level of visual impairment at which eligibility for special consideration, services, or funding is set. Defined as 20/200 in the better eye after correction or vision that does not exceed 20° in the visual field.

lens (of eye) The transparent component of the eye between the posterior chamber and the vitreous body that functions in focusing light rays and images on the retina.

Lesch-Nyhan syndrome An inborn error of metabolism, characterized by retardation and negative behaviors.

life-space interview A procedure in which a trained professional helps a child work out responses to situations; one aspect of the psychoeducational approach to emotional disturbance.

longitudinal study Research that follows a case or situation over a considerable time, usually a number of years.

low-incidence disability A classification of impairments that are few in number in relation to other disabilities of the general population (e.g., those involving vision, hearing, or orthopedic impairments).

low vision Educationally, refers to severe visual impairment after correction but with the potential to increase visual functioning through optical aids, nonoptical aids, environmental modifications, and specific techniques.

macula The small area near the center of the retina, responsible for detailed vision.

mainstreaming The practice of educating exceptional children in regular educational settings. Generally involves placement in regular classrooms and providing support services when necessary. Used most often with students who have mild disabilities.

mandate A requirement that specific tasks or steps are to be carried out (i.e., federal and state laws mandating that educational services be provided to all disabled children and youth).

manual communication A system sometimes used by deaf individuals employing sign language or a code expressed primarily through the hands.

manually-coded English (MCE) A communication option for deaf individuals; combines American Sign Language vocabulary with some pragmatic English structures; fingerspelling supplements ASL signs.

medical model One approach to emotional disturbance, viewing present behaviors as symptoms of an underlying cause.

meningitis Inflammation of the membranes that surround the brain and spinal cord.

meningomyelocele A sac-like membranous pouch that protrudes through an opening in the skull or spinal column; the sac contains cerebrospinal fluid but no spinal nerves. Often occurs in conjunction with spina bifida.

mental age The level of intellectual functioning based on the average for individuals of the same chronological age.

mental retardation A broadly used term that refers to significantly subaverage general intellectual functioning manifested during the developmental period and existing concurrently with impairment in adaptive behavior. At present, definitions indicate a person having an IQ of 70 or less and showing impairment in adaptation or social ability.

metacognition Refers to self-knowledge about how one learns and the regulation of one's own cognition.

microcephalus (microcephaly) A condition in which the head size is small because of an inherited defect that causes reduced brain size and severe mental retardation.

middle ear The part of the ear consisting of the eardrum, the three bones of the hearing mechanism, and the eustachian tube.

minimal brain dysfunction (MBD) A term referring to the functional limitation of children of near average, average, or above average intelligence who show learning or behavior disorders as a result of diagnosed or suspected deviations in functions of the central nervous system. The preferred term at present is learning disability.

mobility The process of moving about safely and effectively within the environment. An especially important ability for blind persons, who must coordinate mental orientation and physical locomotion to achieve safe, effective movement. Mobility aids such as canes, guide dogs, sighted guides, or electronic devices help them move about.

modeling A teaching technique in which the teacher performs a desired behavior and encourages the pupil to try the same behavior, using the teacher's demonstrated behavior as an example.

monitoring Activities conducted to ensure that particular requirements or procedures are carried out. For example, states may establish monitoring procedures to determine the degree to which local districts fulfill the IEP requirements of PL 94–142.

monoplegia Paralysis involving one limb.

morphology The form of a single word, in language. A morpheme is the smallest unit of language that has meaning.

multidisabilities Concomitant impairments, the combination of which causes problems in learning.

multifactorially inherited disorders Conditions resulting from the combined effects of genetic and environmental components.

muscular dystrophy (MD) A hereditary disorder that causes loss of vitality and progressive deterioration of the body as a result of atrophy, or the replacement of muscle tissue with fatty tissue.

myelomeningocele See *meningomyelocele*.

myofunctional therapy The training of tongue movements to aid speech production.

myopia (nearsightedness) Condition in which distance vision is poor, usually because of a lengthened diameter of the eyeball from front to back, causing the image to come in focus at a point in front of the retina. Myopia usually is corrected by eyeglasses having a concave lens.

native language The language an individual uses most naturally and learned first.

neonatal Refers to time between the onset of labor and 6 weeks following birth.

neurologically impaired or **disabled** Pertaining to any of a number of conditions resulting from injury or malformation of the central nervous system. Conditions such as cerebral palsy, epilepsy, and the Strauss syndrome are examples.

NIMH Acronym for the National Institute of Mental Health.

noncategorical Refers to programs or philosophies that do not label or differentiate among the various disabilities or exceptionalities except in providing services.

nondiscriminatory testing The use of assessment instruments that allow the individual being tested to perform maximally on those skills or behaviors being assessed. A test discriminates against an individual when the norms are inappropriate, the content does not relate to the individual's cultural background, the examinee does not understand the language of the test items or of the person administering the test, or when sensory problems interfere with performance.

norm A standard based on the performance of a representative group with which the performance of others on similar tasks can be compared.

normalization An ideology that has been emphasized as a principle of human service; addresses the provision of patterns of life for the disabled that are as close as possible to those of members of society in general. This principle has received particular support in reference to improving services for persons with mental retardation.

norm-referenced tests Instruments used to ascertain an individual's performance compared to others' performance on the same instrument.

nystagmus Continuous, involuntary movement of the eyeball; usually affects both eyes and is associated with visual impairment.

occupational therapy Engaging individuals or groups in activities designed to enhance their physical, social, psychological, and cognitive development. A major service provided by most rehabilitation centers.

ophthalmologist A physician (M.D.) specializing in diagnosis and treatment of defects and diseases of the eye who can perform surgery, prescribe drugs, and determine the proper lenses.

optician A technician who grinds lenses, fits them into frames, and adjusts frames to the wearer.

optic nerve The cranial nerve that carries nerve impulses of sight to the brain.

optometrist A licensed doctor of optometry (O.D.) who specializes in measurement of refractive errors of the eye and prescribes glasses or contact lenses to correct these errors. Those specializing in low vision prescribe optical aids such as telescopic lenses.

oral Pertaining to, surrounding, or done by the mouth, as in speech.

organic Refers to factors within the body, particularly the central nervous system, that can cause a disabling condition.

orthopedic disability A disabling condition caused by physical impairments, especially those related to the bones, joints, and muscles.

orthosis An appliance used to support, correct, or align a physical deformity; a brace.

osteogenesis imperfecta A condition characterized by defective development of bone tissue.

otitis media Inflammation of the middle ear, possibly accompanied by pain, fever, interference with hearing, and vertigo. The condition can result in conductive hearing loss or impairment.

pacing Regulating the rate at which material is presented to a student according to how rapidly he or she can learn it.

paralysis Loss of voluntary movement or sensation in a part of the body; caused by disease or injury.

paraplegia Paralysis involving the lower half of the body (both legs).

paraprofessional A person trained as an assistant to a professionally qualified teacher. Some states have certification requirements for paraprofessionals.

parent-to-parent group A program designed to allow parents of disabled children the opportunity to discuss their feelings about their children, which can be highly beneficial.

partially seeing Having visual acuity greater than 20/20 but not greater than 20/70 in the better eye with correction; this term is no longer used by practitioners in the field.

perceptual disorders Difficulties or deficiencies in using the sense of sight, touch, smell, taste, or hearing to correctly recognize the various objects or situations within the environment. This type of disorder may become apparent in a student's poor performance in activities such as drawing, writing, and recognizing forms, sizes, or shapes.

perinatal Refers to the general time period shortly before, during, or immediately after birth.

peripheral vision Perception of objects, color, or motion by portions of the eye other than the macula. The images perceived are at the extreme edges of the visual field.

Perthes (Legg-Calve-Perthes) disease Degeneration of the growth center of the thigh bone; intervention can reverse its effects.

pervasive developmental disorders Distortions in the whole range of psychological functions during childhood development including attention, perception, learning abilities, language, social skills, reality contact, and motor skills.

petit mal A mild form of seizure occurring in epileptic conditions; characterized by dizziness and momentary lapse of consciousness.

phenylketonuria (PKU) A hereditary condition in which the absence of an enzyme essential for digesting protein affects the metabolism of the body and results in a gradual buildup of toxic substances in the blood and urine of infants having this condition. Interferes with normal development and function of the brain and is possibly the most widely known abnormality of metabolism that causes mental retardation.

phonology The concept relating to the production and comprehension of speech sounds. Phonemes comprise the sound categories.

physical therapy Manipulation, massage, and exercise of body parts to assist an individual with motor control for optimal functioning.

postnatal Occurring after birth.

precision teaching A systematic procedure of continuous and direct recording of behavior, espoused by Ogden Lindsley and others. Precision teaching employs the techniques of behavior modification and task analysis for management of instruction and behavior.

prenatal Occurring during gestation; prior to birth.

prevalence As applied to exceptional children, the number of exceptional children who exist at the present time.

profound mental retardation A term originated by the American Association on Mental Retardation referring to a level of intellectual functioning comparable to the educational classification of severe retardation. The individual requires supervision throughout life. The intellectual level, when assessed with an individual intelligence test, is estimated at IQ scores below 20.

projective technique A relatively unstructured method used to study and diagnose certain problems of personality. A product or response (such as a drawing, interpretation of a picture, or completion of a sentence) is secured from an individual and analyzed in an effort to gain an understanding of the total personality.

prosthesis An artificial body part.

protective safeguards Procedures established to ensure that the rights of the individual are protected.

psychoanalytic approach See *intrapsychic approach*.

psychological processes Covert cognitive behaviors that transform and manipulate information.

psychomotor seizure An epileptic activity in which the individual appears to be conscious during the attack but behaves in an unusual or bizarre way, after which he or she does not remember what happened during the episode. Some indications of psychomotor seizure may be chewing, lip smacking, ringing in ears, abdominal pains, dizziness.

psychosis A term of medical origin referring to a type of severe behavior disorder. Characteristics include loss of reality contact and abnormal acts, thoughts, and feelings.

Public Law 93–380 Educational Amendments of 1974, passed August 21, 1974.

Public Law 93–516 An amendment passed by Congress broadening the application of Section 504 of the Rehabilitation Act of 1973 to include educational services.

Public Law 94–142 The Education for All Handicapped Children Act of 1975.

Public Law 99–457 Amended and reauthorized the Education for All Handicapped Children Act and appropriated more monies for preschool intervention; also provided specific guidelines, including those for the individualized family service plan (IFSP). Passed in 1986.

pupil (of eye) The contractible opening in the center of the iris of the eye, through which light enters.

quadriplegia Paralysis involving all four limbs.

receptive language The aspect of communication that involves an individual's receival and comprehension of information from others.

referent An object, idea, or event in the real world symbolized by words.

regular education initiative (REI) An effort starting in about 1985 to combine regular education and special education into one system. REI would provide maximum mainstreaming for students with disabilities.

rehabilitation Literally, restoration. Most often used in reference to physical problems.

reinforcement Any consequence of behavior that increases the probability of that behavior being repeated in the future.

remediation Correction of a deficiency. Often used in reference to correction of academic deficits (e.g., problems in reading).

resource room A program option involving placement of a student in a regular class plus assignment to a special teacher for remedial or supplemental instruction. The special teacher may be referred to as a resource teacher, and the room in which special instruction is offered is referred to as a resource room.

retina The innermost component of the eye, which contains sensitive nerve fibers that connect to the optic nerve to produce sight. Retinal detachment is the loosening or pulling away of the retina from its normal position in the eye. In children, this condition usually is caused by accidents and may start with a slight loss of vision that might progress to almost complete blindness.

retrolental fibroplasia (retinopathy of prematurity) A disease of the eyes that results from excessive oxygen while a baby is in an incubator. The condition causes a retinal overgrowth that limits vision. The disease was common among premature babies of the 1940s but was drastically reduced in incidence until recent years, when medicine began to save very small infants.

rigidity State of continuous tension of the muscles; seen in some types of cerebral palsy.

rubeola The "old-fashioned" 10-day measles, or red measles, which is accompanied by a red rash and fever. The disease can be prevented with vaccine, and is far less threatening to the unborn fetus than is rubella.

schizophrenia A severe mental disorder characterized by a fragmented personality involving fantasies, illusions, delusions, and, in general, being out of touch with reality.

school social work services School social workers provide a major communication link between school staff and families. Casework services include assistance in interpreting evaluation reports and making recommendations. In some districts social workers chair child-study committees. They are a major resource for special educators working with community agencies.

screening Abbreviated testing procedures by a variety of disciplines conducted on a large scale to locate children requiring more detailed testing or specialized teaching.

SEA An abbreviation for state education agency, the department in state government with primary responsibility for public school education.

Section 504 Refers to Section 504 of the Rehabilitation Act of 1973. Contains requirements designed to guarantee the civil rights of persons with disabilities.

self-contained class A program in which pupils with similar needs and skills are assigned and taught by the same teacher throughout the school day.

semantics The study of the significance or meaning of words.

sensorineural (sensory-neural) hearing loss A condition involving impairment in the inner ear or the central nervous system. Also referred to as neural or nerve deafness.

sheltered workshop A facility that offers individuals who are not able to work in competitive employment an opportunity to work in a controlled environment at their level of functioning.

shunt (shunting) A technique involving implantation of a tube to drain or provide a bypass for excess cerebrospinal fluid, as in hydrocephalus.

sickle cell anemia A hereditary blood disorder most commonly seen in the black population; red blood cells are crescent-shaped and cannot pass readily through blood vessels.

soft neurological signs Mild or slight neurological abnormalities that are difficult to detect.

spastic Refers to muscular incoordination resulting from muscle spasms, opposing contractions of muscles, and paralytic effects. Also denotes one form of cerebral palsy having the above characteristics.

special class A program option for exceptional children involving assignment of children with similar instructional needs to a class taught by a certified special teacher. Special classes sometimes are referred to as self-contained classes.

special education A broad term covering programs and services for children who deviate physically, mentally, or emotionally from the normal to an extent that they require unique learning experiences, techniques, or materials in order to be maintained in the regular classroom, and specialized classes and programs if the problems are more severe. As defined by PL 94–142, special education is specifically designed instruction, at no cost to the parent, to meet the unique needs of a child with disabilities, including classroom instruction, physical education, home instruction, and instruction in hospitals and institutions.

special-purpose school A term frequently applied to schools that serve only exceptional children. Such schools may offer programs for one or more types of exceptional children. Sometimes called special schools.

special teacher A teacher certified to teach exceptional children. Historically the term has been applied primarily to teachers of self-contained classes for exceptional children. Currently the term is applied to certified teachers assigned to teach exceptional children.

speech The realization of language through a sound system, including articulation, fluency, and voice parameters.

speech-language pathologist A trained specialist who works with students who have articulation, fluency, voice, and/or language problems. Therapy services may be provided in individual therapy sessions, group therapy sessions, or, in many cases, through consultation with the student's regular classroom teacher.

speechreading Formerly called "lipreading," a technique for decoding verbal information using visible movements of the speaker's mouth in conjunction with context and auditory cues.

spina bifida A congenital malformation of the spine characterized by lack of closure of the vertebral column, which often allows protrusion of the spinal cord into a sac at the base of the spine. The degree of severity may vary, but this condition often causes paralysis of the lower extremities, changes in tactile and thermal sensations, and a lack of bowel and bladder control. Whenever possible, surgery is performed at an early age to reduce the disabling effects. Spina bifida frequently is associated with hydrocephalus and a reduction of intelligence.

standard deviation A measure of expressing the variability of a set of scores or attributes. Small standard deviations mean the scores are distributed close to the mean; large standard deviations mean the scores are spread over a wider range.

standardized tests Tests for which norms and specific directions for administration are available.

state aid Funds from the state treasury allocated to local districts. Most states provide extra funds to local districts to help cover the additional costs incurred in educating exceptional children.

state institutions Residential programs supported by public tax sources; most states operate institutions for persons with mental retardation and emotional/behavioral problems.

state plan A stipulation of Public Law 94–142 requiring state departments of education to submit a planned program for implementation and administration of the law, following the guidelines for content and structure.

stereotyped behavior Seemingly purposeless motor activity or body posturing. Seen commonly in persons with severe disabilities.

stimulus Any object or happening that excites a response from an organism.

strabismus A condition in which a person's eyes cross as a result of weakness of one or more of the eye muscles; prevents the eyes from focusing on the same object simultaneously.

structure-of-intellect Guilford's model, used extensively in gifted education.

stuttering Slang term for dysfluency; speech characterized by blocking, hesitation, or repetition of single sounds, words, and sometimes sentences.

support services Special services provided to exceptional children beyond their basic educational program. May include speech-language therapy, occupational therapy, physical therapy, music therapy, tutoring, and psychological services.

surrogate parent A person other than an individual's natural parent who has legal responsibility for the person's welfare.

syntax (or **grammar**) The linguistic rules of word order for meaningful sentences; rules governing sentence structure and word/phrase sequence.

Tay-Sachs disease A condition characterized by a defect in the metabolism of fats. Leads to blindness, paralysis, convulsions, and mental retardation.

telescoping An instructional option in gifted education that involves covering the same amount of material in less than the usual amount of time.

teratogens Outside agents or conditions that cause malformations in developing embryos.

therapeutic recreation A form of treatment that employs leisure activities of a mildly physical nature as corrective measures.

time-out A behavior management technique that eliminates possible reinforcing events for undesirable behaviors for a given time. For example, a child may be moved from classmates to a corner of the room.

total communication A system of expressive/receptive language in which manual signs and fingerspelling are combined with speech, speechreading, and listening in the way deemed most beneficial to a hearing impaired individual.

trainable mentally retarded (TMR) A term introduced in state educational codes to define children who are not able to profit suitably from regular classes or classes for educable mentally retarded students. Most criteria in state codes stipulate that the intellectual level would involve IQ scores ranging from 35 to 55, along with other characteristics that indicate the potential for profiting from a program designed to help pupils with social adjustment, self-help skills, and controlled work settings.

transdisciplinary approach Involves sharing expertise and responsibilities among team members who are involved in the assessment process and development of the educational program.

trauma Generally, a physical or psychological blow.

traumatic brain injury Injury to the head that produces severe memory disorder. Individuals will express some characteristics similar to those of individuals with learning disabilities and may be placed in such programs, but this may not be the most appropriate placement.

tremor Rhythmical movement or shaking; often associated with cerebral palsy.

triplegia Paralysis involving three limbs.

Turner's syndrome An inherited disorder affecting the chromosome that determines sex characteristics, resulting in retarded mental, physical, and sexual development.

underachiever An individual who does not perform at a level expected for his or her age and ability level.

value system The underlying motives, goals, and expectations that influence others' actions and philosophy.

visual efficiency The degree to which one can perform specific visual tasks with ease, comfort, and minimum time; cannot be measured or predicted clinically with any accuracy by medical, psychological, or educational personnel.

visual functioning How people use whatever vision they have. Some children and youth have limited visual capacity and are still extremely visually oriented; others with similar visual potential are not responsive to visual stimuli at all.

visual impairment A measured loss of any of the visual functions such as acuity, visual fields, color vision, or binocular vision.

vitreous humor The fluid in the back chamber of the eye that fills that space between the retina and the lens.

vocational education Educational programs designed to prepare individuals for employment.

vocational rehabilitation The service of providing diagnosis, guidance, training, physical restoration, and placement to disabled persons for the purpose of preparing them for and involving them in employment that helps them to live with greater independence. The preferred term is now rehabilitation services.

VSTM Acronym for very short-term memory.

work-study programs The teaching of vocational skills combined with actual on-the-job experience.

world view A shared pattern of basic beliefs and assumptions about the nature of the world and how it works.

zero reject One of the principles upon which PL 94–142 and numerous court cases have been based. Essentially, it says that no child, regardless of the degree of disability, may be refused a free appropriate public education if other children of that age are served.

*A*UTHOR *I*NDEX

S*UBJECT* I*NDEX*

A

AAMD Adaptive Behavior Scale: Public School Version, 427
Ability groups, 380–381, 793
Absence seizures, 544
Absenteeism, 719
Abstract information processing, 398
Academic achievement
  difficulties affecting, 185, 186, 188
  in emotionally disturbed students, 299–300
  in hearing impaired students, 465
  intelligence tests as predictor of, 299
  in learning disabled students, 198
  measurement of discrepancies between potential and, 195–197
  reform proposals and, 11–13
Academic potential
  measurement of discrepancies between achievement and, 195–197
  of physically disabled students, 550–551, 554–555
Acceleration
  explanation of, 793
  for gifted students, 399–400
Accommodation, eye, 793
Acoustic trauma, 462
Active listening, 793
Adaptive behavior
  assessment of, 245–246, 427
  explanation of, 793

mental retardation and, 218, 222, 237
in severely disabled children, 431–433
Adaptive equipment
  explanation of, 793
  for physically disabled students, 557–558
  for severely disabled children, 439
Adaptive physical education, 793
Adhocracy, 763–765, 773
Adolescents. *See also* Youths
  gifted female, 388, 400, 408–409
  interventions for learning disabled, 193, 198
  needs of physically disabled, 559
  role of family and, 162
  services for mentally retarded, 254–255
Adults, learning disabled, 193
Adventitious deafness, 793
Advocacy, 793
Advocacy movement
  contributions of, 55–56
  evolution and developments of, 40, 107
  goals of, 7
African Americans
  attitudes toward school among, 719–720
  educational equality for, 54–55
  poverty among, 716–717
  racial conflict and, 721, 722
  school failure among, 718–719
Age norms, 793
Aggression, 300–301
Agraphia, 793

AIDS, 47, 793. *See also* HIV infection
Air conduction, 793
Akinetic seizures, 544
Albinism, 503, 793
Alternative certification, 18, 20
Alternative response forms, 440
Ambiopia, 793
American Association on Mental Retardation (AAMR), 217–219, 223
American Sign Language (ASL). *See also* Manually coded English (MCE)
  debates regarding oral *vs.,* 455–456
  explanation of, 475, 793
  use of, 462
  view regarding use of, 475
Americans with Disabilities Act (ADA) (Public Law 101–336)
  background of, 40
  explanation of, 35, 39
  provisions of, 69–70, 420
Amniocentesis, 230, 793
Amplification, 477
Anecdotal method, 793
Aniridia, 503, 793
Annual goals, 793
Annual reporting, 52–53
Anoxia, 229, 462, 793
Antifoundationism, 594–596
Aphasia, 794
Apraxia, 794
Aptitude-treatment interaction (ATI), 178
Aqueous humor, 794
Architectural barriers, 698, 794
Articulation
  explanation of, 794